Consumer
Behaviour

Martin Evans
Ahmad Jamal
Gordon Foxall

John Wiley & Sons, Ltd

Copyright © 2006   John Wiley & Sons Ltd, The Atrium, Southern Gate, Chichester,
West Sussex PO19 8SQ, England

Telephone: (+44) 1243 779777

Email (for orders and customer service enquiries): cs-books@wiley.co.uk
Visit our Home Page on www.wiley.com
Reprinted June 2006

Other Wiley Editorial Offices

John Wiley & Sons Inc., 111 River Street, Hoboken, NJ 07030, USA

Jossey-Bass, 989 Market Street, San Francisco, CA 94103-1741, USA

Wiley-VCH Verlag GmbH, Boschstr. 12, D-69469 Weinheim, Germany

John Wiley & Sons Australia Ltd, 42 McDougall Street, Milton, Queensland 4064, Australia

John Wiley & Sons (Asia) Pte Ltd, 2 Clementi Loop #02-01, Jin Xing Distripark, Singapore 129809

John Wiley & Sons Canada Ltd, 22 Worcester Road, Etobicoke, Ontario, Canada M9W 1L1

Wiley also publishes its books in a variety of electronic formats. Some content that appears
in print may not be available in electronic books.

Library of Congress Cataloging-in-Publication Data

Evans, Martin (Martin J.)
    Consumer behaviour / Martin Evans, Ahmad Jamal, Gordon Foxall.
        p. cm.
    Includes bibliographical references and index.
    ISBN-13 978-0-470-09352-8 (alk. paper)
    ISBN-10 0-470-09352-8 (alk. paper)
        1. Consumer behavior. I. Title: Consumer behavior. II. Jamal, Ahmad, 1965- III. Foxall, G. R. IV. Title.
    HF5415.32.E933 2006
    658.8′342—dc22

                                                                                2005025623

British Library Cataloguing in Publication Data

A catalogue record for this book is available from the British Library

ISBN-13 978-0-470-09352-8
ISBN-10 0-470-09352-8

Typeset in 10/13pt Plantin by Laserwords Private Limited, Chennai, India
Printed and bound by Grafos S.A., Barcelona, Spain
This book is printed on acid-free paper responsibly manufactured from sustainable forestry
in which at least two trees are planted for each one used for paper production.

CONTENTS

DETAILED CONTENTS

PREFACE

Strangely, perhaps, you and the three authors of this book have something in common. We are all consumers. We all *think* about buying things, we *talk* about buying things and we *buy* and *use* things (things meaning products and services). We also use the things we buy to say something about ourselves to others and even to ourselves. 'We are what we have and possess' (Tuan Yi-Fu 1980) and pretty well everything we have has been purchased by someone at sometime.

It is probably no great surprise that a book with a title like Consumer Behaviour would be about these sorts of issues. It is concerned with the variety of consumer buying behaviours which most of us experience. The book analyses these experiences, using consumer behaviour theory and provides application of theories and concepts via practical examples of such experiences. Our concern is also to contextualize the study of consumer behaviour within marketing, so we offer many insights and guidelines for marketing practice.

Not that all these experiences are necessarily 'good'. Some consumers might think that marketers encourage them to consume more and more and that they won't be happy until they consume the next thing. Often this doesn't work either: consumers feel the need to consume again and again. So the book is not entirely uncritical of marketers' efforts to get consumers to keep on consuming.

Sometimes consumers might indulge in a bit of shoplifting or buy counterfeit brands. As a result the book presents an innovative chapter on consumer *mis*behaviour.

Because consumer behaviour is a sub area of the study of human behaviour, it necessarily draws from psychology and social psychology in order to inform what many people enjoy: people watching. No exception here, the book explores how consumer behaviour can be understood and explained by these underpinning disciplines and what the implications are for marketers (who always want to influence consumers).

STRUCTURE

The book is structured around three Parts. In Part 1 we focus on the consumer as an individual: what motivates consumers to buy what they do buy and how their cognitive processes operate. This Part also explores the role and nature of consumer demographics (age, gender, social grade) and the implications of these for consumption behaviour and for marketers. In addition, consumer psychographics (personality, lifestyle and self-concept) can similarly provide useful insights for both consumer behaviour and for marketing activity. So Part 1 is essentially concerned with consumers as *individuals*.

Part 2 broadens the analysis to explore more *social* dimensions of consumer behaviour. All consumers are influenced by people around them: friends, family and reference groups. But the societies in which consumers live have their own culture and indeed subcultures, so Part 2 explores the buying and marketing implications of these social aspects of consumer behaviour. There is much discussion at present of tribal and postmodern consumption patterns and Part 2 includes an analysis of these as well.

The final Part of the book integrates many of the theories and concepts from Parts 1 and 2 into more holistic topics. These include how consumers interact with new products, how they become repeat purchasers and loyal consumers. Another highly topical issue is relationship marketing, and Part 3 explores this from the perspective of relational consumption and how recent phenomena such as loyalty schemes and the use of enormous amounts of very personal consumer data are being used to explain consumer behaviour and indeed to target us as individuals. The coverage of misbehaviour also forms a component of Part 3 because it, too, draws from some of the earlier concepts to explain why consumers are not always angels.

ADDED VALUE

All three authors have extensive experience of teaching and researching consumer behaviour and know the strengths and weaknesses of the many consumer behaviour texts that are available. We have produced a book which is very much based on how most students learn this subject: through the application of theory. It is all well and good to learn lots of theories and reproduce 'the words' in assignments and examinations, but this is not sufficient for real understanding or for the development of the ability to use and apply concepts in different contexts – not least in the real world of marketing.

So, we provide plenty of **Examples** of how the theories and concepts we present can be used to explain consumer behaviour. Many are from the perspective of the consumer and many from that of the marketer, again reflecting our positioning of the book as a practical one for both consumer researchers and for marketers.

We are strong advocates that best practice is informed by good theory, so we are thorough in the use of theory and the research findings of others. An innovative feature here is the inclusion of some actual **research articles** within the text. We feel that once students experience some research findings in the form of the original source, not just someone else's summary, they will develop a hunger to explore more of what the academic journals can offer.

In each chapter we include what we call **Think Boxes**. These are little stop-off points that encourage engagement with the issues dealt with at that point, so the reader can bring their own experiences and thoughts on the matter into play – so going beyond a more passive way of learning.

The style is deliberately student-friendly and concise, so it doesn't overwhelm the reader. It is accessible and indeed manageable for a one- or two-semester module. The Think Boxes and **end of chapter questions** provide plenty of scope for insightful and fun engagement with the material and for seminar exercises.

There are also links to useful and relevant **web sites** at different stages throughout the book and these allow the reader to discover more about the issue to which they refer.

Talking of web sites, the book has its own sizeable web site at **www.wiley.com/go/evans**. Throughout the text we refer to some additional **journal articles** and these are available for you to read online. The web site contains **links** to other useful sites, an online **glossary** and **multiple choice quizzes** for you to test your understanding.

For lecturers, the web site provides comprehensive **PowerPoint presentations** for each chapter and suggested **solutions** for the end-of-chapter questions.

ACKNOWLEDGEMENTS

We are very grateful for the help, support and encouragement of all at John Wiley & Sons, Ltd: especially Anneli Anderson, Sarah Booth, Deb Egleton, Rachel Goodyear and Steve Hardman. Thanks also to Jean Foxall, Anne Bassett Evans and Victoria James for their help at various stages of writing.

We thank students on the courses we have taught, over several decades. They have given us encouragement and inspiration to produce a student-friendly book and they have shown us how to achieve this.

We have also had extremely thorough reviews of draft material by five reviewers and we have been able to improve the book as a result of their very constructive feedback. Thank you kindly.

Last but certainly not least, we offer our thanks and love to our families for encouraging us, but also our apologies for neglecting them during the writing process. Your support, as always, keeps us going.

Martin Evans
Ahmad Jamal
Gordon Foxall
Cardiff Business School
July 2005

All reasonable efforts have been made to trace the copyright owners of third party material included in this book. In the event of any omission of acknowledgement, copyright owners are invited to contact the Higher Education Division at John Wiley & Sons Ltd so that they can be acknowledged in future editions of the book or request that such material be removed from future editions.

ABOUT THE AUTHORS

Martin Evans is a Senior Fellow at Cardiff Business School. He previously held professorial posts at the Universities of Portsmouth, Glamorgan and West of England. His industrial experience was with Hawker Siddeley and then as a consultant to a variety of organizations over 30 years. Martin's specialist areas include direct marketing, consumer behaviour and marketing research and information and he has over 180 publications including eight books, mostly in these areas. He is an academic prize winner at the International Marketing Communications Conference, the Academy of Marketing, the Learning and Teaching Support Network (ITSN) and Institute of Direct Marketing. He is a Fellow of both the Chartered Institute of Marketing and Institute of Direct Marketing.

Ahmad Jamal is a Senior Lecturer in Marketing and Strategy and the Coordinator for the Ethnic Marketing Research Group at Cardiff Business School. He received his PhD in Consumer Behaviour from University of Bradford. Ahmad is a former Deputy Secretary of the Academy of Marketing UK, a member of Association of Consumer Research and a Deputy Senior Examiner for Marketing Planning at the Chartered Institute of Marketing. His research interests include cross-cultural consumer behaviour, self-concept, service quality, brand evaluations and customer satisfaction, and he has published 15 articles in various publications. His major areas of teaching include consumer behaviour, advertising and other forms of marketing communications.

Gordon Foxall is a Distinguished Research Professor at Cardiff University. His chief research interests lie in psychological theories of consumer choice and consumer innovativeness and their relationships to marketing management and strategy. He has published some 16 books and over 250 articles and papers on these and related themes and has previously held professorial appointments at the Universities of Strathclyde, Birmingham and Keele. He is a Fellow of both the British Psychological Society (FBPsS) and the British Academy of Management (FBAM) and was recently elected an Academician by the Academy of Learned Societies for the Social Sciences (AcSS).

PART 1
INDIVIDUAL ASPECTS OF
CONSUMER BEHAVIOUR

We open the book with an exploration of consumers as individuals. That is, we use many theories and concepts from psychology to explain how consumers behave.

We start (Chapter 1) with an exploration of what motivates consumers and for this we explain the difference between needs and wants. For this we draw from theories of motivation based on the work of, for example, Maslow and Freud. We also critically examine concerns over marketing's role in exploiting the human condition, which tends to aspire for more and more.

The next three chapters (Chapters 2, 3 and 4) also draw mainly from psychology as we take you through a sequential model of how consumers can respond to marketing activities. We explore, for example, consumers' perceptual and learning processes, how they develop attitudes toward products and services and indeed how marketers can use a knowledge of all this in their promotional campaigns. What happens after purchase is also of great relevance. We examine how post-purchase doubt can occur and also how markets can reassure consumers that they have indeed bought the right thing. Much depends on the level of involvement consumers have with the product or service concerned, so we explore aspects of low and high involvement from both a consumer and marketer perspective.

We then turn (in Chapter 5) to demographic characteristics of individuals and how these can influence their buying behaviour. There are many implications for marketers as well, of age/generational cohorts, gender, sexuality and social grade. We provide evidence of how consumers of different ages are interested in different things and how their mindsets need to be taken on board by marketers while targeting them. Gender is an interesting factor in consumer behaviour – men and women behave differently as consumers – and marketers often use gender stereotypes but not always in ways that are appreciated by their targets. We also introduce sexuality here because many marketers are keen to appeal to what they see as relatively lucrative gay market segments. Social grade (based on occupational groups) has long been used by marketers but we are critical of this classification on a number of grounds, despite its continued use.

Part 1 also covers what we call consumer psychographics (Chapter 6). This includes personality, lifestyle and self-concept theory. There was initial and probably fairly obvious excitement about the prospect of matching brand personalities with consumer personalities, the logic being that consumers buy things that reflect their personalities. However, we show that many consumers want to hide aspects of their real personality and portray different traits. As a result, self-concept theory has some mileage in explaining consumer behaviour because it shows how some consumers buy brands which are congruent with how they see themselves or how they want others to see them. Some specific traits, however, such as innovativeness and inner-directedness, do hold useful clues for marketing activity. We explore consumer lifestyles as researched via anonymized market research, which attempts to uncover consumer activities, interests and opinions.

We conclude Part 1 with the inclusion of a full research article on symbolic consumption among teenagers. This extends the introductory coverage of the role of symbolism in buying behaviour.

Throughout Part 1, there are practical examples and references to material, including other academic research articles, which can be accessed via the accompanying web site.

CHAPTER 1

CONSUMER MOTIVES AND VALUES

INTRODUCTION

The understanding of customer **needs and wants** is one of the major underpinning constructs of the **marketing concept**. The nature of being **market-orientated** rather than **product-orientated** requires organizations to consider who their (best) customers might be, where they are, how to target them and with what and an important starting point is to understand what it is they really 'want'. This is not as easy as it might sound. A company might be making 8 mm drills and at first sight it might seem logical for the company to focus on 'selling' 8 mm drills. However, customers don't buy 'drills' so much as 'holes': that is, what the product (or service) can do for them, rather than what it is in its tangible form. Indeed the DIY store *Homebase* has used the slogan: 'Make a house a home.'

EXAMPLE 1.1

The concept of market orientation can be illustrated in many ways. Charles Revson, the founder of Revlon cosmetics stated, 'In the factory we make cosmetics; in the drugstore we sell hope.'

In other words it isn't the physical composition or features that are being purchased, but rather the benefits consumers might derive from their purchase. An advertisement for Canon microcomputers depicted a variety of situations in the life of a man. Each box in the press advertisement showed, variously, the man at the office working on business plans, with employees in a negotiating situation, with clients in a selling situation, on the squash court and at home with his family. This multifaceted way of life fits very well in this **postmodern** era of persons fulfilling many roles. Each of these boxes had captions: forward planning, employee relations, clinching the deal, playing hard, and being a dad. The implication of course was that a prospective Canon computer buyer would not be buying RAMs, ROMs and hard disks, but would be buying something that takes over the tedious and time-consuming chores, thus allowing the buyer more time for the important things in life, and therefore being more successful at them, including being a better squash player and parent!

A Sainsbury's television commercial featured a mother and young son at the checkout. When the items were rung up on the till, the display did not show prices but, for example: 'mum's night off' for a pizza, 'breakfast in bed' for a packet of croissants.

Throughout all this the son looked glum: they had perhaps had a row. When the gingerbread man was rung up the display was 'peace offering'!

The classic way for marketing to focus on the 'benefits approach' is to identify needs of the target and to match one or more product or service features that are in some way relevant with each need. Then each feature can be converted, using a 'which means' approach, into a benefit that can satisfy that need (Table 1.1).

Customer needs and requirements should not, however, be totally satisfied: business is not altruistic because it needs to make a profit in order to stay in business and grow. What is needed is a crucial

Table 1.1 Needs, features, benefits

Needs	Features	Benefits
Identify needs	**Select relevant features**	**Convert features into benefits that satisfy needs**
Newly married couple who have just moved into a newly built house	This drill-bit set includes a set of masonry and wood/metal bits	This drill-bit set can help you turn your house into a home by allowing you to personalize it by hanging shelves, pictures, etc.
Shy and retiring 18-year-old who has just started university and wants to make some new friends	Designer-label jacket	This jacket will help you fit in and become part of the in-crowd
A young woman who wants to experience life to the fullest and wishes to make a statement about her individuality	A navel-piercing service	Piercing your navel makes a statement. It says something about who you are and you've never before experienced anything like the feeling it gives you.

compromise of satisfying organizational goals and satisfying customer needs, which can lead to competitive advantage in increasingly crowded marketplaces. This chapter explores how marketing can interpret and use motivation theories in these respects and provides practical examples of their application. We start with a discussion of **motivation** and motivation theories, then extend this into coverage of **values**. The chapter closes with a brief exploration of research approaches to investigating consumer motives and values.

MOTIVATION

Motivation is a basic concept in human behaviour and thus, also in consumer behaviour. Motivation can be described as the driving force within individuals that moves them to take a particular action. This driving force is produced by a state of tension, which exists as a result of an unfulfilled need that moves us away from psychological equilibrium or **homeostasis** (Figure 1.1).

Indeed, motivated behaviour is activity that is directed towards the attainment of a goal or objective. As we have indicated, not all **motives** derive from physical drives. Having satisfied their hunger and other physical needs, people may be found buying such items as fashionable clothes or cosmetics. Evidently, the motives behind this behaviour originate quite separately from those that involve the satisfaction of the physiological drives (also called **biogenic drives**) of, for example, keeping warm and 'needing' to eat and drink in order to live. A whole range of **psychogenic** drives (e.g. the desire to be appreciated or to have status or feel 'at one with oneself') stem from our social environment, **culture** and social group interactions. Many such as Belk *et al.* (2003) even argue that **want** (or desire), which is fundamentally social in nature, is the major driving force or motivation behind much of our contemporary consumption.

Every individual has the same need structure, but different specific needs will be to the fore in different individuals at various points in time and according to different cultural and social contexts. In critical mode, Mishan (1971) argued that marketing adds to dissatisfaction, rather than satisfaction:

> Advertising, taken as a whole, conspires first to make men feel that the things that matter to them are the material things of life: the goods, services and opportunities provided by the economy. Second, it conspires to make men dissatisfied with what they have – so goading them into efforts to increase their 'real' earnings so as to acquire more of the stuff produced by modern industry. (p 244)

Need satisfaction   Deprivation

Homeostasis

- We strive for a state of equilibrium (*Homeostasis*)

- Physiological needs (e.g. hunger) move us away from this

- But so do *social* and *psychological* needs

Figure 1.1   The homeostasis see-saw

He also maintained that the plethora of versions of products and services, with relatively little differentiation (apart from the 'emotional') again added to consumer anxiety and dissatisfaction. He preferred less choice but greater real differentiation.

So, marketers are often accused of creating a need for a product or a service that would not exist except due to some aggressive and repetitive marketing activities that educate, inform and even persuade consumers to buy those products and services. For example, most advertisements strive to portray products in such an emotional and persuasive manner that consumers start to think that they ought to buy those products even if that specific brand is not a necessity for sustaining life. However, our proposition is that marketing does not create needs, rather it encourages us to want or desire brand X by associating its acquisition with the satisfaction of a latent need.

Indeed Marx (1867/1967) wrote:

> A commodity is, in the first place, an object outside us, a thing that by its properties satisfies human wants of some sort or another. The nature of such wants, whether for instance they spring from the stomach or from fancy, makes no difference.

However, he was not convinced about them satisfying our needs because he also said that the danger of continual aspirations to *have* things was that it creates the illusion that *having* is a way to happiness. We just want more and more and are constantly distant from happiness.

Tangible and practical uses of products are often subordinated to more symbolic values. In a useful chapter on how consumers use *the things* we buy to communicate more symbolic meaning with others, Gabriel and Lang (1995, chapter 3) draw from Theodor Adorno's philosophical thinking of post-war Germany. Adorno and others from what became known as the **Frankfurt School** saw social symbolism of products often outweighing their more practical use values. The work of Vance Packard (1957) extended this to assert that as the *practical* is subordinated in favour of the more frivolous, we are unduly influenced by the persuasive powers of marketing.

Various forms of marketing communications (e.g. advertising, personal selling, branding, sales promotions, direct marketing, packaging) contribute by conveying **symbolic meanings** about who we are and the way we can relate to ourselves and to others in the society. On this basis, products and services can be strategically positioned in competitive marketplaces and marketing communications (in particular) can, at an operational level, benefit from an understanding of the key aspects of motivation theory because specific message appeals can be based on such analysis.

www.	For more on symbolic consumption, read the article by Piacentini and Mailer (2004), Symbolic Consumption in Teenagers' Clothing Choices, which follows Part 1 and also appears on the accompanying web site at www.wiley.com/go/evans.

Furthermore, marketers can restructure and shape how human needs are manifested by introducing and producing products that did not exist before (Firat *et al.*, 1995). For instance, the need for transportation and mobility has been restructured and reshaped in recent times by the production and consumption of cars and televisions. Due to the modern organization of life and the relationships of work and home, we have witnessed a reorganization of the transportation and entertainment systems at both the society and individual levels leading to changes in our consumption and expenditure patterns (Firat *et al.*,1995).

Might consumer's buying behaviour not only reflect their desire to buy benefits but that the aggregation of their purchases even define them? Are we what we buy (Belk, 1988)?

McAlexander *et al.* (2002) propose that, from a marketers' perspective, it is worth exploiting consumers' desire not only to buy benefits but also an experience. They suggest that this can gain competitive advantage by focusing: 'not merely on the product and its positioning but also on the *experience* of ownership and consumption'. The concept of experiential consumption is explored in Chapter 10.

THINKBOX

Our central proposition, then, is that marketing does not create needs but shapes the manifestation of these via wants for specific brands and types of products.

Do you think that marketing creates needs? Explain your position.

How do you feel about the proposition that many of the things we buy lack real use value and are merely bought for their symbolism to ourselves and to others?

Positive and Negative Motivation

Positive and negative motivation may be distinguished as **approach** and **avoidance**, respectively. As positive motivation, people are looking for positive situations, positive mood, pleasure, sensory gratification, intellectual stimulation, social approval and comfort: things that may enrich their lives and are worthwhile to strive for and goals that they want to reach (Figure 1.2). Holidays and entertainment are examples of products and services appealing to a positive motivation.

With negative motivation, people are motivated to escape from negative situations, negative mood, pain, illness and discomfort such as a headache: they want to avoid and remove problems. For example,

Figure 1.2   Positive motivation
It's not how you really are, but how the advertisement suggests you might become. But does marketing sometimes promise the undeliverable, leading to consumer discontent?
Source: Swish Jeans

people do not like to be stranded on a motorway when their cars break down suddenly and hence the motivation to purchase the breakdown cover. Similarly, a consumer while buying a washing machine may opt to buy an extended warranty for up to five years to avoid inconvenience and pain associated with calling and paying for expensive repairs if the machine breaks down.

We discuss **cognitive dissonance** later in this chapter (and in Chapter 4) and this is another exam of how we are motivated to avoid states of disequilibrium.

Internal and External Motivation

Motivation is either internal ('from within a person') or external ('from the environment'). Internal motivation is concerned with instinct, need, drive or emotion. It often has a physiological base, e.g. hunger, thirst, sexual needs and need for stimulation. We explore aspects of deep-seated inner drives in the later section on **Freudian motivation**. **External motivation** is based on an attractiveness of environmental stimuli such as products and services and often becomes **internal motivation** in the form of preference for products, services, and situations.

Operant conditioning and **vicarious learning** (explored in more detail in Chapter 3) are based on the attractiveness of goods and services and the reinforcements these goods provide for consumers through their benefits. Operant conditioning is concerned with the strengthening of behaviour through **reinforcement**. If consumers select a brand or product type they may be positively reinforced by the benefits of the product. But if these benefits are absent, there can be a 'negative' reinforcement of not repeating the same buying experience. Vicarious learning (Chapters 3, 7 and 9) relates to the imitation drive of people. Many will try to imitate celebrities and fashion models. They imitate the clothing, movements and typical characteristics of these role models and in this way external motivational drives are often triggered. Combining positive and negative motivation with internal and external motivation gives the four types of motivation of Table 1.2.

At this point we turn to specific theories of motivation and how the work of the marketer and consumer researcher can be informed by these.

Table 1.2   Different kinds of motivation

Motivation	Internal	External
Positive	pleasure, comfort	attractive goods and services, attractive situations
Negative	pain, discomfort	unattractive goods and services, unattractive situations

MASLOW'S HIERARCHY OF NEEDS

Perhaps the most widely cited theory of motivation is that of Maslow which is represented as a hierarchy of needs (Figure 1.3). Maslow's proposition is that needs at one level must be at least partially satisfied before those at the next level become important in determining our actions. The satisfaction of a lower-order need triggers the next level of needs into operation, demanding new patterns of behaviour on the part of the individual. Naturally the basic needs must be met first

Figure 1.3 Maslow's hierarchy of needs

(adequately, if not completely). But once the physiological (**biogenic**) needs have been satisfied, the individual turns their attention to the fulfilment of more advanced **psychogenic** requirements such as social acceptance and self-esteem. People may also have needs for 'cognition', that is to know and to understand things, and Maslow's level 5 reflects this. Many will have a need for learning for its own sake, for example. There can also be a need for creativity and for outlets for artistic, creative and aesthetic drives (level 6). The final stage in the motivational hierarchy is the need for what Maslow calls **self-actualization**. While he does not define this term with any real degree of precision, it appears to represent the attainment of what other psychologists call *self-realization*, the process in which the individual has the opportunity to invest all their talents and abilities in activities which they find meaningful: activities which help develop **personality**, e.g. through leisure activities and creative pastimes.

The significance of the hierarchy to marketing is great. It clearly demonstrates that a need refers to more than mere physiological essentials. Other forces driving our behaviour can come from a concern for our safety, social integration, personal recognition, learning, appreciation of our surroundings or from the perceived importance of spiritual satisfaction.

WWW.	**Take a look at this web site for more on Maslow's theory:**
	http://www.businessballs.com/maslow.htm

The hierarchy can be criticized; for example, Maslow suggested that as societies develop they move further up the hierarchy in terms of their most relevant needs to tackle. It could be argued here that not everyone will move up the ladder in quite the same way, perhaps missing some levels and perhaps moving back down to lower level needs. An illustration of this would be where, in Western industrialized countries, at the same time as attempting to satisfy social and higher levels of the hierarchy, many will be heavily orientated to, for example, safety and security as a result of fears about criminality, the violent society and terrorism. An advertisement by the Discovery Television channel for documentary programmes about terrorism pictured an airplane flying close to two tower blocks of flats. The copy headline was: 'Terrorism has changed the way we view the world.' Marketing clearly recognizes how even the most developed societies have strong and rekindled safety needs. This is evidenced by the plethora of advertisements for personal alarms, life assurance policies and home and car security devices. Chubb locks, for example, use the copy: 'Pick your own lock before a burglar does . . . and lock out unwelcome visitors.'

Some expensive products will target lower-level needs. Prior to the slightly more trendy Volvo advertising of today, the company promoted 'safety' as a key benefit of its cars for many decades (Figure 1.4). So, in the context of the discussion of consumer motivation, such criticisms are relatively pedantic. We present Maslow to reinforce the point that consumers can be motivated by more than the 'essentials' of physiology and that there can be changes, over time, to what motivates individuals. Maslow's theory makes a distinction between what may be termed physical/inherited needs and learned needs. The latter are not innate but acquired by the individual through social interaction.

Identifying which needs are especially salient within different market segments is a task for marketers and market researchers. To demonstrate this, a useful illustration is the toothpaste market. Many of us might think, 'Toothpaste is toothpaste' and that we all use it in similar quantities for similar reasons. Table 1.3 adapts a classic piece of research into an apparently non-differentiated market. It shows consumers may be assigned to different segments for a variety of reasons and can, on this basis, be targeted with different marketing mixes.

So, whereas brands of fluoride toothpaste may be tangibly and chemically very similar, they will often be targeted at different market segments. Even the brand *names* used can suggest this, on the basis of varying benefits being sought: Close Up, Aquafresh, Ultrabrite and Macleans. The imagery surrounding the advertising of these brands similarly suggests the difference between 'features' and 'benefits'. Some might show two mothers with their children in a dentist's waiting room. One child has to have several

Figure 1.4 Example of how marketers have targeted Maslow's 'safety' needs
Reproduced by permission of Volvo Car UK Ltd and Abbott Mead Vickers BBDO.

Table 1.3   Toothpaste consumer benefit segments

	Sensory segment	Sociable segment	Worrier segment	Independent segment
Main benefit	flavour	bright teeth	decay prevention	price
Demographic factors	children young people	teens	large families	men
Lifestyle factors	hedonistic	active	conservative	concerned with value

Adapted from Haley (1968)

fillings and the other does not. Explicitly there might be references to the brand used by the child who has no cavities, suggesting that this is the brand for 'you', if you want to prevent tooth decay and hence satisfy a need or value to safeguard yourself (needs at level 2). Implied, however, is an even stronger benefit that if you don't use this brand as a parent, in some way you are not such a good parent (needs at levels 2, 3 and perhaps 4).

Recently, Colgate, in Figure 1.5, heavily promoted the benefit of fresh breath.

Figure 1.5   Toothpaste 'benefits'
Example of a marketer recognizing that different market segments will be motivated by different needs and therefore providing a basis for 'benefit segmentation'.
©Colgate-Palmolive Company 2005. Designed by Jim Richards, addicted2tv.com

EXAMPLE 1.2

Direct mailings for pensions aimed at the 18–35s have shown that in order to secure an assured future, a second pension is increasingly desirable (level 2). BUPA has used the advertising strapline: 'You're amazing, we want to keep you that way.' This and campaigns for life assurance, especially covering family members, can be linked with level 2 but also, because of the implied concerns for loved ones, we can see level 3 being activated (i.e. social needs) and additionally, more personal esteem needs from level 4 (our self-esteem can be enhanced by feeling we are looking after those for whom we have some responsibility). Social needs are also portrayed by BT's 'Friends and Family' and 'It's Good to Talk' campaigns. Perhaps, rather incredulously, we can see a possible use of self-actualization and its 'utopian' nature in Bounty Bar (a chocolate bar) advertisements claiming 'a taste of paradise'?

There is evidence of a trend toward self-actualization as reflected in **individualism**. We explore this further in Chapters 6 and 11 but it is worth a brief mention here. During the 1970s in the UK and the USA this trend was identified and led, among other things, to the Regan and Thatcher election campaigns from the late 1970s and into the 1980s, based on 'self-reliance' (BBC, 2002; McNulty and McNulty, 1987). 'Standing on one's own feet' and 'freeing the individual from the state' were the sorts of mantras of those elections and were manifestations of research at the time that was put forward as evidence of the self-actualizing consumer, by the creator of the VALS life style research in USA and confirmed more recently (McNulty, 2002). Indeed in UK, research reported by Publicis (1992) suggests that from 1973 to 1989 there had been a shift in motivators from 'level 1 and 2' functional and rational factors (40% to 27% of the population) and 'level 3' other-directedness (static at 35%) to more **inner-directedness** levels 4 to 7 (25% to 38% of the population). So although we started by suggesting a criticism of Maslow that not all societies will continue to progress up the hierarchy, there is evidence to suggest this can happen within some.

While keeping Maslow's theory in mind, one can think of some other theories that have tended to explain individual differences in motivation. For instance, consumers are likely to be different in their need for achievement (McClelland, 1961), their need for cognition (Cohen *et al.*, 1955) and their need for affiliation and power (Atkinson, 1958). Similarly, McGuire classified motives into two broad categories: cognitive and affective. **Cognitive motives,** as per McGuire (1974, 1976), reflected motives that emphasized an individual's need for being adaptively orientated towards the environment and for achieving a sense of meaning. **Affective motives** emphasized an individual's need to achieve satisfying feeling states and to obtain emotional goals.

FREUDIAN THEORY OF MOTIVATION

Consider the following: owners of sports cars verbalize reasons for purchase as being able to accelerate safely during overtaking manoeuvres. This, however, might just be a *good* reason, and the underlying *real* reason might be that the sports car helps attract the opposite sex or is even a substitute mistress. This is not as far-fetched as it might sound and was actually the theme of a classical advertising for the MGB GT car in the early 1980s. The copy headline for that advertisement read: 'Psychologists say a saloon car is a wife and a sports car is a mistress.' The MGB advertisement played on the proposition that not only are consumers buying benefits rather than features, but also that the benefits can sometimes satisfy more deeply seated needs. In this case, the sports car would be considered to be a subconscious symbol.

Sigmund Freud's psychoanalytic theory underpins this thinking and distinguishes three basic structures of the mind: **Id, Ego** and **Superego** (Table 1.4).

Table 1.4   Id, ego and superego

Structure	Level
Superego	Conscious
Ego	Subconscious
Id	Unconscious

The id is unconscious, instinctive source of our impulses: a source of psychic energy. It is a beast looking for immediate hedonistic gratification (pleasure), self-interest and a short-term perspective. Freud argued that the libido, sexuality, is the driving force of the id but the more general interpretation is that the id is the reservoir of 'base' instincts and these could be sexually or violence-related or even be traumatic experiences from the past which linger in the unconscious and exert influence on conscious and subconscious processes. There is a large degree of 'internal' motivation here, based on deeply seated instinctive drives.

Many people believe that consumers may be influenced at the unconscious level with 'subliminal' advertising. Subliminal advertising is supposed to exert influence on behaviour while consumers are not aware of the influence attempt of this type of advertising. Examples of subliminal advertising are short flashes, such as 'Eat popcorn' or 'Drink Coca-Cola' inserted in a film in New Jersey. These flashes were too short to be consciously observed (Packard, 1957). Subliminal images may also be inserted in pictures, in a scrambled or hidden way, e.g. the word 'sex' to be read in the ice cubes in a glass of whisky (Key, 1973). The suggestion is that these hidden flashes or pictures are being unconsciously observed and processed and, without any cognitive defence or screening by the superego, transmitted to the mind of consumers. These subliminal messages exert a strong effect on behaviour without people knowing that they are influenced. Recent research, however, does not support this view and there is conflicting evidence for its effectiveness. But if subliminal advertising should work, it would bring many ethical questions to the fore whether this type of advertising would be allowed or not.

Superego

However, the **superego** represents the internalized representation of the morals and values of those important to us in society and operates at the conscious level. In this way the superego is more of an 'external' motivator. It consciously controls our behaviour by seeking to make it fit with these internalized norms. It is our social conscience and can conflict with the id.

Ego

The **ego**, on the other hand, responds to the real world and acts in a mediating role between the id and reality. It does not operate at the conscious level but neither is it submerged into the unconscious; instead it is a subconscious mediator between the other two elements. Thus it controls our instinctive drives and tries to find a realistic means by which we can satisfy our impulses, or socially acceptable (to satisfy the superego) outlets that will adequately address the id drives (Figure 1.6).

Figure 1.6   The Freudian see-saw

THINKBOX

In Figure 1.7, the id suggests what we 'really' want to wear or see, but which might not be entirely socially acceptable in public. Our superego reflects our social conscience and is what we see as being socially acceptable, but which probably doesn't satisfy the id enough. The ego comes up with styles which satisfy the id acceptably but which are also socially acceptable in public.

Id   Superego   Ego

Figure 1.7   Naughty, nice, naughty but nice

Source: Ann Summer's, www.annsummers.com (id); Freemans plc, www.freemans.com (Superego and Ego).

EXAMPLE 1.3

If a main tenet of the theory is the conflict and ultimate compromise between the id, the superego and the ego, consider the effects of alcohol. In a classic television anti-drink advertising campaign, the same scene was played twice, through the perceptions of the two main characters. First, a man was drinking more and more and (through his eyes) becoming more sophisticated, suave and attractive to the women around him. Then the same episode was played as if through her eyes: a drunk was getting more and more obnoxious. What this nicely demonstrates is the effect that alcohol can have on reducing the constraints of the superego.

Indeed, in a series of advertisements for Pernod, the copy, in a variety of different settings, read 'Pernod: free the spirit'. Apart from the obvious play on words, it could also be equated with the notion of freeing the id. When on holiday in a foreign country we often don't know of the local norms and some will deliberately ignore them so that there is little perception of social constraints at all. Again the id can be free and this might explain the **misbehaviour** (see Chapter 12) of binge drinkers in Spanish resorts and elsewhere.

Even ice cream has been promoted with a similar 'free the id' appeal (Figure 1.8).

Tapping the id, but in a way that can ultimately be manifested in a socially acceptable way, is the key to this approach. Consider the following: 'Why do people take so much pleasure in immersing themselves in warm water? One theory is that it awakens distant memories of floating in the comfort of the womb.' This was actually part of the copy for a British Gas advertisement!

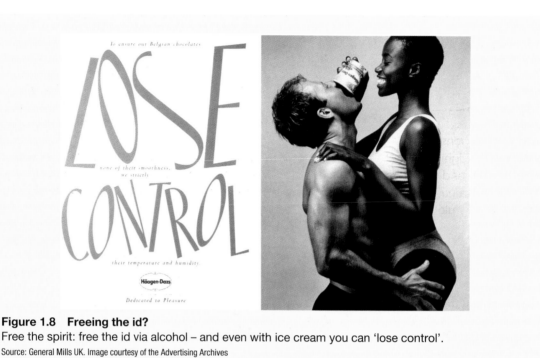

Figure 1.8   Freeing the id?
Free the spirit: free the id via alcohol – and even with ice cream you can 'lose control'.
Source: General Mills UK. Image courtesy of the Advertising Archives

Referring back to the use of **subliminal messages** to reach the subconscious. Early experiments were based on editing in a single-frame insert to cinema films. As we know, although films appear convincingly as movement, they are composed of a series of still frames. The speed through the projector gives the impression of movement. The point is that our senses are not quick enough to distinguish each single frame. The idea behind the experiments was to use this knowledge and it was thought that the single-frame insert would not be consciously noticed but, because it did physically appear on the screen for a fraction of a second, there would be a chance that the receivers' subconscious might accept the message. Indeed, for the test products, Coca-Cola and popcorn, more was sold during the commercial break (after the 'subliminal' message in the form of this additional single frame was shown) than was the case in 'control' audiences where the insets were not projected.

The approach was pounced on by the media and, as a result of general public concern, subliminal advertising was made illegal in many countries. However, other experiments attempting to replicate the results were not entirely conclusive about its effectiveness. Nevertheless there was sufficient concern for the legislation to remain.

Lasswell's (1948) **theory of the triple appeal** is useful for practical implementation of Freud-based marketing messages. This states that to be successful the message must appeal to all three elements of the mind. If not and it appeals only to the id, for instance, its effects will be immediately negated by the superego. If the appeal is purely to the superego, the social conscience it is in danger of being too 'goody-goody' and won't address what really motivates us, and if the appeal is pure 'ego' it can be too logical and therefore lacks 'appeal'. So, Lasswell would opt for an appeal that was a touch 'naughty' but also 'nice'.

EXAMPLE 1.4

It might be suggested that appeals to the id can be made in other subconscious ways. Pack designs could trigger subconscious sets of associations; for example, when there is phallic and other symbolism in the designs, shapes, textures and materials. Also, consider the scope for 'voice under' messages as part of in-store music tracks declaring you must not steal, but which (at the conscious level) are inaudible.

Marketers might attempt to tap the Id in such a way as to encourage what some might regard as rather dubious purposes. The purchase of a camcorder, for example, might be explained via a number of 'good' reasons but the 'real' reason might not be one that all **purchasers** would verbalize (Figure 1.9)!

Figure 1.9   'Good' and (dubious) 'real' motives
Good and real reasons for buying a camcorder . . .
© Sanyo Europe Ltd. Reproduced by permission

Other messages might attempt to tap the subconscious id drives with what superficially would appear to be rather obscure references. Take, for instance, an advertisement in which a woman is about to eat a toffee apple. She wears a bracelet on her wrist in the form of a snake and the copy reads: 'Adam just cured my fear of snakes.' The advertisement is actually for gold jewellery, but there is plenty of Freudian symbolism here (Adam and Eve, 'forbidden fruit' and the phallic symbolism of snakes!). This might go completely over the heads of the target market, at least at the conscious level, but if it reaches the id then it might well be doing what was intended.

The problem with the subconscious, of course, is that it is very difficult to identify and research – even its very existence. Different psychoanalysts might well interpret research findings in different ways and so the whole approach attracts critical attention.

However, new developments in **direct marketing** might increase the use of id appeals. For example, Club 18–30 targeting of what they see as the 'real' reason for young people to go on their holidays (i.e. sex on holiday) is barely disguised ('Beaver Espania', 'One swallow doesn't make a summer', 'the summer of 69'). We suggest that this sort of 'id' appeal would generally not be acceptable in mass media communications that reach the mass of the population with little targeting. But the direct approach perhaps allows for this, providing these risqué messages are targeted at the 'like-minded' in a discreet and confidential way; for example, through direct mail. In one mailing, Club 18–30 portrayed a couple of dolls having sex with the headline, 'coming soon'. In this way, the more 'private' message, which direct communications provide, could give added momentum for Freudian messages which are almost *all* id.

MEMETICS

We wonder if a new consumer motivator is in the process of being identified and exploited. **Memetics** has recently attracted significant attention (Dawkins, 1989; Blackmore, 1999; Marsden, 1998, 1999; Williams, 2002). Whereas a gene passes forms of behaviour down (vertically) through the generations, a meme acts as a sort 'horizontal' communicator of how to behave. The difference, however, is that memes work more like a viral contagion. A good example of the principle is how it is often difficult not to start yawning if others are yawning (Marsden, 1998). Could memes go some way to explaining the spread of extreme xenophobia, Nazism or ethnic cleansing? It might be an unconscious communication, thus having some relationship with the Freudian paradigm discussed above and be one which might be most enduring if instilled at an early age. Will it become possible to 'create' a meme that marketers can use to communicate through societies, with consumers becoming infected with a mind virus that is not recognized consciously, but which results in them suddenly joining the next fad or fashion? Some say this is nearly possible, and research is being conducted to 'design and engineer highly infectious memes that could be used in marketing campaigns' (Marsden, 1998).

WWW.   **Take a look at this website for more on memes and memetics:**

www.geocities.com/persistentmemes/articles.html

THINKBOX

In 1957,with respect to what we might see today as straightforward mass media advertising such as TV advertising, Vance Packard raised concerns about its 'hidden persuasion' potential. He wrote: 'Eventually – say by AD 2000 – perhaps all this depth manipulation of the psychological variety will seem amusingly old-fashioned. By then perhaps the biophysicists will take over "biocontrol", which is depth persuasion carried to its ultimate' (Packard, 1957:195).
What do you think?

COGNITIVE DISSONANCE AS MOTIVATOR

The final motivation theory we have space to explore here is the need to avoid or reduce cognitive dissonance (Festinger, 1957). This is discussed in more detail in Chapter 4 but, briefly, it is a condition reflecting a tendency towards mental unease (the homeostasis see-saw again) which occurs when an individual holds two attitudes, ideas, beliefs or other cognitions that are not in harmony with each other. In this situation the person tries to reduce dissonance – perhaps by dropping a cognition, perhaps by strengthening one. Dissonance is therefore a factor in motivation because it leads the individual to change their opinion, attitudes or behaviour in order to reach a state of 'consonance' or homeostasis.

For example, there is dissonance in a smoker who knows that smoking is dangerous to health. The smoker is motivated to reduce the dissonance, perhaps by stopping or reducing the smoking behaviour or by not reading (or screening out) the messages conveying the dangers of smoking. Another well-known example of cognitive dissonance theory concerns the post-decisional doubt expressed by purchasers of new cars. The existence of dissonance among such customers was deduced from their tendency to seek further information about the model just bought despite having previously considered several alternatives. There is a degree of reassurance that many buyers seek, to confirm their choice. Marketing responds with 'welcome packs' for new customers (especially for new customers of mobile phone companies), 'congratulations' messages on joining the 'family' of owners, after-sales service and the use of comparative advertising in which competitors offerings are not seen in such good light as their own. Chapter 4 explores dissonance as a **post-purchase** phenomenon in more detail, but in this chapter we submit that dissonance reduction and/or avoidance as a clear motivator for many consumers.

MOTIVATION AND SHOPPING

In a shopping context, we can think of motivation as the driving force within consumers that makes them shop. Table 1.5 presents some of the shopping motives identified by previous research. The

Table 1.5   Shopping motives

Tauber (1972)

- **Diversion** highlights shopping's ability to present opportunities to the shopper to escape from the routines of daily life and therefore represents a type of recreation and escapism.
- **Self-gratification** underlines shopping's potential to alleviate depression as shoppers can spend money and buy something nice when they are in a down mood.
- **Physical activity** focuses on consumers' need for engaging in physical exercise by walking in spacious and appealing retail centres, particularly when they are living in urban and congested environments.
- **Sensory stimulation** emphasizes the ability of the retail institutions to provide many sensory benefits to consumers as they can enjoy the physical sensation of handling merchandise, the pleasant background music and the scents.
- **Social and communication** motives feature shopping's potential to provide opportunities to socialize, meet and communicate with others with similar interests.
- **Peer group attraction** stresses consumers' desires to be with their reference group.
- **Status and authority** reflect shopping's ability to provide opportunities for consumers to command attention and respect from others.
- **Pleasure of bargaining** reflects consumers' desires and abilities to make wiser decisions by engaging in comparison shopping and special sales.

Westbrook and Black (1985)

- **Anticipated utility**–the benefits provided by the product acquired via shopping.
- **Role enactment**–identifying and assuming culturally prescribed roles.
- **Negotiation**–seeking economic advantage via bargaining.
- **Choice optimization**–searching for and securing precisely the right products to fit one's demands.
- **Affiliation**–with others directly or indirectly.
- **Power and authority**–attainment of elevated social position.
- **Stimulation**–seeking novel and interesting stimuli.

Arnold and Reynolds (2003)

- **Adventure shopping**–to seek stimulation, adventure, and feelings of being in a different world.
- **Social shopping**–for enjoyment of shopping with friends and family, socializing while shopping and bonding with others.
- **Gratification shopping**–for stress relief, to alleviate a negative mood and as a special treat to oneself.
- **Idea shopping**–for keeping up with trends and new fashions and to seek new products and innovations.
- **Role shopping**–for getting enjoyment as a consequence of shopping for others.
- **Value shopping**–reflecting shopping for sales, looking for discounts, and hunting for bargains.

well-known work of Tauber (1972) concerns the identification of a number of shopping motivations with the premise that consumers are motivated by a number of personal and social needs. The personal motives include the needs for role-playing, diversion, self-gratification, learning about new trends, physical activity and sensory stimulation. The social motives identified by Tauber (1972) include the needs for social experiences, communication with others, peer group attractions, status and authority, and pleasure in bargaining. Similarly, Westbrook and Black (1985) and Arnold and Reynolds (2003) identify a number of interesting shopping motivations. It is worth noting that, for some consumers, a shopping experience can be potentially entertaining, playful and fun, emotionally involving and a mechanism of escaping from the daily routines. In this way it reinforces the earlier view that we buy less for tangible functionality than for social and psychological symbolism that satisfy higher-level needs. Even the *process* of buying can be more important than the resulting product acquisition itself. We explore negative dimensions of this (for example, **compulsive buying**) in our chapter on **consumer misbehaviour** (Chapter 12).

For other consumers, however, *shopping* can obviously be task-orientated (e.g. I have to buy this as part of my day-to-day routine) and is a very rational activity to satisfy more physiological needs.

By knowing and exploring consumers' motivations for shopping, researchers have been able to profile shoppers into different segments and have examined similarities and differences among these segments. Table 1.6 presents characteristic features of different shopper segments based on Sproles and Kendall's (1986) work on mental orientations that characterize consumers' approaches to making shopping choices. Marketers can improve their targeting efforts by developing marketing communications that emphasize key features of the shopping experience (e.g. depict the shopping experience as a delightful adventure or emphasize value for money). They can also improve store designs and store layouts (e.g. tailor store atmospherics to the needs of a particular segment).

Table 1.6 Classification of shoppers based on Sproles and Kendall's (1986) consumer decision-making styles

Shopper category	Characteristics
Quality-consciousness shoppers	They look for highest possible quality while shopping; like to shop carefully, systematically and may not feel satisfied with just-good-enough brands.
Brand-conscious shoppers	They seek out more expensive and famous brands; like to perceive price–quality link, have positive attitudes towards departmental and speciality stores selling expensive and popular brands and may prefer best-selling, heavily advertised brands.
Novelty-fashion-conscious shoppers	They seek to buy novel and fashionable items; like to seek pleasure and excitement out of discovering new things, want to keep up to date with new styles and trends.
Recreational shoppers	They look for pleasure, fun, recreation and entertainment out of shopping.
Value-conscious shoppers	They seek bargains and look for deals; are concerned about getting best value for money; engage in comparison-shopping.
Impulsive shoppers	They tend to buy on impulse; do not like to plan their shopping; remain unconcerned about how much they spend.
Confused shoppers	They tend to get confused by over-choice of brands and information; likely to experience information overload.
Brand-loyal shoppers	They to tend to like and buy same brands again and again; likely to have developed particular behaviours and habits.

www.   **Addis and Holbrook (2001) on the conceptual link between mass customization and experiential consumption: An explosion of subjectivity, Journal of Consumer Behaviour, Vol 1 No 1 pp 50–66 can be found on the accompanying web site and it explores a variety of issues relevant to the current chapter: hedonistic versus utilitarian consumption, experiential consumption as well as aspects of relational consumption, relevant to Chapter 10.**

www.wiley.com/go/evans

VALUES

Higher-level needs approach the status of **values**, which are critical determinants of behaviour (Baier, 1969). Rokeach (1968) regarded a value as 'an enduring belief that a specific mode of conduct or end-state of existence is personally or socially preferable to an opposite or converse mode of conduct or end-state of existence'. For Schwartz and Bilsky (1987) values transcend specific situations and one of the most widely accepted value inventory is the Rokeach Value Survey (RVS). The RVS measures 18 **instrumental values** and the same number of **terminal values** (Table 1.7). Instrumental values are related to preferred modes of conduct such as honesty and friendliness which people know can lead to being accepted by others and to having good relations with others. Instrumental values are thus means to reach a goal. Terminal values are more related to end-state goals such as wisdom, happiness and freedom. Products and services may also be related to terminal values; for example, Coca-Cola and its connotation with US values.

Vinson and Lamont (1977) devised a model of consumer value systems by arranging values at three different levels and giving a hierarchical arrangement to them (Figure 1.10).

Table 1.7   The Rokeach Value Survey

Instrumental Values	Terminal Values
Ambitious	A Comfortable Life
Broad-minded	An Exciting Life
Capable	A Sense of Accomplishment
Cheerful	A World at Peace
Clean	A World of Beauty
Courageous	Equality
Forgiving	Family Security
Helpful	Freedom
Honest	Happiness
Imaginative	Inner Harmony
Independent	Mature Love
Intellectual	National Security
Logical	Pleasure
Loving	Salvation
Obedient	Self-respect
Polite	Social Recognition
Responsible	True Friendship
Self-controlled	Wisdom

Source: Adapted from Rokeach (1973)

www. Chapter 6 explores lifestyles that reflect consumer values. As a link between consumer values, Maslow's hierarchy of needs and our coverage of personality in Chapter 6, take a look at this web site:

http://www.realmotivations.co.uk/

This is the site of the Wegener company which researches values and lifestyles based on Maslow. You can complete a version of their questionnaire yourself and get a personal profile – see if it matches your view of yourself!

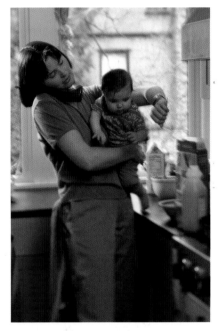

In different cultures, different values have been found and we discuss this in more detail in Chapter 8. However, it is worth introducing Hofstede's (1980) study on work-related cultural values in 40 countries. This identified four major dimensions: power distance, uncertainty avoidance, femininity/masculinity and individualism/collectivism. The power-distance emphasis refers to the extent to which a particular society or its members tolerate an unequal distribution of power in the society. In cultures with large power distance, people tend to have their rightful places in the society. They also tend to respect old age, and status is valued to show off power. People in low power-distance cultures try to look younger than they are and the powerful people try to look less powerful. The uncertainty-avoidance emphasis refers to the extent to which people tend to feel threatened by uncertain, risky and ambiguous situations. People in cultures with large uncertainty-avoidance tend to appreciate the need for rules and formality to structure their lives. They also tend to value competence, which leads them to value experts. In masculine cultures, people tend to value achievement and success and there is a significant role differentiation between males and females. In feminine cultures, people tend to value caring for others and quality of life and there is less role differentiation. People in individualist cultures tend to look after themselves and their immediate family only whereas, in collectivist cultures, people tend to value belonging to groups that look after them in exchange for loyalty.

Similarly, Western values are characterized by 'separatedness' in the sense of people being relatively independent and individualistic (as the Publicis [1992] research above suggested). The Harley Davidson strapline, 'We don't care how everyone does it ... we prefer to go our own way' encapsulates this, whereas non-Western cultures are more 'connected' in terms of being more interdependent and collective. The Fuji Bank in Japan has used the strapline, 'Meeting clients' needs is half the story, meeting society's needs is the other half.' Furthermore, Harris Research (1998) has found differing values within Europe as summarized in Table 1.8. Similarly, Caillat and Mueller (1996) compared the cultural variables manifest in US and UK commercial messages for beer advertising, including dominant cultural values. The study found that the US commercials perpetuated predominantly US cultural values (e.g. achievement, individualism/independence, and modernity/newness) whereas UK commercials presented

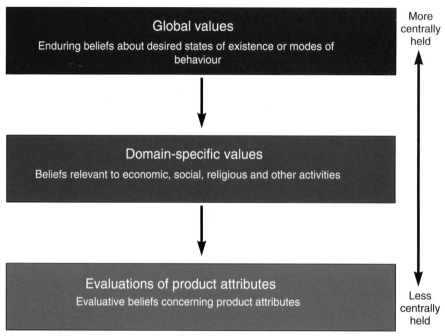

Figure 1.10   Consumer value systems

Source: D. Vinson, J. Scott and L. Lamont, 'The Role of Personal Values in Marketing and Consumer Research', *Journal of Marketing* 41 (April 1977), pp. 45–50. Reproduced by permission of American Marketing Association

Table 1.8   European values

Country	Values
UK	Singularity, difficult to express feelings, not tactile
France	Search for quality of life/well being
Italy	Religious idealism, community, curiosity
Spain	Human interaction, sharing, harmony
Germany	Tangible reality, concrete pleasure

Source: Adapted by the authors from Harris Research (1998) European Values Research
Report, London

predominantly UK cultural values (e.g. tradition/history and eccentricity). Their findings led them to conclude a standardized message strategy among the US and UK beer markets might not be very effective, because of differences in cultural values.

People are not born with their values. Rather, values are passed from one generation to another; they are learned. Engel *et al.* (1986) point out that some values are relatively constant while others are subject to change. They propose that the triad of families, religious institutions and school plus early lifetime experiences leads to a model of **intergenerational value transmission** (Figure 1.11).

This analysis is developed in the next section discussing motivation research methods because it provides a framework for research; namely, to explore a hierarchical sequence of how consumers perceive product **attributes**, their **consequences** and what these then reveal about their values (**means–end chains**).

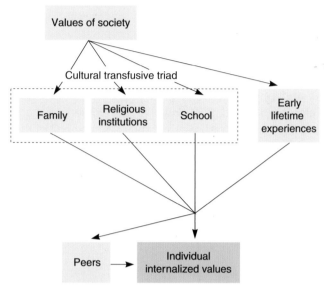

Figure 1.11   Intergenerational value transmission
Source: Adapted from Engel *et al.* (1986)

MOTIVATION RESEARCH

It is apparent from the foregoing that the identification of consumers' motives is a complex business. The difficulties involved in discovering directly the precise motivating factors that shape buying behaviour led some marketers and consumer researchers to devise techniques for exposing hidden motives. Such techniques sometimes need to reveal suppressed and repressed motives and some are briefly discussed below. Most marketing research textbooks will provide more detailed expositions.

Projective Techniques

If persons are relieved of direct responsibility for their expressions, they will tend to answer more freely and truthfully. **Projective tests** are designed to achieve this end. These are called 'projective tests' because respondents are required to project themselves into someone else's place or into some ambiguous situation. Consider the following examples of projective tests:

Third-Person Tests

In **third-person tests,** the respondent is encouraged to reply through some third party. The rationale is that there are both 'good' and 'real' reasons for behaviour. 'Good' reasons are socially acceptable (e.g. to buy environmentally friendly products). 'Real' reasons are sometimes not socially accepted. While 'good' reasons will probably be given in response to a direct questioning approach, such as 'Why did you buy this?', these answers may only be partially true. There may be a 'real' reason for behaviour that either the respondent is unwilling to admit or unable to recognize. An indirect question – for example, 'What sort of people buy this?' or 'Why do people buy these?' – might be sufficient to reveal 'real' reasons for behaviour.

EXAMPLE 1.5

A classic piece of market research years ago investigated the reasons for poor sales of the newly introduced instant coffee. The widely quoted study of instant coffee usage illustrates that there can be 'good' and 'real' reasons for behaviour (Haire, 1950). The indirect questioning approach employed in this project was to ask women what sort of housewife would have compiled the shopping lists shown in Table 1.9. One half of the sample had list 1, which differed from list 2 only by having instant coffee included. The instant-coffee shopping list was seen to have been drawn up by a lazier, less well-organized woman who was described as not being a good housewife. Direct questioning, on the other hand, revealed good reasons for preferring real coffee, which revolved around the product not tasting as good as drip-grind coffee. Respondents were considered to be unwilling or unable to reveal their true (real) reasons for not buying instant coffee.

Table 1.9   Haire's shopping list

Shopping list 1	Shopping list 2
$1\frac{1}{2}$ lb hamburger	$1\frac{1}{2}$ lb hamburger
2 loaves Wonderbread	2 loaves Wonderbread
Bunch of carrots	Bunch of carrots
1 can Rumfords baking powder	1 can Rumfords baking powder
1 lb Nescafé instant coffee	1 lb Maxwell House drip-grind coffee
2 cans Del Monte peaches	2 cans Del Monte peaches
5 lb potatoes	5 lb potatoes

Source: Haire (1950)

Word Association Test

This type of test, also known as 'free association', involves firing a series of words at respondents who must state immediately which other words come into their minds. Word association tests can be used to determine consumer attitudes towards products, stores, advertising themes, product features and brand names. A frequent association with 'Volvo', for many years, was 'safety'.

Psychodrama

Here, the respondent is asked to play a role and, to do so, they are given a complete description of the circumstances. For instance, the role-playing of respondents to depict two alternative painkillers with other respondents playing the role of the pain. How the 'painkiller' tackles the 'pain' might lead to the copy strategy in direct response and other advertising campaigns (Cooper and Tower, 1992).

Cartoon Test

Informants are presented with a rough sketch showing two people talking. One of them has just said something represented by words written into a 'speech balloon' as in a comic strip. The other person's balloon is empty and the respondent is asked how this other person might reply (Figure 1.12). The idea is that the respondent's *own* feelings are *projected* through that reply.

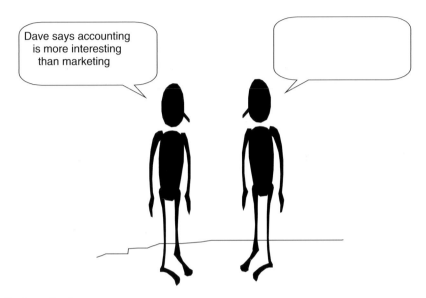

Figure 1.12   Cartoon test

MEANS–END CHAIN ANALYSIS AND LADDERING

As mentioned in the 'Values' section, a useful technique is repeatedly to ask the respondent (words to the effect of) 'What does that mean to you?' For example, it is typical to start with product or service attributes such as those shown in Figure 1.13 and to encourage the respondent to work through a series of 'consequences' towards their own motives and values. Product features or attributes are thus 'creating' benefits, and these benefits are contributing to the realization of consumer needs and values. The sequence of 'attributes → benefits → values' is called a 'ladder' or a means–end chain (Gutman, 1982; Reynolds and Gutman, 1988).

> **www.** **Take a look at the article by Woodside (2004), Advancing Means-End Chains by Incorporating Heider's Balance Theory and Fournier's Consumer Brand Relationship Typology, which is accessible from the accompanying web site: www.wiley.com/go/evans. We refer to this again in Chapters 3 and 11 because it integrates concepts from those chapters with the means–end chain approach.**

Figure 1.13   Means–end chains using laddering

SUMMARY

■ It might be tempting to assume that a 'need' would be for the necessities of life whereas a 'want' would be for something that is merely desired in, perhaps, a 'luxury' sense. This is *not* the marketing view. Marketing sees 'needs' as being any motivator that encourages some sort of behavioural response. In this way, a need can certainly be for the necessities like food and drink, but can equally be for more social and psychological reasons. Needs are motivational forces providing direction and intensity of behaviour: both approach and avoidance behaviours. Approach behaviour results from a positive motivation (sensory gratification, intellectual stimulation and social approval). Avoidance behaviour results from a negative motivation (problem avoidance and problem removal).

■ Motivated behaviour occurs when an individual perceives an external goal (incentive) and experiences internally a need or drive which stimulates them to reach that goal. Motives can be classed as biogenic (psychological and safety needs) or sociogenic (affective, esteem and actualization needs). Both of these types of motive are useful in marketing planning. Cognitive dissonance may also motivate.

■ Maslow provides a view of human motivation which is hierarchical, moving from physiological to social, psychological and spiritual needs. Freud on the other hand suggests we are motivated by deep-seated drives, which we do not always recognize at a conscious level.

■ Satisfaction of needs and wants is a major emphasis of the marketing concept and they are often activated through social interaction, observation, vicarious learning (imitation), advertising and just due to the presence of products. Marketing may make latent needs manifest (through specific wants and desires) but it does not create needs in people. People are not always aware of the 'real' needs determining their behaviour, so advertising may sometimes appeal to these subconscious and unconscious needs.

■ Marketers can improve the effectiveness of their targeting activities by investigating the reasons consumers go shopping. Consumers can be motivated to shop by personal and social motives, hedonistic and utilitarian motives and cognitive and affective motives.

■ Values are more enduring and can be gleaned from means–end chain research. Other forms of research are important for exploring what motivates consumers, such as projective techniques.

QUESTIONS

1. **Find some examples of Freudian symbolism in advertising and packaging.**

2. **Using your course as a product/service, create a needs–features–benefits framework and discuss its use in marketing the course.**

3. **Discuss the reasons why consumers go shopping.**

4. **Find *three* press advertisements and for each of these:**
   a. Decide what are the likely target market and promotional objectives, based on media and message used and your knowledge of competition within such markets.
   b. What do Maslow and Freud contribute to explaining the message used and motivational factors in the target market?

5. **Choose a product or service, and then design projective techniques to explore why consumers do or do not buy it.**

FURTHER READING

Elliott R (1999) Symbolic Meaning and Postmodern Consumer Culture, in **Brownlie** D *et al.* (eds) (1999) Rethinking Marketing, Sage. This chapter concisely summarizes the key issues in symbolic consumption and contextualizes them within **postmodern society**.

Packard V (1957) The Hidden Persuaders, McKay, New York. No marketing student should miss this one. It might be old and some of the content will seem dated, but the critical analysis of the use of consumer psychology for marketing purposes will still provide food for thought.

Woodruffe-Burton *et al.* (eds) (2005) Toward a Theory of Shopping, Journal of Consumer Behaviour, Vol 4 No 4. This Special Issue of *JCB* is an excellent amalgam of research for a number of countries. These papers contribute much to our understanding of consumer shopping behaviour.

CHAPTER 2

CHAPTER OBJECTIVES

After engaging with the material presented in this chapter and its associated exercises and reading, you should be able to:

■ Integrate the application of concepts from psychology within the first stages of a model of how consumers respond to marketing activity

■ Explain why consumer exposure to marketing activity is selective and suggest ways for marketers to overcome this

■ Examine ways of creating conditions for a greater likelihood that consumers will attend to the marketing message/offering

■ Apply some of the principles of the psychology of perception to increase the likelihood that consumers will interpret the message/offering in the intended manner.

CONSUMER RESPONSE TO MARKETING ACTIONS: 1
EXPOSURE, ATTENTION, PERCEPTION

INTRODUCTION

In this chapter we introduce a model of how consumers respond to marketing activities with a view to providing some theoretical and practical implications. The model is called the **hierarchy (or sequence) of communication effects: exposure, attention, perception, learning, attitude, action,** and **post-purchase** (Figure 2.1). This is not necessarily a sequence that consumers follow in all situations, but it provides a logical framework for integrating concepts from psychology to explain how consumers can respond to marketing activity. We will be discussing these *staged* responses in the current chapter and the next two chapters. You need to bear in mind that there are several other sequential models such as: 'AIDA' (attention–interest–desire–action) (Tosdal, 1925; St Elmo Lewis, circa 1900); the slightly more expanded model proposed by Lavidge and Steiner (1961) and labelled by Palda (1968) the **'hierarchy of effects'**. This includes the following stages: awareness, knowledge, liking, preference, conviction and purchase. There are also the stages leading from awareness to adoption (Robertson, 1971), which are discussed in Chapter 9 on new product buying.

- Post-purchase
- Action
- Attitude
- Learning
- *Perception*
- *Attention*
- *Exposure*

Figure 2.1 Sequential effects of response to marketing

In order to understand consumer response to marketing activity, we need to start from what is known as **exposure**. Consumers do not watch every TV advertisement or read every marketing message in store or in the print media. Indeed many consumers will 'channel hop' while watching TV in order to avoid advertisements (**zapping**) or fast-forward through the advertisements in programmes they have recorded (**zipping**). As a result, consumers' exposure to marketing activity is selective. However, when an advertising message comes into contact with a consumer's **senses** (see 'Sensory Systems', under 'Perception and Interpretation' later in this chapter), we say that the consumer is being exposed to the message. In other words, now the message has a *chance* of being noticed by the consumer. There are many forms of marketing activities – such as branding, packaging, point of sale materials, in-store displays, web sites and sales promotional offers etc. – all of which must be placed within the range of a consumer's senses in order to get a chance of being noticed. Obviously, without being exposed, there is no chance that a consumer will respond to any sort of marketing activity. The trouble is that not all consumers expose themselves to all marketing activities, advertising, media and distribution channels, so there are significant implications here for media and distribution channel selection.

But even if the marketing message or offering is in the right place, there is no guarantee that the target group will see it. The marketer's main concern is then to attract the attention of consumers. **Attention** is the stage when the consumer simply notices or sees the message. There are particular techniques that can be employed here, as the section on attention explores.

After being exposed to the message and after paying attention to it, the consumer makes sense of the message. At this **perception** stage, the consumer recognizes, selects, organizes and interprets the message (Harrell, 1986). They may not do so in the way marketers would like them to, but this fact reinforces the value of exploring the psychology of perception here, because it is from this that shared ways of interpretation can be encouraged.

Learning is the stage whereby the consumer remembers the message by storing it in **memory**. This stage is characterized by applications from the psychology of learning. Although the intended meaning of the message might be understood and remembered, this is not the same as the development of a favourable predisposition. At the **attitude** stage, the consumer responds *affectively*, taking a more or less favourable position on the message and thereby establishes a positive or a negative attitude towards it. Thus the attitude stage is, as the name suggests, concerned with attitude theory and how consumer attitudes develop and can be changed. We explore learning and attitudes in the next chapter.

These stages in the hierarchy determine whether an **action** will take place and what kind of action (trial, purchase, usage, asking for more information).

However, once a purchase has been made, this is not the end of the process. At the **post-purchase** stage, the consumer responds by expressing satisfaction or dissatisfaction towards the advertised brand or engages in positive or negative **word-of-mouth** communication with others. One solitary transaction is not the purpose of marketing, which is concerned with regular and mutually satisfying transactions. The study of **cognitive dissonance** can be of benefit in this regard. Action and cognitive dissonance are explored in Chapter 4. Satisfaction with the purchase is a good starting point for repeat purchasing, which could be cultivated to develop **loyalty, advocacy** and even relational interaction between the organization/brand and consumer. Later chapters explore **repeat purchasing** (Chapter 9), loyalty and relational marketing (Chapter 10).

For the current chapter, we start by exploring the initial sequence of exposure–attention–perception. These are sometimes described as being subsets of the perceptual process.

EXPOSURE

In order to be effective, marketers have to make sure that consumers are exposed to their marketing activities. From the marketing point of view, exposure is ensuring that the marketing offering or message is in the right place, at least potentially, for the target market to have access to it. Exposure is a basic requirement if marketers want to change consumer perceptions, attitudes or behaviour.

For instance, while making media choices, marketers have to decide about the proportion of the target audience that should see, read or hear their promotional message during a campaign. While keeping in mind the profile of their target audience and budgetary constraints, they want to make sure that a large proportion of their target market is exposed to their message. Their decisions are based on what is known as **reach**. Reach is the percentage of target audience that would be exposed at least once to your advertised message if you advertised in a medium (such as a newspaper or a magazine). However, exposing consumers to a message just once may not be enough for understanding or acceptance of the message. Therefore, a message is often repeatedly delivered during a particular time period. **Frequency** is the number of times a message is placed or shown during a particular period of time. For example, a high-profile TV advertisement may be shown 60 times or more during just one month. In many media plans, the reach and a minimum or average number of exposures is the objective.

When it comes to television audiences and their exposure to commercials, it is commonplace to calculate television ratings (TVRs). This is a measure of how far a communications channel 'reaches' into the target market. For example, specific TV commercial time slots might reach 100% of the target audience. It might also be thought that to make an 'impact', three exposures would be needed. This is known as 'opportunities to see' (OTS). In this case, the calculation to determine TVRs would be $100 \times 3 = 300$ TVRs. But is it realistic to expect 100% of target market to be reached? Would they all be watching these specific commercials? Probably not, so different calculations can be made based on experience or further research.

Perhaps 50% of target audience might more realistically be reached and it might be thought that there should be more exposures of the commercial to make an impact (often six have been found appropriate). So now the TVR calculation would be $50 \times 6 = 300$ TVRs.

Clearly this adds cost because each exposure is costing air time (often £50 000 per 30-second commercial). So this has to be balanced against the realistic 'reach' of time slots and the estimated number of needed OTSs.

The reach of a newspaper or magazine is different from the number of copies sold. Since more than one reader may read a newspaper copy, the reach of a newspaper is usually larger than the number of copies sold. Similarly, reach of a medium is different from the reach of a part of the medium. Not all readers see all pages of a newspaper and thus miss several advertisements. TV viewers do not see all programmes and commercials. Advertising reach is thus generally lower than medium reach.

EXAMPLE 2.1

An interesting example of advertising reach concerns the audiotape producers Maxell. Rather than selecting media according to the traditional television ratings approach, they asked tape **users** directly what their favourite programmes were. The result was a six-week TV campaign leading up to Christmas with many slots at slightly unconventional times such as 2 a.m. The campaign cost £330 000, which was very inexpensive for a six-week television campaign of the intensity employed.

A number of years ago Lea and Perrins sauce ran a campaign which incorporated door drops of free samples, a small bottle of sauce banded onto magazine covers and sales of the bottle through Tesco for a loss leading price of 19p (Lovell, 1997). In all cases targets were invited to send for a recipe book in exchange for providing data about themselves (nine questions' worth). The exercise was designed to gather data for targeting purposes. By matching the data collected with lifestyle profiles (see Chapter 11) it was found that Lea and Perrins customers were absolutely 'average', nothing peculiar to them seemed to emerge. However, one of the specific questions enquired about television viewing habits; 43% of the Lea and Perrins users said they watched morning programmes on ITV. Had the company relied solely on their demographic and lifestyle profiling, they would not have selected this particular scheduling (i.e. off-peak television advertising) and thus they saved valuable resources and satisfied exposure criteria very effectively.

The society in which we live is characterized by **fragmentation** of media, which poses some serious concerns about the ability of marketers to reach large number of consumers using a mass medium such as TV (Rust and Oliver, 1994). Therefore, achieving the right level of exposure may not be as simple as it sounds. Rather than relying on a single mass medium, marketers can still reach their target audiences by using multiple media (Magrath, 1992).

THINKBOX

In order to appreciate the difficulties marketers have in putting their messages in front of you, consider the number of ways in which *you* avoid them. For example, think of the number of TV advertisements you deliberately zip or zap, the number of print messages you won't even look at and the range of publications you do not read but which would be logical ones in which to advertise to reach people like you.

ATTENTION

Even if the marketing offering is in the right place, there is no guarantee that the market will see it or pay attention to it. Therefore, while exposure is important, it is not enough to ensure that consumers will respond to a marketing activity such as an advertising message. Consumers often scan the media to see whether there is something interesting on TV or in the newspaper. As such, they focus on what is relevant to them. They continue to focus their attention on relevant messages, be they editorial or news (**initial attention**). If the message is not really important for them they continue scanning the medium for what might be (**persistent attention**).

Attention reflects the amount of mental energy or effort that we allocate to stimuli. We normally pay selective attention to marketing stimuli and are often unaware of most of such stimuli in our environment. Marketers, though, want us to pay **focal attention** to their advertised messages to utilize more of our cognitive processes while responding to their marketing efforts. The probability that we will pay focal attention to marketing activities goes up if they have some relevance and are of interest to us.

For example, consider the case of a print advertisement for a washing machine. Most of the advertisement may go unnoticed by us (that is, we will ignore reading the detailed part of the message) if we do not need to buy a washing machine. However, we are likely to pay focal attention to the details of the message (e.g. washing speed, washing load, energy ratings, etc.) if we are already considering buying a new washing machine. Similarly a mobile phone enthusiast will consciously and voluntarily make use of mental ability to process the information and pay focal attention to most mobile phone advertisements.

Although not an entirely reliable estimate, there are several suggestions that every UK consumer is exposed to at least 2000 promotional messages a day but that they probably notice less than 5%. Americans are exposed to 18 million unsolicited telephone calls daily and receive 3000 coupons each per year (Hallberg, 1995). Davidson (1997) suggests that the average consumer in Spain and Italy is exposed to over 20 000 commercials per year. He also submits that £1 m worth of advertising probably only buys 0.1% share of consumer exposure. Goddin (1999) suggests that in the USA there are over 3000 marketing messages per day and that, on average, each US citizen had $1000 spent on them via direct targeting in 1998.

All of this suggests that there is an increase in what is known as advertising **clutter** (too many messages bombarded at consumers). A cumulative effect of clutter is that consumers can become sceptical and can employ advertising avoiding strategies (such as zipping and zapping) to maintain control over their psychic space (Speck and Elliott, 1997). This poses an additional challenge for marketers because they have to make sure that their message is noticed by consumers.

Four aspects of attention may be distinguished:

1. **Gaining attention:** This is important but a difficult task given the clutter of commercial messages.
2. **Holding attention:** Once gained, attention needs to be held in order for the actual message to be conveyed.
3. **Leading attention:** Attention must be guided toward the message and not to peripheral elements in the communication.
4. **Distracting attention:** This is usually ineffective, unless the arguments of the message are weak, in which case distraction might prevent consumers from discovering the weakness of the arguments.

Techniques to Gain and Hold Attention

At the attention stage, marketers are concerned with attracting and maintaining attention and there are particular techniques that can be employed to accomplish this. Among these is the use of colour, movement, position of the message, size, conditioned response, novelty, humour and participation.

Use of Colour

On a general level, colour tends to arrest the attention more than monochrome and indeed different colours have different attention values. The warm colours (orange and red) advance toward us, having the effect of making whatever it is appear larger, whereas the cooler colours (blue) recede, making the message appear smaller. On this basis red is often cited as having the highest attention value. Having said this there can be problems associated with the use of red. The Royal Mail's automated sorting machines cannot read addresses printed in black on a red background and this presents enormous difficulties every Valentine's Day when the use of red envelopes is commonplace.

Using colour in packaging to gain attention is particularly useful for fast-moving consumer goods where a consumer often has to make an instant choice at the point of purchase. A clever use of colour in packaging can draw attention to the brand and can break through the competitive clutter. It can symbolize brand values and can send a powerful emotional signal to consumers.

Different colours have been found to affect search times in store. Jansson *et al.* (2004) investigated a variety of colours and hues and found that basic colours can reduce consumer search times more than non-basics and that there could be real benefits in employing these issues when designing point of sale materials.

It has been found that primary colours particularly attract children, and yellow especially attracts young children (Littlewood, 1999). Furthermore, in studies it is proposed that women are more likely to be attracted to colourful direct mail envelopes than are men (see Chapter 5 and our discussion of 'gender').

EXAMPLE 2.2

In a classic case in the USA, a whisky company supplied display racks to a department store. Whenever a customer physically got close to the rack, a mechanism in the rack released a bottle so it fell, only a short way, to be held again by the rack. This was wonderfully successful at gaining attention; nearly all the customers lunged forward to try to catch the falling bottle. However, although this achieved the aims of the attention stage, it had negative effects on subsequent stages, being thought of as a rather 'sneaky' trick. There is an important message here. Whatever happens in one stage can affect other stages. In this case the attitudes formed were somewhat negative, even though the attention was supremely achieved.

Movement

Movement is another technique used to gain attention. Thus advertising on television or in the cinema is often considered more effective at generating attention than static press or direct mail messages. However, it is possible to simulate movement in a still picture and this is often done effectively with blurred backgrounds suggesting a moving foreground (Figure 2.2). Video cassettes within direct mailings

Figure 2.2   Speeding sports car
BMW: The simulation of movement in print advertising to attract attention.
Source: BMW. Image courtesy of the Advertising Archives

allowing the use of movement are becoming more popular for communicating messages. Similarly there are interactive communications via the Internet and multimedia messaging services (MMS) via mobile phones which can incorporate graphics, music and video clips.

A variation on *movement* is the use of sound and modern technology, which enables the marketer to send 'speaking brochures' containing a 'chip' allowing personalization of each message.

Position

The position of the message is also important in gaining attention. The outside back cover of a magazine, for example, means that the advertising message can be noticed even without opening the magazine at all. Some marketers might include the main component of the message on the envelope of a mailing to increase the chances of it being noticed. Others, however, believe that by doing this, recipients might be more likely to discard the piece before opening because it would be clear it was a piece of direct mail. Variations on this theme include letting an enticing part of the message (e.g. the incentive) show through the window of the envelope. Some believe that the right-hand page attracts more attention than the left because as we browse through the pages from the beginning, it is the right page that is uncovered first. Those, however, who start with the sports page on the rear of a newspaper may well disagree and argue that the left-hand page is the one that is usually noticed first. If a double-page spread is employed then there are no competing messages and so attention could be more likely because of this. A compromise is to cover a double-page spread with a message but using just half of each page.

The 'golden section' technique or 'law of thirds', known by architects and artists, can also be employed. This suggests that if a rectangle is divided into thirds, both vertically and horizontally, then the eye goes to the points of intersection (Figure 2.3). Placing important parts of the copy or graphics at these points might therefore make them more prominent. Additionally, in the context of direct mail, if some of the message is moved to the postscript or 'PS', it is often the case that this will be the part of the letter that is especially noticed and remembered.

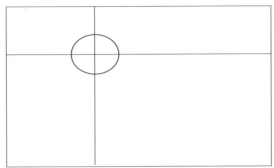

Figure 2.3   The golden section

The 'eye camera' is useful for tracing the path that the eye takes over a 'space' such as a mailing or advertisement (Figure 2.4). In this way different colour combinations or different positions of copy headline can be tried out to find the most effective version for attracting attention to the key parts of the message.

Size

The size of the message has also been the focus of marketing discussion. This is not, however, a straightforward matter. Doubling the size of a message is unlikely to double attention. A suggestion is that attention increases as the square root of the message size increases (Rudolph, 1947).

Conditioned Response

Yet another approach to gaining attention uses known conditioned responses. We attend, almost automatically, to the sound of a telephone ringing and this approach is used to good effect in direct response radio advertising. Other examples include the introduction to a radio advertisement with a statement such as 'Here is a news flash'. A major direct marketer, Avon Cosmetics, uses a ringing door bell and the 'Avon calling' slogan in its promotional approach. See Chapter 3 for a discussion of the theory behind conditioning. The work of Pavlov underpins much of this.

Figure 2.4   Eye camera
The eye camera traces the path the eye takes. This can help determine the best positioning for a poster or even the main message within an advertisement, in order for it to be noticed. This can also help in 'leading attention' to what the marketer hopes will be noticed.
Photograph: Martin Evans

Novelty

If a message is in some way different it may stand out and thus attract more attention. For instance, a monochrome TV advertisement is likely to gain attention because people are not as accustomed to them as they are to colour advertisements. An unusual and distinct message can elicit feelings of surprise due to what is known as **schema discrepancy**. When the contents of a marketing communication message are different from generally expected beliefs, attitudes and/or behaviours, then they are likely to be perceived as incongruent, followed by feelings of surprise. For example, Alden *et al.* (2000) report that as the familiarity with the situation depicted in a message increases, the effect of incongruity on surprise also increases. For example, a TV advertisement may first depict a generally familiar situation to consumers (e.g. people drinking beer in a pub) and then show an unusual event (such as the slamming of the door by a stranger). This increases the effect of incongruity on surprise and thereby gains consumer attention.

The use of surprise in marketing communications can not only gain attention but also encourage consumers to spend more. For instance, while investigating the effect of in-store surprise or unexpected coupons (e.g. electronic shelf coupons, peel-off coupons on product packaging) on consumer behaviour, Heilman *et al.* (2002) reported that the use of the surprise coupon increased the size of the shopping basket and the number of unplanned purchases made on that shopping trip.

In practice many marketers place the distinctiveness of their communications at the top of their priorities. The direct mail industry has a strong track record of employing unusual and attention grabbing mailings. All sorts of items have been sent in mailings and this makes the medium extremely capable of delivering innovative creative ideas (Figure 2.5).

Figure 2.5   Novelty mailings
Telewest mailed a locked safe and a web site address to 2000 IT managers. The web site gave the safe combination access number and the safe included shredded money to reflect a fraction of the sum that the advertiser's secure data transfer system could save.
Photograph: Martin Evans

Certainly, communications do need to stand out from the crowd but because many consumers may be risk averse, communications must also create a sense of familiarity. Thus, the marketer needs to be careful when using novel messages. For example, in an outrageous mailing in USA, Barnes (2001) describes:

> a pigeon in a cage was first trialled … the idea was that recipients would attach their response to the leg of the pigeon which would return 'home'. Surprised at the low response rate, post-campaign research revealed that instead of the birds being released, they were killed and eaten [by some recipients].

Another problem of course is that novelty lasts only a short time so the employment of this approach must be especially dynamic to maintain its distinctiveness. It is clear, though, that marketers are very proactive in this area and they do try different approaches (Figure 2.6).

Humour

The use of humour in marketing communications is often very effective in getting attention and improving brand recognition (Sternthal and Craig, 1973; Weinberger et al., 1995). Weinberger and Gulas (1992) quote prior research to suggest that 94% of advertising practitioners hold the view that humour is an effective attention-getter. In a study involving TV, radio and print advertising, Weinberger et al. (1995) found that the use of humour varied by the media type. TV and radio advertisements used humour two to three times more often than magazine advertisements. Similarly, the use of humour also varied with product type. Humour was used mostly for products such as snack chips, beer, chewing gum, candy, soft drinks, toilet bowl cleaners and laundry detergents whereas it was used least often for high-risk items such sports cars, motorcycles, jewellery and insurance.

Figure 2.6   Novelty
The two cars glued to a poster were advertising Araldite glue, not Ford.
Source: Huntsman LLC. Image courtesy of the Advertising Archives

---

EXAMPLE 2.3

Andruss (2001) quotes a TV ad by FedEx Express that featured a football team's young equipment manager who felt distressed over the whereabouts of five missing boxes of uniforms he had shipped to Madrid for a big match. He was told by an older man that he did not need to worry as long as the boxes were shipped with FedEx (but they were not). The ad then showed a football ground, where a player from the opposing team was about to attempt a penalty kick. As the camera pulled out, viewers saw that the equipment manager's team was defending its goal without uniforms or a stitch of any other kind of clothing. The tagline of the ad stated: 'Let FedEx take the load off your shoulders.' The campaign resulted in an immediate jump in unaided brand awareness levels among the target audience, which in this case consisted of small and medium-size business owners across Latin America.

Participation

Not only is it important to attract the attention of consumers, but also the marketer must hold the attention and convey the message. Attention-getting devices are numerous, but if attention is attracted by methods inconsistent with the message or the situation, this attention is readily lost. Attention may be held by encouraging the audience to participate. Messages which work in this way might be ambiguous or incomplete and for this reason the audience (sometimes through a double take) is encouraged to attend to the message more than would otherwise be the case, in order to complete the message and to make sense of it (the Zeigarnik effect, named after B. Zeigarnik in 1927).

This is known as the **law of closure** (see 'Gestalt Approaches to Perception Organization', below), which suggest that consumers often enjoy 'filling in the gaps' for themselves.

PERCEPTION AND INTERPRETATION

Once noticed, the message/offering should be perceived and interpreted or understood in the intended way. For this stage we draw information from the psychology of perception. Engel *et al.* (1986) understand perception to mean 'the process whereby stimuli are received and interpreted by the individual and translated into a response'.

Sensory Systems

Consumers become aware of their environment through the five senses, as we mentioned at the beginning of the chapter, but we explore sensation here because as well as being the 'receptors' they can also determine how we interpret messages. Table 2.1 summarizes the sort of perceptions that can follow from each 'sense'.

The retail environment provides marketers with many opportunities to play on consumers' senses in order to develop and maintain their relationships with brands (Fulberg, 2003; Jackson and Fulberg, 2003). Often, marketers use the term **store atmospherics** to refer to approaches that tap consumers' senses.

Table 2.1 **Perception and the use of senses**

Perceiving through	Illustration
Vision	Use of colour, pack/product/logo designs are important.
Sound	Music sound tracks to TV advertisements can affect how the advertising message itself is interpreted; use of fast music in-store to speed up the momentum of shopping; pleasant music likely to arouse positive emotions.
Touch	Not well researched, but North Europeans not as tactile as South Europeans (important for face-to-face sales); consumers like to touch fabrics (fabric swatches in fashion catalogues) and this can create problems for on-line marketers.
Taste	Blind tests show importance of brand image (see examples in text).
Smell	Aroma (synthetic or real) of bread baking in store to suggest the bread is really fresh; palm trees in travel agents to conjure up nostalgic memories of holidays in warm climates.

EXAMPLE 2.4

An example of how the law of closure can attract attention in order to 'solve the puzzle' is the use of mobile phone 'text' language. For example, G8 yor M8s. This is being used in advertising to both show a degree of street credibility of brands but also to hold attention for a few more seconds because of its superficial ambiguity.

Posters for Disneyland Paris by Ogilvy Mather Direct are based on capturing images from 8 mm cinefilm before production and end up as 3-D holograms, which are expensive but attention grabbing (Stokes, 1997).

Sometimes the type of participation is not the intended response. One poster advertisement for Levi's jeans actually had a pair of 501s glued to the poster itself. The result was that many people clearly noticed the message because many of them tried to get the jeans, but of course they were positioned too high on the poster for this to be an easy matter (Figure 2.7). This sort of physical participation on the part of the consumer was not intended but demonstrates the attention-grabbing value of the ad as well as the jeans-grabbing aim (of consumers).

Some marketers are experimenting with **multisensory brands**. For example, Nike found that 845 of respondents in a test preferred the trainers in a room infused with a floral scent compared with the same trainers in a non-scented room (Lindstrom, 2005). This is because 'A strong brand appeals to all five senses'. Sounds of products in use are being incorporated in advertising, such as the sound of cereals 'snapping, crackling and popping'. The 'scratch and sniff' technique has of course been used for a long time in magazine adverts for perfumes. As Flynn (2005) states: 'Using multiple senses to create a brand experience can make the experience more powerful and differentiate the brand.'

Figure 2.7   Attention and participation

Source: Levi Strauss

EXAMPLE 2.5

Spies and Hesse (1997), in a study of two furniture stores in Germany with different store atmospheres, found that consumers' moods improved with pleasant, but deteriorated with less pleasant, store atmosphere. Similarly other sensory elements such as sound, often examined as music, can influence consumers' responses to advertising (e.g. attitudes towards the advertisement) and to the retail environments (e.g. spend more money or stay longer in the shop).

One supermarket study found a 38% increase in sales when the supermarket played slow music compared with fast music (Milliman, 1982). In comparison with visual and taste cues, it is often difficult for consumers to recognize and/or label smell cues (Ellen and Bone, 1998). Their ability to recognize odour may be influenced by other cues. For instance, our ability to recognize a lemon scent is much higher if the scent is contained in a yellow rather than, say, a red container (Ellen and Bone, 1998).

Similarly North *et al.* (1999) investigated the extent to which stereotypically French and German music influenced selections of French and German wines by supermarket customers. During a two-week testing period, they placed French and German wines of the same price and sweetness on the shelves with appropriate national flags and played French and German music on alternate days. Findings revealed the sale of French wine increased when French music was played whereas the sale of German wines increased when German music was played.

Figure 2.8 shows a marketer attempting to engage the senses.

It has also been discovered that beers can be perceived as having different taste sensations according to the type of music being played in the background. Apparently the (same) beers tasted stronger when the music harmonized and weak or watery when the music was harsher (Holt-Hansen, 1978). A similar result was obtained in an experiment in which the preference for a ball-point pen was greater when shown with attractive music than with unattractive music (Gorn, 1982).

Figure 2.8   Five senses ice cream
Reproduced by permission of Unilever UK

The development of the Internet as a shopping medium reduces the scope for sensory experiences. However, it has been found that consumers do desire sensory stimuli, yet many on-line retailers do not provide appropriate surrogates (Parsons, 2004).

WWW.   **Take a look at Parsons (2004), Sensory Stimuli and E-Tailers, Journal of Consumer Behaviour, Vol 5 No 1, which can be accessed via the accompanying book web site at www.wiley.com/go/evans.**

How consumers interact with store atmospherics is also relevant and there are three aspects of this: **proxemics, kinesics** and **paralanguage**. Proxemics refer to how people use physical space as a means of conveying information. For example, if the buyer stands far away from the seller, the implication is dislike, thus reducing the likelihood of a transaction. Kinesic behaviour involves the use of body positioning and movement as well as eye contact to indicate one's feelings. Here, greater eye contact between buyer and seller is generally associated with a more positive feeling between the two parties. Realizing this, we would expect the seller to use eye contact as a selling device. One might use various gestures (head nods, hand movements, etc.) to determine effect.

Finally, **paralanguage** refers to the particular choice of words used to transmit information. Yawns, loudness and tempo of voices are also elements of paralanguages. If the consumer felt positively about the sale, they might use words such as 'here' and 'this' as opposed to 'there' and 'that'. When asked about the product at hand, the seller might indulge in an over-inclusion strategy, where responsibility is diffused by attributing it to more than one source.

THINKBOX

Next time you spend time in a shopping mall, make a note of the number of times your various senses are touched by marketing activity.

Sensory Marketing Research

It is interesting to note that market researchers are aware of not only what respondents say but also how they say it. Habershon (2004), for example, is keen to use facial expressions of respondents to supplement their actual words, thus combining both sight and sound within market research. For example, 'The sixty anger expressions share certain core configurational properties which distinguish them from the family of fear expressions, disgust expressions and so forth' (Ekman and Freisen, 2003). In addition, consumer researchers are using brain scans to reveal the nature of brain activity when processing marketing information (Leighton, 2004).

Following from the above-mentioned 'multisensory brands', Lindstrom (2005) describes the need for a measure of consumer reactions that spans the senses – a 'Sensogram'.

Perception Organization

In this section we build up a typology of conventions for perceptual organization, how we make sense of sensory inputs. First, try interpreting the pictures in Figure 2.9.

These pictures were used to demonstrate the importance of *how* messages are presented (Bernstein, 1975). These versions of a hypothetical brand were presented to respondents, who were asked to what sort of product category they might belong. Version 1 produced no uniform reply and nothing very spontaneous was forthcoming. It was seen by different people as being a range of very different categories. Version 2, however, started to produce more rapid replies and ones which were a bit more focused: on a brand stamped on a car tyre or tea chest, presumably because of the stencilled style. Version 3 was stronger again. Most people readily thought of a comic or a powerful cleaner. Version 4 also produced fairly spontaneous and similar responses: a travel company of some kind, such as a ferry operator, airline and so on. The point of Bernstein's experiment was to convey the important message for marketers that

Figure 2.9   KAZON
If each were a brand, in which product category?
Source: D Bernstein, *Creative Advertising* (Harlow: Longman, 1975), p. 128

the way in which something is presented can affect consumers' perception of it. Even the pronunciation of KAZON might influence how consumers perceive it.

Convention 1

Perception is not isolated to the substantive element of a message. Clearly there are important implications here for logo and pack design.

The interpretation of KAZON also shows that if we already hold an image of a brand's logo, a similar logo might be thought to be for a brand in the same product category.

Convention 2

The law of similarity means we are likely to interpret a new message in a similar way to something already in our existing experience.

Figure 2.10 depicts two images in one picture. The experiment here was based on a split sample. One half of the sample was informed that they were going to be shown a picture of an old woman and the other half of the sample a picture of a young woman. Although it did not work with all respondents, most of those expecting to see the old woman saw this image first in the picture (with many going on to see the other image as well) and most of those expecting to see the young woman saw this image first, again with many going on to see the other image as well. To go from one image to the other one has to turn a kind of 'mental switch'.

Convention 3

Our interpretation of a message is often based on 'expectations'.

Gestalt Approaches to Perceptual Organization

Gestalt psychology stresses the fact that perception of a stimulus does not occur in isolation from a host of other variables. The German word *Gestalt* means 'whole' or 'entirety'. This section explores aspects of how we organize our interpretation of messages and sensory inputs. However, rather than producing a list, we invite you to engage with several issues as a way of building up to a series of conventions on perception.

Figure 2.10   The old and the young woman
Which do you see first: an old woman or a young woman? This is a good illustration of an important principle of the psychology of perception. We see what we expect to see.

Figure 2.11   Figure–ground relationships

Have a look at Figure 2.11 and you probably won't have any difficulty in seeing two messages: either a glass or two faces in profile looking at each other, depending whether you use white or black as the 'figure' or the 'background'.

Convention 4

'Figure–ground' relationships can influence how something is interpreted. You can't see both images at the same time.

This was used to great effect in some on the 1930s advertising campaigns by Shell. The classic images were interpreted differently depending on which was taken as the figure or ground.

Earlier we mentioned the law of closure as a way of gaining attention. In that respect, messages which are incomplete and ambiguous can encourage us to take notice just because of their strangeness.

Convention 5

The law of closure can be effective if it encourages consumers to solve the puzzle themselves because they are spending more time interpreting the message.

In Figure 2.13, the two lines are the same length but we are likely to perceive the bottom one to be longer because its 'wings' extend our perception outwards whereas the top line's more inwardly directed wings take our interpretation to a more contracted shorter length. This is an example of the law of continuity.

In Figure 2.14 there is another variation on this process of our minds 'extending' lines. The boxes are the same size and shape but the bottom one might appear taller and thinner if our minds continue the thin vertical lines upwards. This is used in fashion design where, for example, pinstripe suits are supposed to make the wearer appear taller and thinner. Actually the approach does not necessarily produce a 'slimming' effect because where there are extra curves/bulges, the thin lines sometimes are seen to waver, thus accentuating the problems! Larger swirling patterns might be better at disguising such shapes. Conversely, the other 'pack' might appear to be wider and squatter because we continue the wide horizontal band sideways. Perhaps this explains why broad hoop designs on rugby jerseys can make the wearer appear broader than he really is.

EXAMPLE 2.6

The Newcastle Brown poster (Figure 2.12) depicts an irate cat and a bottle of Newcastle Brown. The image here was from a poster in Cardiff and the authors have asked students at Cardiff University if they understand this message. Very few did and complained it was just too ambiguous. Clearly there is another piece of information needed to make sense of this one. As many from Tyneside (more than 300 miles from Cardiff) will know, Newcastle Brown is known as 'the dog'. Armed with this piece of information, the consumer might indeed look twice at the ambiguity but soon fit the pieces together. The ambiguity and its solution can greatly enhance the attention value of marketing messages. But there is no point in assuming the majority of the target audience will have the missing pieces of the advertising jigsaw. This demonstrates that there are different **frames of reference** within a country as well as between countries.

When targeting is more accurate, advertisers and consumers can have fun with messages. For example, another in the Newcastle Brown series pictured a can of the beer with the ring pull having just been opened and the spray forming a speech balloon in which the word 'woof' appeared.

Figure 2.12   Newcastle Brown
Law of Closure – but you need the components in order to make the message 'whole' and make sense: cognitive participation
Reproduced by permission of Scottish and Newcastle. Photograph: Martin Evans

Convention 6

The law of continuity encourages the consumer to continue an element of a stimulus in a particular direction. A core marketing module might well have taken you through the four Ps of marketing (product,

Figure 2.13   Visual illusions

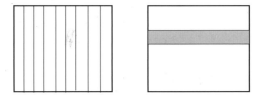

Figure 2.14   Extending lines

price, place and promotion). However, when you, as a consumer, perceive a brand, it is likely that you do not think atomistically in terms of each 'mix' element in isolation from the rest. Instead you probably think of the whole brand experience. Gestalt perceptual processes are ultimately based on the whole being greater than the sum of the parts.

Convention 7

The whole is greater than the sum of the parts.

www.   **Have a look at this web site, which discusses aspects of gestalt perception:**

http://www.cultsock.ndirect.co.uk/MUHome/cshtml/perception/percep4.html

THINKBOX

BMW used the tagline, 'A car is more than the sum of its parts', to encourage a $2 + 2 = 5$ sort of interpretation of the car and The Beatles might have produced pretty good music as individuals after their break-up but the amalgam of all four was a world beating synergy.

How can a brand be more than the sum of its parts ?

Colour

Under 'Attention' we discussed the use of colour in attracting attention. In this perception stage, we return briefly to the use of colour. Different colours can transmit different meanings and emotions. Most colours have both positive and negative meanings and of course different colours are more or less fashionable at different points in time.

For example, Cadbury's use of purple in its packaging is very effective in communicating 'luxury' and 'quality' images to consumers (Figure 2.15). For many years, Virgin has cleverly used the red colour in its logo as well as in most of its packaging materials to send a clear signal to consumers that it is an active, stimulating and energetic brand. The phone company Orange not only uses the colour orange extensively in its branding; it even uses it as its name

Figure 2.15   Use of purple by Cadbury

©Cadbury Schweppes plc. Reproduced by permission

Use of particular colours in communication is like making a fashion statement. Just as fashion and trends change, so does the use of different colours by marketers. That is why most manufacturers of cars change 30% of their colour offerings every year and rely on the expert advice of colour consultants well before a particular colour is introduced (Triplett, 1995).

The meanings associated with colours are culture-specific and hence people in different cultures can associate different meanings to the same colour. For instance, in a cross-cultural study of colour meanings and preferences involving eight different countries, Madden *et al.* (2000) found that red was perceived as active, hot and vibrant across all countries. However, while black and brown were perceived as 'sad' and 'stale' across all cultures, yet the same colours had additional meanings of being 'formal' in Brazil, Colombia, China and Taiwan and of being 'masculine' in Austria, Hong Kong and the United States. The meanings associated with colours can change across cultures but within cultures as well. For instance, in the USA, while black clothing generally conjures up funereal images, in urban markets across America, black clothing is perceived as 'trendy' (Gimba, 1998). Table 2.2 summarizes colour perceptions in the USA as per Kanner (1989).

Table 2.2   Colour perceptions in the USA

Colour	Perceived meanings
Red	Exciting, hot, passionate, strong
Green	Secure, calm, natural
Blue	Authority, commands respect
Black	Sophisticated, mystery, power
Yellow	Warmth, novelty, caution

Summarized by the authors from Kanner (1989).

Marketers also need to take into account the needs of those consumers who have colour-deficient vision and who cannot perceive some of the colours that people with normal colour vision can (Kaufman-Scarborough, 2001). A student was reprimanded while on placement with a company a few years ago. His role was a 'rep' for a cosmetics company and although he knew he was mildly colour-blind, he managed to totally confuse the colour-coded shampoo packs and stocked his retail customers with the wrong product versions.

Convention 8
Colour can influence perception.

www.	Have a look at these web sites, which explore the use of colour in general and in marketing:
	http://www.web-design-uk.biz/web_design/psychology_color_marketing.htm
	http://www.infoplease.com/spot/colors1.html

Sensory Thresholds

A further consideration is that our perceptual senses have limits. These are called **absolute sensory thresholds**. The point here is that, although a message might exist, our senses are not capable of picking up all sensory inputs. Our hearing or sight is not as acute as that in some members of the animal kingdom. One implication of this has already been discussed in a different context – subliminal messages (in Chapter 1). If a message is below our sensory threshold it is just possible that although the message is not perceived consciously it might be subconsciously.

EXAMPLE 2.7

'Veteran' readers may remember the 'run-out' (first pressing only) track of the Beatles' *Sergeant Pepper* album. If played with a dog in the room, this can produce strange behaviour from the animal because, unperceived by the human listener, the police dog whistle on this track would be clearly heard by the dog!

A marketing application of the sensory threshold concept is the use of an audio message as part of supermarket muzak that says something to the effect of 'I must not steal'. The message might be below the sensory threshold to be consciously heard but perhaps it reaches the mind subconsciously (see Chapter 1). If so, by definition, the receiver is not consciously aware of the message so does not put up emotional barriers to the message and may therefore react as intended.

---

www.	Have a look at the following web sites, which explore subliminal perception in greater detail:
	http://www.arts.uwaterloo.ca/~pmerikle/papers/SubliminalPerception.html
	http://www.csicop.org/si/9204/subliminal-perception.html

Sensory Discrimination

A variation on this sensory threshold point concerns sensory discrimination. That is, can we always detect differences between similar sensory inputs? The marketing application here is reflected in the many taste tests that are regularly conducted. A recent group of students, for example, conducted a taste test as part of their marketing research module. Before the test most claimed to like chocolate, and that they preferred one particular brand. Indeed many claimed that they would be able to identify that brand in a blind test (in which all brand identification is removed). Respondents stated which sample of chocolate they preferred and which brand they generally preferred. Most also thought that the sample they liked in the test was also their generally preferred brand, but of course it was not. This sort of experiment demonstrates the importance of branding, advertising imagery, packaging and so on, in affecting consumers' perception of a marketing offering. It again shows the importance of the 'whole' over the components of the marketing mix.

Often, retailer brands try to emulate national brands in terms of packaging. For example, Figure 2.16 shows national and retailer packs of men's cosmetics. This is an attempt to reduce discrimination between brands in the hope that consumers might go for the cheaper own label because it looks the same as the highly advertised national brand. This is another example of the law of similarity.

THINKBOX

We bet that you will probably say that you prefer particular brands of beer, chocolate, fast food, colas etc. but can you *really* identify them in blind tests? Try this with some friends. If you do not always identify your claimed preferred brands, what does this say about:

1. your perceptual process, and
2. the power of branding, packaging and advertising?

Figure 2.16   Attempt to narrow sensory discrimination
The black packs are of the national and retailer versions respectively. Would you mind which you bought?
Photograph: Martin Evans

Just Noticeable Difference

Another dimension of sensory discrimination, concerning the degree to which consumers might or might not notice a change in some marketing message, product design or package, is what is known as the 'just noticeable difference' (JND). Consider the incremental changes in pack design in Figure 2.17.

Many marketers will use their knowledge of this to make changes over time in such a way as not to make it obvious that they are making changes. But minor changes to pack design can keep the brand appearing fresh and up to date even if the changes are not particularly noticed.

The same logic can apply to changes to price levels. Rather than a major change in one move, the product might be moved up or down the price ladder in stages, such that each sequential change is barely noticed by the majority of consumers. Those who are especially involved (see Chapter 4) with the product or service concerned are, however, more likely to spot these incremental changes. Conversely, if a marketer actually wants consumers to notice a price difference – for example, when marking-down stock for a 'sale' – they would try to ensure that the change was above the JND. Miller (1962) has suggested such a price change (for 'sales' to be noticed) should be around 25% of the previous price and anything less would not be effective.

The JND is the degree of change needed for a consumer to notice a difference between two stimuli 50% of the time. Experimentation on JND has a long history and it was Weber in 1834 who found one of the most robust relationships in any psychological concept. Weber found that if a stimulus is initially 'intense' or strong, a greater change is needed for individuals to notice it. He used the senses of sight and sound for his research and came up with a formula for the relationship between the strength of the initial stimulus and the degree of change needed to be noticed:

$$\frac{\Delta I}{I} = K$$

where ΔI = the JND,
I = the strength or intensity of the stimulus, and
K = a constant, which is different for each sense.

Weber's work was applied to marketing by Miller (1962).

For example, consider a change in the weight of a tin of tuna fish. In research it might be found that, from the initial 300 g size, 50% of respondents only noticed a difference in the amount of tuna for their toasted sandwiches when it reached 280 g.

Figure 2.17   Pack design changes
Each change might not always be noticed, even though the cumulative effect over time is significant.
Reproduced by permission of Robert Opie

Therefore, substituting in Weber's formula:

$$\frac{21\,g}{300\,g} = 0.07 \, (\text{a } 7\% \text{ change in tin weight is needed before a change is noticed})$$

In other words, the marketer might 'get away' with reducing the tin to 280 g and consumers would not notice the difference.

The 'constant' means that for other sizes of similar products – e.g. a large 600 g tin of salmon might be reduced to 558 g (600 g – 7% = 558 g) – consumers would not notice the difference in the amount of fish. It has been found that because of different 'constant' values for taste and smell, marketers of ready meals, for example, might need to manipulate the aroma of a 'new improved' dish more than its taste, in order to ensure a difference is noticed.

THINKBOX

Manufacturers of light bulbs could have taken advantage of the JND by selling 95-watt bulbs. As with cars advertised as having a 2-litre engine (when it is really 1975 cc) the light bulb manufacturer might say you are getting the light of a 100-watt bulb for less usage of electricity, assuming the consumer might not be able to tell the difference in brightness between 95- and 100-watt bulbs.

Is this a rip-off?

Selective Attention and Perception

We have already said that consumers are bombarded daily with many thousands of messages. One way of coping with this constant bombardment of information and persuasion with which the individual has to contend is through selection of what is perceived.

The precise manner in which the person allows some messages to penetrate or 'get through' while rejecting others depends on their values, motives and attitudes as well as their social situation, current interests and preoccupations. Messages which are in tune with what the individual already believes stand a much better chance of gaining attention and being perceived than those which are at odds with their preoccupations or tangential to their interests and needs. **Perceptual vigilance** is where consumers are open to what they are interested in and even seek it. **Perceptual defence** is where consumers avoid messages which are not congruent with their view of the world. We discuss this further in Chapter 4.

The fact that different individuals might perceive the same message differently, or selectively, might lead to the conclusion that the above discussion is totally irrelevant, that there is nothing we can do to affect perception. This is very far from the truth because the more we understand about the perceptual process, both generally and of the target market concerned, the more we can ensure that intended receivers of the message will interpret the message in the intended way. The A and B regions in Figure 2.18 are the fields of experience of the sender and the receiver. Region C is the common frame of reference for the message between sender and receiver. If the sender of the message understands the frame of reference of the receiver and puts the message in terms that mean the same to both sender and receiver, there is a greater chance of effective communication. The receiver will then perceive and understand the message in the intended way.

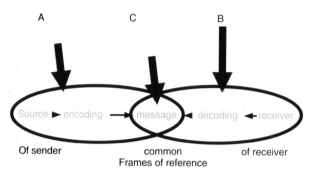

Figure 2.18   Schramm and Roberts' model of communication

Source: W Schramm and D Roberts (eds), *The Process and Effects of Mass Communication.* (Urbana IL: University of Illinois Press, 1971). © Board of Trustees of the University of Illinois. Used with permission

For example, consider a crooked sign in long-hand writing advertising fresh eggs, found along a country lane and outside a rustic country cottage. This would probably be congruent with the receiver's frame of reference for 'happy hens' and free range eggs. The same sign in a city centre probably wouldn't be. Conversely, if the sign read 'flying lessons' then the receiver might be less tempted to ask for further details in the rustic cottage than in a more urban setting!

As we mentioned earlier, there are so many distractions for the consumer these days, such as advertising clutter, all of which constitute **noise** in the communications process and can hinder the message either getting through at all or being interpreted in ways other than the intended.

EXAMPLE 2.8

The recent outsourcing of call centre provision to other countries – for example, India – has seen unusual training of the operatives, in order for them to work within a similar frame of reference to those who call them. They are trained to know about current UK weather and storylines in TV soaps so they can converse more casually.

This shows that the interpretation of meaning is also dependent upon the context of the consumer's own cultural knowledge and understanding. That is why perceptions of reality differ from consumer to consumer as each person interprets social and physical stimuli so that these fit their overall culturally determined world view.

Product Perception

It should be clear by now that it is important to look at things from the consumer's perspective, That is, rather than thinking in terms of what we are *making* and *selling* marketers should empathize more and think in terms of *what benefits* consumers buy and how they perceive products and brands.

How consumers perceive a range of brands can be researched to build **perceptual maps**. How consumers perceive the product in terms of image relative to competing offerings (Ries and Trout, 1986) is extremely important and marketers should use an understanding of this to position their own brands. In this way, brand positioning is not actually something that is done *to* a product – rather it is something that marketers do to the minds of consumers.

EXAMPLE 2.9

Figure 2.19 shows an example of positioning for travel agencies. This suggests that the segments of customers labelled 'specialist', 'price buster' and so on, require differing degrees of control, both over the travel/tour buying process and with the degree of specialized or standardized 'package' the agency provides. Whether this approach would be adopted by travel agencies is debatable, but it could be a significant and worthwhile change in how different known customers are treated in-store.

Figure 2.19 Travel agencies: service needs and perceptual mapping
Source: Forster (1997)

Perception and Evoked Sets

If consumers mapped a range of brands, it is likely that they would not be aware of some of the brands in a product or service category. This is known as their **unawareness set**. They may be aware of some brands and be able to bring to mind some of them which they consider purchasing – this is called the **evoked set**. They may also know some brands but remain indifferent to them. This is called the **inert set**. They can also know and reject brands based on experience or information. This is called the **inept set**. Through the use of marketing communications, marketers aim to make sure that a right kind of brand association (see Chapter 3) is created in consumers' minds (e.g. cool, innovative, trendy). However, becoming part of consumers' evoked set is often a hard task because only few brands get their place here.

Perception and Intangibility of Services

Intangibility means that services cannot be touched or grasped. Intangibility also means that services are incorporeal – that is, they do not have physical bodies and they do not exist in physical space and therefore they cannot be sensed by our physical senses (Mittal, 2002). The intangibility of services poses some additional challenges when it comes to perceiving and comprehending services and developing communication programmes for them (Legg and Baker, 1996; Grove *et al.* 2002). Table 2.3 presents an overview of creative approaches as suggested by the service advertising literature to address the problem of intangibility and other services problems (Legg and Baker, 1996; Mittal, 2002).

Because of the intangible nature of services, it is difficult for a service organization to understand how its customers perceive and evaluate the quality of its services (Parasuraman *et al.*, 1985; Zeithaml, 1981). However, customers make inferences about service quality on the basis of tangibles (the buildings, the physical layout, etc.) that surround the service environment. Support for this argument comes from empirical evidence suggesting that the tangible, physical surroundings of the service environment can have a significant impact on customers' affective responses and their behavioural intentions (Wakefield and

Table 2.3   Creative approaches to improve consumers' perceptions of services

Creative message treatment	Examples
Show the physical components of a service delivery process	The AA van rescuing a stranded customer
Focus on the tangibles	Show physical facilities, equipment, appearance of personnel
Use vivid information	Any information that creates very strong mental image of service
Use specific and concrete language	'Strong research capability', 'Sound analysis', 'Experts in delivery'
Use relevant tangible objects to improve comprehension	'Under the traveller's umbrella'; 'The Nationwide blanket of protection'
Use interactive imagery	Direct Line's use of moving telephone, Lombard Direct's use of talking telephone
Present objectively document data on past performance	The punctuality record of a train company
Show a typical service delivery event	An employee going out of the way to help a customer
Show testimonials from customers about some aspect of service	A letter from a satisfied customer
Show a typical customer experiencing the service	A customer getting a good deal for his home insurance; 'Quote me happy' campaign by Norwich Union Direct
Encourage people to speak positively about the service and use personal endorsement	BT's use of 'It's good to talk' campaign
Educate customers for service process	Easyjet's web site providing information to customers about what they need to do during the service delivery
Communicate backstage operations, rules and policies to improve confidence	A service company showing their backstage operations in a TV ad
Use dramaturgy	AA's dramatic use of service delivery process

Blodgett, 1999). Dabholkar *et al.* (1996) reported similar findings, that the tangible aspects of department stores do influence customers' perceptions of service quality.

Legg and Baker (1996) argue that even when consumers comprehend services and realize that the service is useful in satisfying their needs, they may still experience difficulties in developing a list of potential service providers in their minds. Advertising helps to create brand identities by associating a brand's name with some sensory images (e.g. a symbol, logo, graphics or other visual form). Mittal (2002) argues that creation of brand identity is easier for a physical product because it has a tangible form, which acts alongside the associated visual forms to lead to clear brand identity. However, in the case of services, symbols alone have to do the job of creating brand identity by capturing the core meaning or essence of the service. For example, many service providers use relevant phrases or logos to create a clear brand identity in consumers' minds (e.g. Direct Line, loans4you.com, insure.com).

Mortimer (2001) conducted qualitative interviews of creative directors in the UK and reported that the respondents perceived intangibility to be the most prominent characteristic of services. The respondents suggested a greater emphasis should be placed on personal recommendations and on not promising something that could not be delivered. They also believed services relied upon trust and relationship and therefore clear and consistent branding campaigns to build familiarity and trust were important for service advertisers. The issues of loyalty and relationships are discussed in Chapter 11.

SYMBOLISM IN PERCEPTUAL INTERPRETATION

Marketers are sometimes turning to the study of symbols and signs (**semiotics**). Here, marketing messages will have three elements: the 'object' (e.g. the product/brand itself), the 'sign' (e.g. the imagery used in the message) and the 'meaning' (which is how the recipient interprets the message) as shown in Figure 2.20.

The marketer can:

1. relate signs in the message directly to the product or brand. For example, using an *icon* that is almost as good as a picture of the product, such as a telephone on wheels to promote a telephone-based motor insurance company.
2. relate signs in the message that share common properties. For example, using an *index*, such as depicting scented flowers in the advertising of an air freshener.

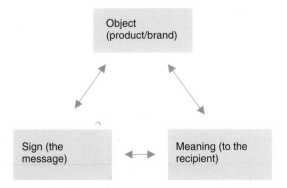

Figure 2.20   Semiotics triad

3. relate signs in the message that have agreed associations. For example, using a *symbol* such as the US cowboy to create the 'rugged' persona for Marlboro cigarettes (that is, before the model died of lung cancer).

The article at the end of Part 1 provides more details on the nature of symbolic consumption, so we will not take this issue further at this point.

SUMMARY

■ The model of pre- and post-purchase buying stages introduced in this chapter is an example of a 'hierarchy of effects' sequential model. Such models allow the discussion of what otherwise might appear to be discrete topics within a more integrated framework. In this chapter we have explored the concepts of exposure, attention and perception.

■ There are important implications for the placing and timing of marketing messages in order to match the intended target market's likely exposure to media. Similarly, there are techniques which marketers can employ to increase the likelihood of their messages being noticed. In order to gain attention, marketers can use movement, or simulated movement, novelty, participation and colour.

■ From the marketer's perspective, it is clearly important for consumers to notice marketing activity and then to respond in the way the marketer intends. Perception, which refers to the reception and interpretation of external stimuli by an individual, begins with the process of sensation and is a selective operation. Without attention being given to a stimulus, perception will not take place; and people give their attention largely to those things in which they have an interest, or which are novel, or from which they derive pleasure and satisfaction. Consumers react to advertisements, products, packages and so on according to their motives, attitudes and social situation, and each individual's perception of these marketing mix elements is unique to him or her.

QUESTIONS

1. **Identify and discuss some of the widely used techniques to gain and hold consumer attention. Conduct an experiment to test your ideas.**

2. **What is perception? What is the role of our five senses in perception? Use some common examples to illustrate.**

3. **Services are characterized by many features, such as their intangibility. Use your own examples to discuss the impact of intangibility on services advertising. How can marketers resolve those problems?**

4. **Select some press advertisements or packages that are good illustrations of the use of any of the following:**

    a. Perception of colour

    b. Use of visual illusions

    c. Ambiguity and participation.

How might theory be applied in each case? What is the likely effectiveness?

5. **Provide examples of the JND principle from price, pack and product changes. Conduct an experiment to measure the JND for a change in the price of a brand of beer.**

FURTHER READING

Foxall G, **Goldsmith** R and **Brown** S (1998) Consumer Psychology for Marketing, 2nd edn, International Thomson Business Press, London. This is a good summary of a number of aspects of psychology within the marketer–consumer context. It examines cognitive processes such as perception, learning and attitudes. There is also coverage of motivation, lifestyles, consumer choice, **postmodern consumers** and consumer behaviour within social and consumption environments.

Jackson M and **Fulberg** P (2003) Sonic Branding, Palgrave, Basingstoke. 'Silence is golden' as the Tremeloes asserted in their 1967 song. However, it isn't, according to this book. There is much to be gained from the use of sound in branding and this is the book from which to learn. It also provides wider coverage of what brands are and how they communicate with consumers.

CHAPTER 3

CONSUMER RESPONSE TO MARKETING ACTIONS: 2
LEARNING, ATTITUDES

CHAPTER OBJECTIVES

After engaging with the material presented in this chapter and its associated exercises and reading, you should be able to:

■ Integrate the application of concepts from psychology within a model of how consumers can respond to marketing activity

■ Apply aspects of behavioural learning to increase the likelihood of consumers remembering and learning about the marketing message/offering

■ Apply aspects of cognitive learning to increase the likelihood of consumers remembering and learning about the marketing message/offering

■ Analyse and evaluate different approaches to explaining the link between attitudes and behaviour

■ Explain different approaches to attitude formation and change

INTRODUCTION

The last chapter focused on exposure, attention and perception stages of our **hierarchy of effects** model. This chapter moves the discussion forward by focusing on the learning and attitude stages of the model (Figure 3.1). If the consumer noticed and interpreted the marketing message in the intended way, we now need to explore ways of encouraging the consumer to learn effectively about the marketing activity, to remember the message and then to develop favourable emotions and intentions toward it.

In this chapter we explore aspects of both learning and attitude and provide examples of how these concepts apply to consumer behaviour. We also show how marketers can benefit from understanding these concepts.

- Post-purchase
- Action
- Attitude
- Learning
- Perception
- Attention
- Exposure

Figure 3.1   Sequential model of response to marketing

LEARNING

Assuming that the marketing offering is interpreted appropriately, learning is concerned with ensuring it is remembered in the intended way. Marketing communication may be considered to be concerned with teaching consumers about various marketing offerings. If this is the case, marketing itself can benefit from knowing about how consumers learn about things.

Indeed, learning is closely associated with perception: learning influences perception and, in turn, depends upon it. Also, both processes are intimately connected with and shaped by the individual's motives (Chapter 1), attitudes (this chapter) and personality (Chapter 6).

Learning can be explored by using either a behavioural or cognitive approach.

Behavioural Learning

The behavioural approach to learning is based on what is known as the stimulus–response model. Within the behavioural school of thought, there are two popular approaches to learning: **associationist learning** (or **classical conditioning**) and **instrumental learning** (or **operant conditioning**). We discuss both of these in the following sections.

Associationist Learning: Classical Conditioning

Associationist learning is based on the early work of the Russian physiologist Ivan Pavlov (1928) and on the work of Skinner (1938). Pavlov considered learning to be essentially concerned with stimulus–response relationships. His experiments included observation of dogs' responses to different stimuli. He observed that the dogs in his experiments salivated when they were presented with food. However, there was nothing exceptional about this. It is a natural and even automatic response to a stimulus like presentation of food. What was really fascinating was that he also observed that the dogs salivated not only when they were given the food but also whenever they heard the footsteps of the assistants who brought the food to them. Pavlov went on to present various other stimuli at the same time as presenting the food. Again the dogs salivated. This process (repeated 'paired stimuli') was also tried with other stimuli (the sound of a tuning fork, light bulb being flashed, etc.). After repeatedly presenting food with these other stimuli, Pavlov again presented 'the other' stimulus by itself and the dogs salivated to just the tuning fork, light bulb and so on, even though no food was present. What he argued was that an unnatural response to the light or sound had been conditioned into the animals. This type of learning became known as **classical conditioning** and is summarized in Figure 3.2 with its application to the car market.

Figure 3.2   Associationist learning: classical conditioning

Marketing might not operate precisely at the level of Pavlov's experiments but the principles are used every day. If marketing understands the target market's **frame of reference** (see Chapter 2) – for example, status appeals/benefits or sex appeals/benefits – it can present that relevant appeal repeatedly and the market is likely to respond favourably to the appeal itself. But then if the brand is presented at the same time, with plenty of repetition of this paired stimuli approach, the market may well learn to associate the brand with that particular appeal/benefit.

In Chapter 1, we argued that marketing does not create needs, but rather encourages a want for a specific product because of the association between the acquisition of the product/service and the satisfaction of a need. This is the basis of the associationist learning approach. The approach explains why consumers learn to associate certain beliefs and feelings with certain brands and many of our preferences are learned this way.

EXAMPLE 3.1

In Figure 3.3, an advertisement for rail travel creates an association between road travel and discomfort. This also reflects the approach of increasing negative emotions toward competing products/services and is explored in more detail in Chapter 4, in our coverage of cognitive dissonance.

Another example of association concerns the use of celebrities in advertising. In Figure 3.4, for example, Madonna's characteristics and what she stands for may well transfer to the brand (Versace) she is endorsing in the advertisement (see Chapter 9). Similarly, through the constant pairing of specific music to a brand in a TV ad, marketers aim to condition the response of consumers.

Although this is not a specific marketing application, especially writing from Cardiff, we cannot resist a rugby example. Some years ago the then Coach of the England rugby team, Geoff Cooke, decided that the support the Wales team received from home supporters in the

Figure 3.3　Associating a competing product with discomfort
Reproduced by permission of Scotrail and DDB London

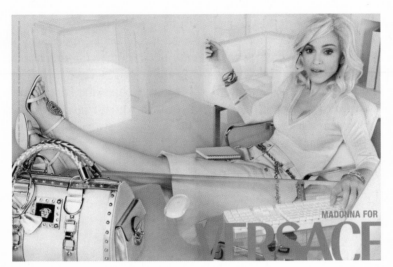

Figure 3.4   Associating a brand with a celebrity

Source: Versace. Image courtesy of the Advertising Archives

Cardiff stadium was so significant that it needed to be counteracted. Specifically, he wanted to reduce the power of the Welsh anthem, before kick-off. He played especially passionate versions of this to the England players but as a soundtrack alongside a film of great England tries against Wales in Cardiff (yes, there have been some!). The idea was to encourage the England players to associate the Welsh anthem with good English play.

THINKBOX

The associations attached to a large number of well-advertised brands can be explained by this process (Table 3.1).

Table 3.1   Some famous brand associations

- Volvo = Safety
- Golf Gti = sporty
- BMW = quality
- Levi's = youth
- Wrangler = cowboys
- Benetton = colourful

Try this for yourself. Get a friend to list some well-known brands and then to ask you to spontaneously come up with what they mean to you. You might be surprised at how your associations match marketers' intentions as reflected in the advertisements for these brands.

Instrumental Learning: Operant Conditioning

This is another behavioural approach to explaining learning and it relates to the consequences that similar responding has produced in the past. Skinner's work resulted in **operant conditioning.** Here, the frequency of occurrence of a specific behaviour is modified by the consequences of the outcome of that behaviour. This learning approach recognizes that learning can be encouraged and even reinforced through the use of positive and negative reinforcers. Generally speaking, marketers want to increase the rate at which learning takes place and to reduce the rate at which consumers' memory decays. For example, several researchers have drawn on studies of the psychology of reinforcement. **Reinforcement** is closely allied to one of the oldest and simplest of laws that psychology has produced – the **laws of effect** – which states that actions that are enjoyed or satisfying are repeated (Figure 3.5).

Figure 3.5   Operant (or instrumental) conditioning

For instance, by offering a price reduction (e.g. 10% off on everything bought) at the time of purchase, marketers can increase the probability that the consumer will repeat their behaviour (e.g. will shop at the store again). Similarly, a customer is likely to walk past a store where their complaints were met with abusive outbursts. Walking past and shopping elsewhere avoid such aversive consequences and are said to be negatively reinforced; i.e. their rate of repetition is increased by avoidance/escape rather than by approach.

Now, it is obvious that a consumer who purchases a particular brand is likely to repeat this buying pattern only if they derive an acceptable minimum level of satisfaction from the purchased item. Consumers who are disappointed in their choices are likely to switch to alternative brands. For this reason, advertising and other promotional efforts must make claims which can be borne out by the consumer's post-purchase experience of the product (see our coverage of cognitive dissonance in the next chapter); the strength and amount of reinforcement are directly related to the number of behavioural repetitions the customer makes. When the outcome of buying the same product/service is similarly rewarding over repeated purchases, the consumer can develop a habit of buying that brand. In this way, operant conditioning can go some way to explaining **habitual buying.**

Continued positive reinforcement from habitual buying may be difficult to break, but at the same time a single disappointing reaction to a particular brand may not be enough to overcome all the reinforcement that has previously taken place.

THINKBOX

Consider your own buying behaviour. To what extent can your buying be explained by operant conditioning? What other factors might be involved?

Repetition is clearly an important dimension of behavioural learning and marketers need to consider the number of 'exposures' of the message that should be used. We have already covered of 'reach and frequency' in Chapter 2, but there are issues that are especially pertinent to the learning process, which we examine here.

Repetition Effects

As we have seen, repetition of 'paired stimuli' can help create associations via classical conditioning but, in a wider context, how many exposures are needed for optimal learning of the message? The concept is also sometimes known as **advertising wearout**. This is where diminishing marginal effects take place after repetition. There is a clear link here with the reinforcement stage of operant conditioning because without repetition it is difficult for solus marketing activity per se to aid retention. It is not valid to state precisely how many exposures are needed because of individual learning characteristics, the nature of the message itself, its timing and influence of competing messages and influences from the environment.

However, a somewhat glib rule of thumb is that four categories of exposures might be needed. The first, to achieve awareness, the second exposure to relate the message to the target consumers' frame of reference (to show relevance), and the third to remind of the benefits of the product or service concerned. As we discuss in the next chapter, it is also the case sometimes that consumers seek reassurance, after they have purchased something, that they have done the right thing. So a fourth category of exposure can be helpful at that stage. We also suggest that there is likely to be a degree of repetition of exposures for each of these four stages, but the precise number depends on the product, the message, the consumer and a host of situational and competitive factors, making a definitive and universally applicable number of exposures difficult to state. The general point is surely pertinent, though, that repetition effectiveness increases over a certain number of exposures, then stabilizes and eventually declines.

www.	Visit the following web site for a summary of classical and operant conditioning:
	http://www.wilderdom.com/personality/L9-1ClassicalConditioning.html

Cognitive Learning

From a cognitive perspective, learning involves more than stimulus–response processes. The latter is sometimes equated with the mind being a black box with a stimulus being the input and a response being the output. With cognitive learning the focus is very much on what happens within the black box (mind) and the nature of the cognitive processes involved in learning.

Consumers also engage in **reasoning** when they encounter some information in their lives (e.g. brand information) and deduce their own conclusions regarding the information's suitability, relevance and importance to them. This may involve integration of new information with existing knowledge already stored in memory or the evaluation of a brand's attributes against some criteria to determine brand suitability. Consumers devote more effort, time and cognitive energy than with behavioural stimulus–response-based learning.

The level of involvement which a consumer has with the situation is important, too. We discuss involvement in the next chapter but it is worth mentioning the **passive learning** theory of Krugman (1965). He stated that when consumers are exposed to mass media, either they lack personal involvement or they exhibit a high degree of involvement. In the low-involvement mode, consumers process very little of the information received, but repeated exposures to the information leaves a basic perceptual structure in the mind leading to low-involvement learning. But even with low-involvement situations, learning is more than a mere stimulus–response sequence.

We can also learn by observing others, thinking about what they are doing and how it might apply to ourselves. The imitation of the behaviours of others is known as **vicarious learning**. Not only can a consumer observe the actions of others – and, when the perceived consequences of their actions are seen to be positive and attractive, the consumer may well imitate that behaviour – but also they can avoid those actions seen to be unattractive. A range of consumer behaviours (such as shopping, interaction with sales assistants, brand selection and consumption) can be modelled for consumers who pattern their future actions on the basis of examples observed.

Gestalt Contributions to Learning

In the previous chapter we discussed gestalt approaches to perceptual organization. The gestalt school of psychology is also relevant here, in terms of explaining learning processes. A major figure within the gestalt school was Kohler, who proposed that learning took place in more of a cognitive way than the behavioural stimulus–response approach could achieve. He demonstrated this with a number of experiments with apes, and one ape in particular displayed **insight** by being able to put the components of a problem together to form a (greater) whole, or a solution. These experiments were conducted around the same time as Pavlov's but Kohler thought there was more to human learning than mere stimulus–response relationships. Kohler presented apes with a variety of puzzles.

One such puzzle involved an ape in an almost bare cage, with a bunch of bananas hanging from the roof. The architecture of the cage made the bananas difficult to reach. Kohler left a table in the corner of the cage. What the apes wanted was to learn how to get the bananas, but they were left to solve the problem on their own. Nothing much happened for some time until one ape, Sultan, eventually moved the table to be underneath the bananas, stood on the table and managed to reach the fruit. Kohler described the extra element of mental processing in the learning process needed to solve problems as 'insight'.

The law of closure, the law of similarity and the law of continuity have already been discussed in Chapter 2 as contributing to how consumers can be encouraged to attend to and then interpret messages. We return to the gestalt approach here because, where consumers need to devote relatively significant amounts of mental processing to learning about a marketing message/offering, that learning can itself be especially effective and enduring. This is because the consumer has to participate in the marketing activity and, as the old adage has it, *learning by doing* is often more effective.

So the marketing implication is that because the 'problem' is not solved at the immediate superficial level, by encouraging participation, marketers are tapping into this process of insight.

EXAMPLE 3.2

An example of encouraging more effective learning through 'doing' was reflected in an Oxfam mailing. This included a tape measure which could be used to measure whether one's child's arm was small enough that they could be classified as suffering from malnutrition, as given in enclosed tables of wrist diameters of malnourished children. The process of comparing a well-fed Western child with a starving one in a poor country adds more to learning about the general issue than a mere copy headline requesting donations to Oxfam.

A somewhat more dubious example comes from France and concerns a poster campaign. The first poster showed a bikini-clad woman and copy to the effect that in two days' time she would remove her top half. Two days later another poster appeared with the woman topless and copy promising the bottom half would be removed in another two days. Sure enough on the appointed day another version appeared with the woman, now naked with her back to the camera! The copy this time merely stated that the company keeps its promises. The objective here was to show potential advertisers (the poster was run by the poster owners themselves) that the poster *medium* could produce more responses than many clients had thought.

In this way, the campaign used the gestalt law of continuity because the images told a story which needed all three, in sequence, to make sense. The approach required the recipient to engage with the story, which tapped insightful learning. Although this would probably have been ambiguous to the consumer, it would make more sense to advertisers who were sceptical about the poster medium being able to be responsive within days rather than the common belief (at the time) that a poster could only be held for a month.

Figure 3.6 shows part of a Volkswagen insert produced for the launch of the new Golf. As well as providing information about the car it also included a cardboard cut-out model which consumers could make. The more time spent experiencing the product (even in model form), the greater the learning about its design and features.

Figure 3.6   Learn by participative 'doing'
Reproduced by permission of Proximity London and Volkswagen Group UK Ltd

> **THINKBOX**
>
> Discuss gestalt psychology and its role in developing 'participative' marketing messages. Does 'tapping insight' work for you, when you are encouraged to 'learn by doing' when marketing activity uses gestalt laws?
>
> It is also suggested that younger segments are more interested in participative marketing messages than are older segments – do you see this among the young people you know? Why, or why not?

Stimulus Generalization and Discrimination

Once learned, a consumer can often extend their response to other similar stimuli. For instance, in the case of a popular brand, consumers are likely to be already familiar with the brand and are likely to hold some favourable, strong and unique brand-related images and associations in memory. On the basis of this, and using the principle of stimulus generalization, the brand name can be extended to new product categories, hoping that consumers will react positively to the new products. This practice is known as 'family branding strategy' and is very popular among marketers. Other marketers encourage stimulus generalization (that is, usually, making their brand look and sound like a competitor), hoping that the consumers' feelings for the competitor's brand will be generalized to their own brand. Also, by using similar packaging to national brands, own label brands can be perceived in a similar light and this can reduce the need for spending as much on promotional activity as is spent on national brands. This is also why some national brands defend their packaging or logos with vigorous litigation against those who copy them.

'Stimulus discrimination' refers to consumers learning to make different responses to similar stimuli. Some consumers have strong brand preferences and learn to discriminate among essentially identical products. Marketers of well-known brands often aim to make their brand distinctive in consumers' minds so that the consumer will discriminate and associate positive feelings only with their brands and not with their look-alikes.

Measurement of Learning

Most measurements of learning involve some verbal response to interviewer questions. The answers indicate the degree of awareness, recognition and/or recall aroused in the respondents by the (e.g.) advertising. What is measured is the proportion of each sample who, upon being shown an advertisement, claim to have noted it (the **recognition method**), or who, upon being shown a brand advertised in a magazine they have read, can 'play back' enough of the advertisement to indicate that they have in fact seen it (the **aided recall method**).

The limitation common to these studies is that the respondent's claim of having been exposed to advertising cannot be taken at face value. Recognition scores do not necessarily decrease with the increase in time since reading, through memory loss, as might have been expected. This suggests that the respondent was 'recognizing', not the advertisement they had actually seen, but the likelihood that this was the kind of advertisement they would have noted, given the opportunity. Recognition could also result from previous purchases rather than be the cause of later ones.

Respondents also sometimes claim to recognize 'control' advertisements they could not have seen. The extent of misclaiming can be related to the respondent's interest in the product advertised, and other personal characteristics. Such studies also appear to be ineffective as predictors of future behaviour. What is retained by respondents may have nothing to do with their subsequent purchases. **Selective retention** operates here as well.

Indeed the selective processes affect all stages so far – **selective exposure**, **selective attention**, **selective perception** and **selective retention**. The techniques and theory on which to base marketing approaches, however, provide potential means for ensuring a reasonable degree of uniformity of response even though there is equally the potential for individualistic responses.

ATTITUDES

If the hierarchy of effects 'sequence' has 'worked' so far, then the message has:

- been communicated via appropriate vehicles to reach the target market,
- gained attention,
- been interpreted the intended way, and
- been remembered in the intended way.

We are now concerned with developing favourable attitudes toward the marketing offering/message. Loudon and Della Bitta (1993) suggest that an attitude is 'an enduring organization of motivational, emotional, perceptual and cognitive process with respect to some aspects of the individual's world'. This is useful, especially at this stage in the book, because it serves to reinforce the integration of some of the concepts explored so far (e.g. motivation, perception and learning).

A person's attitude is a major outcome of the learning processes that we discussed earlier in the chapter. That is, on the basis of whatever is learned about the stimulus or object, an individual develops either a liking or a disliking towards it. More specifically, an attitude refers to a predisposition to respond in a consistent or predictable manner to a stimulus. This explains why attitudes are always towards some stimulus (or 'object'). The stimulus can be anything, such as a physical or a social object (e.g. a brand, a retail store or even a person), an action (e.g. going to watch a football match or make a purchase), an idea (e.g. capitalism) or even advertising.

The Structural Approach to Attitudes and Attitude Change

One of the most enduring approaches to attitudes is the proposition that an attitude has three components: cognitive (beliefs), affective (emotions) and conative (intentions) (Figure 3.7):

- A *cognitive* component – this consists of a person's beliefs or knowledge about an issue or an object, such as the reliability of a car or its fuel consumption. These beliefs might not be accurate in terms of product specifications or objective assessments of reliability, but are in many ways more important because they reflect how the individual perceives the case to be, even if there is a mismatch between their beliefs and reality;

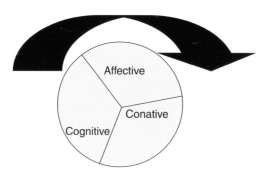

Figure 3.7   Attitude components

- An *affective* component – this consists of a person's feelings or emotions about the issue of the object; these feelings can be 'positive' or 'negative'. These are based on the beliefs about the object that the individual holds; and
- A *behavioural* (conative) component – this consists of how the individual is likely to respond to the object based on what they know about it and how they feel about it; that is, that individual's 'readiness to respond behaviourally' to the object.

This approach has been especially useful in researching attitudes (see later section) because it provides a framework for devising questions that cover each component in order to be able to measure attitudes holistically.

The structural approach also helps in the definition of communications objectives, message creation and campaign evaluation. Objectives can be defined by discovering the nature of beliefs with regard to the marketing 'object', whether 'affect' is favourable or unfavourable, and whether the target audience exhibits any intention to buy. Messages can be tailored depending on what is discovered during this analysis. Campaigns may also evaluated by measuring these same dimensions over the course of the campaign (and before–after it) in order to identify if it changes attitudes.

Balance Theory

Related to the concept of cognitive and affective components is Heider's (1958) balance theory, which argues that consumers try to maintain a degree of balance between cognitive and affective components and in this respect the approach is congruent with **cognitive consistency**. If we experience inconsistency between the components, we will change our attitude in order to create harmony. The theory provides a 'triad' framework of the consumer, the attitude 'object' and some other person (Figure 3.8)

For example, Martin has a somewhat negative attitude toward Microsoft because he perceives it as having a world-dominating and monopolistic marketing strategy. Microsoft introduces a new software product called 'NoMoreRedEye' which automatically eliminates red eye from digital photographs as Windows Explorer opens them. Martin is initially negative toward 'NoMoreRedEye'. However, his friend Gordon is an absolute computer whiz kid and recommends the product highly. Martin's attitude toward Gordon is one of strong friendship over many years. The imbalance needs resolving. Martin could either change his attitude toward Gordon or toward 'NoMoreRedEye'. In this case he changes (but only just) his attitude to being more positive toward 'NoMoreRedEye'.

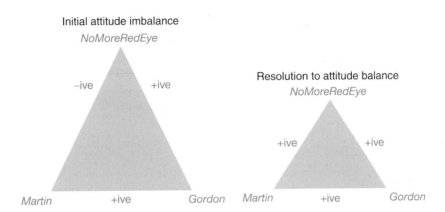

Figure 3.8   Balance theory

The balance theory has important implications for marketers and is yet another explanation of the use of celebrities in marketing messages. A brand toward which a consumer has a slightly negative attitude can be seen in a different light if a celebrity who is especially liked by the consumer is used to endorse it and thereby transfers the positive attitude to the brand.

www.	In Chapter 1 we discussed the means–end chain approach to uncovering motives and values, and recommended an article on this to you. That same article also incorporates Heider's balance theory within the means–end chain method, and is accessed via the accompanying book web site at www.wiley.com/go/evans: Woodside A G (2004) Advancing Means-End Chains by Incorporating Heider's Balance Theory and Fournier's Consumer-Brand Relationship Typology, Psychology and Marketing, Vol 21 No 4 pp 279–294

THINKBOX

Have you ever changed any attitudes in the way implied by Heider's balance theory? Why or why not?
  How else could the theory be used by marketers and consumers?

Attitude Measures

Marketers are often keen to discover consumers' attitudes towards their product offerings or the offering of their competitors. They can measure attitudes using different rating scales. However, measuring attitudes requires special consideration because it is far too easy and superficial to ask a respondent a question like this: 'What is your attitude towards Bloggo Brand?' only to receive a reply along the lines of 'I like it', or 'It's all right'. While such feelings may be important, it would be of greater use to uncover the reasons for such feelings and the type of actions in which they are likely to result; that is, using the tri-component structural approach to attitudes.

If intentions are based on specific elements of knowledge (beliefs) and evaluations, these beliefs and evaluations need to be discovered if the results are to be meaningfully used. Furthermore, such attributes are perceived by respondents with varying degrees of strength, so that the concept of degree in measuring attitudes is unavoidable. While some form of scale is required, the straightforward like/dislike continuum would be of only limited value. A more useful approach is to compile a series of scales, each measuring a different attribute of the same attitude. If a department store wishes to identify any scope for improvement on the one hand and perceived strengths to accentuate on the other hand, there are a variety of attitude scaling methods that can be employed and these are outlined below.

Semantic Differential Scales

The **semantic differential** incorporates a set of five- or seven-point bipolar scales (Figure 3.9). The scales are characterized by opposites such as good/bad, active/passive, hot/cold, rough/smooth and strong/weak.

For example, consumers can be asked to express their attitudes towards the direct mail that they receive by ticking or circling a number on the scale. One advantage of the semantic differential is that it provides a convenient way of comparing attitudes to different elements (e.g. the same scales could be used to elicit responses to mobile phone marketing, interactive television, email marketing, as well as direct mail) on the same scales, and a useful pictorial representation can be produced to compare attitudes to all of these objects.

Likert Scales

Respondents may be presented with a series of statements about the topic concerned, and asked to indicate their degree of agreement with each, according to a five-point scale ranging from 'strongly agree' to 'strongly disagree'. It is important, though difficult in practice, for the range of statements offered to cover the range of cognitive, affective and conative aspects that any given topic involves. Figure 3.10 shows a version of the **Likert scaling** technique, where a mixture of positive and negative statements allows respondents' consistency to be checked.

Both the semantic differential and Likert scales can be used quantitatively by assigning values to each scaling position, and average scores for all respondents' replies can be calculated, either for each scale or in an overall summation.

We have to be very careful with attitude measurement, however. As is often the case with the use of opinion polls to predict voting behaviour, respondents might not always reveal their true attitudes toward political parties or to their voting intentions. Indeed these intentions may change right up to the moment of slipping their voting card into the ballot box.

For the direct mail you receive, in general do you think it is:

Interesting	1	2	3	4	5	Uninteresting
Informative	1	2	3	4	5	Uninformative
Intrusive	1	2	3	4	5	Not intrusive
Entertaining	1	2	3	4	5	Not entertaining
Damaging to the environment	1	2	3	4	5	Not damaging to the environment
Relevant to you	1	2	3	4	5	Not relevant to you

Figure 3.9 Semantic differential

Please indicate your level of agreement or disagreement with the following statements:

	Strongly agree				Strongly disagree
I like having product or service information communicated to me by organizations	1	2	3	4	5
I like to decide for myself when and where to look for product or service information	1	2	3	4	5
The more that organizations know about me, the better they can meet my needs	1	2	3	4	5
I really don't mind about marketers having my personal details	1	2	3	4	5
There is a need for strong laws to control the sharing of personal information	1	2	3	4	5
For the direct mail I receive, marketers have generally got my details correct	1	2	3	4	5
I like to deal with organizations over the phone	1	2	3	4	5
I like to deal with organizations through the post	1	2	3	4	5

Figure 3.10   Likert scaling

Across a range of attitude measurement studies, respondents frequently answer according to how they think the interviewer might like them to respond, or to how they think 'most' people would feel about the issue. The latter is called the **bandwagon effect** (Nancarrow *et al.*, 2004). Also, what people say they intend to do and what they actually do are usually quite different and frequently have no relevance to their attitudes. According to Kauffman *et al.* (1997), 'People lie consistently and people's behaviours are going to lag behind what they say.' Engel *et al.* (1995:394) agree with Kauffman *et al.* (1997) and state that:

> People do distort or hide their true feelings, particularly when the topic is heavily value laden such as alcohol and tobacco consumption, environmentalism and nutrition, yet accurate prediction of specific behaviour requires the use of specific measures that correspond to behaviour.

THINKBOX

Try to analyse the components of your attitudes towards the course you are studying.

How might these be converted into a questionnaire to investigate students' attitudes toward the course?

Fishbein's Multi-Attribute Model (Attitude Toward Object Model)

According to Fishbein (1973), our attitude towards an 'object' (e.g. a product or a brand) is predicated upon what we consider to be an appropriate range of beliefs about that object and how we evaluate these. Respondents might be able to score brands or products along each semantic differential scale (belief) but they might not regard all bipolars as of equal importance or favourableness. So the idea is to elicit not only a rating along each belief scale, but also a favourableness rating of each scale. Multiplying the two for each scale and aggregating the scores provides a more meaningful analysis. The attitude is thus the summation of the weighted belief scores.

For instance, imagine John is an A-level student and that he is going to university next year. He is asked to indicate his beliefs about two universities on a scale of 1 to 5 for each of the attributes such as research quality, teaching quality, library facilities, social environment and computing facilities (Figure 3.11a). John is then asked to indicate the importance *to him* of each of the attributes using a scale of 1 to 5 (Figure 3.11b). The ranking scores for each attribute are reported in the third and fourth columns of Figure 3.11c. The results for attribute importance are reported in the second column of Figure 3.11c. The researcher then multiplies scores for each of the attributes with its corresponding importance score and adds them together. The summed weighted belief scores of 56 and 68 represent John's attitudes towards each university.

Alternative Attitude Models

As we have seen, there are clear uses of the tri-component approach within the structural approach to attitudes but at the same there are criticisms of it and there are different views as to the sequence between cognition, affect and conation.

For example, the conative component is sometimes not seen as a determinant of consumer attitudes, rather attitudes are viewed as *determining* the conative component. That is, a person's behavioural intentions will depend on their attitudes. It is not difficult to find reports that cast doubt on the relationship between consumer attitudes and behaviour in the marketplace (Festinger, 1964; Wicker, 1969; Calder and Ross, 1973).

So, different sequences are available for how cognition, affect and conation operate. Solomon *et al.* (2003) provide a summary of these. They apply the hierarchy of effects specifically to attitudes. They call conation 'behaviour' (but remember this is actually *intention* to behave, not actual behaviour) and, as a result, use the 'ABC' acronym (Figure 3.12).

Thus there is a continuing debate about how attitudes predict behaviour, regardless of their structure and formation. Having said this, it can be assumed that some knowledge of an individual's attitude will increase the likelihood of understanding the individual's intended and actual behaviour. The most significant development in the use of attitudes as a predictor of behaviour has probably been the recognition of additional predicting variables, used to overcome some of the problems. For example, it is also likely that attitudes depend to some extent on the level of the involvement in the topic or purchase issue, by each individual. We recognize this and explore the nature and implications of 'involvement' in the next chapter.

Other such variables might be unpredicted and uncontrollable, such as social or peer pressure. We explore these issues as specific concepts in consumer behaviour in Chapter 7 but they also contribute to another set of attitude models discussed in this chapter. The potential influence of both attitudes and social influences is explicitly recognized in Fishbein and Ajzen's (1975) theories of reasoned action and planned behaviour.

The Theory of Reasoned Action

The theory of reasoned action extends the original tri-component model by the inclusion of what other (relevant) people might be perceived to think about the topic (object). This is the key addition and is called the 'subjective norm'. Figure 3.13 graphically summarizes this theory.

Please place an X on each of the following scales to indicate your beliefs about how these universities rate on these features:

	Strongly Agree	Agree	No View	Disagree	Strongly Disagree
I believe the University of Cardiff has excellent research ranking	5	4	3	2	1
I believe the University of Poppleton has excellent research ranking	5	4	3	2	1
I believe the quality of teaching at the University of Cardiff is good	5	4	3	2	1
I believe the quality of teaching at the University of Poppleton is good	5	4	3	2	1
I believe the social environment at the University of Cardiff is reasonably good	5	4	3	2	1
I believe the social environment at the University of Poppleton is reasonably good	5	4	3	2	1
I believe the University of Cardiff has excellent library facilities	5	4	3	2	1
I believe the University of Poppleton has excellent library facilities	5	4	3	2	1
I believe the University of Cardiff has very good computing facilities	5	4	3	2	1
I believe the University of Poppleton has very good computing facilities	5	4	3	2	1

Figure 3.11a John's beliefs about two universities

Please place an X on each of the following scales to indicate the extent to which each of the following is important to you:

	Strongly Agree	Agree	No View	Disagree	Strongly Disagree
It is important for me to study at a university with excellent research ranking	5	4	3	2	1
It is important for me to study at a university with good teaching quality	5	4	3	2	1
It is important for me to study at a university with a reasonably good social environment	5	4	3	2	1
It is important for me to study at a university with excellent library facilities	5	4	3	2	1
It is important for me to study at a university with very good computing facilities	5	4	3	2	1

Figure 3.11b Attribute importance by John

Attribute	Attribute importance	Attribute score for Poppleton	Attribute score for Cardiff
Quality of research	2	2	5
Quality of teaching	5	3	4
Library facilities	3	2	3
Social environment	5	5	4
Computing facilities	3	2	3
		56	68

Figure 3.11c John's overall attitude towards each of the universities

Figure 3.11   Illustration of Fishbein's multi-attribute model (expectancy value)

Worst score for a single attribute would be (importance) $5 \times$ (rating)$1 = 5$ and best score would be (importance) $5 \times$ (rating)$5 = 25$

Figure 3.12   ABCs
Source: Adapted by the authors from Solomon *et al.*, 2003.

Figure 3.13   Fishbein and Ajzen's theory of reasoned action
Source: M Fishbein and I Ajzen, *Belief, Attitude, Intention and Behavior*, Reading, MA: Addison-Wesley, 1975

The Theory of Planned Behaviour

The theory of planned behaviour states that the influence of your partner or parents will play an important part in your decision, and the amount of knowledge that you have, be it instrumental (i.e. knowledge-based) or experiential (i.e. feelings-based), will also affect your decision. Other factors could affect attitude here, such as a lack of need, a lack of finance, change in circumstances and a lack of motivation.

The theory of planned behaviour is an extension of reasoned action theory (Ajzen, 1988; Ajzen and Madden, 1986). Attitude toward the behaviour and subjective norm are further extended to include perceived control. This factor refers to ease or difficulty in performing the behaviour and it is assumed to reflect past experience as well as anticipated obstacles (Figure 3.14).

This model predicts behaviour by the intention to perform that behaviour. Behavioural intention is then split into three elements: attitude towards the behaviour, subjective norm, and perceived behavioural

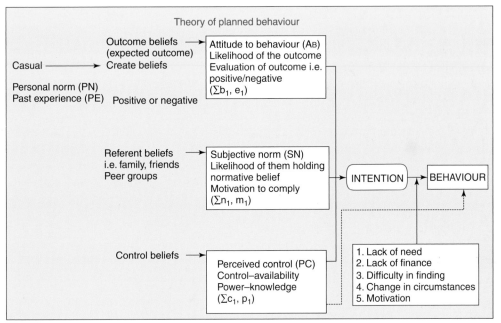

Figure 3.14   Theory of planned behaviour
The correlation is stronger if you have the relevant strength.
Normative salient beliefs determine the thoughts easily brought to mind.
Global measures to cover A_B, SN and PC
Product sum Σb_1, e_1, Σn_1 and $\Sigma c_1 p_1$
Source: M Fishbein and I Ajzen, *Belief, Attitude, Intention and Behavior*, Reading, MA, Addison-Wesley, 1975, p. 48

control. Attitude toward behaviour is predicted by salient beliefs about a behaviour, weighted by the subject's estimation of the likelihood that performing the behaviour will result in a given outcome. Subjective norm is predictive by normative beliefs about what relevant other people (salient others) would advise, modified by the subject's motivation to comply with the advice of those people. Perceived behavioural control is measured through control beliefs that may help or hinder the individual in carrying out that behaviour (Fishbein and Ajzen, 1975).

The Functional Approach to Attitudes

Attitudes can serve many functions for consumers as proposed by Katz (1960) and therefore it is important for marketers to study and understand these functions. He attributes four functions to attitudes:

1. the instrumental function, in which the individual assesses the utility of objects for the attainment of their goals;
2. the ego-defensive function, in which the individual uses attitudes to protect their **self-image** by emphasizing their place in their social world;
3. the value-expressive function, by which the individual expresses their central values and self to others; and
4. the knowledge function, by which the individual constructs the meaning of their world, or gives explanation to both physical and metaphysical phenomena.

Instrumental Function

This is an extension of operant or instrumental learning as discussed earlier in this chapter. If a purchasing experience is satisfying (rewarding), not only are we more likely to repeat it but also we are likely to develop favourable attitudes toward it.

Ego-Defensive Function

There might be an initial desire for a product but a consumer might not be able to afford, for example, a sports car. They might develop unfavourable attitudes toward it by 'defending' their psyche by deciding such a car is, actually, too flashy and ostentatious for someone in middle age. They might also decide that it would be totally unpractical for collecting those shelving units from the local DIY store and indeed someone who has developed a bit of middle-aged spread might find difficulty getting in to the car and even greater difficulty getting out.

Value-Expressive Function

Whereas ego-defensive attitudes actually cover up true feelings (e.g. toward that sports car), value-expressive attitudes deliberately communicate these true feelings, values and self-image (see Chapter 6 for coverage of self-image).

The brands we buy and display or talk about can reflect inner values and our self-image. For example, the purchase of a Harley Davidson motorbike often goes beyond its functions as a mode of transport and allows the values and self-image of the owner to be observable. The consumer who tries to be an ethical consumer might seek a savings account from a financial services company which makes a point about only investing ethically (e.g. not in arms companies or companies which exploit child labour in poor countries, etc.). In such cases, the consumer will display positive attitudes toward Harley Davidson, or the Cooperative Bank, even if their friends don't want to consume the same products/services.

Knowledge Function

As we saw in the previous chapter, we do not 'expose' ourselves to all marketing media/messages and certainly don't 'attend' to the increasing bombardment of marketing activity which is coming through a plethora of media. Indeed attitudes help in the filtering process and extend the 'selective' concepts discussed in the previous chapter. For example, consumers who are especially interested in cars will have favourable attitudes toward almost any new marketing activity concerned with cars.

THINKBOX

How do your attitudes affect your purchasing of durable products?

Changing Attitudes and Behaviour

A great deal of marketing effort is aimed at persuasion, which may be defined for our purposes as 'attempted attitude and behaviour change'. Social psychology has been helpful in this regard in that certain principles of attitude change have been presented in the literature of that discipline. Attitude change remains, none the less, an inexact science.

Attitudes are essentially stable structures and are not easily modified. Thus the first fact on which social psychologists and marketers agree firmly is that attitude change is a difficult and expensive enterprise.

Marketers can think of the attitude components and attempt to focus on one of them in their efforts to change attitudes. For example, in the 2005 UK general elections, the Labour Party produced a leaflet aimed at British Muslims to change their cognitions or beliefs by claiming that Labour's long-standing ties with British Muslims helped Labour deliver a range of benefits for the British Muslim community. The idea here was to change British Muslims' attitudes towards Labour by drawing attention to a number of benefits (which would otherwise go unnoticed) in the context of Labour's controversial involvement in the Iraq war.

Credibility and Discrepancy

Whatever the marketing goals are, the marketing manager endeavours to produce the maximum of attitude change in the market, given budgetary and time constraints. The extent to which this succeeds depends on the credibility attributed to the source of marketing messages by the audience.

Credibility includes both expertise and trustworthiness (Zimbardo and Ebbesen, 1970). In a seminal study into credibility effects, Hovland and Weiss (1951) showed that Americans were more likely to change their attitudes to believe in the possibility of building atomic-powered submarines when a message arguing that this could be done was attributed to a highly credible source, namely J. Robert Oppenheimer, the famous physicist. Persons who were led to believe that the source of the message was the official Russian newspaper *Pravda* were very unlikely to believe that atomic submarines were a feasible proposition! At the time the Americans perceived *Pravda* to be little more than a propaganda tool of (iron curtain) Russia.

Advertisements which feature popular singers, actors, footballers and so on (e.g. Figure 3.4, the use of Madonna in a Versace advertisement) attempt to persuade members of the audience to ascribe the message they receive to a highly credible source. If 'experts' endorse a product, their opinion appears more trustworthy and, especially in view of the fact that many consumers tend to discount much of what persuasive advertising claims, the use of a credible source may be crucial in gaining the audience's attention and in ensuring that selective perception does not cause the message to be screened before it is even considered. (See, also, our coverage of different types of 'power' that social groups can wield, in Chapter 7.)

The exploitation of such methods of opinion change are limited, however. Hovland *et al.* (1953) report that after a few weeks the positive influence of highly credible message sources and the negative effects of low-credibility sources is extinguished. This has important budgetary implications for advertising. Often expensive celebrities are used in advertising as highly credible sources, but their continued use may not only be costly but also may produce diminishing returns relatively quickly in terms of the impact of their credibility.

THINKBOX

It is worth considering a recent development in the role of trust in changing attitudes. One of the hormones found naturally in the body is oxytocin. When subjects inhaled extra oxytocin in an experiment, it was found to have the effect of increasing trust on the part of the person inhaling.

Could it be that the dissemination of oxytocin via, for example, air-conditioning systems in car showrooms might have the effect of enhancing the trust invested in car salespeople? Although it is unlikely that we currently have the technology for achieving this, it raises issues for the future.

Do some research to investigate the current state of this issue, and think about your own position on the value – and ethics – of the approach.

(Kosfeld *et al.*, 2005)

Content and Organization

The content and organization of marketing communications also have implications for the modification of consumers' attitudes. One of the recurrent themes in attitude research is the role that fear plays in persuading people to alter their opinions and behaviour. A considerable body of research findings that relate fear to persuasion has been accumulated, as is shown by a classic review by Sternthal and Craig (1974). First, persuasion through fear is closely related to the credibility of the message's source. The higher the credibility of the originator, the greater the amount of attitude (and, generally, behavioural) change that occurs directly as a result of the fear appeal. This seems to be the case because greater cognitive dissonance (see Chapter 4) can be created when the audience believes that the message source is authoritative than when it is able to deprecate the fear appeal's origin, and cognitive dissonance is resolved through a change in attitude or behaviour or both. Where a low-credibility source is used, message recipients are likely to avoid the fear-inducing message by means of selective attention and perception.

Second, Sternthal and Craig show that characteristics of the message's audience may moderate fear appeals as happens for those whose coping ability is less developed; persons high in self-esteem are vulnerable to fear appeals as are those whose 'perceived vulnerability' is low – e.g. non-smokers or light smokers perceive themselves as having low vulnerability to lung cancer and are more easily persuaded by fear appeals related to cancer than are heavy smokers.

Third, fear appeals are usually effective only when a means of escape from the threatened consequences is clearly depicted in the message. Failure to indicate how the message recipient can avoid the threatened effects of non-compliance with what the message advocates may simply result in the recipient's avoiding the message itself by means of perceptual defence mechanisms. This is important because it has been shown that threats of a social nature (giving offence to others or being ostracized) is more effective than threats of physical consequences. People appear to assume that horrifying things simply will not happen to them and are not easily persuaded to, say, give up smoking, by being shown the physical consequences. It is probably easier in the case of threats of social disapproval to indicate to the audience how the more unpleasant consequences of their behaviour can be avoided.

For example, anti-drink-driving campaigns may be more effective when they portray the effects on family and loved ones of a tragic death of a child due to drink-driving than if the message focuses on the drink-driver.

EXAMPLE 3.3

Saatchi & Saatchi devised a campaign for the Multiple Sclerosis Society to coincide with the London Marathon. The ads appeared in the national press and on cross-track posters in the London Underground. The aim was to contrast the debilitating effects of the disease with the able-bodied runners, using a switch device to show the unpredictable way in which MS can switch off parts of the body (Figure 3.15). Part of the problem for the agency was the recognition that people donate to charities for which they feel empathy, yet relatively few have direct experience of MS. Hitting the right tone was essential to generate that empathy.

This case study demonstrates the sensitive yet powerful use of a fear appeal to change attitudes toward multiple sclerosis (DMA Awards 2003).

Figure 3.16 is an anti-smoking advertisement, targeted mainly at individual smokers, to show what smoking does to their insides.

Figure 3.15   Generating empathy
© MS Society UK/Saatchi & Saatchi. Reproduced by permission

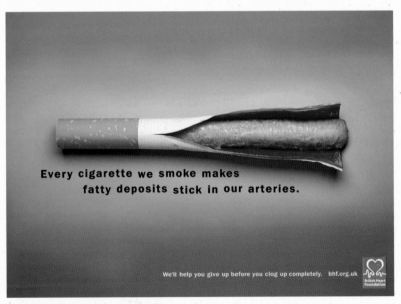

Figure 3.16   A more personal fear appeal
© British Heart Foundation. Reproduced by permission

A consideration which also concerns the content and structuring of advertising messages is that of the one-sided/**two-sided appeal** (Figure 3.17). Should persuasive messages include elements which are unfavourable to the product or service which is being marketed? On the face of it there might appear to be no case for presenting potentially damaging information to any audience, no matter

Figure 3.17 Two-sided appeal
This accepts that attitudes toward Marmite are quite polarized and even plays on this to good effect

how sophisticated and educated it may be, for any amount of damage to the company's image or its brand images must surely result in lost sales and reduced profit. Despite such natural misgivings, there is fairly conclusive evidence that, within a specified context, two-sided appeals (those which incorporate arguments for and against the product or brand) may be more effective than one-sided appeals.

The constraints on this technique are threefold:

1. The market or segment receiving this message must be currently unconvinced of the message's attractiveness (i.e. consumers who are at present not buying the brand and those whose current attitudes make them unlikely to do so in the near future are ideal targets for two-sided appeals).
2. Those most persuaded by the two-sided appeal tend to be highly educated (the academic practice of presenting both sides of an argument seems to appeal to those who have received large amounts of formal education).
3. The technique is advisable where there is a likelihood that the audience will find out about the less attractive (or even unattractive) side of the product anyway (Figure 3.18).

Repetition

As discussed above, with respect to learning, repeating persuasive messages is important and this also helps develop and change attitudes. Indeed learning theory is useful in assessing the extent to which repetition contributes to attitude change. In most cases, repetition certainly appears to be positively related to consumers' expressed intentions to buy, and these are often a good guide to purchasing behaviour. There is always the possibility, however, that constant repetition may lead to boredom and psychological fatigue and that it may then reduce the consumer's intention to buy. The consumer's rate of learning (change in behaviour) is, as we have seen, related to reinforcement through experience of the advertiser's claims

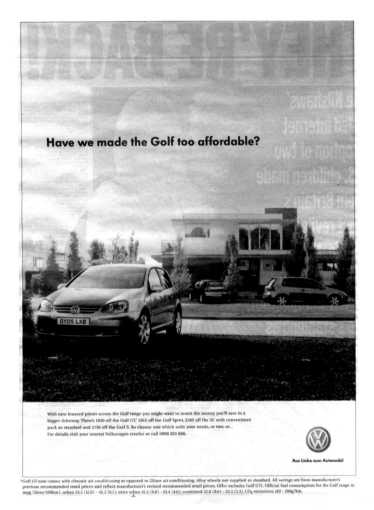

Figure 3.18   Too many Golfs?
This VW advertisement is mildly self-critical in that it questions the company's pricing policy.
Reproduced by permission of Volkswagen UK

and so it is likely that repetition to people who do not buy the product or who have had unfavourable experiences with it may serve only to instil existing negative attitudes.

Attitude Reinforcement

An alternative to changing attitudes is to reinforce those attitudes which already exist among consumers who are favourably disposed to the firm's product brand. There may be scope for increasing sales frequency or for developing new uses for the product. Associated with this is the creative use of word-of-mouth advertising, which will be dealt with in Chapter 9. Denigration of the opposition has also been suggested as an alternative to attitude change (Chapter 4).

Attitude Segmentation

As a final thought on consumers' attitudes and how marketers might benefit from recognizing them, Mitchell (2001) found that consumers could be *segmented* on the basis of their attitudes; in her case, with respect to their engagement with unsolicited direct marketing activity. She identified the following segments:

- **Privacy seekers** – concern themselves with direct mail itself and are concerned that organizations have their personal details;
- **Hostile reactors** – hold negative perceptions about personal selling and telesales;
- **Physical invaders** – concerned about physical invasion of personal selling and telesales;
- **Advertising acceptors** – not concerned about physical invasion in relation to advertising in general;
- **Advertising sufferers** – thought that inappropriate advertising caused them distress;
- **Policy rejecters** – held negative attitudes and rejected the organization's policy suggestions about consumer privacy;
- **Government regulators** – felt that the government should regulate and control unsolicited direct mail and telesales;
- **Individual controllers** – felt that the individual should regulate and control unsolicited direct mail and telesales;
- **Organizational distrusters** – felt that the organization could not be trusted to regulate and control unsolicited direct mail and telesales. (Mitchell, 2001).

This approach could extend the more usual bases for segmenting markets and bring in a more affective dimension, which could be of value to both consumer and marketer.

Our coverage continues in the next chapter with how to encourage the consumer to (positive) 'action' and how to reinforce that action. We also explore levels of involvement with which consumers engage with products and services and show how this affects the sequential model we have explored thus far.

THINKBOX

What factors make you change your attitude toward a company or brand?
Give examples of effective and ineffective attitude changing messages from your own experience.

SUMMARY

■ We have seen that consumer behaviour is a process of learning; it is modified according to the customer's past experience and the objectives they have set.

■ There are a variety of ways of analysing the learning process. We have explored the application within a consumer–marketer context, looking at the behavioural 'classical' and 'operant conditioning' approaches and the more cognitive (e.g. gestalt) approach.

■ Then we examined 'attitudes', which refers to a predisposition to behave in a particular way when presented with a given stimulus, and attitudes towards people, places, products and things are classified as favourable (positive) or unfavourable (negative). Attitudes are composed of three elements or dimensions: cognitive, conative and affective. Behaviour and attitudes are related and each may influence the other, but attitudes and behaviour are not always entirely consistent, and it has even been claimed that attitudes may stem from behaviour rather than vice versa. For marketing, it is usually only important that attitudes and behaviour vary together in some consistent way. There are several ways of testing or measuring attitudes and some examples have been given.

■ Attempts to change attitudes have included methods relating to the credibility of message sources and the amount of discrepancy involved in the communication. Discrepancy may be greater when the source's credibility is high. Fear appeals also work well when source credibility is high. Presenting both sides of an argument may induce more attitude change in an educated audience which is sceptical of the advertiser's claims.

■ The next chapter takes us into the final stages of this model, namely the 'action' stage which serves to convert positive affective and conative attitudinal constructs into a behavioural outcome and then into post-purchase re-evaluation of this action.

QUESTIONS

1. **Find some press advertisements or packages that are good illustrations of the use of associationist learning. How effective are they likely to be? Why?**

2. **Find some press ads or packages that are good illustrations of the use of cognitive learning. How effective are they likely to be? Why?**

3. **How would the theory of reasoned action be applied to a study into consumer attitudes toward the use of mobile telephony by marketers? Design a questionnaire for a marketer wanting to explore 18- to 24-year-old students' attitude towards receiving marketing messages via their mobile phones.**

4. **How would Katz' functions of attitudes apply to your own purchasing behaviour?**

5. **How good at changing attitudes are:**
   a. Fear appeals
   b. Two-sided appeals.
   Find ads that use these approaches. How could you use research findings to judge their effects?

FURTHER READING

Atkinson R L *et al.* (eds) (1999) Introduction to Psychology, 12th edn, Wadsworth. This classic psychology text provides more details of the underpinning psychological concepts we explore in Chapters 1–4. We especially recommend Atkinson *et al.*'s coverage of perception and learning.

East R (1997) Consumer Behaviour: Advances and Applications in Marketing, Prentice Hall. This consumer behaviour text has particularly useful chapters covering attitudes (for this chapter) and loyalty (for Chapter 10).

CHAPTER 4

CHAPTER OBJECTIVES

After engaging with the material presented in this chapter and its associated exercises and reading, you should be able to:

■ Explain techniques that encourage consumers to act upon marketing activities

■ Explain impulse buying and customer satisfaction as important concepts

■ Apply cognitive dissonance theory to help explain how consumers can respond after purchase

■ Explain involvement and discuss implications of levels of involvement for consumer behaviour and for the relevance of sequential models of response to marketing activity

CONSUMER RESPONSE TO MARKETING ACTIONS: 3
ACTION, POST-PURCHASE DISSONANCE, CONSUMER INVOLVEMENT

INTRODUCTION

The two previous chapters have taken us through most of the pre-purchase stages of our sequential model. We now complete these with the 'action' stage followed by what happens post-purchase (Figure 4.1). Marketers are not merely concerned with a one-off purchase but to encourage repeat purchase (as we discuss in Chapter 9, and loyal and even relational buying as we explore in Chapter 10). In this chapter, we provide a discussion and application of a variety of concepts which can help explain not only post-purchase behaviour (such as **cognitive dissonance**) but also involvement which can help marketers determine the extent and nature of the relevance of sequential (**hierarchy of effects**) models.

• *Post-purchase*
• *Action*
• Attitude
• Learning
• Perception
• Attention
• Exposure

Figure 4.1   To the two final stages of the sequential model of response to marketing

ACTION

The whole rationale behind this model is that there is no simple checklist of marketing activities that results in instant action by consumers. The previous stages of response move potential customer through pre-purchase events so that there is a better chance of the conversion of 'intend to buy' into 'buy'.

Impulse Buying

Even the gimmicks aimed at **impulse buying** are to some extent dependent upon some level of prior understanding and interest in the product or service. For example, the point of sale promotions will themselves be building upon the above sequence of events.

Consumers engage in impulse buying when they experience a sudden but powerful and persistent urge to buy a product offering immediately, with diminished regard to the consequences of buying the offering (Rook, 1987). It is often an unplanned decision, which may happen in less than a second and is a common and prevalent feature of the marketplace. We may wrongly assume that impulse buying is associated only with low-value, low-involvement purchases (e.g. soft drinks, chocolates and potato crisps) but as per Rook (1987), it could also be associated with high-value and high-involvement products (e.g. VCRs, microwave ovens, and even a vacation cruise). According to Rook (1987), impulse buying is relatively extraordinary and exciting, emotional rather than rational and is likely to be perceived as bad rather than good.

THINKBOX

Do you normally buy on impulse? Do you think it is a rational or an emotional decision? Share your ideas with a friend who has also bought on impulse.

It might also be assumed that no 'pre-purchase' stages would be relevant with this, but Bayley and Nancarrow (1998) found that there are four styles of impulse buying and we can assume that pre-purchase stages are relevant for some of these: *accelerator impulse, compensatory impulse, breakthrough impulse* and *blind impulse. Accelerator impulse* buying is driven by a desire to stock up for a future need. For example, a housewife may buy on impulse to confirm that she is a good carer for her family. *Compensatory impulse* buying occurs when the buyer either feels 'down' and low in self-esteem and uses sudden purchases as a prop or if purchaser rewards themselves for achieving something or after completing a tedious or difficult chore and use a surprise purchase as a reward. In an old chocolate advertisement, for example, Cadbury depicted people achieving something and then rewarding themselves a medal; a CDM (Cadbury's Dairy Milk).

The *breakthrough impulse* buying is intriguing. It can include some high-value products such as cars and even houses! It appears that the purchaser suddenly decides that whatever underlying emotional conflict with which they have been wrestling can be resolved by a step change in their lives. 'A few years ago Winnie went out to buy a spare set of car keys and signed up for a new car' was how one respondent described an impulse purchase in this category. Another one revealed: 'After a row with his wife he jumped into the car to drive around and cool down. He drove past a house for sale and something made him stop. He put an offer on it there and then and went back to tell his wife the good news'. Finally, *blind impulse* buying is probably what we tend to think of as impulse buying: buying with no underlying purpose and no regard for the fulfilment of any needs of either a functional, social or psychological nature.

An earlier approach to impulse buying, by Stern (1962), identified four forms of impulse buying:

1. **Pure impulse buying,** where the consumer breaks a normal purchasing pattern by buying on sudden grounds of novelty or escapism.
2. **Reminder impulse buying,** where the item is suddenly 'remembered' as being wanted because the consumer recalls that stocks are low or that they intended at some point to buy it.
3. **Suggestion impulse buying,** where the consumer goes through a very rapid evaluation on the spur of the moment without any prior knowledge of the product.
4. **Planned impulse buying,** where the consumer intends to buy, but 'what' is not decided prior to the shopping trip. That is, they know they will buy something, perhaps on the basis of special offers. The 'specials' in stores such as Lidl provide an example of how some consumers know in advance that something from that range will be bought.

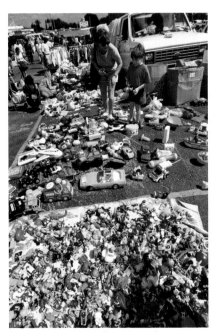

However, within the context of postmodern society, impulse buying can work as an act of freedom allowing consumers to fulfil their desires and feel in full control of their lives (Thompson *et al.*, 1990). It can also allow consumers to reinforce their self-identities. That would probably explain why consumers often end up buying clothes on impulse. One would also imagine that impulse buying is linked to hedonistic shopping experiences whereby sense of adventure and thrill, feelings of excitement and escapism can all lead to a reduction of self-control. Buying on impulse can also be a personality trait (called 'impulsiveness trait'), which refers to a person's tendency to buy spontaneously, unreflectively, immediately and **kinetically** (Rook and Fisher, 1995). That is a consumer with high impulsiveness trait is likely to be more receptive and open towards buying spontaneously.

Certain retail environments such as airports, funfairs, casinos and even car boot sales appear to be particularly suitable for impulse buying. For instance, while waiting at the airport, consumers can engage in impulse buying for a variety of reasons (Table 4.1).

Crawford and Melawar (2003) argued that marketers could take a number of steps to increase the possibility that consumers will buy on impulse in environments such as airports. They suggested reducing stress levels and anxiety (e.g. locate flight screens in visible locations), inducing browsing (e.g. provide open and attractive retail environment) and reducing normative traits (e.g. stress the rationality of impulse buying via promotional materials).

Table 4.1   Impulse buying at the airport

	Illustration
The holiday effect	Consumer is going on a holiday with high levels of excitement and more disposable income is at hand than normal
The family effect	Consumers think of buying gifts for family and friends
The guilt effect	Business travellers buying for spouse and children to compensate for the loss of family time due to business travel
The reward effect	Consumers' self-indulgence
The occasion effect	Easter, Christmas, Mother's Day, Valentine's Day, birthday
The exclusivity effect	You can only buy certain products in specific travel related environment such as airport
The effect of forgetting	I forgot to bring my umbrella
The effect of confusion	Information overload causing impulse buying
The effect of disposing	I need to get rid of some leftover foreign currency

Based on G Crawford and T C Melewar, The Importance of Impulse Purchasing Behaviour in the International Airport Environment, *Journal of Consumer Behaviour*, Vol. 3 No 1 (2003), p. 85 © John Wiley & Sons, Ltd. Reproduced with permission

THINKBOX

Think of a retail setting other than airports. What steps can marketers take to encourage impulse buying given the range of effects identified by Crawford and Melawar (2003)?

Direct Marketing 'Calls to Action'

For *direct* marketing specifically, however, in order for *action* to take place, marketing messages must include a 'proposition', a 'solution' and a 'mechanism' for facilitating response. Unfortunately, many such mechanisms are designed poorly and make it difficult for the target audience to respond (e.g. coupons which are too small to fill out completely or **DRTV** advertisements which do not provide ample time for the telephone number to be recorded).

Indeed direct marketers will be especially interested in the nature of this stage – measuring response rates and the time of response according to individual profiles and so on. It has been found that, if direct mailings are written using 'you' (the consumer) rather than 'us' (the company), response rates are significantly higher. Similarly, adding words like 'now' or 'instantly' at the end of sentences such as 'If you buy this/donate to that' will also usually increase response rates.

POST-PURCHASE

Response or purchase at the action stage does not represent the end of consumer response to marketing efforts. Marketing is concerned with satisfied customers, good relationships with customers, repeat purchasing and/or the spreading of goodwill, as can be the case with loyal advocates. Post-purchase advertising and other product information on packages and labels are important for consumers to structure their product experience. For example, a consumer who buys a bottle of wine would like to learn about the **country of origin** of the wine, the type of grapes and other related information. The wine may even taste better knowing this information. Some wine distributors provide this sort of 'added value' and it can help develop relationships with their customers. There is further coverage of this in Chapter 10, but here we first focus on two important post-purchase phenomena called 'satisfaction' and 'cognitive dissonance'.

Customer Satisfaction

Customer satisfaction is the attitude-like feeling of a customer towards a product or service after it has been used. It is generally described as the full meeting of one's expectations (Oliver, 1980). The concept of satisfaction is important for marketers because it is the essence of success in today's highly competitive world of business. Marketers often try to become market-oriented and customer-focused and in doing so improving customer satisfaction becomes an important corporate goal for them. In fact, satisfaction is a major aim of all of our marketing activities and is a key influence in the formation of future purchase intentions. For instance, a satisfied customer is very likely to share their experiences with others, thereby engaging in what is known as positive **word-of-mouth advertising**. Similarly, a dissatisfied customer is very likely to switch brands and/or complain, thereby engaging in negative **word-of-mouth advertising**.

Related to the concept of satisfaction is anticipated satisfaction (Shiv and Huber 2000). Consider, for example, a consumer who is deciding between two brands of mobile phone. One has the latest digital camera and is really light to carry; the other has a low price. When this consumer approaches this decision with a view to develop anticipated satisfactions, s/he is likely to pay more attention to those attributes that are vivid in nature (attributes which are easy to visualize and construct imagined experiences – in this case, the digital camera and the weight of the phone) than to less vivid attributes (in this case, the price). Therefore, the consumer is more likely to choose the mobile phone with the camera. Thus, anticipated satisfaction is not related to the actual performance or use of the product but rather to consumers' imagined ideas about how the product is going to function.

Antecedents of Customer Satisfaction

In order to understand what causes satisfaction, researchers have widely relied on the **disconfirmation paradigm**, which views satisfaction with products and brands as a result of two cognitive variables: pre-purchase expectations and disconfirmation. According to Peters and Olson (2005), 'pre-purchase expectations are beliefs about anticipated performance of the product; post-purchase perceptions are the consumer's thoughts about how well the product performed. Disconfirmation refers to the differences between the two' (p 403). In other words, post-purchase perceptions are compared with pre-purchase expectations and this comparison process determines disconfirmation. For example, when the perceived performance exceeds a customer's expectations (this is a positive disconfirmation), then the customer feels satisfied. On the other hand, if the perceived performance falls short of customer's expectations (this is a negative disconfirmation), then the customer feels dissatisfied. Empirical research has generally supported this view. For instance, Churchill and Surprenant (1982) reported that when customers perceived the product performing better than expected, they became more satisfied. When actual product performance far exceeds expectations – that is, when there is a big difference between them – then consumers feel delighted (Oliver, 1997). This obviously depends upon initial expectation levels, and if consumers already have higher expectations, then delighting customers can be a very difficult task. Also, when consumers are not familiar with a product category or the brand (if they have never used it before or never heard of it), then they are very likely to have some poorly formed expectations about the product or the brand. So it might be that once consumers' knowledge and familiarity goes up, their expectations go up as well.

Equity and attributions are also considered as determinants of satisfaction judgements. Equity is viewed as a 'fairness, rightness or deservingness judgement that consumers make in reference to what others receive' (Oliver, 1997:194). Consumers are thought to be more satisfied when they perceive fair (i.e. equitable) treatment; also when they attribute favourable outcomes to themselves and negative to others (Oliver, 1993). More recent work argues for taking into account not only cognitions but also affective responses as both coexist and make independent contributions to satisfaction judgements (Mano and Oliver, 1993).

Consequences of Customer Satisfaction

Just as some researchers have looked at the causes of satisfaction, others have looked into consequences of satisfaction, which include complaining behaviour, word-of-mouth advertising and repurchase intentions. We will discuss repurchase intentions in a later chapter. If you are not satisfied, then you have the option of complaining, which is a very good way of getting rid of your anger and frustration. Consumers are very likely to complain when they attribute blame to someone else (rather then themselves), or when they experience a stronger dissatisfying consumption experience. Similarly, if there are greater chances of some kind of redress (e.g. the store will listen to my complaint), then consumers are more likely to complain. It also depends whether you have the right level of ability and motivation (e.g. time, monetary cost, perceived benefit) to complain. In addition to complaining to the service provider, the manufacturer or the retailer, consumers also share their dissatisfying experiences with others and, thus, engage in negative word-of-mouth advertising (Richins 1983). This type of behaviour also allows consumers to release their anger and frustration while regaining control over a bad situation and gaining sympathy from others. When consumers

complain or engage in negative word of mouth, they are actually relieving their cognitive dissonance, which we discuss in detail in the following section.

THINKBOX

Have you ever complained to a manufacturer, retailer or service provider? What was the response? Do you think it was a good idea to complain? As a marketer, what would be your response to consumers' complaints?

Cognitive Dissonance

Post-purchase activities can be better understood with reference to cognitive dissonance theory. Cognitive dissonance is a kind of psychological tension resulting from perceived inconsistencies in cognitions (Festinger, 1957). For example, let us assume that you have just purchased a new car after a fairly extensive pre-purchase search and evaluation of alternatives. Your final choice is probably a bit of a compromise because no car is completely tailored to the requirements of each individual customer. Having said this, you are likely to view your choice as highly satisfactory. However, there may have been other cars available that you believed had some superior design features. These slightly contradictory cognitions can produce dissonance and you may ask yourself if you have made the correct choice. The level of dissonance is a function of the importance of the cognitions to the individual. So, if the point about other design features is very minor, the level of dissonance might be negligible. If, however, you drive your new car home and your next-door neighbour, who you see as being especially knowledgeable about cars, says, 'Why on earth did you buy that? That model has a terrible repair record!', your level of dissonance could be very substantial indeed.

Cognitive dissonance is a motivator in that the individual tries to reduce it. In the above example, a high level of dissonance over the car might lead the buyer to seek supporting evidence for his decision, to reassure himself that he has done the right thing. Indeed, much advertising is aimed at people who have already made a purchase, in order to help them overcome dissonance, reassure them of their purchase decision and to ease the way for a repeat purchase or at least to spread positive messages to others. It is also worth emphasizing that dissonance is not the same as dissatisfaction. Dissatisfaction produces dissonance, yes, but a generally satisfying purchase may also produce cognitive dissonance if some of the cognition's over it are slightly inconsistent with each other.

EXAMPLE 4.1

Take the example reported by Jones (1996), which we also discuss in Chapter 10, concerning the missing ashtray from his BMW. The BMW dealer had forgotten to replace the ashtray after a service but a chance call to a Lexus dealer resulted in them collecting the ashtray from BMW and delivering it to Jones! Even though he had been a loyal BMW owner for 12 years, this seemingly minor incident over the ashtray raised dissonance in his mind. The Lexus dealer's actions suggested to him that there would be less dissonance if he were a Lexus customer, so that's what he became.

Although we are discussing dissonance in the post-purchase phase (because it applies particularly well here), it can occur in the pre-purchase phase as well. We can usually perceive positive and negative cognitions whenever we are faced with alternatives, so the mental processing of these pros and cons can obviously lead to levels of confusion and doubt over the best choice. Therefore, the onus is on the interactive relational marketer to provide the target with information, which will help the individual overcome such dissonance. It might appear obvious to suggest that we emphasize consonant cognitions (positive aspects of the product). However, there are occasions when a slightly negative set of points can be made as well. The use of two-sided arguments has been suggested as being effective for more educated audiences. Charity marketers often draw attention to the 'downside' of, for example, parting with one's hard earned money but (the upside is) for a very good 'cause'. The marketer might also emphasize how many satisfied customers there are. For example, a satellite broadcaster used the copy headline, 'Half a million people can't be wrong.' Marketers can also extend this by targeting specific individuals as endorsers or **opinion leaders**. The targeting of **opinion formers** (e.g. journalists) is also a highly sophisticated business, as we discuss in Chapter 9, with the aim of securing positive and relevant 'editorial' coverage by those who are likely to be perceived as being independent, credible experts. This can 'reassure' customers that they have bought the right product.

Another example of dissonance comes from the cigarette-smoking market and this provides us with something of a framework for overcoming dissonance or avoiding it in the first instance. Smoking cigarettes is initially a positive and rewarding activity. There is initially no dissonance. However, receiving messages about health risks and negative societal reactions to smoking poses a problem and leads to the psychological tension of dissonance. Table 4.2 shows four generalized ways of overcoming dissonance.

The first method looks simpler than it really is. Changing our behaviour by stopping altogether (apart from being easier to say than to achieve) might reduce the dissonance resulting from the health and social warnings. All the positives for the individual (the nicotine, etc.) have gone, and dissonance can arise over not smoking! The individual might turn to eating more, especially mints, and this might lead to dissonance over gaining weight or tooth problems! Less dramatic changes in behaviour, such as to smoking cigars or a pipe, might enable the individual to reassure herself that the health risk might be less and that, although dissonance still exists, it is not at the same level and therefore it might be manageable. Once the cigar smoker, however, realizes that the result from smoking cigars in the same way that he smoked cigarettes (inhaling) can be even more damaging, then dissonance will clearly rocket again!

The second method is to refuse to accept that there is a strong or proven link between cigarette smoking and health problems. It has been found that some smokers rationalize their behaviour in this way. They say there might be a correlation but not necessarily a causal link. The point here is that if dissonance is based on the balance between positive and negative cognitions, by reducing the perceived level of the negative ones, dissonance can thus be reduced to a tolerable level.

Table 4.2 Dissonance reducing strategies in smoking

Strategy	Action
1. Change one's behaviour	Stop smoking
	Change to smoking cigar or pipe
2. Distort the dissonant information	Refuse to accept cancer connection
3. Minimize the importance of the issue	Say there is more chance of death in a car crash
4. Ignore dissonant information and seek consonant information	Seek social support

The third strategy reduces the importance of all of the cognitions. By convincing ourselves that the issue is relatively insignificant in our lives we might still experience dissonance over it, but at a much reduced and acceptable level. We might, of course, increase dissonance over driving, especially if we drive and smoke at the same time!

The fourth approach is a variation on the second. Rather than distorting that which is dissonant, we might seek more of that which is consonant. The argument that our friends are fit and healthy and that they smoke serves to accentuate the positive cognitions to an extent that they outweigh the dissonant cognitions. Early cigarette advertising actually used this approach and depicted young, fit and energetic smokers with the implication that 'You too can be like this if you smoke this brand'! Even sporting heroes were used in such smoking advertisements.

Figure 4.2 shows how marketing messages of that bygone era depicted, somewhat unethically, healthy people to reassure that smoking cigarettes will not do harm. Indeed the copy of one reads 'For your throat's sake, smoke Craven A' and the other implies the endorsement of women (see Chapter 9 for more on endorsement) with a probable aim of encouraging women to take up smoking at a time when it was predominantly a male preserve.

Based on the above discussion we can transfer the general strategies into workable approaches in marketing. It might appear obvious to suggest that we emphasize the consistent cognitions (positive

Figure 4.2   (Unethical) reassurances from marketers
Overcoming dissonance: healthy women smoke (seeking social support) and it's good for you (!) (using positive cognitions).
Reproduced by permission of Robert Opie

aspects of the product) and indeed this is based on the balancing act between the consonant and the dissonant aspects. However, there are occasions when a slightly negative set of points can be made as well. The use of **two-sided arguments** has been suggested as being effective for more educated audiences (see Chapter 3). Another example is the old Volkswagen advertisement which showed the Golf being advertised as slower than a competitor, with the tagline 'Once again, our GTi is about to be left standing'. The small print, however, went on to point out the extra safety and other features that the Golf possessed.

This also takes us to the implication that there are dissonant elements of competing products. This is again based on the balance between the consonant and dissonant. We perhaps try to increase dissonance over competing products. Comparative advertising, although banned in some countries, is used extensively in others. In the UK, for instance, it is not uncommon for advertisements for model X car to show the market leader as well and to emphasize, selectively, only a few features such as the smaller boot that the competitor has. The other car might be the market leader but 'ours' is so much less expensive and still comes with many similar features.

EXAMPLE 4.2

Another good illustration of a two-sided appeal was an advertisement for new homes. The two-column message listed the advantages of buying a new home in one column, such as a ten-year guarantee, the latest fittings, new electrical systems and energy-saving heating. In the other column were the negatives associated with buying a 20-year-old house, e.g. the need to spend money on a new kitchen, electrical rewiring and the replacement of windows.

Figure 4.3 shows a poster for Bird's Eye curries, prompting consumers to investigate what is lurking in their curries, especially artificial ingredients which cannot be identified by simply looking at the product. The effect might be to increase dissonance over these competing brands, hence tipping the balance in favour of Bird's Eye.

Figure 4.3   Increasing dissonance over competing brands
Reproduced by permission of Bird's Eye, a division of Unilever plc. Illustrated by Anthony Burrill

One of the most seminal examples of building dissonance over a competitor occurred during the 1979 UK general election, when the Conservative Party took a swipe at the then incumbent Labour Government (Figure 4.4). The basis was high levels of unemployment but it is interesting to note that after the Conservative win in 1979 unemployment rose.

Figure 4.4   Comparative/negative advertising
Perhaps unfortunately, modern political campaigning seems mostly to 'knock' opposition parties.
Photograph: Martin Evans

THINKBOX

The building dissonance approach is also to be seen in the music industry. Record companies strive to get their CDs into the 'charts', not only because this means they sell more at that stage and get more airplay but also because once a recording can be promoted as 'a hit' it appears to give additional credibility and to reduce potential dissonance. The buyer can think that if they are silly to buy, then millions of others are as well, and that is unlikely!

The same applies to the book market. Faced with rows of novels, the one with 'million seller' on the cover can attract the buyer in the same way.

Music programmes even describe new releases as 'future hits'. Are consumers more likely to buy if the CD is described as a 'hit' or 'future hit' than if there were no 'charts' at all?

What does this say about our buying behaviour?

Related to this is offering reassurance through after-sales service and warranties. This is again very prominent in the car market and reflects the pragmatic view that cars are complicated pieces of machinery and that no car is tailor-made for each individual customer, so there are bound to be both consonant and dissonant cognitions. However, if the marketer emphasizes that, if anything goes wrong, there is nothing for the consumer to worry about, there need be no dissonance after purchase because the company will look after the purchaser. Network Q in 2005 used the copy headline: 'With 114 checks on every Network Q car, peace of mind comes as standard' (Figure 4.5).

Figure 4.5   Reassurance
Consumers know very well that a car is a complicated product and things can go wrong. They seek reassurance that if there are problems, these can be resolved easily.
© Vauxhall Network Q. Reproduced by permission

Another approach is based on the strategy of reducing the importance of the issue. How many of us have bought a garment in a 'sale' and it doesn't fit too well or in daylight the colour is pretty awful? We are sometimes able to reduce this dissonance to a tolerable level and even go back and buy something else from the 'sales', because we rationalize it as 'a bargain' and therefore it doesn't matter so much!

www.	Have a look at this web site for a summary of cognitive dissonance:
	http://en.wikipedia.org/wiki/Cognitive_dissonance

INVOLVEMENT

Before we leave the sequential model it is worth saying that levels of involvement that customers have with the product category or the specific purchase issue can go some way to determining the value of such models. As we have seen through the last two chapters, consumers' response to marketing activity and indeed their decision-making can be depicted as a sequential cognitive process. However, we must take account of the level of involvement that consumers show in the decisions they make, their personal interest and engagement in the process.

Involvement is commonly defined as the consumer's personal interest in buying or using an item from a given product field, an approach which nicely summarizes the individual, experiential and situational components of the relationship. However, consumers can be involved not only with a product category (e.g. mobile phones) but also with a brand (e.g. Nokia), an advertisement (e.g. a print ad for Nokia), a medium (e.g. the Internet) and a purchase decision (e.g. deciding between alternatives when buying a mobile phone). According to Zaichkowsky (1985), consumers respond differently in these various involvement scenarios. For example, when consumers are highly involved with an advertisement, they are likely to develop more counter-arguments to what is being stated through the advertisement. Also, **higher involvement** with purchase decisions leads to consumers spending more time and effort and indulging in extensive information search. A person's level of involvement depends upon personal relevance and the inherent interests, needs and values of the individual, which motivate them towards the object of involvement. Similarly, physical characteristics and situational factors can also influence a person's level of involvement (Zaichkowsky, 1985). Also, involvement affects consumers' cognitive (e.g. information searching, processing, attention, satisfaction) and behavioural (e.g. early adoption of a product) responses.

Consumers can have **enduring involvement**, which continues out of sustained interest in the product category and **situational involvement**, which is short-lived because the interest is related to an event (e.g. buying a dress for a wedding). Consumers can also have response involvement, which refers to the cognitive and behavioural consequences that arise from the associated levels of enduring and situational involvement. For example, a person's enduring involvement with a product category, say mobile phones, and situational involvement with a given situation (e.g. buying one as a birthday present for a daughter) should have significant cognitive and behavioural consequences pertaining to the buying of a mobile phone in this particular context.

When a consumer perceives something to be of personal relevance and of interest, it means that it is self-related and in some way instrumental in achieving certain life goals and values (Celsi and Olson, 1988). There can be some intrinsic sources of personal relevance (e.g. knowledge associations based on experiences with a product and which are stored in the memory); these do not change across situations and remain relatively stable. Therefore, enduring involvement is relatively stable and longer-lasting. However, marketing activities are just one example of situational sources of personal relevance because they help activate self-relevant consequences, goals and values. Since most situational sources of personal relevance are changeable, the **situational involvement** can also change when the situation changes (Celsi and Olson, 1988).

Celsi and Olson (1988) investigated the role of involvement (defined as self-relevant knowledge that is activated in a given situation) in consumers' attention and comprehension processes. Their findings indicated that as consumers' involvement increased, subjects allocated more attention to the advertisements, exerted greater mental effort during comprehension of those ads, increasingly focused on product-related information contained in the ads and engaged in extra elaboration of the product information during comprehension.

Some products, such as high-performance cars, seem inherently involving because of their complexity, risk and cost, while others, such as toothpaste, seem uninvolving by comparison because of their familiarity, low risk and low cost (Laaksonen, 1994). In fact, while this is true in a general way, involvement is actually a relationship rather than a property of this or that product or service. It reflects not only the degree of

	High involvement	Low involvement
Decision-making	Sequential models	Less evidence for sequential models
	Cognitive learning	Passive learning
Habit	Loyalty	Inertia
	Instrumental conditioning	Classical conditioning

Figure 4.6   Involvement and hierarchy of effects (sequential) models

uncertainty experienced by a consumer when they are faced with consideration of a product but also the personal characteristics of the consumer (some people find everything more involving than others) and on the situation in which purchase and consumption take place.

In fact, consumers' motivation to process information is often conceptualized in terms of consumers' involvement with the information stimuli. Figure 4.6 illustrates low and high involvement with decision-making and different types of learning.

In Chapter 3 we referred to the situation under high involvement, where cognitive learning is applicable and low involvement is associated with **passive learning** (Krugman, 1965). Also, consumers go through the sequential model under high-involvement conditions whereas there is less evidence of applicability of sequential models under low-involvement conditions.

> **THINKBOX**
>
> Think of a low-involvement decision and a high-involvement decision that you made recently. To what extent do you think your decision-making differed in the two situations?

In order to move consumers' involvement from low to high, marketers could:

1. Link the brand with an involving issue. For example, high cholesterol is an important issue for some and therefore the clear linking of brands, such as Benecol, which lower cholesterol, can help to increase consumers' involvement with what otherwise might be a rather boring product (margarine).
2. Link the brand with an involving personal situation, such as advertising a satellite car-navigation brand on radio when harried commuters might be struggling through the rush-hour traffic. Figure 4.7 shows a Häagen-Dazs advertisement which links ice cream with even more 'involving situations'!
3. Link the brand with a message style which is itself involving, such as the cinema quality 'blockbuster' advertisements that Guinness often produce.

Information processing and attitude change are determined by involvement and consumers' motivation to process information. High involvement leads to a **central route to persuasion**, which 'views attitude change, resulting from a person's diligent consideration of information that she or he feels is central to the true merits of a particular attitudinal position' (Petty *et al.*, 1983:135). Consumers pay strong attention to the product-related features and other relevant factual information and consciously elaborate potential outcomes. Attitude change here is relatively enduring, predictive of behaviour and is resistant

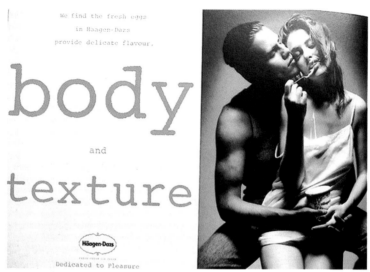

Figure 4.7   Advertisement aiming to increase involvement with a brand
Source: General Mills UK

to counter-persuasion. Under high-involvement conditions, an advertising message is likely to affect cognition, then attitudes and then behaviours (Krugman, 1965).

On the other hand, low involvement leads to a **peripheral route to persuasion** whereby consumers pay limited attention to non-product features and feelings. Here the information processing is largely unconscious with no or very limited elaborative activities. Using some simple cues (e.g. opinion of an expert) consumers make simple inferences about the merits of the advocated position (Petty *et al.*, 1983). Under low-involvement conditions, an advertising message is likely to affect cognition, then behaviours and then attitudes (Krugman, 1965).

The central route deals with the message *content* and the peripheral route with the *execution* of the message (use of humour, celebrities, music and so on). Central route processing depends on much of what we have discussed in the preceding two chapters: attention, perception, learning and then attitude formation. Peripheral route processing, however, can be more spontaneous depending on how the style of the message appeals to the consumer. As the well-known lyrics go: 'It ain't what you do, it's the way that you do it.' These arguments are based on what is known as the **Elaboration likelihood model** (Petty and Cacioppo, 1983). The model argues that, depending upon the likelihood of a message-relevant thought occurring, different methods of inducing persuasion are likely to work best. That is, when the elaboration is high, the central route to persuasion works best, but when the elaboration is low, the peripheral route will work best. The model has significant implication for message strategy and message content. For example, when there is high involvement, attitude change can best be achieved by presenting high-quality argument and presenting a lot of rational and detailed information. On other hand, under low-involvement conditions, attitude change can best be achieved by using some peripheral cues (e.g. attractive models, delightful music, expert persons).

Another related approach is summarized in Figure 4.8, which presents a simple grid model used by **Foote, Cone and Belding**, a major advertising agency, to analyse consumer–product relationships. The grid also shows the typical locations of several different products. The **FCB Grid** (Berger, 1986) is based on two concepts: consumers' involvement and their salient knowledge, meanings and beliefs about the product.

Involvement	Motives	
	Think	Feel
High	Pension scheme	Sports car
	Economy car	Cosmetics
Low	Washing and cleaning products	Soft drinks
		Burgers

Figure 4.8 The FCB grid

Some products are considered primarily in terms of rational factors, such as the functional benefits of using the product. These are termed **think products** in the grid model. Included in this category are such products as investments and car batteries, all products purchased primarily for their functional consequences.

In contrast, **feel products** are considered by consumers primarily in terms of non-verbal (visual or other types) images and emotional factors, such as psychosocial benefits and values. For instance, products purchased primarily for their sensory qualities, such as ice cream and cosmetics, as well as products for which emotional consequences are dominant, such as flowers or jewellery, are feel products in the FCB Grid. An example of the practical application of this concept can be seen on the use of scent strips for perfume products, which allow consumers to experience 'feel' products. Marketing research shows that consumers are more likely to buy products that they have sampled. Scent strips on press advertisements can be a very effective marketing communication device.

THINKBOX

Think about a recent purchase of a product. Was it a 'feel' product or a 'think' product? How do you know? Is the feel/think dichotomy relevant to all products? What about services?

The appropriate message strategy depends on the product's position in the grid. Sometimes, a product can be 'moved' within the grid, from a 'think' to a 'feel' product.

There are, however, some limitations of this model as reported by Rossiter, Percy and Donovan (1991). For example, they criticize the method of conceptualizing involvement for the FCB grid and argue that it does not distinguish brand choices from wider product category choice and this affects the think–feel issue. So both involvement and think–feel constructs are seen to be limited. As a result we have the *Rossiter–Percy Grid* (Figure 4.9), which is claimed to be more robust and provide richer insights. It operates in two ways: first, it recognizes a difference between brand recall and brand recognition, and second, it incorporates positive and negative motivations with high and low involvement.

By understanding how consumers might react to specific brands, the implications of the four quadrants of the Rossiter–Percy Grid are:

1. **Low-involvement/negative motivations** To attack negative motivations a simple-solution approach is suggested and marketers should not worry too much if consumers don't like the style of message. In order to attack the low-involvement dimension, marketers should keep the benefits relatively clear but not in proliferation. They should be easy to learn from a few exposures.

	Type of motivation	
	Informational (negative motivations)	Transformational (positive motivations)
Low-involvement decision-making	Examples: aspirin, light beer, detergent,	Examples: candy, regular beer, fiction novels
High-involvement decision-making	Examples: microwave oven, insurance, home renovations	Examples: vacations, fashion clothing, cars

Figure 4.9   Involvement and motivation

Based on J R Rossiter, L Percy and R J Donovan, A Better Advertising Planning Grid, *Journal of Advertising Research*, October/November 1991, pp. 11–21. Reproduced by permission of Cambridge University Press

2. **Low-involvement/positive motivations**   In order to attack the low-involvement dimension here, marketers should use repetition of exposures in order to 'build up' reinforcement. For positive motivations, the approach should find an emotional appeal, which is relevant to the consumer in order to encourage liking of the message.

3. **High-involvement/negative motivations**   To attack negative motivations here, marketers need to ensure positive reaction to the main point of the message rather than the peripheral issues. In order to exploit the high-involvement dimension, marketers should employ convincing appeals, which do not over-claim benefits. Comparative messages might be useful when consumers perceive relatively similar brand alternatives.

4. **High-involvement/positive motivations**   To exploit positive motivations, marketers relate emotional benefits of the product very clearly to the target segment's lifestyle and motivations and should not be overly concerned whether the style of message is liked. In order to exploit high involvement, marketers should provide useful information for those who are highly involved, and should make relatively strong claims for their product or service.

> **www.**   **Have a look at this article, which is accessible from the accompanying web site at www.wiley.com/go/evans:**
>
> **Hansen T (2005) Perspectives on Consumer Decision Making: An Integrated Approach, Journal of Consumer Behaviour, Vol 4 No 6. It explores relationships between attitudes, involvement and emotional buying and the role that price and quality play in consumer decision-making.**

SUMMARY

In this chapter, we have reviewed ways of encouraging consumers to 'act' and to respond positively after purchase. We have also introduced moderators of the sequential approach, in the form of involvement.

Impulse buying is a pervasive and characteristic feature of the purchasing behaviour of most of us. Consumers can buy all sorts of products on impulse – low and high value, and low and high risk. Impulse buying allows consumers to reflect their self-view and their identities. Certain retail environments, such as airports and casinos, are particularly suitable for impulse buying, and marketers can take a number of steps to improve the probability of impulse purchasing happening.

Customer satisfaction is a post-purchase attitude like feeling and is an important theoretical as well as practical concept. Some of the widely known antecedents of customer satisfaction include expectations, disconfirmation of expectations, performance, affect, equity and attributions, whereas complaining behaviour, negative word-of-mouth advertising and repurchase intention are outcomes of dissatisfaction.

Cognitive dissonance can occur before purchase as well as after purchase. When alternatives are presented there will usually be both consistent and inconsistent cognitions about each. Marketing can help avoid cognitive dissonance and help reduce it if it is experienced. If a purchase is not satisfying, dissonance arises, because of inconsistent cognitions, dissonance can still occur. The objective is to keep dissonance to a minimum and to encourage repeat purchase or at least the spreading of goodwill.

Involvement can help explain the degree to which the pre-/post-purchase sequential model applies to different consumers. Consumers can become involved with product categories, brands, advertisements, communication media and even purchase decisions. Involvement reflects the product's relevance to a consumer and can be enduring, situational and response-driven. Personal relevance can be driven either by some intrinsic personal sources such as knowledge associations based on experiences or by some extrinsic, external sources such as marketing communication activities. Higher levels of involvement often lead to a central route to persuasion whereas lower levels lead to a peripheral route to persuasion. In either case, marketers can aim to employ different strategies to consumers' attitudes. There are other integrating models that build on involvement including the elaboration of likelihood model, the FCB Grid and the Rossiter–Percy Grid. Marketers in general and advertisers in particular can use them to decide brand positioning and spot advertising opportunities.

QUESTIONS

1. **What is impulse buying? Use your own examples to suggest how marketers can encourage impulse buying.**

2. **What is customer satisfaction? How can marketers prepare to offer it? What are its consequences for marketers?**

3. **What is post-purchase dissonance? Give your own examples. Did you go on to buy the same products/services/brands again? What did you tell others about them?**

4. **Choose brands for which you have:**
   a. low involvement, and
   b. high involvement.
   How does theory explain your behaviour with respect to these brands?

5. **Compare and contrast the FCB and Rossiter–Percy models. How do they explain your buying behaviour for some selected brands? How do they suggest marketers should target you?**

FURTHER READING

Festinger L (1957) Cognitive Dissonance, Stanford University Press, California. This is the original and seminal work from which marketers have borrowed and adapted the term 'cognitive dissonance' within the context of consumer behaviour, especially but not exclusively post-purchase.

Rossiter J R, **Percy** L and **Donovan** R J (1991) A Better Advertising Planning Grid, Journal of Advertising Research, October/November, pp 11–21. This paper is also a seminal contribution. It extends the FCB Grid and the concept of involvement to their own Rossiter-Percy Grid. The paper is well worth reading.

CHAPTER 5

CONSUMER DEMOGRAPHICS

CHAPTER OBJECTIVES

After engaging with the material presented in this chapter and its associated exercises and reading, you should be able to:

■ Comprehend how demographics contribute to an understanding of consumer behaviour

■ Analyse and evaluate the role played by age in explaining consumer behaviour

■ Analyse and evaluate the role played by gender in explaining consumer behaviour

■ Analyse and evaluate the role played by social grade in explaining consumer behaviour

INTRODUCTION

Consumer **demographics** are important for marketers because consumers can be targeted using variables such as age, gender and occupation. Consumer behaviour differs with demographic variables. For example, many of our purchases vary by age category. Also, men and women can behave differently as consumers. For instance, because of differences in male and female roles in different cultures, men and women end up performing different tasks and behaviours. Marketing has not, traditionally, explored **social class** but uses a surrogate (**social grade**) based on occupational grouping, but this approach has been severely questioned in recent years. In this chapter, we discuss a number of demographic factors and their relevance to marketers and consumer researchers.

If any of your course projects have involved conducting an analysis of specific markets, it is quite likely that you will have referred to some of the commercial 'market reports' in your library, such as MINTEL, Keynote, the Target Group Index (TGI) or Market Assessment. These profile customers who buy various products according to the demographic characteristics of age, gender and social grade (occupation) (Table 5.1).

Table 5.1   Market report profiling – men's underwear, percentages

	Boxer shorts	Briefs	Vest	Y-fronts
All Men 15+	50	25	12	11
15–24	72	10	9	3
25–34	64	21	4	6
35–44	54	26	8	3
45–54	46	31	11	12
55–64	35	36	14	16
65+	29	25	28	27
AB	42	27	10	14
C1	56	25	11	7
C2	56	24	13	10
D	52	22	15	14
E	41	22	16	9

Gender: 45% of women (63% of married women) buy vests and pants for their men.
Source: Adapted by the authors from MINTEL, March 2004.

THINKBOX

Go through Table 5.1 and try to infer reasons for the figures given. What might explain the age differences for men wearing the different types of underwear?

How might social grade explain these differences and what are the reasons for and implications of so many women buying underwear for their men?

Clearly, demographic factors can differentiate buying behaviour but to what extent do they actually explain differences? That is, it might be relatively easy to infer reasons but is inference a dangerous practice?

Not only are demographic characteristics still found in the commercial market reports from MINTEL, Keynote, Market Assessment and so on but also they are included as important profile questions in many consumer research studies. They are relatively easy to collect and, as a result, they can provide consumer researchers and marketers with very useful data.

In the following sections we explore the traditional demographic characteristics of age, gender and social grade and whether they still provide any value to the process of understanding consumer behaviour. We also discuss consumer sexuality, which is becoming an important base for marketers to segment their markets.

AGE AND GENERATIONAL COHORTS

Rather than looking at the issue of age from only a chronological perspective, we can combine **chronological age** with other age perceptions (Table 5.2). This means biologically we have a physical age; psychologically we grow, learn and mature through what we learn and our experiences (also, the 'spirit

Table 5.2 Age categories

Chronological age	Number of years that you have lived since birth
Biological age	An estimate of your present position with respect to your potential lifespan
Social age	Age in terms of social roles and habits; this is concerned with different roles you take during the life cycle indicating your standing in society
Cognitive age	This is your self-perceived age (the age you perceive yourself to be, related to your self-concept); this can include subjective age and personal age
Subjective age	Your self-perception with reference to other age groups (e.g. middle-aged, elderly, old)
Personal age	This is also based on your self-perceptions and comprises four age dimensions: feel age (how old you feel), look age (how you look), do age (how involved you are in doing things favoured by someone important in your life); and interest age (how similar your interests are to those of a particular age group)
Other perceived age	This is a subjective evaluation of your age status as assessed by others

Source: Based on B Barak and LG Schiffman, Cognitive Age: A Non Chronological Age Variable, *Advances in Consumer Research*, Vol 8 (1981), pp 602–606. Reproduced by permission of the Association for Consumer Research

might be willing but the flesh is weaker'; and socially we develop as a result of our interaction with others, from family to **peer** and **reference group** (Treguer, 2002). Also, certain people (e.g. the elderly) cope very well with age transitions and have a higher tendency to perceive themselves to be younger than their actual age. This influences a range of their behaviours including their satisfaction levels with brands and with others around them. Cognitively young consumers lead active lives, enjoy many of the same goods and services as younger and middle-aged consumers and are a good target for products such as travel services, automobile and recreational services (Stephens, 1991). **Cognitive age** has some very useful implications for advertising because feeling younger than your actual age is important (Stephens, 1991). For instance, while targeting the 55+ age group, marketers can use relatively young actors and spokespersons to improve the effectiveness of their advertising message. Similarly, they can portray the elderly in healthy and activity pursuits and depict more family-related interactions. However, keep in mind that the idea of cognitive age applies not only to the elderly but also to different age groups (e.g. young and middle-aged) who all have a certain cognitive age.

The approach, then, is to consider how those from specific 'generations' behave as consumers. Each cohort will have gone through the same era and will have had similar experiences during their formative years as adults. A major implication of the **generational cohort** approach is that marketers are given clues as to what to say to each cohort segment and how to say it, on the basis of the formative events experienced within each cohort. Indeed Belk (1988) has asserted that 'Possessions are a convenient means of storing the memories and feelings that attach our sense of past' and in this way the consumption patterns of generational cohorts can be predicated on important symbolism.

We start by exploring several specific age segments: the burgeoning 'grey' market, including baby boomers and first, young consumers. However, we will hold back a discussion of children and their buying behaviour and influence to Chapter 7 because this needs to be integrated with wider aspects of **family buying behaviour**.

THINKBOX

The Who sang about 'My generation' and each era has its own music which captures the ethos of the times. This means that the late teen and early twenties phase is significant in our development.

Recently the Gangsta rap genre appears to use stronger and stronger images and extreme lyrics as, perhaps, exemplified by Eminem. In the 1990s, the Spice Girls attempted to sing about post-feminist self-confidence in 'Wannabe'. In the 1980s, Frankie Goes to Hollywood recommended 'Relax', the Undertones advocated 'Teenage kicks' in 1978 and in 1968 the Beatles considered a 'Revolution'. Our personal development as we move from child to adult is full of contradictions and the tensions due to our physical and emotional development. We want to find our own identity yet value the security of the family. At the same time, because of the former, we are prone to rebelling against the latter producing difficult-to-deal-with tensions.

How does your generational cohort interact with the world? What music reflects your formative years? Why?

What do you think your cognitive age is? What should marketers do to satisfy your age requirements? Contrast your views with those of a friend.

It has been suggested that whereas 'adults' define themselves by their occupations, youths are 'defined by their consumption patterns. Brands and products are therefore of critical importance to teenagers' (Gillespie, 2003) and this is clearly congruent with the multiple roles of self-expressive behaviour discussed in the next chapter and the phenomenon of tribal behaviour (in Chapter 7) which facilitates a degree of individualism and even narcissism but within the safety of a group.

A major generational cohort, and in some sense the first to be especially recognized as such, was the generation born in the years following the Second World War; that is, between 1945 and 1965. This explains the subsequent divisions of generations based on a 20-year generational span (i.e. allowing individual development to about age 20) and the mid-decade periods. However, we 'work backwards' here, from the most recent adult/young adult generation, those born between 1977 and 1994.

Generation Y (or 'N')

Those born between 1977 and 1994 have been termed **Generation Y** or the Millennial Generation (Adam Smith Institute, 1998). Sometimes this cohort is labelled the 'N-Gen' after 'the net' and the 'information revolution' which has been such a major impact on their development (Schewe and Meredith, 2004). Many in this category have been found to be materialists, brand-orientated, risk-takers, keen on business, hedonism and illegal drugs and having a disrespect for politics. But they are not as cynical as their predecessor, **Generation X** (see below). The Future Foundation (2000) extended this research and found Generation Y to be more accepting of multi-nationals and less interested in protesting. Further analysis of Generation Y has been conducted by Shepherdson (2000) and Gofton (2001). If this group were targeted, this profile could provide useful clues as to the sort of message and media to use and reach them.

Davidson (2003) discusses them as being introspectively and self-expressively motivated:

> They are only interested in their personal lives, the parties they go to, the clothes they wear … the absence of community … the cult of celebrity provides an exciting surrogate community … celebrity (provides) a real identity in a sea of mock individuality.

Generation X (or Baby Busters)

This group was born approximately from 1966 to 1976 and the name 'Generation X' was coined by Coupland (1991). Indeed he probably started the sequence of 'alphabetical' generations because Gen X was the first so labelled back in the early 1990s. They have become important spenders – demanding their own products and searching for their own identity. A complicating factor is that this group has been found to be especially individualistic and sceptical of marketing activity. O'Donohoe and Tynan (1998), for example, found that young adults are indeed advertising-literate. This doesn't make them difficult to reach, but it is proving harder to influence them. Coupland (1991), Bashford (2000) and Ritchie (1995) have analysed their behaviour and attitudes. Ritchie, for example, declares that 'Xers' have known much more advertising all their lives, compared with older generations but that they do not

> dislike advertising … they dislike hype … overstatement, self importance, hypocrisy and the assumption that anyone would want to be disturbed at home by a salesman on the telephone [but] they do not reject the concept of conspicuous consumption. (Ritchie, 1995:159)

Research International (1996) also found these young adults (by then in their 20s) to be dismissive of advertising that insults intelligence, knocks competitors or tries too hard to be 'hip'. Coupland provides a series of values of Xers, some of which are reproduced in Table 5.3.

Xers might also be more interested in engaging with marketing rather than being passive receivers of it. If so, marketing can provide some of what Generation X might be looking for – that is, greater interactivity and participation in marketing communications.

THINKBOX

Consider the difference between a (passive) advertising message for Marlboro cigarettes and a more participative approach which involved a 'treasure hunt'. Here, an advertisement announced a competition and gave a telephone number that entrants should call. The telephone contact involved asking the caller various questions and it gathered some personal data for a company database. If the quiz questions were correctly answered, a mail pack was sent; this included a letter, a map and a video. Each contained 'clues' as to where the 'hidden treasure' could be found and the recipient played the role of a treasure hunter.

Are younger market segments more likely to engage with this sort of participative marketing message than older segments?

Table 5.3 Xers

Value	Definition
Divorce assumption	A form of *safety net-ism*, the belief that if a marriage doesn't work out, then there is no problem because partners can simply seek a divorce.
Anti-sabbatical	A job taken with the sole intention of staying only for a limited period of time (often one year). The intention is usually to raise enough funds to partake in another, more personally meaningful activity such as water-colour sketching in Crete or designing computer-knit sweaters in Hong Kong. Employers are rarely informed of intentions.
Legislated nostalgia	To force a body of people to have memories they do not actually possess: 'How can I be a part of the 1960s generation when I don't even remember any of it?'
Spectacularism	A fascination with extreme situations.
Cult of aloneness	The need for autonomy at all costs, usually at the expense of long-term relationships. Often brought about by overly high expectations of others.
Voter's block	The attempt, however futile, to register dissent with the current political system by simply not voting.
Yuppie Wannabes	An X Generation sub-group that believes the myth of a yuppie lifestyle being both satisfying and viable. Tend to be highly in debt, involved in some form of substance abuse and show a willingness to talk about Armageddon after three drinks.
Me-ism	A search by an individual, in the absence of training in traditional religious tenets, to formulate a personally tailored religion alone. Most frequently a mishmash of reincarnation, personal dialogue with a nebulously defined god figure, naturalism and a karmic eye-for-eye attitude.
Strangelove reproduction	Having children to make up for the fact that one no longer believes in the future.
2 + 2 = 5-ism	Caving in to a target marketing strategy aimed at oneself after holding out for a long period of time. 'Oh, all right, I'll buy your stupid cola. Now leave me alone.'
Down-nesting	The tendency of parents to move to smaller, guest-room-free houses after the children have moved away so as to avoid children aged 20 to 30 who have boomeranged home.

Source: Adapted by the authors from D Coupland *Generation X: Tales for an Accelerated Culture*, London, Abacus, 1991. Reproduced by permission of Time Warner Book Group UK

Indeed, in their interpretation of their research in 35 countries, Research International (1996) suggested that practical implications of the young adult perspective would lead to 'interactive, challenging relationships' between advertiser and consumer. This is congruent with the **postmodern** (see Chapter 7) construct of **hyperreality** (Firat and Schultz, 1997).

THINKBOX

You are quite likely to be within Generation Y. How do the above descriptions 'fit' your outlook and consumption behaviour, and those of your contemporaries?

Between X and Boomer

From a major research programme, Taylor Nelson Sofres (2004) found the 35 to 50 age group to 'dip in and out' of things. They switch their pursuits and relationships and want relatively immediate results from their activities. 'They enjoy watching do-it-yourself and cookery programmes on TV (rather than doing it themselves).' This reinforces research about the *cellular household*: 'Family viewing is extremely rare with family members spread around the house, watching different TV sets' (Collins, 2004). Marketers will be heartened by the findings that 35- to 50-year-old men are very interested in clothes, appearance and brands and enjoy shopping (Taylor Nelson Sofres, 2004).

Baby Boomers

We turn now to consider the first of the generational cohorts identified as such, those born between 1945 and 1965. The **baby boomers** – those born in the years following the Second World War – have very distinctive attributes and have became a very important target for marketers. They were involved in a massive social revolution which changed music, fashions, political thought and social attitudes forever (Fifield, 2002). They were the generation to grow up in the 1960s when the term 'teenager' hadn't been used previously. They were not 'small adults' who, in previous generations, had worn similar clothes to their parents. The new generation, however, wanted their own culture, their own fashions and music, and their own social attitudes, which rejected the values of their parents. Coupled with this desire for ownership of their thoughts and lives, the baby boomer generation was the most affluent (generally) of any 'youth market' until their era, so they were able to engage in the consumer market, and marketers responded with a fashion and music explosion which we had previously not experienced.

They had their formative years in the 1960s and 1970s and saw and engaged with significant developments such as rock and pop music, youth fashion, the women's 'liberation' movement, the freedom that 'the pill' gave to sexual behaviour and world events such as 'Vietnam' and the 'Cold War'.

This cohort is now turning 50 and there are over 20 million people aged over 50 in the UK, and this figure will approach 25 million by 2021 (Ahmad, 2002). Such a consumerism-literate market should be extremely attractive. Indeed in USA a baby boomer turned 50 every 6.8 seconds in 2001. The large segment coupled with its purchasing power – it was the first to become empowered as consumers – means it is a favourite target for marketers.

Overall, they are relatively wealthy, in terms of inheritance from their parents. That previous generation was 'blessed' with low house prices when they bought and a lifestyle which was much less materialistic. As a result their estates have often (but clearly not always) been cascading down to the new over-50 market. Many have a 'cognitive age' less than their 'chronological' age' and therefore act much more youthfully than their age might suggest (Szmigin and Carrigan, 2000, 2001). In other words they have a youthful **self-concept** (Moschis, 2003), and we explore self-concept theory in the next chapter.

The Over-50s

The over-50s in the UK hold 80% of the country's wealth and 40% of spending (£145 billion pa) and is not only the only segment that is growing but also the one that has more disposable income than all the others combined (Cummins, 1994; Bond, 1997). Worldwide there are 600 million people over 60 years

Table 5.4   Over-50s

55–64s
Take more holidays than the average and more than half are planning two or more holidays in the next 12 months.
Certain charities such as blind causes, cancer and the elderly appeal to the over-55s more than the norm.
65–74s
Favourite activities are gardening, crosswords, reading. A significant proportion enjoy classical music, support the National Trust, do voluntary work and play bridge. They have an above-average number of long-term savings plans.
75–84s
Less likely to have travelled abroad in their lives, buy a significant amount of plants and vitamins through the mail but are unenthusiastic about other mail order purchases.
85+
Have fewer interests but continue to favour gardening, classical music and current affairs. They are significant charity supporters despite lower incomes.

Source: Adapted by the authors from the Telegraph Group reported in E. Carling, Grappling with the Grey Market, *Marketing Direct* (1999)

of age, and by 2050 there could be 2 billion. Their growth as a proportion of the population has been cited as a worrying factor in many countries (Moschis, 2003): more pensioners than the smaller workforce will be able to support but, from a consumption perspective, it is obvious that they are very important to marketers. But it is foolish to lump these together in just one segment (Gunter, 1998; Treguer, 2002). There are those in their sixties and seventies and indeed the over-70s who are from other generations with lifestyles and attitudes of their own (Table 5.4).

Research amongst the over-50s has revealed several characteristics. The over-50s don't like to be portrayed as 'old' but at the same time would see through attempts to portray them as 'young', so caution is needed. They often prefer to keep their youthful self concept: 'the notion that a person of a certain age is like a person of any age, can be rather effective' (Moschis, 2003), as suggested in Figure 5.1. But there are times when age catches up as Figure 5.1 also shows.

There has certainly been an explosion of magazine titles aimed at various over-50 groups, demonstrating that the market is not homogeneous and that the various groups can be reached. The profiling in this sector is not merely on the basis of age, however; social grade and geodemographics are also being used and there is a trend toward overlaying this with attitudinal research. An example of this comes from the analysis of the TGI in 1993 (Cummins, 1994) which found, based on shopping attitudes and behaviour, that there are 'astute cosmopolitans', constituting about 19% of the 50 to 75s and who are discerning consumers. There are also the 'temperate xenophobes' (20% of 50 to 75s) who are less likely to go abroad or eat 'foreign food'. The 'thrifty traditionalists' make up 20% and a further 19% are 'outgoing funlovers'. The largest group is the 'apathetic spenders' (21%) who use credit cards to extend their purchasing power beyond what they can really afford (Cummins, 1994). The over-50s can be more loyal: 'The problem with young consumers is that they are "flippy". As soon as someone else targets them they jump ship. The mature consumer tends to be more loyal and they tend to do more business' (Cooper, 2003).

There is another issue for marketers and consumer researchers, here: 'As soon as you target the mature sector, people are worried that it's going to upset their youth market, but not if you use niche channels like direct mail and the internet' (Cooper, 2003). Saga is a major direct marketer, for instance.

Figure 5.1   Baby boomers are as young as they feel and as old as they are
A slight spoof on a classic Wonderbra advertising campaign and is actually an advertisement by Age Concern.
See Evans and Rowland (1996) for a discussion of the semiotics of campaigns.
© Age Concern England. Reproduced by permission. Image courtesy of the Advertising Archives

THINKBOX

Consider this view from within the motor industry:

The car dealers often despair of the marketing initiatives they see. The focus is on the young or the young family, even for the point of sale in showrooms . . . older people often have 2 or 3 cars per family, yet manufacturers get hung up on items like cup holders. (Pulham, 2003)

A major issue, then, surrounding this is that marketers tend to target younger age segments yet the 50 to 60 segment buy two-thirds of all cars, more long-haul holidays than younger segments and even 25% of all toys (Sclater, 2003). Datamonitor (2003) speculates that one reason for the relative neglect is that half the staff in advertising agencies are themselves under 30 and it has been suggested that it is not always seen to be 'cool' for these to design advertising 'creative' for older segments (Cooper, 2003). It probably isn't a case, however, of allocating older staff to older accounts, as Cooper suggests; whatever age group media planners are shouldn't affect what they're planning. They should be experienced enough to target the demographics of their clients irrespective of their own interests.

   Could you design an advertising campaign for package holidays aimed at, say, the 55 to 64s?

www.   **Have a look at the following web site, which provides more on demographics and generational cohorts in particular:**

http://demographics.biography.ms/

   Consumer researchers often joke about their analysis of demographic data being 'broken down by age and sex'. We now turn from age to sex, or at least *gender*.

GENDER

If you revisit Table 5.1, you will notice that women buy a significant proportion of men's underwear, and marketers can target women even if they are not the user of the product. Even where there is a 'joint' use, as in the case of condoms, women are important purchasers. In that market, 95% of purchases traditionally were by men but now, women buy one third of all condoms (Cubitt, 2004). This phenomenon is replicated in many consumer markets and is one of the themes of this section. Another theme is the changing social roles of men and women and how these are reflected by marketers' actions.

Often, such reflection is via **gender stereotyping** but although this has been used extensively over many decades, it hasn't always escaped criticism (Nokes, 1994; Rees, 1995; Murray, 1995). Reliance on 'mother' (Figure 5.2) or 'mistress' or 'career woman' images of women in advertising sometimes attracts complaints on sexist or offensive grounds, as have some more recent demeaning images of men.

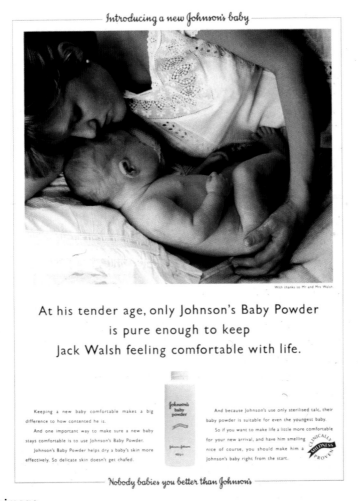

Figure 5.2 Mother image
This image powerfully reflects the strength of maternal instincts.
© Johnson & Johnson Ltd. Reproduced by permission. Image courtesy of the Advertising Archives

Table 5.5   Sex roles not changing fast enough? Percentages

	20–24	45–54	65+
My partner does some housework, less than me and that's OK	33	37	35
Does some but not enough	8	4	4

Source: Woman 2000 Report: Household chores.

Increases in the divorce rate and the 'singles' market (imposed through divorce or by decision) have added to the more general changes in sex roles, with women becoming more individualistic through their own careers rather than being housewives per se. Marketing to women, however, may still be in need of updating.

As female roles change, so do those of men, but perhaps not as fast as women would like (Table 5.5).

EXAMPLE 5.1

Could Figure 5.3, for example, be seen as sexist by men?

Figure 5.3   **Sexist male advertising?**
© Sanyo Europe Ltd. Reproduced by permission

The revolutionary Levi's advertisement of the 1980s saw a 'stripping' Nick Kaman in a launderette. Innocent enough even then, but it introduced new ways to depict men in advertising. Since then we have witnessed an increase in the portrayal of naked or near-naked men in advertising. The use of naked women has often been criticized as sexist, but what about naked men? Are these ads sexist toward men? Why or why not?

We have seen a variety of male stereotypes such as those we might term: 'caring sharing new man', the 'family' man, the 'yob lad', 'modelling' man, 'househusband' man, as well as gay images. Female stereotyping has been criticized for decades but could it be that male images might come in for the same treatment? In a study by Elliott and Elliott (2005), young men did not respond particularly positively to the portrayal of naked/sexual male imagery in advertising, homophobia being one major theme to emerge; as was another, which 'identified body consciousness and vanity as female traits'.

In a broader context, in a study conducted by the market research agency Capibus on behalf of the Chartered Institute of Marketing (CIM) (2000), 48% of a sample of 1013 adults in UK thought women are inaccurately stereotyped in advertising but only 39% thought men were inaccurately so stereotyped. Sex appeals produced interesting results: 59% of 15 to 24s said they enjoy the use of sex to promote a product but this fell to just 23% of the over-65s; and 60% of women disliked the approach compared with just 37% of men.

Marketing cannot afford to assume all women to be homogeneous (and similarly for men). Indeed as we act out multiple roles 'in the post millennial society individuals will be able to pick and choose different gender schemes or choose not to care about gender at all' (Kacen, 2000).

In fact, Cohan (2001) identifies three major ethical issues related to advertising messages targeted at women (Table 5.6) and makes a compelling argument urging the advertising industry to project images and values which women hold as important, and to discontinue the use of stereotypical images. Cohan's argument is not to give up sex appeal altogether but to become more inclusive by showing images of not only young but also older women with less than perfect figures with a more natural look.

However, not all advertising is bad or leads to such consequences. For example, the cosmetics industry has successfully used sensual images of females to convey benefits to consumers. Many also think that if

Table 5.6   Ethical issues in women in advertising

What the advertising does	Illustrations	Why is it bad?
1. Projects sex stereotypes of a weaker role of women in life	Show women as submissive; in constant need of alteration or improvement; feeling ashamed of themselves; dissatisfied in life; confused, childish, contradictory, or generally in need of help.	This leads to beliefs among women that they are or they ought to be weak, mindless and in need of help. Ignores the true role of women in society such as that of successful professional women
2. Redefines attractiveness from something natural to an unattainable ideal; leads to erosion of self-esteem with no room for inner beauty	Show impossible youth, impossible perfection, which is inhuman and (in most cases) can only be accomplished with professional make-up and hairstyles	Encourages women to desire to attain impossible perfection and body figure; it becomes difficult for many women to gain jobs in certain areas (e.g. flight attendants); leads to higher levels of frustration among women as the standard seems unattainable; causes problems among teenagers who wish to look too thin (many eat too little)
3. Portrays women as 'things' or 'mere sex objects'	Use stunningly disordered models, fragmented body parts; women displayed as dolls or animals; a woman's face as a mask, and her body as an object	Leads to destruction of women's true self; may cause violence against women

Source: Based on J A Cohan, Towards a New Paradigm in the Ethics of Women's Advertising, *Journal of Business Ethics*, Vol 33 No 4 (2001), pp. 323–337. Reproduced with kind permission of Springer Science and Business Media

EXAMPLE 5.2

Figure 5.4   Things appear to have changed
Packaging suggesting 'the weaker sex', and a 1900 advertisement for what appears to be little more than a face mask. This was aimed at men to control their wives smoking in public – and even their 'excessive talking'!

© Alcoa Inc. Reproduced by permission. Image courtesy of the Advertising Archives

Figure 5.5   But have they . . . sexy or sexist?
Is this demeaning to women because she is in a state of undress? Is it demeaning to men because she is dominating him with a whip? Or is it merely reflecting mutual sexuality positively?

© Skechers Footwear USA/Phil Mucci Photography LLC. Reproduced by permission the message is targeted at a suitable audience using an appropriate medium (e.g. a specialist magazine), then there is less chance that the contents of the message will be perceived as offensive by someone. Jaffe and Berger (1994) argued that, due to a rise in number of working women, advertisers were already using modern images of women. An example that was quoted included the projection of a superwoman image, where they manage the demands of their jobs and their homes with little help from others. For example, advertisers often project an egalitarian women image in the advertisements where woman and husband (both working) share the household chores together. Jaffe and Berger (1994) investigated the effect of these modern female role portrayals in print ads for food products, and found that the egalitarian portrayal was the most effective role portrayal among many segments of the female market.

THINKBOX

What is your view on the ethical issues raised by Cohan (2001)? Do you think it is appropriate to use female or even male sex objects in advertising?

Do you think advertisers need to be more accountable in terms of their advertising practices? If yes, how can you achieve this without compromising creativity in advertising?

Understanding Consumer Behaviour via Information Processing Styles

This is concerned with the idea that the male and female brains might 'work' differently. Information processing style has been generally reviewed by Kitchen and Spickett-Jones (2003) but the point in the current section concerns possible gender differences as identified by Moir and Moir (1998). Males tend to be selective processors of information and use heuristics cues, whereas females tend to be comprehensive processors of information paying attention to all of the information (Darley and Smith, 1995; Meyers-Levy and Maheswaran, 1991).

Neurolinguistic programming – NLP, as it is termed – is already being used in practice to target consumers; for example, Tunney (1999) explains the use by Marketing Focus of NLP to identify 14 different types of information processing styles. Ford is also using brain scans to detect which car designs prompt different responses, and the Open University with London Business School evaluate TV commercials via brain scans. As Steven Rose, director of brain and behaviour research at the Open University states,

> What would be worrying if marketers, governments or police felt they could control people's thoughts by manipulating brain processes in this way ... I am not sure marketing are going to be looking at this ... but I would be surprised if they don't. (Leighton, 2004)

Previous research also suggests that females are more likely to communicate their internal emotional states than males, who are normally reluctant to disclose their intimate feelings such as those that imply any weakness or dependence on others or vulnerability (Kring and Gordon, 1998). The gift-giving literature in consumer behaviour suggests that women are the primary gift-givers because of their greater concern to show care and love to others (Cheal, 1988). Similarly, Fischer and Arnold's (1990) study of Christmas gift-giving among men and women found that women, in comparison with men, were more involved in this sort of activity.

EXAMPLE 5.3

For example, Evans *et al.* (1999, 2000) drew from findings in neurology based on MRI scans of male and female brains as they processed information (by reading). Female brains generated more activity from more areas of the brain than did male brains. The researchers propose that women were using more elements of messages (colour, imagery, words, etc.) to form meaning and as a result left and right, front and back areas of their brains 'lit up' when reading material. As for men, their brains showed less activity, and the supposition was that they were focusing more on fewer specific elements of the messages, mostly the words, to make sense of it (Figure 5.6). Consumer behaviour based on neurolinguistics therefore suggests that women respond well to bright colours, photographs and images, and men respond well to bold headlines, bullet points and graphs.

Inattention   Attention

Female mail pack   Male mail pack

Figure 5.6   Brain activity and male and female mail packs

Brain activity: P Laybourne and D Lewis, Neuromarketing: The Future of Consumer Research?, *Admap* (May 28–30 2005), pp 28–30. Reproduced with permission of Admap, the world's primary source of strategies for effective advertising, marketing and research. For more information visit www.admapmagazine.com. © World Advertising Research Center. Mail packs: © Target Direct. Reproduced by permission

The exception within this study concerned cars. Women appeared more interested in the facts such as running costs, safety features and fuel consumption, and men more concerned with image and appearance (Figure 5.7) and, perhaps in a Freudian sense (see Chapter 1), whether the car has a long red bonnet!

Figure 5.7   Boys and their toys
© Target Direct. Reproduced by permission

THINKBOX

Does marketing accurately reflect male and female buying behaviour? Why, or why not?
    Do male and female brains 'work' differently?

So – as with age – gender, although being an apparently straightforward demographic characteristic, hides a multitude of implications for the marketer.

SEXUALITY

An extension of gender is **sexual identity**. Most of us are male or female (there are some who are transgender/transsexual) but the concepts of masculinity and femininity are aligned along a continuum based to a large extent on:

- the socialization of our culture (men kiss each other in some cultures but not others) (Solomon, 2004);

- our own self-image (see the next chapter);
- how we use our bodies to reflect this and indeed how we clothe, enhance and even physically modify our bodies to achieve the image we wish to project to others.

Androgyny and bisexuality are mixes of the two poles of the continuum. Marketers can appeal to our opposite pole in appropriate circumstances (Figure 5.8).

Marketing is also increasingly interested in the gay market segments. Gay men, for example, spend twice as much on clothing and four times as much on grooming as straights do. Dodd *et al.* (2005) have explored the extent to which young gay men are 'dependent' on clothing purchases and whether marketing exploits this too far. They are often relatively more affluent, in higher socio-economic groups (see next section) and have few dependants (MINTEL, 2001). The segment is easier to reach nowadays because there are more gay magazines and TV programmes as well as access via the Internet (MINTEL, 2001) and sponsorship of gay events (e.g. by Smirnoff, Levi's and Virgin). Even as far back as 1994, Time-Warner considered introducing a magazine for gay men (Ritchie, 1995:158).

Gay men have also been found to be more responsive to new products and might be a good target in the early stages in the life of new products and services, in terms of the early adopter and opinion leadership constructs discussed in Chapter 9.

The significance of the gay market cannot be underestimated – Middleton (1997) said it was worth around £12 million. Gay women earn around £3000 pa more than is average for women and '40% of gay men are estimated (in 1997) to have an annual income in excess of £25 000' (Middleton, 1997). In research conducted by Rainbow TV, it was found that 46% of the gay population had taken a foreign holiday in the previous year compared with 29% of the entire population (Rainbow TV, 1997) and 80% take two or more holidays each year (Table 5.7).

As is discussed in Chapter 11, with reference to geodemographics, the gay market can potentially be identified and profiled from census data. But in the meantime we turn to one of the consumer researchers' most used profile characteristics, social grade.

Figure 5.8   Masculine self
Masculinity–feminity is not just a biological issue but is also a cognitive continuum.
© Jim Beam Brands Co. Reproduced by permission

Table 5.7　Gay consumer behaviour

£1.4 billion spent on leisure each year
£730 million spent on the home each year
90% eat out regularly
79% take more than two holidays per year
Lesbians earn £3000 more than the average UK woman
27% have higher education
42% spend more than £500 pa on clothes
50% gay men wear Levis
More than 30% spend between £50 and £100 on CDs pa
35% visit a gay club or pub each week
65% claim they will boycott gay-unfriendly places
Bass's portfolio of gay clubs/pubs turned over £8.7 million
　　in 1995–1996: up 18% year on year.

Source: Adapted by the authors from Rainbow TV (1997).

EXAMPLE 5.4

In a recent Levi's ad, one woman is 'kissing' another and has her hand in the pocket of yet another. The woman on the left tries to pull her away. According to Levi's America: 'The image is actually of the same girl and is intended to depict a "virtual reality" of her expressing different aspects of her personality. The Australian marketing team said that the campaign was designed to position women as confident, sassy and self-empowered. The ad also fits with our long tradition of respecting and celebrating diversity and freedom of expression.' (http://www.commercialcloset.org/cgi-bin/iowa/portrayals.html?record=1144).

Figure 5.9　This Diesel clothing advertisement used an overtly gay image
© Diesel. Reproduced by permission. Image courtesy of the Advertising Archives

www. Take a look at Oakenfull and Greenlee (2005), Queer Eye for a Gay Guy: Using Market Specific Symbols in Advertising to Attract Gay Consumers without Alienating the Mainstream, Psychology and Marketing, Vol 22 No 5 pp 421–440, accessed via the accompanying book web site at www.wiley.com/go/evans.

www. Have a look at the following web sites, which provide more on the 'gay market' and the 'pink pound':

http://www.gaytoz.com/bResearch.asp

http://www.commercialcloset.org/cgi-bin/iowa/index.html

and:

http://www.commercialcloset.org/cgi-bin/iowa/index.html

which provides a critique of what the site regards as positive and negative gay advertisements.

SOCIAL GRADE

Especially in the past, marketers have acknowledged that there is a degree of social stratification, but they have long avoided researching possible segments on the basis of social class in any true sociological sense. This would involve rather complicated assessment of income, wealth, power and skill.

In the UK, instead of this, social grade is determined via the occupation of the 'chief income earner' in the household. A sixfold **classification** results: A, B, C1, C2, D, E (Table 5.8). The main 'dividing line' is between C1 and C2, above which there are non-manual occupations and below which there are manual ones (Market Research Society, 2004). Many commercial market research programmes have found significant differences in buying behaviour between respondents in the various social grades: have a look at the MINTEL or other such reports in your library (and in Table 5.1 where briefs would appear to have a more up-market profile and vests more down-market).

The traditional justification for the continued use of social grade is basically twofold (Market Research Society, 1981). First, it is simple to research. All that is required is for data to be analysed according to the occupation of the 'chief income earner in the household'. Second, social grade appears to have been a reasonably good discriminator of buying behaviour as you will find in many (but not all) product-markets profiled in MINTEL-type reports. Social grade also reflects lifestyle patterns and is used widely by advertisers while profiling consumers.

Table 5.8 Social grade based on Occupation of chief income earner, percentages

Grade	Description	1991	2004
A	Top of profession	3	3.5
B	Middle management	10	21.5
C1	Teachers/students	24	29.1
C2	Skilled manual	30	20.9
D	Semi-skilled manual	25	6.2
E	L/R unemployed, state pensioners	8	9.1

During the 1980s in particular, a number of significant criticisms of social grade were made. There are inevitable anomalies in its use. For example, significant proportions of those earning above the national average are C2DE, so the traditionally strong correlations between social grade and income have been destroyed. Some in C2, such as highly skilled manual workers, will be earning more than some middle managers in group B and some full time students in C1 will be earning less than some manual workers in D.

It has also been shown that of 400 respondents to earlier surveys who were re-interviewed to confirm their social grade, 41% had been allocated to the wrong group, and this is an indication of instability of the system (O'Brien and Ford, 1988).

Another problem concerning social grade is that although there might be some correlations between social grade and purchase, how can this be used? Certainly it is relevant for selecting appropriate advertising media based on the matching of segment social grade with the social grade profiles for different media. But there could be dangers in inferring values and attitudes of those in each social grade in order to create marketing communications messages. These more *affective* dimensions might not be caused by occupation. Furthermore, in the context of the urban industrialized environments where social networks can be complex and fluid in nature, it is often difficult to think of a group of consumers as a community of individuals who are bound together by a common social grade or social status (Henry, 2005).

Recent attempts to improve social classification do not bode well, either. The census of 2001 has produced eight (rather than the previous six) categories but excludes the over-75s (Zelin, 2003). Indeed the new system has been found to be as good a discriminator of purchase activity as the 'ABC1' system, but Rose (1999) could not recommend it as a replacement for social grade. However, the previous system was based on households (occupation of chief income earner in the household) whereas the new system is at individual level, so the marketer might be tempted to at least experiment with this because of the stronger potential of data at individual level. However, in comparative research, the Market Research Society (2004) concluded that the old social grade model was a better discriminator than the new socio-economic classification (SEC) and indeed the latter 'would have none of the advantages we would look for in a new system' (Market Research Society, 2004). It is, therefore, perhaps not surprising that the 2001 census output included both the new SEC and the standard (ABC1) social gradings (Market Research Society, 2004); but maybe it is surprising that it attracts such criticism itself.

Although family circumstances and ethnicity are usually discussed under the 'demographics' heading, we explore these in other chapters ('family' within Chapter 7 along with children's involvement with consumption issues; and ethnicity in Chapter 8).

SUMMARY

■ In this chapter, we explored some of the relevant and meaningful demographic variables and their implications for marketers. In particular, we looked into the roles of age, gender, sexuality and social grade in explaining consumer behaviour.

■ An age is something we all possess but equally it is inevitable that we all 'age'. The notion of generational cohorts is important in marketing because it identifies the key outlooks possessed by people within different age groups, and this knowledge can inform marketing communications messages greatly.

■ Gender leads to male and female stereotypes in marketing activity but there are more involved issues. Masculinity and femininity are not absolute but are positioned differently along a continuum for each individual. Information processing styles can vary according to this, and the whole area is further complicated by sexuality and self-image (which can change in different social circumstances).

■ Marketing's widespread use of social grade has come under critical scrutiny in recent years and, although it can apparently reveal differences in buying behaviour, we need to be wary of the accuracy of the data and also need to ask ourselves why such differences are there. That is, does social grade explain behaviour? Or is there merely a coincidental link? Nevertheless, social grade is an important indicator of consumer lifestyle and is widely used in marketing communications for profiling consumers.

QUESTIONS

1. **How will Generations Y and X differ in consumer behaviour and favourite marketing style?**

2. **Baby boomers are significant in terms of their numbers and affluence? How good is the marketing aimed at them?**

3. **What do you think of the way marketers use gender stereotyping in advertising?**

4. **Should marketers use sexuality as a targeting base? Why (and how)? Or why not?**

5. **From which social grade do you come? How far does this explain your buying behaviour?**

FURTHER READING

Gunter B (1998) Understanding the Older Consumer, Routledge and **Treguer** J P (2002) 50+ Marketing, Palgrave. The 'average' student (if there is such a creature), is not usually over 50. However, the 'older' consumer is becoming very important to marketers, yet relatively few marketers who devise campaigns for the over-50s are themselves over 50. These two books provide important and interesting perspectives on these older consumers.

Market Research Society (2004) Occupation Groupings: A Job Dictionary, Market Research Society, London ISBN 0906117275. Our coverage of social grade in UK in this chapter showed that the occupation of the chief income earner in a household determines the social grade to which they belong. This short work by the MRS lists pretty well every occupation and the corresponding social grade.

Moir A and **Moir** B (1998) Men Don't Iron: The Real Science of Gender Studies, HarperCollins, London. This book distils a great deal of research from around the world about the differences between men and women. What about feminism or equality, you say. Well, read on and you will discover that gender differences are more than the result of social or cultural pressure. The science of the brain is examined and applied in this book and adds much to the ongoing debate.

CHAPTER 6

CONSUMER PSYCHOGRAPHICS

INTRODUCTION

Our coverage of **psychographics** includes **lifestyle, personality** and **self-image.** As the 'psycho' component suggests, the approach is more concerned with trying to get beneath the skin of consumers and to be able to explain their behaviour in greater depth than the 'profiling' approach of demographics can. This chapter examines each of these psychographics dimensions in turn but also reflects upon the relative and synergistic contributions of psychographics and demographics to understanding consumer behaviour and for the targeting of marketing activity.

LIFESTYLE

Lifestyle is a mode of living as reflected in consumers' unique patterns of attitudes, interests and opinions. Lifestyle is important because one can develop deeper insights into consumer behaviour by looking at how consumers spend their time and what they think of various elements of their environment. One can also get a closer idea of consumers' motives, feelings and beliefs because lifestyles are reflections of self-concept.

Table 6.1   Examples of lifestyle statements

- I buy clothes for comfort, not for style
- Once I find a brand I like, I tend to stick to it
- I always buy British whenever I can
- I dress to please myself
- My family rarely sits down to a meal together at home
- I enjoy eating foreign food
- I like to do a lot when I am on holiday

Source: British Market Research Bureau (1987), Target Group Index.

There are two approaches to lifestyle: what we term **traditional lifestyle** and **contemporary lifestyle**. It is the former that we concentrate on in this chapter because the latter, which is discussed in Chapter 11, is less to do with 'psycho' dimensions of consumer behaviour and more with what consumers claim they actually do. Indeed the latter is mainly used to create lists of named consumers who claim to buy specific brands. But our focus in this chapter, on traditional lifestyle marketing, is to explore consumer activities, interests and opinions (**AIO analysis**) using market research techniques which do not reveal individual consumer identities.

'Traditional lifestyle' is based typically on the presentation to respondents of a series of statements. Traditional lifestyle research has been based typically on the presentation to respondents of a series of statements (**Likert scales**). Table 6.1 reproduces a short selection of the (246) lifestyle statements used in the Target Group Index (TGI) annual research programme (British Market Research Bureau, 1988).

Respondents are presented with these statements and asked to give their degree of agreement with each. From this there are two main alternative ways of analysing the data.

First, because the Target Group Index also provides an extremely comprehensive profiling of the sorts of consumers, in demographic terms, who buy a range of products and brands, it is possible to cross-tabulate the sort of consumer who buys 'Bloggo' brand not only with age, gender and social grade but also with any or all of the attitudes, interests and opinions (AIOs) reflected in the lifestyle questions.

For example, the buying of a particular brand of lager might be associated with young males from C1 and C2 social grades. By cross-tabulating with the lifestyle questions, it might be revealed that these buyers tend *not* to like healthy eating, but do enjoy the hedonism of sun, sea and sex package holidays.

www.	**Have a look at the following web site, which provides more on the Target Group Index and its lifestyle component:**
	http://www.tgisurveys.com/

The second main way of using the data, whether it be TGI or other traditional lifestyle data, is to explore the full range of lifestyle answers in order to group consumers into segments within which there is a strong degree of homogeneity in terms of their activities, interests and opinions.

EXAMPLE 6.1

In the 1980s, Levi Strauss in USA went through a new product development programme concerning a range of upmarket men's suits. The market research programme that was involved, revolved around an attempt to discover 'lifestyles'. This included eliciting degrees of agreement with statements such as:

- 'Dressing right is a complete mystery to me'
- 'I dress to please my friends'
- 'I think of myself as very fashionable in the clothes I wear'
- 'I dress to conform to what others seem to expect'
- 'Others often ask my advice when it comes to clothes buying'

Each emerging 'cluster' would then be allocated a somewhat glib title. In the Levi lifestyle research programme, for example, the main clothing segments were labelled as: the 'classic independent', the 'mainstream traditionalist', the 'price shopper', the 'trendy casual' and so on. This sort of profile would not only help determine appropriate product/service features but also help to arrive at an advertising message which is congruent with the segment's lifestyle.

In the UK a lifestyle typology was compiled by Taylor Nelson's Applied Futures (McNulty and McNulty, 1987) and identified the following segments: the belonger, the survivor, the experimentalist, the conspicuous consumer, the social resistor, the self-explorer and the aimless (Table 6.2). The self-explorer group was the fastest growing, which further reinforces one of the propositions of this chapter – namely that some markets have become more

Table 6.2   Taylor Nelson's lifestyle typology

Lifestyle category	Characterized by	Percentage of population
Belonger	Place great store by home, family, country, the establishment, etc.	19
Survivor	Disposed towards identification with groups and accepting of authority. Self-expression and creativity are irrelevant.	16
Experimentalist	Attracted to all that is new and different, always looking for new ideas, items and experiences	12
Conspicuous consumer	Energy is directed toward the consumer dream via material possessions, take their cues from reference groups, non-critical of advertisers, followers of fashion	18
Social resister	Seeks to maintain the status quo, controlling self, family, society, suppressing self in favour of duty and moral obligation	15
Self-explorer	Self-aware and self-concerned people, self-expression important	14
Aimless	Uninvolved and alienated, aggressive towards the system, resentful of its failure to provide employment	6

orientated to **self-expression** and individualism. This traditional form of lifestyle (AIO) segmentation provides useful insight into what makes people 'tick'. It is based upon traditional market research – administering Likert scaled statements concerned with activities, interests and opinions to a sample of consumers. The data is anonymized and the resulting profiles are very useful for determining the style and mood of promotional messages.

The Applied Futures typology in the UK was derived from the 'values and lifestyle' research programme in USA (VALS) and the latest version of this is summarized in Figure 6.1 with the sorts of research questions shown via the link on the accompanying web site. At the time of writing you could even answer these questions online and be profiled accordingly.

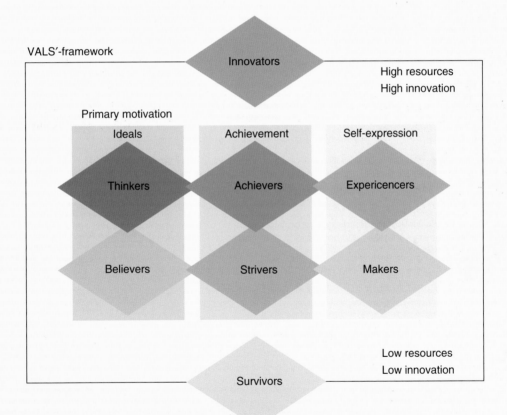

Figure 6.1   VALS

Source: http://www.sric-bi.com/VALS/presurvey.shtml

Figure 6.2 summarizes a current profiling of the UK according to this form of lifestyle research.

SELF-ACTUALIZERS Seeking the highest levels of personal development, they are people- and relationship-oriented and consequently are tolerant and empathetic. Innovative and experimental by nature, they are open, sociable, far-sighted and non-materialistic. They have the self-confidence to back their own judgement and the vitality to sweep others along with them. *18% of UK population*

INNOVATORS Self-confident risk-takers, they seek out the new and the different and set their own targets to achieve. *8% of UK population*

ESTEEM-SEEKERS Acquisitive and materialistic they aspire to what they see as the symbols of success, both in terms of 'possessions' and 'experiences'. *23% of UK population*

 STRIVERS Looking towards outer-directedness, image and status are important but only to provide acceptance from their peer group so hold on to traditional values. *10% of UK population*

CONTENTED CONFORMERS Want to be 'normal' so go along with the herd. Accepting of their lot, they are comfortable and contented in the secure world they have created. *24% of UK population*

 TRADITIONALISTS Risk-averse, they look to traditional values and behaviours for guidance. Quiet and reserved, they hang back and try to blend in with the crowd. *11% of UK population*

DISCONNECTED Stand apart and are embittered, and therefore apathetic. Tend to live in the ever-present now, not thinking of tomorrow's consequences. *7% of UK population*

Figure 6.2   Consumer Insight's 'Social Value Groups' 2005

Reproduced by permission of Consumer Insights: http://www.insightmc.com/insightmc_groups3.htm

www.   **Have a look at this web site, which provides more on the VALS Lifestyle and Values Group and allows you to respond to a version of the survey itself:**

http://www.sric-bi.com/VALS/presurvey.shtml

The following web site provides more on the Consumer Insights UK Social Value Groups:

http://www.insightmc.com/insightmc_groups3.htm

EXAMPLE 6.2

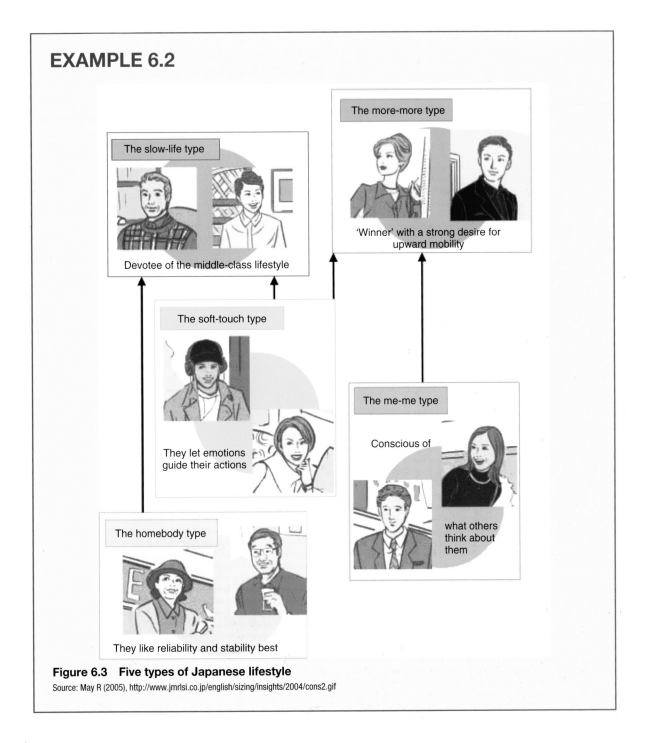

Figure 6.3   Five types of Japanese lifestyle

Source: May R (2005), http://www.jmrlsi.co.jp/english/sizing/insights/2004/cons2.gif

Referring back to Chapter 1, we discussed means–end chains to uncover underpinning values. With lifestyle research, there is a progression the other way; that is, interests, activities and opinions can help explain behaviour and buying activities, which in turn can inform target marketing approaches (Orth *et al.*, 2004).

Before we leave traditional lifestyle research it is worth linking this with our coverage of demographics in the previous chapter. The nearby Think Box provides a short case study, which demonstrates the combined use of these methods of understanding consumers in order for marketers to devise marketing mixes.

THINKBOX

Dragon Foods Ltd (DFL) is about to introduce a new, instant breakfast food. The product requires no preparation, and can be used as a meal substitute or as a snack, and as a dietary or nutritional food. According to a recent study of lifestyles and food consumption needs conducted by DFL, the following **lifestyle segments** could be considered potential buyers of the product:

1. Harried commuters – busy career people who need a source of energy and nutrition but who don't have time to prepare and eat a complete breakfast meal.
2. Career women – women whose work prevents them from making sure that their children eat a full and balanced breakfast.
3. Snack-servers – housewives who ensure that their children do eat a full and balanced breakfast, but who also want to provide them with good-tasting snacks as an added source of energy.
4. Calorie-counters – dieters looking for tasty, filling and nutritious meal substitutes.

Additional **demographic** data reveals the following:

1. Harried commuters – young career people, single or married with no children, mostly college-educated, employed in ABC1 occupations.
2. Career women – married women, aged 25 to 45 with two or three children of school age, employed in mostly B and C1 occupations.
3. Snack-servers – married women, aged 23 to 40 with one or two children of school age or younger, husbands employed in C1C2 occupations.
4. Calorie-counters – men and women, aged 18 to 49, from all walks of life, with no other distinguishing characteristics other than the common perceived need to diet.

Suppose DFL decided to select the harried commuters as its target market.

1. Recommend a suitable marketing mix, showing how the demographic and lifestyle profiles respectively could contribute to determining on each element of the mix.
2. How far can Dragon Foods combine all segments with a marketing mix?

www. Take a look at the following web site, which provides more on the Target Group Index and its fusion with customer data:

http://www.firstt.co.uk

Personality Variables

The word 'personality' is frequently used to refer to the capacity of a person for popularity, friendliness or charisma. However, these might be specific personality dimensions that an individual might possess. Someone who is unpopular, aloof and unfriendly still has a personality. We all have a personality and it is this that provides the essential differences between one individual and another. Personality, according to this interpretation, consists of the mannerisms, habits and actions that make a person an individual and thereby serve to make them distinct from everyone else. Eysenck *et al.* (1975) define personality as 'the relatively stable organisation of a person's motivational dispositions arising from the interaction between biological drives and the social and physical environment'. Personality is thus a function of innate drives, learned motives and experience. The various themes in definitions of personality are brought together by Kempner (1976) where the term is explained as 'that integrated organisation which determines each individual's pattern of behavioural responses to the environment', so that 'the study of personality is essentially the study of differences between people'. Like lifestyle, marketers can use some **personality traits** as the basis of segmenting their target market.

Psychoanalytic Theory

One of the first major ideas to inform personality research was provided by Sigmund Freud, who proposed that our personality is the result of the polarizing forces of the id and superego and the intervening and balancing mechanism of the ego. We discussed the implications of this for understanding consumer behaviour and for marketing activity in Chapter 1.

Trait Theory

Traits are an individual's characteristic ways of responding to the social and physical environment. Examples are aggression, honesty, anxiety, **independence** and sociability. You might think that for marketers it is an attractive segmenting approach to match brands with consumers' personalities, the logic being that we buy products and services that in some way reflect or extend our personality traits.

EXAMPLE 6.3

Two classic studies, which attempt to link traits with product use, concern the ownership of cars. Both were carried out in the United States and, among other things, involved car owners' preferences towards buying either a Ford or a Chevrolet. Evans (1959) cites as the stimulus for his research the fact that, while mechanically and in designer terms these types of car were almost identical, advertisers had tried to create very different brand images for them based on what they assumed to be profiles of car buyers. Likely Ford owners were popularly portrayed as independent, impulsive, masculine and self-confident, while probable

Chevrolet buyers were presented as conservative, thrifty, prestige-conscious, less masculine and moderate. A standard personality test (the Edwards Personal Preference Schedule) was used to measure these personality traits and others which might be relevant. The test was administered to owners of one or other make of car.

In a first trial based solely on the personality test scores of subjects, Evans was able to predict successfully whether an individual owned a Ford or Chevrolet in 63% of cases, 13% more than would have been the case in a purely chance situation. In a second experiment, using only socio-economic measures of the individual, these predicted correctly in 70% of tries. In a third experiment where a combination of both sets of consumer characteristics were used, Evans failed to improve his accuracy beyond that of his first try. Clearly, none of these results is sufficiently reliable to be of much value to the car manufacturer who wants to segment his market on the basis of consumer personality. A replication of part of this work by Westfall (1962), which used the Thurstone Temperament Schedule in place of the Edwards scale, also failed to distinguish satisfactorily between Ford and Chevrolet owners by personality traits, though it succeeded in distinguishing convertible owners from non-convertible owners; persons who scored low on the measures of activity, vigour, impulsiveness and sociability had a lower-than-average chance of owning a convertible.

Although cars have figured in a number of surveys, a wide range of products and brands have now been covered by tests, as is shown in the accompanying tables. Table 6.3 shows

Table 6.3   Personality and product choice: some examples

	Product/Brand	Traits	Results
(a)	**Fords/Chevrolets**	Achievement, deference, exhibition, autonomy, affiliation, intraception, dominance, abasement, change, heterosexuality, aggression	Allowed correct prediction of 13% more buyer's choices than chance alone would give
(b)	**Car types**	Activeness, vigour, impulsiveness, dominance, stability, sociability, reflectiveness	'No personality differences between Ford and Chevrolet owners.' Low activity related to low convertible ownership.
(c)	**Magazines**	Sex, dominance, achievement, assistance	Less than 13% of purchase behaviour variance explicable in terms of personality for
	Cigarettes	Dominance, aggression, change, autonomy	magazines or cigarettes.
(d)	**Toilet tissue**	45 traits	Personality of no value in prediction of brand loyalty, number of units purchased or colour of tissue.
(e)	**Private brands**	Enthusiasm, sensitivity, submissiveness	Less than 5% of purchase variance explained by these three traits; other traits of no value.

Source: Derived from (a) Evans (1959); Westfall (1962); (c) Koponen (1960); (d) Advertising Research Foundation (1964); (e) Myers (1967).

that research has involved a variety of traits. The results can be briefly summed up as follows: there is a mass of evidence that personality traits are linked with product and brand choice but the associations are, in the main, very weak. Correlation coefficients of the order of 0.3 or below are very common in these studies, showing that the proportion of variability in consumer purchase patterns that can be explained in terms of personality traits is quite small.

Type Theory

Another approach to personality analysis involves the classification of various **types** of personality. The classification of people as introverts and extroverts is a well-known example, which stems from Carl Jung's psychoanalytical theories.

The possibility that trait theorists have been looking in the wrong place for applicable information on the links between consumers' personalities and their consumption habits has led some researchers to substitute **personality type** variables in their marketing investigations: but the results have only been a little more encouraging than those for trait research discussed above.

For instance, we might consider the work of Cohen (1967). He used the research paradigm advanced by Horney (1950) (classifying consumers into compliant, aggressive or detached types). Compliant individuals are anxious to be with others, to receive love, recognition, help and guidance. Such needs may make them over-generous and over-sensitive so that they shy away from criticism and allow others to dominate them. They are essentially conformists. Aggressive people tend to be achievement-orientated, desire status and see life as a competitive game. They seek the admiration of others through being outgoing in their behaviour and may exhibit what are often called 'leadership qualities'. Finally, detached individuals try to separate themselves from others both emotionally and behaviourally; they do not seek responsibility or obligations and do not try to impress other people. Each of these personality types contains sufficient unique traits to be conceptually distinct from the others, though in practice it is probable that many individuals possess elements of more than one.

In consumer tests, Cohen was able to match these personality types with product/brand preferences and usage rates. For instance, highly compliant people were more likely than less compliant types to use mouthwash, prefer 'Dial' soap, and drink wine at least several times per month. Those respondents scoring high on aggression bought more men's deodorant than low-aggression types. The compliant and detached persons drank tea at least several times a week while the others drank it much less frequently.

Fruitful as these results appear to be, it is important to note that Cohen presents only selected data and that no statistically significant relationships were found for a wide range of products including cigarettes, dress shirts, men's hairdressing, toothpaste, beer, diet products and headache remedies. Nevertheless, this particular study tends to give encouragement to the use of personality type as a meaningful concept for consumer behaviour research. Preferences for media offerings were also discovered, taking the personality/consumer choice relationship beyond brand selection and usage rates. Aggressive individuals, for example, preferred exciting television programmes, and magazines like *Playboy*. Compliant persons more readily chose more homely programmes and typically read *Readers Digest*. The detached subjects had more mixed and ambivalent preferences.

Brand Personality

As we saw in Chapter 1, consumers buy benefits and even a degree of emotional engagement with brands. Just as humans have personality traits, brands are also sometimes invested with personality dimensions. For instance, Aaker (1997) identified five brand personality dimensions – sincerity, excitement, competence, sophistication and ruggedness – using 631 respondents who rated 37 brands on 114 personality traits. However, while there may be apparent similarities between human personality traits and those associated with a brand, there are some differences in the way in which they are formed (Aaker, 1997). For instance, we infer human traits on the basis of our observation of a person's behaviour, physical attributes, attitudes, beliefs and other demographics. In contrast, our perceptions of brand personality traits are formed due to our interactions (both direct and indirect) with the brand. For example, consumers normally have stereotypical perceptions of brand users, those who are associated with the brand (e.g. employees working for a brand) and brand endorsers (e.g. expert spokespersons or celebrities). McCracken (1988) argued that the images associated with these persons identified with a brand are transferred directly to the brands, leading to some distinct perceptions of brand personalities in our minds. Similarly, marketing efforts including advertising styles, product features and attributes, brand names and logos also contribute indirectly towards the formation of distinct perceptions of brand personalities in our minds.

A related approach views human personality as being the meanings constructed by an individual to describe the inner features and characteristics of another individual, based on observations of that individual's behaviour (Allen and Olson, 1995; Aaker and Fournier, 1995). Transferring this to brands, consumers can make attributions about the brand's personality (its inner characteristics) on the basis of behaviours and actions performed by the brand. This means that to create a meaningful and effective brand personality in consumer minds, marketers need to make sure that their brand is perceived to be doing things actively (e.g. use of animations or use of brands as characters in a story). There is also a relationship approach to brand personality research (Fournier, 1995; Aaker and Fournier, 1995). It is postulated that consumers develop trait inferences on the basis of their observation of behaviours undertaken by a brand in its capacity as an active, meaningful and a contributing dyadic partner. The trait inferences which are generated in this manner collectively summarize our perceptions of brand personality (Fournier, 1995).

> **www.** Woodside (2004) was commended in Chapter 1 in discussing the means–end chain approach to uncovering motives and values, and in Chapter 3 because it also incorporates Heider's balance theory within the means–end chain method. It incorporates Fournier's brand relational constructs as well.
>
> AG Woodside, Advancing Means-End Chains by Incorporating Heider's Balance Theory and Fournier's Consumer-Brand Relationship Typology, can be accessed via the accompanying book web site at www.wiley.com/go/evans.

> **www.** http://www.realmotivations.co.uk
>
> allows you to try out a lifestyle survey and to receive a brief outline of your personality characteristics. Please note that the lifestyle survey is not of the traditional anonymous type, but aims to produce lists of named consumers, as discussed in Chapter 11 (contemporary lifestyle).

Social Character Research

Inner-/Other-Directedness

A related approach to personality and consumer choice research derives from the behavioural categories put forward by Riesman in *The Lonely Crowd* (1950). Riesman uses social character to sum up the individual's personality type. His system has three categories: tradition-direction, other-direction and inner-direction, each of which has implications for attitudes and behaviour. Tradition-directed are those whose values and behaviour stem from the past. Inner-directeds have a strong personal sense of what sort of behaviour is correct and other-directeds' values, attitudes and behaviour are largely acquired from others. Table 6.4 summarizes a possible approach to target inner- and other-directed people.

Table 6.4   Inner- and other-directed appeals

Product	Inner-directed approach	Other-directed approach
Painkiller	Don't spoil your leisure time Showing individual involved with DIY	Don't spoil your leisure time Showing a group in a pub

If you consider the 'inner-directed' category, you may well remember our earlier discussion of lifestyles and the emerging prevalence of the self-explorer and other 'inner-directeds'. This is also of relevance later in this chapter where we discuss further implications of consumers whose inner-directedness is manifested in being self-expressive through their consumption.

> **www.**   Take a look at the following web site, which offers a link to an article summarizing Riesman's *Lonely Crowd* work.
>
> http://www.robertfulford.com/LonelyCrowd.html

Self-Monitoring

Self-monitoring is the degree to which persons adapt themselves to their social environment. Persons high in self-monitoring behave chameleon-like and are always trying to make good impressions on others. It is important for them to be accepted by others. They tend to buy products and brands that contribute to making favourable impressions on their reference group. Persons low in self-monitoring behave more according to their own beliefs and attitudes, and are less influenced by the perceived or actual approval of their social environment. Inner- and other-directedness looks similar to self-monitoring, but is somewhat different. Inner-directed people are concerned with their own thoughts and problems. Other-directed people are more social and looking for contacts with other people.

To distil much of the research into the use of personality in understanding consumer behaviour for marketing targeting purposes, there are some personality traits that offer much scope and these are: **innovativeness**, and **inner-** versus **outer-directedness** and the **self-concept**. Innovativeness is discussed in more detail in Chapter 9 on new product buying.

Perhaps one of the problems with personality in explaining consumer behaviour is that an objective personality test might reveal our true personality but we might not know that this is how we are or we may not agree with it. Second, we might want to disguise our true personality and therefore buy brands that in some way extend those traits we want to portray, and perhaps different traits at different times in different social circumstances. This leads us to a consideration of how we might want to be and how we think we are, rather than how we actually are, according to some externally determined personality tests and criteria. This is self-concept theory.

Self-Concept

This variation on the personality theme in consumer psychographics is based not on what sort of personality consumers possess, as identified through administering standardized personality inventory tests, but on how consumers perceive themselves.

Self-concept refers to all of the subjective thoughts and feelings that a person has about himself or herself as an object (Rosenberg, 1979). It is formed in an interaction process between a person and others in which the person strives for self-enhancement (Grubb and Grathwohl, 1967). It can encompass different things such as 'role identities, personal attributes, relationships, fantasies, possessions, and other symbols that individuals use for the purpose of self-creation and self-understanding' (Schouten, 1991:413). You can view self-concept from different perspectives (Sirgy, 1982). For instance, taking a psychoanalytical approach, you can consider it to be a self-system inflicted with conflict (recall the discussion about tensions between the id and the superego). Take a cognitive perspective and you can describe self-concept in terms of information processing about the self. Take a more symbolic route and you can treat self-concept as a function of interpersonal interactions. Whatever the case, the self-concept develops over time, is not innate (you have to learn it), has the purpose of protecting and enhancing your ego, is unique (it propels individualism in your mind) and it includes self-related knowledge and beliefs that are stored in your memory (Graeff, 1996; Onkvisit and Shaw, 1987).

Dimensions of Self

Self-concept is a multidimensional concept and can include actual self, ideal self, social self and ideal social self (Figure 6.4). The variants of 'self' are based on the actual self and the more aspirational ideal self (sometimes referred to as the **looking-glass self**). These variations are also based on whether consumption is private or more conspicuous with social connotations. In Chapter 5 we discussed gender and sexuality and provided examples of how some consumers will identify with sexual identities which might not obviously reflect their physiological gender. Perhaps the most appropriate variants of 'self' for the respective buying contexts are the actual self in the private context and the ideal self in the social context.

Multiple Selves

There is a discussion about whether self-concept is stable and consistent over time or whether it changes in different situations (Markus and Kunda, 1986). Since we are influenced by others and want to influence

	Actual self	Ideal self
Private context	How I see myself now	How I would like to see myself
Social context (looking-glass self)	How I think others see me	How I would like others to see me

Figure 6.4   Actual and ideal self in a private and social context

others in return, plus the fact that we are with different 'others' on different types of occasions, the general view is that we can all have 'multiple selves' or **multiple identities**. In other words, self-relevant thoughts and feelings can change once you change the social context or situation. For example, when you are talking to your boyfriend or girlfriend in private, you have a different set of feelings and thoughts about yourself than when you appear in a job interview. These multiple selves coexist in our memory and we tend to activate a particular self, making it more salient depending upon a particular situation or context. For example, Jamal and Chapman (2000) reported that respondents in their study experienced multiple selves and identities, revealing their differences and similarities with other groups.

This means a consumer is likely to subscribe to several self-images within their life sphere depending upon the situational context. The implication is that marketers need to facilitate the co-presence and aggregation of individuals having a multiple sense of being by emphasizing the experiential qualities of their products and by reinforcing feelings of consumers in different contexts (Jamal, 2003). A related concept is the notion of **possible selves**, which is a kind of self-relevant knowledge pertaining to how individuals think about their potential and about their future. These are the sorts of selves that you could become or you are afraid of becoming (Markus and Nurius, 1986).

Extended Self

Extended self is based on the idea that we can value certain possessions to the extent that they become part of ourselves (Belk, 1988). The possessions could include external objects, such as brands and collections, but also animals (e.g. pets), persons (e.g. children, partners), places (e.g. a religious monument), body parts and vital organs – everything that could be viewed as 'mine'. Citing the work of McClelland (1961), Belk (1988) argued that possessions become part of ourselves when we are able to exercise some degree of control and power over them. Just as valuing possessions leads to them becoming part of ourselves, losing them also leads to a loss or lessening of ourselves.

Our purchases become an extension of ourselves and the ultimate of this process is where we buy 'modifications' to our body such as tattoos, plastic surgery or body piercings (Figure 6.5). There are serious social responsibilities arising from this that marketers are not always keen to address (see Chapter 12). The 'ideal' **body image** as marketers stereotype it in their advertising or on fashion catwalks (yes, that's just as much 'marketing' as a advertisement) is often difficult for all to achieve. It can lead to eating disorders and body mutilation. It is further complicated by the fact that what is culturally seen to be a desirable body shape varies across cultures, so this reinforces the power of others (see Chapter 7).

Figure 6.5   Extending our self-image by modifying our body

The approach is based on an interaction between our self-image and symbols in our environment and is referred to as **symbolic interactionism**. This is based on the idea that we and our behaviour are influenced by our interactions with the society at large and with our reference groups. We will discuss the influence of reference groups in a later chapter, but it is important to note here that symbolic interactionism leads to an interesting form of research. Rather than investigating single products and consumers' self-concepts, it might be more meaningful to explore groupings of products which symbolize similar things (even if the products themselves are totally unrelated). For example, consider a selection of designer labels across product categories and whether this portfolio might reflect self-concept synergistically. Marketers often depict upmarket cars in advertisement for upmarket jewellery and vice versa.

THINKBOX

Along with all the variations of the self-concept discussed so far, consider also that we all act out multiple roles. Think about how different you are in today's 2 p.m. lecture from how you were in the club at 2 a.m. on Saturday – or how you are with your family and various other people. Indeed we might be with the same people but in different circumstances and will act out different selves each time.

What are the implications for marketing of your multiple selves?

Self-Image Congruence

The importance of self-concept lies in the fact that consumers tend to buy products (or at least some) that are perceived to be similar to their own self-concept. In other words, we have our own self-image and we can psychologically compare that with those of a typical user of a brand (Sirgy, 1982). Consider, for example, the case of a university student who views herself as a modern, trendy, flexible and cool person. She may be influenced by a particular brand of a computer that she views as being used by individuals who are also modern, trendy, flexible and cool. During such a psychological comparison, the product-user image interacts with the consumer's self-concept, generating a subjective experience referred to as **self-image congruence** (Sirgy *et al.*, 1997). When the comparison is between a consumer's actual self and brand/product-user image, it is known as **actual self-image congruence**. Similarly, consumers can have **ideal self-image congruence** and **social self-image congruence** depending upon the type of self-concept used in the comparison process. The self-image congruence influences our behaviour through certain motives such as the needs for self-consistency (i.e. the tendency to behave consistently with one's own view of self) and self-esteem (i.e. the tendency to seeks experiences that enhance one's self-concept), and is regarded as an important predictor of consumer behaviour (Sirgy, 1982).

Self-image congruence is important because research has shown that it affects a number of consumer behaviours (e.g. brand preferences and evaluations, purchase intentions, attitudes toward brands, satisfaction). For instance, Jamal and Goode (2001) investigated the effects of self-image congruence on brand preference and satisfaction using a questionnaire, which was sent to 500 consumers of precious jewellery in five major cities of the UK. A total of 118 completed questionnaires were received back and their analysis led to the conclusion that self-image congruence was a very strong predictor of consumers' brand preferences and a good predictor of consumer satisfaction. It was also found that individuals with higher levels of self-image congruence were more likely to prefer the brand and enjoy higher levels of satisfaction with the brand as compared to those with lower levels of self-image congruence.

Self-image congruence is of high relevance to advertisers also because they can tailor the contents of their messages depending upon the degree of self-image congruence experienced by their target consumers. For instance, Graeff (1996) conducted an experiment among 100 consumers to test whether advertising messages could be used to activate a person's self-concept and whether this activation had any effect on product evaluations and attitudes towards brands. Their general hypothesis was that the effect of self-image congruence would be greater for those who viewed advertisements that encouraged them to think about their self-concept than for those who viewed advertisements that encouraged them to think about functional attributes of the product (e.g. physical product quality). Their findings revealed that activating self-concept through advertisements had a significant effect and led to the generation of more favourable attitudes towards the brand and the ad. Similarly, advertisements that encouraged customers to focus on functional product quality reduced the effect of self-image congruence on brand and ad attitude.

Similarly, the effects of self-image congruence are likely to be stronger for products that are conspicuous in nature and are publicly consumed (e.g. cars and jeans) than those that are less conspicuous in nature and are privately consumed (e.g. soap and underwear). Marketers can, however, remedy this situation by bringing the privately consumed products out and making them more conspicuous through advertising (Onkvisit and Shaw, 1987).

Self-Concept Research Mechanics

The self-concept approach can be based on semantic differential scales showing series of bipolar adjectives, on which respondents may be asked to position how they see various brands, and/or themselves and/or

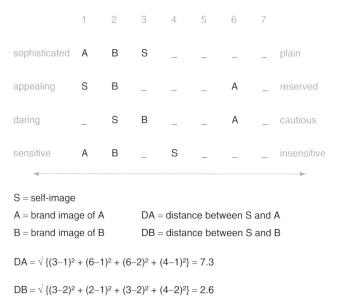

Figure 6.6 Self-concept distance scores (seven-point scale)
The smaller the distance score, the greater the degree of congruence between brand and self-images. Brand preferences can be predicted on the basis of such congruence.

their ideal self-concept. The brand preferred would then be the one closest to (having the greatest degree of congruence with) the segment's self-image or ideal self-image. With distance scores this degree of congruence is calculated and this helps to identify appropriate brand images to create and project (Figure 6.6).

An Alternative Approach for Measuring Self-Image Congruence

Sirgy *et al.* (1997) proposed an alternative method of measuring self-image congruence. Rather than using product-user images and self-images, they suggested measuring self-image congruence experience directly using Likert-type scales (Table 6.5). The method induces subjects to conjure up the product-user image right at the moment of response rather than through the use of some predetermined images. Sirgy *et al.* (1997) then compared the predictive validity of the two methods (old and new) in six studies involving different customer groups, products, consumption settings and dependent variables. Their findings provided support for the high predictiveness of the new method over and beyond the old one.

Inner-Directedness, Self-Concept and Self-Expression

As an expression of self-perception and inner-directedness, this approach could be of further significance because of the evidence that suggests that people are becoming more orientated to self-expression and 'inner direction' as opposed to following mass social movements. There appears to be greater pluralism in the market today (Henley Centre for Forecasting, 1992; Evans, 1989). The concept of postmodernism also includes a greater individualism, **pluralism** and even fragmentation (Van Raaij and Schoonderbeek, 1993).

Research reported by Publicis (Block, 1992) suggests that from 1973 to 1989 there has been a shift in 'motivators' from functional and rational factors (40% to 27% of the population) and 'outer-directedness' (static at 35%) to more 'inner-directedness' (25% to 38% of the population).

Table 6.5 Alternative method for measuring self-image congruence

- First, ask your respondents to think about a particular product (e.g. athletic shoes or women's apparel and clothing style).
- Then ask them to think about the kind of person who typically uses that product. Ask them to imagine that person in their minds and describe the person using some personal adjectives (e.g., stylish, classy, modern, sexy etc.,).
- Once they have done this, ask the respondents to indicate their agreement or disagreement to the following statements*:
  - This product (brand X) is consistent with how do I see myself (in situation X).
  - Using this product (in situation X) reflects who I am.
  - People similar to me use this product (brand X in situation X).
  - This product (brand X) is a mirror image of me (in situation X).
  - The kind of person who typically uses this product (in situation X) is very much like me.
- Ask your respondents to mark their responses on a Likert-type scale ranging from 1 to 5 or 1 to 7.

* Statements included here are for illustration only. See Sirgy *et al*. (1997) for their use of different statements in different contexts.
Source: Based on JM Sirgy *et al*., Assessing the Predictive Validity of Two Methods of Measuring Self-Image Congruence, *Journal of the Academy of Marketing Science*, Vol 25 No 3 (1997), pp. 229–241. © 1997. Reprinted by permission of Sage Publications Inc.

EXAMPLE 6.4

Some group discussions conducted for Levi Strauss in the mid-1980s revealed general praise for Levi's advertising in which rock music soundtracks were used. Many in the groups, however, expressed their own personal music tastes to be orientated towards different specific music styles of the time. The result was a poster campaign that showed 12 head shots of different young people who clearly had different fashion tastes, many of them music-based (Figure 6.7). The copy subheading reads: 'Blue jeans cut twelve ways'.

Figure 6.7 Levi individualism poster
Source: Levi Strauss

Figure 6.8 gives a further example of marketers' use of self-expression and individualism in their understanding of and subsequent targeting of consumers.

Figure 6.8   Self-expression
Individualized car number plates appeal to many who want to personalize their cars and allow others to see the link between themselves and the car they drive
© DVLA. Reproduced by permission

The Undesired Self

In the same way that within 'motivation' there are 'avoidance' motives, because of negative consequences, Hogg and Bannister (2001) describe the **undesired self**. Here the 'image congruence' approach is modified to allow exploration of undesired end states and undesired self-images. Hogg and

Bannister (2001) report qualitative research which reinforces the importance of significant others in determining what is 'undesirable'. An implication is to link negative consequences of, say, drink-driving with negative consumer stereotypes in order to discourage that behaviour (see Chapter 12). A UK TV advertisement showed how social embarrassment can be an undesired end state when an individual enters a fancy dress party as an elf only to find all the others are all dressed as Elvis (claiming that he thought his invite had stated elves!).

WWW. **Have a look at Todd (2001) Self-Concept: A Tourism Application, Journal of Consumer Behaviour, Vol 1 No 2 pp 184–196, accessed via the accompanying book web site at www.wiley.com/go/evans.**

SUMMARY

■ Lifestyle can be researched in different ways. This chapter has explored traditional lifestyle, which is researched via traditional market research techniques using anonymized samples of consumers giving their degree of agreement with a series of Likert statements covering activities, interests and opinions. The approach can be especially helpful in getting beneath the consumer's skin in order to devise relevant promotional messages, which fit with their outlook in life.

■ Personality refers either to an extensive range of separate behavioural traits (honesty, perseverance and hostility, for instance) or to overall types of character and response (extrovert and introvert). In spite of some high hopes and prima facie evidence that aspects of consumers' purchase behaviour might be closely related to their personality traits, empirical verification of this association is still lacking. Some traits are of value to marketers, however, such as innovativeness and inner-directedness/self-expression.

■ Self-concept theory overcomes some of the problems with personality in that this is concerned more with how individuals think of themselves (or want others to see them) than with how they actually are. This is important because much consumption is to do with covering up personality aspects we don't want others to see and with extending those traits we do want others to think we possess.

QUESTIONS

1. **Consider the following situation:**
   A self-concept study was conducted for a cosmetics company with a view to creating a marketing mix for a new perfume based on matching brand images with self-images. The cosmetics company had recently taken over another company and, among other products, had acquired a perfume. This was to be relaunched on the basis of their self-concept study findings.

Respondents were shown three 'advertisements' for perfume. The advertised 'brands' were given three different themes. One used a prestigious, sophisticated theme (the possible brand name here was 'La Vogue'); the second a sensual, slightly naughty theme ('Vamp'); and the third a romantic theme ('Romano')' Each 'advertisement' included appropriate narrative, picture sequences and models.

The results are shown in Tables 6.6, 6.7, 6.8 and 6.9. Respondents were asked to position their reactions on each of the scales. In Table 6.6 we see how respondents perceived the three 'brands'. There was, of course, no difference between the perfumes in a chemical sense – the three advertisements were merely three different ways of marketing the same product.

Table 6.6 shows their perceptions of their preferred 'brand'. Table 6.7 shows how the respondents see themselves and Table 6.8 shows how the respondents want other people to see them – that is, their 'aspirational' self-image in a social context.

Table 6.6 Brand Images

```
 1   luxurious       |__L__|___|___|__VR_|___|___|____| plain
 2   lustful         |__V__|___|___|___|__L__|___|__R_| innocent
 3   classical       |___|___|_LR__|___|___|__V__|____| fashionable
 4   sophisticated   |__L__|___|___|__R__|___|__V__|___| unsophisticated
 5   unadventurous   |___|__L__|___|___|___|__VR_|____| adventurous
 6   discriminating  |___|__L__|___|_R__|___|___|__V_| undiscriminating
 7   shy             |___|__LR__|___|___|___|__V__|___| unreserved
 8   prestigious     |__L__|___|___|___|__R__|__V__|___| not prestigious
 9   sensitive       |___|__R__|___|__L__|___|__V__|___| insensitive
10   inhibited       |___|__L__|__R__|___|___|___|__V_| uninhibited
11   romantic        |__R__|___|__L__|___|___|__V__|___| unromantic
12   sexy            |__V__|___|___|___|__R__|__L__|___| unsexy
```

L = La Vogue, V = Vamp, R = Romano.

Table 6.7 Self-Images

```
 1   luxurious       |___|___|___|___|___|_✓_|___|___| plain
 2   lustful         |___|___|_✓_|___|___|___|___|___| innocent
 3   classical       |___|___|___|_✓_|___|___|___|___| fashionable
 4   sophisticated   |___|___|___|___|_✓_|___|___|___| unsophisticated
 5   unadventurous   |___|___|_✓_|___|___|___|___|___| adventurous
 6   discriminating  |___|___|___|___|___|___|_✓_|___| undiscriminating
 7   shy             |___|___|_✓_|___|___|___|___|___| unreserved
 8   prestigious     |___|___|___|___|___|___|_✓_|___| not prestigious
 9   sensitive       |___|_✓_|___|___|___|___|___|___| insensitive
10   inhibited       |___|___|_✓_|___|___|___|___|___| uninhibited
11   romantic        |___|___|_✓_|___|___|___|___|___| unromantic
12   sexy            |___|___|___|_✓_|___|___|___|___| unsexy
```

Table 6.8   Self-Ideal Images

1	luxurious	|___|___|___|_✓_|___|___|___|	plain
2	lustful	|___|___|___|___|___|___|_✓_|	innocent
3	classical	|_✓_|___|___|___|___|___|___|	fashionable
4	sophisticated	|___|___|_✓_|___|___|___|___|	unsophisticated
5	unadventurous	|___|___|___|___|___|_✓_|___|	adventurous
6	discriminating	|___|_✓_|___|___|___|___|___|	undiscriminating
7	shy	|_✓_|___|___|___|___|___|___|	unreserved
8	prestigious	|___|_✓_|___|___|___|___|___|	not prestigious
9	sensitive	|✓_|___|___|___|___|___|___|	insensitive
10	inhibited	|___|___|___|___|_✓_|___|___|	uninhibited
11	romantic	|_✓_|___|___|___|___|___|___|	unromantic
12	sexy	|___|_✓_|___|___|___|___|___|	unsexy

Table 6.9   Demographic profile of respondents

socio-econ	age			
	18–25	26–35	36–49	50+
A	14	8	8	5
B	22	11	7	3
C1	21	10	9	2
C2	19	8	5	—
D	9	2	—	—
E	7	1	—	—
Totals	92	40	29	10

a. Calculate the distance scores for each brand against each of the two variants of self-concept. On this basis, decide which brand image you will select and with which version of 'self' it will be matched.

b. Decide which of the image dimensions you will select for the 'brand-self' matching determined in question 1a. Also, use the demographics in Table 6.9 to determine the demographic segment you intend to target. (Table 6.9 shows the profile of those respondents who actually preferred the brand you selected in question 1a).

c. Have a go at compiling a marketing mix for this brand. Explain the relative contributions of the self-concept and demographic information in devising each mix element. Be specific over these contributions, to produce a detailed 'mix' including: product range, package design, size, colours, on-pack information, brand name, price levels, selection of retail outlet type and location, promotional media and details of any TV or print promotional messages (not just 'copy headlines').

2. **Draw up a lifestyle questionnaire to measure your fellow students' activities, interests and opinions. Conduct some interviews and see if an analysis of the data produces well-defined homogenous clusters.**

3. **Do we 'buy things that extend our real personality'?**

FURTHER READING

Baudrillard J (1999) The Consumer Society: Myths and Structures, Sage. This is a work which emanates more from sociology than marketing. It provides a very insightful – and critical – examination of consumption within contemporary society. It extends our coverage of self and individualism, of lifestyles and consumption as affected by the media (in our terms, marketing).

Willmott M and **Nelson** W (2003) Complicated Lives: Sophisticated Consumers, Intricate Lifestyles, Simple Solutions, John Wiley & Sons, Chichester. The Future Foundation is a major research organization and think tank which explores changes in society as they affect companies and markets. This book brings together much of their recent work and is recommended highly. It extends our coverage of individualism, demographics and emerging lifestyles.

PART 1: JOURNAL ARTICLE

Symbolic Consumption in Teenagers' Clothing Choices

M Piacentini and G Mailer

Reproduced from Journal of Consumer Behaviour, Vol 3 No 39 (2004) 231–264.

Introduction and Theoretical Background

Research Context

It is generally accepted by marketing and consumer researchers that individuals consume products and brands for their symbolic properties as much as for functional benefits (Levy, 1959; Elliott, 1999). Individuals use products and brands as materials with which to cultivate and preserve their identities. Consumer goods are capable of serving consumers in this way because of the symbolic meaning that is embedded in them (Belk, 1988; Solomon, 1983; Leigh and Gabel, 1992). Contained within the symbolism are the messages that an individual may wish to transmit to other socially significant people. Goods are part of what Douglas and Isherwood (1996) call a 'live information system', and their meaning is grounded in their social context. For young people, these symbols are especially pertinent, as they are often in stages of uncertainty, gathering material possessions as a way of establishing their identity and gaining much-needed prestige (Belk, 1988). The goal of the current study is to learn more about the ways in which young people use clothes, and to develop understanding of why they use these symbols in this way.

Symbolic Consumption

Individuals use consumer goods and practices in a number of ways. First, individuals use goods as materials with which to create, foster and develop their identity (Elliott and Wattanasuwan, 1998). Here, the symbolic meaning of goods is used as an outward expression of their self-concept and connection to society (Elliott, 1999). Recent research into self-concept has focused on the premise that consumers develop a sense of who they are over time, through a long, continuous process of self-examination and observation. Thompson (1995) described the self-concept as a 'symbolic project' that is actively constructed and preserved through symbolic consumption behaviour. Individuals can develop a repertoire of symbolic consumption objects that can be collectively used in the construction of self-identity.

Related to the use of goods in the development of self-identity, is the use of goods as symbols for communicating with other consumers. There is evidence that people use consumption as a means to encode messages to others through their consumption, and also for decoding messages from others' consumption practices (Holman, 1980; Belk *et al.*, 1982). How successfully these processes are carried out depends upon the individual's knowledge of the codes involved (McCracken and Roth,

1989). These messages will only be successfully communicated if the symbolism in the offering is socially recognized (Grubb and Grathwohl, 1967).

The degree of product conspicuousness also influences the communication of self-identity messages through consumption symbols (Hwan Lee, 1990). Socially consumed products are utilized most often in instances of symbolic consumption (Hyatt, 1992), consumers being more likely to use products that are socially visible to others to communicate their identity (Hwan Lee, 1990). Where there is a high degree of social visibility, perceived risk is also high. As product conspicuousness increases, an individual's own choices are more likely to be contingent upon the consumption choices of socially significant others (Hwan Lee, 1990). In situations of high perceived social risk individuals are more likely to anticipate the likely evaluations of others and make consumption choices accordingly. It is therefore important for individuals to determine how other people in their social group might interpret the meanings of certain products and brands (Ligas and Cotte, 1999). Individuals can then use the symbolic content of chosen consumption objects to reflect their affiliation or connection to a particular social group (Elliott and Wattanasuwan, 1998). Similarly, they might reject certain products on the basis of their symbolic meanings if they prove to be incongruent with the consumption choices of significant referents (Elliott, 1999). In this way, symbolic purchasing behaviour also encompasses aspects of aversive consumer choice (Hogg, 1998).

A final aspect of consumer's use of these symbols encompasses both these earlier facets of symbolic consumption and the use of consumption to signify social distinction. According to Bourdieu (1984), people draw on three different types of resources (economic, social and cultural capital) to compete for status, referred to as symbolic capital (Holt, 1998). Economic capital relates to the financial resources available to the individual, while social capital covers the relationships and social networks that influence individual behaviour (Trigg, 2001). Bourdieu (1984) wrote about 'cultural capital' as knowledge that is accumulated through upbringing and education, and that confers social status. Cultural capital consists of a set of 'socially rare and distinctive tastes, skills, knowledge and practices' (Holt, 1998:3). According to Bourdieu, cultural capital is the lynchpin of a system of distinction in which cultural and social hierarchies correspond and people's tastes are predominantly a marker of class. Although an individual may have economic capital that can be used to consume certain brands and products that may confer social standing, without the necessary skills associated with high cultural capital, they will not occupy a higher social position. Cultural capital is critical to the communication of social position through symbolic consumption.

Young People and Consumption Symbolism

When consumers enter new phases of their lives, or take on new roles, they tend to be insecure and feel uncertain about how to behave. Understanding the important rites of passage in people's lives can lead to an improved understanding of consumer behaviour. Rites of passage are personal and social experiences that are partially constructed through the use of material objects (Fischer and Gainer, 1993), and are generally characterized by separation, transition or reintegration with former roles (Van Gennep, 1960). As consumers experience these rites of passage they enter a period of disequilibrium, and begin to assimilate a new status and make appropriate role adaptations (Rosow, 1976; Van Gennep, 1960). For consumers in role transition, there is a reliance on the symbolic properties of goods to assist them in performing the desired role (Leigh and Gabel, 1992). Ambiguity and uncertainty about their new role leads to symbolic buying behaviour.

The transition from childhood to adulthood is a major rite of passage in all societies, and involves a significant change in status and behaviours (Hill, 1992:399). In the absence of initiation rites, consumption habits take on a greater role in distinguishing the pre-adult from the adult (Ozanne, 1992:396). Young people, particularly in the West, tend to have a strong desire to communicate their maturity and 'adultness' to their peers through their consumption. Gathering material possessions is a way of establishing their identity and gaining much-needed prestige (Belk, 1988), especially at this time of 'identity crisis' for many. adolescents,

This phenomenon is not exclusive to young people immersed in consumer culture. Elliott and Wattanasuwan (1999) studied the ways in which young Thai Buddhists use symbolic consumption in the construction of self. They found evidence that these teenagers formed attachments to material goods in their endeavours to construct their religious selves (interestingly, contrary to the central concept of 'no self' in this particular Buddhist sect). Of great importance in the development of self and social symbols were social interactions with others in the religious sect. Here, the teenagers validated the symbolic meanings attached to consumption practices and experiences through discursive elaboration, i.e. through discussion, description and argument. The communication of symbolic meaning relies on the shared knowledge, language and understanding with others in the particular social group.

Methods

The research aimed to discover how teenagers use the symbolic properties of clothes and brands, and to develop understanding of why they use these goods in this way. Given the exploratory nature of the research questions, a theory-driven qualitative approach (Smith, 1987) was used. Clothes are a socially consumed product category, with strong social norms affecting individual behaviour. A number of authors advise that in research situations where there are strong social norms surrounding the subject or when there are a variety of personal tastes, it is preferable to use individual interviews for data collection (Morgan, 1988; Easterby-Smith *et al.*, 1991). Since both these criteria apply in the case of fashion choices, the individual interview was chosen as the data collection tool.

The sample was teenagers and the selection criteria for participation in the study were age, social class and sex. The study included two age groups: young teenagers (aged 12 to 13) and older teenagers (aged 15 to 17). Young teenagers, in the transition from childhood to adolescence, are known to be insecure about their appearance and identity, preoccupied with issues relating to how they compare with others (Odlum, 1978). Older teenagers, on the cusp of adulthood, have additional concerns related to leaving school and the responsibilities of entering the adult world.

The second selection criteria used in this study was social status. As discussed earlier, one function of the consumption of the product symbols is as an indicator of social position, and this is something we were interested to explore in this context. Teenagers were recruited to participate from two schools in Glasgow: a state comprehensive school and a fee-paying school. The comprehensive school was in a predominantly working-class area, housing families in the C1, C2 and D social class groupings. The fee-paying school had pupils attending from a wide catchment area and, although scholarships for less privileged children are available, the majority of the pupils come from families in the A and B social groups.

Finally, there is some limited evidence that boys and girls differ in the way they form their self-concept. Boys primarily want to achieve and maintain a high position in a status hierarchy (the emphasis is on doing, achievement and success). Girls place greater emphasis on forming and preserving relationships and this is the main impact on their self-esteem (Rose *et al.*, 1998). Given these differences, it was thought that there might be significant differences between the groups in terms of how they consumed clothing symbols.

Within the schools, several teachers took responsibility for recruiting the sample (quota guidelines were given by researchers), and all participants volunteered. All children participating in the study completed written consent forms. A total of 38 in-depth interviews were conducted between 22 January and 20 February 2001.

Participants were interviewed in their school, and were assured of the anonymity and confidentiality of the interviews. A topic guide was used, developed from the literature review and covering the main themes. These main areas of interest were noted and sub-divided, and a list of possible questions was identified to explore each sub-topic and formed the basis of the research interview. During each interview the interviewer adopted an active listening approach, reacting and responding to the particular issues raised.[1] Prompts and probing were used, to encourage elaboration. Third-person projective techniques were also used in an attempt to prompt the participant into projecting their feelings into the situation (Proctor, 1997).

For data analysis a systematic coding via content analysis was used (Morgan, 1988). A coding scheme was created from the conceptual framework and research questions stemming from the literature. This scheme was expanded as the analysis progressed, with emergent concepts coded and included (Coolican, 1994). This systematic approach to coding, combined with an inductive element, led to a comprehensive coding scheme, which was context-sensitive (Miles and Huberman, 1994).

Results

The research aimed to discover how teenagers use the symbolic properties of clothes and brands. We found that the clothes choices made by young people are closely bound to their self-concept, and are used both as a means of self-expression and as a way of judging the people and situations they face. There are a number of aspects to this, each of which will be taken in turn below.

First, clothes act as signals that they are similar to other people who wear similar clothes, an important issue when meeting new people. Throughout our interviews, participants consistently returned to the link between clothing symbols and the personality and interests of individuals, and the fact that they relied on these 'stereotypes' when meeting people for the first time. In this respect, clothes have a particular importance when meeting others and trying to establish friendships. While nearly all involved in this study were uncomfortable with the idea that clothes were the main determinant when choosing friends, they did agree that clothing was a good initial indicator of the personality and interests of potential friends.

> Interviewer: Do you think you pick your friends on the basis of what they wear?
>
> Participant: I wouldn't say I did, I'd say it was more on personality but in a way I think that goes with what they wear. But I wouldn't say 'Oh my goodness, I'm not speaking to her' because she's wearing a certain thing.
>
> (Female, 15 years old, comprehensive school)
>
> Interviewer: Do people at school form groups on the basis of their tastes, lifestyles or what they wear?
>
> Participant: Yes, I would say definitely but I think that lifestyles, what you wear and tastes all kind of go together as one. There are people who like certain bands who dress a certain way and they all stick together. There's the academics and they tend to stick together.
>
> (Female, 17 years old, private school)

In this context, young people use clothes to identify those who may have something in common with them. Clothes are important as they signify many different aspects of the character of the individual wearing them. Musical taste, social roles, occupation, social class, lifestyle, group membership, past times and personality were all cited to a greater or lesser extent. While there is a wide variety of factors that influence the way people dress, music in particular emerged as an important factor. The importance of music is unsurprising, given the central role of music to youth culture. One boy, who early on in our discussion stated that he did not choose friends based on their clothes, agreed that he did make judgements about musical taste (which was important to him) on the basis of clothes.

> Interviewer: What would you think about a new bass guitarist who joined your band who was wearing a tracksuit?
>
> Participant: (Laughs) I'd tell him to go home! You can tell an awful lot about someone's taste in music from what they wear. It may seem as if I'm generalizing here, but the simple fact of the matter is, I've never met anyone who wears Kappa tracksuits all the time who is into good music or could ever play the bass.
>
> (Male, 17 years old, private school)

This was a fairly typical position for the young people in this study to take. While they would play down the importance of clothing symbols in relation to meeting new people, many conceded later on in the discussion that these material symbols did occupy a central role in their social judgements.

Clothes are also used as a way of signalling that they 'fitted in' to the broad social group, as a means of ensuring that they are wearing clothing that is socially acceptable to their wider community, and not just in terms of their immediate friendship group.

> Interviewer: Do you think your attitudes towards clothes have changed since first or second year?
>
> Participant: Yes, definitely. I think back in first or second year you were more concerned with making an impression and the way you could do that was through clothes. You wanted to conform to what others thought was nice, rather than what you yourself wanted.
>
> Interviewer: Why do you think this has changed?
>
> Participant: I think now you are more independent and you're more stable with what you think and you don't feel as influenced by other people.
>
> (Female, 17 years old, private school)

> Interviewer: Do you think different groups of people tend to all wear the same clothes?
>
> Participant: Yes, I was talking to my friends about this. There's the group of people that are draped in gold, and they've got all the gold bangles and the gold earrings. I mean I like gold but not that much of it. And the big name tags and everything. And there's people in 'joggies' and 'trackies' and then there's people in the school uniform who have other things they wear outside of school. But there is groups and they're all going about with duffle coats, dolly shoes and draw string bags and me and my friends just look at them and think, 'I'm glad I'm not like them'.
>
> (Female, 12 years old, comprehensive school)

Within our interviews there was extensive discussion of the issues associated with conforming to the expectations of the wider community, and the importance of wearing clothes that were deemed to be acceptable. Clothes are used as material symbols of economic, social and cultural role in society, and we found evidence of Veblen's (1899) snob effect and of some using clothes as a symbol of their rejection of mainstream society.

The use of clothes to indicate affluence was mainly observed among children at the private school – unsurprising given their family's typically higher social and economic status. There were two strands to this. First, clothes were used as a way to compete socially, where it was important to be an 'early adopter' of elite and scarce brands.

Interviewer: You say you play a lot of football. Why did you buy the boots you have now?

Participant: I bought my boots because I loved them and someone else wore them. Silver Predators, I got them in Italy and they did cost a lot of money and I did buy them because someone else had them.

Interviewer: So who had them?

Participant: Del Piero. He had they boots. Barthez has them and so does Beckham. So I thought, 'they'll do me'.

Interviewer: So how do you feel when you wear them?

Participant: They actually are the comfiest shoes in the world.

Interviewer: Is comfort more important than the brand name?

Participant: I think it's less important. Even if they weren't comfortable I'd still have bought them.

Interviewer: Do they make you more confident when you're playing?

Participant: It does in a way. If you play against someone that you've not played against and they see you with these boots on they think, 'he's going to be a good player' and you tend to get more people watching you or looking at you.

(Male 17 years old, private school)

As this quote reveals, consumption of elite brands demonstrates wealth and shows commitment to the purpose for which the brand was purchased (in this case, football). There is also an associated 'halo effect', where individuals who are seen as wealthy and successful are also assumed to be clever and attractive, and better at performing their role in a specific context.

The other aspect of this effect is the use of clothing to indicate affluence. However, the private school children sought to distance themselves from this.

Interviewer: Why do you think some people want to show off how expensive their clothes are?

Participant: Some people think that it shows they have money and that that makes them a better person.

Interviewer: Would it impress you if someone came into school with a brand new pair of expensive trainers or a top of the range jacket?

Participant: In my opinion, I think it makes them look quite sad that they've went to all that trouble just to come to school.

(Female, 12 years old, private school)

Participant: I think there's an alternative fashion going on with all these skate-punk being anti-fashion and it's become a fashion itself. I think that's very funny. I do try and shy away from brands and what not, it's just advertising how much money you've got, which I don't think is necessary.

(Male, 17 years old, private school)

These views suggest a confidence in their social and economic position, where they do not believe that it is necessary to use the material symbols attached to clothes to demonstrate their wealth. These are teenagers in a position where they have economic capital, but they also have cultural capital that leads them to believe that such displays of economic wealth are distasteful, and inappropriate for them.

A different picture emerged at the comprehensive school, where most of the children came from families of lower socio-economic position. Here, there was evidence of a 'bandwagon effect', where clothing was used as a way of keeping up with others in the school. Buying branded clothes was important to demonstrate that they were not poor. These participants were aware of the symbolic value of their clothes and, while unable or unwilling to purchase the most expensive clothes, they did look for acceptable and affordable high-street brands.

Interviewer: Is it important for you to have branded clothes?

Participant: Not really but I'd prefer to have it because it makes you mix in. You don't want to be any worse than what your friends have got and you don't want to be any better so you just get the same logos as your friends just to keep up with them . . . I wouldn't want to stand out of the crowd; I just want to be part of it. I wouldn't want to be the big man.

(Male, 15 years old, comprehensive school)

Interviewer: Why do you think so many people are into brand names?

Participant: I'm not like that. But I think it does have an influence on people. I know from talking to people that if you say 'I bought a top from Matalan' they go 'Oh, cheapskate!'

Interviewer: Do a lot of people pay more attention to the price than what it looks like?

Participant: Yes, definitely.

Interviewer: Do you think people are impressed with expensive clothing?

Participant: Yes. If I do buy something from a cheaper shop I try not to tell them (my friends) about it so that people won't start slagging me off.[2]

(Female, 15 years old, comprehensive school)

Buying branded clothes was an important aspect of conforming to group norms. The discussion around this topic showed that it is not acceptable to these young people to be wearing cheap clothes. If the choice was made to wear these clothes, then the consensual view was that the child could expect to be teased by the others in the group, and it was unlikely that they would 'fit in' with the group. In this context, brands are important as signals to others of social position, but this is primarily indicated in terms of economic capital (i.e. that child was not too poor to purchase the latest brands/clothes). In addition, the brands signalled product knowledge (i.e. you know what brands are acceptable and fashionable). Buying these branded goods helped prevent the child from being the focus of any social punishment such as bullying or name-calling.

Finally, clothes were used to enhance role performance. Careful consideration was clearly given to clothes in different situations, dependent on the message that the individual wished to communicate. This relates closely to the different roles that they are performing, and the associated identities developed to coincide with those roles. The 'school disco', a separate event occurring at both schools, exemplifies this. The disco was an infrequent occurrence, where they had the chance to socialize with each other, free from the restrictions of school and its dress code. For some, this was a fraught time, requiring a great deal of thought and preparation in the clothing choices made.

> Interviewer: Can you think of any special occasions that you really think a lot about what you wear?
>
> Participant: If I'm going to a school disco or anything like that I think, 'I better put something nice on' because I don't want people staring at me. There's nice girls going to the disco as well.
>
> Interviewer: Do you want to try and impress them?
>
> Participant: Yes.
>
> (Male, 12 years old, private school)
>
> Participant: A lot of people are going to see you and if they see you looking like a complete state then they're not going to think a lot of you.
>
> (Female, 12 years old, private school)

This new and unfamiliar social situation presents challenges and those interviewed emphasized the importance of clothes in impression management. Clothes have the dual function of ensuring that they are dressed in a socially acceptable way (often conforming to the group norms), but also in marking their individuality in order that they may be attractive to others there. In more familiar situations, the symbols are not so important.

The study also provided evidence of clothing being used to facilitate fluent role transition. One example is the girl who has felt her clothing tastes change as her time to start university draws near, with her attire becoming more 'studenty'. Clothing was also used to mark the dissolution of certain life stages or roles.

> Interviewer: What kind of clothes do you wear? Do you wear sports clothes?
>
> Participant: I did when I was younger, wearing trainers, joggies, sweatshirts, it's not really me any more.
>
> Interviewer: What do you mean 'it's not me any more'?

Participant: I don't know, I can't say that they are kids clothes but if I was going out and I was going to spend money, I'd rather spend it on a nice shirt or coat than a football top. My tastes have changed. It's the same as most of my friends. I think as you get older you tend to wear less sports clothes unless you're involved in that sort of area with your employment or hobbies.

(Male, 17 years old, comprehensive school)

Participant: I've noticed that recently, because I'm going to Uni next year, I've changed the way I dress. I buy more cheaper things than I used to ... I don't like names showing, it looks tacky.

(Female, 17 years old, private school)

By adapting the clothing symbols they consume teenagers can and do compensate for the uncertainty that comes with a role transition. The symbols are used both internally, to make the individual more comfortable, and externally, to tell others who they are and what group they belong to.

The other main examples of clothes impacting on role performance come from sports. For those who were active in sports, comments were made about the role of the football strip and club tracksuit as an aid to performance.

Interviewer: How do you feel when you have your club uniform on?

Participant: You've got to represent the club. You look smart, you look like a team. You look the part.

Interviewer: What about the first time you put it on?

Participant: I felt good. It was the first time I had put on a strip before and I felt as if I was part of a team, that I was actually good at the sport. Especially if you had new boots, I always got new boots if I was starting a team.

Interviewer: Do you think you play better with new boots on?

Participant: I always thought inside before the game that I was going to play better, but it just really depends on how good you are and how fit you are.

(Male, 16 years old, comprehensive school)

There were also a few examples where the participants felt that wearing certain clothes improved their sporting performance. For example wearing the Karate training outfit *gi* made the wearer feel that:

Interviewer: Do you think that you perform your moves better with the proper outfit on?

Participant: Yes, I think it's a psychological thing. When you're in normal clothes you don't feel as important. It does give you a wee edge.

Interviewer: Can you think back to the first time you put it on? How did you feel?

Participant: Great, I just felt I was really getting into it, it was a way of clarifying that I was a karate person. Whereas before I was just doing it in my joggies and it didn't feel as if I was doing it properly.

(Female, 15 years old, comprehensive school)

Wearing her *gi* had a positive effect on how successful she was in carrying out her moves. The outfit also had a symbolism attached beyond that relating to performance, where this girl felt the outfit symbolised to others her commitment to the sport.

Discussion

Our research found that young people symbolically use clothing in many different ways. The level of importance attached to the symbolic qualities of clothes by each respondent varied, which affected how they consumed clothes. Factors such as their knowledge of clothing codes (McCracken and Roth, 1989), their level of self-monitoring (Auty and Elliott, 1998) and their attitudes towards materialism (Browne and Kaldenberg, 1997) all influenced this to some extent. Despite the variations among the sample, adolescents used clothes, as symbols, for many different purposes, and the extent to which they did depended on both the individual and the situation.

Clothing was found to be useful as an aid for managing first impressions (Holman, 1980), and acted as a signal that they are like other people who wear similar clothes. While some teenagers were more judgemental than others were, most felt that clothes provided useful information about a person in some way or another. Consumer stereotyping was the term given to this by Hyatt (1992) and many individuals felt that they were relatively successful at being able to base their judgements on this process.

Clothing symbols are also a useful mechanism for conforming, a theme throughout our discussions. A key dilemma for an adolescent is weighing up the costs and benefits of either conforming to social norms or expressing individuality. The findings suggest that 'fitting in' with the peer group is still of great importance to many adolescents and clothing is used to symbolize the link between the individual and the group they wish to be accepted by. In some cases displaying the appropriate symbols shields the insecure teenager from teasing and name-calling. Equally, by rejecting the symbols worn and recognized by the majority, clothing can be used to express someone's individuality. In our study, second-hand clothing was consumed for its symbolic qualities in a similar way that high fashion clothing is consumed. However, the desired message being transmitted is very different. Often, sub-groups within a school are formed by like-minded individuals who ironically conform, by not conforming.

Different perspectives also emerged about the role of clothes in communication about social position. For these young people, clothing choices are clearly distinctive and reflect their social position, in terms of economic and cultural capital (as anticipated from Bourdieu's work in this area). We found that the participants at the two schools had quite different understandings of the role of clothing in signifying their social position. For those attending the comprehensive school there was evidence that clothing choices were made to demonstrate economic competence. Buying branded clothes was important to demonstrate that they were not poor, and brands were a useful way of 'keeping up' with others in the school. In contrast, those participants attending the private school expressed distaste for heavily branded clothes, and generally distanced themselves from such clothes. These perspectives are the product of social conditioning, and will be determined by family, school and neighbourhood, reflecting the material conditions that are experienced as a result of one's position in society (Allen and Anderson, 1994). Taste in clothing and ways of dressing are based on distinctions, and enable people to judge and classify one another (Holt, 1998).

This echoes Bourdieu's ideas about the cultural elite, where 'aesthetic distancing' occurs as a way of marking an elite grouping (1984:34–35). The high aesthetic is defined as 'against the popular' and informs the tastes and preferences of those in this group. In the context of the current study, adopting an 'anti-brand' position in their clothing choices (and therefore not making 'popular' clothing choices), demonstrated a higher level of cultural, rather than economic, capital. There was evidence of a confidence underpinning these participants' tastes and preferences, learned effortlessly and unconsciously through their social world. For the participants in the comprehensive school (where clothing as a display of 'economic capital' was an important theme) the emphasis was on acceptance by peers, and social learning occurred via friends, through the media and popular culture.

A final role task that clothing is required to perform is making the wearer feel more confident, and better equipped to fulfil certain roles. Wearing certain clothes can have the psychological effect of reducing insecurities. Some authors (Jensen and Ostergaard, 1998) suggest that the more insecure an individual was the more conscious they will be concerning their dress. The findings of this study suggest that this may be the case, especially for teenagers. Respondents from both schools admitted that they 'enjoyed' wearing branded clothes, and that they benefit in a private and personal sense rather than benefiting from the consumption socially. This was apparent in the discussions indicating that branded goods are often preferred even when others will not see them. Here the symbols are not only used to communicate with others but also for the purposes of conversing with yourself, to reinforce self-identity, the 'symbolic self-completion' (Solomon, 1996), which tends to occur after a role transition has taken place. Adolescents, who are in the process of change, are expected to show signs of this and the research verified this.

It is clear then that the clothes young people wear have many functions. Teenagers are trying to satisfy many (often conflicting) goals through the consumption of clothes. This study has shown how complicated this process can be and has highlighted some of the decisions that have to be weighed up by the average teenager.

The findings also provide evidence to suggest that there is a link between clothing and self-concept. It was difficult to determine whether people define themselves and then choose their clothes based on that definition or whether their clothes and consumption provided them with a definition of who they are. Nevertheless, clothing consumption has a more significant effect upon the self or is influenced more by the self than most product decisions. The findings from this study tell us about the specific consumption practices of a particular group of consumers, and it may be difficult to extend the findings to other consumption contexts. Clothing, however, may only be part of a portfolio of products that adolescents use to maximize their role performance. Although it would be difficult to find a type of good that is consumed more conspicuously than clothing by adolescents, it may be worthwhile to conduct a similar study for mobile phones, which have become a status symbol for many teenagers in recent years. The same individuals who use their clothes to make a statement may use their mobile phone and branded food and beverage products to communicate a similar message.

Notes

1. The second author conducted all interviews.
2. A colloquial term to refer to continuous teasing, often quite hurtful.

REFERENCES

Allen D E and **Anderson** P F (1994) Consumption and Social Stratification: Bourdieu's Distinction, Advances in Consumer Research, Vol 21 pp 70–74

Auty S and **Elliott** R (1998) Fashion Involvement, Self-Monitoring and the Meaning of Brands, Journal of Product and Brand Management, Vol 7 No 2 pp 109–123

Belk R, **Mayer** R and **Bahn** K (1982) The Eye of the Beholder: Individual Differences in Perceptions of Consumption Symbolism, Advances in Consumer Research, Vol 9 pp 523–530

Belk R W (1988) Possessions and the Extended Self, Journal of Consumer Research, Vol 15, pp 139–168

Bourdieu P (1984) Distinction: A Social Critique of the Judgement of Taste, trans. R Nice, Routledge, London

Browne B A and **Kaldenberg** D O (1997) Conceptualizing Self-Monitoring: Links to Materialism and Product Involvement, Journal of Consumer Marketing, Vol 14 No 1 pp 31–44

Coolican H (1994) Research Methods and Statistics in Psychology, 2nd edn, Hodder & Stoughton, London

Douglas M and **Isherwood** B (1996) The World of Goods: Towards an Anthropology of Consumption, Routledge, London and New York

Easterby-Smith M, **Thorpe** R and **Lowe** A (1991) Management Research: An Introduction, Sage, London

Elliott R (1999) Symbolic Meaning and Postmodern Consumer Culture, in **Brownlie** D, **Saren** M, **Wensley** R and **Whittington** R (eds), Rethinking Marketing, Sage, London

165

Elliott R and **Wattanasuwan** K (1998) Brands as Symbolic Resources for the Construction of Identity, International Journal of Advertising, Vol 17 No 2 pp 131–145

Fischer E and **Gainer** B (1993) Baby Showers: A Rite of Passage in Transition, Advances in Consumer Research, Vol 20 pp 320–324

Grubb E L and **Grathwohl** H L (1967), Consumer Self-Concept, Symbolism and Market Behaviour: A Theoretical Approach, Journal of Marketing, Vol 31 No 4 pp 22–27

Hill R (1992) Transition in Turmoil: When Becoming an Adult Involves Criminal Behaviour, Advances in Consumer Research, Vol 19 pp 399–401

Hogg M K (1998) Anti-Constellations: Conceptualization and Content, European Advances in Consumer Research, Vol 3 pp 44–49

Holman R H (1980) Clothing as Communication: An Empirical Investigation, Advances in Consumer Research, Vol 7 pp 372–377

Holt D B (1998) Does Cultural Capital Structure American Consumption?, Journal of Consumer Research, Vol 25 pp 1–25

Hwan Lee D (1990) Symbolic Interactionism: Some Implications for Consumer Self Concept and Product Symbolism Research, Advances in Consumer Research, Vol 17 pp 386–393

Hyatt E M (1992) Consumer Stereotyping: The Cognitive Bases of the Social Symbolism of Products, Advances in Consumer Research, Vol 19 pp 299–303

Jensen A F and **Ostergaard** P (1998) Dressing for Security or Risk? An Exploratory Study of Two Different Ways of Consuming Fashion, European Advances in Consumer Research, Vol 3 pp 98–103

Leigh J H and **Gabel** T G (1992) Symbolic Interactionism: Its Effects on Consumer Behaviour and Implications for Marketing Strategy, Journal of Consumer Marketing, Vol 9, Winter, pp 27–38

Levy S (1959) Symbols for Sale, Harvard Business Review, Vol 37, July/August, pp 117–124

Ligas M and **Cotte** J (1999), The Process of Negotiating Brand Meaning: A Symbolic Interactionist Perspective, Advances in Consumer Research, Vol 26 pp 609–614

McCracken G and **Roth** V J (1989) Does Clothing Have a Code? Empirical Findings and Theoretical Implications in the Study of Clothing as a Means of Communication, International Journal of Research in Marketing, Vol 6 pp 13–33

Miles H B and **Huberman** A M (1994) Qualitative Data Analysis: An Expanded Sourcebook, Sage, Thousand Oaks, California

Morgan D L (1988) Focus Groups as Qualitative Research, Sage, Newbury Park, California

Odlum D (1978) Adolescence, 3rd edn, Wayland, London

Ozanne J L (1992) The Role of Consumption and Disposition During Classic Rites of Passage: The Journey of Birth, Initiation and Death, Advances in Consumer Research, Vol 19 pp 396–397

Proctor T (1997) Essentials of Marketing Research, 1st edn, Pitman, London

Rose M R, **Boush** D M and **Friestad** M (1998) Self-Esteem, Susceptibility to Interpersonal Influence, and Fashion Attribute Preference in Early Adolescents, European Advances in Consumer Research, Vol 3 pp 197–203

Rosow I (1976) Status and Role Change Through the Life Span, in **Binstock** R H and **Shanas** E (eds), Handbook of Aging and the Social Sciences, Van Nostrand Reinhold, New York

Smith M L (1987) Publishing Qualitative Research, American Education Research Journal, Vol 24 No 2 pp 173–183

Solomon M R (1983) The Role of Products as Social Stimuli: A Symbolic Interactionism Perspective, Journal of Consumer Research, Vol 10 pp 319–329

Solomon M R (1996) Consumer Behaviour, 3rd edn, Prentice Hall, New Jersey

Thompson J B (1995), The Media and Modernity: A Social Theory of the Media, Polity, Cambridge

Trigg A B (2001) Veblen, Bourdieu, and Conspicuous Consumption, Journal of Economic Issues, Vol 3 No 1, March, pp 99–116

Van Gennep A (1960) The Rites of Passage, trans. Vizedom M B and Caffee G L, University of Chicago

Veblen T (1899) The Theory of the Leisure Class, 1st edn, Macmillan, New York

Questions on this article

1. Conduct a review of the literature on symbolic consumption and discuss how this might explain your clothes purchasing.
2. Explore the relationship between symbolic consumption and self-concept theory.

PART 2

SOCIAL AND GROUP ASPECTS OF CONSUMER BEHAVIOUR

Having explored a number of individual aspects of consumers and how these can explain their buying behaviour, we turn, in Part 2, to social influences on consumers.

Here, there are powerful forces exerted by various social groups on consumers to conform to various group norms. We therefore analyse (in Chapter 7) the role of reference groups in this process and the types of social power they exert. A recent phenomenon is postmodernism and we examine the implications of this for consumer buying behaviour. This is sometimes reflected in the emergence of tribes and tribal buying behaviour. Another recent development is the virtual group. People are increasingly interacting via the superhighway rather than face-to-face. This includes interaction as consumers, either with other consumers (to exchange buying experiences) or with organizations.

We then turn to the family (also in Chapter 7). This is obviously the first 'group' that individuals experience and it exerts important influences over buying behaviour. We examine the changing nature of many Western families as manifested in, for example, an increase in the singles market. Families change over time and the family life cycle concept is very useful for explaining and even predicting consumer behaviour over time. Within families, there can be significant division of labour in terms of the buying process and we explore not only the roles of men and women but also that of children. The latter are increasingly influential and marketers are well aware of this. It is, however, not only the children themselves who can 'pester' but also parents can sometimes be targeted to buy expensive 'image brands' for their children. This is not necessarily because their children want them but because the parents want their children to portray certain images.

Chapter 8 is concerned with other aspects of social influence: culture and subculture. Here, we explore aspects of cultures, cultural meaning rituals. It is clear that many marketers are keen to globalize their marketing. But sometimes this can lead to problems because different cultures view the world in different ways. Marketers need to recognize such differences in how they target international markets if they are not to offend cultural traditions and values. It is all too easy to offend when communications media cross international boundaries so readily, as the Internet does. We also examine aspects of ethnicity here and show how these subcultures are a growing and important component of many societies. Marketers are increasingly targeting ethnic segments and we explore some of the implications of this.

Our 'reading' for Part 2 is a paper which explores how the roles of men and women in families have changed over several decades. The article also provides useful and practical clues for how markets should be targeting men and women.

Throughout Part 2, there are practical examples and references to material, including other actual research articles, which can be accessed via the accompanying web site.

CHAPTER 7

SOCIAL GROUP, TRIBAL AND HOUSEHOLD BUYING INFLUENCES

CHAPTER OBJECTIVES

After engaging with the material presented in this chapter and its associated exercises and reading, you should be able to:

■ Understand the nature of social group influence in consumer behaviour

■ Apply different types of group influence to consumer behaviour and marketing

■ Appreciate the dynamic nature of society and its effects on groups such as tribalism, postmodernism and virtual groups

■ Analyse and evaluate how families buy through different stages of development and change

■ Assess relative contributions of family members to the buying process

■ Explore the nature of pester and parent power and discuss some of the ethical issues in targeting to children.

INTRODUCTION

Homo sapiens is a social species. As a result we interact with others constantly. Each of us is a member of a family and may belong to a great variety of social groups such as university, work, leisure-related and friendship groups. We don't all need to be extrovert or 'soul of the party' types: others in a group often influence us and we can also be the influencers within these groups. There are also groups to which we aspire to belong or at least identify with even if they are not membership groups.

Through societal developments including what is referred to as postmodernism, there are significant changes in the nature of groups. We now have a plethora of constantly changing groups (sometimes referred to as **tribes**) and some groups operate virtually, via the Internet, yet they all hold powerful implications for consumer behaviour and marketing.

Many of the decisions made by consumers are taken within the environment of the family and are thus affected by the desires and attitudes of other family members. Many products are purchased on behalf of other members of the buyer's household, perhaps as gifts, and these purchases inevitably reflect some degree of **joint decision-making**. Even the most personal of purchases can be influenced in some details by the behaviour of the buyer's family and this social group demands special attention from consumer researchers. The family has also been affected by modern and postmodern factors, resulting in a number of different 'models' of the family, such as the single-parent household and indeed the single household.

This chapter explores these aspects of groups within a consumer behaviour context and with implications for marketing.

SOCIAL GROUPS

In many cases, group influence is instrumental in determining an individual's buying behaviour. Sprott back in 1958 wrote that a group is 'a plurality of persons who interact with one another in a given context more than they interact with anyone else'. In essence, a human group involves several persons who share common goals or purposes and who interact in pursuance of these objectives; each member of the group is perceived by others as a group member and all members are bound together by patterns and networks of interaction over time. The interdependence of group members is made enduring by the evolution of a group ideology which cements the beliefs, values, attributes and norms of the group (Kassarjian and Robertson, 1973).

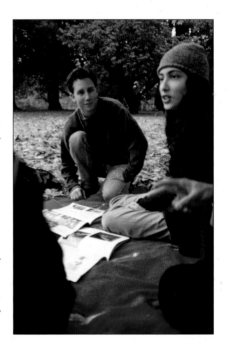

Behavioural scientists also refer to primary groups and secondary groups. Primary groups are characterized by their size and by the close relationships that take place within them. Examples of primary groups are the family (discussed later in this chapter), a seminar/tutorial group of students, and the 'mile-high hang-gliding society' at your university. Secondary groups are made up of more than one primary group and examples include your students' union, and the wider social system within a company or university.

Consumer research is also concerned with informal groups, which occur 'spontaneously' on the basis of common interests and the geographical closeness of members rather than formal groups, which are usually officially organized groups with a more rigid structure. Informal organization occurs, however, within formal organizations and is inevitably influenced by the 'official' structure of its environment.

Reference Groups

Any individual or a group of individuals that can significantly influence your behaviour could be called your 'reference group' (Bearden and Etzel, 1982). Consumers use them as sources of attitudes, beliefs, values or behaviours (even a single person, for example a celebrity, who carries out this function is also known as a reference *group*). These groups perform certain important functions for consumers. For instance, the reference group can provide settings and can enforce standards of behaviour. It can also act as a point of comparison against which consumers evaluate themselves. This is particularly useful because by social comparison we are able to judge the consequences of our behaviour. Three distinct uses of the term 'reference group' can be traced in the sociological literature and all of them are useful in consumer research. They are:

1. Groups with which the individual compares himself, his attitudes, his behaviour, his performance; this could be a formal contractual group (e.g. the person is a member of the group, approves the group values and has a regular interaction with the group) or an informal group or person.
2. Groups to which the individual aspires to belong; and
3. Groups whose social perspectives are assumed by the individual as a framework of reference for his own actions (Shibutani, 1955).

According to Park and Lessig (1977), reference group influence can be manifested in three main ways. First, an **information influence** when, for example, a consumer is considering buying a product and seeks information about brands in that product category, from family, friends, perceived experts (including those who belong to an association and those who work with the product as a profession). In doing so, the individual can also make inferences by watching the behaviour of others (e.g. endorsement or a seal of approval from an expert, or by observing the type of products used by others). This type of influence works because we aim to seek information in order to be able to make informed decisions. Second, there is a **utilitarian influence** which concerns a degree of conformity (see below) with the behaviour or norms of a group with which the consumer wants to identify. For example, an individual may purchase a brand because they want to comply with the expectations of others (e.g. family members or workmates or those with whom they interact regularly). This influence works well if the individual perceives that their behaviour is visible or known to others and that the significant others in the group can mediate some rewards or punishment. Third, there is a **value expressive influence** which is where the consumer buys, for example, a brand, which they think will enhance their image among others in the group. This influence works particularly well when the individual likes those in the reference group.

As consumers, we wish to be psychologically associated with others in order to enhance our self-concept. Many organizations offer 'affinity' credit cards which some consumers will see as a way of visibly projecting their own affinity with that organization and its values. Many charities, for example, offer such a credit card.

THINKBOX

Provide examples from your own experience or that of people you know, of each of the following: information, utilitarian and value expressive influence.

You need to note that reference group influence varies depends upon whether the product category/brand is a **publicly consumed luxury**, a **privately consumed luxury**, a **publicly consumed necessity** or a **privately consumed necessity** (Bearden and Etzel, 1982). We say a product/brand is public if other people know that you have got the product/brand and they can identify it with little or no difficulty. A product/brand is said to be private when you use it at home in such a way that others (except your immediate family) are not aware of it. There are some similarities here with our discussion of self-concept theory in Chapter 6, where we explored private and social contexts for consumption. Figure 7.1 summarizes the effects of different contexts on reference group influences.

Publicly consumed luxury	Privately consumed luxury
Examples: golf clubs, snow skis, sailboats	Examples: TV games, bread maker, paper security shredder
Strong reference group influence on both whether or not the product is owned and the specific brand which is purchased (because both the product and the brand are visible to others)	**Strong reference group influence** on product (everyone has it, so you have to have it) but a **weaker influence** on specific brand (because the brand consumption is hidden from public gaze)
Publicly consumed necessity	**Privately consumed necessity**
Examples: wrist watches, clothing, cars	Examples: mattresses, duvets, freezers
There is a **weak reference group influence** on whether or not the product is owned (because you have to have it as everyone has it) but **a strong reference group influence** on the specific brand which is purchased (because everyone will see it)	There is a **weak reference group influence** on **both** whether or not the product is owned and on the specific brand which is purchased (neither product nor brand is visible to others)

Figure 7.1   The context of consumption and reference group influence

Based on WO Beardon and MJ Etzel, Reference Group Influence on Product and Brand Purchase Decisions, *Journal of Consumer Research*, Vol 9 (1982), pp. 183–194. Reproduced by permission of the University of Chicago Press

Conformity and Independence

Group membership involves the individual in the acceptance of a degree of conformity and that the group itself evolves norms of behaviour which specify the ideal actions to which members should conform. Social groups also tend to have a system of rewards and sanctions through which adherence to group norms is reinforced positively and thereby encouraged, and deviance is punished and thus discouraged. Ultimately groups may exclude members who flout the norms which other group members accept and to which they conform. Figure 7.2 reflects marketers' understanding that pressure to conform can be a useful advertising appeal.

While conformity is an inevitable feature of social groups, absolute compliance is never found. Independence is also a valued trait for many people. Even in buying situations where people choose the same brands of a product as their friends, they often select an alternative colour or display their independence in some way. The motive, which is responsible for this desire to maintain freedom, has been called **reactance** and there is experimental evidence to suggest that, where compliance is forced, individuals will do their best to achieve some degree of autonomy and independence (Venkatesan, 1966).

EXAMPLE 7.1

Several interesting experiments have shown that, under laboratory conditions at least, individuals tend to shape their judgements so that they fit in with the opinions and behaviour of others. Asch (1955) reports a series of tests which relate expressed opinions to **social pressure** and which confirm that there is a strong desire in most people to conform to group judgements. Groups of about eight people were asked to match a single line on one white card with a line of similar length on another card which contained several lines. Each member of the group selected the corresponding line individually in a prearranged order. All of the group members except the last to report his answer were working for the experimenter, however, and gave patently false answers. The point of the experiments was to ascertain the reaction of the final group member to report – he alone was the subject of the tests. He could either trust his senses and refuse to conform with the majority or he could go along with the rest of the group despite the evidence of his visual sense.

In almost 37% of the cases, subjects chose to conform to group pressures even though the chosen line was clearly unequal to the reference line. This occurred despite the fact that in control tests – where no groups contained stooges and where no one was under any pressure to do anything other than what his senses suggested – less than 1% of cases resulted in mistakes being made.

Individual subjects varied considerably; some were willing to conform all the time to group pressures while others consistently refused to do so, and few subjects changed their minds after showing initial conformity or independence. Further trials were conducted to find out whether the size of the majority was more important than its unanimity. Groups ranging from two persons to 15 were used in these tests but, beyond a group size of three, increases in size had little further effect on conformity. Whatever the group's size though, the presence of a disturbing element – another person in league with the experimenter who chose to disagree with the majority, sometimes agreeing with the subject, sometimes not – reduced the majority of a great deal of its power and made it easier for the subject to disagree with the group.

Venkatesan conducted an experimental study of consumer behaviour which was intended to throw light on the questions of conformity to social pressure and the possibilities of reactance occurring in consumer decision-making situations. One hundred and forty-four college students were asked to select and evaluate one of three men's suits which were identical in style, colour and size and which were denoted simply by letters of the alphabet: A, B and C. Information provided for the subjects included the suggestions that the suits were from different manufacturers, that there were differentials in quality from one suit to another, that previous studies carried out at a prestigious research centre had established that the best suit could be identified by experts, and that the study in which the subjects were taking part was to determine whether buyers were capable of selecting the best suit.

For purposes of comparison, three experimental conditions were created:

Condition 1

This involved a control group in which subjects evaluated the suits independently, reported separately on them, and received no group pressures to conform or comply.

Figure 7.2 A conformity appeal
Buy this and you'll have great hair like me.
Reproduced by permission of Wella ShockWaves

Condition 2

This involved groups of four subjects, three of whom were in league with the experimenter. The seating arrangements were manipulated so that the confederates reported first, orally, that the best suit was B, thus establishing a group norm for the naive subject to conform or reject.

Condition 3

This was similar to Condition 2 but there was an attempt by the experimenter at engineering reactance, and the responses of the three confederates in each group were accordingly specified thus:

Confederate 1: I am not sure if there is a difference – it is not great; but if I have to choose then B is the *best* suit.

Confederate 2: (Looking at Confederate 1) You say B . . . Well, I cannot see any difference either – I will 'go along with you' – B is the *best* suit for me.

Confederate 3: Well you guys chose B. Although I am not sure, I am *just going along* to be a good guy. I choose B too.

When it came to the real subject's turn, the situation had already been structured so as to reduce his choice.

Table 7.1   Conformity and independence in consumer choice

Suit	Condition 1	Condition 2	Condition 3
A	17	11	14
B	10	22	14
C	20	9	19

The results, which are displayed in Table 7.1, are consistent with the hypothesis that consumers generally conform to group norms when making brand choices but reject attempts at inducing them to make particular brand decisions.

In Condition 1, where no social influence attempt was made, the distribution of responses did not differ from what chance would have predicted by a significant amount. In Condition 2, where conformity was promoted, the proportion of choices cast in favour of suit B was greater by a significant amount than chance would suggest (i.e. than one third), which indicates that conformity to a group norm is to be expected. However, in Condition 3, where compliance was induced, the proportion of choices of suit B was not significantly different from one third, indicating that consumers who realize they are being forced to conform to the group's standards may react by deliberately asserting their independence.

It is worth a reminder about 'individualism' here. In Chapter 6 we explored the trend toward greater degrees of self-expression and pluralism in society and this can lead to increased independence but, even with this, the individual will usually want the security and accepted behaviour norms which groups can provide.

THINKBOX

Consider the clothing market. To what extent do people wear garments to reflect their individualism and/or desire to conform?

Conformity is not the only dimension of group dynamics that has interested social researchers. Group cohesiveness has also attracted attention. Cohesiveness has been described as 'the overall level of attraction towards the group' which 'can be equated with "loyalty"' (Argyle, 1969). It is this factor of cohesiveness which makes a group something more than a mere collection of individuals; it involves feelings of belongingness and integrity, and develops as the group fulfils the interpersonal needs of its members.

Cohesiveness is also closely connected with the affective nature of the group and this suggests a method of measuring cohesiveness in terms of the likings and dislikings of one member for the rest of the group. Moreno (1953) introduced the method of sociometry to measure cohesiveness in groups; this method essentially involves asking group members which other person(s) they would prefer to share some activity with or to select those who would surely be unsuitable for that activity.

The results of a sociometric approach produce a sociogram, such as in Figure 7.3. This indicates the respondent pictured at the centre is a popular individual with whom everyone wishes to interact, and the bottom right is an 'isolate' individual with whom no one wishes to interact in the context specified. The triangle formed by (1), (2) and (3) represents a clique.

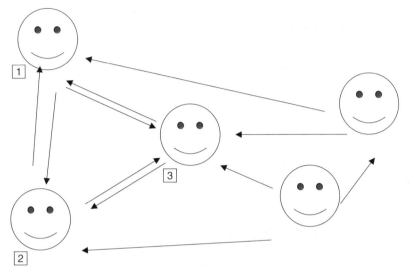

Figure 7.3   A sociogram

Leadership

The third and final facet of group dynamics that is useful for understanding consumer behaviour is the evolution of positions of leadership within groups and the formation of hierarchies. Leaders are usually defined as those who most frequently initiate action within the group, though this activity must, of course, be clearly relevant to the goals of the group whether formal or informal. Argyle (1969) comments that the emergence of hierarchies in groups is a universal human phenomenon and that, whatever the size of the group, some people communicate more than others. Other group members, perhaps less sure of their opinions, tend to look to the leader for ideas and inspiration. The person with most ideas, and who puts them forward persuasively, inevitably assumes a position in the hierarchy which reflects this while others delegate the propagation of ideas to them. Leadership may also be based on popularity and there is a tendency for the 'best-liked group member' to have some degree of leadership. In this case, they are then instrumental in releasing tensions, and questioning the role of the group and its members.

We explore two specific aspects of group hierarchies in Chapter 9: **opinion leadership** and **opinion forming**.

EXAMPLE 7.2

Stafford (1966) carried out an experiment involving ten already existing groups of housewives each with approximately four members. The groups were ranked on the basis of cohesiveness tests from one to ten, the first group being the most cohesive, the tenth, the least. The housewives were asked to select one of four brands of bread over a period of time and to obtain all of their bread from the source indicated by the experimenter. The four 'brands' of bread were, in reality, identical save that their wrappers were identified by a single letter of the alphabet: H, L, M or P. Analysis of the housewives' choices at the end of the experimental period indicated that the group's favourite brand was identical with the leader's best-liked brand for the five most cohesive groups. After that, the relationship broke down but the study demonstrates the influence of the group and its leader and suggests that this is strongest where loyalty and belongingness are highest. Although this was an experimental test, the housewives were unaware of the nature of the test, and the conclusion that primary groups affect brand choice appears to be a valid one.

Social Power

Group influence is determined by the power the group wields. There are different types of **social power** as proposed by French and Raven (1959):

- **Referent power** operates when a consumer identifies with or admires the group or person. Examples of this are (as we discuss in Chapter 9) when celebrity endorsers are used effectively in advertising.
- **Information power** operates when a consumer perceives someone as possessing knowledge about the issue. This also relates to examples in Chapter 9 where we discuss opinion-forming journalists. For example, motoring journalists writing in motoring magazines might seem to be knowledgeable about cars. The knowledge may or may not be real – just perceived to be there.
- **Legitimate power** is where a consumer thinks that the position of the referent confers authority in the context concerned; for example, police officers in the law enforcement context. Sometimes it is possible to simulate legitimate power in advertising, by portraying someone who might not in reality be a policemen or doctor, but the uniform/white coat they wear gives them assumed authority. In a cross-cultural context, members of a collectivist culture normally associate legitimate power with groups like the family elders.
- **Expert power** is where there really is a good degree of expert knowledge on the part of the referent. Here, well-known experts can be especially influential, such as a world famous astronomer advertising a telescope.
- **Reward power** is similar to what Park and Lessig describe as 'utilitarian influence', because it operates when responding favourably to the referent results in positive reinforcement (Chapter 3) by the group. For example, the purchase of the trendiest trainers might be rewarded by the approbation of the individual by their group, if trendy trainers are part of their credo.
- **Coercive power** can be the opposite of reward power. It encourages conformity by explicitly or implicitly threatening some form of intimidation. Fear appeals in advertising can be based on this, as can the more personal intimidation of the less desirable forms of 'foot in the door' personal selling.

Negative Reference Groups

The discussion so far has referred mainly to groups with which the consumer positively identifies and in many cases will aspire to have some sort of link with. Such groups are therefore termed

Table 7.2 Reference group influence

Product valency	Brand valency	Examples
Strong (+)	Strong (+)	Cars, cigarettes, beer, drugs
Strong (+)	Weak (−)	Air conditioners, instant coffee, black and white TV
Weak (−)	Strong (+)	Clothing, furniture, magazines, refrigerator (type), toilet soap
Weak (−)	Weak (−)	Soap, canned peaches, laundry soap, refrigerator (brand), radios

Source: Adapted by the authors from FS Bourne, *Group Influence in Marketing and Public Relations*, Foundation for Research on Human Behaviour, 1956, p. 8

aspirational groups. The notion of negative reference groups or **avoidance** or **disassociative groups** is also relevant here. These are groups or individuals whose behaviour, beliefs and values the individual deliberately avoids adopting as their own. It is probable that consumers select reference groups which are compatible with their self-images and ideal self-images, and that the use of inconsistent distant others in advertisements will elicit a positive response only in consumers who have already adopted the appropriate groups as personal reference points. Any distant reference group is bound to affect some segment of the market in this way and care must be taken to measure the possible extent of this before marketing plans are operationalized.

Non-Membership Reference Groups

A related framework for studying the reference effects of **non-membership groups** has been put forward by Bourne (1956) who identified conspicuousness as the most pervasive product attribute involved in reference group influence. Conspicuousness, however, can mean two things: not only must the product be capable of being seen and perceived by others; it must also stand out and command attention.

Bourne recognized that the influence of reference groups varies from product to product and set out to isolate those product areas where reference group influence was particularly strong. He claimed that the strongest influence occurred in relation to those products and brands about which people had evolved strong norms specifying ideal behaviour on usage patterns, brand preferences, and so on.

Further empirical work allowed Bourne to attach 'valencies' to the brands of certain products and to product groups themselves, denoting high or low reference group influence. Four possibilities exist: strong product valency with either strong or weak brand valency, and weak product valency with either strong or weak brand valency. Table 7.2 shows the products which Bourne allocated to each of these four categories.

TRIBAL AND POSTMODERN CONSUMER BEHAVIOUR

Consumers can express individuality but within the safety of groups – such is postmodern consumer behaviour. The examples in Figure 7.4 imply that consumers might want to identify with style or behaviour groups and this leads us into the area of tribal behaviour. Indeed this is the logical blending of

Goths *Indie*

Numetal *Pop princess* *Rude Boy*

Soulstress *Teenclubber*

Figure 7.4 Teenage tribes

© BBC Radio & Music Interactive. Reproduced by permission

extension of individualism and group conformity as explored by Patterson's (1998) tribes or the style groups of Evans and Blythe (1994).

For teenagers, especially, the search for individuality is manifested in a 'search for identity and belonging' (Davidson, 2003) thus supporting the importance of tribes: 'The majority tend to be more transient and consumer led. Kids can buy a look, an identity and an attitude' (Davidson, 2003). Perhaps the first teenage tribe was the 'Teddy boy' group. In the 1950s, for the first time, teenagers had more disposable income than teenagers of earlier generations and they wanted to display their independence from parents in the way they dressed, the music they liked and the behaviour they displayed. No longer did teenagers look like younger versions of their parents; they had their own and different dress codes.

THINKBOX

When you were a teenager to which tribes did you belong? What were the norms and buying behaviour involved?

It is also worth pausing to consider the multiple and fluid groups to which we all now belong and postmodernism can, to some extent, explore this. Consider the music market. 'Modernism' resided in the relatively few 'boxes' of the modern era, for example, rock, progressive, R&B, etc. But in the postmodern era there is tremendous pluralism, for many confusing pluralism. There are now multiple music pastiches as reflected in the sampling by current bands of earlier clips and the result is gangsta rap, jungle, hiphop, house, hardcore, acid jazz, boogie woogie, trance, world fusion . . .

–you try to complete the list and relate each to your own tribal subculture!

Table 7.3 summarizes some of the conditions operating within postmodernism. **Hyperreality** reflects a postmodern desire for experiencing man-made theme parks rather than nature-made natural environments. Even shopping malls might include themed areas reflecting, for example, Disney World. There is a degree of fragmentation in that consumption is frenetic. We have multiple roles, as discussed earlier, and this means our group membership is not only varied but also constantly changing. We have

Table 7.3 Postmodern conditions

Condition	Illustration
Openness/tolerance	Acceptance of difference (different styles, ways of being and living) without prejudice or evaluations of superiority or inferiority
Hyperreality	Constitution of social reality through hype or simulation that is powerfully signified and represented
Perpetual present	Cultural propensity to experience everything (including the past and the future) in the present, 'here and now'
Paradoxical juxtapositions	Cultural propensity to juxtapose anything with anything else, including oppositional, contradictory and essentially unrelated elements.
Fragmentation	Omnipresence of disjointed and disconnected moments and experiences in life and sense of self – and the growing acceptance of the dynamism which leads to fragmentation in markets
Lack of commitment	Growing cultural unwillingness to commit to any single idea, project or grand design
Decentring of the subject	Removal of the human being from the central importance she or he held in modern culture – and the increasing acceptance of the potentials of their objectification
Reversal of consumption and production	Cultural acknowledgement that value is created not in production (as posited by modern thought) but in consumption – and the subsequent growth of attention and importance given to consumption
Emphasis on form/style	Growing influence of form and style (as opposed to content) in determining meaning and life
Acceptance of disorder/chaos	Cultural acknowledgement that, rather than order, chaos and disequilibria are the common states of existence – and the subsequent acceptance and appreciation of this condition

Source: AF Firat and CJ Shultz, From Segmentation to Fragmentation, *European Journal of Marketing*, Vol 31, Nos 3–4 (1997), p. 186. Republished with permission, Emerald Group Publishing Ltd.

disconnected lifestyles and are happy to switch brands as suggested or implied by different groups and their memberships. Furthermore, consumers are no longer passive receivers of marketing. They interact with it and, via group interaction, make their own meaning of advertisements and brands.

As Table 7.3 illustrates, some argue that our postmodern society is characterized by social dissolution, extreme individualization of taste and consumption patterns and a fragmentation of collective meanings (Firat and Shultz, 1997). The point is that the traditional bonds of community are gradually destroyed by the shift towards a more abstract and rationalized society composed of lonely and isolated individuals. However, others such as Maffesoli (1996), Bauman (1992) and Cova and Cova (2001, 2002) argue for a reverse movement in which consumers are joining together by developing strong emotional bonds (e.g. sharing of same tastes, habits, intellectual pursuits or participating in events like animal rights protests or anti-capitalism campaigns). This ephemeral and unstable grouping of consumers who are joined together by sharing emotions, feelings and passions on a relatively small scale is termed as a **tribe**. However, unlike the archaic tribes, a consumer can belong to many tribes at a time because the boundaries of such a grouping are conceptual rather than physical (Cova and Cova, 2002). Also, membership of such a group transcends traditional cultural, national and race barriers – anyone sharing the same space and a common sentiment can join the tribe, which has a less articulated but differentiated form (Cova, 1997).

EXAMPLE 7.3

Figure 7.5 shows an example of marketers attempting to exploit consumers' desires to conform to the norms of tribal groups. Sometimes apparent individualism is actually tribal social group behaviour: different enough, but within the safety of a group.

Figure 7.5   Tribal group influence
Source: Versace

Unlike a market segment, the tribe consists of heterogeneous consumers with different demographic features who are capable of collective action and act as advocates for their causes (Cova and Cova, 2002). This has some important implications because marketers may not be able to treat consumers as a homogeneous market segment. However, the problem can be resolved by paying attention 'to the tacit and the visceral, especially the feelings of the consumers' (Firat and Shultz, 1997:198) which unite consumers in the tribes. Rather than focusing on building relationships between consumers and the firm directly, marketers can position their brand as a supporter of tribal links among consumers aiming to develop more *affective* consumer loyalty (Cova and Cova, 2001, 2002).

There are instances of where the tribe is not only a rallying point for shared values but these are expressed specifically through a brand. In Chapter 10 we discuss the case of the exceptional loyalty that some consumers have to Harley Davidson motorbikes. We also show that there are organized 'brandfests' at which Harley Owners Group (HoGs) members can share common passions (see Chapter 11). This leads to the notion of brand community, which is defined as a 'specialized, non-geographically bound community, based on a structured set of social relations among admirers of a brand' (Muniz and O'Guinn, 2001:412).

VIRTUAL GROUPS

With the growth of the World Wide Web interface, the potential has been unleashed for the widespread creation of online virtual groups (communities) on a commercial basis. As Loader (1998) has observed:

> The global communication networks which make up cyberspace are claimed to be altering almost every facet of our lifestyles, including patterns of work and leisure, entertainment, consumption, education, political activity, family experience and community structures. (p 3)

> Cyberspace has become a new kind of social terrain, crowded with 'virtual communities', in which people come together for sexual flirtation, business, idle gossip, spiritual exploration, psychological support, political action, intellectual discourse on all kinds of subjects – the whole range of human interests and needs. (Anderson, 1999)

Fundamentally, new technologies permit people to make direct connections with others by the elimination of the middleman, a process known as disintermediation.

Further, the like-minded come together irrespective of time and space issues to form groups and a variety of networks, a process known as 'aggregation'. Howard Rheingold (1993) has observed that:

> The future of the Net is connected to the future of community, democracy, education, science, and intellectual life – some of the human institutions people hold most dear, whether or not they know or care about the future of computer technology. (p 6)

Research by Robert Kozinets (1999) points towards Internet user experience as a key determinant – at least so far – of participation within a virtual community. People use networked computers for social relating and whether termed 'virtual communities' (Rheingold, 1993), 'brand communities' (Muniz, 1997), 'communities of interest' (Armstrong and Hagel, 1996), or Internet cultures (Jones, 1995) research reveals that online groups are often market-oriented in their interests. Kozinets (1998) refers to 'virtual communities of consumption'.

There are a specific sub-group of virtual communities that explicitly centre upon consumption-related interests. They can be defined as 'affiliative groups whose online interactions are based upon shared enthusiasm for, and knowledge of, a specific consumption activity or related group of activities' (Kozinets, 1998) and in this way are online versions of the **brand community** discussed above.

EXAMPLE 7.4

Muniz and O'Guinn (2001) studied the consumption habits, family and leisure activities, interests, use of computer-mediated communications and what was perceived as important by some families and users of Saab cars and Macintosh computers in a small neighbourhood in the USA. Their findings revealed that members of the brand communities shared a strong sense of consciousness (e.g. 'we-ness') which transcended geographical boundaries (e.g. members used the Internet to communicate with other Saab and Mac users). Similarly, members developed a strong sense of oppositional brand loyalty (e.g. deriving important aspects of community experience from opposition to users of competing brands like BMW and IBM). Members shared brand stories and felt a sense of moral responsibility towards others.

Kozinets's research outlines four distinct virtual community 'types'. The first of the four types are the tourists who lack strong social ties to the group, and maintain only a superficial or passing interest in the consumption activity. Next are the minglers, who maintain strong social ties, but who are only perfunctorily interested in the central consumption activity. Devotees are opposite to this: they maintain a strong interest in and enthusiasm for the consumption activity, but have few social attachments to the group. Finally, insiders are those who have strong personal ties to the consumption activity.

McWilliam (2000) argues that online communities thrive because they offer the participants a number of benefits. First, the online community acts as a platform or a forum for exchanging of common interests. For example, there can be discussion groups, regular forums on some topical issues, a research databases which members can browse and use, a job exchange forum and a daily newsletter to keep members informed. Second, consumers get a sense of 'place', with codes of behaviour (e.g. shared rules and values) by using the online communities. Third, online communities promote dialogues and relationships among members through the use of discussion groups and other mechanisms. Fourth, online communities encourage active participation by everyone (not by just a few) as thousands of consumers can read the messages and post their responses on a bulletin board or a newsgroup.

In a research project funded by the European Social Fund and the Direct Marketing Association (Evans, Wedande *et al.*, 2001) significant benefits emerged for those marketers who provide virtual communities on their commercial sites. In this study companies did, so were likely to be perceived more positively by at least a quarter of the users. Indeed, when asked directly, more than half of all respondents say they think it is a good idea for companies to provide virtual communities on their web sites. A third of respondents would also like to use a virtual community to communicate with the company itself. Providing such facilities on a web site may also strengthen the relationship that consumers have with an organization. The concept of relational interaction between companies and consumers is discussed in Chapter 11.

From the same study (Evans, Wedande *et al.*, 2001), a third of respondents claimed to have purchased something via a virtual community site and 50% used the sites to find more information about products and services.

So, we propose several benefits of online communities that marketers can exploit:

- For the majority of virtual community participants, interacting within a virtual community is an effective way of connecting to a diverse group of people.
- Individuals can choose their level of interaction, gather and give information and advice and express their opinions – all while maintaining an important, perceived, level of control over the interaction.
- It helps them find information.
- They enjoy the interaction with other people and feel that they 'get something out of participating'.
- It's an opportunity to discuss topics that they are interested in.
- The majority of enthusiasts like to receive advice from other people. A smaller proportion like to give advice. This may be a good indicator for companies to use bulletin boards for posting product/service advice.

The *relational* potential of such communities is clear and because the locus of control is nearer the consumer, there is great scope for the online relational community (Figure 7.6). Consumers can take more of the initiative and be proactive in their interactions with other consumers and with companies.

www. The following web site provides regular papers on a great variety of online communities:

http://www.onlinecommunityreport.com/

Figure 7.6 Consumer control over marketer–consumer interaction can increase via online communities

THINKBOX

What virtual groups/communities do you belong to?
What is your relationship with them and do they influence your buying behaviour
in any way?
Explore some company web sites and the virtual communities they provide.
How effective are these in developing greater relational interaction with their
consumers?

FAMILY INFLUENCES ON CONSUMER BEHAVIOUR

The traditional form of the family in industrial societies is the *nuclear*
or two-generation family, which consists usually of a mother,
father and their children. Extended family comprises mother
and father, numerous mature siblings who have spouses and who
all live in one large joint-family arrangement (Childers and Rao,
1992). Extended families exist in collectivist cultures such as India,
Pakistan, Thailand, Japan and China, whereas nuclear families
prevail mostly in individualistic cultures such as the UK. A child
in an individualistic culture is socialized to become a distinct,
autonomous individual with emphasis on self and being different from others whereas a child in a
collectivist culture is socialized to become an inherently integrated person with others who attach great
deal of value to conformity to others in the group (Rose, 1999). However, in individualistic societies we
see a trend toward different and often smaller families. There are now, for example, many more single
households, single-parent households and childless couples than ever before, and Table 7.4 also reports
on the rise in the divorce rate in UK which has an effect on the 'singles' market.

Table 7.4   Household composition in UK

People in the household	1971	2004
	%	%
Couple, no children	19	25
Couple, dependent children	52	37
Lone parent	4	12
	1950	2003
Marriages	408 000	306 000
Divorces	around 30 k	167 k

Source: Social Trends, 2005.

Table 7.5   Household consumption

11% of households earning   £100–320 per week own a dishwasher
56% of households earning   >£700 per week own a dishwasher

	Lone Parent %	Other families %
Ownership of satellite TV:	27	43
Access to Internet at home:	39	73

Source: General Household Survey, 2004.

Consumer Behaviour by Family Type

The General Household Survey, published annually by the Office for National Statistics in UK, provides a wealth of data on household behaviour, including product ownership, consumption of social services and so on. Table 7.5 provides a glimpse into the Aladdin's cave of household data.

> **www.**   **Have a look at the following web site, which provides more on the General Household Survey:**
>
> **http://www.statistics.gov.uk/ssd/surveys/general_household_survey.asp**

Intergenerational Influence

We learn our norms, attitudes and values from our families as part of our socialization and the effect of the family in our socialization is known as **intergenerational influence** (Childers and Rao, 1992). It is stated by Childers and Rao (1992) that a number of our behaviours including brand preferences, brand loyalties, information search, media usage and dependency and price sensitivity can be influenced by intra-family communications. In their study of US and Thai subjects, Childers and Rao (1992) found that intergenerational influence in Thailand was stronger for both luxuries and necessities whereas in the USA the influence was stronger for necessities than for luxuries. They concluded that the influence of family members was stronger in extended families (Thailand) than in nuclear families (USA). In a classic study, Young and Wilmott (1975) clearly demonstrated the influence of extended kin (e.g. grandparents, uncles) on the overall family's behaviour and decisions.

While some like Childers and Rao (1992) have compared the effect of different family types on consumer behaviours, it is still useful to explore the nuclear form of the family because it provides a good initial framework in the Western societies such as the UK.

The Family Life Cycle

The concept of a family life cycle shows how the family unit's interests and buying behaviour changes over time due to the progression from the single bachelor stage, to newly married, married with children, married with children who no longer live in the parental home ('empty nest'), and finally to the solitary survivor stage (Table 7.6).

Table 7.6   Modern family lifecycle

Life cycle stage
Bachelor
Newly married couples
Full nest 1 (with pre-school children)
Full nest 1 (lone parent)
Middle age, no children (aged 35–44)
Full nest 2 (school-aged children)
Full nest 2 (lone parents)
Launching families (with non-dependent children)
Launching families (lone parent)
Empty nest 1 (childless aged 45–60)
Empty nest 2 (retired)
Solitary survivor (under 65)
Solitary survivor (retired)
Total

Source: RW Lawson, The Family Life Cycle: A Demographic Analysis, *Journal of Marketing Management*, Vol 4 No 1 (1988), pp. 13–32. Reproduced by permission of Westburn Publishers Ltd.

THINKBOX

It is clear that each of these stages has its own implications for consumers' income and expenditure patterns. Family needs and the ability to satisfy them can be uniquely associated with each life cycle phase.

How would a family's needs change over time, for furniture, clothes, food, cars, financial services and holidays?

EXAMPLE 7.5

A recent promotional campaign by Barclays Bank depicted the life stages through which their customers go, by picturing a young single man, then a couple with a family and an older couple whose children had left home, and suggesting that the bank has financial service products to suit not just each stage 'now' but each individual as they progress through these stages of the life cycle.

The concepts here have been extended and applied within practical market analysis programmes such as SAGACITY (Research Services Ltd, 1981) given in Table 7.7. SAGACITY combines an abbreviated family life cycle with income and occupation. The result is a series of 12 categories based on life stage, whether both partners are working or not, and on 'blue collar' or 'white collar' occupations.

Table 7.7 Twelve SAGACITY categories

1	Dependent			1.1	White collar
				1.2	Blue collar
2	Pre-family			2.1	White collar
				2.2	Blue collar
3	Family	3.1	Better off	3.11	White collar
				3.12	Blue collar
		3.2	Worse off	3.21	White collar
				3.22	Blue collar
4	Empty nest	4.1	Better off	4.11	White collar
				4.12	Blue collar
		4.2	Worse off	4.21	White collar
				4.22	Blue collar

Source: Research Services Ltd (1981).

Roles and Decision-Making in the Family

As some of the traditional functions of the family have declined, others have taken on increased significance. Consumption planning has become a central function of the modern family in industrial societies and the different purchasing roles of various family members have become more important.

A variety of role players, both within and external to the family, affect purchase decision-making. Thus Kotler (1972) distinguishes five **buying roles**, which must be taken into account in analyses of family buying behaviour. These are the **initiator** (the person from whom the idea of buying a certain product first comes), the **influencer**, (who consciously or unconsciously affects the purchase in some way, perhaps as an opinion leader), the **decider** (who makes any of the decisions or sub-decisions that determine the precise nature of the purchase), the **purchaser** (who actually carries out the final purchase), and the *user* (who makes practical use of the item bought).

Almost all family decisions are affected by more than one of these consumer roles. For example, the selection of a venue for a family trip, although paid for and purchased by the parents, may be initiated and strongly influenced by children (see the **pester power** section, later in this chapter).

Husband–Wife Decision Making

A considerable amount of empirical consumer research has concerned the role behaviour of family decision units and within this research, the theme of husband–wife interaction in the decision-making process has predominated.

Komarovsky (1961) hypothesized that the amount of communication between husbands and wives varies directly with the egalitarianism and sharing of tasks displayed in the family. If one of the joint tasks is shopping, then the very scale and complexity of the operation demands considerable discussion between partners.

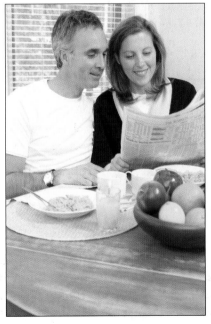

Summarizing the empirical evidence on husband–wife interaction, which might help confirm or refute this hypothesis, Komarovsky concluded that:

1. There is a tendency for wives to have more influence in decision-making in the lower socio-economic groups (and this suggests that the symmetrical type of family is to be found more in the middle classes);
2. There appears to be a curvilinear relationship between the family's social class and the extent of joint involvement in its decision processes: both low- and high-income groups show low joint involvement whereas middle-income families tend to be high in joint decision-making; and
3. Joint involvement is greater among younger couples than among older ones.

The possibility that either husbands or wives may predominate in decisions relating to particular products is confirmed by a well-known investigation of husband–wife relationships carried out by Kenkel (1961). The products mentioned by the couples were classified into five separate categories as shown in Table 7.8.

Table 7.8   Kenkel's division of labour

1.	Wife personal	e.g. clothes, jewellery
2.	Wife household	e.g. washing machine, cooking utensils
3.	Husband	e.g. books, clothes, watch
4.	Joint family	e.g. furniture, TV, car
5.	Children	e.g. toys, clothes.

Davis and Rigaux (1974) analysed the influence exerted by husbands and wives at differing stages in the process of consumption planning and decision-making. Their investigation was designed to determine whether there are differences in partners' roles at different stages of the decision-making process and how husbands and wives perceive their roles at each stage of the process.

Husbands and wives in 73 households in Belgium were asked to provide information on their decision-making relative to 25 products and services. Each respondent was required to specify the person who had been dominant in making the overall decision with regard to each of the 25 areas (Table 7.9).

According to Davis and Rigaux (1974), decisions can be classified in one of four ways for the families as a whole: **husband-dominant**, **wife-dominant**, **syncratic** and **autonomic decisions**. The last two categories require further explanation. When more than half the families made a joint decision with respect to an item, the decision was classified as syncratic; when fewer than half the families made the decision jointly, it was classed as autonomic.

Table 7.9   Davis and Rigaux's family decision-making roles

Husband-dominant	life insurance, other insurance
Wife-dominant	Cleaning products, kitchenware, child clothing, wife clothing, food, other furnishings
Autonomic	cosmetics, non-prescription drugs, appliances, housing upkeep, husband clothing, alcoholic beverages, garden tools, saving objectives, forms of saving, car
Syncratic	Children's toys, living-room furniture, outside entertainment, vacation, school, housing, TV

Having demonstrated that purchase decision can be classified in this way Davis and Rigaux turned to the question of the nature of **husband–wife** interactions at three stages in the decision-making process. The selected stages are:

1. problem recognition
2. search for information, and
3. final decision.

Figure 7.7 shows that **marital roles** appear to vary from phase to phase in the decision process but it has to be added that the differences are by no means large, and may not be statistically significant.

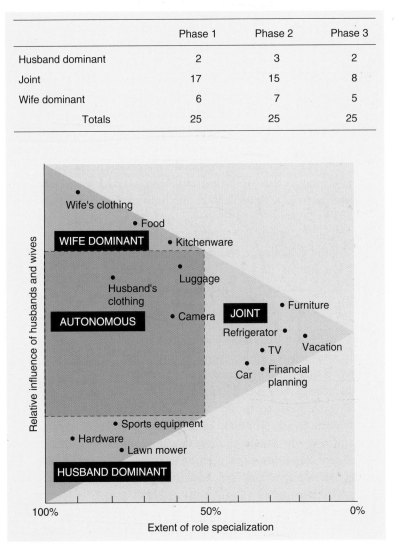

	Phase 1	Phase 2	Phase 3
Husband dominant	2	3	2
Joint	17	15	8
Wife dominant	6	7	5
Totals	25	25	25

Figure 7.7   Marital roles and decision process phases

Source: HL Davis and BP Rigaux, Perceptions of Marital Roles in Decision Processes, *Journal of Consumer Research*, Vol 1 No 1 (1974). Reproduced by permission of the University of Chicago Press

The focus on husband and wife roles tends to neglect the growing influence of children in consumption decisions and we now turn our attention to this.

Children and Pester Power

The influence of children on family expenditure has long been recognized and advertisers have frequently made use of this fact to persuade parents to buy certain products through appeals to their children. The market for children's products has itself grown rapidly in the last several decades and the teenage market in particular is a very attractive segment for many manufacturers and marketers, as we have seen.

What some marketers do is to target their advertising at a slightly older age group so that the 'trickle down' theory operates – younger kids see the product being used by their elders and want to follow their lead. By the time it has trickled down to them the older ones have been enticed to the next craze.

When children are of primary school age it is often school friends who become more important product influencers than parents. Observation and word of mouth are then very important in developing children's preferences.

Many marketers have really taken this on board and have started to get into schools with various sponsorship and 'educational' ventures. Schools need the help to ease financial hardship associated with their budgets but some teachers might be uncomfortable with this way of getting to the children's market.

Any viewing of TV at 'children's' times will confirm saturation of commercials aimed at children. Younger children may merely watch these as entertainment but as they grow, the brand and image become important and salient in children's minds as a result of associative learning processes and vicarious learning (see Chapter 3).

Children's TV viewing (which of course includes advertisement viewing), is significant. In one study (Annenberg Public Policy Centre, 1999) it was estimated that children spend 60% more time per year in watching television than they spend in school.

As well as child related-consumption, we are also concerned here with the role of children in determining more adult purchases, for example, which car the parents will buy and where to go on holiday and so on. The family is a decision-making unit, which means that there are different roles for each member. There will be deciders, influencers, buyers, users, gatekeepers (holders of information) and different members can play each of these roles at different times – including children. Indeed Lindstrom (2004) suggests that 8- to 14-year-olds are the most powerful gatekeepers of consumption information in many families. Children are increasingly influencing choice of housing, durables, clothes, TV, video, cars and holidays as well as in the more conventional areas such as sweets. Tinson and Nancarrow (2005) found that children thought of themselves as influencing 73% of family trips to the cinema, 63% of family holidays and 37% of family car purchase.

John (1999) reviewed 25 years of consumer socialization research dealing with what is known about children's development as consumers and the way they respond to marketing stimuli in different age groups. It was found that children pass through various stages of cognitive development whereby during the initial years (aged four to five) they tend to focus on surface aspects of product and brand information, learn to identify TV ads and distinguish them from other forms of programming and tend to see the ads as a form of entertainment (e.g. the ad is funny). By the age of seven to eight, they start to understand the intent of advertising (e.g. ads are trying to make you buy something). At the age of eight, children can also recognize whether the advertising is telling the truth and whether there is a bias in the message leading to a general lack of trust and less liking of advertising in general. In later years (ages nine to ten) they are able to focus on deeper aspects of stimuli and become even more sceptical of advertising. When children are 11 and 12, they may start to behave very much like grown-ups (e.g. may have good knowledge about products/brand features). However, at this age, they still lack specific knowledge of what tactics and advertising appeals are used by an advertisement.

In this context, one can argue that young children (aged eight and less) can be at risk for being easily misled or deceived by the advertising message as they do not have enough cognitive defence mechanisms to interpret and comprehend the truth behind a commercial message (John, 1999; see also Zhang and Sood, 2002). Clearly there are ethical issues here. Children have not fully matured, by definition, yet marketers heavily target children, often in very subtle ways with a view to nurture brand preferences among children.

Although there is evidence to suggest that brands are not as stable as they used to be – we switch more regularly in many product-markets – once a brand has become a clear preference it may well remain within the repertoire of acceptable brands for a considerable period. Think of the effort that the banks make to target just one age 'year' – 18-year-olds. As these go off to university their business is courted by most of the banks with offers such as discounts off CDs, free stationery, low bank charges and so on.

THINKBOX

There are anecdotal stories of 10-year-olds mugging and even killing for the 'right' brand of trainers in some urban areas of USA. How important for UK 10-year-olds are 'brands'?

Most UK marketing trade bodies outlaw practices, which exploit minors. How effective do you think these regulations are?

Many parents have succumbed to youth culture and look to their children for what is 'hip' to buy. In a survey for the BBC *Money Programme* (1997) it was found that 72% of parents admitted to £20 of their weekly spending being influenced by their children, 22% of parents thought up to £50 of weekly spending to be a result of pester power and even 4% thought that up to £100 of their weekly spending was based on this! This would amount to £5 billion per year if averaged across the UK. Lindstrom (2004) estimates that 'tweens' (8- to 14-year-olds) influence and even control $1.18 trillion pa. It has even been suggested that up to 80% of brand choices (even those aimed at parents) are 'controlled' by tweens (Millward-Brown, 2002).

EXAMPLE 7.6

The targeting of children to encourage pester power is not new, as Figure 7.8 shows; a 1950s advertisement for Bovril was aimed at both parents and children and the McDonald's bus will encourage children to want to eat more fast food (Figure 7.9).

Figure 7.8   Old and new examples of encouraging pester power
A similar approach was adopted by Rowntrees: 'Don't forget the fruit gums, Mum!'
Reproduced by permission of Robert Opie

Figure 7.9   Reminding children and parents of the 'fun' to be had as well as the food at McDonald's
Photograph: Martin Evans

THINKBOX

Next time you are in a supermarket, watch what happens as parents with young children go around the store.

Do the children pick up any items? Do they sometimes ask nicely for them, sometimes scream if they don't get them and sometimes surreptitiously put them in the basket – perhaps especially at the supermarket checkout?

Parent Power

Turning pester power on its head, there are marketers who recognize that some parents want their children to project a certain image (Brown, 2004). This is not the same as the children themselves saying what they want. Lego has promoted its kindergarten brick, Duplo, with a £5 million campaign through direct mail, plus advertisements in magazines sent to mothers of pre-school children.

THINKBOX

Advertisements for very expensive designer childrenswear often appear in magazines aimed at 30–50-year-old ABC1 women, thereby not directly targeting children but their parents instead. Such a strategy exploits adults wanting to 'live through their children' and express their own self-concept vicariously through their children.

What are the implications of this for consumers (children and parents), marketers and society as a whole?

www. Schaninger and Lee (2002) A New Full Nest Classification Approach, *Psychology and Marketing*, Vol 19 No 1 pp 25–58, which explores family life cycle issues, especially the full nest stage, appears on the web site that accompanies this book: www.wiley.com/go/evans

SUMMARY

■ Groups are specifically defined in behavioural science to refer to collections of individuals brought together to achieve a particular purpose. Primary groups are characterized by face-to-face interaction and evolve norms, which influence the behaviour of their members. Reference groups are social artefacts, which the individual uses for purposes of comparison, aspiration and to obtain values and perspectives. Group membership usually imposes a degree of conformity on the person.

■ Consumers are vitally influenced by their group memberships and by their reference groups. Brand choice, conformity and independence depend to an extent on group affiliations, and reference group influences vary from product to product and brand to brand. Socially distant reference groups also have relevance for marketing but some segments of the population must be expected to regard them as negative reference points.

■ Reference group influence can be manifested in the form of information influence, utilitarian influence or value expressive influence and the extent to which these are effective depends upon the product type. There are some characteristic features of living in postmodern society including fragmentation, lack of commitment, hyperreality, and emphasis on form and style. While some argue that we now live in a society of isolated individuals, others argue for a reverse movement in which we join with others on the basis of sharing common passions, feelings and interest. Such a group of consumers is called a 'tribe' and there are many manifestations of tribal behaviour including the teenage groupings. Related to the idea of tribe is the notion of brand communities and online communities whereby consumers participate as groups.

■ The family is the context within which many consumer decisions are made and there is thus wide scope for the attitudes and behaviour of one family member to influence the purchase behaviour of another. The effect of the family in our socialization process is known as 'intergenerational influence' and some of our brand choices and brand preferences may be guided by such an influence. Consumer needs and the ability to satisfy them vary from stage to stage of the family life cycle. Shopping behaviour for some products varies significantly with life cycle stage. The roles of husbands and wives appear to vary from phase to phase of the decision-making process; specific products and decision areas can be classified as husband-dominant, wife-dominant, autonomic or syncratic. Children can influence family expenditure in the form of pester power but there are some ethical concerns regarding the targeting of children by marketers. This is particularly so in the context of young children who lack cognitive defence mechanisms to understand and comprehend the advertising intent and the use of persuasion, deception and bias in commercial messages.

| www. | Read the article which follows Part 2: Belch and Willis (2002), Family Decision at the Turn of the Century, Journal of Consumer Behaviour, Vol 2 No 2. This can also be accessed via the web site at www.wiley.com/go/evans. |

QUESTIONS

1. **How do advertisers try to use 'group influence'? Think about this through relevant theories of group behaviour and influence. Give specific examples. for illustration.**

2. **Give examples of marketing activity that reflect French and Raven's typology of social power.**

3. Thinking about postmodernism, explain special groupings of consumers such as tribes, brand communities and online communities. Why do marketers need to study them?

4. Discuss family buying behaviour. How does the family decision-making unit change over time, and why?

5. What ethical issues are there for marketers if they recognize the importance of pester (and parent) power?

FURTHER READING

Firat A F and **Venkatesh** A (1993), Postmodernity: The Age of Marketing, International Journal of Research in Marketing, Vol 10 pp 227–249

Moore E S, **Wilkie** W L and **Lutz** R J (2002), Passing the Torch: Intergenerational Influences as a Source of Brand Equity, Journal of Marketing, Vol 66 No 2 pp 17–38. This is a very useful paper which convincingly explores the nature of intergenerational influences and identifies intergenerational influences for various products and brands.

Tajfel H (1981), Human Groups and Social Categories: Studies in Social Psychology, Cambridge: Cambridge University Press. This is a classic book on human groups and the social categories.

CHAPTER 8

CULTURE AND SUBCULTURE

CHAPTER OBJECTIVES

Having engaged with the material in this chapter you should be able to:

■ Explain what is meant by culture, cultural meaning and the role of shared consumption rituals

■ Examine the nature of differing consumer values across cultures and their implications for national and international marketing and standardization versus customization.

■ Explore the nature and implications of 'country of origin' for marketers and consumers.

■ Explain what are subcultures, ethnic subcultures, ethnicity and ethnic identity and the implications of these for targeting.

■ Explain acculturation and the way it applies to the understanding of consumer behaviour of ethnic minority consumers.

INTRODUCTION

It might be a cliché to say that the world is getting smaller in terms of travel, communication, trade and population movements, but because more marketers are targeting more markets, this reinforces the importance of recognizing whatever **diversity** there is in these markets. There are plenty of examples of companies' international marketing strategies failing where this was not the case. Later in the chapter you will find some examples of brand names, which have not 'converted' well to international markets and other examples of a lack of understanding of how to interact with people in different societies. So, as markets and marketing become more international and in some cases global, it is increasingly important to recognize cultural differences and to respect different consumers' values, traditions and ways of life.

We need to bear in mind that societies differ radically, such that apparently homely materialities can assume startlingly different meanings as one passes from one social context to another. It is also the case that within a particular society, such as a country, there are often different **subcultures** reflecting a growing cosmopolitan mix within populations. Subcultures often differ in their place in, and understanding of, patterns of class, status, ethnicity and the like. With greater opportunities for travel, communication and immigration/emigration, many societies see original indigenous populations being enriched by the experiences and knowledge of those from different cultures. The resulting 'minorities' can be of significant and growing proportion and will retain their own values and lifestyles but within their new environments. Marketers need to respect them and to understand the consumption behaviour of these ethnic segments.

This chapter is structured around these issues. We start by exploring culture: its meaning and implications for consumers and marketers and then narrow the focus to examine the characteristics of subcultural behaviour.

CULTURE

There are many definitions and descriptions of **culture** in the literature, many going as far back as the beginning of the twentieth century. Few provide as helpful a 'classification' as Johnson (1962). To him, culture comprises:

- **Cognitive elements and beliefs:** These are what a society 'knows' (and transmits from generation to generation) about the physical and social worlds and the way in which society works and its religious beliefs.
- **Values and norms:** These inform how the majority in the society are expected to behave. Non-normative behaviour is how the individual responds and reacts to these more generalized societal norms.
- **Sign, signals and symbols:** These include language and the variety of conventions in a society for conveying meaning. In terms of language, it is sometimes said, jokingly, that the US and UK cultures are separated by a common language.

It is worth pointing out that culture is dynamic; it changes as new ideas come along and as the environment changes, for example as a result of climate change or technological change which in turn can effect changes in lifestyles. Marketing can also impact upon cultural change. In the UK, before McDonald's fast food restaurants opened, market research revealed a liking for waiter/waitress service and a dislike of brightly lit venues. But as the US style format appeared in UK, the British soon changed their lifestyles to fit and so one aspect of their culture was changed. Indeed 'McDonaldization' is a term used to reflect the spread of American culture across other societies. The advent of the microwave and 'instant' meals provided impetus in many Western societies for the harried lifestyles of fragmented households and there is a 'chicken and egg' debate about which came first.

Culture and Meaning

Culture can also be defined as the **meaning system** that members of any specific group use to inform their lives. This meaning system provides us with a sense of identity (who we are) and rationale for our actions (how we should behave and what we should be doing in different contexts). It also helps us to make sense of what other people and even objects stand for and how and in what sense we should deal with them. Consumer products are a part of this system of meaning, which is often culturally specific and shared, learned and transmitted through generations. The food we eat, the clothes we wear, the type of transport we use every day and the possessions we love all serve as a media for the expression of our cultural meaning.

McCracken (1986) argues that culture is the lens through which people see their world. It is also a blueprint of human activity. As a lens, culture determines how we see our world and as a blueprint, it determines how the world is fashioned by our efforts. However, culture cannot exist without perception, without the attribution of meaning (Chapman 1992). There can be no outsider accounts, no extra-cultural observers; we are all in cultures of our own, and a recognition of this is a step to understanding it (Jamal, 1997).

EXAMPLE 8.1

This point can be illustrated through an example. Imagine you are in India and you see two adolescent Hindu boys walking together holding their hands. You may instantly get the impression that the two boys are homosexuals. However, to the boys and to everyone around them in the Indian culture, the same act signifies friendship and solidarity with each other (Spradley and McCurdy, 1977). Similar examples of differences in classification and meaning systems can be found in family and kinship patterns around the world.

McCracken (1986) uses the term cultural category to represent the basic distinctions that a culture utilizes to divide up its world of everyday experiences. Examples of cultural categories include time (e.g. leisure vs. work time), space (e.g. personal vs. public) and person (e.g. gender). Such categorizations and distinctions help us understand and comprehend our world of everyday experiences. These categorizations are often culturally specific and could be subject to change. For instance, we in the West have a strong sense of private space, which requires some distance between us as individuals and others. However, such a distinction may not be that significant in some other cultures where conformity to group is more important than valuing one's own individual self. The notion that culture is concerned with meaning implies that we should be mostly concerned with the study of people in groups, since meaning is a shared phenomenon and plays an important role in group life.

One aim of studying culture is then to find a way of understanding and describing the 'lenses' and 'blueprints' to which McCracken refers. We are also encouraged to investigate various cultural categories and cultural meanings that are important to each culture. In order to get a better understanding of cultural categories and meanings, marketers as well as consumer researchers need to think about adopting some qualitative and interpretive methods of investigation. One such interpretive approach is an ethnographic account of people and their meanings where time is spent observing and participating in consumption experiences of consumers in natural settings (Arnould and Wallendorf, 1994). Sufficient time should be spent (e.g. couple of months) meeting a sample of consumers on a regular basis and researchers should communicate with them through their language, from the 'native's point of view' (Geertz, 1973). You may find some other methods such as focus groups and long interviews (McCracken, 1988) to be quite effective as well.

According to the **meaning-transfer model** (Figure 8.1) suggested by McCracken (1986), the meaning originally resides in the *culturally constituted world*, which is the world of everyday experiences in which consumers live and make sense of marketing stimuli. The meaning is then disengaged and transferred

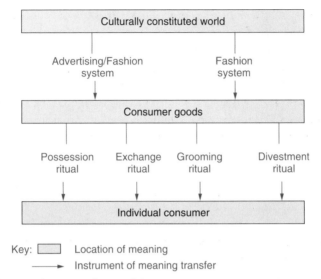

Figure 8.1   McCracken's meaning-transfer model
Source: G McCracken, Culture and Consumption, *Journal of Consumer Research*, Vol 13 (June 1986), pp. 71–84. Reproduced by permission of the University of Chicago Press

to consumer goods via macro mechanisms such as advertising and fashion systems. The meaning is finally transferred to individual consumers through a range of *symbolic actions* such as gift exchange rituals, possession rituals, grooming rituals and divestment rituals. Since **rituals** play an important part in consumers' lives and the way consumers make sense of the world around them, we will discuss them in the next section.

It is important at this stage to note that the underlying assumptions of the meaning transfer model are that: cultural meaning is attached to consumer goods; cultural meaning can be communicated by goods; and consumers turn to consumer goods as a source of cultural meaning. This implies that consumers do not simply consume products for their material benefits but consume the symbolic meaning of those goods as portrayed in their images (Elliott, 1997). Consumption of products and brands thus becomes the very arena in which 'culture is fought over and licked into shape' (Douglas and Isherwood, 1980:57).

Cultural Rituals

In our daily lives, we normally engage in a number of repetitive and apparently simple behaviours – **cultural rituals**. For example, most of us go to work/study on a fairly regular basis. We also have to eat our food (sometimes alone and sometimes with the family) and go shopping (sometimes more than once a week). Although they look simple, these types of repetitive behaviours link us to our physical, temporal, social and cultural environments. In order to reflect many of our everyday as well as extraordinary experiences, Rook (1985:252) defined ritual as:

  a type of expressive, symbolic activity constructed of multiple behaviours that occur in a fixed, episodic sequence, and that tend to be repeated over time. **Ritual behaviour** is dramatically scripted and acted out and is performed with formality, seriousness, and inner intensity. (emboldening added)

Some important features of a ritual could include **scripted behaviour**, the use of artefacts, a serious and intense atmosphere, an audience, evocative and stylized staging, a community of believing participants and the symbolic meanings of actions (Gainer, 1995). Rituals involve a variety of social and psychological processes, which perform many individual and societal functions (Werner *et al.* 1988).

A significant underlying feature of a ritual is that it can be *public* or *shared* with others in some ways (Gainer, 1995). For instance, when we observe rituals associated with many of our communal events (e.g. communal feasts, weddings), we find that these events and their rituals convey a sense of collective identity, which mainly exists in the context of these events. An important function of these events is 'to instil and to celebrate a sense of group cohesiveness' (Werner *et al.*, 1988:205). Such events draw us into groups, whereby our participation can be both a privilege and an obligation. Wallendorf and Arnould's (1991) study of Thanksgiving in the USA identified several behavioural patterns, including following prescribed rules of food preparation, fasting or eating very little prior to the meal, consuming abundant amounts of food at the meal, and enacting togetherness through storytelling and viewing photographs. However, we need to bear in mind that a consumer's distinctive personal identity can also be conveyed through rituals associated with communal events such as birthdays, puberty rites and other rites of passage, including death. In these ceremonies, an individual's identity is highlighted through others including family members, friends and kin who also participate. Thus, the purpose of the shared consumption rituals can be to establish the self to oneself and to others.

Therefore, by studying ritualistic consumer behaviours, marketers can gain some really interesting insights into the way consumers view themselves and others around them. For instance, Gainer (1995) investigated how different features of a ritual characterized an art attendance (e.g. live performing arts) and reported three major findings. First, consumers undertook art attendance in order to pursue some interpersonal goals. For instance, while some had the desire to attend with others to socialize with them, others also wanted to express 'an image of themselves as sensitive and intellectual individuals' (p. 255). Second, consumers undertook art attendance in order to build bridges to socially distant acquaintances. For instance, by attending the art performances, consumers had the opportunity to build and strengthen close ties and develop a sense of attachment with other people (such as work acquaintances and neighbours). Third, consumers undertook art attendance in order to manage individual and community identities. For instance, art attendance gave participants an opportunity to world of connected individuals to another' (Gainer, 1995:257).

Using Goffman's (1959) notion of public behaviour as a performance and Turner's (1969, 1984) notion of social drama, Gainer (1995) conceptualized rituals of art performance as a social performance whereby symbolic meanings involving both the actors and the observers were communicated and confirmed. This allowed Gainer to go beyond the apparent meaning of the staged performance to individual consumers and to examine the art attendance as the provision of a venue whereby consumers established and maintained their membership in a small social world by communicating and sharing their values with others. Gainer went further and viewed art attendance as **rituals of reproduction** (Cheal, 1989) in which 'individuals in a dislocated and impersonalized post-industrial world participate in order to establish and maintain the bonds of a particular small world' (Gainer, 1995:254). That is, art attendance, in Gainer's view, served the function of constructing the relationships of a future social life in a specific small world. Other studies such as those by Errington (1987, 1990) reinforce the view that in shared consumption rituals, the self is established symbolically, not only through material objects, but also in terms of **social connections** to others (Gainer, 1995). The social connections are becoming quite explicit nowadays as an increasing number of people are joined together by strong emotional bonds such as the sharing of same tastes, habits, intellectual pursuits or participating in events like animal rights protests or anti-capitalism campaigns (Maffesoli, 1996).

VALUES

In Chapter 1, we explored consumer **values** in the context of what motivates consumers to buy as they do; and in Chapter 6, consumer lifestyles were shown to reflect (at least in part) the values that consumers hold. As we have seen (Chapter 1) **Western values** are characterized by 'separatedness' in the sense of people being relatively independent and individualistic. The individualistic Harley Davidson strapline reflects this, as does the other example in Figure 8.2. Non-Western cultures are more 'connected' (interdependent and collective) than Western ones.

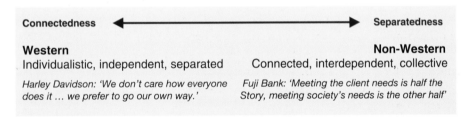

Figure 8.2   Social values continuum

Individualistic cultures (e.g. UK) tend to hold an independent view of the self, which emphasizes separateness, internal attributes and uniqueness of individuals. However, **collectivist cultures** (e.g. Japan) tend to hold an interdependent view of the self that stresses connectedness, social context and relationships. Both cultures have different time orientations. For instance, within an individualistic culture, time is viewed as a past/present continuum whereby it can be experienced and used in a linear way. Here time is also regarded as a tangible commodity, which can be spent, saved, wasted and lost. In other words, time is prioritized in such a way that the relative importance of promptness of schedules is greater than the relative importance of social relationships. On the other hand, within a collectivist culture, time is treated as less tangible and more as a way of building relationships with others. Time is non-linear here (e.g. time is structured according to the seasons of the year, which come back every year) and relates to social processes and to conceptualization of the ordering of social life.

Connectedness–separatedness, or collectivism–individualism, is one continuum developed by Hofstede (1980) who also identified other values-related cultural constructs such as:

- **Power distance:** for example, the relatively informal culture of many Western societies compared with a more structured set of interpersonal relationships in some Asian societies.
- **Uncertainty avoidance:** the extent to which ambiguity is overcome by belief structures and societal institutions, for example organized religion and how significant an element of that society is.

- **Long-term orientation:** also termed 'Confucian dynamism' reflects the importance a society attaches to perseverance and values associated with preparing for and shaping the future, as opposed to a short-term, living-for-today orientation. In theory at least, the former should be more conducive to relationship marketing than the alternative short-term, profit-seeking cultures.
- **Masculinity vs. feminity:** this concerns the degree of assertiveness, doing and acquiring in societies such as the USA compared with more nurturing and thinking cultures such as some Asian societies. It also relates to sex roles in society. In some societies the role of women is to be the child-bearer and housewife. Singer Sewing Machines, for example, decided that in order to be successful in some Middle Eastern countries some years ago, they could not target women, so they appealed to men, with the message that the sewing machine would make their wives more efficient.

THINKBOX

It is interesting to reflect upon Hofstede's framework in the light of research conducted to evaluate its applicability. For example, research conducted by Pressey and Selasse (2003) reports aspects of culture as being less important in buyer–seller relationships than perhaps expected. The study used face-to-face interviews with senior import and export managers and a postal questionnaire distributed for 11 countries.

Do you think Hofstede's **cultural dimensions** can influence buyer–seller relationships in a business-to-business context? If yes, how and in what sense can culture have an impact? What is the best method to find out the impact of culture on buyer–seller relationships?

CULTURAL DIFFERENCES AND SIMILARITIES

On the one hand there is the proposition that due to the recent developments in technology and consumer tastes, **a global market** for **global brands** has emerged. Levitt (1983) argued that technology was a significantly powerful force that drove the world towards a converging commonality as consumers across the world wanted all of the brands that they had heard about, seen or experienced via the new technologies (e.g. the Internet, cable TV). The main argument was that the world's needs and desires were becoming 'homogenized' and that the entire world could be treated as one large marketplace. Organizations could create competitive advantage by benefiting from huge economies of scale in production, distribution, marketing and management, and translating these benefits into reduced world prices. Where consumers are seen to act in a relatively homogenous way in the consumption context, marketers have attempted to globalize the marketing mix as much as possible by **standardizing** products, promotion campaigns, brands, prices and distribution channels for all markets. The economic and competitive pay-offs for global marketing strategies are certainly great. Brand name, product characteristics, packaging and labelling are among the easiest marketing mix variables to standardize; media allocation, marketing communications, retail outlets and price may be more difficult. In the end, the degree of similarity among the various environmental and market conditions determines the feasibility of globalization for global marketers, or standardization for international marketers.

Many, however, argue that there are important language and **cultural differences** (e.g. traditions, norms, customs, habits, attitudes and perceptions differ across cultural groups) and therefore one needs to

Table 8.1   Different perspectives in different countries, 1981 and 1990

	UK		Rep. of Ireland		France		Italy	
	'81	'90	'81	'90	'81	'90	'81	'90
Confidence in:								
Companies	48	46	49	51	42	60	33	62
Press	29	13	44	36	31	37	31	40
More important:								
Freedom	69	63	46	45	54	48	43	42
Equality	23	31	38	52	32	42	45	44
Happy	38	38	39	43	19	25	10	16
Proud to be	55	52	66	76	33	32	41	41

Source: Adapted by the authors from Heald (1982, 1993).

use a customized approach. In international marketing, **customization** refers to products and marketing activities being modified according to cultural, regional and national differences.

Table 8.1 reflects some attitudinal differences between nations according to an international Gallup survey (Heald, 1982, 1993). The survey revealed different attitudes in different countries to such issues as:

- confidence in companies and the press in each country;
- pride in being a national of each country; and
- whether freedom or equality were seen to be more important to the inhabitants.

The relevance of this is that marketers need to understand the **frame of reference** (Chapter 2) of the people in the countries they intend to target. The style of communications messages must acknowledge that people can hold different views.

'Think global, act local' is a popular marketing phrase and it serves to reinforce the importance of not ignoring local culture. For example, a recent HSBC TV commercial includes an example from Thailand where feet should not be exposed. This was included in Winick's 1961 study of cultural taboos.

Nonetheless, it should be remembered that there are degrees of both customization and globalization. Neither strategy is implemented in its pure form. The debate will doubtless continue over which products can be fully globalized. For some products – such as soft drinks – a global marketing strategy, including advertising, seems to work well; while for other products – such as beer – strategies must accommodate local, regional, religious and national differences.

When a new product is developed, most companies will attempt to make it a global product with a common name and position. The pressure for standardization is particularly strong in Europe, where there is now considerable media overlap and fewer distinct distribution systems. However, a more difficult issue is whether or not to create a global brand when regional brands are in place.

When a brand is already established in a country, for example, it commands high awareness levels and will often have developed a set of associations that can be very valuable. Changing the name and/or position in order to simply conform to a standardized global brand may be extremely costly. The effort to change the Datsun name to the global brand Nissan in the United States in the early 1980s probably cost more than $1 billion. Five years after the name change, the Datsun name was still as strong as the Nissan name.

A new name also kills any associations that the old name might have developed. Heinz does not put its name on the products it acquires outside the United States because it wants to retain their associations.

EXAMPLE 8.2

Many international marketing blunders occur because of a failure on the part of marketers to understand the language and cultural differences in values, traditions, customs and norms. Even when the markets are apparently similar (e.g. the USA and the UK), there can be cultural differences that can influence the way message is received and interpreted by consumers. For example, Caillat and Mueller (1996) compared cultural variables reflected in beer advertising messages developed in the USA and the UK. Findings revealed that different cultural values were represented differently in the two countries. While the US advertisements perpetuated values such as achievement, independence, modernity and newness, the UK ads perpetuated values such as tradition and history. Similarly, while the UK sample used *humour appeals* almost exclusively (89.5%), the US sample relied on *emotional* and *sex appeals* (78.9%). The two samples also differed in the way alcohol consumption was depicted through the advertising. UK advertisements more often presented characters drinking beer on ordinary occasions. However, the US ads tended to show characters drinking beer during special occasions or even tended to avoid representing the product being consumed at all. This suggested a difference in cultural attitudes towards drinking; the UK being more liberal and the USA being more conservative. Their research concluded that a standardized approach for the two countries was not appropriate because of differences in **cross-cultural values**.

www.   **Have a look at the following web site, which provides more examples of such branding strategies :**

     www.heinz.com

THINKBOX

If an existing name has **weak associations**, of course, it has little to lose by changing. In the late 1980s in the US market, Mars successfully changed the name of its Kal Kan dog food to 'Pedigree' and its Kal Kan cat food to 'Whiskas' to create worldwide names. In contrast to Kal Kan, which was mainly associated with cans, the name 'Pedigree' was associated with a quality, expensive pet that would only be served the best food, and the name 'Whiskas' was feline-sounding and likeable. Some brands are positioned quite differently in different countries. Clearly, it would be foolish to force a common position on such brands in order to achieve a standardized global brand.

You can probably think of a number of other brand names that have changed in recent years to reflect greater standardization across countries (Marathon chocolate bars became Snickers, Oil of Ulay cosmetics became Oil of Olay, Jif became Cif, etc.).

Did these name changes work for you and how do you think the names change worked in different countries?

Table 8.2 shows the paradox of often needing to be relatively standardized across cultures because of high costs of new product development and at the same time the need to respond to more local differences in taste.

Table 8.2   Standardization vs. customization

	Japan	Poland	USA	Holland
Appearance	****	**	****	***
Interior	*****	****	*	****
Handling	***	****	*	***
Comfort	*****	****	***	**

Car clinic in different countries, product testing a new car (the more *s the more that country, on average, likes the relevant dimension of the car being evaluated) Implications for world cars – satisfy *some* well or *everyone* poorly?

THINKBOX

For each of the following, consider the arguments for and against a standardized marketing approach across countries:

Cars
Beer
Fast food
Lingerie
Credit cards

Earlier in the chapter we referred to Johnson's classification of the essential elements of culture. These included *signs*, *signals* and *symbols*. Examples of these are shown in Table 8.3.

Table 8.3   Signs and symbols

Society	Symbol	Meaning
Iran	Blue	Funeral/mourning
Japan	White	Funeral/mourning
Latin America	Purple	Death

EXAMPLE 8.3

'Come alive, you are in the Pepsi generation' – means 'Come alive out of the grave' (in Germany) and 'Pepsi brings your ancestors back from the grave' (in China).
Chevy Nova – in Spain means 'Doesn't go'.
Esso – phonetically the name means 'stalled car' in Japan.
Kellogg's Bran Buds – 'burned farmer' in Sweden.
A Chinese brand, 'Pansy', did not do well in USA (it was a brand of men's underwear).
'Fanny fish' and 'Krapp toilet paper' might be greeted with a different reaction outside their countries and so might 'Bonka coffee' outside Spain – actually there were three variations of Bonka!

USE OF HUMOUR

Since consumers are bombarded with so many commercial messages (we call this 'clutter'), many marketers use humour as a way of getting attention. Use of humour can be particularly effective when it comes to products that we buy on a fairly regular and repeated basis and so do not allocate much of our mental energies to evaluating information before making a purchase. As many of us enjoy watching humorous advertisements, it is possible that we may develop a liking for the advertisement and/or for the advertised brand. Research on comparing television advertising in the USA and the UK reveal that advertisers in the UK rely more on humorous advertisements than their counterparts in the USA (Weinberger and Spotts, 1989).

Humour involves the generation of some pleasurable feelings that can be triggered by the experiencing of some forbidden feelings, violating some uniform social standards or the social context in which it occurs (Spotts et al., 1997). While humour is very effective in drawing consumers' attention and improving the likeability of the message, it may not always be effective in increasing the probability that the message will be properly understood and comprehended by consumers.

When it comes to conveying humour in different countries, marketers need to be careful in choosing the themes, situations and settings. In a cross-national study of TV ads in Germany, Thailand, South Korea and the United States, Alden et al. (1993) found that a substantial number of humorous advertisements in the four countries appeared to rely on expected/unexpected or possible/impossible contrasts. The study also found that the number of humorous advertisements portraying group-oriented situations (e.g. use of three or more characters) in Korea and Thailand was much higher than the number of similar humorous advertisements found in Germany and USA. This reflects Hofstede's collectivist–individualist dimension as Korea and Thailand are collectivist cultures whereas Germany and the USA are more individualistic cultures. Similarly, the number of humorous advertisements portraying characters of unequal status was much higher in Korea and Thailand than in Germany and the USA. This reflects Hofstede's power distance dimension, as both Thailand and Korea are low on this dimension in comparison with Germany and the USA.

THE INTERNET CROSSING CULTURES

Consider the Internet. Clearly this can have global reach and indeed everything which the marketer puts on an Internet site is accessible from anywhere in the world unless access controls are put in place.

Because Internet sites can be accessed from anywhere, the law in many countries considers things done on the Internet as being within their jurisdiction no matter where the computer hardware is sited. Many countries therefore apply their own laws, not the laws of the country where the computer hardware is or from where the Internet communications originate.

Clearly marketers must consider the legality of what they wish to do under the laws of every country, not just their own.

EXAMPLE 8.4

1. Virgin Atlantic Airways maintained a web site, which included details of its trans-Atlantic airfares. The web site described a return airfare of under $500, but when a prospective passenger asked for one of these tickets he was told that this special price was no longer available and the alternative was a ticket costing a little over $500. Under US law the airline was obliged to keep the information up-to-date, and as it had inadvertently failed to do so it ended up paying the US Department of Transport $14,000.

2. The Italian company Tattilo Editrice SpA made erotic pictures available over the Internet. The milder pictures were made available to all visitors to the web site, whether or not they had a subscription. More explicit pictures were available to those who wished to subscribe to a special service. Tattilo is an Italian company, based in Italy and both services were made available from computer equipment located in Italy. The domain name (that is the Internet address) of the Web site was playmen. Playboy Enterprises Inc – the publisher of *Playboy* magazine – had failed to obtain protection for its Playboy trade mark in Italy in a previous case brought against Tattilo. However, Playboy brought proceedings against Tattilo in the New York courts claiming that Tattilo had infringed Playboy's US registration of the Playboy trade mark by – among other things – its use of the playmen site address because the service was available to US citizens. The court agreed and ordered Tattilo to either refuse subscriptions from US customers or shut down its Internet site, even though that site was in Italy. Tattilo was also ordered to pay to Playboy the gross profits it had earned from subscriptions to the service by US customers and all gross profits earned from the sale of goods and services advertised on the playmen site. Interestingly, the court stated that 'Cyberspace is not a safe haven.'

Evans *et al.* (2004)

Country of Origin Effects

We normally hear comments that certain products from certain countries are better than others in one way or another. For example, we may hear comments such as 'Japanese cars are more reliable' or 'Belgian chocolates are the best.' These comments represent well-developed stereotypical beliefs that consumers have about products that originate from other countries (Hong and Wyer, 1989). Consumers often use the **country of origin** as an information cue to make inferences about products and their attributes such as quality and reliability. They can treat country of origin as an important product attribute during product evaluation when more specific information relevant to the product is not readily available (Han and Terpstra, 1988). In this sense, country of origin serves an informational function by providing cues to the consumers regarding product attributes when consumers are unfamiliar with a product (Han and Terpstra, 1988).

Country of origin works as an *image variable*, which influences consumers' perceptions of a brand or a product to the extent that the evaluation of other salient and important attributes is affected (Janda and Rao, 1997). Furthermore, consumers can utilize country of origin as **heuristics** (these are quick rules of thumb, Chaiken, 1980) as a basis for evaluating products without considering other attribute information.

However, country of origin cues can also relate directly to a consumer's sense of affiliation with a nation or country and can reinforce a sense of national identity (Bruning, 1997). For instance, a less nationalistic and ethnocentric consumer is more likely to prefer a foreign product to domestic substitutes than a more nationalistic and ethnocentric consumer. Ethnocentric consumers have a tendency to feel proud of and attached to products originating from their own culture and a tendency to reject culturally dissimilar products.

SUBCULTURES

Subcultures refer to groups within a society which possess distinctive characteristics. Widely quoted examples include cultural groupings on the basis of geographical region, religion and ethnicity. However, the term **subculture** can also be used to refer to 'a distinctive subgroup of society that self selects on the basis of a shared commitment to a particular product class, brand, or consumption activity' (Schouten and McAlexander, 1995:43). We can therefore use the term 'subculture' to refer to, for example, the teenage subculture or that of the postmodern consumer and even that of 'tribes' or 'communities' (Chapter 7).

It is important for marketers to study subcultures because consumer behaviour often varies from one to another and some subcultures are based almost entirely on *cultural artefacts*, which are obtained in the marketing system. For example, a three-year ethnographic study of Harley-Davidson motorcycle owners classified them as a 'subculture of consumption' because they appeared to be a distinctive subgroup within the society with a shared commitment to the brand and a visible hierarchical social structure. This subculture also shared unique set of beliefs and values and used unique jargons and rituals to express their identity (Schouten and McAlexander, 1995). The nearby Think Box will help you understand some of the emerging sub-groupings in our society, such as online communities.

We discussed tribal and postmodern behaviour in Chapter 7 and Generation X and Y in Chapter 5. Here we focus on some of the ethnic minority groups in the UK but first we will look at what is meant by ethnicity and ethnic identity.

THINKBOX

Many of the leading brands host online **brand communities** through bulletin boards, forums and chat rooms. McWilliam (2000) says that brands which are built around the idea of hosting and building **online communities** are community brands. An example is the Geocities web site, which is home to millions of community members 'living' in different 'neighbourhoods'.

Would you say that the online community is an example of a subculture?

Can you think of reasons why consumers join such communities?

What are the implications for building strong relationships with consumers and what happens if a consumer in real life feels dissatisfied with a brand and spreads a negative word of mouth via online communities?

How can marketers respond to such challenges?

Ethnic Subcultures

There have been immigrant groups in the UK throughout its existence, although these have varied in size and provenance; among the recent arrivals are, for example, South Asians (Indians, Pakistanis and Bangladeshis), Chinese, Black-Caribbean, Irish, Poles, Central European Jews, Cypriots and Turks. We find that *cultural diversity* in the UK is already affecting and shaping many institutions (e.g. the educational institutions have to cope with a multicultural student body and staff) and culinary habits (e.g. the assimilation of a variety of ethnic foods into British cuisine – Jamal, 1996). You may note that cultural diversity brings many marketing opportunities as marketers can target new segments with suitable products but it also presents some challenges. In order to be successful, marketers need to look at differences in subcultures that drive differences in consumption patterns, responses to advertising and direct marketing efforts, media usage, brand choices and decision-making styles.

Ethnicity and Ethnic Identity

Within the British context we normally use the term 'ethnic' to describe groups of relatively recent immigrants who are perceived to be sufficiently different from the mainstream Anglo-Saxon group. However, the term could be used to describe any social group (mainstream or minority), irrespective of their cultural and social background. Therefore, a study of an ethnic group does not necessarily mean a study of an ethnic minority group. The term **ethnicity** implies many dimensions including 'a sense of common customs, language, religion, values, morality, and etiquette' (Webster, 1994:321). In other words, ethnicity can be viewed as a characteristic of racial group membership on the basis of some commonly shared features. You can also describe ethnicity in terms of biological make-up of consumers and the extent to which genetic factors play their role in conveying aspects of ethnicity including consumption behaviour.

It is important to note that ethnicity exists 'in a context of oppositions and relativities' (Tonkin *et al.*, 1989:17). In other words,

the basis of ethnicity is self-identification of the members mediated by the perceptions of the others. There are two sets of principles that operate within ethnicity: the **inclusionary–exclusionary principle** and the **difference–identity principle**. By excluding, one establishes difference. By including, one establishes identity. Both are, therefore, closely related (Venkatesh, 1995:33; emboldening added).

Hence what we are allows us to understand what we are not. That is why an increasing number of consumer researchers draw our attention to the fact that *intercultural contact* and the way we adapt and respond to other cultural groups can be a defining feature of a society. Ethnicity can be best understood by exploring the ways in which consumers interact with one another and with other important players in the society, such as marketers and businesses (Penaloza and Gilly, 1999). We can also get a better understanding of ethnicity by 'looking at situations in which groups or group members present themselves to, and interact with, other groups and the outside society' (Costa and Bamossy, 1995:9).

In a study involving two ethnic subcultures – English Canadians and French Canadians in Montreal – Laroche *et al.* (2003) reported that English Canadians demonstrated more positive perceptions towards the UK and its products than did the French Canadians. Similarly, French Canadians demonstrated more positive perceptions towards France and its products than did the English Canadians. This shows that consumers' subcultures and their perceptions of cultural similarity with other countries can influence their attitudes towards them (Laroche *et al.*, 2003).

You may note that the terms 'ethnicity' and 'ethnic identity' are often used interchangeably. This is because ethnicity can also be defined as a process of self-identification whereby individuals define themselves and others into specific groups using ethnic labels (Rossiter and Chan, 1998). At the individual level, the process of self-identification or ethnic identity is part of one's self-concept which is based on knowledge of membership in a social group(s) together with emotional significance and value that is attached to that membership (Tajfel, 1981). This discussion links up with our discussion of self in Chapter 6. You can say that a person's ethnic identity involves their sense of belonging to a group, as well as the feelings and thoughts that go with being part of that group. In this sense, ethnic identity could be viewed as a complex psychological process that involves perceptions, cognition, affect and knowledge structures about how a person thinks and feels about himself and others in the society (Cuellar *et al.*, 1997; Tajfel, 1981).

The processes of thinking and feeling could play an important role in the lives of **ethnic minority consumers**. For instance, in an ethnographic study of British-Pakistanis in Bradford, Jamal and Chapman (2000) reported the coexistence of both positive and negative perceptions among the participants towards their own group as well as towards the mainstream society. These perceptions were important because they guided their thoughts and actions in terms of developing a sense of who they were, and who they were not. The perceptions also informed their consumer decision-making processes regarding which products to buy, where to buy and on what basis to buy. The nearby Think Box will help you comprehend the notion of situational, multiple but often coexisting identities.

THINKBOX

Bouchet (1995) argues that ethnicity is like a bricolage whereby one builds self-identity on the basis of heterogeneous elements taken from a diversity of *cultural representations* and practices. Oswald (1999) provided empirical evidence to support the coexistence of consumers' mixed emotions and their implications for ethnicity and ethnic identity, arguing that 'in consumer culture, ethnicity can be bought, sold and worn like a loose garment' (p 304). Stayman and Deshpande (1989) made a related argument by suggesting that ethnicity is not just about one's identification with a particular ethnic group but also about how strongly one identifies with that group in a particular situation. According to them, 'ethnicity is not just who one is, but how one feels in and about a particular situation' (p 361). They argued that social situation and one's perception of that situation influenced their felt ethnic identity. They concluded that persons in multicultural societies were likely to have a set of ethnic and other identities that might be differentially salient. In other words, they are expected to have multiple selves whereby they act differently in different situations and with different individuals (see also Markus and Kunda, 1986; Markus and Nurius, 1986).

On the basis of this, Donthu and Cherian (1994) cited the example of some Hispanics in the USA who behaved very much like the mainstream population all year round except while celebrating Cindo de Mayo or while visiting a Hispanic restaurant with family and friends. Similarly, Jamal (2003) argued that consumers not only feel a stable sense of identity but also a fluid sense of identity whereby they can play with different images of themselves. The discussion implies that one can experience or feel multiple and coexisting identities that can inform one's buying behaviours in different contexts and locations (Jamal and Chapman, 2000).

As a consumer, have you ever felt a sense of multiple identities in different situations?

As a marketer, what role you can play in facilitating the coexistence of a variety of modes of consumption and a sense of being?

Ethnicity and Acculturation

Initially social researchers expected immigrants (mostly in North America, particularly in the USA) to abandon their own *cultural heritage* and conform to what was dominant in America at the time of their arrival there. It was assumed that over a period of time, immigrants would blend into a national whole (like a melting pot) and abandon their distinctive cultural features. However, a quick glance at many Western societies suggests that ethnic subcultures do not abandon their cultural features. Rather they recreate their own small cultural worlds in their own ways (like a salad bowl where ingredients can coexist with one another). Therefore, consumer researchers now use the term **consumer acculturation** to describe changes in consumer behaviours of ethnic subcultures.

Acculturation refers to the 'phenomena which result when groups of individuals having different cultures come into continuous first hand contact, with subsequent changes in the original culture patterns of either or both groups' (Redfield *et al.*, 1936, cited in Berry, 1980:9). Another way of looking at acculturation is to say that it is 'the general process of movement and adaptation to the cultural environment in one country by persons from another country' (Penaloza, 1994:33). An implicit assumption here is that the immigrant consumers can maintain some aspects of their original cultural values and traditions in addition to moving towards the culture of the host society. The nearby Think Box will help you understand some important features of acculturation as they apply to all of us.

THINKBOX

An important feature of acculturation is that it recognizes the fact that the process of cultural change is a reciprocal one because we are talking about contact and interactions among different cultural groups (one being the immigrant group and the other being 'every other' group in the society). Hence, changes can and do happen among *any* of the groups including the mainstream consumers. Think, for example, the popularity of ethnic foods (in particular the Asian cuisine) both inside and outside the home in the UK. The total expenditure on ethnic eating, including restaurants and takeaways, is expected to be over £1 billion annually. There are an estimated 6000 Chinese restaurants, 5500 Indian restaurants and 300 Thai restaurants. These figures suggest a significant change in the dietary habits of the UK population. According to Jamal (1996), such changes happened partly due to frequent cultural encounters between the cultural categories of mainstream population and those of ethnic subcultures and ethnic minority businesses such as restaurants and corner shops.

In your view, what other factors count for such massive and visible cultural change among the UK population?

In terms of acculturation, Berry (1980) raised two important questions. First, to what extent does an individual or a group have a sense of identification with their culture of origin; in other words, does an individual or a group feel it important to retain identification with the culture of origin? Second, to what extent does the individual or group want to have positive relations with the dominant society? On the basis of this, Berry (1980) identified four possible varieties of acculturation.

The first one is called assimilation, which refers to the situation where an immigrant consumer or group relinquishes their cultural identity over time and moves into the larger society. The second one is called integration, which refers to a situation when an immigrant consumer or group not only maintains their original cultural integrity but also makes a move to become an integral part of a larger societal framework. The third one is named as **rejection**, which refers to a situation where an immigrant consumer or group rejects the mainstream society while maintaining identity with the culture of origin. And the fourth is called deculturation, where an immigrant consumer or group rejects movement into the mainstream society as well as any identification with the culture of origin.

Consumer behaviour of ethnic minority consumers is likely to be influenced by a dual set of acculturation agents: one which is aligned with their country of origin and one which is aligned with the country of destination. In both cases, the acculturation agents include family, friends and media, and commercial, educational and religious institutions (Penaloza, 1994). Through the process of learning, these consumers can adapt and adjust to the mainstream cultural environment in the way that they exhibit consumption patterns associated with the mainstream culture, their original culture or a hybrid combination of the two cultures. For example, Jamal and Chapman (2000) found that consumption patterns of British-Pakistanis in Bradford, UK, were a reflection of their Pakistani culture, UK culture and a combination of both.

The extent to which an ethnic minority consumer feels associated with their culture of origin can be an important predictor of some of their consumer behaviour. For instance, Deshpande *et al.* (1986) found that Hispanic-Americans who identified strongly with their culture of origin tended to use Spanish language media heavily, held a positive attitude towards advertising, were brand-loyal and were likely to buy brands advertised to their ethnic group as compared to those who identified weakly with their culture of origin.

One should also expect **intergenerational differences** when it comes to understanding consumer behaviours of ethnic minority consumers. For instance, Jamal (1997, 1998) reported strong generational differences in shopping orientations of British-Pakistanis who were born and raised in the UK in comparison with those who belonged to the first generation.

EXAMPLE 8.5

Ethnic identification can be expressed via shopping behaviours. This can be reflected through the choice of specific stores or preference for particular brands. For example, Herche and Balasubramaian (1994) looked into how ethnic minority consumers from different ethnic backgrounds varied in their shopping orientations. Their study involved 6000 respondents belonging to six ethnic minority consumer groups (i.e. Black, Hispanic, Chinese, Japanese, Italian and Korean) in the USA. They found that Black consumers had the highest level of ethnic identification as compared to other ethnic minority groups with respect to their buying attitudes and preferred to buy from Black-owned businesses.

EXAMPLE 8.6

Similarly, the behaviour of ethnic minority consumers can differ from that of their mainstream counterparts. For example, Chudry and Pallister (2002) reported some significant differences in British-Pakistani and native consumers' attitudes towards direct mail. The British-Pakistani group felt positive about the idea of direct mail but took personal involvement in direct mail much less seriously. The group did not want to reveal personal information and desired the direct mail to be accurately targeted and to be engaging. The group also depended much more heavily on advice from family and workmates than its counterpart. Similarly Jamal (1996, 1998) studied the food consumption experiences of British-Pakistani and mainstream consumers in Bradford, UK. His study found that there were significant differences between the food consumption experiences of both groups.

   Also, Shim and Gehrt (1996) reported findings in relation to the shopping approaches of Hispanic, White and Native adolescents in the USA. They found that the Hispanic adolescents depicted a greater tendency to the *social/hedonistic shopping orientation* than did the White and Native American adolescents. The White adolescents, on the other hand, manifested a greater tendency toward the *utilitarian approach to shopping* than did Hispanic and Native American adolescents. Hispanic adolescents also manifested a greater tendency towards novelty/fashion consciousness, recreational and brand-loyal orientations as compared to their White and Native American counterparts. Hispanic adolescents were the most likely to interact with parents while making purchase choices. They were also the most likely to enjoy printed media, to be receptive to television advertising, and to believe that school is a good source of consumer education.

The Need for Understanding Ethnic Subcultures in the UK

There are a number of reasons for developing a better understanding of consumer behaviour of ethnic minority consumers in the UK. First, irrespective of the country of origin, the ethnic minority community (as a whole) has been the fastest-growing segment of the total population in the UK (Clegg, 1996; Suzman,

1996) about 30% of London's population is expected to come from the ethnic minorities in 15 years' time (Timmins, 1995). 'Ethnic minorities will make up the majority in half of London's boroughs. The country's ethnic population as a whole is growing by 2.5% annually and is set to double over the next 50 years' (Sclater, 2002). For many marketers, the growing number of ethnic minority consumers could soon mean some important market niches to target. However, to target them effectively, marketers need to have a good understanding of the way ethnic minority consumers live and construct their lives in the UK.

> **www.** **Have a look at the following web site:**
>
> **www.raceforopportunity.org.uk**
>
> **This provides information on the 'Race for Opportunity' survey conducted in 2002. The survey found that banks and building societies filled six of the top ten private sector organizations in terms of enlightened approaches to ethnic minorities.**

Second, marketers are always interested in instilling brand loyalties in their target customers particularly when they are relatively young; children are likely to develop strong brand loyalties over time. In the case of ethnic minority consumers, they already enjoy a significant share in the school-age population of many urban areas of the UK (e.g. London, Birmingham, Bradford). Furthermore, some recent media reports suggest that some of the cleverest kids in the UK's schools today are likely to be of ethnic minority origin as they are increasingly outperforming their mainstream counterparts.

Third, marketers are also interested in targeting customers that are relatively affluent. In the case of the ethnic minority consumers, positive attitudes towards hard work and family life have led to the creation of many millionaires owning high street brands like Joe Bloggs Clothing, Horne Brothers, Ciro Citterio fashion shops, Colorama, Time computers and Binatone telephones. Furthermore, many of the ethnic minority consumers are self-employed, leading to a stable stream of income.

Fourth, marketers of health products (such as GPs, the NHS and pharmaceutical companies) are strongly interested in exploring the consumption patterns of ethnic minority consumer groups because of their different health patterns as compared to mainstream consumers. For instance, ethnic minority consumer groups from the Indian subcontinent are more likely to have diabetes and coronary heart disease than mainstream consumers.

Targeting Ethnic Subcultures

There is a debate about whether mainstream marketers should target ethnic segments differently or go for 'inclusive marketing'. The latter is exemplified by an advertising campaign by the British Navy, featuring people of different racial origins. The idea is not to exclude but rather to attract as many as possible from different ethnic segments.

As we have seen, ethnic segments have their own cultures, languages, religions and distinct requirements. It is not always appropriate for them to be targeted with more general products and services by merely changing advertisements for them. Different coloured skin, for example, has different moisture content, and the formulation of cosmetics should be different (as they are in the Revlon range in USA), not merely suggesting how people of different colours can select from existing ranges to arrive at appropriate colour combinations. There are examples of differentiating product ranges, such as the organic baby food range from Boots the Chemist which includes halal-approved food for Muslims (according to Islamic law for food preparation).

There could be two main effects of not targeting ethnic minority consumers properly. First, the ethnic minority consumers may feel alienated by large companies and their marketing and advertising campaigns, leading to a sense of exclusion from mainstream society (Suzman, 1996). Second, marketers of mainstream brands can miss out opportunities to take advantage of the £10 billion ethnic minorities spend every year, because of misplaced marketing and advertising drives (Suzman, 1996). However, there are some small businesses that have been very active in identifying and serving the needs of ethnic minority consumers. One can look at their marketing practices because they have been quite successful in establishing a variety of commercial enterprises such as corner shops, grocery stores, cash and carrys, restaurants, takeaways, ethnic supermarkets, food wholesaling, electronics and textiles. Some of these businesses particularly target specific ethnic minority consumer groups; others target both the ethnic minority consumers as well as the mainstream population in the UK. However, what makes them significantly different from mainstream marketers is that they do understand the needs and requirements of ethnic minority consumers.

For instance, in a recent study of ethnic minority enterprises such as grocery stores, corner shops, mini-supermarkets and restaurants, Jamal (2005) reported that the enterprises successfully adapted their marketing mixes to suit the needs of their co-ethnic consumers. This meant they provided a full range of ethnic as well as non-ethnic products for the needs of their consumers and followed a differential pricing strategy, offering special discounts to opinion leaders and formers in the community. They also promoted

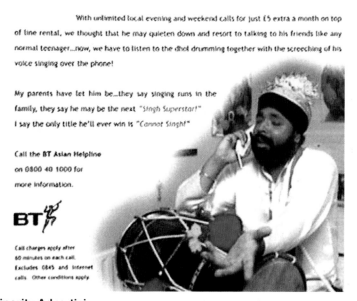

Figure 8.3 Ethnic minority Advertising
Reproduced by permission of British Telecommunications plc

themselves not only via traditional media (newspapers, radio) but also via the extensive use of word of mouth advertising and by participating in community events.

There are now market research agencies that offer specialized services to research ethnic segments, so the argument of a decade or so ago that they are difficult to research is not as strong as it once was. Indeed the 2001 Census included additional questions about ethnicity and these led to the more accurate identification of the locations and characteristics of ethnic communities in UK (the Census being available for commercial purposes). Also, with the developing ethnic minority media it is equally possible to reach ethnic minority segments with marketing messages. There are newspapers, magazines and now, of course, an expanding range of dedicated radio and TV channels (via cable and satellite) together with the Internet not only communicate with ethnic segments in their own language (see Figures 8.3 and 8.4) and using the same frame of reference, but do this interactively.

Figure 8.4　Lynx advertisement

© Unilever UK Home & Personal Care Ltd. Illustrated by Mike Koelsch. Reproduced by permission. Image courtesy of the Advertising Archives

THINKBOX

Figure 8.5   Communicating with a multiracial society
© Commission for Racial Equality (CRE). Reproduced by permission

If ethnic segments differ in their needs and values, they should be treated differently. But if they are, is that discrimination?

Also, is the targeting of ethnic segments in any way racist?

However, many marketers are reluctant to target ethnic communities. Indeed a research project was proposed (by one of the authors), believing that direct mail campaigns would benefit from understanding ethnic communities' reaction to the medium. Although a number of direct marketing agencies agreed, they stated that they were wary of how the research might be portrayed in 'the media'. The feeling was that it would be taken to be racist.

Crossing Cultures

An interesting variation on the analysis so far concerns the behaviour and opinions of those who move from one culture to another – for example, foreign students going to study in another country. For instance, Davies and Fitchett (2003) found some emotional, symbolic and pragmatic issues related to crossing of cultures. *Emotional factors* included loneliness and being unable to feel part of a group. *Symbolic issues* included difficulty in understanding and interpreting social rules in the new society, especially in social situations and overcoming communication problems. *Pragmatic issues* included, for example, getting used to public transport, getting used to new food and eating habits, and sorting out personal financial arrangements. Overall a significant majority of their sample reported experiencing 'culture shock'. Less than 2% said that their experiences in the UK matched exactly with expectations held prior to arrival, so marketers need to be aware of the disorientation of culture-crossers. This will especially apply where there are large concentrations of foreign visitors, such as university towns with significant numbers of foreign students.

> **www.** **Have a look at the following article, which is accessible from the accompanying web site at www.wiley.com/go/evans:**
>
> **Keillor, D'Amico and Horton (2001) Global Consumer Tendencies, Psychology and Marketing, Vol 18 No 1 pp 1–19**
>
> **This paper provides some evidence to suggest the emergence of a global consumer.**

SUMMARY

■ Culture could be defined in numerous ways but it can refer to what a society knows about its physical and social world including its religious beliefs, what it considers to be appropriate forms of conduct, and the language and other forms of conveying meanings that it uses for communication. Culture is dynamic and continuously in the process of changing and is transmitted from one generation to another. It can also refer to the overall meaning system that a group of people uses to inform their lives and to make sense of the world around them. Brands and services are part of this system of meaning, which acts as a lens through which people see their world and make sense of it. We realize the power of our own culture when we encounter a different one. Cultural categories are the distinctions that a culture uses to divide up its world of everyday experiences. There are many examples of such distinctions, including time and space.

■ Meaning originally resides in the culturally constituted world and can be transferred to consumer brands and goods via advertising and fashion systems. Meaning is transferred at an individual level through a range of ritualistic behaviours. Rituals are repetitive behaviours, which help us link up with our environment including brands and services. While some rituals are private and personal, others are shared, conveying a sense of collective identity and belonging to a group.

■ Different cultures have different values, with Western cultures often emphasizing individualism with focus on the individual self and Eastern cultures emphasizing collectivism with focus on conformity to the group. However, some argue that due to the recent developments in technology, global trade and migration, consumers are becoming homogenized and hence a standardized approach to target them is effective. Others argue that there exist very strong cultural differences (e.g. differences in norms, values, beliefs, attitudes and languages) and therefore one should adopt a customized approach. Companies often use a middle-of-the-road approach combining some elements from both approaches.

■ Since consumers are exposed to large number of marketing stimuli, use of humour can be very effective in getting their attention. However, it is important to bear in mind that cross-cultural differences exist in the way humour is interpreted and that extra care is needed in choosing the themes, situations and settings while using humour. Some consumers have a stereotypical belief about products that originate from other countries and thus country of origin can act as important information cue (or a heuristic) during the product evaluation stage of consumer decision-making. Some consumers have ethnocentric tendencies as they tend to favour products made or processed in their own cultures and countries.

■ Subcultures refer to smaller groups within a society which possess certain distinctive features (e.g. teenage subculture or ethnic minority subculture). Many of the Western societies can be described as culturally diverse where ethnic minority subcultures are growing in size and have increased purchasing power accompanied by heightened political and cultural awareness and ethnic pride. Ethnicity can be viewed as a characteristic of racial group membership on the basis of some commonly shared features. It can also be described in terms of the biological make-up of individuals and the extent to which genetic factors play their role in conveying aspects of ethnicity including consumption behaviour. However, for many, ethnicity is also a process of self-identification whereby individuals define themselves and others into specific groups using ethnic labels. Ethnicity exists in the context of oppositions and relativities and the process of self-identification is mediated by the perceptions of others. Acculturation is the approach utilized by many to understand the consumer behaviour of ethnic minority consumers. The extent to which ethnic minority consumers feel attached to their original culture can influence their decision-making and shopping behaviours. Marketers can respond to consumer differences with differentiation and segmentation strategies and adapt their marketing mix according to the cultural aspirations, needs and wants of the target group.

QUESTIONS

1. What is meant by 'culture'? What do you think of the idea that culture is the meaning system that members of any specific group use to inform their lives?

2. Using examples of your own, discuss the meaning transfer model suggested by McCracken (1986).

3. What issues are involved in adopting a standardized vs. customized approach to targeting consumers around the globe? Which are most important? Use examples to illustrate.

4. What are the effects of country of origin and the use of humour in consumer behaviour?

5. What is 'acculturation'? How does it help to understand consumer behaviour of ethnic minority consumers?

FURTHER READING

Arnould E J and **Thompson** C J (2005) Consumer Culture Theory (CCT): Twenty Years of Research, Journal of Consumer Research, Vol 31 No 4 pp 868–883. This paper provide a very good overview of the past 20 years of consumer research dealing with socio-cultural, experiential, symbolic and ideological aspects of consumption.

Mick D G (1986) Consumer Research and Semiotics: Exploring the Morphology of Signs, Symbols, and Significance, Journal of Consumer Research, Vol 13 No 2 pp 196–213. This is a classic paper which comprehensively outlines the emergence and principal perspectives of semiotics (the study of meanings and symbols) and then discusses its applications and implications for consumer research.

Wallendorf M and **Reilly** M (1983) Ethnic Migration, Assimilation, and Consumption, Journal of Consumer Research, Vol 10, December, pp 292–302. This is a classic article in consumer research dealing with issues of ethnicity and assimilation.

Family Decision at the Turn of the Century: Has the Changing Structure of Households Impacted the Family Decision-Making Process?

A M Belch and L A Willis

Reproduced from Journal of Consumer Behaviour, Vol 2 No 2 (2002) 111–124.

Introduction

Following the publication of the often-cited study of family decision-making by Davis and Rigaux (1974), a number of researchers began to focus their attention on multiple facets of family decision-making within the household. In fact, scores of articles were published in the 1970s and 1980s examining the decision-making processes of adults, adolescents and children. In the 1990s, however, less attention has been allocated to family decision-making research, particularly the roles of husbands and wives. As a result, the literature may not be reflective of current family decision-making situations (a view supported by Lackman and Lanasa, 1993).

Thus, a need exists to examine the effect that changes that have occurred within the traditional US household may have had on husbands' and wives' decision-making processes in the year 2000 – over a decade since this topic has been examined in depth.

Literature Review and Hypotheses Development

In order to address the question of whether changes in the American family over the last two decades have significantly affected husband and wife decision-making, it is necessary to review literature in two areas. First, the extant literature on the changing American household is reviewed to provide justification for hypothesizing that the nature of decision-making in the household may have also changed. Second, the literature on family decision-making and the role of husbands and wives is reviewed to provide a comparative base of evaluation and prediction.

The Changing American Household

A number of studies have concluded that the traditional family structure prevalent in the 1970s is no longer representative of all American families. A study by the Population Reference Bureau concludes that the family structure has changed significantly in the past few decades, and that these changes have taken place at a frantic pace (Ahlburg and DeVita, 1992). The study indicates that as many as one in three Americans is now a member of a blended family (step family), and that blended families will continue to be a dominant force in the lives of children for the future. Noting that marriage rates are falling, divorce rates are rising and that 25% of babies are now born to unmarried mothers (compared to 10% in 1970), the article concludes that responsibilities of family members will become more complex, more ambiguous and more open to dispute.

Similarly, Clulow (1993) contends that the organization of families in industrial countries (for example, Australia, United States and most Western European countries) has changed dramatically in the past quarter of a century as a result of increases in divorce rates, falling marriage rates, co-habitation without marriage, single parenting and increased women in the work force. He notes that the organization of the family has been affected by (1) a shift from the command to the negotiation method for family decision-making; and (2) the two income family (which has increased the status and options for women and has generated uncertainty about gender roles and responsibilities). Clulow suggests that new families incorporate non-traditional family structures as well as traditional ones operating under changed circumstances in their decision-making processes.

Reports by Jacques (1998) and Hamburg (1993), citing many of the same reasons, also demonstrate that the family has changed. In the former study, Jacques notes that many relationships are now fluid and uncertain. Citing Stacey (1996), he notes that many families lament the passing of the traditional family. Hamburg also provides evidence that the family of the 1990s is quite different from the father-dominated structure of the 1960s. Numerous other studies (Ellwood, 1993; Pearl, 1995; Powers, 1994), suggest that families – and the ways these families make decisions regarding the household unit – are significantly different than they were in the past.

Family Decision-Making: Husbands and Wives

Research on the roles of husbands and wives in family decision-making dates back at least to the 1960s when Davis (1970) first conducted a study on the relative influence of husbands and wives. Since that time, several studies have examined aspects of marital roles and family decision-making. While highly prevalent in the 1970s and 1980s, Mangleburg (1989); Foxman, Tansuhaj and Ekstrom (1989); Belch, Belch and Ceresino (1985); Foxman and Tansuhaj (1988); Corfman and Lehmann (1987), Davis (1971), Davis and Rigaux (1974), Filiatrault and Ritchie (1980), Park (1982), Qualls (1987), Rosen and Granbois (1983), Spiro (1983) and Wilkes (1975), among others, much less attention has been given to this topic in the decade of the 1990s – Talpade (1990); Beatty and Talpade (1994); Corfman (1990).

In a landmark study, Davis and Rigaux (1974) concluded that husbands and wives had different role specializations and varying degrees of relative influence for various products and at various stages in the purchase decision process. Wives were found to be more dominant during the problem recognition and information search stages for household furnishings and, to a lesser degree, appliances; whereas, husbands were more dominant at the information search stage for autos and to a lesser degree, at the problem recognition and final decision stages. Much less role specialization was shown for housing decisions, which tended to be more syncratic in nature.

In a similar study, but extended to include the role of adolescents, Belch *et al.* (1985), concluded that family members' influence varied by product, by stages of the decision-making process, and by various decision areas, with the husbands and wives clearly dominating the decision process. The husband's influence was strongest for automobiles and television sets, whereas the wife was more dominant in decisions for household appliances, furniture and breakfast cereal.

More recent studies reflect some changes in the decision-making process, suggesting a movement toward more joint decision-making. Putnam and Davidson (1987) replicated the Davis and Rigaux (1974) study and found significant changes occurring in the household. Household decisions to purchase automobiles, televisions, and financial planning shifted from husband-dominated product decisions to joint decisions. Final decisions to purchase stereos, financial planning, automobiles, carpet, and living room furniture were all jointly made. Further, it was shown that couples demonstrated increasing role specialization (or more joint decision-making) as the couple moved from information search to a final decision for all product categories.

Additional support for the changing roles of husbands and wives was reported by Qualls (1982). Qualls studied product contexts in which few joint decisions were traditionally made and found a profound shift toward joint decision-making for children's education and housing. Other studies support the notion that husbands are exerting greater influence in decisions in which the wife was historically dominant and wives are exerting greater influence in areas that were traditionally the husband's domain. For example, husbands were found to be making greater than half of the household decisions to purchase soaps, cereals, soft drinks, and snack foods (Anonymous, 1980). In addition, in 1992, men were purchasing a quarter of household groceries, an increase of 17% from 1987 (Zinn, 1992). In addition, 80% of men were found to do some major food shopping every month (Zinn, 1992). Women, on the other hand, were shown to be taking a larger role in decisions to purchase insurance, automobiles, and financial services (Candler, 1981).

In summary, studies suggest that the roles of husbands and wives in the family decision-making process are changing. However, none of these more recent studies have examined the process as the earlier studies of Davis, and Belch *et al.* Thus there remains a need to examine how these changes have affected the decision-making process in the year 2000. Given that there have been changing family values and roles, it would benefit marketers to have a more current understanding of the family decision-making process. This research will update well cited previous studies (e.g. Davis and Rigaux (1974) and Belch *et al.* (1985)) to examine current practices in family decision-making. These earlier studies will also serve as a basis for comparison for these changes (if they do, in fact, exist).

Theory

The literature on family decision-making is extensive, as the area has received attention in such diverse areas as consumer behaviour, sociology, economics, cultural anthropology, and rural sociology. In addition, both macro (the observation and investigation of households) and micro (observation of individual members of the household) approaches have been taken.

From a theoretical perspective, fewer theories seem to be relied upon. The most common of these are resource theory (Blood and Wolf, 1960) and social power theory (French and Raven, 1959; Raven, Center and Rodrigues, 1975) – both of which assume a micro perspective. According to resource theory, the individual's personal resources relative to others are the basis for power. Relative income, education, available time, and social status are examples of factors that contribute to power. Thus, male-dominant families of the pre World War II and earlier years, were a result of the fact that the husband was more likely to be the sole worker outside of the home, and was also more likely to have higher status within the household as a result of his social status, relative income and (most often) higher education. The wife's power, to the limited degree of its existence, resulted from more time availability. As noted by Blood and Wolf, two of the primary factors leading to an increase in family influence of women commencing in the 1950s, were the fact that they were now being employed outside of the home as well as furthering their education (p 18). As women became more educated and provided more income to the family on a relative basis, the more egalitarian the decision-making process became. Since the turn of the century the number of women in the workforce increased from 20% to over 60% in 1999. The percentage of women making more than $20,000/year has risen from 14% in 1968 to over 43% by the end of the 20th century, and the labour market participation rate for women 25–44 has increased to over 75% (Cohn, 2000). Following the theory of Blood and Wolf, then, there should be an even more egalitarian relationship among household decision-making as the wife's level of education and income increase.

Raven, Centers and Rodrigues (1975) examined the bases of conjugal power from the perspective of social power theory. Six bases for power were considered responsible for relative influence levels. One of these, expert power – the belief that one family member has superior knowledge or ability which will result in the best possible outcome – was shown to be particularly relevant to family decision-making. In turn, the attribution of expert power was shown to increase with education and social class, with more syncratic decision-making occurring in more egalitarian households.

The Changing American family

In examining these theoretical explanations in light of the changing American family, one might expect that as more women work outside the home, and improve their education and social class standings, the family decision-making structure would change as well. Simply put, we are hypothesizing that given that the American family has changed, and based on the theories of Blood and Wolf and French and Raven, we would expect a corresponding change in the family decision-making process as well, with women gaining an increased say in previously male-dominated product decisions.

Purpose and Hypotheses

Given that over ten years have passed since the publication of the last articles that specifically examined the variation of husbands' and wives' influence across stages in the family decision-making process and across product categories (Putnam and Davidson 1987, Belch *et al.*, 1985) and the fact that numerous changes have been documented within the household, it is imperative to re-examine the dynamics of the family decision-making process. More specifically, this study will attempt to examine today's family decision-making process to determine how family decisions are made in 2000 and to provide currency to our understanding of the process.

Three specific hypotheses were examined. The first two of these were identical to those in the Belch *et al.* (1985) study, while the third hypothesis changes as a result of the changing family structure.

H_1: Family members' influence will vary as a function of the product category and the stage of the decision-making process, with women gaining more input into previously male-dominated products (for example, automobiles).

H_2: Family members' influence in the decision-making process will vary as a function of specific decision areas for each product category, with women gaining more input into all decision stages.

H_3: The degree of influence of each family member at each stage of the decision-making process and for specific decision areas will have changed since the 1970s and 1980s, reflecting changes in the structure and roles of the modern family. Men will have relinquished control over previously dominated decisions, and women will have increased input into all decision areas. Women will also have gained input into previously male-dominated product decisions.

Methodology

Research Design

The research employed a self-administered survey with convenience sampling in the Southwestern geographic of the United States. A field survey questionnaire designed to very closely match that employed in an earlier published study (Belch *et al.*, 1985), but focusing only on the adults (as in Davis and Rigaux) gathered information on family members' influence across three stages of the decision-making process, as well as within specific decisions for seven products and services. Respondents were asked complete the surveys separately (with no input from the other spouse) and to indicate the amount of influence both adults had in each of the three stages of the decision process (initiation, search and evaluation, and the final decision), using a six-point scale ranging from no influence at all to all of the influence. A similar scale was used to measure the amount of influence each had in specific decision areas. Questions regarding when and where to purchase, how much money to spend, style, make and model decisions, etc., constituted this segment of the survey.

Similar to previous studies, the products included automobile, television, household appliances, household furniture and family vacation. Two additional products, food and insurance, were added, as the more recent literature indicates that there have been changes in the decision-making process for both, with each reflecting moderate or high levels of individual involvement and syncratic decision-making properties.

Sample and Data Collection

In an attempt to replicate the Belch *et al.* (1985) study as closely as possible, the same data collection method was employed. Self-administered surveys were distributed to approximately 242 households in southwestern United States. Quotas were established to ensure adequate representation of families. In order to qualify to participate, each couple was required to have been living together and functioning as a family for a minimum of one year. (Again, a slight modification to the previous studies which only included husbands and wives. As the rate of cohabiting, unmarried adults has increased, we found it necessary to include this category to reflect currency.) Each adult was provided with a questionnaire with instructions to complete it separately from the other adult in order to avoid any possible collaboration.

After elimination of those surveys that did not meet the established criteria or that were not accurately completed, a final usable sample of 229 couples (458 individuals) constituted the final sample. Sample statistics are summarized in Table A2.1.

Table A2.1 Sample demographics (n = 458)

Descriptor	Percentage
Respondent's age	
20–29	28.4
30–39	15.8
40–49	26.1
50–59	23.8
60+	5.9
Highest level of education completed	
High school graduate	8.0
Some college	32.6
Associate, vocational or occupational degree	15.6
Bachelor's degree	22.5
Some post-graduate	7.6
Post-graduate degree	13.6
Marital status	
Not married	20.2
Married less than 5 years	17.2
Married 6–10 years	12.4
Married 11–15 years	8.0
Married 16–20 years	4.1
Married 21–25 years	13.6
Married 26–30 years	14.0
Married 31–35 years	5.3
Married 36+ years	5.1
Years living in same household	
Less than 5 years	37.7
6–10 years	16.1
11–15 years	9.9

(continued overleaf)

Table A2.1 *(continued)*

Descriptor	Percentage
16–20 years	5.3
21–25 years	12.4
26–30 years	9.2
31–35 years	5.3
36+ years	4.1
Income	
Under $15,000	16.6
$15,000–$24,999	15.4
$25,000–$34,999	15.7
$35,000–$44,999	17.3
$45,000–$54,999	10.5
$55,000–$64,999	5.9
$65,000 and above	18.5
Employment status	
Full-time employed	69.0
Part-time employed	17.7
Retired	4.8
Homemaker	5.7
Unemployed	2.8
Occupation status	
Not employed outside the home	8.7
Semi-skilled or labour	8.4
Skilled trade or vocation	13.6
Technical or clerical	23.7
Professional	45.7

Results

Family Member Influence across Decision Stages

The first hypothesis suggests that family members' influence should vary across the stages of the decision-making process and across product categories. To test this hypothesis, the relative influence scores of husbands and wives[1] across the stages of the decision-making process for each product category were examined. These mean scores represent the average of husbands' and wives' perceptions (see Table A2.2).

As with previous studies, results indicate that husbands' and wives' influence varies by product and decision-making stage. The husband tends to have more influence in all phases of the decision-making process for televisions, automobiles and insurance. In contrast, wives have more influence across all stages of the decisions to purchase household appliances, household furniture and food. Husbands and wives share more equal influence in decisions regarding vacations; however, the wives' influence in the initiation and evaluation stages for vacations is less than it is in the final decision. All differences are significant at $p < 0.01$. (A comparison to earlier studies will be provided later in this section.)

Family Member Influence by Decision Area

The second hypothesis suggests that the influence of family members in specific decision areas will vary across product categories. As indicated by Table A2.3,

Table A2.2   Mean influence by stages in the decision process

	Stages		
	Initiation	Search and evaluation	Final decision
Television			
Husband	4.31 (1.17)	4.34 (1.23)	4.60 (1.03)
Wife	3.35 (1.17)	3.02 (1.22)	3.56 (1.16)
Automobile			
Husband	4.37 (1.01)	4.60 (1.05)	4.62 (1.03)
Wife	3.79 (1.08)	3.27 (1.20)	3.82 (1.13)
Vacation			
Husband	3.87 (0.97)	3.76 (1.23)	4.06 (1.02)
Wife	4.19 (0.96)	4.22 (1.15)	4.30 (1.03)
Household Appliances			
Husband	3.35 (1.12)	3.45 (1.27)	3.54 (1.17)
Wife	4.43 (1.02)	4.20 (1.12)	4.49 (0.96)
Household Furniture			
Husband	3.47 (1.40)	3.26 (1.21)	3.57 (1.14)
Wife	4.51 (0.96)	4.34 (1.11)	4.59 (0.88)
Insurance			
Husband	4.37 (1.29)	4.35 (1.41)	4.53 (1.28)
Wife	3.53 (1.44)	3.45 (1.51)	3.55 (1.48)
Food			
Husband	3.44 (1.14)	3.22 (1.25)	3.38 (1.19)
Wife	4.60 (0.95)	4.54 (1.07)	4.66 (0.93)

Scale: 1 = no input
        6 = all of input
Each score represents the average of husbands' and wives' perception of family influence. Numbers in parentheses are standard deviations.

Table A2.3   Mean influence for specific decision areas

Product	Husband	Wife
Automobile		
When to purchase	4.30 (1.08)	3.56 (1.11)
How much money	4.36 (1.03)	3.69 (1.16)
Make	4.26 (1.11)	3.67 (1.15)
Model	4.23 (1.12)	3.70 (1.17)
Colour	3.67 (1.21)	4.11 (1.17)
Where to purchase	4.32 (1.19)	3.24 (1.19)
Television		
When to purchase	4.17 (1.10)	3.47 (1.12)
How much money	4.23 (1.02)	3.70 (1.12)
Brand	4.33 (1.07)	3.30 (1.12)
Model	4.31 (1.09)	3.31 (1.12)
Colour versus black/white	4.37 (1.08)	3.29 (1.12)
Where to purchase	4.26 (1.13)	3.32 (1.19)
Vacation		
Where to go	3.81 (0.91)	4.24 (0.95)

(continued overleaf)

Table A2.3 (*continued*)

Product	Husband	Wife
How much money	3.99 (0.93)	4.00 (0.97)
How much time	3.97 (0.86)	3.99 (0.97)
Where to stay	3.82 (0.97)	4.14 (1.03)
When to go	3.98 (0.94)	4.00 (1.04)
Household appliances		
What appliance	3.28 (1.06)	4.41 (0.87)
How much money	3.46 (1.07)	4.23 (0.94)
Where to purchase	3.30 (1.19)	4.17 (1.11)
Style	2.99 (1.11)	4.47 (0.98)
Colour	2.87 (1.07)	4.56 (0.98)
Brand	3.12 (1.18)	4.36 (1.05)
Household furniture		
What furniture	3.37 (0.96)	4.41 (0.89)
How much money	3.63 (1.00)	4.19 (0.95)
Where to purchase	3.30 (1.12)	4.26 (1.04)
Style	3.20 (1.05)	4.46 (0.93)
Colour	3.15 (1.06)	4.52 (0.90)
Fabric	3.15 (1.10)	4.51 (0.93)
Insurance		
How much to spend	4.32 (1.29)	3.42 (1.33)
Where to purchase	4.27 (1.34)	3.37 (1.39)
When to purchase	4.25 (1.30)	3.42 (1.36)
Type of coverage	4.35 (1.28)	3.44 (1.37)
Coverage amount	4.37 (1.29)	3.47 (1.39)
Food		
How much to spend	3.14 (1.20)	4.55 (0.99)
Where to purchase	2.90 (1.24)	4.69 (1.02)
When to purchase	2.92 (1.21)	4.70 (0.98)
What to purchase	3.16 (1.13)	4.64 (0.93)
Brands to purchase	2.89 (1.23)	4.70 (0.99)

Scale: 1 = no input
  6 = all of input
Each score represents the average of husbands' and wives' perception of family influence. Numbers in parentheses are standard deviations.

results for the specific decision areas strongly support the findings for influence by decision-making stages. First, findings suggest that the husband's influence is greater for all aspects of the automobile purchase except colour, where the wife is more influential. (All significant at $p < 0.01$). In addition, husbands were more influential across all aspects of both television and insurance purchases. (All significant at $p < 0.01$). In contrast, wives were more influential in all decisions regarding household appliances, household furnishings and food. (All significant at $p < 0.01$). Finally, results for vacation decisions demonstrated more joint decision-making. Husbands and wives had approximately equal input into deciding how much money, how much time, and when to go on vacations; however, the wife was more influential in deciding where to go and where to stay for a vacation. The only significant difference ($p < 0.01$) was for the decision on where to go, with the wife demonstrating the most influence.

Table A2.4   Mean influence by stages in the decision process

			Stages			
	Initiation 1985	Initiation 1999	Search and evaluation 1985	Search and evaluation 1999	Final 1985	Final 1999
Television						
Husband	4.14 (1.34)	4.31 (1.17)	4.34 (1.41)	4.34 (1.23)	4.53 (1.32)	4.60 (1.03)
Wife	3.60 (1.22)	3.35 (1.17)	3.12 (1.38)	3.02 (1.22)	3.63 (1.40)	3.56 (1.16)
Automobile						
Husband	4.70 (1.19)[1]	4.37 (1.01)[1]	4.88 (1.23)[2]	4.60 (1.05)[2]	4.91 (1.16)[1]	4.62 (1.03)[1]
Wife	3.52 (1.32)[2]	3.79 (1.08)[2]	2.98 (1.38)	3.27 (1.20)	3.53 (1.41)	3.82 (1.13)
Vacation						
Husband	4.16 (1.20)[1]	3.87 (0.97)[1]	4.07 (1.32)[2]	3.76 (1.23)[2]	4.29 (1.25)	4.06 (1.02)
Wife	4.04 (1.18)	4.19 (0.96)	3.99 (1.33)	4.22 (1.15)	4.12 (1.29)	4.30 (1.03)
Household appliances						
Husband	3.48 (1.28)	3.35 (1.12)	3.49 (1.38)	3.45 (1.27)	3.73 (1.33)	3.54 (1.17)
Wife	4.58 (1.17)	4.43 (1.02)	4.34 (1.37)	4.20 (1.12)	4.60 (1.22)	4.49 (0.96)
Household furniture						
Husband	3.63 (1.26)	3.47 (1.40)	3.53 (1.36)	3.26 (1.21)	3.84 (1.29)[2]	3.57 (1.14)[2]
Wife	4.58 (1.15)	4.51 (0.96)	4.43 (1.28)	4.34 (1.11)	4.58 (1.16)	4.59 (0.88)

[1] $p < 0.01$
[2] $p < 0.05$
scale: 1 = no input at all
         6 = all of the input
Each score represents average of husbands' and wives' perceptions of influence.

Family Members Influence Changes

Comparisons of the means from the Belch *et al.* (1985) study and the current study reveal several notable changes (see Table A2.4). A number of significant differences exist in the decision to purchase an automobile, reflecting changes since the 1985 study. While the husband still has more influence in the initiation of the decision to buy an automobile, the relative degree of influence has significantly decreased, and the wife's influence has significantly increased. In addition, in comparison to 1985, husbands have significantly less influence in the search and evaluation and final decision stages of the automobile purchase. Specifically, as shown in Table A2.5, husbands have less influence in the decisions of when to purchase and how much money to pay for automobiles. In addition, wives have more influence in the decisions regarding make, model, colour and where to purchase automobiles.

Significant differences also exist for decisions regarding vacations. Overall, husbands have less influence than they did in 1985, with significantly less influence in the initiation and search and evaluation stages (Table A2.4). In addition, husbands have less influence in the decisions of where to go, how much money to spend, how much time to spend, where to stay, and when to go on a vacation. Wives have significantly more influence in the decision of when to go than in the 1985 study (Table A2.5).

In respect to decisions regarding household furniture, husbands were found to have less influence in the final decision for household furnishings and less influence in the decision of how much to spend on both household furnishings

Table A2.5 Mean influence for specific decision areas

Product	Husband 1985	Husband 1999	Wife 1985	Wife 1999
Automobile				
When to purchase	4.62(1.30)[2]	4.30(1.08)[2]	3.41(1.29)	3.56(1.11)
How much money	4.66(1.25)[2]	4.36(1.03)[2]	3.43(1.32)	3.69(1.16)
Make	4.52(1.31)	4.26(1.11)	3.31(1.35)[2]	3.67(1.15)[2]
Model	4.42(1.35)	4.23(1.12)	3.40(1.38)[2]	3.70(1.17)[2]
Colour	3.80(1.45)	3.67(1.21)	3.73(1.47)[2]	4.11(1.17)[2]
Where to purchase	4.62(1.38)	4.32(1.19)	2.86(1.38)[2]	3.24(1.19)[2]
Television				
When to purchase	4.27(1.34)	4.17(1.10)	3.67(1.31)	3.47(1.12)
How much money	4.43(1.31)	4.23(1.02)	3.59(1.34)	3.70(1.12)
Brand	4.30(1.33)	4.33(1.07)	3.41(1.32)	3.30(1.12)
Model	4.18(1.35)	4.31(1.09)	3.47(1.35)	3.31(1.12)
Colour versus black/white	4.30(1.37)	4.37(1.08)	3.83(1.36)[1]	3.29(1.12)[1]
Where to purchase	4.20(1.46)	4.26(1.13)	3.31(1.46)	3.32(1.19)
Vacation				
Where to go	4.04(1.22)[2]	3.81(0.91)[2]	4.04(1.18)	4.24(0.95)
How much money	4.28(1.28)[2]	3.99(0.93)[2]	3.83(1.26)	4.00(0.97)
How much time	4.35(1.27)[1]	3.97(0.86)[1]	3.89(1.23)	3.99(0.97)
Where to stay	4.08(1.24)[2]	3.82(0.97)[2]	3.94(1.23)	4.14(1.03)
When to go	4.31(1.31)[1]	3.98(0.94)[1]	3.72(1.31)[2]	4.00(1.04)[2]
Household appliances				
What appliance	3.39(1.20)	3.28(1.06)	4.50(1.13)	4.41(0.87)
How much money	3.79(1.27)[1]	3.46(1.07)[1]	4.15(1.19)	4.23(0.94)
Where to purchase	3.46(1.31)	3.30(1.19)	4.17(1.24)	4.17(1.11)
Style	3.06(1.23)	2.99(1.11)	4.58(1.14)	4.47(0.98)
Colour	2.89(1.23)	2.87(1.07)	4.66(1.13)	4.56(0.98)
Brand	3.30(1.35)	3.12(1.18)	4.47(1.26)	4.36(1.05)
Household furniture				
What furniture	3.51(1.17)	3.37(0.96)	4.46(1.13)	4.41(0.89)
How much money	3.98(1.24)[1]	3.63(1.00)[1]	4.11(1.17)	4.19(0.95)
Where to purchase	3.50(1.25)	3.30(1.12)	4.25(1.20)	4.26(1.04)
Style	3.24(1.19)	3.20(1.05)	4.63(1.11)	4.46(0.93)
Colour	3.14(1.21)	3.15(1.06)	4.67(1.12)	4.52(0.90)
Fabric	3.09(1.26)	3.15(1.10)	4.66(1.17)	4.51(0.93)

[1] $p < 0.01$
[2] $p < 0.05$
scale: 1 = no input at all
6 = all of the input
Each score represents average of husbands' and wives' perceptions of influence.

and household appliances than they did 15 years ago (Tables A2.4 and A2.5 respectively). No significant changes were shown between the two studies in regard to household appliances and television purchases by stages. Interestingly, the husband has seemingly lost influence regarding how much money to spend on household appliances. Comparative values for food and insurance purchases were not available, as information on these items was not acquired in the Belch *et al.* (1985) study.

Discussion and Implications

In summary, these results bear out what might be expected intuitively. While one might argue that practitioners have known this for some time, the fact remains that this research is the first to document these effects empirically. The changes that have occurred in the American family as a result of dual working relationships and other changes have also been reflected in changes in the family decision-making process. Overall, women have gained more influence in most of the decision-making areas, gaining significantly more influence in the initiation stage, and increased influence regarding search and evaluation and the final decision for automobile purchases – a previously husband-dominated product. The husband's influence in all decision areas regarding this purchase has significantly decreased since the 1985 study. The husband has also lost influence in all stages of decisions regarding vacations while the wife has gained substantial influence in all of these decision-making stages. Interestingly, the only product area in which the husband has gained influence over the past 15 years is in regard to the purchase of a television. In all stages from initiation to final decision, the level of influence exerted by the husband has increased, while that of the wife has decreased. However, closer examination of specific decision areas shows that women have increased their influence in regard to how much money to spend, while the husband's influence has increased in all other areas. Similarly, the only area in which significant differences are reflected for household appliances and household furniture is in regard to this same decision (how much to spend) – in each case the husband losing influence. In all other decision areas, changes are mixed, indicating that it may be that the decisions are being deferred to the spouse thought to have more involvement and/or expertise with the product.

The findings of this research have important strategic implications. As practitioners have suspected, the woman has gained independence and importance in almost every area of the family decision-making process. As contributors to the household income, and as a result of changing cultural values, women are taking on more roles in the household. Companies wishing to compete successfully must now target this segment, appealing to their specific needs and wants. Most automobile companies have instituted programs targeted specifically at women, including educational programs, sales training programs for salespersons, and the hiring of female sales people in an attempt to better satisfy the needs of this segment. Numerous Internet sites like iVillage.com and Woman.com have achieved success by appealing specifically to this segment.

Another important implication is the changing role structure of the husband. Men are increasingly taking on roles once classified as feminine (Zinn, 1992). As a result of this change in the American family, marketing efforts must also change. For example, Campbell's soup, in recognition of the influence of husbands in grocery purchasing, has begun purchasing advertising space in male-oriented magazines such as Sports Illustrated, Field and Stream, and Rolling Stone. Similarly, Procter and Gamble now portrays the husband in advertisements in roles that were traditionally more feminine, including child care and grocery selection. These are just a few examples of how the market is responding to the shift toward joint decision-making in the household.

Finally, work and leisure activities have resulted in extreme time changes in the availability of time for either spouse. Between work, leisure activities of either spouse and/or their children, etc., families seem to be increasingly time poor. One method of coping with these time constraints may be the allocations of family decisions – particularly those of relatively less importance. The decision as to which television or household appliance to purchase may now be relegated to the party more involved or more expert, while more critical decisions – automobile and vacation decisions, how much money the family can afford, etc. – have increasingly become a decision of interest and concern to both parties.

From a theoretical perspective, two possible explanations as to these changes might be offered. Blood and Wolf (1960) argued that the spouse with the greater amount of resources would have the most power in the decision-making process. At that time, men generally had more power due to their greater resource contribution to the household. By the end of the decade, however, studies found that wives gained power when they were working wives, as their occupational status relative to the husband's increased, and as their contribution to household income increased (Lupri, 1969). Thus, these findings may be the result of the fact that women are contributing more, and thus have gained power. For what might be considered major expenditure decisions, as well for how much to spend for appliances and televisions, the female now has more influence, likely reflecting her increased resource contribution. The same would certainly seem to hold true for decisions regarding vacations, as the woman has gained the right to decide based on her increased resource contribution.

A second perspective is that decision-making might be influenced by the relative expertise of individuals (French and Raven, 1959). It is possible that as more women join the workforce and engage in other activities outside of the home, their expertise in different areas may have increased. Whereas in the past, the husband may have been considered the expert in many of the decision areas considered here, the modern woman may have now gained experience as well as confidence in these areas, due, at least in part, to increased involvement. For example, the majority of dual working families in the US now own two automobiles – sometimes considered his and hers, or one for work and one for the family. These results may reflect women's knowledge and preferences regarding specific products and/or brands. Likewise, more experiences outside of the home may lead to increased expertise in other product areas as well. Women may be as, or more, knowledgeable in many of these areas as their spouse. This increased expertise would then contribute to her increased role in the decision process.

Limitations

As noted, this research was designed to approximately replicate the Belch *et al.* study of 1985 to determine if changes in the American family have resulted in changes in the family decision-making process as well. While the hypothesis that such changes have occurred was supported, there were limitations that should be noted. Like the previous study, the sample for this research was based on a specific geographical area of families. The study, therefore, is limited in the extent that this sample can be projected to the entire USA or foreign countries. Research employing a national sample would be of great interest and offer validations for many of the conclusions made herein. Finally, the 1985 study also examined the role of children in the family decision-making process, which this study did not. Thus, comparisons can be made only in regard to the roles of adults living in the household, rendering this study less than a replication of household decision-making. Nevertheless, these limitations not withstanding, the research provided here has validated the belief that the family decision-making process has changed since 1985. Thus, it makes a contribution to the academic literature by providing more updated insights into the family decision-making process – insights that reflect the changing structures in US households.

Note

1. The terms husband and wife are used to represent the male and female members of the household. It should be noted that all respondents are not legally married, although they reside in the same household and share the roles of decision-making.

REFERENCES

Ahlburg D A and **DeVita** C J (1992) New Realities of the American Family, Population Bulletin

Anonymous (1980) Large Numbers of Husbands Buy Household Products, Do Housework, Marketing News, Vol 14 No 7 p 1

Beatty S E and **Talpade** S (1994) Adolescent Influence in Family Decision Making: A Replication with Extension, Journal of Consumer Research, Vol 21 pp 331–341

Belch G, **Belch** M A and **Ceresino** G (1985) Parental and Teenage Influences in Family Decision Making, Journal of Business Research, Vol 13, April, pp 163–176

Blood R O Jr and **Wolfe** D M (1960) Husbands and Wives: The Dynamics of Married Living, Free Press, Glencoe, IL

Candler J (1981) A Long Drive for Recognition, Advertising Age, Vol 52 No 26 p 2

Clulow C (1993), New Families? Changes in Societies and Family Relationships, Sexual and Marital Therapy, Vol 8 No 3 pp 269–273

Cohn L (2000) Women in the Workforce: They Have Come a Long Way, Business Week, February

Corfman K P (1990) Methodological Problems in Survey and Experimental Research on Family Choice Processes, Advances in Consumer Research, Vol 17 pp 520–523

Corfman K P and **Lehmann** D R (1987) Models of Cooperative Group Decision-Making and Relative Influence: An Experimental Investigation of Family Purchase Decisions, Journal of Consumer Research, Vol 14, June, pp 1–13

238

Davis H L (1970) Dimensions of Marital Roles in Consumer Decision Making, Journal of Marketing Research, Vol 7, May, pp 168–177

Davis H L (1971) Measurement of Husband-Wife Influence in Consumer Purchase Decisions, Journal of Marketing Research, Vol 8, August, pp 305–312

Davis H L and **Rigaux** B P (1974) Perception of Marital Roles in Decision Processes, Journal of Consumer Research, Vol 1, June, pp 51–62

Ellwood D T (1993) The Changing Structure of American Families: The Bigger Family Planning Issue, Journal of the American Planning Association, Vol 59 No 1 pp 3–8.

Ferber R and **Lee** L (1974) Husband-Wife Influence in Family Purchasing Behavior, Journal of Consumer Research, Vol 1 pp 43–50

Filiatrault P and **Ritchie** J R B (1980) Joint Purchasing Decisions: A Comparison of Influence Structure in Family and Couple Decision-Making Units, Journal of Consumer Research, Vol 7, September, pp 131–140.

Foxman E R and **Tansuhaj** PS (1988) Adolescents and Mothers' Perceptions of Relative Influence in family Purchase Decisions: Patterns of Agreement and Disagreement, Advances in Consumer Research, Vol 15 pp 449–853

Foxman E R, **Tansuhaj** P S and **Ekstrom** K M (1989) Family Members' Perceptions of Adolescents' Influence in Family Decision Making, Journal of Consumer Research, Vol 15 pp 482–491

French J Jr and **Raven** B (1959) The Bases of Social Power, in Studies in Social Power, Institute for Social Research, Ann Arbor, MI, pp 150–165

Hamburg D A (1993) The American Family Transformed: Changes in Social Structure Since the 1960's, Society, Vol 30 No 2 pp 69–70

Jacques J M (1998) Changing Marital and Family Patterns: A Test of the Post-Modern Perspectives, Sociological Perspectives, Vol 41 No 2 pp 381–413

Lackman C and **Lanasa** J M (1993) Family Decision-Making Theory, An Overview and Assessment, Psychology and Marketing, Vol 10 No 2 pp 81–93

Lavin M (1993) Husband-Dominant, Wife-Dominant, Joint: A Shopping Typology for Baby Boom Couples? Journal of Consumer Marketing, Vol 10 pp 33–42

Lupri E (1969) Contemporary Authority Patterns in the West German: A Study in Cross-National Validation, Journal of Marriage and the Family, Vol 31 pp 134–144

Mangleburg T F (1990) Children's Influence in Purchase Decisions, Advances in Consumer Research, Vol 17, pp 813–825

Park C W (1982) Joint Decisions in Home Purchasing: A Muddling-Through Process, Journal of Consumer Research, Vol 9, September, pp 151–162

Pearl K N (1995), Portrait of the Changing Family, Scholastic Update, Vol 127 No 11 pp 4–6

Powers M (1994), Families, They Are A-changin', Human Ecology Forum, Vol 22 No 1, Winter, pp 20–23

Putnam M and **Davidson** W R (1987) Family Purchasing Behavior: II Family Roles by Product Category, Management Horizons, Inc., Columbus, Ohio

Qualls W J (1982) Changing Sex Roles: Its Impact Upon Family Decision Making, Advances in Consumer Research, Vol 9 pp 267–270

Qualls W J (1987) Household Decision Behavior: The Impact of Husbands' and Wives' Sex Role Orientation, Journal of Consumer Research, Vol 14, September, pp 264–279

Raven B H, **Centers** R and **Rodrigues** A (1975) The Bases of Conjugal Power, in **Cromwell** R E and **Olson** D H (eds), Power in Families, John Wiley & Sons Ltd, New York, pp 217–232

Rosen D L and **Granbois** D H (1983) Determinants of Role Structure in Family Financial Management, Journal of Consumer Research, Vol 10, September, pp 253–258

Spiro R L (1983) Persuasion in Family Decision-Making, Journal of Consumer Research, Vol 9, March, pp 393–402

Talpade S (1990) Teenager Influence in Family Decision Making: Theoretical Foundations, Scale Development and Empirical Analysis, Dissertation, Department of Marketing, University of Alabama

Wilkes R E (1975) Husband-Wife Influence in Purchase Decisions – A Confirmation and Extension, Journal of Marketing Research, Vol 12, May, pp 224–227

Zinn L (1992) Real Men Buy Paper Towels, Too, Business Week, 9 November, pp 75–77

Questions on this article

1. The composition of families in Western societies is changing. Using the literature and examples, discuss the nature of such change and provide illustrations of how family members' buying roles are often complex.
2. Compare and contrast the nature of family purchasing behaviour in Western societies with that in other cultures.

PART 3
INTEGRATED APPROACHES TO
CONSUMER BEHAVIOUR

Part 3 of the book extends the coverage of some of the distinct concepts which we introduced in Parts 1 and 2, within integrating approaches to explaining consumer behaviour.

We start (Chapter 9) with an exploration of how consumers react to new products and services. We show that there are different market segments that adopt new products in different ways over time. There are further important implications here, in the recognition that some can be used to 'spread the word' to others. The use of multi-step flows of communication by markets is a reflection of this as they often use celebrities or journalists to endorse a product as a way of encouraging its adoption.

This analysis is furthered in Chapter 10 with coverage of repeat buying and the extent to which marketers can encourage and exploit loyal and even relational buying. Models of repeat and loyal buying are presented along with marketers' attempts to capture loyalty through, for example, loyalty schemes. Whether the same sort of relationship can exist between companies and consumers as between people is analysed and evaluated. What is certain, though, is that marketers want to develop relationships with their best consumers. We present examples of how this has been done but we also show the difficulties of achieving relational consumption.

Chapter 11 takes this even further. The relatively recent use of consumers' personal details has led to more personalized targeting by marketers. Sources of data include consumers' transactional data and geodemographics. In addition consumers can be 'tracked' via new radio frequency identification (RFID) tags in the products they buy, and via global positioning satellites (GPS), which can monitor the location of their mobile phones. There are new ways of analysing consumer data and sophisticated data-mining software is presented here. As well as clear benefits to marketers, for example, in being able to target individual consumers with offers for products and services in which they are known to have an interest, the extent of personal details available to marketers (and others?) leads some consumers to be concerned about 'big brother' privacy issues.

If there are any concerns over marketers' behaviour, Chapter 12 delves into the darker aspects of consumer (mis)behaviour. Consumers can indulge in shoplifting, they might not always own up to being given too much change at the checkout, they can illegally download music and buy bootleg copies of films. This chapter examines a large range of such behaviour along with some of the reasons why consumers misbehave. Marketers might also consider anticonsumption as misbehaviour on the part of consumers. But there can be philosophical reasons why some are concerned about the proliferation of planet-damaging products and people-damaging marketing techniques. As a result some consumers consume little and others will react negatively toward marketing techniques and even act as consumer terrorists.

Part 3 is concluded with a research paper into the use of illicit drugs.

The accompanying web site houses many other articles, along with links to relevant web sites which provide further coverage and examples of the issues, theories and concepts that we explore in the text.

CHAPTER 9

NEW PRODUCT BUYING

INTRODUCTION

Introducing new products is important for marketers because it allows them to compete effectively in a highly competitive marketplace. That is why all marketing texts deal with new product development and **product life cycle** (PLC) strategies. The key proposition behind the product life cycle concept is that marketers should adapt their marketing as products go through various stages (e.g. 'introduction', 'growth', 'maturity' and 'decline') of their life. This is predicated on the facts that: markets usually become increasingly competitive over the life cycle; and that customers change over time – the more innovative will be the earlier adopters and the less innovative will be later adopters. The latter is the starting point for this chapter. There are also issues of how consumers perceive new products and the factors that can lead to acceptance or rejection of these. In addition, the nature of flows of communication concerning new products is relevant, especially when both the marketer and the consumer use **opinion formers** or **opinion leaders** to disseminate and receive information respectively. These topics hold many implications for marketing generally, for introducing new products and services and for explaining new and repeat purchasing behaviour.

This chapter explores these areas, starting with some foundation theory (**diffusion-adoption of innovations**) and follows this through to current research into 'innovative' and 'adaptive' behaviour by consumers. There are strong links with other topics covered elsewhere in the book, notably 'personality' in Chapter 6, 'sequential models' of consumer response to marketing (Chapters 2, 3 and 4) and 'involvement' (Chapter 4). The issues are then furthered by coverage in Chapter 10 of loyal, switching and relational behaviour.

FOUNDATION THEORY

Diffusion-Adoption of Innovations

The processes of spreading innovations through a society and how individuals 'adopt' these, is the domain of **diffusion-adoption of innovations** theory. **Diffusion** refers to how the innovation is communicated and distributed through society over time – it is a macro concept concerned with aggregated **adoption** behaviour. We will describe each component in turn:

Innovation and its Types

An **innovation** is anything (e.g. idea, concept, product or service) perceived as being new in the marketplace. Robertson (1967) categorized innovations in terms of the amount of disruption and behavioural change they cause in existing consumption patterns (Figure 9.1).

Discontinuous Innovations

Radically new products which have maximum disruptive effect are termed 'discontinuous innovations'. In their day, the internal combustion engine and television came into this category. 'Disruption' is not necessarily a problem to be overcome: the internal combustion engine provided revolutionary, convenient transportation for work and leisure, and the TV dramatically changed entertainment and informational and educational media, which in turn changed lifestyles. As time moves on, of course, a new version of one of these products, today, creates less disruption and would be called a 'continuous innovation'.

Dynamically Continuous Innovations

This is the 'in-between' type of innovation, creating some change in how consumers behave but not perceived to be dramatically important changes by those individuals. Electric lawnmowers, for instance, do the same job as manual versions but faster and with less effort and therefore do a known job differently. This is called a 'dynamically continuous innovation': the result is evolutionary, not revolutionary.

Discontinuous innovations ⬅	Dynamically continuous innovations	Continuous innovations ➡
High level of disruption and behavioural change		Low level of disruption and behavioural change
Internal combustion engine in the first car	The first hatchback car	Car fitted with satellite navigation and pollen filter
Personal computer	Portable laptop PC	Faster 'chips' and larger memory

Figure 9.1 Degrees of disruption: more of a continuum than categories

Continuous Innovations

These are variations on familiar products: 'new improved' shampoos, 'mark 2' models of cars, for which the radiator grill has been slightly redesigned and perhaps fuel economy improved, and second editions of successful textbooks. These are minimally disruptive of established consumption patterns; they allow life to go on much as before but provide the benefits of the most recent developments in technology and thought. These are continuous innovations and most of the new product launches each year tend to fit into this category.

Genuinely discontinuous innovations are few and far between. When such an item is introduced it is the first brand in a wholly new product class, right at the beginning of the product life cycle (Howard and Moore, 1982).

Alternative Types of Innovation

An alternative to the continuum approach (Figure 9.1) has been suggested by Hoyer and McInnes (2001). They suggest that innovations can also be 'functional innovations', 'aesthetic or hedonistic innovations' and 'symbolic innovations'. The first of these, *functional innovations*, have functional performance benefits over existing products. Examples are often technology-driven, such as the combined shampoo/conditioner or ever more powerful laptop computers. Successful aesthetic or hedonistic innovations appeal to consumers' more sensory, creative, pleasure-seeking or creative needs (such as Maslow's levels 5, 6 and 7). Symbolic innovations are related to new associations with, for example, social groups or tribes (see Chapter 7). Symbolic innovations can be invested with other symbolic meanings as well because 'a complete ensemble of consumption objects may be able to repeat the diverse and possibly incongruous aspects of the total self' (Belk, 1988). As a result, our possessions, including the brands we buy, extend our self-image (see Chapter 6) to others and to ourselves. So some new products and services will be especially relevant to consumers' self-concept.

Criteria for Acceptance of Innovations

People are often suspicious of radical innovations and Rogers (1959, 1983) proposed several criteria useful for determining the likely success of new products. Some of these dimensions are more directly involved with facilitating trial, while others both facilitate trial and encourage brand loyalty. We discuss each in turn.

Compatibility

'Compatibility' refers to the degree to which a product is consistent with consumers' current values, cognitions and behaviours. Other things being equal, a product that does not require an important change in consumer values, beliefs, purchase or use behaviours is more likely to be tried by consumers. For example, a shampoo and conditioner in one bottle requires little change on the part of consumers to try the product, and both 'features' are congruent with consumers' behaviours.

Relative advantage

'Relative advantage' refers to the degree to which an item has a sustainable, competitive, differential advantage over other product classes, product forms and brands. There is no question that relative advantage is a most important product characteristic not only for obtaining trial, but also for continued purchase and the development of brand loyalty. The main question raised by this characteristic is: 'Which attribute makes this product better than competitive products'? The shampoo/conditioner, providing it does the job as well as separate products, requires less effort and time.

Relative advantage is a most important element of successful product strategies. However, such an advantage can seldom be sustained through technology or modifications of product attributes alone. One of the most important sources of sustainable relative advantage is product symbolism (as discussed in Chapters 1 and 2 and in the article at the end of Part 1).

Trialability

'Trialability' refers to the degree to which a product can be tried on a limited basis or divided into small quantities for an inexpensive trial. Other things being equal, a product that facilitates a non-purchase trial or limited-purchase trial is more likely to influence the consumer to try the product. Test-driving a car, trying on a sweater, tasting bite-sized pieces of a new snack bar, trying the free sample-sized bottle of a new shampoo 'banded' onto a magazine are ways that consumers can try products on a limited basis with reduced risk.

Observability

'Observability' refers to the degree to which a product or its effects can be sensed by other consumers. New products that are public and frequently discussed or seen are more likely to be adopted rapidly. For example, many clothing styles become popular after consumers see celebrities wearing them, and new cars are also highly observable. There is tremendous importance here, as is discussed shortly, in using opinion formers and opinion leaders to communicate the new product.

Speed

'Speed' refers to how fast the benefits of the product are experienced by the consumer. Because many consumers are orientated towards immediate rather than delayed gratification, products that can deliver benefits sooner rather than later have a higher probability of at least being tried. For example, diets that promise results within the first week are more likely to attract consumers than are those that promise results in six months (but 'hype' can be exposed by the 'observability' characteristic, in this instance).

Simplicity

'Simplicity' refers to the degree to which a product is easy for a consumer to understand and use. Other things being equal, a product that does not require complicated assembly and extensive training for the consumer to use it, has a higher chance of trial. For example, many computer products are promoted as being 'user-friendly' to encourage purchase. The trial or adoption of a new cooking sauce might be delayed if it involved complicated preparation and cooking, especially when many consumers tend to expect 'convenience' in such products.

Perceived Risk

If the perceived (physical, financial or social) risk of the new product is low, it is more likely to be adopted. Products with a high level of perceived risk, such as dangerous or expensive sports, will generally have a lower adoption rate, as can Internet banking if security of personal data or finance is perceived to be at risk.

Product Symbolism

Product symbolism refers to what the product or brand means to the consumer and what the consumer experiences in purchasing and using it. Consumer researchers recognize that some products possess symbolic features, and that consumption of them may depend more on their social and psychological meaning than on their functional utility (see Chapter 1). For example, the jeans market is dominated by major brands but there are functional and even design similarities among these. It seems clear that jeans branding and imagery have meanings and symbolize different values for consumers.

Indeed, Hoyer and MacInnis (2001) include 'symbolic innovations' in their framework for categorizing innovations, as mentioned above. To them, symbolic innovations are those that convey some sort of associative meaning such as belonging to a peer or reference group (see Chapter 7). It might not always be a new product in the conventional sense, but rather new symbolic meaning, such as when a long-established drink brand which had an 'old-fashioned' image is repackaged and relaunched and aimed at a young, trendy market.

Aesthetic or Hedonistic Innovations

Aesthetic or hedonistic innovations are also cited by Hoyer and MacInnis (2001) in their categorization of innovations and we can consider them as being important in determining likely acceptance of new products. They appeal to our sensory or pleasure-seeking needs, and include such things as new clothing styles, new forms of dance, new food flavours and textures, so for those who really want to try new things and are motivated by new experiences (see 'Adopter Categories', below) these will be further dimensions that can facilitate trial and adoption.

Innovation Overload

We can add a more general factor: innovation overload (Schiffman and Kanuk, 2000) which is where consumers are faced with a bewildering array of new products across many categories and the increase in the number of, and speed of change within, categories leaves the time-hungry consumer unable to make informed decisions or even any decisions. This can help explain resistance to a new product but is not so much to do with that new product per se, but rather with a general marketing and consumption environment that might be seen to be too active.

The Communication of Innovation

This element of the diffusion process is concerned with direct and deliberate personal forms or less formal, indirect ones that perhaps allow some of the natural opinion leadership flows of information to take their usual course. This can be of crucial importance – often a local opinion leader will be more persuasive than a paid-for expensive advertising campaign. But how to 'influence the influencers' is the inevitable question here. Because different adopter categories have varying characteristics in terms of the sources of information – and even type of message – to which they will respond, different communications approaches will be required: sometimes direct and personal approaches such as personal selling, sometimes less personal such as advertising, and sometimes of the 'article' type – for example as produced through press releases. These aspects are discussed in more detail later in this chapter.

The Social System

Innovations are targeted at specific segments (the 'social system' in terms of the constructs of innovation theory). Again based on adopter category characteristics, some consumers will be more influential within their particular social system (segment) than others, and a later section discusses in some detail the role of opinion formers and opinion leaders and the implications of targeting these in order to speed up the diffusion process.

Time

Some adopters go through the sequence of pre- and post-purchase stages in ways that lead to adoption more quickly than others do, so the time element is an important variable in determining the innovativeness of adopters and in turn who to target and on what basis.

Another aspect of time relates to how quickly the 'new behaviour' required becomes accepted and therefore how quickly discontinuous innovations become dynamically continuous and then continuous innovations.

Adoption

The **adoption** process is really the other side of the same coin: indeed the same dimensions of 'innovation', 'time', 'social system' and 'communication' operate here. Adoption is not merely purchase (that can happen during 'trial') but rather it is more regular or committed purchase behaviour. The adoption process is often shown to be reflected in a series of stages through which consumers progress:

$$\text{Awareness} \Rightarrow \text{interest} \Rightarrow \text{evaluation} \Rightarrow \text{trial} \Rightarrow \text{adoption}$$

There are variations on the theme here and such sequences are also known as 'hierarchy of effects models' (see Chapters 2 to 4). The one above makes no allowances for skipping stages and feedback is not catered for. Another early model was proposed by Lavidge and Steiner (1961), as mentioned in Chapter 2 and this includes the following stages:

$$\text{Awareness} \Rightarrow \text{Knowledge} \Rightarrow \text{Liking} \Rightarrow \text{Preference} \Rightarrow \text{Conviction} \Rightarrow \text{Purchase}$$

This was possibly the first adoption model to be based on an 'information–attitude–behaviour' theory of the communications effect (see Chapter 3).

Another problem-solving model lists four stages:

$$\text{knowledge} \Rightarrow \text{persuasion} \Rightarrow \text{discussion} \Rightarrow \text{confirmation (Rogers and Shoemaker, 1971)}$$

These hierarchy of effects models have been criticized by Ehrenberg (1975) in the context of well-established and regularly advertised brands. In such circumstances, Ehrenberg proposes that consumer behaviour is more to do with habit. Even in his 'Awareness, Trial, Reinforcement' (ATR) model (Figure 9.2) the focus is on reinforcement which can lead to repeat purchase. This would be based on the operant conditioning approach discussed in Chapter 3.

Whichever model is favoured, an important implication is that the more innovative consumers go through the sequence at a speedier rate than those who are less innovative. As we say, the same elements as for diffusion are appropriate here: the progression through these stages 'over *time*' due to individuals'

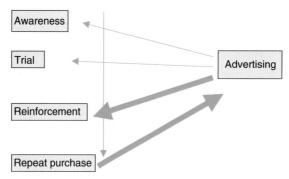

Figure 9.2   Ehrenberg ATR model
The heavy lines denote the major effects.

innovativeness, which in turn can be related to their position in *society* and how they influence others and/or are influenced by others and the *communications* sources they seek and are influenced by.

Most prefer to wait and see what happens to the first adopters before they themselves make a purchase. The consumers who do buy at this stage are usually highly involved in the product field. They are heavy users of whatever preceded the innovation (e.g. radio and films in the case of television). In Chapter 6, we discussed rather inconclusive attempts to link consumer personalities with the products and services they buy. One problem with that approach was that consumers do not always recognize the totality of their personalities and, even if they do, some will want to disguise certain traits and project other traits in different social contexts. However, research is much more affirmative over one particular trait: an apparent 'need for newness' or **innovativeness**. Some want to be the first to try novel ideas and thereby to communicate them to others, whereas more cautious consumers buy later, if at all. The more innovative often display a strong personal interest in the product field, which links with 'involvement' as covered in Chapter 4.

A major focus of consumer research has been to identify the characteristics of the more innovative consumers and their differences from other consumers. A review of this research found that the more innovative tend to be more highly educated and younger, and to have greater social mobility, more favourable attitudes towards risk (more venturesome), greater social participation, and higher opinion leadership than other consumers (Gatignon and Robertson, 1985).

It should be noted that the five adopter categories and the percentages in Table 9.1 are somewhat arbitrary. Their validity has not been fully supported in consumer research, particularly not for **low-involvement** products (Gatignon and Robertson, 1985). It is a useful framework, however, in indicating the relative incidence of the different adopter segments.

Table 9.1   Adopter categories

Segment	Proportion of eventual total adopters
Innovators	The first 2.5% of the total number of eventual adopters of a new product
Early adopters	The next 13.5% to adopt
Early majority	The next 34% to adopt
Late majority	The next 34% to adopt
Laggards	The last 16% to adopt

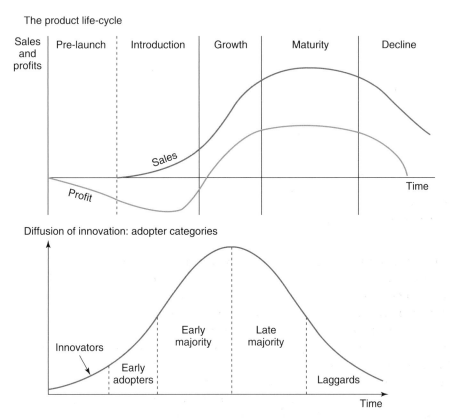

Figure 9.3   Relationship between the product life cycle and adopter categories

The idea that different types of consumers become adopters of products in different stages of the product's life cycle does have important implications for marketing strategy (Figure 9.3). Promotion and other elements of marketing strategy should change across time to appeal to different types of consumers. Remember our reference to the product life cycle at the beginning of this chapter. We believe that identifying different adopting segments over time provides more marketing value than the PLC in its more narrow sense and indeed we consider it to be an important base for segmenting markets.

Adopter Categories

The characteristics of adopter categories were well summarized by McCarthy (1977) approximately 30 years ago:

Innovators are eager to try new ideas. They do not need much persuasion. They are fairly well off and are willing to take risks. They tend to be younger and to have higher status and education. Their reading goes beyond 'local' and mass media communications. They have the closest contact with scientific and specialist sources of information and in general rely on impersonal sources. They seek social relationships outside their local peer circle. They are extrovert in a jet-set sense. They have a broad range of interests and are socially mobile.

Early adopters tend to have the greatest contact with salespeople and local people and are often leaders in local clubs and organizations. They exhibit the greatest opinion leadership and are highly 'localite'.

They have a high status and are fairly well off. They are highly respected in local society and are often asked for their opinions and advice.

Early majority have contact with mass media and salespeople, but also with early adopters. They do not exhibit so much opinion leadership and they deliberate over adoption decisions.

Late majority tend to be sceptical and need much pressure from peers before they adopt. They are below average in terms of income, status and education, etc. They adopt when they perceive little risk, perhaps when they see others like themselves using an innovative product.

Laggards are bound in tradition and often use other laggards as sources of information. The past is their frame of reference. Some are semi-isolates who do not use the mass media or salespeople as information sources. They tend to be older and from lower socio-economic groups and are less wealthy. They might become adopters when innovators are adopting the next innovation.

 Some consumers may appear to be almost laggardly *non-adopters* but instead do not adopt because they are actively against the usage of a product; for instance anti- or non-smokers, vegetarians, or people that do not possess a car for pro-environmental reasons. These could, in some cases, be innovators in the sense of adopting an (e.g.) anti-materialistic stance.

It becomes clear, on considering this description of the various adopters, how there can be **segmentation over time**, because each category is quite different from the others in terms of innovativeness, demographic profile and sources of information used. It is worth pointing out that the earliest innovator is not incredibly young, wealthy and well-educated, but is more so than others in the market concerned. In other words, if we are concerned with the over-50s market, innovators are usually nearer 50 than 90 and more affluent than most within the over-50s market, and so on.

What is also evident, however, is that there is a reasonably logical 'cascading' sequence from innovators through to early majority consumers. The 'big divide' could be between early and late majority. For the latter, the 'newness' appeal is precisely why these people are not already adopters. So it means the appeals should change to being less based on newness, even turning this around to state a degree of longevity in the market, 'tried and tested' and so on. It might also mean prices falling a little, to appeal to the late majority. If so, then the whole character of the brand is being changed – perhaps too much for the earlier adopters?

However, for Moore (1991) the big divide (or 'chasm') is between the early adopters and early majority in the market for hi-tech products: 'the difficulty . . . in accepting a new product if it is presented in the same way as it was to the (preceding) group'.

THINKBOX

Tec Shoes is a specialist manufacturer of high-quality athletic footwear. The company has been manufacturing scientifically designed specialist shoes for top runners, racket-sports players and other athletes for several years.

Now the company feels that most people interested in sport could benefit from wearing this footwear because of the increased care and protection of the feet they can provide, because of the contribution that the medical profession as well as experienced footwear and fashion designers make to the creation of the products.

Tec Shoes has been concerned only with top sportspeople on a personal basis and is unsure about how to reach a wider target market. One company executive suggests that different promotional approaches be used to reach different adopter categories over the products' life cycle.

What promotional mixes (advertising, publicity, sales promotion, direct marketing, personal selling) should be used to reach each of these market segments which adopt in different ways 'over time' ? How should the 'message' change for each segment?

ADAPTERS VS. INNOVATORS

Cognitive style is concerned with how individuals make decisions and solve problems. The **Kirton Adaption Innovation Inventory** (KAI [1994]) scales can identify individuals' positions along one particular continuum of cognitive styles: an adapter–innovator continuum.

The extreme innovator is easily bored by routine and seeks novelty and stimulation in discontinuous change. Innovators' solutions generally transcend the context in which the problem has arisen. The identification of the earlier adopter (market initiator in this context) is strategically important for four reasons (Goldsmith and Flynn, 1992). First, they represent the immediate source of cash flow to the company eager to start retrieving the expenses of new product development; the fact that initiators are usually heavy users of the product class in question means that they play a disproportionate role in recouping developmental costs. Second, they may provide market leadership and help set up barriers to new competition that prevent other firms making a fast entry into the market. Third, they provide important feedback to the company on further new product development. And, fourth, they communicate the innovation to the less active sections of the market, the bulk of the market who will eventually provide the high levels of sales and profits.

However, the results of an investigation of the cognitive styles of initial adopters of general new food brands were enigmatic given the expectation that these market initiators would be innovators (Foxall, 1995). KAI scores of respondents did not correlate with the number of new brands purchased and 40% of the sample were adapters. Most intriguing of all was the finding that the consumers who bought the largest number of new brands were adapters. A similar pattern of results was apparent from a second study, this time of 'healthy' food products (Foxall, 1995).

A possible reason for this unanticipated result emerged from further consideration of adaption–innovation theory. Innovators are likely to purchase novel items impulsively, independently and perhaps haphazardly. By their very nature, they will probably choose a number of innovative products just to try them out. But, while these sensation-seekers are more likely to try many new products, they are also likely to retain few of them in their repertoires (Mittelstaedt *et al.*, 1976). Adapters, however, will presumably show two patterns of behaviour. Those who are not much interested in the product field will, as we might think, be suspicious of new products; in both studies the buyers of fewest brands or products were adapters. Yet those adapters who have a high level of personal involvement with a product field will act quite differently.

A third study explored this (Foxall, 1995). This time, respondents were asked to indicate their level of personal involvement with 'healthy' foods. The instrument used to measure this construct was the Zaichkowsky (1987) Personal Involvement Inventory (PII) which measures ego-involvement or the personal interest shown by individuals in a named product field. Once again, no correlation was found between the number of innovations bought and KAI, and well over half the sample were adapters. More importantly, the results confirmed the hypothesis: the highest level of purchase was shown by more-involved adapters.

Let us pause a moment to consider the implications of these findings. It appears that the post-launch market for new foods is not a homogeneous collection of innovators whose personalities predispose them to be venturesome, risk-taking, flexible and self-assured *early adopters*, as our earlier framework within this chapter suggested. Rather, the market consists of three psychographic segments, each with its own personality profile: less-involved adapters (who buy least), innovators (who buy an intermediate number regardless of their level of involvement), and more-involved adapters (who buy most). Moreover, each of these segments has its own distinctive style of decision-making. Each segment is likely to become aware of new brands/products in a different fashion, to search and evaluate information in its own way, to choose uniquely and to have a distinctive post-decisional reaction. The launch marketing strategy for a new product needs to accommodate all three.

Two further investigations have taken the use of personal computers as their focal interest: the use of a range of software is usually thought to be highly involving; personal computers are well past the introduction stage of their product life cycle; the research involved consumption rather than purchasing, and it allowed situational variables to be examined (Foxall, 1995).

Whereas in the case of new foods adapters buy most; for software applications innovators were found the most likely to adopt most applications. Involvement is a crucial factor in each case and overall the conventional wisdom is sometimes correct, but unsophisticated, and our conclusion is that marketing strategies must thus be multifaceted. In particular the general involvement level engendered by the product is very important. The market for new 'healthy' foods contains innovators, more-involved adapters, and a significant group of less-involved adapters. That for new software applications contains more-involved adapters, more-involved innovators, plus groups of less-active, less-involved adapters and innovators. Because new product marketing relies on the diffusion sequence over time, none of these can be ignored, even at the launch stage. What consumers absorb about an innovation at that stage may colour their impressions for a long time to come.

Marketing strategies should, therefore, be sensitive to the coexistence of adapters and innovators in both the initial and established markets for new products. A marketing strategy directed towards, say, the adapters is likely to alienate the innovators. Perhaps the failure of marketing campaigns which aimed principally at innovators, and ignored the fact that initial adopters and use-initiators may be adapters, have contributed to the high failure rates of new consumer products. But the crucial question now is the likely implications of adaptive–innovative cognitive styles for future marketing campaigns.

The conventional wisdom provides easy prescriptions for managerial action: just focus on the more innovative, but the research indicates that there are three problems with that. First, each launch segment has a unique decision-making style. Second, each active segment, therefore, requires its own launch marketing mix, reflecting the decision style and involvement level of its members. Third, post-launch markets – the markets for imitators – are also segmented by decision style and require multifaceted marketing. Further exploration of these complex issues is beyond the scope of this book but we recommend further reading (Foxall *et al.*, 1998).

In the meantime we return to another of the tenets of diffusion-adoption theory: the nature of multi-step flows of communication via opinion formers and opinion leaders.

TWO- AND MULTI-STEP FLOWS OF COMMUNICATIONS

As will have been deduced from the initial framework, a major factor in speeding up the diffusion process is the use of 'recommendations' by those who are seen to have **source credibility**, which can involve perceived expertise and trustworthiness. **Source attractiveness** is where the consumer perceives the source of a message to be similar to themselves and this has been found to increase the persuasiveness of the source (Woodside and Davenport, 1974).

Consumers receive information about new products from a variety of sources including from those who are thought to possess special knowledge and expertise. These intervening participants are often regarded as credible because they are perceived to be trustworthy and because they are believed to have expertise in a particular product area. This is Lazarsfeld's (1944) proposition, and led to his 'two-step' flow of communications model (Figure 9.4).

Katz and Lazarsfeld (1955) presented these initial ideas following research into the voting and purchase behaviour of Americans. They identified individuals who not only received information but also processed and re-presented the information to others and in doing so were able to influence their decision-making. Therefore, information received directly from personal influence channels is regarded as generally more persuasive than information received through mass media. Those people who influence others are usually referred to as **opinion leaders**, and are often product class- or domain-specific. Those who are opinion leaders across categories are known as **market mavens** (see later section).

Some people have status conferred upon them by their peer group (Raven and French, 1959; and see Chapter 7). Through recognition of their expertise, prowess or particular knowledge or skills, these opinion leaders are able to guide and lead the thoughts of others in particular product areas. Opinion leaders often rely on word-of-mouth communications to influence others and often do so, as Kingdom (1970) says, passively, by being observed. Bristow *et al.* (2005) reaffirm the importance of opinion leaders who do not just communicate by **word of mouth** (WOM) but by being observed. They refer to such opinion leaders as **opinion shapers**. In this way, the key point is that they are change agents however they communicate with others. Featherstone (1991) describes symbol specialists, style leaders, taste makers and leading edge consumers, but it all amounts to the same general paradigm of influence.

However, the model can be enhanced. Some influencers have a status of expertise bestowed upon them by the nature of their employment or training (e.g. journalists). These are referred to as **opinion formers:** people who are actively and deliberately involved in the process of shaping and forming the thoughts of others with regard to specific products and services. Very often they will use the mass media to communicate their reprocessed information (journalists) while all can be regarded as active influencers, or talkers (Kingdom, 1970).

Opinion Formers and Opinion Leaders

To illustrate the difference between the two types of influencer, an accountant who has particular taxation skills may be an opinion former to their clients. Communications might be expected to be more formal

Sender - - - - - - ▶ Opinion leader - - - - - - ▶ Receiver

Figure 9.4 Two-step model of communication

and direct. To their peers they may be an important advisory/influential person and thus be an opinion leader. Communications in these circumstances may be more informal and indirect (word-of-mouth).

Just as the role of the influencer can be considered to be relatively complex, so can the role of the receivers or **opinion followers**. Some actively seek information from the social networks within which they participate (two-step) while others prefer to rely on mass media communications (one-step) for information and guidance (Robinson, 1957).

The **two-step model of communication** has a number of strengths and weaknesses. Opinion formers and leaders are assumed to pass on positive information, but communication planners need to be sure that they will not reprocess and transmit the information in a negative manner and so reverse the intentions of the source of the message. Furthermore, not only can opinion leaders be difficult to identify but also it can be difficult to measure the degree of impact they have in influencing opinion followers. Opinion formers, on the other hand, are more easily identified but potentially less effective than opinion leaders.

Opinion Formers

Broadcast entertainment programmes are sometimes used to convey messages. An example of this is the Russian radio 'soap' *House Seven, Entrance 4* which is part funded by the EU Know-How Fund with the aim of giving advice on living in a market economy (Bailey, 1997). The then British Prime Minister, Tony Blair, even appeared on this programme as an opinion former conveying a message about the importance of education. Other similar programmes are also used in this way. The BBC's *The Archers* has been used as an opinion former to convey messages about farming practice and indeed one of its original aims when launched was to educate farmers about new methods after the Second World War.

Other UK 'soaps' frequently portray issues which have been either influenced by, or worked through in conjunction with, a sponsor of some kind. For example, a storyline concerned with euthanasia was prompted by a press release from the Morphine Information Service, demonstrating the multi-step flow model. The show's producer has stated, 'We cannot get away from the fact that people will have an interest in putting a message across in (our) stories' (Mellis, 1997). Other 'soap' stories have originated from the UK government (adult literacy) and the National Schizophrenia Fellowship (a storyline concerning schizophrenia). These are strong examples of how opinion formers, albeit 'simulated' opinion formers (the characters exist only in fiction), can be powerful formers of opinion.

THINKBOX

Next time you listen to a 'news' programme, count the number of times phrases like: 'X is likely to announce Y today' occur. In such cases, news is not being reported, but press releases are. Should we therefore have two categories of 'news': *actual* news and *future* news? We even hear music being announced as a 'future hit'. Such reports by credible news or music presenters are examples of opinion-forming.

Could it be that 'news is something someone, somewhere doesn't want printed, the rest is just public relations' (Humphries, 1995) and that, with or without regulation among the ranks of 'invisible persuaders', influence over the media is as 'powerful as it remains utterly unnoticed' (Michie, 1998:316)?

What do *you* think?

Since consumers perceive some celebrities as highly trustworthy, believable, persuasive and likeable, marketers often rely on them to endorse their products. In the UK, for example, the image of Sainsbury's supermarkets has been greatly enhanced by its use of a TV chef (Jamie Oliver) in its advertising messages, and Oliver spearheaded a campaign to improve school dinners in 2005. His expertise as a chef invested him with opinion-forming powers.

In 1979 when Sony introduced the Walkman, the company gave samples of the product to film stars and models, who were thus used as opinion formers to show that there was a fashion benefit as well as functionality. As the company's public relations manager states, 'The most powerful way of telling someone that something is a good product is if someone who is credible tells you that it is' (Goodman, 1997).

EXAMPLE 9.1

A problem with this approach is that the celebrity might do something to dilute or even degrade the association. For example, Adidas pulled out of campaign using the athlete Dwain Chambers when he was found guilty of using banned drugs. Even if they are good boys and girls, it can cost the marketers large sums. For example, in 2003 David Beckham was reported to be earning, from such endorsements: £2 million from Vodafone, £1 million from Marks & Spencer, £1 million from Rage Software, £1 million from Police brand sunglasses, £1 million from Brylcreem and £5 million from Adidas (among others) (Hopkins, 2003). This is not to say that he isn't an effective opinion former, but how cost-effective?

However, the use of celebrities to endorse brands is not new. Figure 9.5 shows the use of Shirley Temple, a child actress of the 1930s, being portrayed on a cereal pack. Note that her film company also gets a mention.

THINKBOX

Are you influenced to think of a brand differently if promoted using a well known celebrity (be honest)?

Generally there should be a degree of congruity between the celebrity used and the brand itself (Kamins, 1990; and Misra and Beatty, 1990) but congruence can be on different levels: some logical link, such as a sports person endorsing sporting equipment; or merely emotional, where a comedian endorses a relatively frivolous or 'wacky' brand.

A related issue is the number of different product types a celebrity is endorsing at a given time. For instance, Tripp *et al.*, (1994) investigated the effects of number of products endorsed by a celebrity on consumer attitudes and purchase intentions. Their findings revealed a negative link between multiple products endorsed by a celebrity and consumer attitudes towards the advertisement.

Perhaps it is an example of the cynical and marketing-savvy environment in which we all now live that consumers know that companies might want to make some sort of relevant association (see Chapter 3)

Figure 9.5   Shirley Temple
Reproduced by permission of Robert Opie

between the product and the endorser but that the endorser may or may not even use the product, never mind like it. Silvera and Austad (2004) concluded from their experimental research into the effectiveness of celebrity endorsement, that marketers could pay more attention than they do to 'making strong and believable explanations for why endorsers truly do like the products they endorse'. This is based on their findings that consumers can be persuaded more if they believe the endorser likes what they are endorsing.

Another issue concerns how well celebrities 'travel' in global marketing campaigns. Research is less well developed in this area and Chao et al.'s (2005) exploratory study advocates further research.

The use of celebrities can be further explained with reference to types of social power: social power, referent power, information power, legitimate power, expert power, reward power and coercive power (Raven and French, 1959; and see Chapter 7).

Small businesses have scarce resources and cannot really afford to compete with the large advertising budgets of some of their powerful competitors. So, rather than booking expensive television advertising campaigns to target the final consumer, it is often recommended that they consider targeting business correspondents of the local newspapers and magazines as opinion formers, so that they might achieve some editorial coverage of their new ranges or other aspects of their business.

These correspondents are read as if they possess a degree of knowledge and credibility regarding the subject matter and act as opinion formers, sometimes in a far more persuasive way than a paid-for advertising campaign. On a larger scale, this is why, for example, the top fashion designers are keen to 'show' at the major fashion shows in order to get editorial coverage in the leading fashion and women's magazines and national newspapers. The 'saleability' of their collections is often only secondary to achieving 'exposure' via the opinion-forming fashion journalists. In this way there is a multi-step flow of communications: designers to opinion-forming journalists to buyers in chain stores and their designers, then to opinion-leading consumers and on to the following 'majority' in the market place.

Similar methods are employed in the motor market (Evans and Fill, 2000) where public relations (PR) people possess databases of motoring correspondents and categorize these in terms of their opinion-forming credentials with the consumer – or at least in terms of circulation figures for their newspapers and magazines.

Some PR managers said they targeted a few carefully selected motoring journalists, with some going more for blanket coverage of the motoring press and others recognizing the different levels of likely persuasion possible from regional and national newspapers and the motoring magazines. Some even recognize more of a pecking order among named journalists, such as one who has a list of 1700 motoring journalists but selects 600 of the 'top' journalists for some events and just six for other events.

Selected journalists might be taken, via first-class travel, to (for example) South Africa (in the case of one car launch) where they road-tested the new car, enjoyed the sunshine, food and hospitality (and even partners were paid for, though only at second-class rates!) and were given a 'press release'. Now, this is not merely a list of technical specifications but will usually be full of favourable adjectives, many of which can reappear in road reports in the press. Most car manufacturers employ in-house PR specialists, many having previously been motoring journalists themselves.

The consumer will read these road reports as if from some totally objective and independent source. An editor of one such magazine has admitted that there is pressure on editors by the advertisers. If less glowing reports are published, he says, there have been occasions when the advertiser has informed the editor that they will advertise elsewhere for a while.

This goes even further. A PR consultant confessed that they regularly check the daily press and estimate that two-thirds to three-quarters of the news/editorial (that is, ignoring all advertising content) originates from some PR source or another. This type of publicity isn't advertising, it comes from an (objective) business journalist, so again the cognitive defences on the part of the readership are not raised.

The findings confirmed that, in the case of motor industry PR personnel, nearly all of their campaigns targeted journalists, that this approach was important to their strategy and that it was very effective. This confirms the general multi-step flow proposition. The main methods of so targeting journalists is via press releases and 'events' such as launches.

'Real' Opinion Leaders

As for using real opinion leaders, an early experiment conducted by Mancuso (1969) demonstrates the potential influence they can exert. A pop record was produced, but not distributed widely. In some university towns, sociometric research was conducted. This entailed asking each student, in isolation from the rest of the group, with which other members of the class they would most like a conversation about buying music (sociometric research, see Figure 7.3). Those students mentioned by many others were identified as possessing a degree of credibility in terms of music

and records. They were then thought to be higher in opinion leadership than others. A copy of the record was mailed to these opinion leaders, as a token of appreciation.

As a 'control group', a copy of the record was mailed to other students in other universities. In this case, however, student names were selected at random from class lists. Some may have been opinion leaders, but this would have been a coincidence and it is assumed that fewer of them would be opinion leaders than those selected in the other universities through sociometric research. Distribution for the record was set up in the university towns that were used as both experimental and control groups. For those towns in which 'real' opinion leaders were selected, the record moved into the charts, but in the control towns, where few opinion leaders were targeted, the record was not a 'hit'.

This research demonstrates the potential power of targeting opinion leaders. It also indicates the complexity that is often encountered when attempting to identify real opinion leaders, by name and address.

As mentioned earlier, Bristow *et al.* (2005) use the term 'opinion shapers' because, to them, this extends word of mouth (WOM) influence to non-verbal communication such as that which vicarious learning (Chapter 3) would explain. They also report an interesting study which found that opinion shapers in the financial services market (consumers) were twice as likely to say that they sought out finance TV programmes as the rest of the respondents. Financial services marketers should clearly either 'buy into' such programme's advertising 'spots' or even sponsor the programme (or perhaps try to influence the content?). The same research found that opinion shapers in the 16- to 34-year-old group were more than 1.3 times the average likely to watch US entertainment and fashion programmes. So again there are useful clues for the marketers wishing to reach opinion leaders/shapers in the consumer market.

EXAMPLE 9.2

Another example is the marketing of the Tamagotchi (virtual pet) in the late 1990s. In Japan, teenagers were recruited to 'spread the word' to their friends about the new product and even to form queues outside stores to simulate strong demand (Murphy, 1997).

In pharmaceutical markets, for example, the approach was described by a medic, Michael Rawlins (1984) in the *Lancet* – in somewhat critical terms. He described how medics in UK are targeted by the pharmaceutical industry and are classified as either 'conservatives' or 'risk takers'. The more innovative are identified by sales representatives who discuss doctors' prescribing habits with local pharmacists. This information can be used to target the more innovative when a new drug is being launched. To their peers these are opinion leaders and are invited to various 'events', seminars, lunches and so on. The effect is for a substantial proportion of them to start prescribing the new drug. Their behaviour is observed by the less innovative and is emulated, thus demonstrating the two-step flow of communication. Rawlins is critical of the industry for the approach but also lays a charge of potential corruption at the door of some medics. They expect such rewards in return for sometimes needless prescribing habits.

To take this further, some years ago the drug Flosint was launched. It treated rheumatoid arthritis and the launch was based on selected medics (opinion leaders among peers in their field) being taken to Switzerland for a weekend 'conference' with plenty of food and drink and an all-expenses paid trip on the *Orient Express*. Many went back to prescribe Flosint and they were copied by the followers. The approach can clearly be effective in speeding up the diffusion rate. The final twist to this particular case history was that, within a few months of its launch, Flosint was associated with several deaths and it was banned.

It has even been reported that some medical test results on drugs have been affected by the drug company that sponsored the academic research with some research articles being ghostwritten by the company and therefore bringing into question the validity of the research paper, even though it appears in a reputable medical journal (Healy, 2004).

Political lobbying is also based on the general principle here. PR companies maintain computerized databases of all Members of Parliament, their political and non-political interests. When the small print of proposed legislation is scrutinized by these companies on behalf of their clients and something is discovered that might affect the client, the PR agents set to work on opinion-leading politicians. Often it will not be members of the Cabinet who are targeted but those known to have an interest in and credibility over the issue. These Members of Parliament will be dined and receive a presentation in favour of the PR consultant's client. If they go back to Parliament and set up 'working committees', they will probably be more influential because they are seen to have greater credibility than other Members of Parliament in the issue concerned.

THINKBOX

Does the use of opinion leaders in medical and political areas raise concerns over the ethics of such approaches? Why, or why not?

The use of opinion polls has also been called into question recently in this respect (Nancarrow *et al.*, 2004). Pressure groups increasingly want to convince legislators of their cause and sometimes use biased question wording in their opinion polls, encourage supporters of the cause to 'pile in' as respondents or distort the statistical data so the results are more favourable to the cause than they really are. This can be a sort of reverse opinion-forming, where (supposed) public opinion is used in attempts to influence politicians.

www. Have a look at this web site, which provides more on pressure groups in politics:

http://www.historylearningsite.co.uk/pressure_groups.htm

We feel that the addition of the opinion former transforms the original two-step flow model into a multi-step flow model. Here the sender will target opinion formers directly and deliberately and may or may not target opinion leaders (perhaps depending on the complexity involved with identification). Opinion leaders may receive information from the sender and/or from opinion formers, as suggested in Figure 9.6.

Figure 9.6   Multi-step flows of communication and the integration of opinion-forming and opinion-leading

Source: M Evans and C Fill Extending the Communication Process, *International Journal of Advertising*, Vol 19 No 3 (2000), pp 377–396. Reproduced by permission of the World Advertising Research Center

www.   Take a look at the article by Nancarrow, Nancarrow and Page (2002) An Analysis of the Concept of *Cool* and its Marketing Implications, Journal of Consumer Behaviour, Vol 1 No 4 pp 311–322 on the web site at www.wiley.com/go/evans.

This paper explores cultural capital and cultural intermediaries within the context of investigating style leaders' consumption.

Simulating Opinion Leaders

As was seen earlier, those in the early adopter category are more likely to be higher in opinion leadership, and they possess certain demographic characteristics. This means that with some further research into specific markets, it is usually possible to identify the *sort* of people who are opinion leaders. These characteristics can then be depicted in promotional campaigns. Levi's employ different advertising campaigns for the 15- to 19-year-olds in the style press in order to 'reach the key opinion leaders in that age group' (Edmonson, 1993).

In the study of the motor market (Evans and Fill, 2000) reported above, relatively few motor PR campaigns target opinion-leading consumers. The closest this appears to get is the use of celebrities, selected according to availability, cost and some estimation of 'image congruence'. The familiar concern was expressed about using celebrities, in that there is a risk, if the celebrity is recruited only to be prosecuted for drink driving offences, or some similarly embarrassing misdemeanour.

EXAMPLE 9.3

An example is a totally mythical character, Roy of the Rovers. The comic of this name was bought by a sportswear company and whereas there was little advertising in the publication the sporting hero, Roy, was always wearing that company's brand of sportswear.

Many films and television programmes are subject to 'product placement', where brands are shown or mentioned in the film. Viewers do not put up their cognitive defence to the same extent as they might if the same products appeared in commercials. The suppliers pay for the privilege, of course. A classic example concerns the James Bond series (Figure 9.7). Many products are mentioned or shown, often just once, and part of the idea is that James Bond is some sort of aspirational reference point for some of the audience, an opinion former in effect, and if he wears a Seiko watch, shaves with a Philishave, and drinks Bollinger champagne and drives an Aston Martin, BMW or even a Citroen 2CV, then followers should do so as well! This is a classic example of a simulated opinion former.

Some years ago the brewing industry wanted to change the image of lager as being a feminine drink. The approach was to advertise more macho images of men drinking lager and to associate, through sponsorship, lager with energetic and aggressive sports. All of this probably contributed to the 'lager lout' image but certainly demonstrated effective campaigns. The simulated opinion leadership approach was prohibited in that anything vaguely communicating a lager lout stereotype could not be used. One company took the simulation even further and introduced George the bear who was only a stone's throw away from being a lager lout himself. Even this approach was banned, serving to reinforce its potential effectiveness.

Figure 9.7 Simulated opinion leaders
He's not real but James Bond can lead opinion.
Reproduced by permission of Omega SA

The overall implication is to communicate with the opinion leaders first (by formal marketing activities) and then through a two-step or even multi-step flow of communication and influence, the 'followers' are persuaded.

Market Mavens

Feick and Price (1987) identify an extension of the gatekeeper role (see Chapter 7). **Market mavens** not only hold useful information for others about products but also they are so interested in buying and consumption generally that they can provide information about prices and availability at different stores as well as details of the products themselves. They may not, however, have purchased these products themselves – they are almost 'consumerist hobbyists'. Transferred to the Internet they are termed **infomediaries** and act in a similar 'agony aunt ' role for other consumers. Indeed they have been found to be motivated by a desire to share information, to help others and by the joy of disseminating information about products (Walsh *et al.*, 2004).

Such sharing and dissemination can be orchestrated by marketers via viral or network marketing campaigns in which the targeted consumer is encouraged to send the message (chain letter-like) on to many of their friends. Thomas (2004) extends network, pyramid and viral marketing into 'buzz marketing'. He defines this as where marketers' initial efforts are 'amplified by third parties'. The Internet facilitates this via chat rooms and online communities and he shows how even irate consumers can be used positively if their problems can be sorted out, because they are often more involved and are likely to share experiences. So again we have the importance of involvement in the influence process.

> **www.** **Have a look at the following web site, which provides more on opinion leaders and followers in the 15- to 24-year-old group:**
>
> **http://www.roar.org.uk/press54.htm**

Diffusion Patterns

In some markets – for example, fashion – it is typical for marketing to use multi-step flows of communication; in this instance from designers to fashion shows, to fashion editors and journalists, to retail buyers to consumer fashion opinion leaders to fashion followers, in early and late 'majority' categories. Again in this instance, fashion opinion leaders are characterized as young, gregarious and high in status (Katz and Lazarsfeld, 1955). However, fashion opinion leaders can be found at both the top and bottom of the socio-economic scale (Midgeley and Wills, 1979). If they are so spread for a single fashion then there can be difficulties in maintaining consistent marketing communications. Other researchers have come up with theories of 'trickle down' (from designers to the general public), 'trickle across' (spreading within social strata) and even 'trickle up' (especially punk fashions in 1970s).

SUMMARY

■ The manner in which a new innovation is communicated and distributed in a society is called 'diffusion' and there can be many types of innovations such as discontinuous, dynamically continuous and continuous innovations. Important characteristics of innovations include compatibility, relative advantage, triability, observability, speed, simplicity, perceived risk, product symbolism, hedonism and innovation overload. This chapter has shown that some consumers progress through unawareness to repurchase sequences more quickly than others. It is also clear that there are several different categories of adopters and that this helps greatly in understanding how consumers behave toward new products.

■ The concept of two- or multi-step flows of communication (from more innovative opinion leaders to the followers) is especially helpful in speeding up the diffusion rates for new products and services. There are also, however, some ethical concerns over some uses of this knowledge.

It is probably not generally realized how much of the editorial and news content of our media is derived from publicity sources. Such sources target opinion formers, especially, based on their pivotal and powerful role in multi-step flows of communications.

■ Conventional wisdom, which assumes a uniform process of consumer decision-making, should, it appears, be modified to include considerations not only of level of involvement but also of consumers' differing cognitive styles as measured by such methods as the KAI inventory.

QUESTIONS

1. **Which discontinuous innovations, dynamically continuous innovations and continuous innovations have you personally experienced?**

2. **How much have you influenced others and how much have you been influenced by others in a buying context? Did any of the roles of market maven, opinion leader, or opinion former apply?**

3. **What ethical issues are involved with the targeting journalists or politicians via the model of multi-step flows of communication?**

4. **Explore the issues involved with Kirton's Adapter-Innovator paradigm in the context of innovative buying.**

FURTHER READING

Foxall G R (2003) Consumer Decision Making: Process, Level and Styles, in Baker M (ed.), The Marketing Book, Butterworth Heinemann. This chapter is an excellent summary of the extension of innovation theory to take account of different consumer decision styles. The work draws from Kirton's original 'adaptive-innovative' theory and reports more recent research. Integrated with this is involvement theory and there are cautionary words about over-emphasizing consumers' cognitive processes in their consumption behaviour.

Moore G (1995) Crossing the Chasm, Harper Business, New York. This important work extends the traditional concept of the normal curve of adopter categories by adding a significant gap or 'chasm' between the early adopters and early majority of adopters of technological products.

CHAPTER 10

CHAPTER OBJECTIVES

After engaging with the material presented in this chapter and its associated exercises and reading, you should be able to:

■ Extend the concepts of adoption processes and repeat purchase into prediction models of new product buying

■ Explain the nature, characteristics and measurement of switching, defection and repeat purchasing

■ Critically examine what 'loyalty' means in theory and practice and how it should be measured and encouraged

■ Analyse and evaluate the nature and benefits of relational interaction between consumers and organizations

REPEAT, LOYAL AND RELATIONAL BUYING

INTRODUCTION

From a marketer's point of view, customer loyalty is an important concept because greater **loyalty** can lead to a number of benefits such as reduction in marketing costs, increased opportunities for brand extensions and an improved market share. Loyal customers are a good source for spreading positive **word of mouth** and the most positive are **advocates**. They also offer greater resistance to competitive offerings. More and more companies now realize the significance of retaining their existing customers and increasingly develop marketing programmes (e.g. relational marketing activities) to improve **retention** rates. They are aiming to improve customer loyalty and encourage customer–firm dialogue and relationships as a way of creating competitive advantage. From consumers' perspective, greater levels of loyalty may mean they have a great deal of passion and **commitment** to the brand and reduction in search costs, **perceived risk** and enhancement of **self-concept**.

Beyond loyalty there is the possibility of relational buying where consumers engage with brands on such emotional levels that the interaction between consumer and brands/companies involves reciprocated affective relationships. Some consumers experience consumption in holistic ways if all their senses are involved along with their emotions, as a result of the symbolic nature of their consumption.

In this chapter we cover **repeat purchasing** behaviour, **loyalty** and **relational buying** behaviours from both the consumer and marketer perspective.

REPEAT PURCHASING BEHAVIOUR

One of the earlier approaches to customer loyalty includes looking at the **repeat buying** of low priced, frequently bought products, which appears to be a well defined act and tends to be easy to measure using **consumer panel** data. Here, repeat purchasing behaviour is what matters, irrespective of any **affective** dimensions of what goes on in consumers' minds.

> ## THINKBOX
>
> In a number of product categories (e.g. groceries) consumers often buy the same products or brands on a repeated basis either on the same purchase occasion or as several distinct purchases in a given time period.
>
> Consider your own grocery shopping. To what extent do you repeat buy the same brands?
>
> Does this make you loyal to those brands?

Repeat purchasing behaviour can be explained using the **operant conditioning** learning model (see Chapter 3). If the purchasing of the same product or service is reasonably rewarding it can become repetitive. There is a **stimulus–response** sequence here and, together with methods of quantifying sequential purchases, it is possible to use **probability theory** to predict which brand will be purchased next, after whatever sequence of brands was previously bought. Models using this 'probability' approach based on purchase sequence are termed **stochastic models**. These models make predictions about repeat purchasing using consumer panel data. Consumer panels involve households that agree to report on their buying behaviour or media habits over a period of time. Panel households are often asked to go through their shopping baskets when they return home and 'scan' all their purchases (Figure 10.1). The point that the same households report over a period of time is significant: it means individual household buying patterns can be monitored, including levels of repeat buying.

Landmark approaches to repeat buying using consumer panels date back to the 1950s and 1960s and include works by Brown (1952–1953) and Parfitt and Collins (1968). The *Chicago Tribune* ran a consumer panel and Brown studied the behaviour of 100 of the panel members. He found marked consistencies in the patterns in which brands of various products were bought, and on this basis, proposed four 'patterns' of loyalty:

- **Undivided loyalty:** within a product category, the consumer buys just one of the brands;
- **Divided loyalty:** the consumer buys from a repertoire of alternative brands in a product category on different buying occasions;
- **Unstable loyalty:** which is really brand switching because the consumer switches from 'undivided' loyalty to one brand to a similarly regular pattern for another brand;
- **No loyalty:** the consumer doesn't even buy from a repertoire of brands, but appears to buy haphazardly from all the brands available.

The Parfitt–Collins model also utilized panel data, in their case to calculate the penetration of the market and the repeat purchasing rate in order to estimate eventual brand share. It is thus a predictive model. Figure 10.2 shows how panel households bought different brands (T, R, and S) in the same

Figure 10.1 Consumers scan their purchases

product category, from the time (week 1) that new brand (T) was launched. In week 1, two households purchased this brand for the first time, so this is the cumulative number of new buyers for week 1. In the second week, household numbers 3 and 4 buy T for the first time, bringing the cumulative number of new buyers to four in week 2 and so on. When expressed as a percentage of those buying in the product category, this provides the market penetration rate.

In Figure 10.3 the cumulative number of buyers for the first few weeks was projected forward as an estimate of what the eventual penetration percentage would be. In this case, it was estimated that 34% of those buying in the product category would have tried T once. Figure 10.3 shows only seven households from a panel that might have comprised several thousands. From the entire panel an average period for repurchase is calculated. Some buyers in this category will buy every week, some every two weeks, and others less frequently. The average repurchasing period in this case was estimated to be a fortnight. The first repeat purchase period is not weeks 2 and 3 for every household, but the two-week period immediately following the time of first purchase by each household: weeks 3 and 4 for households 3 and 4, weeks 4 and 5 for households 5, 6 and 7, and weeks 2 and 3 for the first two households.

In each repeat purchase period, the percentage of all purchases in the product category that were of brand T, is calculated. This is the repeat purchase rate. As can be seen from the first repeat purchase period: of ten purchases, six were of T, and of ten purchases in the second repeat purchase period, five were of T and so on. This figure is projected forward after calculating it for just a few weeks, to give an estimate of the eventual stable level of repeat purchase. In this case the prediction is for a 25% repeat purchase rate (Figure 10.3). Thus, 34% of the market will (it is estimated) eventually have bought T once, and 25% of these will go on to buy it on a repeat purchase basis (which in this instance means every fortnight).

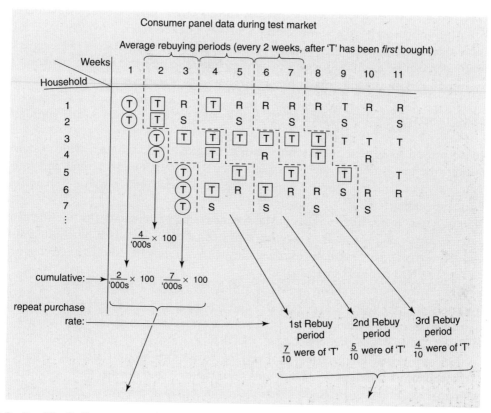

Figure 10.2   Parfitt–Collins model: calculation of repeat purchase rates

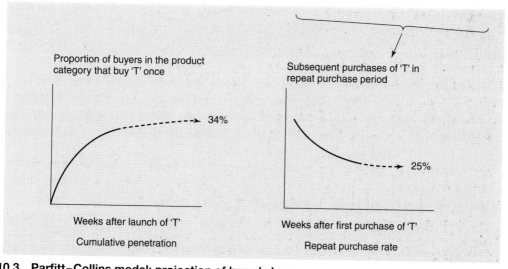

Figure 10.3   Parfitt–Collins model: projection of brand share

Source: JH Parfitt and BJK Collins. The Use of Consumer Panels for Brand-Share Prediction, *Journal of Marketing Research*, Vol 5 (1968), pp 131–145.

If T is consumed at average levels for the product category (i.e. that is, once every fortnight), the prediction for its eventual brand share will be 25% of 34% of the market (which is 8.5%). If T is consumed more than other brands, obviously more will be sold and it will have a higher market share. A buying level index can be calculated, again from the panel data, for the level of usage of T. If it is purchased more than every fortnight, on average, a corresponding 'weight' of something more than 1 will increase the estimated 8.5% to an appropriate level. Likewise, if T is bought only (say) half as frequently as other brands, then a buying level index of 0.5 will weight the 8.5% down to the appropriate level (4.25%).

This approach proved to be extremely robust as a conceptual underpinning, which informed later models. However, there are more variables at work than those monitored by time and frequency of purchase. As we saw in Chapter 3 (operant conditioning), if a purchase is rewarding there is a greater chance of repeat purchasing.

There is also a 'habit' factor in repurchase. Many consumers will continue to buy the same brand merely because of inertia, unless and until they are activated to reconsider their purchasing. Sometimes the advertising of a new brand or temporary unavailability of the existing brand can trigger a re-evaluation, which may or may not lead to brand switching.

Following from the logic of the above approaches, Ehrenberg and various collaborating researchers have extensively explored the prediction of repeat brand purchase and it is worth referring to Ehrenberg (1988). The major theory to emerge from this work is what is known as the negative binomial distribution theory (NBD). The mathematics of the theory are beyond the scope of this book but briefly, the proposition is that the probability of making 'x' number of purchases of a brand within a time period is a function of purchase frequency and penetration of the market and the function reflects a negative binomial statistical distribution. Ehrenberg developed a computer programme (Program NBD) to analyse penetration, purchase frequency and time period data in order to predict repurchase rates.

| **www.** | **Take a look at the following article, which provides another approach to the acceptance of new products – the Bass model:** |
| | **www.pdma.org/visions/oct02/diffusion.html** |

Returning to Figure 10.3, households 2 and 7, for example, have purchased different brands but we might predict that they are more likely to buy S next time. This is only an estimate in the Parfitt–Collins model, which does not take the **reinforcement** construct into account. But if we also knew that these households were pleased with their recent purchases of S, the likelihood of repurchase could be strengthened. As a result another approach has been developed.

BEYOND REPEAT PURCHASING: LOYALTY

Whereas stochastic models are relatively mechanistic and based on probabilities of recurring behaviour, **deterministic models** are based more on cognitive processes. Here, it is presumed that repeat purchase 'loyalty' involves **commitment** and a stronger **affective** motivator. Even if a cheaper alternative is available, the consumer would continue to buy the first brand because of greater commitment and/or **trust**. More variables will be involved here to explain regular buying patterns.

Figure 10.4   Acquisition and retention

Source: M Evans, L O'Malley and M Patterson, *Exploring Direct and Customer Relationship Marketing*, Thomson Learning, London, 2004. Reproduced by permission of Thomson Publishing Services

One approach is to consider stages of decision-making based on a progression from when organizations acquire consumers through to the processes involved with how consumers are retained (and therefore become regular buyers).

The 'awareness through to adoption' (Chapter 9) sequence is one of several such 'sequential models' (Chapters 2, 3 and 4) of consumer response to marketing activity. Here we present another sequential model but one which is especially relevant to the theme of this chapter. Figure 10.4 depicts the progression that consumers make from being attracted to a brand/company through to not only being regular buyers/patrons of it, but also to feeling they are in a relationship with that brand/company. This also shows that, as with the product life cycle (and indeed some human relationships) there can be 'decline' stages and perhaps a degree of recovery of the relationship as well. We summarize these stages but focus more on the later ones which move us onto *affectively* positive repeat purchasing, which is predicated on attitudinal loyalty and relational buying.

Attraction

Here, consumers and organizations see each other as potential 'partners' in terms of buying and selling. Organizations might see the consumer as being a likely prospect because, for example, they match the profile of existing good customers. The main criterion for the organization relates more to the financial value that the consumer might contribute to profitability than anything particularly attitudinal or emotional on the part of the organization. (See the next chapter for more on the new 'metrics' which are underpinning interaction between organization and consumer.)

Consumers are perhaps attracted to a particular organization's advertising, which seems to promise the benefits they seek to derive. In turn consumers are probably more concerned with getting the value they seek than in a desire to have a relationship per se with the organization. There will be some consumers, however, who undoubtedly develop strong bonds with the brands they buy.

EXAMPLE 10.1

'Pre-consumers', that is school-aged children who might be interested in joining the British Army when old enough, were encouraged to join a 'club'. This involved receiving a magazine several times a year and receiving emails about events, exhibitions and competitions to engage their interest even before they were old enough to join the Army. There was also a web site with which the teenagers could engage. Many of those *attracted* (before they could 'buy' into the service) were indeed converted into enlisters. (DMA Award, 2001)

Interaction

Consumers interact with organizations in a variety of ways; via telephone, mail, the Internet and, most powerful of all, face-to-face with service providers. These interactions can occur before, during and after product/service delivery and the resulting expectations can help determine whether consumers move to the next stage.

EXAMPLE 10.2

Kitten owners *interacted* with Pedigree Masterfoods before they were customers. The company advertised free kitten care packs and the result was that 30% of kitten-owning consumers were recruited. (DMA Award, 2001)

Progression

Potential customers now become customers. Because the relationship between the consumer and the organization reflects a degree of collaboration providing benefits for both sides, the relationship 'progresses' to variously enduring degrees. Efforts to strengthen relationships with satisfied customers include inviting their participation in consumer clubs and providing exclusive services for high-value customers.

Deterioration

All things must pass. Relationships rarely move directly from a state of progression to dissolution, but deteriorate gradually. Deterioration is where commitment and loyalty fade perhaps because the consumer becomes attracted to an even more enticing organizational offering elsewhere, or because their own circumstances change (a new stage of their family life cycle (Chapter 7)) or maybe because the organization repositions itself, perhaps after a merger or takeover.

EXAMPLE 10.3

Personalization is particularly important to Amazon.co.uk. Consumers are able to edit the personalized recommendations they receive (Figure 10.5) by rating their purchases to build a picture of what they like. A 'wish list' service allows customers to tell their friends and family what they would like for Christmas and birthdays, while the site's 1-Click ordering system means consumers can buy products with one click of the mouse without having to fill in order forms. Updates are sent to consumers during the steps of the ordering process. As a result there is not merely a purchase–sale transaction, but *progression* is facilitated by the personalized offers based on interests gleaned from transactional records.

Figure 10.5   Progression personalization

Source: www.amazon.co.uk

EXAMPLE 10.4

Older female consumers were found to be feeling somewhat alienated by the style of Lever Brothers' advertising of the Persil washing powder brand, which targeted young women. Many of these older consumers were therefore becoming less enthusiastic about the brand. But they had not entirely defected.

   The company targeted 'modern grandmas' with a mailing which asked for their laundry tips, based on their wider and fuller experience of life. Eight thousand tips were sent in. In this way they were encouraged to feel 'wanted' and this helped stave off *deterioration* of their interaction with Persil. (DMA Award, 2001)

Cessation

It is probably inevitable that many relationships between consumers and organizations will end. The organization, for example, might eliminate the product/service concerned or the consumer's new circumstances might mean the product simply isn't relevant any more (e.g. in the case of Mothercare and the woman whose children have grown up).

Reclamation

However, organizations should not always totally forget these consumers. Telecoms companies, for example, are realizing the benefits of regaining profitable customers. They must analyse the reasons behind relationship cessation in order to assess the possibility of reclaiming the consumer and estimate the costs of doing so.

EXAMPLE 10.5

The rather quaint tradition in UK of having one's milk delivered in the morning has come under pressure as more consumers include milk in their supermarket shopping trips and because more have already left home for work before the milk is delivered.

Associated Co. Creameries recognized this trend and tried to stop the decline. The company left empty milk bottles on the doorsteps of lapsed customers with a note proclaiming the benefits of having milk delivered (Figure.10.6). The *reclamation* programme produced a 26% increase in milk delivery customers on those milk rounds that employed the technique at a cost of just 49p per customer. (DMA Award, 2001)

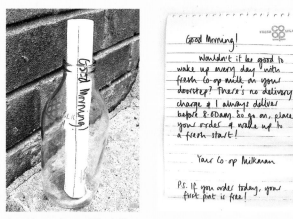

Figure 10.6   Reclaiming doorstep milk delivery consumers
Courtesy of Dairy Farmers of Britain

Loyalty programmes are another device used to retain customers. These are proving increasingly popular with both consumers and organizations and therefore are deserving of greater attention within a conceptual framework of *loyalty*, to which we now turn.

LOYALTY

Reichheld (1988) argued that consumers' repeat purchase patterns may not reveal their true loyalty behaviour as they may be trapped by inertia or they may be indifferent to brands or there may be high exit barriers imposed by the brand. Also, a consumer who is actually a loyal one may not buy on a repeated basis because of a reduced need for a given product or brand.

Dick and Basu (1994) also propose a framework that conceptualizes loyalty as combining both behavioural and attitudinal approaches to the understanding of loyalty. They conceptualized loyalty as the relationship between the **relative attitude** shown by a person towards a brand/product/store and their patronage behaviour. Relative attitudes take into consideration the notion that we all compare brands relevant to a given consumption context in which our perceptions and attitudes towards brands coexist in our minds. Therefore, our attitude towards a given entity is always in relation to some other entity. A person's relative attitude is said to be at its highest when the person associates the target brand with a strong attitude and clearly differentiates this from other brands with which the consumer has weaker attitudes. Similarly, a person may have a weak attitude but if that attitude is strongly differentiated from competitors, then it also leads to a high relative attitude and may contribute towards loyalty. On the contrary, a person may have a positive attitude but they do not perceive the target brand to be much different from competition. In this case, the person is likely to show a multi-brand loyalty because all alternatives are perceived as equally good. So the key points here are the extent to which a person perceives a focal brand to be different from other brands in the marketplace and the strength of attitude. As long as the consumer perceives significant differences among competing brands, their relative attitude towards a focal brand is likely to be high and this may contribute towards loyalty.

The conceptualization which linked relative attitudes with repeat patronage led to four categories of loyalty, each of which has managerial implications (Table 10.1). The four categories of loyalty provide a far richer conceptualization of loyalty than previously existed. The first one is **loyalty,** which exists when consumers have high relative attitude and high repeat patronage behaviour. Very often, marketers aim to create this form of loyalty whereby consumers like their brand much more than any other brand and buy the brand on a regular basis. The second one is **latent loyalty**, which exists when consumers have high relative attitude but low repeat patronage. The low repeat patronage may be due to some normative or situational influences and marketers need to tackle them through marketing communication efforts. The third one is **spurious loyalty**, which exists when consumers have low relative attitude but high repeat patronage. This reflects typical repeat buying of low-value, low-involvement and frequently purchased items. This behaviour may be driven by habit or inertia or by some situational cues (e.g. familiarity with a shelf position). The fourth one is **no loyalty**, which exists when consumers have a low relative attitude and a low repeat patronage.

Table 10.1 Loyalty segments

		Repeat patronage	
		High	**Low**
Relative attitude	**High**	Loyalty	Latent loyalty
	Low	Spurious loyalty	No loyalty

Source: AS Dick and K Basu Customer Loyalty: Toward an Integrated Framework, *Journal of the Academy of Marketing Science*, Vol 22 No 2 (1994), pp 99–113. Reproduced by permission of Sage Publications Inc.

Loyalty and Satisfaction

It would be logical to expect loyalty to depend to at least some extent, on 'satisfaction'. As a result, measures of consumer satisfaction have been widely used as proxy measures for loyalty. However, research from the Ogilvy Loyalty Centre suggests that 85% of automotive industry users report being satisfied but only 40% repurchase, while for **FMCG** goods, 66% of people who identified a favourite brand admitted to having bought another brand most recently (McKenzie, 1995). As a result, satisfaction measures have proved to be ineffective measures of loyalty (Reichheld, 1988). But are marketers really wrong in assuming that satisfied customers will automatically be loyal?

As we might expect, the picture is more complicated. In extensive research in a number of different product markets, Jones (1996) reported that the degree of claimed satisfaction is critical to levels of repeat purchase (Figure 10.7). In other words, those who claimed to be completely satisfied were more loyal than those who stated that they are merely satisfied. Figure 10.7 presents the satisfaction scale whereby consumers are asked to rank their satisfaction levels using a five-point scale from very satisfied (5) to very dissatisfied (1). The difference between repeat purchase behaviour for someone who scores '4' on a five-point satisfaction survey and those who score '5' is sixfold. That is, mere satisfaction (e.g. '4') is manifested in repeat purchasing far less than when it is extremely high satisfaction (e.g. a score of '5'). It is not enough, therefore to satisfy customers, but to 'delight' them.

Jones and Sasser (1995) in fact propose another version of a loyalty grid, which groups consumers into four distinct groups on the basis of their satisfaction and loyalty levels (Figure 10.8):

- **Group 1 Loyalists** These are completely satisfied consumers who claim to have high levels of satisfaction and loyalty. They stay with firms and remain supportive of the firm's activities. Some of these can even turn into advocates (those who are so satisfied and delighted that they share their experiences with others by engaging in positive word of mouth).
- **Group 2 Defectors** They have low to medium levels of satisfaction and loyalty. These include those who claim to be completely dissatisfied, quite dissatisfied and even neutral when asked about their satisfaction levels. They normally switch brands due to unsatisfactory experiences. Some of them can even become **consumer terrorists**. These have such a bad experience that they can't wait to tell others about their bad and frustrating experiences. They will be positioned at the left of the horizontal

Figure 10.7   The need to 'delight' consumers

Source: TO Jones, Why Loyal Customers Defect, Keynote Presentation, IDM Symposium, 6 June 1996. © T. Jones. Reproduced by permission

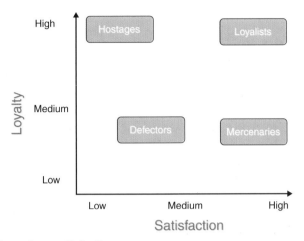

Figure 10.8   Loyalty grid based on satisfaction

Source: TO Jones and WE Sasser, Why Loyal Customers Defect, Harvard Business Review (1995), pp 88–99. Reproduced by permission of Harvard Business School Publishing

axis and anywhere along the vertical. When the bad word of mouth spreads, it gets worse each time a story is told and the actual facts become distorted. They can spread ill will concerning the organization or even play games such as swapping loyalty cards to be awkward or to see what happens to their 'targeted' offers (see Chapter 12).

- **Group 3 Mercenaries**   These show high levels of satisfaction but low to medium levels of loyalty. They normally do not stay with the firm long enough to become profitable customers for the firm.
- **Group 4 Hostages**   They show low to medium levels of satisfaction but high levels of loyalty. These consumers are stuck with the companies (due to lack of choice or the monopolistic position of firms, such as those in the telecommunications and airline industries).

Customer Switching Behaviour

Many consumers routinely defect from brands and companies and this may happen for a variety of reasons. Sometimes we are simply not happy with our experiences with a brand, whereas on other occasions we get a better deal or better alternative elsewhere. Keaveney (1995) identified more than 800 critical behaviours of service firms that led customers to switch their service providers. On the basis of this, Keaveney grouped reasons for customer defection into the following eight categories:

1. **Core service failure**   Consumers defect due to mistakes (e.g. billing errors) or other technical problems with the service itself.
2. **Service encounter failure**   Consumers defect because in their interactions with employees they found employees to be uncaring, impolite, unresponsive and lacking sufficient knowledge.
3. **Employee responses to service failures**   Consumers defect because service providers were unable to handle the situation properly (e.g. reluctant response, failure to respond or negative response).
4. **Pricing**   Consumers defect because the existing service provider charges a high price, has high service charges or has increased the price recently.
5. **Inconvenience**   Consumers defect due to inconvenient location, working hours or waiting time to get an appointment.

6. **Attracted by a competitor**   Consumers defect because a competitor makes a better offer.
7. **Ethical issues**   Consumers defect because of perceived illegal, immoral, unsafe or other unhealthy behaviours of the firms.
8. **Involuntary switching**   caused by factors that are beyond consumers' control (e.g. customer moving house).

Also, DeSouza (1992) cited following reasons for customer defections:

1. Defection in order to purchase a superior product from a competitor.
2. Defection due to market related factors – defecting to a different market. For example, a transport company which has moved out of road haulage therefore no longer needs to buy trailers.
3. Defection due to technology related reasons – a consumer who has converted from using one technology to another. Customers who abandoned high street banks in favour of banks that provide dedicated telephone or Internet banking would fall into this category.
4. Defection due to organizational related factors – switching as a result of ethical or political pressures. For example, many customers who switched to the Co-Operative Bank did so because they preferred to support the ethical position held by that bank.

Reichheld (1996) argues that the longer a customer stays with a firm, the better it is for the firm because the customer is likely to buy more and become less sensitive to price. Furthermore, in certain industries, if companies can manage to reduce their customer defections from, say 15% to 10%, they can double their profits (Reichheld, 1996).

EXAMPLE 10.6

Revisit Example 4.1 concerning Professor Jones (the same one as cited in this chapter) and his BMW ash tray. He became an 'advocate' for Lexus after being *satisfied* with BMW for over a decade, but clearly not *delighted*.

Do you or does anyone you know have any similar experiences – in any product/service context ?

What are the implications for consumers and for marketers?

Customer Loyalty and Loyalty Programmes

A loyalty programme (Figure 10.9) normally aims to build customer loyalty by rewarding consumers for their cumulative purchasing over time. In most cases, the aims of loyalty programmes are:

- to retain customers by providing them value and satisfaction;
- to increase spending by existing customers; and
- to cross-sell other products that the existing customers might not be aware of.

There are many examples of loyalty programmes but a very famous one is that of Tesco Club card, which was introduced in 1995 to retain existing customers and to increase spending by them. The card is swiped at the point of sale, earning points for each pound spent, and the transaction details are then

Figure 10.9   Nectar loyalty scheme
It has been suggested that the Nectar scheme is a template for the UK State ID scheme (Ambler, 2002).
© Loyalty Management UK Ltd. Reproduced by permission

fed into a centralized database overnight. Consumers then get vouchers on a quarterly basis. In this case, consumers get rewarded after a time period (a quarter). However, there are other loyalty schemes, which reward your behaviour immediately (e.g. an instant scratch card). Similarly, you can have direct rewards (product related) and indirect rewards (non-product related). Yi and Jeon (2003) found that, under high-involvement conditions, direct rewards were perceived to be more valuable than indirect rewards. Under low-involvement conditions, immediate rewards were perceived to be more valuable than delayed rewards.

The Nectar scheme is an example of one that operates across partner companies. These started with the four named on the card in Figure 10.9. but continues to expand, including (at the time of writing): Threshers, Vodafone, Adams, Ford, Hertz, Brewsters, Blockbusters, EDF Energy, Winemark, Magnet, Beefeaters, eBookers and American Express (who replaced BarclayCard).

Today many organizations are being forced into running a loyalty programme, simply because their competitors are offering them. However, loyalty programmes represent a considerable investment, and take at least two to three years to achieve any return on investment. Often there can be 'loyalty' to the programme rather than the organization and as soon as a more attractive offer – or scheme – comes along, the consumer might defect (or at least keep multiple loyalty cards – which would suggest an oxymoron).

THINKBOX

Consider this: a consumer is on a diet – or at least his wife thinks he is. He uses his loyalty card at the supermarket for most of the groceries but pays cash for the chocolate biscuits because he doesn't want to be sent offers for similar goodies, because such offers might be a 'give-away' to his wife about his lack of self control (Sasse, 2005).

A study investigating supermarket loyalty schemes (Evans *et al.*, 1997) based on qualitative group discussions found that irrespective of demographic profile through the groups there was a high degree of similarity in the main issues raised. These themes were as follows;

1. The schemes were widely used.
2. The schemes were seen to be potentially money saving, but even among some of the adopters this potential was not always seen to be fully realized and was not enough to prevent switching behaviour between schemes.
3. There were very clear concerns over revealing personal details. Many (especially, but not exclusively) women participants did not like divulging personal details such as marital status, age, household numbers, telephone numbers, bank accounts, type of dwelling or home contents. This was seen to be intrusive. They were unhappy about the fact that their personal details and their purchases could be linked together on databases for various ulterior purposes. (We explore the use [and abuse] of consumers' personal details and transactional data in Chapter 11.)

THINKBOX

You personally may have at least one loyalty card, which might encourage you to frequent that store more often but does it engender a feeling of greater emotional attachment with the store?

Is it the convenient location of the store or the fact that you can get what you want there?

So, do you have any *affective* feelings of loyalty to the organization?

What, for you, *is* 'loyalty'?

---

www.   **Have a look at the following web sites:**

http://www.nectar.com/NectarHome.nectar

This is the web site for the major loyalty scheme, Nectar, which is a partnership between many well known companies.

http://www2.acnielsen.com/issues/loyalty.shtml

This is a link to the international market research agency, AC Nielsen's research on loyalty.

BEYOND LOYALTY: RELATIONAL CONSUMPTION

Can loyal consumers go even further with their interaction with organizations and develop 'relationships' with them? This is an area of particular interest in recent years and many organizations have appointed 'relationship marketing managers' and claim to have developed relationship marketing programmes. So what is **relational consumption** (at least normatively)?

Based on the Evans *et al.* (2004) definition of *relationship marketing*; relational consumption involves the identification, specification, initiation, maintenance and (where appropriate) dissolution of long-term relationships between consumers and brands/organizations through mutual exchange, fulfilment of promises and adherence to relationship norms in order to satisfy the objectives and enhance the experience of the parties concerned.

For customers, true relational interaction can be very satisfying:

- They feel an affinity with the organization beyond mere repeat purchase and this can add the 'experiential' nature of much current consumer behaviour (see section below). They can feel 'known' to the organization, not just as an anonymous consumer but akin to the personal interaction of restaurateur and regular consumer.
- They often receive special treatment and extra pampering by the organization.
- They are likely to receive timely and relevant communications of offers that would be of interest to them at that moment.

Combining organizational and consumer motivations, it becomes clear that the successful implementation of *relational marketing* would also make marketing more efficient because (wasteful) expenditure on advertising and promotion could be reduced.

The template that is most generally (but not necessarily appropriately) employed to explore relationships, is that of marriage. In the early 1980s Theodore Levitt made a striking comparison between business relationships and contemporary marriage. According to Levitt (1983): 'The sale merely consummates the courtship. Then the marriage begins. How good the marriage is depends on how well the relationship is managed by the seller.'

In talking about commercial relationships as marriages, we assume that the parties in the relationship are on an equal footing, and there are certain values that we implicitly rely upon. For example, we assume that relationships involve partners who should be committed and loyal. The long-term nature of the relationship is emphasized compared with the one-night stand, and there is an underlying suggestion that such relationships should be monogamous. But as with many 'theories' in (especially) economics and other disciplines, over-qualification (of 'we assume') can lead to unreality.

From a relationship perspective, Fournier (1998) views customer loyalty as a committed and affect-laden partnership between consumers and their brands which grows and evolves over time. Fournier (1998) identified many attributes of brand-relationship quality including the following, many of which have appeared in different guises elsewhere in the book:

- **Love/passion** – this describes the emotional attachment of consumers with brands – consumers often have a passion to possess a brand and will feel anxiety if the brand is not available (Chapter 1).
- **Self-concept connection** – brands provide a mechanism for connecting to the self and to the notions of who one is (Chapter 6).
- **Interdependence** – brands play a central role in consumers' day-to-day lives and routine (Chapters 1 and 5). Consider Figure 10.10, where Tesco is not just concerned with 'selling groceries' but with engagement within consumers' daily lives.
- **Commitment** – as consumers pass through different stages of their life cycles, they stick with the brands (both in good times and bad times; see Chapters 9 and 10).
- **Intimacy** – consumers feel a sense of extensive familiarity with brands and very good understanding of their attributes (this chapter).
- **Partner quality** – consumers perceive brands to have qualities that they normally associate with their partners (e.g. dependability, credibility, trustworthiness and reliability). Brands are perceived as active, contributing members of the dyadic relationship (this chapter).

Figure 10.10   Interdependence with Tesco

© Tesco Stores Ltd. Reproduced by permission

- **Nostalgic attachment** – brands allow consumers to imagine their past. They can bring back vivid memories of the past as brands remind consumers of their past consumption contexts and situations (Belk, 1988). (We discussed this aspect in Chapter 5 where we explored generational cohorts.)

---

www. | **Have a look at the following web site:**

http://www.tesco.com/

This is the web site for Tesco but have a look at the range of products and services the company provides. Many people need venture little further for their purchases across most product/service categories: books, CDs, DVDs, electricals, DIY, flowers, gardening, music downloads, credit cards, loans, mortgages, savings, insurance, telecoms (broadband, dial-up Internet), advice on diets and healthy eating, holidays, flights, games, delivered wine, legal advice, gas and electricity – oh, and food.

Does this represent an all-pervasive relational interaction?

www. Take a look at the article by Woodside (2004), which is accessible from the accompanying web site at www.wiley.com/go/evans. We referred to the same article in Chapters 1 and 3 because it integrates concepts from those chapters with Fournier's relational typology.

Key Relational Constructs

There are a number of concepts commonly employed to explain and describe successful relationships.

Trust

Trust is considered to be the basis for exchange and the glue that holds a relationship together. Conversely, in the absence of trust, exchange becomes increasingly difficult. Scott (2002) highlights that it is useful to:

> Think of trust as a natural resource, like water. It oils the machinery of human interaction in everything from marriage and friendship to business and international relations. There are reserves of trust, in a perpetual state of replenishment or depletion. And in this parched and suddenly sweltering spring, it is not just water supplies that are looking ominously low.

Unless there is a minimum level of trust between parties, it is unlikely that a relationship will be initiated at all. Similarly, if trust breaks down the relationship is likely to be dissolved. Furthermore, it remains difficult to identify exactly why trust intensifies or decreases. In practice, trust may be a function of the reputation and perceived expertise of the organization and its employees. Organizational reputation is communicated to customers through corporate and brand image, through advertising, through product and service quality and through the behaviour of its employees.

Trust is particularly important for services, which by their nature are highly intangible (for example, banks and insurance companies) because there is a need for a minimum level of consumer trust before service delivery is initiated (Liljander and Strandvick, 1995). As a result, organizations must carefully consider the implications of the promises they make. Equally, visible elements of the organization's activities (e.g. personalized communications) signal to customers the quality of other, less visible, organizational activities. Thus, engendering trust also involves paying attention to the details that matter to customers.

Commitment

In addition to trust, commitment is also considered to be central to successful relationship marketing (Morgan and Hunt, 1994). An initial level of commitment is required to initiate the relationship and, as the relationship deepens, so too does the existence and evidence of commitment. Moreover, without commitment, no relationship is believed to exist. Referring to consumer markets, De Wulf *et al.* define commitment as 'a consumer's desire to continue a relationship ... accompanied by this consumer's willingness to make efforts at maintaining it' (De Wulf *et al.*, 2001). Furthermore, commitment involves behavioural, attitudinal, affective and calculative components (Geyskens *et al.*, 1996).

- **Behavioural commitment**   refers to the actual behaviour of parties in the relationship, the efforts they make and the choices they take. The earlier discussion of repeat purchase rates is an example of consumers' behavioural commitment and the level of organizational investment in helping and interacting with individual consumers is a reflection of their behavioural commitment.
- **Attitudinal commitment**   refers to 'an implicit or explicit pledge of relational continuity' between relational partners (Oliver, 1999).
- **Affective commitment**   relates to positive feelings towards the organization. As a result of these feelings, the consumer is not tempted to seek alternatives or to engage in any cost-benefit analytical schemes. Affectively committed customers voice strong intentions to remain in the relationship and are willing to invest in that relationship (Samuelsen and Sandvik, 1997).
- **Calculative commitment,** in contrast, is partly instrumental. In this case, calculative commitment may be the outcome of a perceived lack of alternatives or estimation that the switching costs might outweigh likely benefits. Customers who remain in a relationship as a result of calculative commitment will only do so as long as their cost-benefit analysis provides no incentive to leave. However, such customers are only loyal while it is instrumentally rewarding for them to be loyal (Samuelson and Sandvik, 1997).

Mutual Goals

Mutual goals are important because they explain the motivation for relationship development. However, the goals of relational partners do not have to be the same. Rather, both parties must simply have the possibility to achieve their goals through the relationship. For example, an organization wishes to engender loyalty among its customers because it has been proven that it is more profitable to service existing customers than to constantly attract new ones. (Reichheld and Sasser, 1990). Similarly, customers may wish to reduce the time and effort (search costs) of shopping around and this is possible by remaining loyal to a good supplier. Customers may also accrue the extra benefits of shopping in a familiar environment and having the product or service customized to their requirements at no extra cost (Sheth and Parvatiyar, 2000).

Satisfaction

Customers are not motivated to engage in relationships unless they are satisfied with the offer made by the organization (Tzokas and Saren, 1997). However, buyers evaluate satisfaction on other criteria also. For example, economic satisfaction refers to an 'evaluation of the economic outcomes that flow from the relationship' and social satisfaction to the 'psychological aspects of [the] relationship' (Geyskens *et al.*, 2000). Thus, satisfaction is a multidimensional construct that must include the quality of the core product or service as well as the economic and social aspects of the relationship. Linked to this is the comparison level of alternatives, which simply acknowledges that satisfaction is always relative. That is, customers are happy to remain in any given relationship so long as they believe there are no better alternatives out there. To a large extent, this concept explains why individuals remain in relationships in which they express unhappiness.

Cooperation

Cooperation is another variable that recognizes the interdependent and interactive nature of relationships. Relational partners must be willing and able to work together to improve relational outcomes. Cooperation is essential for achieving mutual goals and is a necessary prerequisite for any adaptations to products, services, systems or processes to occur.

It is interesting to note that research in the B2B sector suggests that relational partnerships with suppliers or client companies can sour over time and that it can be the very relational constructs that, over time, deteriorate (Anderson and Jap, 2005; Grayson and Amber, 1999).

> ## THINKBOX
>
> It is interesting that one of the architects of customer relationship programmes, Clive Humby – of DunnHumby, the company that manages the loyalty schemes for a number of organizations including Tesco – has actually questioned the appropriateness of 'relationships' in the business context. In the keynote speech at the IDM's annual lecture, Humby (2004) said that it would be more appropriate to use the 'R' word to mean 'relevance' rather than relationship.
> What do you think?

Guanxi

It is worth pausing to consider a different relational paradigm; that from within Chinese culture, called *Guanxi*.

This is similarly concerned with connections but at the face-to-face level. The relationships are not based on written agreements as might be the case in Western society, with, for example opt-in/permission marketing, but rather on personal trust. The connections require reciprocal obligation (Brunner and Koh, 1988). Wong and Leung (2001:5) succinctly provide the underpinning for *Guanxi*: 'The traditional Confucian concept of the group taking precedence over the individual ... the five relationships, emperor–subject, father–son, husband–wife, brother–brother and friend–friend, perpetuate its influence in modern China.' They show how gifts and hospitality can be used at what we would refer to as the attraction and interaction stages of acquisition. But emotional relationships (*ganqing*) evolve with further bonding so that the outsider actually becomes an insider and this is when and how business deals work effectively.

Experiential Consumption

We introduced the concept of experiential consumption in Chapter 1 where we posited an extension beyond the buying of benefits to the buying of experiences. In terms of consumer behaviour theory, this is informed by several of the concepts we have also introduced, such as gestalt psychology (Chapter 3) because there is a synergy of the four Ps of marketing (product, price, place and promotion) with how the product engages with a range of the consumer's senses (Chapter 2). From this we learn that our perceptual processes and senses are important. We have now explored the relational approach in the current chapter, as this advocates reciprocal interactive involvement between company/brand/product and consumer.

> **www.** Take a look at following articles, which are accessible from the accompanying web site at www.wiley.com/go/evans:
>
> Addis and Holbrook (2001) On the Conceptual Link between Mass Customisation and Experiential Consumption: An Explosion of Subjectivity, Journal of Consumer Behaviour, Vol 1 No 1 pp 50–66
>
> Caru and Cova (2006) How to Facilitate Immersion in a Consumption Experience: Appropriation Operations and Service Elements, Journal of Consumer Behaviour Vol 5 No 1
>
> These papers explore a variety of issues relevant to the current chapter: relational and experiential consumption as well as aspects of utilitarian versus hedonistic consumption, relevant to Chapter 1.

Marketers refer to **experiential marketing** and we consider this from the consumer's perspective as **experiential consumption.** This can be **sense consumption**, which targets several of the consumer's senses.

EXAMPLE 10.7

An example of using consumers' senses in an experiential marketing campaign is afforded by the Coca-Cola Magic Ride campaign. Here, consumers watched a three-dimensional show during which they *heard* the (digitized) sound of fizzing cola, *smelt* the aroma of the cola, *felt* cold air bubbles and then *tasted* the product itself.

Feel consumption exploits consumers' emotions.

EXAMPLE 10.8

When the VW Beetle was relaunched, the early campaigns emotionally portrayed feelings of nostalgia for the 1960s version. If you remember what we have said about possessions defining consumers and especially the nostalgic role that possession can play (Belk, 1988) you will see the logic of this approach.

Then there is **think consumption**, which is a form of experiential marketing that 'appeals to the intellect with the objective of creating cognitive, problem solving experiences that engage consumers creatively' (Schmitt, 1999). We refer you back to our coverage of the **FCB grid** in Chapter 4 because this involves 'think' and 'feel' products.

Relate consumption encompasses all and incorporates the brand within the consumer's core existence, and in this way is closest to the relational marketing paradigm discussed here.

Such approaches can have a clear edge over other, non-participatory, campaigns in encouraging trial of the product. Some researchers even suggest that experiential marketing will not only be a major plank for gaining competitive advantage but also for increasing brand loyalty (Barrett, 2003).

EXAMPLE 10.9

It was back in 1983 that Harley Davidson introduced their relationship marketing strategy, via the owners club (Harley Owners Group – HOG). The brand has long been an icon in the motorcycle world and this has been reinforced by the strong associations of its appearance in such films as *Easy Rider* and *Terminator II*. Harley's relationship strategy was kick-started by the informal meetings held by Harley fans. They nicknamed the bikes 'HOGS' in any case, so it wasn't a huge jump to set up the 'HOG' relationship club.

To add a more social slant to the image of bikers, Harley Davidson associated the company with the Muscular Dystrophy Foundation and hold events to promote the charity. Now Harley owners hold rallies and rides for quite a range of charities. The strength of emotion toward the brand is reflected in the feeling that it is driveway jewellery. Indeed, via the Owners Group, this is supported by the range of bike merchandising including accessories, jackets and caps. It all adds to a way of life that HOG members have bought into and there are few relationship strategies that are so 'affectively' based. There are tangible retention devices as well: customers can up-grade to a bigger model one year after purchase with trade-in at full value.

Now, potential owners of second and even third bikes are targeted for relational treatment. The channels of relational interaction are also extensive:

multi-lingual customer care will be provided through a newly centralized call centre, allowing the delivery of dedicated bespoke service to HOG's 70 000 strong user base. Customers can use telephone, fax, e-mail, or mail to find out about forthcoming rides, event tours and merchandise with a view to offering a web and SMS service in future. (Rubach, 2003a)

Consider the emotional, symbolic and experiential consumption aspects of the potential relational consumption that are afforded HOGs.

This brings us a long way from the starting point of this chapter, which focused on behavioural repeat purchasing. It shows how marketers and consumers can benefit from reciprocal engagement beyond the mere sale–purchase exchange.

SUMMARY

■ Customer loyalty is important as it provides benefits to both consumers and to firms. One of the earlier approaches to loyalty included measuring repeat purchasing behaviour using panel data and researchers predicted consumer behaviour using stochastic models. A deterministic, cognitive-based approach to explaining loyalty is also suggested and the concept of retention strategy might be a relevant one to integrate in this respect. Repeat purchasing may not always lead to loyalty and the much-hyped loyalty scheme is sometimes in danger of being little more than short-term sales promotion or even an oxymoron.

■ Loyalty as opposed to repeat purchasing includes attitudinal constructs in addition to the behaviour of just buying repeatedly. Customer satisfaction is an important antecedent to customer loyalty but one should note the effects of those who are merely satisfied and those who are completely satisfied or delighted with a firm's offering. Those who are delighted can become advocates and can recommend the brand to others whereas merely satisfied and dissatisfied customers are likely to switch brands.

■ Relational consumption is an important concept and many have advocated its principles of reciprocal affective interaction. Indeed brands are not lifeless entities: the amalgam of consumers' purchases can even define them – they can be perceived as being a live and active central part of consumers' lives. Consumers often show a great deal of involvement, passion, love and commitment towards them. It is important to consider the relationship that develops, grows and evolves over time between a consumer and the brands they buy.

QUESTIONS

1. **What is repeat buying? How is this different from the loyalty models proposed by Dick and Basu (1994) and Jones and Sasser (1995)? Use examples to illustrate.**

2. **What must organizations do to overcome criticisms that their loyalty programmes are nothing more than sophisticated sales promotions?**

3. **For the following contexts, which key relational constructs are likely to be most important for a consumer: financial services company, supermarket, mail order firm, expensive restaurant.**

4. **What parallels are there between the elements of 'relationship' you have with people close to you and any relationship you have with brands or companies?**

5. **How much do you engage in experiential consumption? Can this approach lead to relational buying? Why, or why not?**

FURTHER READING

Ehrenberg A S C (1988) Repeat Buying, 2nd edn, Charles Griffin, London. This is a seminal monograph which reports extremely extensive empirical research into consumer repeat purchasing behaviour.

Humby C, **Hunt** T and **Phillips** T (2003) Scoring Points: How Tesco Is Winning Customer Loyalty, Kogan Page. This text takes repeat purchasing into the twenty-first century with an in-depth discussion of how Tesco's loyalty scheme operates. It is a rich source of insights into the use of customer data for marketing purposes.

CHAPTER 11

CHAPTER OBJECTIVES

After engaging with the material presented in this chapter and its associated exercises and reading, you should be able to:

■ Explain the trend toward behavioural-based knowledge of consumer behaviour via transactional data and the emergence of biographics

■ Evaluate the role and relevance of a variety of consumer surveillance approaches available to marketers to track consumers' behaviour

■ Analyse and evaluate the role and nature of geodemographics and *contemporary* lifestyle research in understanding and profiling consumer behaviour

■ Elucidate how consumers react to individualized consumer–organization interaction

DATA-BASED CONSUMER BEHAVIOUR

INTRODUCTION

The two previous chapters discussed how a greater understanding of new and repeat buying can move toward loyal and even relational buying behaviour. This chapter continues this theme by analysing how consumer behavioural information and further sources of individualized profile data can be used not only to explain and predict consumers' behaviour but also to facilitate individualized consumer–organization interaction.

First, we explore personalized behavioural data and its contribution to understanding how consumers behave. These data include consumers' **transactional data** such as are gathered via loyalty cards or on-line purchases. But there is also an increasing range of other sources of **behavioural data**, including: **radio frequency identification 'tags' (RFID)**, **Internet cookies**, **global positioning satellites (GPS)** and even **genetic data**. Some of this might sound a bit sinister, but these are personalized behavioural data sources used by some current and probably by many future marketers, to understand and target consumers.

We then turn to personalized (or near personalized) **profiling** databases, such as **geodemographics** and **contemporary lifestyle research**, which claim to provide further explanations of consumer behaviour.

The trend toward trying to understand consumers as individuals means that marketers are increasingly targeting them as such (or at least within smaller and smaller segments). This goes further, as our discussion of relational consumption in Chapter 10 proposed, because it has the potential for individualized consumer–organizational interaction.

The chapter then concludes with an exploration of wider social implications of the **'data-based consumer'** and indeed how consumers themselves are reacting to being targeted more precisely.

UNDERSTANDING CONSUMER BEHAVIOUR FROM PERSONALIZED BEHAVIOURAL DATA

Transactional Data

When companies are able to track individual buying behaviour, via loyalty schemes (chapter 10) or on-line transactions, they collect transactional data.

These data are used to help explore consumer behaviour in two main ways: to identify and predict what will be bought; and to identify the 'better' consumers.

Identifying and Predicting What Will be Bought

By linking items purchased with specific named consumers, their patterns of consumption can be tracked in order to target them, as individuals or small segments.

EXAMPLE 11.1

An inspection of a retail loyalty scheme database revealed, for a certain 'Mrs Brown', her address and a variety of behavioural information including: she shops once per week, usually on a Friday, has a baby (because she buys nappies), spends £90 per week on average and usually buys two bottles of gin every week (Mitchell, 1996). By knowing what individual consumers buy, the retailer might be able to target them with relevant offers while the consumer saves money at the same time.

Transactional data provides scope for analysing who buys what, when and through what form of payment. Purchase patterns can be revealed for different geographic locations, store branches, seasons of the year and all of this for each customer. Inferences about consumer interests and likely future buying behaviour can be made from transactional data over a period of time. Such inferences can lead the organization to targeting individual consumers at what are hoped to be appropriate times with relevant offers. If consumers do indeed see this as timely and relevant and there are repeated and reciprocated personalized interactions, a relationship between consumer and organization/brand might develop.

Identifying the 'Better' Consumers

Personalized consumer researchers can identify the **recency, frequency and monetary value (RFM)** of customer orders. Recency – just knowing they have purchased from us in the past is important but not sufficient; we are probably less interested in those who bought from us 10 years ago and not since. Frequency – a one-off purchase may also make a customer less attractive (depending, of course, on the product

THINKBOX

Next time you are in a supermarket queue at a checkout, have a look at the items in the trolley in front of you (surreptitiously and without causing offence, of course!). In the meantime, consider Figure 11.1.

Figure 11.1   Transactional data

Photographs: Martin Evans

What does this say about the household it will be going to?

If you had details of what this consumer bought from this store every week for a year and indeed for several years, would you be able to build up a good picture of what they liked?

Could you also start to *predict* what will be on their shopping list?

market in which we operate). So knowing how often they buy from us is an important measure. Monetary value – small orders are usually less attractive than larger ones, so this is yet another measure of significance. Indeed marketers are increasingly concentrating on their 'better' customers – those who have the highest monetary value (and frequency) of purchase and are segmenting on the basis of 'volume' because in this way they are more cost-effective, because they concentrate on those who bring greater returns.

Vilfredo Pareto's theory of income distribution has been transferred and borrowed by marketers to support the proposition that 80% of sales come from just 20% of customers – in many markets the ratio

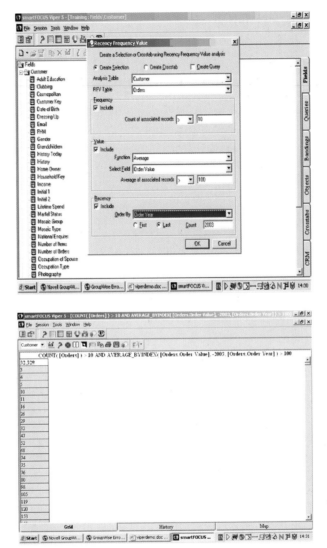

Figure 11.2 VIPER data-mining
VIPER can identify RFM categories
© SmartFocus Group plc. Reproduced by permission

can be even more polarized (95:5 is not uncommon). For RFM analysis transactional data must be tracked by the database – actual purchase history is needed. Figure 11.2 shows a screenshot from the RFM tool within the **Viper** data-mining software product. Actually names and addresses (withheld here, but IDs shown) of those customers who have ordered more than 10 times in 2003 (the most recent year for that dataset) with an average order value of over £100 are extracted very quickly from the customer database.

However, those consumers who do *not* contribute as much to profit as the company might wish and have a low RFM, might be **excluded**. This might lead to some disaffection among the less attractive segments when they realize that others are being presented with the 'better' offers. It has been suggested, even from within the industry, that alienated customers might even see this as something 'Orwellian in nature' (Wright, 1999).

Personalized 'Surveillance' Data

RFID Tags

To date, the tracking of transactional data in the 'bricks and mortar' shopping environment has been via bar-coded items linked with some mechanism for identifying the individual consumer (e.g. loyalty cards). In the future, bar codes might be replaced by radio frequency identification tags (RFID) which are extremely small (grain of sand) radio transmitters embedded within products or their packaging. They emit radio signals which can be collected by hand-held or static scanners. Their main current use is to track goods as they move through supply chains and help in the stock control and ordering processes. However, they are being used in experiments by various retailers, such as Marks & Spencer, House of Fraser and Tesco, to track items in-store. Not only can this lead to more accurate shelf-stacking, but also to in-store personalized targeting. Here, consumers will soon be able to push their **smart trolleys** around supermarkets. Smart trolleys will be able to access consumers' transactional profiles once their loyalty cards are swiped (on *entry* to the store) in order to target relevant offers in real time and indeed in the right location within the store.

Another application is in tackling theft. As items are taken off the shelves, they can be tracked through (and out of) the store and matched with what was actually paid for. Some tags will even incorporate a miniature camera that can help identify thieves (BBC, 2003).

EXAMPLE 11.2

The film *Minority Report* demonstrated real-time recognition of customers as they entered a store or even just walked around a shopping mall. Recognition was via automatic retina identification (biometrics) and on this basis customer transactional and profile records were accessed and relevant promotions and offers delivered at the same time. This might have been futuristic at the time of the film's release (in 2002) but the technology is certainly available and perhaps RFID will even replace this. A London department store and a casino have already introduced biometric recognition (facial recognition software) so that their 'special' customers can be recognized as soon as they enter and then quickly greeted personally by a manager (Steiner, 2002), RFID could be an alternative way of identifying customers – as long as they didn't swap clothes! Invasion of privacy is a possible implication of this new trend, as suggested by London (2003) and Shabi (2003), but what is invasion of privacy to some is not to others.

GPS and Cookies

The future use of such tags might be much broader, however, and could include tracking whereabouts after purchase (or theft) and even through to disposal and **global positioning satellite (GPS)** tracking of the tags can even be used. Global positioning satellites (GPS) can also track the location of mobile phones to within several metres without the owner knowing. This can lead to personalized targeting (in real time) by marketers who are geographically in close proximity to the individual consumers; for example, as a consumer approaches a particular store.

There is also the covert surveillance of web traffic, via technology such as **cookies**: the 'surfing' behaviour of those visiting web sites can provide valuable information about how prospects and customers behave on the Internet.

Credit Cards

Even the humble credit card has moved into a new era. The 'chip and pin' card carries a computer chip which can hold a great deal of consumer data: 'Never before have customers carried around in their pocket their own database of all the brands they have bought or all the promotions they have responded to' (Shaw, 2004). While at the checkout till, the 'PIN screen' can show personalized offers for the next shopping trip.

EXAMPLE 11.3

Mobile telephony is also a major new medium. The film company Twentieth Century Fox has a 'home entertainment' unit and for the launch of the DVD version of the film *Minority Report*, they used a sound clip from the film. Receivers of this telephone message were surprised to hear a man drawing breath and then saying, 'Where's my *Minority Report*?' and then screaming: 'Do I even have one?' The voice was that of Tom Cruise, the star of the film. The message ended: 'Don't miss out on your *Minority Report*. Buy it now on DVD and video.' This led to complaints to the Advertising Standards Authority (ASA) based on the phone message being offensive and that it could have caused distress and indeed that it did not make clear it was an advertisement. Some people who received the message had to pay to call their answer phone to retrieve the message if they had not been able to answer their phone when it was initially sent. Twentieth Century Fox Home Entertainment justified this by saying that it was only sent to those who had registered their details on the company's web site (30 000 of them) and had actually asked for communications concerning films and DVDs. So the company considered it appropriate to communicate with those who had 'opted-in' for relational interaction. The company also thought that most people who had expressed this sort of interest would be familiar with Tom Cruise's voice. However, the ASA upheld the complaints on the basis that when consumers are out of the film context and going about their daily routine they would not necessarily be thinking of receiving a message from Tom Cruise and the nature of the message could indeed be seen to be somewhat menacing and could therefore cause offence. (Rosser, 2003).

THINKBOX

Does the prospect of being tracked every minute of the day, through the items we carry or wear, represent an invasion of personal privacy?
  Why, or why not?

UNDERSTANDING CONSUMER BEHAVIOUR VIA PERSONALIZED PROFILE DATA

Geodemographic Profiles

We need to start with the national census, here. Originally the census was devised to help government and social planners determine infrastructural, community and social requirements for the next few years. But more recently it has also been used by companies to understand consumers. The first commercial use of the census was a marketing watershed and from 1981, in the UK, the national census has been available for marketing purposes.

The use of the national census in the UK led to the development of geodemographic systems and was a major catalyst in providing alternatives to anonymized market research samples. Although names and addresses cannot be revealed from the census, a link via the postal code system with the electoral roll means that it is possible to identify individual households and their characteristics. In November 2001 a member of the public won his case against Wakefield Council after that council had not been able to confirm that his electoral roll data (name and address) would not be supplied to third parties (such as marketers) without his consent (Acland, 2001). This had been a worry of the Information Commissioner who had been concerned that the electoral roll is compiled for voting purposes and should not be used for another purpose (one of the principles of the data protection legislation). The result has been the inclusion of opt-out options for electoral roll submissions and this should help to alleviate privacy concerns. But this means that only a smaller and, by definition, an incomplete electoral roll can be used. Even within months of the electoral roll opt-out being introduced, over 10 million people had opted out (Larkins, 2003) and by 2004 this had risen to over 29% of the population (indeed over 70% in some individual local authority areas) (May, 2005). So there are problems for marketers in the database's lack of geographical coverage. The reduced completeness of the roll could lead to an increase in poor (junk) targeting (Rubach, 2003b).

There are several geodemographic products but two leading ones are **Acorn** and **Mosaic** from the companies Consolidated Analysis Centres Incorporated (CACI) and Experian respectively. They overlay analyses of census data with a variety of data sources including financial data such as county court judgements (CCJs) for bad debt, electoral roll and Royal Mail (post code and address) data. The result is a profile of neighbourhoods, often at full postcode level of around 15 households. The basic rationale behind geodemographics is that 'birds of a feather flock together', making neighbourhoods relatively homogenous. An easy criticism in riposte, however, is that 'I am not like my neighbour'.

Geodemographic systems are not restricted to the UK, and a number of similar systems have been operating around the world for many years. In other European countries similar systems exist and several geodemographic companies now operate throughout many European countries and even, recently (in the case of Mosaic) into China.

It is straightforward to profile the area around a postcode in terms of geodemographic categories (Gonzalez-Benito and Gonzalez-Benito(2005). This could be the catchment area of an existing retail outlet, bank, pub and so on, or it could be the profiling of a 'drive time' area of one of several possible locations to site a new branch of a multiple retailer. It is likely that the retailer (in this case) would know the geodemographic profile of existing best customers and from the geodemographic profile of the new area would be able to purchase (from Experian or CACI, for example) the names and addresses of those who match this profile, for potential for direct mail or telemarketing contact.

EXAMPLE 11.4

Figure 11.3 depicts the sort of neighbourhood profiling offered by geodemographic systems (MOSAIC in this case). The 11 groups here are further subdivided into 61 'types'. To illustrate

Group A: Symbols of success

Group B: Happy families

Group C: Suburban comfort

Group D: Ties of community

Group E: Urban intelligence

Group F: Welfare borderline

Group G: Municipal dependency

Group H: Blue collar enterprise

Group I: Twilight subsistence

Group J: Grey perspective

Group K: Rural isolation

Figure 11.3 Geodemographic groups

© Experian Ltd. Reproduced by permission

Table 11.1   Mosaic type 16: conservative values

Consumer values *Conservative values* appreciates personal contact rather than impersonal transaction channels. Here people will naturally turn to professional advisors when key decisions need to be made. They like to discuss with shopkeepers or their sales assistants the relative merits of different brands and products, assuming that they will get unbiased advice. They use financial advisors. By contrast they are not very IT-literate and are not people to purchase over the Internet. However, having time at their disposal, many residents take very seriously the opportunities for searching out information on different products and will be well informed on new consumer issues such as the use of chemicals and ingredients in foods, and genetically modified crops. Preferences in food and fashion are conservative, and the opening of a local branch of Marks & Spencer would be seen as a major benefit.

Nevertheless residents are willing to support local shopkeepers and local suppliers, particularly if they can establish a personal relationship with them. Range, freshness and quality of service are more important than price and conformity with latest fashion trends. These people are likely to support their local church and give generously to charities. Perhaps on account of its age, this type has remained loyal to the Conservative Party notwithstanding its recent electoral vicissitudes.

Consumption patterns *Conservative values* represents a good market for the financial services industry and for long-haul travel. Much money is also spent on gardening products, on personal services such as laundry, dry-cleaning and hairdressing, and on quality food brands. By contrast, relatively little is spent on home improvement, on home furnishing or on clothing. People in these areas seldom smoke and prefer visits to country restaurants to evenings at the local pub.

Culture and consumer psychology *Conservative values* represents a very mainstream type in terms of tastes, values and lifestyle. These people are as practical and pragmatic in their consumption decisions and choices, as they probably are in all aspects of daily life. Unlikely to hold strong views on major issues, they are nevertheless 'switched on' to world and local events, through reading the better-quality papers and watching national and regional TV news programmes. They are likely to be careful with money even to the point of thriftiness but have developed money management skills over the years and are likely to be quite financially astute. They keep a close eye on the stock market and other investments, to stretch their savings and maintain financial security. There may also be some interest here in the possibility of raising cash from the equity in their homes.

Conservative with a small 'c', their attitude towards and engagement with consumption is confined to routine provisioning. These consumers are not likely to be tempted into trying new products which they have seen advertised, and will tend to stick with familiar brands. Even though they are careful with the pennies, they are not bargain hunters and, indeed, shopping holds no particular interest for them. Probably the type of people who maintain values dating from a time when things were bought to last, they will tend not to see the point of buying new clothes or household furnishings when those they have are still perfectly adequate. The same goes for new gadgets and appliances. These consumers are not likely to try any new-fangled equipment and may simply have no need for them in their traditional homes and lifestyles. In consumer behaviour terms, these are the 'laggards' when it comes to new products and brands. Appearances are not important, either, although their interest in their neat and pleasant gardens suggests their homes are neat and pleasant inside, albeit in a dated kind of way.

Moderate TV viewing is likely to revolve around informative programmes such as *Antiques Roadshow* and *Gardeners' World*, with a little *University Challenge* to keep the grey cells ticking over and *Songs of Praise* for spiritual edification. Grandchildren feature highly among this type, and it may be that the *conservative values* consumers are likely to splash out a little more where they are concerned.

Table 11.1

They do enjoy a comfortable and cosy lifestyle, however, and will indulge themselves to some extent with frequent holidays and short breaks – possibly coach tours or even cruises–which they may well take with a group of like-minded friends. For the rest of the time, however, they lead orderly lives, moving into old age in a comfortable and familiar daily routine.

the depth of consumer behaviour 'knowledge' that can be gleaned from just one of these types. Table 11.1 provides a summary.

There is now a full geodemographic analysis of the Target Group Index (TGI), which is an annual report in 34 volumes of buyer profiles in most product markets, based on samples of over 20 000. From this, each geodemographic category's interest in the product concerned can be determined. In fact the TGI sample design is now based on geodemographic categories and so sample design is an application of geodemographics. In addition, the National Readership Survey is similarly analysed by geodemographics and this can provide readership profiles for media selection purposes. The TGI is fused with BARB TV panel data in order to estimate media habits, lifestyle, product purchase and geodemographic profiles of the population, hence the depth of analysis in Table 11.1.

Figure 11.4 demonstrates how geodemographics can profile a catchment area (for example) for the potential citing of a retail outlet. The Mosaic (in this case) category overlays of the local map show where different segments live. If, for example, the retailer is mainly targeting the 'stylish single' segment, the map shows the area of greatest concentration of this segment. Indeed names and addresses of those in this segment can be purchased in order to target these potential customers personally. This particular map shows a five-minute off-peak drive time from Cardiff Business School (CF10 3 EU). Table 11.2 then shows how market potential can be estimated from a geodemographic profile of a (potential) catchment area.

Most geodemographic systems are also now heavily fused with financial data so it is not surprising, therefore, that such consumer data is of interest to government departments. CACI, for example, have an entire department dealing exclusively with government contracts for Acorn and related products. The Inland Revenue would have particular interests in the financial details of households to check financial details and trends against tax returns from those they want to investigate further.

It is interesting to note that for the 2001 census, the British Government, for the first time 'officially added commercial business to the list of users' of the census (Exon, 1998). New questions potentially relevant to the marketer and market researcher were added, including a clever question revealing the sexuality of partners (Exon, 1999; Brindle, 1999). The question wording asked for names of partners in the household and presumably marketers will assume same or different sex partners to indicate sexuality – the gay market being an important one for many marketers to target (see 'Sexuality' in Chapter 5).

However extensive the census becomes, the major limitation of census data relates to the difficulties associated with updating information, particularly because in the UK the census is only carried out every ten years and the 2011 census might be the last of its kind in the UK. It is likely that a range of data sources from different government departments and elsewhere will form the basis of the census after that date.

Figure 11.4   Five-minute off-peak drive time from CF103EU

Another issue concerns the generic nature of geodemographics. These have traditionally been off-the-shelf systems from which marketers can profile their existing customers according to postcode or select a sample of certain geodemographic clusters for research purposes. But all this is fine as long as the underpinning clustering of the specific data included is relevant to the marketer's purposes. If *different* census questions are analysed and overlaid with *different* financial and other details, to form more tailored clusters relevant to specific marketer's needs, then the customized geodemographic system might be even more useful in uncovering consumer behaviour.

Also, as sophisticated as geodemographics might be, it *profiles* consumers; it does not in itself explain why they behave as they do and neither does it provide individualized information on what they buy: remember it is based on aggregated data for neighbourhoods.

WWW.   **Take a look at the following web site, which takes you to Experian's new site and includes information about the new Mosaic, the 2001 census and much more:**

www.business-strategies.co.uk/BSHome.asp

Table 11.2   Market potential

The following shows how the area around a car dealership can be analysed by geodemographics.

Geodemographic group	% of area	×	Model X index	=	Area sales potential
			Table Catchment area analysis		
1	1.4	×	61	=	−0.85
2	–	×	108	=	–
3	9.7	×	84	=	8.15
4	7.9	×	39	=	2.92
5	–	×	41	=	–
6	11.4	×	53	=	6.04
7	–	×	34	=	–
8	13.9	×	124	=	17.80
9	29.4	×	230	=	66.93
10	22.5	×	217	=	48.82
11	3.1	×	84	=	2.60
Total					154.11

If Model X would be bought by 5% of the national population and the catchment area is 10 000, a sales potential of 10 000 × 5% = 500 would be expected. But the index here is 154.11, so for this catchment area the sales potential is 500 × 1.5411 = 770.

www.   Take a look at the following article, which can be accessed via the accompanying book web site at www.wiley.com/go.evans:

Duchessi, Schaninger and Nowak (2004) Creating Cluster-Specific Purchase Profiles from Point of Sale Scanner Data and Geodemographic Clusters: Improving Category Management at a Major US Grocery Chain, Journal of Consumer Behaviour, Vol 4 No 2 pp 97–117

Lifestyle Profiles

We explored traditional (anonymized) lifestyle research in Chapter 6. Here, however, we review an alternative approach to lifestyle research which has developed since around the late 1980s.

Contemporary lifestyle research, as we term this, asks respondents to tick those responses that apply in terms of products and services in which they claim an interest or actual purchase. Table 11.3 demonstrates some typical questions, some of which will be sponsored by specific companies.

Table 11.3 reflects just a portion of typical current lifestyle surveys. Many more questions are included, covering claimed buying behaviour across many different product and service categories. Some questions will be sponsored by specific companies; for example, a car insurance company might sponsor a question asking for the month in which the car insurance is renewed. Because these surveys are not anonymized (the data will be filed in a database by name and address of respondent) it is likely that in the month prior to that respondent's renewal date, they are very likely to receive direct mailings soliciting defection to the sponsoring company.

The difference between the more traditional form of lifestyle segmentation discussed in chapter 6 and the current approach is that the former builds psychographic profiles from segments from relatively small

Table 11.3   Contemporary lifestyle research

Please indicate your marital status:
single
married
divorced/separated
widowed
What is your name and address?.........
What is your partner's full name?........
Holidays:
How much are you likely to spend per person on your next main holiday?
up to £500 ☐   £501–£999 ☐   £1000–1499 ☐   £1500–£2000 ☐
£2000+ ☐

In which country are you likely to take your next main holiday?.........

In which month are you likely to take your main holiday?.........

(anonymized) data sets and expands these to generalize patterns within the larger population. The latter, however, has the ability to list specific names and addresses of those who claim to be interested in specific products, brands and services.

---

www. www.prospectlocator.com is Experian's online 'list' site. It shows how consumers can be selected (by name and address and even telephone number), according to a variety of characteristics including geodemographics and specific factors from lifestyle lists.

www.firstt.co.uk is part of DunnHumby and shows how TGI lifestyle data is being fused with customer data.

Genetic Profile Data

Further issues arise in the realm of genetic data and assessing insurance risk (Specter, 1999). Clearly, for financial services companies, it would be useful to be able to assess risks on the basis that gene patterns can indicate individuals' future potential susceptibility to illness or disease (Borna and Avila, 1999). In the UK some patient data is available in the NHSnet database that can be accessed by healthcare professionals (Introna and Powloudi, 1999). In a survey of 3000 UK households, three quarters were against genetic tests for insurance underwriting, 85% against insurance companies rejecting applicants on this basis and 78% against insurance companies charging higher premiums on the basis of genetic tests. Indeed, 68% of the sample thought that this use of genetic data should be prohibited by law (Borna and Avila, 1999). Introna and Powloudi (1999) report that medics have expressed concern over this trend. The logical extension of the scenario is that those who don't need insuring will be insured and the rest will be excluded. This is an example of the corollary of the RFM type of metrics introduced above: it can result in those consumers who are less valuable or more costly to a service being excluded.

BIOGRAPHICS AND INDIVIDUALISM

Biographics

The fusion of transactional and profile data leads to a significant trend in consumer behaviour research, namely **biographics**. Consumers are being analysed in ever more sophisticated and detailed ways and this is leading to the identification and targeting of smaller but better defined (at least in theory) segments. But although this gives the impression that we have moved to one-to-one marketing, this is not the norm and perhaps is more rhetoric than reality. There might be personalized targeting, in the sense that the individual is addressed by name, and there might be some data-driven offer that matches the data-mining outcome for the segment to which the individual is allocated, but this is not the same as understanding customers on a truly individual basis as we would in a human relationship context.

---

www. | **Take a look at the following web sites:**

www.dunnhumby.com, the company that deals with the loyalty scheme data for several organizations, including Tesco.

www.talkingnumbers.com, which is the web site of a company that specializes in data-driven solutions – there are case studies and other useful information here.

THINKBOX

'Data' can become a surrogate for consumer insight. For example Mitchell (2001) recently quoted a director of one of the largest retailers in the UK:

We've given up trying to understand our customers ... helping us cut a lot of complexity from our business. The academic's instinct is to gather a large amount of information, formulate a theory, and apply it to a situation ... (this) creates waste in the form of the wrong information at the wrong time, leading to the wrong decisions ... or ... fruitless attempts to predict or alter customer behaviour.

The favoured approach by this company, 'sense and respond' (Haeckel, 2001), is to react quickly on the basis of customer contact via call centres, Internet, interactive digital TV and infomediaries. This is understandable in the current context of pressure to achieve short-term profit in order to provide shareholder value. However, it can lead to a subordination of the key component of the marketing concept itself – namely, customer satisfaction – to over-emphasis on tracking transactional data. Another example concerns a major data consortium, Jigsaw, which is run by Cadbury, Kimberley Clark and Unilever. This consortium has announced the scrapping of attitudinal data in favour of transactional data (Walker, 2001).

Might this even lead to companies 'dictating' what we put in our shopping baskets because they know what we have bought previously and think they understand us so well? (Richardson, 2000)

In other words, marketers have so much data on individual consumers – their personal details, profile and purchase patterns – that there is less of a need for the kind of market research which tries to answer the 'why' questions of consumer purchase or non-purchase behaviour.

What do you think about this?

Individualism

The Henley Centre (1978) predicted the trend toward individualism as far back as the 1970s when they discussed household behaviour as being **cellular** rather than **nuclear** – households were beginning to do things together less and less and beginning to behave more independently: families were not eating together as often and were having TV and sound systems in their 'own' rooms.

One reason for such fragmentation of markets is consumers' desire to be treated more as individuals (see Chapter 6). Evidence of the trend toward individualism was uncovered during the 1970s and led, among other things, to the Regan and Thatcher election campaigns from the late 1970s and into the 1980s based on 'self-reliance' (BBC, 2002). 'Standing on one's own feet' and 'freeing the individual from the state' were the sorts of mantras of those elections and were manifestations of research at the time that revealed individualism (McNulty, 2002).

THINKBOX

Individualism is manifested in greater pluralism within society, evident in the high street where pluralism in clothing styles is observable.

Is the logical extension of this that if more consumers want to express individuality then it provides marketers with opportunities to treat them individually and not only offer more self-expressive products but also to target them as individuals?

CONSUMER REACTION TO INDIVIDUALIZED CONSUMER–ORGANIZATION INTERACTION

As society continues to be time-poor due to long working hours (see Figure 11.5) many consumers seek time-saving purchasing methods, such as via direct mail, telephony and the Internet, which are the manifestations of the new personalized and data-informed consumer–organization interaction.

However, Evans *et al.* (2001) found that the situation is complex. At the same time as participating in direct reciprocal interaction, consumers also express various concerns. They are, for example, simultaneously, street-wise and cynical. Various dimensions of privacy were revealed, as we summarize below.

Figure 11.5 Time-hungry cash-rich commuters
Harried commuters interact with companies via phone, mail and Internet
Source: Digital Vision. Reproduced with permission

Physical/Interaction Privacy

Although direct personalized targeting is clearly a convenience to the time-constrained contemporary consumer, it can also be its own worst enemy because the consumer can be bombarded by unwanted or untimely (junk) information (Evans *et al.*, 2001).

'Physical/interaction privacy' relates to the physical intrusion of marketing communications (for example, direct mail, telesales, emails) into the daily lives of consumers. The 'hottest' prospects are, somewhat obviously, targeted most heavily, such as those with the highest spending power. Ungoed-Thomas and Nuki (1998) reported their uncovering of a 'Midas' list of those between 25 and 45, earning more than £50 000 pa, who own lots of electronic products and engage in relatively expensive leisure activities. They 'are being sent 250 mailshots a year, five times the national average'. If these people enjoy receiving information about even more things they can spend their money on, then there probably isn't a problem, as long as they can sustain such expenditure levels. However, many will feel this is just too much – as one consumer reported: 'Every day it comes through the door ... it's relentless ... I don't read it on principle because Britain is turning into a huge buying experience and I hate it' (Rule, 1998).

Information Privacy

Evans *et al.* (2001) also reveal a 'privacy paradox' in that some consumers are somewhat cynical about 'relational' interaction and concerned about divulging personal information but are participants nevertheless. There might be a desire on the part of organizations to develop relationships with customers but customers do not always want to reciprocate. It is likely that the cynicism is predicated upon a lack of trust resulting from business scams, unfulfilled promises and marketing hype.

'Information privacy' refers to the extent to which individuals can **control** who holds their data, and what is done with those data (Westin, 1967). In the USA, many consumers already believe that they have lost all control over how information about them is used, with some even suggesting that if they could, they would add privacy to their constitutional rights to life, liberty and the pursuit of happiness (Schroeder, 1992). Indeed there has been a plethora of books written on this issue in the USA in recent years (Rothfeder, 1992; Chesbro 1999; Rosen, 2001; Larson, 1994; Charrett, 1999).

EXAMPLE 11.5

In the UK the Information Commissioner's office ran a hard-hitting advertising campaign aimed at marketers who deal with personalized consumer databases (Figure 11.6).

Figure 11.6   Information Commissioner's advertisement to database marketers
© Information Commissioner's Office. Reproduced by permission

The marketers themselves might delight in having access to this sort of data on the consumers they want to target, but how might they feel about their own data being available like this?

As a result of these privacy conflicts between consumers and organizations, Westin envisages a rise in what he calls 'consensual databases' (**permission marketing**), where consumers consent to information surrender in return for some type of reward such as coupons, samples or money (Westin, 1992). However, as Mitchell states,

Permission isn't enough ... is ticking a box once, permission to spam me for the rest of my life ... there's only one way out: to put consumers in the driving seat, empowering them to specify what sort of messages they are looking for by time, place and category. (Mitchell, 2002)

In reality there may be no easy solution.

For a fuller discussion of the wider social implications of personalized data-informed marketing, see Evans (2005).

THINKBOX

How do *you* feel about reciprocal personalized interaction with companies?
Do you have concerns in terms of physical and information privacy?
Why or why not?

SUMMARY

■ Transactional data provide the means to assess consumer behaviour in terms of what they buy, when, how and where. This is personalized when linked with loyalty schemes or online cookies. There is a range of other data sources, such as RFIDs, NLPs, cookies and genetics, all of which have specific implications for explaining consumer behaviour.

■ A major catalyst in consumer-profiling research was the marketing use in 1981 of the census which led to the first geodemographic product in UK. These are now widespread around the world and census data is overlaid with data from a variety of other sources such as financial and lifestyle data.

■ The combination of data profiles with transactional data provides the new biographics which marketers often claim can help generate the sort of relational interaction discussed in the previous chapter. However, there are concerns that 'data' drives too much and becomes the surrogate for real consumer insight, which might be derived from a more psychologically and socially informed consumer behaviour paradigm.

■ New metrics can be applied to this data to identify the best – and worst – consumers in order to focus on the former and (often) to exclude the latter. New media facilitate personalized interaction between consumer and organization and allow individualism to be manifested.

■ However, there are wider social concerns over the use and potential misuse of personal data and consumers and marketers need to come to a mutually amicable arrangement over how such data is used.

QUESTIONS

1. **What are the implications for consumers and marketers of the trend toward biographics?**

2. **What is meant by 'geodemographics'? How might the approach explain consumer behaviour?**

3. **As a consumer, are you comfortable knowing that marketers have lots of your personal details?**

4. **What consumer data is a car dealership likely to hold? What external sources might it fruitfully buy in? How could this data explain consumer behaviour?**

5. **The coverage in this chapter of the *Minority Report* film reports:**
   a. How consumers can be biometrically recognized, individually, as they enter a shopping mall; and
   b. How consumers can be targeted as individuals via mobile phones.
   What are the issues for both marketers and consumers that these two developments present?

FURTHER READING

Evans M, **O'Malley** L and **Patterson** (2004) Exploring Direct and Customer Relationship Marketing, Thomson Learning, p 544. This is an extensive exploration of what some refer to as 'the new marketing' based around the use of very personalized consumer data for segmenting and targeting purposes.

Lace S (ed.) (2005) The Glass Consumer: Life in a Surveillance Society, Policy Press/National Consumer Council. This is a collection of readings which critically examines the use of personal consumer data in public and private sectors. The readings are not only concerned with marketing applications, but also with wider issues of technology and society, social policy as well as consumption.

CHAPTER 12

CONSUMER MISBEHAVIOUR

CHAPTER OBJECTIVES

After engaging with the material presented in this chapter, its associated exercises and reading, you should be able to:

■ Appreciate that we can all misbehave as consumers

■ Explore a range of misbehaviours and their consequences for the company, the consumers and society

■ Differentiate between illegal and abnormal consumer behaviour

■ Be aware of some of the reasons for consumer misbehaviour

■ Appreciate how consumer misbehaviour can be related to each aspect of marketing activity and indeed toward capitalism, multi-nationals and the materialistic society.

INTRODUCTION

This final chapter recognizes that consumers themselves are not always angels. They might indulge in consumption behaviours that might harm themselves or others in some ways. According to Fullerton and Punj (2004), consumer misbehaviour refers to 'behavioural acts by consumers which violate the generally accepted norms of conduct in consumption situations and thus disrupt the consumption order'. This could be extended to include consumption and related behaviours which also disrupt other consumers, the environment and society at large (even though they may be generally accepted forms of behaviours). While a simple example would be queue-jumping at checkouts, a more delicate example would be the case of purchasing products that can harm our environment.

The American term 'jaywalker' (someone who dangerously crosses streets; for example, when not indicated to do so by the pedestrian crossing lights) has been adapted to refer to consumers who misbehave. Lovelock (1994) uses the phrase **jaycustomer** to refer to consumers who:

- Do not pay for goods or do not pay the full price;
- Break the rules of consumer–organization interaction, by, for example, queue-jumping at theme parks or in supermarkets;
- Are overly angry with company personnel;

- Vandalize company property or equipment;
- Fail to pay for goods or services not because of criminal intent but just due to lack of concern or interest.

As discussed in Chapter 10, there are also **consumer terrorists**: those who are dissatisfied with a particular company or brand and spread ill will about it and who generally try to undermine its credibility and even its activities (Jones and Sasser, 1995).

An otherwise well-behaved person might misbehave while on board a plane with a group of friends. A minority of football fans act as a hooligans before, during and after matches. Both of these are examples of consumption misbehaviours. More obvious instances would be shoplifting, illegal drug-use, under-age drinking and binge-drinking. Some consumers dispose of plastic shopping bags in ways that litter our streets and pollute the environment (they may take up to 500 years to decompose when buried in a landfill site). We use cars even though we know that cars seriously pollute our environment and contribute towards global warming.

Sometimes consumer misbehaviour is encouraged by marketers, such as eating disorders induced by the sort of unrealistic body images portrayed in advertising, as discussed in Chapter 6. Could it be that the entire marketing industry is guilty of encouraging shallow materialism?

We focus here on misbehaviours that violate the generally accepted norms of conduct and that are of concern or threat to others and to the environment.

THINKBOX

It is likely that many who are now good citizens engaged in petty shoplifting or vandalism as teenagers. Does this mean that you think such youth misbehaviour to be harmless? Why, or why not?

CONSUMER MISBEHAVIOUR TYPOLOGIES

Consumers can misbehave in many ways. Table 12.1 summarizes some of the more obvious forms of misbehaviour. It classifies misbehaviour into four categories depending on whether the behaviour is abnormal or illegal and whether the misbehaviour occurs during the acquisition stage of consumption or is related to the use of the products and services (Hoyer and McInnes, 2001).

Table 12.1 Consumer misbehaviour typologies

	Misbehaviour in acquiring products	Product misuse
Abnormal consumer behaviour	**Excessive buying**	**Addictive**
	To compensate for psychological problems	Buying drugs
		Alcohol
	Sometimes over-stretching financial resources leading to bad debt or bankruptcy cases	Gambling
		Binge-eating/drinking
		Smoking
Illegal consumer behaviour	Theft, shoplifting, black markets, bootlegging, counterfeiting brands	Under-age drinking
		Under-age smoking
		Under-age sex
		Related products and services misuse
		Drug use and abuse

Source: Adapted by the authors from WD Hoyer and DJ MacInnes, *Consumer Behavior*, 2nd edn, Houghton Mifflin, Boston, 2001. Copyright ©2001 by Houghton Mifflin Company. Adapted with permission

Misbehaviour in Acquiring Products

Abnormal Behaviour

One type of abnormal behaviour is known as 'compulsive consumption behaviour' and is defined by O'Guinn and Faber (1989) as a 'response to an uncontrollable drive or desire to obtain, use, or experience a feeling, substance, or activity that leads an individual to repetitively engage in a behaviour that will ultimately cause harm to the individual and/or to others' (p148). Examples include: drug abuse, excessive eating, alcoholism, excessive sexuality and gambling. By definition, compulsive behaviour is repetitive in nature and carries negative consequences for the individual even though there can be some short-term rewards. Once a consumer fully develops this behaviour and becomes used to it, they face great difficulty in controlling it even though they are fully aware of the negative consequences. According to O'Guinn and Faber (1989), physiological, genetic, psychological, social and cultural factors contribute towards the development of such behaviour by a person. Compulsive buyers have low levels of self-esteem and a high ability to fantasize, which allows them to escape reality (O'Guinn and Faber, 1989). Some consumers may have 'obsessive personalities' which contribute to this behaviour. Anecdotally, one teenager spends around 10% of her gross weekly wage on nail varnish alone. The effects on finances and social relationships can be devastating if such buying cannot be sustained.

A survey of young adults (aged 20 to 32) in the USA revealed that family structure is related to compulsive buying and to materialism (Rindfleisch *et al.*, 1997). Those whose parents were divorced or separated showed much higher levels of compulsive buying and materialistic values than those whose parents were not divorced. Moreover, family resources (e.g. household income, parental support, role modelling and guidance) and family stressors (e.g. lack of stability, parental conflict, loss of friends and relatives, and changes of adult caregivers) appeared partially to mediate the relationship between family structure and compulsive buying.

Illegal Behaviour

There are many instances in which consumers seek products through illegal means (e.g. shoplifting or illegal use of products). Some goods are especially prone to being stolen in-store. Razor blades and DVDs have been among the first to be RFID-tagged (see Chapter 11) and there is also the possible use of subliminal audio messages in store ('I must not steal') in an attempt to reduce pilferage.

Product Misuse

Abnormal Product Use

Addictions, here, are examples of what can happen when compulsive behaviour gets out of hand after purchase. Drink, gambling and drugs can lead to dependency which in turn can lead to other social and personal disasters such as financial ruin, job loss and family break-up.

Binge-drinking has been a social evil for several years. The damage that 40 or more units of alcohol in one night can do to the individual, those around them, the police and health services is clearly not a worry for those concerned, at the time of bingeing, but there are consequences nonetheless.

Illegal Product Use

There are several activities which are regulated by law. These include smoking, driving and sexual intercourse. Teenagers, however, are 'finding themselves': they are developing their own identity, which means becoming more distant from parents and even rebelling against them and 'the establishment'. Hence there is always a clash between 'teenage kicks' and the law.

In terms of illegal drug use, this can lead to crime, to violent gangs vying for catchment areas for 'dealing', and personal misery, ill-health and even death. As with crime in general, there can be a deliberation over the costs of being caught and the benefits of success (Becker, 1968; and Wilson and Hernstein, 1985).

> **WWW.** **Take a look at the article that follows this chapter, Fitchett and Smith (2002) Consumer Behaviour in an Unregulated Market. This can also be found on the accompanying web site at www.wiley.com/go/evans.**

THINKBOX

Under-age smoking, drinking and sex are illegal and the consumption of many products related to these activities (by the under-aged) represents consumer misbehaviour.

Do you agree?

What issues are raised by this?

IDEALISTIC RATIONALE FOR MISBEHAVIOUR

The postmodern era sees consumption as integral to societal behaviour and norms. This contrasts with earlier times (e.g. 1960s and 1970s) when materialism and capitalism were rebelled against

(Gabriel and Lang, 1995). It was also possible to use legitimate consumption behaviour as a manifestation of misbehaviour. For example, the punk era of the late 1970s saw teenagers dressing in bin bags with safety pins through their ears as symbols of rebellion against the 'prescribed' fashions of expensive fashion designers and marketers. The current version of this is the battle between massive multinational corporate power and anti-corporation activism on the part of some sections of consumers (Klein, 2001).

Sometimes consumers boycott a company's products because they feel the company operates in unethical ways. Examples are Nestlé and the controversy surrounding its selling of powdered milk to poor African communities, or L'Oréal and its use of animals to test its cosmetics. Such consumer behaviour could be construed as *mis*behaviour by the companies concerned, but sections of society could see this to be highly ethical behaviour which sometimes manages to reverse what they see as *company* misbehaviour.

Some argue that business and marketing activities have a macro effect in shaping attitudes and values which lead to consumer misbehaviour (Fullerton and Punj, 2002). In other words, most of the misbehaviour is an 'unintended consequence of the marketing activities of firms, which seek to promote a philosophy of consumption so that consumers will buy more' (p 240). This reflects the **cultural authority perspective** in which marketers are viewed as cultural engineers with strong abilities and techniques (e.g. use of persuasive communications, segmentation and targeting techniques) to shape consumer desires, feelings and actions and to promote a consumer culture in which consumers implicitly grant authority to the marketers to organize their tastes (Holt, 2002). We explored some of these dimensions in Chapter 1 where we raised questions about marketing's exploitation of human drives. These motivate us to aspire to more and more, without necessarily satisfying us, regardless of how much we buy and own.

In such a context, some consumers fight back by allocating products with oppositional meanings, by using them in more idiosyncratic ways (which may be viewed as misbehaviour by others) and by seeking out social spaces in which to produce their own culture and identities (Firat and Venkatesh, 1995; Holt, 2002). Holt (2002) argues that conflict between consumers and marketers arises 'when firms attend to their internal interests rather than seek to meet consumer wants and needs' (p 70). Consumers can feel rebellious when there is huge perceived 'social distance' between a large, multinational organization and the consumer. They also have negative attitudes towards large organizations because there can be a big gap between the GDP figure for many underdeveloped countries and the profits of big multinational corporations. It might be due to the multinational imposing its own values and/or practices on other countries. In some cases it might be because there is not the personal contact between organization and consumer that might have existed in previous eras.

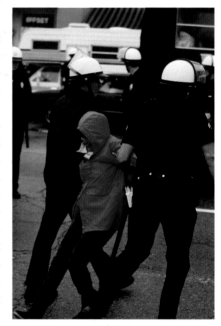

For example, the 'corner shop' catchment area and its inhabitants were well known by the shopkeeper on a personal basis but the more impersonal retail chains can't achieve this even through their attempts of loyalty scheme surrogacy (as discussed in the two previous chapters). As a result, social distance is even greater and might lead to the view that some forms of misbehaviour are almost legitimate (Houston and Gassenheimer, 1987).

---

www. | **Have a look at the following web sites:**

http://www.corporatewatch.org/

http://www.adbusters.org

These are good examples of anti-corporate online communities for consumers to exchange views and negative experiences of company and marketing activity.

THINKBOX

Sometimes there can be a rejection of the consumption and materialistic world. Some consumers 'make do' from cheap supplies or charity shops.
   Could either of these phenomena be considered 'consumer misbehaviour'?

CONSUMER MISBEHAVIOUR WITH RESPECT TO MARKETING ACTIVITIES

Whatever the motive, consumer misbehaviour influences not only consumers themselves but also other consumers, marketers and the environment in which we all live. Consumers can display misbehaviour in the way that they interact with, and react to, specific marketing activities.

THINKBOX

Whereas some behaviour is clearly unethical, such as those which break the law or seriously affect other people, there is perhaps, a grey area depending on our personal stance.
   From Figure 12.1 and Table 12.2, which do you think are *not* examples of consumer misbehaviour? Why do you think so?

Fullerton and Punj (2002) report a range of consumer misbehaviour directed against marketer's merchandise, their physical and electronic premises, financial assets and even employees. They report seven important motives for such misbehaviour.

EXAMPLE 12.1

Table 12.2 summarizes consumer misbehaviours with respect to a number of marketing activities including the ones in which we as consumers, either consciously or unconsciously, cause trouble to the environment and to others.

Table 12.2   Consumer misbehaviour and marketing activities

Marketing activity	Consumer misbehaviour
Products and services	Anti-social product use and misuse, such as in Figure 12.1
	Abuse of services, such as 'bad behaviour' when travelling on planes or when on holiday
	Use of environmentally damaging products such as cars, airline travel, fur garments, TV and sound systems with remote control
	Disposal of products in an environmentally damaging manner
	Knowingly investing in companies which exploit child labour and use other socially undesirable practices
	Purchase pornography products which exploit and damage women in particular and sometimes children
	Damaging brand reputation of companies perceived to be politically or socially irresponsible
	Buying products to indulge in sports which damage the environment, such as non-degradable fishing lines which can kill birds, guns to shoot wildlife
	Consumption of foods we know will damage our health
Price	Avoidance of paying, not owning up to being undercharged or given too much change, or falsely claiming the reverse
	Knowingly taking advantage of loans and credit when financial position won't sustain these
	Credit card fraud
Distribution	Vandalism of shops and shopping malls
	Illegal or unethical distribution of counterfeit goods
	Use of unauthorized distribution to sell bootleg products
	Physically damaging in-store displays and carpets
Promotion	Adding graffiti to posters
	Distorting (via word of mouth or online communities) advertising messages to damage the reputation of a brand out of spite
	Relationship marketing
	Deliberately distorting purchase details in loyalty and marketing database schemes by, for example, swapping loyalty cards
	Identity theft, abuse of personal details of other consumers
Relationship marketing and marketing databases	Misusing or stealing consumers' personal information and credit card details from marketing databases for fraudulent use
Market research	Poll rigging
	Deliberately mis-responding
Marketers' employees and other consumers	Being abusive to front-line marketing staff such as call centre operatives, complaints departments, store-till operators and service staff
	Double standards adopted by the same individual in their capacity as a marketer and consumer

Figure 12.1   Fur misbehaviour
Why kill—for vanity?
© People for the Ethical Treatment of Animals (PETA). Reproduced by permission

1. When consumers are unable to fulfil their consumption goals through legitimate means, they are likely to engage in misbehaviours such as theft and fraud.
2. Some consumers find the act of misbehaving to be a thrilling experience in which they defy basic legal and moral strictures and hence they misbehave.
3. An absence of moral constraint can lead to misbehaviour. In other words, the acts of misbehaviours may not be perceived as bad or undesirable.
4. In certain groups (e.g. teenagers), misbehaviour may be perceived as a way of promoting a group's identity by positioning itself differently from others in the society. Here, an act of misbehaviour reinforces one's sense of belonging to the group.
5. Strong negative attitudes towards large institutions and particular ownership of businesses can trigger misbehaviour.
6. Certain situational factors (e.g. crowding, unsettling amount of heat and noise) can trigger powerful impulses to misbehave.
7. Some consumers engage in rational weighting of the risks and rewards associated with misconduct, which can trigger misbehaviour.

Consumer Misbehaviour with Respect to Products and Services

Table 12.2 lists several examples of misbehaviour with respect to product purchasing. Is it misbehaviour to buy products which damage our planet and the life it supports? Consider, for example, the case of buying of fur and cars. Figure 12.1 summarizes the problems with buying fur garments. From mid-2000, fur is back in fashion and as a result more than 30 000 baby seals were shot, speared and clubbed to death in Canada in March 2005. Over a thousand hunters were employed to strip the pups of their fur.

Figure 12.2 A consumer's struggle against car usage
Why worship the car?
© IEESDS. Photograph: Thierry David. http://www.decroissance.org

They are helpless, 'can't swim or get away' (Beeston, 2005) and some are 'still alive after they had been skinned' (Aldworth, 2005).

Figure 12.2 shows Car Buster's co-founder who set across the countryside of southern France on foot in July 2004, with a donkey at his side, to highlight the need for an alternative to consumerism (in this case car travel) and economic growth, and to promote conviviality along the way. But to what extent are consumers willing to buy cars that wouldn't pollute the environment or even consider alternatives to having a car in the first place?

Similarly, consider the case of holidays. Are we as consumers willing to forego our beloved foreign holidays because planes damage the Earth's environmental balance? Indeed, do we misbehave too much on holidays anyway? Club 18–30's recent campaigns are an interesting example of marketing's encouragement of misbehaviour on holiday.

This links with our coverage of Freudian motivation in Chapter 1 where we explored the superego-diminishing effect of alcohol and different societal constraints when on holiday. Should youth market segments indulge so much in sex, alcohol and drugs while on holidays? These can damage their country's reputation, physically damage the holiday destination's infrastructure, and violence and rape can sometimes be consequences of certain sorts of holiday purchase.

Consumer Misbehaviour with Respect to Price

If a consumer has a standard rail ticket, yet occupies a seat in a first-class compartment, this is misuse of a service but it also is an example of use without paying, which, in many guises, is misbehaviour over price. There are a great many reasons why consumers misbehave over price. One of the earliest is the gap between their consumption/ownership aspirations and the financial means to realize these (Merton, 1968; Brokaw, 1993).

Perhaps one of the most obvious examples here is shoplifting. But as Fullerton and Punj (2004) also state, it can include returning goods such as clothing or DIY tools after one use only in order to get a refund. They also cite the switching of price tags in an attempt to get an item for much less than should be paid for it. Daspin (2000) also cites driving away from a petrol station without paying and this is again theft, as is leaving a restaurant without paying.

Another example of misbehaviour which in effect means that proper prices have not been paid includes failing to own up to a cashier's error and leaving with more change than is due. Steenhaut and Van Kenhove (2005) found that this depends on the level of the consumer's commitment to the retailer; if there is high commitment and large amounts of change involved, the consumer is more likely to 'own up'. But if the consumer has low commitment and large excess of change, they are less likely to own up. Steenhaut and Van Kenhove (2005) say this can be explained by opportunism on the consumer's part.

If a consumer submits a fraudulent insurance claim hoping to be reimbursed for items not stolen or destroyed, then this is a further example of misbehaviour, which in effect means that proper prices have not been paid.

Are consumers, who acquire tickets for a concert by the latest and trendiest rock band and then sell to other consumers at several times their face-value price, abusing price? Black markets do not represent normality even if they have become commonplace.

The downloading of music has largely been illegal and the artist does not get paid when it occurs. Increasingly though, provision is made for royalty payments, as iPods, Internet-enabled mobile phones and MP3 players (and indeed music web sites) become more common and the industry recognizes that rather than see downloading as a threat it can turn it into an opportunity.

THINKBOX

Is there any parallel between consumer misbehaviour with respect to music piracy (the unauthorized downloading of music or buying of pirated music) and the buying of counterfeit brands?

For this, read: Chiou, Huang and Lee (2005); and Gentry, Putrevu and Shultz (2006).

The latter is accessed via the accompanying web site. It explores the implications of increasingly 'convincing' counterfeits and suggests, among other things, that consumers might buy a counterfeit brand as part of the 'trial' stage of the adoption process (Chapter 9) and if it is rewarding enough may go on to buy the 'real thing'.

www. Take a look at the article on consumer misbehaviour by Tonglet (2002) Consumer Misbehaviour: An Exploratory Study of Shoplifting, Journal of Consumer Behaviour, Vol 1 No 4 pp 336–354, which can be accessed via the accompanying web site at www.wiley.com/go/evans.

Consumer Misbehaviour with Respect to Distribution

The examples listed in Table 12.2 under this heading include the vandalism of shops and shopping centres. 'Bootlegging' is where illegal copies of, for example, DVDs or videos are made and sold, so it can be a distribution misbehaviour as well as a pricing one, as discussed above. Counterfeiting of brands is also distribution misbehaviour as well as pricing misbehaviour. Some people go to inordinate lengths to produce, sell and consume fake brands. Before the Iron Curtain came down, Levi's jeans labels were smuggled into the Soviet Union and sewn into 'ordinary' jeans. Consumers were more than happy to buy these: the jeans were cheaper than the real thing but conveyed the same image. However, Levi's branding, advertising and merchandising was 'ripped off' in the process.

Consumer Misbehaviour with Respect to Promotion

Consumers can be incredibly powerful. Consider the following:

> Whether directed against customers, employers or entire organizations, satirical messages created by activist organizations and even disapproving comments posted by customers can be quite damaging. Consumers weigh negative word of mouth far more heavily than they do positive comments about a product or service. According to a study by the White House Office of Consumer Affairs, 90% of *unhappy* customers will not do business with a company. Each of them is likely to share their grievance with at least nine other people and 13% of these disgruntled customers will go on to tell more than thirty people of their negative experience. (Solomon, 2003)

In terms of consumers defacing marketing messages, the addition of graffiti to posters is fairly common. This might reflect random attacks of mindless vandalism, if the posters are conveniently located and relatively easy to write on (compared with brick, for example). Or there could be some deeper reason for the graffiti, such as a political or another activist slogan, targeting the specific brand or company concerned (Figure 12.3). Examples of consumers defacing posters can be seen around the country. Following the

Figure 12.3　Activist poster graffiti
© JP Defaut/eyevine. Reproduced by permission

earlier mention of some consumers' perception that Nestlé operates unethically, a poster for Nescafé was defaced with the graffiti: 'Nescafé kills babies.'

Consumer Misbehaviour with Respect to Relationship Marketing and Marketing Databases

The previous chapter discussed aspects of consumer misbehaviour with respect to relationship marketing and marketing databases. It is a possibility, for example, that marketing databases could be used to target burglaries. That is, the destination of goods could be gleaned from customer databases in order to determine premises to burgle.

Some consumers engage in other illegal activities relating to personal data and its electronic storage. For example, the increase in credit card fraud and identity theft has been fuelled by the availability of personal details stored electronically by marketers.

In Chapter 10 we mentioned the consumer who hid his chocolate biscuit consumption from his wife. He did this by paying cash, for these items only, and putting the rest of the grocery purchases on his wife's loyalty card. He felt that without doing this she might be targeted with chocolate offers as a result of the company's analysis of the transactional records. Is this consumer misbehaviour? Or is it an example of marital misbehaviour?

Consumer Misbehaviour with Respect to Market Research

Some pressure groups are becoming adept at using opinion polls to influence policy decisions. They can orchestrate the 'piling in' (Nancarrow *et al.*, 2004) by other like-minded consumers to, for example, online polls. You may consider the following questions:

- Is it respondent misbehaviour to give answers which you think the interviewer wants to hear?
- Is it respondent misbehaviour to give any old answer just to get the interview over?
- Is it respondent misbehaviour to give answers which are generally known to be public opinion even if you yourself feel differently about the issue?
- Is it respondent misbehaviour to give a deliberately 'outlying' response out of bloody-mindedness?

Consumer Misbehaviour with Respect to Marketers' Employees and Other Consumers

Fullerton and Punj (2002) summarize several examples of this form of misbehaviour, including verbal abuse by consumers of marketing staff and in some cases the physical abuse of them. Harris and Reynolds (2004) extend this to include vindictive revenge and sexual predation of front-line marketing staff. They also reinforce the view that misbehaving consumers do not represent the minority but indeed the majority of consumers. In another study, Harris and Reynolds (2003) provide clear evidence of the damaging effects on marketing front-line staff of the abusive and aggressive consumer: 'More than 93% of employees interviewed indicated that dysfunctional customer behaviour negatively affected their emotional state.' They also found that few companies had policies to deal with the problem. There is even a web site – customerssuck.com – which is set up by some front-line employees as a forum for employees to share their grievances about awkward consumers.

> ## THINKBOX
>
> Might the 'exclusion' of some consumers on the grounds of not contributing much to sales or profit (as discussed in the previous chapter) be extended to exclusion based on misbehaviour?
>
> Could it be that a manifestation of 'the customer is always right' perspective is that a degree of misbehaviour is tolerated? There might be a pragmatic view that a certain level of abuse is tolerated even if the same abuse might not be in a different social setting. Does this encourage even more abuse by consumers?

BEHAVIOUR BALANCES

We have norms and expectations which might determine the extent to which behaviour is perceived as misbehaviour (Fullerton and Punj, 2002). In a marketing context, consumers have expectations of how firms and their employees should behave whereas marketers also expect their consumers to behave in certain ways. Furthermore, consumers have certain expectations regarding the behaviour of *other* consumers in a particular situation. Figure 12.4 suggests that the wider societal perspective of

Figure 12.4   Impersonal Trust and consumer behaviour

consonant behaviour requires that the three components of the 'exchange triangle' interact smoothly. Any dissonance between them can violate **impersonal trust**. Impersonal trust is where people who do not normally interact have faith in each other. Where there is either no misbehaviour or that which does exist has relatively minimal impact on the other parties, there is a consonant exchange environment. But where there is significant misbehaviour and/or it impinges upon the lives of the other parties more dramatically, there is a dissonant exchange environment and misbehaviour has a wider and negative effect on society.

THINKBOX

What were your motives for any consumer misbehaviour in which you might have indulged ?

Should marketers do anything to address consumer misbehaviour? Why, or why not? And if 'yes', what sort of measures would be effective?

SUMMARY

■ Consumer misbehaviour has serious consequences for all: those who indulge in such behaviours as well as others including members of the society, marketers and even the environment. Consumer misbehaviour occurs when someone violates the socially accepted norms of conduct in a consumption situation. However, it can also be extended to include other behaviours that have some negative consequences for consumers or society or the environment. Consumer misbehaviour can be categorized as abnormal and illegal behaviours. Compulsive buying behaviour is one form of abnormal behaviour and it can make a person repeatedly engage in the behaviour in such a way that it would eventually cause some harm to the person.

■ There are many motives for consumer misbehaviour including the temptation to fulfil some unfulfilled aspirations, the desire to seek thrill and adventure, lack of moral constraint, some perceived coherence and affiliation with a group, strong and negative attitudes against capitalism and firms working within it, situational factors like crowding or being in a group of people and some rationalistic assessment of risks and rewards.

■ We live in a society which is dominated by a consumerist culture. Sometimes, though, marketing activities may be perceived as too controlling, too intrusive and being too powerful in shaping our desires, feelings, attitudes and consumption habits. Some consumers do not like the idea of not being in control of their lives and rebel against corporate and marketing culture. There are many instances in which consumers misbehave towards the marketing activities involving product, price, distribution, marketing communication, marketing research and even employees of the firm.

QUESTIONS

1. What is consumer misbehaviour? Why do consumers engage in such behaviour?

2. Does marketing encourage consumption so far as to make it damaging to the individual and to society?

3. Have you ever engaged in any of the activities summarized in Tables 12.1 and 12.2? To what extent do you consider this to be misbehaviour? Why, or why not? What are the implications of your stance for marketing, for consumers and for society?

4. Is marketing at fault for, for example, making shoplifting easy, for encouraging binge-drinking, for encouraging aspirations to unrealistic self-images?

5. Are we all too willing to buy things which damage the planet (e.g. cars, fur, etc.)? What shall we do as consumers and as marketers to stop such misbehaviour?

FURTHER READING

Klein N (2001) No Logo, Flamingo, London. A wonderfully irreverent – but not irrelevant – exposition on anti-capitalism. This one will make you think as much as Packard's *Hidden Persuaders* (Chapter 1).

Gabriel Y and **Lang** T (1995) The Unmanageable Consumer, Sage, London. As well as exploring consumer's behaviour in terms of 'chooser', 'communicator', hedonist' and so on, Gabriel and Yang also delve into the darker side of consumer behaviour: 'consumer as rebel', 'consumer as activist'.

PART 3: JOURNAL ARTICLE

Consumer Behaviour in an Unregulated Market: The Satisfactions and Dissatisfactions of Illicit Drug Consumption

J A Fitchett and A Smith

Reproduced from Journal of Consumer Behaviour, Vol 1 No 4 (2002) 355–368.

Introduction

> Opium! dread agent of unimaginable pleasure and pain! What solemn chords does it now strike upon my heart! What heart-quaking vibrations of sad and happy remembrances! (Thomas De Quincey, 1971)

There are few products currently available to today's mass consuming public that can ever hope to have conferred upon them the favourable recommendations and testimonials equivalent to those expressed by illicit drug users when describing their consumption experiences. Were it not for the potentially undesirable and unpleasant consequences that can occur as a result of their consumption, illicit drugs could be said to constitute an ideal, almost perfect consumer product in the sense that they offer potential consumers immense gratification and satisfaction. But satisfaction from drug consumption can never be guaranteed, regardless of the precautions and safeguards users may try to establish. The structure of the illicit drug market and the type of satisfaction sought by users means that dissatisfaction always remains a very real and likely outcome of use.

This discussion presents some recent findings from an on-going project into consumption practices in illicit markets, which has come to focus mainly on the supply, distribution and consumption of illicit recreational drugs. The data highlighted a number of issues relating to contemporary aspects of consumer behaviour research, especially issues regarding responses to satisfactory and dissatisfactory consumption experiences. Whilst many respondents described their experiences with recreational drugs as highly pleasurable and satisfying, there were also number of occasions when experiences were reported as disappointing, dissatisfying and in some cases highly unpleasant. There are several explanations that can be used to account for variations in terms of levels of satisfaction gained from such experiences. The market for illicit drugs remains unpredictable and inconsistent which means that users have to accept that a degree of uncertainty is inherent to supply and consumption. The manner in which this disparity was dealt with and explained amongst the user group illustrates many of the complex behavioural responses that individuals employ to deal with such uncertainties.

The potential levels of satisfaction and dissatisfaction that can result from drug consumption are extreme, exceeding those normally sanctioned in legitimate marketing contexts. Analysis of the consumer behaviour of drug consumption thus stretches the dichotomy of satisfaction and dissatisfaction beyond conventional limits and boundaries. Satisfaction for most consumer products is usually a somewhat sedate and moderate experience. Consumers do not usually expect products to alter their mental states physiologically and psychologically in order to evaluate them as satisfactory. As long as products perform adequately and consumers are content and happy, the outcome can said to be satisfactory. For instance, consumers do not typically expect to feel elation and immense pleasure from the cleaning qualities of their soap-powder, just as it is unlikely to find consumers who expect to be psychologically aroused by the standard of service received from a financial service provider. Equally, whilst consumers may express disappointment and in some cases anger with products and services that fail to live up to expectations, few product failures require consumers to confront the prospect of physical harm and pain, criminal prosecution or even death.

To further complicate the issue, satisfaction and dissatisfaction of illicit drug use are so closely aligned to one another that the two cannot be easily separated or considered discrete. As DeQuincey's opening confession testifies, obtaining the feelings of immense pleasure and satisfaction from drug consumption also requires the user to anticipate and expect the possibility of experiencing potentially intense feelings of displeasure and dissatisfaction. The fact that recreational drug consumption is illicit, potentially dangerous and prohibited can for some groups (such as young people) add to the overall expected value of the experience (Preeble and Casey, 1987). Users do not necessarily perceive the risks associated with use to be sources of dissatisfaction, but rather conceptualize them as part of the expected satisfaction. Consequently, any policies that are seen to make drug use 'safer' or more acceptable could potentially result in the level of expectation and satisfaction decreasing for some users.

Consumer Satisfaction and Dissatisfaction (CS/D)

As the majority of articles and books dedicated to the topic eagerly remark, consumer satisfaction is a particularly significant area for consumer research. Satisfaction is considered to be the most preferable outcome of a market exchange for all concerned. Maddox (1982) comments that 'The satisfaction of consumer wants is the ultimate purpose of all economic and marketing processes', the logic of which implies that dissatisfaction is a most undesirable outcome for all concerned and consequently should be avoided if at all possible. Early explorations into the measurement and conceptualization of consumer satisfaction and dissatisfaction (CS/D) produced the disconfirmation model (Anderson, 1973; Oliver, 1977, 1980), in which consumer satisfaction is said to be achieved when pre-purchase expectations are fulfilled or excelled, dissatisfaction ensuing when expectations remain unfulfilled. Although much has been done to expand and modify this model of CS/D, the basic idea of disconfirmation remains the dominant concept is CS/D research. Cadotte et al. (1987) conclude that their findings support the disconfirmation paradigm although like many others propose that more attention is needed to improve the techniques used to measure CS/D (Peterson and Wilson, 1992). Beardon and Teel (1983) also found expectations and disconfirmation to be plausible determinants of satisfaction.

Since considerable attention has been given to the refinement of disconfirmation models it is difficult to summarize the main assumptions without some inevitable oversimplification. In the majority of its numerous forms the model assumes that consumers form expectations of products and services which they then use to evaluate outcome. There is much debate on how consumers establish these expectations, Gardinal (1994) proposing that consumers draw upon an aggregated or generic ideal formed by previous experiences, whereas Olsen and Dover (1979) suggest that expectations are manifestations of product specific beliefs. The model further assumes that consumers, once having considered the discrepancy between their expectations and experienced outcome, will make a positive or negative judgement and potentially use this judgement to inform future consumption decisions. Satisfaction may therefore lead to subsequent purchases, brand loyalty and a generally positive evaluation of the firm and its products, whereas dissatisfaction can lead complaining behaviour or taking business elsewhere (Hirschman, 1970). Although both Levesque and McDougall (1996) and Gronhaug and Gilly (1991) show that many dissatisfied customers remain loyal and do not change their behaviours, the model nevertheless remains predicated on the assumption that outcome (satisfaction or dissatisfaction) will influence future intentions and behaviour.

Conventional behaviourist readings of consumer action have developed a number of interpretations in an effort to explain why individuals may not cease to undertake those consumer activities that they have previously experienced as dissatisfactory. Post-purchase dissonance theory, for instance, suggests that when there is a large discrepancy between expected outcome and actual outcome individuals are in fact less likely to change their activities and subsequent consumer behaviour. Consumers deal with dissonance in a number of ways, including ignoring or distorting dissonant information as well as changing behaviour. However, whilst behaviourist readings may seem to provide an explanation for why consumers of illicit recreational drugs continue to consume despite negative and dissatisfactory consequences, there remains a question as to whether discrepancy between expectations and outcome are either large or unexpected in this context. Illicit drug users may not perceive a gap between possible negative outcomes and positive expectations, and if they do they may not perceive the gap to be larger than that present in any other 'everyday' consumption context. In fact consumers may well expect negative outcomes whilst simultaneously anticipating pleasurable ones. The prospect of uncertain, even negative outcomes may also be a contributory factor in the formation of positive expectations. The notion that illicit drug users are either ill informed or totally ignorant of potential outcomes of drug consumption does not seem credible. The assumption that users consider this type of consumption exotic is also questionable. The imposition of clearly demarcated boundaries of behavioural causes and determined responses, and the belief that consumers are rationally motivated to achieve satisfactory outcomes relative to preconceived and separate expectations, does not appear to adequately describe the illicit drug consumption experience.

The case of recreational drug use thus presents an interesting level of complexity to the generally accepted notion of disconfirmation. Assuming that recreational drug consumption is embarked upon freely and that the user can choose to cease or continue consumption at any time, one might assume that repeated inconsistency in terms of the likelihood of satisfactory and dissatisfactory outcomes would eventually lead to fewer and less habitual consumers. However, challenging this assumption reveals some of the more subtle and perhaps irrational aspects of consumer choice.

Recreational Drug Consumption

We will resist the temptation to either condemn or condone illicit drug consumption. The consumption of illicit substances does of course have some singular, perhaps even unique characteristics that sets it apart from other consumption situations and in this respect it is not totally comparable to the implications of the majority of everyday consumption decisions and choices. However, in terms of consumer behaviour theory there would appear to be little justification in isolating and distinguishing recreational drug consumption from other consumption scenarios. Recreational drugs are commodities like any other which are desired, purchased and consumed in much the same way as mass consumer goods (Merton, 1982; Hirschman, 1992). Accepting this premise implies that the same theoretical assumptions and conceptual frameworks that are applied by consumer researchers to investigate 'normal' consumption behaviour are equally applicable to an analysis of illicit drug use. As Henderson (1997) comments:

> Although young people cannot be regarded as an homogeneous group and there is distinct segmentation in the market for their leisure services, young people approach soft drugs in the same rational, matter-of-fact way they deal with other consumer goods. (Henderson, 1997)

Existing theories of consumer behaviour do not justify considering recreational drug use as fundamentally different to other types of product use. Distinctions that differentiate illicit drug use from other types of consumption have validity in the context of prevailing social and moral beliefs rather than to the effects and consequences of use (Hoffman, 1990; D'Angelo, 1994). The categorization of substances as 'illicit/illegal', whilst perhaps being socially and morally defensible, does not adequately represent the reality of their consumption or indeed the similarities and differences between different types of illicit drug and other substances freely and legally available to consumers (Henderson, 1997). In terms of effect, dependency and lifestyle for instance, amphetamine use should probably be considered more akin to alcohol consumption rather than to heroin or cocaine use although this distinction tends not to be acknowledged either legally or culturally.

The study intentionally avoids considering the consumption of substances that are widely acknowledged to be physically addictive because the dependency consumers have to these substances has a dramatic effect on the capacity to make positive and controlled choices about future consumption. This study limits its enquiry to specific types of drug consumption, namely those involving the use of Cannabis, '*Acid*', amphetamines, '*Ecstasy*'[1] or a combination of these substances. There is little evidence to suggest that these 'soft' drugs physically addictive, unlike drugs such as heroin or crack cocaine which can induce physical dependence in the user (Printz, 1997). Contrary to many popular media portrayals, in the majority of cases recreational drug users maintain socially integrated lifestyles (Frey, 1997; Miron and Zwiebel, 1987) that are comparable to their non-drug taking peers. The issue of addiction is, however, far from straightforward or clearly defined. Many 'legal' substances such as alcohol and tobacco can be considered 'addictive' and the notion of addiction has also been applied to compulsive behaviour associated with non-narcotic substances such as food, as well as activities such as shopping and excessive eating (Faber and O'Guinn, 1992; Elliott, 1994; Elliott *et al.*, 1996). But whilst the compulsive eater or shopper (or amphetamine user) may experience distress upon deprivation, it is not directly comparable to that suffered by the narcotic addict (Schur, 1963), and can be attributable to socio-economic or personality characteristics (Rindfleisch *et al.*, 1997) rather than to physical dependency. Whilst there are cases in which users of recreational drugs have developed what appear to be compulsive dependencies, the vast majority of users are able to sustain their drug consumption without any signs of addiction, just as the majority of individuals do not develop an addiction to shopping or eating.

Recreational Drug Use in a Society of Desire

Although it is arguably more difficult to guarantee and expect satisfactory experiences from recreational drug use than from other consumption-related pursuits, it is worth noting that dissatisfaction can be interpreted as not only a prolific characteristic of consumer society, but one of its necessary and inevitable conditions. Campbell (1987) and Falk (1994) both suggest that consumer society operates through the promotion of a social code in which individuals perceive and anticipate ideal future states which are then attempted to be achieved through consumer-related pursuits. This position is closely related to Lacan's notion of desire, where the self is defined by a basic sense of lack and a drive to pursue and find reconciliation.

For Campbell (1987) disparity between ideal anticipation and material realization is inevitable simply because individual ideal expectations are by their very nature specific and unbounded by material reality and temporality. Modern consumption is not only constrained in this regard but also principally designed around mass standardization of products and services. Consumer culture constructs and represents commodity consumption as a principle source of pleasure and satisfaction by promoting the sign and the image over material referents. The relationship between the material basis of commodities and the images that surround them is in many cases virtually non-existent (Baudrillard, 1998). However, rather than abandoning consumption as a tenable source of satisfaction, consumers attribute dissatisfaction to specific commodities rather than to the system of objects itself (Baudrillard, 1996). Consequently consumers are in a continual cycle of lack, followed by desire, anticipation, realization, dissatisfaction and lack. This suggests that the pursuit of satisfaction in any consumption context is destined to fail. Consumer culture is fuelled by the institutionalization of desire and dissatisfaction, and it is therefore of little consequence whether consumers seek to satisfy their insatiable desires in illicit or legitimate market contexts.

One might conclude that such arguments imply that recreational drug users are in fact more socially aware than those consumers who choose to pursue their desires through legitimate channels because of an acceptance of the inevitable likelihood that consumption experiences might be dissatisfactory and unfulfilling. However, whilst it may be true that consumption and consumer society invoke dissatisfaction, it is also true that most consumers act as if satisfaction of desire is possible. The key issue is not whether consumers can ever be satisfied but rather why some seek to maximize satisfaction by the use of recreational drugs despite the increased risk of dissatisfaction and other potentially physical and social consequences.

In light of these considerations, the purpose of the present enquiry is to establish consumers expectations of illicit recreational drug consumption, and more specifically, to consider the relevance of existing prevailing assumptions concerning CS/D in this type of consumption. In order to achieve this, the manner in which illicit drug users respond to and deal with dissatisfactory and satisfactory outcomes needs to be considered, as well the impact such outcomes have on consumers' future intentions regarding use.

The main objective of the field research was to collect the experiences, opinions and views of recreational drug users in order to establish some of their motivations and expectations for drug consumption, together with some of the considerations taken into account when deciding to cease or continue using recreational drugs. Through the assistance of a community youth scheme organizer, access was gained to a youth group in a town on the Clyde estuary near Glasgow in Scotland. The group provided a venue where young people in the local area could go during the evenings and where they could socialize, play pool and table tennis, and talk informally to the group organizers. The youth group was not intended to directly tackle drugs-related issues and those attending were not necessarily involved with recreational drug consumption although the prevalence of drug use in the local area (Hammersley *et al.*, 1997) was such that the vast majority of young people attending the group indicated that they frequently used recreational drugs and had done so for some time.

Three group discussions were held with members of the youth group over a period of two months. Two experienced qualitative researchers led the sessions and the roles of facilitator and observer were interchanged in accordance with the flow of social discourse that emerged during the session. During each session between eight and 16 members of the youth group voluntarily joined in the discussion for varying amounts of time. Some members joined the group and discussed their opinions and views for over an hour, whereas other joined in only for a few moments at a time. The sensitivity of the topic area and the informal nature of the group meant that no more structure could be imposed upon the data collection than this. During each session, each lasting for approximately four hours, most of the young people present joined in the discussion for varying lengths of time. At the request of the young people present the session was tape recorded rather than video recorded. No attempt was made to collect personal details or demographics from the participants. Discussions from each session were transcribed as accurately as possible, although accurate transcription of group conversation from the audio tapes was at times difficult. In addition to the transcript data, notes and transcripts from debrief sessions undertaken by the researchers after each session were used to enhance understanding of session transcripts.

For obvious reasons, the opinions and views of recreational drug users was an important source of data for the project. There are, however, many groups other than the users themselves that have knowledge and experience of recreational drug consumption, and who could provide valuable data for the project. The descriptive depth of the collected data was enhanced by consulting and interviewing representatives of these other interest groups. Qualitative research can be greatly enhanced by triangulating and collaborating different sources with one another because the focus of study is often complex and multi-dimensional (Wilson and Hutchinson, 1991). The differences and similarities in the accounts given, both within and between different groups, enables this 'thickness' to be represented in analysis (Geertz, 1979). To provide the much needed context for the comments expressed during the youth group sessions, a series of three one-hour interviews was also conducted with two police officers involved with drugs education in Scotland, and two drugs squad officers. Three representatives of government health promotion departments were also interviewed who had responsibility for young people and addiction in various areas of Scotland. Interview length varied between one and two hours depending on time constraints and the amount of depth respondents were willing to give. These groups were used to enhance the descriptive depth of the interpretations and to help prioritize relevant issues and themes although are not explicitly referred to here in the analysis.

General Findings

Consistent with a disconfirmation model of CS/D, user comments indicated that the decision to take recreation drugs was predicated on the expectation that use would result in a pleasurable and satisfying outcome. Some descriptions of previously satisfactory experiences with drug use were expressed in generic terms such as 'getting of your head' and 'feeling great', although satisfaction was also expressed in relation of the specific effects of the substance consumed. Acid, for instance, was generally considered satisfying because of the resulting hallucinogenic effects, whereas Ecstasy was valued for having the effect of reducing social inhibitions and generally making the user feel more sociable and friendly.

The findings suggest that users tend to emphasize positive experiences of drug consumption, preferring to recall pleasurable outcomes rather than those that were unpleasant. This is consistent with other CS/D research (Peterson and Wilson, 1992) showing that consumer self-reports invariably exhibit a positive bias. On several occasions during the interviews however, users openly acknowledged that some of their previous experiences had been disappointing and dissatisfying. Although the type of interview data collected does not enable the proportion of dissatisfactory outcomes to satisfactory ones to be determined, members of the group frequently referred to past occasions when drug use had resulted in unpleasant and dissatisfactory experiences. This would suggest that dissatisfaction is not an uncommon or unlikely outcome of drug use but accepted as an inevitable and unavoidable risk of consumption (Kalichman *et al.*, 1996; Schmid, 1998; Lee *et al.*, 1998).

Dealing with Dissatisfaction

Although drug consumers' behaviour would appear consistent with the disconfirmation model of CS/D when experiences are satisfactory and expectations are fulfilled by outcome, reactions to dissatisfying experiences when expectations are unfilled are not consistent with the model. Contrary to Hirschman's (1970) findings for instance, users do not react by complaining to suppliers (voice), or by showing any inclination to seek out alternative suppliers in future (exit).

Whilst the availability and supply of recreational drugs in the area studied seemed to be extensive and widespread, and none of the users indicated that they had any difficulty in obtaining drugs, the illicit nature of the market means that users are more reluctant to approach unknown dealers for drugs if existing dealers supply poor quality substances. This may in part provide some explanation for a lack of supplier switching behaviour.

> Interviewer: So who do you buy your Acid and Ecstasy from?
>
> Female 1: You'll buy it anywhere you can get it, but usually from someone you know and who you've got it from in the past . . .
>
> Interviewer: Why do you use the same . . . .
>
> Female 1: I'm not going to just go up to any [body] in the street and say 'you got any acid pal'. Even if he was dealing he'd probably give you shite anyway. You don't know him and he don't know you.
>
> Male 1: You'll have a dealer that you know, and he'll say, 'I've got two cuts of hash; this one's shite, this one's OK, you should take that one'. Whereas if you didn't know them they wouldn't do that. They'd probably give you shite.

Supply is informal and relies upon tacit knowledge of local dealers (see Soref, 1981). Users typically purchase drugs from acquaintances and occasionally undertake to supply small quantities to their friends themselves. The fact that distribution and supply is structured in this way may have considerable influence of relative judgements of risk. The willingness to trust family and friends above more 'credible' sources of information, is well documented in relation to consumption

(Smith *et al.*, 1996; Frewer *et al.*, 1996), and since illicit drug supply is a particularly uncertain and risky context of exchange, this effect would be expected to be heightened.

The specific and tacit nature of distribution means that consumer response to satisfaction and dissatisfaction in this market differs in some key respects to comparable responses in legitimate markets. Users do not have the same opportunity to change suppliers as they would in conventional marketing contexts and as a consequence users tended to show tolerance towards suppliers that occasionally provide drugs that are dissatisfactory because finding alternative sources was risky. The apathetic reaction to suppliers who may supply low-quality drugs can also be explained by the fact that there is no guarantee that alternative suppliers would be capable of providing drugs of any higher quality since there is no reliable measure that users (or dealers) can apply to determine the quality of consistency of the substances being sold (Jacobs *et al.*, 1987). Recreational drugs are typically passed down a long chain of dealers and suppliers before reaching the user and at each stage the substance can be modified and diluted with potentially any number of non-narcotic substitutes. By the time the dealer sells the drug to the user it is highly unlikely that either party can say with any degree of certainty what the substance being bought actually contains. Users are aware of this uncertainty and consequently do not necessarily attribute poor-quality drugs with particular suppliers and dealers but rather accept it as an unavoidable and uncontrollable risk of drug use.

> Interviewer: How do you know which is the good stuff to buy?
>
> Female 1: After a while you get to know whose giving good stuff and whose giving you shite . . .
>
> Female 2: No I don't agree, that's shite, you don't know anything, you don't know what they are putting in sulph, or f*****g[2] eccy, and to be honest you don't care . . .
>
> Male 2: It's wicked, you never know what they are putting in it.
>
> Male 1: How the f**k are you going to know what you're getting when the c**t selling it to you probably hasn't got a f*****g clue anyway?
>
> Female 3: You just take it.
>
> Female 2: You just don't care.

There would therefore seem to be little reason for the consumer to believe that changing suppliers will necessarily improve the chance of purchasing drugs of a higher quality and which are more likely to produce more satisfying experiences. Taking the implicit nature of supplier–consumer relationships together with the inconsistency of the product itself into account, it thus becomes problematic to assume that drug users will respond to dissatisfaction in the exactly the same way as consumers in legitimate/legal markets.

Despite the obvious differences between illicit and legitimate markets, the manner in which drug users cope with, and respond to dissatisfaction illustrates some of the problems with the disconfirmation model of CS/D when applied to more general instances of consumer behaviour. Because of the above-mentioned conditions of the market for illicit recreational drugs, users do not necessarily expect a satisfactory outcome every time they undertake consumption but rather accept that dissatisfaction is a very real and likely eventuality. Reactions to dissatisfaction may not therefore have any bearing on future behavioural intentions as the disconfirmation model suggests. Considering drug users' behavioural and attitudinal responses to various outcomes of drug consumption shows some of the strategies and belief systems that consumers develop to deal with dissatisfactory consumption outcomes which go beyond the limited reactions allowed for in the disconfirmation model of CS/D.

During the group discussion users drew on several discourses to justify continued drug consumption despite the likelihood of unpleasant and dissatisfactory outcomes. The various justifications for future use can be grouped into roughly two categories, the first involving some form of denial and the second involving deferment of effects to other causes.

Denial

The most common reaction to the interviewer's questions regarding the inevitability of dissatisfaction was to adopt a fatalistic attitude towards continued drug use. Although none of the users interviewed denied that they were aware of the potentially dissatisfactory outcomes of drug consumption, in practice they often disregarded this knowledge, preferring instead to take their chances with continued use.

Interviewer: What about the chances of taking bad Acid?

Female 2: You don't think about it, you think that it won't happen to me.

Female 1: What's the point in worrying about it – you can't do f**k all about it so why worry?

Male 3: ... I think that – I am still here after I have taken it so it can't be that bad.

Interviewer: Do you worry about the possibility of it being ...

Male 3: No, it is basically, 'f**k it I'll try it': If it f**ks you up – too bad.

Female 3: You see when you have acid and you have a bad trip you are like that [gesture: freaked out] and you think o' shit, I am never taking that shit again, it f**ks your head up. You get paranoid. Sometimes you say to yours self 'if you have a bad experience with it you don't go and take it again' but sometimes you don't. Other times you think 'f**k it' it wasn't that bad I'll take it again.

Interviewer: What about longer term effects?

Female 2: That doesn't bother you, you just don't think about it. You don't care. You don't care until it happens to you. The only people that tell you about these ill effects are people who have never taken drugs before. They're all just making up all these things. They say to you 'just say no'. They don't really know what it is doing and how it makes you feel.

Since the user is incapable of controlling the outcome of drug use to a great extent, he or she seems to react by abdicating personal responsibility for these negative consequences, giving them no little consideration when contemplating further use. Instead of making reasoned and balanced judgement to construct future expectations, users only take into account those aspects that they consider to have some notion of personal control in determining and since the quality and effect of the drugs themselves are uncontrollable, users tend to dismiss or deny this effect when forming expectations for further use.

Deferment and Displacement

One of the most significant contradictions in the interview data is the manner in which users attribute the causes of dissatisfactory and satisfactory outcomes. When users described previously pleasurable and satisfying experiences with recreation drug use, they tended to associate the cause of this satisfaction with the narcotic effect of the drug being consumed. When users took an Ecstasy tablet and felt sociable, friendly, in a good mood, or other satisfactory outcomes, this was attributed to the Ecstasy tablet itself. However, when dissatisfactory experiences occurred as a consequence of taking a tablet, users did not apply the same reasoning in attributing the cause of this dissatisfaction. The assumption of disconfirmation models of CS/D that dissatisfying experiences will result in consumers re-evaluating their consumption expectations and refrain from further consumption is not supported by these findings. As Burns and Perkins (1996) suggest, consumers can draw on several strategies when dealing with sub-optimal outcomes that deflect the attribution of dissatisfaction from the products performance. Rather than associating sub-optimal or dissatisfying outcomes with the product, consumers can employ several post-purchase rationalizations such as attributing dissatisfaction to uncontrollable external factors, claiming that they expected and anticipated that dissatisfaction would be a likely outcome, blaming their own state of mind, and if all such strategies seem inappropriate denying that the outcome was in fact dissatisfactory. Users seemed to draw upon a range of these strategies to rationalize dissatisfactory outcomes of recreation drug consumption rather than attributing the dissatisfaction to the drug itself. In the following excerpt for instance, the user identifies her own mental and physical condition as the most likely cause of variation in the effects of Ecstasy consumption, rather than attributing different experiences to the unreliability of the substance being consumed.

> Female 1: You get different feelings on different tabs and Eccy. On some you will feel like, hyper, and dead honest and friendly, and on others you feel. *(Imitating comatose, drowsiness)* and you just want to take it easy, you think 'I just want my bed'. Some eccy's you take and you are like this, and others you take are like that, that's just how it is.
>
> Interviewer: Do the different effects you feel make you think that they are different substances?

Female 2: It depends what mood you are in when you take it. If you're feeling out of it then eccy will just make you feel more out of it and it will probably be shite, but if you're O.K and want a laugh then it's great fun.

Here the user (female 2) is displacing the cause of the negative effects of use away from the substance being consumed and locates it elsewhere, despite being aware that ecstasy tablets can contain several substances other than MDMA and which may have the effect of a stimulant, a suppressant or some other kind of effect altogether.

Satisfaction in Expectation

Many of the discussions developed contradictory lines of argument which to a certain extent inhibited clear and explicit interpretation. Of primary significance, however, was the lengths users were prepared to go to maintain positive expectations toward future occasions of drug consumption. The confused logic and blurred premises on which these denials were founded indicated that the belief that drug consumption was expected to be rewarding and satisfying was in itself something the users valued and sought to maintain, regardless of the actual outcomes of drug consumption – whether satisfying or dissatisfying.

Female 2: My favourite is acid, if I could get it I would take it every f*****g day, I love the f*****g stuff. You see, round here, sometimes you can't get acid, nobody has got any, but that doesn't stop you wanting it! And when you get it you think that it's f*****g great.

Interviewer: Are you ever disappointed . . .

Female 2: It depends, sometimes its great and other times it just – you know – O.K. But you're still going to take it. You never know.

The expectations that users had for further drug consumption were not primarily determined by their actual previous experiences with drugs but by a somewhat idealized expectation. In short, users seemed to believe that future drug use was more than likely to be satisfying because they expected and wanted it to be so, rather than because their experiences indicated that it would be. Although users' responses to dissatisfaction would seem to be inconsistent with a disconfirmation model of CS/D they correspond to several theories of consumer culture (Campbell, 1987; Baudrillard, 1998) which propose that much of the pleasure of modern consumption stems from the anticipation of future satisfaction rather than from actual experiences in the market (Fournier and Guiry, 1993). Falk (1994) for instance, comments that since consumer expectations are developed independently of consumer goods, that is, they are formed as hypothetical outcomes to idealized situations, dissatisfaction is an inevitable and likely outcome of consumption because products are rarely able to meet the diverse and individual requirements of consumers' imagined expectations.

Conclusions

The findings of this preliminary investigation into the satisfactions and dissatisfactions of recreational drug use suggest that alternative models are required to frame and understand consumers reactions to dissatisfaction. Contrary to the prevailing assumptions underpinning the dominant paradigm in CS/D, dissatisfaction cannot be represented solely in terms of a notional evaluative judgement made by the consumer regarding a product's performance. In the case of recreational drug consumption dissatisfaction would seem to be as likely an expected outcome as satisfaction and it may well be the case that similar consumer evaluations structure other, more mainstream consumption encounters. The reality of consumer society is that consumers' desired expectations are often not realized in the marketplace (Campbell, 1987). Occasionally recreational drugs will inevitably fail to supply the desired effect, just as a new car or outfit will not always radically improve lifestyle. The nature of contemporary consumption requires individuals to invest and associate their hopes, dreams and desires in consumer products, regardless of actual outcome and product performance. Consumption dreaming is in itself a valuable and satisfactory pastime which is often quite discreet and separate to actual outcomes of consumption and it would appear, at least with recreational drugs, that consumers are aware of this disparity. What is of primary interest for consumer researchers is the manner in which consumers cope with this occasional inevitable dissatisfaction. As the CS/D disconfirmation paradigm suggests, in some instances consumers may complain or change future behaviour if products fail to perform to a desired standard but there are also many other responses to dissatisfaction that the consumer can adopt. When consumption situations are less formal and less regulated and the consumer cannot reasonably expect to exercise any evaluative judgement that can improve the likelihood of a satisfactory outcome, consumers may simple resign themselves to the possibility of dissatisfaction. When the consumer has some notional level of control over outcome then they will probably adopt a set of behaviours that seek to maximize the chances of satisfaction but in many consumption situations the consumer has no such control and must place themselves at the mercy of the market and the conditions of consumption if they wish to experience satisfactory outcomes. Perhaps the most interesting implication of this research project has been the insight it has provided into consumers deferment and denial behaviours regarding dissatisfaction. Whatever the effects of the Ecstasy and Acid have been like in the past, there is always the chance that the next hit will be great fun. The potential rewards will always outweigh previous dissatisfactions and there are several strategies that we as consumers can employ to ensure that we do not let past failures overly inhibit the opportunity to experience the satisfactions of our preferred consumer products in the future.

Notes

1. The group from which the present data was collected did not refer to recreational drugs by their clinical or pharmaceutical names but used various slang

terms. They tended to refer to Cannabis as *Dope, Weed* or *Blow. Acid* is the common term for Lysergic Acid Diethylamide (LSD). *Ecstasy* or *Eccy* refers to Methylenedioxyamphetamine (MDMA), and *Sulph, powder, whizz* or *Speed* refers to amphetamines.

2. Respondents used a number of expletives when describing their experiences with illicit drugs. So as not to offend readers, these expletives have been removed from the excerpts.

REFERENCES

Anderson R E (1973) Consumer Dissatisfaction: The Effect of Disconfirmed Expectancy on Perceived Product Performance, Journal of Marketing Research, Vol 10 pp 38–44

Baudrillard J (1996) The System of Objects, Blackwell Verso, London

Baudrillard J (1998) Consumer Society: Myths and Structures, Sage, London

Beardon W O and **Teel** J E (1983) Selected Determinants of Consumer Satisfaction and Complaint Reports, Journal of Marketing Research, Vol 20 pp 21–28

Burns D J and **Perkins** D S (1996) Accounts in Post-Purchase Behaviour: Excuses Justifications and Meta Accounts, Journal of Consumer Satisfaction, Dissatisfaction and Complaining Behaviour, Vol 9 pp 144–157

Cadotte E R, **Woodruff** R B and **Jenkins** R L (1987) Expectations and Norms in Models of Consumer Satisfaction, Journal of Marketing Research, Vol 24 pp 305–314

Campbell C (1987) The Romantic Ethic and Spirit of Modern Consumerism, Blackwell, Oxford

D'Angelo E (1994) The Moral Culture of Drug Prohibition, Humanist, September/October, pp 3–7

De Quincey T (1971) Confessions of an English Opium Eater, Penguin

Elliott R (1994) Addictive Consumption: Function and Fragmentation in Postmodernity, Journal of Consumer Policy, Vol 17 pp 159–179

Elliott R, **Eccles** S and **Gourney** K (1996) Revenge, Existential Choice and Addictive Consumption, Psychology and Marketing, Vol 13 No 8 pp 753–768

Faber R J and **O'Guinn** T (1992) A Clinical Screener for Compulsive Buying, Journal of Consumer Research, Vol 19 pp 459–469

Falk P (1994) The Consuming Body, Sage, London

Fournier S and **Guiry** M (1993) An Emerald Green Jaguar, A House on Nantucket and an African Safari: Wish Lists and Consumption Dreams in a Materialist Society, Advances in Consumer Research, Vol 20

Frewer L J, **Howard** C, **Hedderley** D and **Shepherd** R (1996) What Determines Trust in Information about Food-Related Risks? Underlying Psychological Constructs, Risk Analysis, Vol 16 No 4 pp 473–486

Frey B S (1997) Drugs, Economics and Policy, Economic Policy, October

Gardinal S R, **Clemons** D S, **Woodruff** R B, **Schuman** D W and **Burns** M J (1994) Comparing Consumers' Recall of Prepurchase and Postpurchase Product Evaluation Experiences, Journal of Consumer Research, Vol 20, March, pp 548–560

Geertz C (1973) The Interpretation of Cultures, Fontana Press, London

Gronhaug K and **Gilly** M C (1991) A Transaction Cost Approach to Consumer Dissatisfaction and Complaint Actions, Journal of Economic Psychology, Vol 12 pp 165–183

Hammersley R, **Ditton** J and **Main** D (1997) Drug-Use and Sources of Drug Information in a 12–16 year old school sample, Drugs, Education, Prevention and Policy, Vol 4 No 3 pp 231–241

Henderson S (1997) Ecstasy: Case Unsolved, Pandora, Glasgow

Hirschman A O (1970) Exit, Voice and Loyalty, Harvard University Press, Cambridge MA

Hirschman E C (1992) The Consciousness of Addiction: Towards a General Theory of Compulsive Consumption, Journal of Consumer Research, Vol 19 pp 155–179

Hoffman J P (1990) Ideology, Racism and Morality: Investigating the Structural Origins of Drug Prohibition, Free Inquiry in Creative Sociology, Vol 18 No 2 pp 127–138

Jacobs M R, **Leblanc** A E and **Marshman** J A (1987) Understanding Drug Use, in: **Heller** T, **Gott** M and **Jeffery** C (eds), Drug Use and Misuse: A Reader, John Wiley & Sons, pp 43–49

Kalichman S, **Heckman** T and **Kelly** J (1996) Sensation Seeking as an Explanation for the Association between Substance Abuse and HIV-Related Risky Sexual Behavior, Archives of Sexual Behavior, Vol 25 No 2 pp 141–154

Lee C; **Yang** S and **Hazard** B (1998) The Contingent Effects of Risk Perception on Risk-Taking Behavior: Adolescent Participation Orientation and Marijuana Use, Journal of Youth and Adolescence, Vol 27 No 1 pp 17–27

Levesque T J and **McDougall** G H G (1996) Customer Dissatisfaction: The Relationship between Types of Problems and Customer Response, Canadian Journal of Administrative Sciences, Vol 13 No 3 pp 264–276

Maddox R N (1982) The Structure of Consumers' Satisfaction: Cross Product Comparisons, Journal of the Academy of Marketing Science, Vol 10 No 1 pp 37–53

Merton R K (1982) Social Theory and Social Structure, Macmillan

Miron J A and **Zwiebel** J (1995) The Economic Case Against Drug Prohibition, Journal of Economic Perspectives

Oliver R L (1977) Effect of Expectation and Disconfirmation on Postexposure Product Evaluations: An Alternative Interpretation, Journal of Applied Psychology, Vol 64 No 2 pp 480–486

Oliver R L (1980) A Cognitive Model of the Antecedents and Consequences of Satisfaction Decisions, Journal of Marketing Research, Vol 17 pp 460–469

Olsen J C and **Dover** P A (1979) Disconfirmation of Consumer Expectations Through Product Trial, Journal of Applied Psychology, Vol 64 No 2 pp 179–189

Peterson R A and **Wilson** W R (1992) Measuring Customer Satisfaction: Fact and Artifact, Journal of the Academy of Marketing Science, Vol 20 No 1 pp 61–71

Preeble E and **Casey** J J (1987) Taking Care of Business – The Heroin User's Life on the Street, in: **Heller** T, **Gott** M and **Jeffery** C (eds), Drug Use and Misuse: A Reader, John Wiley & Sons, pp 104–112

Printz A (1997) Do European Drugs Policies Matter? Economic Policy, October

Rindfleisch A, **Burroughs** J E and **Denton** F (1997) Family Structure, Materialism, and Compulsive Consumption, Journal of Consumer Research, Vol 23 pp 312–325

Schmid H (1998) Female and Male Students' Intention to Accept Illicit Drugs as a Function of Their Risk Perception and Risk Taking, Swiss Journal of Psychology, Vol 57 No 1 pp 47–56

Schur E M (1963) Narcotic Addiction in Britain and America, Tavistock, London

Smith A P, **Young** J A and **Gibson** J (1997) Consumer Information and BSE: Credibility and Edibility, Risk Decision and Policy, Vol 2 No 1 pp 1–11

Soref M J (1981) The Structure of Illegal Drug Markets: An Organizational Approach, Urban Life, Vol 10 No 3 pp 329–352

Wilson H S and **Hutchinson** S A (1991) Pearls, Pith and Provocation: Triangulation of Qualitative Methods: Heideggarian Hermeneutics and Grounded Theory, Qualitative Health Research, Vol 1 No 2 pp 263–276

PART 3: JOURNAL ARTICLE

Advancing Means–End Chains by Incorporating Heider's Balance Theory and Fournier's Consumer–Brand Relationship Typology

A G Woodside

Reproduced from Psychology and Marketing, Vol 21 No 4 (2004) 279–294.

In consumer research on means–end chains, the meanings that a consumer associates with a product, service, or specific brand are represented hierarchically. The lowest level depicts an object's attributes – those that are physical or concrete, and those that are abstract (e.g. a brand's image). The remaining levels are consumers' outcomes including functional and psychosocial consequences, followed by consumers' instrumental and terminal values (see Gutman, 1997).

Laddering is a frequently used research method for electing means–end chains. Traditionally, laddering is a metaphor representing a respondent's answers to a series of 'why' probes, typically starting with the attributes that distinguish more-desired from less-desired alternatives. Asking for successive elicitations creates a chain of elements leading from a product's attributes to one or a few terminal values: Each successive concept learned becomes a subgoal for the final goal. Gutman and Reynolds (1978) illustrate a resulting ladder elicited from a respondent in a study of breakfast cereal: crunchy : has body : stays with me : avoid snack : aids weight loss : improves appearance : romance. In the empirical research the present article describes, the questions, 'what makes you say that?' and 'what does that lead to?' are used in place of why probes. Becker (1998) emphasizes that 'why' requires a 'good' answer, one that makes sense and can be defended. Such answers are unlikely to reveal logical flaws and inconsistencies. Becker recommends using 'How?' questions.

> When I asked them [such questions] gave people more leeway, were less constraining, invited them to answer in any way that suited them, to tell a story that included whatever they thought the story ought to include in order to make sense. They didn't demand a 'right' answer, didn't seem to be trying to place responsibility for bad actions or outcomes anywhere. (Becker, 1998:59)

Because the scientific literature is compelling that most thinking is unconscious and consumers typically are unable to surface and report unconscious processes (unconscious processes often drive behaviour that consumers are unaware that they performed, e.g. see Bargh, 2002; Zaltman, 2003), advancing theory and research that inform knowledge of consumer unconscious processes is worthwhile. Heretofore, the value for consumer theory and research of means–end chains and the laddering method relates only implicitly to unconscious mental processes – and how laddering may help to surface unconscious thoughts. For example, direct questioning of how a cereal being crunchy aids a consumer's love life may cause a scoffing

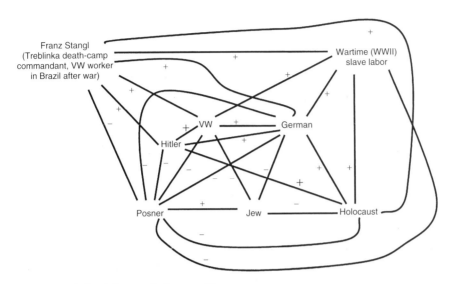

Figure A3.1   A Jewish couple buys a German car

response from the consumer. Asking the consumer a sequence of probing questions is a form of auto driving (cf. Heisley and Levy, 1991) research that may enable the consumer to surface unconscious thoughts that rarely enter conscious processing. Surfacing unconscious processes may result in tension and stress because unbalanced associations occur among concepts now in a consumer's working memory (cf. Heider, 1958). The thought, 'a Jewish couple buys a German car' (see Figure A3.1 and Woodside and Chebat, 2001) implies an example of such stress resulting from a surfacing of negatively valued concepts and images – some held unconsciously – with the positive experiences associating with buying a car highly prized for its design features. Advancing Heider's balance theory to person, brand and attribute (and attribute-to-benefit-to-instrumental and terminal values) enables more robust means–end chain laddering research because the resulting ladders may uncover and display stress and stress resolution, as well as harmonious associations.

Pieters *et al.* (1988) advocate following an alternative empirical method for means–end chains versus the more well-known laddering approach that Gutman and Reynolds (1978) demonstrate. Pieters *et al.* (1988) elicit people's reasons for wanting to do something or to pursue a goal rather than to name concrete features that they associate with a product. Bagozzi and Dabholkar (2000) apply the approach of Pieters *et al.* for mapping persons' cognitive schemas regarding a specific target, President Clinton. Whereas the Pieters *et al.* (1998) and Bagozzi and Dabholkar (2000) refinements are useful for describing how specific schemas accurately predict attitudes and intentions regarding future events, the advances below focus on framing means–end theory and research by consumers' recent lived experiences.

Heider's Balance Theory

Heider (1958, Chapter 7) distinguishes two types of relations between separate entities: unit and sentiment relations. 'Separate entities comprise a unit when they are perceived as belonging together. For example, members of a family are seen as a unit; a person and his deed belong together' (p 176). 'U denotes the cognitive unit between two entities, and notU the fact that the two entities are segregated' (p 201). A sentiment relation refers to the positive (L or_) or negative (DL or_) feelings or valuation that one gives to an entity, such as a person, activity or object.

These relations may be for dyads, triads or more complex cases, but all relations are from the perceiver's subjective point of view. Thus, although a brand may possess a given attribute or provide a specific benefit, if a consumer perceives the opposite, a notU relation results between a brand and such an attribute or benefit.

Heider (1958) describes the two relation concepts to result in four possibilities between two entities: 'U, notU, L, and DL'. He emphasizes:

> By a balanced state is meant a situation in which the relations among the entities fit together harmoniously; there is no stress toward change. A basic assumption is that sentiment relations and unit relations tend toward a balanced state. This means that sentiments are not entirely independent of the perceptions of unit connections between entities and that the latter, in turn, are not entirely independent of sentiments. Sentiments and unit relations are mutually interdependent. It also means that if a balanced state does not exist, then forces toward this state will arise. If a change is not possible, the state of imbalance will produce tension. (Heider, 1958, p. 201)

Unit and sentiment relations represent independent theoretical and empirical propositions grounded in cognitions (i.e. units) and affections (i.e. sentiments). When tension caused by imbalance arises in the mind of the individual, then the individual is likely to exercise some mental and physical effort to eliminate the tension.

> Unbalanced situations stimulate us to further thinking; they have the character of interesting puzzles, problems which make us suspect a depth of interesting background ... Stories in which the stress is laid on unbalanced situations are felt to have a deep psychological meaning. Dostoevski, for instance, describes again and again feelings full of conflict resulting from just such situations. (Heider, 1958:180–181)

Figure A3.2 summarizes the application of Heider's balance theory and related extensions to means–end chain laddering research. Note the grounding in Figure A3.2 includes 'prequel to action' to emphasize that if consumer research focuses on existing consumer–brand relationships (cf. Fournier, 1998), such relationships depend on specific purchase or use situations. A situation is defined as a conjunction of time, place, objects and person(s). Consequently, the lived experiences and top-of-mind attributes and benefits that a consumer identifies (to him- or herself and the interviewer) are contingent on the structure of the situation leading to brand purchase or use. Consequently, the situation informs the attributes–benefits–value associations.

The implication for research design is that means–end chains data for a given respondent should be collected for multiple situations some of which may be

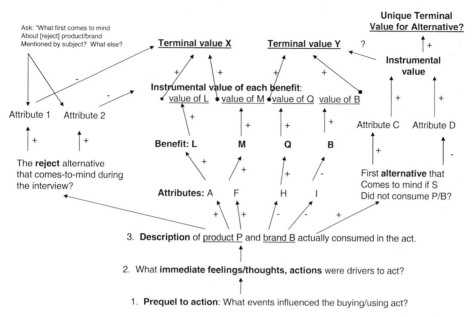

Figure A3.2 **Laddering sentiments**

relevant to the focal brand. A focal brand is defined as the one that the consumer names as used most often or identifies as the one used most recently; alternatively, a focal brand may be defined as the specific target chosen by the researcher – the primary focus of the study for which the researcher asks a respondent to describe – its product features and consequences in experiencing such product features and how these experiences relate to personal values. Asking informants individually to identify a focal brand for a given product category is a less reactive procedure comparatively; the researcher naming a target brand indicates possible self-validation problems – informants report perceptions about the brand mentioned by the researcher that may not relate much to the informants' past or future lives (cf. Feldman and Lynch, 1988). Thus, asking the informant to report on her most recent consumption behaviour and collecting means–end data with respect to Situation X as well as for Situation Y may be more relevant for the informant and reduces the occurrence of self-validity problems.

Figure A3.2 includes the assignment of sentiments (positive and negative signs) to associations in the resulting laddering steps. In Figure A3.2, note that Product P and Brand B associate negatively with Attribute I, and lack of I relates negatively with Benefit B (e.g. assume Benefit B is an informant's comment, 'good tasting mouthwash,' for a mouthwash attribute I). Figure A3.2 advances means–end chains by suggesting collecting data on the first alternative that comes to mind for the consumer for the recent lived experience in the focal situation. For example, 'If you had not consumed Brand B in Situation X, what might you have consumed instead?'

Figure A3.2 also asks for reject alternative information and implies the proposition that the respondent is easily able to surface a product/brand that would have been unacceptable for consumption in his or her recent lived experience.

Such rejection brand data are then followed by means–end probes to surface brand–attributes–values associations for unacceptable alternatives for use in the given situation. The brand strategist might ask here: how often, and for what situations, does my product and brand surface as the reject alternative? When rejection occurs, what attributes and personal values surface in the respondent's mind?

Fournier's Consumer–Brand Relationship Typology

Fournier (1998) extends the two-party social relationship metaphor to encompass the consumer and brands. She develops the consumer–brand relationship proposition, including anthropomorphizing the brand as an active relationship partner – at the level of consumers' lived experiences with their brands. Her proposal of 15 consumer–brand relationships include arranged marriages, casual friend, marriages of conveniences, committed partnerships, best friendships, compartmentalized friendships, kinships, rebounds, childhood friendships, courtships, dependencies, flings, enslavements, enmities, and secret affairs.

Using the advanced means–end chain laddering research that Figure A3.2 summarizes serves to complement and inform Fournier's consumer–brand relationship typology: Multiple consumer–brand relationship types are uncovered by collecting data within given situations of consumer–brand lived experiences, acceptable alternatives to these lived experiences, as well as rejected alternatives. Equally valuable are the data uncovering association streams of the three laddering paths (done, alternative, and rejected) to terminal values.

Applying the Advances in Means-End Chain Laddering Research

The following four case studies illustrate applications of advances in means–end chain laddering research. The four cases report two lived experiences for each of two subjects (Ss).

Method

In order to collect the data to examine the propositions, two subjects, Eric and Peter, were chosen to participate in two separate interviews each. Each subject is a senior in college in his early twenties living in an apartment on campus at a large university in the eastern USA. The interviews were conducted at the residences of the respondents at two different times during the day. The two situations under consideration for this study were the consumption of a beverage in the morning after waking up and the beverage consumption between eight o'clock and midnight on a Friday night. For the means–end chain laddering process described previously, each respondent was asked a series of 34 questions for each situation. The questions were designed to elicit responses that would provide the perceived attributes, benefits and consequences of the products consumed.

The respondents were also asked to provide alternative products that they might have chosen in each situation, as well as rejected products that would not be considered. The subjects were also asked questions pertaining to prior actions to the consumption of the beverage and about the situation itself, such as where it occurred and if anyone else was around. With the responses gathered from each subject an extended means–end chain (MEC) was created for each subject in each situation with the use of the theoretical model shown in Figure A3.2.

The extended MEC begins at the bottom with the prequel to the action discussed. This prequel is the event(s) that is believed to influence the action to occur. From this prior event there must be some sort of recognition, or immediate feelings or thoughts that act as drivers to act. Stemming from the driver is the action itself, or the product usage. The consumer describes of the product (what it was, how much was consumed, and what brand), and provides a brief description of the situation (when and where the action occurred, others present at the time). From these steps the entire MEC develops and builds up to the terminal values.

Identifying a specific lived consumption experience and situation provides theoretical ground for developing means–end chains based on the proposition that the consumption of a specific product and brand is acceptable in only certain situations. In fact, the same brand and product form may associate positively to one situation and negatively to alternative situations for the same consumer. Also, different attributes and benefits may come to mind for consumers of the same brand, depending on the usage situation that the consumer is thinking about (cf. Bearden and Woodside, 1978; Belk, 1974). Consequently, resulting means–end chains may be expected to vary contingent on the focal situations being described in consumers' lived experiences.

From the description of the product and the situation come the three distinct series of the extended MEC. On the left is the reject alternative and on the right is the alternative that would be considered. The centre of the model focuses on the product that was actually used or consumed. The separate attributes of the product or brand are laid out in order to get an idea of the benefits or consequences of each. This same questioning process is used to collect information for the alternative and reject products. After the benefits of the attributes is where the MEC begins to probe for the instrumental beliefs and values of the respondent. These beliefs are often unconsciously stored thoughts that the consumer may not connect but that actually play a role in their decision-making process. Some benefits may lead to the same values, and benefits from the alternative and the reject products can also tie into these same values. The model shows that the alternative and reject products may tie in with the entire means–end chain, which is why they should be considered when one is looking at the unconscious thinking of consumers. Finally, the chain concludes with terminal values or their core values and beliefs in the S's life.

Findings

Beverage Consumed on Monday Morning

For this situation each respondent answered questions about the first beverage they consumed on the day that the interviews took place. Eric went to bed around

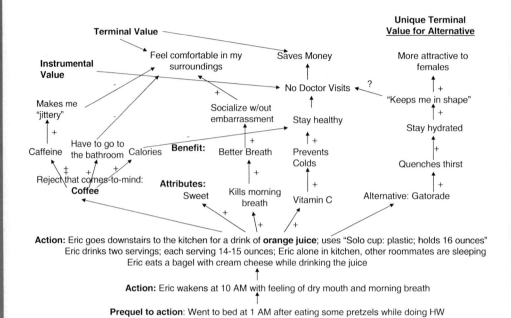

Action: Eric goes downstairs to the kitchen for a drink of **orange juice**; uses "Solo cup: plastic; holds 16 ounces"
Eric drinks two servings; each serving 14-15 ounces; Eric alone in kitchen, other roommates are sleeping
Eric eats a bagel with cream cheese while drinking the juice

Action: Eric wakens at 10 AM with feeling of dry mouth and morning breath

Prequel to action: Went to bed at 1 AM after eating some pretzels while doing HW

Figure A3.3   Tropicana Ladder

1:00 a.m. and did not have anything to drink before going to sleep. After waking up at 10:00 a.m. on Monday morning with a dry mouth and morning breath he went down to the kitchen in his apartment and poured a 16-ounce glass of Tropicana orange juice. Eric proceeded to have another glass of orange juice while he ate a bagel alone at the table. The attributes that he associates with Tropicana orange juice are that it tastes sweet, kills morning breath and contains vitamin C (see Figure A3.3).

No benefit was linked with the sweet taste, but sweet taste is an attribute that Eric remarked that he prefers. The benefit of killing morning breath was having better breath throughout the day, which was also a benefit that he did not believe any alternative drinks offered. Eric explained that he had always been told by his mother that he should drink a lot of orange juice to prevent getting a cold, which is the benefit of the product containing vitamin C. By preventing illness he believes that he would not have to visit the doctor, which was a positive relationship because he does not like paying the extra money or dealing with doctors in general. As an alternative Eric suggested that he also likes to drink Gatorade because it quenches his thirst and keeps him hydrated. Again, by staying hydrated he believes that he will be able to stay in better shape and remain healthier, which ties in with the benefits of the vitamin C in orange juice.

Having good breath is important for Eric because one of his main goals is to feel comfortable in his surroundings. By not having bad breath he felt that he could socialize with others and not worry about others smelling his breath.

Coffee is the product that Eric reports that he rejects because of caffeine, calories and causing him to have to go to the bathroom. The consequences of all of these attributes negatively connected with the value of feeling comfortable because each one posed a problem with comfort. Interestingly there were two other benefits that surfaced in this interview stemming from staying healthy and staying in shape. Eric felt that a result of staying in shape was that this would make him more attractive to females, which seemed to be a common theme with the four different situations. Saving money came up as a core value because in the interview he explained that he bought Tropicana orange juice even though it tended to be more expensive. He was willing to pay the price premium for the brand but overall he is looking to save money.

Peter spent Sunday night watching movies and eating popcorn with his girlfriend until about 2:00 a.m. when they went to bed. When he woke up around 11:00 a.m. on Monday morning his mouth was very dry from the popcorn and he had bad breath. He got out of bed and went to the refrigerator in the bedroom and pulled out the gallon jug of orange juice. He drank three 10-ounce servings directly from the jug while his girlfriend and roommate were asleep in the room. Peter does not recall the brand because he bought whatever was cheapest at the store, but he does know that it was not a major brand like Tropicana. His alternative product was apple juice and the rejected product was cranberry juice (see Figure A3.4).

The attributes that Peter described for the orange juice were that it was refreshing, it killed germs, and that it contained vitamin C. In the interview he remarked that he was not sure if the orange juice actually killed germs but this was what he guessed gave him better breath after drinking it. As a result of having better breath he said that he would actually be able to kiss his girlfriend because she did not like to taste his bad breath. Besides the fact that Peter does not like the taste of cranberry juice in general he also felt that it stained teeth with its red colouring, and caused saliva build-up that made him spit. These consequences can be negatively linked

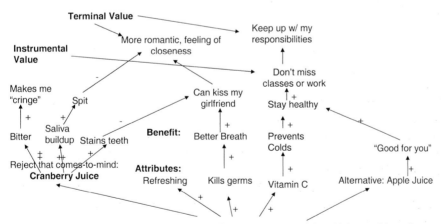

Action: Peter goes to the refrigerator in the bedroom for a drink of **orange juice**; drinks out of the gallon container Peter drinks three servings; each serving 8-10 ounces; Girlfriend and roommate are asleep in the room

Action: Peter wakens at 11 AM with feeling of dry mouth and bad breath

Prequel to action: Went to bed at 2 AM after eating popcorn and watching a movie w/ his girlfriend

Figure A3.4   Juice Ladder

with Peter being able to kiss his girlfriend. All of this leads up to the core value of romance and the feeling of closeness that Peter believes is important.

Peter mentioned that he believed that vitamin C prevents colds and would help him to stay healthy. He also felt that the alternative, apple juice, could help to stay healthy because it is 'good for you'. Staying healthy is important to Peter because another core value is that he likes to keep up with his responsibilities in life. He does not like to fall behind in schoolwork or to miss days at his job. Both respondents chose the same beverage for quite similar reasons but it did not turn out that their core values were also the same. There was the similarity of staying healthy but that is one of the only similarities. Also each respondent had a different relationship with their brand of choice. Using the relationships developed by Fournier (1998), Eric is in a committed partnership with the Tropicana brand, whereas Peter is a 'casual friend/buddy' with his brand of orange juice. Eric is in a long-term, voluntary union with Tropicana even though it is higher priced, because it is a brand that he knows and trusts. Peter buys more based on price; so as long as a certain brand is the cheapest he will continue to purchase it, but if a competitor suddenly becomes cheaper he will now buy that brand. There is no long-term commitment in the brand relationship.

Beverage Consumed Last Friday Night between 8:00 p.m. and Midnight

Both Eric and Peter describe themselves as heavy drinkers, drinking 10 beers on average four or five nights a week. This consumption has increased somewhat over the last couple of years but all throughout they have been 'beer drinkers'. Eric's situation on Friday night began when he invited friends over for pizza and to watch the game on TV (Figure A3.5). He had gone out earlier and bought two 30-packs of Busch Light for the evening, and his friends were expecting to drink when they arrived.

As the night progressed the group began to play drinking games and consume even greater amounts of beer. By midnight Eric recalls having about 12 cans of beer before going to sleep.

The attributes suggested for Busch Light beer are a smooth taste, it contains alcohol, and that it contains calories. The fact that the beverage contained alcohol seemed to be the most prominent reason for consuming the beer. The benefit of the alcohol is that it gets the person drunk, which makes it easier to socialize, but much like the calories in the beer the alcohol is also not healthy. The calories lead to getting fat and being less attractive to females. The alternative product to drink on a Friday night for Eric was vodka. Vodka was an alternative because it was stronger than beer, which would get him drunker, but this leads to having a hangover. The negative consequence of being so very drunk leads to being unattractive to females and conflict with the core values of feeling good both physically and emotionally.

The rejected product for Eric was wine; no specific brand, just wine in general. He reports not liking the taste of wine and he also perceives wine as a 'girly' drink. The bitter taste of the wine causes him to feel sick to his stomach, which has a negative relation to the core value of feeling good physically. The alcohol in beer,

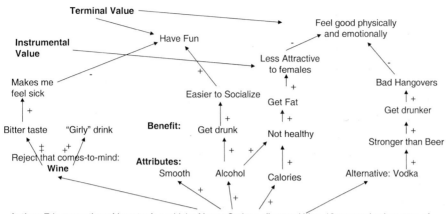

Figure A3.5   Beer, Pizza, TV, Friends (Eric)

which makes it easier to socialize, has a positive relationship with the value of having fun. Eric stressed that at his age he was more concerned with having a good time than with worrying about too many responsibilities, but he did see this mentality changing in the near future because of graduation.

The situation for Peter was different because of the setting but for the most part the MEC looked similar to that of Eric (see Figure A3.6). Peter had taken a test

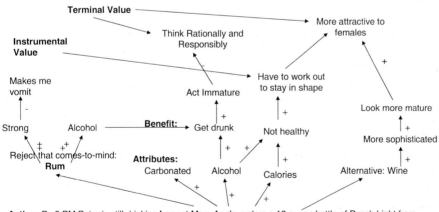

Figure A3.6   Beer, Pizza, TV, Friends (Peter)

earlier in the afternoon that he did not believe had gone very well. After the test he went down to the local bar, Mary Ann's, for happy hour. He met up with friend at the bar and they began to drink beer. By 8:00 p.m. Peter was still at the bar and he was still drinking bottles of Busch Light beer. He had about eight beers between 8:00 p.m. and the time he left the bar at 10:00 p.m. The attributes that Peter describes in Busch Light beer are that it is carbonated, and that it contains alcohol and calories. He could not explain what he thought the benefits of carbonation are, but this could be investigated in a follow-up interview if one was performed. Alcohol was the major attribute that Peter described in beer. The alcohol led to getting drunk and acting immature, which was negatively related to his core value of thinking rationally and responsibly. Peter mentioned rum as the rejected beverage because of a bad experience that he had in the past. Due to this bad experience he cannot drink any rum because it makes him vomit.

Calories were not a major concern for Peter, but he did acknowledge that they are not healthy. Because of this he would need to workout to be more attractive to females. Wine was given as an alternative to beer as a beverage to consume on a Friday night. Peter felt that wine is more of a sophisticated drink and makes him look more mature. He felt that this would make him more attractive to females – in this case, one of his core values.

The brand relationships for both Peter and Eric are about the same for Busch Light beer. Both respondents remarked that Busch Light beer was popular with them because it was cheaper than most beers but that it was not the cheapest. This is a 'casual friendship/buddy' type of relationship because there is not a long-term commitment with the brand. The consumers are loyal but they do buy other brands and will likely not stay with this brand after graduation because of their increased financial situation. Another brand relationship can be seen between Peter and rum. This is an enmities relationship because he has a desire to avoid the product due to its negative effects.

Applying Advanced Means–End Chain Laddering to Learn Unconscious Processes

Research on consumer thinking processes (see Zaltman, 2003) indicates multiple levels of mental processing. Figure A3.7 summarize five levels of thinking processes that serve to inform means–end chain laddering research. Level 1 represents conscious thinking that is verbalized between two or more parties. Level 2 thinking includes conscious handling of thoughts before and after verbalizing thoughts and surfacing thoughts.

Level 3 thinking includes surfacing thoughts that are mostly not under conscious control. Level 4 thinking represents unconscious thinking between two or more persons. Level 5 thinking represents unconscious processing, including spreading activation of relationships among concepts that the individual is unaware are occurring.

Other empirical findings (see Bargh, 2002; Wegner, 2002) support a core proposition about how the mind thinks: The most processing occurs unconsciously

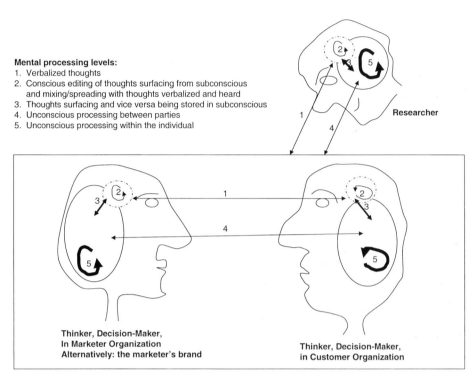

Mental processing levels:
1. Verbalized thoughts
2. Conscious editing of thoughts surfacing from subconscious and mixing/spreading with thoughts verbalized and heard
3. Thoughts surfacing and vice versa being stored in subconscious
4. Unconscious processing between parties
5. Unconscious processing within the individual

Researcher

Thinker, Decision-Maker,
In Marketer Organization
Alternatively: the marketer's brand

Thinker, Decision-Maker,
in Customer Organization

Figure A3.7 Five levels of thinking processes

(indicated by the thicker line 5 in Figure A3.7). Such unconscious thinking influences consumers' actions in ways mostly unknown to the consumers themselves.

Such observations are likely to cause stress among consumer researchers who mainly apply the currently (early 21st century) dominating logic of asking fixed-point (e.g. seven-point scale items) questions because such questioning mostly reaches only Level 1 processing, that is, verbalized thoughts (cf. Zaltman, 2003). Some deeper form of questioning is necessary to reach into Levels 2 to 5 mental processing. The advances in means–end chain laddering research that this article has proposed may help achieve this objective.

Limitations and Suggestions for Future Research

The four MEC laddering cases serve to inform theory development and are not intended as representative of college students in general or for specific segments of beverage consumers. This report of empirically applying the advances in the MEC laddering is limited by not taking the step of describing the results in follow-up interviews with the two case study Ss and having the Ss confirm and elaborate on the researcher's interpretations (Hirschman, 1986, argues for such a validation step). Such an additional auto driving step will likely prove useful for achieving further advances in MEC laddering theory and research.

352

REFERENCES

Bagozzi R P and **Dabholkar** P A (2000) Discursive Psychology: An Alternative Conceptual Foundation to Means–End Chain Theory, Psychology and Marketing, Vol 17 pp 535–586

Bargh J A (2002) Losing Consciousness: Automatic Influences on Consumer Judgment, Behavior, and Motivation, Journal of Consumer Research, Vol 29 pp 280–285

Bearden W O and **Woodside** A (1978) Consumption Occasion Influence on Consumer Brand Choice, Decision Sciences, Vol 9 pp 274–281

Becker H S (1998) Tricks of the Trade: How to Think about Your Research While You're Doing it, University of Chicago Press, Chicago

Belk R (1974) An Exploratory Assessment of Situational Effects in Buyer Behavior, Journal of Marketing Research, Vol 11 pp 156–163

Feldman J M and **Lynch** J G Jr (1988) Self-Generated Validity and Other Effects of Measurement on Belief, Attitude, Intention, and Behavior, Journal of Applied Psychology, Vol 73 pp 421–435

Fournier S (1998) Consumers and Their Brands: Developing Relationship Theory in Consumer Research, Journal of Consumer Research, Vol 24 pp 343–373

Gutman J (1997) Means–End Chains as Goal Hierarchies, Psychology and Marketing, Vol 14 pp 545–560

Gutman J and **Reynolds** T J (1978) An Investigation of the Levels of Cognitive Abstraction Utilized by Consumers in Product Differentiation, in **Eighmey** J (ed.), Attitude Research Under the Sun, American Marketing Association, Chicago, pp 57–64

Heider F (1958) The Psychology of Interpersonal Relations, John Wiley & Sons, New York

Heisley D D and **Levy** S J (1991) Autodriving: A Photoelicitation Technique, Journal of Consumer Research, Vol 18 pp 257–272

Hirschman E C (1986) Humanistic Inquiry in Marketing Research: Philosophy, Method, and Criteria, Journal of Marketing Research, Vol 23 pp 237–249

Pieters R, **Baumgartner** H and **Allen** D (1995) A Means–End Chain Approach to Consumer Goal Structures, International Journal of Research in Marketing, Vol 12 pp 227–244

Wegner D M (2002) The Illusion of Conscious Will, Bradford Books, Cambridge, MA

Woodside A G and **Chebat** J C (2001) Updating Heider's Balance Theory in Consumer Behavior, Psychology and Marketing, Vol 18 pp 475–496

Zaltman G (2003) How Consumers Think, Harvard Business School, Cambridge, MA

Questions on these articles

1. Select a form of consumer misbehaviour. Provide a proposal as to how you would research how and why consumers might or might not engage in such behaviour.
2. What individual and social factors help to explain why young people use illicit drugs?
3. Write a critique of Woodside's approach to:
   a. means–end chain laddering research with Heider's balance theory; and
   b. means–end chain laddering research by applying Fournier's consumer–brand relationships.

GLOSSARY

Absolute sensory thresholds. Physiological limits to sensory perception.

Acculturation refers to the phenomena which result when a particular ethnic or cultural group come into continuous first-hand contact with another group and the subsequent changes that occur in the original culture patterns of either or both groups.

Acculturation agents refer to institutions or mechanisms such as family, friends, media and commercial, educational and religious institutions that can facilitate the cultural changes occurring among an ethnic or immigrant group.

Acorn. A classification of residential neighbourhoods – the first geodemographic system in UK, introduced by Consolidated Analysis Centres Incorporated. This, as with other geodemographic systems, is based on analysis of census data at postcode level. All UK households are profiled according to a clustering of similarities. Acorn profiles are now supplemented by a range of other data sources but the census is the key source. Links with the electoral roll allow individual addresses to be identified.

Action. Consumer behaviour as a result of information processing, which may take the form of trying the product, adopting it, consuming it, searching for information about it, and so on.

Adoption. Regular or committed purchase behaviour. A one-off purchase is not sufficient for adoption. The adoption process is often shown to be reflected in a series of stages through which consumers progress: awareness ⇒ interest ⇒ evaluation ⇒ trial ⇒ adoption.

Advertising wearout. The effect of an advertisement's repetition such that each additional exposure to it has a less than proportionate influence on consumers.

Advocacy. Consumers recommending a brand/store/company.

Affective motives. Motives whose achievement results in satisfying emotional states.

Aided recall method. A technique of advertising research that involves asking respondents to reproduce or 'play back' sufficient of the ad to show that they have seen it.

AIO Analysis. Traditional lifestyle analysis, referring to activities, interests and opinions.

Approach. Behaviour directed towards a goal or object. This may include physical movement or thinking or feeling about an entity.

Aspirational group is a group to which a person aspires to belong.

Assimilation refers to the phenomena that result when an immigrant consumer or group relinquishes their cultural identity over time and adapts the cultural values and traditions of the larger mainstream society.

Associationist learning. *See* **Classical conditioning.**

Attention. The stage in the persuasion process at which the consumer merely notices the message.

Attitude. A consumer's evaluative response to an object or person; their feelings or affective reaction towards it.

Attributes. Any elements or features of a product or service judged salient by a consumer to their purchase behaviour.

Autonomic decisions refer to those decisions that are spontaneous and are involuntary in nature.

Avoidance. Behaviour that involves moving away from an object or goal; this may be physical or mental.

Baby boomers. The generation born following the Second World War; usually regarded as those born between 1945 and 1965.

Bandwagon effect. The tendency of respondents in attitude research to give the answers they imagine the interviewer wants them to give.

Behavioural data. Data which provide personalized facts about how consumers behave. The main source is transactional data, but Internet **cookies** can track consumers' paths through the Internet, global positioning satellites (**GPS**) can locate where a consumer's mobile phone is geographically, and radio frequency identification 'tags' (**RFID**), if not 'switched off' at the checkout, can track consumers' purchases into use and even disposal.

Biogenic drives. Needs that are biological in origin, e.g. for food, water, sex.

Biographics. The combination of behavioural data and profile data. Analogous to the 'biography' in literature, biographics can provide a 'buying biography' of individual consumers.

Body image. How consumers perceive their bodies and how they would like their bodies to be. Can be influenced (not always positively or healthily) by idealized images as shown in marketing messages. Sometimes leads to physical alteration of one's body via cosmetic surgery, piercing and tattooing.

Brand attributes refer to brand-related features such as price, quality and durability.

Brand community is a grouping of individuals which is specialized, non-geographically bound and has a structured set of social relations among participants.

Buying roles refer to different roles that a consumer can play in the buying process.

Cellular household. The notion that many households, especially in Western cultures, are more fragmented than used to be the case. Household members have their own 'cells': children have their TVs and computers in their bedrooms and there is less communal activity than in more integrated households.

Central route to persuasion. Attitude change that is the result of the consumer's deliberative involvement with information.

Chronological age. Number of years that a person has lived since birth.

Classical conditioning. The process in which an initially neutral stimulus, through constant pairing with an unconditioned stimulus that elicits a given, unconditioned, response, acquires the capacity to elicit a similar response itself even in the absence (for a time) of the unconditioned stimulus. The hitherto neutral stimulus is now known as the conditioned stimulus and the similar response is the conditioned response.

Classification system is the systematic grouping of objects, thoughts and ideas into categories on the basis of structural relationships between them.

Clutter. Bombardment of consumer with information to the extent that they cannot distinguish one message from another.

Coercive Power encourages conformity by explicitly or implicitly threatening some form of intimidation.

Cognitive age. The consumer's self-perceived age, the age they feel. It is related to the consumer's self-concept.

Cognitive consistency. The theory that consumers attempt to maintain a degree of balance between the cognitive and affective elements of their attitudes. Attitude change results from the homeostatic modification of one or other element.

Cognitive dissonance. A person who holds two or more contradictory cognitions (beliefs, attitudes, intentions, etc.) is said to experience cognitive dissonance, an emotional state that motivates them to drop or modify one of the cognitions in order to reduce the dissonance.

Cognitive motives. Motives whose fulfilment engenders a sense of meaning in the individual.

Collectivist cultures tend to hold an interdependent view of the self that stresses connectedness, social context and relationships with others.

Commitment. A component of reciprocal relationship consumption which means that both parties are so comfortable with the relationship that they don't feel the need to look for alternative partners.

Compulsive buying. Buying products or brands one had not planned to purchase.

Conformity to group is one's tendency to follow the norms, traditions, rules and regulations prescribed by the group.

Consequences. The outcomes of behaviour that determine the rate at which that and similar behaviours are subsequently performed: usually conceptualized as rewards (reinforcers) and punishments (punishers).

Conspicuousness refers to something which is obvious, easy to notice or attracts attention by being unusual.

Consumer acculturation refers to the overall process of movement and adaptation to the cultural environment in one country by persons from another country.

Consumer misbehaviour is consumption behaviour that can have adverse effects on themselves or others in some way. Such misbehaviour infringes accepted societal norms.

Consumer panels. A form of marketing research in which the same respondents report over a period of time. The resulting longitudinal data can be especially useful in identifying trend over time. Typical consumer panels report on media habits or the consumption of fast-moving consumer goods such as groceries.

Consumer terrorists. Consumers who have such a bad experience that they tell others about their bad and frustrating experiences. They might also be subversive and swap loyalty cards in order to damage the integrity of consumer databases.

Contemporary lifestyle. Based on personalized surveys which ask respondents to 'tick' those responses that apply in terms of products and services in which they claim an interest or actual purchase. The data is attributed to the respondent's name and address and is used to compile lists for contact via mail, telephony or email.

Cookies. Web messages which can identify visitors to web sites. Repeated visits can lead to customized web pages being developed for the consumer.

Country of origin refers to the place or country where the brand or product is manufactured or assembled.

Country of origin effect refers to the stereotypical beliefs that consumers have about products or brands originating from specific countries.

Cultural authority perspective. Marketing is not so much a mirror of society as a shaper of consumer culture and an organizer of consumer tastes.

Cultural category represents the basic distinctions that a culture utilizes to divide up its world of everyday experiences.

Cultural rituals refer to repetitive and expressive behaviours that are shared by a group of people.

Culture refers to socially learned behavioural patterns, arts, beliefs, institutions, and all other products of human work and thought. The term also refers to the meaning system that people use to inform their lives, providing them a sense of identity and rationale for their actions. Culture helps people to make sense of what other people and even objects stand for, and how and in what sense one should deal with them.

Customer satisfaction. The degree of positive or negative affect a consumer feels towards a product, store or brand at the post-purchase stage of the buying cycle.

Customization refers to products and marketing activities being modified according to cultural, regional and national differences.

Decider is the person who makes any of the decisions or sub-decisions which determine the precise nature of the purchase.

Deculturation refers to the phenomena that result when an immigrant consumer or group rejects movement into the mainstream society as well as any identification with their own culture of origin.

Demographics. Consumer characteristics which are objective: age, gender, marital status and occupation.

Deterministic models. Models of repeat purchase and loyalty, based on cognitive processes. Repeat purchase 'loyalty' here involves commitment and affective dimensions, not just behavioural repeat purchasing.

Diffusion. How an innovation is communicated and distributed through society over time.

Diffusion-adoption of innovations. The conceptual framework for how new products and ideas are spread through society and how they are received, accepted and adopted.

Disconfirmation paradigm. A means of understanding the causes of consumer satisfaction in terms of pre-purchase expectations and their subsequent confirmation or disconfirmation.

Disintermediation is the process of taking away any middleman or intermediary.

Diversity refers to variety. The term is often used to mean the existence of a variety of ethnic groups in a marketplace or a society.

DRTV is direct response television advertising. Some form of response mechanism is included in the advertisement itself, such as a telephone number or web site address.

Ego. *See* **Freudian motivation.**

Elaboration likelihood model. The theory that advertising messages provoke different likelihoods of the consumer becoming involved and therefore of highly elaborating the message by taking the central route to persuasion or failing to become involved and thus taking the peripheral route.

Emphasis on form/style refers to the condition of Western society in which there is a growing influence of form and style (as opposed to content) in determining meaning and life.

Enduring involvement. Sustained interest in a particular product category.

Ethnic identity refers a set of behavioural or personal characteristics by which an individual is recognizable as a member of a group. This reflects a person's knowledge of membership in a social group(s) together with emotional significance and value that is attached to that membership.

Ethnic media refers to the media that communicate in a particular ethnic language and is normally targeted at a particular ethnic group.

Ethnic segment refers to a grouping of ethnic consumers that may potentially be targeted by marketers.

Ethnicity can be viewed as a characteristic of racial group membership on the basis of some commonly shared features such as common customs, language, religion and values.

Ethnocentric consumer refers to a consumer who believes in the superiority of their own ethnic group or culture or country over others.

Evoked set. Brands within a particular category that consumers bring to mind, some of which they consider purchasing (the 'consideration set').

Expert power is where there really is a good degree of generally known expert knowledge on the part of the referent.

Extended family normally consists of a patriarchal or matriarchal figure and some mature siblings who have spouses and children and who all live in one joint family system.

External motivation. Motivation generated by the possibility of acquiring extrapersonal things such as products.

Family buying behaviour is the buying behaviour of a family as a unit.

FCB grid. A framework reflecting consumers' involvement and their salient knowledge, meanings and beliefs about the product. Some products are considered primarily in terms of rational factors, such as the functional benefits of using the product ('think' products) in the grid model. In contrast, 'feel' products are considered by consumers primarily in terms of non-verbal images and emotional factors. The grid was originally used by the Foote, Cone and Belding (FCB) Advertising Agency.

Feel products. Products that the consumer considers primarily in terms of emotional factors such as their putative psychological and social benefits.

Felt ethnic identity refers to one's sense of belonging to a group and the feelings and thoughts that go with being part of that group in a particular situation.

FMCG. Fast-moving consumer goods, such as groceries.

Focal attention. Deeper cognitive engagement with a persuasive message.

Formal group is an officially organized group of people having a proper structure and procedures to be followed.

Fragmentation refers to the condition of Western society in which disjointed and disconnected moments and experiences in life and a sense of self are omnipresent and there is a growing acceptance of the dynamism which leads to fragmentation in markets.

Fragmentation of collective meanings refers to the demise of collective meanings.

Frame of reference. The framework into which consumers perceive a particular product or brand as fitting or belonging.

Frankfurt School. A group of social thinkers in Germany who saw social symbolism of products often outweighing their more practical use values.

Frequency. The number of times a message is placed or shown during a given period of time.

Freudian motivation. The motivating states realized in the individual as the result of conflict among the id and superego as they are regulated by the ego. The id is the unconscious and instinctive source of selfish motivation, immediate gratification. The idea that comes closest to that of the superego is that of the conscience, a socially learned device that regulates one's motives; in Freudian motivation it tends to inhibit the antisocial influences that have their origin in the id. The ego is the seat of reason, the self, which attempts to create a balance between id and superego so that the individual can function effectively.

Generation X. The generational cohort following the **baby boomers** and born approximately between 1966 and 1976. The name 'Generation X' was coined by Douglas Coupland in 1991.

Generation Y. The generational cohort following **Generation X** and born between 1977 and 1994. Sometimes also called the Millennial Generation or the 'N-Gen' after 'the net' and the 'information revolution' which were such significant technological events of the time.

Generational cohort. Division of age groups based on a 20-year span to allow individuals to develop.

Genetic data. Data on an individual's evolutionary development, for example, their family medical history.

GPS. Global positioning system. When signals are beamed (e.g. from mobile phones) to a number of satellites, the triangulation of that signal can position the source of the signal.

Group cohesiveness refers to a condition of cohering in which group members show their attraction to and attachment with a group.

Group conformity refers to the notion of acting or behaving in correspondence with socially accepted standards, conventions, rules or laws prescribed by the group.

Habitual buying. The apparently unthinking behaviour of consumers in repeatedly selecting a particular product, store or brand.

Hierarchy (or sequence) of communication effects. The cumulative sequential effects of advertising or other persuasive messages in generating consumers' exposure to the message, their giving their attention to it, followed by perception, cognitive learning, attitude formation and change, intentionality and action. It may also include post-purchase behaviours such as cognitive dissonance reduction.

Homeostasis. A process that promotes balance and harmony of working. Initially employed to denote autonomous physiological processes that reduce irregularities in blood pressure or body temperature, the term is also used somewhat metaphorically to refer to social and psychological processes that generate equilibrium.

Husband-dominant decisions are those decisions in which the husband is the decision-maker and/or exerts a major influence in the joint decision-making process.

Husband–Wife decision-making refers to the notion that both spouses can engage in joint decision-making.

Hyperreality. An especially postmodern phenomenon which translates 'hype' into consumer desires to experience simulation more than reality: e.g. man-made theme parks rather than nature-made natural environments.

Id. *See* **Freudian motivation.**

Independence from group is a person's tendency to break away from the group or show some defiance of the group by not explicitly following the norms, traditions, rules and regulations prescribed by the group.

Individualism is the tendency to hold an independent view of the self, which emphasizes separateness, internal attributes and uniqueness of individuals.

Individualistic cultures tend to hold an independent view of the self, which emphasizes separateness, internal attributes and uniqueness of individuals.

Inept set. Known brands that consumers reject as purchase possibilities because of poor experience with them or negative information towards them.

Inert set. Brands consumers know but to which they are indifferent.

Influencer refers to the person who consciously or unconsciously affects the purchase in some way, perhaps as an opinion leader.

Infomediaries. Provide a sort of brokerage service to consumers by collecting information about their buying patterns and requirements and providing information about different potential suppliers.

Informal group is a grouping of people on the basis of common interests and geographical proximity with no formalities or rigid structure.

Information influence occurs when an individual enhances their knowledge of the environment and their ability to cope with some aspect of this environment (e.g. purchasing a brand) by seeking specific information from their reference group (e.g. family, experts).

Information power operates when a consumer perceives someone as possessing knowledge about the issue.

Initial attention. First scanning of information to determine its relevance.

Initiator refers to the person from whom the idea of buying a certain product first comes.

Inner-directed. Riesman used social character to explain personality type. Inner-directeds have a strong personal (inner) sense of what sort of behaviour is correct.

Innovation. A product, service or idea which is perceived as new by a significant proportion of consumers in a market.

Innovativeness. A personality trait which reflects the individual's interest in trying and using new products.

Insight. The capacity of the untrained person or animal to structure information in order to produce effective behaviour.

Instrumental learning. *See* **Operant conditioning.**

Instrumental values. Things that are desired only because they lead to wanted consequences.

Integration refers to the phenomena that result when an immigrant consumer or group not only maintains their original cultural integrity but also makes a move to become an integral part of a larger societal framework.

Intergenerational influence is the effect of the family in the socialization of a person.

Intergenerational value transmission. The cultural passing on of desires, usually from parents to their children but conceivably from children to grandparents (or within any other combination of generations).

Internal motivation. Intrapersonally generated motivation.

Internet cultures are cultures that exist in the context of the Internet.

Interpretive approach refers to a variety of non-traditional perspectives on the study of consumer behaviour. Generally speaking, an interpretive approach to consumer research aims to understand the meaning of consumer behaviour by focusing on the context and by utilizing qualitative data and qualitative analysis, and by frequently using an emergent research design and procedures.

Jaycustomer. Lovelock's transfer of the jaywalker concept to those consumers who are over-awkward or malicious toward companies, brands and/or marketers.

Joint decision-making refers to two or more consumers making decisions jointly. Within the household context, it could be husband and wife engaging in joint decision making.

Kinesics. The use of body and movement as well as eye positioning to indicate feelings.

Kirton Adaption Innovation Inventory. Developed by Kirton to measure individuals' self-perceived cognitive styles. The main application in consumer research is to identify innovators who try different ways of solving problems and adaptors who do things in ways which are more familiar to them.

Lack of commitment refers to the condition of Western society in which individuals are increasingly unwilling to commit to any single idea, project or grand design.

Law of effect. Behaviours which have pleasant consequences are repeated; those that have unpleasant outcomes are not.

Learning (cognitive). The storing of a message in **memory** and the processing of message information by memory.

Legitimate power is where a consumer thinks that the position of the referent confers authority in the context concerned, for example, police officers in the law enforcement context.

Likert scaling. The presentation of a series of attitude statements to respondents and asking for their degree of agreement with each statement.

Long interview refers to an in-depth face-to-face interview lasting for around an hour and a half during which the interviewer tries to understand what things mean to the person who is being interviewed.

Long-term orientation reflects the importance a society attaches to perseverance and values associated with preparing for and shaping the future, as opposed to a short-term, living-for-today orientation.

Loyalty. The tendency to repurchase a particular brand, variously conceived as a behavioural phenomenon (simply the rate at which the consumer chooses Brand A over other brands) and/or as an attitudinal phenomenon (the amount of positive affect the consumer has towards the brand, which may manifest itself behaviourally when an opportunity to purchase presents itself).

Mainstream marketers refer to marketers of mainstream brands and products.

Marital roles in decision-making refer to the role played by husband and wife in the decision-making process.

Market mavens. Consumers who transmit information about new products and services to others. They may or may not be early adopters themselves but act more as active gatekeepers of information about a range of new products.

Market-orientated. An extrovert attitude on the part of the firm which (logically, if not always chronologically) begins by establishing what consumers want and are willing to pay for before commencing production and distribution.

Marketing concept. The business philosophy that sees the consumer as the final arbiter of commercial success which leads the firm to orientate all of its functions and efforts towards the profitable satisfaction of consumer wants.

Means–end chains. The sequence in which consumers' perceptions of product attributes and outcomes reveal their basic values.

Memetics. The theory that humans' imitative behaviour can be explained in terms of ideas (memes) that 'jump from brain to brain' as people observe others' behaviour. Just as the gene is the replicator in natural selection, so memes are cultural replicators that communicate socially acceptable practices.

Memory. The storing of information and its processing by association with other mental information such as attitudes, motivations and ideas.

Mosaic. The brand name of Experian's geodemographic system, developed by Richard Webber after he moved from CACI where he had pioneered **Acorn**, the first geodemographic system in UK.

Motivation. The energizing state that arises from internal needs and drives and orients the individual's behaviour towards achieving an appropriate goal. A complete state of motivation requires both the inner drive and the external means of satisfying it to be present. Positive motivation is that which leads to **approach** behaviour; negative motivation that which leads to **avoidance**.

Motives. *See* **Motivation**.

Multiple identities refer to the notion that a person can experience many identities at a given time.

Multisensory brands. Brands that appeal to two or more senses rather than a single modality.

Needs and wants. A need can be understood as an internal state of an organism that it will strive to fulfil *or* as whatever will serve to overcome that inner state of deprivation. Needs in the first sense are often treated as drives that arise biologically (e.g. towards food or sex) or as resulting from social pressures (e.g. for status). Hence they are often referred to as biogenic or socio- (or psycho-) genic. In either case, they denote what the organism requires in order to function as a biological or social entity. Wants, which are whatever the individual desires and demands, are generally thought to arise entirely from acquired social and psychological considerations. Hence, we may be born with a need for food but develop a taste or want for chocolate chip cookies as a result of social experience.

Negative reference group is a group or individual whose behaviour, beliefs or values the individual deliberately avoids adopting as their own.

Neurolinguistic programming. How individuals think, process information and experience their world.

Noise. Distraction from an advertising message as a result of clutter.

Nuclear family normally consists of two spouses and a small number of children living together and representing one family unit.

Online communities refer to communities that exist in the virtual environment, like the Internet.

Operant conditioning. An operant is an behavioural response that *operates* on the environment to produce positive or aversive consequences ('rewards' and 'punishments') that control the rate of future emission of the response. Operant conditioning is the process in which an operant response is controlled by its being followed by a reinforcer or punisher. Any feature of the environment that is present when this conditioning occurs may come to control the response, even when the reinforcer or punisher is not presented. Operant conditioning is said to be complete when this (discriminative) stimulus alone controls the rate of the response.

Opinion formers. Individuals who actively and deliberately shape and form the thoughts of others, from a (usually impersonal) position of some perceived level of expertise, for example, motoring journalists or TV personalities.

Opinion leaders. Individuals who are seen, usually at a more local peer group level, to be knowledgeable about a specific product category and from whom others are willing to take advice.

Oppositional brand loyalty refers to loyalty towards a specific brand, based on a perceived opposition and dislike of competing brands.

Outer-directed. Riesman used social character to explain personality type. Other-directeds' values, attitudes and behaviour are largely acquired from others.

Paralanguage. The conscious and deliberate choice of words in conveying information.

Passive learning. The effects of information on consumers' mental structures which take place even though they are not involved with the message.

Perceived risk. This is where consumers see some less desirable consequences of a purchase or product and can often, but not always, be greater when the purchase is expensive and the product more complex.

Perceptual defence. The avoidance of messages which are incongruent with one's current world view.

Perceptual maps. The mental dimensions on which consumers construe brands in order to categorize and compare them.

Perceptual vigilance. Being open to what one is interested in to the extent of seeking information about it.

Peripheral route to persuasion. Attitude change that results from the individual's limited level of involvement with the message.

Permission marketing. The equivalent of an 'opt-in', where consumers agree to specific elements of a relationship with an organization.

Persistent attention. Continued scanning of information once its relevance has been established.

Personality. The amalgam of an individual's physical, psychological and social characteristics as reflected in their natural and acquired behaviour, opinions and ideals.

Personality traits. Specific characteristics which individuals possess and display in responding to the social and physical environment. Examples are aggression, honesty, anxiety, independence and innovativeness.

Personality types. Classifications of individuals into groups, such as extrovert or introvert.

Pester power refers to the influences exerted by children on the decision-making of parents.

Pluralism refers to the notion that many different distinct ethnic, religious and cultural groups coexist and are tolerated within a society and considered to be desirable and socially beneficial.

Postmodern. The late twentieth century and early twenty-first century have seen a dramatic expansion of communications and the trend away from standardization of mass production. There is also pluralism in society and as a result there is a fragmentation of society and many different ways for consumers to behave.

Postmodern consumer is a consumer showing or revealing the cultural tendencies associated with postmodernity.

Postmodern consumer behaviour is consumer behaviour showing or revealing the cultural tendencies associated with postmodernity.

Postmodern society refers to the Western society with all the features and characteristics associated with postmodernity.

Post-purchase. The stage in the buying process in which the consumer evaluates what they have bought and reaches a level of satisfaction or dissatisfaction with it.

Power distance is the extent to which less powerful members of a society or country accept the fact that power is not distributed equally in the society.

Primary group is normally the immediate group to which one belongs, such as family and friends.

Privately consumed luxuries are those products that are not visible to others when consumed, are exclusive and conspicuous in nature and are not commonly owned.

Privately consumed necessities are products that are not observed when being consumed and are also commonly owned by others.

Probability theory. The statistics of calculating the likelihood of an event occurring.

Product attributes refer to features such as price, quality and durability.

Product life cycle. Products and services are seen to ape the biological time clock and have stages of development, maturity and decline.

Product-orientated. A tendency of firms to look inwardly towards what they are capable of producing rather than outwardly towards what consumers want to buy.

Profiling. Data about the characteristics of consumers can help categorize them into different segments for targeting.

Projective tests. Methods of revealing consumers' underlying motivations and understandings by requiring them to project themselves into situations of purchase and consumption in which they role-play or describe the behaviour of others, explaining what is going on in the situation and why.

Proxemics. How people use physical space to convey information.

Psychogenic drives. Needs that are socially inculcated, e.g. for prestige.

Psychographics. The identification, analysis and use of consumer personality, lifestyle and self-concept characteristics to understand consumer behaviour.

Publicly consumed luxuries are those products that are visible to others when consumed, are exclusive and conspicuous in nature and are not commonly owned.

Publicly consumed necessities are products that are observed when being consumed and are also commonly owned by others.

Purchaser is the person who actually carries out the final purchase.

Reasoning. The process in which consumers deduce conclusions form information.

Recognition method. A technique of advertising research that involves showing an advertisement to consumers and asking whether they have seen it before.

Reference group refers to any individual or a group of individuals that can significantly influence one's behaviour.

Referent power operates when a consumer identifies with or admires a group or person.

Reinforcement. A behavioural consequence that increases the frequency with which the behaviour is subsequently enacted.

Relational buying. Reciprocally favourable emotional engagement between company and consumer in the buying context.

Repeat purchasing. Degrees of purchase recurrence.

Retention. Retaining customers over a period of time. It is often cheaper to develop strategies to keep customers than to acquire new customers.

Reward power operates when responding favourably to the referent results in positive reinforcement by the group.

RFID. Radio frequency identification (tags) which emit a radio signal which can be decoded by relevant radio receivers. Used mostly to track items through the supply chain.

RFM. Recency, frequency and monetary value of individual consumers' buying patterns with a specific company.

Ritual refers to a kind of expressive, symbolic activity constructed of multiple behaviours that occur in a fixed, episodic sequence, which is repeated over time.

Schema discrepancy. The capacity of a message to evoke surprise by being unusual or discrepant.

Secondary group is made up of more than one primary group such as a students' union.

Selective attention. Consumers can notice certain messages but even if exposed to others they can screen them out and avoid attending to them.

Selective exposure. Consumers, consciously or subconsciously, avoid some media but not others.

Selective perception. Consumers can extract from a message certain elements which fit their own frame of reference, even if they tend to distort the intention of the message.

Selective retention. Consumers retain elements of a message which might not reflect the intention of that message, but which are congruent with the consumer's frame of reference.

Self-actualization. The state of having fulfilled all of one's potential capacities. In Maslow's hierarchy of needs system, this is the final stage of development, achievable only after the individual has fulfilled all their biogenic and sociogenic needs.

Self-image. How we see ourselves.

Self-concept refers to the totality of thoughts and feelings that a person has of himself or herself as an object.

Self-expression refers to an individual expressing personality, feelings and ideas (within the marketing context, this is said to happen via brand consumption).

Semantic differential. A method of attitude assessment that requires respondents to place an object on a seven- or nine-point scale bounded by antonyms.

Senses. Usually taken to include the modalities of vision, hearing, smell, taste and touch, but sometimes including also balance.

Situational involvement. Interest in a product category that is sustained only by the current situation and which dissipates when the situation changes.

Social class. The stratification of society.

Social grade. Marketing's surrogate for social class in UK, based on occupation of the chief income earner in a household.

Social power is the ability or official capacity to exercise control and authority by a group of individuals acting together.

Social pressure is a type of pressure exerted on an individual by members of their social group.

Socialization is the process by which a person, beginning at infancy, acquires the habits, beliefs and accumulated knowledge of society through education and training for adult status.

Sociogram is a sociometric chart plotting the structure of interpersonal relations in a group situation.

Sociometry is the quantitative study of interpersonal relationships in populations, especially the study and measurement of preferences.

Source attractiveness. This is where the consumer perceives the source of a message to be similar to himself or herself. This has been found to increase the persuasiveness of the source.

Source credibility. This is when the source of a message is perceived as having relevant expertise and to be trustworthy.

Standardization refers to products and marketing activities being modified according to cultural, regional and national differences.

Stochastic models. These models make predictions, usually based on probabilities, about repeat purchasing using longitudinal data.

Subcultures refer to groups within a society, which possess distinctive characteristics. The term can also be used to refer to a distinctive subgroup of society that self selects on the basis of a shared commitment to a particular product class, brand, or consumption activity.

Subliminal messages. Persuasive influences that affect behaviour at the unconscious level without the individual who is subject to them registering that they have impinged upon them.

Superego. *See* **Freudian motivation.**

Symbolic interactionism. There is meaning that consumers attach to many things, often at a symbolic level. The meaning of any product or consumption situation is dependent upon how the consumer interprets the symbols.

Syncratic decisions refer to those decisions that are taken out of mutual consent with a second party.

Terminal values. Things desired as ends in themselves.

Theory of the triple appeal. The view that in order to be successful in persuading an audience, a message must appeal simultaneously to the **id, ego** and **superego.** A message that appeals only to the id will provoke a counter-appeal from the superego which will render the message unpersuasive. It is necessary therefore that the message assuage the superego as well as making a guarded appeal to the id. An appeal only to the superego will tend to invite conformity to it which will not arouse any of the want-generating mechanisms controlled by the id; such a message is unlikely to be persuasive unless the advertiser is promoting a very socially acceptable behaviour, such as altruism. An appeal to the ego (reason) alone is likely to be ineffective because it engenders neither an id-related desire nor the mental conflict whose resolution is likely to be achieved by buying the product advertised.

Think products. Products that the consumer considers primarily by reasoning about them, e.g. in terms of their functional benefits.

Third-person tests. Methods of revealing consumers' motivations and understandings by involving the idea of a typical consumer of a particular product or brand about whom the respondent is asked such questions as 'What is she like? 'Why does she buy this?' In this way, the respondent may more readily provide access to her own feelings and motives than if she is asked 'head-on' what she thinks.

Traditional lifestyle. Anonymized market research which presents a series of attitude (**Likert**) statements reflecting the respondent's activities, interests and opinions. Generalized clusters of similar responses lead to the identification of the 'sorts' of consumers who fit the profile of each lifestyle segment but names and addresses are not available, in contrast to contemporary lifestyle research.

Transactional data. Data from individual purchase transactions with a company. Over time, what a consumer buys from a company can provide useful information to predict future purchasing behaviour. It can also identify the RFM scores of each consumer.

Tribe is a collection grouping of heterogeneous consumers, with different demographic features, who are capable of collective action and act as advocates for their causes.

Trust. The mutual favourable confidence between company and consumer. Each sees the other as being reliable and not likely to damage the other.

Two-sided arguments (two-sided appeals). Advertisements that provide counter as well as positive arguments about the pros and cons of buying a brand.

Unawareness set. Brands within a product or service category of which consumers do not know.

Uncertainty avoidance is the extent to which people in a country or society feel threatened by uncertainty and ambiguity and try to avoid them.

Undesired self. Marketing and other consumers can influence an individual's perception of self and some consumers will try to avoid appearing in particular ways as a result.

User is the person who makes practical use of the item bought.

Utilitarian influence occurs when a person complies or conforms to the aspirations and expectations of reference group because they perceive that their behaviour is visible or known to the group members and that the group can mediate some rewards or punishment.

Value expressive influence occurs when an individual uses reference group to express their image and self-concept.

Values are enduring beliefs that a particular action or mode of conduct is personally or socially acceptable and desirable. Values include abstract social entities such as justice and mercy, as well as socially and marketing-contrived desires like fresh breath confidence and being a 'good' parent.

Vicarious learning. Learning as a result of observing the behaviour of others, especially when they are overtly rewarded or punished for their actions.

Viper. A data-mining package from SmartFocus, Bristol.

Virtual communities refer to communities that exist in the virtual environment, like the Internet.

Virtual groups refer to groups that exist in the virtual environment, like the Internet.

Wants. *See* **Needs and wants.**

Wife-dominant decisions are those decisions in which wife is the decision-maker and/or exerts a major influence in the joint decision-making process.

Word-of-mouth advertising. Consumers pass on information about brands, stores and companies to others, orally, or by others observing their behaviour.

Zapping. Channel-surfing or -hopping to avoid advertisements.

Zipping. Fast-forwarding through advertisements.

REFERENCES

Aaker J (1997) Dimensions of Brand Personality, Journal of Marketing Research, Vol 35, August, pp 347–356

Aaker J and **Fournier** S (1995) A Brand as a Character, a Partner, and a Person: Three Perspectives on the Question of Brand Personality, Advances in Consumer Research, Vol 22 pp 391–395

Acland H (2001) Ruling Puts DM Industry Firmly on Back Foot, Marketing Direct, December

Adam Smith Institute (1998) The Millennial Generation, London

Addis M and **Holbrook** M B (2001) On the Conceptual Link between Mass Customisation and Experiential Consumption: An Explosion of Subjectivity, Journal of Consumer Behaviour, Vol 1 No 1 pp 50–66

Advertising Research Foundation (1964) Are There Consumer Types?

Ahmad R (2002) The Older or Aging Consumer in UK, International Journal of Market Research, Vol 44 No 3 pp 337–361

Ajzen I (1988) Attitudes, Personality and Behavior, Milton Keynes: Open University Press

Ajzen I and **Fishbein** M (1970) The Prediction of Behaviour from Attitudinal and Normative Variables, Journal of Experimental Social Psychology, Vol 6, pp 466–487

Ajzen I and **Madden** T J (1986) Prediction of Goal-Directed Behaviour: Attitudes, Intentions and Perceived Behavioural Control, Journal of Experimental Social Psychology, Vol 22 No 5 pp 453–474

Alden D A, **Hoyer** W D and **Lee Chol** (1993) Identifying Global and Culture-Specific Dimensions of Humour, Journal of Marketing, Vol 57 No 2 pp 64–73

Alden D A, **Mukherjee** A and **Hoyer** W D (2000) The Effects of Incongruity, Surprise and Positive Moderators on Perceived Humor in Television Advertising, Journal of Advertising, Vol 29 No 2 pp 1–14

Aldworth R (2005) in **Beeston** R (2005) Killing in the Name of Fashion, The Times, 31 March p 3

Allen D E and **Olson** J (1995) Conceptualising and Creating Brand Personality: A Narrative Theory, Advances in Consumer Research, Vol 22, pp 391–395

Ambler T (2002) Why Big Brother Believes Loyalty is Good for You, Marketing, 17 October, p 10

Anderson E and **Jap** S D (2005) The Dark Side of Close Relationships, MIT Sloan Management Review, Spring, pp 75–82

Anderson W T (1999) Communities in a World of Open Systems, Futures, Vol 31 pp 457–463

Andruss P L (2001) FedEx Kicks up Brand through Humor, Soccer and Line of Naked Men, Marketing News, 30 July, Vol 35 No 16 pp 4–5

Annenberg Public Policy Centre (1999) reported in **Lindstrom** M (2004) Child's Play, The Marketers, CIM, Maidenhead, July/August, pp 23–24

Argyle M (1969) Social Interaction, Methuen, p 220

Armstrong A and **Hagel** J (1996) The Real Value of On-Line Communities, Harvard Business Review, May/June, pp 134–141

Arnold M J and **Reynolds** K E (2003) Hedonic Shopping Motivations, Journal of Retailing, Vol 79 No 2 pp 1–20

Arnould E J and **Thompson** C J (2005) Consumer Culture Theory (CCT): Twenty Years of Research, Journal of Consumer Research, Vol 31 No 4 pp 868–883

Arnould E J and **Wallendorf** M (1994) Market-Oriented Ethnography: Interpretation Building and Marketing Strategy Formulation, Journal of Marketing Research, Vol 31 No 4 pp 484–504

Asch S (1955) Opinions and Social Pressure, Scientific American, November

Atkinson J W (1958) Motives in Fantasy, Action, and Society, Van Nostrand, Princeton, NJ

Atkinson R L *et al.* (eds) (1999) Introduction to Psychology, 12th edn, Wadsworth

Baier K (1969) What is Value?: An Analysis of the Concept, in **Baier** K and **Resher** E (eds), Values and the Future, Free Press, New York

Bailey J (1997) Tune in to the Power of the Viewing Public, PR Week, 17 October

Barak B and **Schiffman** L G (1981) Cognitive Age: A Nonchronological Age Variable, Advances in Consumer Research, Vol 8 pp 602–606

Barnes R (2001) High Impact Mail, Marketing Direct, November, pp 51–53

Barrett L (2003) Getting Touch-Feely with UK Consumers, Marketing Week, 26 July p 22

Bashford S (2000) Generation X Uncovered, Marketing Direct, October, pp 17–19

Baudrillard J (1999) The Consumer Society: Myths and Structures, Sage

Bauman Z (1992) A Sociological Theory of Postmodernity, in **Beilharz** P, **Robinson** G and **Rundell** J (eds), Between Totalitarianism and Postmodernity, MIT Press, Cambridge, MA, pp 149–162

Bayley G and **Nancarrow** C (1998) Impulse Purchasing: A Qualitative Exploration of the Phenomenon, Qualitative Market Research, Vol 1 No 2 pp 99–114

BBC (1997) Money Programme, 16 October

BBC (2002) Century of the Self, November

BBC (2003) Beyond the Bar Code, In Business Series, Radio 4, 2 October

Bearden W O and **Etzel** M J (1982) Reference Group Influence on Product and Brand Purchase Decisions, Journal of Consumer Research, Vol 9 pp 183–194

Becker G S (1968) Crime and Punishment, Journal of Political Economy, Vol 762 pp 169–217

Beeston R (2005) Killing in the Name of Fashion, The Times, 31 March p 3

Belk R W (1988) Possessions and the Extended Self, Journal of Consumer Research, Vol 15 pp 139–168

Belk R W, **Ger** G and **Askegaard** S (2003) The Fire of Desire: A Multisited Inquiry into Consumer Passion, Journal of Consumer Research, Vol 30 No 3 p 326

Berger D (1986) Theory into practice: The FCB Grid, European Research, January, pp 35–46

Bernstein D (1975) Creative Advertising, Longman, Harlow, p 128

Berry W J (1980) Acculturation as Varieties of Adaptation, in **Padilla** A M (ed.), Acculturation: Theory, Models and Some New Findings, Westview Press, Boulder, Colorado, pp 9–46

Blackmore S (1999) The Meme Machine, Oxford University Press

Block, R (1992) Sales Talk, BBC Radio 4, January

Bond C (1997) Frightened and Fifty, Marketing, 22 May, pp 27–28

Borna S and **Avila** S (1999) Genetic Information: Consumers' Right to Privacy Versus Insurance Companies' Right to Know: A Public Opinion Survey, Journal of Business Ethics, Vol 19 pp 355–362

Bouchet D (1995) Marketing and the Redefinition of Ethnicity, in **Costa** J A and **Bamossy** G J (eds), Marketing in a Multicultural World, Sage, London, pp 68–104

Bourne F S (1956) Group Influence in Marketing and Public Relations, Foundation for Research on Human Behaviour, p 8

Brindle D (1999) Census Check on Partners, Guardian, 5 March, p 12

Bristow L, **Tinson** J and **Nancarrow** C (2005) How to Target Movers and Shakers, Admap, May, pp 40–42

British Market Research Bureau (1988) The Target Group Index

Brokaw T (1993) The Lost Generation, The Brokaw Report, Livingston, Burelle's Information Services, New Jersey

Brown C (2004) Top Brands Wake up to the Rise of 'Parent Power', Precision Marketing, 1 January, p 11

Brown G H (1952–1953) Brand Loyalty – Fact or Fiction, Advertising Age, 23 June 1952 – January 1953 (series)

Bruning E R (1997) Country of Origin, National Loyalty and Product Choice: The Case of International Air Travel, International Marketing Review, Vol 14 No 1 pp 59–74

Brunner J A and **Koh** A C (1988) Negotiations in the People's Republic of China, Journal of Global Marketing, Vol 2 No 1 pp 33–55

Buttle F and **Burton** J (2002) Does Service Failure Influence Customer Loyalty?, Journal of Consumer Behaviour, Vol 1 No 3 pp 217–227

Caillat Z and **Mueller** B (1996) Observations: The Influence of Culture on American and British Advertising: An Exploratory Comparison of Beer Advertising, Journal of Advertising Research, May/June, pp 79–85

Calder B J and **Ross** M (1973) Attitudes and Behaviour, General Learning Press, Morristown, NJ

Carling E (1999) Grappling with the Grey Market, Marketing Direct

Caru A and **Cova** B (2006) How to Facilitate Immersion in a Consumption Experience: Appropriation Operations and Service Elements, Journal of Consumer Behaviour, Vol 5 No 1

Celsi R L and **Olson** J C (1988) The Role of Involvement in Attention and Comprehension Processes, Journal of Consumer Research, Vol 15 No 2 pp 210–224

Chaiken S (1980) Heuristics Versus Systematic Information Processing and the Use of Source Versus Message Cues in Persuasion, Journal of Personality and Social Psychology, Vol 39, November, pp 752–766

Chao P, **Wuhrer** G and **Werani** T (2005) Celebrity and Foreign Brand Names as Moderators of Country of Origin Effects, International Journal of Advertising, Vol 24 pp 2173–2192

Chapman M (1992) Social Anthropology and International Business: Some Suggestions, paper presented at the AIB Conference, Brussels, 20–22 November

Charret S (1999) Identity, Privacy and Personal Freedom: Big Brother V New Resistance, Paladin Press, Boulder, Colorado

Chaudhuri A (2002) A Study of Emotion and Reason in Products and Services, Journal of Consumer Behaviour, Vol 1 No 3 pp 267–279

Cheal D (1988) The Gift Economy, Routledge, London

Cheal D (1989) The Postmodern Origin of Ritual, Journal of Theory of Social Behavior, Vol 18 No 3 pp 269–290

Chesbro M (1999) Privacy for Sale: How Big Brother and Others are Selling Your Private Secrets for Profit, Paladin Press, Boulder, Colorado

Childers T L and **Rao** A R (1992) The Influence of Familial and Peer-Based Reference Groups on Consumer Decisions, Journal of Consumer Research, Vol 19 No 2 pp 198–211

Chiou J S, **Huang** C Y and **Lee** H H (2005) The Antecedents of Music Piracy Attitudes and Intentions, Journal of Business Ethics, Vol 57 pp 161–174

Chudry F and **Pallister** J (2002) The Importance of Ethnicity as a Segmentation Criterion: The Case of the Pakistani Consumers' Attitudes towards Direct Mail Compared with the Indigenous Population, Journal of Consumer Behaviour, Vol 2 No 2 pp 125–137

Churchill G A and **Suprenant** C (1982) An Investigation into the Determinants of Customer Satisfaction, Journal of Marketing Research, Vol 19, November, pp 491–504

CIM (2000) Consumer Research: Advertising and Gender, Chartered Institute of Marketing, Maidenhead

Clark R A and **Goldsmith** R E (2005) Market Mavens: Psychological Influences, Psychology and Marketing Vol 22 No 4 pp 289–312

Clegg A (1996) Marketing Week: Cover Story: Colour Blind, 21 June

Cleveland M, **Barry** J B, **Laroche** M, **Ward** P and **Bergeron** J (2003) Information Search Patterns for Gift Purchases: A Cross National Examination of Gender Differences, Journal of Consumer Behaviour, Vol 3 No 1 pp 20–47

Cohan J A (2001) Towards a New Paradigm in the Ethics of Women's Advertising, Journal of Business Ethics, Vol 33 No 4 pp 323–337

Cohen A, **Stotland** E and **Wolfe** D (1955) An Experimental Investigation of Need for Cognition, Journal of Abnormal and Social Psychology, Vol 51 pp 291–294

Cohen J B (1967) An Interpersonal Orientation to the Study of Consumer Behaviour, Journal of Marketing Research, Vol 6 pp 270–278

Collins A (2004) reported in **Taylor Nelson Sofres**, Are You a Member of Your Kid's Generation? (http://www.tns-global/corporate/doc/0/2vmqq3513e0419caj02jk5176f/247) accessed 23 March 2004

Consumer Insight (2005) http://www.insightmc.com/insightmc_groups3.htm, last accessed 6 June 2005

Cooper P (2003) in **Sclater** I, Challenging Perceptions, Marketing Business, February, pp 16–17

Cooper P and **Tower** R (1992) Inside the Consumer Mind, Journal of the Market Research Society, Vol 34 No 4 pp 299–311

Cooper S, **McLoughlin** D and **Keating** A (2005) Individual and Neo-Tribal Consumption: Tales from the Simpsons of Springfield, Journal of Consumer Behaviour, Vol 4 No 5

Costa J A and **Bamossy** G J (1995) Perspectives on Ethnicity, Nationalism, and Cultural Identity, in **Costa** J A and **Bamossy** G J (eds) Marketing in a Multicultural World, Sage, London, pp 26–67

Coupland D (1991) Generation X: Tales for an Accelerated Culture, Abacus

Cova B (1997) Community and Consumption: towards a Definition of the Linking Value of Product or Services, European Journal of Marketing, Vol 31 No 3/4

Cova B and **Cova** V (2001) Tribal Aspects of Postmodern Consumption Research: The Case of French In-Line Roller Skaters, Journal of Consumer Behaviour, Vol 1 No 1 pp 67–76

Cova B and **Cova** V (2002) Tribal Marketing: The Tribalisation of Society and its Impact on the Conduct of Marketing, European Journal of Marketing, Vol 36 No 5/6 pp 595–618

Crawford G and **Melewar** T C (2003) The Importance of Impulse Purchasing Behaviour in the International Airport Environment, Journal of Consumer Behaviour, Vol 3 No 1 p 85

Cubitt E (2004) Battle Erupts to Exploit Joy of Sex, Precision Marketing, 23 April, p 12

Cuellar I, **Nyberg** B and **Maldonado** R E (1997) Ethnic Identity and Acculturation in a Young Adult Mexican-Origin Population, Journal of Community Psychology, Vol 25 No 6 pp 535–549

Cummins B (1994) Time Pundits, Marketing Week, 8 April, pp 29–31

Dabholkar P A, **Thorpe** D I and **Rentz** J O (1996) A Measure of Service Quality for Retail Stores: Scale Development and Validation, Journal of the Academy of Marketing Science, Vol 24 pp 3–16

Darley W K and **Smith** R E (1995) Gender Differences in Information Processing Strategies: An Empirical Test of the Selectivity Model in Advertising Response, Journal of Advertising, Vol 24 No 1 pp 41–56

Daspin E (2000) The Cheater Principle, Wall Street Journal, August, pp 1–16

Datamonitor (2003) Report on the Grey Market, reported by **Sclater** I, Challenging Perceptions, Marketing Business, February, pp 16–17

Davidson A (2003) From Why to Z, Research, February, pp 31–33

Davies A and **Fitchett** J A (2003) Crossing Culture: A Multi-Method Enquiry into Consumer Behaviour and the Experience of Cultural Transition, Journal of Consumer Behaviour, Vol 3 No 4 pp 315–330

Davis H L and **Rigaux** B P (1974) Perceptions of Marital Roles in Decision Processes, Journal of Consumer Research, Vol 1 No 1

Dawkins R (1989) The Selfish Gene, Oxford University Press

De Wulf K, **Odenkerken-Schroder** G and **Iacobucci** D (2001) Investments in Consumer Relationships: A Cross Country and Cross Industry Exploration, Journal of Marketing, Vol 65 pp 33–50

Deshpande R, **Hoyer** W D and **Donthu** N (1986) The Intensity of Ethnic Affiliation: A Study of the Sociology of Hispanic Consumption, Journal of Consumer Research, Vol 13, September, pp 214–220

DeSouza G (1992) Designing a Customer Retention Plan, Journal of Business Strategy, March/April, pp 24–28

Dick A S and **Basu** K (1994) Customer Loyalty: Toward an Integrated Framework, Journal of the Academy of Marketing Science, Vol 22 No 2 pp 99–113

DMA (2001) Camouflage Case, Book of the Night, Direct Marketing Association, London

Dodd C, **Linaker** A and **Grigg** N P (2005) He's Gotta Have It: Shopping Dependency and the Homosexual Male Clothing Consumer, Journal of Consumer Behaviour, Vol 4 No 5

Donthu N and **Cherian** J (1994) Impact of Strength of Ethnic Identification on Hispanic Shopping Behaviour, Journal of Retailing, Vol 70 No 4, pp 383–393

Douglas M and **Isherwood** B (1980) The World of Goods: Towards an Anthropology of Consumption, New York

Duchessi P, **Schaninger** C M and **Nowak** T (2004) Creating Cluster-Specific Purchase Profiles from Point of Sale Scanner Data and Geodemographic Clusters: Improving Category Management at a Major US Grocery Chain, Journal of Consumer Behaviour, Vol 4 No 2 pp 97–117

East R (1997) Consumer Behaviour: Advances and Applications in Marketing, Prentice Hall

Edmonson R (1993) reported in Levi Zips into Youth Market with Hip Ads, Marketing, 17 June

Ehrenberg A S C (1988) Repeat Buying: Theory and Applications, 2nd edn, Charles Griffin, London

Ekman P and **Freisen** V (2003) Unmasking the Face, A Guide to Recognising Emotions from Facial Expressions, Major Books

Ellen P S and **Bone**, P F (1998) Does It Matter if It Smells? Olfactory Stimuli as Advertising Executional Cues, Journal of Advertising, Vol 27 No 4 pp 29–40

Elliott R (1997) Existential Consumption and Irrational Desire, European Journal of Marketing, Vol 31 No 3/4 pp 285–296

Elliott R and **Elliott** C (2005) Idealised Images of the Male Body in Advertising: A Reader-Response Exploration, Journal of Marketing Communications, Vol 11 No 1 pp 3–20

Engel J F, **Blackwell** R D and **Miniard** P W (1986) Consumer Behaviour, 5th edn, Dryden Press, Chicago; 8th edn, 1995

Errington F (1987) Reflexivity Deflected: The Festival of Nations as an American Cultural Performance, American Ethnologist, Vol 14 pp 654–667

Errington F (1990) The Rock Creek Rodeo: Excess and Constraint in Men's Lives, American Ethnologist, Vol 17 pp 628–645

Evans F B (1959) Psychological and Objective Factors in the Prediction of Brand Choice, *Journal of Business*, p 39

Evans M (1989) Consumer Behaviour Toward Fashion, European Journal of Marketing, Vol 23 No 7 pp 7–16

Evans M (2005) The Data Informed Marketing Model and its Social Responsibility, in Lace S (ed.) The Glass Consumer: Life in a Surveillance Society, Policy Press/National Consumer Council

Evans M and **Blythe** J (1994) Fashion: A Paradigm of Consumer Behaviour, Journal of Consumer Studies and Home Economics, Vol 18 No 3, September, pp 229–237

Evans M and **Fill** C (2000) Extending the Communication Process, International Journal of Advertising, Vol 19 No 3 pp 377–396

Evans M, **Nairn** A and **Maltby** A (1999) Gender Differences for Financial Services Direct Mail, Journal of Financial Services Marketing, Vol 4 No 2 pp 139–162

Evans M, **Nairn** A and **Maltby** A (2000) The Hidden Sex Life of the Male and Female Shot, International Journal of Advertising, Vol 19 No 1, February, pp 43–65

Evans M, **O'Malley** L and **Patterson** M (2001) Bridging the Direct Marketing-Direct Consumer Gap: Some Solutions from Qualitative Research, Qualitative Market Research: An International Journal, Vol 4 No 1 pp 17–24

Evans M, **O'Malley** L and **Patterson** M (2004) Exploring Direct and Customer Relationship Marketing, Thomson Learning, London

Evans M, **Patterson** M, **O'Malley** L and **Mitchell** S (1997) Consumer Reactions to Database-Based Supermarket Loyalty Programmes, Journal of Database Marketing, Vol 4 No 4 pp 307–320

Evans M and **Rowland** G (1996) Semiotic Contexts: on Reading Bar Codes, Research, February, pp 12–13

Evans M, **Wedande** G, **Ralston** L and **van t'Hul** S (2001) Consumer Interaction in the Virtual Era: Some Solutions from Qualitative Research, Qualitative Market Research: An International Journal, Vol 4 No 3 pp 150–159

Eysenck H Y *et al.* (1975) An Encyclopaedia of Psychology, Fontana

Exon M (1998) The Moral Marketing Maze, Precision Marketing, 28 September, p 12

Experian (2004) MOSAIC Multimedia CD ROM Guide, Nottingham

Featherstone M (1991) Consumer Culture and Postmodernism, Sage, London

Feick L F and **Price** L L (1987) The Market Maven: A Diffuser of Marketplace Information, Journal of Marketing, Vol 51, pp 83–97

Festinger L (1957) A Theory of Cognitive Dissonance, Stanford University Press, California

Festinger L (1964) Behavioural Support for Opinion Change, Public Opinion Quarterly, Vol 28 pp 404–417

Fifield P (2002) New Age Marketing, Marketing Business, December/January, pp 34–37

Firat A F, **Dholakia** N and **Venkatesh** A (1995) Marketing in a Postmodern World, European Journal of Marketing, Vol 29 No 1 pp 40–56

Firat A F and **Schultz II** C J (1997) From Segmentation to Fragmentation: Markets and Marketing Strategy in the Postmodern Era, European Journal of Marketing, Vol 31, No 3–4 pp 183–207

Firat A F and **Venkatesh** A (1993), Postmodernity: The Age of Marketing, International Journal of Research in Marketing, Vol 10 pp 227–249

Firat A F and **Venkatesh** A (1995) Liberatory Postmodernism and the Reenchantment of Consumption, Journal of Consumer Research, Vol 22, December, pp 239–267

Fischer E and **Arnold** S J (1990) More than a Labor of Love: Gender Roles and Christmas Gift Shopping, Journal of Consumer Research, Vol 17 No 3 pp 333–345

Fishbein M (1973) The Search for Attitudinal-Behaviour Consistency, in **Kassarjian** H H and **Robertson** T S (1973) Perspectives in Consumer Behaviour, Scott Foresman, pp 210–220

Fishbein M and **Ajzen** I (1975) Belief, Attitude, Intention and Behavior: An Introduction to Theory and Research, Addison–Wesley, Reading, MA

Fitchett J A and **Smith** A (2002) Consumer Behaviour in an Unregulated Market: The Satisfactions and Dissatisfactions of Illicit Drug Consumption, Journal of Consumer Behaviour, pp 355–368

Flynn M (2005) How to Use the Senses for a Better Brand Experience, Admap, May, pp 31–33

Forster S (1997) Direct Marketing in the Travel and Tourism Sector, IDM lecture, UWE, Bristol, May

Fournier S (1995) The Brand as Relationship Partner: An Alternative View of Brand Personality, Advances in Consumer Research, Vol 22 pp 391–395

Fournier S (1998) Consumers and Their Brands: Developing Relationship Theory in Consumer Research, Journal of Consumer Research, Vol 24, pp 343–373

Foxall G R (1995) Cognitive Styles of Consumer Initiators, Technovation, Vol 15 pp 269–288

Foxall G R (2003) Consumer Decision Making: Process, Level and Styles, in Baker M (ed.), The Marketing Book, Butterworth Heinemann

Foxall G R, **Goldsmith** R E and **Brown** S (1998) Consumer Psychology for Marketing, 2nd edn, International Thomson Business Press, London and New York

French J R P and **Raven** B (1959) The Bases of Social Power, in **Cartwright** D (ed.), Studies in Social Power, MI Institute for Social Research, pp 150–167

Fulberg P (2003) Using Sonic Branding in the Retail Environment: An Easy and Effective Way to Create Consumer Brand Loyalty While Enhancing the In-Store Experience, Journal of Consumer Behaviour, Vol 3 No 2, December, pp 193–198

Fullerton R A and **Punj** G (2002) Repercussions of Promoting an Ideology of Consumption: Consumer Misbehaviour, Journal of Business Research, Vol 57, pp 1239–1249

Future Foundation (2000) Responding to the Future, London

Gabriel Y and **Lang** T (1995) The Unmanageable Consumer, Sage, London

Gainer B (1995) Ritual and Relationships: Interpersonal Influences on Shared Consumption; Journal of Business Research, Vol 32 No 3, March, pp 253–261

Gatignon H and **Robertson** T S (1985) A Propositional Inventory for New Diffusion Research, Journal of Consumer Research, March, pp 849–867

Geertz C (1973) The Interpretation of Cultures, Basic Books

General Household Survey (2004) Social Survey Division of the Office of National Statistics, London

Gentry H J W, **Putrevu** S and **Shultz** C J (2006) The Effects of Counterfeiting on Consumer Search, Journal of Consumer Behaviour, Vol 5 No 6

Geyskens I and **Steenkamp** J-B (2000) Economic and Social Satisfaction: Measurement and Relevance to Marketing Channel Relationships, Journal of Retailing, Vol 76 No 1 p 13

Gillespie M (2003) In Search of Lost Youth, Research February, pp 28–29

Gimba G J (1998) Color in Marketing: Shades of Meaning, Marketing News, 16, Vol 38 No 6, March, p 6

Goddin S (1999) Permission Marketing, Simon & Schuster, New York

Goffman E (1959) The Presentation of Self in Everyday Life, Doubleday, New York

Gofton K (2001) Firms Fail to Relate to Customers, Marketing Direct, January, p 10

Goldsmith R E and **Flynn** L R (1992) Identifying Innovators in Consumer Product Markets, European Journal of Marketing, Vol 26 No 12 pp 42–55

Gonzalez-Benito O and **Gonzalez-Benito** B J (2005) The Role of Geodemographics in Retail Location Strategy, International Journal of Market Research, Vol 47 No 3 pp 295–316

Goodman S (1997) as reported by **Murphy** D in Money Where your Mouth Is, P R Week, 9 October, pp 35–36

Gorn G J (1982) The Effects of Music in Advertising on Choice Behavior: A Classical Conditioning Approach, Journal of Marketing, Vol 46 pp 94–101

Graeff T R (1996) Using Promotional Messages to Manage the Effects of Brand and Self-Image on Brand Evaluations, Journal of Consumer Marketing, Vol 13

Grayson K and **Amber** T (1999) The Dark Side of Long Term Relationships in Marketing Services, Journal of Marketing Research, February, pp 132–141

Green H (1995) Welcome to Your Over-Friendly Supermarket, Independent on Sunday, 20 August, pp 10–11

Grove S J, **Carlson** L and **Dorsch** M J (2002) Addressing Services' Intangibility through Integrated Marketing Communication: An Exploratory Study, Journal of Services Marketing, Vol 16 No 5 pp 393–411

Grubb E L and **Grathwohl** L H (1967) Consumer Self-Concept, Symbolism and Market Behaviour: A Theoretical Approach, Journal of Marketing, Vol 31 No 4 pp 22–27

Gunter B (1998) Understanding the Older Consumer, Routledge

Gutman J (1982) A Means-End Chain Model Based on Consumer Categorisation Processes, Journal of Marketing, Vol 46, Spring, pp 60–72

Habershon J (2004) in Need to Know, Research, MRS, June, p 10

Haeckel (2001) reported in **Mitchell** A, Playing Cat and Mouse Games with Marketing, Precision Marketing, 16 March, p 14

Haire M (1950) Projective Techniques in Marketing Research, Journal of Marketing, Vol 14 pp 649–656

Haley R I (1968) Benefit Segmentation: A Decision Oriented Research Tool, Journal of Marketing, July, pp 30–35

Hallberg G (1995) All Consumers Are Not Created Equal, John Wiley & Sons

Han C (1989) Country Image or Summary Construct?, Journal of Marketing Research, Vol 26 No 2 pp 222–229

Han C and **Terpstra** V (1988) Country-of-Origin Effects for Uni-National and Bi-National Products, Journal of International Business Studies, Vol 19 No 2 pp 235–255

Hansen T (2005) Perspectives on Consumer Decision Making: An Integrated Approach, Journal of Consumer Behaviour, Vol 4 No 6

Harrell G (1986) Consumer Behaviour, Harcourt Brace Jovanovich

Harris L and **Reynolds** K (2003) The Consequences of Dysfunctional Customer Behaviour, Journal of Service Research, Vol 6 No 2 pp 144–161

Harris L and **Reynolds** K (2004) Jaycustomer Behaviour: An Exploration of Types and Motives in the Hospitality Industry, Journal of Services Marketing, Vol 18 No 5 pp 339–357

Harris Research (1998) European Values Research Report, London

Heald G (1982) A Comparison between American, European and Japanese Values, World Association for Public Opinion Research Annual Meeting, Maryland, USA, 21 May

Heald G (1993) Changing Values 1981–1990, Market Research Society Annual Conference, Birmingham

Healy D (2004) Select Committee on the Influence of the Pharmaceutical Industry, Westminster, October

Heider F (1958) The Psychology of Interpersonal Relations, John Wiley & Sons, New York

Heilman C M, **Nakamoto** K and **Rao** A G (2002) Pleasant Surprises: Consumer Responses to Unexpected In-Store Coupons, Journal of Marketing Research, Vol 39 No 2 pp 242–252

Henley Centre for Forecasting (1978) Planning Consumer Markets, London

Henley Centre for Forecasting (1992) Presentation to Market Research Society, 5 March, Bristol

Henry P C (2005) Social Class, Market Situation, and Consumers' Metaphors of (Dis)Empowerment, Journal of Consumer Research, Vol 31 No 4 pp 766–778

Herche J and **Balasubramanian** S (1994) Ethnicity and Shopping Behaviour, Journal of Shopping Centre Research, Vol 1 No 1, Fall, pp 65–80

Hofstede G (1980) Culture's Consequences, Sage, Thousand Oaks, CA

Hogg M K and **Bannister** E N (2001) Dislikes, Distastes and the Undesired Self: Conceptualising and Exploring the Role of the Undesired End State in Consumer Experience, Journal of Marketing Management, Vol 17 No 1–2 pp 73–104

Holbrook M B and **Schindler** R M (2003) Nostalgic Binding: Exploring the Role of Nostalgia in the Consumption Experience, Journal of Consumer Behaviour, Vol 3 No 2 pp 107–128

Holt D B (2002) Why Do Brands Cause Trouble? A Dialectical Theory of Consumer Culture and Branding, Journal of Consumer Research, Vol 29 No 1 pp 70–91

Holt-Hansen K (1971) Perceptual and Motor Skills, Vol 33 No 3 pp 101–103

Hong S T and **Wyer** R S Jr (1989) Effects of Country-of-Origin and Product Attribute Information on Product Evaluation: An Information-Processing Perspective, Journal of Consumer Research, Vol 16 No 2 pp 175–187

Hopkins N (2003) Advertisers Reject Thrills and Spills of the Race to Promote Programmes for Third World, Time Business, 19 April, p 55

Horney K (1950) Neurosis and Human Growth, Norton, New York

Houston F S and **Gassenhemer** J B (1987) Marketing and Exchange, Journal of Marketing, Vol 51 pp 3–18

Hovland C I, **Janis** I L and **Kelley** H H (1953) Communication and Persuasion, Yale, New Haven, CT

Hovland C I and **Weiss** W (1951) The Influence of Source Credibility on Communication Effectiveness, Public Opinion Quarterly, Vol 15

Howard J A and **Moore** W L (1982) Changes in Consumer Behavior over the Product Life Cycle, in **Tushman** M L and **Moore** W L (eds) Readings in the Management of Innovation, Pitman, Boston, MA, pp 122–130

Hoyer W D and **MacInnes** D J (2001) Consumer Behavior, 2nd edn, Houghton Mifflin, Boston

Humby C (2004) R is for Relevance, Annual IDM Lecture, London

Humby C, **Hunt** T and **Phillips** T (2003) Scoring Points: How Tesco Is Winning Customer Loyalty, Kogan Page

Humphries J (1995) Institute of Management Conference

Introna L and **Powloudi** A (1999) Privacy in the Information Age: Stakeholders, Interests and Values, Journal of Business Ethics, Vol 22 pp 27–38

Jackson M and **Fulberg** P (2003) Sonic Branding, Palgrave, Basingstoke

Jaffe L and **Berger** P (1994) The Effect of Modern Female Sex Role Portrayals on Advertising Effectiveness, Journal of Advertising Research, Vol 34 No 4 pp 32–42

Jamal A (1996) Acculturation: The Symbolism of Ethnic Eating among Contemporary British Consumers, British Food Journal, Vol 98 No 10 pp 14–28

Jamal A (1997) Acculturation and Consumer Behaviour: A Study of Cross Cultural Differences, Inter-Ethnic Perceptions and Consumption Experiences in Bradford, unpublished PhD thesis, University of Bradford, United Kingdom

Jamal A (1998) Food Consumption among Ethnic Minorities: The Case of British-Pakistanis in Bradford, UK, British Food Journal, Vol 100 No 5 pp 221–228

Jamal A (2003) Marketing in a Multicultural World: The Interplay of Marketing, Ethnicity and Consumption, European Journal of Marketing, Vol 37 No 11/12 pp 1599–1620

Jamal A (2005) Playing to Win: An Explorative Study of Marketing Strategies of Small Ethnic Retail Entrepreneurs in the UK, Journal of Retailing and Consumer Services, Vol 12 No 1 pp 1–13

Jamal A and **Chapman** M (2000) Acculturation and Inter-Ethnic Consumer Perceptions: Can You Feel What We Feel?, Journal of Marketing Management, Vol 16 pp 365–391

Jamal A and **Goode** M (2001) Consumers and Brands: A Study of the Impact of Self-Image Congruence on Brand Preference and Satisfaction, Marketing Intelligence and Planning, Vol 19 No 7 pp 482–492

Janda S and **Rao** C P (1997) The Effect of Country-of-Origin Related Stereotypes and Personal Beliefs on Product Evaluation, Psychology and Marketing, Vol 14 No 7 pp 689–703

Jansson C, **Marlow** N and **Bristow** M (2004) The Influence of Colour on Visual Search Times in Cluttered Environments, Journal of Marketing Communications, Vol 10, September, pp 183–193

Japan Consumer Marketing Research Institute Tokyo http://www.jmrlsi.co.jp/english/sizing/insights/2004/cons2.gif

John D R (1999) Consumer Socialization of Children: A Retrospective Look at Twenty Five Years of Research, Journal of Consumer Research, Vol 26, December, pp 183–213

Johnson H M (1962) Sociology, Routledge & Kegan Paul, pp 86–95

Jones S (1995) Understanding Community in the Information Age, in **Jones** S G, Cybersociety: Computer-Mediated Communication and Community, Sage, Thousand Oaks, CA, pp 10–35

Jones T O (1996) Why Loyal Customers Defect, Keynote Presentation, IDM Symposium, 6 June London

Jones T O and **Sasser** W E (1995) Why Loyal Customers Defect, Harvard Business Review, pp 88–99

Kacen J J (2000) Girrl Power and Boyyy Nature: The Past, Present and Paradisal Future of Consumer Gender Identity, Marketing Intelligence and Planning, Vol 18 No 6/7 pp 345–355

Kamins M A (1990) An Investigation into the 'Match-Up' Hypothesis in Celebrity Advertising: When Beauty May Only be Skin Deep, Journal of Advertising, Vol 19 No 1 pp 4–13

Kanner B (1989) Color Schemes, New York Magazine, 22–23 April

Kassarjian H H and **Robertson** T S (1973) Perspectives in Consumer Behaviour, Scott Foresman, p 292

Katz E (1960) The Functional Approach to the Study of Attitudes, Public Opinion Quarterly, Vol 24 pp 163–204

Katz E and **Lazarsfeld** P F (1955) Personal Influence, Free Press, New York

Kauffman S E, **Silver** P and **Poulin** J (1997) Gender Differences in Attitudes toward Alcohol, Tobacco and Other Drugs, Social Work, Vol 42 No 3 pp 231–241

Kaufman-Scarborough C (2001) Accessible Advertising for Visually-Disabled Persons: The Case of Color-Deficient Consumers, Journal of Consumer Marketing, Vol 18 No 4/5 pp 303–318

Keaveney S M (1995) Customer Switching Behaviour in Service Industries: An Exploratory Study, Journal of Marketing, Vol 59 pp 71–82

Keillor B D, **D'Amico** M and **Horton** V (2001) Global Consumer Tendencies, Psychology and Marketing, Vol 18 No 1 pp 1–19

Kempner T (1976) A Dictionary of Management, Penguin

Kenkel W F (1961) Husband Wife Interaction in Decision-Making and Decision Choices, Journal of Social Psychology, Vol 54

Key W B (1973) Subliminal Seduction, Signet, Englewood Cliffs, NJ

Kingdom J W (1970) Opinion Leaders in the Electorate, Public Opinion Quarterly, Vol 34 pp 256–261

Kirton M J (1994) A Theory of Cognitive Style, in **Kirton** M J (ed.), Adaptors and Innovators: Styles of Creativity and Problem-Solving, 2nd edn, Routledge, London pp 1–36

Kitchen P and **Spickett-Jones** G (2003) Information Processing: A Critical Literature Review and Future Research Directions, International Journal of Market Research, Vol 45 No 1 pp 73–98

Klein N (2001) No Logo, Flamingo, London

Komarovsky M (1961) Class Differences in Family Decision-Making, in **Foote** N N (ed.), Household Decision-Making, New York University Press

Kosfeld M, **Heinrichs** M, **Zak** P J, **Fischbacher** U and **Fehr** E (2005) Oxytocin Increases Trust in Humans, Nature, Vol 435 No 7042, 1 June, pp 673–676

Kotler P (1972) Marketing Management, Prentice-Hall, p 113

Kozinets R (1998) On Netnography: Initial Reflections on Consumer Research Investigations of Cyberculture, in **Alba** J and **Hutchinson** W (eds), Advances in Consumer Research, Vol 25 pp 366–371

Kozinets R (1999) E-Tribalized Marketing? The Strategic Implications of Virtual Communities of Consumption, European Management Journal, Vol 17 No 3 pp 252–264

Kring A M and **Gordon** A H (1998) Sex Differences in Emotion: Expression, Experience, and Physiology, Journal of Personality and Social Psychology, Vol 74, March, pp 686–703

Krugman H E (1965) The Impact of Television Advertising: Learning without Involvement, Public Opinion Quarterly, Vol 29 pp 349–356

Laaksonen P (1994) Consumer Involvement: Concepts and Research, Routledge, London and New York

Lace S (ed.) (2005) The Glass Consumer: Life in a Surveillance Society, Policy Press/National Consumer Council

Larkins V (2003) 10 Million Tick Electoral Roll Opt-Out Box, Marketing Business, February, p 6

Laroche M, **Papadopoulos** N, **Heslop** L and **Bergeron** J (2003) Effects of Subcultural Differences on Country and Product Evaluations, Journal of Consumer Behaviour, Vol 2 No 3 pp 232–247

Larson E (1994) The Naked Consumer: How Our Private Lives Become Public Commodities, Penguin, New York

Lasswell H D (1948) The Analysis of Political Behaviour, Routledge & Kegan Paul

Lavidge R J and **Steiner** G A (1961) A Model for Predictive Measurements of Advertising Effectiveness, Journal of Marketing, Vol 25 pp 59–62

Lawson R W (1988) The Family Life Cycle: A Demographic Analysis, Journal of Marketing Management, Vol 4 No 1 pp 13–32

Laybourne P and **Lewis** D (2005) Neuromarketing: The Future of Consumer Research?, Admap, May, pp 28–30

Lazarsfeld P *et al.* (1944) The People's Choice, Duell, Sloan & Pearce Inc., New York

Legg D and **Baker** J (1996) Advertising Strategies for Service Firms, in **Lovelock** C H (ed.), Services Marketing, 3rd edn, Prentice Hall

Leighton N (2004) They're Reading Our Minds, Sunday Times, 25 January, p 9

Levitt T (1983) The Marketing Imagination, Free Press, New York

Liljander V and **Strandvick** T (1995) The Nature of Customer Relationships in Services, Advances in Marketing and Management, Vol 4 pp 141–167

Lindstrom M (2004) Child's Play The Marketers, CIM, Maidenhead, July-August, pp 23–24

Lindstrom M (2005) Sensing an Opportunity, Sensory Appeal, The Marketers, CIM, Maidenhead, No 10, February, pp 6–11

Littlewood F (1999) Attention Seekers, Marketing, 13 May, p 31

Loader B (ed.) (1998) Cyberspace Divide: Equality, Agency and Policy in the Information Society, Routledge, London, pp 3–16

London S (2003) Radio ID Tags Spread Waves of Anger among Privacy Activists, Financial Times, 1 March, p 1

Louden D L and **Della Bitta** A J (1993) Consumer Behaviour, McGraw Hill, New York

Lovell C (1997) IDM Guest Lecture, University of the West of England, 30 January, Bristol

Lovelock C (1994) Product Plus, McGraw Hill, New York

Madden T J, **Hewett** K and **Roth** M S (2000) Managing Images in Different Cultures: A Cross-National Study of Color Meanings and Preferences, Journal of International Marketing, Vol 8 No 4 pp 90–107

Maffesoli M (1996) The Time of the Tribes: The Decline of Individualism in Mass Society, Sage, London

Magrath A J (1992) The Death of Advertising has been Greatly Exaggerated, Sales and Marketing Management, Vol 144 No 2, February, pp 23–24

Mancuso J R (1969) Why Not Create Opinion Leaders for New Product Introductions?, Journal of Marketing, Vol 33 pp 20–25

Mano H and **Oliver** R L (1993) Assessing the Dimensionality and Structure of the Consumption Experience: Evaluation, Feeling and Satisfaction, Journal of Consumer Research, Vol 20, December, pp 451–466

Manyiwa S and **Crawford** I (2002) Determining Linkages between Consumer Choices in a Social Context and the Consumer's Values: A Means-End Approach, Journal of Consumer Behaviour, Vol 2 No 1 pp 54–70

Market Research Society (1981) Working Party Report on Social Grade, MRS, London

Market Research Society (2004) Occupation Groupings: A Job Directory, 5th edn, Market Research Society, London

Markus H R and **Kunda** Z (1986) Stability and Malleability of the Self Concept, Journal of Personality and Social Psychology, Vol 51 No 4 pp 858–866

Markus H R and **Nurius** P (1986) Possible Selves, American Psychologist, Vol 41 No 9 pp 954–969

Marsden P S (1998) Memetics: A New Paradigm for Understanding Customer Behaviour and Influence, Marketing Intelligence and Planning, Vol 16 No 6

Marsden P S (1999) Help Advertising Evolve: Clone Consumer Thought-Patterns, Admap, March, pp 37–39

Marx K (1867/1967) Capital, Vol 1, International Publishers, New York

May M (2005) Electoral Roll Reveals Final Opt-Out, Marketing Direct, February, p 7

May R (2005) Consumer White Paper 2004: Changing Consumption Patterns, Japan Consumer Marketing Research Institute, Tokyo, http://www.jmrlsi.co.jp/english/sizing/insights/2004/cons2.gif

McAlexander J H, **Schouten** J W and **Keonig** H F (2002) Building Brand Community, Journal of Marketing, Vol 66 No 1 pp 38–55

McCarthy E J (1977) Basic Marketing Learning Aid, Irwin, Homewood, IL

McClelland D C (1961) The Achieving Society, Van Nostrand, Princeton, NJ

McCracken G (1986) Culture and Consumption: A Theoretical Account of the Structure and Movement of Cultural Meaning of Consumer Goods, Journal of Consumer Research, Vol 13, June, pp 71–84

McCracken G (1988) The Long Interview, Sage

McGuire W (1974) Psychological Motives and Communication Gratification, in **Blummer** J F and **Katz** E (eds) The Uses of Mass Communications: Current Perspectives on Gratification Research, Sage, Beverly Hills, pp 106–167

McGuire W (1976) Some Internal Psychological Factors Influencing Consumer Choice, Journal of Consumer Research, Vol 2 No 4 pp 302–319

McKenzie S (1995) Distinguishing Marks, Marketing Week, 17 November, pp 13–15

McNulty C (2002) interview on BBC, Century of the Self, November

McNulty C and **McNulty** R (1987) Applied Futures: Social Value Groups, Taylor Nelson

McWilliam G (2000) Building Stronger Brands through Online Communities, Sloan Management Review, Vol 41 No 3 pp 43–54

Mellis R (1997) as quoted in **Bailey** J, Tune in to the Power of the Viewing Public, P R Week, 17 October, p 7

Merton R K (1968) Social Theory and Social Structure, Free Press New York

Meyers-Levy J and **Maheswaran** D (1991) Exploring Differences in Males' and Females' Processing Strategy, Journal of Consumer Research, Vol 18, June, pp 63–70

Michie D (1998) Invisible Persuaders, Bantam Press

Mick D G (1986) Consumer Research and Semiotics: Exploring the Morphology of Signs, Symbols, and Significance, Journal of Consumer Research, Vol 13 No 2 pp 196–213

Middleton T (1997) The Pink Pound, Direct Response, February, pp 49–53

Midgely D and **Wills** G (1979) Fashion Marketing Lateral Marketing Thoughts, Bradford: MCB Prem, p 131

Miller R L (1962) Dr Weber and the Consumer, Journal of Marketing, January, pp 57–62

Milliman R E (1982) Using Background Music to Affect the Behavior of Supermarket Shoppers, Journal of Marketing, Vol 46, Summer, pp 86–91

Millward-Brown (2002) Brand Child Study, reported in **Lindstrom** M (2004) Child's Play, The Marketers, CIM, Maidenhead, July-August, pp 23–24

MINTEL, (2004) Men's Underwear, March

Mishan E J (1971) 21 Popular Economic Fallacies, Pelican, Harmondsworth

Misra S and **Beatty** S E (1990) Celebrity Foundations of the Endorsement Process, Journal of Consumer Research, Vol 16 No 1 pp 310–321

Mitchell A (1996) You and Yours, Interview transcribed from BBC Radio 4, January

Mitchell A (2001) Playing Cat and Mouse Games with Marketing, Precision Marketing, 16 March, p 14

Mitchell A (2002) Permission to Target in Not a Licence to Spam, Precision Marketing, 12 July, p 14

Mitchell V W and **Walsh** G (2004) Gender Differences in German Consumer Decision-Making Styles, Journal of Consumer Behaviour, Vol 3 No 4 pp 331–346

Mittal B (2002) Services Communications: From Mindless Tangibilization to Meaningful Messages, Journal of Services Marketing, Vol 16 No 5 pp 424–431

Mittelstaedt R A, **Grossbart** S L, **Curtis** W W and **DeVere** S P (1976) Optimal Stimulation Level and the Adoption Decision Process, Journal of Consumer Research, Vol 3, pp 84–94

Moir A and **Moir** B (1998) Why Men Don't Iron: The Real Science of Gender Studies, Harper-Collins, London

Molesworth M and **Suortti** J P (2002) Buying Cars on Line: The Adoption of the Web for High Involvement, High Cost Purchases, Journal of Consumer Behaviour, Vol 2 No 2 pp 155–168

Moore E S, **Wilkie** W L and **Lutz** R J (2002), Passing the Torch: Intergenerational Influences as a Source of Brand Equity, Journal of Marketing, Vol 66 No 2 pp 17–38

Moore G (1991) Crossing the Chasm, Harper Business, New York

Moreno J L (1953) Who Shall Survive?, Beacon House

Morgan R M and **Hunt** S D (1994) The Commitment–Trust Theory of Relationship Marketing, Journal of Marketing, Vol 58 pp 20–38

Mortimer K (2001) Services Advertising: The Agency Viewpoint, Journal of Services Marketing, Vol 15 No 2 pp 131–140

Moschis G P (2003) Marketing to Older Adults: An Updated Overview of Present Knowledge and Practice, Journal of Consumer Marketing, Vol 20 No 6 pp 516–525

⇒**Muniz** A M (1997) Brand Community and the Negotiation of Brand Meaning, in **Brucks** M and **MacInnis** D J, Advances in Consumer Research, Vol 24, Association for Consumer Research, Provo, UT, pp 308–309

Muniz A M and **O'Guinn** T C Jr (2001) Brand Community, Journal of Consumer Research, Vol 27 No 4 pp 412–431

Murphy D (1997) Money Where your Mouth Is, P R Week, 9 October, pp 35–36

Murray I (1995) Bare Faced Cheek of a Naked Butt, Marketing Week, 17 November, Vol 94

Myers J G (1967) Determinants of Private Brand Attitude, Journal of Marketing Research, Vol 4

Nancarrow, C, **Nancarrow** P and **Page** J (2002) An Analysis of the Concept of *Cool* and its Marketing Implications, Journal of Consumer Behaviour, Vol 1 No 4 pp 311–322

Nancarrow C, **Tinson** J and **Evans** M (2004) Polls as Marketing Weapons: Implications for the Market Research Industry, Journal of Marketing Management, Vol 20 No 5–6 pp 639–655

Nokes B (1994) The Good the Bad and the Sexist, Marketing Week, Vol 11, February, pp 50–51

North A C, **Hargreaves** D J and **McKendrick** J (1999) The Influence of In-Store Music on Wine Selections, Journal of Applied Psychology, Vol 84 pp 271–276

O'Brien S and **Ford** R (1988) Can We at Last Say Goodbye to Social Class?, Journal of the Market Research Society, Vol 30 pp 289–332

O'Donahoe S and **Tynan** C (1998) Beyond Sophistication: Dimensions of Advertising Literacy, International Journal of Advertising, Vol 17 pp 467–482

Oakenfull G K and **Greenlee** T B (2005) Queer Eye for a Gay Guy: Using Market-Specific Symbols in Advertising to Attract Gay Consumers without Alienating the Mainstream, Psychology and Marketing, Vol 22 No 5 pp 421–440

O'Guinn T C and **Faber** R J (1989) Compulsive Buying: A Phenomenological Exploration, Journal of Consumer Research, Vol 16 No 2 pp 147–158

Oliver R L (1980) Cognitive Model of the Antecedents and Consequences of Satisfaction Decisions, Journal of Marketing Research, Vol 17, November, pp 460–469

Oliver R L (1993) Cognitive, Affective, and Attribute Bases of the Satisfaction Response, Journal of Consumer Research, Vol 20 No 3 pp 418–430

Oliver R L (1997) Satisfaction: A Behavioural Perspective on the Consumer, McGraw-Hill, New York

Oliver R L (1999) Whence Consumer Loyalty, Journal of Marketing, Vol 63 pp 33–44

Onkvisit S and **Shaw** J (1987) Self-Concept and Image Congruence: Some Research and Managerial Implications, Journal of Consumer Marketing, Vol 4 No 1 pp 13–23

Orth U R, **McDaniel** M, **Shellhammer** T and **Lopetcharat** K (2004) Promoting Brand Benefits: The Role of Consumer Psychographics and Lifestyle, Journal of Consumer Marketing, Vol 21 No 2 pp 97–108

Oswald R L (1999) Culture Swapping: Consumption and the Ethnogenesis of Middle-Class Haitian Immigrants, Journal of Consumer Research, Vol 25, March, pp 303–318

Packard V (1957) The Hidden Persuaders, McKay, New York

Palda K S (1968) The Hypothesis of a Hierarchy of Effects: A Partial Solution, Journal of Marketing Research, May, pp 131–145

Parasuraman A, **Zeithaml** V and **Berry** L (1985) A Conceptual Model of Service Quality and its Implications for Future Research, Journal of Marketing, Vol 49, Fall, pp 41–50

Parfitt J H and **Collins** B J K (1968) The Use of Consumer Panels for Brand-Share Prediction, Journal of Marketing Research, Vol 5 pp 131–145

Park G W and **Lessig** V P (1977) Students and Housewives: Differences in Susceptibility to Reference Group Influence, Journal of Consumer Research, Vol 4 pp 102–110

Parsons A (2004) Sensory Stimuli and E-Tailers, Journal of Consumer Behaviour, Vol 4 No 6

Patterson M (1998) Direct Marketing in Postmodernity: Neo-Tribes and Direct Communications, Marketing Intelligence and Planning, Vol 16 No 1 pp 68–74

Pavlov I P (1928) Lectures on Conditioned Reflexes: The Higher Nervous Activity of Animals, 1, trans. Gantt H, Lawrence & Wishart, London

Penaloza L (1994) Atravesando Fronteras/Border Crossings: A Critical Ethnographic Exploration of the Consumer Acculturation of Mexican Immigrants, Journal of Consumer Research, Vol 21, June, pp 289–294

Penaloza L and **Gilly** M C (1999) Marketer Acculturation: The Changer and the Changed, Journal of Marketing, Vol 63, July, pp 84–104

Peters J P and **Olson** J C (2005) Consumer Behaviour and Marketing Strategy, McGraw Hill, New York

Petty R E and **Cacioppo** J T (1983) Central and Peripheral Routes to Persuasion: Application to Advertising, in **Percy** L and **Woodside** A G, Advertising and Consumer Psychology, Lexington Books, Lexington

Petty R E, **Cacioppo** J T and **Schumann** D (1983) Central and Peripheral Routes to Advertising Effectiveness: The Moderating Role of Involvement, Journal of Consumer Research, Vol 10 No 2 pp 135–146

Piacentini M and **Mailer** G (2004) Symbolic Consumption in Teenagers' Clothing Choices, Journal of Consumer Behaviour, Vol 3 No 3 pp 231–264

Pincus J (2004) The Consequences of Unmet Needs: The Evolving Role of Motivation in Consumer Research, Journal of Consumer Behaviour, Vol 3 No 4

Pressey A D and **Selassie** H G (2003) Are Cultural Differences Overrated? Examining the Influence of National Culture on International Buyer-Seller Relationships, Journal of Consumer Behaviour, Vol 2 No 4 pp 354–368

Pringle H and **Binet** L (2005) How Marketers Can Use Celebrities to Sell More Effectively, Journal of Consumer Behaviour, Vol 4 No 3 pp 201–214

Publicis (1992) presented by **Block**, R, Sales Talk, BBC Radio 4, January

Pulham A (2003) reported in **Sclater** I, Challenging Perceptions, Marketing Business, February, pp 16–17

Rainbow TV (1997) research reported in **Middleton** T, The Pink Pound, Direct Response, February, pp 49–53

Raven J R P and **French** B (1959) The Bases of Social Power, in **Cartwright** D (ed.), Studies in Social Power, MI Institute for Social Research, pp 150–167

Rawlins M (1984) Doctors and Drug Makers, Lancet, Vol 4, August, pp 276–278

Redfield R, **Linton** R and **Herskovits** M J (1936) Memorandum on the Study of Acculturation, American Anthropologist, Vol 38 No 2 pp 149–152

Rees J (1995) Calvin Klein Makes 'Offensive' Ads Pay, Marketing Week, 8 September, Vol 23

Reichheld F F (1988) Loyalty and the Renaissance of Marketing, Marketing Management, Vol 2 No 4 pp 10–21

Reichheld F F (1996) Learning from Customer Defections, Harvard Business Review, Vol 74 No 2, March/April

Reichheld F F and **Sasser** W E (1990) Zero Defects: Quality Comes to Service, Harvard Business Review, September/October, pp 105–111

Research International (1996) Materialism or New Realism, Research International Ltd, London

Research Services Ltd (1981) SAGACITY: A tool for more Effective Market Analysis and Media Planning, London

Revolution Awards (2002) Haymarket, London

Reynolds T J and **Gutman** J (1988) Laddering Theory, Method, Analysis and Interpretation, Journal of Advertising Research, February/March, pp 11–31

Rheingold H (1993) The Virtual Community: Homesteading on the Electronic Frontier, Addison–Wesley, Reading, MA

Richardson L (2000) You Can Run But You Can't Hide, Revolution, September, pp 12–15

Richins M L (1983) Negative Word-of-Mouth by Dissatisfied Customers: A Pilot Study, Journal of Marketing, Vol 47, Winter, pp 68–78

Ries A and **Trout** J (1986) Positioning: The Battle for Your Mind, McGraw Hill, New York

Riesman D (1950) The Lonely Crowd, Yale University Press, New Haven, Conn.

Rindfleisch A, **Burroughs** J E and **Denton** F (1997) Family Structure, Materialism, and Compulsive Consumption, Journal of Consumer Research, Vol 23 No 4 pp 312–325

Ritchie K (1995) Marketing to Generation X, Lexington Books, New York

Robertson T S (1967) The Process of Innovation and the Diffusion of Innovation, Journal of Marketing, Vol 31 pp 14–19

Robertson T S (1971) Innovative Behaviour and Communication, Holt, Rhinehart & Winston

Robinson J P (1957) Inter-Personal Influence in Election Campaigns: Two-Step Flow Hypothesis, Public Relations Quarterly, Vol 40 pp 304–319

Rogers E M (1959, 1983) Diffusion of Innovations, Free Press, New York

Rogers E M and **Shoemaker** F (1971) Communication of Innovation, Macmillan, p 103

Rokeach M (1968) Beliefs, Attitudes and Values, Jossey-Bass, San Francisco

Rokeach M (1973) The Nature of Human Values, Free Press, New York

Rook D W (1985) The Ritual Dimension of Consumer Behaviour, Journal of Consumer Research, Vol 12, December, pp 218–240

Rook D W (1987) The Buying Impulse, Journal of Consumer Research, Vol 14 No 2 pp 189–200

Rook D W and **Fisher** R J (1995) Trait and Normative Aspects of Impulsive Buying Behaviour, Journal of Consumer Research, Vol 22 No 3 pp 305–313

Rose G (1999) Consumer Socialisation, Parental Style and Development Timetables in US and Japan, Journal of Marketing, Vol 63 No 3 pp 105–119

Rosen J (2001) The Unwanted Gaze: The Destruction of Privacy in America, Vintage Books, New York

Rosenberg M (1979) Conceiving the Self, Basic Books, New York

Rosser M (2003) 20th Century to Persist with Voicemail Ads, Precision Marketing, 14 February, p 1

Rossiter J R and **Chan** A M (1998) Ethnicity in Business and Consumer Behaviour, Journal of Business Research, Vol 42, pp 127–134

Rossiter J R, **Percy** L and **Donovan** R J (1991) A Better Advertising Planning Grid, Journal of Advertising Research, October/November, pp 11–21

Rothfeder J (1992) Privacy for Sale: How Computerisation Has Made Everyone's Private Life an Open Secret, Simon & Schuster, New York

Rubach E (2002) Up Close and Too Personal, Precision Marketing, 1 February, p 12

Rubach E (2003a) Harley Gears up for Euro Loyalty Assault, Precision Marketing, January, p 1

Rubach E (2003b) Industry Hail Robertson Defeat, Precision Marketing, 23 May, p 1

Rudolph H J (1947) Attention and Interest Factors in Advertising, Funke Wagnalls, New York

Rule J (1998) reported in **Ungoed-Thomas** J and **Nuki** P, Mailshot Firms Blitz 'Midas' Consumers, Sunday Times, 17 May

Rust R T and **Oliver** R W (1994) The Death of Advertising, Journal of Advertising, Vol 23 No 4, December, pp 71–77

Samuelsen B and **Sandvik** K (1997) The Concept of Customer Loyalty, in 26th Annual EMAC Conference: Progress, Prospects and Perspectives, Warwick Business School, Coventry, England

Sasse A (2005) Effective Security and Privacy: Protecting People Not Just Data, International Symposium on Confidentiality, Privacy and Disclosure in the 21st century, University of Manchester, UK, 3 May

Schaninger C M and **Lee** D H (2002) A New Full Nest Classification Approach, Psychology and Marketing, Vol 19 No 1 pp 25–58

Schewe C D and **Meredith** G (2004) Segmenting Global Markets by Generational Cohorts: Determining Motivations by Age, Journal of Consumer Behaviour, Vol 4 No 1 pp 51–63

Schiffman L G and **Kanuk** L Z (2000) Consumer Behaviour, 7th edn, Prentice Hall, NJ

Schmitt B H (1999) Experiential Marketing: How to Get Customers to Sense, Feel, Think, Act and Relate to Your Company and Brands, Free Press, New York

Schouten J W (1991) Selves in Transition: Symbolic Consumption in Personal Rites of Passage and Identity Reconstruction, Journal of Consumer Research, Vol 17 No 4 pp 412–425

Schouten J W and **McAlexander** J H (1995) Subcultures of Consumption: An Ethnography of the New Biker, Journal of Consumer Research, Vol 22 No 1 pp 43–62

Schramm W and **Roberts** D (eds) (1971) The Process and Effects of Mass Communication, University of Illinois Press, Urbana, IL

Schroeder D (1992) Life, Liberty and the Pursuit of Privacy, American Demographics, June, Vol 20

Schwartz S H and **Bilsky** W (1987) Toward a Universal Psychological Structure of Human Values, Journal of Personality and Social Psychology, Vol 53, pp 550–562

Sclater I (2002) Race Relations, Marketing Business, September, pp 31–33

Sclater I (2003) Challenging Perceptions, Marketing Business, February, pp 16–17

Scott J (2002) Once Bitten, Twice Shy: A World of Eroding Trust, New York Times, 21 April, p 5

Shabi R (2003) The Card Up Their Sleeve, Guardian Weekend Magazine, 19 July, pp 14–19

Shaw D, **Grehan** E, **Shui** E, **Hasaan** L and **Thomson** J (2005) An Exploration of Values in Ethical Consumer Decision Making, Journal of Consumer Behaviour, Vol 4 No 3 pp 185–200

Shaw J (2004) Chip and Pin, Campaign Supplement, 9 April, p 7

Shepherdson N (2000) Life's a Beach 101, American Demographics, May

Sheth J N and **Parvatiyar** A (eds) (2000) Handbook of Relationship Marketing, Sage, Thousand Oaks, CA

Shibutani T (1955) Reference Groups as Perspectives, American Journal of Sociology, Vol 60

Shim S and **Gehrt** K C (1996) Hispanic and Native American Adolescents: An Exploratory Study of Their Approach to Shopping, Journal of Retailing, Vol 72 No 3 pp 307–324

Shiv B and **Huber** J (2000) The Impact of Anticipating Satisfaction on Consumer Choice, Journal of Consumer Research, Gainesville, Vol 27 No 2, September, pp 202–217

Silvera D H and **Austad** B (2004) Factors Predicting the Effectiveness of Celebrity Endorsement Advertisements, European Journal of Marketing, Vol 38 No 11/12 pp 1509–1526

Sirgy J M (1982) Self-Concept in Consumer Behaviour: A Critical Review, Journal of Consumer Research, Vol 9 No 3 pp 287–300

Sirgy J M, **Grewal** D, **Mangleburg** F T, **Park** J-O, **Chon** K-S, **Claiborne** C B, **Johar** J S and **Berkman** H (1997) Assessing the Predictive Validity of Two Methods of Measuring Self-Image Congruence, Journal of the Academy of Marketing Science, Vol 25 No 3 pp 229–241

Skinner B F (1938) The Behaviour of Organisms, Appleton-Century-Crofts, New York

SmartFocus (2004) Viper Print Out, Bristol

Smigel E O (1956) Public Attitudes toward Stealing as Related to the Size of the Organisation, American Sociology Review, Vol 21 pp 320–327

Social Trends (2005) Office for National Statistics, London

Solomon M (2003) Conquering Consumerspace; Marketing Strategies for a Branded World, Amacom, New York

Solomon M (2004) Consumer Behaviour: Buying, Having and Being, Pearson, Upper Saddle River, New Jersey

Solomon M, **Bamossy** G and **Askegaard** S (2003) Consumer Behaviour, Prentice Hall

Speck P S and **Elliott** M T (1997) Predictors of Advertising Avoidance in Print and Broadcast Media, Journal of Advertising, Vol 26 pp 61–76

Specter M (1999) Cracking the Norse Code, Sunday Times Magazine, 21 March, pp 45–52

Spies K and **Hesse** F (1997) Store Atmosphere, Mood and Purchasing Behavior, International Journal of Research in Marketing, Vol 14 pp 1–17

Spotts H E, **Weinberger** M G and **Parsons** A L (1997) Assessing the Use and Impact of Humor on Advertising Effectiveness: A Contingency Approach, Journal of Advertising, Vol 26 No 3 pp 17–33

Spradley J P and **McCurdy** D W (1977) Conformity and Conflict: Readings in Cultural Anthropology, 3rd edn, Boston, Little Brown

Sproles G B and **Kendall** E L (1986) A Methodology for Profiling Consumers' Decision-Making Styles, Journal of Consumer Affairs, Vol 20 No 2 pp 267–280

Sprott W H (1958) Human Groups, Penguin Books, p 9

St Elmo Lewis E (circa 1900) cited in **Barry** T E and **Howard** D J, A Review and Critique of the Hierarchy of Effects in Advertising, International Journal of Advertising, Vol 9 pp 121–135

Stafford J E (1966) Effects of Group Influences on Consumer Brand Preferences, Journal of Marketing Research, Vol 3

Stayman D M and **Deshpande** R (1989) Situational Ethnicity and Consumer Behaviour, Journal of Consumer Research, Vol 16, December, pp 361–371

Steenhaut S and **Van Kenhove** P (2005) Relationship Commitment and Consumer Behaviour in a Retail Setting: The Case of Recovering Too Much Change at the Checkout, Journal of Business Ethics, Vol 56 pp 335–353

Steiner R (2002) Watch Out, Big Spenders, Big Brother is Watching You, Sunday Times Business, 11 August, p 1

Stephens N (1991) Cognitive Age: A Useful Concept for Advertising?, Journal of Advertising, Vol 20 No 4 pp 37–48

Stern H (1962) The Significance of Impulse Buying Today, Journal of Marketing, Vol 26 pp 59–62

Sternthal B and **Craig** C S (1973) Humor in Advertising, Journal of Marketing, Vol 37 No 4 pp 12–18

Sternthal B and **Craig** C S (1974) Fear Appeals: Revisited and Revised, Journal of Consumer Research, Vol 1 No 3

Stokes D (1997) cited in **Darby** I, Printing Gets all Creative, Marketing Direct, January, pp 52–56

Suzman M (1996) Advertisers Miss Out on Ethnic Minority Market, Financial Times, November, Vol 19

Szmigin I and **Carrigan** M (2000) The Older Consumer as Innovator: Does Cognitive Age Hold the Key?, Journal of Marketing Management, Vol 16 No 5 pp 505–528

Szmigin I and **Carrigan** M (2001) Learning to Love the Older Consumer, Journal of Consumer Behaviour, Vol 1 No 1 pp 22–34

Tajfel H (1981) Human Groups and Social Categories: Studies in Social Psychology, Cambridge University Press, Cambridge

Tauber E M (1972) Why Do People Shop?, Journal of Marketing, Vol 36 No 4 pp 46–49

Taylor Nelson Sofres (2004) Are You a Member of Your Kid's Generation? (http://www.tns-global/corporate/doc/0/2vmqq3513e0419caj02jk5176f/247) accessed 23 March 2004

Telegraph Group (1999) reported in **Carling** E (1999) Grappling with the Grey Market, Marketing Direct

Thomas G (2004) Building the Buzz in the Hive Mind, Journal of Consumer Behaviour, Vol 4 No 1

Thompson C J, **Locander** W B and **Pollio** H R (1990) The Lived Meaning of Free Choice: An Existentialist-Phenomenological Description of Everyday Consumer Experiences of Contemporary Married Women, Journal of Consumer Research, Vol 17

Timmins N (1995) London's Ethnic Balance Shifting, Independent, 12 December

Tinson J and **Nancarrow** C (2005) The Influence of Children on Purchases, International Journal of Market Research, Vol 47 No 1 pp 5–28

Todd S (2001) Self-Concept: A Tourism Application, Journal of Consumer Behaviour, Vol 1 No 2 pp 184–196

Tonglet M (2002) Consumer Misbehaviour: An Exploratory Study of Shoplifting, Journal of Consumer Behaviour, Vol 1 No 4 pp 336–354

Tonkin E, **Chapman** M and **McDonald** M (eds.) (1989) History and Ethnicity, Routledge, London

Tosdal H (1925) Principles of Personal Selling, Shaw, Chicago, p 61

Treguer J P (2002) 50+ Marketing, Palgrave

Triplett T (1995) Carmakers Driven by Quest to Find Tomorrow's Color, Marketing News, Vol 29 No 18, 28 August, pp 38–39

Tripp C, **Jensen** T D and **Carlson** L (1994) The Effects of Multiple Product Endorsement by Celebrities, Journal of Consumer Research, Vol 20 No 4 pp 535–548

Tuan Yit Fu (1980) The significance of the Artefact, Geographical Review, Vol 70 No 4 p 472

Tunney D (1999) Harnessing the Subconscious to Bolster Sales, Marketing, 13 May, p 20

Turner V (1969) The Ritual Process, Aldine, Chicago

Tzokas N and **Saren** M (1997) Building Relationship Platforms in Consumer Markets: A Chain Approach, Journal of Strategic Marketing, Vol 5 No 2 pp 105–120

Ungoed-Thomas J and **Nuki** P (1998) Mailshot Firms Blitz 'Midas' Consumers, Sunday Times, 17 May

VALS (2005) http://www.sric-bi.com/VALS/presurvey.shtml, last accessed 6 June 2005

van Raaij W F and **Schoonderbeek** W M (1993) Meaning Structure of Brand Names and Extensions, European Advances in Consumer Research, Vol 1, pp 479–484

Venkatesan M (1966) Consumer Behaviour: Conformity and Independence, Journal of Marketing Research, Vol 3

Venkatesh A (1995) Ethnoconsumerism: A New Paradigm to Study Cultural and Cross-Cultural Consumer Behaviour, in **Costa** J A and **Bamossy** G J (eds), Marketing in a Multicultural World, Sage, London, pp 26–67

Vinson D J S and **Lamont** L (1977) The Role of Personal Values in Marketing and Consumer Research, Journal of Marketing, Vol 41, April, pp 45–50

Wakefield K L and **Blodgett**, J G (1999) Customer Response to Intangible and Tangible Service Factors, Psychology and Marketing, Vol 16 No 1 pp 51–68

Walker C (2001) US Threat to Axe Data Treaty Puts Multinationals on Alert, Precision Marketing, 6 April, p 1

Wallendorf M and **Arnould** E J (1991) We Gather Together: Consumption Rituals of Thanksgiving Day, Journal of Consumer Research, Vol 18, June, pp 13–31

Wallendorf M and **Reilly** M (1983) Ethnic Migration, Assimilation, and Consumption, Journal of Consumer Research, Vol 10, December, pp 292–302

Walsh G, **Gwinner** K P and **Swanson** S R (2004) What Makes Mavens Tick? Exploring the Motives of Market Mavens' Initiation of Information Diffusion, Journal of Consumer Marketing, Vol 21 No 2 pp 109–122

Webster C (1994) Effects of Ethnic Identification on Marital Roles in the Purchase Decision Process, Journal of Consumer Research, Vol 21, September, pp 319–331

Weinberger M G and **Gulas** C S (1992) The Impact of Humor in Advertising: A Review, Journal of Advertising, Vol 21 No 4, December, pp 35–60

Weinberger M G and **Spotts** H E (1989) Humor in US Versus UK TV Commercials: A Comparison, Journal of Advertising, Vol 18 No 2 pp 39–44

Weinberger M G, **Spotts** H, **Campbell** L and **Parsons** A L (1995) The Use and Effect of Humor in Different Advertising Media, Journal of Advertising Research, Vol 35 No 3, May/June, pp 44–56

Werner C M, **Haggard** L M, **Altman** I and **Oxley** D (1988) Temporal Qualities of Rituals and Celebrations: A Comparison of Christmas Street and Zuni Shalako, in **McGrath** J E (ed.), The Social Psychology of Time: New Perspectives, Sage, London, pp 203–254

Westbrook R A and **Black** W C (1985) A Motivation-Based Shopper Typology, Journal of Retailing, Vol 61 No 1 pp 78–103

Westfall R (1962) Psychological Factors in Predicting Brand Choice, Journal of Marketing, Vol 26

Westin A (1967) Privacy and Freedom, Atheneum, New York

Westin A (1992) Consumer Privacy Protection: Ten Predictions, Mobius, February, pp 5–11

Wicker A (1969) Attitudes Versus Actions: The Relationship of Overt Responses to Attitude Objects, Journal of Social Issues, Vol 25 pp 24–32

Williams R (2002) Memetics: A New Paradigm for Understanding Customer Behaviour, Marketing Intelligence and Planning, Vol 20 No 3 pp 162–167

Willmott M and **Nelson** W (2003) Complicated Lives: Sophisticated Consumers, Intricate Lifestyles, Simple Solutions, John Wiley & Sons, Chichester

Wilson J Q and **Hernstein** R J (1985) Crime and Human Nature, Simon & Schuster, New York

Winick C (1961) Anthropology's Contributions to Marketing, Journal of Marketing, Vol 25

Wong Y H and **Leung** T K P (2001) Guanxi: Relationship Marketing in a Chinese Context, International Business Press, New York

Woodruffe-Burton H, **Eccles** S and **Elliott** R (2002) Towards a Theory of Shopping Behaviour, Journal of Consumer Behaviour, Vol 1 No 3 pp 256–266

Woodruffe-Burton H, **Eccles** S and **Elliott** R (eds) (2005) Special issue: Toward a Theory of Shopping, Journal of Consumer Behaviour, Vol 4 No 4

Woods R (2004) Exploring the Emotional Territory for Brands, Journal of Consumer Behaviour, Vol 3 No 4 pp 388–403

Woodside A and **Davenport** W (1974) The Effect of Salesman Similarity and Expertise on Consumer Purchasing Behaviour, Journal of Marketing Research, May, pp 198–202

Woodside A G (2004) Advancing Means-End Chains by Incorporating Heider's Balance Theory and Fournier's Consumer-Brand Relationship Typology, Psychology and Marketing, Vol 21 No 4 pp 279–294

Wright B (1999) reported in **Beenstock** S (1999) Supermarkets Entice the Ultra Customer, Marketing, 15 April, p 15

Yi Y and **Jeon** H (2003) Effects of Loyalty Programs on Value Perception, Program Loyalty, and Brand Loyalty, Academy of Marketing Science, Vol 31 No 3 pp 229–240

Youjae Y and **Hoseong** J (2003) Effects of Loyalty Programs on Value Perception, Program Loyalty, and Brand Loyalty, Academy of Marketing Science Journal, Greenvale, Vol 31 No 3, Summer, pp 229–241

Young M and **Wilmott** P (1975) Family and Kinship in East London, Routledge & Kegan Paul

Zaichkowsky J L (1985) Measuring the Involvement Construct, Journal of Consumer Research, Vol 12 No 3 pp 341–352

Zaichkowsky J L (1987) The Personal Involvement Inventory: Reduction, Revision and Application to Advertising, Discussion Paper number 87-08-08, Simon Fraser University, Faculty of Business Administration

Zavestoski S (2002) Anticonsumption Attitudes, Psychology and Marketing (Guest Editorial), Vol 19 No 2 pp 121–126

Zeithaml V A (1981) How Consumer Evaluation Processes Differ between Goods and Services in **Donnelly** J and **George** W (eds), Marketing of Services, American Marketing, Chicago, pp 186–190

Zelin A (2003) Good Housekeeping, Research, February, pp 24–25

Zhang S and **Sood** S (2002) Deep and Surface Cues: Brand Extension Evaluations by Children and Adults, Journal of Consumer Research, Vol 29 No 1 pp 129–142

Zimbardo P and **Ebbesen** E B (1970) Influencing Attitudes and Changing Behaviour, Addison–Wesley, p 20

INDEX

Note: page numbers in *italics* refer to figures, tables, thinkboxes or example boxes.

Global Marketing
Global Edition

EDITION

6

Global Marketing

Global Edition

Warren J. Keegan

Lubin Graduate School of Business
Pace University—New York City and Westchester, New York

Mark C. Green

Department of Business Administration and Economics
Simpson College—Indianola, Iowa

PEARSON

Boston   Columbus   Indianapolis   New York   San Francisco   Upper Saddle River
Amsterdam   Cape Town   Dubai   London   Madrid   Milan   Munich   Paris   Montreal   Toronto
Delhi   Mexico City   Sao Paulo   Sydney   Hong Kong   Seoul   Singapore   Taipei   Tokyo

Editorial Director: Sally Yagan
Editor in Chief: Eric Svendsen
Executive Editor: Melissa Sabella
Acquisitions Editor, Global Edition: Steven Jackson
Assistant Editor: Kierra Kashickey
Director of Marketing: Patrice Lumumba Jones
Senior Marketing Manager: Anne Fahlgren
Marketing Manger, International: Dean Erasmus
Marketing Assistant: Melinda Jensen
Senior Managing Editor: Judy Leale
Senior Production Project Manager: Kelly Warsak
Senior Operations Supervisor: Arnold Vila
Operations Specialist: Ilene Kahn
Senior Art Director: Janet Slowik
Art Director: Steven Frim
Interior Designer: Wanda Espana
Cover Designer: Jodi Notowitz
Cover Art: © StanOd–Fotolia.com
Permissions Project Manager: Shannon Barbe
Manager, Visual Research: Beth Brenzel
Image Permission Coordinator: Annette Linder
Manager, Cover Visual Research & Permissions: Karen Sanatar
Media Project Manager: Lisa Rinaldi
Media Editor: Denise Vaughn
Full-Service Project Management: Jennifer Welsch/BookMasters, Inc.
Composition: Integra Software Services
Printer/Binder: Courier/Kendallville
Cover Printer: Lehigh-Phoenix Color/Hagerstown
Text Font: Times 10/12

Credits and acknowledgments borrowed from other sources and reproduced, with permission, in this textbook appear on appropriate page within text.

This is a special edition of an established title widely used by colleges and universities throughout the world. Pearson published this exclusive edition for the benefit of students outside the United States and Canada. If you purchased this book within the United States or Canada you should be aware that it has been imported without the approval of the Publisher or the Author.

10 9 8 7 6 5 4 3 2

ISBN 10:   0-13-704268-X
ISBN 13: 978-0-13-704268-5

To Bergin, Hunter, Cian, and Hannah
—WJK

To the memory of my father
—MCG

Brief Contents

Contents

Preface

Dear Students,

Our goal in *Global Marketing,* Sixth Edition, is to bring you an understanding of global marketing as a whole, as well as to focus on the importance of emerging nations in contemporary global marketing.

We take an environmental and strategic approach by outlining the major dimensions of the global business environment. The conceptual and analytical tools will prepare you to successfully apply the 4Ps to global marketing.

Our goal for all six editions has been the same: to write a book that is authoritative in content yet relaxed and assured in style and tone. Here's what students have had to say:

- "The textbook is very clear and easy to understand;"
- "An excellent textbook with many real-life examples;"
- "The authors use simple language and clearly state the important points;"
- "This is the best textbook that I am using this term;"
- "The authors have done an excellent job of writing a text than can be read easily."

When *Principles of Global Marketing* first appeared in 1996, we invited you to "look ahead" to such developments as the ending of America's trade embargo with Vietnam, Europe's new currency, Daimler AG's Smart car, and Whirlpool's expansion into emerging markets. Those topics represented "big stories" in the global marketing arena and continue to receive press coverage on a regular basis.

Guided by our experience using the text in undergraduate and graduate classrooms and in corporate training seminars, we have revised, updated, and expanded *Global Marketing,* Sixth Edition. We have benefited tremendously from your feedback and input; we also continue to draw on our direct experience in the Americas, Asia, Europe, Africa, and the Middle East. The result is a text that addresses your needs and the needs of instructors in every part of the world. *Global Marketing* has been adopted at scores of colleges and universities in the United States; international adoptions of the English-language edition include Australia, Canada, China, Ireland, Japan, Malaysia, South Korea, Spain, and Sri Lanka. The text is also available in Chinese (simplified and traditional), Japanese, Portuguese, and Spanish editions.

Warren Keegan   *Mark C. Green*

WHAT'S NEW TO THE SIXTH EDITION

As David Byrne once sang, "It's not yesterday anymore." The global economic crisis provided the main backdrop for this revision. Virtually every industry sector, company, and country has been affected by the downturn. The signs are everywhere: Cash-strapped consumers have cut back on spending. Companies are scaling back production and laying off workers. Spooked lenders have tightened credit, squeezing companies and consumers. Merger and acquisition activity has slowed dramatically. Real estate values are plummeting. Although the story continues to unfold as this edition goes to press, we have tried to offer up-to-date, original insights into the complexities and subtleties of the economic situation and their implications for global marketers. Other specific updates and revisions include:

- Each chapter-opening vignette is now linked to an end-of-chapter case with discussion questions. Fifty percent of the chapter-opening vignettes and related end-of-chapter cases are new to the Sixth Edition. Holdover cases have been revised and updated.
- All tables containing key company, country, and industry data have been updated. Examples include Table 1-4 "The World's Largest Corporations;" all the income and population tables in Chapter 3 and Chapter 7; Table 10-2, "The World's Most Valuable Brands;" Table 13-1 "Top 25 Global Marketers;" and Table 13-2 "Top 20 Global Advertising Organizations."
- "Global Marketing and the Digital Revolution," which appeared in *Global Marketing,* Fifth Edition, as Chapter 17, is now Chapter 15. This sequencing places the chapter in Part IV with chapters devoted to the marketing mix. The change is based on adopter feedback as well as the authors' desire to better integrate content pertaining to Web 2.0, digital distribution, and related topics.
- The impact of Web 2.0 on global marketing activities has increased dramatically since *Global Marketing*, Fifth Edition, was published in 2008. New discussion of social media is integrated throughout the Sixth Edition. Specific examples include the French Ministry of Agriculture's efforts to promote French cheese and wine in the United States (Chapter 14). To supplement their use of *Global Marketing*, Sixth Edition, faculty and students can access author updates and comments on Twitter, the micro-blogging Web site, as well as Delicious.com, the social bookmarking site (www.delicious.com/MarkCGreen).
- We've gone color! With a new full color design, you can see how vibrant and exciting the world of international marketing is.
- New maps section provides students with more global context.

Despite the ill winds blowing through the world economic scene in 2009, time marches on. China celebrated the 60th anniversary of the founding of the People's Republic. Barbie turned 50; 30 years have passed since Sony introduced the Walkman to the world. Also in 2009, Germany commemorated twenty years of unification, NAFTA turned 15, and the euro celebrated its 10th anniversary.

The central theme in the Fifth Edition was the growing impact of emerging nations in general and Brazil, Russia, India, and China in particular. The Sixth Edition contains expanded coverage of emerging markets as a whole. Prior to the world economic downturn, Mexico, Indonesia, Nigeria, Turkey, and a handful of other emerging nations were rapidly approaching the "tipping point" in terms of both competitive vigor and marketing opportunity. Emerging giants such as Embraer (Brazil), Cemex (Mexico), Lenovo (China), and India's Big Three—Wipro, Infosys, and Tata—have faced a variety of challenges brought on by the recession. Even so, they will become increasingly visible on the global stage. That these companies are likely to stand alongside established global giants such as Coca-Cola, Nestlé, and Toyota is one measure of how, as Thomas L. Friedman has noted, the world has flattened.

Current research findings have been integrated into each chapter of *Global Marketing*, Sixth Edition. For example, we have incorporated key insights from Arindam K. Bhattacharya and David C. Michael's 2008 *Harvard Business Review* article, "How Local Companies Keep Multinationals at Bay." Robyn Meredith's recent book *The Elephant and the Dragon* was a valuable resource for our coverage of India and China. Similarly, our thinking about global market segmentation and targeting has been influenced by David Arnold's recent book, *The Mirage of Global Markets*. We have added scores of current examples of global marketing practice as well as quotations from global marketing practitioners and industry experts. Throughout the text, organizational Web sites are referenced for further student study and exploration.

Each chapter contains several illustrations that bring global marketing to life. Chapter-opening vignettes introduce a company, a country, a product, or a global marketing issue that directly relates to chapter themes and content. More than half the opening vignettes in the Sixth Edition are new, including: "The Global Economic Crisis: Is America the 'Market of Last Resort?'" (Chapter 2); "Suzlon Energy" (Chapter 10); "Global Marketers Discover Social

Media" (Chapter 15); and "Unilever" (Chapter 17). In addition, every chapter contains one or more boxes on three themes: Emerging Markets Briefing Book; Strategic Decision Making in Global Marketing, and Culture Watch.

CASES

The case set in *Global Marketing*, Sixth Edition, strikes a balance between revisions of earlier cases (e.g., Case 1-1 "McDonald's Expands Globally While Adjusting Its Local Recipe" and Case 17-2 "Boeing and Airbus: A Twenty-First Century Dogfight"), and entirely new cases (e.g., Case 2-3 "One Laptop Per Child," and Case 15-1 "Global Marketers Discover Social Media." The cases vary in length from a few hundred words to more than 2,600 words, yet they are all short enough to be covered in an efficient manner. The cases were written with the same objectives in mind: to raise issues that will encourage student interest and learning, to stimulate class discussion, and to enhance the classroom experience for students and instructors alike. Every chapter and case has been classroom tested.

One of our challenges is the rate of change in the global business environment. Yesterday's impossibility becomes today's reality; new companies explode onto the scene; company leadership changes abruptly. In short, any book can be quickly outdated by events. Even so, we set out to create a compelling narrative that captures the unfolding drama that is inherent in marketing in the globalization era. The authors are passionate about the subject of global marketing; if our readers detect a note of enthusiasm in our writing, then we have been successful. We believe that you will find *Global Marketing*, Sixth Edition, to be the most engaging, up-to-date, relevant, useful text of its kind.

Acknowledgments

We are grateful to the reviewers of this book for their many insights and helpful suggestions.

Michael Mayo, Kent State University

Carol Johanek, Washington University in St. Louis

Ronald N. Borrieci, Embry-Riddle Aeronautical University

Robert Badowski, Thiel College

Catherine Giunta, Seton Hill University

Deborah Gaspard, Southeast Community College

Phil Corse, Northwestern, Kellogg School of Management

Kathy Bohley, University of Indianapolis

Prema Nakra, Marist College

This book reflects the contributions, labor, and insights of many persons.

I would like to thank my students, colleagues, associates, and clients for sharing their insights and understanding of global marketing theory and practice. It is impossible to single out everyone who has contributed to this edition, but I would especially like to thank:

Steve Burgess, John Dory, Stephen Blank, Lawrence G. Bridwell, Bob Fulmer, Pradeep Gopalakrisna, Donald Gibson, Jim Gould, David Heenan, Hermawan Kartajaya, Suren Kaushik, Bodo B. Schlegelmilch, Barbara Stöttinger, John Stopford, Jim Stoner, Martin Topol, Robert Vambery, Dominique Xardel, and Michael Szenberg.

I also wish to acknowledge the many contributions of the students in my doctoral seminar on global strategic marketing. The Pace doctoral students are a remarkable group of experienced executives who have decided to pursue a doctoral degree while working full time.

My associates at Keegan & Company, Eli Seggev, Mark Keegan, and Anthony Donato, are outstanding expert consultants. Their backgrounds include collectively doctoral degrees in marketing, law, and a masters degree in public administration. The cross-fertilization of their training and experience and challenging client assignments addressing contemporary marketing issues is a continuing source of new ideas and insights on global strategic marketing.

My research assistants, Kandarp Shah and Nitin Singula, provided invaluable research assistance in many areas, including the very difficult task of creating the global income and population data that appears in this edition. My secretary Mary O'Connor at the Pace Graduate Center, and Sally Basso at Keegan & Company have provided support above and beyond the call of duty.

Special thanks are due to the superb librarians at Pace University: Michelle Lang, head, Graduate Center Library, and Anne B. Campbell, reference librarian, have a remarkable ability to find anything. Like the Canadian Mounties who always get their man, Michelle and Anne always get the document. My admiration for their talent and appreciation for their effort is unbounded.

Elyse Arno Brill, my coauthor of *Offensive Marketing* (Butterworth Heinemann) has provided invaluable assistance in research, writing, and teaching. Her energy and creativity are unbounded. I am in awe of her ability to juggle a large and growing family, community service, and a working farm with our joint projects. She is an original and creative thinker with an impressive ability to identify important new directions and insights in marketing.

Melissa Sabella, Executive Editor and Associate Vice President, Pearson/Prentice Hall, was quick to endorse and support the sixth edition. Kierra Kashickey, Editorial Project Manager, Kelly Warsak, Production Project Manager, and Karin Williams, Editorial Assistant, kept the revision process on track and on schedule. Beth Brenzel, Visual Research Manager, located many of the new photo images that appear in the Sixth Edition. Denise Vaughn, Media Editor, helped us assemble a top-notch video supplement package. As on previous editions, we were fortunate to work with Jennifer Welsch, Senior Project Manager at BookMasters, Inc., on the final stages of the publication process. We are grateful for the continuity of support at Pearson/ Prentice Hall.

Finally, I wish to thank my wife, Dr. Cynthia MacKay, who is a constant source of inspiration, support, and delight, as well as my companion in global market field research trips (many by motorcycle).

Warren J. Keegan
October 2009

I am indebted to the many colleagues and friends who carefully read and critiqued individual manuscript sections and chapters. Their comments improved the clarity and readability of the text. In particular, I would like to thank Hillary Brown, Hunter Clark, Frank Colella, Dave Collins, Diana Dickinson, Wendy Foughty, Mark Freyberg, Alexandre Gilfanov, Carl Halgren, Kathy Hill, Mark Juffernbruch, David Kochel, Peter Kvetko, Keith Miller, Gayle Moberg, James Palmieri, Alexandre Plokhov, Brian Steffen, David Wolf, Nathan Wright, and Thomas Wright.

A large number of individuals were instrumental in helping us secure permissions, and I want to acknowledge everyone who "went the extra mile" in supporting this revision. I would especially like to thank Kirk Edmondson, Lexus Advanced Business Development; Travis Edmonson, Pollo Campero; Cherie Gary, Sony Ericsson; Leena Handi, Bang & Olufsen; Adam Huening, *Greensburg (Ind.) Daily News;* Lou Ireland, Pioneer Hi-Bred International; Mary Jubb, Kikkoman; Daniel McDonnell, Forrester Research; Pat McFadden, Nucor; Morgan Molinoff, Edelman; Jenni Moyer, Consumer Electronics Association; Naomi Starkman, Slow Food Nation; Ciarra O'Sullivan, Global Call to Action Against Poverty; Sarah Shoraka, Greenpeace UK; Kathleen Tepfer, Scottish Development International; Peter VanVaalen, *Greensburg (Ind.) Daily News;* Terri Wilsie, CSX; and Jeff Wilson, Firestone Agricultural Tire.

The authors are indebted to Keith Miller, Ellis and Nelle Levitt Distinguished Professor of Law at Drake University Law School, for contributing Case 5-2 "Internet Gambling." Hunter R. Clark, also of the Drake University Law School, contributed valuable updates to Case 5-1 "America's Cuban Conundrum."

I would also like to thank the many present and former students at Simpson College and the University of Iowa who have offered feedback on previous editions of *Global Marketing* and suggested improvements. Emily Beckmann contributed a new case about marketing the Galápagos; Kelli Herzberg wrote the case about India's Suzlon Energy. Simpson alumna Beth Dorrell graciously offered her expertise on export documentation. Mikkel Jakobsen wrote about his first job in global marketing for Case 8-2; Mikkel also provided source material on Denmark for the "Culture Watch" box in Chapter 4. Thanks also to Alanah Davis for her work on Case 1-3 "Acer Inc." and to Caleb Hegna for supplying important data about the white goods market in Germany. Jing Hao, my research assistant at Simpson College, and Chao-Hsiang Cheng (University of Iowa) offered useful insights about China; they also contributed English-to-Chinese and Chinese-to-English translations to this edition. My conversations with Benedikt Schwoll helped shaped the text discussion of marketing practices in Germany.

It was a great pleasure working with the Prentice Hall team that managed the production of this edition. Let me echo Warren's thanks to all members of the Pearson team, and especially to Kierra Kashickey and Kelly Warsak. Kudos also to our photo researcher, Beth Brenzel, for demonstrating once again that "every picture tells a story," and to Karyn Morrison for permissions research on ads and other illustrations. Thanks also to Michelle O'Brien for her great work on marketing support materials, and to the entire PH sales team for helping promote the book in the field. Daniel Wells, my PH's publishers representative, also gets a heartfelt "thank you" for his support and encouragement. I also want to acknowledge the contributions of the supplement authors for their fine work on the ancillary material that is available with this book.

Last, but not least, my love and appreciation to my kids for understanding and supporting what dad is trying to do during those long hours he spends in the office.

Mark C. Green
October 2009

About the Authors

Dr. Warren J. Keegan

Warren J. Keegan is Professor Emeritus of Marketing and International Business and Director of the Institute for Global Business Strategy at the Lubin School of Business, Pace University, New York City and Westchester. He is the founder of Warren Keegan Associates, Inc., a consulting consortium of experts in global strategic management and marketing, and Keegan & Company LLP, a firm specializing in litigation support.

Dr. Keegan is the author of many books. His text, *Global Marketing Management*, Seventh Edition (Prentice Hall, 2002), is recognized as the leading global marketing text for M.B.A. courses around the world. His other books include *Global Marketing*, Fourth Edition (Prentice Hall, 2005); *Offensive Marketing: An Action Guide to Gaining the Offensive in Business* (with Hugh Davidson) (Elsevier, Butterworth Heinemann, 2004); *Marketing Plans That Work*, Second Edition (with Malcolm McDonald) (Butterworth-Heinemann, 2002); *Marketing*, Second Edition (Prentice Hall, 1995); *Marketing Sans Frontieres* (InterEditions, 1994); *Advertising Worldwide* (Prentice Hall, 1991); and *Judgments, Choices and Decisions* (Wiley, 1984). He has published in the leading business journals including the *Harvard Business Review, Journal of Marketing, Journal of International Business Studies, Administrative Science Quarterly,* and the *Columbia Journal of World Business.*

He is a former MIT Fellow in Africa where he served as Assistant Secretary, Ministry of Development Planning, and Secretary of the Economic Development Commission for the Government of Tanzania. He was a consultant with Boston Consulting Group and Arthur D. Little, and Chairman of Douglas A. Edwards, a New York corporate real estate firm.

Dr. Keegan holds an M.B.A. and doctorate from the Harvard Business School. He has been a visiting professor at New York University, INSEAD (France), IMD (Switzerland), the Stockholm School of Economics, Emmanuel College of Cambridge University, and the University of Hawaii. He is a former faculty member of Columbia Business School, Baruch College, and the School of Government and Business Administration of The George Washington University.

He is a Lifetime Fellow of the Academy of International Business, Individual Eminent Person (IEP) Appointed by Asian Global Business Leaders Society (other awardees include: Noel Tichy, Rosabeth Moss Kanter, and Gary Wendt). His biography is listed in *Who's Who in America* (A. N. Marquis). He is a member of the International Advisory Board of École des Hautes Études Commerciales (HEC), Montreal; the Editorial Advisory Board, Cranfield School of Management and *Financial Times* Management Monograph Series; and is a current or former director of The S.M. Stoller Company, Inc.; The Cooper Companies, Inc. (NYSE); Inter-Ad, Inc.; American Thermal Corporation, Inc.; Halfway Houses of Westchester, Inc.; Wainwright House; and The Rye Arts Center.

He is an enthusiastic global traveler and enjoys teaching and learning, motorcycle touring, tennis, reading, theatre, movies, museums, swimming and rowing, loafing and working, home improvements, and life.

Dr. Mark C. Green

Mark C. Green is Professor of Management and Marketing at Simpson College in Indianola, Iowa, where he teaches courses in management, marketing, advertising, international marketing, and entrepreneurship and innovation. He is also a Visiting Professor at the University of Iowa's Tippie College of Business. Dr. Green earned his B.A. degree in Russian literature from Lawrence University, M.A. and Ph.D. degrees in Russian linguistics from Cornell University, and an M.B.A. degree in marketing management from Syracuse University.

In addition to co-authoring *Global Marketing*, Sixth Edition, with Warren Keegan, Dr. Green has also contributed case studies and chapter materials to several other textbooks published by

Prentice Hall. These include: *Advertising Principles and Practices*, Fourth Edition, by William Wells, John Burnett, and Sandra Moriarty (1997); *Behavior in Organizations*, Sixth Edition, by Jerald Greenberg and Robert Baron (1996); *Business*, Fourth Edition, by Ricky Griffin and Ronald Ebert (1995); and *Principles of Marketing* by Warren Keegan, Sandra Moriarty, and Thomas Duncan (1992). Dr. Green has also written essays on technology and global business that have appeared in the *Des Moines Register* and other newspapers.

Dr. Green has traveled to the former Soviet Union on numerous occasions. In 1995 and 1996, he participated in a grant project funded by the U.S. Agency for International Development (USAID) and presented marketing seminars to audiences in Nizhny Novgorod. In addition, Dr. Green has served as a consultant to several Iowa organizations that have business and cultural ties with Russia and other former Soviet republics. Dr. Green has lectured in Russia and Ukraine on topics relating to emerging market economies. His 1992 monograph, *Developing the Russian Market*, received an award from the Iowa-based International Network on Trade.

In 1997, Dr. Green was the recipient of Simpson College's Distinguished Research and Writing Award. Dr. Green also received the 1995 Distinguished Teaching Award for senior faculty. In 1990, he was the recipient of Simpson's Excellence in Teaching Award for junior faculty. He also received the 1988 Outstanding Faculty of the Year awarded by the Alpha Sigma Lambda adult student honorary at Simpson College.

Dr. Green enjoys playing bass and guitar with the Sonny Humbucker Band; the members include Simpson colleagues David Wolf (associate professor of English) and Mark Juffernbruch (associate professor of accounting). Rounding out the lineup are David Kochel, a political consultant with Red Wave Communications, and Thom Wright, an architect with RDG Planning & Design. Dr. Green blogs about music on the band's Web sites: www.myspace.com/thesonnyhumbuckerband; and www.sonnyhumbucker.com. Dr. Green also manages tenor saxophone jazz great Dave Tofani, who records for the SoloWinds label.

Pearson wishes to acknowledge and thank the following people for their work on the Global Edition:

Dr. Serap Atakan, Department of Business Administration, Istanbul Bilgi University, Turkey.

Dr. Melodena Stephens Balakrishnan, Associate Professor, University of Wollongong in Dubai, Dubai.

Dr. Sebnem Burnaz, Department of Management Engineering, Istanbul Technical University, Turkey

Dr. Bulent Dumlupinar, Management and Marketing Department, Bang College of Business, Republic of Kazakhstan.

Mohammed El-Adly (Ph.D.) Abu Dhabi University, United Arab Emirates.

Dr Tunji Gbadamosi, Senior Lecturer in Marketing Royal Docks Business School, University of East London, United Kingdom.

See Kwong Goh, TAR College, Malaysia.

Mrs Martina Hoffmann, Fontys International School of Economics, Netherlands.

Dr Yusniza Kamarulzaman, University of Malaya, Malaysia.

Andrew Ng, Adjunct Associate Professor, NUS Business School, National University of Singapore, Singapore.

Chris Pentz, Department of Business Management, Stellenbosch University, South Africa.

Jon and Diane Sutherland

Selected Maps for Global Marketing, 6e

Map 1

Nestlé's Global Holdings (Nestlé; transnational company); see Chapter 1, p. 41; p. 54; Chapter 2, p. 87.

Map 2

Exchange Arrangements (currency/global finance); see Chapter 2, pp. 96–100; Chapter 11, pp. 374–377.

Map 3

Changes in Currency Values Relative to U.S. dollar (currency/global finance); Chapter 2, pp. 96–100; Chapter 11, pp. 374–377.

Map 4

Foreign Trade Zone on Mauritius (FTZ); see Chapter 3, pp. 132–136; Chapter 8, p. 275.

Map 5

Countries' Relative Political Riskiness (political risk); see Chapter 5, pp. 172–175.

Map 6

Social Responsibility Hot Spots (corruption; corporate social responsibility); Chapter 5, pp. 192–194; Chapter 17, pp. 569–575.

Map 7

The Region Surrounding the Malacca Strait (piracy); see Chapter 12, pp. 422–424.

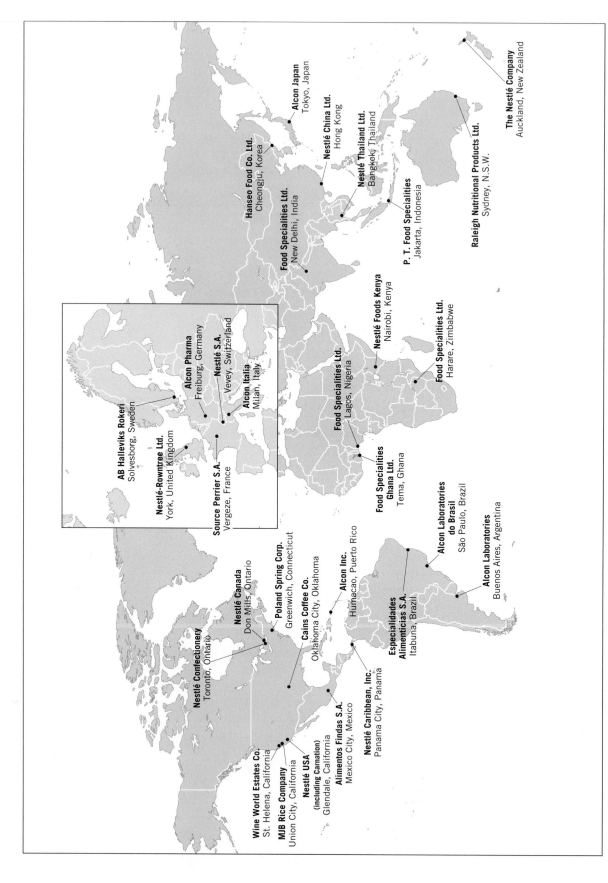

A Sampling of Nestlé's Global Holdings, Subsidiaries, and Affiliates

Alcon Japan
Tokyo, Japan

Nestlé China Ltd.
Hong Kong

Nestlé Thailand Ltd.
Bangkok, Thailand

The Nestlé Company
Auckland, New Zealand

Hanseo Food Co. Ltd.
Cheongju, Korea

Food Specialities Ltd.
New Delhi, India

P. T. Food Specialities
Jakarta, Indonesia

Raleigh Nutritional Products Ltd.
Sydney, N.S.W.

Nestlé Foods Kenya
Nairobi, Kenya

Food Specialities Ltd.
Harare, Zimbabwe

Alcon Pharma
Freiburg, Germany

Nestlé S.A.
Vevey, Switzerland

Alcon Italia
Milan, Italy

AB Halleviks Rokeri
Solvesborg, Sweden

Nestlé-Rowntree Ltd.
York, United Kingdom

Source Perrier S.A.
Vergeze, France

Food Specialities Ltd.
Lagos, Nigeria

Food Specialities
Ghana Ltd.
Tema, Ghana

Alcon Laboratories
do Brasil
São Paulo, Brazil

Alcon Laboratories
Buenos Aires, Argentina

Nestlé Confectionery
Toronto, Ontario

Nestlé Canada
Don Mills, Ontario

Poland Spring Corp.
Greenwich, Connecticut

Cains Coffee Co.
Oklahoma City, Oklahoma

Alcon Inc.
Humacao, Puerto Rico

Especialidades
Alimenticias S.A.
Itabuna, Brazil

Wine World Estates Co.
St. Helena, California

MJB Rice Company
Union City, California

Nestlé USA
(including Carnation)
Glendale, California

Alimentos Findas S.A.
Mexico City, Mexico

Nestlé Caribbean, Inc.
Panama City, Panama

28

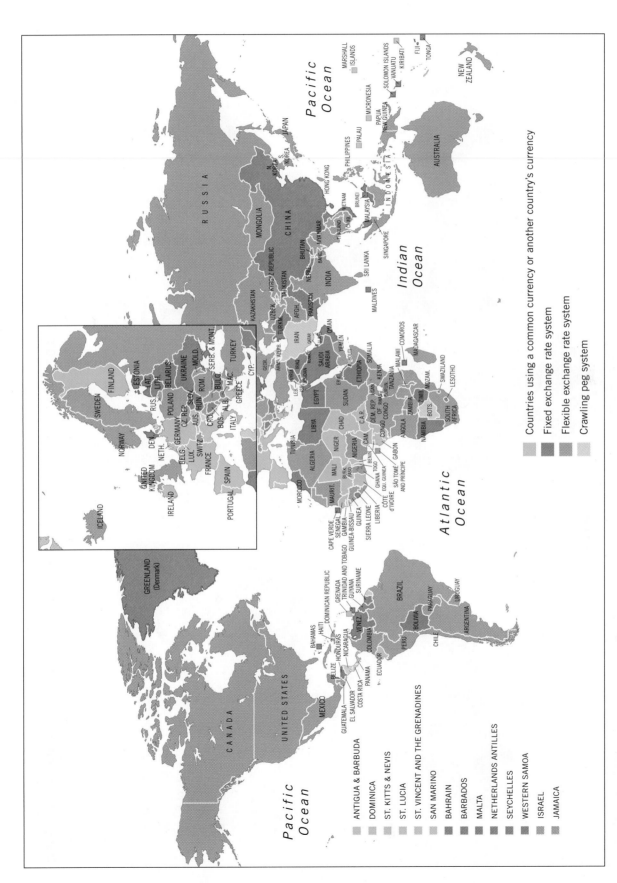

Exchange Rate Arrangements as of 2007

Source: IMF, www.imf.org, September 2, 2008.

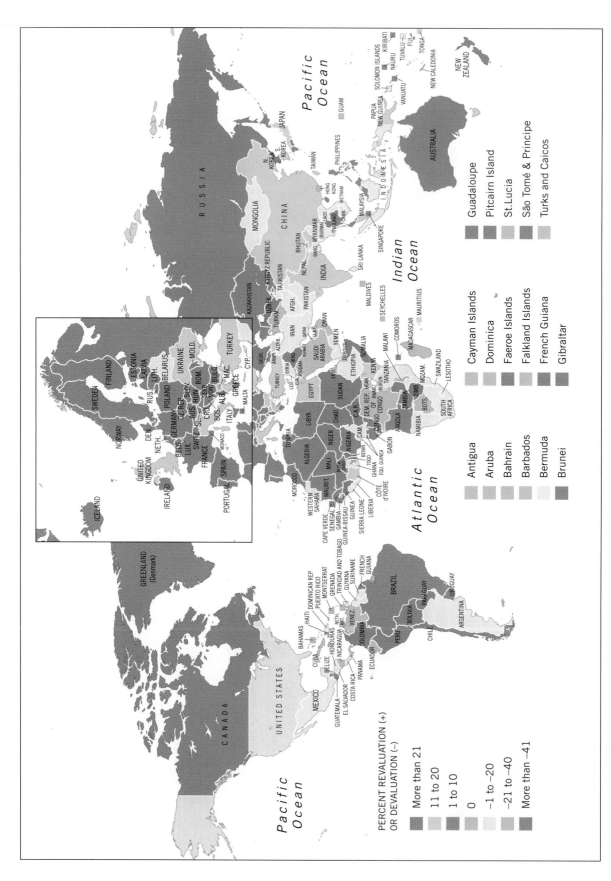

Changes in Currency Values Relative to the U.S. Dollar, July 2008 Versus July 2003

PERCENT REVALUATION (+)
OR DEVALUATION (−)

- More than 21
- 11 to 20
- 1 to 10
- 0
- −1 to −20
- −21 to −40
- More than −41

Antigua
Aruba
Bahrain
Barbados
Bermuda
Brunei

Cayman Islands
Dominica
Faeroe Islands
Falkland Islands
French Guiana
Gibraltar

Guadaloupe
Pitcairn Island
St.Lucia
São Tomé & Principe
Turks and Caicos

Mauritius has created a foreign trade zone (FTZ) to diversify its economy and encourage manufacturing. Today the country exports over $1.6 billion worth of textiles, apparel, and other goods to Europe and the United States. Because of the FTZ's success, the country's economy has enjoyed 5 percent annual growth during the last decade.

Goodlands

Centre de Flacq

Beau Bassin

Quatre Bornes

Curepipe

Mahebourg

Chemin Grenier

Port Louis

Mauritius, which was once a French naval base, is a tropical island, roughly $10\frac{1}{2}$ times the area of Washington, D.C. For much of its history Mauritius's 1.2 million residents depended on sugarcane, and even today 90 percent of its cultivated land is devoted to this crop.

Foreign Trade Zone on Mauritius

Countries' Relative Political Riskiness, 2008

Source: Euromoney's Survey of Country Risk, *Euromoney*, March 2008, p. 14ff.

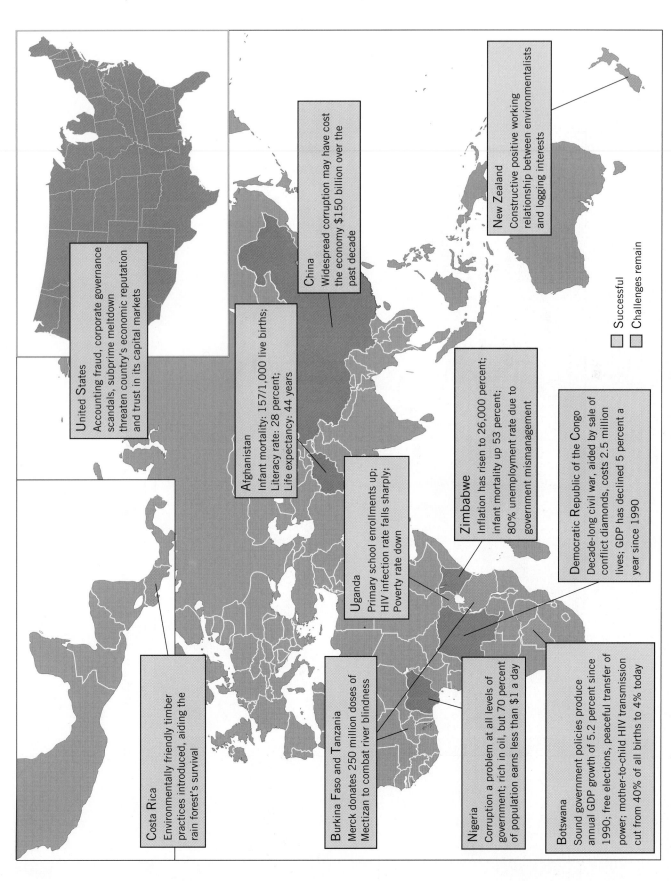

Social Responsibility Hot Spots: Some Successes, But Many Challenges Remain

United States
Accounting fraud, corporate governance scandals, subprime meltdown threaten country's economic reputation and trust in its capital markets

China
Widespread corruption may have cost the economy $150 billion over the past decade

New Zealand
Constructive positive working relationship between environmentalists and logging interests

Afghanistan
Infant mortality: 157/1,000 live births;
Literacy rate: 28 percent;
Life expectancy: 44 years

Costa Rica
Environmentally friendly timber practices introduced, aiding the rain forest's survival

Uganda
Primary school enrollments up;
HIV infection rate falls sharply;
Poverty rate down

Zimbabwe
Inflation has risen to 26,000 percent;
infant mortality up 53 percent;
80% unemployment rate due to government mismanagement

Democratic Republic of the Congo
Decade-long civil war, aided by sale of conflict diamonds, costs 2.5 million lives; GDP has declined 5 percent a year since 1990

Burkina Faso and Tanzania
Merck donates 250 million doses of Mectizan to combat river blindness

Nigeria
Corruption a problem at all levels of government; rich in oil, but 70 percent of population earns less than $1 a day

Botswana
Sound government policies produce annual GDP growth of 5.2 percent since 1990; free elections, peaceful transfer of power; mother-to-child HIV transmission cut from 40% of all births to 4% today

Successful
Challenges remain

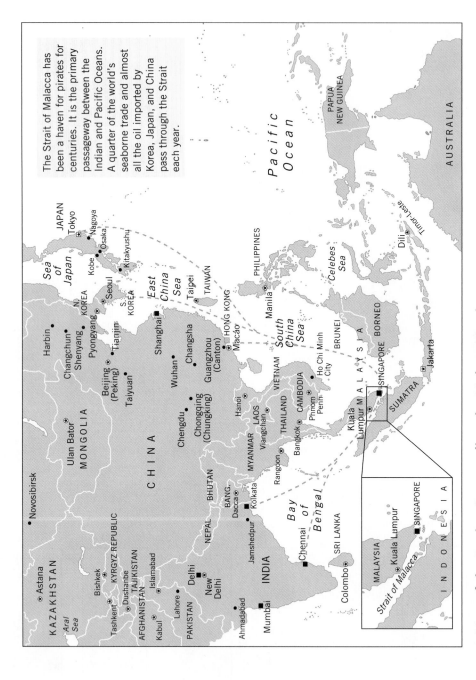

The Strait of Malacca has been a haven for pirates for centuries. It is the primary passageway between the Indian and Pacific Oceans. A quarter of the world's seaborne trade and almost all the oil imported by Korea, Japan, and China pass through the Strait each year.

A Map of the Region Surrounding the Malacca Strait

Global Marketing
Global Edition

Introduction to Global Marketing

Case 1-1
The Global Marketplace Is Also Local

Consider the following proposition: *We live in a global marketplace*. McDonald's restaurants, Sony digital TVs, LEGO toys, Swatch watches, Burberry trench coats, and Caterpillar earthmoving equipment are found practically everywhere on the planet. Global companies are fierce rivals in key markets. For example, American auto industry giants General Motors and Ford are locked in a competitive struggle with Toyota, Hyundai, and other global Asian rivals as well as European companies such as Volkswagen. U.S.-based Intel, the world's largest chip maker, competes with South Korea's Samsung. In the global cell phone market, Nokia (Finland), Ericsson (Sweden), Motorola (United States), and Samsung are key players. Appliances from Whirlpool and Electrolux compete for precious retail space with products manufactured and marketed by China's Haier Group and LG of South Korea.

Now consider a second proposition: *We live in a world in which markets are local*. In China, for example, Yum Brands' new East Dawning fast-food chain competes with local restaurants such as New Asia Snack.[1] France's domestic film industry generates about 40 percent of local motion picture box office receipts; U.S.-made movies account for about 50 percent. In Turkey, local artists such as Sertab account for more than 80 percent of recorded

Exhibit 1-1: England's Burberry Group celebrated its 150th anniversary in 2006. Burberry's trademark is registered in more than 90 countries. The company's signature plaid pattern—often referred to as "the check"—is incorporated into a wide range of apparel items and accessories. The Burberry brand is enjoying renewed popularity throughout the world; sales in Asia are particularly strong.

CEO Angela Ahrendts wants to broaden the brand's appeal. To do this, she reintroduced a vintage company logo: an equestrian knight holding a flag emblazoned with the Latin word Prorsum ("forward"). Burberry recently launched a Web site, www.artofthetrench.com. The company also has a presence on social media Web sites such as Facebook and Twitter.
Source: China Photos/Getty Images, Inc.

music sales. *Kiki*, a Japanese magazine for teenage girls, competes for newsstand sales with *Vogue Girl, Cosmo Girl*, and other titles from Western publishers. In Germany, children's television powerhouse Nickelodeon competes with local broadcaster Super RTL. In Brazil, many consumers are partial to Antarctica and other local soft drink brands made from guaraná, a berry that grows in the Amazon region.

The "global marketplace versus local markets" paradox lies at the heart of this textbook. In later chapters, we will investigate the nature of local markets in more detail. For now, however, we will focus on the first part of the paradox. Think for a moment about brands and products that are found throughout the world. Ask the average consumer where this global "horn of plenty" comes from, and you'll likely hear a variety of answers. It's certainly true that some brands—McDonald's, Corona Extra, Swatch, Waterford, Benetton, and Burberry, for instance—are strongly identified with a particular country. In much of the world, McDonald's is the quintessential American fast-food restaurant, just as Burberry is synonymous with British country life (see Exhibit 1-1).

However, for many other products, brands, and companies, the sense of identity with a particular country is becoming blurred. Which brands are Japanese? American? Korean? German? Where is Nokia headquartered? When is

a German car *not* a German car? Can a car be both German *and* American? Consider:

- An American-built Ford Mustang has 65 percent American and Canadian content; an American-built Toyota Sienna XLE minivan has 90 percent American and Canadian content.[2]
- China's Shanghai Automotive (SAIC) owns the rights to the MG, the legendary two-seat British sports car. SAIC plans to manufacture MGs in a new factory in Oklahoma; it is already producing MG's TF model at a plant in Longbridge, UK. India's Tata Group recently paid $2.4 billion to acquire Land Rover and Jaguar from Ford.
- German carmaker BMW exports the X5 sport utility vehicle that it builds in Spartanville, South Carolina, to more than 100 countries.

At the end of this chapter, you will find the rest of Case 1-1. Taken together, the two parts give you the opportunity to learn more about the global marketplace and test your knowledge of current issues in global marketing. You may be surprised at what you learn!

[1]Janet Adamy, "East Eats West: One U.S. Chain's Unlikely Goal: Pitching Chinese Food in China," *The Wall Street Journal* (October 20, 2006), pp. A1, A8.
[2]Jathon Sapsford and Norihiko Shirouzu, "Mom, Apple Pie and . . . Toyota?" *The Wall Street Journal* (May 11, 2006), p. B1.

INTRODUCTION AND OVERVIEW

As the preceding examples illustrate, the global marketplace finds expression in many ways. Some are quite subtle; others are not. While shopping, you may have noticed more multi-language labeling on your favorite products and brands. Your local filling station may have changed its name from Getty to Lukoil, reflecting the Russian energy giant's expanding global reach. On the highway, you may have seen a semitrailer truck from FedEx's Global Supply Chain Services fleet. Or perhaps you took advantage of Radiohead's offer to set your own price when you downloaded *In Rainbows* from the Internet. When you pick up a pound of whole-bean Central American coffee at your favorite coffee café, you will find that some beans are labeled Fair Trade Certified. Your toll-free telephone call to a software technical support service or an airline customer service center may be answered in Bangalore or Mumbai. *Slumdog Millionaire*, which received an Oscar in 2009 for Best Picture, was filmed on location in and around Mumbai. Possibly you heard or read recent news accounts of antiglobalization protesters disrupting meetings of the World Trade Organization in Cancún, London, or some other major city.

The growing importance of global marketing is one aspect of a sweeping transformation that has profoundly affected the people and industries of many nations during the past 160 years. International trade has existed for centuries; beginning in 200 B.C., for example, the legendary Silk Road connected the East with the West. Even so, prior to 1840, students sitting at their desks would not have had any item in their possession that was manufactured more than a few miles from where they lived—with the possible exception of the books they were reading. From the mid-1800s to the early 1920s, with Great Britain the dominant economic power in the world, international trade flourished. A series of global upheavals, including World War I, the Bolshevik Revolution, and the Great Depression, brought that era to an end. Then, following World War II, a new era began. Unparalleled expansion into global markets by companies that previously served only customers located in their home country is one hallmark of this new global era.

Three decades ago, the phrase *global marketing* did not exist. Today, savvy businesspeople utilize global marketing for the realization of their companies' full commercial potential. That is why, no matter whether you live in Asia, Europe, North America, or South America, you may be familiar with the brands mentioned in the opening paragraphs. However, there is another, even more critical reason why companies need to take global marketing seriously: survival. A management team that fails to understand the importance of global marketing risks losing its domestic business to competitors with lower costs, more experience, and better products.

But what is global marketing? How does it differ from "regular" marketing? **Marketing** is an organizational function and a set of processes for creating, communicating, and delivering value to customers and for managing customer relationships in ways that benefit the organization and its stakeholders.[3] Marketing activities center on an organization's efforts to satisfy customer wants and needs with products and services that offer competitive value. The **marketing mix** (product, price, place, and promotion) comprises a contemporary marketer's primary tools. Marketing is a universal discipline, as applicable in Argentina as it is in Zimbabwe.

This book is about *global marketing*. An organization that engages in **global marketing** focuses its resources and competencies on global market opportunities and threats. A fundamental difference between regular marketing and global marketing is the scope of activities. A company that engages in global marketing conducts important business activities outside the home-country market. The scope issue can be conceptualized in terms of the familiar product/market matrix of growth strategies (see Table 1-1). Some companies pursue a *market development strategy*; this involves seeking new customers by introducing existing products or services into new geographical markets. For example, as Walmart expands into Guatemala and other Central American countries, it is implementing a market development strategy.

Global marketing may also take the form of a *diversification strategy* in which a company creates new products or services and introduces them into new geographical markets. This is the strategy that South Korea's LG Electronics has used to target the American home appliance market. LG's product offerings include a stylish, high-tech refrigerator priced at $3,000; the unit features a built-in flat-panel LCD television. LG's commitment to innovative products prompted Home Depot to start carrying the LG appliance line.[4] Japan's Kirin Holdings is also pursuing a diversification strategy; the company recently acquired Australia's biggest milk processor, Dairy Farmers. Kirin is experiencing soft demand at home, but executives anticipate increased demand for dairy products in China and India. When successfully formulated and implemented, a globally oriented growth strategy can result in increased revenues for a company.

Companies that engage in global marketing frequently encounter unique or unfamiliar features in specific countries or regions of the world. In China, for example, product counterfeiting and piracy are rampant. Companies doing business there must take extra care to protect their

TABLE 1-1 Product/Market Growth Matrix

		Product Orientation	
		Existing Products	New Products
Market Orientation	**Existing markets**	1. Market penetration strategy	2. Product development strategy
	New markets	3. Market development strategy	4. Diversification strategy

[3]American Marketing Association.
[4]Cheryl Lu-Lien Tan, "The New Asian Import: Your Oven," *The Wall Street Journal* (June 22, 2005), pp. D1, D4.

intellectual property and deal with "knockoffs." In some regions of the world, bribery and corruption are deeply entrenched. A successful global marketer understands specific concepts and has a broad and deep understanding of the world's varied business environments. He or she also must understand the strategies that, skillfully implemented in conjunction with universal marketing fundamentals, increase the likelihood of market success. This book concentrates on the major dimensions of global marketing. A brief overview of marketing is presented next, although the authors assume that the reader has completed an introductory marketing course or has equivalent experience.

PRINCIPLES OF MARKETING: A REVIEW

As defined in the previous section, marketing is one of the functional areas of a business, distinct from finance and operations. Marketing can also be thought of as a set of activities and processes that, along with product design, manufacturing, and transportation logistics, comprise a firm's **value chain**. Decisions at every stage, from idea conception to support after the sale, should be assessed in terms of their ability to create value for customers.

For any organization operating anywhere in the world, the essence of marketing is to surpass the competition at the task of creating perceived value—that is, a superior value proposition—for customers. The **value equation** is a guide to this task:

$$Value = Benefits/Price \text{ (money, time, effort, etc.)}$$

The marketing mix is integral to the equation because benefits are a combination of the product, promotion, and distribution. As a general rule, value, as the customer perceives it, can be increased in two basic ways. Markets can offer customers an improved bundle of benefits or lower prices (or both!). Marketers may strive to improve the product itself, to design new channels of distribution, to create better communications strategies, or a combination of all three. Marketers may also seek to increase value by finding ways to cut costs and prices. Nonmonetary costs are also a factor, and marketers may be able to decrease the time and effort that customers must expend to learn about or seek out the product.[5] Companies that use price as a competitive weapon may scour the globe to ensure an ample supply of low-wage labor or access to cheap raw materials. Companies can also reduce prices if costs are low because of process efficiencies in manufacturing or because of economies of scale associated with high production volumes.

Recall the definition of a market: *people or organizations that are both able and willing to buy.* In order to achieve market success, a product or brand must measure up to a threshold of acceptable quality and be consistent with buyer behavior, expectations, and preferences. If a company is able to offer a combination of superior product, distribution, or promotion benefits *and* lower prices than the competition, it should enjoy an extremely advantageous position. Toyota, Nissan, and other Japanese automakers made significant gains in the American market in the 1980s by creating a superior value proposition: They offered cars with higher quality and lower prices than those made by General Motors, Ford, and Chrysler. Today, the auto industry is shifting its attention to emerging markets such as India and Africa. Renault and its rivals are racing to offer middle-class consumers a new value proposition: high-quality vehicles that can sell for the equivalent of $10,000 or less. On the heels of Renault's success with the Dacia Logan comes the $2,500 Nano from India's Tata Motors (see Case 11-1).

Some of Japan's initial auto exports were market failures. In the late 1960s, for example, Subaru of America began importing the Subaru 360 automobile and selling it for $1,297. After *Consumer Reports* judged the 360 not acceptable sales ground to a halt. Similarly, the Yugo automobile achieved a modest level of U.S. sales in the 1980s (despite a "don't buy" rating from a consumer magazine) because its sticker price of $3,999 made it the cheapest new car available. Low quality was the primary reason for the market failure of both the Subaru 360 and the Yugo.[6] Walmart's recent departure from the German market was due in part to the fact that Germans

---

[5]With certain categories of differentiated goods, including designer clothing and other luxury products, higher price is often associated with increased value.
[6]The history of the Subaru 360 is documented in Randall Rothman, *Where the Suckers Moon: The Life and Death of an Advertising Campaign* (New York: Vintage Books, 1994), p. 4.

could find lower prices at stores known as "hard discounters." In addition, many German consumers prefer to go to several small shops rather than seek out the convenience of a single "all-in-one" store.

Competitive Advantage, Globalization, and Global Industries

When a company succeeds in creating more value for customers than its competitors, that company is said to enjoy **competitive advantage** in an industry.[7] Competitive advantage is measured relative to rivals in a given industry. For example, your local laundromat is in a local industry; its competitors are local. In a national industry, competitors are national. In a global industry—consumer electronics, apparel, automobiles, steel, pharmaceuticals, furniture, and dozens of other sectors—the competition is, likewise, global (and, in many industries, local as well). Global marketing is essential if a company competes in a global industry or one that is globalizing.

The transformation of formerly local or national industries into global ones is part of a broader process of *globalization*, which Thomas L. Friedman defines as follows:

> Globalization is the inexorable integration of markets, nation-states and technologies to a degree never witnessed before—in a way that is enabling individuals, corporations and nation-states to reach around the world farther, faster, deeper and cheaper than ever before.[8]

From a marketing point of view, globalization presents companies with tantalizing opportunities—and challenges—as executives decide whether or not to offer their products and services everywhere. At the same time, globalization presents companies with unprecedented opportunities to reconfigure themselves; as John Micklethwait and Adrian Wooldridge put it, the same global bazaar that allows consumers to buy the best that the world can offer also allows producers to find the best partners.[9] Globalization is presenting significant marketing opportunities for professional sports organizations such as the National Football League and Major League Soccer (Exhibit 1-2).

Exhibit 1-2: National Football League (NFL) Europe and Major League Soccer (MLS) are dedicated to promoting, respectively, American football globally and soccer in the United States. The NFL is focusing on a handful of key markets: Canada, Germany, Japan, Mexico, the United Kingdom, and China. Placekicker Gao Wei had hoped to be in the Seattle Seahawks lineup for a 2008 exhibition game at Worker Stadium in Beijing. However, the game did not take place because of the Beijing Olympics.

Soccer United Marketing, an MLS offshoot, has purchased English-language TV rights for several World Cup championships. As MLS's Don Garber notes, "In the global culture the universal language is soccer. That's the sweet spot. If it weren't for the shrinking world caused by globalization, we wouldn't have the opportunity we have today."[10]

Source: Ryan Pyle.

---

[7]Jay Barney notes that "a firm is said to have a competitive advantage when it is implementing a value-creating strategy not simultaneously being implemented by any current or potential competitors." See Jay Barney, "Firm Resources and Sustained Competitive Advantage," *Journal of Management* 17, no. 1 (1991), p. 102.

[8]Thomas L. Friedman, *The Lexus and the Olive Tree* (New York: Anchor Books, 2000), p. 9.

[9]John Micklethwait and Adrian Wooldridge, *A Future Perfect: The Challenge and Hidden Promise of Globalization* (New York: Crown Publishers, 2000), p. xxvii.

[10]Grant Wahl, "Football vs. Fútbol," *Sports Illustrated* (July 5, 2004), pp. 68–72.

Is there more to a global industry than simply "global competition?" Definitely. As defined by management guru Michael Porter, a **global industry** is one in which competitive advantage can be achieved by integrating and leveraging operations on a worldwide scale. Put another way, an industry is global to the extent that a company's industry position in one country is interdependent with its industry position in other countries. Indicators of globalization include the ratio of cross-border trade to total worldwide production, the ratio of cross-border investment to total capital investment, and the proportion of industry revenue generated by companies that compete in all key world regions.[11] Figure 1-1 ranks several industries in terms of degree of globalization. The figure was created by calculating the ratio of the annual value of global trade in the sector—including components shipped to various countries during the production process—to the annual value of industry sales.

Achieving competitive advantage in a global industry requires executives and managers to maintain a well-defined strategic focus. **Focus** is simply the concentration of attention on a core business or competence. The importance of focus for a global company is evident in the following comment by Helmut Maucher, former chairman of Nestlé SA:

> Nestlé is focused: We are food and beverages. We are not running bicycle shops. Even in food we are not in all fields. There are certain areas we do not touch. For the time being we have no biscuits [cookies] in Europe and the United States for competitive reasons, and no margarine. We have no soft drinks because I have said we either buy Coca-Cola or we leave it alone. This is focus.[12]

However, company management may choose to initiate a change in focus as part of an overall strategy shift. Even Coca-Cola has been forced to sharpen its focus on its core beverage brands. Following sluggish sales in 2000 and 2001, former chairman and chief executive Douglas Daft formed a new alliance with Nestlé that jointly developed and marketed coffees and teas. Daft also set about the task of transforming Coca-Cola's Minute Maid unit into a global division that markets a variety of juice brands worldwide. As Daft explained:

> We're a network of brands and businesses. You don't just want to be a total beverage company. Each brand has a different return on investment, is sold differently, drunk for different reasons, and has different managing structures. If you mix them all together, you lose the focus.[13]

Examples abound of corporate executives addressing the issue of focus, often in response to changes in the global business environment. In recent years Fiat, Volvo, Electrolux, Toshiba, Colgate, Royal Philips Electronics, Henkel, Bertelsmann, and many other companies have stepped up efforts to sharpen their strategic focus on core businesses. Specific actions can take a number of different forms besides alliances, including mergers, acquisitions, divestitures, and folding some businesses into other company divisions.[14]

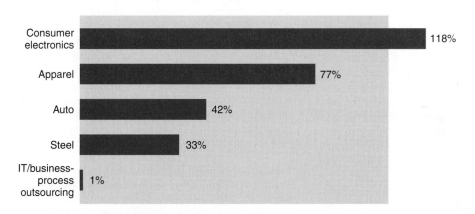

FIGURE 1-1

Degree of Industry Globalization

Source: Diana Farell, "Assessing Your Company's Global Potential," *Harvard Business Review* 82, no. 12 (December 2004), p. 85. Used by permission.

---

[11]Vijay Govindarajan and Anil Gupta, "Setting a Course for the New Global Landscape," *Financial Times—Mastering Global Business,* part I (1998), p. 3.

[12]Elizabeth Ashcroft, "Nestlé and the Twenty-First Century," Harvard Business School Case 9-595-074, 1995. See also Ernest Beck, "Nestlé Feels Little Pressure to Make Big Acquisitions," *The Wall Street Journal* (June 22, 2000), p. B4.

[13]Betsy McKay, "Coke's 'Think Local' Strategy Has Yet to Prove Itself," *The Wall Street Journal* (March 1, 2001), p. B6.

[14]Robert A. Guth, "How Japan's Toshiba Got Its Focus Back," *The Wall Street Journal* (December 12, 2000), p. A6.

Although the English Channel (La Manche) separates England and France by just 21 miles, the countries have been rivals for generations. Historically, there have been innumerable wars, disputes over territories, a multitude of thrones, and a plethora of quests for supremacy in Europe. English and French armies have battled against each other in North America and in India.

From around 1900, a feeling of mutual respect began to dawn between the two countries. Francophiles in Britain and Anglophiles in France attempted to mend the rift with the initiative known as the Entente Cordiale. However, despite being allies in both world wars, France under De Gaulle attempted to exclude Britain from any place in the European community.

Recent relations have been much friendlier in recent times, but differences can come to a head. The two countries were on opposite sides in the debate that led up to the removal of Saddam Hussein in 2003, clashing in the UN Security Council meetings. Both countries are contemptuous of one another's cooking and culture. Stereotyping is still all too common and for both sides there is a lack of understanding of cultural differences. The rivalry often emerges once again in sport, notably in rugby and in soccer. Yet the two countries are still far apart on a number of global issues.

The cities of London and Paris found themselves as rivals in 2005, when deliberations were underway as to which of the cities would be granted the honor of being the venue for the 2012 Olympics. Under International Olympic Committee rules, the bidding cities were expected to refrain from criticizing their competitors. Both London and Paris behaved impeccably throughout.

Yet despite these rivalries, considerable numbers of French and Britons are clearly not xenophobic and reject the complicated relationship between the countries. Over 50,000 Britons have second homes in France, and the number of Britons living in France is around 600,000. Nearly 300,000 French people are registered as living in Britain.

Nicolas Sarkozy, the French president elected in 2007, began to make attempts to forge a closer relationship and overcome the rivalries between the two countries, believing that both countries could become stronger if they stood together. Tensions still remain; until recently the Eurostar service, which connected the French and British capitals by train, terminated at Waterloo Station in London. In 1998, French politician Florent Longuepée claimed it was upsetting for the French to be reminded of Napoleon's defeat when they arrive in London by Eurostar. It was hardly a tactful decision by the British, but the Eurostar service now mercifully terminates at the King's Cross St. Pancras station in London.

The countries' rivalry can sometimes surface in the most peculiar ways. In early 2008, the popular children's cartoon series *Mister Men*, created back in 1971 by Roger Hargreaves, introduced a new character, Mister Rude. The new bright orange character was the first to have a foreign accent—French. An estimated 100 million *Mr Men* books have been sold in 22 countries. A source at the French Embassy in London was quoted in the

Exhibit 1-3: Britain and France have been great political, economic, and military rivals for centuries despite close proximity.
Source: © photogl - Fotolia.com.

Daily Telegraph, a popular British newspaper, accepted that it was lighthearted, but also conceded that it would not improve Anglo-French relations.

Relations on many fronts are still lukewarm. Old stereotypes show little sign of disappearing, although France is Britain's largest supplier, and British exports to France are worth over $30 billion per year, nearly 10 percent of Britain's visible exports worldwide. Britain is also the largest overseas investor in France. There are 1,700 French businesses, subsidiaries, and branches in Britain employing 330,000 people. There are 2,000 British firms operating in France. Despite the years of rivalry, Prime Minister Gordon Brown described the bilateral relationship between the two countries in 2009 as being the "entente formidable," by working together to be a greater force in the world. France's presidency of the European Union and an Anglo-French summit in Evian in July 2009 have seen an improvement in relations between the two countries, at least for now.

Sources: Robert Tombs and Isabelle Tombs, *That Sweet Enemy: The French and the British from the Sun King to the Present*, (New York: Knopf, 2007); Alan Sharp and Glyn Stone (eds.), *Anglo-French Relations in the Twentieth Century: Rivalry and Cooperation* (London: Routledge, 2002); Philippe Chassaigne and Michael L. Dockrill (eds.), *Anglo-French Relations 1898 to 1998: From Fashoda to Jospin* (Basingstoke: Palgrave, 2001); Richard Davis, *Anglo-French Relations Before the Second World War: Appeasement and Crisis* (Basingstoke: Palgrave, 2001); UK Trade and Investment, www.uktradeinvest.gov.uk.

Value, competitive advantage, and the focus required to achieve them are universal in their relevance and they should guide marketing efforts in any part of the world. Global marketing requires attention to these issues on a worldwide basis and utilization of a business intelligence system capable of monitoring the globe for opportunities and threats. A fundamental premise of this book can be stated as follows: Companies that understand and engage in global marketing can offer more overall value to customers than companies that do not have that understanding. There are many who share this conviction. In the mid-1990s, for example, C. Samuel Craig and Susan P. Douglas noted:

> Globalization is no longer an abstraction but a stark reality. . . . Choosing not to participate in global markets is no longer an option. All firms, regardless of their size, have to craft strategies in the broader context of world markets to anticipate, respond, and adapt to the changing configuration of these markets.[16]

Evidence is mounting that companies in a range of industries are getting the message. For example, three Italian furniture companies have joined together to increase sales outside of Italy and ward off increased competition from Asia. Luxury goods purveyors such as LVMH and Prada Group provided the model for the new business entity, which unites Poltrona Frau, Cassina, and Cappellini.[17] Hong Kong's Tai Ping Carpets International is also globalizing. Top managers have been dispersed to different parts of the world; while the finance and technology functions are still in Hong Kong, the marketing chief is based in New York City and the head of operations is in Singapore. As company director John Ying noted, "We're trying to create a minimultinational."[18]

GLOBAL MARKETING: WHAT IT IS AND WHAT IT ISN'T

The discipline of marketing is universal. It is natural, however, that marketing practices will vary from country to country, for the simple reason that the countries and peoples of the world are different. These differences mean that a marketing approach that has proven successful in one country will not *necessarily* succeed in another country. Customer preferences, competitors, channels of distribution, and communication media may differ. An important managerial task in global marketing is learning to recognize the extent to which it is possible to extend marketing plans and programs worldwide, as well as the extent to which adaptation is required.

The way a company addresses this task is a reflection of its **global marketing strategy (GMS)**. Recall that in single-country marketing, strategy development addresses two fundamental issues: choosing a target market and developing a marketing mix. The same two issues are at the heart of a firm's GMS, although they are viewed from a somewhat different perspective (see Table 1-2). *Global market participation* is the extent to which a company has operations in major world markets. *Standardization versus adaptation* is the extent to which each marketing mix element is standardized (i.e., executed the same way) or adapted (i.e., executed in different ways) in various country markets. For example, Nike recently adopted the slogan "Here I am" for its pan-European clothing advertising targeting women. The decision to drop the famous "Just do it" tagline in the region was based on research indicating that college-age women in Europe are not as competitive about sports as men are.[19]

GMS has three additional dimensions that pertain to marketing management. First, *concentration of marketing activities* is the extent to which activities related to the marketing mix

> "We believe a company can only think in one set of terms. If you are premium, you have to focus on it."
>
> Helmut Panke, former Chairman Bayerische Motoren Werke (BMW) AG[15]

[15]Scott Miller, "BMW Bucks Diversification to Focus on Luxury Models," *The Wall Street Journal* (March 20, 2002), p. B4.

[16]C. Samuel Craig and Susan P. Douglas, "Responding to the Challenges of Global Markets: Change, Complexity, Competition, and Conscience," *Columbia Journal of World Business* 31, no. 4 (Winter 1996), pp. 6–18.

[17]Gabriel Kahn, "Three Italian Furniture Makers Hope to Create a Global Luxury Powerhouse," *The Wall Street Journal* (October 31, 2006), p. B1.

[18]Phred Dvorak, "Big Changes Drive Small Carpet Firm," *The Wall Street Journal* (October 30, 2006), p. B3.

[19]Aaron O. Patrick, "Softer Nike Pitch Woos Europe's Women," *The Wall Street Journal* (September 11, 2008), p. B6.

TABLE 1-2 Comparison of Single-Country Marketing Strategy and Global Marketing Strategy (GMS)

Single-Country Marketing Strategy	Global Marketing Strategy
Target Market Strategy	Global Market Participation
Marketing Mix Development	Marketing Mix Development
Product	Product adaptation or standardization
Price	Price adaptation or standardization
Promotion	Promotion adaptation or standardization
Place	Place adaptation or standardization
	Concentration of Marketing Activities
	Coordination of Marketing Activities
	Integration of Competitive Moves

(e.g., promotional campaigns or pricing decisions) are performed in one or a few country locations. *Coordination of marketing activities* refers to the extent to which marketing activities related to the marketing mix are planned and executed interdependently around the globe. Finally, *integration of competitive moves* is the extent to which a firm's competitive marketing tactics in different parts of the world are interdependent. The GMS should enhance the firm's performance on a worldwide basis.[20]

Some brands are found in virtually every country; Coke is a case in point. Coke is the best-known, strongest brand in the world; its enviable global position has resulted in part from the Coca-Cola Company's willingness and ability to back its flagship brand with a network of local bottlers and a strong local marketing effort. However, companies that engage in global marketing do not necessarily conduct business in every one of the world's 200-plus country markets. For example, in the $30 billion market for recorded music, 12 countries—including the United States, Japan, the United Kingdom, and France—account for 70 percent of sales. Global marketing *does* mean widening business horizons to encompass the world in scanning for opportunity and threat. The decision to enter one or more particular markets outside the home country depends on a company's resources, its managerial mind-set, and the nature of opportunities and threats. Today, most observers agree that Brazil, Russia, India, and China—four emerging markets known collectively as BRIC—represent significant growth opportunities. Throughout this text, marketing issues in these countries are highlighted in "Emerging Markets Briefing Book" boxes.

The issue of standardization versus adaptation has been at the center of a long-standing controversy among both academicians and business practitioners. Much of the controversy dates back to Professor Theodore Levitt's 1983 article in the *Harvard Business Review,* "The Globalization of Markets." Levitt argued that marketers were confronted with a "homogeneous global village." He advised organizations to develop standardized, high-quality world products and market them around the globe by using standardized advertising, pricing, and distribution. Some well-publicized failures by Parker Pen and other companies that tried to follow Levitt's advice brought his proposals into question. The business press frequently quoted industry observers who disputed Levitt's views. As Carl Spielvogel, chairman and CEO of the Backer Spielvogel Bates Worldwide advertising agency, told *The Wall Street Journal* in the late 1980s, "Theodore Levitt's comment about the world becoming homogenized is bunk. There are about two products that lend themselves to global marketing—and one of them is Coca-Cola."[21]

[20]Shaoming Zou and S. Tamer Cavusgil, "The GMS: A Broad Conceptualization of Global Marketing Strategy and Its Effect on Performance," *Journal of Marketing* 66, no. 4 (October 2002), pp. 40–56.

[21]Joanne Lipman, "Ad Fad: Marketers Turn Sour on Global Sales Pitch Harvard Guru Makes," *The Wall Street Journal* (May 12, 1988), p. 1.

Global marketing made Coke a worldwide success. However, that success was *not* based on a total standardization of marketing mix elements. For example, Coca-Cola achieved success in Japan by spending a great deal of time and money to become an insider; that is, the company built a complete local infrastructure with its sales force and vending machine operations. Coke's success in Japan is a function of its ability to achieve global localization, being as much of an insider as a local company but still reaping the benefits that result from world-scale operations.[22] Similarly, in India, the company's local Thums Up cola brand competes with—and even outsells—the flagship cola.[23]

What does the phrase *global localization* really mean? In a nutshell, it means that a successful global marketer must have the ability to "think globally and act locally." Kenichi Ohmae recently summed up this paradox as follows:

> The essence of being a global company is to maintain a kind of tension within the organization without being undone by it. Some companies say the new world requires homogeneous products—"one size fits all"—everywhere. Others say the world requires endless customization—special products for every region. The best global companies understand it's neither and it's both. They keep the two perspectives in mind simultaneously.[24]

As we will see many times in this book, *global* marketing may include a combination of standard (e.g., the actual product itself) and nonstandard (e.g., distribution or packaging) approaches. A global product may be the same product everywhere and yet different. Global marketing requires marketers to think and act in a way that is both global *and* local by responding to similarities and differences in world markets. As shown in Exhibit 1-4, HSBC uses this understanding to position itself as "The World's Local Bank."

The Coca-Cola Company has convincingly demonstrated that the ability to think globally and act locally can be a source of competitive advantage. Because the company is adept at adapting sales promotion, distribution, and customer service efforts to local needs, Coke has become a billion-dollar-plus brand in six markets outside the United States: Brazil, Germany, Great Britain, Japan, Mexico, and Spain. This type of success does not happen overnight. For example, Coca-Cola managers initially did not understand the Japanese distribution system. However, with considerable investment of time and money, they succeeded in establishing a sales force that was as effective in Japan as it was in the United States. The Japanese unit has also created numerous new beverage products expressly for the Japanese market; these include Georgia-brand canned coffee and Qoo, a noncarbonated juice drink. Although the company has experienced a recent sales decline in Japan, it remains a key market that accounts for about 20 percent of the Coca-Cola Company's total worldwide operating revenues (see Exhibit 1-5).[25]

The Coca-Cola Company supports its Coke, Fanta, and Powerade brands with marketing mix elements that are both global and local. Dozens of other companies also have successfully pursued global marketing by creating strong global brands. This has been accomplished in various ways. The Altria Group (formerly Philip Morris), for example, made Marlboro the world's number one cigarette by identifying the brand with a cowboy. By creating distinctive, user-friendly handset designs, Nokia has become the world's leading cell phone brand. In automobiles, Daimler AG's Mercedes-Benz nameplate enjoys global recognition thanks to Germany's reputation for excellence in automotive engineering. Virtually all Nokia phones are manufactured in Finland; by contrast, some Mercedes models are manufactured outside

[22]Kenichi Ohmae, *The Borderless World: Power and Strategy* (New York: Harper Perennial, 1991), pp. 26, 27.

[23]Nikhil Deogun and Jonathan Karp, "For Coke in India, Thums Up Is the Real Thing," *The Wall Street Journal* (April 29, 1998), pp. B1, B2.

[24]William C. Taylor and Alan M. Webber, *Going Global: Four Entrepreneurs Map the New World Marketplace* (New York: Penguin Books USA, 1996), pp. 48, 49.

[25]Chad Terhune, "Coke Tries to Pop Back in Vital Japan Market," *The Wall Street Journal* (July 11, 2006), pp. C1, C3.

Germany. Gillette uses the same packaging for its flagship Mach3 razor everywhere in the world. Italy's Benetton utilizes a sophisticated distribution system to quickly deliver the latest fashions to its worldwide network of stores. The backbone of Caterpillar's global success is a network of dealers who support a promise of "24-hour parts and service" anywhere in the world. As these examples indicate, there are many different paths to success in global markets. In this book, we do *not* propose that global marketing is a knee-jerk attempt to impose a totally standardized approach to marketing around the world. A central issue in global marketing is how to tailor the global marketing concept to fit particular products, businesses, and markets.[26]

---

[26]John A. Quelch and Edward J. Hoff, "Customizing Global Marketing," *Harvard Business Review* 64, no. 3 (May–June 1986), p. 59.

Exhibit 1-5: Some of Coke's many faces around the world. Although the basic design of the label is the same (white letters against a red background), the Coca-Cola name is frequently transliterated into local languages. In the left-hand column, the Arabic label (second from top) is read from right to left; the Chinese label (fourth from the top) translates to "delicious/happiness."
Source: The Coca Cola Company.

As shown in Table 1-3, McDonald's global marketing strategy is based on a combination of global and local marketing mix elements. For example, a vital element in McDonald's business model is a restaurant system that can be set up virtually anywhere in the world. McDonald's offers core menu items—hamburgers, French fries, and soft drinks—in most countries, and the company also customizes menu offerings in accordance with local eating customs. The average price of a Big Mac in the United States is $3.54. By contrast, in China, Big Macs sell for the equivalent of $1.83. In absolute terms, Chinese Big Macs are cheaper than American ones. But is it a fair comparison? Real estate costs vary from country to country, as do per capita incomes. McDonald's prices can be understood in terms of the length of time a person must work to earn enough money to buy a Big Mac. Each year UBS, a Swiss bank, publishes a study of purchasing power based on a weighted average of hourly wages across 13 occupations. For example, in Los Angeles and Tokyo, earnings from about 10 minutes of work can buy a Big Mac; by contrast, in Bogotá and Nairobi, the corresponding figures are, respectively, 97 minutes and 91 minutes.[27]

TABLE 1-3 Examples of Effective Global Marketing—McDonald's

Marketing Mix Element	Standardized	Localized
Product	Big Mac	McAloo Tikka potato burger (India)
Promotion	Brand name	Slang nicknames, for example Mickey D's (USA, Canada), Macky D's (UK, Ireland), Macca's (Australia), Mäkkäri (Finland), MakDo (Philippines)
	Advertising slogan "i'm lovin' it"	*McJoy* magazine "Hawaii Surfing Hula" promotion (Japan)
Place	Free-standing restaurants in high-traffic public areas	McDonald's Switzerland operates themed dining cars on the Swiss national rail system; McDonald's is served on the Stena Line ferry from Helsinki to Oslo; home delivery (India)
Price	Average price of Big Mac is $3.54 (United States)	$5.79 (Norway); $1.83 (China)

[27]"Working Time Required to Buy . . . ," *Prices and Earnings,* 2006 Edition (UBS), p. 11.

The particular approach to global marketing that a company adopts will depend on industry conditions and its source or sources of competitive advantage. For example:

- Harley-Davidson's motorcycles are perceived around the world as *the* all-American bike. Should Harley-Davidson start manufacturing motorcycles in a low-wage country such as Mexico?
- The success of Honda and Toyota in world markets was initially based on exporting cars from factories in Japan. Now, both companies have invested in manufacturing and assembly facilities in the Americas, Asia, and Europe. From these sites, the automakers supply customers in the local market and also export to the rest of the world. For example, each year Honda exports tens of thousands of Accords and Civics from U.S. plants to Japan and dozens of other countries. Will European consumers continue to buy Honda vehicles exported from America? Will American consumers continue to snap up American-built Toyotas?
- As of 2007, Gap operated 2,692 stores in the United States and more than 450 stores internationally. The company sources most of its clothing from apparel factories in Honduras, the Philippines, India, and other low-wage countries. Should Gap open more stores in Asia?

The answer to these questions is: It all depends. Because Harley's competitive advantage is based in part on its "Made in the USA" positioning, shifting production outside the United States is not advisable. The company has opened a new production facility in Kansas and taken a majority stake in Buell Motorcycle, a manufacturer of "American street bikes." Toyota's success in the United States is partly attributable to its ability to transfer world-class manufacturing skills to America while using advertising to inform prospective customers that American workers build the Avalon, Camry, and Tundra models with many components purchased from American suppliers.

As noted, several hundred Gap stores are located outside the United States; key country markets include Canada, the United Kingdom, Japan, and France. Japan may present an opportunity for Gap to increase revenues and profits in a major non-U.S. market. A recent annual report noted that, in terms of sales revenues, the apparel market outside the United States is twice as large as that within the United States. Also, "American style" is in high demand in Japan and other parts of the world. Gap's management team has responded to this situation by selectively targeting key country markets—especially areas with high population densities—while continuing to concentrate on trends in the U.S. fashion marketplace. However, operating difficulties in the core U.S. market has led to the departure of several executives in recent years; CEO Paul Pressler left Gap early in 2007 after five years at the helm. This situation suggests that management's top priority at this time should be the domestic market (see Exhibit 1-6).[28]

Exhibit 1-6: Gap is a global brand, but recently the company has struggled to connect with customers in the United States. Despite these problems, the company continues to expand overseas. Gap's first Asian stores outside of Japan opened recently. The Singapore GAP, with 9,000 square feet of floor space, is located in the Wisma Atria mall; the opening of the Singapore store, and another in Malaysia, mark the first time the company has used franchising as an expansion strategy. Joshua Schulman, Gap's managing director of international strategic alliances, explained, "As we have a strong following of customers from these markets who shop at Gap while abroad, these markets will be ideal for the Gap brand's franchise debut."
Source: Monica Almeida/ *The New York Times.*

[28]Gap's transformation into a global brand is chronicled in Nina Munk, "Gap Gets It," *Fortune* (August 3, 1998), pp. 68–74+; see also Jayne O'Donnell and Mindy Fetterman, "Can Gap Be Saved?" *USA Today* (January 24, 2007), pp. 1B, 2B.

THE IMPORTANCE OF GLOBAL MARKETING

The largest single market in the world in terms of national income is the United States, representing roughly 25 percent of the total world market for all products and services. U.S. companies that wish to achieve maximum growth potential must "go global" because 75 percent of world market potential is outside their home country. Management at Coca-Cola clearly understands this; about 75 percent of the company's operating income and two-thirds of its operating revenue are generated outside North America. Non-U.S. companies have an even greater motivation to seek market opportunities beyond their own borders; their opportunities include the 300 million people in the United States. For example, even though the dollar value of the home market for Japanese companies is the second largest in the world (after the United States), the market *outside* Japan is 85 percent of the world potential for Japanese companies. For European countries, the picture is even more dramatic. Even though Germany is the largest single country market in Europe, 94 percent of the world market potential for German companies is outside Germany.

Many companies have recognized the importance of conducting business activities outside their home country. Industries that were essentially national in scope only a few years ago are dominated today by a handful of global companies. In most industries, the companies that will survive and prosper in the twenty-first century will be global enterprises. Some companies that fail to formulate adequate responses to the challenges and opportunities of globalization will be absorbed by more dynamic, visionary enterprises. Others will undergo wrenching transformations and, if the effort succeeds, will emerge from the process greatly transformed. Some companies will simply disappear. Table 1-4 lists the top 25 of *Fortune* magazine's 2008 ranking of the 500 largest service and manufacturing companies by revenues.

TABLE 1-4 The *Fortune* Global 500: Largest Corporations by Revenues

Company	Revenues (US$ millions)
1. Walmart Stores (USA)	$378,799
2. Exxon Mobil (USA)	372,824
3. Royal Dutch/Shell Group (UK/Netherlands)	355,782
4. BP (Britain)	291,438
5. Toyota Motor (Japan)	230,201
6. Chevron (USA)	210,783
7. ING Group (Netherlands)	201,516
8. Total (France)	187,280
9. General Motors (USA)	182,347
10. ConocoPhillips (USA)	178,558
11. Daimler (Germany)	177,167
12. General Electric (USA)	176,656
13. Ford Motor (USA)	172,468
14. Fortis (Belgium/Netherlands)	164,877
15. AXA (France)	162,762
16. Sinopec (China)	159,260
17. Citigroup (USA)	159,229
18. Volkswagen (Germany)	149,054
19. Dexia Group (Belgium)	147,648
20. HSBC Holdings (UK)	146,500
21. BNP Paribas (France)	140,726
22. Allianz (Germany)	140,618
23. Crédit Agricole (France)	138,155
24. State Grid (China)	132,885
25. China National Petroleum (China)	129,798

TABLE 1-5 How Big Is the Market I? Consumer Products

Product or Service	Size of Market	Key Players and Brands
Cigarettes	$295 billion	Philip Morris International (USA); British American Tobacco (UK); Japan Tobacco (Japan)
Luxury goods	$230 billion	LVMH Group (France); Richemont (Switzerland); PPR (France)
Cosmetics	$200 billion	L'Oréal SA (France); Estée Lauder (USA); Shiseido (Japan); Procter & Gamble (USA)
Personal computers	$175 billion	Hewlett-Packard (USA); Dell (USA); Acer (Taiwan); Lenovo (China)
Flat-screen TVs	$100 billion	Samsung (South Korea); Sony (Japan); LG (South Korea)
Bottled water	$100 billion	Nestlé (Switzerland); Groupe Danone (France); Coca-Cola (USA); PepsiCo (USA)
White goods (major appliances)	$85 billion	Whirlpool (USA); Electrolux (Sweden); Bosch-Siemens (Germany)
Cell phones	$60 billion	Nokia (Finland); Motorola (USA); Ericsson (Sweden); Samsung (South Korea)
Video games	$43 billion	Nintendo (Japan); Sony (Japan); Microsoft (USA)
Recorded music	$32 billion	Sony BMG (Japan); Warner Music (USA); EMI (UK); Universal Music Group (France)

Source: Compiled by the authors.

Two of the companies in the top 10 are giants in the global auto industry: GM and Toyota. Measured by market capitalization, Toyota (ranked fifth in revenue) is the world's most valuable car company. Today, Toyota sells more cars worldwide than GM; its market capitalization (roughly $200 billion) is nearly equal to the *combined* valuations of the eight leading Western automakers! Clearly, Toyota is doing something right. Oil companies occupy half of the spots in the top 10 rankings by revenues; ExxonMobil also ranked first in profitability in the *Fortune* Global 500. This showing is not surprising given the recent surge in oil prices. Walmart, the world's biggest retailer, rounds out the top 10 ranks. Walmart currently generates only about one-third of revenues outside the United States. However, global expansion is the key to the company's growth strategy over the next few years.

Examining the size of individual product markets, measured in terms of annual sales, provides another perspective on global marketing's importance. Many of the companies identified in Table 1-4 are key players in the global marketplace. Annual sales in select global industry sectors markets are shown in Tables 1-5 and 1-6. Table 1-7 shows annual sales in individual countries for select product categories. Table 1-8 lists annual unit sales for select product categories in various countries and world regions.

TABLE 1-6 How Big Is the Market II? Industrial Products and Services

Product or Service	Size of Market	Key Players and Brands
Container shipping	$150 billion	Maersk (Denmark); Evergreen Marine (Taiwan)
Construction equipment	$90 billion	Caterpillar (USA); Komatsu (Japan); Volvo (Sweden)
LCD display screens	$70 billion	Samsung (South Korea); Sharp (Japan); LG Display (South Korea)
Services outsourcing	$47 billion	Tata Consultancy Services (India); Infosys Technologies (India); Wipro (India); Tech Mahindra (India)
Crop seeds	$30 billion	Monsanto (USA); DuPont (USA)
DRAM chips	$26 billion	Samsung (South Korea); Infineon Technologies AG (Germany); Hynix Semiconductor (South Korea)
Customer relationship management (CRM) services	$6 billion	Oracle (USA); SAP (Germany)
Regional jet aircraft	$5.9 billion	Bombardier (Canada); Embraer (Brazil)

Source: Compiled by the authors.

TABLE 1-7 How Big Is the Market III? Individual Country/Regional Markets

Country	Category	Annual Sales
United States	Online retail	$172 billion
	White goods	$22.4 billion
	Wood furniture	$23 billion
	Video game consoles and games	$10 billion
	Toothpaste	$1.5 billion
	Ringtones	$600 million
Japan	Pharmaceuticals	$50 billion
	Luxury goods	$10.5 billion
India	Total retail	$370 billion
	Soft drinks	$2.3 billion
	Chocolate	$157 million
Europe	Online retail	$48 billion
	Cigarettes	$18 billion
	Home appliances (wholesale)	$25 billion
China	Consumer electronics	$85 billion
	Home appliances	$38 billion
	Cosmetics and toiletries	$10.3 billion
	Auto parts	$19 billion
	Pharmaceuticals	$11.7 billion

Source: Compiled by the authors.

TABLE 1-8 How Big Is the Market IV? Country/Region/World Markets by Product Category and Total Annual Units Sold

Country/Region	Category	Annual Sales
Japan	Cell phone handsets	50 million
United States	Cars and light trucks	13 million vehicles
India	Cell phone subscribers	270 million
Latin America	Automobiles	4 million vehicles
European Union	Shoes	2.5 billion pairs
Worldwide	Flat-panel TV sets	50 million units
Worldwide	Cigarettes	5.2 trillion cigarettes
Worldwide	Cell phone handsets	1.2 billion handsets
Worldwide	HDTV sets	200 million units
Worldwide	Cars and light trucks	70 million vehicles

Source: Compiled by the authors.

MANAGEMENT ORIENTATIONS

The form and substance of a company's response to global market opportunities depend greatly on management's assumptions or beliefs—both conscious and unconscious—about the nature of the world. The world view of a company's personnel can be described as ethnocentric, polycentric, regiocentric, and geocentric.[29] Management at a company with a prevailing ethnocentric

---

[29]Adapted from Howard Perlmutter, "The Tortuous Evolution of the Multinational Corporation," *Columbia Journal of World Business* (January–February 1969).

orientation may consciously make a decision to move in the direction of geocentricism. The orientations are collectively known as the EPRG framework.

Ethnocentric Orientation

A person who assumes that his or her home country is superior to the rest of the world is said to have an **ethnocentric orientation**. Ethnocentrism is sometimes associated with attitudes of national arrogance or assumptions of national superiority; it can also manifest itself as indifference to marketing opportunities outside the home country. Company personnel with an ethnocentric orientation see only similarities in markets, and *assume* that products and practices that succeed in the home country will be successful anywhere. At some companies, the ethnocentric orientation means that opportunities outside the home country are largely ignored. Such companies are sometimes called *domestic companies.* Ethnocentric companies that conduct business outside the home country can be described as *international companies;* they adhere to the notion that the products that succeed in the home country are superior. This point of view leads to a **standardized** or **extension approach** to marketing based on the premise that products can be sold everywhere without adaptation.

As the following examples illustrate, an ethnocentric orientation can take a variety of forms:

- Nissan's earliest exports were cars and trucks that had been designed for mild Japanese winters; the vehicles were difficult to start in many parts of the United States during the cold winter months. In northern Japan, many car owners would put blankets over the hoods of their cars. Nissan's assumption was that Americans would do the same thing. As a Nissan spokesman said, "We tried for a long time to design cars in Japan and shove them down the American consumer's throat. That didn't work very well."[30]
- Until the 1980s, Eli Lilly and Company operated as an ethnocentric company: Activity outside the United States was tightly controlled by headquarters and the focus was on selling products originally developed for the U.S. market.[31]
- For many years, executives at California's Robert Mondavi Corporation operated the company as an ethnocentric international entity. As former CEO Michael Mondavi explained, "Robert Mondavi was a local winery that thought locally, grew locally, produced locally, and sold globally. . . . To be a truly global company, I believe it's imperative to grow and produce great wines in the world in the best wine-growing regions of the world, regardless of the country or the borders."[32]
- The cell phone divisions of Toshiba, Sharp, and other Japanese companies prospered by focusing on the domestic market. When handset sales in Japan slowed a few years ago, the Japanese companies realized that Nokia, Motorola, and Samsung already dominated key world markets. Atsutoshi Nishida, president of Toshiba, noted, "We were thinking only about Japan. We really missed our chance."[33]

In the ethnocentric international company, foreign operations or markets are typically viewed as being secondary or subordinate to domestic ones. (We are using the term *domestic* to mean the country in which a company is headquartered.) An ethnocentric company operates under the assumption that "tried and true" headquarters knowledge and organizational capabilities can be applied in other parts of the world. Although this can sometimes work to a company's advantage, valuable managerial knowledge and experience in local markets may go unnoticed. Even if customer needs or wants differ from those in the home country, those differences are ignored at headquarters.

Sixty years ago, most business enterprises—and especially those located in a large country like the United States—could operate quite successfully with an ethnocentric orientation. Today, however, ethnocentrism is one of the major internal weaknesses that must be overcome if a company is to transform itself into an effective global competitor.

[30]Norihiko Shirouzu, "Tailoring World's Cars to U.S. Tastes," *The Wall Street Journal* (January 1, 2001), pp. B1, B6.
[31]T. W. Malnight, "Globalization of an Ethnocentric Firm: An Evolutionary Perspective," *Strategic Management Journal* 16, no. 2 (February 1995), p. 125.
[32]Robert Mondavi, *Harvests of Joy: My Passion for Excellence* (New York: Harcourt Brace & Company, 1998), p. 333.
[33]Martin Fackler, "A Second Chance for Japanese Cell Phone Makers," *The New York Times* (November 17, 2005), p. C1.

Polycentric Orientation

The **polycentric orientation** is the opposite of ethnocentrism. The term *polycentric* describes management's belief or assumption that each country in which a company does business is unique. This assumption lays the groundwork for each subsidiary to develop its own unique business and marketing strategies in order to succeed; the term *multinational company* is often used to describe such a structure. This point of view leads to a **localized** or **adaptation approach** that assumes products must be adapted in response to different market conditions. Examples of companies with a polycentric orientation include the following:

- Until the mid-1990s, Citicorp operated on a polycentric basis. James Bailey, a former Citicorp executive, explains, "We were like a medieval state. There was the king and his court and they were in charge, right? No. It was the land barons who were in charge. The king and his court might declare this or that, but the land barons went and did their thing."[34] Realizing that the financial services industry was globalizing, then-CEO John Reed attempted to achieve a higher degree of integration between Citicorp's operating units.
- Unilever, the Anglo-Dutch consumer-products company, once exhibited a polycentric orientation. For example, its Rexona deodorant brand had 30 different package designs and 48 different formulations. Advertising was also executed on a local basis. Top management has spent the last decade changing Unilever's strategic orientation by implementing a reorganization plan that centralizes authority and reduces the power of local country managers.[35]

Regiocentric Orientation

In a company with a **regiocentric orientation**, a region becomes the relevant geographic unit; management's goal is to develop an integrated regional strategy. What does "regional" mean in this context? A U.S. company that focuses on the countries included in the North American Free Trade Agreement (NAFTA)—namely, the United States, Canada, and Mexico—has a regiocentric orientation. Similarly, a European company that focuses its attention on Europe is regiocentric. Some companies serve markets throughout the world, but do so on a regional basis. Such a company could be viewed as a variant of the multinational model discussed previously. For decades, a regiocentric orientation prevailed at General Motors: Executives in different parts of the world—Asia-Pacific and Europe, for example—were given considerable autonomy when designing vehicles for their respective regions. Company engineers in Australia, for example, developed models for sale in the local market. One result of this approach: A total of 270 different types of radios were being installed in GM vehicles around the world. As GM Vice Chairman Robert Lutz told an interviewer in 2004, "GM's global product plan used to be four regional plans stapled together."[37]

Geocentric Orientation

A company with a **geocentric orientation** views the entire world as a potential market and strives to develop integrated global strategies. A company whose management has adopted a geocentric orientation is sometimes known as a *global* or *transnational company.*[38] During the past several years, longstanding regiocentric policies at GM such as those previously

"What unites us through our brands, markets, and businesses is the group's identity, which we refer to as 'a worldwide business with local presence.' Everywhere we operate, our priority is to create or develop a strong brand that reflects consumer needs in that market as closely as possible."[36]
Franck Riboud, Chairman and CEO Groupe Danone

---

[34]Saul Hansell, "Uniting the Feudal Lords at Citicorp," *The New York Times* (January 16, 1994), Sec. 3, p. 1.

[35]Deborah Ball, "Too Many Cooks: Despite Revamp, Unwieldy Unilever Falls Behind Rivals," *The Wall Street Journal* (January 3, 2005), pp. A1, A5.

[36]Franck Riboud, "Think Global, Act Local," *Outlook* no. 3 (2003), p. 8.

[37]Lee Hawkins, Jr., "New Driver: Reversing 80 Years of History, GM Is Reining in Global Fiefs," *The Wall Street Journal* (October 6, 2004), pp. A1, A14.

[38]Although the definitions provided here are important, to avoid confusion we will use the term *global marketing* when describing the general activities of global companies. Another note of caution is in order: Usage of the terms *international*, *multinational*, and *global* varies widely. Alert readers of the business press are likely to recognize inconsistencies; usage does not always reflect the definitions provided here. In particular, companies that are (in the view of the authors as well as numerous other academics) global are often described as *multinational enterprises* (abbreviated MNE) or *multinational corporations* (abbreviated MNC). The United Nations prefers the term *transnational company* rather than *global company*. When we refer to an "international company" or a "multinational," we will do so in a way that maintains the distinctions described in the text.

discussed have been replaced by a geocentric approach. Among other changes, the new policy calls for engineering jobs to be assigned on a worldwide basis; a global council based in Detroit determines the allocation of the company's $7 billion annual product development budget. One goal of the geocentric approach: Save 40 percent in radio costs by using a total of 50 different radios.

It is a positive sign that, at many companies, management realizes the need to adopt a geocentric orientation. However, the transition to new structures and organizational forms can take time to bear fruit. As new global competitors emerge on the scene, management at long-established industry giants such as GM must face up to the challenge of organizational transformation. A decade ago, Louis R. Hughes, a GM executive, said, "We are on our way to becoming a transnational corporation." Basil Drossos, former president of GM de Argentina, echoed his colleague's words, noting, "We are talking about becoming a global corporation as opposed to a multinational company; that implies that the centers of expertise may reside anywhere they best reside."[39] For the moment, GM is still the world's number one automaker in terms of revenue. Table 1-9 compares the two companies just prior to the onset of the global economic crisis; even then, Toyota surpassed GM in terms of profitability and market value. In 2008, Toyota sold more vehicles worldwide than GM. As GM teetered on the brink of bankruptcy in 2009, it was clear that it would have to be remade as a smaller, leaner company.

A global company can be further described as one that pursues either a strategy of serving world markets from a single country, or one that sources globally for the purposes of focusing on select country markets. In addition, global companies tend to retain their association with a particular headquarters country. Harley-Davidson and Waterford serve world markets from the United States and Ireland, respectively. By contrast, Gap sources its apparel from low-wage countries in all parts of the world; a sophisticated supply chain ensures timely delivery to its network of stores. Although Gap is a global brand, it focuses primarily on the key U.S. market. Harley-Davidson, Waterford, and Gap all may be thought of as global companies.

Transnational companies both serve global markets and utilize global supply chains; in addition, there is often a blurring of national identity. A true transnational would be characterized as "stateless." Toyota and Honda are two examples of companies that exhibit key characteristics of transnationality (see Exhibit 1-7). At global and transnational companies, management uses a combination of standardized (extension) and localized (adaptation) elements in the marketing program. A key factor that distinguishes global and transnational companies from international or multinational companies is *mind-set*: At global and transnational companies, decisions regarding extension and adaptation are not based on assumptions. Rather, such decisions are made on the basis of ongoing research into market needs and wants.

One way to assess a company's "degree of transnationality" is to compute an average of three figures: sales outside the home country to total sales; assets outside the home country to total assets; and employees outside the home country to total employees. Viewed in terms of these metrics, Nestlé, Unilever, Royal Philips Electronics, GlaxoSmithKline, and the News

"These days everyone in the Midwest is begging Honda to come into their hometown. It is no longer viewed as a 'Japanese' company, but a 'pro-American-worker corporation' flush with jobs, jobs, jobs."

Douglas Brinkley, Professor of History, Tulane University[40]

TABLE 1-9 GM and Toyota Compared

	General Motors	Toyota
Revenue	$205 billion	$185 billion
Profit or <Loss>	<$11.3 billion>	$12.6 billion
Market value*	$17.5 billion	$197 billion
Worldwide car production	9.2 million	8.3 million
Percentage of worldwide workforce in United States	45	11
Percentage of U.S. light-vehicle sales	24.8	15

*Share price × number of outstanding shares

[39]Rebecca Blumenstein, "Global Strategy: GM Is Building Plants in Developing Nations to Woo New Markets," *The Wall Street Journal* (August 4, 1997), p. A4.
[40]Douglas Brinkley, "Hoosier Honda," *The Wall Street Journal* (July 18, 2006), p. A14.

Exhibit 1-7: In 2006, Honda Motor announced plans to build a new $550 million auto assembly plant in the Midwest. Michigan, Ohio, and other job-hungry states were under consideration as potential sites. To encourage Honda to build the plant in their town, 200 residents of Greensburg, Indiana, posed for this photo while standing in the shape of Honda's "H" logo. Jordan Fischer, a photographer for the *Greensburg Daily News,* captured this image from the roof of a nearby building. Honda eventually did choose Greensburg as the site for its plant; production began in fall 2008. The plant's 2,000 employees produce 16,000 Honda Civics each month.
Source: Jordan Fischer/*Greensburg Daily News.*

Corporation are all transnational companies. Each is headquartered in a relatively small home country market, a fact of life that has compelled management to adopt regiocentric or geocentric orientations to achieve revenue and profit growth.

The geocentric orientation represents a synthesis of ethnocentrism and polycentrism; it is a "world view" that sees similarities and differences in markets and countries and seeks to create a global strategy that is fully responsive to local needs and wants. A regiocentric manager might be said to have a world view on a regional scale; the world outside the region of interest will be viewed with an ethnocentric or a polycentric orientation, or a combination of the two. However, recent research suggests that many companies are seeking to strengthen their regional competitiveness rather than moving directly to develop global responses to changes in the competitive environment.[41]

The ethnocentric company is centralized in its marketing management, the polycentric company is decentralized, and the regiocentric and geocentric companies are integrated on a regional and global scale, respectively. A crucial difference between the orientations is the underlying assumption for each. The ethnocentric orientation is based on a belief in home-country superiority. The underlying assumption of the polycentric approach is that there are so many differences in cultural, economic, and marketing conditions in the world that it is futile to attempt to transfer experience across national boundaries. A key challenge facing organizational leaders today is managing a company's evolution beyond an ethnocentric, polycentric, or regiocentric orientation to a geocentric one. As noted in one highly regarded book on global business, "The multinational solution encounters problems by ignoring a number of organizational impediments to the implementation of a global strategy and underestimating the impact of global competition."[42]

EMERGING MARKETS BRIEFING BOOK

⮞ Global Market Growth in the Twenty-First Century

Executives at Boeing forecast that Chinese airline companies will order up to 2,300 aircraft valued at more than $180 billion between now and 2025. Chinese carriers—which include Air China and China Southern Airlines—will operate a total of 2,800 aircraft, making China the second largest aviation market in the world. Boeing (USA) will face tough competition from Airbus (EU).[43]

---

[41]Allan J. Morrison, David A. Ricks, and Kendall Roth, "Globalization Versus Regionalization: Which Way for the Multinational?" *Organizational Dynamics* (Winter 1991), p. 18.

[42]Michael A. Yoshino and U. Srinivasa Rangan, *Strategic Alliances: An Entrepreneurial Approach to Globalization* (Boston: Harvard Business School Press, 1995), p. 64.

[43]Don Phillips and David Lague, "Airbus Jet Deal May Put an Assembly Line in China," *The New York Times* (December 6, 2005), p. C3.

FORCES AFFECTING GLOBAL INTEGRATION AND GLOBAL MARKETING

The remarkable growth of the global economy over the past 65 years has been shaped by the dynamic interplay of various driving and restraining forces. During most of those decades, companies from different parts of the world in different industries achieved great success by pursuing international, multinational, or global strategies. During the 1990s, changes in the business environment presented a number of challenges to established ways of doing business. Today, despite calls for protectionism as a response to the economic crisis, global marketing continues to grow in importance. This is due to the fact that, even today, driving forces have more momentum than restraining forces. The forces affecting global integration are shown in Figure 1-2.

Regional economic agreements, converging market needs and wants, technology advances, pressure to cut costs, pressure to improve quality, improvements in communication and transportation technology, global economic growth, and opportunities for leverage all represent important driving forces; any industry subject to these forces is a candidate for globalization.

Multilateral Trade Agreements

A number of multilateral trade agreements have accelerated the pace of global integration. NAFTA is already expanding trade among the United States, Canada, and Mexico. The General Agreement on Tariffs and Trade (GATT), which was ratified by more than 120 nations in 1994, has created the World Trade Organization (WTO) to promote and protect free trade. In Europe, the expanding membership of the European Union is lowering boundaries to trade within the region. The creation of a single currency zone and the introduction of the euro are also expected to expand European trade in the twenty-first century.

Converging Market Needs and Wants and the Information Revolution

A person studying markets around the world will discover cultural universals as well as differences. The common elements in human nature provide an underlying basis for the opportunity to create and serve global markets. The word *create* is deliberate. Most global markets do not exist in nature; marketing efforts must create them. For example, no one *needs* soft drinks, and yet today in some countries per capita soft drink consumption *exceeds* the consumption of water. Marketing has driven this change in behavior, and today, the soft drink industry is a truly global one. Evidence is mounting that consumer needs and wants around the world are converging today as never before. This creates an opportunity for global marketing. Multinational companies pursuing strategies of product adaptation run the risk of falling victim to global competitors that have recognized opportunities to serve global customers.

The information revolution—what Thomas L. Friedman refers to as the *democratization of information*—is one reason for the trend toward convergence. The revolution is fueled by a variety of technologies, products, and services, including satellite dishes, globe-spanning TV networks such as CNN and MTV, widespread access to broadband Internet, and Facebook, Twitter, YouTube, and other social media. Taken together these communication tools mean that people in the remotest corners of the globe can compare their own lifestyles and

FIGURE 1-2

Driving and Restraining Forces Affecting Global Integration

→ STRATEGIC DECISION MAKING IN GLOBAL MARKETING
Philips Electronics Changes Its Global Marketing Strategy

Royal Philips Electronics is a $37 billion consumer-electronics company headquartered in the Netherlands. Philips manufactures a vast array of products. For example, Philips Lighting is the largest manufacturer of light bulbs in the world; in Western Europe alone, the Philips brand commands more than one-third of the light bulb market. At the beginning of the twenty-first century, Philips's other divisions included domestic appliances, consumer electronics, industrial electronics, semiconductors, and hospital medical systems.

Philips has changed with the times. For example, to meet the challenge of Japanese consumer electronics manufacturers such as Sony and Matsushita, Philips executives abandoned the company's polycentric, multinational approach and adopted a more geocentric orientation. A first step in this direction was to create industry groups in the Netherlands responsible for developing global strategies for research and development (R&D), marketing, and manufacturing. The change paid off in Europe, where Philips became the number-one selling color television brand.

Despite such successes, the company lost $3.4 billion in 2002. Part of the problem was the fact that the company's U.S. consumer electronics division had been losing money for years. Even though Philips was a pioneer in developing new product categories such as CD players, the company was mostly known for Philips-Magnavox, a low-end TV brand. Philips stepped up its marketing efforts in the key North American market, which accounts for about 26 percent of overall consumer electronics sales. In 2001, Larry Blanford, formerly president of Maytag Corporation's appliance division, was assigned the task of revitalizing Philips's U.S. business. The stakes were high: Soon after Blanford took the job, the word was passed along from headquarters that if the U.S. unit didn't show a profit for 2004, it would be shut down.

Blanford mapped out a strategy designed to position Philips as a premium, high-tech brand and to boost sales of high-margin, must-have digital products such as wide-screen flat-panel HDTV monitors, DVD recorders, and portable MP3 music players. The U.S. sales team was quadrupled in size to 50 people; Blanford also instituted a policy requiring salespeople to visit at least two retail stores each week. Even as Philips worked to improve relations with specialty electronics retailers, it spent $100 million on a consumer brand awareness advertising campaign keyed to the theme "Getting Better." Some industry observers warned that Blanford had his work cut out for him. As a Dutch consumer electronics analyst noted, "In the U.S., Philips has been seen as a clunky brand, not at all sexy. They have a long road ahead to change people's minds."

Despite his efforts, and faced with strong competition from Sony and other Asian companies, Blanford did not succeed in turning around the electronics business in the United States. Now Gerard Kleisterlee, Philips's chief executive, is charting a new path. He closed most of the company's electronics factories; Philips TVs will now be manufactured by licensees. The semiconductor business was sold to a group of private-equity investors for €7.4 billion. Kleisterlee envisions high growth in health-related products and services that can be marketed directly to consumers. Focus group research helped Philips's marketers identify a need for "independent living" among the elderly. The company has responded to the opportunity by creating products such as the HeartStart Home Defibrillator. Kleisterlee also engineered the acquisition of Lifeline, a Massachusetts-based company that provides medical-alert services and systems.

Sources: Leila Abboud, "Philips Widens Marketing Push in India," *The Wall Street Journal* (March 20, 2009), p. B3; Leila Abboud, "Philips's Medical Malady," *The Wall Street Journal* (December 24, 2007), p. A7; Leila Abboud, "New Treatment: Electronics Giant Seeks a Cure in Health Care," *The Wall Street Journal* (July 11, 2007), pp. A1, A11; Dan Bilefsky, "Lost in Translation: A European Electronics Giant Races to Undo Mistakes in U.S.," *The Wall Street Journal* (January 7, 2004), pp. A1, A10; Gregory Crouch, "Philips Electronics Reports Best Profit in Three Years," *The New York Times* (October 15, 2003), p. W1; Gregory Crouch, "Philips Electronics Lost $3.4 Billion Last Year," *The New York Times* (February 12, 2003), p. W1; Dan Bilefsky, "Famed Philips Tries to Raise U.S. Profile," *The Wall Street Journal* (October 3, 2002), p. B4; Dave Pringle and Dan Bilefsky, "Philips Plans to Unveil Digital Videodisc Recorder," *The Wall Street Journal* (August 24, 2001), p. B7.

standards of living with those in other countries. In regional markets such as Europe and Asia, the increasing overlap of advertising across national boundaries and the mobility of consumers have created opportunities for marketers to pursue pan-regional product positionings. The Internet is an even stronger driving force: When a company establishes a site on the Internet, it automatically becomes global. In addition, the Internet allows people everywhere in the world to reach out, buying and selling a virtually unlimited assortment of products and services.

Transportation and Communication Improvements

The time and cost barriers associated with distance have fallen tremendously over the past 100 years. The jet airplane revolutionized communication by making it possible for people to travel around the world in less than 48 hours. Tourism enables people from many countries to see and experience the newest products sold abroad. In 1970, 75 million passengers traveled internationally; according to figures compiled by the International Air Transport Association, that figure increased to nearly 540 million passengers in 2003. One essential characteristic of the effective global business is face-to-face communication among employees and between the company and its customers. Modern jet travel made such communication feasible. Today's information technology allows airline alliance partners such as United and Lufthansa to sell seats on each other's flights, thereby making it easier for travelers to get from point to point. Meanwhile, the cost of international telephone calls has fallen dramatically over the past several decades. That fact, plus the advent of new communication technologies such as e-mail, fax, video teleconferencing, Wi-Fi, and broadband Internet, means that managers, executives, and customers can link up electronically from virtually any part of the world without traveling at all.

A similar revolution has occurred in transportation technology. The costs associated with physical distribution, both in terms of money and time, have been greatly reduced as well. The per-unit cost of shipping automobiles from Japan and Korea to the United States by specially designed auto-transport ships is less than the cost of overland shipping from Detroit to either U.S. coast. Another key innovation has been increased utilization of 20- and 40-foot metal containers that can be transferred from trucks to railroad cars to ships.

Product Development Costs

The pressure for globalization is intense when new products require major investments and long periods of development time. The pharmaceuticals industry provides a striking illustration of this driving force. According to the Pharmaceutical Research and Manufacturers Association, the cost of developing a new drug in 1976 was $54 million. Today, the process of developing a new drug and securing regulatory approval to market it can take 14 years; the average total cost of bringing a new drug to market is estimated to exceed $400 million.[44] Such costs must be recovered in the global marketplace because no single national market is likely to be large enough to support investments of this size. Thus Pfizer, Merck, GlaxoSmithKline, Novartis, Bristol-Myers Squibb, Sanofi-Aventis, and other leading pharmaceutical companies have little choice but to engage in global marketing. As noted earlier, however, global marketing does not necessarily mean operating everywhere; in the pharmaceutical industry, for example, seven countries account for 75 percent of sales. As shown in Table 1-10, demand for pharmaceuticals in Asia is expected

TABLE 1-10 World Pharmaceutical Market by Region

	2008	2003–2008	2008–2013
	Market Size US$ bn	CAGR %	Forecast CAGR %
North America	311.8	5.7%	−1% to 2%
Europe	247.5	6.4%	3% to 6%
Asia/Africa/Australia	90.8	13.7%	11% to 14%
Japan	76.6	2.7%	1% to 4%
Latin America	46.5	12.7%	11% to 14%
Total world	773.1	6.6%	3% to 6%

Source: Based on IMS Health Market Prognosis. Courtesy of IMS Health.

---

[44]Joseph A. DiMasi, Ronald W. Hansen, and Henry G. Grabowski, "The Price of Innovation: New Estimates of Drug Development Costs," *Journal of Health Economics* 22, no. 2 (March 2003), p. 151.

to exhibit double-digit growth in the next few years. In an effort to tap that opportunity and to reduce development costs, Novartis and its rivals are establishing research and development centers in China.[45]

Quality

Global marketing strategies can generate greater revenue and greater operating margins, which, in turn, support design and manufacturing quality. A global and a domestic company may each spend 5 percent of sales on R&D, but the global company may have many times the total revenue of the domestic because it serves the world market. It is easy to understand how Nissan, Matsushita, Caterpillar, and other global companies have achieved world-class quality (see Exhibit 1-8). Global companies "raise the bar" for all competitors in an industry. When a global company establishes a benchmark in quality, competitors must quickly make their own improvements and come up to par. For example, the U.S. auto manufacturers have seen their market share erode over the past four decades as Japanese manufacturers built reputations for quality and durability. Despite making great strides in quality, Detroit now faces a new threat: Sales, revenues, and profits have plunged in the wake of the economic crisis. Even before the crisis, the Japanese had invested heavily in hybrid vehicles that are increasingly popular with eco-conscious drivers. The runaway success of the Toyota Prius is a case in point.

World Economic Trends

Prior to the global economic crisis that began in 2008, economic growth had been a driving force in the expansion of the international economy and the growth of global marketing for three reasons. First, economic growth in key developing countries creates market opportunities that provide a major incentive for companies to expand globally. Thanks to rising per capita

In the Shanxi Province of China, coal miners and their families will be able to breathe a little easier, thanks in part to Caterpillar. Using 60 methane-gas-powered generator sets, the mine authority will collect toxic methane gas from the mine sites and use it to provide over 120 megawatts of clean electricity for the local power grid. The largest methane gas power project of its kind when completed, it is expected to seriously reduce greenhouse emissions, while providing power for schools, hospitals and businesses in the region. Turning toxic gas into the lifeblood of a city is one of many stories of progress being written every day, on every continent, by the people of Caterpillar. Whether it's helping India build superhighways to support its booming economy or developing technology for self-guiding robots—everything we do is guided by one goal: that the world be better tomorrow, because of the work we're doing today.

CATERPILLAR
成就今日 · 创造未来

Exhibit 1-8: Caterpillar is the world's largest manufacturer of construction and mining equipment, diesel and natural gas engines, and industrial gas turbines. Caterpillar is also the technology leader in construction, transportation, mining, forestry, energy, logistics, and electric power generation. In countries around the world, Caterpillar turns on the lights, builds the roads, and brings the financing, the technology, and the experience to create lasting change. Caterpillar's goal is "to make sure the world will be better tomorrow, because of the work we're doing today." This ad highlights Caterpillar's role in making progress possible in China by converting toxic methane gas into clean electric power. *Source:* Reprinted courtesy of Caterpillar, Inc.

---

[45]Nicholas Zamiska, "Novartis to Establish Drug R&D Center in China," *The Wall Street Journal* (November 11, 2006), p. A3.

incomes in India, China, and elsewhere, the growing ranks of middle-class consumers have more money to spend than in the past. At the same time, slow growth in industrialized countries has compelled management to look abroad for opportunities in nations or regions with high rates of growth.

Second, economic growth has reduced resistance that might otherwise have developed in response to the entry of foreign firms into domestic economies. When a country such as China is experiencing rapid economic growth, policymakers are likely to look more favorably on outsiders. A growing country means growing markets; there is often plenty of opportunity for everyone. It is possible for a "foreign" company to enter a domestic economy and establish itself without threatening the existence of local firms. The latter can ultimately be strengthened by the new competitive environment. Without economic growth, however, global enterprises may take business away from domestic ones. Domestic businesses are more likely to seek governmental intervention to protect their local positions if markets are not growing. Predictably, the current economic crisis creates new pressure by policymakers in emerging markets to protect domestic markets.

The worldwide movement toward free markets, deregulation, and privatization is a third driving force. The trend toward privatization is opening up formerly closed markets; tremendous opportunities are being created as a result. In a recent book, Daniel Yergin and Joseph Stanislaw described these trends as follows:

> It is the greatest sale in the history of the world. Governments are getting out of businesses by disposing of what amounts to trillions of dollars of assets. Everything is going—from steel plants and phone companies and electric utilities to airlines and railroads to hotels, restaurants, and nightclubs. It is happening not only in the former Soviet Union, Eastern Europe, and China but also in Western Europe, Asia, Latin America, and Africa—and in the United States.[46]

For example, when a nation's telephone company is a state monopoly, the government can require it to buy equipment and services from national companies. An independent company that needs to maximize shareholder value has the freedom to seek vendors that offer the best overall value proposition, regardless of nationality. Privatization of telephone systems around the world created significant opportunities for telecommunications equipment suppliers such as Sweden's Ericsson; Alcatel-Lucent, a Franco-American company; and Canada-based Nortel Networks. After years of growth, however, most telecom suppliers are experiencing slower growth as customers cut spending in the face of the global recession. As this book went to press, Nortel Networks was on the brink of bankruptcy.

Leverage

A global company possesses the unique opportunity to develop leverage. In the context of global marketing, **leverage** means some type of advantage that a company enjoys by virtue of the fact that it has experience in more than one country. Leverage allows a company to conserve resources when pursuing opportunities in new geographical markets. In other words, leverage enables a company to expend less time, less effort, or less money. Four important types of leverage are experience transfers, scale economies, resource utilization, and global strategy.

EXPERIENCE TRANSFERS A global company can leverage its experience in any market in the world. It can draw upon management practices, strategies, products, advertising appeals, or sales or promotional ideas that have been market-tested in one country or region and apply them in other comparable markets. For example, Whirlpool has considerable experience in the United States dealing with powerful retail buyers such as Sears and Circuit City. The majority of European appliance retailers have plans to establish their own cross-border "power" retailing

[46]Daniel Yergin and Joseph Stanislaw, *The Commanding Heights* (New York: Simon & Schuster, 1998), p. 13.

systems; as former Whirlpool CEO David Whitwam explained, "When power retailers take hold in Europe, we will be ready for it. The skills we've developed here are directly transferable."[47]

Chevron is another example of a global company that gains leverage through experience transfers. As H. F. Iskander, general manager of Chevron's Kuwait office, explains:

> Chevron is pumping oil in different locations all over the world. There is no problem we have not confronted and solved somewhere. There isn't a rock we haven't drilled through. We centralize all that knowledge at our headquarters, analyze it, sort it out, and that enables us to solve any oil-drilling problem anywhere. As a developing country you may have a national oil company that has been pumping your own oil for twenty years. But we tell them, "Look, you have twenty years of experience, but there's no diversity. It is just one year of knowledge twenty times over." When you are operating in a multitude of countries, like Chevron, you see a multitude of different problems and you have to come up with a multitude of solutions. You have to, or you won't be in business. All those solutions are then stored in Chevron's corporate memory. The key to our business now is to tap that memory, and bring out the solution that we used to solve a problem in Nigeria in order to solve the same problem in China or Kuwait.[48]

SCALE ECONOMIES The global company can take advantage of its greater manufacturing volume to obtain traditional scale advantages within a single factory. Also, finished products can be manufactured by combining components manufactured in scale-efficient plants in different countries. Japan's giant Matsushita Electric Company is a classic example of global marketing in action; it achieved scale economies by exporting VCRs, televisions, and other consumer electronics products throughout the world from world-scale factories in Japan. The importance of manufacturing scale has diminished somewhat as companies implement flexible manufacturing techniques and invest in factories outside the home country. However, scale economies were a cornerstone of Japanese success in the 1970s and 1980s.

Leverage from scale economies is not limited to manufacturing. Just as a domestic company can achieve economies in staffing by eliminating duplicate positions after an acquisition, a global company can achieve the same economies on a global scale by centralizing functional activities. The larger scale of the global company also creates opportunities to improve corporate staff competence and quality.

RESOURCE UTILIZATION A major strength of the global company is its ability to scan the entire world to identify people, money, and raw materials that will enable it to compete most effectively in world markets. For a global company, it is not problematic if the value of the "home" currency rises or falls dramatically because there really is no such thing as a home currency. The world is full of currencies, and a global company seeks financial resources on the best available terms. In turn, it uses them where there is the greatest opportunity to serve a need at a profit.

GLOBAL STRATEGY The global company's greatest single advantage can be its global strategy. A global strategy is built on an information system that scans the world business environment to identify opportunities, trends, threats, and resources. When opportunities are identified, the global company adheres to the three principles identified earlier: It leverages its skills and focuses its resources to create superior perceived value for customers and achieve competitive advantage. *The global strategy is a design to create a winning offering on a global scale.* This takes great discipline, much creativity, and constant effort. The reward is not just success, it's survival. For example, French automaker Renault operated for many years as a regional

[47]William C. Taylor and Alan M. Webber, *Going Global: Four Entrepreneurs Map the New World Marketplace* (New York: Penguin USA, 1996), p. 18.

[48]Thomas L. Friedman, *The Lexus and the Olive Tree* (New York: Anchor Books, 2000), pp. 221–222.

company. During that time, its primary struggle was a two-way race with Peugeot Citroën for dominance in the French auto industry. However, in an industry dominated by Toyota and other global competitors, Chairman Louis Schweitzer had no choice but to formulate a global strategy. Initiatives include acquiring a majority stake in Nissan Motor and Romania's Dacia. Schweitzer has also invested $1 billion in a plant in Brazil and is spending hundreds of millions of dollars in South Korea.[49]

A note of caution is in order: A global strategy is no guarantee of ongoing organizational success. Companies that cannot formulate or successfully implement a coherent global strategy may lose their independence. InBev's acquisition of Anheuser-Busch at the end of 2008 is a case in point. Some globalization strategies do not yield the expected results, as seen in the unraveling of the DaimlerChrysler merger and the failure of Deutsche Post's DHL unit to penetrate the U.S. domestic package delivery market.

The severe downturn in the business environment in the early years of the twenty-first century has wreaked havoc with strategic plans. This is proving true for established global firms as well as newcomers from emerging markets that only recently came to prominence on the world stage. For example, at Swiss-based ABB and Mexico's Cemex, the ambitious global visions of the respective chief executives were undermined by expensive strategic bets that did not pay off.[50] Although both companies survived, they are smaller, more focused entities than they were previously.

RESTRAINING FORCES Despite the impact of the driving forces identified previously, several restraining forces may slow a company's efforts to engage in global marketing. In addition to the market differences discussed earlier, important restraining forces include management myopia, organizational culture, national controls, and opposition to globalization. As we have noted, however, in today's world the driving forces predominate over the restraining forces. That is why the importance of global marketing is steadily growing.

MANAGEMENT MYOPIA AND ORGANIZATIONAL CULTURE In many cases, management simply ignores opportunities to pursue global marketing. A company that is "nearsighted" and ethnocentric will not expand geographically. Myopia is also a recipe for market disaster if headquarters attempts to dictate when it should listen. Global marketing does not work without a strong local team that can provide information about local market conditions. Executives at Parker Pen once attempted to implement a top-down marketing strategy that ignored experience gained by local market representatives. Costly market failures resulted in Parker's buyout by managers of the former UK subsidiary. Eventually, the Gillette Company acquired Parker.

In companies where subsidiary management "knows it all," there is no room for vision from the top. In companies where headquarters management is all-knowing, there is no room for local initiative or an in-depth knowledge of local needs and conditions. Executives and managers at successful global companies have learned how to integrate global vision and perspective with local market initiative and input. A striking theme emerged during interviews conducted by one of the authors with executives of successful global companies. That theme was the respect for local initiative and input by headquarters executives, and the corresponding respect for headquarters' vision by local executives.

NATIONAL CONTROLS Every country protects the commercial interests of local enterprises by maintaining control over market access and entry in both low- and high-tech industries. Such control ranges from a monopoly controlling access to tobacco markets to national government control of broadcast, equipment, and data transmission markets. Today, tariff barriers have been largely removed in the high-income countries, thanks to the WTO, GATT, NAFTA, and other economic agreements. However, **nontariff barriers** (**NTBs**) are still very much in evidence. NTBs are non-monetary restrictions on cross-border trade such as the proposed "Buy American"

---

[49]John Tagliabue, "Renault Pins Its Survival on a Global Gamble," *The New York Times* (July 2, 2000), Section 3, pp. 1, 6; Don Kirk and Peter S. Green, "Renault Rolls the Dice on Two Auto Projects Abroad," *The New York Times* (August 29, 2002), pp. W1, W7.

[50]Joel Millman, "The Fallen: Lorenzo Zambrano; Hard Times for Cement Man," *The Wall Street Journal* (December 11, 2008), p. A1.

provision in Washington's economic stimulus package, food safety rules, and other bureaucratic obstacles. NTBs have the potential to make it difficult for companies to gain access to some individual country and regional markets.

OPPOSITION TO GLOBALIZATION To many people around the world, globalization and global marketing represent a threat. The term *globaphobia* is sometimes used to describe an attitude of hostility toward trade agreements, global brands, or company policies that appear to result in hardship for some individuals or countries while benefiting others. Globaphobia manifests itself in various ways, including protests or violence directed at policymakers or well-known global companies (see Exhibit 1-9). Opponents of globalization include labor unions, college and university students, national and international nongovernmental organizations (NGOs), and others. *Shock Doctrine* author Naomi Klein has been an especially outspoken critic of globalization.

In the United States, some people believe that globalization has depressed the wages of American workers and resulted in the loss of both blue-collar and white-collar jobs. Protectionist sentiment has increased in the wake of the ongoing economic crisis. In many developing countries, there is a growing suspicion that the world's advanced countries—starting with the United States—are reaping most of the rewards of free trade. As an unemployed miner in Bolivia put it, "Globalization is just another name for submission and domination. We've had to live with that here for 500 years and now we want to be our own masters."[51]

OUTLINE OF THIS BOOK

This book has been written for students and businesspersons interested in global marketing. Throughout the book, we present and discuss important concepts and tools specifically applicable to global marketing.

Exhibit 1-9: Concerns about surging Chinese imports and possible job losses have fueled antiglobalization sentiment in America. Some products that are "Made in China" have come under even closer scrutiny following revelations about tainted baby formula and pet food, toothpaste that may contain chemical toxins, defective drywall, and toys contaminated with lead paint.
Source: "Labor Day," Mike Thompson/Copley News Service.

---

[51]Larry Rohter, "Bolivia's Poor Proclaim Abiding Distrust of Globalization," *The New York Times* (October 17, 2003), p. A3.

The book is divided into five parts. Part I consists of Chapter 1, an overview of global marketing and the basic theory of global marketing. Chapters 2 through 5 comprise Part II, in which we cover the environments of global marketing. Chapters 2 and 3 cover economic and regional market characteristics, including the location of income and population, patterns of trade and investment, and stages of market development. In Chapter 4, we examine social and cultural elements; and in Chapter 5 we present the legal, political, and regulatory dimensions.

We devote Part III to topics that must be considered when approaching global markets. We cover marketing information systems and research in Chapter 6. Chapter 7 discusses market segmentation, targeting, and positioning. Chapter 8 surveys the basics of importing, exporting, and sourcing. We devote Chapter 9 to various aspects of global strategy, including strategy alternatives for market entry and expansion.

We devote Part IV to global considerations pertaining to the marketing mix. The application of product, price, channel, and marketing communications decisions in response to global market opportunity and threat is covered in detail in Chapters 10 through 14. Chapter 15 explores the ways that the Internet, e-commerce, and other aspects of the digital revolution are creating new opportunities and challenges for global marketers.

The two chapters in Part V address issues of corporate strategy, leadership, and the impact of the digital revolution on global marketing. Chapter 16 includes an overview of strategy and competitive advantage. Chapter 17 addresses some of the leadership challenges facing the chief executives of global companies. In addition, the chapter covers the organization and control of global marketing programs and examines the issue of corporate social responsibility.

Summary

Marketing is an organizational function and a set of processes for creating, communicating, and delivering value to customers and for managing customer relationships in ways that benefit the organization and its stakeholders A company that engages in **global marketing** focuses its resources on global market opportunities and threats. Successful global marketers such as Nestlé, Coca-Cola, and Honda use familiar **marketing mix** elements—the four Ps—to create global marketing programs. Marketing, R&D, manufacturing, and other activities comprise a firm's **value chain**; firms configure these activities to create superior customer value on a global basis. The **value equation** (V = B/P) expresses the relationship between value and the marketing mix.

Global companies also maintain strategic **focus** while relentlessly pursuing **competitive advantage**. The marketing mix, value chain, competitive advantage, and focus are universal in their applicability, irrespective of whether a company does business only in the home country or has a presence in many markets around the world. However, in a **global industry**, companies that fail to pursue global opportunities risk being pushed aside by stronger global competitors.

A firm's **global marketing strategy (GMS)** can enhance its worldwide performance. The GMS addresses several issues. First is the nature of the marketing program in terms of the balance between a **standardized (extension) approach** to the marketing mix elements and a **localized (adaptation) approach** that is responsive to country or regional differences. Second is the *concentration of marketing activities* in a few countries or the dispersal of such activities across many countries. Companies that engage in global marketing can also engage in *coordination of marketing activities*. Finally, a firm's GMS addresses the issue of *global market participation.*

The importance of global marketing today can be seen in the company rankings compiled by *The Wall Street Journal, Fortune, Financial Times*, and other publications. Whether ranked by revenues or some other measure, most of the world's major corporations are active regionally or globally. The size of global markets for individual industries or product categories helps explain why companies "go global." Global markets for some product categories represent hundreds of billions of dollars in annual sales; other markets are much smaller. Whatever the size of the opportunity, successful industry competitors find that increasing revenues and profits means seeking markets outside the home country.

Company management can be classified in terms of its orientation toward the world: **ethnocentric**, **polycentric**, **regiocentric**, or **geocentric**. The terms reflect progressive levels of development or evolution. An ethnocentric orientation characterizes *domestic* and *international companies*; international companies pursue marketing opportunities outside the home market by extending various elements of the marketing mix. A polycentric worldview predominates at a *multinational company*, where country managers operating autonomously adapt the marketing mix. When management moves to integrate and coordinate activities on a regional basis, the decision reflects a regiocentric orientation. Managers at *global* and *transnational companies* are geocentric in their orientation and pursue both extension and adaptation strategies in global markets.

The dynamic interplay of several driving and restraining forces shapes the importance of global marketing. Driving forces include market needs and wants, technology, transportation and communication improvements, product costs, quality, world economic trends, and a recognition of opportunities to develop **leverage** by operating globally. Restraining forces include market differences, management myopia, organizational culture, and national controls such as **nontariff barriers** (**NTBs**).

Discussion Questions

1. What are the basic goals of marketing? Are these goals relevant to global marketing?
2. What is meant by "global localization"? Is Coca-Cola a global product? Explain.
3. A company's global marketing strategy (GMS) is a crucial competitive tool. Describe some of the global marketing strategies available to companies. Give examples of companies that use the different strategies.
4. UK-based Burberry is a luxury fashion brand that appeals to both genders and all ages. To improve Burberry's competitiveness in the luxury goods market, CEO Angela Ahrendts recently unveiled a new strategy that includes all the elements of the marketing mix. The strategy also addresses key markets that Burberry will participate in, as well as the integration and coordination of marketing activities. Search for recent articles about Burberry and write a brief summary that outlines Burberry's GMS.
5. How do the global marketing strategies of Harley-Davidson and Toyota differ?
6. Describe the difference between ethnocentric, polycentric, regiocentric, and geocentric management orientations.
7. Identify and briefly describe some of the forces that have resulted in increased global integration and the growing importance of global marketing.
8. Define *leverage* and explain the different types of leverage available to companies with global operations.
9. Each August, *Fortune* magazine publishes its survey of the Global 500. The top 25 companies for 2008 are shown in Table 1-4. Browse through the list and choose any company that interests you. Compare its 2008 ranking with the most recent ranking (which you can find either by referring to the print version of *Fortune* or by visiting www.fortune.com). How has the company's ranking changed? Consult additional sources (e.g., magazine articles, annual reports, the company's Web site) to get a better understanding of the factors and forces that contributed to the company's move up or down in the rankings. Write a brief summary of your findings.
10. There's a saying in the business world that "nothing fails like success." In this chapter, you read about some of Gap's recent problems. How can a fashion retailer that was once *the* source for wardrobe staples such as chinos and white T-shirts suddenly lose its marketing edge? Motorola has also fallen victim to its own success. The company's Razr cell phone was a huge hit, but Motorola struggled to leverage that success. Also, Starbucks CEO Howard Shultz recently warned that his company and brand risk becoming commoditized. If you were to make separate recommendations to management at each of these companies, what would you say?

Now that you have an overview of global marketing, it's time to test your knowledge of global current events. Some well-known companies and brands are listed in the left-hand column. The question is: In what country is the parent corporation located? Possible answers are shown in the right-hand column. Write the letter corresponding to the country of your choice in the space provided; each country can be used more than once. Answers follow.

_____ 1. Firestone Tire & Rubber	a. Germany
_____ 2. Ray-Ban	b. France
_____ 3. Rolls-Royce	c. Japan
_____ 4. RCA televisions	d. Great Britain
_____ 5. Budweiser	e. United States
_____ 6. Ben & Jerry's Homemade	f. Switzerland
_____ 7. Gerber	g. Italy
_____ 8. Miller Beer	h. Sweden
_____ 9. Rollerblade	i. Finland
_____ 10. Case New Holland	j. China
_____ 11. Weed Eater	k. Netherlands
_____ 12. Holiday Inn	l. Belgium
_____ 13. Wild Turkey bourbon	m. India
_____ 14. Thinkpad	
_____ 15. Wilson Sporting Goods	
_____ 16. Right Guard	
_____ 17. B.F. Goodrich	
_____ 18. Jaguar	

Answers:

1. Japan (Bridgestone)   2. Italy (Luxottica SpA)   3. Germany (Volkswagen)   4. China (TTE)   5. Belgium (InBev; now Anheuser-Busch InBev)   6. Great Britain/Netherlands (Unilever) 7. Switzerland (Nestlé)   8. Great Britain (SABMiller)   9. Italy (Benetton)   10. Italy (Fiat)   11. Sweden (AB Electrolux) 12. Great Britain (InterContinental Hotels Group PLC) 13. France (Groupe Pernod Ricard)   14. China (Lenovo) 15. Finland (Amer Group)   16. Germany (Henkel)   17. France (Michelin)   18. India (Tata Motors)

Case 1-1 Discussion Questions

1. Anheuser-Busch, which has been described as "an American icon," is now under the ownership of a company based in Belgium. Responding to reports that some consumers planned to boycott Bud products to protest the deal, one industry observer said, "Brand nationality is all about where it was born, and also the ingredients of that beer and how they make the beer. Basically, it doesn't matter who owns it. We are in a global world right now." Do you agree?

2. Anheuser-Busch (A-B) has long enjoyed a reputation as a very desirable place to work. Executives were awarded well-appointed corporate suites and traveled on corporate jets; many had secretaries as well as executive assistants. When managers took commercial flights, they flew first class. Most employees received beer for free and could count on donations of beer and merchandise for community events. Tickets to Cardinals home games were also used as a marketing tool. A-B spent heavily on advertising and promotion; various advertising agencies produced about 100 new ads for A-B each year. Given these facts, what changes, if any, would you expect A-B's new owners to make? Why?

3. In 2009, Italy's Fiat acquired a 20 percent stake in Chrysler, another iconic American company. Are you familiar with Fiat? What do you think CEO Sergio Marchionne hopes to accomplish with this deal? How might Chrysler benefit from the alliance?

4. Ben & Jerry's Homemade is a quirky ice cream marketer based in Burlington, Vermont. Founders Ben Cohen and Jerry Greenfield are legendary for enlightened business practices that include a three-part mission statement: product mission, financial mission, and social mission. When the company was acquired by consumer products giant Unilever, some of the brand's loyal customers were alarmed. What do you think was the source of their concern?

McDonald's Corporation is a fast-food legend whose famous golden arches can be found in 118 different countries. The company is the undisputed leader in the quick service restaurant (QSR) segment of the hospitality industry, with more than twice the systemwide revenues of Burger King. McDonald's built its reputation by promising and delivering three things to customers: inexpensive food with consistent taste regardless of location; quick service; and a clean, familiar environment. The company was also a pioneer in the development of convenience-oriented features such as drive-through windows and indoor playgrounds for children. Today, thanks to memorable advertising and intensive promotion efforts, McDonald's is one of the world's most valuable brands. The golden arches are said to be the second most recognized symbol in the world, behind the Olympic rings. In the United States alone, McDonald's typically spends about twice as much on advertising as Burger King and Wendy's.

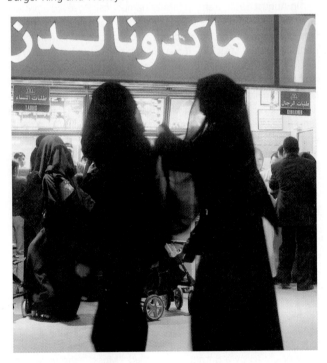

Source: AP Wide World Photos.

Today, however, the company faces competitive attacks from several directions. During the 1990s, a wide range of upscale food and beverage purveyors arrived on the scene. For example,

consumers began flocking to Starbucks coffee bars where they spent freely on lattes and other coffee-based specialty drinks. The "fast-casual" segment of the industry that includes companies such as Panera Bread, Cosi, and Baja Fresh is attracting customers seeking higher-quality menu items in more comfortable surroundings. Meanwhile, Subway overtook McDonald's as the restaurant chain with the most outlets in the United States. Some industry observers suggested that, in terms of both food offerings and marketing, McDonald's was losing touch with modern American lifestyles.

Until recently the picture appeared brighter outside the United States. Thanks to changing lifestyles around the globe, more people are embracing the Western-style fast-food culture. McDonald's responded to the opportunities by stepping up its rate of new unit openings. As shown in Table 1, McDonald's International is organized into three geographic regions: (1) Europe; (2) Asia/Pacific, Middle East, and Africa (APMEA); and (3) Other Countries. In 2005, the offices of the country heads for Europe and Asia were moved from headquarters to their respective regions; now, for example, the head of APMEA manages his business from Hong Kong. Commenting on the change, Ken Koziol, vice president of worldwide restaurant innovation, explained, "McDonald's was built on a strong foundation of a core menu that we took around the world but we need to make sure we are more locally relevant. Taste profiles and desires are changing."

Asia-Pacific

The Indian market appears to hold huge potential for McDonald's. In fall 1996, the company opened its first restaurants in New Delhi and Bombay. In Delhi, the golden arches competes with Nirula's, a quick-service restaurant chain with several dozen outlets; in addition, there are hundreds of smaller regional chains throughout India. The U.S.-based Subway chain opened its first Indian location in 2001; Pizza Hut, KFC, and Domino's Pizza have also entered the market. The Pizza Hut on Juhu Road in Bombay is housed in a three-story-tall building with large plate glass windows and central air conditioning; on most nights a long line of customers forms outside.

Indian demand for meals from the major food chains is growing at a double-digit rate; annual total sales exceed $1 billion. With those trends in mind, McDonald's identifies strategic locations in areas with heavy pedestrian traffic such as the shopping street in Bandra in the Bombay suburbs. Other restaurant locations include a site near a college in Vile Parle and another opposite the Andheri train station. Prices are lower than in other countries; most sandwiches cost about 40 rupees (less than $1). Drinks cost 15 rupees,

TABLE 1 Total Number of Systemwide Restaurants

	United States	Europe	APMEA	Other Countries and Corporate	Total
2007	13,862	6,480	7,938	3,097	31,377
2006	13,774	6,403	7,822	3,047	31,046
2005	13,727	6,352	7,692	2,995	30,766

Source: McDonald's *Annual Report*, 2007.

and a packet of French fries is 25 rupees. A complete meal costs the equivalent of about $2.

Because the Hindu religion prohibits eating beef, McDonald's developed the lamb-based Maharaja Mac specifically for India. Despite protests from several Hindu nationalist groups, the first McDonald's attracted huge crowds to its site near the Victoria railway terminal; customers included many tourists from across India and from abroad as well as locals commuting to and from work. In short order, however, Hindu activists renewed their protests, this time accusing the company of using beef tallow in its cooking. Management responded by posting signs reading "No beef or beef products sold here," but the doubts raised by the controversy kept many potential customers away.

Since that time, McDonald's has worked steadily to prove that it is sensitive to Indian tastes and traditions. As is true throughout the world, McDonald's emphasizes that most of the food ingredients it uses—as much as 95 percent—are produced locally. In addition, to accommodate vegetarians, each restaurant has two separate food preparation areas. The "green" kitchen is devoted to vegetarian fare such as the spicy McAloo Tikka potato burger, Pizza McPuff, and Paneer Salsa McWrap. Meat items are prepared on the red side. Even the mayonnaise is made without eggs. Some of the new menu items developed for India are being introduced in Europe and the United States.

> *"The tastes of the urban, upwardly mobile Indian are evolving, and more Indians are looking to eat out and experiment. The potential Indian customer base for a McDonald's or a Subway is larger than the size of entire developed countries."*
>
> **Sapna Nayak, food analyst at Raobank India**

China is currently home to the world's largest McDonald's. The first Chinese location opened in mid-1992 in central Beijing, a few blocks from Tiananmen Square. Despite having a 20-year lease for its first store, McDonald's found itself in the middle of a dispute between the central government and Beijing's city government. City officials decided to build a new $1.2 billion commercial complex in the city center and demanded that McDonald's vacate the site. However, central government officials had not approved the city's plans. McDonald's was forced to abandon the location; despite the turbulent start, McDonald's now has more than 800 restaurants in China. The restaurants purchase 95 percent of their supplies, including lettuce, from local sources.

In Asia and elsewhere, McDonald's protects itself from currency fluctuations by purchasing as much as possible from local suppliers. For example, the company's Singapore locations now buy chicken patties from Thailand rather than from the United States. However, French fries must still be imported from Australia or the United States. To help offset higher costs, McDonald's offers customers the choice of rice as a side dish at a lower price.

Western Europe

The golden arches are a familiar sight in Europe, particularly in England, France, and Germany; there is even a four-star Golden Arch hotel in Zurich. Overall, Europe contributes about 40 percent of both revenue and operating income, making it a key world region. However, at the end of the 1990s, Europe operations posted sales declines linked to consumer concerns about mad cow disease. The chain's British business was hit especially hard; the public health scare about mad cow disease resulted in bans on

British beef exports to continental Europe. Responding to public concerns, McDonald's immediately substituted imported beef at its British restaurants. By mid-1997, convinced that British beef was safe, McDonald's put it back on the menu. Ironically, no sooner had the beef furor subsided than Burger King brought its aptly named Big King sandwich ("20 percent more beef than a Big Mac") to England. In 2000 and 2001, concerns over the safety of the meat supply surfaced again amid an outbreak of hoof-and-mouth disease and ongoing media reports about mad cow disease. The public's reduced appetite for beef was reflected in decreases in systemwide sales, revenues, and operating income for McDonald's European division in 2000.

France's tradition of culinary excellence makes it a special case in Europe; dining options range from legendary three-star Michelin restaurants to humble neighborhood bistros. From the time McDonald's opened its first French outlet in 1972, policymakers and media commentators have voiced concerns about the impact of fast food on French culture. Even so, with nearly 1,000 outlets, France today represents McDonald's third-largest market in Europe. However, controversy has kept the company in the public eye. For example, some French citizens objected when McDonald's became the official food of the World Cup finals that were held in France in 1998.

In August 1999, a sheep farmer named Jose Bové led a protest against construction of the 851st French McDonald's near the village of Millau. The group used construction tools to dismantle the partially finished structure. Bové told the press that the group had singled out McDonald's because, in his words, it is a symbol of America, "the place where they not only promote globalization and industrially produced food but also unfairly penalize our peasants." In 2002, executives at McDonald's France even ran an ad in *Femme Actuelle* magazine suggesting that children should eat only one meal at McDonald's per week.

McDonald's French franchisees experience some of the same competitive pressures facing the U.S. units; there are also key differences. For example, local bistro operators have enjoyed great success selling fresh-baked baguettes filled with ham and brie, effectively neutralizing McDonald's advantage of fast service and low prices. In response, executives hired an architecture firm to develop new restaurant designs and reimage the French operations.

A total of eight different themes were developed; many of the redesigned stores have hardwood floors and exposed brick walls. Signs are in muted colors rather than the chain's signature red and yellow and the golden arches are displayed more subtly. Overall, the restaurants don't look like McDonald's elsewhere. The first redesigned store is located on the Champs Elysées on a site previously occupied by a Burger King; called "Music," the restaurant provides diners with the opportunity to listen to music on iPods and watch music videos on TV monitors. In some locations, lime green Danish designer armchairs have replaced plastic seats. As McDonald's locations in France undergo style makeovers, some franchisees report sales increases of 10 to 20 percent. Encouraged by these results, McDonald's has embarked on an ambitious program to refurbish several thousand outlets in various countries.

Central and Eastern Europe

On January 31, 1990, after 14 years of negotiation and preparation, the first Bolshoi Mac went on sale in what was then the Soviet Union; by the end of the decade, there were more than two dozen McDonald's restaurants in Russia. The first Moscow McDonald's was built on Pushkin Square, near a major metro station just a few blocks from the Kremlin. It has 700 indoor seats and another 200 outside. It boasts 800 employees and features a 70-foot counter with 27 cash registers, equivalent to 20 ordinary McDonald's rolled into one. At present, there are more than 180 McDonald's locations in 40 Russian cities, and the original Pushkin Square store enjoys the distinction of being the world's second-busiest McDonald's. To ensure a steady supply of high-quality raw materials, the company built McComplex, a huge $45 million processing facility on the outskirts of Moscow. McDonald's also worked closely with local farmers to boost yields and quality; today the company sources 75 percent of its ingredients from a network of 100 in-country suppliers.

The turmoil stemming from the dissolution of the Soviet Union and Russia's sometimes tortuous journey toward a market economy during the 1990s has presented the management of McDonald's Russia with a number of challenges. Although massive public demonstrations followed a failed coup attempt in August 1991, the protesters did not target McDonald's. Perhaps management's biggest challenge to date was the currency crisis that began in the summer of 1998 when the Russian government devalued the ruble and defaulted on its foreign debt. Many companies immediately raised prices to compensate for the precipitous drop in the ruble's value, and customers stopped buying.

Ukraine and Belarus are among the other members of the Commonwealth of Independent States with newly opened restaurants. The first Ukrainian McDonald's opened in Kiev in 1997; by 2007, the chain had expanded to 57 locations in 16 cities. Plans call for up to 100 restaurants, for a total investment of $120 million. McDonald's has also set its sights on Central Europe, where plans call for hundreds of new restaurants to be opened in Croatia, Slovakia, Romania, and other countries.

Refocusing on the U.S. Market

By the late 1990s, McDonald's strategy of growing its U.S. business by opening new restaurants was not yielding the desired results. In 1998, McDonald's struggles led to a management shakeup: Chairman and CEO Michael R. Quinlan relinquished the top position to Jack M. Greenberg, who had headed McDonald's USA. Greenberg immediately launched a range of new growth-oriented initiatives, including the company's first forays outside the core business. For example, McDonald's acquired a majority stake in the Chipotle Mexican Grill chain. The move signaled McDonald's recognition both of the increasing popularity of ethnic foods and of heightened interest among consumers in healthy eating. McDonald's also acquired Aroma, a coffeehouse chain in London.

The acquisition spree continued as McDonald's snapped up Donatos Pizza and Boston Market, a floundering chain featuring home-style cooking. As Greenberg conceded, "There are pieces of the business we can't do under the arches. When you're out with friends on a Saturday night for pizza and wine, you don't go to McDonald's." Greenberg envisioned that these partner brands would add at least 2 percent to McDonald's growth rate within a few years. In addition McCafé, a gourmet coffee shop modeled on a successful Australian concept, was tested in downtown Chicago, and a McTreat ice cream parlor had a trial run in Houston.

"McDonald's comes off as uncool. If you want to be chic, you eat sushi. Indian food is even more cutting edge. McDonald's is like white bread."

Daniel, a 26-year-old architectural draftsman in San Francisco

In 2002, Greenberg resigned and Jim Cantalupo became CEO. Cantalupo was a retired vice chairman whose 28-year career at McDonald's included considerable international experience. He vowed to get the company back on track by focusing on the basics, namely customer service, clean restaurants, and reliable food. Unhappy with the company's recent "Smile" advertising theme, Cantalupo took the extraordinary step of calling a summit meeting of senior creative personnel from 14 advertising agencies representing McDonald's 10 largest international markets. Foremost among them was New York–based DDB Worldwide, the lead agency on the McDonald's account that handles advertising in 34 countries including Australia, the United States, and Germany. In addition, Leo Burnett is responsible for ads targeting children. McDonald's marketing and advertising managers from key countries were also summoned to the meeting at company headquarters in Oakbrook, Illinois.

As Larry Light, then-global chief marketing officer for McDonald's, noted:

> Creative talent is a rare talent, and creative people don't belong to geographies, to Brazil or France or Australia. We're going to challenge our agencies to be more open-minded about sharing between geographies.

Charlie Bell, a former executive at McDonald's Europe who was promoted to chief operating officer, didn't mince words about the company's advertising. "For one of the world's best brands, we have missed the mark," he said before the summit meeting. In June, the company announced that it had picked the phrase "i'm lovin' it" as its new global marketing theme; the idea was proposed by Heye & Partner, a DDB Worldwide unit located in Germany. Tragically, within a few months, both Cantalupo and Bell died unexpectedly. Jim Skinner, the company's current chief executive officer, instituted a "Plan to Win" initiative to increase McDonald's momentum.

Even as McDonald's executives attempted to come to grips with the problems facing their company, various business experts were offering advice of their own. In the mid-1990s, one market analyst said, "McDonald's is similar to Coca-Cola ten years ago. It's on the verge of becoming an international giant, with the United States as a major market, but overseas as the driving force." Adrian J. Slywotzky, author of *Value Migration*, noted, "McDonald's needs to move the question from 'How can we sell more hamburgers?' to 'What does our brand allow us to consider selling to our customers?'" Mark DiMassimo, chief executive of a New York–based company that specializes in brand advertising, called McDonald's "a large lost organization that is searching for a strategy." In his view, "The company must focus, focus, focus, and stand for one thing."

There is evidence that, several years on, the "Plan to Win" strategy is gaining traction. *Consumer Reports* lauded the company's efforts to upgrade its coffee program. Consumers have embraced "better-for-you" menu items such as salads and sandwiches. The company is also seeking ways to be more environmentally conscious by using less plastic packaging and recycling more. Denis Hennequin, the executive in charge of European operations, is pleased with the results of his plan to redefine McDonald's image. He said, "I'm changing the story. We've got to be loyal to our roots, we have to be affordable, we have to be convenient . . . but we have to add new dimensions." In 2007, bolstered in part by strong sales growth in Europe, McDonald's stock price reached its highest level in years.

Discussion Questions

1. Identify the key elements in McDonald's global marketing strategy. In particular, how does McDonald's approach the issue of standardization?

2. Do you think government officials in developing countries such as Russia, China, and India welcome McDonald's? Do consumers in these countries welcome McDonald's? Why or why not?

3. At the end of 2003, McDonald's announced it was selling the Donatos Pizza unit. Then, in 2006, the Chipotle chain was spun off. In light of these strategic actions, assess McDonald's prospects for success beyond the burger-and-fries model.

4. Is it realistic to expect that McDonald's—or any well-known company—can expand globally without occasionally making mistakes or generating controversy? Why do antiglobalization protesters around the world frequently target McDonald's?

Visit the Web site

www.mcdonalds.com includes a directory to country-specific sites

Sources: Janet Adamy, "As Burgers Boom in Russia, McDonald's Touts Discipline," *The Wall Street Journal* (October 16, 2007), pp. A1, A17; Jenny Wiggins, "Burger, Fries, and a Shake-Up," *Financial Times* (January 27, 2007), p. 7; Steven Gray, "Beyond Burgers: McDonald's Menu Upgrade Boosts Meal Prices and Results," *The Wall Street Journal* (February 18–19, 2006), pp. A1, A7; Jeremy Grant, "Golden Arches Bridge Local Tastes," *Financial Times* (February 9, 2006), p. 10; Saritha Rai, "Tastes of India in U.S. Wrappers," *The New York Times* (April 29, 2003), pp. W1, W7; Bruce Horovitz, "It's Back to Basics for McDonald's," *USA Today* (May 21, 2003), pp. 1B, 2B; Sherri Day, "After Years at Top, McDonald's Strives to Regain Ground," *The New York Times* (March 3, 2003), pp. A1, A19; Sherri Day and Stuart Elliot, "At McDonald's, an Effort to Restore Lost Luster," *The New York Times* (April 8, 2003), pp. B1, B4; Shirley Leung and Suzanne Vranica, "Happy Meals Are No Longer Bringing Smiles at McDonald's," *The Wall Street Journal* (January 31, 2003), p. B1; Shirley Leung and Ron Lieber, "The New Menu Option at McDonald's: Plastic," *The Wall Street Journal* (November 26, 2002), pp. D1, D2; Shirley Leung, "McHaute Cuisine: Armchairs, TVs and Espresso—Is It McDonald's?" *The Wall Street Journal* (August 30, 2002), pp. A1, A6; Bruce Horovitz, "McDonald's Tries a New Recipe to Revive Sales," *USA Today* (July 10, 2001), pp. 1A, 2A; Geoff Winestock and Yaroslav Trofimov, "McDonald's Reassures Italians About Beef," *The Wall Street Journal* (January 16, 2001), pp. A3, A6; Kevin Helliker and Richard Gibson, "The New Chief Is Ordering Up Changes at McDonald's," *The Wall Street Journal* (August 24, 1998), pp. B1, B4; Bethan Hutton, "Fast-Food Group Blows a McBubble in Slow Economy," *Financial Times* (May 8, 1998), p. 24; Bruce Horovitz, "My Job Is Always on the Line," *USA Today* (March 16, 1998), p. 8B; David Leonhardt, "McDonald's: Can It Regain Its Golden Touch?" *Business Week* (March 9, 1998), pp. 70–74+; Richard Tomkins, "When the Chips Are Down," *Financial Times* (August 16, 1997), p. 13; Yumiko Ono, "Japan Warms to McDonald's Doting Dad Ads," *The Wall Street Journal* (May 8, 1997), pp. B1, B12.

Case 1-3
Acer Inc.

Acer Inc. is a leading marketer of notebook and desktop PCs. The company, which posted sales of $11.3 billion in 2006, also produces other products such as flat-screen monitors and personal digital assistants. As Taiwan gained a reputation as the "tech workshop of the world," Acer was able to become Taiwan's number one exporter by manufacturing and marketing computers sold under its own brand name. Acer also produced equipment on an original equipment manufacturer (OEM) basis for well-known global companies such as IBM, Dell, and Hitachi. As company founder, chairman, and CEO, Stan Shih built Acer Inc. into one of Taiwan's most successful companies.

Despite Acer's success, the company had trouble breaking into the American market. Between 1995 and 1997, Acer's U.S. market share dropped from 15 to 5 percent. In the late 1990s, Shih noted, "In the United States and Europe, we are relatively weak. The local players there are very strong. The problem is that we don't have good experience in marketing in those regions. It's a people issue, not a product issue." Shih has discovered that building brands in the business-to-business market is easier than building brands in the business-to-consumer market. "Business-to-consumer brands have more value but also face more challenges. People involved in business-to-business are usually rational, but consumers in business-to-consumer are usually emotional in choosing their brands," he says.

Source: Dan Hartung/Getty Images.

In 2000, in a major restructuring, Acer spun off its manufacturing operations. The reason: Shih wanted to transform Acer from a top 10 global PC manufacturer into a "marketing and services powerhouse." Shih also refocused Acer's distribution and marketing on the vast, fast-growing China market. Acer and other key

70

players in Taiwan's high-tech industry stand to benefit from closer economic ties with the mainland giant, which joined the WTO in 2001. WTO rules require that both China and Taiwan eliminate limitations on foreign investment. As a result, the Taiwan-based producers from which Acer now sources its products have most of their factories in China.

Shih envisions building a solid market base in greater China (mainland China, Taiwan, and Hong Kong) and expanding from there to the rest of the world. "The market in China is very critical for Taiwanese companies to become global companies," Shih says. "Innovation is not necessarily related to whether you are smart or not. The reality is that if you don't have a big market it's not easy to innovate because the return on investment is too low. The potential of China is not just big markets and low-cost labor. Actually, it's also for highly educated engineers or professionals." Shih believes that, if greater China becomes the company's "home" market (as opposed to just Taiwan), Acer will capture critical economies of scale that will allow it to develop innovative new products that will succeed in China as well as the rest of the world.

Shih understands that it is crucial for Acer to develop a strong brand image in China. "The challenge for this region is really the poor image that is often associated with products here," says Shih. Shih believes that it is necessary for all companies to be stable and secure in the local market before pursuing regional, then global markets. He continues, "Another important feature is also the government and the general public. They have to understand the role of supporting activities for local brands. If they do not support or use the locally made products, there will be no improvement in this area."

Ronald Chwang, Acer's chief technology officer, anticipates that Acer's knowledge of China's market will help the company achieve its growth and market share objectives; as he puts it, "Now we have a market where we understand the culture and the people's needs. That should enable Acer to move a lot of hardware." As Acer Group CEO J.T. Wang noted recently, "China and Taiwan share not just the same language and culture, but a lot of our Taiwanese suppliers are already there. We can take our brand global by building a strong home market."

Still, Acer faces tough competition in China. Lenovo, a local mainland brand, dominates with about one-third of the market. Wang believes Acer is well positioned to overtake Lenovo and other local mainland firms to become the leader in PC sales in China. Shih believes Acer will have an advantage compared to local PC makers because Acer is "more global." At the same time, Shih is convinced his company will be able to compete with better-known global companies that are entering China because Acer is more "local" than they are. Acer's international identity gives the company access to advanced business practices, technology, and economies of scale that companies like Lenovo do not have. "We have more technology. . . . We have more global exposure. . . . We have more international know-how. . . . We can gradually gain more market share," Shih says.

Shih admits that sales of Acer's desktop PCs in China have developed more slowly than he expected. He attributes this to Acer's poor brand recognition in the mainland. However, Shih made a strategic bet that the company's notebook computers would help Acer establish a quality name and high-end image. Meanwhile, Lenovo acquired IBM's Thinkpad notebook business in a move that catapulted the company into third place among the world's computer makers. Keenly aware of the importance of scale in the global computer market, Acer acquired U.S.-based Gateway in 2007.

Shih had promised his wife he would retire at the end of 2004 when he turned 60. He kept his promise, stepping down in December of that year. Why? "This way the company can have new blood," he said. "Acer is solid and stable, but a little bit old-fashioned. Sometimes we are not aggressive enough among the middle and high level managers." The move is paying off: Acer is currently the top notebook brand in Europe, and its low prices are a crucial selling point in key emerging markets such as India and Eastern Europe. With the Gateway acquisition completed, Acer was on track to surpass Lenovo and become the world's third largest PC marketer by the end of 2007. Will the new leadership team headed by J.T. Wang be able to replicate Acer's European success in the United States and Asia?

Discussion Questions

1. Acer's strategy has been described as "divide and conquer." Explain.
2. How did the "global markets/local markets" paradox figure into Stan Shih's strategy for China?
3. Can Acer become the world's third largest PC company, behind Dell and Hewlett-Packard?
4. Even before the current economic crisis deepened, growth in the U.S. PC market had begun slowing. Despite strong competition from Dell and Hewlett-Packard, Acer's U.S. market share increased from 1 percent in 2004 to 3.3 percent by the end of 2006. What are Acer's prospects for gaining further share in the United States?

This case was prepared by Research Assistant Alanah Davis under the supervision of Professor Mark Green.

Sources: Jason Dean and Christopher Lawton, "Acer Buys Gateway, Bulks Up for Global Fight," *The Wall Street Journal* (August 28, 2007), pp. B1, B4; Jason Dean and Jane Spencer, "Acer Seeks Happiness in Its 'Land of Sorrow,'" *The Wall Street Journal* (April 5, 2007), pp. B1, B6; Jane Spencer, "Taiwan's Acer May Take Bronze," *The Wall Street Journal* (November 16, 2006), p. B6; Jason Dean, "PC Underdog Raises Its Sights," *The Wall Street Journal* (September 20, 2005), p. C6; "Special Report—Stars of Asia—Managers," *Business Week* (July 12, 2004); Bruce Einhorn, Amy Reinhardt, and Maureen Kline, "Acer: How Far Can It Ride This Hot Streak?" *Business Week* (May 17, 2004), p. 52; Hiawatha Bray, "Acer Embodies Taiwanese Climb Up Manufacturing Food Chain," *The Boston Globe* (June 24, 2002); Simon Burns and Kathy Wilhelm, "Acer Who?" *Far Eastern Economic Review* (May 24, 2001), pp. 47; Wai-Chan Chan, Martin Hirt, and Stephen M. Shaw, "The Greater China High-Tech Highway," *The McKinsey Quarterly* no. 4 (October 11, 2002); Charles S. Lee, "Acer's Last Stand?" *Fortune* (June 10, 2002); Yu Wui Wui, "Marketing Asian Brands," *New Straits Times—Management Times* (October 4, 2000).

The Global Economic Environment

Case 2-1
The Global Economic Crisis

In his 1997 book *One World, Ready or Not,* William Greider described the United States as "the buyer of last resort." Greider explained that, for many years, the United States was the only nation that was willing to absorb production surpluses exported by companies in Europe, Asia, and Latin America. Greider asked: "Who will buy the surpluses when the United States cannot?" The conventional wisdom has long held that strong spending by consumers in other nations would keep the world economy humming.

However, by 2008, Greider's question was taking on a new urgency and the conventional wisdom was being tested. An economic crisis that had its roots in lax subprime mortgage lending practices began to spread around the globe. In the United States, where the crisis began, economic misery was widespread: The housing market collapsed, real estate values plummeted, credit tightened, and job growth slowed (see Exhibit 2-1). As the price of oil passed the $100 per barrel benchmark, the average price of a gallon of gasoline rose to $4. American consumers were, indeed, less willing and less able to buy.

However, the crisis was not confined to the United States alone. Consumer-goods exporters in Asia, which

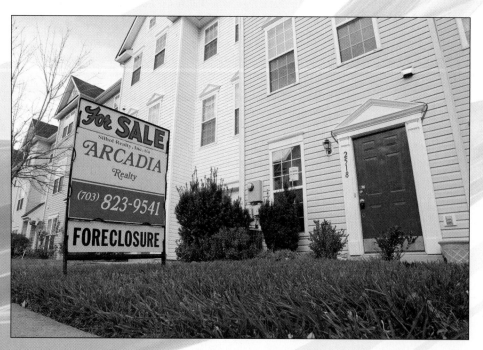

Exhibit 2-1: The bursting of the global real estate bubble was only one aspect of the worst recession in decades. The ripple effects from the economic turmoil were felt around the world. In 2007, just before the onset of the crisis, Mexico's Cemex SAB acquired an Australian company, Rinker Materials, for $15.3 billion. Unfortunately, one of Rinker's primary sources of revenue was the United States housing market. With that market collapsing, Cemex chief Lorenzo Zambrano was forced to sell assets and cut spending in an effort to trim his company's debt load.
Source: Paul J. Richards/AFP/Newscom.

had prospered as Americans snapped up autos, electronics, and other products, faced flagging demand. By contrast, Brazil and Russia, two nations that had experienced economic turmoil in the 1990s, were buoyed by soaring demand for commodities such as gas and oil. Demand for raw materials was particularly strong in India and China. Then, as the economic crisis deepened, prices for oil and other commodities plummeted. Case 2-1 describes the challenges of the current economic environment in more detail. When you are done reading the chapter, study the case and answer the discussion questions. Needless to say, the current economic downturn is creating both challenges and opportunities for global marketers.

The global economic crisis vividly illustrates the dynamic, integrated nature of today's economic environment. Recall the basic definition of a market: people or organizations with needs and wants and both the willingness and ability to buy or sell. As noted in Chapter 1, many companies engage in global marketing in an effort to reach new customers outside their home countries and thereby increase sales, profits, and market share. Brazil, Russia, India, and China deserve special mention; collectively referred to as **BRIC**, these four country markets are particularly dynamic and represent important opportunities.[1] The BRIC nations and other emerging markets are also home to companies that are challenging established global giants at home and abroad. This chapter will identify the most salient characteristics of the world economic environment, starting with an overview of the world economy, a survey of economic system types, a discussion of stages of market development, and balance of payments. Foreign exchange is discussed in the final section of the chapter. Throughout the chapter, we will discuss the implications of the worldwide economic downturn on global marketing strategies.

"As the saying goes, if you are not manufacturing in China or selling in India, you are as good as finished."[2]

Dipankar Halder, Associate Director,
KSA Technopak, India

THE WORLD ECONOMY—AN OVERVIEW

The world economy has changed profoundly since World War II.[3] Perhaps the most fundamental change is the emergence of global markets; responding to new opportunities, global competitors have steadily displaced or absorbed local ones. Concurrently, the integration of the world economy has increased significantly. Economic integration stood at 10 percent at the beginning of the twentieth century; today, it is approximately 50 percent. Integration is particularly striking in the European Union (EU) and the North American Free Trade Area.

Just 65 years ago, the world was far less integrated than it is today. As evidence of the changes that have taken place, consider the automobile. Cars with European nameplates such as Renault, Citroën, Peugeot, Morris, Volvo, and others were radically different from the American Chevrolet, Ford, or Plymouth, or Japanese models from Toyota or Nissan. These were local cars built by local companies, mostly destined for local or regional markets. Even today, global and regional auto companies make cars for their home-country car buyers that are not marketed abroad. However, it is also true that the world car is a reality for Honda and Toyota. Product changes reflect organizational changes as well: The world's largest automakers have, for the most part, evolved into global companies. Ford is a case in point: In 2008, the company unveiled an updated version of the Fiesta that will be marketed throughout the world. As Mark Fields, an executive vice president at Ford, explained, "We've had cars with the same name, like Escort and

[1]The "BRIC" designation first appeared in a 2001 report published by Goldman Sachs, the New York–based investment bank, hedge fund, and private equity firm.
[2]Saritha Rai, "Tastes of India in U.S. Wrappers," *The New York Times* (April 29, 2003), p. W7.
[3]Numerous books and articles survey this subject, for example, Lowell Bryan et al., *Race for the World: Strategies to Build a Great Global Firm* (Boston: Harvard Business School Press, 1999).

Focus, but the products themselves were very regional. This is a real shift point for us in that it's a real global car."[4]

During the past two decades, the world economic environment has become increasingly dynamic; change has been dramatic and far-reaching. To achieve success, executives and marketers must take into account the following new realities:[5]

- Capital movements have replaced trade as the driving force of the world economy.
- Production has become "uncoupled" from employment.
- The world economy dominates the scene; individual country economies play a subordinate role.
- The struggle between capitalism and socialism that began in 1917 is largely over.
- The growth of e-commerce diminishes the importance of national barriers and forces companies to reevaluate their business models.

The first change is the increased volume of capital movements. The dollar value of world trade in goods and services was $16.9 trillion in 2007. However, the London foreign exchange market turns over $450 billion each working day; overall, foreign exchange transactions worth approximately $1.5 trillion are booked every day—far surpassing the dollar volume of world trade in goods and services.[6] There is an inescapable conclusion in these data: Global capital movements far exceed the dollar volume of global trade. This explains the paradoxical combination of U.S. trade deficits and a strong dollar during the first half of the 1980s and again in the early twenty-first century. According to orthodox economic theory, when a country runs a deficit on its trade accounts, its currency should depreciate in value. Today, it is capital movements and trade that determine currency value.

The second change concerns the relationship between productivity and employment. To illustrate this relationship, it is necessary to review some basic macroeconomics. **Gross domestic product (GDP)**, a measure of a nation's economic activity, is calculated by adding consumer spending (C), investment spending (I), government purchases (G), and net exports (NX):

$$C + I + G + NX = GDP$$

Economic growth, as measured by GDP, reflects increases in a nation's productivity. Until the recent economic crisis, employment in manufacturing had remained steady or declined while productivity continued to grow. Now, because of the global recession, both employment and productivity are declining. The historical pattern is especially clear in American agriculture, where fewer farm employees produce more output. In the United States, manufacturing's share of GDP declined from 19.2 percent in 1989 to 13 percent in 2004.[7] In 2001, manufacturing employment accounted for about 13 percent of the U.S. workforce; in 1971, the figure was 26 percent. During that 30-year period, productivity has increased dramatically. Similar trends can be found in many other major industrial economies as well. One recent study of 20 large economies found that, between 1995 and 2002, more than 22 million factory jobs have been eliminated. Manufacturing is not in decline—it is *employment* in manufacturing that is in decline.[8]

---

[4]Bill Vlasic, "Ford Introduces One Small Car for a World of Markets," *The New York Times* (February 15, 2008), p. C3.
[5]William Greider offers a thought-provoking analysis of these new realities in *One World, Ready or Not: The Manic Logic of Global Capitalism* (New York: Simon & Schuster, 1997).
[6]Alan C. Shapiro, *Multinational Financial Management*, 7th ed. (Hoboken, NJ: John Wiley & Sons, 2003), p. 137. A Eurodollar is a U.S. dollar held outside the United States. U.S. dollars are subject to U.S. banking regulations; Eurodollars are not.
[7]Another economic indicator, gross national income (GNI), is comprised of GDP plus income generated from nonresident sources. A third metric, gross national product (GNP), is the total value of all final goods and services produced in a country by its residents and domestic business enterprises, plus the value of output produced by citizens working abroad, plus income generated by capital held abroad, minus transfers of net earnings by global companies operating in the country. GDP also measures economic activity; however, GDP includes *all* income produced within a country's borders by its residents and domestic enterprises as well as foreign-owned enterprises. Income earned by citizens working abroad is *not* included. For example, Ireland has attracted a great deal of foreign investment, and foreign-owned firms account for nearly 90 percent of Ireland's exports. This helps explain the fact that, in 2005, Ireland's GDP totaled €161 billion while GNP was €135 billion. However, as a practical matter, GNP, GDP, and GNI figures for many countries will be roughly the same.
[8]Jon E. Hilsenrath and Rebecca Buckman, "Factory Employment Is Falling World-Wide," *The Wall Street Journal* (October 20, 2003), p. A2. Some companies have cut employment by outsourcing or subcontracting nonmanufacturing activities such as data processing, accounting, and customer service.

EMERGING MARKETS BRIEFING BOOK

⬆) Russia's Economic Roller-Coaster Ride

In August 1998, the Russian economy imploded. The ruble plunged in value and the government defaulted on its foreign debt obligations. Many Russians faced wage cuts and layoffs; savings were wiped out as banks collapsed. The meltdown sent shock waves through global financial markets. Russia was down, but it was not out; in the years since the crisis, Russia's economy has experienced substantial growth. By 2006, a country that had teetered on the brink of bankruptcy had posted four consecutive years of 6 percent economic growth and had amassed $250 billion in foreign currency reserves. The dramatic economic recovery can be attributed in part to record world prices for oil and gas; the energy sector is Russia's most important source of export revenue.

A second explanation for the rebounding economy was politics. In 2000, Vladimir Putin succeeded Boris Yeltsin as president. Putin initiated a reform program that included a new tax code. He also streamlined customs regulations, slashed subsidies to state-owned enterprises, and made other improvements in the business climate. A third factor in Russia's economic rebound was the fact that price increases for imports caused by the ruble's devaluation stimulated local production of a wide range of goods. As one economist noted, "The crash of '98 really cleaned out the macro-economy." Putin confidently predicted that national income in Russia would double by 2010.

Will Putin's vision for economic growth in Russia be realized? Can the current recovery be sustained? Some indicators are positive; for example, foreign investment topped $13 billion in 2005, more than three times the 2002 level. Negotiations are ongoing to gain Russia admittance to the WTO. From the American perspective, issues such as market access for U.S. financial services companies and intellectual property protection are top priorities. Software, music, and video piracy are well-entrenched; annual losses from illegal software alone are estimated to be about $1.5 billion. Resolving those issues would pave the way for a lifting of U.S. economic restrictions known as the Jackson-Vanik amendment and the granting of permanent normal trade relations with Russia.

Putin hosted the 2006 Group of Eight Summit in St. Petersburg, further enhancing Russia's status on the world stage. Despite the positive publicity, however, other recent events have raised concerns in the world community. There is concern in Washington that Putin is suppressing the growth of democratic institutions. The phrase *managed democracy* describes what some call the arbitrary exercise of state power. Russia plans to limit foreign investment in strategic industries such as oil; the term *renationalization* has been applied to the process by which state-owned enterprises are acquiring rivals. *Kleptocracy* refers to rampant corruption and bribery.

Russia is so dependent on revenues from the fuel and energy sectors that some feared the major decline in world oil prices that began in 2008 would have a destabilizing effect. A related problem is the fact that Russia's energy industry is dominated by a handful of huge conglomerates. The men who run these companies are known as oligarchs; at one time, Yukos Oil's Mikhail Khodorkovsky, Sibneft's Roman Abramovich, and their peers were among Russia's ultra-rich elite. However, there was widespread resentment among the Russian citizenry about the manner in which the oligarchs gained control of their respective companies. In July 2003, the Putin government sent a message to the oligarchs by arresting billionaire businessman Platon Lebedev on charges of paying too little for a fertilizer plant that he acquired in 1994. Khodorkovsky was also arrested and his Yukos empire was forced into bankruptcy.

There are other problems as well. Putin's tax reform program was relatively easy to implement; however, further reforms may face more opposition. Russia's entrenched bureaucracy is a barrier to increased economic freedom. The banking system remains fragile and in need of reform. Tragically, in the fall of 2006, Andrei Kozlov, Russia's top banking regulator, was shot to death on the streets of Moscow. Yevgeny Yasin, a former economy minister and an advocate of liberal reforms, noted recently, "The Russian economy is constrained by bureaucratic shackles. If the economy is to grow, these chains must be dropped. If we can overcome this feudal system of using power, we will create a stimulus for strong and sustainable economic growth and improve the standards of living."

A number of global companies took note of Russia's improved economic climate. For example, IKEA, the global furniture retailer, has opened dozens of new stores across Russia. France's Auchan and German retail chains Rewe and Metro are targeting the grocery market (see Exhibit 2-2). By contrast, Walmart, Carrefour, and UK-based Tesco do not yet have a market presence; management at these companies believes the risks and difficulties of doing business in Russia are too great.

In 2008, Dimitri Medvedev was elected president; Putin was named prime minister. The price of a barrel of oil fell from $200 to less than $50, and Russia's economy began to sputter. As the global recession deepened, Russia's dependence on a single commodity for the bulk of its export earnings turned out to be a liability. Only time will tell how long it will be until the good times return.

Sources: Neil Buckley, "From Shock Therapy to Retail Therapy: Russia's Middle Class Starts Spending," *The Financial Times* (October 31, 2006), p. 13; David Lynch, "Russia Brings Revitalized Economy to the Table," *USA Today* (July 13, 2006), pp. 1B, 2B; Guy Chazan, "Kremlin Capitalism: Russian Car Maker Comes under Sway of Old Pal of Putin," *The Wall Street Journal* (May 19, 2006), pp. A1, A7; Greg Hitt and Gregory L. White, "Hurdles Grow as Russia, U.S. Near Trade Deal," *The Wall Street Journal* (April 12, 2006), p. A4; Chazan, "Russia Is Flush—For Now," *The Wall Street Journal* (November 17, 2004), p. A14; Peter Weinberg, "Russia Merits a Welcome into the Trade Fold," *Financial Times* (October 27, 2003), p. 13; Mark Medish, "Russia's Economic Strength Begins at Home," *Financial Times* (September 22, 2003), p. 15; Andrew Jack and Stefan Wagstyl, "In 1998, Russia Was Nearly Bankrupt. Today It Has Reserves of $60 Bn. but Its Economic Future Remains Insecure," *Financial Times* (August 18, 2003), p. 9; Gregory L. White and Jeanne Whalen, "Why Russian Oil Is a Sticky Business," *The Wall Street Journal* (August 1, 2003), p. A7; Marshall Goldman, "Russia Will Pay Twice for the Fortunes of Its Oligarchs," *Financial Times* (July 26/27, 2003), p. 10.

Exhibit 2-2: Russia is being transformed by economic change. In Moscow, for example, affluent Russians can shop at boutiques that offer Versace, Burberry, Bulgari, and other exclusive brands. Although per capita gross national income (GNI) in Russia is only $5,770, Russian shoppers spend an estimated $4 billion each year on luxury goods. Flush with dollars from oil exports, in 2006 the Russian government lifted all currency controls, making the ruble freely convertible in world markets.
Source: Alexander Nemenov/ AFP/Getty Images, Inc. AFP.

The third major change is the emergence of the world economy as the dominant economic unit. Company executives and national leaders who recognize this have the greatest chance of success. For example, the real secret of the economic success of Germany and Japan is the fact that business leaders and policymakers focus on world markets and their respective countries' competitive positions in the world economy. This change has brought two questions to the fore: How does the global economy work, and who is in charge? Unfortunately, the answers to these questions are not clear-cut.

The fourth change is the end of the Cold War. The demise of communism as an economic and political system can be explained in a straightforward manner: Communism is not an effective economic system. The overwhelmingly superior performance of the world's market economies has given leaders in socialist countries little choice but to renounce their ideology. A key policy change in such countries has been the abandonment of futile attempts to manage national economies with a single central plan. This policy change frequently goes hand in hand with governmental efforts to foster increased public participation in matters of state by introducing democratic reforms.[9]

Finally, the personal computer revolution and the advent of the Internet era have in some ways diminished the importance of national boundaries. Worldwide, an estimated 1 billion people use personal computers. In the so-called Information Age, barriers of time and place have been subverted by a transnational cyberworld that functions "24/7." Amazon.com, eBay, Facebook, Google, iTunes, MySpace, Priceline, Twitter, and YouTube are just a few of the companies that are pushing the envelope in this brave new world.

> "Only an outbreak of protectionist policies or a sharp rise in international shipping costs could slow or temporarily reverse manufacturing's declining share of employment in the United States."[10]
> Steven J. Davis, Professor of Economics, University of Chicago

> "Ask one billion people, and 99 percent of them are going to say they want a car. The problem is, how many can afford it?"[11]
> Jagdish Khattar, Managing Director, Maruti Suzuki India

ECONOMIC SYSTEMS

Traditionally, economists identified four main types of economic systems: market capitalism, centrally planned socialism, centrally planned capitalism, and market socialism. As shown in Figure 2-1, this classification was based on the dominant method of resource allocation (market versus command) and the dominant form of resource ownership (private versus state). Thanks to

[9]Marcus W. Brauchli, "Poll Vaults: More Nations Embrace Democracy—and Find It Can Often Be Messy," *The Wall Street Journal* (June 25, 1996), pp. A1, A6.
[10]Tracey Taylor, "A Label of Pride That Pays," *The New York Times* (April 23, 2009), p. B4.
[11]Heather Timmons, "In India, a $2,500 Pace Car," *The New York Times* (October 12, 2007), p. C1.

FIGURE 2-1

Economic Systems

Resource Allocation

	Market	Command
Private	Market capitalism	Centrally planned capitalism
State	Market socialism	Centrally planned socialism

Resource Ownership

globalization, however, economic systems are harder to categorize within the confines of a four-cell matrix. Alternatively, more robust descriptive criteria include the following:[12]

- *Type of economy* Is the nation an advanced industrial state, an emerging economy, a transition economy, or a developing nation?
- *Type of government* Is the nation ruled by a monarchy, a dictatorship, or a tyrant? Is there an autocratic one-party system? Is the nation dominated by another state, or is it a democracy with a multi-party system? Is it an unstable or terrorist nation?
- *Trade and capital flows* Is the nation characterized by almost completely free trade or incomplete free trade, and is it part of a trading bloc? Is there a currency board or exchange controls? Is there no trade, or does the government dominate trade possibilities?
- *The commanding heights* (e.g., the transportation, communications, and energy sectors). Are these sectors state owned and operated? Is there a mix of state and private ownership? Are they all private, with or without controlled prices?
- *Services provided by the state and funded through taxes* Are pensions, health care, and education provided? Pensions and education but not health care? Do privatized systems dominate?
- *Institutions* Is the nation characterized by transparency, standards, the absence of corruption, and the presence of a free press and strong courts? Or is corruption a fact of life and the press dominated by the government? Are standards ignored and the court system compromised?
- *Markets* Does the nation have a free market system characterized by high risk/high reward entrepreneurial dynamism? Is it a free market that is dominated by monopolies, cartels, and concentrated industries? Is it a socialized market with cooperation between business, government, and labor (but with little entrepreneurial support)? Or is planning, including price and wage controls, dominated by the center?

Market Capitalism

Market capitalism is an economic system in which individuals and firms allocate resources and production resources are privately owned. Simply put, consumers decide what goods they desire and firms determine what and how much to produce; the role of the state in market capitalism is to promote competition among firms and ensure consumer protection. Today, market capitalism is widely practiced around the world, most notably in North America and the European Union (see Table 2-1).

It would be a gross oversimplification, however, to assume that all market-oriented economies function in an identical manner. Economist Paul Krugman has remarked that the United States is distinguished by its competitive, "wild free-for-all" and decentralized initiative. By contrast, outsiders sometimes refer to Japan as "Japan Inc." The label can be interpreted in different ways, but it basically refers to a tightly run, highly regulated economic system that is also market oriented.

---

[12]The authors are indebted to Professor Francis J. Colella, Department of Economics, Simpson College, for suggesting these criteria.

TABLE 2-1 Western Market Systems

Type of System	Key Characteristics	Countries
Anglo-Saxon Model	Private ownership; free enterprise economy; capitalism; minimal social safety net; highly flexible employment policies	United States, Canada, Great Britain
Social Market Economy Model	Private ownership; "social partners" orientation that includes employer groups, unions, and banks; unions and corporations are involved in government, and vice versa; inflexible employment policies	Germany, France, Italy
Nordic Model	Mix of state ownership and private ownership; high taxes, some market regulation, generous social safety net	Sweden, Norway

Centrally Planned Socialism

At the opposite end of the spectrum from market capitalism is **centrally planned socialism**. In this type of economic system, the state has broad powers to serve the public interest as it sees fit. State planners make "top-down" decisions about what goods and services are produced and in what quantities; consumers can spend their money on what is available. Government ownership of entire industries as well as individual enterprises is characteristic of centrally planned socialism. Because demand typically exceeds supply, the elements of the marketing mix are not used as strategic variables.[13] Little reliance is placed on product differentiation, advertising, or promotion; to eliminate "exploitation" by intermediaries, the government also controls distribution.

The clear superiority of market capitalism in delivering the goods and services that people need and want has led to its adoption in many formerly socialist countries. An ideology developed in the nineteenth century by Marx and perpetuated in the twentieth century by Lenin and others has been resoundingly refuted. As William Greider writes:

> Marxism is utterly vanquished, if not yet entirely extinct, as an alternative economic system. Capitalism is triumphant. The ideological conflict first joined in the mid-nineteenth century in response to the rise of industrial capitalism, the deep argument that has preoccupied political imagination for 150 years, is ended.[14]

For decades, the economies of China, the former Soviet Union, and India functioned according to the tenets of centrally planned socialism. All three countries are now engaged in economic reforms characterized, in varying proportions, by increased reliance on market allocation and private ownership. Even as China's leaders attempt to maintain control over society, they acknowledge the importance of economic reform (see Exhibit 2-3). At a recent assembly, the Communist Party said that reform "is an inevitable road for invigorating the country's economy and promoting social progress, and a great pioneering undertaking without parallel in history."

Centrally Planned Capitalism and Market Socialism

In reality, market capitalism and centrally planned socialism do not exist in "pure" form. In most countries, to a greater or lesser degree, command and market resource allocation are practiced simultaneously, as are private and state resource ownership. The role of government in modern market economies varies widely. An economic system in which command resource allocation is utilized extensively in an overall environment of private resource ownership can be called **centrally planned capitalism.** A fourth variant, **market socialism**, is also possible. In such a system, market allocation policies are permitted within an overall environment of state ownership.

In Sweden, for example, where the government controls two-thirds of all expenditures, resource allocation is more "command" oriented than "market" oriented. Also, as indicated in Table 2-2, the Swedish government has significant holdings in key business sectors. Thus, Sweden's so-called "welfare state" has a hybrid economic system that incorporates elements

---

[13]Peggy A. Golden, Patricia M. Doney, Denise M. Johnson, and Jerald R. Smith, "The Dynamics of a Marketing Orientation in Transition Economies: A Study of Russian Firms," *Journal of International Marketing* 3, no. 2 (1995), pp. 29–49.

[14]William Greider, *One World, Ready or Not: The Manic Logic of Global Capitalism* (New York: Simon & Schuster, 1997), p. 37.

Exhibit 2-3: In 2003, the Rolling Stones' *40 Licks* CD went on sale in China. However, some of the band's most famous hits—"Brown Sugar," "Beast of Burden," "Honky Tonk Women," and "Let's Spend the Night Together"—were left off because officials viewed them as promoting social permissiveness. The Stones were scheduled to bring their fortieth anniversary tour to Beijing and Shanghai in 2003. However, the concerts were postponed due to the SARS outbreak. When Mick, Keith, and company finally did perform in China in 2006, government officials ordered the band to omit five songs from its set list.
Source: AP Wide World Photos.

of both centrally planned socialism and capitalism. The Swedish government is embarking on a privatization plan that calls for selling its stakes in some of the businesses in Table 2-2.[15] In 2008, Vin & Spirit was sold to France's Pernod Ricard for $8.34 billion.

As noted previously, China is an example of centrally planned socialism. However, China's Communist leadership has given considerable freedom to businesses and individuals in the Guangdong Province to operate within a market system. Today, China's private sector accounts for approximately 70 percent of national output. Even so, state enterprises still receive more than two-thirds of the credit available from the country's banks.

Market reforms and nascent capitalism in many parts of the world are creating opportunities for large-scale investments by global companies. Indeed, Coca-Cola returned to India in 1994, two decades after being forced out by the government. A new law allowing 100 percent foreign ownership of enterprises helped pave the way. By contrast, Cuba stands as one of the last bastions of the command allocation approach. Daniel Yergin and Joseph Stanislaw sum up the situation in the following way:

> Socialists are embracing capitalism, governments are selling off companies they had nationalized, and countries are seeking to entice multinational corporations expelled just two decades earlier. Today, politicians on the left admit that their governments can no

"Countries with planned economies have never been part of economic globalization. China's economy must become a market economy."[16]
Long Yongtu, chief WTO negotiator for China

TABLE 2-2 Examples of Government Resource Ownership in Sweden

Company	Industry Sector	State Ownership %
TeliaSonera	Telecom	45
SAS	Airline	21
Nordea	Banking	20
OMX	Stock Exchange	7
Vin & Spirit	Alcohol	100*

*Sold in 2008.

[15]Joel Sherwood and Terence Roth, "Defeat of Sweden's Ruling Party Clears Way for Sales of State Assets," *The Wall Street Journal* (September 19, 2006), p. A8.
[16]Nicholas R. Lardy, *Integrating China into the Global Economy* (Washington, D.C.: The Brookings Institution, 2003), p. 21.

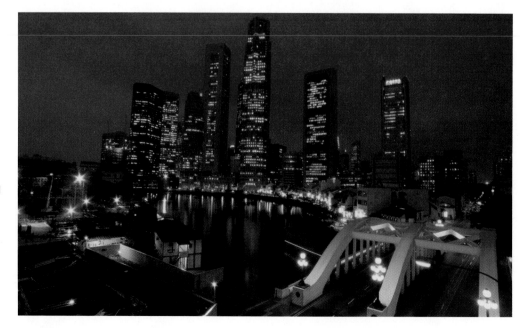

Exhibit 2-4: For decades, Singapore has been an important trade hub in Asia. The city-state is now being remade as a cultural destination. Leaders have embarked upon an ambitious real estate development program designed to keep Singapore up-to-date and competitive with Doha, Dubai, and other popular tourist centers. Sentosa Cove, a mixed-use, integrated resort, features thousands of apartments and villas, as well as hotels, a casino complex, and numerous retail shops. Unfortunately, many development projects are now in jeopardy, victims of the global recession.
Source: Tim Hall/Getty Images, Inc.–Photodisc/Royalty Free.

longer afford the expansive welfare state. . . . The decamping of the state from the "commanding heights" marks a great divide between the 20th and 21st centuries. It is opening the doors of many formerly closed countries to trade and investment, and vastly increasing the global market.[17]

The Washington, D.C.–based Heritage Foundation, a conservative think tank, takes a more conventional approach to classifying economies: It compiles a survey of more than 175 countries ranked by degree of economic freedom (Table 2-3). A number of key economic variables are considered: trade policy, taxation policy, government consumption of economic output, monetary policy, capital flows and foreign investment, banking policy, wage and price controls, property rights, regulations, and the black market. Hong Kong and Singapore are ranked first and second in terms of economic freedom; Cuba, Zimbabwe, and North Korea are ranked lowest (see Exhibit 2-4).

There is a high correlation between the degree of economic freedom and the extent to which a nation's mixed economy is heavily market oriented. However, the validity of the ranking has been subject to some debate. For example, author William Greider has observed that the authoritarian state capitalism practiced in Singapore deprives the nation's citizens of free speech, a free press, and free assembly. For example, in 1992, Singapore banned the import, manufacture, and sale of chewing gum, because discarded wads of gum were making a mess in public places. Today, gum is available at pharmacies; before buying a pack, however, consumers must register their names and addresses. Greider notes, "Singaporeans are comfortably provided for by a harshly autocratic government that administers paranoid control over press and politics and an effective welfare state that keeps everyone well housed and fed, but not free."[18] As Greider's observation makes clear, some aspects of "free economies" bear more than a passing resemblance to command-style economic systems.

STAGES OF MARKET DEVELOPMENT

At any point in time, individual country markets are at different stages of economic development. The World Bank has developed a four-category classification system that uses per capita **gross national income (GNI)** as a base. The income definition for each of the stages is based on the World Bank's lending categories, and countries within a given category generally have a

---

[17]Daniel Yergin and Joseph Stanislaw, "Sale of the Century," *Financial Times Weekend* (January 24–25, 1998), p. I.
[18]William Greider, *One World, Ready or Not: The Manic Logic of Global Capitalism* (New York: Simon & Schuster, 1997), pp. 36–37. See also John Burton, "Singapore's Social Contract Shows Signs of Strain," *Financial Times* (August 19–20, 2006), p. 3.

TABLE 2-3 Index of Economic Freedom—2009 Rankings

1. Hong Kong	47. Malta	93. Tanzania	140. Djibouti
2. Singapore	48. Qatar	94. Montenegro	141. Syria
3. Australia	49. Mexico	95. Lebanon	142. Equatorial Guinea
4. Ireland	50. Kuwait	96. Ghana	143. Maldives
5. New Zealand	51. Jordan	97. Egypt	144. Guinea
6. United States	52. Jamaica	98. Tunisia	145. Vietnam
7. Canada	53. Portugal	99. Azerbaijan	146. Russia
8. Denmark	54. United Arab Emirates	100. Bhutan	147. Haiti
9. Switzerland	55. Panama	101. Morocco	148. Uzbekistan
10. United Kingdom	56. Bulgaria	102. Pakistan	149. Timor-Leste
11. Chile	57. Peru	103. Yemen	150. Laos
12. The Netherlands	58. Malaysia	104. The Philippines	151. Lesotho
13. Estonia	59. Saudi Arabia	105. Brazil	152. Ukraine
14. Iceland	60. Saint Vincent and the Grenadines	106. Cambodia	153. Burundi
15. Luxembourg		107. Algeria	154. Togo
16. Bahrain	61. South Africa	108. Zambia	155. Guyana
17. Finland	62. Albania	109. Serbia	156. Central African Republic
18. Mauritius	63. Uganda	110. Senegal	157. Liberia
19. Japan	64. France	111. Sri Lanka	158. Sierra Leone
20. Belgium	65. Romania	112. The Gambia	159. Seychelles
21. Macau	66. Belize	113. Mozambique	160. Bangladesh
22. Barbados	67. Thailand	114. Mali	161. Chad
23. Austria	68. Slovenia	115. Benin	162. Angola
24. Cyprus	69. Mongolia	116. Croatia	163. Solomon Islands
25. Germany	70. Dominica	117. Nigeria	164. Kiribati
26. Sweden	71. Namibia	118. Gabon	165. Guinea-Bissau
27. The Bahamas	72. Colombia	119. Côte d'Ivoire	166. Republic of Congo
28. Norway	73. Madagascar	120. Moldova	167. Belarus
29. Spain	74. Kyrgyz Republic	121. Papua New Guinea	168. Iran
30. Lithuania	75. Turkey	122. Tajikistan	169. Turkmenistan
31. Armenia	76. Italy	123. India	170. São Tomé and Príncipe
32. Georgia	77. Cape Verde	124. Rwanda	171. Libya
33. El Salvador	78. Macedonia	125. Suriname	172. Comoros
34. Botswana	79. Paraguay	126. Tonga	173. Democratic Republic of Congo
35. Taiwan	80. Fiji	127. Mauritania	
36. Slovak Republic	81. Greece	128. Niger	174. Venezuela
37. Czech Republic	82. Poland	129. Malawi	175. Eritrea
38. Uruguay	83. Kazakhstan	130. Bolivia	176. Burma
39. Saint Lucia	84. Nicaragua	131. Indonesia	177. Cuba
40. South Korea	85. Burkina Faso	132. China	178. Zimbabwe
41. Trinidad and Tobago	86. Samoa	133. Nepal	179. North Korea
42. Israel	87. Guatemala	134. Bosnia and Herzegovina	
43. Oman	88. Dominican Republic	135. Ethiopia	**NOT RANKED**
44. Hungary	89. Swaziland	136. Cameroon	Afghanistan
45. Latvia	90. Kenya	137. Ecuador	Iraq
46. Costa Rica	91. Honduras	138. Argentina	Liechtenstein
	92. Vanuatu	139. Micronesia	Sudan

Source: Terry Miller, "Freedom Is Still the Winning Formula," *The Wall Street Journal* (January 13, 2009), p. A17.

TABLE 2-4 **Stages of Market Development**

Income Group by per Capita GNI	2006 GNI ($ millions)	2006 GNI per Capita($)	% of World GNI	2006 Population (millions)
High-income countries GNI per capita ≥ $11,456	37,731,702	36,608	77.49	1,031
Upper-middle-income countries GNI per capita ≥ $3,706 but ≤ $11,455	4,797,291	5,913	9.85	811
Lower-middle-income countries GNI per capita ≥ $936 but ≤ $3,705	4,639,790	2,038	9.53	2,276
Low-income countries GNI per capita ≤ $935	1,570,841	649	3.23	2,420

number of characteristics in common. Thus, the stages provide a useful basis for global market segmentation and target marketing. The categories are shown in Table 2-4.

A decade ago, a number of countries in Central Europe, Latin America, and Asia were expected to experience rapid economic growth. Known as *big emerging markets* (BEMs), the list included China, India, Indonesia, South Korea, Brazil, Mexico, Argentina, South Africa, Poland, and Turkey.[19] Today, much attention is focused on opportunities in Brazil, Russia, India, and China. As previously noted, these four countries are collectively known as BRIC. Microsoft's experience illustrates the nature of the market opportunity in these countries: In fiscal 2008, the software giant's collective revenues from BRIC grew 54 percent, compared with overall global revenue growth of 18 percent. Experts predict that the BRIC nations will be key players in global trade even as their track records on human rights, environmental protection, and other issues come under closer scrutiny by their trading partners. The BRIC government leaders will also come under pressure at home as their developing market economies create greater income disparity. For each of the stages of economic development discussed here, special attention is given to the BRIC countries.

Low-Income Countries

Low-income countries have a GNI per capita of less than $936. The general characteristics shared by countries at this income level are:

1. Limited industrialization and a high percentage of the population engaged in agriculture and subsistence farming
2. High birth rates
3. Low literacy rates
4. Heavy reliance on foreign aid
5. Political instability and unrest
6. Concentration in Africa south of the Sahara

About 40 percent of the world's population is included in this economic category. Many low-income countries have such serious economic, social, and political problems that they represent extremely limited opportunities for investment and operations. Some are low-income, no-growth countries such as Burundi and Rwanda that are beset by one disaster after another. Others were once relatively stable countries with growing economies that have become divided by political struggles. The result is an unstable environment characterized by civil strife, declining income, and often considerable danger to residents. Haiti is a case in point. Countries embroiled in civil wars are dangerous areas; most companies find it prudent to avoid them.

Other low-income countries represent genuine market opportunities. Bangladesh is a case in point: Per capita GNI is approximately $450, and the garment industry is enjoying burgeoning exports. Finished clothing exports totaled $9 billion in 2007; the president of the Bangladesh

---

[19]For an excellent discussion of BEMs, see Jeffrey E. Garten, *The Big Ten: The Big Emerging Markets and How They Will Change Our Lives* (New York: Basic Books, 1997).

Garments Manufacturers and Exporters Association expects that figure to reach $25 billion by 2013. An estimated 1.8 million Bangladeshis—mostly women—work in the industry for an average monthly wage of about $35. Bangladesh received preferential treatment under the Multifiber Arrangement (MFA), an international pact dating to the mid-1970s that established import quotas to regulate the global trade in garments. The MFA expired at the end of 2004; some observers expected that a shakeout in the garment industry would lead to widespread unemployment and social and political unrest. However, this has not happened. The garment sector's vigor is due in part to Bangladesh's extremely low labor costs and new limits on Chinese textile exports to the United States.[20]

The newly independent countries of the former Soviet Union present an interesting situation: Income is declining, and there is considerable economic hardship. The potential for disruption is certainly high. Are they problem cases, or are they attractive opportunities with good potential for moving out of the low-income category? These countries present an interesting risk-reward trade-off; many companies have taken the plunge, but many others are still assessing whether to take the risk. Table 2-3 rates two low-income former Soviet republics—Belarus and Turkmenistan—quite low in terms of economic freedom. This is one indication of a risky business environment. Russia itself, whose economy is in the upper-middle income category, has slipped significantly in the most recent ranking (number 146). As evidenced by the Kremlin's recent actions, which include cutting off supplies of natural gas to some former Soviet republics and launching a military action in Georgia, economic and political instability are present here as well.

With 2006 per capita GNI of $820, India is the sole low-income country in the BRIC grouping. In 2007, India commemorated the sixtieth anniversary of its independence from Great Britain. For many decades, economic growth was weak. As the 1990s began, India was in the throes of economic crisis: Inflation was high, and foreign exchange reserves were low. Country leaders opened India's economy to trade and investment and dramatically improved market opportunities. Manmohan Singh was placed in charge of India's economy. Singh, former governor of the Indian central bank and finance minister, noted, "For years, India has been taking the wrong road." Accordingly, he set about dismantling the planned economy by eliminating import licensing requirements for many products, reducing tariffs, easing restrictions on foreign investment, and liberalizing the rupee.

The results were impressive: Foreign exchange reserves jumped to $13 billion in 1993 from $1 billion in 1991. However, the political climate remains unpredictable. The nationalistic Bharatiya Janata Party (BJP) has been a vocal and powerful opponent of reform; in 2004, the BJP was ousted in national elections and the left-leaning Congress party came to power. Manmohan Singh, India's former finance minister and the architect of the country's economic reforms, is the new prime minister. Financial markets reacted negatively to uncertainty over India's future direction; as one analyst put it, "This feels like the Asia crisis and the Mexico crisis times again."[21]

Despite such concerns, Yashwant Sinha, the country's former finance minister, declared that the twenty-first century will be "the century of India." His words appear prescient; India is home to a number of world-class companies with growing global reach, including Infosys, Mahindra & Mahindra, Tata, and Wipro. Meanwhile, the list of companies operating in India is growing longer. They include Benetton, Cadbury, Coca-Cola, DuPont, Ericsson, Fujitsu, IBM, L'Oréal, MTV, Staples, Unilever, and Walmart. India's huge population base also presents attractive opportunities for automakers. Suzuki, Hyundai, General Motors, and Ford are among the global car manufacturers doing business in India.

> "It may feel like the temperature has only risen a couple of degrees so far, but this heralds the end of India's economic Ice Age."[22]
>
> Vivek Paul, Vice Chairman, Wipro

Lower-Middle-Income Countries

The United Nations designates 50 countries in the bottom ranks of the low-income category as **least-developed countries (LDCs)**; the term is sometimes used to indicate a contrast with **developing** (i.e., upper ranks of low-income plus lower-middle and upper-middle-income) **countries** and **developed** (high-income) **countries. Lower-middle-income countries** are those with a GNI per capita between $936 and $3,705. Consumer markets in these countries are expanding rapidly. Countries such as China, Indonesia, and Thailand represent an increasing competitive

---

[20]Mahtab Haider, "Defying Predictions, Bangladesh's Garment Factories Thrive," *The Christian Science Monitor* (February 7, 2006), p. 4. See also Peter Fritsch, "Looming Trouble: As End of a Quota System Nears, Bangladesh Fears for Its Jobs," *The Wall Street Journal* (November 20, 2003), pp. A1, A12.
[21]Sara Calian, "In India, Plunges and Protest," *The Wall Street Journal* (May 18, 2004), p. C16.
[22]Manjeet Kirpalani, "The Factories Are Humming," *Business Week* (October 18, 2004), pp. 54–55.

threat as they mobilize their relatively cheap—and often highly motivated—labor forces to serve target markets in the rest of the world. The developing countries in the lower-middle-income category have a major competitive advantage in mature, standardized, labor-intensive industries such as making toys and textiles.

With per capita GNI of $2,000, China is the BRIC nation in the lower-middle-income category. China represents the largest single destination for foreign investment in the developing world. Attracted by the country's vast size and market potential, companies in Asia, Europe, and North and South America are making China a key country in their global strategies. Shenzhen and other special economic zones have attracted billions of dollars in foreign investment. Despite ongoing market reforms, Chinese society does not have democratic foundations. Although China has joined the World Trade Organization, trading partners are still concerned about human rights, protection of intellectual property rights, and other issues. The country's leaders must deal with China's sprawling bureaucracy while reforming the state enterprise sector. To ensure that the nation's export-led economic transformation is sustained, policymakers have launched hundreds of infrastructure projects. These include airports, cargo ports, highways, and railroads. Avon, the Coca-Cola Company, Dell, Ford, General Motors, Honda, HSBC, JP Morgan Chase, McDonald's, Motorola, Procter & Gamble, Samsung, Siemens AG, Toyota, and Volkswagen are among the scores of global companies that are actively pursuing opportunities in China.

Upper-Middle-Income Countries

Upper-middle-income countries, also known as industrializing or developing countries, are those with GNI per capita ranging from $3,706 to $11,455. In these countries, the percentage of population engaged in agriculture drops sharply as people move to the industrial sector and the degree of urbanization increases. Malaysia, Chile, Hungary, Venezuela, and many other countries in this stage are rapidly industrializing (see Exhibit 2-5). They have high literacy rates and strong education systems; wages are rising but they are still significantly lower than in the advanced countries. Innovative local companies can become formidable competitors and help contribute to their nations' rapid, export-driven economic growth.

Russia and Brazil, with per capita GNI of $5,770 and $4,710, respectively, are the two BRIC nations that currently fall into the upper-middle-income category. As noted elsewhere in the chapter, Russia's economic situation improved and declined again as the price of oil reached record levels and then collapsed. Strong local companies have appeared on the scene, including Wimm-Bill-Dann Foods, Russia's largest dairy company. However, the Kremlin's recent use of military force in Georgia has many observers worried. Corruption is pervasive, and the bureaucracy often means a mountain of red tape for companies such as Diageo, Mars, McDonald's, Nestlé, and SAB Miller. Still, the market opportunity is enticing: Wages have increased dramatically in recent years, and consumers are showing a tendency to spend rather than save.[24]

Brazil is the largest country in Latin America in terms of the size of its economy, population, and geographic territory. Brazil also boasts the richest reserves of natural resources in the hemisphere. Brazil has tamed hyperinflation, and liberalized trade is replacing tariff protection and an import quota system. Global companies doing business in Brazil include Electrolux, Fiat, Ford, General Motors, Nestlé, Nokia, Raytheon, Toyota, Unilever, and Whirlpool.

Typical of countries at this stage of development, Brazil is a study in contrasts. Grocery distribution companies use logistics software to route their trucks; meanwhile, horse-drawn carts are still a common sight on many roads. To help them keep pace with the volatile financial environment, many local retailers have invested in sophisticated computer and communications systems. They utilize sophisticated inventory management software to maintain financial control. Thanks to Brazil's strength in computers, the country's outsourcing sector is growing rapidly.[25] Former French president Chirac underscored Brazil's importance on the world trade scene when he noted, "Geographically, Brazil is part of America. But it's European because of its culture and global because of its interests."[26]

"In a global market, you're going to gain your profit not by sitting tight in the United States in a flat and declining market. You're going to make your money in China and Russia and India and Brazil."[23]

Tom Pirko, President, BevMark, commenting on InBev's acquisition of Anheuser-Busch

[23]Sarah Theodore, "Beer Has Big Changes on Tap," *Beverage Industry* (September 2008), p. 24.

[24]Jenny Wiggins, "Brands Make a Dash into Russia," *Financial Times* (September 4, 2008), p. 10.

[25]Antonio Regalado, "Soccer, Samba and Outsourcing?" *The Wall Street Journal* (January 25, 2007), p. B1.

[26]Matt Moffett and Helene Cooper, "Silent Invasion: In Backyard of the U.S., Europe Gains Ground in Trade, Diplomacy," *The Wall Street Journal* (September 18, 1997), pp. A1, A8.

SHARING THE WARMTH OF THE SEASON

VENEZUELA IS WARMING UP THE HOLIDAYS IN NEW YORK

When temperatures dip – and heating oil prices rise, the best holiday gift for a low-income family is to help them stay warm.

To help keep those in need warm this winter, CITGO– a major supplier of heating oil to the Northeast– is reaching out to help these families enjoy a warm holiday and safe winter.

Working with non-profit housing and community organizations, CITGO is offering a significant amount of gallons of heating oil at deeply discounted prices to qualified residents of the Bronx, Queens and Harlem.

Why would an oil company give such a gift? Because we're not just any oil company. CITGO is a subsidiary of Petróleos de Venezuela S.A. (PDVSA), the oil company owned by the people of Venezuela, whose traditional solidarity is expressed once again through this heating oil program. This initiative is a simple humanitarian act to help people weather high fuel costs and the economic aftermath of the hurricanes this fall.

The United States is Venezuela's long-time trading partner and friend. The U.S. has been there for others in need; now it's our turn.

What better way to embrace the holiday spirit?

Exhibit 2-5: With per capita GNI of $6,070, Venezuela is considered an upper-middle-income country. Venezuela is one of the world's top oil-producing nations, and an important source of U.S. oil imports. A state-owned company, Petróleos de Venezuela S.A. (PDVSA), has operations in many different countries. For example, its CITGO Petroleum subsidiary operates 13,000 filling stations in the United States. The collapse in oil prices has had a direct impact on Venezuela's economy. *Source:* Citgo.

Upper-middle-income countries that achieve the highest rates of economic growth are sometimes referred to collectively as **newly industrializing economies (NIEs)**. Hungary is a case in point: Scores of manufacturing companies have received ISO-9000 certification for documenting compliance with recognized quality standards. The influx of technology, particularly the computer revolution, creates startling juxtapositions of the old and the new in these countries.

Marketing Opportunities in LDCs and Developing Countries

Despite many problems in LDCs and developing countries, it is possible to nurture long-term market opportunities. Today, Nike produces and sells only a small portion of its output in China, but when the firm refers to China as a "two-billion-foot market," it clearly has the future in mind.

C. K. Prahalad and Allen Hammond have identified several assumptions and misconceptions about the "bottom of the pyramid" (BOP) that need to be corrected:[27]

- Mistaken assumption #1: *The poor have no money.* In fact, the aggregate buying power of poor communities can be substantial. In rural Bangladesh, for example, villagers spend considerable sums to use village phones operated by local entrepreneurs.
- Mistaken assumption #2: *The poor are too concerned with fulfilling basic needs to "waste" money on nonessential goods.* In fact, consumers who are too poor to purchase a house do buy "luxury" items such as television sets and gas stoves to improve their lives.
- Mistaken assumption #3: *The goods sold in developing markets are so inexpensive that there is no room for a new market entrant to make a profit.* In fact, because the poor often pay higher prices for many goods, there is an opportunity for efficient competitors to realize attractive margins by offering quality and low prices.
- Mistaken assumption #4: *People in BOP markets cannot use advanced technology.* In fact, residents of rural areas can and do quickly learn to use cell phones, PCs, and similar devices.
- Mistaken assumption #5: *Global companies that target BOP markets will be criticized for exploiting the poor.* In fact, the informal economies in many poor countries are highly exploitative. A global company offering basic goods and services that improve a country's standard of living can earn a reasonable return while benefiting society.

Despite the difficult economic conditions in parts of Southeast Asia, Latin America, Africa, and Eastern Europe, many nations in these regions will evolve into attractive markets. One of marketing's roles in developing countries is to focus resources on the task of creating and delivering products that are best suited to local needs and incomes. Appropriate marketing communications techniques can also be applied to accelerate acceptance of these products. Marketing can be the link that relates resources to opportunity and facilitates need satisfaction on the consumer's terms.

An interesting debate in marketing is whether it has any relevance to the process of economic development. Some people believe that marketing is relevant only in affluent, industrialized countries, where the major problem is directing society's resources into ever-changing output or production to satisfy a dynamic marketplace. In the less-developed country, the argument goes, the major problem is the allocation of scarce resources toward obvious production needs. Efforts should focus on production and how to increase output, not on customer needs and wants.

Conversely, it can be argued that the process of focusing an organization's resources on environmental opportunities is a process of universal relevance. The role of marketing—to identify people's needs and wants and to focus individual and organizational efforts to respond to these needs and wants—is the same in all countries, irrespective of the level of economic development. When global marketers respond to the needs of rural residents in emerging markets such as China and India, they are also more likely to gain all-important government support and approval.

For example, pursuing alternative energy sources is important for two reasons: the lack of coal reserves in many countries and concerns that heavy reliance on fossil fuels contributes to global warming. Similarly, people everywhere need affordable, safe drinking water. Recognizing this fact, Nestlé launched Pure Life bottled water in Pakistan. The price was set at about 35 cents a bottle, and advertising promised "Pure safety. Pure trust. The ideal water." Pure Life quickly captured 50 percent of the bottled water market in Pakistan; the brand has been rolled out in dozens of other low-income countries (see Exhibit 2-6).[28] The Coca-Cola Company recently began to address dietary and health needs in low-income countries by developing Vitango, a beverage product that can help fight anemia, blindness, and other ailments related to malnutrition.

There is also an opportunity to help developing countries join the Internet economy. Intel chairman Craig Barrett has been visiting villages in China and India and launching programs to provide Internet access and computer training. One aspect of Intel's World Ahead initiative is the development of a $550 computer that is powered by a car battery. Similarly, Hewlett-Packard engineers are working to develop solar-powered communication devices that can link remote areas to

---

[27]C.K. Prahalad and Allen Hammond, "Serving the World's Poor, Profitably," *Harvard Business Review* 80, no. 9 (September 2002), pp. 48–57.
[28]Ernest Beck, "Populist Perrier? Nestlé Pitches Bottled Water to World's Poor," *The Asian Wall Street Journal* (June 18, 1999), p. B1.

Exhibit 2-6: According to the World Bank, approximately 25 percent of the world's population lives on less than $2 per day. In Brazil, Latin America's largest market, low-income consumers comprise 87 percent of the population and account for 512 billion reals—$240 billion—in annual income. The balance of Brazil's population accounts for 454 billion reals. Nestlé's competitors in Brazil include both local and global brands. Sales of Nestlé's Bono brand cookies increased 40 percent in Brazil after both the serving size and the price were decreased.
Source: Reprinted with permission of *The Wall Street Journal,* © 2007 Dow Jones & Company, Inc. All Rights Reserved Worldwide.

the Internet.[29] Meanwhile, an initiative called One Laptop Per Child has the goal of developing a laptop computer that governments in developing countries can buy for $100 (see Case 2-2).

Global companies can also contribute to economic development by finding creative ways to preserve old-growth forests and other resources while creating economic opportunities for local inhabitants. In Brazil, for example, Daimler AG works with a cooperative of farmers who transform coconut husks into natural rubber to be used in auto seats, headrests, and sun visors. French luxury-goods marketer Hermès International has created a line of handbags called "Amazonia" made of latex extracted by traditional rubber tappers. Both Daimler and Hermès are responding to the opportunity to promote themselves as environmentally conscious while appealing to "green"-oriented consumers. As Isabela Fortes, director of a company in Rio de Janeiro that retrains forest workers, notes, "You can only prevent forest people from destroying the jungle by giving them viable economic alternatives."[30]

High-Income Countries

High-income countries, also known as advanced, developed, industrialized, or postindustrial countries, are those with GNI per capita of $11,456 or higher. With the exception of a few oil-rich nations, the countries in this category reached their present income level through a process of sustained economic growth.

The phrase *postindustrial countries* was first used by Daniel Bell of Harvard to describe the United States, Sweden, Japan, and other advanced, high-income societies. In his 1973 book *The Coming of the Post-Industrial Society,* Bell drew a distinction between the industrial and the postindustrial stages of country development that went beyond mere measures of income. Bell's thesis was that the sources of innovation in postindustrial societies are derived increasingly from the codification of theoretical knowledge rather than from "random" inventions. The service sector

"Sustainable energy pioneers who focus on the base of the pyramid could set the stage for one of the biggest bonanzas in the history of commerce, since extensive adoption and experience in developing markets would almost certainly lead to dramatic improvements in cost and quality."[31]

Stuart L. Hart and Clayton M. Christensen

[29]Jason Dean and Peter Wonacott, "Tech Firms Woo 'Next Billion' Users," *The Wall Street Journal* (November 3, 2006), p. A2. See also David Kirkpatrick, "Looking for Profits in Poverty," *Fortune* (February 5, 2001), pp. 174–176.
[30]Miriam Jordan, "From the Amazon to Your Armrest," *The Wall Street Journal* (May 1, 2001), pp. B1, B4.
[31]Stuart L. Hart and Clayton M. Christensen, "The Great Leap: Driving Innovation from the Base of the Pyramid," *MIT Sloan Management Review* 44, no. 1 (Fall 2002), p. 56.

accounts for more than half of national output, the processing and exchange of information becomes increasingly important, and knowledge trumps capital as the key strategic resource. In addition, in a postindustrial society, intellectual technology is more important than machine technology, and scientists and professionals play a more dominant role than engineers and semiskilled workers. Postindustrial societies exhibit an orientation toward the future and stress the importance of interpersonal relationships in the functioning of society. Taken together, these forces and factors spell big sociological changes for the work and home lives of the residents of postindustrial nations.

Product and market opportunities in a postindustrial society are heavily dependent upon new products and innovations. Ownership levels for basic products are extremely high in most households. Organizations seeking to grow often face a difficult task if they attempt to expand their share of existing markets. Alternatively, they can endeavor to create new markets. Today, for example, global companies in a range of communication-related industries are seeking to create new e-commerce markets for interactive forms of electronic communication. A case in point is Barry Diller's IAC/InterActiveCorp, which includes Ask.com, Expedia.com, Hotels.com, and other Internet businesses.

South Korea occupies a unique position among the high-income countries in that it is the only one classified as an emerging market by influential stock market indexes. South Korea is home to Samsung Electronics, LG Group, Kia Motors Corporation, Daewoo Corporation, Hyundai Corporation, and other well-known global enterprises. In place of substantial barriers to free trade, South Korea has initiated major reforms in its political and economic system in response to the "Asian flu." Even so, investors note the political risk posed by North Korea. Another concern is inconsistent treatment of foreign investors by the government. For example, authorities recently raided the local offices of French retailer Carrefour. If the indexes do eventually reclassify South Korea as a "developed" market, the change would trigger a wave of investment inflows.[32]

Seven high-income countries—the United States, Japan, Germany, France, Britain, Canada, and Italy—comprise the **Group of Seven (G-7)**. Finance ministers, central bankers, and heads of state from the seven nations have worked together for more than a quarter of a century in an effort to steer the global economy in the direction of prosperity and to ensure monetary stability. Whenever a global crisis looms—be it the Latin American debt crisis of the 1980s or Russia's struggle to transform its economy in the 1990s—representatives from the G-7 nations gather and try to coordinate policy. Starting in the mid-1990s, Russia began attending the G-7 summit meetings. In 1998, Russia became a full participant, giving rise to the **Group of Eight (G-8)** (see Exhibits 2-7 and 2-8).

Exhibit 2-7: When Russian president Vladimir Putin hosted the Group of Eight Summit in Saint Petersburg in 2006, he took advantage of the opportunity to show his country to the world in a positive light. The PR effort included a two-hour television broadcast during which Putin answered questions submitted from around the world via the Internet. The figure on Putin's laptop depicts the Bronze Horseman, a statue near St. Isaac's Cathedral that faces the Neva River. The monument was commissioned by Catherine the Great in tribute to Peter the Great, who founded Saint Petersburg as Russia's "Window on the West." Putin was *Time* magazine's 2007 "Person of the Year." Despite Putin's public efforts, some observers fear that, behind the scenes, the Kremlin is attempting to reassert state control over Russia's energy sector and other strategic assets.
Source: Dmitry Astakhove/Getty Images, Inc. AFP.

[32]Ian McDonald and Karen Richardson, "For South Korea, 'Emerging' Label Can Be a Burden," *The Wall Street Journal* (July 12, 2006), p. C1.

G8 LEADERS:
THE WORLD'S WISHES ARE IN FRONT OF YOU

Keep your aid promises

Healthcare and Education for all

Climate change: stop harming, start helping

DON'T CUT THEM DOWN

Today, the G8 summit begins – and so does the Tanabata festival, when people in Japan write their wishes for the year ahead and tie them to bamboo trees. In the last month, more than 1,000,000 citizens from around the world have sent virtual Tanabata wishes to the G8 leaders:

- More and better aid
- Education for all
- Free health service for all and delivery on HIV/AIDS commitments
- Act now to stop climate catastrophe and support adaptation
- End the food crisis

It is time to honour the world's wishes. Don't let us down!

Exhibit 2-8: When the world's leaders meet to discuss policy issues, non-governmental organizations (NGOs) often take advantage of the opportunity to make their voices heard. This print ad was timed to coincide with the 2008 G-8 summit in Japan. The ad was paid for by Oxfam International, Whiteband, Save the Children, One, and Avaaz.org. The copy urges G8 leaders to keep their aid promises, to provide health care and education for everyone, and to address the issue of climate change. *Source:* Used by permission.

Another institution comprised of high-income countries is the **Organization for Economic Cooperation and Development (OECD**; www.oecd.org). The 30 nations that belong to the OECD believe in market-allocation economic systems and pluralistic democracy. The organization has been variously described as an "economic think tank" and a "rich-man's club"; in any event, the OECD's fundamental task is to "enable its members to achieve the highest sustainable economic growth and improve the economic and social well-being of their populations." Today's organization

The term *tiger* has frequently been used to describe fast-growing economies in Asia. For years, Hong Kong, Singapore, Taiwan, and South Korea were considered tigers because they posted double-digit rates of economic growth. As the decade of the 1990s came to an end, however, the Asian "economic miracle" had given way to hard times. Concurrently, some observers began calling Ireland the "Celtic Tiger." Riding the wave of the technology boom of the late 1990s, Ireland's economy grew at an annual rate of 9.6 percent. Lured by low corporate tax rates and a skilled work-force, companies from the United States, the United Kingdom, Germany, and Japan established subsidiaries in Ireland. The country best known for exports such as Waterford crystal, Guinness stout, Riverdance, and U2 had been transformed into a preferred location for high-tech manufacturing (see Exhibit 2-9).

More than 500 U.S. companies created tens of thousands of jobs as Intel, Motorola, and Gateway built factories to keep pace with burgeoning global demand for personal computers and other high-tech products. Before long, however, there were signs that Ireland's economic bubble might burst. The country's infrastructure was showing signs of stress, labor was in short supply, and inflation soared. By mid-2000, the pot of gold at the end of the rainbow gave way to gray and gloom. As the U.S. economy slowed and the technology sector slumped, the impact on Ireland was immediate. Exports fell as foreign companies severely curtailed operations in Ireland or even closed down altogether.

Irish officials had high hopes for Media Lab Europe, which opened in July 2000 in Dublin in a building that once was the site of a Guinness brewery. Media Lab Europe was an offshoot of the original Media Lab that was established at the Massachusetts Institute of Technology (MIT) more than 25 years ago. The Irish government allocated nearly $50 million in funding to establish the organization. In addition, global companies such as BT, Intel, the LEGO Group, and Swatch AG paid for sponsorships that entitled them to a first look at the lab's innovations in such areas as robotic design, speech synthesis, and holographic imaging.

Irish officials hoped the investment would pay off by strengthening Ireland's position in advanced information-technology research. However, there were problems. For one thing, some researchers at MIT were reluctant to move their work to Ireland. By mid-2001, only six researchers and about two dozen research associates, assistants, and graduate students were working in a facility designed to accommodate 250 people. In 2005, the Media Lab Europe was closed down after MIT and the Irish government failed to reach agreement on future funding.

"We're transitioning the nation from being a supplier and producer of other people's ideas to a place where you can actually do that development."

Enda Connolly, Industrial Development Agency of Ireland

The Media Lab Europe generated a fair amount of controversy during its short existence. Some academics were offended by the notion that Ireland needs outside help; critics also questioned whether the lab would contribute to economic growth to the extent envisioned by the government. To placate such critics, the government increased funding for local research efforts. For example, Science Foundation Ireland (SFI) is a government-funded initiative funded to create an economic base in information technology, telecommunications, and biotechnology. A typical SFI research grant provides €1 million in annual support for five years. The Irish government hopes that, attracted by the skills and talents of students graduating from local universities, global companies currently operating in Ireland will increase their level of investment. Ultimately, the government hopes to create its own world-class companies. In 2007, Ireland launched a National Development Plan. The theme is "Transforming Ireland: A Better Life for All."

Meanwhile, the economic downturn is directly affecting some of Ireland's oldest and most iconic brands. Citing falling global demand and the real estate bust, Guinness canceled plans to invest €650 ($1 billion) to build a superbrewery on the site of its 250-year-old St. James's Gate facility. And Waterford, the venerable crystal and fine-china company, violated its credit obligations. The company entered insolvency administration and its owners put its assets up for sale.

Visit the Web site

www.sfi.ie

Sources: Charles Forelle, "Ireland's Boom Falls Hard in Global Crisis," *The Wall Street Journal* (February 7–8, 2009), p. A6; Jeanne Whalen, "Waterford Wedgewood Succumbs," *The Wall Street Journal* (January 6, 2009), p. B3; Jeffrey Stinson, "Ireland's Economy Not Roaring Back," *USA Today* (November 20, 2008), p. 10; Quentin Peel, "Cowen Must Revive the Celtic Tiger," *Financial Times* (April 8, 2008), p. 2; Glenn R. Simpson, "Wearing of the Green: Irish Subsidiary Lets Microsoft Slash Taxes in U.S. and Europe," *The Wall Street Journal* (November 11, 2005), pp. A1, 10; John Murray Brown, "Ireland Extends Its Hospitality to Top Scientists," *Financial Times* (November 8, 2003), p. 12; Alana Cowell, "Ireland, Once a Celtic Tiger, Slackens Its Stride," *The New York Times* (February 19, 2003), pp. C1, C4; Saritha Rai, "Rift in India Leads M.I.T. to Abandon a Media Lab," *The New York Times* (May 8, 2003), p. C4; David Armstrong, "Many Irish Eyes Aren't Smiling on MIT Import," *The Wall Street Journal* (July 5, 2001), p. B1, B4; Jeffrey R. Young, "MIT's Media Lab, a Media Darling, Seeks Global Role and New Missions," *The Chronicle of Higher Education* (October 12, 2001), pp. A41–A43; Christopher Rhoads, "U.S. Slowdown Muffles the Volume of Ireland's Boom," *The Wall Street Journal* (March 6, 2001), p. A18; Mike Burns, "High-Tech Shudders for the Celtic Tiger," *Europe*, no. 406 (May 2001), pp. 14–15; Stewart Brand, *The Media Lab: Inventing the Future at M.I.T.* (New York: Viking Penguin, 1988).

Exhibit 2-9: U2's Bono is a key figure in several advocacy organizations. DATA (debt, AIDS, trade, Africa) helped influence the G-8's decision to provide an additional $25 billion in aid to sub-Saharan Africa by 2010. ONE (The Campaign to Make Poverty History) is a constellation of several NGOs united in an effort to generate grassroots interest in policy issues via alternative media such as YouTube and MySpace. EDUN Apparel's garments are designed in New York City and sewn in developing countries. Finally, Bono was instrumental in launching Project (RED), a marketing initiative with Apple, GAP, and other corporate partners. A percentage of profits from sales of RED-branded product is donated to the Global Fund to Fight AIDS.
Source: Amy Sancetta/AP Wide World Photos.

is based in Paris and evolved from a group of European nations that worked together after World War II to rebuild the region's economy. Canada and the United States have been members since 1961; Japan joined in 1964. Evidence of the increasing importance of the BRIC group is the fact that Brazil, Russia, India, and China have all formally announced their intention to join the OECD. Applicants must demonstrate progress toward economic reform.

Representatives from OECD member nations work together in committees to review economic and social policies that affect world trade. The secretary-general presides over a Council that meets regularly and has decision-making power. Committees comprised of specialists from member countries provide a forum for discussion of trade and other issues. Consultation, peer pressure, and diplomacy are the keys to helping member nations candidly assess their own economic policies and actions. The OECD publishes country surveys and an annual economic outlook. Recently, the OECD has become more focused on global issues, social policy, and labor market deregulation. For example, the OECD has addressed the vexing problem of bribery; in 1997, it passed a convention that requires members to cooperate when pursuing bribery allegations. In the decade since the agreement entered into force, Germany, France, and other countries have adopted antibribery laws. Prosecutors from various countries are doing a better job of collaborating across borders; one recent case against Siemens AG resulted in a record €201 million fine.[33]

The Triad

The ascendancy of the global economy has been noted by many observers in recent years. One of the most astute is Kenichi Ohmae, former chairman of McKinsey & Company Japan. His 1985 book *Triad Power* represented one of the first attempts to develop a coherent conceptualization of the new emerging order. Ohmae argued that successful global companies had to be equally strong in Japan, Western Europe, and the United States. These three regions, which Ohmae collectively called the **Triad,** represented the dominant economic centers of the world. Today, nearly 75 percent of world income as measured by GNP is located in the Triad. Ohmae has recently revised his view of the world; in the **expanded Triad,** the Japanese leg encompasses the entire Pacific region; the American leg includes Canada and Mexico; and the boundary in Europe is moving eastward. Coca-Cola is a perfect illustration of a company with a balanced revenue stream. Approximately one-quarter of the company's revenues are generated in Asia; another 25 percent come from Europe, Eurasia, and the Middle East. North America accounts for about 40 percent.

---

[33]Russell Gold and David Crawford, "U.S., Other Nations Step Up Bribery Battle," *The Wall Street Journal* (September 12, 2008), pp. B1, B6.

Marketing Implications of the Stages of Development

The stages of economic development described previously can serve as a guide to marketers in evaluating **product saturation levels**, or the percentage of potential buyers or households who own a particular product. In countries with low per capita income, product saturation levels for many products are low. For example, India's teledensity—a measure of ownership of private telephones—is only about 20 percent of the population. In China, saturation levels of private motor vehicles and personal computers (PCs) are quite low; there is only one car or light truck for every 43,000 Chinese, and only one PC for every 6,000 people. In Poland in 2001, there were 21 cars per 100 compared with 49 in the 15-nation European Union; in 2002 Poland had 11 PCs

---

➔ STRATEGIC DECISION MAKING IN GLOBAL MARKETING
Mexico's "Tequila Crisis"

On December 20, 1994, the Bank of Mexico embarked on a course of action that sent shock waves around the world. A combination of circumstances, including a $28 billion current-account deficit, dwindling reserves, the murder of presidential candidate Donaldo Colosio, and eroding investor confidence, forced the Bank of Mexico to devalue the peso. The Clinton administration quickly arranged $20 billion in loans and loan guarantees, secured in part by some of Mexico's $7 billion in annual oil export revenues. Opponents of NAFTA—notably Ross Perot—seized the opportunity to denounce both the loans and the trade agreement. The devalued peso, critics predicted, would make U.S. exports to Mexico more expensive and reduce America's $2 billion trade surplus with Mexico. NAFTA opponents also noted that increased imports of Mexican goods into the United States would constitute a new threat to U.S. jobs.

The Bank of Mexico attempted to devalue the peso gradually; in fact, the Mexican currency declined nearly 40 percent relative to the dollar and other key currencies. As expected, one immediate effect of the devaluation was a sharp decline in Mexican purchases of U.S. imports. For example, Westinghouse and Lennox had been aggressively selling air conditioners after NAFTA reduced tariffs; sales quickly slowed down after the devaluation. McDonald's, KFC, Dunkin' Donuts, and other U.S. restaurant chains were also hard hit as they were forced to raise prices. Many franchisors had contracted to pay rent for their facilities in dollars; after the devaluation, franchisors who couldn't pay the rent were forced to shut down. Simply put, the purchasing power of Mexican consumers was cut nearly in half. To reduce the risk of inflation, the Mexican government pledged to cut spending and allow interest rates to rise. Meanwhile, investors who had poured money into Mexico since the late 1980s, lured by the promise of low inflation and a stable currency, faced huge declines in the value of their holdings.

For many manufacturing companies, the weaker peso wreaked havoc with 1995 sales forecasts. GM, for example, had hoped to export 15,000 vehicles to Mexico in 1995, a goal rendered unattainable by the financial crisis. Ford raised vehicle prices in Mexico; the increases applied to vehicles built in Mexico as well as those imported from Canada and the United States. Shares of Avon Products, whose Mexican sales comprise 11 percent of the company's $4 billion in annual revenue, declined

sharply on Wall Street. Hoping to calm investors' fears, company executives predicted that a decline in Mexican sales would be offset in 1995 by gains in other countries.

Supporters and opponents of NAFTA debated the long-term effects of the devaluation. Harley Shaiken, a labor professor at the University of California and NAFTA critic, noted, "It will have a dual impact: It will diminish the market for U.S. goods in Mexico, but the more sizable impact will be the transfer of production to Mexico. It's going to make Mexico less desirable as a place to sell things and far more desirable as a place to make things." Persons holding opposing views acknowledged that the devaluation cut Mexican wages in dollar terms. However, NAFTA supporters pointed out that labor's percentage of total cost in autos and auto parts, which constitute Mexico's largest export sector, was relatively low. Despite the devaluation, NAFTA supporters denied that there would be a "giant sucking sound" caused by an exodus of U.S. jobs south of the border. In 2009, the fifteenth anniversary of NAFTA's implementation, policymakers and the general public were still divided. Perhaps the best assessment came from a recent report by the Carnegie Endowment of International Peace, which noted, "NAFTA has been neither the disaster its opponents predicted nor the savior hailed by its supporters."

As policymakers around the global tried to respond to the financial crisis of 2008, some looked to Mexico's Tequila Crisis for answers. Several lessons could be discerned. First, it is important to stay flexible and act decisively before the market loses confidence. This may require policymakers to take unprecedented steps such as restructuring mortgages. As part of Mexico's rescue plan, the government assumed bad loans from banks in order to ease the credit crisis. Although the government expected to break even, in the end the government lost three times the amount of money it expected the bailout to cost.

Sources: David Luhnow, "Mexican Crisis Holds Lessons for U.S.," *The Wall Street Journal* (October 13, 2008), p. A2; James Cox, "10 Years Ago, NAFTA Was Born," *USA Today* (December 31, 2003), p. 3B; Craig Torres, "Headed South: Mexico's Devaluation Stuns Latin America—and U.S. Investors," *The Wall Street Journal* (December 22, 1994), pp. A1, A12; "Ford Lifts Prices, Avon Tries to Calm Holders, Dina Estimates Loss as Peso Fallout Continues," *The Wall Street Journal* (January 13, 1995); Michael Clements and Bill Montague, "Will Peso's Fall Prove Perot Right?" *USA Today* (January 17, 1995), pp. B1, B2.

per 100 people. In the EU, the ratio was 34 PCs per 100 people.[34] In India, just 8 out of every 1,000 adults own a car.[35] In Russia, 188 people out of 1,000 own cars; in Germany, the figure is 565 out of 1,000.[36]

BALANCE OF PAYMENTS

The **balance of payments** is a record of all economic transactions between the residents of a country and the rest of the world. U.S. balance of payments statistics for the period 2003 to 2007 are shown in Table 2-5. International trade data for the United States is available from the U.S. Bureau of Economic Analysis (www.bea.gov); the bureau's interactive Web site enables users to generate customized reports. The International Monetary Fund's *Balance of Payments Statistics Yearbook* provides trade statistics and summaries of economic activity for all countries in the world.[37]

The balance of payments is divided into the current and capital accounts. The **current account** is a broad measure that includes **merchandise trade** (i.e., manufactured goods) and **services trade** (i.e., intangible, experience-based economic output) plus certain categories of financial transfers such as humanitarian aid. A country with a negative current account balance has a **trade deficit**; that is, the outflow of money to pay for imports exceeds the inflow of money for sales of exports. Conversely, a country with a positive current account balance has a **trade surplus**. The **capital account** is a record of all long-term direct investment, portfolio investment, and other short- and long-term capital flows. The minus signs signify outflows of cash; for example, in Table 2-5, line 2 shows an outflow of $1.97 trillion in 2007 that represents payment for U.S. merchandise imports. (Other entries not shown in Table 2-5 represent changes in net errors and omissions, foreign liabilities, and reserves.) These are the entries that make the balance of payments balance. In general, a country accumulates reserves when the net of its current and capital account transactions shows a surplus; it gives up reserves when the net shows a deficit. The important fact to recognize about the overall balance of payments is that it is always in balance. Imbalances occur in subsets of the overall balance. For example, a commonly reported balance is the trade balance on goods (line 3 in Table 2-5).

A close examination of Table 2-5 reveals that the United States regularly posts deficits in both the current account and the trade balance in goods. The United States' growing trade deficit

TABLE 2-5 U.S. Balance of Payments, 2003–2007 (US$ millions)

	2003	2004	2005	2006	2007
A. Current Account	**–527,514**	**–665,286**	**–791,508**	**–811,477**	**–731,214**
1. Goods Exports (BOP basis)	713,415	807,516	894,631	1,023,109	1,148,481
2. Goods Imports (BOP basis)	–1,260,717	–1,472,926	–1,677,371	–1,861,380	–1,976,853
3. Balance on Goods	*–547,302*	*–665,410*	*–782,740*	*–838,271*	*–819,373*
4. Services: Credit	302,681	344,426	380,614	422,594	497,245
5. Services: Debit	–250,276	–290,312	–314,604	–342,845	–378,130
6. Balance on Services	*52,405*	*54,114*	*66,011*	*79,749*	*119,115*
7. Balance on Goods and Services	*–494,897*	*–611,296*	*–716,730*	*–758,522*	*–700,258*
B. Capital Account	**–3,480**	**–2,369**	**–4,036**	**–3,880**	**–1,842**

Source: www.bea.gov.

---

[34]Stefan Wagstyl, "The Next Investment Wave: Companies in East and West Prepare for the Risks and Opportunities of an Enlarged EU," *Financial Times* (April 27, 2004), p. 13.
[35]Amy Chozik, "Nissan Races to Make Smaller, Cheaper Cars," *The Wall Street Journal* (October 22, 2007), p. A12.
[36]Will Bland and Katharina Becker, "Oil-Rich Russia Acquires a Taste for Gas Guzzlers," *The Wall Street Journal* (September 18, 2008), p. B4.
[37]Balance of payments data are available from a number of different sources, each of which may show slightly different figures for a given line item.

TABLE 2-6 U.S. Goods and Services Trade with Brazil, India, and China 2007 (US$ millions)

	China	India	Brazil
1. U.S. Goods Exports to	65,073	17,516	24,497
2. Goods Imports from	−321,685	−24,102	−25,650
3. Balance on Goods	*−256,611*	*−6,586*	*−1,153*
4. U.S. Services Exports to	14,205	9,506	9,924
5. Services Imports from	−8,791	−9,663	−4,051
6. U.S. Balance on Services	*5,413*	*−157*	*5,873*
7. U.S. Balance on Goods and Services	*−251,198*	*−6,743*	*4,720*

Source: www.bea.gov.

reflects a number of factors, including increased imports from China, a seemingly insatiable consumer demand for imported goods, and the enormous cost of military operations in the Middle East. Table 2-6 shows a record of goods and services trade between the United States and Brazil, India, and China for 2007. A comparison of lines 4 and 5 in the two tables shows a bright spot from the U.S. perspective: The United States has maintained a services trade surplus with the rest of the world. Overall, however, the United States posts balance of payments deficits while important trading partners such as China have surpluses.

China has more than $1 trillion in foreign reserves, more than any other nation. It offsets its trade surpluses with an outflow of capital, while the United States offsets its trade deficit with an inflow of capital. China and other countries with healthy trade surpluses are setting up *sovereign wealth funds* to invest some of the money. As trading partners, U.S. consumers and businesses own an increasing quantity of foreign products, while foreign investors own more U.S. land, real estate, and government securities. Foreign-owned U.S. assets total $2.5 trillion; in 2005, the United States borrowed 6 percent of its output in goods and services from foreign countries.[38] As Ha Jiming, an economist with China's largest investment bank, noted, "One trillion [in reserves] is a big amount, but it is also a hot potato." Some policymakers in Washington are alarmed about the U.S. trade deficit with China, which reached $250 billion in 2007.

TRADE IN MERCHANDISE AND SERVICES

Thanks in part to the achievements of GATT and the WTO, world merchandise trade has grown at a faster rate than world production since the end of World War II. Put differently, import and export growth has outpaced the rate of increase in GNI. According to figures compiled by the WTO, the dollar value of world merchandise trade in 2007 totaled $13.9 trillion. However, as the world slipped into recession in 2008, annual world trade growth slowed to about 6 percent. The top exporting and importing countries are shown in Table 2-7.

In 2003, Germany surpassed the United States as the world's top exporter. German manufacturers of all sizes have benefited from global economic growth because they provide the motors, machines, vehicles, and other capital goods that are required to build factories and country infrastructures; worldwide, machinery and transport equipment constitute approximately one-third of global exports. Overall, about two-thirds of Germany's exports go to other EU nations; France is the number one country destination, while the United States ranks second. Today, exports generate 40 percent of Germany's gross domestic product, and 9 million jobs are export related. In addition, annual sales by the foreign subsidiaries of German-based companies are $1.5 billion.[39]

China's third place in the export rankings underscores its role as an export powerhouse. Even in the face of Asia's economic downturn in the late 1990s and the SARS outbreak, China demonstrated continued economic strength by achieving double-digit export growth. Chinese exports to the United

---

[38]David Wessel, "Counting on a Miracle with U.S. Debt," *The Wall Street Journal* (September 29, 2005), p. A2.
[39]Bertrand Benoit and Richard Milne, "Germany's Best-Kept Secret: How Its Exporters are Beating the World," *Financial Times* (May 19, 2006), p. 11.

TABLE 2-7 Top Exporters and Importers in World Merchandise Trade, 2004 (US$ billions)

Leading Exporters	2004	Leading Importers	2004
1. Germany	912	1. United States	1,526
2. United States	819	2. Germany	717
3. China	593	3. China	561
4. Japan	566	4. France	466
5. France	449	5. Great Britain	464
6. Netherlands	358	6. Japan	455
7. Italy	349	7. Italy	351
8. Great Britain	347	8. Netherlands	319
9. Canada	317	9. Belgium	286
10. Belgium	307	10. Canada	280

Source: WTO.

States have surged since China joined the WTO in 2001; in fact, policymakers in Washington are pressuring Beijing to boost the value of the yuan in an effort to stem the tide of imports.

Table 2-8 provides a different perspective on global trade. The European Union is treated as a single entity with imports and exports that exclude intra-regional trade among the 25 countries that were EU members at the end of 2006. South Korea, Mexico, and Russia appear in the top 10 exporter rankings; South Korea and Mexico also rank in the top 10 importers table. Figures are cited as a percentage of the world total.

The fastest-growing sector of world trade is trade in services. Services include travel and entertainment; education; business services such as accounting, advertising, engineering, investment banking, and legal services; and royalties and license fees that represent payments for intellectual property. One of the major issues in trade relations between the high- and lower-income countries is trade in services. As a group, low-, lower-middle, and even upper-middle-income countries are lax in enforcing international copyrights and protecting intellectual property and patent laws. As a result, countries that export service products such as computer software, music, and video entertainment suffer a loss of income. According to a recent Global Software Piracy Study conducted by the Business Software Association, annual worldwide losses due to software piracy amount to approximately $29 billion. In China alone, software piracy cost the industry an estimated $3.6 billion in lost sales in 2005.

The United States is a major service trader. As shown in Figure 2-2, U.S. services exports in 2007 totaled nearly $500 billion. This represents about one-third of total U.S. exports. The U.S.

TABLE 2-8 Top Exporters and Importers in World Merchandise Trade, 2004 (percentage of total)

Leading Exporters	2004	Leading Importers	2004
1. European Union	18.1	1. United States	21.8
2. United States	12.3	2. European Union	18.3
3. China	8.9	3. China	8.0
4. Japan	8.5	4. Japan	6.9
5. Canada	4.8	5. Canada	4.0
6. South Korea	3.8	6. South Korea	3.2
7. Mexico	2.8	7. Mexico	3.0
8. Russia	2.8	8. Taiwan	2.4
9. Taiwan	2.7	9. Switzerland	1.6
10. Malaysia	1.9	10. Australia	1.6

Source: WTO.

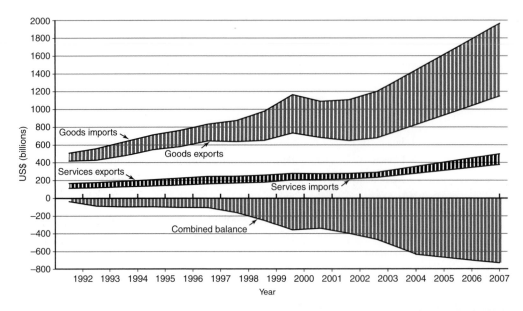

services surplus (service exports minus imports) stood at $119 billion. This surplus partially offset the U.S. merchandise trade deficit, which reached a record $819 billion in 2007. American Express, Walt Disney, IBM, and Microsoft are a few of the U.S. companies that have experienced rapid growth in demand for their services around the world.

OVERVIEW OF INTERNATIONAL FINANCE

Foreign exchange makes it possible for a company in one country to conduct business in other countries with different currencies. However, foreign exchange is an aspect of global marketing that involves certain financial risks, decisions, and activities that are completely different than those facing a domestic marketer. Moreover, those risks can be even higher in developing markets such as Thailand, Malaysia, and South Korea. When a company conducts business within a single country or region with customers and suppliers paying in the same currency, there is no exchange risk. All prices, payments, receipts, assets, and liabilities are in the given currency. However, when conducting business across boundaries in countries with different currencies, a company is thrust into the turbulent world of exchange risk.

The foreign exchange market consists literally of a buyer's and a seller's market where currencies are traded for both spot and future delivery on a continuous basis. The *spot* market is for immediate delivery; the market for future delivery is called the *forward* market. This is a true market where prices are based on the combined forces of supply and demand that come into play at the moment of any transaction. Who are the participants in this market? First, a country's central bank can buy and sell currencies in the foreign exchange market and government securities in an effort to influence exchange rates. For example, in the five-year period between 2001 and 2006, China bought more than $250 billion in U.S. Treasury bonds. Such purchases help ensure that China's currency is relatively weak compared to the U.S. dollar.[40] Second, some of the trading in the foreign exchange market takes the form of transactions needed to settle accounts for the global trade in goods and services. For example, because Porsche is a German company, the dollars spent on Porsche automobiles by American car buyers must be converted to euros. Finally, currency speculators also participate in the foreign exchange market.

Devaluation can result from government action that decrees a reduction in the value of the local currency against other currencies. In 1994, for example, the Chinese devalued the yuan (also known as *renminbi* or "people's money"). The immediate result was to ensure the low-cost position of Chinese exporters. However, the action also set the stage for the 1997 devaluations of the Thai baht, Malaysian ringgit, and Indonesian rupiah; the expression "beggar thy neighbor" is sometimes used to describe devaluations designed to increase export competitiveness.

---

[40]Mark Whitehouse, "U.S. Foreign Debt Shows Its Teeth as Rates Climb," *The Wall Street Journal* (September 25, 2006), p. A9.

TABLE 2-9 Exchange Risks and Gains in Foreign Transactions

Foreign Contract Exchange Rates	$1,000,000 Contract		€1,100,000 Contract	
	U.S. Seller Receives	European Buyer Pays	U.S. Seller Receives	European Buyer Pays
€1.25 = $1	$1,000,000	€1,250,000	$880,000	€1,100,000
€1.10 = $1	$1,000,000	€1,100,000	$1,000,000	€1,100,000
€1.00 = $1	$1,000,000	€1,000,000	$1,100,000	€1,100,000
€0.85 = $1	$1,000,000	€850,000	$1,294,118	€1,100,000

To the extent that a country sells more goods and services abroad than it buys, there will be a greater demand for its currency and a tendency for it to appreciate in value—unless government policymakers do not allow the currency to fluctuate. In 2005, the Chinese government responded to pressure from its trading partners by adopting a policy of **revaluation** to strengthen the yuan against the dollar and other currencies. A stronger yuan would make China's exports to the United States more expensive while making U.S. exports to China less expensive. The net result would be a reduction in China's trade surplus with the United States. The initial 2.1 percent increase in the yuan's value was not expected to have much impact on prices; some experts believe the yuan is undervalued by 20 percent or more (see the Emerging Markets Briefing Book: Is China's Currency Too Weak? feature).[41]

Table 2-9 shows how fluctuating currency values can affect financial risk, depending on the terms of payment specified in the contract. Suppose, at the time a deal is made, the exchange rate is €1.10 equals $1.00. How is a U.S. exporter affected if the dollar strengthens against the euro (e.g., trades at €1.25 equals $1.00) and the contract specifies payment in dollars? What happens if the dollar weakens (e.g., €0.85 equals $1.00)? Conversely, what if the European buyer contracts to pay in euros rather than dollars?

Purchasing Power Parity

Given that currencies fluctuate in value, a reasonable question to ask is whether a given currency is over- or undervalued compared with another. Recall from the previous discussion that the currency's value could reflect government policy (as in the case of China) or market forces. One way to answer the question is to compare world prices for a single well-known product: McDonald's Big Mac hamburger. The so-called Big Mac Index is a "quick and dirty" way of determining which of the world's currencies are too weak or strong. The underlying assumption is that the price of a Big Mac in any world currency should, after being converted to dollars, equal the price of a Big Mac in the United States. (Similar indexes have been proposed based on the price of Starbucks coffee and IKEA furniture.)

A country's currency would be overvalued if the Big Mac price (converted to dollars) is higher than the U.S. price. Conversely, a country's currency would be undervalued if the converted Big Mac price is lower than the U.S. price. Economists use the concept of **purchasing power parity (PPP)** when adjusting national income data to improve comparability. Table 2-10 shows the Big Mac Index for selected countries in 2008. The first column of figures shows the price of a Big Mac converted from the local currency to dollars at the prevailing exchange rate. Thus, we can see that the Chinese yuan is undervalued against the dollar by about 58 percent. In other words, based on the U.S price for a Big Mac, the yuan/dollar exchange rate ought to be 3.53/$1 rather than 6.84 to $1.[42] India is not included in the Index. Can you explain why?

Economic Exposure

Economic exposure reflects the impact of currency fluctuations on a company's financial performance. Economic exposure can occur when a company's business transactions result in sales or purchases denominated in foreign currencies. Diageo, for example, faces transaction exposure to the

---

[41]Sue Kirchhoff, "First Step: China Will Stop Pegging Yuan to Dollar," *USA Today* (July 22, 2005), p. 1B, 2B.
[42]The authors acknowledge that the PPP theory-based Big Mac Index is simplistic; as noted in this section, exchange rates are also affected by interest rate differentials and monetary and fiscal policies—not just prices.

TABLE 2-10 The 2008 Big Mac Index

Country	Big Mac Price Converted to $	Official Exchange Rate	Over- or Undervaluation of Local Currency (%)
Switzerland	5.60	1.16/$1	+58
U.S.	3.54	–	–
Brazil	3.45	2.27/$1	–2
Euro zone	3.42	1.28/$1	+24
Japan	3.23	89.9/$1	–9
Russia	1.73	35.7/$1	–51
China	1.83	6.84/$1	–48

Source: Adapted from "Big Mac Index," Economist.com, accessed May 1, 2009. Used by permission.

extent that it accepts payment for exports of Scotch whisky at one exchange rate but actually settles its accounts at a different rate of exchange.[43] Obviously, currency exposure is a critical issue for Nestlé, with 98 percent of annual sales taking place outside Switzerland. Among countries in the euro zone, GlaxoSmithKline, Daimler AG, BP, Sanofi-Aventis, Royal Dutch Shell, AstraZeneca, and SAB Miller all generate more than one-third of total sales in the U.S. market. Given the current weakness of the dollar relative to the euro, all of these companies face potential economic exposure. By comparison, GE generates more than 50 percent of its revenues in the domestic U.S. market, so the relative extent of GE's exposure is less than that of the European companies previously listed. Even so, as noted in its annual report, GE does face economic exposure:

> When countries or regions experience currency and/or economic stress, we often have increased exposure to certain risks, but also often have new profit opportunities. Potential increased risks include, among other things, high receivable delinquencies and bad debts, delays or cancellations of sales and orders principally related to power and aircraft equipment, higher local currency financing costs and slowdown in established financial services activities.[44]

In dealing with the economic exposure introduced by currency fluctuations, a key issue is whether the company can use price as a strategic tool for maintaining its profit margins. Can the company adjust prices in response to a rise or fall of foreign exchange rates in various markets? That depends on the price elasticity of demand. The less price-sensitive the demand, the greater the flexibility a company has in responding to exchange rate changes. In the late 1980s, for example, Porsche raised prices in the United States three times in response to the weak dollar. The result: Porsche's U.S. sales dropped precipitously, from 30,000 vehicles in 1986 to 4,500 vehicles in 1992. Clearly, U.S. luxury car buyers were exhibiting elastic demand curves for pricey German sports cars!

Managing Exchange Rate Exposure

It should be clear from this discussion that accurately forecasting exchange rate movements is a major challenge. Over the years, the search for ways of managing cash flows to eliminate or reduce exchange rate risks has resulted in the development of numerous techniques and financial strategies. For example, it may be desirable to sell products in the company's home country currency. When this is not possible, techniques are available to reduce both transaction and operating exposure.

Hedging exchange rate exposure involves establishing an offsetting currency position such that the loss or gain of one currency position is offset by a corresponding gain or loss in some other currency. The practice is common among global companies that sell products and maintain operations in different countries. Today, for example, Porsche relies on currency hedging rather than price increases to boost pretax profits on sales of its automobiles. Porsche manufactures all

---

[43]John Willman, "Currency Squeeze on Guinness," *Financial Times—Weekend Money* (September 27–28, 1997), p. 5.
[44]*General Electric 2004 Annual Report*, p. 58.

EMERGING MARKETS BRIEFING BOOK

⇒ Is China's Currency Too Weak?

In July 2005, the Peoples Bank of China announced the end of a 10-year effort to peg the value of the Chinese currency, the yuan, to the value of the U.S. dollar. Instead, the yuan would be linked to a basket of several foreign currencies. The announcement signaled Beijing's decision to abandon a policy of fixed exchange rates, according to which 8.28 yuan equaled $1, and adopt a policy of flexible rates. In short, by ending the peg, China's central bank was finally allowing the yuan to float.

The United States and other key trading partners had been urging such an action for years. *The New York Times* called the Chinese central bank's decision "the most hotly anticipated event for the foreign-exchange world in years." Many economists believed that the yuan had been undervalued relative to the dollar and other currencies by as much as 40 percent, and this weakness was cited as one of the factors contributing to growing trade deficits with China. For example, the U.S. trade deficit with China was more than $200 billion in 2006. This had occurred, it was argued, because the Chinese government had deliberately manipulated its currency to give Chinese exports a price advantage compared to goods from the United States and other countries.

Some observers favored a quick change in the yuan's value; others argued for a go-slow, gradualist approach. The immediate result of the revaluation was a 2.1 percent increase in the yuan's value, to 8.11 yuan equals $1. The stronger yuan was expected to have a ripple effect on the economies of China's top trading partners. For one thing, it was likely to result in increased prices for Chinese exports to the United States and elsewhere. This would be good news to some of the 12,000 members of the National Association of Manufacturers (N.A.M.). Many small factory owners in the United States are worried about competing with low-priced Chinese goods. However, a stronger yuan could be bad news for Walmart and other retailers that buy billions of dollars worth of goods from China each year. Likewise, global companies based in the West such as Whirlpool that source manufactured goods in China might be forced to raise prices.

By mid-2007, the yuan had appreciated about 8.5 percent against the dollar. However, that was not enough to satisfy some policymakers. Impatient with the slow pace of the revaluation, some members of the U.S. Congress introduced legislation designed to punish China for its currency policy. One bill, co-sponsored by Senate Finance Chairman Max Baucus, a democrat, and Charles Grassley, the republican senator from Iowa, was contingent on the U.S. Treasury Department determining that a "currency misalignment" had occurred. Following such a finding, the United States would impose fines in the form of antidumping penalties and the Chinese government would have six months to make the required currency adjustments. If China didn't take action, the U.S. trade representative would request dispute settlement at the WTO. A final ruling would be issued in 2010.

The introduction of the Congressional bill raised several questions. For example, it was unclear whether a dispute involving currency issues was a legitimate trade issue that the WTO would agree to hear. Another issue was whether it was possible to determine exactly how much the yuan would have to appreciate for it to be fairly aligned with the dollar.

Some observers warned that the Baucus-Grassley bill and others like it could undermine the trade relationship between the United States and China and actually harm U.S. companies that do business with China. Since joining the WTO in 2001, China has become America's fourth-largest export market. According to a study by the American Chamber of Commerce in China, American companies sold $61 billion worth of goods to China in 2005. Chamber chairman James Zimmerman noted, "A revalued yuan will not force the Chinese to buy American goods and services." Others warned that Chinese companies could diversify their export base by expanding trade with other countries. A trade war was another possibility. Scott Miller, director of trade policy for Procter & Gamble, said, "You can't rule out a backlash. That ought to be part of the calculus that lawmakers should consider." Some observers raised concerns that, in retaliation for trade sanctions, China might restrict market access for American goods.

Sources: John McCary and Andrew Batson, "Punishing China: Will It Fly?" *The Wall Street Journal* (June 23–24, 2007), p. A4; Wu Yi, "It's Win-Win on U.S. China Trade," *The Wall Street Journal* (May 17, 2007), p. A21; Martin Wolf, "How China Has Managed to Keep the Renminbi Pinned Down," *Financial Times* (October 11, 2006), p. 13; Louis Uchitelle, "What to Do About China and the Yuan," *The New York Times* (October 12, 2005), p. C1; E. S. Browning, "Yuan Move Might Stir Big Ripples," *The Wall Street Journal* (July 25, 2005), pp. C1, C4; Sue Kirchhoff, "First Step: China Will Stop Pegging Yuan to Dollar," *USA Today* (July 22, 2005), pp. 1B, 2B; Keith Bradsher, "A Chinese Revaluation May Not Help U.S.," *The New York Times* (January 4, 2005), pp. C1, C5.

of its cars in Europe, but generates about 45 percent of its sales in the United States. Thus, Porsche faces economic exposure stemming from the relative value of the dollar to the euro. Porsche is "fully hedged"; that is, it takes currency positions to protect all earnings from foreign-exchange movements.[45]

If company forecasts indicate that the value of the foreign currency will weaken against the home currency, it can hedge to protect against potential transaction losses. Conversely, for predictions that the foreign currency will appreciate (strengthen) against the home currency, then a gain, rather than a loss, can be expected on foreign transactions when revenues are converted

---

[45]Stephen Power, "Porsche Powers Profit with Currency Play," *The Wall Street Journal* (December 8, 2004), p. C3.

into the home currency. Given this expectation, the best decision may be not to hedge at all. (The operative word is "may"; many companies hedge anyway unless management is convinced the foreign currency will strengthen.) Porsche has profited by (correctly) betting on a weak dollar.

External hedging methods for managing both transaction and translation exposure require companies to participate in the foreign currency market. Specific hedging tools include forward contracts and currency options. *Internal hedging methods* include price adjustment clauses and intra-corporate borrowing or lending in foreign currencies. The **forward market** is a mechanism for buying and selling currencies at a preset price for future delivery. If it is known that a certain amount of foreign currency is going to be paid out or received at some future date, a company can insure itself against exchange loss by buying or selling forward. With a forward contract, the company can lock in a specific fixed exchange rate for a future date and thus immunize itself from the loss (or gain) caused by the exchange rate fluctuation. By consulting sources such as *Financial Times, The Wall Street Journal,* or www.ozforex.com, it is possible to determine exchange rates on any given day. In addition to spot prices, 30-, 60-, and 180-day forward prices are quoted for dozens of world currencies.

Companies use the forward market when the currency exposure is known in advance (e.g., when a firm contract of sale exists). In some situations, however, companies are not certain about the future foreign currency cash inflow or outflow. Consider the risk exposure of a U.S. company that bids for a foreign project but won't know if the project will be granted until sometime later. The company needs to protect the dollar value of the contract by hedging the *potential* foreign currency cash inflow that will be generated if the company turns out to be the winning bidder. In such an instance, forward contracts are not the appropriate hedging tool.

A foreign currency **option** is best for such situations. A **put option** gives the buyer the right, not the obligation, to sell a specified number of foreign currency units at a fixed price, up to the option's expiration date. (Conversely, a **call option** is the right, but not the obligation, to buy the foreign currency.) In the example of bidding the foreign project, the company can take out a put option to sell the foreign currency for dollars at a set price in the future. In other words, the U.S. company locks in the value of the contract in dollars. Thus, if the project is granted, the future foreign currency cash inflow has been hedged by means of the put option. If the project is *not* granted, the company can trade the put option in the options market without exercising it; remember, options are rights, not obligations. The only money the company stands to lose is the difference between what it paid for the option and what it receives upon selling it.

Financial officers of global firms can avoid economic exposure altogether by demanding a particular currency as the payment for its foreign sales. As noted, a U.S-based company might demand U.S. dollars as the payment currency for its foreign sales. This, however, does not eliminate currency risk; it simply shifts that risk to the customers. In common practice, companies typically attempt to invoice exports (receivables) in strong currencies and imports (payables) in weak currencies. However, in today's highly competitive world market, such practice may reduce a company's competitive edge.

Summary

The economic environment is a major determinant of global market potential and opportunity. In today's global economy, capital movements are the key driving force, production has become uncoupled from employment, and capitalism has vanquished communism. Based on patterns of resource allocation and ownership, the world's national economies can be categorized as **market capitalism**, **centrally planned capitalism**, **centrally planned socialism**, and **market socialism**. The final years of the twentieth century were marked by a transition toward market capitalism in many countries that had been centrally controlled. However, there still exists a great disparity among the nations of the world in terms of economic freedom.

Countries can be categorized in terms of their stage of economic development: **low income, lower-middle income, upper-middle income,** and **high income. Gross domestic product (GDP)** and **gross national income (GNI)** are commonly used measures of economic development. The 50 poorest countries in the low-income category are sometimes referred to as **least-developed countries (LDCs)**. Upper-middle-income countries with high growth rates are often called **newly industrializing economies (NIEs)**. Several of the world's economies are notable for their fast growth; the **BRIC** nations include Brazil (lower-middle income), Russia (upper-middle-income), India (low income), and China (lower-middle income). The **Group of Seven (G-7)**, **Group of Eight (G-8)**, and **Organization for Economic Cooperation and Development (OECD)** represent efforts by high-income nations to promote democratic ideals and free-market policies throughout the rest of the world. Most of the world's income is located in the **Triad**, which is comprised of Japan, the United States, and Western Europe. Companies with global aspirations generally have operations in all three areas. Market potential for a product can be evaluated by determining **product saturation levels** in light of income levels.

A country's **balance of payments** is a record of its economic transactions with the rest of the world; this record shows whether a country has a **trade surplus** (value of exports exceeds value of imports) or a **trade deficit** (value of imports exceeds value of exports). Trade figures can be further divided into **merchandise trade** and **services trade** accounts; a country can run a surplus in both accounts, a deficit in both accounts, or a combination of the two. The U.S. merchandise trade deficit was $819 billion in 2007. However, the United States enjoys an annual service trade surplus. Overall, the United States is a debtor; Japan enjoys an overall trade surplus and serves as a creditor nation.

Foreign exchange provides a means for settling accounts across borders. The dynamics of international finance can have a significant impact on a nation's economy as well as the fortunes of individual companies. Currencies can be subject to **devaluation** or **revaluation** as a result of actions taken by a country's central banker. Currency trading by international speculators can also lead to devaluation. When a country's economy is strong or when demand for its goods is high, its currency tends to appreciate in value. When currency values fluctuate, global firms face various types of economic exposure. Firms can manage exchange rate exposure by **hedging**.

Discussion Questions

1. Explain the difference between market capitalism, centrally planned capitalism, centrally planned socialism, and market socialism. Give an example of a country that illustrates each type of system.

2. The seven criteria for describing a nation's economy introduced at the beginning of this chapter can be combined in a number of different ways. For example, the United States can be characterized as follows:

   - *Type of economy:* Advanced industrial state
   - *Type of government:* Democracy with a multi-party system
   - *Trade and capital flows:* Incomplete free trade and part of trading bloc
   - *The commanding heights:* Mix of state and private ownership
   - *Services provided by the state and funded through taxes:* Pensions and education but not health care
   - *Institutions:* Transparency, standards, corruption is absent, a free press and strong courts
   - *Markets:* Free market system characterized by high risk/high reward entrepreneurial dynamism

   Use the seven criteria found on pp. 76–77 to develop a profile of one of the BRIC nations, or any other country that interests you. What implications does this profile have for marketing opportunities in the country?

3. Why are Brazil, Russia, India, and China (BRIC) highlighted in this chapter? Identify the current stage of economic development for each BRIC nation.

4. Turn to the Index of Economic Freedom (Table 2-3) and identify where the BRIC nations are ranked. What does the result tell you in terms of the relevance of the index to global marketers?

5. The Heritage Foundation's Index of Economic Freedom is not the only ranking that assesses countries in terms of successful economic policies. For example, the World

Economic Forum (WEF; www.weforum.org) publishes an annual Global Competitiveness Report; in the 2006–2007 report, the United States ranks in sixth place according to the WEF's metrics. By contrast, Sweden is in third place. According to the Index of Economic Freedom's rankings, the United States and Sweden are in sixth and twenty-sixth place, respectively. Why are the rankings so different? What criteria does each index consider?

6. When the first edition of this textbook was published in 1996, the World Bank defined "low-income country" as one with per capita income of less than $501. In 2003, when the third edition of *Global Marketing* appeared, "low income" was defined as $785 or less in per capita income. As shown in Table 2-4 of this chapter, $935 is the current "low income" threshold. The other stages of development have been revised in a similar manner. How do you explain the upward trend in the definition of income categories during the past 15 years?

7. A manufacturer of satellite dishes is assessing the world market potential for his products. He asks you if he should consider developing countries as potential markets. How would you advise him?

8. A friend is distressed to learn that America's merchandise trade deficit hit $819 billion in 2007. You want to cheer your friend up by demonstrating that the trade picture is not as bleak as it sounds. What do you say?

Singapore and the Philippines rely heavily on exports of electronics. As U.S. consumer spending slowed in 2007–2008, exports from these nations began to slump. Moreover, Singapore's ambitious goal to reinvent itself as a regional financial and entertainment destination had attracted a massive influx of bankers, lawyers, and other professionals from all over the world. The resulting housing boom turned out to be short-lived; with the global economic crisis deepening, thousands of foreign workers departed and Singapore's real estate market collapsed

By contrast, Indonesia, Malaysia, and Thailand were experiencing strong demand for exports of crude oil, natural gas, and other commodities. Thailand and Malaysia are key sources of palm oil, which can be used both for cooking and as a biodiesel fuel. Who was buying? Simply put, China's booming economy continued to exhibit strong demand.

Japan, the world's second-largest economy, became less dependent on exports to the United States during the first decade of the twenty-first century. Although Europe and the United States were still key markets for HDTVs and luxury cars, a weak yen and strong demand in emerging markets for Japanese-built machine tools and construction equipment meant that companies such as Komatsu booked increased sales to China and Southeast Asia that offset slowing sales elsewhere.

However, the weak yen also meant that many Japanese manufacturers operated production facilities at home rather than shifting production abroad. For example, Sharp manufactured all the display panels for its LCD TVs in Japan. However, as the yen strengthened from 123¥ to $1 in July 2007 to about 100¥ to $1 over the next 18 months, exports declined sharply. As Sharp's CFO said early in 2009, "The past way of using our own money to build all our factories in Japan and exporting to overseas markets is something that we have to rethink."

The ripple effect from the global recession was felt especially strongly in Canada, America's top trading partner. As the U.S. housing market collapsed, exports of Canadian hardwood fell. With U.S. homeowners feeling pinched and credit terms tightening, auto sales took a nosedive. GM, Ford, and Chrysler announced production slowdowns in their Canadian assembly plants; however, industry observers noted that it was small auto parts makers in Ontario and elsewhere that would be particularly vulnerable. The pain is being felt in other industry sectors as well. Nortel Networks, once the most valuable company listed on the Toronto Stock Exchange, filed for bankruptcy. Accounting scandals diverted management's attention while aggressive competitors and new technologies changed the industry landscape.

Compounding Canada's problem was the fact that its currency, the "loonie," had strengthened considerably against the U.S. dollar. That meant that auto parts shipped to the United States—$18.1 billion worth in 2007—were more expensive. Not surprisingly, many Canadian firms are diversifying geographically to reduce their dependence on the U.S. market. For example, Samco Machinery, an automotive equipment maker, has won orders from India's Tata Motors. Samco sells 20-ton machines that represent cutting-edge metal-bending technology.

Europe's economy was also mired in recession; some observers noted that the lack of ambitious stimulus proposals in the region meant that a recovery would take more time than in the United States or Asia. As in other parts of the world, credit restrictions and tighter lending policies meant that it was harder for retailers and distributors to finance inventories.

As the economic crisis deepened in the fall of 2008, world leaders offered a variety of perspectives and proposals. Some denounced "American-style capitalism" at the annual General Assembly meeting at the United Nations. French president Nicolas Sarkozy called for greater oversight of the global financial system. "Let us rebuild together a regulated capitalism in which whole swatches of financial activity are not left to the sole judgment of market operators," he said. Brazilian president Luiz Inácio Lula da Silva, a former labor leader, called for the global community to create a new foundation for the world economic system that would prevent abuses and shrink the gap between the rich and poor. Mahmoud Ahmadinejad, president of Iran, told the Assembly that the financial crisis was a sign that the American empire is "reaching the end of its road."

Case 2-1 Discussion Questions

1. Does the global economic crisis signal that the American model of free market capitalism is fundamentally flawed?
2. Policymakers in Japan, the world's second-largest economy, must transition their nation away from a manufacturing-dependent model for growth. What industry sectors might emerge as the new drivers of economic growth?
3. Do you think that the economic stimulus programs in the United States, Asia, and elsewhere are the right approach to pulling the world out of recession?

Sources: Yuka Hayashi and John Murphy, "As Factories Vanish, Japan Seeks to Fashion a New Economy," *The Wall Street Journal* (April 14, 2009), p. A8; Jason Dean and Marcus Walker, "Crisis Stirs Critics of Free Markets," *The Wall Street Journal* (September 25, 2008), p. A3; Jay Solomon, "Leaders Seek Global Response to Financial Crisis," *The Wall Street Journal* (September 24, 2008), p. A10; James Hookway, "Commodities Exporters Look to China for Growth as the West Sags," *The Wall Street Journal* (June 5, 2008), p. A12; Marcus Walker, James Hookway, John Lyons, and James T. Areddy, "U.S. Slump Takes Toll Across Globe," *The Wall Street Journal* (April 3, 2008), pp. A1, A13; David J. Lynch, "Woe, Canada: Catching Canada's Economic Chill," *USA Today* (February 26, 2008), p. 1B; Peter S. Goodman, "Trading Partners Fear U.S. Consumers Won't Continue Free-Spending Ways," *The New York Times* (January 25, 2008), pp. C1, C4; Keith Bradsher, "Throughout Asia, Exporters Brace for Tremors from a U.S. Pullback," (January 25, 2008), pp. C1, C4.

As director of the prestigious Media Lab at the Massachusetts Institute of Technology (MIT), Nicolas Negroponte had a unique opportunity to immerse himself in cutting-edge technology development projects. Robotic design, artificial intelligence, holographic video, and educational applications for PCs were just some of the areas the Lab's various departments explored. In 2005, after 20 years at the Lab, Negroponte announced he was leaving to pursue an ambitious vision: bridging the digital divide between developed and developing nations by providing powerful PCs to schoolchildren in sub-Saharan Africa and other impoverished parts of the world. Negroponte named his initiative One Laptop Per Child (OLPC); his goal was to develop a $100 laptop that governments could buy in large quantities and distribute to schools. As Negroponte said, "My goal is not selling laptops. OLPC is not in the laptop business. It's in the education business." In April 2007, Negroponte announced that he hoped to have between 50 and 150 million children using the new computer by the end of 2008.

"We do not view kids as a market, but as a mission."

Nicolas Negroponte, founder OLPC

The OLPC design team, which included Media Lab veteran Walter Bender, created a computer known as the XO that is rugged enough to stand up to heavy use and abuse. The XO is dust- and waterproof; a small solar panel can be used to recharge the battery. The laptop's high-resolution screen displays bright images even in sunlight; other features include a built-in video camera. Wi-Fi connectivity is provided by two small antennas on either side of the screen; some observers have commented that the antennas look like ears on a friendly alien-type creature.

To keep the cost down, each computer is loaded with an open-source operating system known as Linux. Linux is non-proprietary; that is, it is available for free to anyone who wants to use it. Moreover, Linux users are encouraged to make improvements to it. The user interface, dubbed Sugar, can also be modified by the children using the computers. As described by its creators, Sugar captures students' "world of fellow learners and teachers as collaborators, emphasizing the connections within the community, among people, and their activities." The design team believes that Linux and Sugar will foster collaborative learning among schoolchildren, in line with OLPC's core mission. The laptops are powered by microprocessors from Advanced Micro Devices (AMD); these cost less than components from Intel.

Another factor affecting the final cost is the volume of production. Negroponte needs firm purchase commitments so that production can be scaled up quickly. Government officials in Libya and Nigeria pledged to buy about one million computers each for their respective citizens; however, by mid-2007 both countries had backed off those pledges. As a result, the manufacturer, Taiwan's Quanta Computer, only achieved an initial production volume of 300,000 units. The lower volume, plus microprocessor upgrades, translated into a higher per-unit cost. The $100 price—a key selling point—would have to be abandoned. The new price target would be in the $180 to $190 range.

The higher price was one reason that initial enthusiasm for OLPC did not translate into firm commitments for orders. Other issues surfaced as well. For example, some potential buyers worried about the lack of Microsoft's Windows operating system. Meanwhile, OLPC had attracted the attention of several industry heavyweights. In 2006, Intel officials demonstrated a laptop prototype called the Classmate that was designed to sell for $230 to $300. The Classmate features Microsoft's Windows XP operating system, has four hours of battery life, and uses a solid-state flash drive. In 2007, Microsoft chairman Bill Gates announced that his company would offer developing countries a $3 software package that includes Windows, Office, and educational software. The low-priced software was offered through Unlimited Potential Group, the Microsoft unit that targets developing countries; early customers included the governments of Libya and Egypt.

Negroponte accused Intel officials of trying to undermine his nonprofit's efforts; for example, reports surfaced that Intel's sales force had made head-to-head comparisons between the Classmate and the OLPC laptop during presentations in Mongolia and Nigeria. Even so, Intel made a substantial financial contribution to OLPC and an Intel official joined the organization's board.

In November 2007, in an effort to increase production, OLPC announced a promotion called "Give One. Get One." Consumers in the United States and Canada were offered the opportunity to buy two OLPC computers for $399. Each buyer would keep one laptop; the second would go to a student in Haiti or another developing country.

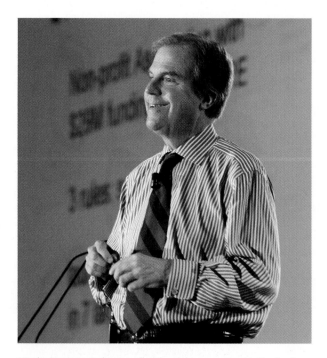

Nicolas Negroponte has travelled the globe promoting his One Laptop Per Child initiative.
Source: William B. Plowman/AP Wide World Photos.

In 2008, faced with disappointing sales, Negroponte struck a deal with Microsoft. Starting in 2010, the OLPC laptops would be delivered with both the Microsoft Windows operating system and the nonproprietary Linux OS. Microsoft would provide the software for about $3 per computer, bringing the total selling price of each laptop to $199.

Discussion Questions

1. Why are Microsoft, Intel, and other leading for-profit companies interested in low-cost computers for the developing world?
2. Do you agree with Negroponte's decision to partner with Microsoft?

3. Assess the thinking behind the "give one, get one" promotion. Do you think this is a good marketing tactic?

Sources: Steve Stecklow, "Laptop Program for Kids in Poor Countries Teams Up with Microsoft's Windows," *The Wall Street Journal* (May 16, 2008), pp. B1, B2; Steve Stecklow and James Bandler, "A Little Laptop with Big Ambitions: How a Computer for the Poor Got Stomped by Tech Giants," *The Wall Street Journal* (November 24–25, 2007), pp. A1, A7; David Pogue, "$100 Laptop a Bargain at $200," *The New York Times* (October 4, 2007), pp. C1, C8; Kevin Maney, "The Latest Cool Tool You Can't Have: Laptops So Cheap They're Disposable," *USA Today* (February 28, 2007), p. B8; John Markoff, "At Davos, the Squabble Resumes on How to Wire the Third World," *The New York Times* (January 29, 2007), pp. C1, C2.

Case 2-3
From Communism to Capitalism: Vietnam's Economic Transformation

In October 2001, U.S. President George Bush signed an agreement that created a U.S.–Vietnam free trade area. The signing marked yet another milestone along Vietnam's path toward a more open market, the timeline for which includes the following:

- In February 1994, U.S. President Bill Clinton ended America's 19-year economic embargo of Vietnam and opened the door for U.S. companies to target the world's twelfth most populous country.
- In July 1995, President Clinton reestablished diplomatic relations with Vietnam. In the absence of diplomatic relations, many Vietnamese manufactured exports to the United States faced prohibitive tariffs.
- In 1995, Vietnam joined the Association of Southeast Asian Nations (ASEAN).
- In 1998, the White House announced that it would exempt Vietnam from the Jackson-Vanik amendment. The exemption meant that, pending congressional approval, American companies investing in Vietnam could apply for financial assistance from the Overseas Private Investment Corporation (OPIC) and the Export-Import Bank.
- In July 2000, U.S. President Bill Clinton signed a trade pact with Vietnam.
- The Asia-Pacific Economic Cooperation (APEC) Summit was held in Hanoi in November 2006.
- Vietnam joined the World Trade Organization in 2007.

After being ratified by Congress, President Clinton's actions in the mid-1990s established normal trading relations (NTR) between the two countries. In particular, Vietnam benefited from an immediate lowering of duties on a number of goods produced by its light industry sector (see Figure 1). Vietnamese tariffs and quotas on imports from the United States would be lowered more gradually. U.S. companies immediately seized the opportunity. As Brian Watson, a Hong Kong–based deputy regional director for the McCann-Erickson advertising agency, said in the mid-1990s, "Vietnam is the next great frontier. There is an enormous amount of interest among clients. Every meeting starts with a question about going into Vietnam."

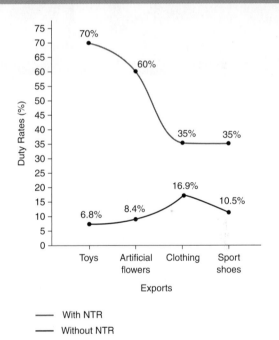

— With NTR
— Without NTR

FIGURE 1

Duty Rates on Vietnamese Exports to the United States with and Without NTR

Source: Based on *Vietnam Economic Times.*

While the U.S. business community hailed Washington's initiatives, many American firms found themselves playing catch up; by the early 1990s, many non-U.S. global companies had preceded the Americans into Vietnam. For example, South Korean industrial giant Daewoo was a key investor; other companies with major commitments included Sony, Toshiba, Honda, Peugeot, and British Petroleum. Carrier was among the first U.S. companies to legally market in Vietnam in 1994; the company's window air conditioners appeared in stores in Hanoi and Ho Chi Minh City. Gillette

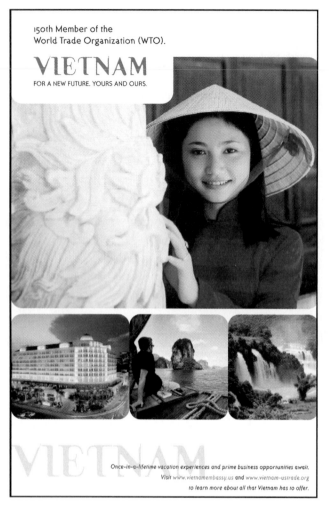

Source: Vietnam Embassy.

began shipping razor blades and disposable razors, and AT&T began selling home and office telephone products through a distributor in Taiwan. Mobil began exploring for oil, Caterpillar set up equipment-leasing operations, and the Otis Elevator division of United Technologies joined in the construction boom. J. Walter Thompson, Ogilvy & Mather, and Backer Spielvogel Bates Worldwide became the first Western ad agencies to open liaison offices in Vietnam.

Considering that 60 percent of Vietnam's population is under the age of 25, it is no surprise that PepsiCo and the Coca-Cola Company also responded proactively to the new market opportunity. At the time of the official announcement about ending the embargo, McCann-Erickson had already produced a TV commercial for Coca-Cola that included the global slogan "Always"; likewise, Ogilvy & Mather had a Pepsi ad ready for TV. Coca-Cola announced plans for a $20 million bottling plant outside of Hanoi, but was denied permission to build in Ho Chi Minh City (formerly Saigon). Pepsi's joint venture with a Vietnamese firm in Ho Chi Minh City is bottling Pepsi; local production began within hours of President Clinton's 1994 announcement. To supply the market in the south, Coca-Cola imported canned soda from Singapore. For a short period of time, a can of Coke cost twice as much as a bottle of Pepsi.

Experts agree that the Vietnamese market holds tremendous potential over the long term. It may be two decades before Vietnam reaches the level of economic development found in Thailand today. Meanwhile, the country's location in the heart of Asia and the presence of an ample low-wage workforce are powerful magnets for foreign companies. By the end of 1999, France ranked first in foreign investment while Japan was the top trading partner. Overall foreign direct investment peaked at about $3.1 billion in 1997 after rising steadily since the early 1990s (see Figure 2). After falling to about $2.1 billion in 1999, investment rebounded to $2.3 billion in 2002. As encouraging as those figures are, however, investment levels in China are much higher.

There are still many challenges for companies seeking to invest in Vietnam. The population is very poor, with 2006 annual per capita GNI of only about $700. However, urbanites with savings estimated at $1 to $2 billion comprise one quarter of the population. The infrastructure is undeveloped: Only 10 percent of roads are paved, electricity sources are unreliable, there is less than one telephone per 100 people, and the banking system is undeveloped. The Communist Party of Vietnam (CPV) is struggling to adapt to the principles of a market economy, and the layers of bureaucracy built up over decades of communist rule slow the pace of change. A key agency is the State Committee for Cooperation and Investment (SCCI); as Vu Tien Phuc, a deputy director of the agency, explained, "Every authority would like to have the last say. We have to improve the investment climate." William Ratliff, an analyst with the Hoover Institute, points out that the question for Vietnam is "whether it's possible to carry on free-market reforms and maintain absolute political power."

Yvonne Gupwell, a business consultant who was born in Vietnam, believes that "The biggest mistake companies make is they think because the Vietnamese are so polite, they're a little bit dim. The Vietnamese are poor, but they are not mentally poor at all." Statistics support this view; for example, adult literacy is nearly

FIGURE 2

Foreign Direct Investment in Vietnam, 1992–2002

90 percent. In fact, an emerging entrepreneurial class has developed a taste for expensive products such as Nikon cameras and Ray-Ban sunglasses, both of which are available in stores. Notes Do Duc Dinh of the Institute on the World Economy, "There is a huge unofficial economy. For most people, we can live only 5 days or 10 days a month on our salary. But people build houses. Where does the money come from? Even in government ministries, there are two sets of books—one for the official money and one for unofficial."

> *"In 1996, you were told where to invest, and you also had to build the road, the school, the hospital. You said, 'Thank you very much; my new address is Malaysia.'"*
>
> A foreign businessman in Vietnam

Euphoria over Vietnam's potential showed signs of waning at the end of the 1990s. Part of the problem was the "currency contagion" that struck Asia in mid-1997; Asian countries that had been major investors were forced to scale back their activities in Vietnam. More generally, many companies were finding it difficult to make a profit. Cross-border smuggling from Thailand depressed legitimate sales of products produced locally by Procter & Gamble, Unilever, American Standard, and other companies. Foreign companies were also frustrated by the shallow pool of qualified local managers. It was also clear that China was attracting a great deal of foreign investment away from other countries in the region.

Today, many companies are discovering that Vietnam is an excellent source of low-cost labor. Burgeoning apparel and textile exports to the United States led to an agreement on export quotas in 2003. The fledgling tech sector also appears to hold great promise. Vietnam's universities turn out graduates who are highly trained in information technology. One company, Glass Egg Digital Media, provides software-writing services to leading global video-game developers such as France's Infogames and U.S.-based Electronic Arts. Glass Egg founder Phil Tran pays programmers annual salaries of about $4,000, tens of thousands less than programmers in the United States are paid.

Although still strongly influenced by Communist hard-liners, the bureaucrats in Hanoi have demonstrated an increased willingness to adopt much-needed reforms to foreign investment laws. In January 2000, for example, the regulatory environment improved with the enactment of an enterprise law that streamlined the process of market entry and setting up a business; a stock market was also opened. Increasingly, decisions about foreign investment are being made at the provincial level, and local officials are offering incentives and issuing import licenses more quickly. Investors in many industry sectors are now able to set up wholly foreign-owned firms; previously, the government rarely approved such arrangements. Instead, foreign companies were encouraged to form joint ventures with state-owned enterprises. The improved investment climate helps explain why a number of foreign carmakers, including Ford, GM, and Toyota, have established operations in Vietnam. Noted one local businessman approvingly, "In the past, it was absolutely horrendous to set up a private company. Now 99 percent of the difficulties are gone."

> *"The reform is definitely irreversible. Any attempt to come back to a centrally planned economy, to overplay the state sector, is economically irrational, inefficient and, psychologically, is counterproductive."*
>
> Le Dang Doanh, advisor to the government of Vietnam

Vietnam's free trade area agreement with the United States entered into force in December 2001. The effect was immediate: The value of U.S. imports from Vietnam more than doubled in 2002, to nearly $2.4 billion. At the end of 2003, the two nations signed an air services agreement that made it easy for travelers to book flights to Vietnam. The agreement came as Vietnam's government began marketing the country as an attractive vacation destination. Despite such positive news, however, many problems remain. For example, Vietnam's legal system is still bewildering, and regulations can change on a moment's notice. Relations between the new trading partners have shown some signs of strain, as evidenced by U.S. charges that Vietnam has been dumping catfish in the U.S. market at artificially low prices.

Visit the Web site

www.vietnam-ustrade.org

Discussion Questions

1. Assess the market opportunities in Vietnam for both consumer products companies and industrial-products companies. What is the nature of the opportunity?
2. Nike and several other well-known American companies are sourcing some of their production in Vietnam, thereby taking advantage of a labor force that is paid the equivalent of $2 per day or less. Are goods labeled "Made in Vietnam" likely to find widespread acceptance among American consumers?
3. Some critics have argued that Cuba is more deserving of diplomatic and trade relations with the United States than Vietnam. What are some of the factors behind this argument?

An excellent video overview is found in "Visions of a New Vietnam." The program was originally aired on the Nightly Business Report; *we recommend viewing the DVD in conjunction with the case discussion.*

Sources: Keith Bradsher, "Vietnam's Roaring Economy Is Set for World Stage," *The New York Times* (October 25, 2006), pp. A1, C4; Joseph Erlich, "Vietnam's Trade-War Wounds," *The Wall Street Journal* (August 26, 2005), p. A10; Dan Reed, "Ex-Enemies Make a Deal," *USA Today* (December 9, 2003), p. 5B; Reginald Chua and Margot Cohen, "Vietnamese Tiger Growls Again; Investors Want a Change of Stripes," *The Wall Street Journal* (March 13, 2003), p. A10; Margot Cohen, "Foreign Investors Take New Look at Vietnam and Like What They See," *The Wall Street Journal* (January 28, 2003), p. A14; Amy Kamzin, "Vietnam's Change of Heart," *Financial Times* (August 28, 2002), p. 13; Bruce Knecht, "Vietnam Taps Videogame Talent," *The New York Times* (October 21, 2001), p. B5; Frederik Balfour, "Back on the Radar Screen," *Business Week* (November 20, 2000), pp. 56–57; Wayne Arnold, "Clearing the Decks for a Trade Pact's Riches," *The New York Times* (August 27, 2000), sec. 3, pp. 1, 12; Samantha Marshall, "Vietnam Pullout: This Time, Investors Pack Up Gear, Stymied by Bureaucracy, Lack of Reforms," *The Wall Street Journal* (June 30, 1998), p. A15; Marshall, "P&G Squabbles with Vietnamese Partner," *The Wall Street Journal* (February 27, 1998), p. A10; Reginald Chua, "Vietnam Frustrates Foreign Investors as Leaders Waffle on Market Economy," *The Wall Street Journal* (November 25, 1996), p. A10; "Vietnam," *The Economist* (July 8, 1995), pp. 1–18 (survey); William J. Ardrey, Anthony Pecotich, and Clifford J. Schultz, "American Involvement in Vietnam, Part II: Prospects for U.S. Business in a New Era," *Business Horizons* 38 (March/April 1995), pp. 21–27; Edward A. Gargan, "For U.S. Business, a Hard Road to Vietnam," *The New York Times* (July 14, 1995), p. C1; Marilyn Greene, "Very Soon, Vietnam Will Be Very Good," *USA Today* (April 1, 1994), p. 8A; Robert Keatley, "Vietnam, Despite Promise, Faces Climb," *The Wall Street Journal* (August 18, 1994), p. A8; Philip Shenon, "Vietnam: Behind a Red-Tape Curtain," *The New York Times* (November 13, 1994), sec. 3, p. 6; James Cox, "Vietnamese Look Forward to Trade, Jobs," *USA Today* (July 12, 1995), pp. 1A, 2A; Kevin Goldman, "Agencies Get Ready for Vietnam Business," *The Wall Street Journal* (February 7, 1994), p. B10.

3

Regional Market Characteristics and Preferential Trade Agreements

Case 3-1
The United States and South Korea Sign a Free Trade Agreement

Why do nations trade? Presumably, each trading partner has something to gain, such as access to more goods and services and lower prices. For example, the money that consumers save by buying low-cost food imports can be spent on other products, resulting in a higher standard of living. Open markets are one way that globalization has led to economic integration. The United States and South Korea recently completed negotiations on the world's largest bilateral trade agreement. The deal reduces tariffs on about 90 percent of product categories; prior to the agreement, South Korea's tariffs on imported food averaged about 52 percent. Overall, its import tariffs averaged about 11.2 percent. By comparison, the United States has a 12 percent tariff on food and overall tariffs of about 3.7 percent.

Observers expect that a reduction in South Korea's tariffs will boost two-way trade from $78 billion in 2006 to $100 billion by 2010. General Motors, Ford, and Chrysler are some of the U.S. companies that stand to benefit from improved access to a market with 48 million people: Each year, only about 5,000 American cars are sold in South Korea, compared with 800,000 Korean cars sold in the United States. In fact, the trade gap in autos accounts for about 80 percent of South Korea's trade deficit with the United States, which stood at $13 billion in 2006. American farmers and ranchers also anticipate increased demand for beef and other agricultural exports as import tariffs of 40 percent are phased out over 15 years. For its part, the United States will reduce tariffs on automobile and electronics imports; this will be

Exhibit 3-1: South Korean protesters march with a banner reading "Let's keep away the Korean-US FTA that threatens our life" during a rally against U.S. beef imports in central Seoul on June 8, 2008. South Korean street protests against U.S. beef imports showed no sign of abating despite former President George W. Bush's pledge to help ease food safety concerns here.
Source: Jung Yeon-Je/AFP/Newscom.

a boon for Hyundai, Samsung, LG, and other industry leaders in South Korea. On paper, it appears that both sides will benefit from the free trade agreement. If that is true, why are some people adamantly opposed to the agreement (see Exhibit 3-1)? When you have finished reading Chapter 3, turn to Case 3-1 for more discussion of the pros as well as possible "cons."

Since World War II, there has been a tremendous interest among nations in furthering the cause of economic cooperation and integration. The agreement between the United States and South Korea illustrates the fact that trade deals can be limited to two nations; however, trade negotiations and trade agreements also occur at the regional and global levels. Our survey of the world trade environment begins at the global level with the WTO and its predecessor, the GATT. Next, the four main types of bilateral and regional preferential trade agreements are identified and described. An introduction to individual countries in the world's major market regions follows; each section also includes detailed discussion of the specific preferential trade agreements in which those countries participate. Important marketing issues in each region are also discussed. Several important emerging country markets were described in Chapter 2; in this chapter, special attention will be given to individual country markets that were not previously discussed.

THE WORLD TRADE ORGANIZATION AND GATT

The year 2007 marked the sixtieth anniversary of the **General Agreement on Tariffs and Trade (GATT)**, a treaty among nations whose governments agree, at least in principle, to promote trade among members. GATT was intended to be a multilateral, global initiative, and GATT negotiators did succeed in liberalizing world merchandise trade. GATT was also an organization that handled 300 trade disputes—many involving food—during its half century of existence. GATT itself had no enforcement power (the losing party in a dispute was entitled to ignore the ruling), and the process of dealing with disputes sometimes stretched on for years. Little wonder, then, that some critics referred to GATT as the "General Agreement to Talk and Talk."

The successor to GATT, the **World Trade Organization (WTO)**, came into existence on January 1, 1995. From its base in Geneva, the WTO provides a forum for trade-related negotiations among its 150 members. The WTO's staff of neutral trade experts also serve as mediators in global trade disputes. The WTO has a Dispute Settlement Body (DSB) that mediates complaints concerning unfair trade barriers and other issues between the WTO's member countries. During a 60-day consultation period, parties to a complaint are expected to engage in good-faith negotiations and reach an amicable resolution. If that fails, the complainant can ask the DSB to appoint a three-member panel of trade experts to hear the case behind closed doors. After convening, the panel has nine months within which to issue its ruling.[1] The DSB is empowered to act on the panel's recommendations. The losing party has the option of turning to a seven-member appellate body. If, after due process, a country's trade policies are found to violate WTO rules, it is expected to change those policies. If changes are not forthcoming, the WTO can authorize trade sanctions against the loser. Table 3-1 lists some recent cases that have been brought to the WTO.

Trade ministers representing the WTO member nations meet annually to work on improving world trade. It remains to be seen whether the WTO will live up to expectations when it comes to additional major policy initiatives on such vexing issues as foreign investment and agricultural

---

[1]Scott Miller, "Global Dogfight: Airplane Battle Spotlights Power of a Quirky Court," *The Wall Street Journal* (June 1, 2005), pp. A1, A14.

TABLE 3-1 Recent WTO Cases

Countries Involved in Dispute	Nature of Dispute and Outcome
United States, European Union, Canada versus China	In 2006, the complainants asked the DSB to consider Chinese tariffs on imported auto parts. The complainants argued that their auto manufacturers were at a disadvantage because Beijing required them to buy components locally or pay high tariffs. In 2008, the WTO ruled that China had violated trade rules.
United States versus Brazil	In 2003, Brazil filed a complaint against the United States charging that cotton subsidies depressed prices and disadvantaged producers in emerging markets. In 2004, the DSB, in its first-ever ruling on agricultural subsidies, agreed that cotton subsidies violate international trade rules.
Antigua and Barbuda versus the United States	In 2003, Antigua filed suit charging that, by prohibiting Internet gambling, the United States was violating global trade agreements. In 2004, the WTO ruled in favor of Antigua.
United States versus European Union	In 2002, U.S. President Bush imposed 30 percent tariffs on a range of steel imports for a period of three years. The EU lodged a protest, and in 2003, the WTO ruled that the tariffs were illegal. President Bush responded by lifting the tariffs.

"For the WTO process to work, countries have to start liberalizing policies in politically sensitive sectors."[2]
Daniel Griswold, Center for Trade Policy Studies, Cato Institute

subsidies. The current round of WTO negotiations began in 2001; the talks collapsed in 2005 and attempts to revive them in the years since have not been successful. For more on the trade talks, turn to the Strategic Decision Making box on page 113.

PREFERENTIAL TRADE AGREEMENTS

The GATT treaty promotes free trade on a global basis; in addition, countries in each of the world's regions are seeking to liberalize trade within their regions. A **preferential trade agreement** is a mechanism that confers special treatment on select trading partners. By favoring certain countries, such agreements frequently discriminate against others. For that reason, it is customary for countries to notify the WTO when they enter into preferential trade agreements. In recent years, the WTO has been notified of approximately 300 preferential trade agreements. Few fully conform to WTO requirements; none, however, has been disallowed.

Free Trade Area

A **free trade area** (FTA) is formed when two or more countries agree to eliminate tariffs and other barriers that restrict trade. When trading partners successfully negotiate a **free trade agreement** (also abbreviated FTA), the ultimate goal of which is to have zero duties on goods that cross borders between the partners, it creates a free trade area. In some instances, duties are eliminated on the day the agreement takes effect; in other cases, duties are phased out over a set period of time. Countries that belong to an FTA can maintain independent trade policies with respect to third countries. **Rules of origin** discourage the importation of goods into the member country with the lowest external tariff for transshipment to one or more FTA members with higher external tariffs; customs inspectors police the borders between members.

For example, because Chile and Canada established an FTA in 1997, a Canadian-built Caterpillar grader tractor imported into Chile would not be subject to duty. If the same piece of equipment was imported from a factory in the United States, the importer would pay about $13,000 in duties. Could Caterpillar send the U.S.-built tractor to Chile by way of Canada, thereby allowing the importer to avoid paying the duty? No, because the tractor would bear a "Made in the U.S.A." certificate of origin indicating it was subject to the duty. Little wonder, then, that the U.S. government negotiated its own bilateral free trade agreement with Chile that entered into force in 2003.

According to the Business Roundtable, to date more than 300 free trade agreements have been negotiated globally; roughly 50 percent of global trade takes place among nations linked by FTAs (see Table 3-2). Additional examples of FTAs include the European Economic Area, a free trade area that includes the 27-nation EU plus Norway, Liechtenstein, and Iceland; the Group of

[2]Scott Miller, "Trade Talks Twist in the Wind," *The Wall Street Journal* (November 8, 2005), p. A14.

TABLE 3-2 **Free Trade Agreements Around the World**

FTAs negotiated globally	300 (approx.)
FTAs negotiated since 2002 in Asia Pacific	119
Percentage of world trade occurring through FTAs	50%
Countries with which China is negotiating or has proposed FTAs	28
EU FTAs	21
U.S. FTAs	10

Source: Business Roundtable, March 2007. Reprinted by permission of Business Roundtable.

Three (G-3), an FTA encompassing Colombia, Mexico, and Venezuela; and the Closer Economic Partnership Agreement, a free trade agreement between China and Hong Kong. As noted in the chapter introduction, the United States is currently negotiating an FTA with South Korea; negotiations are also ongoing with Panama and Colombia (see Exhibit 3-2).

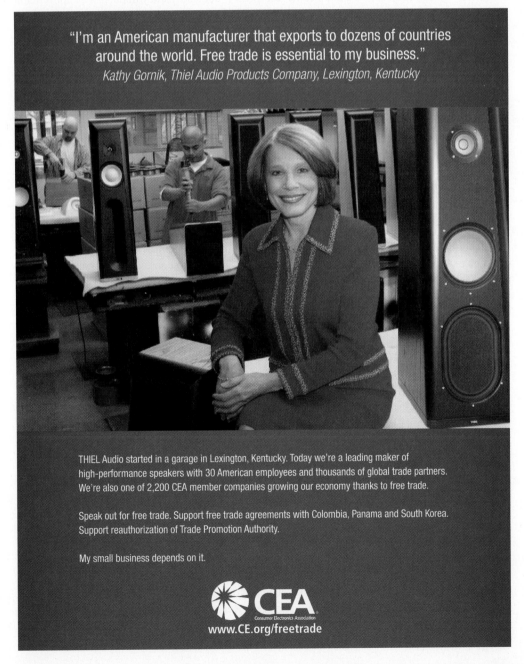

Exhibit 3-2: Many small business owners are advocates of free trade agreements. Speaking on behalf of the Consumer Electronics Association, the CEO of electronics manufacturer Thiel notes, "Today we're a leading maker of high-performance speakers with 30 American employees and thousands of global trade partners. We're also one of 2,200 CEA members growing our economy thanks to free trade. Speak out for free trade. Support free trade agreements with Colombia, Panama, and South Korea."
Source: Used by permission of Consumer Electronic Association.

TABLE 3-3 Forms of Regional Economic Integration

Stage of Integration	Elimination of Tariffs and Quotas Among Members	Common External Tariff (CET) and Quota System	Elimination of Restrictions on Factor Movements	Harmonization and Unification of Economic and Social Policies and Institutions
Free Trade Area	Yes	No	No	No
Customs Union	Yes	Yes	No	No
Common Market	Yes	Yes	Yes	No
Economic Union	Yes	Yes	Yes	Yes

Customs Union

A **customs union** represents the logical evolution of a free trade area. In addition to eliminating internal barriers to trade, members of a customs union agree to the establishment of **common external tariffs** (CETs). In 1996, for example, the European Union and Turkey initiated a customs union in an effort to boost two-way trade above the average annual level of $20 billion. The arrangement called for the elimination of tariffs averaging 14 percent that added $1.5 billion each year to the cost of European goods imported by Turkey. Other customs unions discussed in this chapter are the Andean Community, the Central American Integration System (SICA), Mercosur, and CARICOM.

Common Market

A **common market** is the next level of economic integration. In addition to the removal of internal barriers to trade and the establishment of common external tariffs, the common market allows for free movement of factors of production, including labor and capital. The Andean Community, the SICA, and CARICOM, which currently function as customs unions, may ultimately evolve into true common markets.

Economic Union

An **economic union** builds upon the elimination of the internal tariff barriers, the establishment of common external barriers, and the free flow of factors. It seeks to coordinate and harmonize economic and social policy within the union to facilitate the free flow of capital, labor, and goods and services from country to country. An economic union is a common marketplace not only for goods but also for services and capital. For example, if professionals are going to be able to work anywhere in the EU, the members must harmonize their practice licensing so that a doctor or lawyer qualified in one country may practice in any other. The full evolution of an economic union would involve the creation of a unified central bank, the use of a single currency, and common policies on agriculture, social services and welfare, regional development, transport, taxation, competition, and mergers. A true economic union requires extensive political unity, which makes it similar to a nation. The further integration of nations that were members of fully developed economic unions would be the formation of a central government that would bring together independent political states into a single political framework. The EU is approaching its target of completing most of the steps required to become a full economic union, with one notable setback. Despite the fact that 16 member nations ratified a proposed European Constitution, the initiative was derailed after voters in France and the Netherlands voted against the measure. Table 3-3 compares the various forms of regional economic integration.

NORTH AMERICA

North America, which includes Canada, the United States, and Mexico, comprises a distinctive regional market. The United States combines great wealth, a large population, vast space, and plentiful natural resources in a single national economic and political environment and presents unique marketing characteristics. High product-ownership levels are associated with high income

STRATEGIC DECISION MAKING IN GLOBAL MARKETING
Sixty Years of Trade Negotiation

Between 1947 and 1994, the member countries of GATT completed eight rounds of multilateral trade negotiations. Tariffs have been reduced from an average of 40 percent in 1945 to 5 percent today. The result has been a tremendous growth in trade: In the three decades from 1945 to 1975, the volume of world trade expanded by roughly 500 percent. The seventh round of negotiations was launched in Tokyo and ran from 1973 to 1979. These talks succeeded in cutting duties on industrial products valued at $150 billion by another 30 percent so that the remaining tariffs averaged about 6 percent. In terms of agricultural trade, there was a standoff between the United States, Europe, and Japan. The confrontation pitted the interests of the American farm lobby against the equally politically powerful farmers of Europe and Japan. Deep-rooted differences resulted in little change in the agricultural area during the Tokyo round. The most notable feature of the Tokyo round was not the duty cuts, but rather a series of nine new agreements on nontariff trade barriers.

GATT officials also devoted considerable attention to the services industry, addressing market-entry barriers in banking, insurance, telecommunications, and other sectors. The services issue was so contentious that the opening of the Uruguay round was delayed from 1982 until 1986. In addition to trade in services, these negotiations revisited the issue of nontariff measures that restrict or distort trade, including agricultural trade policy, intellectual property protection, and restrictions on foreign investment.

Agricultural subsidies and quotas that developed outside the multilateral framework remain a divisive issue. Critics argue that trade patterns are distorted when affluent countries protect and subsidize farm production. While home-market consumers pay higher prices, surplus output is sold abroad at artificially low prices. According to the Organization for Economic Cooperation and Development, in the mid-1990s, the total cost of these subsidies to rich-country taxpayers and consumers was more than $200 billion a year. Critics also believe that subsidies deny poor countries a natural path out of poverty, namely food exports. For example, in a 2002 report, Oxfam International estimated that U.S. cotton subsidies cost cotton farmers in Africa $300 million in lost exports each year.

The Uruguay negotiations were suspended in December 1990 after 30,000 French farmers took to the streets of Brussels to protest a proposed 30 percent cut in agricultural export subsidies. Negotiations resumed a few months later against the background of the united Western war effort in the Persian Gulf War. Negotiators finally succeeded in reaching an agreement by the December 15, 1993, deadline. A stalemate over agricultural subsidies was broken, with France and the EU nations agreeing to reductions. The U.S. Congress voted in favor of GATT at the end of 1994.

Competitive companies will benefit as tariffs are cut or eliminated entirely. The Triad nations agreed to end tariffs in pharmaceuticals, construction and agricultural equipment, Scotch whisky, furniture, paper, steel, and medical equipment.

Also, U.S. restrictions on textile and apparel imports from developing countries were phased out over a 10-year period. Major issues remain unresolved in the entertainment industry; France has insisted on preferences and subsidies for French producers of television programming and motion pictures in order to limit what they feel is "cultural imperialism." Talks aimed at reducing European broadcast restrictions on U.S.-produced movies and television programming were unsuccessful.

Efforts to break the deadlock over agriculture have met with some success. For one thing, the EU's Common Agricultural Policy (CAP) is distinctly different than it was two decades ago. In 1999, EU governments agreed on Agenda 2000 reforms that have resulted in price support reductions and increased attention to environmental issues. In 2003, the EU undertook further reform of CAP by decoupling agricultural income support from production. In 2004, Brazil successfully challenged the EU sugar regime at the WTO. In 2005, the EU proposed cutting subsidies for agricultural exports; it also agreed to cut sugar subsidies by 36 percent over a four-year period. Meanwhile, industry trade groups such as the Committee of Professional Agriculture Organizations and the General Confederation of Agricultural Cooperatives (COPA-COGECA) in the EU are steadfast in their efforts to serve the interests of farmers and provide input to policymakers; COPA-COGECA also is an advocate for sustainable development and related issues.

For its part, the U.S. government has proposed capping subsidies at a maximum of $250,000 per farmer per year. In 2005, the WTO ruled in favor of Brazil's challenge to U.S. cotton subsidies; meanwhile, a grassroots anti-subsidy movement is gaining traction. As Jerry Moran, a Republican congressman from Kansas, told the *Wall Street Journal*, "There are a growing number of people who want to weigh in on farm policy. They care about Africa. They care about the environment. They care about nutrition."

Sources: Alan Beattie, "Weight of Expectation Buries Deal," *Financial Times* (July 25, 2006), p. 2; Scott Killman and Roger Thurow, "Pork Chops: In Fight Against Farm Subsidies, Even Farmers Are Joining Foes," *The Wall Street Journal* (March 14, 2006), pp. A1, A16; Keith Bradsher, "Trade Talks Now Expected to Focus on Exports of Poorest Nations," *The New York Times* (December 12, 2005), pp. C1, C3; Noelle Knox, "French Rally Around Farmers at WTO Talks," *USA Today* (November 30, 2005), p. 5B; Scott Miller, "Trade Talks Twist in the Wind," *The Wall Street Journal* (November 8, 2005), pp. A14, A15; Shailagh Murray, "Subsidies Shackle EU Competitiveness," *The Wall Street Journal* (October 28, 1996), p. A13; "GATT's Last Gasp," *Economist* (December 1, 1990), p. 16; Joseph A. McKinney, "How Multilateral Trade Talks Affect the U.S.," *Baylor Business Review* (Fall 1991), pp. 24–25; Bob Davis, "Squeaky Wheels: GATT Talks Resume, with France and India Calling Many of the Shots," *The Wall Street Journal* (January 31, 1992), pp. A1, A13; "Free Trade's Fading Champion," *Economist* (April 11, 1992), p. 65; Davis and Lawrence Ingrassia, "Trade Acceptance: After Years of Talks, GATT Is at Last Ready to Sign Off On a Pact," *The Wall Street Journal* (December 15, 1993), pp. A1, A7.

and relatively high receptivity to innovations and new ideas both in consumer and industrial products. The United States is home to more global industry leaders than any other nation in the world. For example, U.S. companies are the dominant producers in the computer, software, aerospace, entertainment, medical equipment, and jet engine industry sectors.

In 1988, the United States and Canada signed a free trade agreement (U.S.-Canada Free Trade Agreement, or CFTA); the Canada-U.S. Free Trade Area formally came into existence in 1989. This helps explain the fact that more than $400 billion per year in goods and services flows between Canada and the United States, the biggest trading relationship between any two single nations. Canada takes 20 percent of U.S. exports and the United States buys approximately 85 percent of Canada's exports. Figure 3-1 illustrates the economic integration of North America: Canada is the number one trading partner of the United States, Mexico is second, and China ranks third. American companies have more invested in Canada than in any other country. Many U.S. manufacturers, including GE and IBM, use their Canadian operations as major global suppliers for some product lines. By participating in the Canadian auto market, U.S. automakers gain greater economies of scale. The CFTA, which was fully implemented when all duties were eliminated effective January 1998, is creating a true continental market for most other products.

In 1992, representatives from the United States, Canada, and Mexico concluded negotiations for the **North American Free Trade Agreement (NAFTA)**. The agreement was approved by both houses of the U.S. Congress and became effective on January 1, 1994. The result is a free trade area with a combined population of roughly 430 million and a total GNI of almost $14 trillion (see Table 3-4 and Figure 3-2).

Why does NAFTA create a free trade area as opposed to a customs union or a common market? The governments of all three nations pledge to promote economic growth through tariff

FIGURE 3-1

U.S. Trade Partners 2008

Source: U.S. Bureau of the Census, www.census.gov.

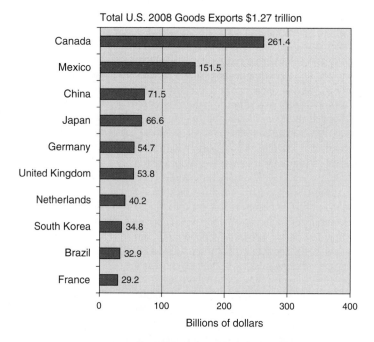

Total U.S. 2008 Goods Exports $1.27 trillion

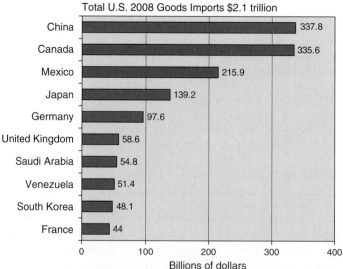

Total U.S. 2008 Goods Imports $2.1 trillion

TABLE 3-4 **NAFTA Income and Population**

	2006 GNI (in millions)	2006 Population (in thousands)	2006 GNI per Capita
United States	$13,386,875	299,398	$44,710
Canada	1,196,626	32,649	36,650
Mexico	815,841	104,221	7,830
Total/Mean GNI per capita	$15,399,342	436,268	$35,298*

*Indicates mean

Source: Reprinted by permission of Warren Keegan Associates, Inc.

elimination and expanded trade and investment. At present, however, there are no common external tariffs nor have restrictions on labor and other factor movements been eliminated. The issue of illegal immigration from Mexico into the United States remains a contentious one. The benefits of continental free trade will enable all three countries to meet the economic challenges of the decades to come. The gradual elimination of barriers to the flow of goods, services, and investment, coupled with strong protection of intellectual property rights (patents, trademarks, and copyrights), will further benefit businesses, workers, farmers, and consumers.

The agreement does leave the door open for discretionary protectionism, however. For example, California avocado growers won government protection for a market worth $250 million; Mexican avocado growers can only ship their fruit to the United States during the winter months, and only to states in the northeast. Moreover, Mexican avocados are subject to quotas so only $30 million worth of avocados reach the United States each year. Mexican farmer Ricardo Salgado complained, "The California growers want to control all of the supply—that way they get the best prices. We'd love to have a bigger selling season, but right now we have to wait for the U.S. Congress to give us permission."[3] Mexico engages in some protectionism of its own; for example, in 2003, a 98.8 percent tariff was imposed on chicken leg quarters beyond the first 50,000 metric tons imported. In addition, Mexico imposed a 46.6 percent tariff on red and golden delicious apples.

FIGURE 3-2

Map of NAFTA Countries

---

[3]Joel Millman, "Bitter Fruit: Spats Persist Despite NAFTA," *The Wall Street Journal* (June 19, 2000), p. A23.

The United States and Canada are bound together by many things, including a trade agreement, a shared border, and a common language. Still, the two nations do not always see eye-to-eye, as evidenced by various trade-related issues that have arisen in recent years. Take, for example, U.S. exports of items related to popular culture. On one side is the American entertainment industry. Exports of music, print publications, television shows, and Hollywood movies all contribute to the U.S. trade surplus in services. In Canada, policymakers, arts organizations, and cultural activists point with concern to statistics indicating that 95 percent of the movies shown in theaters are not Canadian and that 84 percent of the recorded music that Canadians buy is foreign.

Competition is one facet of the issue; Canadians fear that their own national industries will not be able to survive the global juggernaut originating south of the border. Canadians are also concerned about cultural preservation. In the late 1990s, Arthur C. Eggleton, Canada's minister for international trade, said, "There is a very strong dominance in the cultural industries of the Canadian marketplace by the United States. We come at this from the point of preserving culture and identity, while the U.S. comes at it from the standpoint of wanting to do business in our country."

Since the 1960s, Canada has enacted various pieces of legislation that restrict foreign ownership in the book publishing, telecommunications, and broadcasting industries. There are also regulations governing the percentage of Canadian programming that is broadcast by radio and television stations. In the negotiations leading to NAFTA, Canada was successful in excluding culture industries from the liberalized trade and investment framework. The issue came to a head in 1995, when Canada's Parliament imposed an 80 percent excise tax on advertising in the Canadian edition of Time Warner's *Sport's Illustrated.* The dispute focused on split-run magazines, in which the U.S. and Canadian editions are virtually identical in terms of editorial content but carry different advertising. Canadian publishers complained that Time Warner and other U.S. media companies possessed the resources to dominate Canadian culture. The United States took the matter to the World Trade Organization; a trade panel ruled that Canada's actions violated international trade agreements. After the initial ruling was issued, Canada filed an appeal but did not receive a favorable ruling. The U.S. trade representative Charlene Barshefsky hailed the decision, saying it "makes clear WTO rules prevent government from using 'culture' as a pretense for discriminating against imports."

Despite the WTO's ruling in this case, France and other nations share Canada's concerns. OECD member nations have conducted meetings to discuss a multilateral agreement on investment (MAI) that would eliminate barriers to foreign investment; France, Canada, and other nations are seeking to exclude cultural industries from the pact. In 1998, Canada convened a conference of 20 culture ministers in Ottawa in the hope of drafting a trade agreement that would ensure that culture industries received special treatment in trade rules. The agreement would be negotiated in Geneva at the World Trade Organization. Sheila Copps, Canadian heritage minister and host of the meeting, said attendees had agreed to establish a permanent network. In the future, she said, steps would be taken so that "culture is not treated simply like every other commodity." Copps also noted that the United States was not invited to take part in the conference because it does not have a culture minister.

Sources: Roger Ricklefs, "Canada Fights to Fend Off American Tastes and Tunes," *The Wall Street Journal* (September 24, 1998), pp. B1, B8; Anthony DePalma, "Happy 4th of July, Canada!" *The New York Times* (July 5, 1998), p. 3; Rosanna Tamburri, "Canada to Promote Pact to Curb U.S.'s Cultural Exports," *The Wall Street Journal* (June 29, 1998), p. B5; Tamburri, "Canada Considers New Stand Against American Culture," *The Wall Street Journal* (February 4, 1998), p. A18; Bernard Simon, "Canada Scrambles to Protect Magazines," *Financial Times* (July 2, 1997), p. 6; John Urquhart, "Canada Appealing Panel Ruling Backing U.S. Complaints on Magazines," *The Wall Street Journal* (March 17, 1997), p. B8; Anthony DePalma, "Trade vs. Cultural Identity in Canada," *The New York Times* (October 7, 1996), p. D9.

LATIN AMERICA: SICA, ANDEAN COMMUNITY, MERCOSUR, CARICOM

Latin America includes the Caribbean and Central and South America (because of NAFTA, Mexico is grouped with North America). The allure of the Latin American market has been its considerable size and huge resource base. After a decade of no growth, crippling inflation, increasing foreign debt, protectionism, and bloated government payrolls, the countries of Latin America have begun the process of economic transformation. Balanced budgets are a priority and privatization is underway. Free markets, open economies, and deregulation have begun to replace the policies of the past. In many countries, tariffs that sometimes reached as much as 100 percent or more have been lowered to 10 to 20 percent.

With the exception of Cuba, most elected governments in Latin America are democratic. However, there is widespread skepticism about the benefits of participating fully in the global economy. As left-leaning politicians such as Venezuela's President Hugo Chávez become more popular, concern is growing that free-market forces may lose momentum in the region. Global corporations are watching developments closely. They are encouraged by import liberalization, the prospects for lower tariffs within subregional trading groups, and the potential for establishing more efficient regional production. Many observers envision a free trade area throughout the hemisphere. The four most important preferential trading arrangements in Latin America are the Central American Integration System (SICA), the Andean Community, the Common Market of the South (Mercosur), and the Caribbean Community and Common Market (CARICOM).

Central American Integration System

Central America is trying to revive its common market, which was set up in the early 1960s. The five original members—El Salvador, Honduras, Guatemala, Nicaragua, and Costa Rica—decided in July 1991 to reestablish the Central American Common Market (CACM). Efforts to improve regional integration gained momentum with the granting of observer status to Panama. In 1997, with Panama as a member, the group's name was changed to the Central American Integration System (Sistema de la Integración Centroamericana or SICA; see Figure 3-3). Table 3-5 shows the income and population data in the region.

The Secretariat for Central American Economic Integration, headquartered in Guatemala City, helps to coordinate the progress toward a true Central American common market. Common rules of origin were also adopted, allowing for freer movement of goods among SICA countries. SICA countries agreed to conform to a common external tariff (CET) of 5 to 20 percent for most goods by the mid-1990s; many tariffs had previously exceeded 100 percent. Starting in 2000, import duties converged to a range of 0 to 15 percent.

Implementation of the Central American Free Trade Agreement with the United States created a free trade area known as DR-CAFTA that includes five SICA members (El Salvador, Honduras, Guatemala, Nicaragua, and Costa Rica; Panama is excluded) plus the Dominican Republic. Implementation has been slow but some changes have already taken effect. For example, 80 percent of U.S. goods and more than half of U.S. agriculture products can now be imported into Central America on a duty-free basis. Benefits to Central American companies include a streamlining of export paper work and the adoption of an online application process. The region will attract more direct foreign investment as foreign companies see reduced risk

FIGURE 3-3

Map of SICA Countries

TABLE 3-5 SICA Income and Population

	2006 GNI (in millions)	2006 Population (in thousands)	2006 GNI per Capita
Costa Rica	$21,894	4,399	$4,980
El Salvador	18,096	6,762	2,680
Guatemala	33,725	13,029	2,590
Honduras	8,844	6,969	1,270
Nicaragua	5,163	5,532	930
Panama	16,442	3,288	5,000
Total/Mean GNI per capita	$104,164	39,979	$2,605*

*Indicates mean

Source: Reprinted by permission of Warren Keegan Associates, Inc.

thanks to clearer rules. In addition, a significant number of companies in Central America operated in the "shadow economy" with many commercial transactions going unreported. Government tax revenues should increase as companies join the formal economy to take advantage of CAFTA's benefits.[4]

Despite progress, attempts to achieve integration in Central America have been described as uncoordinated, inefficient, and costly. There are still tariffs on imports of products—sugar, coffee, and alcoholic beverages, for example—that are also produced in the importing country. As one Guatemalan analyst remarked, "Only when I see Salvadoran beer on sale in Guatemala and Guatemalan beer on sale in El Salvador will I believe that trade liberalization and integration is a reality."[5]

Andean Community

The Andean Community (Comunidad Andina de Naciones or CAN; see Figure 3-4 and Table 3-6) was formed in 1969 to accelerate the development of member states Bolivia, Colombia, Ecuador, Peru, and Venezuela through economic and social integration. Members agreed to lower tariffs on intragroup trade and to work together to decide what products each country should produce. At the same time, foreign goods and companies were kept out as much as possible. One Bolivian described the unfortunate result of this lack of competition in the following way: "We had agreed, 'You buy our overpriced goods and we'll buy yours.'"[6]

In 1988, the group members decided to get a fresh start. Beginning in 1992, the Andean Pact signatories agreed to form Latin America's first operating subregional free trade area. The pact abolished all foreign exchange, financial and fiscal incentives, and export subsidies at the end of 1992. Common external tariffs were established, marking the transition to a true customs union. Overall, the region's rural residents and urban poor have become frustrated and impatient with the lack of progress. As one Andean scholar put it, "After 10 or 15 years of operating with free-market policies, paradise hasn't come. People start wondering if the gospel was as good as advertised."[7]

Within the Andean group members, individual country situations vary. Ecuador, for example, has experienced years of economic and political instability. In 2000, in an attempt to bring rampant inflation under control, the government adopted the U.S. dollar as Ecuador's official currency.

Venezuela is reaping the rewards of booming demand for oil; oil revenues account for 75 percent of its exports. President Hugo Chávez is a self-proclaimed revolutionary firebrand;

---

[4]Adam Thomson, "Trade Deal Has Hidden Qualities," *Financial Times Special Report: Central America Finance & Investment* (September 19, 2008), p. 3.
[5]Johanna Tuckman, "Central Americans Start to Act Together," *Financial Times* (July 9, 1997), p. 4.
[6]"NAFTA Is Not Alone," *The Economist* (June 18, 1994), pp. 47–48.
[7]Marc Lifsher, "The Andean Arc of Instability," *The Wall Street Journal* (February 24, 2003), p. A13.

FIGURE 3-4

Map of Andean Community and MERCOSUR

Andean Group and Mercosur

Mercosur

Andean Group

TABLE 3-6 Andean Community Income and Population

	2006 GNI (in millions)	2006 Population (in thousands)	2006 GNI per Capita
Bolivia	$10,293	9,354	$1,100
Colombia	141,982	45,558	3,120
Ecuador	38,481	13,202	2,910
Peru	82,201	27,589	2,980
Venezuela	163,959	27,021	6,070
Total/Mean GNP per capita	$436,916	122,724	$3,560*

*Indicates mean

Source: Reprinted by permission of Warren Keegan Associates, Inc.

after being elected in 1998, he proclaimed that his vision for Ecuador is "socialism for the twenty-first century." Even so, there are significant market opportunities for global companies. General Motors produces vehicles at a plant in Valencia; even running three shifts per day, it is unable to meet demand. Procter & Gamble's Latin American headquarters are located in Caracas. Other global companies with operations in Venezuela include Cargill, Chevron, Exxon Mobil, Ford, Kellogg, 3M, and Toyota.[8]

---

[8]David J. Lynch, "Venezuelan Consumers Gobble Up U.S. Goods," *USA Today* (March 28, 2007), pp. 1B, 2B.

Common Market of the South (Mercosur)

March 2006 marked the fifteenth anniversary of the signing of the Asunción Treaty. The treaty signified the agreement by the governments of Argentina, Brazil, Paraguay, and Uruguay to form the Common Market of the South (Mercado Común del Sur or Mercosur; see Figure 3-4 and Table 3-7). The four countries agreed to begin phasing in tariff reform on January 1, 1995. Internal tariffs were eliminated, and CETs of 20 percent or less were established. In theory, goods, services, and factors of production will ultimately move freely throughout the member countries; until this goal is achieved, however, Mercosur will actually operate as a customs union rather than a true common market. Today, about 90 percent of goods are traded freely; however, individual members of Mercosur can change both internal and external tariffs when it suits the respective government.

Much depends on the successful outcome of this experiment in regional cooperation. The early signs were positive, as trade between the four full member nations grew dramatically during the 1990s. The region has experienced a series of financial crises; for example, Brazil's currency was devalued in 1995 and again in 1999.

Argentina provides a case study in how a country can emerge from an economic crisis as a stronger global competitor. Argentina's economy minister responded to the financial crisis of 2001–2002 by implementing emergency measures that included a 29 percent currency devaluation for exports and capital transactions. Argentina was allowed to break from the CET and raise duties on consumer goods. The crisis had a silver lining: virtually overnight, Argentina's wine exports to the United States were worth four times more when dollar revenues were converted into pesos. The currency devaluation also makes Argentine vineyard property cheaper for foreign buyers. Low prices for land, inexpensive labor, and ideal growing conditions for the Malbec grape have combined to make Argentina's wine industry a major player in world markets. As one winemaker noted, "You can make better wine here for less money than anywhere in the world." A new challenge looms, however; the dollar's weakness relative to the euro means that winemakers are paying 25 percent more for oak aging barrels imported from France.[9]

The trade agreement landscape in the region continues to evolve. In 1996, Chile became an associate member of Mercosur. Policymakers opted against full membership because Chile already had lower external tariffs than the rest of Mercosur; ironically, full membership would have required raising them. (In other words, Chile participates in the free trade area aspect of

TABLE 3-7 Mercosur Income and Population

	2006 GNI (in millions)	2006 Population (in thousands)	2006 GNI per Capita
Argentina	$201,347	39,134	$5,150
Bolivia*	10,293	9,354	1,100
Brazil	892,639	189,323	4,710
Chile*	111,869	16,433	6,810
Ecuador*	38,481	13,202	2,910
Paraguay	6,016	8,461	1,410
Peru*	82,201	27,589	2,980
Uruguay	17,591	3,314	5,310
Venezuela	163,959	27,021	6,070
*Total/Mean GNI per capita***	$1,524,396	333,831	$4,050**

*Associate members that participate in free trade area only
**Indicates mean
Source: Reprinted by permission of Warren Keegan Associates, Inc.

---

[9]David J. Lynch, "Golden Days for Argentine Wine Could Turn a Bit Cloudy," *USA Today* (November 16, 2007), pp. 1B, 2B.

EMERGING MARKETS BRIEFING BOOK

➔ Brazil

As the figures in Table 3-7 clearly show, Brazil is an economic powerhouse in South America. Brazil has the largest geographical territory and the largest population in the region. Between 1994 and 2004, Brazil's exports grew at an annual rate of 8.78 percent; rapid economic growth has given policymakers, including President Lúiz Inácio Lula da Silva, a greater presence on the global stage and more clout at global trade talks.

One symbol of Brazil's new role in the global economy: Embraer, a jet aircraft manufacturer (see Exhibit 3-3). Specializing in regional jets that seat fewer than 100 passengers, Embraer has won orders from JetBlue, Air Canada, Saudi Arabian Airlines, and other carriers. Embraer shared the cost of developing new models such as the E-170/175 with more than one dozen partners, including General Electric and Honeywell. In order to sell more regional jets to China, Embraer has also established a $50 million joint venture with China Aviation Industry Corporation.

Brazil's agricultural sector is also a leading exporter. Brazil is the world's number one exporter of beef, coffee, orange juice (check the label on your orange juice carton), and sugar. Brazil is rapidly gaining a reputation as a producer of sugar-based ethanol, which can serve as a sustainable substitute for expensive gasoline. Industry observers expect Brazil to double its sugar cane processing capacity by 2010. As Ermor Zambello, manager of the Grupo Farias sugar mill, notes, "Globalization has made us think more about foreign markets. Now, we have more of a global outlook, and we are concerned about global production."

The central issue in the Doha Round is agriculture. Brazil and India are taking the lead of a so-called Group of 20 developing nations calling for agricultural sector reform. For example, the average tariff on Brazil's exports to the 30 OECD nations is 27 percent. Government subsidies are also a key issue. In the EU, government spending accounts for about one-third of gross farm receipts; in the United States, the government provides about one-quarter of gross farm receipts. By contrast, Brazil's spending on farm support amounts to only about 3 percent of farm receipts.

Moving forward, Brazil faces a number of other challenges. Steady appreciation of Brazil's currency, the real, may require exporters to raise prices. Embraer faces tough competition from Canada's Bombardier. The country's infrastructure remains woefully underdeveloped; significant investment is required to improve highways, railroads, and ports. Businesspeople speak of "the Brazil cost," a phrase that refers to delays related to excessive red tape. Trade with China is presenting both opportunities and threats. From 1995 to 2005, Brazil's total two-way trade with China increased from $2.2 billion to $12.2 billion. China's explosive economic growth has created great demand for iron ore and other Brazilian commodity exports. However, Brazilian manufacturers in light-industry sectors such as toys, eyeglasses, and footwear are facing increased competition from low-priced Chinese imports.

Sources: Antonia Regalado, "Soccer, Samba, and Outsourcing?" *The Wall Street Journal* (January 25, 2007), pp. B1, B8; David J. Lynch, "Brazil Hopes to Build On Its Ethanol Success," *USA Today* (March 29, 2006), pp. 1B, 2B; Lynch, "China's Growing Pull Puts Brazil in a Bind," *USA Today* (March 21, 2006), pp. 1B, 2B; Lynch, "Comeback Kid Embraer Has Hot New Jet, and Fiery CEO to Match," *USA Today* (March 7, 2006), pp. 1B, 2B; Lynch, "Brazil's Agricultural Exports Cast Long Shadow," *USA Today* (March 10, 2006), pp. 1B, 2B.

Exhibit 3-3: Embraer is the world's fourth-largest aircraft manufacturer; however, in the regional aircraft sector, Embraer is second only to Canada's Bombardier.
Source: Alexandre Meneghini/AP Wide World Photos.

Mercosur, not the customs union.) Chile's export-driven success makes it a role model for the rest of Latin America as well as Central and Eastern Europe. In 2004 Mercosur signed a cooperation agreement with the Andean Community; as a result, Bolivia, Colombia, Ecuador, and Peru have also become associate members. Venezuela became a full Mercosur member in 2006. The EU is Mercosur's number one trading partner; Mercosur has signed an agreement with the EU to establish a free trade area. Germany and France are opposed to such an agreement on the grounds that low-cost agricultural exports from South America will harm farmers in Europe.

Caribbean Community and Common Market (CARICOM)

CARICOM was formed in 1973 as a movement toward unity in the Caribbean. It replaced the Caribbean Free Trade Association (CARIFTA) founded in 1965. The members are Antigua and Barbuda, Bahamas, Barbados, Belize, Dominica, Grenada, Guyana, Haiti, Jamaica, Montserrat, St. Kitts and Nevis, St. Lucia, St. Vincent and the Grenadines, Suriname, and Trinidad and Tobago. The population of the entire 15-member CARICOM is about 15 million; disparate levels of economic development can be seen by comparing GNI per capita in Dominica and Grenada with that of Haiti (see Table 3-8).

To date, CARICOM's main objective has been to achieve a deepening of economic integration by means of a Caribbean common market. However, CARICOM was largely stagnant during its first two decades of existence. At its annual meeting in July 1991, member countries agreed to speed integration; a customs union was established with common external tariffs. At the 1998 summit meeting, leaders from the 15 countries agreed to move quickly to establish an economic union with a common currency. A recent study of the issue has suggested, however, that the limited extent of intraregional trade would limit the potential gains from lower transaction costs.[10]

TABLE 3-8 CARICOM Income and Population

	2006 GNI (in millions)	2006 Population (in thousands)	2006 GNI per Capita
Antigua and Barbuda	$929	84	$11,050
Bahamas	4,684	327	15,100
Barbados	na	293	na
Belize	1,114	298	3,740
Dominica	262	72	3,670
Grenada	397	108	3,750
Guyana	849	739	1,150
Haiti	4,044	9,446	430
Jamaica	9,504	2,667	3,560
Montserrat	na	na	na
St. Kitts and Nevis	326	48	6,980
St. Lucia	684	166	4,180
St. Vincent and Grenadines	403	120	3,400
Suriname	1,918	455	4,210
Trinidad and Tobago	16,612	1,328	12,500
Total/Mean GNI per capita	$33,788	15,006	$2,293*, a

*Indicates mean
aExcludes Barbados and Montserrat

Source: Reprinted by permission of Warren Keegan Associates, Inc.

---

[10]Myrvin L. Anthony and Andrew Hughes Hallett, "Is the Case for Economic and Monetary Union in the Caribbean Realistic?" *World Economy* 23, no. 1 (January 2000), pp. 119–144.

If the original 1973 treaty were revised, CARICOM nations could qualify for membership in a proposed Free Trade Area of the Americas (FTAA). As Owen Arthur, then prime minister of Barbados, explained, "The old treaty limited the movement of capital, skills, and business in the region. The treaty has to be changed so that regional trade policy can be widened to deal with the FTAA and the EU, and such matters as bilateral investments treaties, intellectual property rights, and trade in services."[11]

The English-speaking CARICOM members in the eastern Caribbean are also concerned with defending their privileged trading position with the United States. That status dates to the Caribbean Basin Initiative (CBI) of 1984, which promoted export production of certain products by providing duty-free U.S. market access to 20 countries, including members of CARICOM. Recently, CBI members requested that the CBI be expanded. The Caribbean Basin Trade Partnership Act, which went into effect on October 1, 2000, exempts textile and apparel exports from the Caribbean to the United States from duties and tariffs. CARICOM is shown in Figure 3-5.

Current Trade-Related Issues

One of the biggest trade-related issues in the Western Hemisphere is the creation of a Free Trade Area of the Americas (FTAA). However, leaders in several Latin American countries—Brazil in particular—are frustrated by Washington's tendency to dictate trade terms that will benefit special interests in the United States. For example, a bipartisan coalition of U.S. policymakers favors the inclusion of labor and other non-trade-related requirements in trade treaties such as the FTAA. Labor law enforcement was included in the texts of the free trade agreements that the United States signed with Jordan and Morocco. However, Brazilian President Luiz Icácio Lula da Silva and other Latin American leaders are opposed to including labor standards in the FTAA. Now Brazil and its Mercosur partners are advocating a slower, three-stage approach to negotiations with the United States. The first stage would include discussions on business facilitation issues such as standardized customs forms and industry deregulation; the second would focus on dispute settlement and rules of origin; and the third would focus on tariffs. Meanwhile, as previously noted, Mercosur, CARICOM, SICA, and the Andean Community are taking steps toward further intra-regional integration and also aligning with Europe.

FIGURE 3-5

CARICOM

---

[11]Canute James, "Caribbean Community Grapples with Challenge of Creating a Single Market," *Financial Times* (July 10, 1998), p. 7.

ASIA-PACIFIC: THE ASSOCIATION OF SOUTHEAST ASIAN NATIONS (ASEAN)

The Association of Southeast Asian Nations (ASEAN) was established in 1967 as an organization for economic, political, social, and cultural cooperation among its member countries. Brunei, Indonesia, Malaysia, the Philippines, Singapore, and Thailand were the original six members. Vietnam became the first Communist nation in the group when it was admitted to ASEAN in July 1995. Cambodia and Laos were admitted at the organization's thirtieth anniversary meeting in July 1997. Burma (known as Myanmar by the ruling military junta) joined in 1998, following delays related to the country's internal politics and human rights record (see Figure 3-6 and Table 3-9).

Individually and collectively, ASEAN countries are active in regional and global trade. ASEAN's top trading partners include Japan ($161.8 billion in total 2006 trade), the United States ($161.2 billion in total 2006 trade), the EU ($160.6 billion in total 2006 trade), and China ($140 billion in total 2006 trade). A few years ago, ASEAN officials realized that broad common goals were not enough to keep the association alive. A constant problem was the strict need for consensus among all members before proceeding with any form of cooperative effort. Although the ASEAN member countries are geographically close, they have historically been divided in many respects. In 1994, economic ministers from the member nations agreed to implement an ASEAN Free Trade Area (AFTA); recent progress at reducing intra-regional tariff reductions means that the free trade area has finally become a reality.

Recently, Japan, China, and Korea were informally added to the member roster; some observers called this configuration "ASEAN plus three." When the roster expanded again to include Australia, New Zealand, and India, it was dubbed "ASEAN plus six." The latter is working to establish an East Asian Community, with the first step being the establishment of an East Asian Free Trade Area.[12] Although China's participation has met with some opposition, China's dynamic growth and increasing power in the region required a response. As ASEAN Secretary General Rodolfo Severino noted, "You can either close yourself off from China and crouch in

FIGURE 3-6

Map of ASEAN

---

[12]Bernard Gordon, "The FTA Fetish," *The Wall Street Journal* (November 17, 2005), p. A16.

TABLE 3-9 ASEAN Income and Population

	2006 GNI (in millions)	2006 Population (in thousands)	2006 GNI per Capita
Brunei	na	366	na
Cambodia	$6,990	14,197	$490
Indonesia	315,845	223,042	1,420
Laos	2,279	5,792	390
Malaysia	146,754	26,114	5,620
Myanmar	na	48,379	na
Philippines	120,190	86,264	1,390
Singapore	128,816	4,484	28,730
Thailand	193,734	63,444	3,050
Vietnam	58,506	84,108	700
Total/Mean GNI per capita	$770,756[a]	544,155	$1,561[*, a]

*Indicates mean
[a]Excluding Brunei and Myanmar
Source: Reprinted by permission of Warren Keegan Associates, Inc.

fear or engage more closely. Although some industries will get hurt, the overall impact on both China and ASEAN would be beneficial."[13]

Singapore represents a special case among the ASEAN nations. In fewer than three decades, Singapore transformed itself from a British colony to a vibrant, 240-square-mile industrial power. Singapore has an extremely efficient infrastructure—the Port of Singapore is the world's second-largest container port (Hong Kong's ranks first)—and a standard of living second in the region only to Japan. Singapore's 4.2 million citizens have played a critical role in the country's economic achievements by readily accepting the notion that "the country with the most knowledge will win" in global competition. Excellent training programs and a 93 percent literacy rate help explain why Singapore has more engineers per capita than the United States. Singapore's Economic Development Board has also actively recruited business interest in the nation. The manufacturing companies that have been attracted to Singapore read like a who's who of global marketing and include Hewlett-Packard, IBM, Philips, and Apple; in all, more than 3,000 companies have operations or investments in Singapore.

Singapore alone accounts for more than one-third of U.S. trading activities with ASEAN countries; U.S. exports to Singapore in 2007 totaled $26.2 billion, while imports totaled $18.3 billion. Singapore is closely tied with its neighbors; more than 32 percent of imports are re-exported to other Asian countries. Singapore's efforts to fashion a civil society have gained the country some notoriety; crime is nearly nonexistent, thanks to the long-ruling People's Action Party's severe treatment of criminals.

Marketing Issues in the Asia-Pacific Region

Mastering the Japanese market takes flexibility, ambition, and a long-term commitment. Japan has changed from being a closed market to one that's just tough. There are barriers in Japan in terms of attitudes as well as laws. Any organization wishing to compete in Japan must be committed to providing top-quality products and services. In many cases, products and marketing must be tailored to local tastes. Repeat visits and extended socializing with distributors are necessary to build trust. Marketers must also master the *keiretsu* system of tightly knit corporate alliances.

On the lighter side, it is worth noting that many consumer packaged goods marketed in Japan—including items that are not imported—have English, French, or German on the labels to suggest a cosmopolitan image and Western look. A Westerner may wonder, however, what the actual communication task is. For example, the label of City Original Coffee proclaims "Ease

---

[13]Amy Kazmin, "ASEAN and China Sign Deal for Free Trade Area," *Financial Times* (November 5, 2002), p. 6.

Your Bosoms. This coffee has carefully selected high quality beans and roasted by our all the experience." The intended message: Drinking our coffee provides a relaxing break and "takes a load off your chest." Casual wear and sports apparel are also emblazoned with fractured messages. Japanese retailers do not seem at all concerned that the messages are syntactically suspect. As one shopkeeper explained, the point is that a message in English, French, or German can convey hipness and help sell a product. "I don't expect people to *read* it," she said.[14]

WESTERN, CENTRAL, AND EASTERN EUROPE

The countries of Western Europe are among the most prosperous in the world. Despite the fact that there are significant differences in income between the north and the south and obvious differences in language and culture, the once-varied societies of Western Europe have grown remarkably alike. Still, enough differences remain that many observers view Western Europe in terms of three tiers. Many Britons view themselves as somewhat apart from the rest of the continent; Euro-skepticism is widespread, and the country still has problems seeing eye-to-eye with historic rivals Germany and France. Meanwhile, across the English Channel, Portugal, Italy, Greece, and Spain have struggled mightily to overcome the stigma of being called "Club Med" nations and other derogatory nicknames by their northern neighbors.[15] Still, as they enter the first decade of the twenty-first century, the governments of Western Europe are achieving hitherto unprecedented levels of economic integration.

The European Union (EU)

The origins of the European Union (EU) can be traced back to the 1958 Treaty of Rome. The six original members of the European Community (EC), as the group was called then, were Belgium, France, Holland, Italy, Luxembourg, and West Germany. In 1973, Great Britain, Denmark, and Ireland were admitted, followed by Greece in 1981, and Spain and Portugal in 1986. Beginning in 1987, the 12 countries that were EC members set about the difficult task of creating a genuine single market in goods, services, and capital; in other words, an economic union. Adopting the Single European Act by the end of 1992 was a major EC achievement; the Council of Ministers adopted more than 200 pieces of legislation and regulations to make the single market a reality.

The objective of the EU member countries is to harmonize national laws and regulations so that goods, services, people, and eventually money can flow freely across national boundaries. December 31, 1992, marked the dawn of the new economic era in Europe. Finland, Sweden, and Austria officially joined on January 1, 1995. (In November 1994, voters in Norway rejected a membership proposal.) Evidence that this is more than a free trade area, customs union, or common market is the fact that citizens of member countries are now able to freely cross borders within the union. The EU is encouraging the development of a community-wide labor pool; it is also attempting to shake up Europe's cartel mentality by handing down rules of competition patterned after U.S. antitrust law. Improvements to highway and rail networks are now being coordinated as well. Further EU enlargement is the big story in this region today. Cyprus, the Czech Republic, Estonia, Hungary, Poland, Latvia, Lithuania, Malta, the Slovak Republic, and Slovenia became full EU members on May 1, 2004. Bulgaria and Romania joined in 2007. Today, the 27 nations of the EU represent 490 million people and a combined GNI of nearly $15 trillion (see Table 3-10). The map in Figure 3-7 shows the EU member nations.

During the two decades between 1979 and 1999, the European Monetary System (EMS) was an important foundation of Western European commerce. The EMS was based on the European currency unit (ECU), a unit of account comprised of a hypothetical basket of "weighted" currencies. The ECU did not take the form of an actual currency; it existed physically in the form of checks and electronically in computers. Some companies priced their raw materials and products in ECU, thereby saving the time and cost of exchange transactions. The 1991 Maastricht Treaty set the stage for the transition from the EMS to an economic and monetary union (EMU) that includes a

---

[14]Howard W. French, "To Grandparents, English Word Trend Isn't 'Naisu,'" *The New York Times* (October 23, 2002), p. A4.
[15]Thomas Kamm, "Snobbery: The Latest Hitch in Unifying Europe," *The Wall Street Journal* (November 6, 1996), p. A17; Kyle Pope, "More Than Water Divides UK, Europe," *The Wall Street Journal* (June 30, 1995), p. A12.

TABLE 3-10 The 27 Nations of the EU—Income and Population

	2006 GNI (in millions)	2006 Population (in thousands)	2006 GNI per Capita
Austria	$329,183	8,281	$39,750
Belgium	405,419	10,541	38,460
Bulgaria	30,669	7,693	3,990
Cyprus	17,948	771	23,270
Czech Republic	131,404	10,270	12,790
Denmark	283,316	5,437	52,110
Estonia	15,302	1,342	11,400
Finland	217,803	5,266	41,360
France	2,306,714	61,257	36,560
Germany	3,032,617	82,375	36,810
Greece	305,308	11,147	27,390
Hungary	109,461	10,067	10,870
Ireland	191,315	4,268	44,830
Italy	1,882,544	58,843	31,990
Latvia	18,525	2,288	8,100
Lithuania	26,917	3,395	7,930
Luxembourg	32,904	462	71,240
Malta	6,216	406	15,310
Netherlands	703,484	16,340	43,050
Poland	312,994	38,129	8,210
Portugal	189,017	10,589	17,850
Romania	104,382	21,590	4,830
Slovak Republic	51,807	5,390	9,610
Slovenia	37,445	2,007	18,660
Spain	1,206,169	44,121	27,340
Sweden	395,411	9,084	43,530
United Kingdom	2,455,691	60,550	40,560
Total/Mean GNI per capita	$14,799,965	491,909	$30,087*

*Indicates mean

Source: Reprinted by permission of Warren Keegan Associates, Inc.

European central bank and a single European currency known as the euro. In May 1998, Austria, Belgium, Finland, Ireland, the Netherlands, France, Germany, Italy, Luxembourg, Portugal, and Spain were chosen as the 11 charter members of the *euro zone*.

The single currency era, which officially began on January 1, 1999, has brought many benefits to companies in the euro zone, such as eliminating costs associated with currency conversion and exchange rate uncertainty. The euro existed as a unit of account until January 1, 2002, when actual coins and paper money were issued and national currencies such as the French franc were withdrawn from circulation. Greece joined in 2001; Slovenia became the thirteenth member on January 1, 2007. Cyrus and Malta joined in 2008, and Slovakia adopted the euro on January 1, 2009 (see Exhibit 3-4).

Marketing Issues in the European Union

The European Commission establishes directives and sets deadlines for their implementation by legislation in individual nations. The business environment in Europe has undergone considerable transformation since 1992, with significant implications for all elements of the marketing mix. Table 3-11 summarizes some of the marketing mix issues that must be addressed in Europe's single market. For example, **harmonization** means that content and other product standards that varied

FIGURE 3-7

MAP of EU

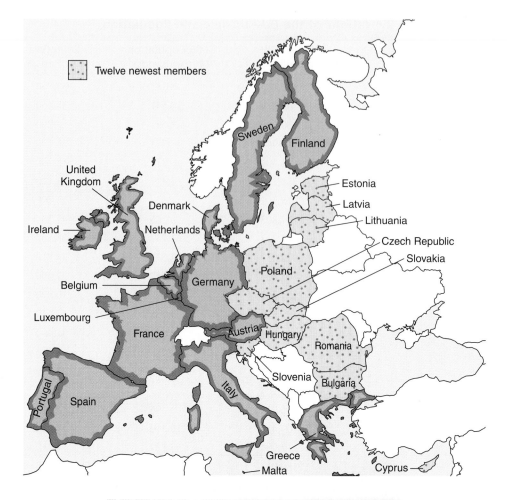

Twelve newest members

Exhibit 3-4: Fireworks exploded over the Danube as Slovakia became the sixteenth member of the euro zone on January 1, 2009. Slovakia qualified for membership because the government has kept inflation low and the budget deficit below 3 percent of GDP. Tiny Slovenia (population 2 million) joined on January 1, 2007; Cyprus and Malta joined the euro zone in 2008.
Source: Newscom.

among nations have been brought into alignment. As a result, companies may have an opportunity to reap economies by cutting back on the number of product adaptations.

Case Europe, for example, manufactures and markets farm machinery. When it introduced the Magnum tractor in Europe in 1988, it offered 17 different versions because of country regulations regarding placement of lights and brakes. Thanks to harmonization, Case offers the current model,

TABLE 3-11 Marketing Strategies in the European Union

	Changes Affecting Strategies	Threats to Marketers' Planning	Management's Strategic Options
Product Strategies	Harmonization in product standards, testing, and certification process Common patenting and branding Harmonization in packaging, labeling, and processing requirements	Incorporating changes mandated by EC directives Complying with rules of origin Local content rules Differences in marketing research	Consolidate production Seek marketing economies Shift from brand to benefit segmentation Standardize packaging and labeling where possible
Pricing Strategies	More competitive environment Lifting of restrictions on foreign products Antimonopoly measures Opening up of the public procurement market	Parallel importing Different taxation of goods Less freedom in setting transfer prices	Exploit different excise and value-added taxes Understand price elasticity of consumer demand Emphasize high-margin products Introduce low-cost brands
Promotion Strategies	Common guidelines on TV broadcasting Deregulation of national broadcasting monopolies Uniform standards for TV commercials	Restrictions on alcohol and tobacco advertising Limits on foreign TV production Differences in permissible promotional techniques	Coordinate components of promotional mix via integrated marketing communications (IMC) Exploit advantage of pan-European media Position products according to local market preferences
Distribution Strategies	Simplification of transit documents and procedures Elimination of customs formalities	Increase in distributors' margins Lack of direct marketing infrastructure Restrictions in the use of computer databases	Consolidate manufacturing facilities Centralize distribution Develop nontraditional channels (direct marketing, telemarketing)

Source: Reprinted from *Long Range Planning*, Vol. 5, G. Guido, "Implementing a Pan-European Marketing Strategy," p. 32, 1991, with permission from Elsevier.

the Magnum MX, in one version. However, because different types of implements and trailers are used in different countries, the MX is available with different kinds of hitches.[16]

The advent of the euro on January 1, 1999, brought about more changes. Direct comparability of prices in the euro zone will force companies to review pricing policies. The marketing challenge is to develop strategies to take advantage of opportunities in one of the largest, wealthiest, most stable markets in the world. Corporations must assess the extent to which they can treat the region as one entity and how to change organizational policies and structures to adapt to and take advantage of a unified Europe.

The music industry is a case in point; long before online music distribution and MP3 file swapping had become issues, the major record companies faced a number of challenges. The single market meant that, for the first time, music retailers in Europe were allowed to buy CDs and tapes from distributors throughout the EU. This practice, known as transshipment, had not been permitted prior to the single market. Now, for example, a music retailer in Germany is no longer tied to a local supplier in Germany if better prices are available elsewhere. The change means that EMI, Sony BMG, Universal Music Group, and Warner have been forced to adopt more uniform pricing policies across Europe. This, in turn, has required them to find ways to cut costs without compromising the need to respond quickly to consumer demand. One solution has been to realign distribution via joint ventures or other arrangements; previously, each company had maintained its own distribution system. In 1998, however, Warner and Sony merged their distribution facilities in the United Kingdom.[17]

---

[16]George Russel, "Marketing in the 'Old Country': The Diversity of Europe Presents Unique Challenges," *Agri Marketing* 37, no. 1 (January 1999), p. 38.

[17]Jeff Clark-Meads, "The Year in Europe: Union Members Confront Parallel Imports and Universes," *Billboard* 107 (December 23, 1995), p. YE14; Alice Rawsthorn, "Music's 'Big Five' Dip Toes in Common Distribution Pool," *Financial Times* (August 14, 1998), p. 60.

The enlargement of the EU will further impact marketing strategies. For example, food safety laws in the EU are different from those in some Central European countries. As a result, Coca-Cola had to delay launching its Powerade sports drink and other beverage products. Specifically, Polish and EU food law require the use of different ingredients. In addition to the harmonization of laws, the very size of the expanded EU offers opportunities. For example, Procter & Gamble executives foresee that, in the event of shortages in a particular country, they will be able to shift products from one market to another. A 27-nation EU also allows for more flexibility in the placement of factories. There will also be challenges. For example, South American banana growers now face 75 percent tariffs on exports to the new EU countries; previously, tariffs on bananas were virtually nonexistent. Also, because tariffs and quotas protect sugar production in the EU, both consumers and food producers such as Kraft will face rising costs.[18]

Because they are in transition, the markets of Central and Eastern Europe present interesting opportunities and challenges. Global companies view the region as an important new source of growth, and the first company to penetrate a country market often emerges as the industry leader. Exporting has been favored as a market entry mode, but direct investment in the region is on the rise; with wage rates much lower than those in Spain, Portugal, and Greece, the region offers attractive locations for low-cost manufacturing. For consumer products, distribution is a critical marketing mix element because availability is the key to sales.

One study examined the approaches utilized by 3M International, McDonald's, Philips Electronics, Henkel, Südzucker AG, and several other companies operating in Central Europe. Consumers and businesses in the region are eagerly embracing well-known global brands that were once available only to government elites and others in privileged positions. The study found a high degree of standardization of marketing program elements; in particular, the core product and brand elements were largely unchanged from those used in Western Europe. Consumer companies generally target high-end segments of the market and focus on brand image and product quality; industrial marketers concentrate on opportunities to do business with the largest firms in a given country.[19]

THE MIDDLE EAST

The Middle East includes 16 countries: Afghanistan, Bahrain, Cyprus, Egypt, Iran, Iraq, Israel, Jordan, Kuwait, Lebanon, Oman, Qatar, Saudi Arabia, Syria, the United Arab Emirates (which include Abu Dhabi and Dubai), and Yemen (see Exhibit 3-5). The majority of the population is Arab, a large percentage is Persian, and a small percentage is Jewish. Persians and most Arabs share the same religion, beliefs, and Islamic traditions, making the population 95 percent Muslim and 5 percent Christian and Jewish.

Despite this apparent homogeneity, many differences exist. Middle Eastern countries are distributed across the index of economic freedom discussed in Chapter 2; Bahrain ranks the highest in terms of freedom, at 16. Kuwait, Saudi Arabia, and the United Arab Emirates are clustered in the mid-50s. Moreover, the Middle East does not have a single societal type with a typical belief, behavior, and tradition. Each capital and major city in the Middle East has a variety of social groups that can be differentiated on the basis of religion, social class, education, and degree of wealth.

The price of oil drives business in the Middle East. Seven of the countries have high oil revenues: Bahrain, Iraq, Iran, Kuwait, Oman, Qatar, and Saudi Arabia hold significant world oil reserves. Oil revenues have widened the gap between poor and rich nations in the Middle East, and the disparities contribute to political and social instability in the area. Saudi Arabia, a monarchy with 22 million people and 25 percent of the world's known oil reserves, remains the most important market in this region.

In the past, pan-Arabism, a form of nationalism and loyalty that transcends borders and amounts to anti-Western dogma, characterized the region. During the Persian Gulf War in the early 1990s, this pan-Arabism weakened somewhat. To defeat Iraq, the Gulf Arabs and their allies broke many of their unwritten rules, including the acceptance of help from the United States, a traditional ally of Israel. However, anti-Americanism was ignited in 2003 following

[18]Scott Miller, "Trading Partners Meet New EU," *The Wall Street Journal* (May 4, 2004), p. A17.
[19]Arnold Shuh, "Global Standardization as a Success Formula for Marketing in Central Eastern Europe," *Journal of World Business* 35, no. 2 (Summer 2000), pp. 133–148.

Exhibit 3-5: Dubai is one of the seven emirates that make up the United Arab Emirates (U.A.E.). Compared to its neighbors, Dubai's economy is relatively diversified: It is an important business hub for the manufacturing, IT, and finance sectors. Dubai has also become a popular tourism destination in the region. The global economic crisis has had a major impact on Dubai. Following six years of economic growth fueled by a building boom and lavish consumer spending, real estate prices have collapsed and major construction projects have been canceled. Workers—many of whom are expatriates—are losing their jobs and visas.
Source: Kamran Jebreili/AP Wide World Photos.

President George W. Bush's decision to invade Iraq and remove Saddam Hussein from power. The repercussions of America's military action continue to be felt throughout the region. The world community is watching to see whether political and social reform can take root in Iraq.

Cooperation Council for the Arab States of the Gulf

The key regional organization is the Gulf Cooperation Council (GCC), which was established in 1981 by Bahrain, Kuwait, Oman, Qatar, Saudi Arabia, and the United Arab Emirates (Table 3-12 and Figure 3-8). These six countries hold about 45 percent of the world's known oil reserves, but production is only about 18 percent of world oil output. Ironically, Saudi Arabia and several other Middle Eastern countries post current-account deficits, largely because they must import most of the goods and services that their citizens consume. The countries are heavily dependent on oil revenues to pay for their imports; efforts toward economic diversification are underway. For example, Saudi Arabia has developed new businesses in the petrochemical, cement, and iron industries; Bahrain is expanding its banking and insurance sectors; and the United Arab Emirates is focusing on information technology, media, and telecommunications.[20]

The organization provides a means of realizing coordination, integration, and cooperation in all economic, social, and cultural affairs. Gulf finance ministers drew up an economic cooperation

TABLE 3-12 GCC Income and Population

	2006 GNI (in millions)	2006 Population (in thousands)	2006 GNI per Capita
Bahrain	$10,288	739	$14,370
Kuwait	55,255	2,599	22,470
Oman	22,994	2,546	9,070
Qatar	na	821	na
Saudi Arabia	331,041	23,679	13,980
United Arab Emirates	102,693	4,248	23,770
Total/Mean GNI per capita	$434,169[a]	34,757	$12,777[*, a]

*Indicates mean
[a]Excluding Qatar
Source: Reprinted by permission of Warren Keegan Associates, Inc.

[20]Moin A. Siddiqi, "GCC: A Force to Be Reckoned With," *Middle East* (December 2003).

FIGURE 3-8

Map of GCC Countries

agreement covering investment, petroleum, the abolition of customs duties, harmonization of banking regulations, and financial and monetary coordination. GCC committees coordinate trade development in the region, industrial strategy, agricultural policy, and uniform petroleum policies and prices. Current goals include establishing an Arab common market and increasing trade ties with Asia.

The GCC is one of three newer regional organizations. In 1989, two other organizations were established. Morocco, Algeria, Mauritania, Tunisia, and Libya banded together in the Arab Maghreb Union (AMU); Egypt, Iraq, Jordan, and North Yemen created the Arab Cooperation Council (ACC). Many Arabs see their new regional groups—the GCC, ACC, and AMU—as embryonic economic communities that will foster the development of inter-Arab trade and investment. The newer organizations are more promising than the Arab League, which consists of 21 member states and has a constitution that requires unanimous decisions.

Marketing Issues in the Middle East

Connection is a key word in conducting business in the Middle East. Those who take the time to develop relationships with key business and government figures are more likely to cut through red tape than those who do not. A predilection for bargaining is culturally ingrained, and the visiting businessperson must be prepared for some old-fashioned haggling. Establishing personal rapport, mutual trust, and respect are essentially the most important factors leading to a successful business relationship. Decisions are usually not made by correspondence or telephone. The Arab businessperson does business with the individual, not with the company. Most social customs are based on the Arab male-dominated society. Women are usually not part of the business or entertainment scene for traditional Muslim Arabs.

AFRICA

The African continent is an enormous landmass with a territory of 11.7 million square miles; the United States would fit into Africa about three and a half times. It is not really possible to treat Africa as a single economic unit. The 54 nations on the continent can be divided into three distinct areas: the Republic of South Africa, North Africa, and sub-Saharan or Black Africa, located between the Sahara in the north and the Zambezi River in the south. With 1.3 percent of the world's wealth and 11.5 percent of its population, Africa is a developing region with an average per capita income of less than $600. Many African nations are former colonies of Europe, and the EU remains the continent's most important trading partner.

The Arabs living in North Africa are differentiated politically and economically. The six northern nations are richer and more developed, and several—notably Libya, Algeria, and Egypt—benefit from large oil resources. The Middle East and North Africa are sometimes viewed as a regional entity known as "Mena"; as oil prices have soared, the International Monetary Fund (IMF) is encouraging Mena policymakers to invest the petrodollar windfall in infrastructure improvements as a way of sustaining economic growth.[21] Most governments in the area are working to reduce their reliance on oil revenues and their public aid levels. The economies of non-oil, "emerging Mena" countries, which include Jordan, Lebanon, Morocco, and Tunisia, have also performed well in recent years.

Economic Community of West African States (ECOWAS)

The Treaty of Lagos establishing the Economic Community of West African States (ECOWAS) was signed in May 1975 by 16 states with the object of promoting trade, cooperation, and self-reliance in West Africa. The members are Benin, Burkina Faso, Cape Verde, Côte d'Ivoire, The Gambia, Ghana, Guinea, Guinea-Bissau, Liberia, Mali, Mauritania, Niger, Nigeria, Senegal, Sierra Leone, and Togo (see Table 3-13 and Figure 3-9). In 1980, the member countries agreed to establish a free trade area for unprocessed agricultural products and handicrafts. Tariffs on industrial goods were also to be abolished; however, there were implementation delays. By January 1990, tariffs on 25 items manufactured in ECOWAS member states had been eliminated. The organization installed a computer system to process customs and trade statistics and to calculate the

FIGURE 3-9

Map of ECOWAS and SADC Countries

---

[21]Victoria Robson, "Window of Opportunity," *Middle East Economic Digest* 49, no. 18 (May 6, 2005), p. 6.

TABLE 3-13 ECOWAS Income and Population

	2006 GNI (in millions)	2006 Population (in thousands)	2006 GNI per Capita
Benin	$4,665	8,760	$530
Burkina Faso	6,249	14,359	440
Cape Verde	1,105	519	2,130
Côte d'Ivoire	16,578	18,914	880
The Gambia	488	1,663	290
Ghana	11,778	23,008	510
Guinea	3,713	9,181	400
Guinea-Bissau	307	1,646	190
Liberia	469	3,579	130
Mali	5,546	11,968	460
Mauritania	2,325	3,044	760
Niger	3,665	13,737	270
Nigeria	90,025	144,720	620
Senegal	9,117	12,072	760
Sierra Leone	1,353	5,743	240
Togo	2,265	6,410	350
Total/Mean GNI per capita	$159,648	279,323	$572*

*Indicates mean

Source: Reprinted by permission of Warren Keegan Associates, Inc.

loss of revenue resulting from the liberalization of inter-community trade. In June 1990, ECOWAS adopted measures that would create a single monetary zone in the region by 1994. Despite such achievements, economic development has occurred unevenly in the region. In recent years, the economies of Benin, Côte d'Ivoire, and Ghana have performed impressively, while Liberia and Sierra Leone are still experiencing political conflict and economic decline.

East African Cooperation

In 1996, the presidents of Kenya, Uganda, and Tanzania established a formal mechanism to promote free trade and economic integration. Tariff issues will be resolved and prospects for a customs union are being explored. Efforts are also underway to develop regional ties in tourism and coordinate energy projects. Although Kenya is the most developed of the three nations, Francis Muthaura, the executive secretary of the secretariat of the Commission of East African Cooperation, expressed optimism that all three will benefit: "A free market is going to generate competition and already we are seeing a lot of cross-border investment. If you have free movement of capital and goods and labor, imbalances will be sorted out in the long term."[22]

Southern African Development Community (SADC)

In 1992, the South African Development Community (SADC) superseded the South African Development Coordination Council as a mechanism by which the region's black-ruled states could promote trade, cooperation, and economic integration. The members are Angola, Botswana, Democratic Republic of Congo (formerly Zaire), Lesotho, Malawi, Mauritius, Mozambique, Namibia, South Africa, Seychelles, Swaziland, Tanzania, Zambia, and Zimbabwe (see Figure 3-9 and Table 3-14). South Africa joined the community in 1994; it represents about 75 percent of the income in the region and 86 percent of intra-regional exports. The SADC's ultimate goal is a fully developed customs union; in 2000, an 11-nation free trade area was finally established (Angola, the

---

[22]Michael Holman, "Learning from the Past," *Financial Times Survey* (November 5, 1996), p. 1.

TABLE 3-14 SADC Income and Population

	2006 GNI (in millions)	2006 Population (in thousands)	2006 GNI per Capita
Angola	$32,646	16,557	$1,970
Botswana	10,358	1,858	5,570
Democratic Republic of Congo	7,742	60,644	130
Lesotho	1,957	1,995	980
Malawi	3,143	13,571	230
Mauritius	6,812	1,253	5,430
Mozambique	6,453	20,971	310
Namibia	6,573	2,047	3,210
Seychelles	751	85	8,870
South Africa	255,389	47,391	5,390
Swaziland	2,737	1,138	2,400
Tanzania	13,404	39,459	350
Zambia	7,413	11,696	760
Zimbabwe	8,016	13,228	620
Total/Mean GNI per capita	$239,724	218,940	$1,095*

*Indicates mean

Source: Reprinted by permission of Warren Keegan Associates, Inc.

Democratic Republic of Congo, and Seychelles are not participants). South Africa has been in discussions with the EU about the formation of a free trade area; other SADC members are concerned that such an arrangement would provide European global companies with a base from which to dominate the continent. South Africa, Botswana, Lesotho, Namibia, and Swaziland also belong to the Southern African Customs Union (SACU). Another concern is war in the Congo, which threatens to have a severe impact on economic growth in the region.[23]

Marketing Issues in Africa

In 2000, U.S. President George W. Bushed signed the African Growth and Opportunities Act (AGOA) into law (see www.agoa.gov). Created with the theme of "Trade, not Aid," the law is designed to support African nations that make significant progress toward economic liberalization. Companies will find it easier to gain access to financing from the U.S. Export-Import Bank; AGOA also represents a formal step toward a U.S.-Africa free trade area. One of the Act's key provisions grants textile and apparel manufacturers in Kenya and Mauritius free access to the U.S. market up to a limit of $3.5 billion in exports each year. As Benjamin Kipkorir, Kenya's ambassador to the United States, observed a decade ago, "Every country that has industrialized, starting from England in the eighteenth century, began with textiles. We'd like to do the same thing."

Under the Agreement on Textiles and Clothing negotiated during the Uruguay Round of GATT negotiations, global textile quotas were eliminated in 2005. Nevertheless, the textile provision in AGOA is controversial. The United States imports about $50 billion in textiles and apparel each year, much of it from Asia, Latin America, and Africa. Wary legislators from textile-producing states fear job losses among their constituents.

Despite such initiatives, only about 3 percent of annual foreign direct investment goes to Africa. Still, some Persian Gulf states are creating closer ties with Africa, investing billions of dollars in key sectors such as infrastructure, agriculture, and telecommunications. For example, Dubai World, a state-owned company, is negotiating a deal in Nigeria's energy sector that could be valued at several billion dollars. Dubai also funded construction of a container terminal that opened recently in

---

[23]Tony Hawkins and Michael Holman, "Trade Tensions Send Southern Africa Regional Link-Up Reeling," *Financial Times* (September 2, 1998), p. 4.

Djibouti. The largest terminal of its kind in sub-Saharan Africa, it will be managed by DP World, a subsidiary of Dubai World. Such investments are welcome at a time when investors in Europe, stung by losses in the developed world, are cutting spending. As Djibouti President Ismail Guelleh noted, "What the Arabs are doing for us is what colonialists should have done for Africa."[24]

Summary

This chapter examines the environment for world trade, focusing on the institutions and regional cooperation agreements that affect trade patterns. The multilateral **World Trade Organization**, created in 1995 as the successor to the **General Agreement on Tariffs and Trade**, provides a forum for settling disputes among member nations and tries to set policy for world trade. The world trade environment is also characterized by **preferential trade agreements** among smaller numbers of countries on a regional and subregional basis. These agreements can be conceptualized on a continuum of increasing economic integration.

Free trade areas such as the one created by the **North American Free Trade Agreement** (NAFTA) represent the lowest level of economic integration. The purpose of a **free trade agreement** is to eliminate tariffs and quotas. **Rules of origin** are used to verify the country from which goods are shipped. A **customs union** (e.g. Mercosur) represents a further degree of integration in the form of **common external tariffs**. In a **common market** such as the Central American Integration System (SICA), restrictions on the movement of labor and capital are eased in an effort to further increase integration. An **economic union** such as the EU, the highest level of economic integration, is achieved by unification of economic policies and institutions. **Harmonization**, the coming together of varying standards and regulations, is a key characteristic of the EU.

Other important cooperation arrangements include the Association of Southeast Asian Nations (ASEAN) and the Cooperation Council for the Arab States of the Gulf (GCC). In Africa, the two main cooperation agreements are the Economic Community of West African States (ECOWAS) and the South African Development Community (SADC).

Discussion Questions

1. Explain the role of the World Trade Organization. Why has the Doha Round of trade talks stalled?
2. Describe the similarities and differences between a free trade area, a customs union, a common market, and an economic union. Give an example of each.
3. The creation of the Single Market in Europe has led to harmonization. What does this mean? How does harmonization affect a company's global marketing strategies?
4. What are the criteria for joining the euro zone?
5. Identify a regional economic organization or agreement in each of the following areas: Latin America, Asia/Pacific, Western Europe, Central Europe, the Middle East, and Africa.
6. Several key dates mentioned in the chapter are listed here. Can you identify the event associated with each? (The answers follow.)
   > January 1, 1994
   > January 1, 1995
   > January 1, 1999
   > January 1, 2002
   > May 1, 2004
   > January 1, 2009

Answers: January 1, 1994—NAFTA becomes effective; January 1, 1995—WTO becomes the successor to GATT; January 1, 1999—introduction of the euro as unit of account; January 1, 2002—euro currency goes into circulation; May 1, 2004 —EU enlargement to 25 members; January 1, 2009—Slovakia becomes the sixteenth member of the euro zone

---

[24]Margaret Coker, "Persian Gulf States Bet on Africa Despite Downturn," *The Wall Street Journal* (February 24, 2009), p. A9.

Trade deals require all parties to make concessions, and the negotiations between the United States and South Korea are a case in point. American beef exports plunged after an outbreak of BSE (mad-cow disease) in 2003. Before the mad cow scare, the Asian nation was the third-largest market for U.S. beef exports. In the spring of 2008, a few weeks after taking office, President Lee Myung-bak decided to lift a ban on U.S. beef; in return, the United States agreed to exclude South Korea's rice industry from the trade agreement.

Why? Rice represents about half of South Korea's agricultural output; a high import tariff means that local rice farmers can charge much higher prices for their crops than farmers in other rice-producing nations such as China. Even though they pay up to three times more for rice than consumers in other Asian countries, many Koreans sympathize with the farmers' concerns; domestic rice production is a source of pride and a symbol of self-sufficiency. As one activist noted, "It is a right for a country to feed its own people and a right for a country to produce its own food."

After President Lee's decision was made public, news reports suggested that mad cow disease could still be present in U.S. herds. Opposition politicians from the United Democratic Party, whose candidate was defeated in the most recent presidential election, took advantage of the negative publicity to suggest that Mr. Lee had caved in to demands by American trade negotiators. The rumors fueled a backlash that included rumors that American consumers don't eat the type of beef that is exported and that consumer products such as mascara contain beef by-products and could be tainted. In May 2008, thousands of people gathered in Seoul to protest.

For U.S. President George W. Bush, the trade pact with South Korea was an important political victory. Suspicion and doubt about trade and globalization was growing among Congressional Democrats. Proposed trade pacts with Colombia and Panama had been given a cool reception. Although the accord with South Korea was concluded in April 2007, it still had to be ratified by lawmakers in both countries. In 2009, a South Korean parliamentary committee approved the FTA; the U.S. Congress was scheduled to act on the measure in 2009 as well. However, Ford, Chrysler, and the United Auto Workers opposed the deal. Hyundai and Kia, the stars of Korea's auto industry, were enjoying great success in the United States despite the recession. Overall sales of both foreign and domestic cars were down by nearly forty percent in the U.S. market. By contrast, sales for Hyundai and Kia were only down 3.6 percent.

Meanwhile, South Korea was also pursuing a trade agreement with the EU. Agriculture was not a key issue in the negotiations; however, regulations that protect Korea's auto industry needed to be addressed. Some observers have suggested that the backlash against Korea's trade accord with the United States would spill over and affect Seoul's negotiations with Brussels. As Richard Baldwin, a professor at the Graduate Institute of International Studies in Geneva, noted, "This shows that the idea that regionalism is easy and multilateralism is hard has been massively overblown."

Case 3-1 Discussion Questions

1. When a trade deal is passed, there are winners and losers. Who stands to win if the U.S.-Korea free trade agreement is ratified? Who stands to lose?

2. Trade issues were central to the 2008 U.S. presidential campaign. In a telephone survey conducted in April 2008, 48 percent of respondents indicated that free trade agreements had a negative impact on the United States. Thirty-five percent said FTAs were a "good thing"; 17 percent answered, "Don't know."

   Then-Senator Barack Obama, the Democratic nominee, pledged that, as president, he would renegotiate the North American Free Trade Agreement. He called for enforceable labor and environmental standards that were not included in the original agreement. Senator Obama also opposed the proposed new FTA with Colombia. In one campaign stop, Senator Obama said, "I think we should use the hammer of a potential opt-out as leverage to ensure that we actually get labor and environmental standards enforced."

   Greg Somers, a Canadian lawyer specializing in international trade, takes exception with Senator Obama's position. "What [Obama} is proposing would be far too intrusive on the sovereignty of the laws of a country. That's not the job of a trade deal," he said. Senator John McCain, Obama's Republican opponent, had this response: "You know what that message sends? That no agreement is sacred if someone declares that as president of the United States they would unilaterally renegotiate it."[25]

   Which candidate's views on trade correspond most closely to yours?

Sources: Chris Woodyard, "Cars Hold Up S. Korean Trade Deal," *USA Today* (May 13, 2009), p. 3B; Alan Beattie, "Hard Bargains," *Financial Times* (June 17, 2008), p. 9; Evan Ramstad, "Korea's Beef with the U.S.," *The Wall Street Journal* (June 6, 2008), p. A11; Evan Ramstad and Julie Yang, "South Korea Answers Uproar on U.S. Beef," *The Wall Street Journal* (May 3/4, 2008), p. A8; Choe Sang-hun, "U.S. and South Korea Agree to Sweeping Trade Deal," *The New York Times* (April 3, 2007), pp. C1, C8; Evan Ramstad, "Korea Trade Focus: Cars," *The Wall Street Journal* (March 29, 2007), p. A8; Evan Ramstad, "South Korea Ready to Open Up," *The Wall Street Journal* (March 28, 2007), p. A6.

[25]Amy Chozick, "Trade Stance Weighs on Obama's Plan to Strengthen Foreign Ties," *The Wall Street Journal* (July 9, 2008), p. A6.

U.A.E. is a new nation, founded in 1971. Though located in the harsh desert land, it is full of unique wildlife, and the focus in recent years for this country known for its oil and unique construction projects is now slowly turning to conservation and sustainability. The founder and ruler of the nation, the late Sheikh Zayed bin Sultan Al Nahyan, established a unique wildlife sanctuary consisting of over 54 miles in 1971. This legacy continues. Near Abu Dhabi, the capital of U.A.E., is an archipelago of 200 islands. Since 2001, it forms part of the Marawah Marine Biosphere Reserve, the largest marine protected area in the country, with a territory of more than 2,700 square miles. This is the first marine biosphere reserve recognized by UNESCO in the region.

Among the unique islands is the Bu Tinah Island and its shoals, a contender in the search for the new seven natural wonders of the world by the New7Wonders Foundation, a nonprofit Swiss-based organization. It was one of 77 nominees, voted for out of 261 contestants in the first round, and it has made it to the final 28. For the next two years, the Environment Agency–Abu Dhabi will be educating the general public about Bu Tinah. Besides educating about conservation, research, and environmental sustainability in this country's fragile marine environment, it is hoped that Bu Tinah becomes one of the final seven natural wonders. What makes Bu Tinah so unique and worthy of conservation is the fact it is not accessible to all visitors except those with special permits, such as particular scientists. It is a low-lying shoal with the most elevated point within the archipelago no higher than 9 feet above sea level. Bu Tinah is a feeding and breeding ground for the

In 2009 the Bu Tinah Shoals became one of the contenders in the New Seven Wonders of Nature, a global initiative fronted by the New Open World Corporation. The natural wonder found itself in great company with the Amazon, the Dead Sea, the Grand Canyon, Maldives, and Galapagos Islands.

Source: © electroshot - Fotolia.com.

second largest population of dugongs, a highly endangered species according to the International Union for Conservation of Nature. Bu Tinah is also unique because of the corals growing there. These corals are growing in extreme harsh conditions as the Gulf waters are among the most saline in the world with temperatures reaching 95°F in summer. Most corals grow in cooler water (73–82°F). This gives researchers around the world an insight about methods to tackle global warming.

Another reason why this area is in need of conservation is that the sea grass and mangroves, which support a multitude of marine life, and the dugong population is easily destroyed by human interaction. The dugong, a gentle herbivore, is probably the source of old mermaid stories. It eats up to 132 pounds of sea grass a day. There are over 600 dugongs in that region. This means conservation is dependent on limiting visitors and any sort of human disturbance or interference.

In fact, dugongs have been historically associated with U.A.E. In Akab Island (Umm al Qaywayn, U.A.E.) a site of dugong bones have been found that date back to more than 6,000 years. The government has also taken proactive action protecting dugongs for over 20 years by a Law of the President of the U.A.E. (Federal Law No. 23) and Article 28/2000 Amiri Decree, and through recent initiatives like banning drift net fishing. Dugongs can hold their breath for 8 minutes, therefore, abandoned fishing nets are a threat to these creatures! The oil spills after the Iraq war have taken its toll on the sea grass, which affects the dugong population. Because the waters are so shallow, it will take 5 years for the waters of the gulf to be flushed and hence pollutants do not easily disperse. Protection of Bu Tinah Shoals needs international support.

U.A.E. is expecting around 11 million visitors in 2010. To encourage preservation of this jewel of nature in a highly misunderstood international area has its challenges. One method is surrogate tourism. The nearby Sir Bani Yas Island is an option for helping educate the public about conservation and protection of Bu Tinah. Sir Bani Yas was one of the homes of the late Sheikh Zayed and now opened to the public in the form of a desert resort managed by Anantara. It is one of eight islands that will be open to the public. There is an Arabian wildlife sanctuary with species like the Arabian onyx. It has one of the world's largest salt-dome hilltops created between 5 and 10 million years ago. An Outward Bound–type camp is being developed by 2010 to facilitate nonprofit adventure education. New technologies that will explore alternate energies are being explored by Masdar, which is building the world's first carbon-neutral city. To date, over 17,000 visitors have taken part in mangrove plantation since its opening in October 2008. Every visitor who leaves a note gets a mangrove planted in remembrance of their visit. It is the Abu Dhabi Tourism Authority, TDIC—the master developer of this project—that must balance tourism numbers with conservation efforts. It is hoped that through this and the New7Wonders campaign that this rare jewel of the Gulf, Bu Tinah, will get the spotlight and the support it needs for its conservation.

Discussion Questions

1. What are some of the challenges in maintaining conservation education especially considering the New7Wonders competition?
2. What are some strategies you can suggest to (1) protect the reserve from too much commercialization, (2) maintain the good work they are doing, and (3) gain international support?

Sources: This case was prepared by Dr. Melodena Stephens Balakrishnan, Associate Professor, University of Wollongong in Dubai, Dubai. *Additional Sources:* Desert Island Resorts, http://desertislands.anantaracom; "Bu Tinah—Wonder in the Making," www.uaeinteract.com/docs/Bu_Tinah,_a_%E2%80%98wonder%E2%80%99_in_the_making/36593.htm. Accessed July 5, 2009; "Bu Tinah Islands," www.visitabudhabi.ae/en/what.to.do/islands.aspx; Ahmed AbdulRehman Al Janahi, "Dugong's Waning Populace in Arabian Gulf: A Chronicle," www.uae.gov.ae/uaeagricent/fisheries/Dugong_e.stm; A. Preen, *Technical Report, Dugongs, Volume 1: The Status and Conservation of Dugongs in the Arabian Region,* MEPA Coastal and Marine Management Series, Saudi Arabia, 1989; A. Preen, "Observations of Mating Behaviour in Dugongs (*Dugong dugon*)," *Marine Mammal Science* 5, no. 4 (1989): 382–387. E. Landais, "Excavation Uncovers Ritual Site," *Gulf News* (November 6, 2009), http://gulfnews.com/news/gulf/uae/general/excavation-uncovers-ritual-site-1.523925; WCMC (World Conservation Monitoring Centre), "Protected Areas Programme," www.wcmc.org.uk/protected_areas/data/wh/ald abra.html. Accessed 2009; "U.A.E. to Attract 11.2 million tourists by 2010," *Travel Daily News* (2008), www.traveldailynews.com/pages/show_page/26920-U.A.E.-to-attract-112-million-tourists-by-2010; Desert Islands-Explore More, www.desertislands.com/EN. Accessed 2009.

Social and Cultural Environments

Case 4-1
Disney Learns to "Act Local" on the Global Stage

The Walt Disney Company, home to Mickey Mouse, Donald Duck, and other iconic characters, has a stellar reputation in many parts of the world for its family-friendly entertainment offerings. The company's parks and resorts division operates theme parks in five global locations, including a recent $1.8 billion park in Hong Kong. Disney's fabled studio entertainment unit has an illustrious history in both animation and live-action features. *The Lion King*, released in 1994, is the highest grossing animated film of all time, selling more than $300 million worth of tickets around the world. More recently, Disney has enjoyed massive hits with live-action features.

These include *The Pirates of the Caribbean* and its sequels as well as classic American fare such as the TV show *High School Musical*.

However, despite high worldwide awareness levels of the Disney brand, as of 2006, only 25 percent of the company's revenues came from outside the United States. Historically, the Disney team has created products at its headquarters in Burbank, California, and then exported them to the rest of the world. Now, as the company targets China, India, South Korea, and other emerging markets, it is departing from its "one size fits all" approach. One factor driving the strategy change:

Exhibit 4-1: Hong Kong Disneyland opened its gates for the first time on September 12, 2005. China's central government recently approved a second Disney resort/theme park location. The new project, in the Pudong district of Shanghai, will carry a price tag of about $3.5 billion.
Source: Alamy Limited.

disappointing first-year attendance for the latest Disney theme park in Hong Kong. Despite planners' attempts to adapt to Chinese culture, the first-year visitor count fell short of the target figure of 5.6 million people. This prompted company executives to step up efforts to educate the Chinese about Mickey Mouse, Donald Duck, and other Disney characters. As Bill Ernest, managing director, told the *Financial Times*, "If you haven't grown up with the brand, the stories, or the theme, you are not quite sure what you are walking into" (see Exhibit 4-1).

The changes underway at the Walt Disney Company illustrate how differences in the social and cultural environments impact marketing opportunities and dynamics around the globe. This chapter focuses on the social and cultural forces that shape and affect individual, group, and corporate behavior in the marketplace. We start with a general discussion of the basic aspects of culture and society and the emergence of a twenty-first century global consumer culture. Next, several useful conceptual frameworks for understanding culture are presented. These include Hall's high- and low-context culture concept, Maslow's hierarchy, Hofstede's cultural typology, the self-reference criterion, and diffusion theory. The chapter includes specific examples of the impact of culture and society on the marketing of both consumer and industrial products. Clearly, the cultural environment of global marketing has a big impact on Disney. At the end of Chapter 4, you will find more about Disney's global marketing strategy in Case 4-1. The discussion questions at the end of the case will give you a chance to reflect further on "lessons learned."

SOCIETY, CULTURE, AND GLOBAL CONSUMER CULTURE

Both differences and similarities characterize the world's cultures, meaning that the task of the global marketer is twofold. First, marketers must study and understand the country cultures in which they will be doing business. Second, they must incorporate this understanding into the marketing planning process. In some instances, strategies and marketing programs will have to be adapted; however, marketers should also take advantage of shared cultural characteristics and avoid unneeded and costly adaptations of the marketing mix.

Any systematic study of a new geographic market requires a combination of tough-mindedness and generosity. While marketers should be secure in their own convictions and traditions, generosity is required to appreciate the integrity and value of other ways of life and points of view. People must, in other words, overcome the prejudices that are a natural result of the human tendency toward ethnocentricity. Although "culture shock" is a normal human reaction to the new and unknown, successful global marketers strive to comprehend human experience from the local point of view. One reason cultural factors challenge global marketers is that many of them are hidden from view. Because culture is a learned behavior passed on from generation to generation, it can be difficult for the inexperienced or untrained outsider to fathom. As they endeavor to understand cultural factors, outsiders gradually become insiders and develop cultural empathy. There are many different paths to the same goals in life. The global marketer understands this and rejoices in life's rich diversity.

Anthropologists and sociologists have offered scores of different definitions of culture. As a starting point, **culture** can be defined as "ways of living, built up by a group of human beings, that are transmitted from one generation to another." A culture acts out its ways of living in the context of *social institutions*, including family, educational, religious, governmental, and business institutions. Those institutions, in turn, function to reinforce cultural norms. Culture includes both conscious and unconscious values, ideas, attitudes, and symbols that shape human behavior and that are transmitted from one generation to the next. Organizational anthropologist Geert Hofstede defines *culture* as "the collective programming of the mind that distinguishes the members of one category of people from those of another."[1] A particular "category of people" may constitute a nation, an ethnic group, a gender group, an organization, a family, or some other unit.

Some anthropologists and sociologists divide cultural elements into two broad categories: material culture and nonmaterial culture. The former is sometimes referred to as the *physical component* or *physical culture* and includes physical objects and artifacts created by humans such as clothing and tools. Nonmaterial culture (also known as *subjective* or *abstract culture*) includes intangibles such as religion, perceptions, attitudes, beliefs, and values. There is general agreement that the material and nonmaterial elements of culture are interrelated and interactive. Cultural anthropologist George P. Murdock studied material and nonmaterial culture and identified dozens of "cultural universals," including athletic sports, body adornment, cooking, courtship, dancing, decorative art, education, ethics, etiquette, family feasting, food taboos, language, marriage, mealtime, medicine, mourning, music, property rights, religious rituals, residence rules, status differentiation, and trade.[2]

It is against this background of traditional definitions that global marketers should understand a worldwide sociocultural phenomenon of the early twenty-first century.[3] It has been argued that consumption has become the hallmark of postmodern society. As cultural information and imagery flow freely across borders via satellite TV, the Internet, and similar communication channels, new global consumer cultures are emerging. Persons who identify with these cultures share meaningful sets of consumption-related symbols. Some of these cultures are associated with specific product categories; marketers speak of "fast-food culture," "credit card culture," "pub culture," "coffee culture," and so on. This cosmopolitan culture, which is comprised of various segments, owes its existence in large part to a wired world in which there is increasing interconnectedness of various local cultures. It can be exploited by global consumer culture positioning (GCCP), a marketing tool that will be explained in more detail in Chapter 7. In particular, marketers can use advertising to communicate the notion that people everywhere consume a particular brand or to appeal to human universals.

Attitudes, Beliefs, and Values

If we accept Hofstede's notion of culture as "the collective programming of the mind," then it makes sense to learn about culture by studying the attitudes, beliefs, and values shared by a specific group of people. An **attitude** is a learned tendency to respond in a consistent way to a given object or entity. Attitudes are clusters of interrelated beliefs. A **belief** is an organized pattern of knowledge that an individual holds to be true about the world. Attitudes and beliefs, in turn, are closely related to values. A **value** can be defined as an enduring belief or feeling that a specific mode of conduct is personally or socially preferable to another mode of conduct.[4] In the view of Hofstede and others, values represent the deepest level of a culture and are present in the majority of the members of a particular culture.

Some specific examples will allow us to illustrate these definitions by comparing and contrasting attitudes, beliefs, and values. The Japanese, for example, strive to achieve cooperation, consensus, self-denial, and harmony. Because these all represent feelings about modes of conduct, they are *values.* Japan's monocultural society reflects the *belief* among the Japanese that they are unique in the world. Many Japanese, especially young people, also believe that the West is the source of important fashion trends. As a result, many Japanese share a favorable *attitude* toward American brands. Within any large, dominant cultural group, there are likely to be **subcultures**; that is, smaller groups of people with their own shared subset of attitudes,

[1]Geert Hofstede and Michael Harris Bond, "The Confucius Connection: From Cultural Roots to Economic Growth," *Organizational Dynamics* (Spring 1988), p. 5.
[2]George P. Murdock, "The Common Denominator of Culture," in *The Science of Man in the World Crisis*, Ralph Linton, ed. (New York: Columbia University Press, 1945), p. 145.
[3]The following discussion is adapted from Dana L. Alden, Jan-Benedict Steenkamp, and Rajeev Batra, "Brand Positioning through Advertising in Asia, North America, and Europe: The Role of Global Consumer Culture," *Journal of Marketing* 63, no. 1 (January 1999), pp. 75–87.
[4]Milton Rokeach, *Beliefs, Attitudes, and Values* (San Francisco: Jossey-Bass, 1968), p. 160.

beliefs, and values. Values, attitudes, and beliefs can also be surveyed at the level of any "category of people" that is embedded within a broad culture. For example, if you are a vegetarian, then eating meat represents a mode of conduct that you and others who share your views avoid. Subcultures often represent attractive niche marketing opportunities.

Religion

Religion is one important source of a society's beliefs, attitudes, and values. The world's major religions include Buddhism, Hinduism, Islam, Judaism, and Christianity; the latter is comprised of Roman Catholicism and numerous Protestant denominations. Examples abound of religious tenets, practices, holidays, and history directly impacting the way people of different faiths react to global marketing activities. For example, Hindus do not eat beef, which means that McDonald's does not serve hamburgers in India (see Case 1-2). In Muslim countries, Yum Brands has successfully promoted KFC in conjunction with religious observances (see Exhibit 4-2).

In the aftermath of the September 2001 terror attacks in New York and Washington, D.C., and the subsequent American military actions in the Middle East, some Muslims have tapped into anti-American sentiment by urging a boycott of American brands. One entrepreneur, Tunisian-born Tawfik Mathlouthi, launched a soft drink brand, Mecca-Cola, as an alternative to Coca-Cola for Muslims living in the United Kingdom and France. The brand's name is both an intentional reference to the holy city of Islam as well as an ironic swipe at Coca-Cola, which Mathlouthi calls "the Mecca of capitalism." London's *Sunday Times* called Mecca-Cola "the drink now seen as politically preferable to Pepsi or Coke."[5] In 2003, Qibla Cola (the name comes from an Arabic word for "direction") was launched in the United Kingdom (see Exhibit 4-3). Founder Zahida Parveen hopes to reach a broader market than Mecca-Cola by positioning the brand "for any consumer with a conscience, irrespective of ethnicity or religion."[6]

Religious issues have also been at the heart of a dispute about whether references to God and Christianity should be included in a new European constitution that will be adopted now that the EU has expanded its membership from 15 to 27 countries. On one side of the dispute are Europe's Catholic countries, including Ireland, Spain, Italy, and Poland. As Italy's deputy prime minister said, "The Italian government believes that [Europe's] common religious heritage should be explicitly referred to with the values of Judeo-Christian tradition." By contrast, the official position in

Exhibit 4-2: Some global companies have successfully capitalized on the love-hate relationship between Muslims and the United States. In the Islamic world, Ramadan is a month of fasting that begins at the end of October. In Indonesia, home to the world's largest Muslim population, KFC uses Ramadan-themed outdoor advertising to encourage Indonesians to come to the restaurants at buka puasa, the end of each day's fast. Business at KFC Indonesia's 200 units is up as much as 20 percent during Ramadan. *Source:* Rachel Donnan.

---

[5]Bill Britt, "Upstart Cola Taps Anti-War Vibe," *Advertising Age* (February 24, 2003), p. 1. See also Digby Lidstone, "Pop Idols," *Middle East Economic Digest* (August 22, 2003), p. 4.
[6]Meg Carter, "New Colas Wage Battle for Hearts and Minds," *Financial Times* (January 8, 2004), p. 9.

Exhibit 4-3: Qibla Cola was launched in 2003; company executives hope to position Qibla as an alternative to mainstream American brands. As one executive noted, "We want to show that you can develop a brand that is global, ethical, quality, and commercially viable. We are not trying to do so by being anti-American but by being anti-injustice." Currently, Qibla Cola is available in several countries, including the United Kingdom, the Netherlands, Norway, Canada, and Pakistan.
Source: Hugo Philpott/Getty Images.

France and Belgium is one of church–state separation. According to this view, religion has no place in the founding documents of the enlarged EU. In addition, Muslims constitute a politically active minority in France and other countries; Turkey is predominately Muslim. Representatives of Europe's Muslim population are resisting any reference to Christianity in the new constitution.[7]

Aesthetics

Within every culture, there is an overall sense of what is beautiful and what is not beautiful, what represents good taste as opposed to tastelessness or even obscenity, and so on. Such considerations are matters of **aesthetics.** Global marketers must understand the importance of *visual aesthetics* embodied in the color or shape of a product, label, or package. Likewise, different parts of the world perceive *aesthetic styles*—various degrees of complexity, for example— differently. Aesthetic elements that are attractive, appealing, and in good taste in one country may be perceived differently in another. In some cases, a standardized color can be used in all countries; examples include the distinctive yellow color on Caterpillar's earth-moving equipment and its licensed outdoor gear and the red chevron on a pack of Marlboro cigarettes. A number of companies seem to be experiencing a case of the "blues," as evidenced by names such as Bluetooth, Blue Moon, and JetBlue Airways; likewise, Skyy vodka is packaged in a distinctive blue bottle.[8]

Because color perceptions can vary among cultures, adaptation to local preferences may be required. Such perceptions should be taken into account when making decisions about product packaging and other brand-related communications. In highly competitive markets, inappropriate or unattractive product packaging may put a company or brand at a disadvantage. New color schemes may also be mandated by a changing competitive environment. For example, after Walmart entered the German market in the 1990s, local retailer Metro AG added blue, white, and yellow to the logo of its Real hypermarket stores.

There is nothing inherently "good" or "bad" about any color of the spectrum; all associations and perceptions regarding color arise from culture. Red is a popular color in most parts of the world; besides being the color of blood, in many countries red also is tied to centuries-old traditions of viticulture and winemaking. One recent study of perceptions in eight

[7]Richard Bernstein, "Continent Wrings Its Hands Over Proclaiming Its Faith, "*The New York Times* (November 12, 2003), p. A4. See also Brandon Mitchener, "Birth of a Nation? As Europe Unites, Religion, Defense Still Stand in Way," *The Wall Street Journal* (July 11, 2003), pp. A1, A6.
[8]Susan Carey, "More U.S. Companies Are Blue, and It's Not Just the Stock Market," *The Wall Street Journal* (August 30, 2001), pp. A1, A2.

STRATEGIC DECISION MAKING IN GLOBAL MARKETING
Uproar over Danish Cartoons

In 2005, while writing a children's book on the life of the prophet Mohammed, Danish author Kare Bluitgen searched unsuccessfully for an illustrator. The problem: Many of the world's Muslims believe that it is blasphemy to depict images of the prophet. Denmark's conservative *Jyllands-Posten* newspaper picked up the story; concerned that this was a case of self-censorship, the paper's cultural editor challenged dozens of well-known illustrators to "draw Mohammed the way that they see him." In September, *Jyllands-Posten* printed submissions from 12 illustrators in conjunction with articles on freedom of speech; one of the images depicted Mohammed with a bomb in his turban.

A few months later, the cartoons were reprinted in newspapers in France, Germany, Switzerland, and elsewhere. Reaction was swift: Protests erupted in Indonesia and other countries with large Muslim populations. The Danish and Norwegian missions in Damascus were set on fire. Some Arab governments supported boycotts of Danish goods and withdrew their ambassadors from Copenhagen (see Exhibit 4-4). Meanwhile, the Danish government called *its* ambassadors back to Copenhagen, and Danish export marketers such as Arla Foods and the LEGO Group sought to deal with a growing consumer backlash in the Middle East. In the words of one employee at Saudi Arabia's airport, "Anything to do with Denmark is now history in the [Saudi] kingdom. Shops, businesses, imports. It's over." As Finn Hansen, head of

international operations at Arla, noted, "This can happen to anyone, anywhere, at anytime if you don't understand other people's cultures."

The controversy was revived in 2008 when three men were arrested and charged with plotting to murder one of the cartoonists. Following the arrests, several newspapers printed the cartoons a second time. This action provoked another round of diplomatic protests in the Muslim world. As Kurt Westergaard, the cartoonist targeted by the would-be killers, noted, "Cartoons always concentrate and simplify an idea and allow a quick impression that arouses some strong feeling." Westergaard's Danish heritage also figures in. "In Denmark there is a culture of radicalism, a skepticism toward authority and religion. It's part of our national character," Westergaard said.

Sources: Michael Kimmelman, "Outrage at Cartoons Still Tests the Danes," *The New York Times* (March 20, 2008), p. B1; David Ibison, "We Have to Think Differently," *Financial Times* (October 2, 2006), p. 7; Lydia Polgreen, "Nigeria Counts 100 Deaths over Danish Caricatures," *The New York Times* (February 24, 2006), p. A8; Andres Higgins, "Danish Businesses Struggle with Big Dilemma," *The Wall Street Journal* (February 10, 2006), p. A4; "The Cartoons That Shook the World," *The Wall Street Journal* (February 11/12, 2006), p. A7; Michael Kimmelman, "A Startling New Lesson in the Power of Imagery," *The New York Times* (February 8, 2006), p. B1; Bertrand Benoit, "Muslim Anger Spreads Round the World," *Financial Times* (February 4/5, 2006), p. 2.

Exhibit 4-4: In 2006, protesters across the Muslim world demonstrated against the publication of cartoon images of Muhammed in a Danish newspaper. Many supermarkets in Cairo, the largest city in the Arab world, removed Danish products from their shelves.
Source: Khaled Desouki/Getty Images, Inc. AFP.

EMERGING MARKETS BRIEFING BOOK

Marketing Barbie in the Middle East

As Barbie, the iconic doll, celebrated the "Big Five-O" in 2009, she faced some problems familiar to many aging baby boomers. Young girls are spending more time with their cell phones and digital music players. Barbie's fashion credentials had also come into question; she was not as trendy and culturally relevant as she had once been. Barbie's relevance was also being challenged in key global markets. For example, in the Middle East, the hottest-selling doll line, Fulla, is associated with Islamic values such as modesty and respect. Fortunately, there was some good news for Barbie's handlers: Mattel won a lawsuit against a competitor that had marketed the edgier Bratz doll line. It was against this background that Mattel celebrated Barbie's fiftieth anniversary by relaunching the doll amid a worldwide advertising and public relations blitz.

Since being introduced in the Middle East, Barbie has faced opposition on political, religious, and cultural grounds. Parents and religious leaders object to the cultural values that Barbie and Ken portray. Writing in the *Cairo Journal*, Douglas Jehl noted, "To put it plainly, the plastic icon of Western girlhood is seen in the Middle East, where modesty matters, as something of a tramp."

In Egypt and Iran, Barbie faces competition from several new doll brands aimed at providing an Islamic alternative to Barbie. As one Arab toy seller noted, "I think that Barbie is more harmful than an American missile." Barbie's challengers include demure-looking dolls such as Laila, who was designed according to recommendations of participants at the Arab League children's celebrations in 1998. Laila wears simple contemporary clothes such as a short-sleeve blouse and skirt and traditional Arab costumes. Abala Ibrahim, director of the Arab League's Department of Childhood, believes "there is a cultural gap when an Arab girl

plays with a doll like Barbie . . . the average Arab girl's reality is different from Barbie's with her swimming pool, Cadillac, blond hair and boyfriend Ken."

Despite the cultural differences and a price equal to seven times the average monthly salary, Barbie has been highly successful in Iran. It remains to be seen whether Barbie, who is "forbidden by Islam," will struggle against new local competitors Sara and Dara, which have been created expressly to compete against Barbie. The dolls feature traditional clothing and headscarves and are available with family members, thus reinforcing the importance of family for Iranian children. The dolls were launched in 2002 at prices about one-third of Barbie's.

Neither Laila nor Sara has achieved the popularity of Fulla, a doll named after the fragrance of the jasmine plant. Syria-based NewBoy Design Studio introduced Fulla in 2003. Packaged in a shiny pink box, Fulla dolls are clothed in modest "outdoor fashions." These include the hijab, or traditional headscarf, and a long gown known as an abaya; a pink prayer rug is included with each doll. As Fawaz Abidin, Fulla brand manager for NewBoy, explained, "This isn't just about putting the hijab on a Barbie doll. You have to create a character that parents and children will want to relate to. Our advertising is full of positive messages about Fulla's character. She's honest, loving, and caring, and she respects her father and mother."

Sources: Edward Iwata, "How Barbie Is Making Business a Little Better," *USA Today* (March 27, 2006), pp. 1B, 2B; Michael Barbaro, "Breaking Up Was Hard to Do," *The New York Times* (February 9, 2006), pp. C1, C6; Souheila Al-Jadda, "Move over, Barbie," *USA Today* (December 14, 2005), p. 23A.

---

countries found that red is associated with "active," "hot," and "vibrant"; in most countries studied, it also conveys meanings such as "emotional" and "sharp."[9] As such, red has positive connotations in many societies. However, red is poorly received in some African countries. Blue, because of its associations with sky and water, has an elemental connotation with undertones of dependability, constancy, and eternity. White connotes purity and cleanliness in the West, but it is associated with death in parts of Asia. In the Middle East, purple is associated with death. Another research team concluded that gray connotes inexpensive in China and Japan, while it is associated with high quality and expensive in the United States. The researchers also found that the Chinese associated brown with soft drink labels and associated the color with good tasting; South Korean and Japanese consumers associated yellow with soft drinks and good tasting. For Americans, the color red has those associations.[10]

Music is an aesthetic component of all cultures, accepted as a form of artistic expression and source of entertainment. In one sense, music represents a "transculture" that is not identified with any particular nation. For example, rhythm, or movement through time, is a universal aspect of music. However, music is also characterized by considerable stylistic variation with regional or country specific associations. For example, bossa nova rhythms are associated with Argentina, samba with Brazil, salsa with Cuba, reggae with Jamaica, merengue with the Dominican Republic, and blues, driving rock rhythms, hip hop, and rap with the United States. Sociologists

---

[9]Thomas J. Madden, Kelly Hewett, and Martin S. Roth, "Managing Images in Different Cultures: A Cross-National Study of Color Meanings and Preferences," *Journal of International Marketing* 8, no. 4 (2000), p. 98.

[10]Laurence E. Jacobs, Charles Keown, Reginald Worthley, and Kyung-I Ghymn, "Cross-Cultural Colour Comparisons: Global Marketers Beware!" *International Marketing Review* 8, no. 3 (1991), pp. 21–30.

Exhibit 4-5: The March 2006 inaugural issue of *Rolling Stone*'s Chinese edition featured local rocker Cui Jian on the cover. Chinese authorities responded immediately. Mr. Cui is famous for penning an anthem to Chinese students participating in the 1989 Tiananmen Square democracy protests. Moreover, Beijing objected to the large *Rolling Stone* masthead and disapproved of the U.S. magazine's choice of *Audiovisual World* as its local partner. In October 2006, *Rolling Stone* reappeared with a new look and a new publishing partner.
Source: Frederic J. Brown/Getty Images, Inc. AFP.

have noted that national identity derives in part from a country's indigenous or popular music; a unique music style can "represent the uniqueness of the cultural entity and of the community."[11]

Music provides an interesting example of the "think global, act local" theme of this book. Musicians in different countries draw from, absorb, adapt, and synthesize transcultural music influences, as well as country-specific ones, as they create hybrid styles such as Polish reggae or Italian hip hop. Motti Regev describes this paradox as follows:

> Producers of and listeners to these types of music feel, at one and the same time, participants in a specific contemporary, global-universal form of expression *and* innovators of local, national, ethnic, and other identities. A cultural form associated with American culture and with the powerful commercial interests of the international music industry is being used in order to construct a sense of local difference and authenticity.[12]

Because music plays an important role in advertising, marketers must understand what style is appropriate in a given national market. Although background music can be used effectively in broadcast commercials, the type of music appropriate for a commercial in one part of the world may not be acceptable or effective in another part. Government restrictions must also be taken into account. In China, authorities have the power to dictate which songs can be marketed and performed, as the Rolling Stones can attest. Rock music journalism must also conform to state mandates, as the publisher of *Rolling Stone* magazine learned (see Exhibit 4-5).

Dietary Preferences

Cultural influences are also quite apparent in food preparation and consumption patterns and habits. Need proof? Consider the following:

- Domino's Pizza, the world's largest pizza-delivery company, pulled out of Italy because Italians perceived its product to be "too American." In particular, the tomato sauce was too bold and the toppings were too heavy.
- To successfully launch the Subway chain in India, it was necessary to educate consumers about the benefits of the company's sandwiches. Why? Because Indians do not normally consume bread.[13]

---

[11]Martin Stokes, *Ethnicity, Identity, and Music: The Musical Construction of Place* (Oxford: Berg, 1994).
[12]Motti Regev, "Rock Aesthetics and Musics of the World," *Theory, Culture & Society* 14, no. 3 (August 1997), pp. 125–142.
[13]Richard Gibson, "Foreign Flavors," *The Wall Street Journal* (September 25, 2006), p. R8.

These examples underscore the fact that a solid understanding of food-related cultural preferences is important for any company that markets food or beverage products globally. Titoo Ahluwalia, chairman of a market research firm in Bombay, points out that local companies can also leverage superior cultural understanding to compete effectively with large foreign firms. He says, "Indian companies have an advantage when they are drawing from tradition. When it comes to food, drink, and medicine, you have to be culturally sensitive."[14] Companies that lack such sensitivity are bound to make marketing mistakes. When Subway expanded into India, the company chose two U.S.-educated Indian brothers to help open stores and supervise operations.

While some food preferences remain deeply embedded in culture, there is plenty of evidence that global dietary preferences are converging. For example, "fast food" is gaining increased acceptance around the world. There are several explanations. Heads of families in many countries are pressed for time and are disinclined to prepare home-cooked meals. Also, young people are experimenting with different foods, and the global tourism boom has exposed travelers to pizza, pasta, and other ethnic foods. Shorter lunch hours and tighter budgets are forcing workers to find a place to grab a quick, cheap bite before returning to work.[15] As cultural differences become less relevant, such convenience products will be purchased in any country when consumer disposable income is high enough.

As we have seen, such processes can provoke a nationalist backlash. To counteract the exposure of its young citizens to *le Big Mac* and other American-style fast foods, the French National Council of Culinary Arts designed a course on French cuisine and "good taste" for elementary school students. The director of the council, Alexandre Lazareff, recently published *The French Culinary Exception*. Lazareff warns that France's vaunted *haute cuisine* is under attack by the globalization of taste. More generally, Lazareff is speaking out against perceived challenges to France's culinary identity and way of life. His concerns are real enough; while McDonald's continues to open new restaurants in France (today there are more than 1100 outlets) the number of traditional bistros has declined steadily over the past several years. Despite McDonald's success, the French have coined a new buzzword, *le fooding*, to express the notion that the nation's passion for food goes beyond mere gastronomy:

> To eat with feeling in France is to eat with your head and your spirit, with your nose, your eyes, and your ears, not simply your palate. *Le fooding* seeks to give witness to the modernity and new reality of drinking and eating in the 21st century . . . Everything is *fooding* so long as audacity, sense, and the senses mix.[16]

Language and Communication

The diversity of cultures around the world is also reflected in language. A person can learn a great deal about another culture without leaving home by studying its language and literature; such study is the next best thing to actually living in another country. Linguists have divided the study of *spoken* or *verbal* language into four main areas: syntax (rules of sentence formation), semantics (system of meaning), phonology (system of sound patterns), and morphology (word formation). *Unspoken* or *nonverbal* communication includes gestures, touching, and other forms of body language that supplement spoken communication. (Nonverbal communication is sometimes called the silent language.) Both the spoken and unspoken aspects of language are included in the broader linguistic field of *semiotics*, which is the study of signs and their meanings.

In global marketing, language is a crucial tool for communicating with customers, suppliers, channel intermediaries, and others. The marketing literature is full of anecdotal references to costly blunders caused by incorrect or inept translations of product names and advertising copy.

---

[14]Fara Warner, "Savvy Indian Marketers Hold Their Ground," *The Wall Street Journal Asia* (December 1, 1997), p. 8.
[15]John Willman, "'Fast Food' Spreads as Lifestyles Change," *Financial Times* (March 27, 1998), p. 7.
[16]Jacqueline Friedrich, "All the Rage in Paris? Le Fooding," *The Wall Street Journal* (February 9, 2001), p. W11.

book   umbrella   clock

Exhibit 4-6: In China, it is bad luck to give a book, an umbrella, or a clock as a gift. Why? The character for "book" is pronounced *shu*, which sounds like "I hope you lose (have bad luck)". "Umbrella" (*san*) sounds like "to break into pieces or fall apart." And "clock" (*zhong*) sounds like "death" or "the end."

As you can see from Exhibit 4-6, pronunciation subtleties associated with certain Chinese characters can trip up well-meaning gift giving in China. For example, it would be a bad sign to give an umbrella to a business acquaintance because it would be the equivalent of hoping that his or her business fails. When British retail-development firm BAA McArthurGlen set up a U.S.-style factory outlet mall in Austria, local officials wanted to know, "Where's the factory?" To win approval for the project, McArthurGlen was forced to call its development a "designer outlet center."[17] Anheuser-Busch and Miller Brewing both experienced market failures in the United Kingdom; the problem was the phrase "light beer," which was understood as meaning reduced alcohol levels rather than fewer calories. Now Miller Lite is marketed in Europe as "Miller Pilsner."[18]

Before Hearst Corporation launched *Good Housekeeping* magazine in Japan, managers experimented with Japanese translations. The closest word in Japanese, *kaji*, means "domestic duties." However, that word can be interpreted as tasks performed by servants. In the end, the American title was retained, with the word "Good" in much larger type on the front cover than the word "Housekeeping." Inside the magazine, some of the editorial content has also been adapted to appeal to Japanese women; for example, the famous Seal of Approval was eliminated because the concept confused readers. Editor-in-chief Ellen Levine said, "We have no interest in trying to export our product exactly as it is. That would be cultural suicide."[19]

In China, Dell had to find a meaningful interpretation of "direct sales," the phrase that describes the company's powerful business model. A literal translation results in *zhi xiao*, which is the Chinese term for illegal pyramid marketing schemes. To counteract the negative connotation, Dell's sales representatives began using the phrase *zhi xiao ding gou*, which translates as "direct orders."[20] Similarly, a team of translators was tasked with compiling a dictionary to help fans of American football in China understand the game (Exhibit 4-7).

Phonology and morphology can also come into play; Colgate discovered that, in Spanish, *colgate* is a verb form that means "go hang yourself." Whirlpool spent considerable sums of money on brand advertising in Europe only to discover that consumers in Italy, France, and Germany had trouble pronouncing the company's name.[21] Conversely, Renzo Rosso deliberately chose "Diesel" for a new jeans brand because, as he once noted, "It's one of the few words pronounced the same in every language." Rosso has built Diesel into a successful global youth brand and one of Italy's top fashion success stories; annual sales revenues exceed $1.2 billion.[22]

Technology is providing interesting new opportunities for exploiting linguistics in the name of marketing. For example, young people throughout the world are using mobile phones to send

[17]Ernest Beck, "American-Style Outlet Malls in Europe Make Headway Despite Local Resistance," *The Wall Street Journal* (September 17, 1998), p. A17. A complete account of one man's efforts to bring outlet malls to Europe is found in J. Byrne Murphy, *Le Deal* (New York: St. Martins, 2008).

[18]Dan Bilefsky and Christopher Lawton, "In Europe, Marketing Beer as 'American' May Not Be a Plus," *The Wall Street Journal* (July 21, 2004), p. B1.

[19]Yumiko Ono, "Will Good Housekeeping Translate into Japanese?" *The Wall Street Journal* (December 30, 1997), p. B1.

[20]Evan Ramstad and Gary McWilliams, "Computer Savvy: For Dell, Success in China Tells Tale of Maturing Market," *The Wall Street Journal* (July 5, 2005), pp. A1, A8.

[21]Greg Steinmetz and Carl Quintanilla, "Tough Target: Whirlpool Expected Easy Going in Europe, and It Got a Big Shock," *The Wall Street Journal* (April 10, 1998), pp. A1, A6.

[22]Alice Rawsthorn, "A Hipster on Jean Therapy," *Financial Times* (August 20, 1998), p. 8.

Exhibit 4-7: Thanks to a team of academics who compiled an encyclopedia of American football terms, Chinese sports fans should have a better understanding of NFL games. For example, the Chinese translation for *blitz* is "lightning war against the quarterback." *Onside kick* is rendered "gambling kickoff" or "short kick," while *punt* is "give up and kick it back."

The authors of *The American Football Encyclopedia* also interpreted *sack* as "capture and kill" or "capture the quarterback"; *play action* is "pass after fake run." *Hail Mary pass* translates as "miracle long pass," and *touchdown* is "hold the ball and touch the ground."

blitz

突袭:猛撞
(四分卫)一种
防守技术

gambling kickoff

赌博踢

short kick

短开球

punt

凌空踢球

capture and kill

'擒杀'

successfully capture the quarterback

成功地擒抱四分卫

play action

假跑真传

Hail Mary pass

长传到达阵区

touchdown

持球触地

text messages; it turns out that certain number combinations have meaning in particular languages. For example, in Korean, the phonetic pronunciation of the numerical sequence 8282, "Pal Yi Pal Yi," means "hurry up," and 7179 ("Chil Han Chil Gu") sounds like "close friend." Also, as many digital-savvy young teens in Korea can attest, 4 5683 968 can be interpreted as "I love you."[23] Korean marketers are using these and other numerical sequences in their advertising. After eBay boosted its presence in China by acquiring the EachNet auction site in 2003, it used rebates and other promotions to attract users. For example, EachNet offered credits of 68 yuan on purchases of 168 yuan or more. The figures were chosen for their linguistic properties: In Chinese, the word "six" is a homophone (has the same pronunciation) for the word "safe," and "eight" is pronounced the same as "prosperity."[24]

One impact of globalization on culture is the diffusion of the English language around the globe. Today there are more people who speak English as a foreign language than there are people whose native language is English. Nearly 85 percent of the teenagers in the EU are studying English. Despite the fact that Sony is headquartered in Japan, the company makes it clear to job applicants in any part of the world that it does not consider English to be a "foreign language." The same is true for Finland's Nokia. Matsushita recently introduced a policy that requires all managers to pass an English language-competency test before being considered for promotion. Top management at Matsushita concluded that a staid corporate culture that was exclusively Japanese was eroding the company's competitiveness in the global market. The English-language requirement is a potent symbol that a Japanese company is globalizing.[25]

The challenges presented by nonverbal communication are perhaps even more formidable. For example, Westerners doing business in the Middle East must be careful not to reveal the soles of their shoes to hosts or pass documents with the left hand. In Japan, bowing is an important form of nonverbal communication that has many nuances. People who grow up in the West tend to be verbal; those from Asia exhibit behavior that places more weight on nonverbal aspects of interpersonal communication. There is a greater expectation in the East that people will pick up nonverbal cues and understand intuitively without being told.[26] Westerners must pay close attention not only to what they hear but also to what they see when conducting business in such cultures.

"Global business makes sense, but it's much more difficult to do it than to talk about it. The American manager prides himself or herself on directness, frankness, being in-your-face, being accountable. But that's almost unique in the world."[27]

A. Paul Flask, managing partner, Korn/Ferry International

---

[23]The authors are indebted to Professor Yong Tae Bang, Department of International Trade, College of Business Administration, Paichai University, South Korea, for his comments on this section. See also Meeyoung Song, "How to Sell in Korea? Marketers Count the Ways," *The Wall Street Journal* (August 24, 2001), p. A6.

[24]Mylene Mangalindan, "Hot Bidding: In a Challenging Market, EBay Confronts a Big New Rival," *The Wall Street Journal* (August 12, 2005), p. A1.

[25]Kevin Voigt, "At Matsushita, It's a New Word Order," *Asian Wall Street Journal Weekly* (June 18–24, 2001), p. 1.

[26]See Anthony C. Di Benedetto, Miriko Tamate, and Rajan Chandran, "Developing Strategy for the Japanese Marketplace," *Journal of Advertising Research* (January–February 1992), pp. 39–48.

[27]Robert Frank and Thomas M. Burton, "Side Effects: Cross-Border Merger Results in Headaches for a Drug Company," *The Wall Street Journal* (February 4, 1997), p. A1.

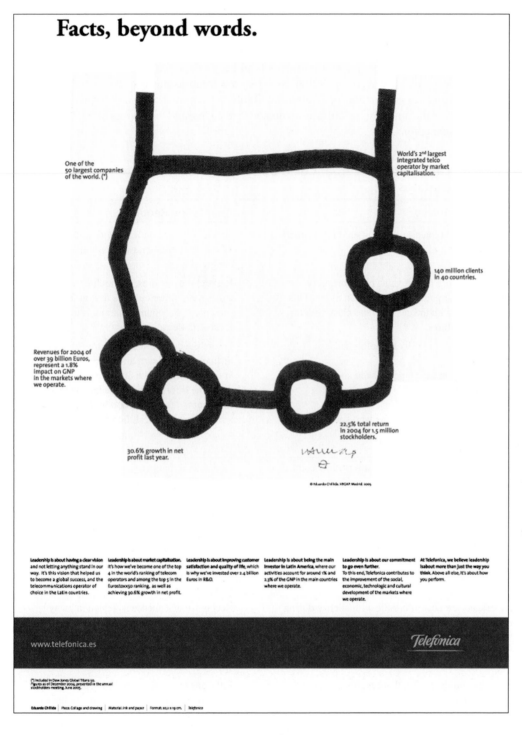

Exhibit 4-8: Spain's Telefónica is a leading provider of both fixed-line and wireless communication services in Spain and Latin America. In Brazil, Telefónica's joint venture with Portugal Telecom commands one-third of the market. Now Telefónica is moving aggressively to provide "triple play" services that include high-speed Internet and video on demand in addition to regular voice communication. The company's UK subsidiary recently launched Look at Me, a service that lets cell phone subscribers create videos with their phones that they can upload and share with others.
Source: Telefonica USA, Inc.

Deep cultural understanding that is based in language can be an important source of competitive advantage for global companies. The aggressive expansion of Spain's Telefónica in Latin America provides a case in point (see Exhibit 4-8). As Juan Villalonga, former chairman of Telefónica, noted, "It is not just speaking a common language. It is sharing a culture and understanding friendships in the same way."[28]

Several important communication issues may emerge. One is *sequencing*, which concerns whether the discussion goes directly from point A to point B or seems to go off on tangents. Another is *phasing*, which pertains to whether certain important agenda items are discussed

---

[28]Tom Burns, "Spanish Telecoms Visionary Beholds a Brave New World," *Financial Times* (May 2, 1998), p. 24.

immediately or after the parties have taken some time to establish rapport. According to two experts on international negotiations, there are 10 distinctly American tactics that frequently emerge during negotiations. These tactics are often effective with other Americans, but may require modification for people from other cultural backgrounds. In any communication situation, speakers offer a variety of verbal cues that can help astute observers understand the speaker's mind-set and mental programming. Table 4-1 summarizes some typical American English cues, the underlying culture-influenced attitudes and behaviors they signify, and suggested adaptations.

TABLE 4-1 American Communication Styles: Verbal Cues, Underlying Realities, and Suggested Adaptations

Verbal Cues	Underlying Reality	Adaptation Required
1. "I can go it alone."	Americans are typically outnumbered in negotiations. Reflects culture of individualism.	Greater reliance on teamwork and division of negotiating labor, especially in collectivist culture.
2. "Just call me 'John.'"	Americans place a high value on informality and equality of participants in negotiations. This may conflict with the customs and class structures of foreign cultures.	Respect the customs, hierarchies, and class structure of other cultures. Learn more via self study; ask country nationals to explain local attitudes and values.
3. "Do you speak English?"	Americans are culturally monolingual. (Old joke: Q: What do you call someone who speaks two languages? A: Bilingual. Q: What do you call someone who speaks one language? A: American!)	Ignore the conventional wisdom about how difficult it is to learn a foreign language; if you have ongoing business in a country, make the effort to study the language. At a minimum, develop a good working relationship with a skilled interpreter.
4. "Get to the point."	Americans' short-term orientation manifests itself as a tendency to be blunt and impatient.	Understand that people from other cultures need to develop a sense of connection and personal trust in order to feel comfortable about doing business. This takes time.
5. "Lay your cards on the table."	Americans like to state the case up front, and are not accustomed to "feeling out" prospective partners.	Slow down, and recognize the need to rephrase the question, several times if necessary. Prepare to spend double the time you think is needed to get the information you seek.
6. "Why doesn't somebody say something?"	Americans are uncomfortable with silence during negotiations and often deal with their discomfort by continuing to speak.	Recognize that silence is golden in many cultures. It can be detrimental to keep up a constant stream of chatter. If there is silence, let it be. Reflect. Take in nonverbal information. *Value* the silence. Take advantage of it.
7. "Don't take 'no' for an answer."	Tenacity and the hard sell are highly valued in the United States.	If the answer is no, stop selling and find out why. Respond to the reasons for the answer "no."
8. "One thing at a time."	Many Americans favor a linear, organized, "left brain" negotiation style. "Point One, Point Two"-style sequencing is not a universal approach.	Recognize your own right brain capability. Embrace a more holistic approach toward negotiations. Be patient if the discussion seems to proceed in loops and spirals.
9. "A deal is a deal."	Expectations and perceptions may not be shared by all parties. Have you agreed on all the points in the contract, or have you agreed to work together?	Accept a more gradual, supplemental view of negotiations and joint effort.
10. "I am what I am."	Americans have a tendency to see things in black-and-white terms.	Adopt a more flexible standpoint. Be willing to change your mind and manner and to adapt to your opposite.

Source: Adapted from John L. Graham and Roy A. Heberger Jr., "Negotiators Abroad—Don't Shoot from the Hip," *Harvard Business Review* 61, no. 4 (July–August 1983), pp. 160–168.

Marketing's Impact on Culture

Universal aspects of the cultural environment represent opportunities for global marketers to standardize some or all elements of a marketing program. The astute global marketer often discovers that much of the apparent cultural diversity in the world turns out to be different ways of accomplishing the same thing. Widespread shared preference for convenience foods, disposable products, popular music, and movies in the United States, Europe, and Asia suggests that many consumer products have broad, even universal, appeal. Increasing travel and improving communications have contributed to a convergence of tastes and preferences in a number of product categories. The cultural change and the globalization of culture have been capitalized upon, and even significantly accelerated, by companies that have seized opportunities to find customers around the world. However, as noted at the beginning of this chapter, the impact of marketing and, more generally, of global capitalism on culture can be controversial. For example, sociologist George Ritzer and others lament the so-called "McDonaldization of culture" that, they say, occurs when global companies break down cultural barriers while expanding into new markets with their products. As Ritzer noted in a recent book:

> Eating is at the heart of most cultures and for many it is something on which much time, attention and money are lavished. In attempting to alter the way people eat, McDonaldization poses a profound threat to the entire cultural complex of many societies.[29]

Fabien Ouaki is living proof that persons outside of academe and government have also joined the battle against McDonaldization. Ouaki is the managing director of Tati, a discount retailer based in France. Ouaki is opening new stores in select countries, including the United States. Ouaki claims that "personal revenge" is one motivation for entering the U.S. market. "As a Frenchman, it makes me sick to see kids crying to go see 'Titanic,' eat at McDonald's, or drink Coke. I want to see New Yorkers crying to have a Tati wedding dress," he said.[30] Similarly, the international Slow Food movement boasts 70,000 members in dozens of countries. Slow Food grew out of a 1986 protest over the opening of a McDonald's on a popular plaza in Rome; every two years, Slow Food stages a Salone del Gusto in Italy that showcases traditional food preparation. As a spokesperson said, "Slow Food is about the idea that things should not taste the same everywhere."[31] In 2008, Slow Food U.S.A. attracted 60,000 people to an event in San Francisco that featured a farmers' market and a speakers series called "Food For Thought" (see Exhibit 4-9).

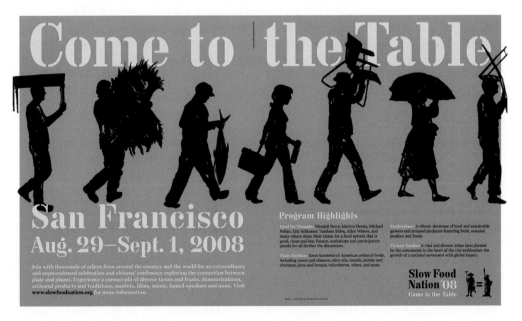

Exhibit 4-9: At Slow Food gatherings, participants can attend forums, workshops, and panels featuring writers such as Eric Schlosser *(Fast Food Nation)* and world famous chefs such as Alice Waters. And, of course, there is the food: artisanal meats, cheeses, breads, and much more.
Source: Used by permission of Slow Food Nation.

[29]George Ritzer, *The McDonaldization Thesis* (London: Sage Publications, 1998), p. 8.
[30]Amy Barrett, "French Discounter Takes Cheap Chic World-Wide," *The Wall Street Journal* (May 27, 1998), p. B8.
[31]Christine Muhlke, "A Slow Food Festival Reaches Out to the Uncommitted," *The New York Times* (September 3, 2008), p. D12. See also Alexander Stille, "Slow Food's Pleasure Principles," *The Utne Reader* (May/June 2002), pp. 56–58.

HIGH- AND LOW-CONTEXT CULTURES

Edward T. Hall has suggested the concept of high and low context as a way of understanding different cultural orientations.[32] In a **low-context culture**, messages are explicit and specific; words carry most of the communication power. In a **high-context culture**, less information is contained in the verbal part of a message. Much more information resides in the context of communication, including the background, associations, and basic values of the communicators. In general, high-context cultures function with much less legal paperwork than is deemed essential in low-context cultures. Japan, Saudi Arabia, and other high-context cultures place a great deal of emphasis on a person's values and position or place in society. In such cultures, a business loan is more likely to be based on "who you are" than on formal analysis of pro forma financial documents.

In a low-context culture, such as the United States, Switzerland, or Germany, deals are made with much less information about the character, background, and values of the participants. Much more reliance is placed upon the words and numbers in the loan application. Similarly, Japanese companies, such as Sony, traditionally paid a great deal of attention to the university background of a new hire; preference would be given to graduates of Tokyo University. Specific elements on a résumé were less important.

In a high-context culture, a person's word is his or her bond. There is less need to anticipate contingencies and provide for external legal sanctions because the culture emphasizes obligations and trust as important values. In these cultures, shared feelings of obligation and honor take the place of impersonal legal sanctions. This helps explain the importance of long and protracted negotiations that never seem to get to the point. Part of the purpose of negotiating, for a person from a high-context culture, is to get to know the potential partner.

For example, insisting on competitive bidding can cause complications in low-context cultures. In a high-context culture, the job is given to the person who will do the best work and whom you can trust and control. In a low-context culture, one tries to make the specifications so precise that the threat of legal sanction forces a builder to do a good job. As Hall has noted, a builder in Japan is likely to say, "What has that piece of paper got to do with the situation? If we can't trust each other enough to go ahead without it, why bother?"

Although countries can be classified as high- or low-context in their overall tendency, there are exceptions to the general tendency. These exceptions are found in subcultures. The United States is a low-context culture with subcultures that operate in the high-context mode. The world of the central banker, for example, is a "gentleman's" world; that is, a high-context culture. Even during the most hectic day of trading in the foreign exchange markets, a central banker's word is sufficient for him or her to borrow millions of dollars. In a high-context culture there is trust, a sense of fair play, and a widespread acceptance of the rules of the game as it is played. Table 4-2 summarizes some of the ways in which high- and low-context cultures differ.

TABLE 4-2 High- and Low-Context Cultures

Factors or Dimensions	High Context	Low Context
Lawyers	Less important	Very important
A person's word	Is his or her bond	Is not to be relied upon; "get it in writing"
Responsibility for organizational error	Taken by highest level	Pushed to lowest level
Space	People breathe on each other	People maintain a bubble of private space and resent intrusions
Time	Polychronic—everything in life must be dealt with in terms of its own time	Monochronic—time is money Linear—one thing at a time
Negotiations	Are lengthy—a major purpose is to allow the parties to get to know each other	Proceed quickly
Competitive bidding	Infrequent	Common
Country or regional examples	Japan, Middle East	United States, Northern Europe

---

[32]Edward T. Hall, "How Cultures Collide," *Psychology Today* (July 1976), pp. 66–97.

HOFSTEDE'S CULTURAL TYPOLOGY

Organizational anthropologist Geert Hofstede was introduced earlier in this chapter in a discussion of his widely quoted definition of culture. Hofstede is also well known for research studies of social values suggesting that the cultures of different nations can be compared in terms of five dimensions.[33] Hofstede notes that three of the dimensions refer to expected social behavior, the fourth dimension is concerned with "man's search for Truth," and a fifth reflects the importance of time. Table 4-3 shows a summary of selected country rankings, plus Hong Kong and Taiwan (for more information, visit www.geert-hofstede.com).

The first dimension, **power distance**, is the extent to which the less powerful members of a society accept—even expect—power to be distributed unequally. To paraphrase Orwell, all societies are unequal, but some are more unequal than others. Hong Kong and France are both high power distance cultures; low power distance characterizes Germany, Austria, the Netherlands, and Scandinavia.

The second dimension is a reflection of the degree to which individuals in a society are integrated into groups. In **individualist cultures**, each member of society is primarily concerned with his or her own interest and those of the immediate family. In **collectivist cultures**, all of society's members are integrated into cohesive in-groups. High individualism is a general aspect of culture in the United States and Europe; low individualism is characteristic of Japanese and other Asian culture patterns.

Masculinity, the third dimension, describes a society in which men are expected to be assertive, competitive, and concerned with material success, and women fulfill the role of nurturer and are concerned with issues such as the welfare of children. **Femininity**, by contrast, describes a society in which the social roles of men and women overlap, with neither gender exhibiting

TABLE 4-3 Hofstede's Cultural Dimension Rankings: Selected Countries

Country	Power Distance (PDI)		Individualism		Masculinity		Uncertainty Avoidance		Long-Term Orientation (LTO)	
	Index	Rank	Index	Rank	Index	Rank	Index	Rank	Index	Rank
Austria	11	53	55	18	79	**2**	70	24–25	31	22–24
Belgium	65	20	75	8	54	22	94	5–6	38	18
Denmark	18	51	74	9	16	50	23	51	46	10
Finland	33	46	63	17	26	47	59	31–32	41	14
France	68	**15–16**	71	10–11	43	35–36	86	10–15	39	17
Germany	35	42–44	67	15	66	9–10	65	29	31	22–24
Greece	60	27–28	35	30	57	18–19	112	**1**	–	–
Ireland	28	49	70	12	68	7–8	35	47–48	43	13
Italy	50	34	76	7	70	4–5	75	23	34	19
Netherlands	38	40	80	4–5	14	51	53	35	44	11–12
Portugal	63	24–25	69	13	31	45	104	2	30	25–26
Spain	57	31	51	20	42	37–38	86	10–15	19	31–32
Sweden	31	47–48	71	10–11	5	52	29	49–50	33	20
UK	65	42–44	89	3	66	9–10	35	47–48	25	28–29
USA	40	38	91	**1**	62	15	41	43	29	27
Japan	54	33	46	22–23	95	**1**	92	7	80	4
Hong Kong	68	**15–16**	25	37	57	18–19	29	49–50	96	**2**
Taiwan	58	29–30	17	44	45	32–33	69	26	87	3

Source: Geert Hofstede, *Culture's Consequences* (Thousand Oaks, CA: Sage, 2001), p. 500. Used by permission of Geert Hofstede.

---

[33]Geert Hofstede and Michael Harris Bond, "The Confucius Connection: From Cultural Roots to Economic Growth," *Organizational Dynamics* (Spring 1988), p. 5.

overly ambitious or competitive behavior. Japan and Austria ranked highest in masculinity; Spain, Taiwan, the Netherlands, and the Scandinavian countries were among the lowest.

Uncertainty avoidance is the extent to which the members of a society are uncomfortable with unclear, ambiguous, or unstructured situations. Members of uncertainty avoiding cultures may resort to aggressive, emotional, intolerant behavior; they are characterized by a belief in absolute truth. Members of uncertainty accepting cultures (e.g., Denmark, Sweden, Ireland, and the United States) are more tolerant of persons whose opinions differ from their own.

Greece and Portugal outrank the others in Table 4-3 in uncertainty avoidance; other Mediterranean countries and much of Latin America rank high in uncertainty avoidance as well. Acceptance of uncertainty generally manifests itself in behavior that is more contemplative, relativistic, and tolerant; these values are evident in Southeast Asia and India.

Hofstede's research convinced him that, although these four dimensions yielded interesting and useful interpretations, they did not provide sufficient insight into possible cultural bases for economic growth. Hofstede was also disturbed by the fact that Western social scientists had developed the surveys used in the research. Because many economists had failed to predict the explosive economic development of Japan and the Asian tigers (i.e., South Korea, Taiwan, Hong Kong, and Singapore), Hofstede surmised that some cultural dimensions in Asia were eluding the researchers. This methodological problem was remedied by a Chinese Value Survey (CVS) developed by Chinese social scientists in Hong Kong and Taiwan.

The CVS data supported the first three "social behavior" dimensions of culture: power distance, individualism/collectivism, and masculinity/femininity. Uncertainty avoidance, however, did not show up in the CVS. Instead, the CVS revealed a dimension, **long-term orientation (LTO)** versus **short-term orientation**, that had eluded Western researchers.[34] Hofstede interpreted this dimension as concerning "a society's search for virtue," rather than a search for truth. It assesses the sense of immediacy within a culture, whether gratification should be immediate or deferred.

Long-term values include *persistence* (perseverance), defined as a general tenacity in the pursuit of a goal. *Ordering relationships* by status reflects the presence of societal hierarchies, and *observing this order* indicates the acceptance of complementary relations. *Thrift* manifests itself in high savings rates. Finally, *a sense of shame* leads to sensitivity in social contacts. Hofstede notes that these values are widely held within high-performing Asian countries such as Hong Kong, Taiwan, and Japan, but that the presence of these values by themselves is not sufficient to lead to economic growth. Two other conditions are necessary: the existence of a market and a supportive political context. Although Hofstede determined that India ranked quite high on the LTO dimension, market restrictions and political forces have, until recently, held back that nation's economic growth.

By studying Hofstede's work, marketers gain insights that can guide them in a range of activities, including product development, interacting with joint venture partners, and conducting sales meetings. For example, understanding the time orientation of one's native culture compared to others' is crucial (see Table 4-2). In Japan, Brazil, and India, building a relationship with a potential business partner takes precedence over transacting the deal. People from cultures that emphasize the short term must adapt to the slower pace of business in some countries. As noted earlier, language can offer some insights into cultural differences. For example, the phrase "in a New York minute" captures the urgent pace of American urban life.

Conversely, the Japanese notion of *gaman* ("persistence") provides insight into the willingness of Japanese corporations to pursue R&D projects for which the odds of short-term success appear low. When Sony licensed the newly invented transistor from Bell Laboratories in the mid-1950s, for example, the limited high-frequency yield (sound output) of the device suggested to American engineers that the most appropriate application would be for a hearing

---

[34]In some articles Hofstede refers to this dimension as "Confucian Dynamism" because it is highest in Japan, Hong Kong, and Taiwan.

aid. However, *gaman* meant that Sony engineers were not deterred by the slow progress of their efforts to increase the yield. As Sony cofounder Masaru Ibuka recalled, "To challenge the yield is a very interesting point for us. At that time no one recognized the importance of it." Sony's persistence was rewarded when company engineers eventually made the yield breakthrough that resulted in a wildly successful global product—the pocket-sized transistor radio.[35]

By understanding the dimension of uncertainty avoidance, global marketers are better equipped to assess the amount of risk with which buyers are comfortable. In Japan and other Asian cultures characterized by a low tolerance for ambiguity, buyers will be conscious of brand names and are likely to exhibit high brand loyalty. Advertising copy in countries with high levels of uncertainty avoidance should provide reassurance by stressing warranties, money-back guarantees, and other risk-reducing features. Hong Kong has an even higher tolerance for ambiguity than the United States; Japan, however, ranks quite high in uncertainty avoidance, as do France and Spain.

The power distance dimension reflects the degree of trust among members of society. The higher the power distance (PDI), the lower the level of trust. Organizationally, high PDI finds expression in tall, hierarchical designs, a preference for centralization, and relatively more supervisory personnel. The PDI dimension also provides insights into the dynamics between superiors and subordinates. In cultures where respect for hierarchy is high, subordinates may have to navigate through several layers of assistants to get to the boss. If so, the latter is likely to be isolated in an office with the door closed. In such cultures, superiors may easily intimidate lower-level employees. Recent research has suggested that, when evaluating alternatives for entering global markets, companies in high PDI cultures prefer sole ownership of subsidiaries because it provides them with more control. Conversely, companies in low PDI cultures are more apt to use joint ventures.[36] In Table 4-3, France and Hong Kong are tied for having the highest PDI. Other countries with high PDI scores are Mexico, India, and Hong Kong.

The masculinity–femininity dimension is likely to manifest itself in the relative importance of achievement and possessions (masculine values) compared with a spirit of helpfulness and social support (feminine values). Overall, an aggressive, achievement-oriented salesperson is better matched to the culture of Austria, Japan, or Mexico than that of Denmark. (Such a salesperson would also have to bear in mind that both Japan and Mexico rank high in LTO, a dimension that can be at odds with transaction-oriented assertiveness.) Similarly, a Western woman who is sent to make a presentation to a Japanese company will undoubtedly find that her audience consists of men. The Japanese managers may react negatively to a woman, especially if she is younger than they are.

The collective–individual orientation deserves special comment because there is wide agreement that it is an important component of culture. Knowing which cultures value the collective and which value the individual can help marketers in various ways. In Japan, for example, the team orientation and desire for *wa* ("harmony") means that singling out one person for distinction and praise in front of peers can be awkward for those involved. Again, language provides important cues about these cultural dimensions; as the saying goes in Japan, "The nail that sticks up gets hammered down." Throughout much of Asia, the collectivist orientation is dominant. In the highly individualist U.S. culture, however, a person whose individual accomplishments are publicly acknowledged is likely to be pleased by the recognition.[37]

Several teams of researchers have attempted to determine whether cross-national collective/individual differences are reflected in print and television advertisements. In theory, a global company's communication efforts should be adapted in accordance with a particular country's orientation. For example, in cultures where individualism is highly valued, ads would

---

[35]James Lardner, *Fast Forward: Hollywood, the Japanese, and the VCR Wars* (New York: NAL Penguin, 1987), p. 45.
[36]Scott A. Shane, "The Effect of Cultural Differences in Perceptions of Transactions Costs on National Differences in the Preference for International Joint Ventures," *Asia Pacific Journal of Management* 10, no. 1 (1993), pp. 57–69.
[37]Adapted from Anne Macquin and Dominique Rouziès, "Selling Across the Culture Gap," *Financial Times—Mastering Global Business,* part 7, 1998, pp. 10–11.

The cultural confrontation between Denmark and the Middle East cast a spotlight on the small European country. What is Denmark really like? The following profile captures Denmark in terms of Hofstede's cultural values framework.

Future Orientation: The extent to which a society encourages and rewards future-oriented behaviors such as planning, investing in the future, and delaying gratification. Denmark scores high.

In the Danish business environment, it is normal to prepare and discuss five-year budgets and business plans that are then adjusted yearly. Also, the Danish population is aware of the importance of saving up for retirement. Minister of Economic Affairs Bendt Bendtsen hopes to establish a world-class innovation center in Denmark. The center would focus on predicting consumer needs and elevate Denmark to the top ranks of countries with consumer-driven innovation. The key areas of study would be economics, anthropology, engineering, design, and psychology.

Gender Differentiation: The extent to which a society maximizes gender role differences. Denmark scores low.

In Denmark, gender role differences are insignificant. Danish women are strong and believe they can do anything that a man can. Because of this, it is very uncommon for men to open doors for women or give them flowers. A few years ago, it was very popular for women to attend "know your car" seminars. Denmark's maternity leave policy provides for a total of 12 months that both the mother and father can use. As is true in the United States, there are great differences between families in Denmark. Generally though, Danish women are very focused on equality both in the home and at work. It is very common for fathers to take equal part in cleaning and other duties around the house.

Uncertainty Avoidance: The extent to which the members of a society are accepting of ambiguous situations or comfortable with unfamiliar situations. Denmark scores low; in other words, it is an uncertainty accepting society.

Danes generally are not afraid of taking chances; they are comfortable doing things that are not carefully thought out or planned. Denmark's "flexicurity" policy combines free labor markets (workers can be fired) with adjustable welfare benefits including financial support and free job training for the unemployed. The Danish social system provides a close-knit safety system to fall back on. In other words, making a mistake may not be very costly, so people are less afraid of taking chances. Society relies on and supports a system that is costly, but provides a constant sense of security. Health care is free for all Danish citizens, so a person doesn't have to worry about losing benefits if he or she changes jobs.

Power Distance: The degree to which members of a society expect power to be unequally shared. Denmark scores low.

This is an area where the countries of Europe differ to the extreme. Denmark scores very low on power distance, which results in very flat and informal organizational structures and the wide use of various matrix models. CEOs and other leaders are directly accessible to the average worker and it is common that leaders are satirized in sketches at company parties. In the Danish workplace it is normal to be paid in accordance to qualifications instead of in accordance to position.

Janteloven, or "the law of Jante," deeply affects how Scandinavian people act and are expected to act. The term originated with writer Aksel Sandemose who wrote a novel about Jante, a village where one is not supposed to believe he or she is better or smarter than anyone else.

Humility is important, and this limits power distance. It is not unusual for the Danish Queen Margrethe II to visit stores in Copenhagen without any visible protection. Also, Prince Felix, son of Prince Joachim and Princess Alexandra, attended a public school in his hometown of Møgeltønder.

Individualism/Collectivism: The degree to which societal institutions encourage individuals to be integrated into groups within organizations and society. Denmark scores high on individualism.

Thanks to Denmark's high tax rates, education—including university and graduate school—is free for everyone. The system is completely based on merit and does not favor people who are well off financially. Students tend to be very competitive.

In-group Collectivism and Institutional Collectivism: The extent to which members of a society take pride in membership in small groups such as their family and circle of close friends and the organizations in which they are employed. Denmark scores high in Institutional Collectivism and low in in-group collectivism.

Denmark's divorce rate is one of the highest in the world. It is difficult to find exact numbers to compare because of the many different ways of calculating it. High uncertainty acceptance may be a factor.

Sources: Mikkel Jakobsen. Also see Justin Fox, "Why Denmark Loves Globalization," www.time.com. Accessed June 1, 2008. Used by permission of Mikkel Jakobsen. Leila Abboud, "Power Play: How Denmark Paved Way to Energy Independence," *The Wall Street Journal* (April 16, 2007), p. A1; Jeffrey Stinson, "Denmark's 'Flexicurity' Blends Welfare State, Economic Growth," *USA Today* (March 7, 2007), pp. 1B, 2B.

typically feature one person; in countries where individualism is less highly valued, ads would feature groups. Although one team[38] claimed to have found a strong correlation, the findings were not confirmed by a later study.[39] However, Cutler argues that print advertising is, by its very nature, designed to communicate to an individual reader. This suggests that the individualism–collectivism distinction may be a moot issue in print advertising.

In highly collectivist cultures, however, products or services that enjoy an early word-of-mouth buzz among influential consumer groups can quickly achieve phenomenon status that then spreads to other countries. The Tamagotchi craze of the late 1990s is a perfect example. The virtual pets were test marketed in central Tokyo in a shopping area frequented by teenage girls. *Kuchikomi* (word of mouth) was so strong among schoolgirls that toymaker Bandai was hard-pressed to keep up with demand. By the time Tamagotchis reached New York toy retailer FAO Schwartz, the prerelease buzz ensured that the initial 10,000-unit shipment sold out immediately. Although Japanese teens also pay attention to print and television advertising, it is clear that marketers can reach this segment by providing selected youngsters with product samples.[40]

THE SELF-REFERENCE CRITERION AND PERCEPTION

As we have shown, a person's perception of market needs is framed by his or her own cultural experience. A framework for systematically reducing perceptual blockage and distortion was developed by James Lee and published in the *Harvard Business Review* in 1966. Lee termed the unconscious reference to one's own cultural values the **self-reference criterion (SRC)**. To address this problem and eliminate or reduce cultural myopia, he proposed a systematic four-step framework:

1. Define the problem or goal in terms of home-country cultural traits, habits, and norms.
2. Define the problem or goal in terms of host-country cultural traits, habits, and norms. Make no value judgments.
3. Isolate the SRC influence and examine it carefully to see how it complicates the problem.
4. Redefine the problem without the SRC influence and solve for the host-country market situation.[41]

The Walt Disney Company's decision to build a theme park in France provides an excellent vehicle for understanding SRC. As they planned their entry into the French market, how might Disney executives have done things differently had they used the steps of SRC?

Step 1 Disney executives believe there is virtually unlimited demand for American cultural exports around the world. Evidence includes the success of McDonald's, Coca-Cola, Hollywood movies, and American rock music. Disney has a stellar track record in exporting its American management system and business style. Tokyo Disneyland, a virtual carbon copy of the park in Anaheim, California, has been a runaway success. Disney policies prohibit sale or consumption of alcohol inside its theme parks.

Step 2 Europeans in general and the French in particular, are sensitive about American cultural imperialism. Consuming wine with the midday meal is a long-established custom.

---

[38]Katherine Toland Frith and Subir Sengupta, "Individualism: A Cross-Cultural Analysis of Print Advertisements from the U.S. and India," paper presented at 1991 Annual Conference of Advertising Division of Association for Education in Journalism and Mass Communication, Boston, MA.

[39]Bob D. Cutler, S. Altan Erdem, and Rajshekhar G. Javalgi, "Advertisers' Relative Reliance on Collectivism-Individualism Appeals," *Journal of International Consumer Marketing* 9, no. 3 (1997), pp. 43–55.

[40]Bethan Hutton, "Winning Word-of-Mouth Approval," *Financial Times* (September 8, 1997), p. 10.

[41]James A. Lee, "Cultural Analysis in Overseas Operations," *Harvard Business Review* (March–April 1966), pp. 106–114.

Europeans have their own real castles, and many popular Disney characters come from European folk tales.

Step 3 The significant differences revealed by comparing the findings in steps 1 and 2 suggest strongly that the needs upon which the American and Japanese Disney theme parks were based did not exist in France. A modification of this design was needed for European success.

Step 4 This would require the design of a theme park that is more in keeping with French and European cultural norms. Allow the French to put their own identity on the park.

The lesson that the SRC teaches is that a vital, critical skill of the global marketer is unbiased perception, the ability to see what is so in a culture. Although this skill is as valuable at home as it is abroad, it is critical to the global marketer because of the widespread tendency toward ethnocentrism and use of the self-reference criterion. The SRC can be a powerful negative force in global business, and forgetting to check for it can lead to misunderstanding and failure. While planning Euro Disney, former Chairman Michael Eisner and other company executives were blinded by a potent combination of their own prior success and ethnocentrism. Avoiding the SRC requires a person to suspend assumptions based on prior experience and success and be prepared to acquire new knowledge about human behavior and motivation.

DIFFUSION THEORY[44]

Hundreds of studies have described the process by which an individual adopts a new idea. Sociologist Everett Rogers reviewed these studies and discovered a pattern of remarkably similar findings. Rogers distilled the research into three concepts that are extremely useful to global marketers: the adoption process, characteristics of innovations, and adopter categories. Taken together, these concepts constitute Rogers' **diffusion of innovation** framework.

An innovation is something new. When applied to a product, "new" can mean different things. In an absolute sense, once a product has been introduced anywhere in the world, it is no longer an innovation because it is no longer new to the world. Relatively speaking, however, a product already introduced in one market may be an innovation elsewhere because it is new and different for the targeted market. Global marketing often entails just such product introductions. Managers find themselves marketing products that may be, simultaneously, innovations in some markets and mature or declining products in other markets.

The Adoption Process

One of the basic elements of Rogers's diffusion theory is the concept of an **adoption process**—the mental stages through which an individual passes from the time of his or her first knowledge of an innovation to the time of product adoption or purchase. Rogers suggests that an individual passes through five different stages in proceeding from first knowledge of a product to the final adoption or purchase of that product: awareness, interest, evaluation, trial, and adoption.

1. *Awareness.* In the first stage the customer becomes aware for the first time of the product or innovation. Studies have shown that at this stage impersonal sources of information such as mass media advertising are most important. An important early communication objective in global marketing is to create awareness of a new product through general exposure to advertising messages.

---

[42]Michael Schuman, "Disney's Great Leap into China," *Time* (July 18, 2005), p. 34.
[43]Matthew Garrahan, "Disney Ventures into Famous Five Territory," *Financial Times* (December 4, 2006), p. 15.
[44]This section draws from Everett M. Rogers, *Diffusion of Innovations* (New York: Free Press, 1962).

2. *Interest.* During this stage, the customer is interested enough to learn more. The customer has focused his or her attention on communications relating to the product and will engage in research activities and seek out additional information.

3. *Evaluation.* In this stage the individual mentally assesses the product's benefits in relation to present and anticipated future needs and, based on this judgment, decides whether or not to try it.

4. *Trial.* Most customers will not purchase expensive products without the "hands-on" experience marketers call "trial." A good example of a product trial that does not involve purchase is the automobile test drive. For health care products and other inexpensive consumer packaged goods, trial often involves actual purchase. Marketers frequently induce trial by distributing free samples. For inexpensive products, an initial single purchase is defined as trial.

5. *Adoption.* At this point, the individual either makes an initial purchase (in the case of the more expensive product) or continues to purchase—adopts and exhibits brand loyalty to— the less expensive product. Studies show that, as a person moves from the evaluation through trial to adoption, personal sources of information are more important than impersonal sources. It is during these stages that sales representatives and word of mouth become major persuasive forces affecting the decision to buy.

Characteristics of Innovations

In addition to describing the product adoption process, Rogers also identifies five major **characteristics of innovations**. These are the factors that affect the rate at which innovations are adopted: relative advantage, compatibility, complexity, divisibility, and communicability.

1. *Relative advantage*: How a new product compares with existing products or methods in the eyes of customers. The perceived relative advantage of a new product versus existing products is a major influence on the rate of adoption. If a product has a substantial relative advantage vis-à-vis the competition, it is likely to gain quick acceptance. When compact disc players were first introduced in the early 1980s, industry observers predicted that only audiophiles would care enough about digital sound—and have the money—to purchase them. However, the sonic advantages of CDs compared to LPs were obvious to the mass market; as prices for CD players plummeted, the 12-inch black vinyl LP was rendered virtually extinct in less than a decade.

2. *Compatibility*: The extent to which a product is consistent with existing values and past experiences of adopters. The history of innovations in international marketing is replete with failures caused by the lack of compatibility of new products in the target market. For example, the first consumer VCR, the Sony Betamax, ultimately failed because it could only record for one hour. Most buyers wanted to record movies and sports events; they shunned the Betamax in favor of VHS-format VCRs that could record four hours of programming.

3. *Complexity*: The degree to which an innovation or new product is difficult to understand and use. Product complexity is a factor that can slow down the rate of adoption, particularly in developing country markets with low rates of literacy. In the 1990s, dozens of global companies developed new interactive multimedia consumer electronics products. Complexity was a key design issue; it was a standing joke that in most households, VCR clocks flashed 12:00 because users didn't know how to set them. To achieve mass success, new products will have to be as simple to use as slipping a prerecorded DVD into a DVD player.

4. *Divisibility*: The ability of a product to be tried and used on a limited basis without great expense. Wide discrepancies in income levels around the globe result in major differences in preferred purchase quantities, serving sizes, and product portions. CPC International's Hellmann's mayonnaise was simply not selling in U.S.-size jars in Latin America. Sales

took off after the company placed the mayonnaise in small plastic packets. The plastic packets were within the food budgets of local consumers, and they required no refrigeration—another plus.

5. *Communicability*: The degree to which benefits of an innovation or the value of a product may be communicated to a potential market. A new digital cassette recorder from Philips was a market failure, in part because advertisements did not clearly communicate the fact that the product could make CD-quality recordings using new cassette technology while still playing older analog tapes.

Adopter Categories

Adopter categories are classifications of individuals within a market on the basis of their innovativeness. Hundreds of studies of the diffusion of innovation demonstrate that, at least in the West, adoption is a social phenomenon that is characterized by a normal distribution curve, as shown in Figure 4-1.

Five categories have been assigned to the segments of this normal distribution. The first 2.5 percent of people to purchase a product are defined as innovators. The next 13.5 percent are early adopters, the next 34 percent are the early majority, the next 34 percent are the late majority, and the final 16 percent are laggards. Studies show that innovators tend to be venturesome, more cosmopolitan in their social relationships, and wealthier than those who adopt later. Early adopters are the most influential people in their communities, even more than the innovators. Thus the early adopters are a critical group in the adoption process, and they have great influence on the early and late majority, who comprise the bulk of the adopters of any product. Several characteristics of early adopters stand out. First, they tend to be younger, with higher social status, and in a more favorable financial position than later adopters. They must be responsive to mass media information sources and must learn about innovations from these sources because they cannot simply copy the behavior of early adopters.

One of the major reasons for the normal distribution of adopter categories is the *interaction effect*; that is, the process through which individuals who have adopted an innovation influence others. Adoption of a new idea or product is the result of human interaction in a social system. If the first adopter of an innovation or new product discusses it with two other people, and each of these two adopters passes the new idea along to two other people, and so on, the resulting distribution yields a normal bell shape when plotted.[45]

FIGURE 4-1

Adopter Categories

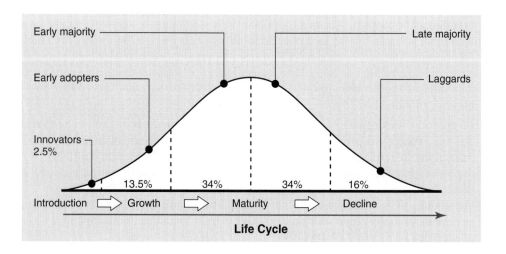

---

[45]For an excellent application and discussion of adopter categories, see Malcolm Gladwell, *The Tipping Point* (New York: Little, Brown, and Company, 2000), chapter 6.

Diffusion of Innovations in Pacific Rim Countries

In a recent cross-national comparison of the United States, Japan, South Korea, and Taiwan, Takada and Jain present evidence that different country characteristics—in particular, culture and communication patterns—affect diffusion processes for room air conditioners, washing machines, and calculators. Proceeding from the observation that Japan, South Korea, and Taiwan are high-context cultures with relatively homogeneous populations and the United States is a low-context, heterogeneous culture, Takada and Jain surmised that Asia would show faster rates of diffusion than the United States. A second hypothesis supported by the research was that adoption would proceed more quickly in markets where innovations were introduced relatively late. Presumably, the lag time would give potential consumers more opportunity to assess the relative advantages, compatibility, and other product attributes. Takada and Jain's research has important marketing implications. They note:

> If a marketing manager plans to enter the newly industrializing countries (NICs) or other Asia markets with a product that has proved to be successful in the home market, the product's diffusion processes are likely to be much faster than in the home market.[46]

As noted before, there are likely to be fewer innovators in Japan and other Asian countries, where risk avoidance is high. However, as the Tamagotchi story illustrated, once consumers become aware that others have tried the product, they follow suit quickly so as not to be left behind.

MARKETING IMPLICATIONS OF SOCIAL AND CULTURAL ENVIRONMENTS

The various cultural factors described earlier can exert important influences on consumer and industrial products marketing around the globe. These factors must be recognized in formulating a global marketing plan. **Environmental sensitivity** reflects the extent to which products must be adapted to the culture-specific needs of different national markets. A useful approach is to view products on a continuum of environmental sensitivity. At one end of the continuum are environmentally insensitive products that do not require significant adaptation to the environments of various world markets. At the other end of the continuum are products that are highly sensitive to different environmental factors. A company with environmentally insensitive products will spend relatively less time determining the specific and unique conditions of local markets because the product is basically universal. The greater a product's environmental sensitivity, the greater the need for managers to address country-specific economic, regulatory, technological, social, and cultural environmental conditions.

The sensitivity of products can be represented on a two-dimensional scale as shown in Figure 4-2. The horizontal axis shows environmental sensitivity, the vertical axis the degree for product adaptation needed. Any product exhibiting low levels of environmental sensitivity—integrated circuits, for example—belongs in the lower left of the figure. Intel has sold more than 100 million microprocessors because a chip is a chip anywhere around the world. Moving to the right on the horizontal axis, the level of sensitivity increases, as does the amount of adaptation. Computers exhibit moderate levels of environmental sensitivity; variations in country voltage requirements require some adaptation. In addition, the computer's software documentation should be in the local language.

---

[46]Hirokazu Takada and Dipak Jain, "Cross-National Analysis of Diffusion of Consumer Durable Goods in Pacific Rim Countries," *Journal of Marketing* 55 (April 1991), pp. 48–53.

FIGURE 4-2

Environmental Sensitivity

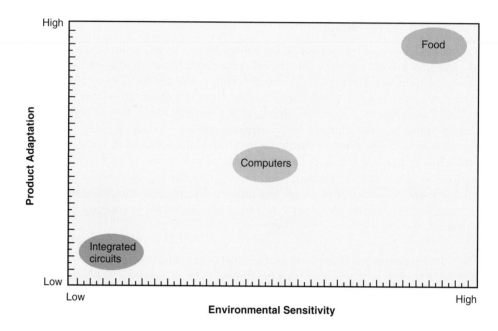

At the upper right of Figure 4-2 are products with high environmental sensitivity. Food sometimes falls into this category because it is sensitive to climate and culture. As we saw in the McDonald's case at the end of Chapter 1, the fast-food giant has achieved great success outside the United States by adapting its menu items to local tastes. GE's turbine generating equipment may also appear on the high-sensitivity end of the continuum; in many countries, local equipment manufacturers receive preferential treatment when bidding on national projects.

Research studies show that, independent of social class and income, culture is a significant influence on consumption behavior and durable goods ownership.[47] Consumer products are probably more sensitive to cultural difference than are industrial products. Hunger is a basic physiological need in Maslow's hierarchy; everyone needs to eat, but what we want to eat can be strongly influenced by culture. Evidence from the front lines of the marketing wars suggests that food is probably the most sensitive category of consumer products. CPC International failed to win popularity for Knorr dehydrated soups among Americans. The U.S. soup market was dominated by the Campbell Soup Company; 90 percent of the soup consumed by households was canned. Knorr was a Swiss company acquired by CPC that had a major share of the European prepared food market, where bouillon and dehydrated soups account for 80 percent of consumer soup sales. Despite CPC's failure to change the soup-eating habits of Americans, the company (now called Bestfoods and a unit of Unilever) is a successful global marketer with operations in more than 60 countries and sales in 110 countries.

Thirst also shows how needs differ from wants. Hydration is a universal physiological need (see Exhibit 4-10). As is the case with food and cooking, however, the particular liquids people *want* to drink can be strongly influenced by culture. Coffee is a beverage category that illustrates the point. On the European continent, coffee has been consumed for centuries. By contrast, Britain has historically been a nation of tea drinkers, and the notion of afternoon tea is firmly entrenched in British culture. In the 1970s, tea outsold coffee by a ratio of 4 to 1. Brits who did drink coffee tended to buy it in instant form, because the preparation of instant is similar to that of tea. By the 1990s, however, Britain was experiencing an economic boom and an explosion of new nightclubs and restaurants. Trendy Londoners looking for a non-pub "third place" found it in the form of Seattle Coffee Company cafés. An instant success after the first store was opened by coffee-starved Americans in 1995, by 1998 Seattle Coffee had

[47]Charles M. Schaninger, Jacques C. Bourgeois, and Christian W. Buss, "French-English Canadian Subcultural Consumption Differences," *Journal of Marketing* 49 (Spring 1985), pp. 82–92.

Exhibit 4-10: In countries where ground water may be contaminated, bottled water is a convenient alternative. The fastest growth in the industry is occurring in developing countries; in the past five years, bottled water consumption has tripled in India and more than doubled in China. However, the Earth Policy Institute views bottled water as an overpriced, wasteful extravagance. The International Bottled Water Association disagrees with that view. A spokesman said, "We're an on-the-go society demanding convenient packaging and consistent quality, and that's what bottled water provides."
Source: Gurinder Osan/AP Wide World Photos.

65 locations around London. Starbucks bought the business from its founders for $84 million. By 2005, Starbucks had overcome the challenge of high real estate prices and had 466 locations in the United Kingdom.[48]

Summary

Culture, a society's "programming of the mind," has both a pervasive and changing influence on each national market environment. Global marketers must recognize the influence of culture and be prepared to either respond to it or change it. Human behavior is a function of a person's own unique personality and that person's interaction with the collective forces of the particular society and culture in which he or she has lived. In particular, **attitudes**, **values**, and **beliefs** can vary significantly from country to country. Also, differences pertaining to religion, **aesthetics**, dietary customs, and language and communication can affect local reaction to a company's brands or products as well as the ability of company personnel to function effectively in different cultures. A number of concepts and theoretical frameworks provide insights into these and other cultural issues.

Cultures can be classified as **high-** or **low-context**; communication and negotiation styles can differ from country to country. Hofstede's social values typology helps marketers understand culture in terms of **power distance, individualism** versus **collectivism, masculinity** versus **femininity, uncertainty avoidance,** and **long-** versus **short-term orientation**. By understanding the **self-reference criterion,** global marketers can overcome the unconscious tendency for perceptual blockage and distortion.

Rogers' classic study on the **diffusion of innovations** helps explain how products are adopted over time by different **adopter categories**. The **adoption process** that consumers go through can be divided into a multi-stage **hierarchy of effects.** Rogers' findings concerning the **characteristics of innovations** can also help marketers successfully launch new products in global markets. Recent research has suggested that Asian adopter categories differ from the Western model. An awareness of **environmental sensitivity** can help marketers determine whether consumer and industry products must be adapted to the needs of different markets.

---

[48]Deborah Ball, "Lattes Lure Brits to Coffee," *The Wall Street Journal* (October 20, 2005), pp. B1, B6. See also Marco R. della Cava, "Brewing a British Coup," *USA Today* (September 16, 1998), pp. D1, D2.

Discussion Questions

1. What are some of the elements that make up culture? How do these find expression in your native culture?
2. What is the difference between a low-context culture and a high-context culture? Give an example of a country that is an example of each type, and provide evidence for your answer.
3. How can Hofstede's cultural typologies help Western marketers better understand Asian culture?
4. Explain the self-reference criterion. Go to the library and find examples of product failures that might have been avoided through the application of the SRC.
5. Briefly explain the social research of Everett Rogers regarding diffusion of innovations, characteristics of innovations, and adopter categories. How does the adoption process in Asia differ from the traditional Western model?
6. Compare and contrast the United States and Japan in terms of traditions and organizational behavior and norms.

In Hong Kong, park officials underestimated the number of guests the park would attract during the 2006 Lunar New Year holiday. Some ticket holders were turned away, prompting complaints that the 310-acre park was too small. Disney officials were slow to recognize that Chinese vacationers who live on the mainland often book package tours. Tour operators choose restaurants, shopping opportunities, and other destinations that generate the highest fees and commissions. Because the tour operators receive a percentage of a group's total dining tab, they may steer tourists away from destinations that do not include dinners in the tour package. At first, Hong Kong Disneyland didn't offer a tour package that included dinners. A new "dining with Disney" program was quickly rolled out. To round out the promotion, individual tour operators were offered a 50 percent individual discount as an incentive to visit Disneyland personally so they would have first-hand experience at the park.

Disney also went to great lengths to capitalize on an astrological coincidence: According to the traditional Chinese calendar, 2008 was the year of the rat. In Hong Kong, Mickey and Minnie Mouse wore special red costumes as Disney proclaimed 2008 to be the "Year of the Mouse." Because the Chinese government tightly controls television and motion picture standards, Disney emphasized affordable consumer products such as plush toys and Disney-themed clothing to generate awareness and interest in the Disney brand.

In 2009, amidst the global economic downturn and ongoing challenges at Hong Kong Disneyland, Disney's Parks and Resorts division announced plans for a new $3.6 billion park in Shanghai. The proposed park would be owned jointly by Disney and the Shanghai municipal government. Consisting of a theme park, hotel, and shops, the development would create 50,000 much-needed jobs. The proposal must be approved by the State Council of China's central government. Shanghai Disneyland is an important element in Disney's strategy for penetrating the local market. However, the proposal does not address Disney's need for increased media exposure; company officials believe that a Chinese Disney TV channel is essential to build awareness of the Disney brand and interest in the new theme park.

Disney's other divisions are also pursuing a more localized approach in key emerging markets. Executives are betting that this strategy will be the key to boosting revenues and profits in emerging markets. As Jason Reed, general manager for Walt Disney Studios International Productions, noted, "We've been very successful with our big global productions, such as *Pirates of the Caribbean* and *National Treasure.* But we think there's a natural way to supplement these films in areas like China, Russia, and India—areas that have built-in film traditions."

For example, in India, Disney is abandoning its go-it-alone policy and partnering with local companies such as Yash Raj Films. Local managers have been given greater autonomy to develop television programming. One new Hindi-language show, *Dhoom Machaao Dhoom,* concerns a girl's quest for identity after living in the United States; another show, *Vicky and Vetal,* concerns a boy's friendship with a 300-year-old ghost. The new approach is clearly paying off. In 2008, Disney released *Roadside Romeo,* its first animated feature developed specifically for India. The film was box-office gold, with the best opening weekend of any Disney feature in India.

Disney is hoping to appeal to India's family-oriented middle-class consumers; core themes include "believe in yourself, express yourself, and celebrate your family." Because the number of cable television subscribers is increasingly rapidly, Disney launched the Disney Channel and Toon Disney. In addition, the company acquired Hugama, a children's channel. Disney is also making Indian versions of its hit movie *High School Musical.* One challenge in India is the number of languages and dialects. *Roadside Romeo* was released in Hindi, Tamil, and Teluga. Future projects may be produced specifically for southern India where movie preferences are markedly different than in the north.

Disney is "going native" in other emerging markets as well. 2009's *Book of Masters* was the company's first live-action film for the Russian market. A Russian version of *High School Musical* is also in the works. Next up: the Middle East. As Disney's Jason Reed says, "There's a really strong affinity between the strong family values in the region and the Disney brand. We want to go out and try to make a film that will play to families from North Africa to the Gulf States."

Case 4-1 Discussion Questions

1. Why is it necessary for Disney to build brand awareness in China and other emerging markets?
2. Do you agree with Disney's decision to pursue a localization approach in emerging markets?
3. Why is *High School Musical* so successful in global markets?

Sources: James T. Areddy and Peter Sanders, "Disney's Shanghai Park Plan Advances," *The Wall Street Journal* (January 10/11, 2009), pp. A1, A7; Matthew Garrahan, "Disney Indian Adventure Rewarded," *Financial Times* (November 12, 2008), p. 18; Geoffrey A. Fowler, "Main Street, H.K.," *The Wall Street Journal* (January 23, 2008), pp. B1, B2; Merissa Marr, "Small World: Disney Rewrites Script to Win Fans in India," *The Wall Street Journal* (June 11, 2007), pp. A1, A10; Geoffrey Fowler and Merissa Marr, "Disney and the Great Wall," *The Wall Street Journal* (February 9, 2006), pp. B1, B2; Paul Wiseman, "Miscues Mar Opening of Hong Kong Disney," *USA Today* (November 10, 2005), p. 5B.

It's a basic law of economics: When supply goes up, price goes down. That is the situation that faced the coffee industry in the early twenty-first century, as a glut of coffee beans led to sharply lower prices on world commodities markets. Historically, coffee has been one of the most lucrative exports in many developing nations. Green, unroasted coffee beans are traded on the London and New York futures markets; Volcafe and Neumann Gruppe are large coffee traders that buy about 25 percent of the world's coffee supply. Other major players include Procter & Gamble (P&G), Kraft, and Nestlé; all three are key suppliers to the grocery industry, where the greatest percentage of coffee is purchased. For example, P&G sells about $1 billion worth of Folgers coffee each year. Specialty coffees such as those marketed by Starbucks are regarded as niche products that account for only about 2 percent of the world's supply of coffee beans.

In 1999, the wholesale price for coffee was about $1.40 per pound; in 2001, the price dropped to $0.42. By the end of 2003, prices had recovered to about $0.50 per pound; however, the cost of producing and processing green coffee beans is between $0.80 and $0.90 per pound. Oversupply is another problem. Between 1990 and 2000, Vietnam's production soared from 84,000 tons to 950,000 tons; Vietnam produces mostly robusta beans, which are cheaper and have a harsher taste than arabica beans. According to the International Coffee Organization, the 2001–2002 harvest yielded 115 million sacks of coffee. However, worldwide consumption only absorbed 105 million bags. Low prices and excess supply all add up to bad news for 25 million coffee farmers in Latin American and Africa.

Since the mid-1990s, Starbucks has pursued a policy of improving working conditions at its suppliers; however, Starbucks' annual coffee purchases amount to only about $180 million. A number of different nongovernmental organizations have begun to address the situation faced by farmers who supply the broader coffee market. For example, the Rainforest Alliance works with big corporations to monitor environmental and working conditions in developing countries. It was a pioneer in certifying lumber sourced from forests in the tropics. It certifies about $12.5 billion worth of coffee beans each year. The Fairtrade Labeling Organization International (FLO; www.fairtrade.net) is a certification authority based in Bonn, Germany, that licenses its trademark to organizations such as the UK's Fairtrade Foundation (www.fairtrade.org.uk). The Fairtrade label on a bag or can of coffee indicates that growers were paid a fair price for their crops. TransFair USA is a fair-trade certification organization in the United States (www.transfairusa.org).

Coffee bearing the Fairtrade label is often marketed with the help of charitable organizations; for example, Oxfam, a private charity in Britain, joined with Equal Exchange, a fair trade distribution company, Traidcraft, and Twin to create a new coffee brand called Cafédirect (www.cafedirect.co.uk). In addition to providing price supports, such organizations also sponsor training and development programs to help growers become more knowledgeable about market prices and learn ways to reach export markets. Catholic Relief Services (CRS)

recently launched an effort to encourage America's 65 million Catholics to buy fair trade coffee (www.crsfairtrade.org/coffee). The CRS Coffee Project is part of a larger organization, the Interfaith Coffee Program of Equal Exchange; the latter includes participants from Lutheran, Presbyterian, and Methodist groups. The bottom line: Wholesale coffee buyers that participate in the fair trade program agree to pay farmers $1.26 per pound for regular coffee beans and $1.41 for higher quality, organic beans.

Source: The Image Works.

Source: Cafedirect.

The Fairtrade coffee movement is gaining momentum among socially conscious consumers. For example, in 2002, the interfaith partnership in the United States sold nearly $1.7 million of fair trade coffee at 7,500 houses of worship; sales in 2003 reached $2.7 million. Although impressive, that figure is a mere drop in the bucket;

annually, Americans spend about $19 billion on coffee. However, as Paul Rice, President and CEO of Transfair, noted, "If we could get every Catholic in the country to drink fair-trade coffee, that would be a huge market right there." He added, "But it's the ripple effect—getting all those people kind of up to speed on what fair trade is all about and getting them to ask for it at their local stores—that's going to have a much broader effect on the market."

"We've been in this business for 100 years and want to be in it for another 100. . . . This is not philanthropy. This is about incorporating sustainable coffee into our mainstream brands as a way to have a more efficient and competitive way of doing business."

Annemieke Wijm, Senior Director for Commodity Sustainability Programs, Kraft Foods

Kraft recently signed an accord with the Rainforest Alliance; Kraft, which buys about 10 percent of the world's coffee crop, agreed to buy beans that are certified as produced with sustainable agricultural practices and blend them into their mass-market brands. The purchases will amount to about $3.1 billion annually and will benefit farmers in Brazil, Colombia, Mexico, and Central America. Tensie Whelen, executive director for the Rainforest Alliance, hailed the accord, noting, "This step by Kraft marks the beginning of transforming the coffee industry. You have a company capable of shaping markets commit to buying a significant amount of coffee and to mainstreaming across their brands and not 'ghettoising' it in one brand."

Meanwhile, industry experts disagree about ways to reduce the supply of low-quality beans. A recent Oxfam report recommended government financing to destroy five million bags of robusta beans currently being stored in warehouses in developing countries. Others would prefer not to ask for government intervention. Peter A. Reiling, president and chief executive of Technoserve, a nonprofit organization that promotes socially responsible entrepreneurship in developing countries, noted, "It's an emotional issue and everyone seems to have a different solution. I'd say there's no one silver bullet, but there are market solutions."

Discussion Questions

1. Is it important for coffee marketers such as Starbucks, Kraft, and Nestlé to create "ethical supply chains"? Why?

2. A recent study by the UK's Institute of Grocery Distribution determined that the majority of consumers do not buy fair trade products. The report noted, "Self-interest is at the center of food choice for most consumers. Few consumers consider the impact of their purchase decisions on anyone or anything but themselves and their family." Do you agree with this finding?

3. What recommendations would you make to help cure the ills of the coffee market?

Sources: Elizabeth Weise, "Fair Trade Sweetens Pot," *USA Today* (February 9, 2005), p. 6D; Mary Beth Marklein, "Goodness—To the Last Drop," *USA Today* (February 16, 2004), pp. 1D, 2D; Tony Smith, "Difficult Times for the Coffee Industry," *The New York Times* (November 25, 2003), p. W1; Sara Silver, "Kraft Blends Ethics with Coffee Beans," *Financial Times* (October 7, 2003), p. 10; Tim Harford, "Fairtrade Tries a Commercial Blend for Coffee," *Financial Times* (September 12, 2003), p. 10; In-Sung Yoo, "Faith Organizations Throw Weight Behind 'Fair Trade' Coffee Movement," *USA Today* (December 2, 2003), p. 7D; Peter Fritsche, "Bitter Brew: An Oversupply of Coffee Beans Deepens Latin America's Woes," *The Wall Street Journal* (July 8, 2002), pp. A1, A10.

The Political, Legal, and Regulatory Environments

Case 5-1
America's Cuban Conundrum

When Barack Obama was sworn in as the 43rd president of the United States, he inherited a situation that had confounded his predecessors in the Oval Office for half a century. The problem was Cuba, the tiny island nation in the Caribbean that, until recently, had been ruled by Fidel Castro (see Exhibit 5-1). His health failing, Castro handed over the levers of power to his brother Raul. And, as President Obama set out an ambitious agenda for sweeping changes, many observers wondered whether it was time for a new era of trade, support, and cooperation with Cuba.

In the decades after Castro took power, America's trade embargo with the island nation was a matter of presidential policy. Then, in 1996, President Bill Clinton signed the Cuban Liberty and Democratic Solidarity Act, also known as the Helms-Burton Act. The president's actions came after Cuban MiGs shot down two U.S. civilian airplanes, killing the four Cuban-Americans who were on board. The act has two key provisions. First, it denies entry into the United States to corporate officers of companies from other countries doing business on U.S. property in Cuba that was confiscated by the Cuban government.

Exhibit 5-1: During nearly 50 years in power, Fidel Castro remained unrepentant and clung to his socialist economic policies. In denouncing "neo-liberal globalization," Castro said, "The more contact we have with capitalism, the more repugnance I feel."
Source: Alejandro Ernesto/Landov Media.

Second, it allows U.S. companies and citizens to sue foreign firms and investors doing business on U.S. property confiscated in Cuba. However, in July 1996, the president ordered a six-month moratorium on lawsuits. Washington pledged to keep the embargo in place until Cuban President Fidel Castro held free elections and released political prisoners. You will learn more about the decision alternatives facing President Obama with respect to Cuba in the continuation of Case 5-1 at the end of this chapter.

America's complex relationship with Cuba illustrates the impact that the political, legal, and regulatory environments can have on international trade and global marketing activities. Each of the world's national governments regulates trade and commerce with other countries and attempts to control the access of outside enterprises to national resources. Every country has its own unique legal and regulatory system that affects the operations and activities of the global enterprise, including the global marketer's ability to address market opportunities and threats. Laws and regulations constrain the cross-border movement of products, services, people, money, and know-how. The global marketer must attempt to comply with each set of national—and, in some instances, regional—constraints. The fact that laws and regulations are frequently ambiguous and continually changing hamper these efforts.

In this chapter, we consider the basic elements of the political, legal, and regulatory environments of global marketing, including the most pressing current issues and some suggested approaches for dealing with those issues. Some specific topics, such as rules for exporting and importing industrial and consumer products, standards for health and safety, and regulations regarding packaging, labeling, advertising, and promotion, are covered in later chapters devoted to individual marketing mix elements.

THE POLITICAL ENVIRONMENT

Global marketing activities take place within the political environment of governmental institutions, political parties, and organizations through which a country's people and rulers exercise power. As we saw in Chapter 4, each nation has a unique culture that reflects its society. Each nation also has a *political culture*, which reflects the relative importance of the government and legal system and provides a context within which individuals and corporations understand their relationship to the political system. Any company doing business outside its home country should carefully study the political culture in the target country and analyze salient issues arising from the political environment. These include the governing party's attitude toward sovereignty, political risk, taxes, the threat of equity dilution, and expropriation.

Nation-States and Sovereignty

Sovereignty can be defined as supreme and independent political authority. A century ago, U.S. Supreme Court Chief Justice Melville Fuller said, "Every sovereign state is bound to respect the independence of every other sovereign state, and the courts in one country will not sit in judgment on the acts of government of another done within its territory." More recently, Richard Stanley, president of the Stanley Foundation, offered the following concise description:

> A sovereign state was considered free and independent. It regulated trade, managed the flow of people into and out of its boundaries, and exercised undivided jurisdiction over all persons and property within its territory. It had the right, authority, and ability to conduct its domestic affairs without outside interference and to use its international power and influence with full discretion.[1]

---

[1] See *Changing Concepts of Sovereignty: Can the United Nations Keep Pace?* (Muscatine, IA: The Stanley Foundation, 1992), p. 7.

Government actions taken in the name of sovereignty occur in the context of two important criteria: a country's stage of development and the political and economic system in place in the country.

As outlined in Chapter 2, the economies of individual nations may be classified as industrialized, newly industrializing, or developing. Many governments in developing countries exercise control over their nations' economic development by passing protectionist laws and regulations. Their objective is to encourage economic development by protecting emerging or strategic industries. Government leaders can also engage in cronyism and provide favors for family members or "good friends." For example, former Indonesian president Suharto established a national car program that granted tax breaks and tariff privileges to a company established in South Korea by his youngest son. The United States, EU, and Japan responded by taking the matter to the WTO.

Conversely, when many nations reach advanced stages of economic development, their governments declare that (in theory, at least) any practice or policy that restrains free trade is illegal. Antitrust laws and regulations are established to promote fair competition. Advanced country laws often define and preserve a nation's social order; laws may extend to political, cultural, and even intellectual activities and social conduct. In France, for example, laws forbid the use of foreign words such as *le weekend* or *le marketing* in official documents. Also, a French law passed in 1996 requires that at least 40 percent of the songs played by popular radio stations must be French. Companies that may be affected positively or negatively by legislative acts often use advertising as a vehicle for expressing their position on the issue (see Exhibit 5-2).

We also noted in Chapter 2 that most of the world's economies combine elements of market and nonmarket systems. The sovereign political power of a government in a predominantly nonmarket economy reaches quite far into the economic life of a country. By contrast, in a capitalist, market-oriented democracy, that power tends to be much more constrained. A current global phenomenon in both nonmarket and market structures is the trend toward privatization, which reduces direct governmental involvement as a supplier of goods and services in a given economy. In essence, each act of privatization moves a nation's economy further in the free-market direction. The trend is clearly evident in Mexico, where, at one time, the government controlled over 1,000 "parastatals." By the early 1990s, most had been sold, as President Carlos Salinas de Gortari presided over the sale of full or partial stakes in enterprises worth $23 billion, including the two Mexican airlines, mines, and banks. Privatization in Mexico and elsewhere is evidence that national governments are changing *how* they exercise sovereign power.

Some observers believe global market integration is eroding national economic sovereignty. Economic consultant Neal Soss notes, "The ultimate resource of a government is power, and we've seen repeatedly that the willpower of governments can be overcome by persistent attacks from the marketplace."[2] Is this a disturbing trend? If the issue is framed in terms of marketing, the concept of the exchange comes to the fore: Nations may be willing to give up sovereignty in return for something of value. If countries can increase their share of world trade and increase national income, perhaps they will be willing to cede some sovereignty. In Europe, the individual EU countries are giving up the right to have their own currencies, ceding the right to set their own product standards, and are making other sacrifices in exchange for improved market access.

Political Risk

Political risk is the possibility of a change in a country's political environment or government policy that would adversely affect a company's ability to operate effectively and profitably. As Ethan Kapstein, a professor at INSEAD, has noted:

> Perhaps the greatest threats to the operations of global corporations, and those that are most difficult to manage, arise out of the political environment in which they conduct their business. One day, a foreign company is a welcome member of the local community; the next day, opportunistic politicians vilify it.[3]

Political risk can deter a company from investing abroad; to put it another way, when a high level of uncertainty characterizes a country's political environment, it may have difficulty in

---

[2]Cited in Karen Pennar, "Is the Nation-State Obsolete in a Global Economy?" *Business Week* (July 17, 1995), p. 80.
[3]Ethan Kapstein, "Avoiding Unrest in a Volatile Environment," *Financial Times—Mastering Uncertainty, Pt I* (March 17, 2006), p. 5.

Motherhood, apple pie and GATT

Quick, name something supported by Presidents Clinton, Bush and Reagan; 450 leading American economists, including four Nobel laureates; the National Governors Association; the Consumers Union; the Business Roundtable, and many others.

Motherhood? Apple pie? Well, probably. But there's no doubt that each of those individuals and organizations supports GATT, the General Agreement on Tariffs and Trade. What's known as the Uruguay Round of GATT, an accord that took 117 countries more than seven years to negotiate, is now awaiting approval by Congress.

The agreement will reduce import tariffs worldwide by an average of 40 percent and cover new areas such as agriculture, intellectual property and some services — areas of importance to the U.S. economy. It could generate as much as $5 trillion in new worldwide commerce by 2005.

In the words of former President Ronald Reagan: "In trade, everyone ends up a winner as markets grow." We've seen evidence of that this year since the North American Free Trade Agreement (NAFTA) went into effect January 1. Despite negative predictions to the contrary, trade is up, consumer prices are down and massive layoffs just haven't happened.

While the GATT tariff reductions are smaller than those for NAFTA, the number of countries involved and the size of their trade flows are much larger. GATT's effect on the U.S. alone will be five times that of NAFTA.

We hope the enacting legislation is approved before Congress adjourns for the year — and without any financing features that would hurt the companies GATT is intended to help.

What will GATT mean for the U.S.?

First, it's important to note that international trade represents about a quarter of U.S. gross domestic product, or GDP — the value of what the nation produces. Over the last five years, exports accounted for half of U.S. economic growth. More than 10.5 million U.S. workers owe their jobs directly or indirectly to the export of goods or services, and another 500,000 to 1.4 million jobs — at higher-than-average pay — are predicted from GATT.

The Treasury Department estimates that the long-range benefits of this GATT accord will amount to $100 billion to $200 billion a year in added income to the U.S., or $1,700 per family. Other studies predict increases to the GDP as high as 1.2 percent. Agricultural exports alone are expected to rise by as much as $8.5 billion a year in the next decade.

What makes GATT such a boon to the U.S.?

■ Foreign countries on average have more trade restrictions and tariffs on U.S. goods than the U.S. does on theirs. GATT will reduce tariffs and level the playing field.

■ GATT will, for the first time, protect "intellectual property" like patents, trademarks and copyrights. That'll help U.S. computer-software, entertainment, high-tech and pharmaceutical industries, to name a few.

■ Also for the first time, GATT will open markets for service industries like accounting, advertising, computer services, construction and engineering.

■ GATT will open markets for U.S. agricultural products.

So let's call our mothers, cut ourselves a slice of apple pie and let our senators and representatives know we want the GATT legislation passed this year.

Mobil®

Exhibit 5-2: Many global companies use corporate advertising to advocate their official position on trade-related issues. In the mid-1990s, Mobil mounted an ad campaign that addressed a number of topics of public interest, including trade issues, clean air, alternative fuels, and health care reform. This ad urged the U.S. Congress to approve GATT. *Source:* ExxonMobil Historical Collection, The Center for American History, The University of Texas at Austin.

attracting foreign investment. However, as Professor Kapstein points out, executives often fail to conceptualize political risk because they have not studied political science. For this reason, they have not been exposed to the issues that students of politics ask about the activities of global companies. (A strong argument for a liberal arts education!) Current events must be part of the information agenda; for example, businesspeople need to stay apprised of the formation and evolution of political parties. Valuable sources of information include *The Economist*, *Financial Times*, and other business periodicals. The Economist Intelligence Unit (EIU; www.eiu.com), the Geneva-based Business Environment Risk Intelligence (BERI SA; www.beri.com), and the PRS Group (www.prsgroup.com) publish up-to-date political risk reports on individual country markets. These commercial sources vary somewhat in the criteria that constitute political risk.

For example, BERI focuses on societal and system attributes, whereas The PRS Group focuses more directly on government actions and economic functions (see Table 5-1).

For example, the political maneuverings of former president Boris Yeltsin's government in Russia created a high level of political risk. Vladimir Putin, Yeltsin's successor, is implementing reforms in an effort to pave the way for Russia's membership in the WTO and to attract foreign investment. The government has a number of bills pending that, if adopted, will strengthen intellectual property and contract law. Medium-term prospects for the transformation of the Russian market appear good. However, as Roland Nash, a Moscow-based investment banker, recently noted, "Political risk is still perceived as being very high here. As an investor in Russia, you have to believe in Putin. You still really can't believe in the rule of law."[4] The current political climate in the rest of Central and Eastern Europe is still characterized by varying degrees of uncertainty. Hungary, Latvia, and Albania represent three different levels of risk. Hungary and Latvia have already achieved upper-middle-income status, although Latvia is projected to grow more slowly. In Albania, the transition to a market economy has been hampered by an ongoing feud between the country's socialist prime minister and the leader of the opposition Democratic party.[5] Diligent attention to risk assessment throughout the region should be ongoing to determine when the risk has decreased to levels acceptable to management.

Companies can purchase insurance to offset potential risks arising from the political environment. In Japan, Germany, France, Britain, the United States, and other industrialized nations, various agencies offer investment insurance to corporations doing business abroad. The Overseas Private Investment Corporation (OPIC; www.opic.gov) provides various types of political risk insurance to U.S. companies; in Canada, the Export Development Corporation performs a similar function. OPIC's activities came under scrutiny in 1997 when the Clinton administration proposed reauthorizing it, along with the Ex-Im Bank. Some legislators wanted to dismantle both agencies

TABLE 5-1 Categories of Political Risk

EIU	Business Environment Risk Intelligence (BERI)	The PRS Group Political Risk Services
War	Fractionalization of the political spectrum	Political turmoil probability
Social unrest	Fractionalization by language, ethnic, and/or religious groups	Equity restrictions
Orderly political transfer	Restrictive/coercive measures required to retain power	Local operations restrictions
Politically motivated violence	Mentality (xenophobia, nationalism, corruption, nepotism)	Taxation discrimination
International disputes	Social conditions (including population density and wealth distribution)	Repatriation restrictions
Change in government/ pro-business orientation	Organization and strength of forces for a radical government	Exchange controls
Institutional effectiveness	Dependence on and/or importance to a major hostile power	Tariff barriers
Bureaucracy	Negative influences of regional political forces	Other barriers
Transparency or fairness	Societal conflict involving demonstrations, strikes, and street violence	Payment delays
Corruption	Instability as perceived by assassinations and guerilla war	Fiscal or monetary expansion
Crime		Labor costs
		Foreign debt

Source: Adapted from Llewellyn D. Howell, *The Handbook of Country and Political Risk Analysis,* 2nd ed. (East Syracuse, NY: The PRS Group, Inc., 1998). Reprinted by permission.

---

[4]David Lynch, "Russia Brings Revitalized Economy to the Table," *USA Today* (July 13, 2006), p. 2B.
[5]Leyla Boulton, "Political Discord Slows EU March," *Financial Times—Albania: Special Report* (May 18, 2004), p. 22.

⇥ STRATEGIC DECISION MAKING IN GLOBAL MARKETING
Microsoft Versus the EU

In 1998, Sun Microsystems filed a lawsuit in U.S. Federal court alleging that Microsoft was restricting the ability of servers marketed by Sun and other companies to interface with PCs running the Windows operating system. More than 90 percent of the world's PCs run Windows as well as other Microsoft software; some of Microsoft's rivals believe the company uses unfair business practices to dominate the global software market.

Although Microsoft settled the U.S. case in 2001, the European Commission had also begun to investigate Sun's complaint; the Commission also launched a separate investigation to determine whether Microsoft was creating a monopoly in digital music downloads and other new market segments by bundling Windows with its Media Player program.

The Commission finally issued a ruling in spring 2004 that Microsoft had violated antitrust laws. Three penalties were imposed. First, Microsoft must allow computer makers to market Windows-equipped PCs equipped with alternative brands of media software for playing music and videos. Second, Microsoft must provide competitors with more information about Windows codes and protocols, spurring innovation in new software products. Finally, Microsoft was ordered to pay a record fine of $602 million (see Exhibit 5-3).

Microsoft had taken the offensive by paying $3 billion to Sun, Novell, and RealNetworks to drop their charges in both the United States and the European Union. Meanwhile, some regulators suggested that Microsoft was intentionally delaying compliance with the commission's orders. A key task was to produce an instruction manual that would help rival companies write Windows-compatible software. Microsoft took the position that doing so amounted to revealing intellectual property. The manual would be especially helpful to companies that service the low-cost, open-source operating system known as Linux. Both copyright and patent law protect Windows source code.

Taking the legal notion of "disclosure" to an extreme, Microsoft sent the regulators boxes containing thousands of pages of documents pertaining to the manual. After the EU team complained, Microsoft sent a lawyer to help sift through the documents. When engineers from Sun, Oracle, Novell, and IBM went to Microsoft headquarters to view the 12,000-page manual, security was tight. The visitors concluded that the manual was disorganized and of no use. The commission ordered Microsoft to improve the manual.

Meanwhile, Neelie Kroes, a former Dutch cabinet minister, became the European commissioner for competition. She met with Microsoft CEO Steve Ballmer to try to settle the matter, but to no avail. After an outside technical consultant determined that the manual was still inadequate, the commissioner formally charged Microsoft with disregarding orders. Microsoft countered that the commission had not made clear exactly what kind of documentation was to be produced.

In July 2006, the commission fined Microsoft an additional €280.5 million for failing to comply with the 2004 antitrust ruling. Kroes also indicated that the precedents in the case would be applied to Vista, Microsoft's forthcoming replacement for Windows. In particular, the concern was that Vista would be bundled with Internet search software that would be an alternative to Google as well as a fixed document reader similar to Adobe Acrobat.

Sources: Tobias Buck, "Microsoft Closer to European Truce," *Financial Times* (July 13, 2006), p. 14; Mary Jacoby, "EU Hits Microsoft with $358.3 Million Penalty," *The Wall Street Journal* (July 13, 2006), p. A3; Mary Jacoby, "Second Front: Why Microsoft Battles Europe Years after Settling with U.S.," *The Wall Street Journal* (May 5, 2006), pp. A1, A12; Adam Cohen, "Microsoft Faces Threat of More Fines in Europe," *The Wall Street Journal* (February 15, 2006), p. B2; Brandon Mitchener, "EU Backs Plans to Punish Microsoft," *The Wall Street Journal* (March 6, 2004), p. B3; Mitchener, James Kanter, and Don Clark, "Regulatory Jolt: EU Warns Microsoft Is Abusing Its Control of Certain Software," *The Wall Street Journal* (August 7, 2003), pp. A1, A2.

---

as part of an effort to reduce government involvement in business. These legislators criticized the agencies for providing unnecessary subsidies to large corporations.[6]

Taxes

Governments rely on tax revenues to generate funds necessary for social services, the military, and other expenditures. Unfortunately, government taxation policies on the sale of goods and services frequently motivate companies and individuals to profit by *not* paying taxes. In China, import duties have dropped since the country joined the WTO. Even so, many goods are still subject to double-digit duties plus a 17 percent value-added tax (VAT). As a result, significant quantities of oil, cigarettes, photographic film, personal computers, and other products are smuggled into China. In some instances, customs documents are falsified to undercount goods in a shipment; the Chinese military has allegedly escorted goods into the country as well. Ironically, global companies can still profit from the practice; it has been estimated, for example, that 90 percent of the foreign cigarettes sold in China are smuggled in. For Philip Morris, this means annual sales of $100 million to distributors in

---

[6]Nancy Dunne, "Eximbank and OPIC Face Survival Test in U.S.," *Financial Times* (May 8, 1997), p. 8.

Exhibit 5-3: Following an antitrust ruling in 2004, Microsoft created Windows XP Edition N, an "unbundled" operating system for the European market that did not include the company's Media Player. In the spring of 2006, attorneys for Microsoft and the European Commission appeared before a 13-judge panel at the European Court of First Instance in Luxembourg. Microsoft's lawyers argued that negligible sales of Edition N constituted evidence that the 2004 ruling was a failure. In September 2007, the Court of First Instance upheld the European Commission's case against the software giant.
Source: Geert Vanden Wijingaert/AP Wide World Photos.

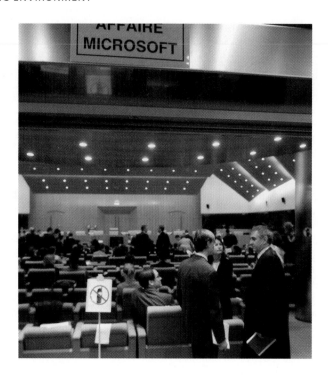

Hong Kong, who then smuggle the smokes across the border.[7] High excise and VAT taxes can also encourage legal cross-border shopping as consumers go abroad in search of good values. In Great Britain, for example, the Wine and Spirit Association estimates that, on average, cars returning from France are loaded with 80 bottles of wine.

Corporate taxation is another issue. The high level of political risk currently evident in Russia can be attributed in part to excessively high taxes on business operations. High taxes encourage many enterprises to engage in cash or barter transactions that are off the books and sheltered from the eyes of tax authorities. This, in turn, has created a liquidity squeeze that prevents companies from paying wages to employees; unpaid, disgruntled workers can contribute to political instability. Meanwhile, the Putin government is pursuing a tough new tax policy in an effort to shrink Russia's budget deficit and qualify for IMF loans. However, such policies should not have the effect of deterring foreign investment. As Bruce Bean, head of the American Chamber of Commerce in Moscow, recently summed up the situation:

> Change the name of the country, change the flag, change the border. Yes, this was done overnight. But build a market economy, introduce a meaningful tax system, create new accounting rules, accept the concept that companies which cannot compete should go bankrupt and the workers there lose their jobs? These things take time.[8]

Meanwhile, global companies are being caught up in the chaos. In July 1998, tax collectors seized dozens of automobiles belonging to Johnson & Johnson's (J&J) Russian division and froze the group's assets. The authorities claimed J&J owed $19 million in back taxes.

The diverse geographical activity of the global corporation also requires special attention to tax laws. Many companies make efforts to minimize their tax liability by shifting the location of income. For example, it has been estimated that tax minimization by foreign companies doing business in the United States costs the U.S. government $3 billion each year in lost revenue. In one approach, called "earnings stripping," foreign companies reduce earnings by making loans to U.S. affiliates rather than using direct investment to finance U.S. activities. The U.S. subsidiary can deduct the interest it pays on such loans and thereby reduce its tax burden.

---

[7]Craig S. Smith and Wayne Arnold, "China's Antismuggling Drive to Hurt U.S. Exporters that Support Crackdown," *The Wall Street Journal* (August 5, 1998), p. A12.
[8]Andrew Higgins, "Go Figure: At Russian Companies, Hard Numbers Often Hard to Come By," *The Wall Street Journal* (August 20, 1998), p. A9.

⋙ CULTURE WATCH
Europe Says "No" to GMOs

In 2008, prior to the onset of the global economic crisis, surging world demand caused the price of oil to spiral upward; cash-strapped consumers felt the economic pain every time they stopped at the gas pump. Adding to consumers' misery: prices for grocery staples were also going up, due in part to rising transportation costs as well as increased demand for food in China and other emerging markets. Meanwhile, the search for alternative fuel sources sparked interest in ethanol and other biofuels. The resulting increase in demand for corn also contributed to record prices for agricultural commodities.

As prices soared, politicians in all parts of the world looked for solutions. Some countries banned food exports to ensure adequate domestic supply. In Asian countries, authorities battled rice hoarding in the face of surging prices. What else could be done? Officials at Bayer, DuPont, Syngenta, Monsanto, and other companies that market genetically modified seeds believe that the answer is, in part, plant biotechnology. Sometimes known as GMOs, the first generation of biotech crops—primarily corn, cotton, soybeans, and canola—demonstrated increased resistance to insect pest and weeds. A new generation of GMOs currently under development could offer different benefits, such as drought and flood resistance, or better water efficiency.

There is a problem, however: A growing number of consumers around the world are deeply concerned about food products that have not been produced naturally. As a result, many are skeptical about GMOs and the benefits of eating food products that incorporate genetically engineered ingredients. As one French citizen noted, "We have a very risk-averse society that has been completely traumatized by food scares."

In Europe, a number of activist groups, including Greenpeace and Friends of the Earth (FoE), have taken up the fight against GMOs (see Exhibit 5-4). They claim that GMOs pose threats to both people and the environment; terms such as *Frankenfoods* have been used to put the point across. The general public, already cynical thanks to perceived governmental mishandling of the "mad cow" scare, has been receptive.

The GMO controversy is not limited to the industrialized world, however. In 2002, Zambia's president rejected a 26,000-ton shipment of genetically modified corn from the United States that was intended for famine relief. Robert Zoellick, the U.S. trade representative at the time, pointed the finger at Europe. "The European antiscientific policies are spreading to other corners of the world," he said. "I find it immoral that people are not being supplied food to live in Africa because people have invented dangers about biotechnology." Concerned that anti-GMO sentiment could spread to Asia, Latin America, and the Middle East, Zoellick hinted that the United States might take its complaint to the WTO. Meanwhile, the EU's executive arm was lobbying several member states to drop opposition to lifting the ban.

Monsanto and other biotech companies have begun to work more closely with government regulators. The companies had already been supplying regulatory agencies with their research; now, the companies are advocating certain changes in the U.S. Food and Drug Administration's policies concerning GMOs. The FDA currently regards most modified crops as identical to conventional ones as long as there is no change in nutrient content or composition. The agribusiness companies are hoping that the FDA can help reassure consumers so that mandatory labeling along the lines of the European model won't be required. American companies are also frustrated by lengthy regulatory delays in Europe, where all EU governments are involved in the process of approving new food products for sale to the public. A product is approved if a qualified majority is reached as a result of a weighted vote. At the European Commission itself, five separate directorates are involved in biotechnology issues, and two—DG Sanco and DG Environment—have responsibility for assessing the safety of the food supply.

Sources: Clive Cookson, "A Time to Sow?" *Financial Times* (July 11, 2008), p. 5; John W. Miller, "Stalk-Raving Mad," *The Wall Street Journal* (October 12, 2006), pp. B1, B5; John Mason and David Firn, "Monsanto Sees Seeds of Food Revolution in Europe," *Financial Times* (March 19, 2004), p. 6; Alison Maitland, "An Ethical Answer to Consumers' Fears," *Financial Times* (December 4, 2003), p. 11; Tony Smith, "Brazil to Lift Ban on Crops with Genetic Modification," *The New York Times* (September 25, 2003), p. W1; Norman E. Borlaug, "Science vs. Hysteria," *The Wall Street Journal* (January 22, 2003), p. A14; Elizabeth Becker, "U.S. Threatens to Act Against Europeans Over Modified Foods," *The New York Times* (January 10, 2003), p. A4.

Seizure of Assets

The ultimate threat a government can pose toward a company is seizing assets. **Expropriation** refers to governmental action to dispossess a foreign company or investor. Compensation is generally provided, although not often in the "prompt, effective, and adequate" manner provided for by international standards. If no compensation is provided, the action is referred to as **confiscation**.[9] International law is generally interpreted as prohibiting any act by a government to take foreign property without compensation. **Nationalization** is generally broader in scope than expropriation; it occurs when the government takes control of some or all of the

---

[9]Franklin R. Root, *Entry Strategies for International Markets* (New York: Lexington Books, 1994), p. 154.

Exhibit 5-4: European consumers have faced a number of food-safety issues in recent years, including outbreaks of hoof-and-mouth disease and mad cow disease. Not surprisingly, many Europeans are skeptical about GMOs (genetically-modified organisms) and the benefits of eating food products that incorporate genetically engineered ingredients. As one French citizen noted recently, "We have a very risk-averse society that has been completely traumatized by food scares."
Source: Pascal Parrot/abacapress.com/Newscom.

enterprises in a particular industry. International law recognizes nationalization as a legitimate exercise of government power, as long as the act satisfies a "public purpose" and is accompanied by "adequate payment" (i.e., one that reflects fair market value of the property).

In 1959, for example, the newly empowered Castro government nationalized property belonging to American sugar producers in retaliation for new American import quotas on sugar. Cuban-owned production sources were not nationalized. Castro offered compensation in the form of Cuban government bonds, which was adequate under Cuban law. The U.S. State Department viewed the particular act of nationalization as discriminatory and the compensation offered as inadequate.[10] More recently, South Korea nationalized Kia, the nation's number three automaker, in the wake of the Asian currency crisis. Some industry observers believe that a much-needed reform of Japan's banking system will require nationalization.

Short of outright expropriation or nationalization, the phrase *creeping expropriation* has been applied to limitations on economic activities of foreign firms in particular countries. These have included limitations on repatriation of profits, dividends, royalties, and technical assistance fees from local investments or technology arrangements. Other issues are increased local content requirements, quotas for hiring local nationals, price controls, and other restrictions affecting return on investment. Global companies have also suffered discriminatory tariffs and nontariff barriers that limit market entry of certain industrial and consumer goods, as well as discriminatory laws on patents and trademarks. Intellectual property restrictions have had the practical effect of eliminating or drastically reducing protection of pharmaceutical products.

In the mid-1970s, J&J and other foreign investors in India had to submit to a host of government regulations to retain majority equity positions in companies already established. Many of these rules were later copied in whole or in part by Malaysia, Indonesia, the Philippines, Nigeria, and Brazil. By the late 1980s, after a "lost decade" in Latin America characterized by debt crises and low GNP growth, lawmakers reversed many of these restrictive and discriminatory laws. The goal was to again attract foreign direct investment and badly needed Western technology. The end of the Cold War and restructuring of political allegiances contributed significantly to these changes.

When governments expropriate foreign property, there are impediments to action to reclaim that property. For example, according to the U.S. Act of State Doctrine, if the government of a foreign state is involved in a specific act, the U.S. court will not get involved. Representatives of expropriated companies may seek recourse through arbitration at the World Bank Investment Dispute Settlement Center. It is also possible to buy expropriation insurance from either a private company or a government agency such as OPIC. The expropriation of copper companies operating

---

[10]William R. Slomanson, *Fundamental Perspectives on International Law* (St. Paul, MN: West Publishing, 1990), p. 356.

in Chile in 1970 to 1971 shows the impact that companies can have on their own fate. Companies that strenuously resisted government efforts to introduce home-country nationals into the company management were expropriated outright; other companies that made genuine efforts to follow Chilean guidelines were allowed to remain under joint Chilean–U.S. management.

INTERNATIONAL LAW

International law may be defined as the rules and principles that nation-states consider binding upon themselves. International law pertains to property, trade, immigration, and other areas that have traditionally been under the jurisdiction of individual nations. International law applies only to the extent that countries are willing to assume all rights and obligations in these areas. The roots of modern international law can be traced back to the seventeenth century Peace of Westphalia. Early international law was concerned with waging war, establishing peace, and other political issues such as diplomatic recognition of new national entities and governments. Although elaborate international rules gradually emerged—covering, for example, the status of neutral nations—the creation of laws governing commerce proceeded on a state-by-state basis in the nineteenth century. International law still has the function of upholding order, although in a broader sense than dealing with problems arising from war. At first, international law was essentially an amalgam of treaties, covenants, codes, and agreements. As trade grew among nations, order in commercial affairs assumed increasing importance. The law had originally dealt only with nations as entities, but a growing body of law rejected the idea that only nations can be subject to international law.

Paralleling the expanding body of international case law in the twentieth century, new international judiciary organizations have contributed to the creation of an established rule of international law: The Permanent Court of International Justice (1920–1945); the International Court of Justice (ICJ; www.icj-cij.org), the judicial arm of the United Nations, founded in 1946; and the International Law Commission, established by the United States in 1947 (see Exhibit 5-5). Disputes arising between nations are issues of *public international law*, and they may be taken before the ICJ (also known as the World Court) located in The Hague. As described in the supplemental documents to the United Nations Charter, article 38 of the ICJ Statute concerns international law:

> The Court, whose function is to decide in accordance with international law such disputes as are submitted to it, shall apply:
>
> **a.** international conventions, whether general or particular, establishing rules expressly recognized by the contesting states;
> **b.** international custom, as evidence of a general practice accepted as law;

Exhibit 5-5: Located in The Hague, the International Court of Justice (ICJ) is the judicial arm of the United Nations. The court's 15 judges are elected to nine-year terms. The primary function of the ICJ is to settle disputes among different countries according to international law. The ICJ also offers advice on legal issues submitted by various international agencies.
Source: U.N./Corbis-NY.

c. the general principles of law recognized by civilized nations;
d. subject to the provisions of Article 59, judicial decisions and the teachings of the most highly qualified publicists of the various nations, as subsidiary means for the determination of rules of law.

Other sources of modern international law include treaties, international custom, judicial case decisions in the courts of law of various nations, and scholarly writings. What happens if a nation has allowed a case against it to be brought before the ICJ and then refuses to accept a judgment against it? The plaintiff nation can seek recourse through the United Nations Security Council, which can use its full range of powers to enforce the judgment.

Common Law Versus Civil Law

Private international law is the body of law that applies to disputes arising from commercial transactions between companies of different nations. As noted, laws governing commerce emerged gradually, leading to a major split in legal systems between various countries.[11] The story of law in the Western world can be traced to two sources: Rome, from which the continental European civil law tradition originated, and English common law, from which the U.S. legal system originated.

A **civil-law country** is one in which the legal system reflects the structural concepts and principles of the Roman Empire in the sixth century.

> For complex historical reasons, Roman law was received differently and at vastly different times in various regions of Europe, and in the nineteenth century each European country made a new start and adopted its own set of national private-law codes, for which the *Code Napoleon* of 1804 was the prototype. But the new national codes drew largely on Roman law in conceptual structure and substantive content. In civil-law countries, the codes in which private law is cast are formulated in broad general terms and are thought of as completely comprehensive, that, is, as the all-inclusive source of authority by reference to which every disputed case must be referred for decision.[12]

In a **common-law country**, many disputes are decided by reliance on the authority of past judicial decisions (cases). A common-law legal system is based on the concept of precedent, sometimes called *stare decisis.* Precedent is the notion that past judicial decisions on a particular issue are binding on a court when that same issue is presented later. This description is somewhat cryptic, as it is easier to observe the operation of precedent than to define it. Nevertheless, precedent and *stare decisis* represent the fundamental principle of common law decision making. Although much of contemporary American and English law is legislative in origin, the law inferred from past judicial decisions is equal in importance to the law set down in codes. Common-law countries often rely on codification in certain areas—the U.S. Uniform Commercial Code is one example— but these codes are not the all-inclusive, systematic statements found in civil-law countries.

The Uniform Commercial Code (UCC), fully adopted by 49 U.S. states, codifies a body of specifically designed rules covering commercial conduct. (Louisiana has adopted parts of the UCC, but its laws are still heavily influenced by the French civil code.) The host country's legal system—that is, common or civil law—directly affects the form a legal business entity will take. In common-law countries, companies are legally incorporated by state authority. In civil-law countries, a contract between two or more parties, who are fully liable for the actions of the company, forms a company.

The United States, 9 of Canada's 10 provinces, and other former colonies with an Anglo-Saxon history founded their systems on common law. Historically, much of continental Europe was influenced by Roman law and, later, the Napoleonic Code (see Exhibit 5-6). Asian countries are split: India, Pakistan, Malaysia, Singapore, and Hong Kong are common-law jurisdictions. Japan, Korea, Thailand, Indochina, Taiwan, Indonesia, and China are civil-law jurisdictions. The legal systems in

---

[11]Much of the material in this section is adapted from Randall Kelso and Charles D. Kelso, *Studying Law: An Introduction* (St. Paul, MN: West Publishing, 1984).
[12]Harry Jones, "Our Uncommon Common Law," *Tennessee Law Review* 30 (1975), p. 447.

Exhibit 5-6: In its origins, the legal system of the United States was substantially influenced by English law. The English and American systems are common law in nature; that is, the law is pronounced by courts when there are no statutes to follow.

Common-law systems are distinguishable from the civil-law systems found in much of Europe. Civil-law systems rely more heavily on statutes and codes, such as the Napoleonic Code of 1804, in deciding cases. From these code provisions, abstract principles are perceived and then applied in specific cases. By contrast, common-law courts find abstract principles in particular cases and then generalize what the law is from those principles.
Source: Lee Snider/The Image Works.

Scandinavia are mixed, displaying some civil-law attributes and some common-law attributes. Today, the majority of countries have legal systems based on civil-law traditions.

As various countries in Eastern and Central Europe wrestle with establishing legal systems in the post-Communist era, a struggle of sorts has broken out; consultants representing both common-law and civil-law countries are trying to influence the process. In much of Central Europe, including Poland, Hungary, and the Czech Republic, the German civil-law tradition prevails. As a result, banks not only take deposits and make loans but also engage in the buying and selling of securities. In Eastern Europe, particularly Russia, the United States has had greater influence. Germany has accused the United States of promoting a system so complex that it requires legions of lawyers. The U.S. response is that the German system is outdated.[13] In any event, the constant stream of laws and decrees issued by the Russian government creates an unpredictable, evolving legal environment. Specialized publications such as *The Russian and Commonwealth Business Law Report* are important resources for anyone doing business in Russia or the CIS.

Islamic Law

The legal system in many Middle Eastern countries is identified with the laws of Islam, which are associated with "the one and only one God, the Almighty."[14] In **Islamic law**, the *sharia* is a comprehensive code governing Muslim conduct in all areas of life, including business. The code is derived from two sources. First is the Koran, the Holy Book written in Arabic that is a record of the revelations made to the Prophet Mohammed by Allah. The second source is the Hadith, which is based on the life, sayings, and practices of Muhammad. In particular, the Hadith spells out the products and practices that are *haram* (forbidden). The orders and instructions found in the Koran are analogous to code laws; the guidelines of the Hadith correspond to common law. Any Westerner doing business in Malaysia in the Middle East should have, at minimum, a rudimentary understanding of Islamic law and its implications for commercial activities. Brewers, for example, must refrain from advertising beer on billboards or in local-language newspapers.

[13]Mark M. Nelson, "Two Styles of Business Vie in East Europe," *The Wall Street Journal* (April 3, 1995), p. A14.
[14]This section is adapted from Mushtaq Luqmani, Ugur Yavas, and Zahir Quraeshi, "Advertising in Saudi Arabia: Content and Regulation," *International Marketing Review* 6, no. 1 (1989), pp. 61–63.

SIDESTEPPING LEGAL PROBLEMS: IMPORTANT BUSINESS ISSUES

Clearly, the global legal environment is very dynamic and complex. Therefore, the best course to follow is to get expert legal help. However, the astute, proactive marketer can do a great deal to prevent conflicts from arising in the first place, especially concerning issues such as establishment, jurisdiction, patents and trademarks, antitrust, licensing and trade secrets, bribery, and advertising and other promotion tools. Chapters 13 and 14 discuss regulation of specific promotion activities.

Jurisdiction

Company personnel working abroad should understand the extent to which they are subject to the jurisdiction of host-country courts. **Jurisdiction** pertains to global marketing insofar as it concerns a court's authority to rule on particular types of issues arising outside of a nation's borders or to exercise power over individuals or entities from different countries. Employees of foreign companies working in the United States must understand that courts have jurisdiction to the extent that the company can be demonstrated to be doing business in the state in which the court sits. The court may examine whether the foreign company maintains an office, solicits business, maintains bank accounts or other property, or has agents or other employees in the state in question. In a recent case, Revlon sued United Overseas Limited (UOL) in U.S. District Court for the Southern District of New York. Revlon charged the British company with breach of contract, contending that UOL had failed to purchase some specialty shampoos as agreed. Claiming lack of jurisdiction, UOL asked the court to dismiss the complaint. Revlon countered with the argument that UOL was, in fact, subject to the court's jurisdiction; Revlon cited the presence of a UOL sign above the entrance to the offices of a New York company in which UOL had a 50 percent ownership interest. The court denied UOL's motion to dismiss.[15]

Jurisdiction played an important role in two recent trade-related disputes. One pitted Volkswagen AG against General Motors. After GM's worldwide head of purchasing, José Ignacio López de Arriortúa, was hired by Volkswagen in 1992, his former employer accused him of taking trade secrets. Volkswagen accepted U.S. court jurisdiction in the dispute, although the company's lawyers requested that the U.S. District Court in Detroit transfer the case to Germany. Jurisdiction was also an issue in a trade dispute that pitted Eastman Kodak against Fuji Photo Film. Kodak alleged that the Japanese government helped Fuji in Japan by blocking the distribution of Kodak film. The U.S. government turned the case over to the WTO, despite the opinion expressed by many experts that the WTO lacks jurisdiction in complaints over trade and competition policy.

Intellectual Property: Patents, Trademarks, and Copyrights

Patents and trademarks that are protected in one country are not necessarily protected in another, so global marketers must ensure that patents and trademarks are registered in each country where business is conducted. A **patent** is a formal legal document that gives an inventor the exclusive right to make, use, and sell an invention for a specified period of time. Typically, the invention represents an "inventive leap" that is "novel" or "nonobvious." A **trademark** is defined as a distinctive mark, motto, device, or emblem that a manufacturer affixes to a particular product or package to distinguish it from goods produced by other manufacturers (see Exhibit 5-7 and Exhibit 5-8). A **copyright** establishes ownership of a written, recorded, performed, or filmed creative work.

Infringement of intellectual property can take a variety of forms. **Counterfeiting** is the unauthorized copying and production of a product. An *associative counterfeit*, or *imitation*, uses a product name that differs slightly from a well-known brand but is close enough that consumers will associate it with the genuine product (see Exhibit 5-9). A third type of counterfeiting is *piracy,* the unauthorized publication or reproduction of copyrighted work. Counterfeiting and piracy are particularly important in industries such as motion pictures, recorded music, computer software, and textbook publishing. Companies in these industries produce products that can be

---

[15]Joseph Ortego and Josh Kardisch, "Foreign Companies Can Limit the Risk of Being Subject to U.S. Courts," *National Law Journal* 17, no. 3 (September 19, 1994), p. C2.

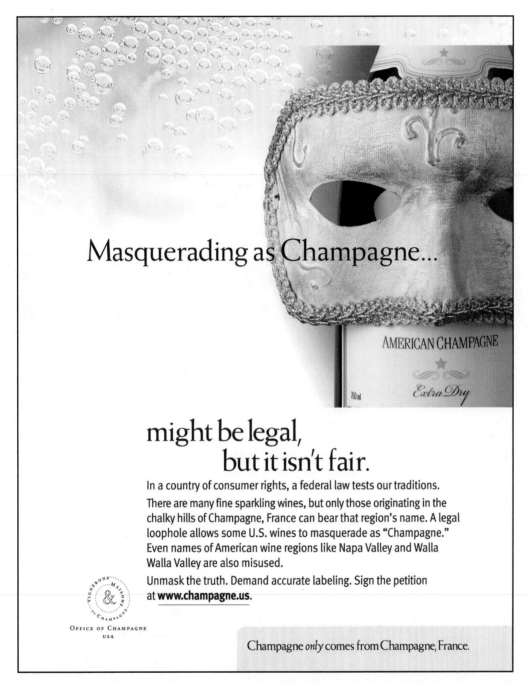

Exhibit 5-7: The Champagne region in France is world famous for producing sparkling wines. However, the word "Champagne" sometimes appears on labels of sparkling wines from the United States and other countries. The European Union recently asked the World Trade Organization for permission to restrict the use of "Champagne" and certain other words associated with traditional European products. Such "geographic indicators" would assure consumers about the origin and authenticity of the products they buy; in other words, a wine labeled "Champagne" would be from Champagne, France. In 2005, representatives from several wine regions in the United States and the EU signed a Joint Declaration to Protect Wine Place & Origin. In addition, a Wine Accord signed by the United States and EU bans the misuse of 16 place names by marketers of wine products that do not originate in those places.
Source: Champagne, USA.

easily duplicated and distributed on a mass basis. The United States in particular has a vested interest in intellectual property protection around the globe because it is home to many companies in the industries just mentioned. However, the United States faces significant challenges in countries such as China. As one expert has noted:

> Current attempts to establish intellectual property law, particularly on the Chinese mainland, have been deeply flawed in their failure to address the difficulties of reconciling legal values, institutions, and forms generated in the West with the legacy of China's past and the constraints imposed by its present circumstances.[16]

In the United States, where patents, trademarks, and copyrights are registered with the Federal Patent Office, the patent holder retains all rights for the life of the patent even if the product is not

---

[16]William P. Alford, *To Steal a Books Is an Elegant Offense: Intellectual Property Law in Chinese Civilization* (Stanford, CA: Stanford University Press, 1995), p. 2.

Exhibit 5-8: Budweiser is a registered trademark of Anheuser-Busch/InBev, the world's largest brewing company. At the present time, however, AB/InBev can't use the Budweiser brand name on a global basis. That's because, in 1895, the Budejovicky Budvar brewery was established in Budweis, Bohemia, and its beer was officially named Budweiser, "the beer of kings." Anheuser-Busch is now suing on a country-by-country basis to win the right to the Budweiser name. It has won cases in Ireland, Portugal, Sweden, and other European countries.
Source: AP Wide World Photos.

produced or sold. The Trademark Act of 1946, also known as the Lanham Act, covers trademarks in the United States. President Reagan signed the Trademark Law Revision Act into law in November 1988. The law makes it easier for companies to register new trademarks. Patent and trademark protection in the United States is very good, and U.S. law relies on the precedent of previously decided court cases for guidance.

To register a patent in Europe, a company has the option of filing on a country-by-country basis or applying to the European Patent Office in Munich for patent registration in a specific number of countries. A third option will soon be available: The Community Patent Convention will make it possible for an inventor to file for a patent that is effective in the 27 signatory nations. Currently, patent procedures in Europe are quite expensive, in part because of the cost of translating technical documents into all the languages of the EU countries; as of mid-2004, the translation issue remained unresolved.[17] In July 1997, in response to complaints, the European

Exhibit 5-9: Luxury goods marketer Louis Vuitton recently sued Carrefour, the French hypermarket operator, in China. Attorneys for Louis Vuitton alleged that a Shanghai Carrefour store sold counterfeit copies of Vuitton's handbags for 50 yuan, the equivalent of about $6. Genuine Louis Vuitton handbags sell for about $1,000 in China. China is experiencing an increase in lawsuits involving patents, trade secrets, and counterfeit goods.
Source: Eugene Hoshiko/AP Wide World Photos.

---

[17]Frances Williams, "Call for Stronger EU Patent Laws," *Financial Times* (May 22, 1997).

Exhibit 5-10: Headquartered in Geneva, Switzerland, the World Intellectual Property Organization (WIPO) is one of 16 specialized subunits of the United Nations. WIPO's mission is to promote and protect intellectual property throughout the world. WIPO views intellectual property as a critical element in economic development; it has created illustrated booklets that explain trademarks, copyright, and other intellectual property issues in a straightforward, easy-to-understand manner. Local agencies can access and print the booklets directly from WIPO's Internet site.
Source: Reprinted with permission from the World Intellectual Property Organization, which owns the copyright.

Patent Office instituted a 19 percent reduction in the average cost of an eight-country patent registration. The United States recently joined the World Intellectual Property Organization (WIPO); governed by the Madrid agreement of 1891 and the more flexible 1996 *Madrid Protocol*, the system allows trademark owners to seek protection in as many as 74 countries with a single application and fee (see Exhibit 5-10).

Companies sometimes find ways to exploit loopholes or other unique opportunities offered by patent and trademark laws in individual nations. Sometimes, individuals register trademarks in local country markets before the actual corporate entity files for trademark protection. For example, Starbucks filed for trademark protection in 1997 in Russia but did not open any cafés there. Sergei Zuykov, an attorney in Moscow, filed a petition in court in 2002 to cancel Starbucks' claim to the brand name because it had not been used in commerce. Technically, Zuykov is merely taking advantage of provisions in Russia's civil code; even though he has been denounced as a "trademark squatter," he is not violating the law. Zuykov has offered to sell Seattle-based Starbucks its name back for $600,000![19]

Then there is the case of singer/songwriter Tom Waits. His distinctive vocal style—a gravelly growl—and songs about losers and dreams have endeared him to his fans. Within the music industry, Waits is distinctive for another reason: Unlike a growing number of musicians, he refuses to license his songs to marketers for use in broadcast commercials. In addition, he aggressively pursues lawsuits against marketers who use "ringers"—soundalikes—in their advertising. Twenty years ago Waits sued Frito-Lay for using a soundalike in a Doritos ad; he was awarded $2.5 million. Recently, the singer has pursued global marketers. For example, he sued Volkswagen's Audi division for a TV commercial that aired in Spain; Waits claimed that the music ripped off his song "Innocent When You Dream" and that the vocalist imitated his vocal style.

"We have confidence in international law. When you invent something, it is necessary immediately to defend your creativity with intellectual patents. Italy has one of the poorest records in Europe with regard to patents. We need to educate businessmen about this."[18]
Mario Moretti Polegato, chairman, Geox (Italy's biggest shoe company)

[18]Tony Barber, "'Patents Are Key' to Taking on China," *Financial Times* (July 25, 2006), p. 2.
[19]Andrew Kramer, "He Doesn't Make Coffee, but He Controls 'Starbucks' in Russia," *The New York Times* (October 12, 2005), pp. C1, C4.

An appeals court in Barcelona awarded Waits $43,000 for copyright infringement and $36,000 for violation of his "moral rights as an artist."

Waits says he does not mind it when another singer imitates him as a form of artistic expression. As Waits explains, "I make a distinction between people who use the voice as a creative item and people who are selling cigarettes and underwear. It's a big difference. We all know the difference. And it's stealing. They get a lot out of standing next to me, and I just get big legal bills."[20]

International concern about intellectual property issues in the nineteenth century resulted in two important agreements. The first is the International Convention for the Protection of Industrial Property. Also known as the Paris Union or Paris Convention, the convention dates to 1883 and is now honored by nearly 100 countries. This treaty facilitates multi-country patent registrations by ensuring that, once a company files in a signatory country, it will be afforded a "right of priority" in other countries for one year from the date of the original filing. A U.S. company wishing to obtain foreign patent rights must apply to the Paris Union within one year of filing in the United States or risk a permanent loss of patent rights abroad.[22]

In 1886, the International Union for the Protection of Literary and Artistic Property was formed. Also known as the Berne Convention, this was a landmark agreement on copyright protection. References to the convention pop up in some unexpected places. For example, as the credits roll at the end of "The Late Show with David Letterman," the following message appears:

> Worldwide Pants Incorporated is the author of this motion picture for purposes of the Berne Convention and all laws giving effect thereto. Unauthorized duplication, distribution, exhibition, or use may result in civil liabilities and/or criminal prosecution.

Two other treaties deserve mention. The Patent Cooperation Treaty (PCT) has more than 100 contracting states, including Australia, Brazil, France, Germany, Japan, North Korea, South Korea, the Netherlands, Switzerland, the Russian Federation and other former Soviet republics, and the United States. The members constitute a union that provides certain technical services and cooperates in the filing, searching, and examination of patent applications in all member countries. The European Patent Office administers applications for the European Patent Convention, which is effective in the EU and Switzerland. An applicant can file a single patent application covering all the convention states; the advantage is that the application will be subject to only one procedure of grant. Although national patent laws remain effective under this system, approved patents are effective in all member countries for a period of 20 years from the filing date.

In recent years, the U.S. government has devoted considerable diplomatic effort to improving the worldwide environment for intellectual property protection. For example, China agreed to accede to the Berne Convention in 1992; on January 1, 1994, China became an official signatory of the PCT. After years of discussion, the United States and Japan have agreed to make changes in their respective patent systems; Japan has promised to speed up patent examinations, eliminate challenges to patent submissions, and allow patent applications to be filed in English.

Effective June 7, 1995, in accordance with GATT, new U.S. patents are granted for a period of 20 years from the filing date. Previously, patents had been valid for a 17-year term effective after being granted. Thus, U.S. patent laws now harmonize with those in the EU as well as Japan. Even with the changes, however, patents in Japan are narrower than those in the United States. As a result, companies such as Caterpillar have been unable to protect critical innovations in Japan because products very similar to those made by U.S. companies can be patented without fear of infringement.[23]

Another key issue is global patent protection for software. Although copyright laws protect the computer code, it does not apply to the idea embodied in the software. Beginning in 1981, the U.S. Patent and Trademark Office extended patent protection to software; Microsoft has more than 500 software patents. In Europe, software patents were not allowed under the Munich Convention; in June 1997, however, the EU indicated it was ready to revise patent laws so they cover software.[24]

"There are two ways to fight piracy in China. The first is the Coca-Cola method. You make your product so well and you distribute it so cheaply that there's no money left for the counterfeiters. The second is the Budweiser approach: Budweiser beer cans in China have fluted edges that are difficult to manufacture. Chinese companies can brew beer and call it Budweiser, but they can't yet put it in a can that looks real. If you don't have an intellectual property rights plan as part of your business plan, you're in trouble."[21]

Thomas Boam, commercial attaché, United States Embassy, Beijing

[20]Ben Sisario, "Still Fighting for the Right to His Voice," *The New York Times* (January 20, 2006), p. B3.
[21]Robyn Meredith, "The Counterfeit Economy," *Forbes* (February 17, 2003), p. 82.
[22]Franklin R. Root, *Entry Strategies for International Markets* (New York: Lexington Books, 1994), p. 113.
[23]John Carey, "Inching Toward a Borderless Patent," *Business Week* (September 5, 1994), p. 35.
[24]Richard Pynder, "Intellectual Property in Need of Protection," *Financial Times* (July 7, 1998), p. 22.

TABLE 5-2 Companies Receiving the Most U.S. Patents, 2005

Company	No. of Patents
1. IBM	2,941
2. Canon Kabushiki Kaisha	1,828
3. Hewlett-Packard	1,797
4. Matsushita Electric Industrial	1,688
5. Samsung Electronics	1,641
6. Micron Technology	1,561
7. Intel	1,549
8. Hitachi	1,271
9. Toshiba	1,258
10. Fujitsu	1,154

Source: U.S. Patent and Trademark Office.

Table 5-2 ranks the 10 companies that received the most U.S. patents in 2005. IBM, which has topped the rankings every year since 1993, generates more than $1 billion in revenues by licensing patents and other forms of intellectual property; Hewlett-Packard has more than 16,000 patents worldwide. As illustrated in Exhibit 5-11, DuPont recently was awarded its 7 millionth patent.

Antitrust

Antitrust laws in the United States and other countries are designed to combat restrictive business practices and to encourage competition. Agencies such as the U.S. Federal Trade Commission, Japan's Fair Trade Commission, and the European Commission enforce antitrust laws (see Exhibit 5-12). Some legal experts believe that the pressures of global competition have

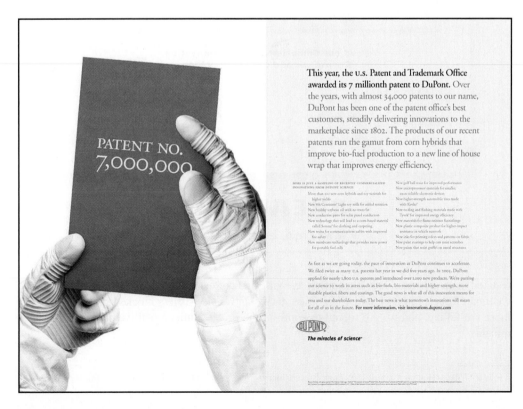

Exhibit 5-11: New products and innovation are the lifeblood of E.I. du Pont de Nemours and Company, better known simply as DuPont. The company's business units include Safety & Protection, Coatings & Color Technologies, and Agriculture & Nutrition. One subsidiary, Pioneer Hi-Bred International, is a biotechnology company headquartered in Iowa. Pioneer develops hybrid seeds that enable farmers in all parts of the world to raise crop yields.
Source: DuPont/Ogilvy & Mather, Phase VI EVA Spacesuit Gloves created by ILC Dover to protect astronauts.

Exhibit 5-12: Advanced Micro Devices (AMD) is the world's second largest supplier of microprocessors for PCs and servers and is recognized as a technology innovation leader. The dominant market leader, Intel, has held its market share constant in the 80–90% range over the years. AMD filed a lawsuit against Intel in U.S. Federal Court, claiming Intel uses its dominant market power to stifle or exclude competition and engage in anticompetitive behavior around the globe. Full-page ads were deployed to describe Intel's conduct as described in the case.
Source: Used with permission by AMD.

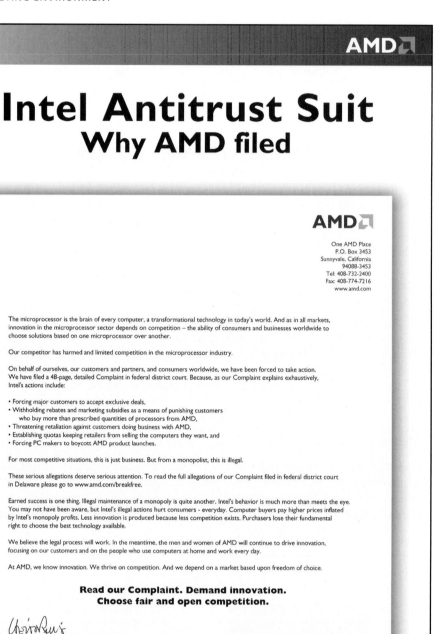

resulted in an increased incidence of price-fixing and collusion among companies. As then-FTC chairman Robert Pitofsky said, "For years, tariffs and trade barriers blocked global trade. Now those are falling, and we are forced to confront the private anticompetitive behavior that often remains."[25]

[25]John R. Wilke, "Hunting Cartels: U.S. Trust-Busters Increasingly Target International Business," *The Wall Street Journal* (February 5, 1997), p. A10.

A recent rash of antitrust actions brought in the United States against foreign companies has raised concerns that the United States is violating international law as well as the sovereignty of other nations. The U.S. antitrust laws are a legacy of the nineteenth-century trust-busting era and are intended to maintain free competition by limiting the concentration of economic power. The Sherman Act of 1890 prohibits certain restrictive business practices, including fixing prices, limiting production, allocating markets, or any other scheme designed to limit or avoid competition. The law applies to the activities of U.S. companies outside U.S. boundaries, as well as to foreign companies conducting business in the United States. In a precedent-setting case, Nippon Paper Industries was found guilty in a U.S. court of conspiring with other Japanese companies to raise fax paper prices in the United States. The Japanese government denounced the U.S. indictment of Nippon Paper in December 1995 as a violation of international law and Japan's sovereignty. The meetings at which pricing strategies were allegedly discussed took place outside the United States; a U.S. federal judge struck down the indictment, ruling that the Sherman Act does not apply to foreign conduct. However, a federal appeals court in Boston reversed the decision. In his opinion, U.S. Circuit Judge Bruce Selya wrote, "We live in an age of international commerce, where decisions reached in one corner of the world can reverberate around the globe."[26]

For the past four decades, the competition authority of the European Commission has had the power to prohibit agreements and practices that prevent, restrict, and distort competition. The commission has jurisdiction over European-based companies as well as non-European ones such as Microsoft that generate significant revenues in Europe. For example, the commission can block a proposed merger or joint venture, approve it with only minor modifications, or demand substantial concessions before granting approval. The commission begins with a preliminary study of a proposed deal; serious concerns can lead to an in-depth investigation lasting several months. Beginning in the mid-1990s, the commission has taken an increasingly activist approach. Mario Monti, an Italian with an economics background, was Europe's antitrust chief during this period. Nicknamed "Super Mario" by the European press, Monti blocked the proposed merger of WorldCom and Sprint in 2000. He also demanded major concessions before allowing America Online to acquire Time Warner.[27] Neelie Kroes recently took over the job from Monti. There have been calls for the EU to revamp its approach to antitrust issues and reduce its caseload. Any proposed changes will pit modernists against traditionalists. As one European attorney complained, "The commission is putting resources into regulating cases that don't actually restrict competition, which means that the cases that do need to be looked at are not being resolved efficiently."[28] Table 5-3 summarizes some recent joint ventures, mergers, and

EMERGING MARKETS BRIEFING BOOK

⬦ Antitrust Issues in Brazil

Although similar antitrust laws are on the books in many countries, they are often weak or loosely enforced. Antitrust is taking on increasing importance in emerging country markets. For example, Colgate-Palmolive's 1995 acquisition of Brazil's Kolynos oral care company for $1 billion was subject to review by that country's Administrative Council of Economic Defense (CADE). Rival Procter & Gamble instigated the review by complaining that the acquisition would give Colgate a 79 percent share of the market. CADE ruled that Colgate must either license the trademark to another company for 20 years or halt sales of the Kolynos brand toothpaste in Brazil for four years; Colgate agreed to the latter.

The Miller Brewing unit of Philip Morris also ran into antitrust problems in Brazil following its 1995 investment of $50 million in a 50/50 joint venture with Cia Cervejaria Brahma SA. CADE ruled that the venture, which produced and distributed Miller Genuine Draft beer, deprived consumers of head-to-head competition between the two brewing companies. CADE also criticized Miller for choosing a market entry strategy that required a relatively low level of investment. Nelio Weiss, a consultant at Coopers & Lybrand's Sao Paulo office, noted, "The message is that foreign companies shouldn't assume that antitrust authorities will be passive."

Sources: Yumiko Ono, "Colgate Purchase Gets Brazil's Blessing but with Restrictions on Brand Name," *The Wall Street Journal* (September 20, 1996), p. A11; Matt Moffett, "Miller Brewing Is Ordered to Sell Its Stake in Brazilian Joint Venture," *The Wall Street Journal* (June 13, 1997), p. A15.

[26]John R. Wilke, "U.S. Court Rules Antitrust Laws Apply to Foreigners," *The Wall Street Journal* (March 19, 1997), p. B5.
[27]Anita Raghavan and Brandon Mitchener, "'Super Mario': EU's Antitrust Czar Isn't Afraid to Say No; Just Ask Time Warner," *The Wall Street Journal* (October 2, 2000), pp. A1, A10.
[28]Emma Tucker, "Europe's Paper Mountain," *Financial Times* (February 11, 1998), p. 21.

TABLE 5-3 Antitrust Rulings

Companies Involved	Global Antitrust Review	Antitrust Review in USA
Acquisition of Anheuser-Busch (United States) by InBev (Belgium/Brazil), 2008, $52 billion	Deal approved in China but company is prohibited from pursuing Huaran Snow or Beijing Yanjing.	Approved; InBev must sell Labatt USA.
Merger of Sony Music (Japan) and BMG (Germany), 2004	Approved by EU.	Approved.
Acquisition of Honeywell (United States) by GE (United States), 2001, $40 billion	Deal was vetoed on grounds that merged firm would be stronger than competitors in aviation equipment.	Deal was on track for approval, subject to conditions.
Joint venture between music businesses of EMI Group PLC (Great Britain) and Time Warner (United States), 2000, $20 billion	EU regulators expressed concern that the new EMI-Time Warner would dominate growing market for digital music distribution.	Deal was scrapped in October 2000 before regulatory review began.

Source: Compiled by the authors.

other global business deals that have been subject to review by antitrust authorities on both sides of the Atlantic.

The interstate trade clause of the Treaty of Rome applies to trade with third countries, so that a company must be aware of the conduct of its affiliates. The commission also exempts certain cartels from Articles 85 and 86 of the treaty in an effort to encourage the growth of important businesses. The intent is to allow European companies to compete on an equal footing with Japan and the United States. In some instances, individual country laws in Europe apply to specific marketing mix elements. For example, some countries permit selective or exclusive product distribution. However, European Community law can take precedence.

In one case, Consten, a French company, had exclusive French rights to import and distribute consumer electronics products from the German Grundig company. Consten sued another French firm, charging the latter with bringing "parallel imports" into France illegally. That is, Consten charged that the competitor bought Grundig products from various foreign suppliers without Consten's knowledge and was selling them in France. Although Consten's complaint was upheld by two French courts, the Paris Court of Appeals suspended the judgment, pending a ruling by the European Commission on whether the Grundig-Consten arrangement violated Articles 85 and 86 of the Treaty of Rome. The commission ruled against Consten on the grounds that "territorial protection proved to be particularly damaging to the realization of the Common Market."[29]

In some instances, companies or entire industries have been able to secure exemption from antitrust rules. In the airline industry, for example, KLM and Northwestern won an exemption from the U.S. government and now share computer codes and set prices jointly. Similarly, the European Commission permitted United International Pictures (UIP), a joint venture between Paramount, Universal, and MGM/UA, to cut costs by collaborating on motion picture distribution in Europe. In 1998, the commission reversed itself and notified the three studios that they must distribute their films independently in Europe.[30] A *cartel* is a group of separate companies that collectively set prices, control output, or take other actions to maximize profits. For example, the group of oil-producing countries known as OPEC is a cartel.

In the United States, most cartels are illegal. One notable exception, however, has a direct impact on global marketing. A number of the world's major shipping lines, including the U.S.-based Sea-Land Service and Denmark's A. P. Moller/Maersk line, have enjoyed exemption from antitrust laws since the passage of the Shipping Act of 1916. The law was originally enacted to ensure reliability; today, it has been estimated that the cartel results in shipping prices that are 18 percent higher than they would be if shippers set prices independently. Attempts in recent years to change the law have not been successful.[31]

[29]Detlev Vagts, *Transnational Business Problems* (Mineola, NY: The Foundation Press, 1986), pp. 285–291.
[30]Alice Rawsthorn and Emma Tucker, "Movie Studios May Have to Scrap Joint Distributor," *Financial Times* (February 6, 1998), p. 1.
[31]Anna Wilde Mathews, "Making Waves: As U.S. Trade Grows, Shipping Cartels Get a Bit More Scrutiny," *The Wall Street Journal* (October 7, 1997), pp. A1, A8.

Licensing and Trade Secrets

Licensing is a contractual agreement in which a licensor allows a licensee to use patents, trademarks, trade secrets, technology, or other intangible assets in return for royalty payments or other forms of compensation. U.S. laws do not regulate the licensing process per se as do technology transfer laws in the EU, Australia, Japan, and many developing countries. The duration of the licensing agreement and the amount of royalties a company can receive are considered a matter of commercial negotiation between licensor and licensee, and there are no government restrictions on remittances of royalties abroad. Important considerations in licensing include analysis of what assets a firm may offer for license, how to price the assets, and whether to grant only the right to "make" the product or to grant the rights to "use" and to "sell" the product as well. The right to sublicense is another important issue. As with distribution agreements, decisions must also be made regarding exclusive or nonexclusive arrangements and the size of the licensee's territory.

To prevent the licensee from using the licensed technology to compete directly with the licensor, the latter may try to limit the licensee to selling only in its home country. The licensor may also seek to contractually bind the licensee to discontinue use of the technology after the contract has expired. In practice, host-government laws and even U.S. antitrust laws may make such agreements impossible to obtain. Licensing is a potentially dangerous action: It may be instrumental in creating a competitor. Therefore, licensors should be careful to ensure that their own competitive position remains advantageous. This requires constant innovation.

As noted, licensing agreements can come under antitrust scrutiny. In one recent case, Bayer AG granted an exclusive patent license for a new household insecticide to S. C. Johnson & Sons. The German firm's decision to license was based in part on the time required for EPA approval, which had stretched to three years. Bayer decided it made better business sense to let the U.S. firm deal with regulatory authorities in return for a 5 percent royalty on sales. However, a class action suit filed against the companies alleged that the licensing deal would allow Johnson to monopolize the $450 million home insecticide market.

At this point, the U.S. Justice Department stepped in, calling the licensing agreement anticompetitive. In a statement, Anne Bingaman, then head of the justice department's antitrust unit, said, "The cozy arrangement that Bayer and Johnson maintained is unacceptable in a highly concentrated market." Bayer agreed to offer licenses to any interested company on better terms than the original contract with Johnson. Johnson agreed to notify the U.S. government of any future pending exclusive licensing agreements for household insecticides. If Bayer is party to any such agreements, the justice department has the right to veto them. The reaction from the legal community was negative. One Washington lawyer who specializes in intellectual property law noted that the case "really attacks traditional licensing practices." As Melvin Jager, president of the Licensing Executives Society, explained, "An exclusive license is a very valuable tool to promote intellectual property and get it out into the marketplace."[32]

What happens if a licensee gains knowledge of the licensor's trade secrets? *Trade secrets* are confidential information or knowledge that has commercial value and is not in the public domain, and for which steps have been taken to keep secret. Trade secrets include manufacturing processes, formulas, designs, and customer lists. To prevent disclosure, the licensing of unpatented trade secrets should be linked to confidentiality contracts with each employee who has access to the protected information. In the United States, trade secrets are protected by state law rather than federal statute; most states have adopted the Uniform Trade Secrets Act (UTSA). The U.S. law provides trade secret liability against third parties that obtain confidential information through an intermediary. Remedies include damages and other forms of relief.

The 1990s saw widespread improvements in laws pertaining to trade secrets. Several countries adopted trade secret statutes for the first time. Mexico's first statute protecting trade secrets became effective on June 28, 1991; China's first trade secret law took effect on December 1, 1993. In both countries, the new laws were part of broader revisions of intellectual property laws. Japan and South Korea have also amended their intellectual property laws to include trade secrets. Many countries in Central and Eastern Europe enacted laws to protect trade secrets. When NAFTA became effective on January 1, 1994, it marked the first international trade agreement with provisions for protecting trade secrets. This milestone was quickly followed by the Agreement on Trade-Related Aspects of

---

[32]Brigid McMenamin, "Eroding Patent Rights," *Forbes* (October 24, 1994), p. 92.

Intellectual Property Rights (TRIPs) that resulted from the Uruguay Round of GATT negotiations. The TRIPs agreement requires signatory countries to protect against acquisition, disclosure, or use of trade secrets "in a manner contrary to honest commercial practices."[33] Despite these formal legal developments, in practice, enforcement is the key issue. Companies transferring trade secrets across borders should apprise themselves not only of the existence of legal protection but also of the risks associated with lax enforcement.

Bribery and Corruption: Legal and Ethical Issues

History does not record a burst of international outrage when Charles M. Schwab, head of Bethlehem Steel at the beginning of the twentieth century, presented a $200,000 diamond and pearl necklace to the mistress of Czar Alexander III's nephew.[34] In return for that consideration, Bethlehem Steel won the contract to supply the rails for the Trans-Siberian railroad. Today, in the post-Soviet era, Western companies are again being lured by emerging opportunities in Central and Eastern Europe. Here, as in the Middle East and other parts of the world, they are finding that bribery is a way of life, and that corruption is widespread. **Bribery** is the corrupt business practice of demanding or offering some type of consideration—typically cash payment—when negotiating a cross-border deal. U.S. companies in particular are constrained in their responses to such a situation by U.S. government policies of the post-Watergate age. Transparency International (www.transparency.org) compiles an annual report ranking countries in terms of a Corruption Perceptions Index (CPI). The "cleanest" score is 10. The 2008 ranking of the highest and lowest countries is shown in Table 5-4.

In the United States, the **Foreign Corrupt Practices Act** (FCPA) is a legacy of the Watergate scandal during Richard Nixon's presidency. In the course of his investigation, the Watergate special prosecutor discovered that more than 300 American companies had made undisclosed payments to foreign officials totaling hundreds of millions of dollars. Congress unanimously passed the act, and President Jimmy Carter signed the act into law on December 17, 1977. Administered by the Department of Justice and the Securities and Exchange Commission, the act was concerned with disclosure and prohibition. The disclosure part of the act required publicly held companies to institute internal accounting controls that would record all transactions. The prohibition part made it a crime for U.S. corporations to bribe an official of a foreign government or political party to obtain

TABLE 5-4 2008 Corruption Rankings

Rank/Country	2008 CPI Score	Rank/Country	2008 CPI Score
1. Denmark	9.3	171. Dem. Rep. of Congo	1.7
1. New Zealand	9.3	171. Equatorial Guinea	1.7
1. Sweden	9.3	173. Chad	1.6
4. Singapore	9.2	173. Guinea	1.6
5. Finland	9.0	173. Sudan	1.6
5. Switzerland	9.0	176. Afghanistan	1.5
7. Iceland	8.9	177. Haiti	1.4
7. Netherlands	8.9	178. Iraq	1.3
9. Australia	8.7	178. Myanmar	1.3
9. Canada	8.7	180. Somalia	1.0

Note: Transparency International's Corruption Perceptions Index measures the perceived levels of public-sector corruption in a given country. The scores range from zero (seen as highly corrupt) to ten (seen as highly clean).

Source: Reprinted from 2008 Corruption Rankings. Copyright 2008 Transparency International: the global coalition against corruption. Used with permission. For more information, visit http://www.trasnsparency.org.

---

[33]Salem M. Katsh and Michael P. Dierks. "Globally, Trade Secrets Laws Are All Over the Map," *The National Law Journal* 17, no. 36 (May 8, 1995), p. C12.
[34]Much of the material in this section is adapted from Daniel Pines, "Amending the Foreign Corrupt Practices Act to Include a Private Right of Action," *California Law Review* (January 1994), pp. 185–229.

or retain business. Payments to third parties were also prohibited when the company had reason to believe that part or all of the money would be channeled to foreign officials.

The U.S. business community immediately began lobbying for changes to the act, complaining that the statute was too vague and so broad in scope that it threatened to severely curtail U.S. business activities abroad. President Ronald Reagan signed amendments to the statutes into law in 1988 as part of the Omnibus Trade and Competitiveness Act. Among the changes were exclusions for "grease" payments to low-level officials to cut red tape and expedite "routine governmental actions" such as clearing shipments through customs, securing permits, or getting airport passport clearance to leave a country.

Although several well-known U.S. companies have pleaded guilty to violations of the antibribery provisions, enforcement of the act has generally been lax. A total of 23 cases were filed between 1977 and 1988. In one such case, a business executive was convicted of giving money and honeymoon airplane tickets to a Nigerian government official in the hopes of securing a contract.[35] There are stiff penalties for violating the law: Convictions carry severe jail sentences and heavy fines (in excess of $1 million). A company cannot pay or reimburse fines, under the theory that individuals commit such crimes. It has also been made clear that the law will not let a person do indirectly (e.g., through an agent, joint venture partner, or other third party) what it prohibits directly.

Some critics of the FCPA decry it as a regrettable display of moral imperialism. At issue is the extraterritorial sovereignty of U.S. law. It is wrong, according to these critics, to impose U.S. laws, standards, values, and mores on American companies and citizens worldwide. As one legal expert points out, however, this criticism has one fundamental flaw: There is no nation in which the letter of the law condones bribery of government officials. Thus, the standard set by the FCPA is shared, in principle at least, by other nations.[36]

A second criticism of the FCPA is that it puts U.S. companies in a difficult position vis-à-vis foreign competitors, especially those in Japan and Europe. Several opinion polls and surveys of the business community have revealed the widespread perception that the act adversely affects U.S. businesses overseas. Some academic researchers have concluded that the FCPA has not negatively affected the export performance of U.S. industry. However, a U.S. Commerce Department report prepared with the help of U.S. intelligence services indicated that in 1994 alone, bribes offered by non-U.S. companies were a factor in 100 business deals valued at $45 billion. Foreign companies prevailed in 80 percent of those deals.[37] Although accurate statistics are hard to come by, the rankings shown in Table 5-4 highlight some areas of the world where bribery is still rampant.

The existence of bribery as a fact of life in world markets will not change because the U.S. Congress condemns it. Bribery payments are considered a deductible business expense in many European countries. According to one estimate, the annual price tag for illegal payments by German firms alone is more than $5 billion. Still, increasing numbers of global companies are adopting codes of conduct designed to reduce illegal activities. Moreover, in May 1997, the OECD adopted a formal standard against bribery by drafting a binding international convention that makes it a crime for a company bidding on a contract to bribe foreign officials. The OECD's antibribery convention (officially known as the Convention on Combating Bribery of Foreign Public Officials in International Business Transactions) went into effect in 1999. The OECD is also working on a smaller scale to create so-called islands of integrity. The goal is to achieve transparency at the level of an individual deal, with all the players pledging not to bribe.[39]

Despite the progress made to date on the new agreement, industry observers have expressed several concerns about the proposed treaty. First, it is unclear whether the new law will be enforced with equal rigor everywhere, and, if not, what sanctions will be imposed. Second, the treaty contains legal loopholes, such as the provision that business contracts can be linked to public aid projects such as building hospitals. Third, there is disagreement on what constitutes a

"Corruption is probably the most immediate threat and difficulty that any business faces in Russia—and the trend is increasing."[38]
Carlo Gallo, business risk consultant

---

[35]Katherine Albright and Grace Won, "Foreign Corrupt Practices Act," *American Criminal Law Review* (Spring 1993), p. 787.

[36]Daniel Pines, "Amending the Foreign Corrupt Practices Act to Include a Private Right of Action," *California Law Review* (January 1994), p. 205.

[37]Amy Borrus, "Inside the World of Greased Palms," *Business Week* (November 6, 1995), pp. 36–38.

[38]Rebecca Bream and Neil Buckley, "Investors Still Drawn to Russia Despite Pitfalls," *Financial Times* (December 1, 2006), p. 21.

[39]José Ángel Gurría, "Rich Must Set the Example of Bribery," *Financial Times* (September 13, 2006), p. 5.

Exhibit 5-13: Anna Politkovskaya, a reporter for Russia's *Novaya Gazeta* ("New Paper"), often filed stories critical of President Vladimir Putin. On October 7, 2006, Politkovskaya was gunned down by assailants as she returned from a shopping trip. Since 2000, more than one dozen journalists have been murdered in Russia. Observers note that Russia's independent press suffered as the Kremlin tightened control in anticipation of the 2008 presidential election.
Source: Yuri Kadobnov/Getty Images, Inc. AFP.

"normal" versus an "abnormal" payment. Finally, it will be necessary to arrive at a workable definition of what constitutes a "public official."[40]

Investigative reporters often file stories regarding bribery or other forms of malfeasance. In emerging countries, journalists may themselves become targets if they criticize the rich or powerful (see Exhibit 5-13). When companies operate abroad in the absence of home-country legal constraints, they face a continuum of choices concerning company ethics. At one extreme, they can maintain home-country ethics worldwide with absolutely no adjustment or adaptation to local practice. At the other extreme, they can abandon any attempt to maintain company ethics and adapt entirely to local conditions and circumstances as they are perceived by company managers in each local environment. Between these extremes, one approach that companies may select is to utilize varying degrees of extension of home-country ethics. Alternatively, they may adapt in varying degrees to local customs and practices.

What should a U.S. company do if competitors are willing to offer a bribe? Two alternative courses of action are possible. One is to ignore bribery and act as if it does not exist. The other is to recognize the existence of bribery and evaluate its effect on the customer's purchase decision as if it were just another element of the marketing mix.

The overall value of a company's offer must be as good as, or better than, the competitor's overall offering, bribe included. It may be possible to offer a lower price, a better product, better distribution, or better advertising to offset the value added by the bribe. The best line of defense is to have a product that is clearly superior to that of the competition. In such a case, a bribe should not sway the purchase decision. Alternatively, clear superiority in service and in local representation may tip the scales.

CONFLICT RESOLUTION, DISPUTE SETTLEMENT, AND LITIGATION

The degree of legal cooperation and harmony in the EU is unique and stems in part from the existence of code law as a common bond. Other regional organizations have made far less progress toward harmonization. Countries vary in their approach toward conflict resolution. The United States has more lawyers than any other country in the world and is arguably the most

---

[40]John Mason and Guy de Jonquières, "Goodbye Mr. 10%," *Financial Times* (July 22, 1997), p. 13.

litigious nation on earth. In part, this is a reflection of the low-context nature of American culture and the spirit of confrontational competitiveness. Other factors can contribute to differing attitudes toward litigation. For example, in many European nations, class action lawsuits are not allowed. Also, European lawyers cannot undertake cases on a contingency fee basis. However, change is in the air, as Europe experiences a broad political shift away from the welfare state.[41]

Conflicts inevitably arise in business anywhere, especially when different cultures come together to buy, sell, establish joint ventures, compete, and cooperate in global markets. For American companies, the dispute with a foreign party is frequently in the home-country jurisdiction. The issue can be litigated in the United States, where the company and its attorneys might be said to enjoy "home court" advantage. Litigation in foreign courts, however, becomes vastly more complex, partly because of differences in language, legal systems, currencies, and traditional business customs and patterns.

In addition, problems arise from differences in procedures relating to discovery. In essence, *discovery* is the process of obtaining evidence to prove claims and determining which evidence may be admissible in which countries under which conditions. A further complication is the fact that judgments handed down in courts in another country may not be enforceable in the home country. For all these reasons, many companies prefer to pursue arbitration before proceeding to litigate.

Alternatives to Litigation for Dispute Settlement[42]

In 1995, the Cuban government abruptly cancelled contracts with Endesa, a Spanish utility company. Rather than seek restitution in a Cuban court, Endesa turned to the International Arbitration Tribunal in Paris, seeking damages of $12 million. Endesa's actions illustrate how alternative dispute resolution (ADR) methods allow parties to resolve international commercial disputes without resorting to the court system. Formal arbitration is one means of settling international business disputes outside the courtroom. **Arbitration** is a negotiation process that the two parties have, by prior agreement, committed themselves to using. It is a fair process in the sense that the parties using it have created it themselves. Generally, arbitration involves a hearing of the parties before a three-member panel; each party selects one panel member, and those two panel members in turn select the third member. The panel renders a judgment that the parties agree to abide by in advance.

The most important treaty regarding international arbitration is the 1958 United Nations Convention on the Recognition and Enforcement of Foreign Arbitral Awards. Also known as the New York Convention, the treaty has 107 signatory countries, including China. Brazil is notable among the big emerging markets for not being a signatory. The framework created by the New York Convention is important for several reasons. First, when parties enter into agreements that provide for international arbitration, the signatory countries can hold the parties to their pledge to use arbitration. Second, after arbitration has taken place and the arbitrators have made an award, the signatories recognize and can enforce the judgment. Third, the signatories agree that there are limited grounds for challenging arbitration decisions. The grounds that are recognized are different than the typical appeals that are permitted in a court of law.

Some firms and lawyers inexperienced in the practice of international commercial arbitration approach the arbitration clauses in a contract as "just another clause." The terms of every contract are different and, therefore, no two arbitration clauses should be the same. Consider, for example, the case of a contract between an American firm and a Japanese one. If the parties resort to arbitration, where will it take place? The American side will be reluctant to go to Japan; conversely, the Japanese side will not want to arbitrate in the United States. An alternative, "neutral" location— Singapore or London, for example—must be considered and specified in the arbitration clause. In what language will the proceedings be conducted? If no language is specified in the arbitration clause, the arbitrators themselves will choose.

In addition to location and language, other issues must be addressed as well. For example, if the parties to a patent-licensing arrangement agree in the arbitration clause that the validity of the patent cannot be contested, such a provision may not be enforceable in some countries. Which country's laws will be used as the standard for invalidity? Pursuing such an issue on a

---

[41]Charles Fleming, "Europe Learns Litigious Ways," *The Wall Street Journal* (February 24, 2004), p. A17.
[42]The authors are indebted to Louis B. Kimmelman of O'Melveny & Meyers LLP, New York City, New York, for his contributions to this section.

country-by-country basis would be inordinately time-consuming. In addition, there is the issue of acceptance: By law, U.S. courts must accept an arbitrator's decision in patent disputes; in other countries, however, there is no general rule of acceptance.

To reduce delays relating to such issues, one expert suggests drafting arbitration clauses with as much specificity as possible. To the extent possible, for example, patent policies in various countries should be addressed; arbitration clauses may also include a provision that all foreign patent issues will be judged according to the standard of home-country law. Another provision could forbid the parties from commencing separate legal actions in other countries. The goal is to help the arbitration tribunal zero in on the express intentions of the parties.[43]

For decades, business arbitration has also been promoted through the International Court of Arbitration at the Paris-based International Chamber of Commerce (ICC; www.iccwbo.org). The ICC recently modernized some of its older rules. However, because it is such a well-known organization, it has an extensive backlog of cases. Overall, the ICC has gained a reputation for being slower, more expensive, and more cumbersome than some alternatives. As U.S. involvement in global commerce grew dramatically during the post–World War II period, the American Arbitration Association (AAA) also became recognized as an effective institution within which to resolve disputes. In 1992, the AAA signed a cooperation agreement with China's Beijing Conciliation Center.

Each year, the AAA uses mediation to help resolve thousands of disputes. The AAA has entered into cooperation agreements with the ICC and other global organizations to promote the use of ADR methods; it serves as the agent to administer arbitrations in the United States under ICC auspices. In one recent case, Toys "R" Us was the losing party in a dispute brought to the AAA. The dispute's origins date back to a 1982 licensing agreement between the toy retailer and Alghanin & Sons regarding toy stores in the Middle East. The AAA ruled that Toys "R" Us was to pay a $55 million arbitration award.

Another agency for settling disputes is the Swedish Arbitration Institute of the Stockholm Chamber of Commerce. This agency frequently administered disputes between Western and Eastern European countries and has gained credibility for its evenhanded administration. However, a favorable ruling from the arbitration tribunal is one thing; enforcement is another. For example, Canada's IMP Group took its case against a Russian hotel development partner to Stockholm and was awarded $9.4 million. When payment was not forthcoming, IMP's representatives took matters into their own hands: They commandeered an Aeroflot jet in Canada and released it only after the Russians paid up![44] Other alternatives have proliferated in recent years. In addition to those mentioned, active centers for arbitration exist in Vancouver, Hong Kong, Cairo, Kuala Lumpur, Singapore, Buenos Aires, Bogotá, and Mexico City. A World Arbitration Institute was established in New York; in the United Kingdom, the Advisory, Conciliation and Arbitration Service (ACAS) has achieved great success at handling industrial disputes. An International Council for Commercial Arbitration (ICCA) was established to coordinate the far-flung activities of arbitration organizations. The ICCA meets in different locations around the world every four years.

The United Nations Conference on International Trade Law (UNCITRAL; www.uncitral. org) has also been a significant force in the area of arbitration. Its rules have become more or less standard, as many of the organizations just named have adopted them with some modifications. Many developing countries, for example, long held prejudices against the ICC, AAA, and other developed-country organizations. Representatives of developing nations assumed that such organizations would be biased in favor of multinational corporations. Developing nations insisted on settlement in national courts, which was unacceptable to the multinational firms. This was especially true in Latin America, where the Calvo Doctrine required disputes arising with foreign investors be resolved in national courts under national laws. The growing influence of the ICCA and UNCITRAL rules, coupled with the proliferation of regional arbitration centers, have contributed to changing attitudes in developing countries and resulted in the increased use of arbitration around the world.

---

[43]Bruce Londa, "An Agreement to Arbitrate Disputes Isn't the Same in Every Language," *Brandweek* (September 26, 1994), p. 18. See also John M. Allen, Jr., and Bruce G. Merritt, "Drafters of Arbitration Clauses Face a Variety of Unforeseen Perils," *National Law Journal* 17, no. 33 (April 17, 1995), pp. C6–C7.
[44]Dorothee J. Feils and Florin M. Sabac, "The Impact of Political Risk on the Foreign Direct Investment Decision: A Capital Budgeting Analysis," *Engineering* 45, no. 2 (2000), p. 129.

THE REGULATORY ENVIRONMENT

The regulatory environment of global marketing consists of a variety of governmental and nongovernmental agencies that enforce laws or set guidelines for conducting business. These regulatory agencies address a wide range of marketing issues, including price control, valuation of imports and exports, trade practices, labeling, food and drug regulations, employment conditions, collective bargaining, advertising content, and competitive practices. As noted in *The Wall Street Journal:*

> Each nation's regulations reflect and reinforce its brand of capitalism—predatory in the U.S., paternal in Germany, and protected in Japan—and its social values. It's easier to open a business in the U.S. than in Germany because Germans value social consensus above risk-taking, but it's harder to hire people because Americans worry more about discrimination lawsuits. It's easier to import children's clothes in the U.S. than Japan because Japanese bureaucrats defend a jumble of import restrictions, but it's harder to open bank branches across the U.S. because Americans strongly defend state prerogatives.[45]

In most countries, the influence of regulatory agencies is pervasive, and an understanding of how they operate is essential to protect business interests and advance new programs. Executives at many global companies are realizing the need to hire lobbyists to represent their interests and to influence the direction of the regulatory process. For example, in the early 1990s, McDonald's, Nike, and Toyota didn't have a single representative in Brussels. Today, each of the companies has several people representing its interests to the European Commission. U.S. law firms and consulting firms also have sharply increased their presence in Brussels; in an effort to gain insight into EU politics and access to its policymakers, some have hired EU officials. In all, there are currently approximately 15,000 lobbyists in Brussels representing about 1,400 companies and nonprofit organizations from around the world.[46]

Regional Economic Organizations: The EU Example

The overall importance of regional organizations such as the WTO and the EU was discussed in Chapter 3. The legal dimensions are important, however, and will be briefly mentioned here. The Treaty of Rome established the European Community (EC), the precursor to the EU. The treaty created an institutional framework in which a council (the Council of Ministers) serves as the main decision-making body, with each country member having direct representation. The other three main institutions of the community are the European Commission, the EU's executive arm; the European Parliament, the legislative body; and the European Court of Justice.

The 1987 Single European Act amended the Treaty of Rome and provided strong impetus for the creation of a single market beginning January 1, 1993. Although technically the target was not completely met, approximately 85 percent of the new recommendations were implemented into national law by most member states by the target date, resulting in substantial harmonization. A relatively new body known as the European Council (a distinct entity from the Council of Ministers) was formally incorporated into the EC institutional structure by Article 2 of the 1987 act. Comprised of heads of member states plus the president of the commission, the European Council's role is to define general political guidelines for the union and provide direction on integration-related issues such as monetary union.[47] Governments in Central and Eastern European countries that hope to join are currently getting their laws in line with those of the EU.

The Treaty of Rome contains hundreds of articles, several of which are directly applicable to global companies and global marketers. Articles 30 through 36 establish the general policy referred to as "Free Flow of Goods, People, Capital and Technology" among the member states. Articles 85 through 86 contain competition rules, as amended by various directives of the 20-member EU

---

[45]Bob Davis, "Red-Tape Traumas: To All U.S. Managers Upset by Regulations: Try Germany or Japan," *The Wall Street Journal* (December 14, 1995), p. A1.

[46]Raphael Minder, "The Lobbyists Take Brussels by Storm," *Financial Times* (January 26, 2006), p. 7. See also Brandon Mitchener, "Standard Bearers: Increasingly, Rules of Global Economy Are Set in Brussels," *The Wall Street Journal* (April 23, 2002), p. A1.

[47]Klaus-Dieter Borchardt, *European Integration: The Origins and Growth of the European Union* (Luxembourg: Office for Official Publications of the European Communities, 1995), p. 30.

Commission. The commission is the administrative arm of the EU; from its base in Brussels, the commission proposes laws and policies, monitors the observance of EU laws, administers and implements EU legislation, and represents the EU to international organizations.[48] Commission members represent the union rather than their respective nations.

The laws, regulations, directives, and policies that originate in the commission must be submitted to the parliament for an opinion and then passed along to the council for a final decision. Once the council approves a prospective law, it becomes union law, which is somewhat analogous to U.S. federal law. Regulations automatically become law throughout the union; directives include a time frame for implementation by legislation in each member state. For example, in 1994 the commission issued a directive regarding use of trademarks in comparative advertising. Individual member nations of the EU have been working to implement the directive; in the United Kingdom, the 1994 Trade Marks Act gave companies the right to apply for trademark protection of smells, sounds, and images and also provides improved protection against trademark counterfeiting.

The Single Market era is one in which many industries face new regulatory environments. The European Court of Justice, based in Luxembourg, is the EU's highest legal authority. It is responsible for ensuring that EU laws and treaties are upheld throughout the union. Based in Luxembourg, it consists of two separate tribunals. The senior body is known as the Court of Justice; a separate entity, the Court of First Instance, hears cases involving commerce and competition (see Table 5-5).

Although the European Court of Justice plays a role similar to that of the U.S. Supreme Court, there are important differences. The European court cannot decide which cases it will hear, and it does not issue dissenting opinions. The court exercises jurisdiction over a range of civil matters involving trade, individual rights, and environmental law. For example, the court can assess damages against countries that fail to introduce directives by the date set. The court also hears disputes that arise among the 27 EU member nations on trade issues such as mergers, monopolies, trade barriers and regulations, and exports. The court is also empowered to resolve conflicts between national law and EU law. In most cases, the latter supersedes national laws of individual European countries.

Marketers must be aware, however, that national laws should always be consulted. National laws may be *stricter* than community law, especially in such areas as competition and antitrust. To the extent possible, community law is intended to harmonize national laws to promote the purposes defined in Articles 30 through 36. The goal is to bring the lax laws of some member states up to designated minimum standards. However, more restrictive positions may still exist in some national laws. Conversely, national laws may be *less* restrictive than community law. Germany, for example, had traditionally placed few restrictions on banana imports (Germany is Europe's top banana-consuming country). When a German court decreed that German companies could import bananas without complying with the EU's 1993 banana regime regulations, the Court of Justice ruled that national courts could not grant interim judicial relief.[49]

TABLE 5-5 Recent and Pending Actions by the European Court of Justice

Country/Plaintiffs Involved	Issue
EU/Microsoft	The Court of First Instance made a preliminary ruling on antitrust sanctions imposed by the European Commission on Microsoft, e.g., the separation of Windows Media from Windows OS. Faced with a fine of more than $350 million, Microsoft filed an appeal with the Court of First Instance.
UK/Airtours	In 1999, the European Commission blocked a takeover by UK-based Airtours of rival travel company First Choice. In 2002, the Court ruled that Airtours could appeal. The court's action marked the first time it overturned an antitrust ruling by the European Commission.
Italy/Monsanto, Syngenta, Pioneer Hi-Bred International	In 2000, fearing risk to human health, Italy banned foods containing four strains of genetically modified corn. The Italian court hearing the plaintiffs' appeal asked for ECJ intervention; in 2003, the ECJ ruled that the ban was not justified. The case was returned to Italy for a final ruling; the Italian court ruled that the government was not entitled to impose the ban.

Source: Adapted from Frank B. Cross, "Lawyers, the Economy, and Society," *American Business Law Journal* (Summer 1998), pp. 477.

---

[48]Klaus-Dieter Borchardt, *The ABC of Community Law* (Luxembourg: Office for Official Publications of the European Communities, 1994), p. 25.
[49]Rikke Thagesen and Alan Matthews, "The EU's Common Banana Regime: An Initial Evaluation," *Journal of Common Market Studies* 35, no. 4 (December 1997), p. 623.

Summary

The political environment of global marketing is the set of governmental institutions, political parties, and organizations that are the expression of the people in the nations of the world. In particular, anyone engaged in global marketing should have an overall understanding of the importance of **sovereignty** to national governments. The political environment varies from country to country, and **political risk** assessment is crucial. It is also important to understand a particular government's actions with respect to taxes and seizure of assets. Historically, the latter have taken the form of **expropriation**, **confiscation**, and **nationalization**.

The legal environment consists of laws, courts, attorneys, legal customs, and practices. **International law** is comprised of the rules and principles that nation-states consider binding upon themselves. The countries of the world can be broadly categorized as having either **common-law** legal systems or **civil-law** legal systems. The United States and Canada and many former British colonies are common-law countries; most other countries are civil-law countries. A third system, **Islamic law**, predominates in the Middle East. Some of the most important legal issues pertain to **jurisdiction**, antitrust, and licensing. In addition, **bribery** is pervasive in many parts of the world; the **Foreign Corrupt Practices Act** (FCPA) applies to American companies operating abroad. Intellectual property protection is another critical issue. **Counterfeiting** is a major problem in global marketing; it often involves infringement of a company's **copyright**, **patent**, or **trademark** ownership. When legal conflicts arise, companies can pursue the matter in court or use **arbitration**.

The regulatory environment consists of agencies, both governmental and nongovernmental, that enforce laws or set guidelines for conducting business. Global marketing activities can be affected by a number of international or regional economic organizations; in Europe, for example, the EU makes laws governing member states. The WTO will have a broad impact on global marketing activities in the years to come. Although all three environments are complex, astute marketers plan ahead to avoid situations that might result in conflict, misunderstanding, or outright violation of national laws.

Discussion Questions

1. What is sovereignty? Why is it an important consideration in the political environment of global marketing?
2. Describe some of the sources of political risk. Specifically, what forms can political risk take?
3. Briefly describe some of the differences between the legal environment of a country that embraces common law and one that observes civil law.
4. Global marketers can avoid legal conflicts by understanding the reasons conflicts arise in the first place. Identify and describe several legal issues that relate to global commerce.
5. You are an American traveling on business in the Middle East. As you are leaving country X, the passport control officer at the airport tells you there will be a passport "processing" delay of 12 hours. You explain that your plane leaves in 30 minutes, and the official suggests that a contribution of $50 would probably speed things up. If you comply with the suggestion, have you violated U.S. law? Explain.
6. "See you in court" is one way to respond when legal issues arise. Why can that approach backfire when the issue concerns global marketing?

Cuba is a communist outpost in the Caribbean where "socialism or death" is the national motto. After Fidel Castro came to power in 1959, his government took control of most private companies without providing compensation to the owners. American assets owned by both consumer and industrial companies worth approximately $1.8 billion were among those expropriated; today, those assets are worth about $6 billion (see Table 1). President Kennedy responded by imposing a trade embargo on the island nation. Five decades later, when Fidel Castro finally stepped down, no significant changes in policy were made.

In 1990, Castro opened his nation's economy to foreign investment; by the mid-1990s, foreign commitments to invest in Cuba totaled more than half a billion dollars. In 1993, Castro decreed that the U.S. dollar was legal tender although the peso would still be Cuba's official currency. As a result, hundreds of millions of dollars are injected into Cuba's economy each year; Cuban exiles living in the United States send much of the money. Cubans can spend their dollars in special stores that stock imported foods and other hard-to-find products. In a country where doctors are among the highest paid workers with salaries equal to about $20 per month, the cash infusions can significantly improve a family's standard of living. In 1994, *mercados agropecuarios* ("farmers markets") were created as a mechanism to enable farmers to earn more money.

Cuba desperately needs investment and U.S. dollars, in part to compensate for the end of subsidies following the demise of the Soviet Union. Oil companies from Europe and Canada were among the first to seek potential opportunities in Cuba. Many American executives are concerned that lucrative opportunities will be lost as Spain, Mexico, Italy, Canada, and other countries move aggressively into Cuba. Anticipating a softening in the U.S. government's stance, representatives from scores of U.S. companies visit Cuba regularly to meet with officials from state enterprises.

Those U.S. companies that are found guilty of violating trade embargoes, including the one on Cuba, are subject to fines of up to $1 million. Cuba remained officially off-limits to all but a handful of U.S. companies. Some telecommunications and financial services were allowed; AT&T, Sprint, and other companies have offered direct-dial service between the United States and Cuba since 1994. Also, a limited number of charter flights were available each day between Miami and Havana. Sale of medicines was also permitted under the embargo. At a state department briefing for business executives, Assistant Secretary of State for Inter-American Affairs Alexander Watson told his audience, "The Europeans and the Asians are knocking on the door in Latin America. The game is on and we can compete effectively, but it will be a big mistake if we leave the game to others." Secretary Watson was asked whether his comments on free trade applied to Cuba. "No, no. That simply can't be, not for now," Watson replied. "Cuba is a special case. This administration will maintain the embargo until major democratic changes take place in Cuba."

Within the United States, the government's stance toward Cuba has both supporters and opponents. Senator Jesse Helms pushed for a tougher embargo and sponsored a bill in Congress that would penalize foreign countries and companies for doing business with Cuba. The Cuban-American National Foundation actively engaged in anti-Cuba and anti-Castro lobbying. Companies that have openly spoken out against the embargo include Carlson Companies, owner of the Radisson Hotel chain; grain-processing giant Archer Daniels Midland (ADM); and the Otis Elevator division of United Technologies. A spokesperson for Carlson noted, "We see Cuba as an exciting new opportunity—the forbidden fruit of the Caribbean." A number of executives, including Ron Perelman, whose corporate holdings include Revlon and Consolidated Cigar Corporation, are optimistic that the embargo will be lifted within a few years.

Meanwhile, opinion was divided on the question of whether the embargo was costing U.S. companies once-in-a-lifetime opportunities. Some observers argued that many European and Latin American investments in Cuba were short-term, high-risk propositions that would not create barriers to U.S. companies. The opponents of the embargo, however, pointed to evidence that some investments were substantial. Three thousand new hotel rooms have been added by Spain's Grupo Sol Melia and Germany's LTI International Hotels. Both companies were taking advantage of the Cuban government's goal to increase tourism. Moreover, Italian and Mexican companies were snapping up contracts to overhaul the country's telecommunications infrastructure. Wayne Andreas, chairman of ADM, summed up the views of many American executives when he said, "Our embargo has been a total failure for 30 years. We ought to have all the Americans in Cuba doing all the business they can. It's time for a change."

The Helms-Burton Era

The Helms-Burton Act brought change, but not the type advocated by ADM's Andreas. The toughened U.S. stance signaled by Helms-Burton greatly concerned key trading partners, even though Washington insisted that the act was consistent with international law. In particular, supporters noted, the "effects doctrine" of international law permits a nation to take "reasonable" measures to protect its interests when an act outside its boundaries produces a direct effect inside its boundaries. Unmoved by such rationalizations, the

TABLE 1 American Companies Seeking Restitution from Cuba

Company	Amount of Claim (millions)
American Brands	$10.6
Coca-Cola	$27.5
General Dynamics	$10.4
ITT	$47.6
Lone Star Cement	$24.9
Standard Oil	$71.6
Texaco	$50.1

Source: U.S. Justice Department.

European Commission responded in mid-1996 by proposing legislation barring European companies from complying with Helms-Burton. Although such a " blocking statute" was permitted under Article 235 of the EU treaty, Denmark threatened to veto the action on the grounds that doing so exceeded the European Commission's authority; its concerns were accommodated, and the legislation was adopted. Similarly, the Canadian government enacted legislation that would allow Canadian companies to retaliate against U.S. court orders regarding sanctions. Also, Canadian companies that complied with the U.S. sanctions could be fined $1 million for doing so.

Meanwhile, executives at Canada's Sherritt International Corp. and Mexico's Grupo Domos received letters from the U.S. government informing them that they would be barred from entering the United States because of their business ties with Cuba. Sherritt operated a Cuban nickel mine, and Grupo Domos owned a 37 percent stake in Cuba's national telephone company. Both assets had been confiscated from U.S. companies. Canada and Mexico initiated arbitration proceedings as provided for under NAFTA. Meanwhile, in the fall of 1996, Canada registered its defiance of Helms-Burton by hosting Cuba's vice president for a four-day visit.

In August 1996, President Clinton signed another piece of legislation designed to put economic pressure on foreign governments. The Iran and Libya Sanctions Act stipulated that foreign governments and companies that invest $40 million or more in the oil or gas industry sectors in Iran or Libya would be subject to U.S. sanctions. Expert opinion was divided as to whether such sanctions would be effective.

In the fall of 1996, the WTO agreed to a request by the EU to convene a three-person trade panel that would determine whether Helms-Burton violated international trade rules. The official U.S. position was that Helms-Burton was a foreign policy measure designed to promote the transition to democracy in Cuba. The United States also hinted that, if necessary, it could legitimize Helms-Burton by invoking the WTO's national security exemption. That exemption, in turn, hinged on whether the United States faced "an emergency in international relations."

Meanwhile, efforts were underway to resolve the issue on a diplomatic basis. Sir Leon Brittan, trade commissioner for the EU, visited the United States in early November with an invitation for the United States and EU to put aside misunderstandings and join forces in promoting democracy and human rights in Cuba. He noted:

> By opposing Helms-Burton, Europe is challenging one country's presumed right to impose its foreign policy on others by using the threat of trade sanctions. This has nothing whatever to do with human rights. We are merely attacking a precedent which the U.S. would oppose in many other circumstances, with the full support of the EU.

In December, senior EU officials approved a resolution sponsored by Spain that formally clarified the EU's intention to step up pressure on Castro. The U.S. State Department hailed the move as "a breakthrough in U.S.–EU relations." The EU insisted that the policy statement did not represent a change in its position or a concession to the United States. Even so, Spain's move surprised Havana, because Spain is Cuba's biggest foreign investor. However, Spain's newly elected conservative government was taking a harder line. Spain's prime minister and Castro even engaged in a bit of public name-calling.

In January 1997, President Clinton extended the moratorium on lawsuits against foreign investors in Cuba. In the months following the Helms-Burton Act, a dozen companies ceased operating on confiscated U.S. property in Cuba. Stet, the Italian telecommunications company, agreed to pay ITT for confiscated assets, thereby exempting itself from possible sanctions. However, in some parts of the world, reaction to the president's action was lukewarm. The EU issued a statement noting that the action "falls short of the European Commission's hopes for a more comprehensive resolution of this difficult issue in trans-Atlantic relations." The EU also reiterated its intention of pursuing the case at the WTO. Art Eggleton, Canada's international trade minister responded with a less guarded tone: "It continues to be unacceptable behavior by the United States in foisting its foreign policy onto Canada, and other countries, and threatening Canadian business and anybody who wants to do business legally with Cuba."

Meanwhile, there was evidence that the U.S. sanctions, combined with other factors, were hurting Cuba. Sherritt and other foreign investors found the going slower than they expected. A number of legal reforms had still not been implemented. Also, the 1997 sugar crop, critical to Cuba's export earnings, was lower than anticipated. Another interesting twist occurred in Canada, where Walmart temporarily removed Cuban-made pajamas from its 136 retail outlets. The issue was whether Walmart was in violation of the Cuban Democracy Act, which makes U.S. global firms responsible for any boycott violations committed by foreign subsidiaries. After spending two weeks studying the matter and consulting with legal experts, Walmart executives ordered the Cuban goods to be returned to the shelves.

In February, the WTO appointed the panel that would consider the dispute. However, Washington declared that it would boycott the panel proceedings on the grounds that the panel's members weren't competent to review U.S. foreign policy interests. Stuart Eizenstat, undersecretary for international trade at the U.S. Commerce Department, said, "The WTO was not created to decide foreign-policy and national-security issues." One expert on international trade law cautioned that the United States was jeopardizing the future of the WTO. Professor John Jackson of the University of Michigan School of Law said, "If the U.S. takes these kinds of unilateral stonewalling tactics, then it may find itself against other countries doing the same thing in the future."

The parties averted a confrontation at the WTO when the EU suspended its complaint in April, following President Clinton's pledge to seek congressional amendments to Helms-Burton. In particular, the president agreed to seek a waiver of the provision denying U.S. visas to employees of companies using expropriated property. A few days later, the EU and the United States announced plans to develop an agreement on property claims in Cuba with "common disciplines" designed to deter and inhibit investment in confiscated property. Washington hoped such a bilateral agreement could be introduced into the negotiations at the OECD pertaining to the Multilateral Agreement on Investment. However, the agreement spelled out the EU's right to resume the trade panel or launch new proceedings if the United States took action against any European companies. The EU had one year to reactivate its complaint; it chose not to, however, and the panel was allowed to lapse in April 1998.

The U.S. stance was seen in a new perspective following the pope's visit to Cuba in January 1998. Many observers were heartened by Cuban authorities' decision to release nearly 300 political prisoners in February. Opinion within the Cuban-American community in Miami, which had historically supported the embargo, now appeared to be divided. In the fall of 1998, several former U.S. secretaries of state called upon President Clinton to create a National Bipartisan Commission on Cuba to review U.S. policy. In the fall of 2000, President Clinton signed a law that permits Cuba to buy unlimited amounts of food and medicine from the United States. The slight liberalization of trade represented a victory for the U.S. farm lobby, although all purchases must be made in cash.

In 2002, several pieces of legislation were introduced in the U.S. Congress that would effectively undercut the embargo. One bill prohibited funding that would be used to enforce sanctions on private sales of medicine and agricultural products. Another proposal would have the effect of withholding budget money earmarked for enforcing both the ban on U.S. travel to Cuba and limits on monthly dollar remittances. Also in 2002, Castro began to clamp down on the growing democracy movement; about 70 writers and activists were jailed.

President George W. Bush responded by phasing out cultural travel exchanges between the United States and Cuba. In 2004, President Bush imposed new restrictions on Cuban Americans. Visits to immediate family members still living in Cuba were limited to only one every three years. In addition, Cuban Americans wishing to send money to relatives were limited to $1,200 per year.

The early months of Barack Obama's administration saw a rollback of various restrictions. In April 2009, for example, the President lifted restrictions on family travel and money transfers. Although reactions to the announcement were mixed, a significant increase in travel on commercial airlines will not be possible until a bilateral aviation agreement is negotiated between the two nations.

At a Summit of the Americas meeting in Trinidad, President Obama declared, "The United States seeks a new beginning with Cuba. I know there is a longer journey that must be traveled in overcoming decades of mistrust, but there are critical steps we can take." Many observers were surprised by the conciliatory tone of Raul Castro's response to the U.S. President's overtures. Castro indicated a willingness to engage in dialog about such seemingly intractable issues as human rights, political prisoners, and freedom of the press. "We could be wrong, we admit it. We're human beings. We're willing to sit down to talk, as it should be done," Castro said.

Raul's initial response to Obama's overture was indeed conciliatory, and in August the United States and Cuba held extended talks for the first time in at least 10 years. These talks included meetings between U.S. and Cuban governmental officials, and also between U.S. officials and Cuban opposition figures. But the official position of the Cuban government, announced in September by Cuban foreign minister Bruno Rodriguez, is that the U.S. trade embargo should be lifted unilaterally without preconditions. Meanwhile, Obama, despite his overtures, appears to be linking any lifting of the embargo to Cuba's making progress on human rights.

Case 5-1 Discussion Questions

1. What was the key issue that prompted the EU to take the Helms-Burton dispute to the WTO?
2. Who benefits the most from an embargo of this type? Who suffers?
3. In light of the overtures U.S. President Barack Obama has made to Raul Castro, what is the likelihood that the United States and Cuba will resume diplomatic and trade relations during the Obama administration?

Sources: The authors are indebted to Hunter R. Clark, Professor of Law, Drake University Law School, for his contributions to this case. *Additional Sources:* Laura Meckler, "Leaders' Comments Auger Warmer U.S.-Cuba Ties," *The Wall Street Journal* (April 18, 2009), p. A3; Alan Gomez, "Obama Could Change Relations with Cuba," *USA Today* (December 8, 2008), p. 4A; Jerry Perkins, "Making American Dollar Legal Tenderizes Tough Cuban Economy," *The Des Moines Register* (April 6, 2003), pp. 1D, 5D; Mary Anastasia O'Grady, "Threshing Out a Deal Between the Farmers and Fidel," *The Wall Street Journal* (September 20, 2002), p. A11; Pascal Fletcher, "Cuba Sees Itself as Shining Example Amid Global Troubles," *Financial Times* (September 19–20, 1998), p. 3; Carl Gershman, "Thanks to the Pope, Civil Society Stirs in Cuba," *The Wall Street Journal* (September 18, 1998), p. A11; Stuart E. Eizenstat, "A Multilateral Approach to Property Rights," *The Wall Street Journal* (April 11, 1997), p. A18; Therese Raphael, "U.S. and Europe Clash over Cuba," *The Wall Street Journal* (March 31, 1997), p. A14; Robert Greenberger, "Washington Will Boycott WTO Panel," *The Wall Street Journal* (February 21, 1997), p. A2; Greenberger, "U.S. Holds Up Cuba Suits, Pleasing Few," *The Wall Street Journal* (January 6, 1997), p. A7; Brian Coleman, "EU to Push for Human Rights in Cuba," *The Wall Street Journal* (December 2, 1996), p. A12; Guy de Jonquières, "Brittan Calls for End to Cuba Row," *Financial Times* (November 7, 1996), p. 10; Julie Wolf and Brian Coleman, "EU Challenges U.S. Plan to Penalize Foreign Firms That Trade with Cuba," *The Wall Street Journal* (July 31, 1996), p. A1; Gail DeGeorge, "U.S. Business Isn't Afraid to Shout *Cuba Si!*" *Business Week* (November 6, 1995), p. 39; Jose De Cordoba, "Cuba's Business Law Puts Off Foreigners," *The Wall Street Journal* (October 10, 1995), p. A14; Sam Dillon, "Companies Press Clinton to Lift Embargo on Cuba," *The New York Times* (August 27, 1995), pp. 1, 4; Thomas T. Vogel, Jr., "Havana Headaches: Investors Find Cuba Tantalizing Yet Murky in Financial Matters," *The Wall Street Journal* (August 7, 1995), pp. A1, A4.

Mankind has engaged in gambling for many centuries. Archeologists have unearthed six-sided dice dating from around 3000 B.C. Ancient Egyptians played a game resembling backgammon. On the Indian subcontinent more than 3500 years ago, there were public and private gambling houses, dice games, and betting on fights between animals. Farther east, Asian cultures also have a rich and long tradition of gambling. As cultural artifacts, playing cards had their primitive origins in Asia.

When Europeans arrived in North America, they found that the native peoples had been gambling in a variety of ways for centuries. Of course, the European settlers and colonists were no strangers to gambling themselves. They brought with them a penchant for gambling in various forms, including card-playing, dice games, and lotteries. Even the Puritan settlers played cards.

Much of America's Revolutionary War was funded from lottery proceeds. Likewise, several of the young nation's new universities, including Columbia, Yale, and Princeton, were founded with substantial financial assistance from lotteries. America's connection to gambling has continued throughout its Civil War, two World Wars, and the emergence of Nevada as the icon of "Las Vegas-style" gambling.

Today, gambling has gone global. This seems logical, given gambling's prevalence through time around the world. The Internet Age is creating new opportunities for gamblers as well as challenges for those wanting to limit the spread of gambling and access to it. No longer is it necessary to physically travel to a casino or horse track to place bets on blackjack, sporting events, and horse racing. "Virtual" casinos have sprung up to engage the gambler in online gaming opportunities. In the 1990s, online casinos proliferated as Internet entrepreneurs sought to satisfy the worldwide demand for online gaming. These companies were based outside the United States because of questions about the legality of such activity under state and federal law. Many of these companies, including Gibraltar-based PartyGaming Plc and 888 Holdings Plc, are publicly traded corporations.

Despite its long history of gambling, the United States has also engaged in strict regulation of the industry. The surge in Internet gaming triggered efforts to ban such activity, and to prosecute those who are the principals of the so-called offshore online casinos. This regulatory action has angered governments in various countries, especially smaller countries where the online casinos are based. One country, Antigua and Barbuda (Antigua), filed a claim with the WTO in 2004 arguing that U.S. laws and policies pertaining to online gambling violate the terms of a fair trade agreement known as the General Agreement on Trade in Services (GATS).

Antigua claimed that the United States discriminated against foreign suppliers of "recreational services," including Internet gaming. The claim was based on the following argument: Even as it maintains a number of federal laws that prohibit offshore Internet gaming, the United States exempts off-track betting on horse races over the Internet from these same federal laws. According to the suit, this situation benefits domestic interests at the expense of offshore casinos.

In 2005, a WTO compliance panel ruled that the United States had, in fact, discriminated between foreign and domestic suppliers of gambling services. But the panel gave the United States an opportunity to show that the prevention of offshore betting was necessary as a means of protecting "public order and public morals." In 2006, U.S. authorities arrested David Caruthers, a British citizen who is the chief executive of Costa Rica–based BetonSports, while he was in the Dallas/Fort Worth airport en route from London to Costa Rica. In a 26-page indictment, the U.S. Department of Justice charged Caruthers and others with 22 counts of racketeering, conspiracy, and fraud.

The debate is far from over. Additional efforts are underway to make Internet gambling in the United States illegal, or at least difficult. In the fall of 2006, U.S. President George W. Bush signed into law the SAFE Port Act, which included the Unlawful Internet Gaming Enforcement Act. This measure prohibits U.S. banks, credit card companies, and other financial intermediaries from sending or receiving money to offshore casinos. Thus, the law makes it difficult for gamblers to fund their offshore accounts. Commenting on the signing of the measure, Michael Bolcerek, president of the Poker Players Alliance (PPA), said, "Today is a dark day for the great American game of poker. Twenty-three million Americans who play the game online will effectively be denied the ability to enjoy this popular form of entertainment, even in the privacy of their own homes."

In March 2007, the WTO ruled again. It found that the continuing exemption for online gambling on horseracing in the United States unfairly discriminated against foreign casinos. The United States can restrict online gambling only so long as its laws are equally applied to American operators as well as foreign operators, the ruling stated. The WTO ruling allows Antigua to seek trade sanctions against the United States. While Antigua may not have the economic muscle to bring about meaningful trade sanctions against the United States, it is possible that other countries affected by the United States ban, including Great Britain, may also petition the WTO for relief.

Discussion Questions

1. Do you think that the Unlawful Internet Gaming Enforcement Act unfairly discriminates against offshore gaming companies?
2. How likely is it that legislative efforts to prevent people who want to gamble from gambling will be successful?
3. At a time when the U.S. government is desperate to generate revenues, would it make sense for policymakers to license, regulate, and tax Internet gambling? Do the results of the 2008 election and the current economic crisis create the conditions for tapping this new revenue source? Or, should concerns about the erosion of social values dominate the discussion of Internet gambling?

Sources: This case was prepared by Keith Miller, Ellis and Nelle Levitt Distinguished Professor of Law, Drake University Law School. Additional sources: Roger Blitz, "The Unlucky Gambler," *Financial Times* (July 23/23, 2006), p. 7; Blitz and Tom Braithwaite, "Online Operators Weigh Up the Odds," *Financial Times* (July 19, 2006), p. 21; Scott Miller and Christina Binkley, "Trade Body Rules Against U.S. Ban on Web Gambling," *The Wall Street Journal* (March 25, 2004), p. A2.

Global Information Systems and Market Research

Case 6-1
Information Technology—The Key to Success for Clicks in South Africa

Clicks Group Limited is a specialist retail group that was founded in 1968 when the entrepreneurial retailer Jack Goldin opened the first Clicks store in Cape Town, South Africa. In 1996, the group was listed on the Johannesburg Stock Exchange of South Africa, and today it operates the retail brands Musica, The Body Shop, and Clicks, boasting more than 540 stores across southern Africa. Musica is the largest retailer of music and entertainment-related merchandise in South Africa, while The Body Shop is a well-known global brand selling naturally inspired beauty products. Clicks Group Limited operates The Body Shop in southern Africa under an exclusive licensing agreement.

Clicks is the leading specialist health, beauty, and lifestyle retailer in South Africa and contributes approximately 66 percent of group profits. Clicks was originally conceived as a drugstore, but established legislation prevented corporate ownership of retail pharmacies in South Africa. Clicks was therefore operated as a drugstore without drugs until regulatory reforms were introduced in 2003, which enabled Clicks to finally fulfill its founding vision. The first Clicks pharmacy was opened in March 2004

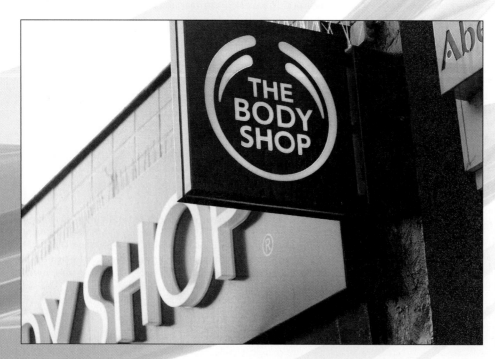

Exhibit 6-1: Clicks Group Ltd has over 540 stores across Southern Africa. It is the southern African franchise holder of The Body Shop brand. The first Body Shop stores opened in South Africa in June 2001 and now have almost 40 stores. The business offers a Body Shop "Love Your Body" clubcard to bolster customer loyalty and to encourage repeat purchases. It is also invaluable in tracking buyer behavior.
Source: © geogphotos/Alamy.

in Sea Point, Cape Town. Today, Clicks operates the largest retail pharmacy chain in South Africa with over 200 in-store dispensaries. Clicks Group Limited furthermore has an increasing presence in the South African health care market through wholesale pharmaceutical distributor New United Pharmaceutical Distributors (UPD), which is the leading full-range pharmaceutical wholesaler in South Africa.

The Clicks brand essentially appeals to consumers in the middle- to upper-income market who appreciate value for money and professional pharmaceutical and health advice as well as consumers who have an interest in health, beauty, and home-trend developments and care about the way they live, look, and feel. Indications are that Clicks is currently trading in the so-called market sweet spot, as the health, beauty, and medicines sector is considered the fastest growing sector of the retail market.

Products supplied by Clicks are mainly targeted at modern South African women, in the age group of 25 to 49. Clicks also serves a secondary target market that includes older women aged 50 and above, as well as younger women, aged between 16 and 24, as well as men. In recent years, Clicks also started to adapt its merchandise range to appeal to consumers of the growing black middle-class market.

Clicks employs a system of sophisticated data-mining techniques that enable the company to reward and up-sell consumers individually, based on their previous buying behavior. After you have finished reading Chapter 6, turn to Case 6-1 which discusses the success Clicks have had with their Clubcard loyalty programme.

INFORMATION TECHNOLOGY AND BUSINESS INTELLIGENCE FOR GLOBAL MARKETING

The phrase **information technology (IT)** refers to an organization's processes for creating, storing, exchanging, using, and managing information. A **management information system (MIS)** provides managers and other decision makers with a continuous flow of information about company operations. MIS is a broad term that can be used in reference to a system of hardware and software that a company uses to manage information. (The term can also be used to describe an IT department; in this case, it refers to people, hardware, and software.) An MIS should provide a means for gathering, analyzing, classifying, storing, retrieving, and reporting relevant data. The MIS should also cover important aspects of a company's external environment, including customers and competitors.

One component of a firm's MIS is a business intelligence (BI) network that helps managers make decisions; its major objective is:

> . . . to enable interactive access to data, enable manipulation of these data, and to provide managers and analysts with the ability to conduct appropriate analysis. By analyzing historical and current data, situations, and performances, decision makers get valuable insights upon which they can base more informed and better decisions.[1]

Global competition intensifies the need for effective MIS and BI that are accessible throughout the company. As Jean-Pierre Corniou, chief information officer (CIO) at Renault, noted recently:

> My vision is to design, build, sell, and maintain cars. Everything I do is directly linked to this, to the urgent need to increase turnover, margins, and brand image. Every single investment and expense in the IT field has to be driven by this vision of the automotive business.[2]

Caterpillar, GE, Boeing, Federal Express, Diageo, Ford, Toyota, and many other companies with global operations have made significant investments in IT in recent years.

[1]Efraim Turban, Ramesh Sharda, Jay E. Aronson, and David King, *Business Intelligence: A Managerial Approach* (Upper Saddle River, NJ: Pearson Education, 2008), p. 9.
[2]Jean-Pierre Corniu, "Bringing Business Technology Out into the Open," *Financial Times—Information Technology Review* (September 17, 2003), p. 2.

Such investment is typically directed at upgrading a company's computer hardware and software. Microsoft, Sun Microsystems, SAP, Oracle, and IBM are some of the beneficiaries of this trend. All are global enterprises, and many of their customers are global as well. Vendors of complex software systems can find it difficult to achieve 100 percent customer satisfaction. Thomas Siebel, founder of Siebel Systems, explains how his company met this challenge:

> Siebel Systems is a global company, not a multinational company. I believe the notion of the multinational company—where a division is free to follow its own set of business rules—is obsolete, though there are still plenty around. Our customers—global companies like IBM, Zurich Financial Services, and Citicorp—expect the same high level of service and quality, and the same licensing policies, no matter where we do business with them around the world. Our human resources and legal departments help us create policies that respect local cultures and requirements worldwide, while at the same time maintaining the highest standards. We have one brand, one image, one set of corporate colors, one set of messages, across every place on the planet.[3]

In 2006, Siebel merged with Oracle.

Unlike the public Internet, an **intranet** is a private network that allows authorized company personnel or outsiders to share information electronically in a secure fashion without generating mountains of paper. Intranets allow a company's information system to serve as a 24-hour nerve center, enabling Amazon.com, Dell, and other companies to operate as *real time enterprises* (RTEs). The RTE model is expected to grow in popularity as wireless Internet access becomes more widely available.

An **electronic data interchange (EDI)** system allows a company's business units to submit orders, issue invoices, and conduct business electronically with other company units as well as outside companies. One of the key features of EDI is that its transaction formats are universal. This allows computer systems at different companies to speak the same language. Walmart is legendary for its sophisticated EDI system; for years, vendors have received orders from the retailer on personal computers using dial-up modems connected to third-party transmission networks. In 2002, Walmart informed vendors it was switching to an Internet-based EDI system. The switch saves both time and money; the modem-based system was susceptible to transmission interruptions, and the cost was between $0.10 and $0.20 per thousand characters transmitted. Any vendor that wishes to do business with Walmart in the future must purchase and install the necessary computer software.[4]

Poor operating results can often be traced to insufficient data and information about events both inside and outside the company. For example, when a new management team took over the U.S. unit of Adidas AG, the German athletic shoe maker, data were not available on normal inventory turnover rates. A new reporting system revealed that archrivals Reebok and Nike turned inventories five times a year, compared with twice a year at Adidas. This information was used to tighten the marketing focus on the best-selling Adidas products. In Japan, 7-Eleven's computerized distribution system provides it with a competitive advantage in the convenience store industry. Every 7-Eleven store is linked with each other and with distribution centers. As one retail analyst noted:

> With the system they have established, whatever time you go, the shelves are never empty. If people come in at 4 A.M. and the stores don't have what they want, that will have a big impact on what people think of the store.[5]

Globalization puts increased pressure on companies to achieve as many economies as possible. IT provides a number of helpful tools. As noted previously, EDI links with vendors enable retailers to improve inventory management and restock hot-selling products in a timely, cost-effective manner. In addition to EDI, retailers are increasingly using a technique known as **efficient consumer response (ECR)** in an effort to work more closely with vendors on stock replenishment. ECR can be defined as a joint initiative by members of a supply chain to work toward improving and optimizing aspects of the supply chain to benefit customers. ECR systems utilize **electronic point of sale (EPOS)** data gathered by checkout scanners to help retailers identify product sales patterns and how

[3]Bronwyn Fryer, "High-Tech the Old-Fashioned Way: An Interview with Tom Siebel of Siebel Systems," *Harvard Business Review* (March 2001), pp. 118–125.
[4]Ann Zimmerman, "To Sell Goods to Walmart, Get on the Net," *The Wall Street Journal* (November 21, 2003), pp. B1, B6.
[5]Bethan Hutton, "Japan's 7-Eleven Sets Store by Computer Links," *Financial Times* (March 17, 1998), p. 26.

consumer preferences vary with geography. Although currently most popular in the United States, the ECR movement is gaining traction in Europe. Companies such as Carrefour, Metro, Coca-Cola, and Henkel have all embraced ECR. Supply chain innovations such as radio frequency identification tags (RFID) are likely to provide increased momentum for ECR.

EPOS, ECR, and other IT tools are also helping businesses improve their ability to target consumers and increase loyalty. The trend among retailers is to develop customer-focused strategies that will personalize and differentiate the business. In addition to point-of-sale scanner data, loyalty programs that use electronic smart cards will provide retailers with important information about shopping habits. A new business model that helps companies collect, store, and analyze customer data is called **customer relationship management (CRM)**. Although industry experts offer varying descriptions and definitions of CRM, the prevailing view is that CRM is a philosophy that values two-way communication between company and customer. Every point of contact ("touchpoint" in CRM-speak) a company has with a consumer or business customer—through a Web site, warranty card or sweepstakes entry, payment on credit card account, or inquiry to a call center—is an opportunity to collect data. CRM tools allow companies such as American Express, Dell, HSBC, Sharp, and Sony to determine which customers are most valuable and to react in a timely manner with customized product and service offerings that closely match customer needs. If implemented correctly, CRM can make employees more productive and enhance corporate profitability; it also benefits customers by providing value-added products and services.

A company's use of CRM can manifest itself in various ways. Some are visible to consumers, others are not; some make extensive use of leading-edge information technology, others do not. In the hotel industry, for example, CRM can take the form of front desk staff who monitor, respond to, and anticipate the needs of repeat customers. A visitor to Amazon.com who buys the latest U2 CD encounters CRM when he or she gets the message "Customers who bought this title also bought Bruce Springsteen's *Working on a Dream.*" CRM can also be based on the click path that a Web site visitor follows. In this case, however, Internet users may be unaware that a company is tracking their behavior and interests.

One challenge is to integrate data into a complete picture of the customer and his or her relationship to the company and its products or services. This is sometimes referred to as a "360-degree view of the customer." The challenge is compounded for global marketers. Subsidiaries in different parts of the world may use different customer data formats, and commercial CRM products may not support all the target languages. In view of such issues, industry experts recommend implementing global CRM programs in phases. The first could focus on a specific task such as *sales force automation* (SFA); this term refers to a software system that automates routine aspects of sales and marketing functions such as lead assignment, contact follow-up, and opportunity reporting. An SFA system can also analyze the cost of sales and the effectiveness of marketing campaigns. Some SFA software can assist with quote preparation and management of other aspects of a sales campaign, such as mass mailings and conference or convention attendee follow-up.

For example, an important first step in implementing a CRM system could be to utilize SFA software from a company such as Oracle or Onyx Software. The objective at this stage of the CRM effort would be to provide sales representatives in all country locations with access via an Internet portal to sales activities throughout the organization. To simplify the implementation, the company could require that all sales activities be recorded in English. Subsequently, marketing, customer service, and other functions could be added to the system.[6]

Privacy issues also vary widely from country to country. In the EU, for example, a Directive on Data Collection has been in effect since 1998. Companies that use CRM to collect data about individual consumers must satisfy the regulations in each of the EU's 27 member countries. There are also restrictions about sharing such information across national borders. In 2000, the U.S. Department of Commerce and the EU concluded a Safe Harbor agreement that establishes principles for privacy protection for companies that wish to transfer data to the United States from Europe. The principles, which are posted in detail at www.export.gov/safeharbor, include:

- The purposes for which information is collected and used and the means by which individuals can direct inquiries to the company
- An "opt out" option to prevent the disclosure of personal information to third parties

> "The major thing is, 'One size fits all' is not true. CRM is designed to support the sales process, and if I develop a system that works in the U.S., it might not work in Europe."
>
> Jim Dickie, Insight Technology Group

---

[6]Gina Fraone, "Facing Up to Global CRM," *eWeek* (July 30, 2001), pp. 37–41.

- An agreement that information can only be transferred to third parties that are in compliance with Safe Harbor Principles
- Individuals must have access to information collected about them and must be able to correct or delete inaccurate information

Databases called **data warehouses** are frequently an integral part of a company's CRM system. Data warehouses can serve other purposes as well. For example, they can help retailers with multiple store locations fine-tune product assortments. Company personnel, including persons who are not computer specialists, can access data warehouses via standard Web browsers. Behind the familiar interfaces, however, is specialized software capable of performing multidimensional analysis by using sophisticated techniques such as linear programming and regression analysis. This enhances the ability of managers to respond to changing business conditions by adjusting marketing mix elements. MicroStrategy, an information services company in the United Kingdom, is one of several companies creating data warehouses for clients. As former vice president Stewart Holness explains, "Many corporations have a vast amount of information which they have spent money accumulating, but they have not been able to distribute it. The Web is the perfect vehicle for it."[7]

As Holness' comment makes clear, the Internet is revolutionizing corporate information processing (see Chapter 15). Companies slow to recognize the revolution risk falling behind competitors. For example, Germany is home to the *Mittelstand*, a group of 3 million small and mid-size manufacturers that have traditionally been focused and successful global marketers. The *Mittelstand* are often cited as an illustration of how small companies can help propel economic growth and sustain prosperity. As Dietmar Hopp, chief executive of Germany's largest software firm, noted in the mid-1990s:

> With globalization there is no difference now between the *Mittelstand* and big companies— the business processes are comparable. It is only a matter of time before foreign competitors use the Internet to strengthen their foothold in Germany. German companies should follow their example and build up their U.S. and Asian activities through electronic marketing and commerce.[8]

There is evidence that *Mittelstand* companies have gotten the message. According to a recent study conducted by IBM Germany and *Impulse*, a German magazine for entrepreneurs, most *Mittelstand* companies now have Web homepages. Approximately one-third use the Web for e-business activities such as ordering and cross-linking with suppliers.[9]

These examples show just some of the ways that IT is affecting global marketing. However, EDI, ECR, EPOS, SFA, CRM, and other aspects of IT do not simply represent marketing issues; they are organizational imperatives. The tasks of designing, organizing, and implementing systems for business intelligence and information must be coordinated in a coherent manner that contributes to the overall strategic direction of the organization. Modern IT tools provide the means for a company's marketing information system and research functions to provide relevant information in a timely, cost-efficient, and actionable manner.

Overall, then, the global organization has the following needs:

- An efficient, effective system that will scan and digest published sources and technical journals in the headquarters country as well as all countries in which the company has operations or customers.
- Daily scanning, translating, digesting, abstracting, and electronic input of information into a market intelligence system. Today, thanks to advances in IT, full-text versions of many sources are available online as PDF files. Print documentary material can easily be scanned, digitized, and added to a company's information system.
- Expanding information coverage to other regions of the world.

---

[7]Vanessa Houlder, "Warehouse Parties," *Financial Times* (October 23, 1996), p. 8. See also John W. Verity, "Coaxing Meaning Out of Raw Data," *Business Week* (February 3, 1997), pp. 134+.
[8]Graham Bowley, "In the Information Technology Slow Lane," *Financial Times* (November 11, 1997), p. 14.
[9]"E-Business in the *Mittelstand*," www.impulse.de (January 23, 2002).

SOURCES OF MARKET INFORMATION

Although environmental scanning is a vital source of information, research has shown that headquarters executives of global companies obtain as much as two-thirds of the information they need from *personal sources*. A great deal of external information comes from executives based abroad in company subsidiaries, affiliates, and branches. These executives are likely to have established communication with distributors, consumers, customers, suppliers, and government officials. A striking feature of the global corporation—and a major source of competitive strength—is the role that executives abroad play in acquiring and disseminating information about the world environment. Headquarters executives generally acknowledge that company executives overseas are the people who know best what is going on in their areas. The following is a typical comment of headquarters executives:

> Our principal sources are internal. We have a very well-informed and able overseas establishment. The local people have a double advantage. They know the local scene and they know our business. Therefore, they are an excellent source. They know what we are interested in learning, and because of their local knowledge they are able to effectively cover available information from all sources.

The information issue exposes one of the key weaknesses of a domestic company: Although more attractive opportunities may be present outside existing areas of operation, they are likely to go unnoticed by inside sources in a domestic company because the scanning horizon tends to end at the home-country border. Similarly, a company with limited geographical operations may be at risk because internal sources abroad tend to scan only information about their own countries or regions.

Direct sensory perception provides a vital background for the information that comes from human and documentary sources. Direct perception gets all the senses involved. It means seeing, feeling, hearing, smelling, or tasting for oneself to find out what is going on in a particular country, rather than getting secondhand information by hearing or reading about a particular issue. Some information is easily available from other sources but requires sensory experience to sink in. Often, the background information or context one gets from observing a situation can help fill in the big picture. For example, Walmart's first stores in China stocked a number of products—extension ladders and giant bottles of soy sauce, for example—that were inappropriate for local customers. Joe Hatfield, Walmart's top executive for Asia, began roaming the streets of Shenzhen in search of ideas. His observations paid off; when Walmart's giant store in Dalian opened in April 2000, a million shoppers passed through its doors in the first week (see Exhibit 6-2). They snapped up

Exhibit 6-2: Joe Hatfield, chief executive of Walmart Asia, is responsible for the retailer's 146 Chinese stores. Hatfield works 17-hour days in his quest to help WalMart edge past Carrefour as China's largest hypermarket operator. Walmart's strategy calls for building a nationwide distribution network; to accomplish this, the company has spent tens of millions of dollars in Kengzi and Shanghai. Industry observers forecast that, by 2015, 200 million Chinese households will have annual incomes of $3,200.
Source: China Photos/Getty Images, Inc.

products ranging from lunch boxes to pizza topped with corn and pineapple.[10] When Jim Stengel was chief marketing officer at Procter & Gamble, he moved his managers away from a preoccupation with research data to a wider view based on direct perception. As Stengel noted recently:

> We often find consumers can't articulate it. That's why we need to have a culture where we are understanding. There can't be detachment. You can't just live away from the consumer and the brand and hope to gain your insights from data or reading or talking to academics. You have to be experiential. And some of our best ideas are coming from people getting out there and experiencing and listening.[11]

Direct perception can also be important when a global player dominates a company's domestic market. Such was the case with Microsoft and its Xbox video game system, which was launched in a market dominated by Sony. Cindy Spodek-Dickey, group manager for national consumer promotions and sponsorships, took Xbox "on the road" with various promotional partners such as the Association of Volleyball Professionals (AVP). At AVP tournaments in different cities, spectators (and potential customers) had the opportunity to visit the Xbox hospitality tent to try out the new system. At one tournament event, Spodek-Dickey explained the importance of informal market research:

> What are the other sponsors doing? What's the crowd into? What brands are they wearing? How are they interacting with our property? I'll stop them as they come out of the tent and say: "What do you think? What do you like about Xbox? What do you think of your PlayStation?" It's mother-in-law research. I wouldn't want to stake a $10 million ad campaign on it, but I think it keeps you credible and real. When you start to hear the same feedback, three, four, five times, you'd better be paying attention. . . . I believe it is part of any good marketer's job to be in touch with their audience and their product. There's no substitute for face-to-face, eye-to-eye, hand-to-hand.[12]

FORMAL MARKET RESEARCH

Information is a critical ingredient in formulating and implementing a successful marketing strategy. As described earlier, a marketing information system should produce a continuous flow of information. **Market research**, by contrast, is the project-specific, systematic gathering of data. The American Marketing Association defines *marketing research* as "the activity that links the consumer, customer and public to the marketer through information."[14] In **global market research**, this activity is carried out on a global scale. The challenge of global market research is to recognize and respond to the important national differences that influence the way information can be obtained. These include cultural, linguistic, economic, political, religious, historical, and market differences.

Michael Czinkota and Ilkka Ronkainen note that the objectives of international market research are the same as the objectives of domestic research. However, they have identified four specific environmental factors that may require international research efforts to be conducted differently than domestic research. First, researchers must be prepared for new parameters of doing business. Not only will there be different requirements, but the ways in which rules are applied may differ as well. Second, "cultural megashock" may occur as company personnel come to grips with a new set of culture-based assumptions about conducting business. Third, a company entering more

> "China and India are very interesting because they are large, fast-growing economies. Indeed, I have a full-time analyst researching the Chinese market for potential acquisitions—on top of a regular market intelligence team that flies in and out of the country as needed. Right now we have terabytes of information on China."[13]
>
> Lorenzo Zambrano, CEO, Cemex

---

[10]Peter Wonacott, "Walmart Finds Market Footing in China," *The Wall Street Journal* (July 17, 2000), p. A31.
[11]Gary Silverman, "How May I Help You?" *Financial Times* (February 4–5, 2006), p. W2.
[12]Kenneth Hein, "We Know What Guys Want," *Brandweek* (November 14, 2002), p. M48.
[13]John Lyons, "Cemex Prowls for Deals in Both China and India," *The Wall Street Journal* (January 27, 2006), p. C4.
[14]Peter D. Bennett, ed., *Dictionary of Marketing Terms,* 2nd ed. (Chicago: American Marketing Association, 1995), p. 169.

than one new geographic market faces a burgeoning network of interacting factors; research may help prevent psychological overload. Fourth, company researchers may have to broaden the definition of competitors in international markets to include competitive pressures that would not be present in the domestic market.[15]

There are two basic ways to conduct market research. One is to design and implement a study with in-house staff. The other is to use an outside firm specializing in market research. In global marketing, a combination of in-house and outside research efforts is often advisable. Many outside firms have considerable international expertise; some specialize in particular industry segments. According to figures compiled by *Marketing News*, global market research revenues for the top 25 research companies totaled $17.5 billion in 2007 (see Exhibit 6-3).[16]

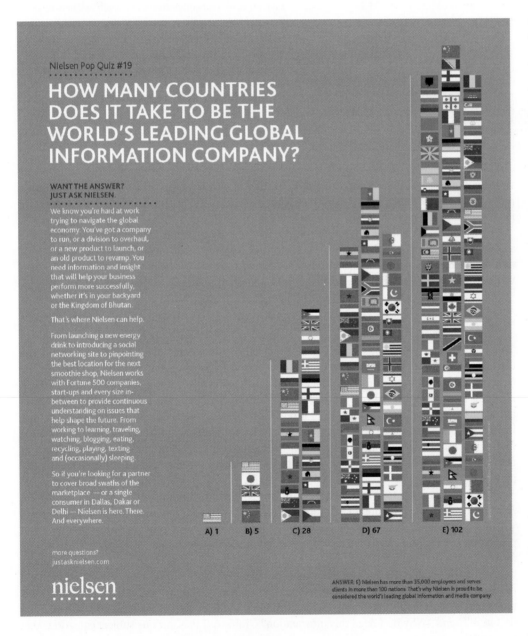

Exhibit 6-3: Nielsen is a global information and media company serving clients in more than 100 countries. As the body copy in this print ad explains, "We know you're hard at work trying to navigate the global economy. You've got a company to run, or a division to overhaul, or a new product to launch, or an old product to revamp. You need information and insight that will help your business perform more successfully, whether it's in your backyard or the Kingdom of Bhutan."
Source: Copyrighted information of The Nielsen Company, licensed for use herein.

---

[15]Michael R. Czinkota and Ilkka A. Ronkainen, "Market Research for Your Export Operations: Part I—Using Secondary Sources of Research," *International Trade Forum* 30, no. 3 (1994), pp. 22–33.
[16]"Top 25 Global Market Research Firms," *Marketing News* (August 15, 2008), pp. H4–H50.

TABLE 6-1 Leading Global Market Research Companies

Company (Home Country)	2007 Research-Only Revenues ($ millions)	Competitive Focus
1. The Nielsen Company (United States; Netherlands)	$4,220.0	Units include ACNielsen, Nielsen Media, Nielsen Connect, Nielsen Mobile, and Spectra. Focus is on media monitoring and business information.
2. IMS Health Inc. (United States)	$2,192.6	Provides market information to pharmaceutical and health care industries.
3. Taylor Nelson Sofres PLC (UK)	$2,137.1	Custom business research; polling and social research; syndicated services.
4. GfK AG (Germany)	$1,593.2	Five business units offer custom research and consumer tracking services, plus research on retail and technology, media, and health care sectors.
5. The Kantar Group (United States; unit of WPP Group)	$1,551.4	Units include Millward Brown and Research International. Focus is on brand awareness and media analysis.

Source: Adapted from "Top 25 Global Market Research Firms," *Marketing News* (August 15, 2008).

The Nielsen Company is the world's largest market research organization; it is the source of the well-known Nielsen TV ratings for the U.S. market. Nielsen Media Research International provides media measurement services in more than 40 global markets. The top global marketing research companies are shown in Table 6-1.

The process of collecting data and converting it into useful information can be quite detailed, as shown in Figure 6-1. In the discussion that follows, we will focus on eight basic steps: information requirement, problem definition, choose unit of analysis, examine data availability, assess value of research, research design, data analysis, and interpretation and presentation.

Step 1: Information Requirement

The late Thomas Bata was a self-described "shoe salesman" who built the Bata Shoe Organization into a global empire that is now based in Switzerland. Legend has it that the Czech-born, Swiss-educated Bata once fired a salesman who, upon returning from Africa, reported that there was no opportunity to sell shoes there because everyone walked around barefoot. According to this story, Bata hired another salesman who appreciated the fact that, in fact, Africa represented a huge untapped market for shoes. This anecdote underscores the fact that direct observation must be linked to unbiased perception and insight. However, as many marketers will acknowledge, it can be difficult to alter entrenched consumer behavior patterns.

Formal research often is undertaken after a problem or opportunity has been identified. A company may need to supplement direct perception with additional information to determine whether a particular country or regional market does, in fact, offer good growth potential. What proportion of potential customers can be converted into *actual* customers? Is a competitor making inroads in one or more important markets around the world? Is research on local taste preferences required to determine if a food product must be adapted? A truism of market research is that a problem well defined is a problem half solved. Thus, regardless of the particular situation that sets the research effort in motion, the first two questions a marketer should ask are "What information do I need?" and "Why do I need this information?" Table 6-2 lists various subject categories that may require research.

Step 2: Problem Definition

As noted in Chapter 4, when a person's home-country values and beliefs influence the assessment of a foreign culture or country, the self-reference criterion (SRC) is at work. The SRC

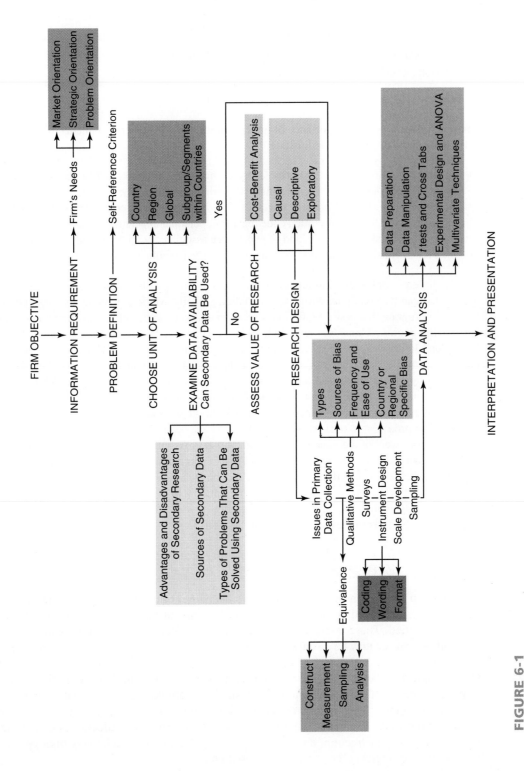

FIGURE 6-1

The International Marketing Resource Process

Source: V. Kumar, *International Marketing Research*, 1st Edition, © 2000. Reprinted by permission of Pearson Education, Inc. Upper Saddle River, NJ.

213

TABLE 6-2 Subject Agenda Categories for a Global Marketing Information System

Category	Coverage
1. Market potential	Demand estimates, consumer behavior, review of products, channels, communication media
2. Competitor information	Corporate, business, and functional strategies; resources and intentions; capabilities
3. Foreign exchange	Balance of payments, interest rates, attractiveness of country currency, expectations of analysts
4. Prescriptive information	Laws, regulations, rulings concerning taxes, earnings, dividends in both host and home countries
5. Resource information	Availability of human, financial, physical, and information resources
6. General conditions	Overall review of sociocultural, political, and technological environments

tendency underscores the importance of understanding the cultural environments of global markets, as the following examples illustrate:

- When Mattel first introduced Barbie in Japan, managers assumed that Japanese girls would find the doll's design just as appealing as American girls did. They didn't.
- When the Walt Disney Company opened Disneyland Paris, park employees were expected to comply with a detailed written code regarding personal appearance. The goal was to ensure that guests receive the kind of experience associated with the Disney name. However, the French considered the code to be an insult to French culture, individualism, and privacy.

As these examples show, assumptions that managers make based on home-country marketing success can turn out to be wrong when applied globally. Marketers might also assume that a marketing program that is successful in one country market can be applied to other country markets in the region. Consider again the case of Disney's theme park business. Although Disneyland Japan was a huge success from opening day, the $3.2 billion Hong Kong Disneyland that opened in 2005 has been less successful. This is due in part to the fact that mainland Chinese have little familiarity with traditional Disney "face characters" such as Snow White. As Jay Rasulo, president of Disney's park and resort division, noted, "People from the mainland don't show up with the embedded 'Disney software' like at other parks."[17]

When approaching global markets, it is best to have "eyes wide open." In other words, marketers must be aware of the impact that SRC and other cross-cultural assumptions can have. Such awareness can have several positive effects. First, it can enhance management's willingness to conduct market research in the first place. Second, an awareness of SRC can help ensure that the research effort is designed with minimal home-country or second-country bias. Third, it can enhance management's receptiveness to accepting research findings—even if they contradict "tried and true" marketing experience in other markets.

Step 3: Choose Unit of Analysis

The next step involves the need to identify in what part(s) of the world the company should be doing business and finding out as much as possible about the business environment in the area(s) identified. These issues are reflected in the subject agenda categories in Table 6-2. The unit of analysis may be a single country; it may also be a region such as Europe or South America. In some instances, the marketer is interested in a segment that is global. Countrywide data are not required for all market entry decisions. Rather, a specific city, state, or province may be the relevant unit of analysis. For example, a company that is considering entering China may focus initially on Shanghai. Located in the Jiangsu province, Shanghai is China's largest city and main seaport. Because Shanghai is a manufacturing center, has a well-developed infrastructure, and is home to a population with a relatively high per capita income, it is the logical focus of a market research effort.

---

[17]Merissa Marr and Geoffrey A. Fowler, "Chinese Lessons for Disney," *The Wall Street Journal* (June 12, 2006), p. B1.

CULTURE WATCH
Bikers Go "Hog" Wild

In 2003, Harley-Davidson (H-D) celebrated its 100th anniversary. The company grew impressively during its first 100 years of operation; as the twenty-first century began, H-D had sales of $2.1 billion, 8,000 employees worldwide, and a network of 1,300 dealerships in 48 countries. Savvy export marketing enabled H-D to dramatically increase worldwide sales of its heavyweight motorcycles. From Australia to Germany to Mexico City, H-D enthusiasts were paying the equivalent of up to $25,000 to own an American-built classic. In many countries, dealers put would-be buyers on a six-month waiting list because of high demand.

H-D's international success came after years of neglecting overseas markets. The company was also slow to react to a growing threat from Japanese manufacturers. Early on, the company used an export-selling approach, symbolized by its underdeveloped dealer network. Moreover, print advertising simply used word-for-word translations of the U.S. ads. By the late 1980s, after recruiting dealers in the important Japanese and European markets, company executives discovered a basic principle of global marketing. "As the saying goes, we needed to think global but act local," said Jerry G. Wilke, vice president for worldwide marketing during that time. Managers began to adapt the company's international marketing to make it more responsive to local conditions.

In Japan, for example, H-D's rugged image and high quality helped make it the best-selling imported motorcycle. Still, Toshifumi Okui, president of H-D's Japanese division, was not satisfied. He worried that the tag line from the U.S. ads, "One steady constant in an increasingly screwed-up world," didn't connect with Japanese riders. Okui finally convinced Milwaukee to allow him to launch a Japan-only advertising campaign juxtaposing images from both Japan and the United States, such as American cyclists passing a rickshaw carrying a geisha. After learning that riders in Tokyo consider fashion and customized bikes to be essential, H-D opened two stores specializing in clothing and bike accessories. Recently H-D has begun catering to Japanese women who enjoy riding (see Exhibit 6-4).

In Europe, H-D discovered that an "evening out" means something different than it does in America. The company sponsored a rally in France, where beer and live rock music were available until midnight. Recalls Wilke, "People asked us why we were ending the rally just as the evening was starting. So I had to go persuade the band to keep playing and reopen the bar until 3 or 4 A.M." Still, rallies are less common in Europe than in the United States, so H-D encourages its dealers to hold open houses at their dealerships. While biking through Europe, Wilke also learned that German bikers often travel at speeds exceeding 100 miles per hour. The company made design changes to create a smoother ride at Autobahn speeds. Harley's German marketing effort began focusing on accessories to increase rider protection. Today, the company has a clear picture of its core European customers; as Klaus Stobel, European affairs director for Harley-Davidson Europe, explained, "The people who buy Harleys in Europe are like the people who buy BMWs in the U.S. They are dentists and lawyers." Even so, in 2002, Europe accounted for just 8 percent of 2002 global revenues.

"Everyone thinks we produce big, showy, custom motorcycles. We actually have a broad range of bikes that well suit European riding habits. We have a perception problem around Harley which is an issue we need to tackle."

John Russell, managing director, Harley-Davidson Europe

Despite high demand from brand-loyal enthusiasts, the company intentionally limits production increases to keep quality high and to keep the product supply limited in relation to demand. In 2006, the company's total annual production volume approached 350,000 motorcycles. Even so, there are not enough bikes to go around, a situation that seems to suit company executives just fine. As former H-D president James H. Paterson once noted, "Enough motorcycles is too many motorcycles."

Sources: Jeremy Grand and Harold Ehren, "Harley-Davidson Eyes Europe," *Financial Times* (July 28, 2003), p. 17; Kevin Kelly and Karen Lowry Miller, "The Rumble Heard Round the World: Harleys," *Business Week* (May 24, 1993), pp. 58, 60; Robert L. Rose, "Vrooming Back: After Nearly Stalling, Harley-Davidson Finds New Crowd of Riders," *The Wall Street Journal* (August 31, 1990), pp. A1, A6; John Holusha, "How Harley Outfoxed Japan with Exports," *New York Times* (August 12, 1990), p. F5; Robert C. Reid, "How Harley Beat Back the Japanese," *Fortune* (September 25, 1989), pp. 155+.

Step 4: Examine Data Availability

The first task at this stage is to answer several questions regarding the availability of data. What type of data should be gathered? Can **secondary data**—for example, data available in company files, the library, industry or trade journals, or online databases—be used? When does management need the information in order to make a decision regarding market entry? Marketers must address these issues before proceeding to the next step of the research process. Using data that

Exhibit 6-4: As Harley-Davison continues to expand globally, it is diversifying its customer base by targeting female riders in key markets such as Japan. In the last few years, H-D has posed double-digit sales increases outside the United States. According to chief executive Jim Ziemer, this is evidence that the company's long-term strategy is working. H-D has replaced many dealers in Europe, acquired its Australian distributor, and is establishing full-service dealerships in China and Thailand.
Source: Charles Pertwee/ Bloomberg News.

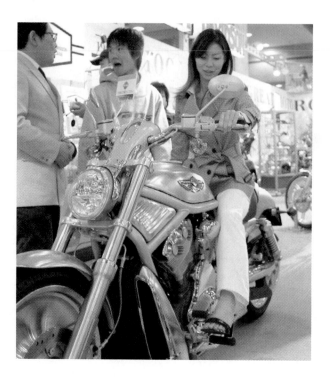

are readily available saves both money and time. A formal market study can cost hundreds of thousands of dollars and take many months to complete.

A low-cost approach to market research and data collection begins with desk research. In other words, "the key to creating a cost-effective way of surveying foreign markets is to climb on the shoulders of those who have gone before."[18] Suppose a marketer wants to assess the basic market potential for a particular product. To find the answer, secondary sources are a good place to start. Personal files, company or public libraries, online databases, government census records, and trade associations are just a few of the data sources that can be tapped with minimal effort and cost. Data from these sources already exist. Such data are known as *secondary data* because they were not gathered for the specific project at hand. *Statistical Abstract of the United States* is just one of the annual publications issued by the U.S. government that contains myriad facts about international markets.

The U.S. government's most comprehensive source of world trade data is the National Trade Data Base (NTDB), an online resource from the Department of Commerce. Another commerce department Web site, STAT-USA/Internet (www.stat-usa.gov), is an excellent online source for merchandise trade, gross domestic product, and other current and historical data. Most countries compile estimates of gross national product (GNP), gross domestic product (GDP), consumption, investment, government expenditures, and price levels. Demographic data indicating the population size, distribution of population by age category, and rates of population growth are also available. Market information from export census documents compiled by the department of commerce on the basis of shippers' export declarations (known as "ex-decs" or SEDs, these must be filled out for any export valued at $1,500 or more) is also available. Another important source of market data is the Foreign Commercial Service.

Many countries have set up Web sites to help small firms find opportunities in world markets. For example, the Virtual Trade Commissioner (www.infoexport.gc.ca) is a service of Canada's Department of Foreign Affairs and International Trade (DFAIT). The site is a computerized database containing the names of Canadian companies that export.

These do not exhaust the types of data available, however. A single source, *The Statistical Yearbook of the United Nations*, contains global data on agriculture, mining, manufacturing,

---

[18]Michael R. Czinkota and Ilkka A. Ronkainen, "Market Research for Your Export Operations: Part I—Using Secondary Sources of Research," *International Trade Forum* 30, no. 3 (1994), p. 22.

construction, energy production and consumption, internal and external trade, railroad and air transport, wages and prices, health, housing, education, communication infrastructure, and availability of mass communication media. The U.S. Central Intelligence Agency publishes *World Factbook,* which is revised yearly. Other important sources are the World Bank, the International Monetary Fund, and Japan's Ministry of International Trade and Industry (MITI). *The Economist* and *Financial Times* regularly compile comprehensive surveys of regional and country markets and include them in their publications. Data from these sources are generally available in both print and electronic form.

How can such data be useful? Take industrial growth patterns as one example. Because they generally reveal consumption patterns, production patterns are helpful in assessing market opportunities. Additionally, trends in manufacturing production indicate potential markets for companies that supply manufacturing inputs. At the early stages of growth in a country, when per capita incomes are low, manufacturing centers on such necessities as food and beverages, textiles, and other forms of light industry. As incomes rise, the relative importance of these industries declines as heavy industry begins to develop.

A word of caution is in order at this point: Remember that data are compiled from various sources, some of which may not be reliable. Even when the sources are reliable, there is likely to be some variability from source to source. Anyone using data should be clear on exactly what the data are measuring. For example, studying income data requires understanding whether one is working with GNP or GDP figures. Also, anyone using the Internet as an information source should evaluate the credibility of the person(s) responsible for the Web site. Moreover, as Czinkota and Ronkainen note,[19] secondary data may support the decision to pursue a market opportunity outside the home country, but it is unlikely to shed light on specific questions: What is the market potential for our furniture in Indonesia? How much does the typical Nigerian consumer spend on soft drinks? If a packaging change is made to ensure compliance with Germany's Green Dot Ordinance, what effect, if any, will the change have on consumer purchasing behavior?

Syndicated studies published by private research companies are another source of secondary data and information (the word *syndicated* comes from the newspaper industry and refers to the practice of selling articles, cartoons, or guest columns to a number of different organizations). For example, MarketResearch.com (www.marketresearch.com) sells reports on a wide range of global business sectors; the company partners with 350 research firms to offer a comprehensive set of reports. A sampling of reports available from MarketResearch.com on topics covered in this textbook is shown in Table 6-3; while a single report can cost thousands of dollars, a company may be able to get the market information it needs without incurring the cost associated with primary research.

TABLE 6-3 Global Market Research Reports from MarketResearch.com

Title of Study	Price	Publisher
Chinese Markets for Cosmetics	$4,000	Asia Market Information & Development Company
Online Music	$3,950	Global Industry Analysts
Whiskies—UK	$3,000	Mintel International Group Ltd.
Luxury Goods Retailing—Global	$2,990	Mintel International Group Ltd.
Pharmaceutical Markets in Brazil, Russia, India, and China	$2,500	Kalorama Information
Economic Crisis Response: U.S. Telecommunications 2008–2012	$2,000	IDC
Automotive Industry	$1,450	Global Industry Analysts
The 2009–2014 World Outlook for Laptop Computers	$795	Icon Group International, Inc.

Source: MarketResearch.com, accessed March 9, 2009.

[19]Michael R. Czinkota and Ilkka A. Ronkainen, "Market Research for Your Export Operations: Part II—Conducting Primary Marketing Research," *International Trade Forum* 31, no. 1 (1995), p. 16.

Step 5: Assess Value of Research

When data are not available through published statistics or studies, management may wish to conduct further study of the country market, region, or global segment. However, collecting information costs money. Thus, the plan should also spell out what this information is worth to the company in dollars (or euro, or yen, etc.) compared with what it would cost to collect it. What will the company gain by collecting this data? What would be the cost of not getting the data that could be converted into useful information? Research requires an investment of both money and managerial time, and it is necessary to perform a cost-benefit analysis before proceeding further. In some instances, a company may pursue the same course of action no matter what the research reveals. Even when more information is needed to ensure a high-quality decision, a realistic estimate of a formal study may reveal that the cost to perform research is simply too high.

The small markets around the world pose a special problem for the researcher. The relatively low profit potential in smaller markets justifies only modest expenditures for marketing research. Therefore, the global researcher must devise techniques and methods that keep expenditures in line with the market's profit potential. There is pressure on the researcher to discover economic and demographic relationships that permit estimates of demand based on a minimum of information. It may also be necessary to use inexpensive survey research that sacrifices some elegance or statistical rigor to achieve results within the constraints of the smaller market research budget.

Step 6: Research Design

As indicated in Figure 6-1, if secondary data can be used, the researcher can go directly to the data analysis step. Suppose, however, data are not available through published statistics or studies; in addition, suppose that the cost-benefit analysis indicated in step 5 has been performed and that the decision has been made to carry on with the research effort. *Primary data* are gathered through original research pertaining to the particular problem identified in step 1. At this point, it is time to establish a research design.

Global marketing guru David Arnold offers the following guidelines regarding data gathering:[20]

- Use multiple indicators rather than a single measure. This approach will decrease the level of uncertainty for decision makers. As the saying goes, "There are three sides to every story: your side, my side, and the truth." A land surveyor can pinpoint the location of a third object given the known location of two objects. This technique, known as *triangulation*, is equally useful in global market research.
- Individual companies should develop customized indicators specific to the industry, product market, or business model. Such indicators should leverage a company's previous experience in global markets. For example, in some developing markets, Mary Kay Cosmetics uses the average wage of a female secretary as a basis for estimating income potential for its beauty consultants.
- Always conduct comparative assessments in multiple markets. Do not assess a particular market in isolation. Comparative assessment enables management to develop a "portfolio" approach in which alternative priorities and scenarios can be developed. For example, to better understand Czech consumers in general, a company might also conduct research in nearby Poland and Hungary. By contrast, if a brewing company wished to learn more about beer consumption patterns in the Czech Republic, it might also conduct research in Ireland and Germany where per capita beer consumption is high.
- Observations of purchasing patterns and other behavior should be weighted more heavily than reports or opinions regarding purchase intention or price sensitivity. Particularly in developing markets, it is difficult to accurately survey consumer perceptions.

With these guidelines in mind, the marketer must address a new set of questions and issues in primary data collection. Should the research effort be geared toward quantitative, numerical data that can be subjected to statistical analysis or should qualitative techniques be used? In global

---

[20]David Arnold, *The Mirage of Global Markets* (Upper Saddle River, NJ: Financial Times Prentice Hall, 2004), pp. 41–43.

market research, it is advisable for the plan to call for a mix of techniques. For consumer products, qualitative research is especially well suited to accomplish the following tasks:[21]

- To provide consumer understanding; to "get close" to the consumer
- To describe the social and cultural context of consumer behavior, including cultural, religious, and political factors that impact decision making
- To identify core brand equity and "get under the skin" of brands
- To "mine" the consumer and identify what people really feel

ISSUES IN DATA COLLECTION The research problem may be more narrowly focused on marketing issues, such as the need to adapt products and other mix elements to local tastes and assessing demand and profit potential. Demand and profit potential, in turn, depend in part on whether the market being studied can be classified as existing or potential. *Existing markets* are those in which customer needs are already being served by one or more companies. In many countries, data about the size of existing markets—in terms of dollar volume and unit sales—are readily available. In some countries, however, formal market research is a relatively new phenomenon and data are scarce. McKinsey & Company, Gartner Group Asia, and Grey China Advertising have been very active in China. For example, using focus groups and other techniques, Grey China gathers a wealth of information about attitudes and buying patterns that it publishes in its Grey ChinaBase Annual Consumer Study. Recent findings point to growing concerns about the future, Westernization of grocery purchases, growing market saturation, increasingly discerning customers, and a rise in consumer willingness to try new products. Even so, data gathered by different sources may be inconsistent. What is the level of soft-drink consumption in China? Euromonitor International estimates consumption at 23 billion liters, whereas Coca-Cola's in-house marketing research team places the figure at 39 billion liters. Likewise, CSM, a Chinese television-rating agency, estimates the TV-advertising market at $2.8 billion per year. According to Nielsen Media Research, the figure is closer to $7.5 billion.[22]

In such situations, and in countries where such data are not available, researchers must first estimate the market size, the level of demand, or the rate of product purchase or consumption. A second research objective in existing markets may be assessment of the company's overall competitiveness in terms of product appeal, price, distribution, and promotional coverage and effectiveness. Researchers may be able to pinpoint a weakness in the competitor's product or identify an under- or unserved market segment. The minivan and sport utility vehicle segments of the auto industry illustrate the opportunity an existing market can present. For years, Chrysler dominated the U.S. minivan segment, for which annual sales at one time totaled about 1.2 million vehicles. Most global marketers compete in this segment, although a number of models have been discontinued due to declining sales. For example, Toyota introduced its Japanese-built Previa in the United States in 1991; critics mocked the teardrop styling and dismissed it as being underpowered. For the 1998 model year, the Previa was replaced with the American-built Sienna. To ensure that Sienna suited American tastes, Toyota designers and engineers studied Chrysler minivans and duplicated key features such as numerous cup holders and a second sliding rear door on the driver's side.

In some instances, there is no existing market to research. Such *potential markets* can be further subdivided into latent and incipient markets. A **latent market** is, in essence, an undiscovered segment. It is a market in which demand would materialize *if* an appropriate product were made available. In a latent market, demand is zero before the product is introduced. In the case of existing markets such as the one for minivans previously described, the main research challenge is to understand the extent to which the competition fully meets customer needs. As J. Davis Illingworth, an executive at Toyota Motor Sales USA, explained, "I think the American public will look at Sienna as an American product that meets their needs."[23] With latent markets, initial success is not based on a company's competitiveness. Rather, it depends on the prime mover advantage—a company's ability to uncover the opportunity and launch a marketing program that taps the latent demand. This is precisely what Chrysler achieved by single-handedly creating the minivan market.

Sometimes, traditional market research is not an effective means for identifying latent markets. As Peter Drucker has noted, the failure of American companies to successfully commercialize fax

[21]John Pawle, "Mining the International Consumer," *Journal of the Market Research Society* 41, no. 1 (1999), p. 20.
[22]Gabriel Kahn, "Chinese Puzzle: Spotty Consumer Data," *The Wall Street Journal* (October 15, 2003), p. B1.
[23]Kathleen Kerwin, "Can This Minivan Dent Detroit?" *Business Week* (February 3, 1997), p. 37.

machines—an American innovation—can be traced to research that indicated no potential demand for such a product. The problem, in Drucker's view, stems from the typical survey question for a product targeted at a latent market. Suppose a researcher asks, "Would you buy a telephone accessory that costs upwards of $1,500 and enables you to send, for $1 a page, the same letter the post office delivers for $0.25?" On the basis of economics alone, the respondent most likely will answer, "No."

Drucker explained that Japanese companies are the leading sellers of fax machines today because their understanding of the market was not based on survey research. Instead, they reviewed the early days of mainframe computers, photocopy machines, cell phones, and other information and communications products. The Japanese realized that, judging only by the initial costs associated with buying and using these new products, the prospects of market acceptance were low. However, each of these products had become a huge success after people began to use them. This realization prompted the Japanese to focus on the market for the *benefits* provided by fax machines, rather than the market for the machines themselves. By looking at the success of courier services such as FedEx, the Japanese realized that, in essence, the fax machine market already existed.[24]

An **incipient market** is a market that will emerge if a particular economic, demographic, political, or sociocultural trend continues. A company is not likely to succeed if it offers a product in an incipient market before the trends have taken root. After the trends have had a chance to gain traction, the incipient market will become latent and, later, existing. The concept of incipient markets can also be illustrated by the impact of rising income on demand for automobiles and other expensive consumer durables. As per capita income rises in a country, the demand for automobiles will also rise. Therefore, if a company can predict a country's future rate of income growth, it can also predict the growth rate of its automobile market.

For example, to capitalize on China's rapid economic growth, Volkswagen, Peugeot, Chrysler, and other global automakers have established in-country manufacturing operations. There is even incipient demand in China for imported exotic cars; in early 1994 Ferrari opened its first showroom in Beijing. Because of a 150 percent import tax, China's first Ferrari buyers were entrepreneurs who had profited from China's increasing openness to Western-style marketing and capitalism. By the end of the 1990s, demand for luxury cars had grown at a faster rate than anticipated.[26] Today, there are 30 million cars and light trucks for China's 1.3 billion people. Clearly, China is a very attractive market opportunity for carmakers.

By contrast, some companies have concluded that China has limited potential at present. For example, in 1998, UK-based retailer Marks & Spencer closed its office in Shanghai and tabled plans to open a store in China. Commenting to the press, a company representative directly addressed the issue of whether or not China represented an incipient market:

> After three years of research, we have come to the conclusion that the timing is not right. The majority of our customers are from middle-income groups. But, our interest is in Shanghai, and the size of the middle-income group, although it is growing, is not yet at a level that would justify us opening a store there.[28]

RESEARCH METHODOLOGIES Survey research, interviews, consumer panels, observation, and focus groups are some of the tools used to collect primary market data. These are the same tools used by marketers whose activities are not global; however, some adaptations and special considerations for global marketing may be required.

Survey research utilizes questionnaires designed to elicit quantitative data ("How much would you buy?"), qualitative responses ("Why would you buy?"), or both. Survey research is often conducted by means of a questionnaire distributed through the mail, by telephone, or in person. Many good marketing research textbooks provide details on questionnaire design and administration.

In global market research, a number of survey design and administration issues may arise. When using the telephone as a research tool, it is important to remember that what is customary

---

"At that time, Japanese women almost never used mascaras because, by nature, they have very straight, short and thin lashes. We designed mascara that was able to lengthen and curl lashes. It was a huge success. We would never have seen that in a focus group."[25]

Jean-Paul Agon, CEO, L'Oréal, discussing the decision to relaunch the Maybelline makeup brand in Japan with mascara

"When we first started, we said there is no existing market for Red Bull, but Red Bull will create it. And this is what finally became true."[27]

Dietrich Mateschitz, creator of Red Bull energy drink, hired a market research firm to test Red Bull. The test indicated a negative reaction to the taste, the logo, and the brand name. Mateschitz ignored the research, and Red Bull is now a $2 billion brand.

---

[24]Peter F. Drucker, "Marketing 101 for a Fast-Changing Decade," *The Wall Street Journal* (November 20, 1990), p. A17.
[25]Adam Jones, "How to Make Up Demand," *Financial Times* (October 3, 2006), p. 8.
[26]Jason Leow and Gordon Fairclough, "Rich Chinese Fancy Luxury Cars," *The Wall Street Journal*, April 12, 2007, pp. B1, B2.
[27]Kerry A. Dolan, "The Soda with Buzz," *Forbes* (March 28, 2005), p. 126.
[28]James Harding, "Foreign Investors Face New Curbs on Ownership of Stores," *Financial Times* (November 10, 1998), p. 7.

STRATEGIC DECISION MAKING IN GLOBAL MARKETING
Iridium

Motorola spent more than a decade and billions of dollars developing Iridium, an ambitious new business that would offer global satellite personal communications services to supplement ground-based wire and cellular telephone services. If it succeeded, Iridium would be a historic first: A business that was truly global from day one of operations. Iridium's first customers were expected to include globetrotting business executives who need to send and receive voice messages and data and who want a single telephone number that will work anywhere on the planet. In addition, the business concept was based on the fact that 90 percent of the world's population lacks access to telephones. Iridium could bring wireless telephone service to rural areas in South America, India, and Africa. (see Exhibit 6-5).

Motorola executives projected that Iridium would attract 5 million users by the year 2002. Each subscriber was expected to contribute $1,000 per year in net revenues to Iridium. In essence, Iridium was a huge bet that the varying technology standards of conventional cellular telephone systems would provide the key to Iridium's success. At the time, cellular phone standards were different in Europe and the United States, so a European businessperson's cell phone unit was rendered inoperable in the United States. Iridium's early customers would have to pay approximately $3,000 for new telephones. Usage fees for satellite telephone calls were set in a range from $1.75 to $7.00 per minute

Industry observers were skeptical. Some wondered whether Motorola could really recoup its investment. One consultant got to the heart of the matter when he asked, "The biggest single issue is, can they sell it? There is no good head count of international businessmen who need this." For their part, Iridium executives reasoned that some 40 million people travel from the United States each year. Even if a small percentage of them became Iridium users, the service would be a success.

Early in 1997, Iridium management announced a number of strategic changes. The company was now aiming to sign up 3 million businesspeople such as contractors, people employed in the oil and gas industries, maritime workers, and employees of heavy construction firms such as Schlumberger and Bechtel. Such professional travelers, it was hoped, would account for about two-thirds of Iridium's revenues. As Dr. Edward Staiano, Iridium's vice chairman and chief executive, said, "The guy who's going to pay for this system is the guy who doesn't look at his phone bill." This change de-emphasized the opportunity in emerging markets with undeveloped telephone systems.

A $140 million global print advertising campaign created by Ammirati Puris Lintas was launched in June 1998. Voice services began on November 1, with paging services available November 15. However, the required number of actual customers never materialized, and by 2000 it appeared that it was all over for Iridium. The apparent lesson: There was no latent market for a premium-priced global satellite telephone service.

However, in late 2000 a group of private investors bought Iridium's assets for the fire-sale price of $25 million. The new owners, doing business as Iridium Satellite LLC, secured a two-year contract with the Pentagon to provide satellite phones to embassy employees and other government agencies. Then Boeing signed an agreement to maintain the satellite network. "We do not see Iridium as a mass consumer service," said Dan Colussy, chairman of the Iridium Satellite LLC. "It is a communications service that addresses the very specific needs of the industrial markets and other specialized segments. Because of our significantly reduced cost structure and Iridium's unique system capabilities, we will be able to serve these markets more effectively than any other existing service." The satellite phone system has proved its worth in the aftermath of natural disasters such as the Asian tsunami in 2004 and Hurricane Katrina in 2005.

Sources: Sarmad Ali, "Reliable Connections Broaden Demand for Satellite Phones," *The Wall Street Journal* (November 3, 2005), p. B1; Paul Davidson, "Satellite Phones Provide Critical Link to Outside World," *USA Today* (September 6, 2005), p. 3B; Quentin Hardy, "Iridium Gets U.S. as First Big Customer of Wireless Communications System," *The Wall Street Journal* (January 26, 1998), p. B6; Sally Beatty, "Iridium Hopes to Ring Up Global Sales," *The Wall Street Journal* (June 22, 1998), p. B8; Hardy, "Iridium Creates New Plan for Global Cellular Service," *The Wall Street Journal* (August 18, 1997), p. B4.

in one country may be impossible in others because of infrastructure differences, cultural barriers, or other reasons. For example, telephone directories or lists may not be available; also, important differences may exist between urban dwellers and people in rural areas. In China, for example, the Ministry of Information Industry reports that 77 percent of households in coastal areas have at least one fixed-line telephone; in rural areas, the number is only 40 percent.

At a deeper level, culture shapes attitudes and values in a way that directly affects people's willingness to respond to interviewer questions. Open-ended questions may help the researcher identify a respondent's frame of reference. In some cultures, respondents may be unwilling to answer certain questions, or they may intentionally give inaccurate answers.

Recall that step 2 of the global market research process calls for identifying possible sources of SRC bias. This issue is especially important in survey research: SRC bias can originate from the cultural backgrounds of those designing the questionnaire. For example, a survey designed and administered in the United States may be inappropriate in non-Western cultures, even if it is carefully translated. This is especially true if the person designing the questionnaire

Exhibit 6-5: Today's Iridium satellite telephone system operates on a much smaller scale than when the service was launched in 1999. Meanwhile, hoping to recover several billion dollars from the failed investment, creditors are suing Motorola in bankruptcy court. Among other things, the plaintiffs alleged that Iridium overpaid Motorola for the satellites that it built. In 2007, a U.S. bankruptcy judge dismissed most of the charges against Motorola.
Source: Odd Andersen/AFP/Getty Images, Inc. AFP.

is not familiar with the SRC. A technique known as *back translation* can help increase comprehension and validity; the technique requires that, after a questionnaire or survey instrument is translated into a particular target language, it is translated once again into the original by a different translator. For even greater accuracy, *parallel translations*—that is, two versions by different translators—can be used as input to the back translation. The same techniques can ensure that advertising copy is accurately translated into different languages.

Personal interviews allow researchers to ask "why?" and then explore answers with the respondent on a face-to-face basis.

A **consumer panel** is a sample of respondents whose behavior is tracked over time. For example, a number of companies, including the Nielsen Media Research unit of Netherlands-based VNU, AGB, GfK, and TNS, conduct television audience measurement (TAM) by studying the viewing habits of household panels. Broadcasters use audience share data to set advertising rates; advertisers such as Procter & Gamble, Unilever, and Coca-Cola use the data to choose programs during which to advertise. In the United States Nielsen has enjoyed a virtual monopoly on viewership research for half a century. For years, however, the four major U.S. television networks have complained that they lose advertising revenues because Nielsen's data collection methods undercount viewership. Nielsen has responded to these concerns by upgrading its survey methodology; the company now uses an electronic device known as a **peoplemeter** to collect national audience data. Peoplemeter systems are currently in use in dozens of countries around the world, including China; Nielsen is also rolling out peoplemeters to collect local audience viewership data in key metropolitan markets such as New York City.

When **observation** is used as a data collection method, one or more trained observers (or a mechanical device such as a video camera) watch and record the behavior of actual or prospective buyers. The research results are used to guide marketing managers in their decision making. For example, after Volkswagen's U.S. sales began to slump, the company launched "Moonraker," an 18-month effort designed to help its engineers, marketers, and design specialists better understand American consumers. Despite the presence of a design center in California, decision makers at headquarters in Wolfsburg, Germany, generally ignored feedback from U.S. customers. As Stefan Liske, director of product strategy at VW, acknowledged, "We needed a totally different approach. We asked ourselves, 'Do we really know everything about this market'?" The Moonraker team visited the Mall of America in Minneapolis and the Rock and Roll Hall of Fame in Cleveland; they also spent spring break in Florida observing college students.

The experience was an eye-opener; as one designer explained, "In Germany, it's all about driving, but here, it's about everything *but* driving. People here want to use their time in other ways,

EMERGING MARKETS BRIEFING BOOK

⇄ Market Research in Brazil

Emerging markets present a number of challenges to anyone conducting market research. First, the technology infrastructure may be undeveloped. In addition, there are geographic issues; in the BRIC nations, for example, many provincial areas are isolated and difficult to reach. Third, researchers may have to adapt their data-gathering methodologies to suit the country environment. Finally, privacy issues can present challenges.

Brazil is a case in point. The technological infrastructure for gathering market data is minimal. Government census reports are a poor source of population data. As a result, it can be difficult to obtain a representative sample; it is expensive to design a national probability sample. Compounding the problem is a lack of telephone penetration. Geographic issues also arise; this is not surprising, given the immensity of Brazil's territory. Marketers often find that, outside of major metropolitan areas, little EPOS data is available. It is very difficult to track what is selling, at what price, and who the customers are. This necessitates the use of field teams to gather data.

A third problem is encountered when designing face-to-face interviews. If the research design calls for interviewing broad socioeconomic groups, the demographics of interviewers should match those of respondent groups. Street or mall-intercept techniques can be used to good effect. Security issues require the use of teams. Researchers may offer a gift rather than cash as an incentive. Finally, privacy issues are very important, especially to affluent Brazilians. Wealthy respondents are unlikely to answer questions about personal finance. To ensure confidentiality, financial services companies may bring in interviewers based on a developed market. To gain trust, interviewers can ask respondents to recommend others.

Sources: Adapted from Arundhati Parmar, "Tailor Techniques to Each Audience in Latin Market," *Marketing News* (February 3, 2003), pp. 4–6. See also Harold L. Sirkin, James W. Hemerling, and Arindam K. Bhattacharya, *Globality: Competing with Everyone from Everywhere for Everything* (New York: Boston Consulting Group, 2008), pp. 117–118.

---

like talk on their cell phone." Another member of the team, an engineer, shadowed a single mom as she took her kids to school and ran errands. The engineer noted that American drivers need a place to store a box of tissues and a place to put a bag of fast food picked up at a drive-through window. "I began thinking about what specific features her car needed. It was about living the customer's life and putting ourselves in their place," he said.[29]

A marketer of breakfast cereals might send researchers to preselected households at 6 A.M. to watch families go about their morning routines. The client could also assign a researcher to accompany family members to the grocery store to observe their behavior under actual shopping conditions. The client might wish to know about the shoppers' reactions to in-store promotions linked to an advertising campaign. The researcher could record comments or discretely take photographs. Companies using observation as a research methodology must be sensitive to public concerns about privacy issues. A second problem with observation is *reactivity*, which is the tendency of research subjects to behave differently for the simple reason that they know they are under study. Additional examples include the following:

- Hoping to gain insights for product and package design improvements, Procter & Gamble sent video crews into 80 households in the United Kingdom, Italy, Germany, and China. P&G's ultimate goal is to amass an in-house video library that can be directly accessed by key word searches. Stan Joosten, an IT manager, noted, "You could search for 'eating snacks' and find all clips from all over the world on that topic. Immediately, it gives you a global perspective on certain topics."[30]
- Michelle Arnau, a marketing manager for Nestlé's PowerBar brand, attended the 2004 New York City Marathon to see how runners were using single-serve packets of PowerGel, a concentrated, performance-boosting gel in a single-serving packet. Ms. Arnau observed that runners typically tore off the top with their teeth and attempted to consume the gel in a single squeeze without breaking their stride. Ms. Arnau was dismayed to see that the long neck of the packet sometimes prevented the gel from flowing out quickly. Designers at Nestlé created an improved package with an upside-down triangular-shaped top that is narrow enough to control the flow of the gel but also fits into the athlete's mouth.[31]

---

[29]Gina Chon, "VW's American Road Trip," *The Wall Street Journal* (January 4, 2006), pp. B1, B9.

[30]Emily Nelson, "P&G Checks Out Real Life," *The Wall Street Journal* (May 17, 2001), pp. B1, B4.

[31]Deborah Ball, "The Perils of Packaging: Nestlé Aims for Easier Openings," *The Wall Street Journal* (November 17, 2005), p. B1.

In **focus group** research, a trained moderator facilitates discussion of a product concept, a brand's image and personality, advertisement, social trend, or other topic with a group comprised of 6 to 10 people. Global marketers can use focus groups to arrive at important insights. For example:

- In the mid-1990s, Whirlpool launched a European advertising campaign that featured fantasy characters such as a drying diva and a washing-machine goddess. The campaign's success prompted management to adapt it for use in the United States and Latin America. First, however, the company conducted focus groups to gauge reaction to the ads. Nick Mote, Whirlpool's worldwide account director at France's Publicis advertising agency, said, "We've had some incredible research results. It was just like somebody switched the lights on."[32]

- In Singapore, focus groups comprised of young teens were used to help guide development of Coca-Cola's advertising program. As Karen Wong, Coke's country marketing director for Singapore, explained, "We tested everything from extreme to borderline boring: body-piercing all over, grungy kids in a car listening to rock music and head-banging all the way. Youth doing things that youth in America do." Some participants found much of Coke's imagery—for example, a shirtless young man crowd surfing at a rock concert and careening down a store aisle on a grocery cart—too rebellious. As one young Singaporean remarked, "They look like they're on drugs. And if they're on drugs, then how can they be performing at school?" Armed with the focus group results, Coca-Cola's managers devised an ad campaign for Singapore that was well within the bounds of societal approval.[33]

- When Blockbuster Video was planning its entry into Japan, the world's number two video rental market, the company convened focus groups to learn more about Japanese preferences and perceptions of existing video rental outlets. In the mid-1990s, most video stores in Japan were tiny operations with limited display space. Video titles were piled up from the floor to the ceilings, making it difficult to find and retrieve individual titles. Acting on the information provided by the focus groups, Blockbuster designed its Japanese stores with 3,000 square feet of floor space and display shelves that were more accessible.[34]

A typical focus group meets at a facility equipped with recording equipment and a one-way mirror behind which representatives of the client company observe the proceedings. The moderator can utilize a number of approaches to elicit reactions and responses, including projective techniques, visualization, and role plays. When using a *projective technique*, the researcher presents open-ended or ambiguous stimuli to a subject. Presumably, when verbalizing a response, the subject will "project"—that is, reveal—his or her unconscious attitudes and biases. By analyzing the responses, researchers are better able to understand how consumers perceive a particular product, brand, or company.

For example, in a focus group convened to assess car-buying preferences among a segment comprised of twenty-somethings, the researcher might ask participants to describe a party where various automotive brands are present. What is Nissan wearing, eating, and drinking? What kind of sneakers does Honda have on? What are their personalities like? Who's shy? Who's loud? Who gets the girl (or guy)? Interaction among group members can result in synergies that yield important qualitative insights that are likely to differ from those based on data gathered through more direct questioning. Focus group research is a technique that has grown in popularity. However, some industry observers caution that the technique has been used so much that participants, especially those who are used on a regular basis, have become overly familiar with its workings.

Focus group research yields qualitative data that does not lend itself to statistical projection. Such data suggests rather than confirms hypotheses; also, qualitative data tends to be directional rather than conclusive. Such data is extremely valuable in the exploratory phase of a project and is typically used in conjunction with data gathered via observation and other methods.

SCALE DEVELOPMENT Market research requires assigning some type of measure, ranking, or interval to a response. To take a simple example of measurement, a *nominal scale* is used to

---

[32]Katheryn Kranhold, "Whirlpool Conjures Up Appliance Divas," *The Wall Street Journal* (April 27, 2000), p. B1.
[33]Cris Prystay, "Selling to Singapore's Teens Is Tricky," *The Wall Street Journal* (October 4, 2002), p. B4.
[34]Khanh T. L. Tran, "Blockbuster Finds Success in Japan that Eluded the Chain in Germany," *The Wall Street Journal* (August 28, 1998), p. A14.

establish the identity of a survey element. For example, male respondents could be labeled "1" and female respondents could be labeled "2." Scaling can also entail placing each response in some kind of continuum; a common example is the Likert scale that asks respondents to indicate whether they "strongly agree" with a statement, "strongly disagree," or whether their attitude falls somewhere in the middle. In a multi-country research project it is important to have *scalar equivalence*, which means that two respondents in different countries with the same value for a given variable receive equivalent scores on the same survey item.

Even with standard data-gathering techniques, the application of a particular technique may differ from country to country. Matthew Draper, vice president at New Jersey–based Total Research Corporation, cites "scalar bias" as a major problem: "There are substantial differences in the way people use scales, and research data based on scales such as rating product usefulness on a scale of 1 to 10 is therefore frequently cluttered with biases disguising the truth." For example, while the typical American scale would equate a high number such as 10 with "most" or "best" and 1 with "least," Germans prefer scales in which 1 is "most/best." Also, while American survey items pertaining to spending provide a range of figures, Germans prefer the opportunity to provide an exact answer.[35]

SAMPLING When collecting data, researchers generally cannot administer a survey to every possible person in the designated group. A sample is a selected subset of a population that is representative of the entire population. The two best-known types of samples are probability samples and nonprobability samples. A probability sample is generated by following statistical rules that ensure that each member of the population under study has an equal chance—or probability—of being included in the sample. The results of a probability sample can be projected to the entire population with statistical reliability reflecting sampling error, degree of confidence, and standard deviation.

The results of a nonprobability sample cannot be projected with statistical reliability. One form of nonprobability sample is a *convenience sample*. As the name implies, researchers select people who are easy to reach. For example, in one study that compared consumer shopping attitudes in the United States, Jordan, Singapore, and Turkey, data for the latter three countries were gathered from convenience samples recruited by an acquaintance of the researcher. Although data gathered in this way are not subject to statistical inference, they may be adequate to address the problem defined in step 1. In this study, for example, the researchers were able to identify a clear trend toward cultural convergence in shopping attitudes and customs that cut across modern industrial countries, emerging industrial countries, and developing countries.[36]

To obtain a *quota sample*, the researcher divides the population under study into categories; a sample is then taken from each category. The term *quota* refers to the need to make sure that enough people are chosen in each category to reflect the overall makeup of the population. For example, assume a country's population is divided into six categories according to monthly income as follows:

Percent of population	10%	15%	25%	25%	15%	10%
Earnings per month	0–9	10–19	20–39	40–59	60–69	70–100

If it is assumed that income is the characteristic that adequately differentiates the population for study purposes, then a quota sample would include respondents of different income levels in the same proportion as they occurred in the population, that is, 15 percent with monthly earnings from 10 to 19, and so on.

Step 7: Data Analysis[37]

The data collected up to this point must be subjected to some form of analysis if it to be useful to decision makers. Although a detailed discussion is beyond the scope of this text, a brief overview is in order. First, the data must be prepared—the term *cleaned* is sometimes used—before further analysis is possible. It must be logged and stored in a central location or database; when research

[35]Jack Edmonston, "U.S., Overseas Differences Abound," *Business Marketing* (January 1998), p. 32.
[36]Eugene H. Fram and Riad Ajami, "Globalization of Markets and Shopping Stress: Cross-Country Comparisons," *Business Horizons* 37, no. 1 (January–February 1994), pp. 17–23.
[37]Parts of this section are adapted from Glen L. Urban, John R. Hauser, and Nikhilesh Dholakia, *Essentials of New Product Management* (Upper Saddle River, NJ: Prentice Hall, 1987), Chapters 6 and 7.

has been conducted in various parts of the world, rounding up data can pose some difficulties. Are data comparable across samples so that multi-country analysis can be performed? Some amount of editing may be required; for example, some responses may be missing or difficult to interpret. Next, questionnaires must be coded. Simply put, coding involves identifying the respondents and the variables. Finally, some data adjustment may be required.

Data analysis continues with *tabulation*, that is, the arrangement of data in tabular form. Researchers may wish to determine various things: the mean, median, and mode; range and standard deviation; and the shape of the distribution (e.g., normal curve). For nominally scaled variables such as "male" and "female," a simple cross-tabulation may be performed. Suppose, for example, Nielsen Media Research surveyed video gamers to determine how they felt about products (e.g., soft drinks) and advertisements (e.g., a billboard for a cell phone) embedded in video games. Nielsen could use cross-tabulation to separately examine the responses of male and female subjects to see if their responses differed significantly. If females were equally or more positive in their responses than males, video game companies could use this information to persuade consumer products companies to pay to have select products targeted at women featured as integral parts of the game. Researchers can also use various relatively simple statistical techniques such as hypothesis testing and chi-square testing; advanced data analysis such as analysis of variance (ANOVA), correlation analysis, and regression analysis can also be used.

If the researcher is interested in the interaction between variables, *interdependence techniques* such as factor analysis, cluster analysis, and multidimensional scaling (MDS) can be used. **Factor analysis** can be used to transform large amounts of data into manageable units; specialized computer programs perform data reduction by "distilling out" a few meaningful factors that underlie attitudes and perceptions from a multitude of survey responses. Factor analysis is useful in psychographic segmentation studies; it can also be used to create perceptual maps. In this form of analysis, variables are not classified as dependent or independent. Subjects are asked to rate specific product benefits on five-point scales; Table 6-4 shows a hypothetical scale that Nokia might use to assess consumer perceptions of a new combination cell phone/digital music player. Although the scale shown in Table 6-4 lists 10 characteristics/benefits, factor analysis will generate *factor loadings* that enable the researcher to determine two or three factors that underlie the benefits. That is why it is said that factor analysis results in data reduction. For the music phone, the researcher might label the factors "easy to use" and "stylish." The computer will also output *factor scores* for each respondent; respondent #1 might have a factor score of .35 for the factor identified as "easy to use"; respondent #2 might have .42, and so on. When all respondents' factor scores are averaged, the position of Nokia's music phone position on a perceptual map can be determined (see Figure 6-2). Similar determinations can be made for other cell phone brands.

TABLE 6-4 Hypothetical Scales for Obtaining Consumer Perceptions of Nokia Music Phone

Instructions: Please rate this product on the following product characteristics or benefits.

Variables (Product Characteristic/Benefit)	Low 1	2	3	4	High 5
1. Long battery life	____	____	____	____	____
2. Many games available	____	____	____	____	____
3. Wireless Internet access	____	____	____	____	____
4. Thin case	____	____	____	____	____
5. Attractive styling	____	____	____	____	____
6. Music file storage capacity	____	____	____	____	____
7. Bright display screen	____	____	____	____	____
8. Fits hand comfortably	____	____	____	____	____
9. Works anywhere in the world	____	____	____	____	____
10. Custom face plates available	____	____	____	____	____

Large number of variables (e.g., "bright display screen" and other key product attributes)—how do they interact? → Computer generates *factor loadings* for each variable so that a smaller number of factors (e.g., "easy to use") can be inferred by the researcher. → Computer generates *factor scores* for each respondent, which are used to create perceptual maps.

FIGURE 6-2

How Factor Analysis Works

Cluster analysis allows the researcher to group variables into clusters that maximize within-group similarities and between-group differences. Cluster analysis shares some characteristics of factor analysis: It does not classify variables as dependent or independent, and it can be used in psychographic segmentation. Cluster analysis is well suited to global market research because similarities and differences can be established between local, national, and regional markets of the world. Cluster analysis can also be used to perform benefit segmentation and identify new product opportunities.

Multidimensional scaling (MDS) is another technique for creating perceptual maps. When the researcher is using MDS, the respondent is given the task of comparing products or brands, one pair at a time, and judging them in terms of similarity. The researcher then infers the dimensions that underlie the judgments. MDS is particularly useful when there are many alternatives from which to choose—soft drink, toothpaste, or automotive brands, for instance—and when consumers may have difficulty verbalizing their perceptions. To create a well-defined spatial map, a minimum of eight products or brands should be used.

Suppose, for example, that a consumer uses an underlying perceptual dimension of "distinct image" in assessing the similarity of pairs of crossover SUVs. Table 6-5 shows a five-point similarity judgment scale for eight current crossover SUV models. Figure 6-3 shows the position of the eight SUV brands on the "distinct image" dimension for a hypothetical respondent. The figure shows that Infiniti and Volvo are the most similar while Infiniti and Buick are the farthest apart. The responses help marketers understand which brands in a particular category—crossover SUV brands in this example—are in direct competition with each other and which are not. The responses are input into a computer running an MDS program; the output is a perceptual map such as that shown in Figure 6-4. Once the computer has generated the map, the marketer examines the positions of different SUV models and infers the dimensions, which in this case are "comfort" and "distinct image." Such a map would be helpful to, say, Kia, when management is designing the next-generation Sportage crossover SUV.

TABLE 6-5 MDS Study Inputs: Similarity Judgment Scales for Pairs of Crossover SUVs

	Very Similar				Very Different
	1	2	3	4	5
Acura MDX/Volvo XC90	____	____	____	____	____
Acura MDX/Infiniti FX45	____	____	____	____	____
Acura MDX/Lexus RX330	____	____	____	____	____
Acura MDX/Honda Pilot	____	____	____	____	____
Acura MDX/Nissan Murano	____	____	____	____	____
Acura MDX/Buick Rendezvous	____	____	____	____	____
Acura MDX/Toyota Highlander	____	____	____	____	____
Volvo XC90/Infiniti FX45	____	____	____	____	____
Volvo XC90/Lexus RX330	____	____	____	____	____
Volvo XC90/Honda Pilot	____	____	____	____	____
Volvo XC90/Nissan Murano	____	____	____	____	____
Volvo XC90/Buick Rendezvous	____	____	____	____	____
Volvo XC90/Toyota Highlander	____	____	____	____	____

FIGURE 6-3

Hypothetical One-Dimensional Illustration of Similarity Judgments

Dependence techniques assess the interdependence of two or more dependent variables with one or more independent variables. Conjoint analysis is an example of a dependence technique that is useful in both single market and global market research. To continue with the SUV example, suppose Kia's new product team has selected an ideal position on Figure 6-3; now the task is to select specific product features that will deliver that positioning. The researchers want to determine the relative importance of a product's *salient attributes* in consumer decision making; that is, the relevance or importance that consumers attach to a product's qualities or properties. If the target position is "smooth, car-like ride while protecting your family," the team must determine relevant physical product characteristics (e.g., 6-cylinder engine, rollover sensors, side-curtain airbags, and onboard global positioning system). The team must also determine other characteristics (e.g., price, mileage, warranty, etc.) that consumers most prefer. Each attribute should be available in different levels, for example, 5-year or 10-year warranty.

Conjoint analysis is a tool that researchers can use to gain insights into the combination of features that will be most attractive to consumers; it is assumed that features affect both perception and preferences. Table 6-6 shows a listing of possible features; a total of 36 combinations are possible. In a full-profile approach, each of these combinations (e.g., 6 cylinder, side-curtain airbags for three rows, 5-year warranty, $27,500) is printed on an index card, and consumers are asked to rank them in order by preference. Conjoint analysis then determines the values or *utilities* of the various levels of product features and plots them graphically. Because the number of combinations can overwhelm subjects and lead to fatigue, it is sometimes preferable to use a pair-wise approach that allows them to consider two attributes at a time.

Better marketing research might have helped Nokia in its struggle to maintain leadership in the highly competitive global cellular phone market. Nokia focused on the functionality and features of its phones, even as consumer tastes and preferences were shifting to trendy styling and features such as cameras and large color screens. For years, Nokia manufactured only so-called

FIGURE 6-4

Hypothetical MDS-based Perceptual Map for Crossover SUVs

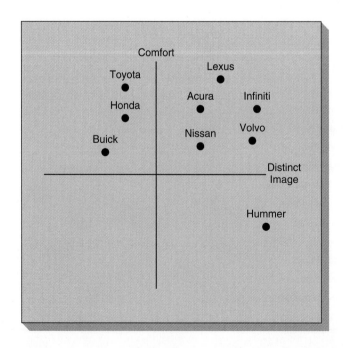

TABLE 6-6 Crossover SUV Product Feature Combinations for Conjoint Analysis

	Engine Size	Side-Curtain Airbags	Warranty	Price
Level 1	—	Side-curtain airbags for front-seat passengers only	—	$22,500
Level 2	6 cylinder	Side-curtain airbags for front-seat and middle passengers	5 years	$27,500
Level 3	8 cylinder	Side-curtain airbags for front, middle, and third-row passengers	10 years	$32,500

"candy bar" phones; because executives believed that the shape was a signature of the Nokia brand, the company did not offer flip (clamshell), slide, or swivel styles. Meanwhile, Sony, LG, Samsung, and Motorola were offering sleek new designs. In Europe, Nokia's market share fell from 51 percent in 2002 to about 33 percent in 2004. "Nokia didn't have the coolness factor," says industry consultant Jack Gold. "They didn't really do flip phones; they were a little late with cameras, and they didn't push them. Coolness in the consumer space is a big deal, and they were stodgy." Ansii Vanjoki, Nokia's head of multimedia, acknowledges, "We read the signs in the marketplace a bit wrong. The competition was emphasizing factors such as color richness and screen size. That's attractive at the point of sale. We missed that one."[38]

COMPARATIVE ANALYSIS AND MARKET ESTIMATION BY ANALOGY One of the unique opportunities in global marketing analysis is to conduct comparisons of market potential and marketing performance in different country or regional markets at the same point in time. A common form of comparative analysis is the intracompany cross-national comparison. For example, general market conditions in two or more countries (as measured by income, stage of industrialization, or some other indicator) may be similar. If there is a significant discrepancy between per capita sales of a given product in the countries, the marketer might reasonably wonder about it and determine what actions need to be taken.

- Soon after George Fisher became CEO of Kodak, he asked for a review of market share in color film on a country-by-country basis. Fisher was shocked to learn that Kodak's market share in Japan was only 7 percent, compared with 40 percent in most other countries. The situation prompted Fisher to lodge a petition with the U.S. trade representative seeking removal of alleged anticompetitive barriers in Japan. The WTO ultimately ruled against Kodak.
- Campbell is the world's largest soup company, commanding about 80 percent of the U.S. canned soup market. However, the company has a presence in only 6 percent of the world's soup markets. Russians eat 32 billion servings of soup each year, and the Chinese consume *300* billion! By contrast, Americans eat 15 billion servings each year. Sensing a huge opportunity, Campbell CEO Douglas Conant has dispatched teams to observe Russian and Chinese habits.[39]
- Catalog sales in the United States represent about 3 percent of overall retail sales. By comparison, catalog sales in Germany account for 5.8 percent of overall sales. This suggests that there is a catalog marketing opportunity in Germany.[40]

In these examples data are, for the most part, available. However, global marketers may find that certain types of desired data are unavailable for a particular country market. This is especially true in developing country markets. If this is the case, it is sometimes possible to estimate market size or potential demand by analogy. Drawing an *analogy* is simply stating a partial resemblance. For example, the advertising and computer industries in the United States both have geographic nicknames. The advertising industry is often referred to as "Madison Avenue," while the phrase "Silicon Valley" is synonymous with California's high-tech industry center. Suppose someone is familiar with the Silicon Valley but has never head of Madison Avenue. One way to explain it is to say that Silicon Valley is to the computer industry as Madison Avenue is to

---

[38]Nelson D. Schwartz and Joan M. Levinstein, "Has Nokia Lost It?" *Fortune* (January 24, 2005), pp. 98–106.
[39]Bruce Horovitz, "CEO Nears 10-Year Goal to Clean Up a Soupy Mess," *USA Today* (January 26, 2009), pp. 1B, 2B.
[40]Cecilie Rohwedder, "U.S. Mail-Order Firms Shake Up Europe," *The Wall Street Journal* (January 6, 1998), p. A15.

the advertising industry. Statements such as this are analogies. Analogy reduces the unknown by highlighting the "commonness" of two different things."[41]

David Arnold notes that there are four possible approaches to forecasting by analogy:[42]

- Data is available on a comparable product in the same country.
- Data is available on the same product in a comparable country.
- Data is available on the same product from an independent distributor in a neighboring country.
- Data is available about a comparable company in the same country.

Time-series displacement is an analogy technique based on the assumption that an analogy between markets exists in different time periods. Displacing time is a useful form of market analysis when data are available for two markets at different levels of development. The time displacement method requires a marketer to estimate when two markets are at similar stages of development. For example, the market for Polaroid instant cameras in Russia at the present time is comparable to the instant camera market in the United States in the mid-1960s. By obtaining data on the factors associated with demand for instant cameras in the United States in 1964 and in Russia today, as well as actual U.S. demand in 1964, one could estimate current potential in Russia.

Step 8: Interpretation and Presentation

The report based on the market research must be useful to managers as input to the decision-making process. Whether the report is presented in written form, orally, or electronically via video, it must relate clearly to the problem or opportunity identified in step 1. Generally, it is advisable for major findings to be summarized concisely in a memo that indicates the answer or answers to the problem first proposed in step 1. Many managers are uncomfortable with research jargon and complex quantitative analysis. Results should be clearly stated and provide a basis for managerial action. Otherwise, the report may end up on the shelf, where it will gather dust and serve as a reminder of wasted time and money. As the data provided by a corporate information system and market research become increasingly available on a worldwide basis, it becomes possible to analyze marketing expenditure effectiveness across national boundaries. Managers can then decide where they are achieving the greatest marginal effectiveness for their marketing expenditures and can adjust expenditures accordingly.

HEADQUARTERS CONTROL OF MARKET RESEARCH

An important issue for the global company is where to locate control of the organization's research capability. The difference between a multinational, polycentric company and a global, geocentric company on this issue is significant. In the multinational company, responsibility for research is delegated to the operating subsidiary. The global company delegates responsibility for research to operating subsidiaries but retains overall responsibility and control of research as a headquarters' function. A key difference between single-country market research and global market research is the importance of comparability. In practice, this means that the global company must ensure that research is designed and executed so as to yield comparable data.

Simply put, *comparability* means that the results can be used to make valid comparisons between the countries covered by the research.[43] To achieve this, the company must inject a level of control and review of marketing research at the global level. The director of worldwide marketing research must respond to local conditions as he or she develops a research program that can be implemented on a global basis. The research director must pay particular attention to whether data gathered is based on emic analysis or etic analysis. These terms, which come from

---

[41]Ikujiro Nonaka and Hirotaka Takeuchi, *The Knowledge-Creating Company* (Cambridge, MA: Harvard Business School Press, 1995), p. 67. As Nonaka and Takeuchi explain, "Metaphor and analogy are often confused. Association of two things through metaphor is driven mostly by intuition and holistic imagery and does not aim to find differences between them. On the other hand, association through analogy is carried out by rational thinking and focuses on structural/functional similarities between two things. . . . Thus analogy helps us understand the unknown through the known."

[42]David Arnold, *The Mirage of Global Markets* (Upper Saddle River, NJ: Financial Times Prentice Hall, 2004), pp. 41–43.

[43]V. Kumar, *International Marketing Research* (Upper Saddle River, NJ: Prentice Hall, 1999), p. 15.

TABLE 6-7 Worldwide Marketing Research Plan

Research Objective	Country Cluster A	Country Cluster B	Country Cluster C
Identify market potential			X
Appraise competitive intentions		X	X
Evaluate product appeal	X	X	X
Study market response to price	X		
Appraise distribution channels	X	X	X

anthropology, refer to the perspective taken in the study of another culture. **Emic analysis** is similar to ethnography in that it attempts to study a culture from within, using its own system of meanings and values. **Etic analysis** is "from the outside"; in other words, it is a more detached perspective that is often used in comparative or multi-country studies. In a particular research study, an etic scale would entail using the same set of items across all countries. This approach enhances comparability but some precision is lost. By contrast, an emic study would be tailored to fit a particular country; inferences about cross-cultural similarities based on emic research have to be made subjectively. A good compromise is to use a survey instrument that incorporates elements of both types of analysis. It is likely that the marketing director will end up with a number of marketing programs tailored to clusters of countries that exhibit within-group similarities. The agenda of a coordinated worldwide research program might look like the one in Table 6-7.

The director of worldwide research should not simply direct the efforts of country research managers. His or her job is to ensure that the corporation achieves maximum results worldwide from the total allocation of its research resources. Achieving this requires that personnel in each country are aware of research being carried out in the rest of the world and are involved in influencing the design of their own in-country research as well as the overall research program. Ultimately, the director of worldwide research must be responsible for the overall research design and program. It is his or her job to take inputs from the entire world and produce a coordinated research strategy that generates the information needed to achieve global sales and profit objectives.

THE MARKETING INFORMATION SYSTEM AS A STRATEGIC ASSET

The advent of the transnational enterprise means that boundaries between the firm and the outside world are dissolving. Marketing has historically been responsible for managing many of the relationships across that boundary. The boundary between marketing and other functions is also dissolving, and the traditional notion of marketing as a distinct functional area within the firm may be giving way to a new model. The process of marketing decision making is also changing, largely because of the changing role of information from a support tool to a wealth-generating, strategic asset.

Many global firms are creating flattened organizations, with less hierarchical, less centralized decision-making structures. Such organizations facilitate the exchange and flow of information between departments that previously may have operated as autonomous "silos." The more information intensive the firm, the greater the degree to which marketing is involved in activities traditionally associated with other functional areas. In such firms there is parallel processing of information.

Information intensity in the firm has an impact on perceptions of market attractiveness, competitive position, and organizational structure. The greater a company's information intensity, the more the traditional product and market boundaries shift. In essence, companies increasingly face new sources of competition from other firms in historically noncompetitive industries, particularly if those firms are also information intensive. Diverse firms now find themselves in direct competition with each other. They offer essentially the same products as a natural extension and redefinition of traditional product lines and marketing activities. Today, when marketers speak of "value added," the chances are they are not referring to unique product features. Rather, the emphasis is on the information exchanged as part of customer transactions, much of which cuts across traditional product lines.

Summary

Information is one of the most basic ingredients of a successful marketing strategy. A company's **management information system** and **intranet** provide decision makers with a continuous flow of information. **Information technology** is profoundly affecting global marketing activities by allowing managers to access and manipulate data to assist in decision making. **Electronic data interchange**, **electronic point of sale** data, **efficient consumer response**, **customer relationship management**, and **data warehouses** are some of the new tools and techniques available. The global marketer must scan the world for information about opportunities and threats and make information available via a management information system.

Formal **market research**—the project-specific, systematic gathering of data—is often required before marketers make key decisions. **Global market research** links customers and marketers through information gathered on a global scale. The research process begins when marketers define the problem and set research objectives; this step may entail assessing whether a particular market should be classified as **latent** or **incipient**. A research plan specifies the relative amounts of qualitative and quantitative information desired. Information is collected using either primary or secondary **data** sources. In today's wired world, the Internet has taken its place alongside more traditional channels as an important secondary information source. In some instances, the cost of collecting primary data may outweigh the potential benefits. Secondary sources are especially useful for researching a market that is too small to justify a large commitment of time and money.

If collection of primary data can be justified on a cost-benefit basis, research can be conducted via **survey research**, **personal interviews**, **consumer panels**, **observation**, and **focus groups**. Before collecting data, researchers must determine whether a probability sample is required. In global marketing, careful attention must be paid to issues such as eliminating cultural bias in research, accurately translating surveys, and ensuring data comparability in different markets. A number of techniques are available for analyzing survey data, including **factor analysis**, **cluster analysis**, **multidimensional scaling (MDS)**, and **conjoint analysis**. Research findings and recommendations must be presented clearly. A final issue is how much control headquarters will have over research and the overall management of the organization's information system. To ensure comparability of data, the researcher should utilize both **emic** and **etic** approaches.

Discussion Questions

1. Explain how information technology puts powerful tools in the hands of global marketers.
2. Assume that you have been asked by the president of your organization to devise a systematic approach to scanning. The president does not want to be surprised by major market or competitive developments. What would you recommend?
3. Outline the basic steps of the market research process.
4. What is the difference between existing, latent, and incipient demand? How might these differences affect the design of a marketing research project?
5. Describe some of the analytical techniques used by global marketers. When is it appropriate to use each technique?
6. Coach has been described as "a textbook lesson on how to revitalize a brand." The same could be said for Burberry, the British fashion goods company discussed in Chapter 1. Locate some articles about Burberry and read about the research its management has conducted and the formula it used to polish the brand. Are the approaches evident at Burberry and Coach similar? Are they competitors?

In 1995, Clicks was the first retailer to start a loyalty program in Africa, the Clicks ClubCard. This program has grown into the largest and most widely used loyalty program in South Africa, with more than 2.6 million active members in 2009.

Membership to the Clicks ClubCard loyalty program is free, and shoppers are awarded with points for every purchase made. ClubCard points are converted into "cash-back" vouchers that are mailed to qualifying members every three months, which can be redeemed for any merchandise within Clicks. The Clicks ClubCard also allows personalized marketing and offers by means of direct mail, e-mail, and cell phone text messages. Double ClubCard points days are also offered and strategically aligned with key promotional events, while ClubCard members also earn additional benefits at Clicks Pharmacy, called PlusPoints.

Electronic newsletters are also distributed to inform customers about promotions and to draw attention to activities in the store, while text messages remind ClubCard members about double points days. The Clicks ClubCard member database is also used to send out coupons, magazines, letters, and targeted special offers.

The primary communication that is used to communicate with ClubCard members is the Clicks ClubCard magazine. This has been a testament to the success of the Clicks customer relationship management program. It is now South Africa's most-read alternate monthly magazine, with a readership of approximately 1,041,000 in 2008.

Even though the Clicks ClubCard loyalty program is widely regarded, management is conscious of the fact that their offerings need to remain at a high level and benefits to Clicks ClubCard members and suppliers need to be frequently updated.

The enormous entry of loyalty programs in the market had resulted in a focus on aspects that are relevant to the consumer. Through the years, Clicks has discovered that shopper insight-driven strategies, based on customer segmentation, are best delivered through collaboration with suppliers. Given this trend, Clicks entered a joint venture operation with 5one, a leading UK marketing services consultancy that specializes in consumer loyalty, database analytics, and technology solutions. The result was the launch of a new marketing solution, the Clicks ClubCard Marketing Service (CCMS), in 2007.

This venture allows Clicks to take full advantage of the potential that exists within the ClubCard database. The combination of communications planning, data analysis services, and the highly advanced customer relationship management technology enables ClubCard Marketing Services to deliver intelligence-driven marketing services to suppliers, which in turn aids it in maximizing a measurable return on investment opportunities.

After conducting a study of ClubCard customers based on transactional data over a period of two years, a Shopper Targeting Model was developed for Clicks ClubCard. The result was that customer selections were optimized resulting in the targeting of multioffer coupon mailings and direct communications to different types of consumers.

The aim is that the Shopper Targeting Model will impel maximum value from Clicks ClubCard communications by engaging with suppliers in programs that merge directly with shopper insight-led activities, resulting in mutually beneficial marketing and commercial activities.

Next is an example of how the Shopper Targeting Approach is used by ClubCard Marketing Services. First, the specific shopper segment (or profile) is identified. For example, a customer who spends considerably more than the average customer spends on beauty and cosmetic products. Then, Clicks would suggest a strategy such as protecting and increasing the customer's spending on beauty and cosmetic products, by rewarding existing shopping behavior. Furthermore, the customer's value could be increased by providing incentives for additional shopping trips on a limited time basis, where new areas, such as hair care and essentials, could also be brought to the attention of the customer.

Finally, personalized offers will be made to Clicks ClubCard members who fall into this shopper segment. Examples of these offers would be reward offers such as free mascara with any purchase of L'Oréal cosmetics, or extra reward points rewarded for purchases of Revlon products.

ClubCard Marketing Services therefore is a targeted marketing and data-planning nucleus, which provides unsurpassed insights into shopper types and behavior based on historic as well as current customer and transaction data from the Clicks ClubCard loyalty program. It also provides a managed solution for optimal targeting of coupon mailings and direct communications to different consumer groups, each communication with relevance to the recipient.

Case 6-1 Discussion Questions

1. The Clicks ClubCard loyalty program is regarded as one of the drivers of growth at Clicks. Explain why you think this program is so successful.
2. Explain why you think Clicks started to adapt its merchandise range to appeal to consumers of the growing black middle-class market in South Africa.
3. Suggest practical marketing strategies which would encourage ClubCard members to make additional trips to Clicks stores.

Sources: This case was prepared by Chris Pentz, Department of Business Management, Stellenbosch University, South Africa. *Additional Sources:* "2008 Sponsors, Clicks ClubCard," www.mpasa.org.za. Accessed November 2, 2009; "Black Women's Spending Power Increases," www.sagoodnews.co.za. Accessed November 10, 2009; "Clicks ClubCard, 2009 Ratecard," www.tppsa.co.za. Accessed September 29, 2009; "Clicks ClubCard Magazine," http://africantime.co.za. Accessed November 2, 2009; "Clicks ClubCard Marketing Services," www.fastmoving.co.za. Accessed October 15, 2009; "Clicks Group Limited, Homepage," www.newclicks.co.za. Accessed November 9, 2009; "Clicks Seeks Pharmacy Role in National Health Insurance," www.busrep.co.za. Accessed November 2, 2009; "Clicks Still on Song," http://secure.financialmail.co.za. Accessed November 9, 2009; "Clicks—The Plan Comes Together," http://secure.financialmail.co.za. Accessed November 2, 2009; "ClubCard Marketing Services," www.nuclicks.co.za. Accessed September 29, 2009; "New Clicks to Focus on Growth," www.fin24.com. Accessed November 2, 2009; D. Olivier, "South Africa Poised to Become a Loyalty Marketing Gem," Journal of Consumer Marketing, 24(3) (2007):180–181; "PICA 2009: Entries Open," www.mpasa.org.za. Accessed November 2, 2009; "SA's Booming Black Middle Class," www.southafrica.info. Accessed November 10, 2009; "The Effectiveness of Retail Loyalty Programmes," www.bizcommunity.com. Accessed September 29, 2009; "You Pay Less—Clicks," www.superbrands. com/za. Accessed October 15, 2009.

Whirlpool Corporation, headquartered in Benton Harbor, Michigan, is the number one appliance company in the United States and number two worldwide. The company sells more than $18 billion worth of "white goods" each year; this category includes refrigerators, stoves, washing machines, and microwave ovens. Whirlpool's success has been achieved in part by offering a brand portfolio comprised of products in different price ranges. These include the premium KitchenAid and Maytag brands as well as the medium-priced Amana and Whirlpool brands.

In part, the impetus for overseas expansion comes from a mature domestic market that is only growing 2 or 3 percent annually. However, Whirlpool is not new to foreign markets; for example, the company has had a presence in Latin America since 1957. Today, it is the market share leader there, offering global brands (Whirlpool, KitchenAid, and Maytag) as well as local (Brastemp) and regional ones (Consul).

At the beginning of 1993, David Whitwam, then-chairman and CEO of Whirlpool Corporation, told an interviewer, "Five years ago we were essentially a domestic company. Today about 40 percent of our revenues are overseas, and by the latter part of this decade, a majority will be." The CEO's comments came three years after he placed his first bet that the appliance industry was globalizing. By acquiring Philips Electronics' European appliance business for $1 billion, Whirlpool vaulted into the number three position in Europe. Whitwam pledged another $2 billion investment in Europe alone. As the decade of the 1990s drew to a close, however, Whitwam's ambitious plans for expanding beyond Europe into Japan and the developing nations in Asia and Latin America hadn't achieved the desired results. Noting that Whirlpool stock underperformed the bull market of the 1990s, analysts began questioning whether Whitwam's global vision was on target. As one analyst put it, "The strategy has been a failure. Whirlpool went big into global markets and investors have paid for it." Others faulted the company on execution. Another analyst said, "I respect Whirlpool's strategy. They just missed on the blocking and tackling."

The challenge facing Whirlpool is rooted partially in the structure of the appliance industry. In Europe, for example, the presence of more than 200 brands and 170 factories makes the appliance industry highly fragmented and highly competitive. Electrolux, a Swedish company, ranks number one. European appliance sales have been flat for years, with sales volumes growing at a mere 1 or 2 percent; industry overcapacity is a major issue. Although analysts expect to see a surge in demand from Central and Eastern Europe within a few years, there will also be an influx of products from low-cost producers in those regions.

To cut costs and bring margins up, Whirlpool has streamlined its European organization. Four regional sales offices replaced sales organizations in 17 separate countries. As president of Whirlpool Europe BV, Hank Bowman trimmed the number of warehouses from 30 to 16 and hopes eventually to have as few as 5 or 6. A global parts-sourcing strategy has helped reduce the number of suppliers by 40 percent. Over the course of several years, Whirlpool invested hundreds of millions of dollars in new-product development. It has already begun marketing a new clothes dryer designed to operate more efficiently and provide higher quality despite containing fewer parts.

Bowman believes that a global market segmentation approach is the key to success in Europe. Whirlpool relies heavily on market research to maintain its leadership in the United States; listening to consumers is important in Europe and Latin America as well. "Research tells us that the trends, preferences and biases of consumers, country by country, are reducing as opposed to increasing," Bowman said recently. He believes that European homemakers fall into distinct "Euro-segments"—traditionalists and aspirers, for example—allowing Whirlpool to duplicate the three-tiered approach to brands that has worked so well in the United States. The Bauknecht brand is positioned at the high end of the market, with Whirlpool in the middle and Ignis at the lower end. For example, appliance shoppers in Germany visiting a department store such as Saturn can choose a Bauknecht Neptun 1400 priced at €699 or a Whirlpool for €369.

Research has also indicated that consumers in different countries prefer different types of features. Thus, Whirlpool has begun emphasizing product platforms as a means to produce localized versions of ovens, refrigerators, and other appliance lines more economically. A platform is essentially a technological core underneath the metal casing of an appliance. The platform—for example, the compressor and sealant system in a refrigerator—can be the same throughout the world. Country or region-specific capabilities can be added late in the production cycle. The goal was to cut 10 percent from Whirlpool's $200 million annual production development budget and achieve a 30 percent productivity increase among the company's 2,000 member product-development staff. Ultimately, the platform project team hopes to reduce the total number of platforms in the company from 135 to 65. Specific goals include reducing the number of dishwasher platforms from 6 to 3, and refrigerator platforms from 48 to 25.

Market research also drives the search for new products that address the specific needs of developing markets. In Brazil, for example, Whirlpool's market entry strategy included acquiring two local established appliance brands, Brastemp and Consul. However, with a basic washer priced at $300, even the low end of Whirlpool's product lines proved to be too expensive for many Brazilians. Economic data indicated that Brazil's 30 million low-income households, many with monthly incomes of about $220, account for about one-third of national consumption. Moreover, studies showed that these households ranked an automatic washer second only to a cell phone as an aspirational purchase. Whirlpool's researchers convened focus groups and made visits to representative low-income households. Marcele Rodrigues is director of laundry technology at Multibrás SA Eletrodomésticos, Whirlpool's Brazilian division. "It wasn't a matter of stripping down an existing model," he noted recently. "We had to innovate for the masses."

Whirlpool's response was to develop what it proudly calls the world's least expensive automatic washer, to be sold under the Consul brand. The company has a strong team of engineers and industrial designers in Brazil, as well as some of its most technologically advanced factories. Despite the fact that Brazil's economy was in turmoil, Whirlpool invested $30 million to develop the new washer, the Ideale, to meet the needs of a large class of consumers who still wash clothes by hand. One cost-saving design breakthrough was a patentable technology that allows the machine to switch from the wash cycle to the spin cycle without shifting gears. The design involves some performance compromises: Compared with more expensive models, the spin cycle takes longer and clothes come out damper. However, research indicated that these were not critical issues for most consumers.

Focus group research also indicated that consumers would find a smaller capacity washer acceptable because low-income families do laundry more often. Because Brazilian housewives like to wash floors underneath furniture, the Ideale sits high on four legs as opposed to resting on the floor as most conventional units do. Perhaps the most significant thing that the Ideale design team learned from its research was that form matters, too. As Emerson do Valle, vice president of Multibrás, explained, "We realized the washer should be aesthetically pleasing; it's a status symbol for these people." The team selected a rounded design with a yellow start button and blue lettering on the control panel. Because white is widely associated with cleanliness in Brazil, the Ideale is only available in white.

Although the Ideale incorporates many design features that appeal to consumers in Brazil, adaptations of the Ideale platform are also being manufactured and marketed in China and India. In India, the color options include green, blue, and white; the setting for delicate fabrics is labeled "sari." Also, the Indian units are mounted on casters so they can be moved easily.

In China, an appliance with a white exterior would be undesirable because of the prevailing belief that white shows dirt easily. For that reason, the Chinese Ideale is available in light blue and gray. In addition, the heavy-duty wash cycle in China is labeled "grease removal" for the simple reason that many Chinese use bicycles for daily transportation. Although the majority of Chinese washing machines have separate tubs for the wash and spin cycles, sales of single-drum washers such as the Ideale and a new frontloading model, the Sunrise, are growing. Overall, washer sales in China totaled 16.5 million units in 2005; Whirlpool expects that number to reach 22.2 million by 2011.

After a decade of losses, Whirlpool China finally posted a profit in 2006. The company first entered the market in the mid-1990s via joint ventures with local partners. Whirlpool called its strategy "T-4": offering refrigerators, washing machines, microwave ovens, and air conditioners, the four most-sought home appliances. Several of the ventures quickly went sour; as one executive recalls, "We quickly jumped into joint ventures without insights into Chinese consumers. We brought in North American know-how, but we also needed to distill local know-how." For one thing, Whirlpool underestimated the speed at which Haier and other local competitors are evolving into world-class manufacturers. Company executives note that, since China joined the World Trade Organization in 2001, it has been easier for Western companies to do business there.

In 2006, Jeff M. Fettig succeeded David Whitwam as Whirlpool's CEO and chairman. If emerging markets are to be drivers of global growth under Fettig's leadership, Whirlpool will have to build brand recognition in countries such as Brazil, India, and China. Also, consumers in emerging markets must be persuaded to move beyond washing machines to purchase some of the company's other appliances. That trend is already gaining traction: Middle-class Chinese consumers are splurging on high-end appliances

Source: Paulo Fridman.

such as a side-by-side Whirlpool refrigerator that costs the equivalent of $2,500. Many of the units find their way into living rooms. As Michael Todman, president of Whirlpool International, noted, "Appliances can be furniture, too. It's a source of pride to own one: 'Gee, look what I can own. I'm doing well.'"

Discussion Questions

1. Describe Whirlpool's global marketing strategy. Does Whirlpool use an extension product strategy or an adaptation product strategy?
2. What is the primary reason people buy and own major appliances such as a washing machine? Is there a *secondary* reason as well?
3. Summarize the role of market research in Whirlpool's globalization strategy. What different types of research methodologies does the company use? What are the advantages of each methodology described in the case?
4. What are the key lessons to be learned from Whirlpool's experience in China?

Sources: Calum MacLeod, "Whirlpool Spins China Challenge into Turnaround," *USA Today* (April 5, 2007), pp. 1B, 2B; Miriam Jordan and Jonathan Karp, "Machines for the Masses," *The Wall Street Journal* (December 9, 2003), pp. B1, B2; Katheryn Kranhold, "Whirlpool Conjures Up Appliance Divas," *The Wall Street Journal* (April 27, 2000), p. B1; Peter Marsh and Nikki Tait, "Whirlpool's Platform for Growth," *Financial Times* (March 26, 1998), p. 8; Peter Marsh and Nikki Tait, "Whirlpool Sticks to Its Global Guns," *Financial Times* (February 2, 1998), p. 4; Greg Steinmetz and Carl Quintanilla, "Tough Target: Whirlpool Expected Easy Going in Europe, and It Got a Big Shock," *The Wall Street Journal* (April 10, 1998), pp. A1, A6; Carl Quintanilla, "Despite Setbacks, Whirlpool Pursues Overseas Markets," *The Wall Street Journal* (December 9, 1997), p. B4; Peter Marsh, "Rough and Tumble Industry," *Financial Times* (July 2, 1997), p. 13; Bill Vlasic, "Did Whirlpool Spin Too Far Too Fast?" *Business Week* (June 24, 1996) pp. 134-136; Patrick Oster, "Call It Worldpool," *Business Week* (November 28, 1994), pp. 98–99; Robert L. Rose, "Whirlpool Is Expanding in Europe Despite the Slump," *The Wall Street Journal* (January 27, 1994), p. B4; Sally Solo, "Whirlpool: How to Listen to Consumers," *Fortune* (January 11, 1993), pp. 77, 79; Gregory E. David, "Spin Dry: Asia Is the Last Phase in Whirlpool's Global Wash Cycle," *Financial World* (October 26, 1993), pp. 30–31.

CHAPTER 7

Segmentation, Targeting, and Positioning

Case 7-1
Global Cosmetics Companies Segment the Market

The world's best-known cosmetics companies are setting their sights on a lucrative new market segment: the emerging middle classes in countries such as Brazil, Russia, India, and China. For example, the Chinese spent $10.3 billion on cosmetics and toiletries in 2005; that figure is expected to increase to $17 billion by 2010. Not surprisingly, marketers at L'Oréal, Procter & Gamble, Shiseido, and Estée Lauder Companies are moving quickly. William Lauder, president and CEO of Estée Lauder, calls China a "$100 billion opportunity."

Noting that there is no "one-size-fits-all" ideal of beauty, cosmetics marketers pride themselves on sensitivity to local cultural preferences. As Jean-Paul Agon,

chief executive of L'Oréal, explains, "We have different customers. Each customer is free to have her own aspirations. Our intention is just to respond as well as possible to each customer aspiration. Some want to be gorgeous, some want to be natural, and we just have to offer them the best quality and the best product to satisfy their wishes and their dreams" (see Exhibit 7-1). For example, many Asian women use whitening creams to lighten and brighten their complexions; in China, white skin is associated with wealth. L'Oréal responded by creating White Perfect; Shiseido offers Aupres White.

The global cosmetics giants' worldwide success is a convincing example of the power of skillful global

Exhibit 7-1: L'Oréal is expanding distribution in China. After successful market tests at Walmart and Carrefour stores, L'Oréal Paris, Maybelline, Garnier, and other brands are now available in retail stores as well as Chinese supermarkets. Recently L'Oréal China launched a new advertising campaign for the Mininurse Professional UV cosmetics line targeting women 18 years of age to 25 years of age. The ads communicate the brand's core benefits: UV protection, daytime skin whitening action, and nighttime hydrating action.
Source: AP Wide World Photos.

market segmentation and targeting. **Market segmentation** represents an effort to identify and categorize groups of customers and countries according to common characteristics. **Targeting** is the process of evaluating the segments and focusing marketing efforts on a country, region, or group of people that has significant potential to respond. Such targeting reflects the reality that a company should identify those consumers it can reach most effectively, efficiently, and profitably. Finally, proper positioning is required to differentiate the product or brand in the minds of target customers. The second part of Case 7-1 (page 266) explores the challenges and issues facing L'Oréal and its competitors as they segment and target the global market for health and beauty products and formulate appropriate positioning strategies.

Consider the following examples of market segmentation and targeting by global companies:

- The personal computer market can be divided into home users, corporate (also known as "enterprise") users, and educational users. Dell originally targeted corporate customers; even today, sales of products for home use account for only 20 percent of revenues. After focusing only on the PC market, Dell then branched out into other computer categories such as servers and storage hardware.

- In 2003, after convening worldwide employee conferences to study women's shaving preferences, Schick-Wilkinson Sword introduced a shaving system for women that features a replaceable blade cartridge. Intuition, as the system is known, incorporates a "skin-conditioning solid" that allows a woman to lather and shave her legs simultaneously. Intuition is a premium product targeted directly at users of Venus, Gillette's three-blade razor system for women.[1]

- Cosmed, a division of Germany's Beiersdorf AG, markets a line of skin care products for women under the NIVEA brand. Recently, the company launched a new brand, NIVEA for Men.

- GM's original market entry strategy for China called for targeting government and company officials who were entitled to a large sedan-style automobile. Today, GM's lineup for China includes the Buick Century, targeted at the country's middle class, and the $10,000 Buick Sail.

As you can see, global markets can be segmented according to buyer category (e.g., consumer, enterprise, government), gender, age, and a number of other criteria. These examples also illustrate the fact that market segmentation and targeting are two separate but closely related activities. These activities serve as the link between market needs and wants and tactical decisions by managers to develop marketing programs and value propositions that meet the specific needs of one or more segments. Segmentation, targeting, and positioning are all examined in this chapter.

GLOBAL MARKET SEGMENTATION

Global market segmentation has been defined as the process of identifying specific segments—whether they be country groups or individual consumer groups—of potential customers with homogeneous attributes who are likely to exhibit similar responses to a company's marketing mix.[2] Marketing practitioners and academics have been interested in global market segmentation for several decades. In the late 1960s, one observer suggested that the European market could be divided into three broad categories—international sophisticate, semi-sophisticate, and provincial—solely on the basis of consumers' presumed receptivity to a common advertising approach.[3] Another writer suggested that some themes—for example, the desire to be beautiful, the desire to be healthy and free of pain, the love of mother and child—were universal and could be used in advertising around the globe.[4]

---

[1]Charles Forelle, "Schick Puts a Nick in Gillette's Razor Cycle," *The Wall Street Journal* (October 3, 2003), p. B7.
[2]Salah S. Hassan and Lea Prevel Katsanis, "Identification of Global Consumer Segments: A Behavioral Framework," *Journal of International Consumer Marketing* 3, no. 2 (1991), p. 17.
[3]John K. Ryans, Jr., "Is It Too Soon to Put a Tiger in Every Tank?" *Columbia Journal of World Business* (March–April 1969), p. 73.
[4]Arther C. Fatt, "The Danger of 'Local' International Advertising," *Journal of Marketing* 31, no. 1 (January 1967), pp. 60–62.

As noted in earlier chapters, four decades ago Professor Theodore Levitt advanced the thesis that consumers in different countries increasingly seek variety, and that the same new segments are likely to show up in multiple national markets. Thus, ethnic or regional foods such as sushi, falafel, or pizza might be in demand anywhere in the world. Levitt suggested that this trend, known variously as the *pluralization of consumption* and *segment simultaneity,* provides an opportunity for marketers to pursue one or more segments on a global scale. Frank Brown, president of MTV Networks Asia, acknowledged this trend in explaining MTV's success in Asia despite a business downturn in the region. "When marketing budgets are tight, advertisers look for a more effective buy, and we can deliver a niche audience with truly panregional reach," he said.[5] Authors John Micklethwait and Adrian Wooldridge sum up the situation this way:

> The audience for a new recording of a Michael Tippett symphony or for a nature documentary about the mating habits of flamingos may be minuscule in any one country, but round up all the Tippett and flamingo fanatics around the world, and you have attractive commercial propositions. The cheap distribution offered by the Internet will probably make these niches even more attractive financially.[6]

Global market segmentation is based on the premise that companies should attempt to identify consumers in different countries who share similar needs and desires. However, the fact that significant numbers of pizza-loving consumers are found in many countries does not mean they are eating the exact same thing. In France, for example, Domino's serves pizza with goat cheese and strips of pork fat known as *lardoons*. In Taiwan, toppings include squid, crab, shrimp, and pineapple; Brazilians can order their pies with mashed bananas and cinnamon. As Patrick Doyle, executive vice president of Domino's international division, explains, "Pizza is beautifully adaptable to consumer needs around the world, simply by changing the toppings."[7]

A. Coskun Samli has developed a useful approach to global market segmentation that compares and contrasts "conventional" versus "unconventional" wisdom (see Table 7-1). For example, conventional wisdom might assume that consumers in Europe and Latin America are interested in World Cup soccer while those in America are not. Unconventional wisdom would note that the "global jock" segment exists in many countries, including the United States.[8] Similarly, conventional wisdom might assume that, because per capita income in India is about $820, all Indians have low incomes. Unconventional wisdom would note the presence of a higher-income, middle-class segment. As Sapna Nayak, a food analyst at Raobank India, noted recently, "The potential Indian customer base for a McDonald's or a Subway is larger than the size of entire developed countries."[9] The same is true of China; the average annual

TABLE 7-1 Contrasting Views of Global Segmentation

Conventional Wisdom	Unconventional Wisdom
1. Assumes heterogeneity between countries.	1. Assumes the emergence of segments that transcend national boundaries.
2. Assumes homogeneity within any given country.	2. Acknowledges the existence of within-country differences.
3. Focuses heavily on cultural differences at a macro level.	3. Emphasizes differences and commonalities in micro-level values, consumption patterns, etc.
4. Segmentation relies heavily on clustering of national markets.	4. Segmentation relies on grouping micro markets within a country or between countries.
5. Within-country microsegments are assigned secondary priority.	5. Micro segments based on consumer behavior are assigned high priority.

Source: Adapted from A. Coskun Samli, *International Consumer Behavior* (Westport, CT: Quorum, 1995), p. 130.

---

[5]Magz Osborne, "Second Chance in Japan," *Ad Age Global* 1, no. 9 (May 2001), p. 28.

[6]John Micklethwait and Adrian Wooldridge, *A Future Perfect: The Challenge and Hidden Promise of Globalization* (New York: Crown Publishers, 2000), p. 198.

[7]Neil Buckley, "Domino's Returns to Fast Food's Fast Lane," *Financial Times* (November 26, 2003), p. 10.

[8]Robert Frank, "When World Cup Soccer Starts, World-Wide Productivity Stalls," *The Wall Street Journal* (June 12, 1998), pp. B1, B2; Daniela Deane, "Their Cup Runneth Over: Ethnic Americans Going Soccer Crazy," *USA Today* (July 2, 1998), p. 13A.

[9]Saritha Rai, "Tastes of India in U.S. Wrappers," *The New York Times* (April 29, 2003), p. W7.

income of people living in eastern China is approximately $1,200. This is the equivalent to a lower-middle-income country market with 470 million people, larger than every other single country market except India.[10]

As we have noted many times in this book, global marketers must determine whether a standardized or an adapted marketing mix is required to best serve those wants and needs. By performing market segmentation, marketers can generate the insights needed to devise the most effective approach. The process of global market segmentation begins with the choice of one or more variables to use as a basis for grouping customers. Common variables include demographics (including national income and size of population), psychographics (values, attitudes, and lifestyles), behavioral characteristics, and benefits sought. It is also possible to cluster different national markets in terms of their environments—for example, the presence or absence of government regulation in a particular industry—to establish groupings.

Demographic Segmentation

Demographic segmentation is based on measurable characteristics of populations such as income, population, age distribution, gender, education, and occupation. A number of global demographic trends—fewer married couples, smaller family size, changing roles of women, higher incomes and living standards, for example—have contributed to the emergence of global market segments. The following are several key demographic facts and trends from around the world:

- Asia is home to 500 million consumers aged 16 and younger.
- India has the youngest demographic profile among the world's large nations. More than half its population is younger than 25; the number of young people below the age of 14 is greater than the entire U.S. population.
- A widening age gap exists between the older populations in the West and the large working-age populations in developing countries.
- In the EU, the number of consumers aged 16 and under is rapidly approaching the number of consumers aged 60 and older.
- Half of Japan's population will be 50 years old or older by 2025.
- By 2030, 20 percent of the U.S. population—70 million Americans—will be 65 years old or older versus 13 percent (36 million) today.
- America's three main ethnic groups—African/Black Americans, Hispanic Americans, and Asian Americans—represent a combined annual buying power of $1 trillion.
- The United States is home to 28.4 million foreign-born residents with a combined income of $233 billion.

Statistics such as these can provide valuable insights to marketers who are scanning the globe for opportunities. As noted in Chapter 4, for example, Disney hopes to capitalize on the huge number of young people—and their parents' rising incomes—in India. Managers at global companies must be alert to the possibility that marketing strategies will have to be adjusted in response to the aging of the population and other demographic trends. For example, consumer products companies will need to convene focus groups consisting of people over 50 years old who are nearing retirement. These same companies will also have to target Brazil, Mexico, Vietnam, and other developing country markets to achieve growth objectives in the years to come.

Demographic changes can create opportunities for marketing innovation. In France, for example, two entrepreneurs began rewriting the rules of retailing years before Sam Walton founded the Walmart chain. Marcel Fournier and Louis Defforey opened the first Carrefour ("crossroads") hypermarket in 1963. At the time, France had a fragmented shop system that consisted of small, specialized stores with only about 5,000 square feet of floor space, such as the *boulangerie* and *charcuterie*. The shop system was part of France's national heritage, and shoppers developed personal relationships with a shop's proprietor. However, time-pressed, dual-parent working families had less time to stop at several stores for daily shopping. The same trend was occurring in other countries. By 1993, Carrefour SA was a global chain with

---

[10]Joseph Kahn, "Made in China, Bought in China," *The New York Times* (January 5, 2003), sec. 3, p. 10.

$21 billion in sales and a market capitalization of $10 billion. By 2008, sales had reached $124 billion; today, Carrefour operates 15,400 stores in 30 countries. As Adrian Slywotzky has noted, it was a demographic shift that provided the opportunity for Fournier and Defforey to create a novel, customer-matched, cost-effective business design.[11]

SEGMENTING GLOBAL MARKETS BY INCOME AND POPULATION   When a company charts a plan for global market expansion, it often finds that income is a valuable segmentation variable. After all, a market consists of those who are willing and *able* to buy. For cigarettes, soft drinks, candy, and other consumer products that have a low per-unit cost, population is often a more valuable segmentation variable than income. Nevertheless, for a vast range of industrial and consumer products offered in global markets today, income is a valuable and important macro indicator of market potential. About two-thirds of world GNI is generated in the Triad; however, only about 12 percent of the world's population is located in Triad countries.

The concentration of wealth in a handful of industrialized countries has significant implications for global marketers. After segmenting in terms of a single demographic variable—income—a company can reach the most affluent markets by targeting fewer than 20 nations: half the EU, North America, and Japan. By doing so, however, the marketers are *not* reaching almost 90 percent of the world's population! A word of caution is in order here. Data about income (and population) have the advantage of being widely available and inexpensive to access. However, management may unconsciously "read too much" into such data. In other words, while providing some measure of market potential, such macro-level demographic data should not necessarily be used as the sole indicator of presence (or absence) of a market opportunity. This is especially true when an emerging country market or region is being investigated.

Ideally, GNI and other measures of national income converted to U.S. dollars should be calculated on the basis of purchasing power parities (i.e., what the currency will buy in the country of issue) or through direct comparisons of actual prices for a given product. This would provide an actual comparison of the standards of living in the countries of the world. Table 7-2 ranks the top 10 countries in terms of 2007 per capita income followed by the respective figure adjusted for purchasing power parity. Although the United States ranks eighth in per capita income, only Norway and Luxembourg surpass its standard of living—as measured by what money can buy.[12] By most metrics, the U.S. market is enormous: nearly $14 trillion in national income and a population that passed the 300 million milestone in 2006. Little wonder, then, that so many non-U.S. companies target and cater to American consumers and organizational buyers!

TABLE 7-2 Per Capita Income, 2007

	2007 GNI Per Capita	2007 Income Adjusted for Purchasing Power
1. Norway	$77,370	$53,650
2. Luxembourg*	$72,430	$61,860
3. Switzerland	$60,820	$44,410
4. Iceland	$57,750	$34,070
5. Denmark	$55,440	$36,800
6. Sweden	$47,870	$37,490
7. Ireland	$47,610	$37,700
8. United States	$46,040	$45,840
9. Netherlands	$45,650	$39,470
10. United Kingdom*	$40,660	$34,050

*2006 data

Source: 2007 World Development Indicators.
Reprinted by permission of Warren Keegan Associates, Inc.

[11]Adrian Slywotzky, *Value Migration* (Cambridge, MA: Harvard Business School Press, 1996), p. 37.
[12]For a more detailed discussion, see Malcolm Gillis et al., *Economics of Development* (New York: Norton, 1996), pp. 37–40.

A case in point is Mitsubishi Motors, which had begun redesigning its Montero Sport SUV with the goal of creating a "global vehicle" that could be sold worldwide with little adaptation. Then the design program changed course; the new goal was to make the vehicle more "American" by providing more interior space and more horsepower. Hiroshi Yajima, a Mitsubishi executive in North America, attributed the change to the vibrancy and sheer size of the American auto market. "We wouldn't care if the vehicle didn't sell outside the U.S.," he said.[13]

Despite having comparable per capita incomes, other industrialized countries are nevertheless quite small in terms of *total* annual income (see Table 7-3). In Sweden, for example, per capita GNI is about $48,000; however, Sweden's smaller population—9 million—means that, in relative terms, its market is limited. This helps explain why Ericsson, IKEA, Saab, and other Swedish companies have looked beyond their borders for significant growth opportunities.

While Table 7-2 highlights the differences between straightforward income statistics and the standard of living in the world's most affluent nations, such differences can be even more pronounced in less-developed countries. A visit to a mud house in Tanzania will reveal many of the things that money can buy: an iron bed frame, a corrugated metal roof, beer and soft drinks, bicycles, shoes, photographs, radios, and even televisions. What Tanzania's per capita income of $410 does not reflect is the fact that instead of utility bills, Tanzanians have the local well and the sun. Instead of nursing homes, tradition and custom ensure that families will take care of the elderly at home. Instead of expensive doctors and hospitals, villagers may utilize the services of witch doctors and healers.

In industrialized countries, a significant portion of national income is the value of goods and services that would be free in a poor country. Thus, the standard of living in low- and lower-middle-income countries is often higher than income data might suggest; in other words, the *actual* purchasing power of the local currency may be much higher than that implied by exchange values. For example, the per capita income average for China of $2,000 equals 16,220 Chinese Renminbi (8.11 Renminbi = US$1.00), but 16,220 Renminbi will buy much more in China than $2,000 will buy in the United States. Adjusted for purchasing power parity, per capita income in China is estimated to be $5,420; this amount is more than twice as high as the unadjusted figure suggests. Similarly, calculated in terms of purchasing power, per capita income in Tanzania is approximately $1,200. Indeed, a visit to the capital city of Dar Es Salaam reveals that stores are stocked with televisions and CD players, and businesspeople can be seen negotiating deals using their cellular phones.[14]

TABLE 7-3 Top 10 Nations Ranked by GNI, 2007

Country	GNI (in millions)
1. United States	13,886,420
2. Japan	4,828,910
3. Germany	3,207,250
4. China	3,126,010
5. United Kingdom*	2,464,280
6. France	2,466,570
7. Italy	1,988,230
8. Spain	1,314,500
9. Canada	1,307,450
10. Brazil	1,122,090

*2006 data

Source: 2007 World Development Indicators.
Reprinted by permission of Warren Keegan Associates, Inc.

---

[13]Norihiko Shirouzu, "Tailoring World's Cars to U.S. Tastes," *The Wall Street Journal* (January 1, 2001), p. B1.
[14]Robert S. Greenberger, "Africa Ascendant: New Leaders Replace Yesteryear's 'Big Men,' and Tanzania Benefits," *The Wall Street Journal* (December 10, 1996), pp. A1, A6.

TABLE 7-4 The 10 Most Populous Countries, 2007

Global Income and Population	2007 Population (millions)	Percent of World Population	2007 GNI (billions)	2007 Per Capita GNI	Percent of World GNI
WORLD TOTAL	6,610.26	100.00%	$52,850.42	$7,995	100.0%
1. China	1,318.31	19.93%	3,126.01	2,000	5.9%
2. India	1,124.79	17.00%	1,071.03	820	2.0%
3. United States	301.62	4.55%	13,386.42	44,710	25.3%
4. Indonesia	225.63	3.40%	372.63	1,420	0.70%
5. Brazil	191.60	2.89%	1,122.09	4,710	2.1%
6. Pakistan	162.48	2.45%	140.24	790	0.26%
7. Russian Federation	142.10	2.14%	1,069.82	5,770	2.0%
8. Bangladesh	158.57	2.39%	74.93	450	0.12%
9. Nigeria	147.98	2.25%	135.33	620	0.3%
10. Japan	127.77	1.94%	4,828.91	37,790	9.1%

Source: 2007 World Development Indicators.
Reprinted by permission of Warren Keegan Associates, Inc.

In 2007, the 10 most populous countries in the world accounted for 47 percent of world income; the 5 most populous accounted for 36 percent (see Table 7-4). Although population is not as concentrated as income, there is, in terms of size of nations, a pattern of considerable concentration. The 10 most populous countries in the world account for roughly 60 percent of the world's population today. The concentration of income in the high-income and large-population countries means that a company can be "global" by targeting buyers in 10 or fewer countries. World population is now approximately 6.5 billion; at the present rate of growth it will reach 12 billion by the middle of the century. Simply put, global population will probably double during the lifetime of many students using this textbook.

As noted previously, for products whose price is low enough, population is a more important variable than income in determining market potential. As former Kodak CEO George Fisher commented over a decade ago, "Half the people in the world have yet to take their first picture. The opportunity is huge, and it's nothing fancy. We just have to sell yellow boxes of film."[15] Thus, China and India, with populations of 1.3 billion and 1 billion, respectively, represent attractive target markets. In a country like China, one segmentation approach would call for serving the existing mass market for inexpensive consumer products. Kao, Johnson & Johnson, Procter & Gamble, Unilever, and other packaged goods companies are targeting and developing the China market, lured in part by the presence of hundreds of millions of Chinese customers who are willing and able to spend a few cents for a single-use pouch of shampoo and other personal-care products.

McDonald's global expansion illustrates the significance of both income and population on marketing activities. On the one hand, as noted in Case 1-2, McDonald's operates in more than 120 countries. What this figure conceals, however, is that 80 percent of McDonald's restaurants are located in nine country markets: Australia, Brazil, Canada, China, France, Germany, Japan, the United Kingdom, and the United States. These nine countries generate about 75 percent of the company's total revenues. Seven of these countries appear in the top 10 GNI rankings shown in Table 7-3; however, only four appear in the Table 7-4 population rankings. At present, the restaurants in the company's approximately 100 non-major country markets contribute less than 20 percent to operating income. McDonald's is counting on an expanded presence in China and other high-population country markets to drive corporate growth in the twenty-first century.

In rapidly growing economies, marketers must take care when using income, population, and other macro-level data during the segmentation process. For example, marketers should keep

---

[15]Mark Maremont, "Kodak's New Focus," *Business Week* (January 30, 1995), p. 63.

in mind that national income figures such as those cited for China and India are averages. Using averages alone, it is possible to underestimate a market's potential; fast-growing, higher-income segments are present in both of these countries. As Harold L. Sirkin and his coauthors point out in *Globality*, the income disparity in China and India is reflected in the diversity of their huge populations. In China, this diversity manifests itself in eight major languages and several dialects and minor languages. The authors write:

> Mandarin is the dominant language in the main cities of northern China, while Cantonese is the dominant language in the south, particularly in Hong Kong. And behind each language is a unique regional history, culture, and economy that collectively give rise to radical differences in tastes, activities, and aspirations.
>
> Such differences present a major challenge for companies in the most fundamental of go-to-market activities: segmenting the population to understand motivations, expectations, and aspirations—and estimating how much spending power each segment has. It makes the term "mass market" almost meaningless. Yes, there is a mass of consumers in the rapidly developing economies, but they can hardly be addressed en masse, at least not through one set of product propositions or one campaign of spoken or written communications.[16]

The same is true in India, where approximately 10 percent of the population can be classified as "upper middle class," with average incomes of more than $1,400. Pinning down a demographic segment may require additional information; according to some estimates, India's middle class totals 300 million people. However, if the middle class segment is defined more narrowly as "households that own cars, computers, and washing machines," the figure would be much lower. According to one Indian expert, India's population can be further segmented to include a "bike" segment of 25 million households in which telephones and motorbikes are present. However, the vast majority of India's population comprises a "bullock cart" segment whose households lack most comforts but typically own a television.[17] The lesson is clear: As Samli has suggested, to avoid being misled by averages, do not *assume* homogeneity.

AGE SEGMENTATION Age is another useful demographic variable in global marketing. One global segment based on demographics is **global teens**, young people between the ages of 12 and 19. Teens, by virtue of their shared interest in fashion, music, and a youthful lifestyle, exhibit consumption behavior that is remarkably consistent across borders. As Renzo Rosso, creator of the Diesel designer jeans brand, explains, "A group of teenagers randomly chosen from different parts of the world will share many of the same tastes."[19] Young consumers may not yet have conformed to cultural norms; indeed, they may be rebelling against them. This fact, combined with shared universal wants, needs, desires, and fantasies (for name brand, novelty, entertainment, trendy, and image-oriented products), make it possible to reach the global teen segment with a unified marketing program. This segment is attractive both in terms of its size (about 1.3 billion) and its multibillion-dollar purchasing power. Coca-Cola, Benetton, Swatch, and Sony are some of the companies pursuing the global teen segment. The global telecommunications revolution is a critical driving force behind the emergence of this segment. Global media such as MTV and the Internet are perfect vehicles for reaching this segment. Satellites such as AsiaSatI are beaming Western programming and commercials to millions of viewers in China, India, and other countries.

Another global segment is the so-called **global elite**: affluent consumers who are well traveled and have the money to spend on prestigious products with an image of exclusivity (see Exhibit 7-2). Although this segment is often associated with older individuals who have accumulated wealth over the course of a long career, it also includes movie stars, musicians, elite athletes, entrepreneurs, and others who have achieved great financial success at a relatively young age. This segment's needs and wants are spread over various product categories: durable goods (luxury automobiles such as Rolls-Royce or Mercedes-Benz), nondurables (upscale beverages such as Cristal champagne or Grey Goose vodka), and financial services (American Express Gold and Platinum cards).

"Urban India is getting saturated. In the cities, everyone who can afford a television has one. If you want to maintain high growth, you have to penetrate into rural India."[18]

K. Ramachandran,
chief executive,
Philips Electronics India

[16]Harold L. Sirkin, James W. Hemerling, and Arindam K. Bhattacharya, *Globality: Competing with Everyone from Everywhere for Everything* (New York: Boston Consulting Group, 2008), p. 117.
[17]Sundeep Waslekar, "India Can Get Ahead if It Gets on a Bike," *Financial Times* (November 12, 2002), p. 15.
[18]Chris Prystay, "Companies Market to India's Have-Littles," *Wall Street Journal* (June 5, 2003), p. B1.
[19]Alice Rawsthorn, "A Hipster on Jean Therapy," *Financial Times* (August 20, 1998), p. 8.

Exhibit 7-2: Rolls-Royce, the automaker whose name is synonymous with exclusive luxury, sells about 1,000 vehicles each year. The United States accounts for about one-third of the overall market. Prices start at $400,000; the company's customers are typically members of the global elite, with more than $30 million in liquid assets. As one industry analyst noted recently, "One of the things that Rolls-Royce has been particularly good at is not corrupting its brand in the name of growth or profit." Rolls-Royce buyers often order customized vehicles; in China, one of the fastest-growing markets for luxury cars, a customer recently paid $2.2 million for a stretch version of the Phantom.
Source: Paul Young/ Reuters/Landov Media.

GENDER SEGMENTATION For obvious reasons, segmenting markets by gender is an approach that makes sense for many companies. Less obvious, however, is the need to ensure that opportunities for sharpening the focus on the needs and wants of one gender or the other do not go unnoticed. Although some companies—fashion designers and cosmetics companies, for example—market primarily or exclusively to women, other companies offer different lines of products to both genders. For example, in 2000, Nike generated $1.4 billion in global sales of women's shoes and apparel, a figure representing 16 percent of total Nike sales. Nike executives believe its global women's business is poised for big growth. To make it happen, Nike is opening concept shops inside department stores and creating free-standing retail stores devoted exclusively to women.[20] In Europe, Levi Strauss is taking a similar approach. In 2003, the company opened its first boutique for young women, Levi's for Girls, in Paris. As Suzanne Gallacher, associate brand manager for Levi's in Europe, the Middle East, and Africa, noted, "In Europe, denim is for girls."[21] The move is part of a broader strategy to boost Levi Strauss' performance in the face of strong competition from Calvin Klein and Gap in the United States and Diesel in Europe. Gallacher predicts that, if Levi's for Girls is a success in France, similar stores will be opened in other European countries.

Psychographic Segmentation

Psychographic segmentation involves grouping people in terms of their attitudes, values, and lifestyles. Data are obtained from questionnaires that require respondents to indicate the extent to which they agree or disagree with a series of statements. Psychographics is primarily associated with SRI International, a market research organization whose original Values and Lifestyles (VALS) and updated VALS 2 analyses of consumers are widely known. Finland's Nokia relies heavily on psychographic segmentation of mobile phone users; its most important segments are "poseurs," "trendsetters," "social contact seekers," and "highfliers." By carefully studying these segments and tailoring products to each, Nokia has captured 40 percent of the world's market for mobile communication devices.[22]

Porsche AG, the German sports car maker, turned to psychographics after experiencing a worldwide sales decline from 50,000 units in 1986 to about 14,000 in 1993. Its U.S. subsidiary, Porsche

[20]Paula Stepanowsky, "Nike Tones Up Its Marketing to Women with Concept Shops, New Apparel Lines," *The Wall Street Journal* (September 5, 2001), p. B19.

[21]John Tagliabue, "2 Sexes Separated by a Common Levi's," *The New York Times* (September 30, 2003), p. W1.

[22]John Micklethwait and Adrian Wooldridge, *Future Perfect: The Challenge and Hidden Promise of Globalization* (New York: Crown Business, 2000), p. 131.

Cars North America, already had a clear demographic profile of its typical customer: a 40-plus-year-old male college graduate whose annual income exceeded $200,000. A psychographic study showed that, demographics aside, Porsche buyers could be divided into several distinct categories. Top Guns, for example, buy Porsches and expect to be noticed; for Proud Patrons and Fantasists, on the other hand, such conspicuous consumption is irrelevant. Porsche used the profiles to develop advertising tailored to each type. As Richard Ford, Porsche vice president of sales and marketing, noted: "We were selling to people whose profiles were diametrically opposed. You wouldn't want to tell an elitist how good he looks in the car or how fast he could go." The results were impressive; Porsche's U.S. sales improved nearly 50 percent after a new advertising campaign was launched.[23]

Honda's recent experience in Europe demonstrates the potential value of using psychographic segmentation to supplement the use of more traditional variables such as demographics. When Honda executives were developing a communication strategy to support the European launch of the company's new HR-V sport utility vehicle in the late 1990s, they brought together a panel of experts from the United Kingdom, Germany, France, and Italy. The goal was to develop a pan-European advertising campaign targeted squarely at a relatively young demographic. The researchers agreed that, irrespective of nationality, European youth exhibit more similarities than differences: They listen to the same music, enjoy the same films, and pursue the same recreational activities. The resulting ad campaign, dubbed "Joy Machine," was targeted at 25- to 35-year-olds. However, the HR-V proved to be popular with Europeans of *all* ages; in fact, one out of six buyers was a grandparent! Reflecting on this turn of events, Chris Brown, an advertising executive at Honda Motor Europe, noted, "The decision within advertising should be about attitudes, not ages. I was recently reminded that [former British prime minister] John Major and Mick Jagger of the Rolling Stones are the same age."[24]

Brown's statement underscores the insight that people of the same age don't necessarily have the same attitudes, just as people in one age bracket sometimes share attitudes with those in other age brackets. Sometimes it is preferable to market to a mind-set rather than a particular age group; in such an instance, psychographic studies can help marketers arrive at a deeper understanding of consumer behavior than is possible with traditional segmentation variables such as demographics.

However, such understanding comes at a price. Psychographic market profiles are available from a number of different sources; companies may pay thousands of dollars to use these studies. SRI International has created psychographic profiles of the Japanese market; broader-scope studies have been undertaken by several global advertising agencies. For example, a research team at D'arcy Massius Benton & Bowles (DMBB) focused on Europe and produced a 15-country study entitled "The Euroconsumer: Marketing Myth or Cultural Certainty?"[25] The researchers identified four lifestyle groups: Successful Idealists, Affluent Materialists, Comfortable Belongers, and Disaffected Survivors. The first two groups represent the elite, the latter two, mainstream European consumers:

Successful Idealists Comprising from 5 percent to 20 percent of the population, this segment consists of persons who have achieved professional and material success while maintaining commitment to abstract or socially responsible ideals.

Affluent Materialists These status-conscious "up-and-comers"—many of whom are business professionals—use conspicuous consumption to communicate their success to others.

Comfortable Belongers Comprising one-fourth to one-half of a country's population, this group, like Global Scan's Adapters and Traditionals, is conservative and most comfortable with the familiar. Belongers are content with the comfort of home, family, friends, and community.

Disaffected Survivors Lacking power and affluence, this segment harbors little hope for upward mobility and tends to be either resentful or resigned. This segment is concentrated in high-crime urban inner-city-type neighborhoods. Despite Disaffecteds' lack of societal status, their attitudes nevertheless tend to affect the rest of society.

The segmentation and targeting approach used by a company can vary from country to country. In Europe Levi Strauss is relying heavily on gender segmentation. By contrast, former CEO Phil

---

[23]Alex Taylor III, "Porsche Slices Up Its Buyers," *Fortune* (January 16, 1995), p. 24.

[24]Ian Morton, "Target Advertising Is Not an Exact Science," *Automotive News Europe* (June 19, 2000), p. 28.

[25]The following discussion is adapted from Rebecca Piirto, *Beyond Mind Games: The Marketing Power of Psychographics* (Ithaca, NY: American Demographics Books, 1991).

EMERGING MARKETS BRIEFING BOOK

⟩ Psychographic Segmentation in Russia

Several years ago, the DMBB agency created a psychographic profile of the Russian market. The study divides Russians into five categories, based on their outlook, behavior, and openness to Western products. The categories include *kuptsy*, Cossacks, students, business executives, and Russian Souls. Members of the largest group, the *kuptsy* (the label comes from the Russian word for "merchant"), theoretically prefer Russian products but look down on mass-produced goods of inferior quality. *Kuptsy* are most likely to admire automobiles and stereo equipment from countries with good reputations for engineering, such as Germany and Scandinavia. Nigel Clarke, the author of the study, notes that segmentation and targeting are appropriate in Russia, despite the fact that its broad consumer market was still in its infancy. "If you're dealing with a market as different as Russia is, even if you want to go 'broad,' it's best to think: 'Which group would go most for my brand? Where is my natural center of gravity?'"

The study's marketing implications became clearer in the late 1990s. Market share growth for many Western brands began to slow; the trend accelerated after the economic crisis of 1998. As Sergei Platinin, director of a Russian company that markets fruit juices, noted, "People used to want only to buy things that looked foreign. Now they want Russian." In the world of fashion, expensive blue jeans from designer Valentin Yudashkin supplanted Armani as *the* hip jeans. At the other end of the price spectrum, McDonald's began offering *pirozhki*—meat and cheese pies. The local Nestlé subsidiary has revived several brands of Russian chocolate candies. According to a survey conducted by Comcon 2, nearly two-thirds of upper-income Russians prefer to buy domestic chocolates, even though they can afford to buy imported brands.

As for behavioral segmentation, Diageo PLC, V&S Vin & Spirit AB, Seagram, and other marketers of distilled spirits know that Russians consume a great deal of vodka. (In fact, the word *vodka* is derived from the Russian word for "water," and Russians believe vodka originated in their country in the fourteenth century.) Annual vodka consumption in Russia is about four billion liters—14.4 liters per capita, the highest in the world. However, as noted previously, Russian consumers have recently shown an increased preference for domestic brands. Production of homemade vodka, known as *samogon*, and illegal bootleg vodka surpasses official production by a ratio of 2 to 1 (see Figure 7-1 and Exhibit 7-3) and the Russian government loses billions in annual tax revenues. As a result of high

duties, as well as the marketing goal of retaining a premium image, imports such as Smirnoff and Absolut are priced significantly higher than local brands. To date, imported vodka brands have captured only a small share of the Russian market.

In the late 1990s, economic uncertainty was high and workers went for months without being paid. In such an environment price is a significant factor. An entrepreneur named Vladimir Dovgan has prospered by launching several different brands of vodka priced between $5 and $10 per bottle. Dovgan's picture is featured on the label, and he also appears in print and television ads. Meanwhile, Diageo PLC began producing Smirnoff in St. Petersburg. Ironically, Smirnoff's heritage is truly Russian, although for decades the brand was produced only in the West. As a company executive noted, "This should make Smirnoff seem more Russian. We want Russians to realize that Smirnoff came to Russia to produce for Russians."

Even as marketers of distilled spirits adjust their strategies, market preferences are changing; young Russians are turning to beer, with demand up 25 percent in the five-year period between 1995–2000. In 2002, expenditures on beer surpassed vodka for the first time. Local brands are favored, as the weak ruble priced imports out of the reach of the average consumer. Some observers attribute the change to the influence of healthier, Western lifestyles. Also, vodka is associated with heavy drinking during Russia's tumultuous transition to a market economy in the 1990s. Even so, vodka is still an $11 billion market in Russia. One of the top-selling brands today is Putinka; the name evokes an association with Russia's economic prosperity under former President Vladimir Putin.

Sources: Andrew Osborn, "Vodkas Reflect Allure of Power," *The Wall Street Journal* (March 10, 2009), p. B4; Nick Paton Walsh, "Russia Lite: Nyet to Vodka, Da to Beer," *The Observer* (October 20, 2002); Ernest Beck, "Absolut Frustration: Why Foreign Distillers Find It So Hard to Sell Vodka to the Russians," *The Wall Street Journal* (January 15, 1998), pp. A1, A9; Betsy McKay, "Vladimir Dovgan Is a Constant Presence in Capitalist Russia," *The Wall Street Journal* (March 20, 1998), pp. A1, A8; Stuart Elliot, "Figuring Out the Russian Consumer," *The New York Times* (April 1, 1992), pp. C1, C19; Betsy McKay, "In Russia, West No Longer Means Best; Consumers Shift to Home-Grown Goods," *The Wall Street Journal* (December 9, 1996), p. A9; John Varoli, "Bored by Vodka, Russians Find More Style in Beer," *The New York Times* (December 19, 1999), sec. 3, p. 7.

Marineau believed that a psychographic segmentation strategy was the key to revitalizing the venerable jeans brand in its home market. Marineau's team identified several different segments, including "fashionistas," trendy teens, middle-aged men, and budget shoppers. The goal was to create different styles of jeans at different price points for each segment and to make them available at stores ranging from Walmart to Neiman Marcus.[26] Likewise, Sony Electronics, a unit of Sony Corp. of America, undertook a reorganization of its marketing function. Traditionally, Sony had approached marketing from a product category point of view. It changed philosophy so that a new unit, the Consumer Segment Marketing Division, would be responsible for getting closer to consumers in the United States (see Table 7-5).[27] What variables did Sony use to develop these categories?

---

[26]Sally Beatty, "At Levi Strauss, Trouble Comes from All Angles," *The Wall Street Journal* (October 13, 2003), pp. B1, B3.
[27]Tobi Elkin, "Sony Marketing Aims at Lifestyle Segments," *Advertising Age* (March 18, 2002), pp. 1, 72.

Official vs. Total Production . . .

. . . And vs. Total Capacity

FIGURE 7-1
Russia's Vodka Industry

Official production and imports
234

Illegally or home-produced vodka
371.8

Production Capacity[a]

Official Production

0   250   500   750   1000
Millions of gallons

Russian vodka consumption, 1997[b]	557.96 million gallons
Money lost on unaccounted-for output[c]	$1.89 billion

[a]For 800 enterprises licensed to produce hard, or 128-proof, liquor
[b]Consumption level is believed to be much higher
[c]Converted to U.S. dollars from rubles at current rate

Exhibit 7-3: Home-brew vodka is a staple in Russia. Consider the following excerpt from Vladimir Voinovich's satirical novel *The Life and Extraordinary Adventures of Private Ivan Chonkin*:

"They clinked glasses. Ivan downed the contents of his glass and nearly fell of his chair. He instantly lost his breath, just as if he'd been punched in the stomach . . .

Gladishev, who had downed his own glass without any difficulty, looked over at Ivan with a sly grin. 'Well, Ivan, how's the home brew?'

'First rate stuff,' praised Chonkin, wiping the tears from his eyes with the palm of his hand. 'Takes your breath away.'"

Source: Oleg Nikishin/Getty Images.

Behavior Segmentation

Behavior segmentation focuses on whether or not people buy and use a product, as well as how often and how much they use or consume. Consumers can be categorized in terms of **usage rates**: for example, heavy, medium, light, and non-user. Consumers can also be segmented according to **user status**: potential users, non-users, ex-users, regulars, first-timers, and users of competitors' products. Marketers sometimes refer to the **80/20 rule** when assessing usage rates. This rule (also known as the *law of disproportionality* or Pareto's Law) suggests that 80 percent of a company's revenues or profits are accounted for by 20 percent of a firm's products or customers. As noted earlier, nine country markets generate about 80 percent of McDonald's revenues. This situation presents McDonald's executives with strategy alternatives: Should the company pursue growth in the handful of countries where it is already well known and popular? Or, should it focus on expansion and growth opportunities in the scores of countries that, as yet, contribute little to revenues and profits?

TABLE 7-5 Sony's U.S. Consumer Segments

Segment	Description
Affluent	High-income consumers
CE Alphas	Early adopters of high-tech consumer electronics products, irrespective of age
Zoomers	55 years old or older
SoHo	Small office/home office
Families	35 to 54 years old
Young professionals/D.I.N.K.S.	Dual income no kids, 25 to 34 years old
Gen Y	Younger than 25 years old (includes tweens, teens, college students)

Benefit Segmentation

Global **benefit segmentation** focuses on the numerator of the value equation: the B in V = B/P. This approach is based on marketers' superior understanding of the problem a product solves, the benefit it offers, or the issue it addresses, regardless of geography. Food marketers are finding success creating products that can help parents create nutritious family meals with a minimal investment of time. Campbell Soup is making significant inroads into Japan's $500 million soup market as time-pressed homemakers place a premium on convenience. Marketers of health and beauty aids also use benefit segmentation. Many toothpaste brands are straightforward cavity fighters, and as such they reach a very broad market. However, as consumers become more concerned about whitening, sensitive teeth, gum disease, and other oral care issues, marketers are developing new toothpaste brands suited to the different sets of perceived needs.

> ## STRATEGIC DECISION MAKING IN GLOBAL MARKETING
> ### Segmenting Europe's Single Market

It may be a single market, but the demographics of twenty-first century Europe still offer ample opportunities for market segmentation. One approach known as "3G" addresses issues pertaining to three distinct segments: people born between 1980 and 2000 (Generation Y), adults 60 years old and older (the Golden Grays), and transnational corporations ("Globerations").

The following trends and traits associated with each have major implications for marketing strategy in the years 2008 and beyond.

GENERATION Y

- share few family activities
- display less reverence toward established authorities
- approach leisure time as "pay-per-play"
- maintain a heavy diet that is heavily weighted toward "convenience food"
- are tech savvy
- are deluged with passive information

GOLDEN GRAYS

- consider it important to mix fun and work
- are relatively affluent, meaning more out-of-home activities
- enjoy high-tech gaming
- expect home health care devices and biotechnology to extend life expectancy
- are deluged with passive information

GLOBERATIONS

- employees will be less inclined to leave their companies as nations gradually reduce the benefits associated with the "social safety net"
- knowledge workers will be challenged finding work-life balance
- customers will want build-to-order solutions
- online auctions will be a significant sales channel
- a few, powerful consumer-to-business buying groups will emerge

Given these trends, which industries will be the winners and which will be the losers? Likely losers in the leisure sector will include general interest consumer magazines and national newspapers; winners will include interactive services, audio books, and social sports such as golf and tennis. Business services losers will likely be newspaper publishers, grocery coupon distributors, and mass-market retailers. Winning services offerings will likely be corporate concierges, personalized telecom networks, and domestic services. Marketers are particularly advised to take the Golden Grays seriously and market brands that provide happiness, convenience, and time savings.

Source: Allyson L. Stewart-Allen, "EU's Future Consumers: Three Groups to Watch," *Marketing News* 35, no. 12 (June 4, 2001), pp. 9–10.

→ CULTURE WATCH
Segmenting the Market for Personal-Care Products

Worldwide, only about 100 million women use tampons; the total market potential is estimated to be 1.7 billion women. In the mid-1990s, Tambrands, marketers of Tampax brand tampons, approached market segmentation in terms of how resistant women are to using tampons. Cluster 1 (the United States, the United Kingdom, and Australia) is comprised of women who use tampons and believe themselves to be well informed about them. Tampon use in Cluster 2 (France, Israel, and South Africa) is limited to about 50 percent of women; some women in this cluster are concerned that tampon use may result in a loss of virginity. Advertising to women in Cluster 2 will focus on endorsements by gynecologists.

Cluster 3, which includes Brazil, Russia, and China, presents the biggest challenge. In these markets, Tambrands must deal with two issues: virginity concerns and the fact that most women in the cluster have little or no experience using tampons. Despite the fact that advertising messages will vary by cluster, each ad will end with the slogan "Tampax. Women Know." Tambrands allocated $65 million for an advertising campaign targeted at the three clusters in 27 countries. One risk: The campaign's frank language would offend women. Commenting on Tambrands' plans, Jeffrey Hill of Meridian Consulting Group commented, "The greatest challenge in the global expansion of tampons is to address the religious and cultural mores that suggest that vaginal insertion is fundamentally prohibited by culture."

Sources: Emily Nelson and Miriam Jordan, "Sensitive Export: Seeking New Markets for Tampons, P&G Faces Cultural Barriers," *The Wall Street Journal* (December 8, 2000), pp. A1, A8; Yumiko Ono, "Tambrands Ads Aim to Overcome Cultural and Religious Obstacles," *The Wall Street Journal* (March 17, 1997), p. B8; Dyan Machan, "Will the Chinese Use Tampons?" *Forbes* (January 16, 1995), pp. 86–87.

The European pet food market represents $30 billion in annual sales. Nestlé discovered that cat owners' attitudes toward feeding their pets are the same everywhere. In response, a pan-European campaign was created for Friskies Dry Cat Food. The appeal was that dry cat food better suits a cat's universally recognized independent nature. Likewise, many Europeans are concerned with improving the health and longevity of their pets. Accordingly, Procter & Gamble is marketing its Iams brand premium pet food as a way to improve pets' health.[28]

Ethnic Segmentation

In many countries, the population includes ethnic groups of significant size. In the United States, for example, there are three major ethnic segments: African/Black Americans, Asian Americans, and Hispanic Americans. Each segment shows great diversity and can be further subdivided. For example, Asian Americans include Thai Americans, Vietnamese Americans, and Chinese Americans, each of whom speak a different language. By contrast, America's Hispanic population includes Mexican Americans, Puerto Rican Americans, Cuban Americans, and others who share a common language. The Hispanic American segment is comprised of more than 40 million people, representing about 14 percent of the population and $560 billion in annual buying power. As a group, Hispanic Americans are hard working and exhibit a strong family and religious orientation. In addition, consider the following statistics:

- Mexican households in California have after-tax income of $100 billion, half the total of all Mexican Americans.
- The number of Hispanic teens is projected to swell from 12 percent of the U.S. teen population to 18 percent in the next decade.

From a marketing point of view, these groups offer great opportunity. Companies in a variety of industry sectors, including food and beverages, consumer durables, and leisure and financial services, are recognizing the need to include these segments when preparing marketing programs for the United States. For example, companies based in Mexico are zeroing in on opportunities to the north. Three Mexican retailers—Famso, Grupo Gigant SA, and Grupo Comercial Chedraui

---

[28]Sarah Ellison and Emily Nelson, "Pet-Food Companies Compete to Be the Pick of the Litter," *The Wall Street Journal* (July 31, 2001), p. B11.

SA—have opened stores in the United States. As Famsa president Humberto Garza Valdez explained at the grand opening of a store in San Fernando, California, "We're not coming to the U.S. to face big companies like Circuit City or Best Buy. Our focus is the Hispanic market."[29]

From 1999 through 2000, new-vehicle registrations by Hispanics in the United States grew 20 percent, twice the overall national growth rate. Honda, Toyota, and other Japanese automakers have been courting U.S. Hispanics for years and have built up a great deal of brand loyalty. Ford and GM are playing catch up, with mixed results; despite large increases in advertising targeting Hispanics, GM's market share is slipping.[30] Sales of Corona Extra beer in the United States have grown dramatically, thanks in part to savvy marketing to the Hispanic segment. In lower-income neighborhoods, imported premium beer brands represent "affordable luxuries." Although a six-pack of Corona typically costs at least a dollar more than Budweiser at a local bodega, it is usually priced lower than Heineken. Marketers must understand, though, that many Hispanic Americans live in two worlds; while they identify strongly with the United States, there is also a sense of pride associated with brands that connect to their heritage.[31]

The preceding discussion outlines the way global companies (and the research and advertising agencies that serve them) use market segmentation to identify, define, understand, and respond to customer wants and needs on a worldwide basis. In addition to the segmentation variables previously discussed, new segmentation approaches are being developed in response to today's rapidly changing business environment. For example, the widespread adoption of the Internet and other new technologies creates a great deal of commonality among global consumers. These consumer subcultures are comprised of people whose similar outlooks and aspirations create a shared mindset that transcends language or national differences. Consumer products giant Procter & Gamble is one company that is attuned to the changing times. As Melanie Healey, president of P&G's Global Health and Feminine Care unit, notes, "We're seeing global tribes forming around the world that are more and more interconnected through technology."[32]

ASSESSING MARKET POTENTIAL AND CHOOSING TARGET MARKETS OR SEGMENTS[33]

After segmenting the market by one or more of the criteria just discussed, the next step is to assess the attractiveness of the identified segments. This part of the process is especially important when sizing up emerging country markets as potential targets. It is at this stage that global marketers should be mindful of several potential pitfalls associated with the market segmentation process. First, there is a tendency to overstate the size and short-term attractiveness of individual country markets, especially when estimates are based primarily on demographic data such as income and population. For example, while China, India, Brazil, and other emerging markets undoubtedly offer potential in the long run, management must realize that short-term profit and revenue growth objectives may be hard to achieve. During the 1990s, Procter & Gamble and other consumer packaged-goods companies learned this lesson in Latin America. By contrast, the success of McDonald's Russia during the same period is a case study in the rewards of persistence and long-term outlook. A second trap that global marketers can set for themselves is to target a country because shareholders or competitors exert pressure on management not to "miss out" on a strategic opportunity. Recall from Chapter 2, for example, the statement by India's finance minister that the twenty-first century will be "the century of India." Such pronouncements can create the impression that management must "act now" to take advantage of a limited window of opportunity. Third,

---

[29]Joel Millman, "Mexican Retailers Enter U.S. to Capture Latino Dollars," *The Wall Street Journal* (February 8, 2001), p. A18.

[30]Eduardo Porter, "Ford, Other Auto Makers Target Hispanic Community," *The Wall Street Journal* (November 9, 2000), p. B4.

[31]Suein L. Hwang, "Corona Ads Target Hispanics in Effort to Hop to Head of U.S. Beer Market," *The Wall Street Journal Europe* (November 21–22, 1997), p. 9; Michael Barone, "How Hispanics Are Americanizing," *The Wall Street Journal* (February 6, 1998), p. A22.

[32]Carol Hymowitz, "Marketers Focus More on Global 'Tribes' Than on Nationalities," *The Wall Street Journal* (December 10, 2007), p. B1.

[33]Parts of the following discussion are adapted from David Arnold, *The Mirage of Global Markets* (Upper Saddle River, NJ: Pearson Education, 2004), Chapter 2.

there is a danger that management's network of contacts will emerge as a primary criterion for targeting. The result can be market entry based on convenience rather than rigorous market analysis. For example, a company may enter into a distribution agreement with a non-national employee who wants to represent the company after returning to his or her home country. The issue of choosing the right foreign distributor will be discussed in detail in Chapter 12.

With these pitfalls in mind, marketers can utilize three basic criteria for assessing opportunity in global target markets: current size of the segment and anticipated growth potential, competition, and compatibility with the company's overall objectives and the feasibility of successfully reaching a designated target.

Current Segment Size and Growth Potential

Is the market segment currently large enough to present a company with the opportunity to make a profit? If the answer is "no" today, does it have significant growth potential to make it attractive in terms of a company's long-term strategy? Consider the following facts about India:

- India is the world's fastest growing cell phone market. The industry is expanding at an annual rate of 50 percent, with 5 to 6 million new subscribers added every month. By mid-2008, India had 261 million cell phone users; that number is expected to increase to 500 million by 2010. Even so, barriers originating in the political and regulatory environments have shackled private-sector growth.[34]
- About 1.3 million cars are sold each year in India; in absolute terms, this is a relatively small number. However, industry observers forecast that the market will expand to 3 million cars within a decade. In 2008, India overtook China as the world's fastest-growing car market.[35]
- 60 million middle-class Indian men and women earn more than $275 per month. The segment is growing rapidly and is expected to number 73 million by 2010. Young, brand-conscious consumers are buying $100 Tommy Hilfiger jeans and $690 Louis Vuitton handbags. Mohan Murjani owns the rights to the Tommy Hilfiger brand in India. Commenting on the country's decade-long economic boom, he notes, "Aspirationally, things changed dramatically. What we were seeing was huge growth in terms of consumers' assets, in terms of their incomes and in terms of their spending power through credit."[36]

As noted earlier, one of the advantages of targeting a market segment globally is that, while the segment in a single-country market might be small, even a narrow segment can be served profitably if the segment exists in several countries. The billion-plus members of the global MTV Generation are a case in point (see Case 7-3). Moreover, by virtue of its size and purchasing power, the global teen segment is extremely attractive to consumer goods companies. In the case of a huge country market such as India or China, segment size and growth potential may be assessed in a different manner.

From the perspective of a consumer packaged goods company, for example, low incomes and the absence of a distribution infrastructure offset the fact that 75 percent of India's population lives in rural areas. The appropriate decision may be to target urban areas only, even though they are home to only 25 percent of the population. Visa's strategy in China perfectly illustrates this criterion as it relates to demographics: Visa is targeting persons with a monthly salary equivalent to $300 or more. The company estimates that currently 60 million people fit that description; by 2010, the number could include as many as 200 million people (see Exhibit 7-4).

Thanks to a combination of favorable demographics and lifestyle-related needs, the United States has been a very attractive market for foreign automakers. For example, demand for sports utility vehicles exploded during the 1990s. From 1990 to 2000, SUV sales tripled, growing from nearly 1 million units in 1990 to 2 million units in 1996 and passing 3 million sold in 2000. Why are these vehicles so popular? Primarily it is the security of four-wheel drive and the higher clearance for extra traction in adverse driving conditions. They also typically have more space for

---

[34]Amol Sharma and Jackie Range, "AT&T, Others Hit by Challenges in India," *The Wall Street Journal* (May 15, 2008), p. B8. See also Eric Bellman, "India's Cell Phone Boom May Lose Charge," *The Wall Street Journal* (August 25, 2006), p. A6.

[35]Heather Timmons, "In India, a $2,500 Pace Car," *The New York Times* (October 12, 2007), p. C1.

[36]Eric Bellman, "As Economy Grows, India Goes for Designer Goods," *The Wall Street Journal* (March 27, 2007), pp. A1, A17. See also Christina Passariello, "Beauty Fix: Behind L'Oréal's Makeover in India: Going Upscale," *The Wall Street Journal* (July 13, 2007), pp. A1, A14.

Exhibit 7-4: In China, only about 1 percent of the population currently owns a credit card. That means roughly 13 million cards for 1.3 billion people. Albert Shiung, China vice president for Visa International Asia Pacific, predicts that 50 million credit cards will be in circulation by 2010. Visa offers cards bearing the Chinese Olympic symbol: a dancing figure based on the Chinese character *jing* that means "capital." The Chinese government stipulated that 60 percent of stores with annual sales of 1 million yuan or more would accept credit cards before the opening ceremonies for the 2008 Olympics Games.
Source: Ng Han Guan/AP Wide World Photos.

hauling cargo. Reacting to high demand for the Jeep Cherokee, Ford Explorer, and Chevy Blazer, manufacturers from outside the United States introduced models of their own at a variety of price points (see Table 7-6). Dozens of SUV models are available as Toyota, Mazda, Honda, Kia, Nissan, Rover, BMW, Mercedes, Volkswagen, and other global automakers target American buyers. Many manufacturers offer various SUV styles, including full-size, mid-size, compact, and crossover SUVs. Even as growth slows in the United States, SUVs are growing in popularity in many other countries. In China, for example, SUVs represent the fastest-growing sector in the auto industry; SUVs account for about 40 percent of auto imports. Officials at GM's Cadillac division are considering exporting the company's popular $50,000-plus Escalade model to China.[37]

Potential Competition

A market segment or country market characterized by strong competition may be a segment to avoid. However, if the competition is vulnerable in terms of price or quality disadvantages, it is possible for a market newcomer to make significant inroads. Over the past several decades, for example, Japanese companies in a variety of industries targeted the U.S. market despite the presence of entrenched domestic market leaders. Some of the newcomers proved to be extremely

TABLE 7-6 Global Automakers Targeting the U.S. Market with SUVs

Automaker	Select SUV Model	Country of Assembly or Manufacture	Year Introduced
Porsche	Cayenne	Germany	2003
Volkswagen	Touareg	Slovakia	2004
Honda	CR-V	Japan	1995
Toyota	RAV-4	Japan	1994
Kia	Sorento	South Korea	2003
BMW	X5	United States	2000
Mercedes-Benz	ML 350	United States	2003

[37]Peter Wonacott and Lee Hawkins Jr., "Saying 'Beamer' in Chinese," *The Wall Street Journal* (November 6, 2003), p. B1. See also Joseph B. White, "Rollback: America's Love Affair with Sport Utilities Is Now Cooling Off," *The Wall Street Journal* (May 30, 2001), pp. A1, A8.

adept at segmenting and targeting; as a result, they made significant inroads. In the motorcycle industry, for example, Honda first created the market for small-displacement dirt bikes. The company then moved upmarket with bigger bikes targeted at casual riders whose psychographic profiles were quite different than that of the hard-core Harley-Davidson rider. In document imaging, Canon outflanked Xerox by offering compact desktop copiers and targeting department managers and secretaries. Similar case studies can be found in earthmoving equipment (Komatsu versus Caterpillar), photography (Fuji versus Kodak), and numerous other industries. By contrast, there are also many examples of companies whose efforts to develop a position in the United States ended in failure. For example, in the computer industry, Acer failed to make headway in a U.S. market dominated by such strong brand names such as Dell (see Case 1-3).

Feasibility and Compatibility

If a market segment is judged to be large enough, and if strong competitors are either absent or deemed to be vulnerable, then the final consideration is whether a company can and should target that market. The feasibility of targeting a particular segment can be negatively impacted by various factors. For example, significant regulatory hurdles may be present that limit market access. This issue is especially important in China today. The company may also encounter cultural barriers, as was the case with Tambrands' efforts to build its feminine-hygiene market. Other marketing-specific issues can arise; in India, for example, three to five years are required to build an effective distribution system for many consumer products. This fact may serve as a deterrent to foreign companies that might otherwise be attracted by the apparent potential of India's large population.[38]

Managers must decide how well a company's product fits the country market in question—or, as noted, if the company does not currently offer a suitable product, can it develop one? To make this decision, a marketer must consider several criteria:

- Will adaptation be required? If so, is this economically justifiable in terms of the expected sales volume?
- Will import restrictions, high tariffs, or a strong home-country currency drive up the price of the product in the target market currency and effectively dampen demand?
- Is it advisable to source locally? In many cases, reaching global market segments requires considerable expenditures for distribution and travel by company personnel. Would it make sense to source products in the country for export elsewhere in the region?

Finally, it is important to address the question of whether targeting a particular segment is compatible with the company's overall goals, its brand image, or established sources of competitive advantage. For example, BMW is one of the world's premium auto brands. Should BMW add a minivan to its product lineup? As former BMW CEO Helmut Panke once explained, "There is a segment in the market which BMW is not catering to and that is the minivan or MPV segment. We don't have a van because a van as it is in the market today does not fulfill any of the BMW group brand values. We all as a team said 'no.'"[39]

A Framework for Selecting Target Markets

As one can infer from this discussion, it would be extremely useful to have formal tools or frameworks available when assessing emerging country markets. Table 7-7 presents a market selection

TABLE 7-7 Market Selection Framework

Market	Market Size	Competitive Advantage		Market Potential	Terms of Access	Market Potential
China (1.3 billion)	100	.07	=	7	.50	3.5
Russia (150 million)	50	.10	=	5	.60	3.0
Mexico (94 million)	20	.20	=	4	.90	3.6

---

[38]Khozem Merchant, "Sweet Rivals Find Love in a Warm Climate," *Financial Times* (July 24, 2003), p. 9.
[39]Neal E. Boudette, "BMW's CEO Just Says 'No' to Protect Brand," *The Wall Street Journal* (November 26, 2003), p. B1.

framework that incorporates some of the elements just discussed. Suppose an American company has identified China, Russia, and Mexico as potential country target markets. The table shows the countries arranged in declining rank by market size. At first glance, China might appear to hold the greatest potential simply on the basis of size. However, the competitive advantage of our hypothetical firm is 0.07 in China, 0.10 in Russia, and 0.20 in Mexico. Multiplying the market size and competitive advantage index yields a market potential of 7 in China, 5 in Russia, and 4 in Mexico.

The next stage in the analysis requires an assessment of the various market access considerations. In Table 7-7 all these conditions or terms are reduced to an index number of terms of access, which is 0.50 for China, 0.60 for Russia, and 0.90 for Mexico. In other words, the "market access considerations" are more favorable in Mexico than in Russia, perhaps in this instance due to NAFTA. Multiplying the market potential by the terms of access index suggests that Mexico, despite its small size, holds greater market potential than China or Russia.

Although the framework in Table 7-7 should prove useful as a preliminary screening tool for inter-country comparisons, it does not go far enough in terms of assessing actual market potential. Global marketing expert David Arnold has developed a framework that goes beyond demographic data and considers other, marketing-oriented assessments of market size and growth potential. Instead of a "top-down" segmentation analysis beginning with, for example, income or population data from a particular country, Arnold's framework is based on a "bottom-up" analysis that begins at the product-market level. The term **product-market** can be used to describe a market defined by a product category; in the automotive industry, for example, phrases such as "luxury car market," "SUV market," and "minivan market" refer to specific product-markets. By contrast, phrases such as "the Russian market" or "the Indian market" refer to country markets.

As shown in Figure 7-2, Arnold's framework incorporates two core concepts: marketing model drivers and enabling conditions. **Marketing model drivers** are key elements or factors required for a business to take root and grow in a particular country market environment. The drivers may differ depending on whether a company serves consumer or industrial markets. Does success hinge on establishing or leveraging a brand name? In Vietnam, for example, Procter & Gamble promotes its Tide detergent brand as "Number 1 in America." Or, is distribution or a tech-savvy sales staff the key element? Marketing executives seeking an opportunity must arrive at insights into the true driving force(s) that will affect success for their particular product-market.

Enabling conditions are structural market characteristics whose presence or absence can determine whether the marketing model can succeed. For example, in India, refrigeration is not widely available in shops and market food stalls. This creates challenges for Nestlé and Cadbury as they attempt to capitalize on Indians' increasing appetite for chocolate confections. Although Nestlé's KitKat and Cadbury's Dairy Milk bars have been reformulated to better withstand heat,

FIGURE 7-2

Screening Criteria for Market Segments

Source: Adapted from David Arnold, *The Mirage of Global Markets* (Upper Saddle River, NJ: Pearson Education, 2004), p. 36.

the absence or rudimentary nature of refrigeration hampers the companies' efforts to ensure their products are in saleable condition.

After marketing model drivers and enabling conditions have been identified, the third step is for management to weigh the estimated costs associated with entering and serving the market with potential short- and long-term revenue streams. Does this segment or country market merit entry now? Or, would it be better to wait until specific enabling conditions are established? The issue of timing is often framed in terms of the quest for **first-mover advantage**. The conventional wisdom is that the first company to enter a market has the best chance of becoming the market leader. Examples from the history of global marketing that appear to support this notion include the Coca-Cola Company, which established itself globally during World War II. However, there are also first-mover *disadvantages*. The first company to enter a market often makes substantial investments in marketing only to find that a late-arriving competitor reaps some of the benefits. There is ample evidence that late entrants into global markets can also achieve success. One way they do this is by benchmarking established companies and then outmaneuvering them, first locally and then globally. Jollibee, the Philippines-based fast-food chain whose business model was influenced by McDonald's, is a case in point.

Late movers can also succeed by developing innovative business models. This approach was used by Stephen Millar, chief executive of Australian wine producer BRL Hardy. Millar's insight was that no leading global brand had emerged in the wine business; in other words, there was no equivalent to Coca-Cola. During the 1990s, Millar established Hardy as a leading global brand. He accomplished this by moving on several fronts. First, he took control of the sales function. Second, he made sure Hardy's wines were crafted to appeal to a broader demographic than "wine snobs" who tend to favor bottles from France and Italy. Third, he supplemented Hardy's line of Australian wines with select brands from other countries. In 2002 Hardy sold 20 million cases of wine worldwide. Today, Hardy is one of the world's top 10 wine companies.[40]

One way to determine the marketing model drivers and enabling conditions is to create a product-market profile. The profile should address some or all of the following basic questions:

1. Who buys our product or brand?
2. Who does not buy our product or brand?
3. What need or function does our product serve? Does our product or brand address that need?
4. Is there a market need that is not being met by current product or brand offerings?
5. What problem does our product solve?
6. What are customers currently buying to satisfy the need, or solve the problem, that our product targets?
7. What price are they paying for the product they are currently buying?
8. When is our product purchased?
9. Where is our product purchased?

PRODUCT-MARKET DECISIONS

The next step in assessing market segments is a company review of current and potential product offerings in terms of their suitability for the country market or segment. This assessment can be performed by creating a product-market grid that maps markets as horizontal rows on a spreadsheet and products as vertical columns. Each cell represents the possible intersection of a product and a market segment. In the case of the candy companies just discussed, both Nestlé and Cadbury determined that a liquid chocolate confection would be one way to address the issue of India's hot weather. The companies are also working to improve the enabling conditions for selling traditional chocolate treats by supplying coolers to merchants.

---

[40]Christopher A. Bartlett and Sumantra Ghoshal, "Going Global: Lessons from the Late Movers," *Harvard Business Review* 78, no. 2 (March–April 2000), pp. 138–140. See also Christopher Lawton, "Aussie Wines Star at Spirits Marketer Constellation Brands," *The Wall Street Journal* (January 16, 2004), pp. B1, B4.

Table 7-8 shows a market-product matrix for Lexus. Toyota launched the Lexus brand in 1989 with two sedan models. In market segmentation terms, the luxury car buyer Lexus hoped to attract is associated with an upper-income demographic. In 1996, Lexus launched its first sport utility vehicle. The decision to enter the SUV product-market represented management's desire to reach upper-income consumers whose lifestyles required something other than a luxury sedan. In 2008, Lexus offered a total of 11 different models in the United States; these include the top-of-the line LX 470 luxury utility vehicle, the LS 430 luxury sedan and, at the entry level, the IS series. Lexus vehicles are marketed in more than 60 countries; the United States is the number one market. Ironically, in Japan the vehicles were sold for years under the Toyota nameplate; the line was relaunched under the Lexus brand in 2005.[41]

TABLE 7-8 2008 Product-Market Grid for Lexus, Select Country Markets

Country Segment	Lexus Brand										
	LS	IS	GS	RX	SC	RX HV	LS HV	GS HV	LX	ES	GX
Asia											
China	X	X	X	X	X	X	X		X	X	
Hong Kong	X	X	X	X	X	X	X				
Taiwan	X	X	X	X	X	X			X	X	
India											
North America											
Canada	X	X	X	X	X	X	X	X	X	X	X
USA	X	X	X	X	X	X	X	X	X	X	X
Latin America											
Brazil	X									X	
Europe											
Austria	X	X	X	X	X	X	X	X			
Belgium	X	X	X	X	X	X	X	X			
Denmark	X	X	X	X		X	X	X			
Finland	X	X	X	X	X	X	X	X			
France	X	X	X	X	X	X	X	X			
Germany	X	X	X	X	X	X	X	X			
Gr. Britain	X	X	X	X	X	X	X	X			
Greece	X	X	X	X	X	X	X	X			
Ireland	X	X	X	X	X	X	X	X			
Netherlands	X	X	X	X	X	X	X	X			
Portugal	X	X				X	X	X			
Russia	X	X	X	X	X	X	X	X	X		
Sweden	X	X	X	X	X	X	X	X			
Switzerland	X	X	X	X	X	X	X	X			
Middle East											
Israel	X	X	X	X	X	X					
UAE	X	X	X	X	X				X	X	
Kuwait	X	X	X	X	X				X	X	
Saudi Arabia	X	X	X	X	X				X	X	

Source: Toyota Motor Corporation.

---

[41]Jathon Sapsford, "Toyota Introduces a New Luxury Brand in Japan: Lexus," *The Wall Street Journal* (August 3, 2005), pp. B1, B5.

The company sold about 50,700 vehicles in Europe in 2006, with the United Kingdom accounting for about 30 percent of those sales. Management intends to build Lexus into a global luxury brand; the goal is to sell 65,000 cars in Europe by the end of the decade. That, in turn, means that Lexus has to target Germany, the largest market in Europe, where 4 in 10 vehicles sold are luxury models. Approximately 15 million cars are sold in Europe each year; Germany accounts for nearly one-quarter of the total. In 2005, Lexus sold about 3,000 cars in Germany; by comparison, Mercedes and BMW sold a combined total of more than 500,000 vehicles. Can Lexus succeed on the home turf of two of the world's leading luxury carmakers? Armed with the understanding that local brands comprise more than 90 percent of German auto sales in the premium segment, Lexus has made significant product adaptations. For example, because Germans want the option of buying vehicles with diesel engines, Lexus developed new diesel models as well as a gas-electric hybrid engine for the RX series. Note that, in Europe, Lexus offers the top-of-the-line LX 470 SUV in only one country: Russia. Can you explain this situation? How do the model offerings vary among the BRIC countries?

TARGET MARKET STRATEGY OPTIONS

After evaluating the identified segments in terms of the three criteria presented, a decision is made whether to pursue a particular opportunity or not. If the decision is made to proceed, an appropriate targeting strategy must be developed. There are three basic categories of target marketing strategies: standardized marketing, concentrated marketing, and differentiated marketing.

Standardized Global Marketing

Standardized global marketing is analogous to mass marketing in a single country. It involves creating the same marketing mix for a broad mass market of potential buyers. Standardized global marketing, also known as *undifferentiated target marketing*, is based on the premise that a mass market exists around the world. In addition, that mass market is served with a marketing mix of standardized elements. Product adaptation is minimized, and a strategy of intensive distribution ensures that the product is available in the maximum number of retail outlets. The appeal of standardized global marketing is clear: lower production costs. The same is true of standardized global communications.

Concentrated Global Marketing

The second global targeting strategy, concentrated target marketing, involves devising a marketing mix to reach a **niche**. A niche is simply a single segment of the global market. In cosmetics, the House of Lauder, Chanel, and other cosmetics marketers have used this approach successfully to target the upscale, prestige segment of the market. Similarly, The Body Shop International PLC caters to consumers in many countries who wish to purchase "natural" beauty aids and cosmetics that have not been tested on animals. Concentrated targeting is also the strategy employed by the hidden champions of global marketing: Companies unknown to most people that have succeeded by serving a niche market that exists in many countries. These companies define their markets narrowly and strive for global depth rather than national breadth. For example, Germany's Winterhalter is a hidden champion in the dishwasher market, but the company has never sold a dishwasher to a consumer, hospital, or school. Instead, it focuses exclusively on dishwashers and water conditioners for hotels and restaurants. As Jürgen Winterhalter noted, "The narrowing of our market definition was the most important strategic decision we ever made. It is the very foundation of our success in the past decade."[42]

"There is a significant difference between the 'mass market' and the premium segment. In the mass market, customers are looking for a good deal. In the premium segment, they are searching for a vehicle that fulfills their expectations and their emotions."[43]
Helmut Panke, former Chairman, BMW

[42]Hermann Simon, *Hidden Champions: Lessons from 500 of the World's Best Unknown Companies* (Boston: Harvard Business School Press, 1996), p. 54.
[43]Helmut Panke and Alex Taylor III, "BMW Turns More American Than Ever," *Fortune* (February 2004), p. 130.

Differentiated Global Marketing

The third target marketing strategy, **differentiated global marketing**, represents a more ambitious approach than concentrated target marketing. Also known as **multisegment targeting**, this approach entails targeting two or more distinct market segments with multiple marketing mix offerings. This strategy allows a company to achieve wider market coverage. For example, in the sport utility vehicle segment described previously, Rover has a $78,525 Range Rover at the high end of the market. A scaled-down version, the Range Rover Sport costs about $20,000 less. At the other end of the price spectrum, the Freelander was launched in Europe in 1997 and quickly became a top seller. The V6 Freelander was available in the United States from 2001 to 2005 with prices starting at $25,000. Today, the lowest-priced model in the line is the LR2, which has a base price of $36,225.

In the cosmetics industry, Unilever pursues differentiated global marketing strategies by targeting both ends of the perfume market. Unilever targets the luxury market with Calvin Klein and Elizabeth Taylor's Passion; Wind Song and Brut are its mass-market brands. Mass marketer Procter & Gamble, known for its Old Spice and Incognito brands, also embarked upon this strategy with its 1991 acquisition of Revlon's EuroCos, marketer of Hugo Boss for men and Laura Biagiotti's Roma perfume. In the mid-1990s, P&G launched a new prestige fragrance, Venezia, in the United States and several European countries. Currently, P&G also markets Envy, Rush, and other Gucci fragrances as a licensee of the Italian fashion house. Conversely, in 1997 Estée Lauder acquired Sassaby Inc., owner of the mass-market Jane brand. This action marked the first move by Lauder outside the prestige segment.[44]

POSITIONING

The term *positioning* is attributed to marketing gurus Al Ries and Jack Trout, who first introduced it in a 1969 article published in *Industrial Marketing* magazine. As noted at the beginning of the chapter, positioning refers to the act of differentiating a brand in customers' minds in relation to competitors in terms of attributes and benefits that the brand does and does not offer. Put differently, positioning is the process of developing strategies for "staking out turf" or "filling a slot" in the mind of target customers.[45] Positioning is frequently used in conjunction with the segmentation variables and targeting strategies discussed previously. For example, Unilever and other consumer goods companies often engage in differentiated target marketing, offering a full range of brands within a given product category. Unilever's various detergent brands include All, Wisk, Surf, and Persil; each is positioned slightly differently. In some instances, extensions of a popular brand can also be positioned in different ways. Colgate's Total toothpaste is positioned as the brand that addresses a full range of oral health issues, including gum disease. In most parts of the world, Total is available in several formulations, including Total Advanced Clean, Total Clean Mint Paste, and Total Whitening Paste. Effective positioning differentiates each variety from the others.

In the decades since Ries and Trout first focused attention on the importance of the concept, marketers have utilized a number of general positioning strategies. These include positioning by attribute or benefit, quality and price, use or user, and competitor.[46] Recent research has identified three additional positioning strategies that are particularly useful in global marketing: global consumer culture positioning, local consumer culture positioning, and foreign consumer culture positioning.

Attribute or Benefit

A frequently used positioning strategy exploits a particular product attribute, benefit, or feature. Economy, reliability, and durability are frequently used attribute/benefit positions. Volvo automobiles are known for solid construction that offers safety in the event of a crash. By contrast,

[44]Tara Parker-Pope, "Estée Lauder Buys Jane Brand's Owner for Its First Venture into Mass Market," *The Wall Street Journal* (September 27, 1997), p. B8.

[45]Al Ries and Jack Trout, *Positioning: The Battle for Your Mind* (New York: Warner Books, 1982), p. 44.

[46]David A. Aaker and J. Gary Shansby, "Positioning Your Product," *Business Horizons* 25, no. 2 (May–June 1982), pp. 56–62.

BMW is positioned as "the ultimate driving machine," a reference that signifies high performance. In the ongoing credit card wars, Visa's long-running advertising theme "It's Everywhere You Want to Be" drew attention to the benefit of worldwide merchant acceptance. In global marketing, it may be deemed important to communicate the fact that a brand is imported. This approach is known as *foreign consumer culture positioning* (FCCP).

Quality and Price

This strategy can be thought of in terms of a continuum from high fashion/quality and high price to good value (rather than "low quality") at a reasonable price. A legendary print ad campaign for Belgium's Stella Artois beer included various executions that positioned the brand at the premium end of the market. One ad juxtaposed a cap pried off a bottle of Stella with a close-up of a Steinway piano. The tagline "Reassuring expensive" was the only copy; upon close inspection of the Steinway, the reader could see that one of the keys was broken because it was used to open the bottle! InBev, the world's biggest brewer in terms of volume, markets the Stella Artois brand. While Stella is regarded as an "everyday" beer in its local market of Belgium, the marketing team at InBev has repositioned it as a premium global brand.[47]

At the high end of the distilled spirits industry, marketers of imported vodkas such as Belvedere and Grey Goose have successfully positioned their brands as super premium entities selling for twice the price of premium ("ordinary") vodka. Ads for several export vodka brands emphasize their national origins, demonstrating how FCCP can reinforce quality and price positioning. Marketers sometimes use the phrase "transformation advertising" to describe advertising that seeks to change the experience of buying and using a product—in other words, the product benefit—to justify a higher price/quality position. Presumably, buying and drinking Grey Goose (from France), Belvedere (Poland), or Ketel One (the Netherlands) is a more gratifying consumption experience than that of buying and drinking a "bar brand" such as Popov (who knows where it's made?).

Use or User

Another positioning strategy represents how a product is used or associates the brand with a user or class of users. For example, to capitalize on the global success and high visibility of the *Lord of the Rings* trilogy, Gillette's Duracell battery unit ran print and TV ads proclaiming that, on location in remote areas of New Zealand, *Rings* director Peter Jackson and his crew used Duracell exclusively. Likewise, Max Factor makeup is positioned as "the makeup that makeup artists use." The Pulsar watch ad shown in Exhibit 7-5 associates the brand with a handsome man who is "addicted to reality TV" and enjoys reading Dostoevsky.

Competition

Implicit or explicit reference to competitors can provide the basis for an effective positioning strategy. For example, when Anita Roddick started The Body Shop International in the 1970s, she emphasized the difference between the principles pursued by "mainstream" health and beauty brands and those of her company. The Body Shop brand stands for natural ingredients, no animal testing, and recyclable containers. Moreover, Roddick abandoned the conventional industry approach of promising miracles; instead, women were given realistic expectations of what health and beauty aids can accomplish.

More recently, Dove's "Campaign for Real Beauty" broke new ground by positioning the brand around a new definition of beauty. The campaign is based on research commissioned by Silvia Lagnado, Dove's global brand director. The research indicated that, worldwide, only 2 percent of women consider themselves beautiful. Armed with this insight, Ogilvy & Mather Worldwide's office in Dusseldorf developed the concept that is the basis of the Campaign for Real Beauty (see Exhibit 7-6). To strengthen the connection between the Real Beauty campaign and Dove's products, Dove launched a new Web community (http://Dove.msn.com) in 2008. Visitors to the site can watch "Fresh Takes," a miniseries that has aired on MTV, as well as seek medical advice on skin care.[48]

---

[47]"Head to Head," *Economist* (October 29, 2005), pp. 66–69.
[48]Suzanne Vranica, "Can Dove Promote a Cause and Sell Soap?" *The Wall Street Journal* (April 10, 2008), p. B6.

Exhibit 7-5: Japan's Seiko Corporation owns the Pulsar watch brand. The global market for timepieces can be segmented in various ways such as benefits sought. For example, many consumers consider a watch to be a fashion accessory. Watchmakers can pursue any or all of the target market strategies discussed here. Pulsar is a mass-market brand; this print ad positions the brand by user.
Source: Seiko Corporation of America.

Global, Foreign, and Local Consumer Culture Positioning[49]

As noted in Chapter 4 and discussed briefly in this chapter, global consumer culture positioning is a strategy that can be used to target various segments associated with the emerging global consumer culture. **Global consumer culture positioning (GCCP)** is defined as a strategy that identifies the brand as a symbol of a particular global culture or segment. It has proven to be an effective strategy for communicating with global teens, cosmopolitan elites, globe-trotting

[49]The following discussion is adapted from Dana L. Alden, Jan-Benedict Steenkamp, and Rajeev Batra, "Brand Positioning through Advertising in Asia, North America, and Europe: The Role of Global Consumer Culture," *Journal of Marketing* 63, no. 1 (January 1999), pp. 75–87.

Exhibit 7-6: The Dove Campaign for Real Beauty supports the mission of the Dove® brand to widen the definition of beauty. The campaign supports the Dove Self-Esteem Fund by developing workshops and education tools that help foster positive self-esteem in girls and young women. The Campaign for Real Beauty has generated a significant amount of favorable publicity worldwide.
Source: Used by permission of Unilever United States, Inc.

laptop warriors who consider themselves members of a "transnational commerce culture," and other groups. For example, Sony's brightly colored "My First Sony" line is positioned as *the* electronics brand for youngsters around the globe with discerning parents. Philips's current global corporate image campaign is keyed to the theme "Sense and Simplicity." Benetton uses the slogan "United Colors of Benetton" to position itself as a brand concerned with the unity of humankind. Heineken's strong brand equity around the globe can be attributed in good measure to a GCCP strategy that reinforces consumers' cosmopolitan self-image.

Certain categories of products lend themselves especially well to GCCP. High-tech and high-touch products are both associated with high levels of customer involvement and by a shared "language" among users.[50] *High-tech products* are sophisticated, technologically complex, and/or difficult to explain or understand. When shopping for them, consumers often have specialized needs or interests and rational buying motives. High-tech brands and products are frequently evaluated in terms of their performance against established objective standards. Portable MP3 players, cell phones, personal computers, home theater audio/video components, luxury automobiles, and financial services are some of the high-tech product categories for which companies have established strong global positions. Buyers typically already possess— or wish to acquire—considerable technical information. Generally speaking, for example, computer buyers in all parts of the world are equally knowledgeable about Pentium microprocessors, 500-gigabyte hard drives, software RAM requirements, and flat-panel displays. High-tech global consumer positioning also works well for special-interest products associated with leisure or recreation. Fuji bicycles, Adidas sports equipment, and Canon cameras are examples of successful global special-interest products. Because most people who buy and use high-tech products "speak the same language" and share the same mind-set, marketing communications should be informative and emphasize performance-related attributes and features to establish the desired GCCP.

By contrast, when shopping for *high-touch products*, consumers are generally energized by emotional motives rather than rational ones. Consumers may feel an emotional or spiritual connection with high-touch products, the performance of which is evaluated in subjective, aesthetic terms rather than objective, technical terms. Consumption of high-touch products may represent an act of personal indulgence, reflect the user's actual or ideal self-image, or reinforce interpersonal relationships between the user and family members or friends. High-touch products appeal to the senses more than the intellect; if a product comes with a detailed user's manual, it's probably high tech. By contrast, the consumption experience associated with a high-touch product probably does not entail referring to an instruction manual. Luxury perfume, designer fashions, and fine champagne are all examples of high-touch products that lend themselves to GCCP. Some high-touch products are linked with the joy or pleasure found in "life's little moments." Ads that show friends chatting over a cup of coffee in a café or someone's kitchen put the product at the center of everyday life. As Nestlé has convincingly demonstrated with its Nescafé brand, this type of high-touch, emotional appeal is understood worldwide.

A brand's GCCP can be reinforced by the careful selection of the thematic, verbal, or visual components that are incorporated into advertising and other communications. For marketers seeking to establish a high-touch GCCP, leisure, romance, and materialism are three themes that cross borders well. By contrast, professionalism and experience are advertising themes that work well for high-tech products such as global financial services. Several years ago, for example, Chase Manhattan bank launched a $75 million global advertising campaign geared to the theme "Profit from experience." According to Aubrey Hawes, a vice president and corporate director of marketing for the bank, Chase's business and private banking clients "span the globe and travel the globe. They can only know one Chase in their minds, so why should we try to confuse them?"[51] Presumably, Chase's target audience is sophisticated enough to appreciate the subtlety of the copywriter's craft—"profit" can be interpreted as either a noun ("monetary gain") or a verb ("reap an advantage").

In some instances, products may be positioned globally in a "bipolar" fashion as both high tech and high touch. This approach can be used when products satisfy buyers' rational criteria while evoking an emotional response. For example, audio-video components from Denmark's Bang & Olufsen (B&O), by virtue of their performance and elegant styling, are perceived as both high tech (i.e., advanced engineering and sonically superior) and high touch (i.e., sleek modern design; see Exhibit 7-7). As former CEO Torben Ballegaard Sørensen explained, "Our brand is about feeling good at home, or where you feel at home—in a car or in a hotel. When daily life is cluttered, you can come home to a system that works and is tranquil. It cocoons you."[52] Nokia has become the world's leading cellular phone brand because the company combines state-of-the-art technical performance with a fashion orientation that allows users to view their phones as extensions of themselves. Likewise, as shown in Exhibit 7-8, Apple positions its products on the basis of both performance ("160GB of storage, holds 40,000 songs") and design (writing in the *Financial Times*, a reviewer called the iPod "an all-time design classic").

To the extent that English is the primary language of international business, mass media, and the Internet, one can make the case that English signifies modernism and a cosmopolitan outlook. Therefore, the use of English in advertising and labeling throughout the world is another way to achieve GCCP. Benetton's tag line "United Colors of Benetton" appears in English in all of the company's advertising. The implication is that fashion-minded consumers everywhere in the world shop at Benetton. English is often used as a marketing tool in Japan. Even though a native English speaker would doubtless find the syntax to be muddled, it is the symbolism associated with the use of English that counts rather than the specific meanings that the words might (or might not) convey. A third way to reinforce a GCCP is to use brand symbols whose interpretation defies association with a specific country culture. Examples include Nestlé's "little nest" logo with an adult bird feeding its babies, the Nike swoosh, and the Mercedes-Benz star.

A second option is **foreign consumer culture positioning (FCCP)**, which associates the brand's users, use occasions, or production origins with a foreign country or culture. A long-running campaign for Foster's Brewing Group's U.S. advertising proudly trumpeted the brand's national origin; print ads featured the tag line "Foster's. Australian for beer" while TV and radio spots were keyed to the theme "How to speak Australian." Needless to say, these ads were not

---

[51]Gary Levin, "Ads Going Global," *Advertising Age* (July 22, 1991), p. 42.
[52]John Gapper, "When High Fidelity Becomes High Fashion," *Financial Times* (December 20, 2005), p. 8.

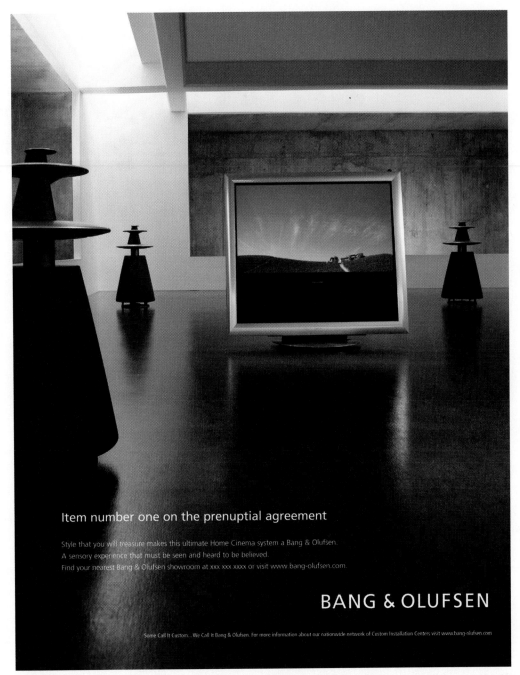

Item number one on the prenuptial agreement

Style that you will treasure makes this ultimate Home Cinema system a Bang & Olufsen.
A sensory experience that must be seen and heard to be believed.
Find your nearest Bang & Olufsen showroom at xxx xxx xxxx or visit www.bang-olufsen.com.

BANG & OLUFSEN

Some Call It Custom... We Call It Bang & Olufsen. For more information about our nationwide network of Custom Installation Centers visit www.bang-olufsen.com

Exhibit 7-7: Renowned worldwide for Danish craftsmanship and innovation, Bang & Olufsen is a textbook example of high-touch, high-tech global brand positioning. This print ad showcases Bang & Olufsen's Home Cinema system, which includes a BeoVision video monitor and BeoLab 5 loudspeakers (price: $19,950 per pair). The headline, "Item number one on the prenuptial agreement," is witty and sophisticated, and underscores the brand's desirability.
Source: Used by permission of Bang & Olufsen.

used in Australia itself! Advertising for Grupo Modelo's Corona Extra brand is identified more generally with Latin America. The "American-ness" of Levi jeans, Marlboro cigarettes, American Apparel clothing, and Harley-Davidson motorcycles—sometimes conveyed with subtlety, sometimes not—enhances their brands' appeal to cosmopolitans around the world and offers opportunities for FCCP.

IKEA, the home furnishings retailer based in Sweden, wraps itself in the Swedish flag—literally. Inside and out, IKEA's stores are decorated in the national colors of blue and yellow. To reinforce the chain's Scandinavian heritage—and to encourage shoppers to linger—many stores feature cafeterias in which Swedish meatballs and other foods are served! Sometimes, brand names suggest an FCCP even though a product is of local origin. For example, the name "Häagen-Dazs" was made up to imply Scandinavian origin even though an American company launched the ice cream. Conversely, a popular chewing gum in Italy marketed by Perfetti bears the brand name "Brooklyn."

Exhibit 7-8: The worldwide success of Apple's iPod digital music player (more than 220 million units sold) can be attributed to a superior global marketing strategy. The iPod product lineup includes the Shuffle, the Nano, the Classic, and the iPod touch. Prices start at $59 and top out at $399. iPods are available directly from www.apple.com and Apple Stores, as wells a variety of other retail sources. Ads reinforce the message that the iPod is the ultimate in high-tech, high-touch "cool." The brand appeals to global teens, the global elite, and everyone in between.
Source: Katsumi Kasahara/AP Wide World Photos.

Marketers can also utilize **local consumer culture positioning (LCCP)**, a strategy that associates the brand with local cultural meanings, reflects the local culture's norms, portrays the brand as consumed by local people in the national culture, or depicts the product as locally produced for local consumers. An LCCP approach can be seen in Budweiser's U.S. advertising; ads featuring the iconic Clydesdale horses, for example, associate the brand with small-town American culture. Researchers studying television advertising in seven countries found that LCCP predominated, particularly in ads for food, personal nondurables, and household nondurables.

Summary

The global environment must be analyzed before a company pursues expansion into new geographic markets. Through **global market segmentation**, a company can identify and group customers or countries according to common needs and wants. **Demographic segmentation** can be based on country income and population, age, ethnic heritage, or other variables. **Psychographic segmentation** groups people according to attitudes, interests, opinions, and lifestyles. **Behavioral segmentation** utilizes **user status** and **usage rate** as segmentation variables. **Benefit segmentation** is based on the benefits buyers seek. **Global teens** and **global elites** are two examples of global market segments.

After marketers have identified segments, the next step is **targeting**: The identified groups are evaluated and compared, and one or more segments with the greatest potential is selected from them. The groups are evaluated on the basis of several factors, including segment size and growth potential, competition, and compatibility and feasibility. Target market assessment also entails a thorough understanding of the **product-market** in question and determining **marketing model drivers** and **enabling conditions** in the countries under study. The timing of market entry should take into account whether a **first-mover advantage** is likely to be gained. After evaluating the identified segments, marketers must decide on an appropriate targeting strategy. The three basic categories of global target marketing strategies are **standardized global marketing**, **niche marketing**, and **multisegment targeting**.

Positioning a product or brand to differentiate it in the minds of target customers can be accomplished in various ways: positioning by attribute or benefit, positioning by quality/price, positioning by use or user, and positioning by competition. In global marketing **global consumer culture positioning (GCCP), foreign consumer culture positioning (FCCP),** and **local consumer culture positioning (LCCP)** are additional strategic options.

Discussion Questions

1. In a recent interview, a brand manager at Procter & Gamble noted, "Historically, we used to be focused on discovering the common hopes and dreams within a country, but now we're seeing that the real commonalities are in generations across geographic borders." What is the significance of this comment in terms of the "conventional" versus "unconventional" approaches to global market segmentation shown in Table 7-1?

2. Identify the five basic segmentation strategies. Give an example of a company that has used each one.

3. Explain the difference between segmenting and targeting.

4. Compare and contrast standardized, concentrated, and differentiated global marketing. Illustrate each strategy with an example from a global company.

5. What is positioning? Identify the different positioning strategies presented in the chapter and give examples of companies or products that illustrate each.

6. What is global consumer culture positioning (GCCP)? What other strategic positioning choices do global marketers have?

7. What is a high-touch product? Explain the difference between high-tech product positioning and high-touch product positioning. Can some products be positioned using both strategies? Explain.

Market research is critical to understanding women's preferences in different parts of the world. According to Eric Bone, head of L'Oréal's Tokyo Research Center, "Japanese women prefer to use a compact foundation rather than a liquid. Humidity here is much higher and the emphasis is on long-lasting coverage." Armed with this knowledge, L'Oréal devotes more development time to compacts rather than liquids. The researchers have also learned that the typical Japanese woman cleanses her face twice.

In China, L'Oréal and its competitors have an opportunity to educate women about cosmetics, which were banned prior to 1982. Each year, L'Oréal observes and films 6,000 Chinese women applying and removing makeup. Alice Laurent, L'Oréal's skincare development manager in Shanghai, says, "In China, the number of products used in the morning and the evening is 2.2." At its Shanghai Innovation Centre, L'Oréal is also studying how to incorporate traditional Chinese medicine into new product lines.

L'Oréal and Procter & Gamble offer a wide range of products in China, including both mass-market and premium brands. By contrast, Estée Lauder's focus is expensive prestige brands such as Estée Lauder, Clinique, and MAC that are sold through upmarket department stores. One research analyst cautions that Estée Lauder's targeting and positioning may be too narrow for China. According to Access Asia, Estée Lauder "is in danger of becoming too exclusively placed at the top end of the market and it may have to reposition itself more in the mass market to compete for a larger part of the Chinese market."

Estée Lauder's Carol Shen disagrees with that assessment. She views her company's brands as aspirational. "Chinese consumers are price sensitive but at the same time are willing to invest in products that are relatively expensive versus their income levels because they are so confident about the future," she says. CEO William Lauder echoes those thoughts. As he explains, "The Estée Lauder brand in China is exploding right now because it represents aspirational luxury but at a price that's much more affordable than Louis Vuitton."

In India, L'Oréal has recently shifted from a low-price, mass-market strategy to a premium price, upscale strategy. Competitor Hindustan Lever rings up nearly $1 billion in annual sales by targeting the hundreds of millions of people who must live on the equivalent of $2 per day. This means body lotion priced at $0.70 and $0.90 bottles of perfume. Upon first entering India in 1991, L'Oréal used a similar strategy. However, its low-priced Garnier Ultra Doux shampoo failed to catch on with consumers. Offering no particular advantage relative to local brands, it was, in the words of Alain Evrard, L'Oréal's managing director for Africa, Orient, and the Pacific, "an absolute flop." Some shopkeepers were stuck with unsold inventories.

In the mid-1990s, Evrard was determined to gain a better understanding of the Indian market. He noted several different trends. The number of working women was increasing dramatically, and consumer attitudes were shifting. Thanks to cable television, CNN and MTV were finding large viewing audiences. To learn more about women's preferences, Evrard spoke with advertising executives and fashion magazine editors as well as L'Oréal's local employees. In doing so, Evrard arrived at a keen insight: Women in their 20s concerned about gray hair were not satisfied with existing do-it-yourself hair color products. Evrard responded by launching L'Oréal Excellence Crème in India. An innovative but expensive product popular in Europe, Excellence Crème was priced at $9 and positioned as a luxury purchase. To gain support among shopkeepers, a local L'Oréal staffer named Dinesh Dayal mounted an education campaign and went door-to-door to promote the product at local shops. Today Excellence Crème is widely available in India. In 2004, after more than a decade of losses, L'Oréal's Indian operations became profitable.

Meanwhile, Shinzo Maeda, president and CEO of Shiseido, does not intend to stay on the sidelines as Western cosmetics marketers penetrate deeper into Asia. Shiseido is Japan's second-largest cosmetics company; however, domestic sales are expected to grow only about 2 percent annually. Maeda notes, "The need to globalize our organization has come at an accelerated pace." Throughout the region, consumers associate the Shiseido brand with a company that understands skin issues specific to Asian women. The company also has a reputation for advanced research and development in key areas such as anti-aging products. In China, Shiseido uses a selling strategy that has been extremely effective in Japan. Highly trained beauty counselors offer advice on color coordination, moisture levels, and related topics. As one beauty counselor said, "It's a real delight to see my customers become happy."

Case 7-1 Discussion Questions

1. How do women's preferences for cosmetics and beauty care vary from country to country?
2. Assess Estée Lauder's strategy for China. Does it make sense to focus on premium brands, or should the company launch a mass-market brand?
3. What is the best positioning strategy for Shiseido as the company expands in Asia? High touch? High tech? Both?

Sources: Miki Tanikawa, "A Personal Touch Counts in Cosmetics," *The New York Times* (February 17, 2009), p. B4; Christina Passariello, "L'Oréal Net Gets New-Market Lift," *The Wall Street Journal* (February 14, 2008), p. C7; Ellen Byron, "Beauty, Prestige, and Worry Lines," *The Wall Street Journal* (August 20, 2007), p. B3; Christina Passariello, "Beauty Fix: Behind L'Oréal's Makeover in India: Going Upscale," *The Wall Street Journal* (July 13, 2007), pp. A1, A14; Beatrice Adams, "Big Brands Are Watching You," *Financial Times* (November 4/November 5, 2006), p. W18; Adam Jones, "How to Make Up Demand," *Financial Times* (October 3, 2006), p. 8; Lauren Foster and Andrew Yeh, "Estée Lauder Puts on a New Face," *Financial Times* (March 23, 2006), p. 7; Rebecca Rose, "Global Diversity Gets All Cosmetic," *Financial Times* (April 11/12, 2004), p. W11.

Case 7-2
KFC China: Targeting Through Localization

When KFC first entered Hong Kong in 1973, it quickly grew to 11 restaurants by the following year. However, the business seriously misjudged the local market and failed to develop a business model that could be sustained. Consequently, by 1975, all 11 of the outlets had been forced to close.

Ten years later, KFC was back. It franchised its operations to Birdland, a company with the backing of local investors. KFC's difficult times in Hong Kong provided the business with vital knowledge when it came to entering China in 1987. At the time, China required overseas businesses to enter into joint ventures with Chinese businesses. KFC China carefully selected local partners with strong government connections.

Localization was also an important aspect of KFC China's approach. The business introduced more new products more frequently than its competitors in China. KFC's core product is chicken, second only in popularity in China to pork. Chicken is also far more popular than beef, giving the business a huge advantage over rival McDonald's. KFC China has worked tirelessly to ensure that it continues to come up with and launch new products that are a better fit for the Chinese consumer. As a result, it is twice as big in China than McDonald's; elsewhere in the world it is the other way around.

The highly localized menu, which includes Chinese-style porridge (congee), Beijing Chicken Roll, Spicy Diced Chicken, and Chinese Dough Fritters, has kept KFC China ahead of McDonald's and Burger King, but other restaurant chains are formidable competitors. Wei Qian La Mian (Ajisen Ramen) is a Japanese chain doing well, as is the Chinese fast-food chain Zhen Gongfu (Real Kung-fu). There are even hi-tech developments in the competition. Recently, the Chinese government agreed to fund a project that centers on a robot capable of preparing a range of popular Chinese dishes at lightning speed.

KFC China is part of the huge Yum! Brands group, which also runs Pizza Hut and Pizza Hut Express in China. Yum! Brands are developing a new brand called East Dawnings in its attempt to fend off competition from local fast-food rivals. It is partly an offensive move and partly a defensive one to ensure that it maintains its position as a market leader in China. East Dawnings is essentially a fusion of the KFC business model with Chinese food. Chinese food is served exclusively, but there is a focus on quick and easy to prepare dishes. Even soft drinks have been replaced with traditional Chinese drinks such as soy plum juice.

East Dawning uses consistent recipes and preparation methods across all of its restaurants. The layout is designed to resemble Chinese homes, and the dining tables are similar to offering tables found in many homes.

KFC has been positioned in Mainland China as a Western brand. It is often perceived as an American brand, but with Chinese characteristics. KFC China's branding strategy was modified through product localization and differentiated marketing practices. McDonald's has remained a recognizable American brand; the TV advertising focuses on being young and hip and has used sports and pop stars in its advertisements. KFC China, on the other hand, has repositioned itself and expanded its target markets to include all ages, family, and friends. As a result, it has seen business volume grow, and the brand has matured in Mainland China.

By 2008, Yum! Brands had opened around 2,500 KFC and Pizza Hut outlets across Mainland China with a combined income

The personal disposable income in Mainland China is anticipated to grow more than twofold in 2012 to reach $2,410 per head, which will increase the amount that the Chinese people spend on fast-food products.
Source: © Lou-Foto/Alamy.

of $2 billion. The fast-food market in Mainland China has been estimated to be worth around $28 billion. In 2009, the group planned to open over 400 new outlets and predicted to eventually have 20,000 outlets in the country.

The targeting and localization approach has clearly worked with the Mainland China operation accounting for over a quarter of Yum! Brands' global operating profit. The group also predicts that this part of the business may well account for 40 percent by 2017. Despite the fact that revenues and profits fell in the U.S. market at the same time, this contribution by KFC China meant that overall shares in the parent company increased in value.

According to the China Cuisine Association, the Chinese fast-food market is maturing. The association sees standardization as being the only way for domestic businesses to compete with the foreign fast-food chains. According to the association, there are over one million outlets of chain fast-food restaurants in China. The fast-food industry is steadily growing and in the China Top 100 catering businesses, the number of fast-food restaurants is increasing year by year.

Again, according to the association, compared to regular fast food, the leisure fast-food market sees consumers willing to pay a higher price, meaning that the average gross profit is higher than in regular restaurants.

Discussion Questions

1. Mainland China is the number one market for Yum! Brands, and KFC China alone has contributed to over 20 percent of global revenue for Yum! Brands. How has KFC China positioned itself differently from the popular McDonald's China franchises that have been successful in other Asian markets like Singapore, but have yet to expand significantly throughout Mainland China?

2. During the localization process, some foreign brands that are low-end in their home markets instead promote themselves as high-end brands in China. How were they able to localize KFC for the Chinese market, having it both suit local tastes yet also position itself as a higher-end alternative to traditional family dining?

3. Other multinationals such as Omega, L'Oréal, and General Motors have enjoyed considerable success in China, while other multinationals have been less successful. What do you think these successful companies have in common with KFC?

Sources: Warren Liu, *KFC in China: Secret Recipe For Success* (Hoboken, NJ: Wiley, 2008); Yum! Brands Inc., www.yum.com; www.chinadaily.co.cn; China Cuisine Association, www.ccas.com.cn; Lisa Takeuchi, "Kentucky Fried Rice," *Cullen Time Magazine* (January 17, 2008).

Case 7-3
The Youth of the World Proclaim, "We Want Our MTV!"

Janet Jackson's "wardrobe malfunction" during the halftime show of the 2004 Super Bowl caused a worldwide sensation. For better or for worse, MTV, which produced the show, demonstrated that it still had the ability to shake things up. Worldwide, musical tastes and trends have changed significantly since MTV first went on the air in 1981. Few current viewers are likely to remember the Buggles, the British duo whose song "Video Killed the Radio Star" was featured in the first clip aired. In some ways, MTV looks the same in the twenty-first century as it did in the 1980s. Today, however, MTV's reach extends far beyond the United States; Viacom's MTV Networks unit, which includes VH1, Comedy Central, and Nickelodeon, comprises the world's largest cable network with nearly 1 billion viewers in 160 countries.

MTV has not prospered by offering the same sights and sounds in every market. Rather, it owes much of its success to the realization that viewer sensibilities and tastes vary on a regional and country-by-country basis. MTV carefully researches those sensibilities and tastes, and then caters to them. MTV is especially popular with persons 15 to 34 years old, with 15-years-olds to 24-year-olds—a pure youth audience, as executives proudly note—as the core consumer. MTV executives are quick to point out that the channel's programming is extremely audience driven; shows like "Total Request Live" (TRL) allowed the channel to stay close to its viewing audience.

Within six years of its launch, MTV had penetrated some 50 million U.S. households, virtually the entire domestic cable audience at the time. Having conquered America, and with support from youth-oriented advertisers such as Coca-Cola, Levi's, and Nike, MTV Europe was launched in Rotterdam in 1987. Today, MTV has 16 local feeds in Europe with coverage stretching from Ireland to Russia. The local feeds are important, because as much as 70 percent of revenues come from advertisers in local markets. One driver of local ad revenues is MTV's commitment to introducing its viewers to local music groups. Despite its sensitivity to local preferences, however, executives and producers still seek economies. As Bill Roedy, president of

Nigerian singer Tuface performed in Johannesburg for the launch of MTV Base. MTV executive Bill Roedy expects that some local artists featured on the channel will achieve broader global recognition. Roedy said, "We are looking to Africa to be a huge contributor. It is going to enrich our channels around the world. We work very hard to develop local artists. It is something we passionately believe in."
Source: Ellen Elmendorp.

MTV Networks International, told *Billboard* magazine in 2000, "MTV looks for format opportunities to make content from one area travel to another with a local look and feel."

The blend of global and local elements in proportions that reflect local preferences is especially clear in Asia. When MTV first entered Japan in 1992, it met with limited success because a licensing agreement with several electronics manufacturers restricted the control that channel executives had over content; the result was an overemphasis on international pop music that was out of sync with viewers. MTV Japan was relaunched with an emphasis on extensive audience research and a new focus on local music and artists.

Today, MTV Asia reaches 125 million households and is comprised of seven channels: Japan, Taiwan, Hong Kong, China, Korea, MTV India, and MTV Southeast Asia (with English-language local feeds for Singapore, Indonesia, Malaysia, Thailand, and the Philippines). In India, the channel presents itself as zany, colorful, and light-hearted. For example, comedian Cyrus Barocha hosts a show called MTV Bakra that plays hidden camera pranks on unsuspecting victims. Programming in Taiwan, by contrast, is similar to that in the United States: edgy and in your face. Overall, MTV Mandarin's playlist contains about 80 percent local music, while MTV Philippines features predominantly international artists.

In 2003, Roedy unveiled a new "gain market scale" strategy. As he noted, "We've built up a big infrastructure. It's now time to leverage our resources and develop programming that can cross borders, regions, and even go global." New programming can cost between $200,000 and $350,000 per 30-minute episode; Roedy hopes to develop shows that will have appeal no matter where the viewers live.

Meanwhile, the global media landscape was rapidly changing. New media forms, including MySpace, YouTube, Facebook, and numerous other Web sites featuring user-generated content, had burst onto the scene. The youth market was fragmenting as consumers downloaded and shared videos and other content using computers, cell phones, and portable music players. In 2005, News Corporation paid $580 million for MySpace; Google acquired YouTube for $1.65 billion. Thanks to new corporate owners with deep pockets, the upstarts were going global in a hurry. For example, MySpace rolled out customized sites in the United Kingdom, Ireland, Australia, Germany, France, and Japan.

In 2006, Viacom Executive Chairman Sumner Redstone fired CEO and president Tom Freston; Redstone believed Freston had not moved aggressively enough to acquire MySpace or a similar hot new media property. Now, as MTV retrenches, Mika Salmi, president of global media at MTV Networks, is confident that his company can reinvent itself. He says, "We have an incredible reach across multiple platforms. We want to go deeper, people want more targeted programming."

Despite such pronouncements, some industry observers question whether MTV can create its own must-have digital content. As media analyst Kaan Yigit put it, "The analogy is the Gap. Both are really Gen X brands with their heyday behind them. . . . They are iconic, well-known, well-liked and respected for their past significance but not central to our culture anymore."

Discussion Questions

1. Describe MTV's global marketing strategy.
2. MTV's original success was based on its reputation as a trendsetter in music and video. How can the company reposition itself in today's new media environment?
3. How can MTV develop a digital strategy that will maintain viewer loyalty and ensure a strong brand presence on the Internet?

Sources: Daisy Whitney, "Retooled MVN Wrestles for Relevance," *Advertising Age* (April 9, 2007), p. S1; Tim Burt, "Veteran Leads MTV's Attack," *Financial Times* (August 12, 2003), p. 6; Charles Goldsmith, "MTV Seeks Global Appeal," *The Wall Street Journal* (January 21, 2003), pp. B1, B3; Anne-Marie Crawford, "MTV: Out of Its Teens," *Ad Age Global* 1, no. 9 (May 2001), pp. 25–26; Magz Osborne, "Second Chance in Japan," *Ad Age Global* 1, no. 9 (May 2001), pp. 26, 28; Claudia Penteado, "MTV Brazil Wins Success with Local Programming," *Ad Age Global* 1, no. 9 (May 2001), p. 29; Mimi Turner, "A Q&A with Bill Roedy," *Billboard* 112 no. 36 (September 2, 2000), pp. 48, 54; Owen Hughes, "MTV Asia's Five Branches," *Billboard* 112, no. 36 (September 2, 2000), pp. 48, 54; Sally Beatty and Carol Hymowitz, "How MTV Stays Tuned In to Teens," *The Wall Street Journal* (March 21, 2000), pp. B1, B4.

Importing, Exporting, and Sourcing

Case 8-1
Chinese and Vietnamese Exports to Europe

Europe is famous as a source for fine leather goods such as handbags and shoes. Each year, consumers in Europe buy 2.5 billion pairs of shoes. Shoes from China currently account for about one-third of the market; since 2001, when China joined the WTO, Chinese imports have increased tenfold. Imports from Vietnam have doubled in the same period (see Exhibit 8-1). The flood of shoe imports from China and Vietnam has been a boon for European retailers and value-conscious consumers.

However, faced with a threat to their business, manufacturers in Italy, Spain, and France sought protection. In an effort to curb the tide of imports, the European Commission imposed tariffs for a period of two years: 16.5 percent on shoes from China and 10 percent on shoes from Vietnam.

Overall, the tariffs will affect 11 percent of the shoes sold in Europe. The vote by representatives of the EU member nations was close: 13 to 12. The narrow margin of victory for the tariffs reflects divergent views in Europe about how to deal with low-cost Asian goods. Countries that advocate free trade, including the United Kingdom, Ireland, and Sweden, oppose the tariffs. A trade group, the European Branded Footwear Coalition, also objected, noting that the tariffs would increase the price of a pair of women's boots by €6.50—more than $8.

The success of Chinese and Vietnamese exporters—and the EU's subsequent imposition of tariffs—serves as a reminder of the impact exporting and importing can have on national and regional economies. You will find the

Exhibit 8-1: Vietnam is home to dozens of state-run textile and apparel manufacturers that export $1 billion in clothing and footwear each year. The country's garment sector produces merchandise for Nike, Zara, The Limited, and other popular brands. Recently, Vietnam's National Textile-Garment Group (Vinatex) began working with Western consultants to transform the structure and culture of its affiliated companies.
Source: Richard Vogel/AP Wide World Photos.

continuation of Case 8-1 on p. 296; you can read more about the debate over European shoe tariffs and make your own recommendations. This chapter provides an overview of import–export basics. We begin by explaining the difference between export selling and export marketing. Next is a survey of organizational export activities. An examination of national policies that support exports and/or discourage imports follows. After a discussion of tariff systems, we introduce key export participants. The next section provides an overview of organizational design issues as they pertain to exporting.

This is followed by a section devoted to material that can be extremely useful to undergraduates who are majoring in international business and international marketing: export financing and payment methods. For many students, that all-important first job may be in the import–export department. A familiarity with documentary credits and payment-related terminology can help you make a good impression during a job interview and, perhaps, lead to a job as an export/import coordinator (see Case 8-2). The chapter ends with a discussion of outsourcing, a topic that is becoming increasingly important as companies in many parts of the world cut costs by shifting both blue-collar and white-collar work to nations with low-wage workforces.

EXPORT SELLING AND EXPORT MARKETING: A COMPARISON

To better understand importing and exporting, it is important to distinguish between **export selling** and **export marketing**. Export selling does not involve tailoring the product, the price, or the promotional material to suit the requirements of global markets. The only marketing mix element that differs is the "place"; that is, the country where the product is sold. This selling approach may work for some products or services; for unique products with little or no international competition, such an approach is possible. Similarly, companies new to exporting may initially experience success with selling. Even today, the managerial mind-set in many companies still favors export selling. However, as companies mature in the global marketplace or as new competitors enter the picture, export *marketing* becomes necessary.

Export marketing targets the customer in the context of the total market environment. The export marketer does not simply take the domestic product "as is" and sell it to international customers. To the export marketer, the product offered in the home market represents a starting point. It is modified as needed to meet the preferences of international target markets; this is the approach the Chinese have adopted in the U.S. furniture market. Similarly, the export marketer sets prices to fit the marketing strategy and does not merely extend home-country pricing to the target market. Charges incurred in export preparation, transportation, and financing must be taken into account in determining prices. Finally, the export marketer also adjusts strategies and plans for communications and distribution to fit the market. In other words, effective communication about product features or uses to buyers in export markets may require creating brochures with different copy, photographs, or artwork. As the vice president of sales and marketing of one manufacturer noted, "We have to approach the international market with *marketing* literature as opposed to *sales* literature."

Export marketing is the integrated marketing of goods and services that are destined for customers in international markets. Export marketing requires:

1. An understanding of the target market environment
2. The use of marketing research and identification of market potential
3. Decisions concerning product design, pricing, distribution and channels, advertising, and communications—the marketing mix

After the research effort has zeroed in on potential markets, there is no substitute for a personal visit to size up the market firsthand and begin the development of an actual export-marketing program. A market visit should do several things. First, it should confirm (or contradict) assumptions regarding market potential. A second major purpose is to gather the additional data necessary to reach the final go or no-go decision regarding an export-marketing program. Certain kinds of information simply cannot be obtained from secondary sources. For example, an export manager or international marketing manager may have a list of potential distributors provided by the U.S. Department of Commerce. He or she may have corresponded with distributors on the list and formed some tentative idea of whether they meet the company's international criteria.

It is difficult, however, to negotiate a suitable arrangement with international distributors without actually meeting face-to-face to allow each side to appraise the capabilities and character of the other party. A third reason for a visit to the export market is to develop a marketing plan in cooperation with the local agent or distributor. Agreement should be reached on necessary product modifications, pricing, advertising and promotion expenditures, and a distribution plan. If the plan calls for investment, agreement on the allocation of costs must also be reached.

One way to visit a potential market is through a **trade show** or a state- or federally sponsored **trade mission**. Each year hundreds of trade fairs, usually organized around a product category or industry, are held in major markets. By attending trade shows and missions, company representatives can conduct market assessment, develop or expand markets, find distributors or agents, or locate potential end users. Perhaps most important, attending a trade show enables company representatives to learn a great deal about competitors' technology, pricing, and depth of market penetration. For example, exhibits often offer product literature with strategically useful technological information. Overall, company managers or sales personnel should be able to get a good general impression of competitors in the marketplace as they try to sell their own company's product.

ORGANIZATIONAL EXPORT ACTIVITIES

Exporting is becoming increasingly important as companies in all parts of the world step up their efforts to supply and service markets outside their national boundaries.[1] Research has shown that exporting is essentially a developmental process that can be divided into the following distinct stages:

1. The firm is unwilling to export; it will not even fill an unsolicited export order. This may be due to perceived lack of time ("too busy to fill the order") or to apathy or ignorance.
2. The firm fills unsolicited export orders but does not pursue unsolicited orders. Such a firm is an export seller.
3. The firm explores the feasibility of exporting (this stage may bypass Stage 2).
4. The firm exports to one or more markets on a trial basis.
5. The firm is an experienced exporter to one or more markets.
6. After this success, the firm pursues country- or region-focused marketing based on certain criteria (e.g., all countries where English is spoken or all countries where it is not necessary to transport by water).
7. The firm evaluates global market potential before screening for the "best" target markets to include in its marketing strategy and plan. *All* markets—domestic and international—are regarded as equally worthy of consideration.

The probability that a firm will advance from one stage to the next depends on different factors. Moving from Stage 2 to Stage 3 depends on management's attitude toward the attractiveness of exporting and their confidence in the firm's ability to compete internationally. However, *commitment* is the most important aspect of a company's international orientation. Before a firm can reach Stage 4, it must receive and respond to unsolicited export orders. The quality and dynamism of management are important factors that can lead to such orders.

---

[1]This section relies heavily on Warren J. Bilkey, "Attempted Integration of the Literature on the Export Behavior of Firms," *Journal of International Business Studies* 8, no. 1 (1978) pp. 33–46. The stages are based on Rogers' adoption process. See Everett M. Rogers, *Diffusion of Innovations* (New York: Free Press, 1995).

TABLE 8-1 Potential Export Problems

Logistics	Servicing Exports
Arranging transportation	Providing parts availability
Transport rate determination	Providing repair service
Handling documentation	Providing technical advice
Obtaining financial information	Providing warehousing
Distribution coordination	**Sales Promotion**
Packaging	Advertising
Obtaining insurance	Sales effort
Legal Procedure	Marketing information
Government red tape	**Foreign Market Intelligence**
Product liability	Locating markets
Licensing	Trade restrictions
Customs/duty	Competition overseas
Contract	
Agent/Distributor Agreements	

Success in Stage 4 can lead a firm to Stages 5 and 6. A company that reaches Stage 7 is a mature, geocentric enterprise that is relating global resources to global opportunity. To reach this stage requires management with vision and commitment.

One study noted that export procedural expertise and sufficient corporate resources are required for successful exporting. An interesting finding was that even the most experienced exporters express lack of confidence in their knowledge about shipping arrangements, payment procedures, and regulations. The study also showed that, although profitability is an important expected benefit of exporting, other advantages include increased flexibility and resiliency and improved ability to deal with sales fluctuations in the home market. Although research generally supports the proposition that the probability of being an exporter increases with firm size, it is less clear that export intensity—the ratio of export sales to total sales—is positively correlated with firm size. Table 8-1 lists some of the export-related problems that a company typically faces.[2]

NATIONAL POLICIES GOVERNING EXPORTS AND IMPORTS

It is hard to overstate the impact of exporting and importing on the world's national economies. In 1997, for example, total imports of goods and services by the United States passed the $1 trillion mark for the first time; in 2008, the combined total was $2.5 trillion. Trends in both exports and imports reflect China's pace-setting economic growth in the Asia-Pacific region. Exports from China have grown significantly; as noted in the chapter introduction, they are growing even faster now that China has joined the WTO. As shown in Table 8-2, Chinese apparel exports to the United States command more than one-third of the overall apparel market. Historically, China protected its own producers by imposing double-digit import tariffs. These will gradually be reduced as China complies with WTO regulations. Needless to say, representatives of the furniture, textile, and apparel industries in the United States are deeply concerned about the impact increased trade with China will have on these sectors. As this example suggests, one word can summarize national policies toward exports and imports: contradictory. For centuries, nations have combined two opposing policy attitudes toward the movement of goods across national boundaries. On the one hand, nations directly encourage exports; the flow of imports, on the other hand, is generally restricted.

[2]Masaaki Kotabe and Michael R. Czinkota, "State Government Promotion of Manufacturing Exports: A Gap Analysis," *Journal of International Business Studies* 23, no. 4 (Fourth Quarter 1992), pp. 637–658.

TABLE 8-2 **Market Share of Top 10 Apparel Exporting Countries to the United States, 2008 (percent)**

1. China	35.4
2. India	5.6
3. Mexico	5.5
4. Vietnam	5.3
5. Indonesia	4.3
6. Bangladesh	3.6
7. Pakistan	3.2
8. Honduras	2.7
9. Cambodia	2.4
10. Italy	2.4

Source: United States Census Bureau.

Government Programs That Support Exports

To see the economic boost that can come from a government-encouraged export strategy, consider Japan, Singapore, South Korea, and the so-called greater-China or "China triangle" market, which includes Taiwan, Hong Kong, and the People's Republic of China. Japan totally recovered from the destruction of World War II and became an economic superpower as a direct result of export strategies devised by the Ministry for International Trade and Industry (MITI). The four tigers—Singapore, South Korea, Taiwan, and Hong Kong— learned from the Japanese experience and built strong export-based economies of their own. Although Asia's "economic bubble" burst in 1997 as a result of uncontrolled growth, Japan and the tigers are moving forward in the twenty-first century at a more moderate rate. China, an economy unto itself, has attracted increased foreign investment from Daimler AG, GM, Hewlett-Packard, and scores of other companies that are setting up production facilities to support local sales, as well as exports to world markets.

Any government concerned with trade deficits or economic development should focus on educating firms about the potential gains from exporting. Policymakers should also remove bureaucratic obstacles that hinder company exports. This is true at the national, regional, and local government levels. In India, for example, leaders in the state of Tamil Nadu recently gave Hyundai permission to operate its plant around the clock, making it the first Hyundai operation anywhere in the world to operate on a 24-hour basis (see Exhibit 8-2).[3] Governments commonly use four activities to support and encourage firms that engage in exporting. These are tax incentives, subsidies, export assistance, and free trade zones.

First, *tax incentives* treat earnings from export activities preferentially either by applying a lower rate to earnings from these activities or by refunding taxes already paid on income associated with exporting. The tax benefits offered by export-conscious governments include varying degrees of tax exemption or tax deferral on export income, accelerated depreciation of export-related assets, and generous tax treatment of overseas market development activities.

From 1985 until 2000, the major tax incentive under U.S. law was the **foreign sales corporation** (**FSC**), through which American exporters could obtain a 15 percent exclusion on earnings from international sales. Big exporters benefited the most from the arrangement; Boeing, for example, saved about $100 million per year, and Eastman Kodak saved about $40 million annually. However, in 2000, the WTO ruled that any tax break that was contingent on exports amounted to an illegal subsidy. Accordingly, the U.S. Congress has set about the task of overhauling the FSC system; failure to do so would entitle the EU to impose up to $4 billion in retaliatory tariffs. Potential winners and

---

[3]Anand Giridharadas, "Foreign Automakers See India as Exporter," *The New York Times* (September 12, 2006), p. C5.

Exhibit 8-2: Chennai (formerly Madras) is both the capital of Tamil Nadu and the automotive capital of India. These Hyundai autos are awaiting export; Daewoo, Fiat, Ford, GM, Honda, Mitsubishi, and Peugeot are among the global automakers with operations in India. India's Automotive Mission Plan calls for sales in the sector to grow 16 percent annually. Before the onset of the global economic crisis, the Ministry of Heavy Industry predicted that vehicle sales would quadruple over the next decade, reaching $145 billion.
Source: Babu/ReutersLandov Media.

losers from a change in the FSC law are lobbying furiously. One proposed version of a new law would benefit GM, Procter & Gamble, Walmart, and other U.S. companies with extensive manufacturing or retail operations overseas. By contrast, Boeing would no longer benefit. As Rudy de Leon, a Boeing executive in charge of government affairs, noted, "As we look at the bill, the export of U.S. commercial aircraft would become considerably more expensive."[4]

Governments also support export performance by providing outright **subsidies**, which are direct or indirect financial contributions or incentives that benefit producers. Subsidies can severely distort trade patterns when less competitive but subsidized producers displace competitive producers in world markets (see the Culture Watch feature). OECD members spend nearly $400 billion annually on farm subsidies; currently, total annual farm support in the EU is estimated at $100 billion. With about $40 billion in annual support, the United States has the highest subsidies of any single nation. Agricultural subsidies are particularly controversial because, although they protect the interests of farmers in developed countries, they work to the detriment of farmers in developing areas such as Africa and India. The EU has undertaken an overhaul of its **Common Agricultural Policy (CAP)**, which critics have called "as egregious a system of protection as any" and "the single most harmful piece of protectionism in the world."[5] In May 2002, much to Europe's dismay, President George W. Bush signed a $118 billion farm bill that actually *increased* subsidies to American farmers over a six-year period. The Bush administration takes the position that, despite the increases, overall U.S. subsidies are still lower than those in Europe and Japan. Congress recently voted to extend the farm bill for another five years.

The third support area is *governmental assistance* to exporters. Companies can avail themselves of a great deal of government information concerning the location of markets and credit risks. Assistance may also be oriented toward export promotion. Government agencies at various levels often take the lead in setting up trade fairs and trade missions designed to promote sales to foreign customers.

The export/import process can entail red tape and bureaucratic delays. This is especially true in emerging markets such as China and India. In an effort to facilitate exports, countries are designating certain areas as **free trade zones (FTZ)** or **special economic zones (SEZ)**. These are geographic entities that offer manufacturers simplified customs procedures, operational flexibility, and a general environment of relaxed regulations.

---

[4]Edmund L. Andrews, "A Civil War Within a Trade Dispute," *The New York Times* (September 20, 2002), pp. C1, C2.
[5]John Micklethwait and Adrian Wooldridge, *A Future Perfect: The Challenge and Hidden Promise of Globalization* (New York: Crown Publishers, 2000), p. 261.

CULTURE WATCH
Cane Growers of Australia?

Australia is the world's number two sugar exporter in the world. Australia is a low-cost producer and has the capacity to produce more than 4.75 million tons of sugar each year. The industry is worth between $1.5 billion to $2 billion in direct revenue, including $1.2 billion in exports. Around 80 percent of Australia's production of sugar goes into the world market.

Australia does not have a protective tariff for the remaining 20 percent of the output that is sold in the domestic market. Instead, the industry has had to learn to compete on an international basis. It has tried to adopt the best practices in production, handling, quality, reliability, and service.

In Queensland there are warehouses that can store 2 million tons of sugar. These are close to the bulk port terminals, so that the sugar can be exported to major customers, including Canada, Japan, Korea, Malaysia, New Zealand, and the United States. The Queensland sugar cane is primarily grown for processing into raw sugar. It is then sold to the refineries. Nearly all of Australia's sugar exports come from Queensland.

Until deregulation on January 1, 2006, all Australian sugar was handled by the sugar marketer, Queensland Sugar Limited. Since then, many of the sugar growers have retained their relationship with the company. It uses its marketing power in order to leverage better prices for Australian sugar on the global market. In other areas of Australia, notably New South Wales and Western Australia, the growers tend to manage their own marketing. The majority of sugar from New South Wales finds its way into the domestic market, while sugar from the Ord area of Western Australia is largely exported to Indonesia.

There are around 4,500 businesses in Australia supplying the 25 sugar mills. During the season, these mills each employ around 150 people and can crush up to 10,000 tons of cane a day. The average time from the cane being cut to it being crushed is less than 12 hours. Some of the sugar mills have been in operation for 100 years. However in 1998 a new mill near Mareeba in Queensland was the first one to be built in 73 years. There are around 500 cane farming operations in New South Wales, 18 in the Ord River area of Western Australia, and 4,000 in Queensland. Most of the cane farms are still family businesses, and only around 2.5 percent are owned by the sugar mills.

All sugar has been handled in bulk since 1964, and it has been harvested mechanically since 1979. The growers have been quick to adopt new farming practices in order to maintain their competitiveness on the world market.

Until 1924, Australia had been a net importer of sugar, but since then not only has Australia been able to produce enough sugar for its own domestic market, but it has also become one of the largest exporters of raw sugar in the world. Brazil has become a dominant force in world sugar production. The European Union subsidizes sugar production, and while Cuba has declined as a producer, Thailand has grown. Some 97 percent of all the Australian sugar exports go to the East Asia region of the world and 3 percent

to North America. This has been a remarkable turnaround in less than 10 years. Back in 1999, 71 percent of exports went to East Asia, 19 percent to North America, 8 percent to the Middle East, and 2 percent to Europe.

In the United States, the total demand for sugar per year is around 10.5 million tons. Around 85 percent of this is supplied by either beet processors or sugar cane refiners from domestically grown sugar. The remaining 15 percent is refined from imported raw cane sugar from 40 different countries, including Australia. Unsurprisingly, the U.S.-based American Sugar Alliance, a national coalition of sugar cane and sugar beet farmers, processors, refiners, and suppliers, is keen to protect its own domestic market. In fact, the U.S. government set certain limits on the amount of sugar that American businesses can import without having to pay tariffs. Due to international trade deals. the United States is committed to import 1.3 million tons of raw cane sugar per year.

Australia was among those that complained in 2005 regarding the European Union's alleged dumping of surplus sugar into the world market. The EU had been producing a surplus of up to 6 million tons per year. Australia, Brazil, and Thailand were among those to be hit by a fall in the world market price for sugar as a result of this surplus. The EU subsidy program was found to be illegal in 2005. Smaller producers in the Caribbean and in Africa had been hit the hardest, although larger producers like Australia were not immune.

The debate over the global sugar industry continues. Australia, for example, provides state and federal subsidies to sugar producers in order to cope with the depressed global prices. The United States sees this as being grossly unfair, as Australia only imports 10,000 tons of sugar a year, while on average the United States imports 1.65 million tons. The U.S. sugar producers believe that their market is already oversupplied with subsidized foreign sugar. They believe that it threatens up to 150,000 U.S. jobs and that businesses involved in the sugar industry are teetering on the brink of ruin.

However, in terms of the importance to Australia of the U.S. market, it is debatable whether subsidized Australian sugar makes any great difference. Only 8 percent of all the sugar that is imported into the United States is Australian. What the U.S. producers object to is the fact that they receive no subsidies from federal or state government and that through trade treaties and obligations related to market access the United States has to accept sugar imports whether the market needs them or not.

Globally, the demand for sugar has never been higher. In fall 2009, strong demand for sugar from India pushed raw sugar prices to a 28-year high. Australian sugar production has failed to rise significantly, mainly due to a lack of investment in heavy agricultural machinery. At best it improves its production by 10 percent per year.

Sources: Cane Growers' Australia, www.canegrowers.com.au; Australian Government's Australian National Resources Atlas, www.anra.au; Australian Government Department of Agriculture, Fisheries and Forestry, www.daff.gov.au; Sugar Australia, www.sugaraustralia.com.au; The American Sugar Alliance, www.sugaralliance.org.

Governmental Actions to Discourage Imports and Block Market Access

Measures such as tariffs, import controls, and a host of nontariff barriers are designed to limit the inward flow of goods. **Tariffs** can be thought of as the "three R's" of global business: rules, rate schedules (duties), and regulations of individual countries. Duties on individual products or services are listed in the schedule of rates (see Table 8-3). One expert on global trade defines **duties** as "taxes that punish individuals for making choices of which their governments disapprove."[6]

As noted in earlier chapters, a major U.S. objective in the Uruguay round of GATT negotiations was to improve market access for U.S. companies with major U.S. trading partners. When the round ended in December 1993, the United States had secured reductions or total elimination of tariffs on 11 categories of U.S. goods exported to the EU, Japan, five of the EFTA nations (Austria, Switzerland, Sweden, Finland, and Norway), New Zealand, South Korea, Hong Kong, and Singapore. The categories affected included equipment for the construction, agricultural, medical, and scientific industry sectors, as well as steel, beer, brown distilled spirits, pharmaceuticals, paper, pulp and printed matter, furniture, and toys. Most of the remaining tariffs were phased out over a five-year period. A key goal of the recent Doha round of trade talks is the reduction in agricultural tariffs, which currently average 12 percent in the United States, 31 percent in the EU, and 51 percent in Japan.

Developed under the auspices of the Customs Cooperation Council (now the World Customs Organization), the **Harmonized Tariff System (HTS)** went into effect in January 1989 and has since been adopted by the majority of trading nations. Under this system, importers and exporters have to determine the correct classification number for a given product or service that will cross borders. With the Harmonized Tariff Schedule B, the export classification number for any exported item is the same as the import classification number. Also, exporters must include the Harmonized Tariff Schedule B number on their export documents to facilitate customs clearance. Accuracy, especially in the eyes of customs officials, is essential. The U.S. Census Bureau compiles trade statistics from the HTS system. Any HTS with a value of less than $2,500 is not counted as a U.S. export. However, *all* imports, regardless of value, are counted.

In spite of the progress made in simplifying tariff procedures, administering a tariff is an enormous problem. People who work with imports and exports must familiarize themselves with the different classifications and use them accurately. Even a tariff schedule of several thousand items cannot clearly describe every product traded globally. The introduction of new products and new materials used in manufacturing processes creates new problems. Often, determining the duty rate on a particular article requires assessing how the item is used or determining its main component material. Two or more alternative classifications may have to be considered. A product's classification can make a substantial difference in the duty applied. For example, is a Chinese-made X-Men action figure a doll or a toy? For many years, dolls were subject to a 12 percent duty when imported into the United States; the rate was 6.8 percent for toys. Moreover, action figures that represent non-human creatures such as monsters or robots were categorized as toys and thus qualified for lower duties than human figures that the Customs Service classifies as dolls. Duties on both categories have been eliminated; however, the Toy Biz subsidiary of Marvel Enterprises spent nearly six years on an action in the U.S. Court of

TABLE 8-3 Examples of Trade Barriers

Country/Region	Tariff Barriers	NTBs
European Union	16.5% antidumping tariff on shoes from China, 10% on shoes from Vietnam	Quotas on Chinese textiles
China	Tariffs as high as 28% on foreign-made auto parts	Expensive, time-consuming procedures for obtaining pharmaceutical import licenses

[6]Edward L. Hudgins, "Mercosur Gets a 'Not Guilty' on Trade Diversion," *The Wall Street Journal* (March 21, 1997), p. A19.

International Trade to prove that its X-Men action figures do not represent humans. Although the move appalled many fans of the mutant superheroes, Toy Biz hoped to be reimbursed for overpayment of past duties made when the U.S. Customs Service had classified imports of Wolverine and his fellow figures as dolls.[7]

A **nontariff barrier (NTB)** is any measure other than a tariff that is a deterrent or obstacle to the sale of products in a foreign market. Also known as *hidden trade barriers*, NTBs include quotas, discriminatory procurement policies, restrictive customs procedures, arbitrary monetary policies, and restrictive regulations.

A **quota** is a government-imposed limit or restriction on the number of units or the total value of a particular product or product category that can be imported. Generally, the quotas are designed to protect domestic producers. In 2005, for example, textile producers in Italy and other European countries were granted quotas on 10 categories of textile imports from China. The quotas, which were scheduled to run through the end of 2007, were designed to give European producers an opportunity to prepare for increased competition.[8]

Discriminatory procurement policies can take the form of government rules, laws, or administrative regulations requiring that goods or services must be purchased from domestic companies. For example, the Buy American Act of 1933 stipulates that U.S. federal agencies and government programs must buy goods produced in the United States. The Act does not apply if domestically produced goods are not available, if the cost is unreasonable, or if "buying local" would be inconsistent with the public interest. Similarly, the Fly American Act states that U.S. government employees must fly on domestic carriers whenever possible. One of the most controversial aspects of U.S. President Barack Obama's $885 billion economic stimulus bill was a proposed provision requiring that all manufactured goods purchased with stimulus money be "Made in the USA" (see Exhibit 8-3). Opponents alleged that the proposal's language violated U.S. trade agreements; the clause elicited strong protests from key trading partners, some of which announced that they would retaliate with protectionist measures of their own. Congress ultimately toned down the protectionist rhetoric, thus averting a possible trade war.[9]

Customs procedures are considered restrictive if they are administered in a way that makes compliance difficult and expensive. For example, the U.S. Department of Commerce might

Exhibit 8-3: In February 2009, U.S. President Barack Obama addressed workers at a Caterpillar plant in Peoria, Illinois. The appearance came one month after Caterpillar officials announced the elimination of 22,000 jobs. The President spoke about his economic recovery and reinvestment plan, noting, "What's happening at this company tells us a larger story about what's happening with our nation's economy—because, in many ways, you can measure America's bottom line by looking at Caterpillar's bottom line." The President added, "Caterpillar has shaped the American landscape, and shown the world what a great American company looks like."
Source: Newscom.

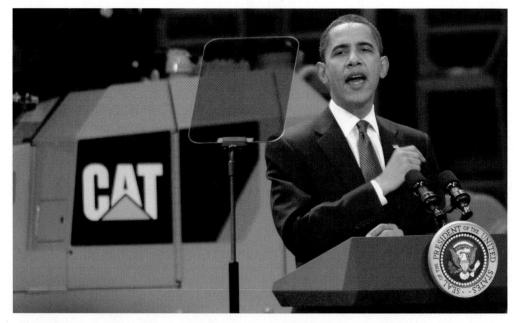

[7]Neil King Jr., "Is Wolverine Human? A Judge Answers 'No'; Fans Howl in Protest," *The Wall Street Journal* (January 20, 2003), p. A1.

[8]Juliane von Reppert-Bismarck and Michael Carolan, "Quotas Squeeze European Boutiques," *The Wall Street Journal* (October 22, 2005), p. A9.

[9]David Lynch, "'Buy American' Clause Stirs Up Controversy," *USA Today* (February 4, 2009), p. 3B.

classify a product under a certain harmonized number; Canadian customs may disagree. The U.S. exporter may have to attend a hearing with Canadian customs officials to reach an agreement. Such delays cost time and money for both the importer and exporter.

Discriminatory exchange rate policies distort trade in much the same way as selective import duties and export subsidies. As noted earlier, some Western policymakers have argued that China is pursuing policies that ensure an artificially weak currency. Such a policy has the effect of giving Chinese goods a competitive price edge in world markets.

Finally, restrictive administrative and technical regulations also can create barriers to trade. These may take the form of antidumping regulations, product size regulations, and safety and health regulations. Some of these regulations are intended to keep out foreign goods; others are directed toward legitimate domestic objectives. For example, the safety and pollution regulations being developed in the United States for automobiles are motivated almost entirely by legitimate concerns about highway safety and pollution. However, an effect of these regulations has been to make it so expensive to comply with U.S. safety requirements that some automakers have withdrawn certain models from the market. Volkswagen, for example, was forced to stop selling diesel automobiles in the United States for several years.

As discussed in earlier chapters, there is a growing trend to remove all such restrictive trade barriers on a regional basis. The largest single effort was undertaken by the EU and resulted in the creation of a single market starting January 1, 1993. The intent was to have one standard for all of Europe's industry sectors, including automobile safety, drug testing and certification, and food and product quality controls. The introduction of the euro has also facilitated trade and commerce.

TARIFF SYSTEMS

Tariff systems provide either a single rate of duty for each item, applicable to all countries, or two or more rates, applicable to different countries or groups of countries. Tariffs are usually grouped into two classifications.

The **single-column tariff** is the simplest type of tariff; a schedule of duties in which the rate applies to imports from all countries on the same basis. Under the **two-column tariff** (Table 8-4), column 1 includes "general" duties plus "special" duties indicating reduced rates determined by tariff negotiations with other countries. Rates agreed upon by "convention" are extended to all countries that qualify for **normal trade relations (NTR)** (formerly most-favored nation or MFN) status within the framework of the WTO. Under the WTO, nations agree to apply their most favorable tariff or lowest tariff rate to all nations—subject to some exceptions—that are signatories to the WTO. Column 2 shows rates for countries that do not enjoy NTR status.

Table 8-5 shows a detailed entry from chapter 89 of the harmonized system pertaining to "Ships, Boats, and Floating Structures" (for explanatory purposes, each column has been identified with an alphabet letter). Column A contains the heading level numbers that uniquely identify each product. For example, the product entry for heading level 8903 is "yachts and other vessels for pleasure or sports; row boats and canoes." Subheading level 8903.10 identifies "inflatable";

TABLE 8-4 **Sample Rates of Duty for U.S. Imports**

Column 1		Column 2
General	Special	Non-NTR
1.5%	Free (A, E, IL, J, MX)	30%
	0.4% (CA)	

A, Generalized System of Preferences
E, Caribbean Basin Initiative (CBI) Preference
IL, Israel Free Trade Agreement (FTA) Preference
J, Andean Agreement Preference
MX, NAFTA Canada Preference
CA, NAFTA Mexico Preference

TABLE 8-5 Chapter 89 of the Harmonized System

A	B	C	D	E	F	G
8903		Yachts and other vessels for pleasure or sports; row boats and canoes				
8903.10.00		Inflatable		2.4%	Free (A, E, IL, J, MX)[a] 0.4% (CA)	
		Valued over $500				
	15	With attached rigid hull.	No			
	45	Other	No			
	60	Other	No			
8903.91.00		Other: Sailboats, with or without auxiliary motors		1.5%	Free (A, E, IL, J, MX) 0.3% (CA)	

A, Generalized System of Preferences
E, Caribbean Basin Initiative (CBI) Preference
IL, Israel Free Trade Agreement (FTA) Preference
J, Andean Agreement Preference
MX, NAFTA Canada Preference
CA, NAFTA Mexico Preference

8903.91 designates "sailboats with or without auxiliary motor." These six-digit numbers are used by more than 100 countries that have signed on to the HTS. Entries can extend to as many as 10 digits, with the last four used on a country-specific basis for each nation's individual tariff and data collection purposes. Taken together, E and F correspond to Column 1 as shown in Table 8-4, while G corresponds to Column 2.

The United States has given NTR status to some 180 countries around the world, so the name is really a misnomer. Only North Korea, Iran, Cuba, and Libya are excluded, showing that NTR is really a political tool more than an economic one. In the past, China had been threatened with the loss of NTR status because of alleged human rights violations. The landed prices of its exports—the cost after the goods have been delivered to a port, unloaded, and passed through customs—would have risen significantly. Thus, many Chinese products would have been priced out of the U.S. market. The U.S. Congress granted China permanent NTR as a precursor to its joining the WTO in 2001. Table 8-6 illustrates what a loss of NTR status would have meant to China.

A *preferential tariff* is a reduced tariff rate applied to imports from certain countries. GATT prohibits the use of preferential tariffs, with three major exceptions. First are historical preference arrangements such as the British Commonwealth preferences and similar arrangements that existed before GATT. Second, preference schemes that are part of a formal economic integration treaty, such as free trade areas or common markets, are excluded. Third,

TABLE 8-6 Tariff Rates for China, NTR Versus Non-NTR

	NTR	Non-NTR
Gold jewelry, such as plated neck chains	6.5%	80%
Screws, lock washers, misc. iron/steel parts	5.8%	35%
Steel products	0–5%	66%
Rubber footwear	0	66%
Women's overcoats	19%	35%

Source: U.S. Customs Service.

industrial countries are permitted to grant preferential market access to companies based in less-developed countries.

The United States is now a signatory to the GATT customs valuation code. U.S. customs value law was amended in 1980 to conform to the GATT valuation standards. Under the code, the primary basis of customs valuation is "transaction value." As the name implies, *transaction value* is defined as the actual individual transaction price paid by the buyer to the seller of the goods being valued. In instances where the buyer and seller are related parties (e.g., when Honda's U.S. manufacturing subsidiaries purchase parts from Japan), customs authorities have the right to scrutinize the transfer price to make sure it is a fair reflection of market value. If there is no established transaction value for the good, alternative methods that are used to compute the customs value sometimes result in increased values and, consequently, increased duties. In the late 1980s, the U.S. Treasury Department began a major investigation into the transfer prices charged by the Japanese automakers to their U.S. subsidiaries. It charged that the Japanese paid virtually no U.S. income taxes because of their "losses" on the millions of cars they import into the United States each year.

During the Uruguay round of GATT negotiations, the United States successfully sought a number of amendments to the Agreement on Customs Valuations. Most important, the United States wanted clarification of the rights and obligations of importing and exporting countries in cases where fraud was suspected. Two overall categories of products were frequently targeted for investigation. The first included exports of textiles, cosmetics, and consumer durables; the second included entertainment software such as videotapes, audiotapes, and compact disks. Such amendments improve the ability of U.S. exporters to defend their interests if charged with fraudulent practices. The amendments were also designed to encourage nonsignatories, especially developing countries, to become parties to the agreement.

Customs Duties

Customs duties are divided into two categories. They may be calculated either as a percentage of the value of the goods (ad valorem duty), as a specific amount per unit (specific duty), or as a combination of both of these methods. Before World War II, specific duties were widely used and the tariffs of many countries, particularly those in Europe and Latin America, were extremely complex. During the past half century, the trend has been toward the conversion to ad valorem duties.

As noted, an *ad valorem duty* is expressed as a percentage of the value of goods. The definition of customs value varies from country to country. An exporter is well advised to secure information about the valuation practices applied to his or her product in the country of destination. The reason is simple: to be price competitive with local producers. In countries adhering to GATT conventions on customs valuation, the customs value is the value of cost, insurance, and freight (CIF) at the port of importation. This figure should reflect the arm's-length price of the goods at the time the duty becomes payable.

A *specific duty* is expressed as a specific amount of currency per unit of weight, volume, length, or other units of measurement; for example, "50 cents U.S. per pound," "$1.00 U.S. per pair," or "25 cents U.S. per square yard." Specific duties are usually expressed in the currency of the importing country, but there are exceptions, particularly in countries that have experienced sustained inflation.

Both ad valorem and specific duties are occasionally set out in the custom tariff for a given product. Normally, the applicable rate is the one that yields the higher amount of duty, although there are cases where the lower is specified. Compound or mixed duties provide for specific, plus ad valorem, rates to be levied on the same articles.

Other Duties and Import Charges

Dumping, which is the sale of merchandise in export markets at unfair prices, is discussed in detail in Chapter 11. To offset the impact of dumping and to penalize guilty companies, most countries have introduced legislation providing for the imposition of **antidumping duties** if injury is caused to domestic producers. Such duties take the form of special additional import charges equal to the dumping margin. Antidumping duties are almost invariably applied to products that are also manufactured or grown in the importing country. In the United States, antidumping duties are assessed after the commerce department finds a foreign company guilty of dumping and the International Trade Commission rules that the dumped products injured American companies.

Countervailing duties (CVDs) are additional duties levied to offset subsidies granted in the exporting country. In the United States, countervailing duty legislation and procedures are very similar to those pertaining to dumping. The U.S. Commerce Department and the International Trade Commission jointly administer both the countervailing duty and antidumping laws under provisions of the Trade and Tariff Act of 1984. Subsidies and countervailing measures received a great deal of attention during the Uruguay GATT negotiations. In 2001, the ITC and commerce department imposed both countervailing and antidumping duties on Canadian lumber producers. The CVDs were intended to offset subsidies to Canadian sawmills in the form of low fees for cutting trees in forests owned by the Canadian government. The antidumping duties on imports of softwood lumber, flooring, and siding were in response to complaints by American producers that the Canadians were exporting lumber at prices below their production cost.

Several countries, including Sweden and some other members of the EU, apply a system of *variable import levies* to certain categories of imported agricultural products. If prices of imported products would undercut those of domestic products, these levies raise the price of imported products to the domestic price level. *Temporary surcharges* have been introduced from time to time by certain countries, such as the United Kingdom and the United States, to provide additional protection for local industry and, in particular, in response to balance-of-payments deficits.

KEY EXPORT PARTICIPANTS

Anyone with responsibilities for exporting should be familiar with some of the entities that can assist with various export-related tasks. Some of these entities, including foreign purchasing agents, export brokers, and export merchants, have no assignment of responsibility from the client. Others, including export management companies, manufacturers' export representatives, export distributors, and freight forwarders, are assigned responsibilities by the exporter.

Foreign purchasing agents are variously referred to as *buyer for export*, *export commission house*, or *export confirming house*. They operate on behalf of, and are compensated by, an overseas customer known as a "principal." They generally seek out the manufacturer whose price and quality match the specifications of their principal. Foreign purchasing agents often represent governments, utilities, railroads, and other large users of materials. Foreign purchasing agents do not offer the manufacturer or exporter stable volume except when long-term supply contracts are agreed upon. Purchases may be completed as domestic transactions with the purchasing agent handling all export packing and shipping details, or the agent may rely on the manufacturer to handle the shipping arrangements.

The **export broker** receives a fee for bringing together the seller and the overseas buyer. The fee is usually paid by the seller, but sometimes the buyer pays it. The broker takes no title to the goods and assumes no financial responsibility. A broker usually specializes in a specific commodity, such as grain or cotton, and is less frequently involved in the export of manufactured goods.

Export merchants are sometimes referred to as *jobbers*. These are marketing intermediaries that identify market opportunities in one country or region and make purchases in other countries to fill these needs. An export merchant typically buys unbranded products directly from the producer or manufacturer. The export merchant then brands the goods and performs all other marketing activities, including distribution. For example, an export merchant might identify a good source of women's boots in a factory in China. The merchant then purchases a large quantity of the boots and markets them in, for example, the EU or the United States.

An **export management company (EMC)** is an independent marketing intermediary that acts as the export department for two or more manufacturers ("principals") whose product lines do not compete with each other. The EMC usually operates in the name of its principals for export markets but it may operate in its own name. It may act as an independent distributor, purchasing and reselling goods at an established price or profit margin. Alternatively, it may act as a commission representative, taking no title and bearing no financial risks in the sale. According to one recent survey of U.S.-based EMCs, the most important activities for export success are gathering marketing information, communicating with markets, setting prices, and ensuring parts availability. The same survey ranked export activities in terms of degree of difficulty; analyzing political risk, sales force management, setting pricing, and obtaining financial information were found to be the most difficult to accomplish. One of the study's conclusions was that the U.S. government should do a better job of helping EMCs and their clients analyze the political risk associated with foreign markets.[10]

Another type of intermediary is the **manufacturer's export agent (MEA)**. Much like an EMC, the MEA can act as an export distributor or as an export commission representative. However, the MEA does not perform the functions of an export department and the scope of market activities is usually limited to a few countries. An **export distributor** assumes financial risk. The export distributor usually represents several manufacturers and is therefore sometimes known as a *combination export manager*. The firm usually has the exclusive right to sell a manufacturer's products in all or some markets outside the country of origin. The distributor pays for the goods and assumes all financial risks associated with the foreign sale; it handles all shipping details. The agent ordinarily sells at the manufacturer's list price abroad; compensation comes in the form of an agreed percentage of list price. The distributor may operate in its own name or in the manufacturer's name.

The **export commission representative** assumes no financial risk. The manufacturer assigns some or all foreign markets to the commission representative. The manufacturer carries all accounts, although the representative often provides credit checks and arranges financing. Like the export distributor, the export commission representative handles several accounts and hence is also known as a combination export management company.

The **cooperative exporter**, sometimes called a *mother hen*, *piggyback exporter*, or *export vendor*, is an export organization of a manufacturing company retained by other independent manufacturers to sell their products in foreign markets. Cooperative exporters usually operate as export distributors for other manufacturers, but in special cases they operate as export commission representatives. They are regarded as a form of export management company.

Freight forwarders are licensed specialists in traffic operations, customs clearance, and shipping tariffs and schedules; simply put, they can be thought of as travel agents for freight. Minnesota-based C.H. Robinson Worldwide is one such company. Freight forwarders seek out the best routing and the best prices for transporting freight and assist exporters in determining and paying fees and insurance charges. Forwarders may also do export packing, when necessary. They usually handle freight from the port of export to the overseas port of import. They may also move inland freight from the factory to the port of export and, through affiliates abroad, handle freight from the port of import to the customer. Freight forwarders also perform consolidation services for land, air, and ocean freight. Because they contract for large blocks of space on a ship or airplane, they can resell that space to various shippers at a rate lower than is generally available to individual shippers dealing directly with the export carrier.

A licensed forwarder receives brokerage fees or rebates from shipping companies for booked space. Some companies and manufacturers engage in freight forwarding or some portion of it on their own, but they may not, under law, receive brokerage from shipping lines.

ORGANIZING FOR EXPORTING IN THE MANUFACTURER'S COUNTRY

Home-country issues involve deciding whether to assign export responsibility inside the company or to work with an external organization specializing in a product or geographic area. Most companies handle export operations within their own in-house export organization. Depending on the company's size, responsibilities may be incorporated into an employee's domestic job description. Alternatively, these responsibilities may be handled as part of a separate division or organizational structure.

---

[10]Donald G. Howard, "The Role of Export Management Companies in Global Marketing," *Journal of Global Marketing* 8, no. 1 (1994), pp. 95–110.

The possible arrangements for handling exports include the following:

1. As a part-time activity performed by domestic employees
2. Through an export partner affiliated with the domestic marketing structure that takes possession of the goods before they leave the country
3. Through an export department that is independent of the domestic marketing structure
4. Through an export department within an international division
5. For multidivisional companies, each of the preceding options is available

A company that assigns a sufficiently high priority to its export business will establish an in-house organization. It then faces the question of how to organize effectively. This depends on two things: the company's appraisal of the opportunities in export marketing and its strategy for allocating resources to markets on a global basis. It may be possible for a company to make export responsibility part of a domestic employee's job description. The advantage of this arrangement is obvious: It is a low-cost arrangement requiring no additional personnel. However, this approach can work under only two conditions: First, the domestic employee assigned to the task must be thoroughly competent in terms of product and customer knowledge; second, that competence must be applicable to the target international market(s). The key issue underlying the second condition is the extent to which the target export market is different from the domestic market. If customer circumstances and characteristics are similar, the requirements for specialized regional knowledge are reduced.

➔ STRATEGIC DECISION MAKING IN GLOBAL MARKETING
Turkish Exports Take Off . . .

The Turkish economy has been one of the fastest growing in the world over the last few years with a stabilized macroeconomic situation and progress regarding the EU accession. The country has been a part of the Custom Union since 1996, and trade barriers continue to decrease. The EU is the major export market for Turkish products, with Germany being the number one export destination. The Turkish government's export incentive programs is a major factor in the success of these export development strategies.

Turkey abandoned its "import substitution" policy in the early 1980s, and an industrialization strategy based on export growth has been adopted to promote internationalization. The main objectives of the new strategy were the promotion of exports, liberalization of foreign trade, and encouragement of private sector activities.

The main driving force behind Turkish export growth after 2000 is increased productivity. In this period, Turkey experienced a major structural change, and its exports shifted from conventional labor-intensive sectors to more technology-capital-intensive sectors with higher value-added goods. High-margin brands contributed to an upgrade in the value chain. In 1996, total exports were $23 billion, whereas in 2007 they reached $107 billion. Today exports exceed 13,000 items produced by 42,000 companies.

Many Turkish firms achieved EU-ISO quality standards, and the perception of quality of Turkish goods has improved in the international marketplace. Turkish firms have won the European Quality Award six times since 1996.

State-owned bank Eximbank Turkey acts as a major export incentive instrument for Turkey by offering specialized financial services like credit, insurance, and guarantee programs. Through Eximbank's subsidized financing for exporters, many SMEs have become successful in highly fragmented global markets.

IGEME (The Export Promotion Centre of Turkey) is the preferred choice by the majority of local companies as their export training provider. After the 1980s, IGEME contributed to the government's efforts to determine bottlenecks for Turkish exports in order to improve the competitive advantage of Turkish firms, especially those of SMEs, for long-term solutions to the structural problems concerning exports.

Another successful model was the establishment of specialized "foreign trade companies" through government incentives. In order to improve the efficiency of SMEs and to increase their competitive capacity, a nonprofit and semiautonomous organization, KOSGEB (The Small and Medium Industry Development Organization), was established by the government in 1990. By providing services at national and international fairs and exhibitions, KOSGEB facilitates the SMEs' entering into new markets.

Local and regional clusters are also expanding through organized industrial zones, including automobile, footwear, leather, textile, and fashion industries. For example, the Fashion and Textile Cluster project was financed by the EU where the beneficiaries, were SMEs. The government supported the "Turquality" project with the aim to promote Turkish brands in textiles, ready-made garments, and leather goods, enhancing Turkey's image in international markets.

Sources: Daniel Workman, "Turkey's Top Imports & Exports 2008," www.suite101.com, Accessed on September 29, 2009; John Gillies, "Turkey: Better Training for Small Exporters," *International Trade Center*, www.tradeforum.com, Issue April 2009; "Bringing Down the Barriers—Chartering a Dynamic Export Development Agenda," World Export Development Forum, Montreux, October 8-11, 2007, UNCTAO/WTO; Murat H. Altintas, Tuncer Tokol, and Talha Harcar, "The Effects of Export Barriers on Perceived Export Performance: An Empirical Research on SMEs in Turkey," *EuroMed Journal of Business*, vol. 2, Issue January 2007, p. 36–56; www.igeme.org.tr; www.eximbank.gov.tr; www.die.gov.tr; www.kosgeb.gov.tr.

Exhibit 8-4: Bucking the trend of downward export income, at the end of 2009 Turkey saw exports increase by nearly 5 percent. By the end of 2009 the total value of exports was worth $94.7 billion, 28 percent down year-on-year compared to 2008. Yet the small monthly increase indicates the strength of the Turkish export market. In recent years the hardest hit has been the agricultural and the mining sectors. Ready to wear and apparel manufacturers, have seen an arrest in the fall of export sales or slight increases.
Source: © dbimages/ Alamy.

The company that chooses not to perform its own marketing and promotion in-house has numerous external export service providers from which to choose. As described previously, these include export management companies (EMCs), export merchants, export brokers, combination export managers, manufacturers' export representatives or commission agents, and export distributors. However, because these terms and labels may be used inconsistently, we urge the reader to check and confirm the services performed by a particular independent export organization.

ORGANIZING FOR EXPORTING IN THE MARKET COUNTRY

In addition to deciding whether to rely on in-house or external export specialists in the home country, a company must also make arrangements to distribute the product in the target market country. Every exporting organization faces one basic decision: To what extent do we rely on direct market representation as opposed to representation by independent intermediaries?

There are two major advantages to direct representation in a market: control and communications. Direct market representation allows decisions concerning program development, resource allocation, or price changes to be implemented unilaterally. Moreover, when a product is not yet established in a market, special efforts are necessary to achieve sales. The advantage of direct representation is that the marketer's investment ensures these special efforts. With indirect or independent representation, such efforts and investment are often not forthcoming; in many cases, there is simply not enough incentive for independents to invest significant time and money in representing a product. The other great advantage to direct representation is that the possibilities for feedback and information from the market are much greater. This information can vastly improve export marketing decisions concerning product, price, communications, and distribution.

Direct representation does not mean that the exporter is selling directly to the consumer or customer. In most cases, direct representation involves selling to wholesalers or retailers. For example, the major automobile exporters in Germany and Japan rely upon direct representation in the U.S. market in the form of their distributing agencies, which are owned and controlled by the manufacturing organization. The distributing agencies sell products to franchised dealers.

In smaller markets, it is usually not feasible to establish direct representation because the low sales volume does not justify the cost. Even in larger markets, a small manufacturer usually lacks adequate sales volume to justify the cost of direct representation. Whenever sales volume is small, use of an independent distributor is an effective method of sales distribution. Finding "good" distributors can be the key to export success.

TRADE FINANCING AND METHODS OF PAYMENT

The appropriate method of payment for a given international sale is a basic credit decision. A number of factors must be considered, including currency availability in the buyer's country, creditworthiness of the buyer, and the seller's relationship to the buyer. Finance managers at companies that have never exported often express concern regarding payment. Many CFOs with international experience know that, in a normal business environment, there are generally fewer collections problems on international sales than on domestic sales, provided the proper financial instruments are used. The reason is simple: A letter of credit can be used to guarantee payment for a product.

Unfortunately, the global financial crisis is undermining the ability of firms of all sizes to get the financing they depend on for trade. Until recently, big lenders such as Citigroup and HSBC had a thriving business setting up lines of credit and then assigning them to smaller banks. However, these smaller banks have become more risk averse and are cutting their exposure to trade financing. Compounding the problem is the fact that trade finance is drying up in key emerging markets—the very markets that have the potential to boost the volume of global trade. In Brazil, for example, even large companies such as Embraer are finding that the cost of dollar-denominated financing has increased dramatically. To remedy the situation, Brazil's development bank and central bank are both making funds available for trade financing.[11]

With the constraints of the current economic environment in mind, we will review the basics of trade financing. The export sale begins when the exporter-seller and the importer-buyer agree to do business. The agreement is formalized when the terms of the deal are set down in a pro forma invoice, contract, fax, or some other document. Among other things, the **pro forma invoice** spells out how much, and by what means, the exporter-seller wants to be paid.

Documentary Credit

Documentary credits (also known as letters of credit) are widely used as a payment method in international trade. A **letter of credit (L/C)** is essentially a document stating that a bank has substituted its creditworthiness for that of the importer/buyer. Next to cash in advance, an L/C offers the exporter the best assurance of being paid. That assurance arises from the fact that the payment obligation under an L/C lies with the buyer's bank and not with the buyer. The international standard by which L/Cs are interpreted is ICC Publication No. 500 of the Uniform Customs and Practice for Documentary Credits, also known as UCP 500.

The importer-buyer's bank is the "issuing" bank; the importer-buyer is, in essence, asking the issuing bank to extend credit. The importer-buyer is considered the applicant. The issuing bank may require that the importer-buyer deposit funds in the bank or use some other method to secure a line of credit. After agreeing to extend the credit, the issuing bank requests that the exporter-seller's bank advise and/or confirm the L/C. (A bank "confirms" an L/C by adding its name to the document.) The seller's bank becomes the "advising" and/or "confirming" bank. Whether it is advised or confirmed, the L/C represents a guarantee that assures payment contingent on the exporter-seller (the beneficiary in the transaction) complying with the terms set forth in the L/C.

The actual payment process is set in motion when the exporter-seller physically ships the goods and submits the necessary documents as requested in the L/C. These could include a transportation bill of lading (which may represent title to the product), a commercial invoice, a packing list, a certificate of origin, or insurance certificates. For most of the world, a commercial invoice and bill of lading represent the minimum documentation required for customs clearance. If the pro forma invoice specifies a confirmed L/C as the method of payment, the exporter-seller receives payment at the time the correct shipping documents are presented to the confirming bank.

The confirming bank, in turn, requests payment from the issuing bank. In the case of an irrevocable L/C, the exporter-seller receives payment only after the advising bank negotiates the documents and requests payment from the issuing bank in accordance with terms set forth in the L/C. Once the shipper sends the documents to the advising bank, the advising bank negotiates those documents and is referred to as the negotiating bank. Specifically, it takes each shipping document and closely compares it to the L/C. If there are no discrepancies, the negotiating or confirming bank transfers the money to the exporter-seller's account.

---

[11]John Lyons, "Trade-Financing Pinch Hurts the Healthy," *The Wall Street Journal* (December 22, 2008), p. A2.

FIGURE 8-1

Flowchart of a Documentary Credit

The fee for an irrevocable L/C—for example, "1/8 of 1 percent of the value of the credit, with an $80 minimum"—is lower than that for a confirmed L/C. The higher bank fees associated with confirmation can drive up the final cost of the sale; fees are also higher when the transaction involves a country with a high level of risk. Good communication between the exporter-seller and the advising or confirming bank regarding fees is important; the selling price indicated on the pro forma invoice should reflect these and other costs associated with exporting. The process described here is illustrated in Figures 8-1 and 8-2.

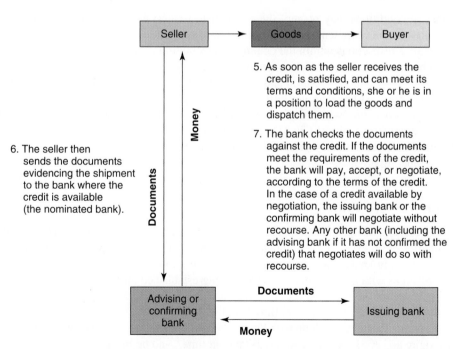

FIGURE 8-2

Flowchart of Documentary Credit Documents

Documentary Collections (Sight or Time Drafts)

After an exporter and an importer have established a good working relationship and the finance manager's level of confidence increases, it may be possible to move to a documentary collection or open-account method of payment. A documentary collection is a method of payment that uses a bill of exchange, also known as a *draft*. A **bill of exchange** is a negotiable instrument that is easily transferable from one party to another. In its simplest form, it is a written order from one party (the *drawer*) directing a second party (the *drawee*) to pay to the order of a third party (the *payee*). Drafts are distinctly different from L/Cs; a **draft** is a payment instrument that transfers all the risk of nonpayment onto the exporter-seller. Banks are involved as intermediaries but they do not bear financial risk. Because a draft is negotiable, however, a bank may be willing to buy the draft from the seller at a discount and thus assume the risk. Also, because bank fees for drafts are lower than those for L/Cs, drafts are frequently used when the monetary value of an export transaction is relatively low.

With a documentary draft, the exporter delivers documents such as the bill of lading, the commercial invoice, a certificate of origin, and an insurance certificate to a bank in the exporter's country. The shipper or bank prepares a collection letter (draft) and sends it via courier to a correspondent bank in the importer-buyer's country. The draft is presented to the importer; payment takes place in accordance with the terms specified in the draft. In the case of a *sight draft* (also known as *documents against payment* or D/P), the importer-buyer is required in principle to make payment when presented with both the draft and the shipping documents, even though the buyer may not have taken possession of the goods yet. *Time drafts* can take two forms. As the name implies, an *arrival draft* specifies that payment is due when the importer-buyer receives the goods; a *date draft* requires payment on a particular date, irrespective of whether the importer has the goods in hand.

Cash in Advance

A number of conditions may prompt the exporter to request cash payment—in whole or in part—in advance of shipment. Examples include times when credit risks abroad are high, when exchange restrictions within the country of destination may delay return of funds for an unreasonable period, or when, for any other reason, the exporter may be unwilling to sell on credit terms. Because of competition and restrictions against cash payment in many countries, the volume of business handled on a cash-in-advance basis is small. A company that manufactures a unique product for which there are no substitutes available can use cash in advance. For example, Compressor Control Corporation is a Midwestern firm that manufactures special equipment for the oil industry. It can stipulate cash in advance because no other company offers a competing product.

Sales on Open Account

Goods that are sold on open account are paid for after delivery. Intracorporate sales to branches or subsidiaries of an exporter are frequently on open-account terms. Open-account terms also generally prevail in areas where exchange controls are minimal and exporters have had long-standing relations with good buyers in nearby or long-established markets. For example, Jimmy Fand is the owner of the Tile Connection in Tampa, Florida. He imports high-quality ceramic tile from Italy, Spain, Portugal, Colombia, Brazil, and other countries. Fand takes pride in the excellent credit rating that he has built up with his vendors. The manufacturers from whom he buys no longer require an L/C; Fand's philosophy is "pay in time," and he makes sure that his payables are sent electronically on the day they are due.

The main objection to open-account sales is the absence of a tangible obligation. Normally, if a time draft is drawn and then dishonored after acceptance, it can be used as a basis of legal action. By contrast, if an open-account transaction is dishonored, the legal procedure may be more complicated. Starting in 1995, the Export-Import Bank expanded insurance coverage on open-account transactions to limit the risk for exporters.

ADDITIONAL EXPORT AND IMPORT ISSUES

In the post–September 11 business environment in the United States, national security concerns have resulted in increased scrutiny for imports. A number of initiatives have been launched to ensure that international cargo cannot be used for terrorism. On such initiative is the Customs Trade Partnership Against Terrorism (C-TPAT). As noted on the U.S. Customs and Border Protection Web site:

> C-TPAT recognizes that U.S. Customs and Border Protection (CBP) can provide the highest level of cargo security only through close cooperation with the ultimate owners of the international supply chain such as importers, carriers, consolidators, licensed customs brokers, and manufacturers. Through this initiative, CBP is asking businesses to ensure the integrity of their security practices and communicate and verify the security guidelines of their business partners within the supply chain.

CBP is responsible for screening import cargo transactions; the goal of C-TPAT is to secure voluntary cooperation from supply chain participants in an effort to reduce inspection delays. Organizations that are C-TPAT certified are entitled to priority status for CBP inspections.

Another issue is *duty drawback*. This refers to refunds of duties paid on imports that are processed or incorporated into other goods and then reexported. Drawbacks have long been used in the United States to encourage exports. However, when NAFTA was negotiated, the United States Trade Representative agreed to restrict drawbacks on exports to Canada and Mexico. As the United States negotiates new trade agreements, some industry groups are lobbying in favor of keeping drawbacks.[12] Duty drawbacks are also common in protected economies and represent a policy instrument that aids exporters by reducing the price of imported production inputs. China was required to remove duty drawbacks as a condition for joining the WTO. As duty rates around the world fall, the drawback issue will become less important.

SOURCING

In global marketing, the issue of customer value is inextricably tied to the **sourcing decision**: whether a company makes or buys its products as well as where it makes or buys its products. **Outsourcing** means shifting production jobs or work assignments to another company to cut costs. When the outsourced work moves to another country, the terms *global outsourcing* or *offshoring* are sometimes used. In today's competitive marketplace, companies are under intense pressure to lower costs; one way to do this is to locate manufacturing and other activities in China, India, and other low-wage countries. And why not? Many consumers do not know where the products they buy—sneakers, for example—are manufactured. It is also true that, as Case 1-1 in Chapter 1 indicated, people often can't match corporate and brand names with particular countries.

In theory, this situation bestows great flexibility on companies. However, in the United States, the sourcing issue became highly politicized during the 2004 presidential campaign. Several Democratic candidates tapped into Americans' fears and concerns over a "jobless" economic recovery. The first wave of nonmanufacturing outsourcing primarily affected *call centers*. These are sophisticated telephone operations that provide customer support and other services to in-bound callers from around the world. Call centers also perform outbound services such as telemarketing (see Exhibit 8-5 and Exhibit 8-6). Now, however, outsourcing is expanding and includes white-collar, high-tech service sector jobs. Workers in low-wage countries are performing a variety of tasks, including completing tax returns, performing research for financial services companies, reading medical CAT scans and X-rays, and drawing up architectural blueprints. American companies that transfer work abroad are finding themselves in the spotlight.

As this discussion suggests, the decision of where to locate key business activities depends on other factors besides cost. There are no simple rules to guide sourcing decisions.

---

[12]R.G. Edmonson, "Drawback Under Attack at USTR," *The Journal of Commerce* (August 11–17), 2003, p. 21.

Exhibit 8-5
Source: Cartoon Features
Syndicate.

The sourcing decision is one of the most complex and important decisions faced by a global company. Several factors may figure into the sourcing decision: management vision, factor costs and conditions, customer needs, public opinion, logistics, country infrastructure, political factors, and exchange rates.

Management Vision

Some chief executives are determined to retain some or all manufacturing in their home country. Nicolas Hayek, head of the Swatch Group, is one such executive. Hayek presided over the spectacular revitalization of the Swiss watch industry. The Swatch Group's portfolio of brands includes Blancpain, Omega, Breguet, Rado, and, of course the inexpensive Swatch brand itself. Hayek demonstrated that the fantasy and imagination of childhood and youth can be translated into breakthroughs that allow mass-market products to be manufactured in high-wage countries

Exhibit 8-6: In Bangalore, India, and other locations, call centers such as this one specialize in "long-distance" or "arm's length" services. India's well-educated workforce and the growing availability of broadband Internet connections mean that more Western service jobs and industries are subject to global outsourcing. Among the tasks being outsourced to India are medical record transcription, tax return preparation, and technical writing. In fact, the book you are reading was typeset in Jawahar Nagar, Pondicherry, India.
Source: CRASTO/Reuters/
Corbis–NY.

side-by-side with handcrafted luxury products. The Swatch story is a triumph of engineering, as well as a triumph of the imagination.

Similarly, top management at Canon has chosen to maintain a strategic focus on high-value-added products rather than manufacturing location. The company aims to keep 60 percent of its manufacturing at home in Japan. The company offers a full line of office equipment, including popular products such as printers and copiers; it is also one of the top producers of digital cameras. Instead of increasing the level of automation in its Japanese factories, it has converted from assembly lines to so-called cell production.[13]

Factor Costs and Conditions

Factor costs are land, labor, and capital costs (remember Economics 101!). Labor includes the cost of workers at every level: manufacturing and production, professional and technical, and management. Basic manufacturing direct labor costs today range from less than $1 per hour in the typical emerging country to $6 to $12 per hour in the typical developed country. In certain industries in the United States, direct labor costs in manufacturing exceed $20 per hour without benefits. German hourly compensation costs for production workers in manufacturing are 160 percent of those in the United States while those in Mexico are only 15 percent of those in the United States. For Volkswagen, the wage differential between Mexico and Germany, combined with the strength of the mark and, most recently, the euro, dictate a Mexican manufacturing facility that builds Golf and Jetta models destined for the United States. The company's Touareg SUV is assembled in Bratislava, Slovakia. Do lower wage rates demand that a company relocate 100 percent of its manufacturing to low-wage countries? Not necessarily. During his tenure as chairman at VW, Ferdinand Piech improved his company's competitiveness by convincing unions to accept flexible work schedules. For example, during peak demand, employees work six-day weeks; when demand slows, factories produce cars only three days per week.

Labor costs in nonmanufacturing jobs are also dramatically lower in some parts of the world. For example, a software engineer in India may receive an annual salary of $12,000; by contrast, an American with the same educational credentials might earn $80,000.

The other factors of production are land, materials, and capital. The cost of these factors depends upon their availability and relative abundance. Often, the differences in factor costs will offset each other so that, on balance, companies have a level field in the competitive arena. For example, some countries have abundant land and Japan has abundant capital. These advantages partially offset each other. When this is the case, the critical factor is management, professional, and worker team effectiveness.

The application of advanced computer controls and other new manufacturing technologies has reduced the proportion of labor relative to capital for many businesses. In formulating a sourcing strategy, company managers and executives should also recognize the declining importance of direct manufacturing labor as a percentage of total product cost. It is certainly true that, for many companies in high-wage countries, the availability of cheap labor is a prime consideration when choosing manufacturing locations; this is why China has become "the world's workplace." However, it is also true that direct labor cost may be a relatively small percentage of the total production cost. As a result, it may not be worthwhile to incur the costs and risks of establishing a manufacturing activity in a distant location.

Customer Needs

Although outsourcing can help reduce costs, sometimes customers are seeking something besides the lowest possible price. Dell Computer recently rerouted some of its call center jobs back to the United States after complaints from key business customers that Indian tech support workers were offering scripted responses and having difficulty answering complex problems. In such instances, the need to keep customers satisfied justifies the higher cost of home-country support operations.

---

[13]Sebastian Moffett, "Canon Manufacturing Strategy Pays Off with Strong Earnings," *The Wall Street Journal* (January 4, 2004), p. B3.

EMERGING MARKETS BRIEFING BOOK

⟫ Furniture Exports from China

Furniture imports are flooding into the United States from China. Until recently, a Chinese-made wooden table might have suffered from obvious flaws such as a warped top or loose legs. Today, however, the situation is quite different: Chinese manufacturers are improving quality and offering designs that appeal to traditional American tastes in décor. The improvements coincided with historically low mortgage rates in the United States; prior to the economic crisis, a record number of Americans were buying new homes or moving into bigger existing ones.

To be sure, there are drawbacks to buying something made halfway around the world. For one thing, oceangoing container ships can encounter delays, and replacement parts can be hard to obtain if a piece breaks. In the case of leather furniture, low prices may be due in part to lower quality leather or a narrower range of color choices. However, China's low labor rates—a typical worker in a furniture factory earns monthly wages equivalent to about $100—translate into reasonable prices that are attractive to budget-conscious American furniture shoppers. For example, some leather sofas from China are priced below $1,000, hundreds less than pieces made in America or Europe. Likewise, an eight-piece dining room set sells for $2,500 to $3,500; a comparable American set would cost twice as much (see Exhibit 8-7).

The furniture industry has become one of the fastest-growing sectors of China's economy. China currently accounts for about 10 percent of global furniture exports, and some industry experts believe exports could increase 30 percent annually through the end of the decade. However, such forecasts are subject to unexpected changes in the business environment. Once such change

was the Asian SARS crisis. New furniture orders fell precipitously as foreign buyers stayed away from Chinese factories and fewer Chinese traveled abroad. At the retail level, many American furniture stores began stocking pieces from non-Asian sources. Some American furniture shoppers were reluctant to buy Chinese-made goods for fear that the disease could somehow be transmitted to humans via inanimate objects. As Lynn Chipperfield, senior vice president at Furniture Brands International, the biggest furniture importer in the United States, noted, "Importing is a constant challenge even under normal circumstances. This doesn't help."

Although the SARS crisis quickly passed, China's export success has caught the attention of American manufacturers and policymakers. American furniture companies, many of which are located in North Carolina and Virginia, have been laying off employees and closing plants. A recent study by an economist at the University of California–Santa Cruz found 500,000 furniture workers lost their jobs between 1979 and 1999; 38 percent were unable to find new jobs. In response, a coalition group called the American Furniture Manufacturers Committee for Legal Trade has petitioned U.S. trade officials. The group is asking investigators to examine whether Chinese furniture prices violate U.S. antidumping statutes.

Sources: Dan Morse and Katy McLaughlin, "China's Latest Export: Your Living Room," *The Wall Street Journal* (January 17, 2003), p. D1; Karby Leggett and Peter Wonacott, "The World's Economy: Surge in Exports from China Jolts Global Industry," *The Wall Street Journal* (October 10, 2002), pp. A1, A8; Jon E. Hilsenrath and Peter Wonacott, "Imports Hammer Furniture Makers," *The Wall Street Journal* (September 20, 2002), p. A2.

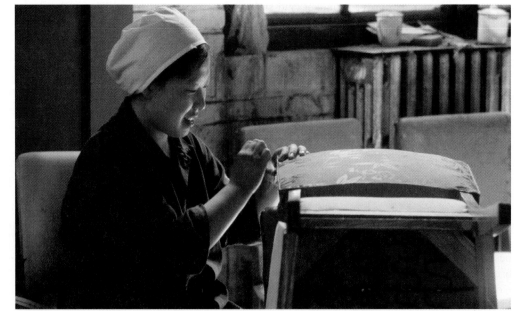

Exhibit 8-7: Lecong, a city in Guangdong Province, can boast that it is the "furniture capital of the world": Approximately 6,000 production facilities are located nearby. The Chinese are adept at carving and other special woodworking skills, and monthly wages are as low as $100. In mid-2004, the U.S. government imposed antidumping duties on wooden bedroom furniture imports to provide some relief for American producers. Meanwhile, Ethan Allen Interiors, Furniture Brands International, Howard Miller Company, and other U.S. manufacturers have little choice but to source at least some of their production in China.
Source: Dean Conger/Corbis–NY.

Logistics

In general, the greater the distance between the product source and the target market, the greater the time delay for delivery and the higher the transportation cost. However, innovation and new transportation technologies are cutting both time and dollar costs. To facilitate global delivery, transportation companies such as CSX Corporation are forming alliances and becoming an important part of industry value systems. Manufacturers can take advantage of intermodal services that allow containers to be transferred among rail, boat, air, and truck carriers. In Europe, Latin America, and elsewhere, the trend toward regional economic integration means fewer border controls, which greatly speeds up delivery times and lowers costs.

Despite these overall trends, a number of specific issues pertaining to logistics can affect the sourcing decision. For example, in the wake of the 2001 terror attacks, importers are required to send electronic lists to the U.S. government prior to shipping. The goal is to help the U.S. Customs Service identify high-risk cargo that could be linked to the global terror network. In the fall of 2002, a 10-day strike on the West Coast shut down 29 docks and cost the U.S. economy an estimated $20 billion. Such incidents can delay shipments by weeks or even months.

Country Infrastructure

In order to present an attractive setting for a manufacturing operation, it is important that a country's infrastructure be sufficiently developed to support manufacturing and distribution. Infrastructure requirements will vary by company and by industry, but minimally, they will include power, transportation and roads, communications, service and component suppliers, a labor pool, civil order, and effective governance. In addition, companies must have reliable access to foreign exchange for the purchase of necessary material and components from abroad. Additional requirements include a physically secure setting where work can be done and from which product can be shipped.

A country may have cheap labor, but does it have the necessary supporting services or infrastructure to support a high volume of business activities? Many countries offer these conditions, including Hong Kong, Taiwan, and Singapore. In scores of other low-wage countries, however, the infrastructure is woefully underdeveloped. In China, a key infrastructure weakness is the "cold chain," a food industry term for temperature-controlled trucks and warehouses. According to one estimate, an investment of $100 billion will be required to modernize China's cold chain.[15] Meanwhile, the Chinese government is spending hundreds of millions of dollars on a superhighway system that will eventually connect all 31 of China's provinces. When the project is completed in 2020, China will have about 53,000 miles of paved expressway—more than the United States.

Infrastructure improvement is a key issue in other emerging markets. In India, for example, it takes eight days for cargo travelling by truck between Kolkata and Mumbai to make the trip of 1,340 miles![16] One of the challenges of doing business in the new Russian market is an infrastructure that is woefully inadequate to handle the increased volume of shipments. The Mexican government, anticipating much heavier trade volume because of NAFTA, has committed billions of dollars for infrastructure improvements.

Political Factors

As discussed in Chapter 5, political risk is a deterrent to investment in local sourcing. Conversely, the lower the level of political risk, the less likely it is that an investor will avoid a country or market. The difficulty of assessing political risk is inversely proportional to a country's stage of economic development: All other things being equal, the less developed a country, the more difficult it is to predict political risk. The political risk of the Triad countries, for example, is quite limited as compared to that of a less-developed country in Africa, Latin America, or

"Supply Chain 101 says the most important thing is continuity of supply. When you establish a supply line that is 12,000 miles long, you have to weigh the costs of additional inventory and logistics costs versus what you can save in terms of lower costs per unit or labor costs."[14]

Norbert Ore, Institute for Supply Management

---

[14]Barbara Hagenbaugh, "Moving Work Abroad Tough for Some Firms," *USA Today* (December 3, 2003), p. 2B.

[15]Jane Lanhee Lee, "China Hurdle: Lack of Refrigeration," *The Wall Street Journal* (August 30, 2007), p. A7.

[16]Harold L. Sirkin, James W. Hemerling, and Arindam K. Bhattacharya, *Globality: Competing with Everyone from Everywhere for Everything* (New York: Boston Consulting Group, 2008), p. 23.

Asia. The recent rapid changes in Central and Eastern Europe and the dissolution of the Soviet Union have clearly demonstrated the risks *and* opportunities resulting from political upheavals.

Other political factors may weigh on the sourcing decision. For example, with protectionist sentiment on the rise, the U.S. Senate passed an amendment that would prohibit the U.S. Treasury and Department of Transportation from accepting bids from private companies that use offshore workers. In a highly publicized move, the state of New Jersey changed a call center contract that had shifted jobs offshore. About one dozen jobs were brought back instate—at a cost of about $900,000.

Market access is another type of political factor. If a country or a region limits market access because of local content laws, balance-of-payments problems, or any other reason, it may be necessary to establish a production facility within the country itself. The Japanese automobile companies invested in U.S. plant capacity because of concerns about market access. By producing cars in the United States, they have a source of supply that is not exposed to the threat of tariff or import quotas. Market access figured heavily in Boeing's decision to produce airplane components in China. China ordered 100 airplanes valued at $4.5 billion; in return, Boeing is making investments and transferring engineering and manufacturing expertise.[17]

Foreign Exchange Rates

In deciding where to source a product or locate a manufacturing activity, a manager must take into account foreign exchange rate trends in various parts of the world. Exchange rates are so volatile today that many companies pursue global sourcing strategies as a way of limiting exchange-related risk. At any point in time, what has been an attractive location for production may become much less attractive due to exchange rate fluctuation. For example, *endaka* is the Japanese term for a strong yen. In 2003, the exchange rate went from ¥122/$1 to ¥107/$1. For every one yen increase relative to the American dollar, Canon's operating income declines six billion yen! As noted earlier, Canon's management is counting on R&D investment to ensure that its products deliver superior margins that offset the strong yen.

The dramatic shifts in price levels of commodities and currencies are a major characteristic of the world economy today. Such volatility argues for a sourcing strategy that provides alternative country options for supplying markets. Thus, if the dollar, the yen, or the mark becomes seriously overvalued, a company with production capacity in other locations can achieve competitive advantage by shifting production among different sites.

Summary

A company's first business dealings outside the home country often take the form of exporting or importing. Companies should recognize the difference between **export marketing** and **export selling**. By attending **trade shows** and participating in **trade missions**, company personnel can learn a great deal about new markets.

Governments use a variety of programs to support exports, including tax incentives, subsidies, and export assistance. Governments also discourage imports with a combination of **tariffs** and **nontariff barriers**. A **quota** is one example of a nontariff barrier. Export-related policy issues include the status of **foreign sales corporations** (**FSCs**) in the United States, Europe's **Common Agricultural Policy** (**CAP**), and **subsidies**. Governments establish **free trade zones** and **special economic zones** to encourage investment.

The **Harmonized Tariff System** (**HTS**) has been adopted by most countries that are actively involved in export-import trade. **Single-column tariffs** are the simplest; **two-column**

---

[17]Jeff Cole, Marcus W. Brauchli, and Craig S. Smith, "Orient Express: Boeing Flies into Flap over Technology Shift in Dealings with China," *The Wall Street Journal* (October 13, 1995), pp. A1, A11. See also Joseph Kahn, "Clipped Wings: McDonnell Douglas's High Hopes for China Never Really Soared," *The Wall Street Journal* (May 22, 1996), pp. A1, A10.

tariffs include special rates such as those available to countries with **normal trade relations (NTR)** status. Governments can also impose special types of duties. These include **antidumping duties** imposed on products whose prices government officials deem too low and **countervailing duties** to offset government subsidies.

Key participants in the export-import process include **foreign purchasing agents**, **export brokers**, **export merchants**, **export management companies**, **manufacturers' export agents**, **export distributors**, **export commission representatives**, **cooperative exporters**, and **freight forwarders**.

A number of export-import payment methods are available. A transaction begins with the issue of a **pro forma invoice** or some other formal document. A basic payment instrument is the **letter of credit (L/C)** that assures payment from the buyer's bank. Sales may also be made using a **bill of exchange (draft)**, cash in advance, sales on open account, or a consignment agreement.

Exporting and importing is directly related to management's **sourcing decisions**. Concern is mounting in developed countries about job losses linked to **outsourcing** jobs, both skilled and unskilled, to low-wage countries. A number of factors determine whether a company makes or buys the products it markets as well as *where* it makes or buys it.

Discussion Questions

1. What is the difference between export marketing and export selling?
2. Why is exporting from the United States dominated by large companies? What, if anything, could be done to increase exports from smaller companies?
3. Describe the stages a company typically goes through as it learns about exporting.
4. Governments often pursue policies that promote exports while limiting imports. What are some of those policies?
5. What are the various types of duties that export marketers should be aware of?
6. How is the current economic crisis affecting financing for global trade?
7. What is the difference between an L/C and other forms of export-import financing? Why do sellers often require L/Cs in international transactions?
8. What criteria should company management consider when making sourcing decisions?

Officially, the EU tariffs on Chinese and Vietnamese shoe imports are known as antidumping duties. In general, such tariffs reflect a finding that products are being sold in export markets for less than the selling price in the exporter's home country. In other words, as explained in the chapter, they are being "dumped." In economic terms, China and Vietnam—both ruled by Communist governments—are considered "nonmarket economies." From the EU's point of view, this means that the two countries' domestic prices are artificial. In such countries, where many enterprises are state-owned, profitability in the Western sense is less of a priority than job creation. To prove dumping, investigators have only to compare the cost of the imported shoes with the prices of shoes produced in true market economies where the laws of supply and demand determine costs and prices. In such a comparison, the Chinese and Vietnamese appear to have a significant price advantage.

The *Financial Times* noted that the tariffs reflect a triumph of the interests of a small number of EU producers at the expense of the region's 450 million consumers. As an editorial in the *Financial Times* observed, antidumping duties are usually used in large-scale, capital-intensive industries such as steel. The editorial noted that, "Shoemaking is not a strategic industry with gigantic economies of scale and barriers to entry where predatory export pricing could deliver an exploitable competitive advantage. [Shoemaking] is an open global market where fierce competition will soon erode large profit margins." The editors continued, "If subsidized shoes are indeed being shipped halfway around the world to be sold off cheaply, more fool their producers. If Beijing and Hanoi want to subsidize European consumers to build their shoe collections, let them."

Shoes are not the only European industry sector protected by antidumping duties. In 2005, prompted by a complaint by the European Bicycle Manufacturers Association, the European Commission raised tariffs on Chinese bicycles from 30.6 to 48.5 percent and imposed a 34.5 percent tariff on bicycles from Vietnam. Some observers believe it was unfair to combine Vietnamese and Chinese bike imports in the same trade suit. They attempted to draw a distinction between the two nations by noting that Chinese bicycles are sold in supermarkets and department stores. By contrast, Vietnamese consumers buy bikes in small shops. According to this line of argument, bicycles from the two countries don't compete with each other in export markets and should therefore not be investigated in the same antidumping suit. However, the European Commission concluded that Vietnam and China produce the same type of bicycles and distribute them through similar channels.

As the deadline for extending the shoe tariffs approached, opposing sides appeared headed for a showdown. The tariffs had, indeed, resulted in lower import levels from China and Vietnam in 2009. However, shoe imports from Indonesia, Thailand, and other emerging markets have surged. Danish shoe manufacturer Ecco is among the coalition of companies that oppose the tariffs. Ecco is a true transnational: it sources its various shoe styles in China, Indonesia, Thailand, Slovakia, and elsewhere. Ecco also markets its shoes globally, including in Asia. As a company vice president noted, "Tariff obstacles in Europe increase the chances that China will close its markets."

Meanwhile, shoe exports from Italy continue to decline. Not surprisingly, many Italian shoemakers support the duties on the grounds that they give domestic producers a chance to rebuild their industry. As the head of the Italian shoemakers' lobby explained, "There's this stereotype of an old man in Tuscany sitting on a park bench sipping wine. That's only part of the picture. A lot of our small businesses are now investing in new technologies."

Case 8-1 Discussion Questions

1. When tariffs are imposed on European imports of shoes from China and Vietnam, who stands to gain? Who stands to lose?
2. European policymakers object to the fact that some Asian shoe production is government subsidized. But, as an editorial in the *Financial Times* noted, "If Beijing and Hanoi want to subsidize European consumers to build their shoe collections, let them." Do you agree?
3. Antidumping duties can be described as a form of protectionism. As the global economic crisis deepened in 2008 and 2009, many countries began implementing protectionist policies. Is this a positive trend, or are such policies likely to prolong the recession?

Sources: John W. Miller, "European Countries Split on Shoe-Tariff Extension," *The Wall Street Journal* (October 9, 2009), p. A12; Miller, "EU Levies Tariffs on China, Vietnam," *The Wall Street Journal* (October 5, 2006), p. A8; Miller, "EU Proposes Duties on Chinese, Vietnamese Shoes," *The Wall Street Journal* (August 31, 2006), p. A4; Juliane von Reppert-Bismarck, "EU Shoe Duty Trips Up Retailers," *The Wall Street Journal* (April 24, 2006), p. A6; "Soft Shoe Shuffle," *Financial Times* (February 27, 2006), p. 12; Raphael Minder, "Mandelson to Defy Shoe Import Furore," *Financial Times* (February 23, 2006), p. 3; Joseph Erlich, "Vietnam's Trade-War Wounds, "*The Wall Street Journal* (August 26, 2005), p. A10.

Case 8-2
A Day in the Life of an Export Coordinator

Mikkel Jakobsen works as an export coordinator with Shipco Transport, a subsidiary of Scan-Group, a major European transportation company. Shipco Transport has offices all over the world, including 12 branches in North America. Shipco has an extensive network of independent agents in most areas of the world. Shipco's core business is Less than a Container Load (LCL) ocean freight, but also offers Full Container Load (FCL) ocean freight services, as well as airfreight. Mikkel and four other coworkers constitute the company's FCL Chicago branch export team.

As a Non-Vessel Operating Common Carrier (NVOCC), Shipco Transport operates similarly to shipping companies such as Maersk Sealand, Mediterranean Shipping Company, and others, with one key difference: Shipco has no vessels of its own. Instead, Shipco relies on favorable contracts with over 40 carriers, enabling them to offer competitive rates on routings to destinations around the world. Most of Shipco's customers are freight forwarders, but the company also deals directly with exporting companies, and on occasion private individuals. Because of its Midwest location, a significant number of containers come through Chicago on a daily basis and are railed to ports around the country.

In 2006, Mikkel earned a BA degree in international management and economics from a small liberal arts college in the Midwest. He is a citizen of Denmark, and currently works in the United States on a J-1 work visa, sponsored by Shipco Transport. How did he get his first job after graduating? Mikkel explains, "In the spring of 2006, I contacted 15 different companies operating in the United States that had a connection to Denmark. I was offered a position in Shipco Transport's Chicago branch."

Mikkel's day begins at 8:30 A.M., and usually ends at 5:30 P.M., depending on the workload. Most customers are located in the Midwest, but overnight, he receives e-mails from overseas that he processes in the morning hours. Mikkel says, "In general, my job consists of quoting out shipping costs to customers, placing bookings with steamship lines, preparing export documentation, and dealing with problems that arise during the container's journey from shipper to consignee."

"A customer contacts me with a rate request on a certain routing," Mikkel continues. "He may wish to ship one 20-foot container with auto parts from Indianola, to the port of Ningbo, China. Based on our carrier contracts, I work up a quote including drayage from Indianola, Iowa, to the appropriate rail hub, rail transportation from hub to port, and ocean freight from U.S port to port of discharge Ningbo. Several things must be considered including what carrier is cheapest on the routing, differences in transit times, if the commodity is covered in the contract, and what profit level is appropriate. If the customer accepts the quote, the booking is placed with the steamship line, and a dispatch is sent to the chosen trucking company. Certain situations need additional attention. If the commodity is hazardous, the hazardous declaration must be approved by the steamship line. Also, certain goods, such as automobiles, must be cleared by customs before leaving the United States to avoid U.S. customs demanding the return of the container for inspection, at the expense of the party at fault.

"Although quoting and setting up bookings takes up a lot of my work day, the majority is spent addressing various problems and issues that arise. Problems such as carriers running out of equipment at their depots, loadings taking longer than expected, or rail delays are common and dealt with regularly. More serious issues are derailments, problems securing payment, and container abandonment. As an example, disposing of scrap materials in the United States can be expensive, and in the past, some have overcome the problem by loading it in a container and sending it to places like India as a collect shipment with a nonexistent consignee. This can become an extremely costly situation as demurrage (storage charges), unloading, and disposal charges may apply.

"In ocean freight, we work with ETDs (Estimated Time of Departure) and ETAs (Estimated Time of Arrival), because vessels crossing oceans tend to deviate from their schedule. Although this is a fact, customers sometimes have a difficult time understanding the concept. In the world of shipping, vessels running late, expected early, or even on time can be a problem. If so, I am contacted by my customer who either needs an explanation or appropriate action taken. As a middleman, I will contact the specific carrier with the same request. Most of the time the problem is that the container hasn't reached its destination according to the ETA.

"Interestingly, sometimes a shipper is interested in a delay, and wants the container held up on its journey. This could be because more time is needed to secure payment, or it could represent an attempt to avoid a holiday in the destination country."

How did Mikkel's college studies prepare him for the job? "Incoterms, Letter of credit, SED (Shippers Export Declaration), and B/L (bill of lading) are just some of the industry jargon used on a daily basis. Working with customers, familiarity is expected. The documentation part of export shipping is important, and demands attention to detail. As an NVOCC, Shipco produces both a House B/L and a Line B/L that holds information on the shipper and the consignee, and on the products shipped. Most of our containers are released on an express release basis, but some require the use of original bills of lading. In these instances, the original B/L must be presented before a container is released. Although I do not get directly involved in the intricacies of L/C (letter of credit) shipments, special attention must be given to the accuracy of B/L information because small deviations can be troublesome. When doing business internationally it is essential to recognize the differences in how business is conducted around the world. South America and Russia in particular are destinations where we rely heavily on our overseas offices and agents and their knowledge of local customs and regulations."

Summing up, Mikkel says, "I enjoy operating on an international level on a daily basis, while doing my part to alleviate the current American trade deficit. Working in the transportation industry, I am sometimes surprised by how many different and obscure items are exported around the world. Although the process may seem overwhelming, with the help of a shipping specialist such as Shipco, any company anywhere can view the entire world as a potential market."

Discussion Questions

1. What knowledge and skills are required to be successful as an export coordinator?
2. What do you think is the best part of Mikkel's job? The worst part?
3. If you were in Mikkel's position, what would your next career move be?

Global Market Entry Strategies: Licensing, Investment, and Strategic Alliances

Case 9-1
Starbucks Expands Abroad

From modest beginnings in Seattle's Pike Street Market, Starbucks Corporation has become a global marketing phenomenon. Today, Starbucks is the world's leading specialty coffee retailer, with 2008 sales of $10.8 billion. Starbucks founder and chairman Howard Schultz and his management team have used a variety of market entry approaches—including direct ownership as well as licensing and franchising—to create an empire of more than 12,000 coffee cafés in 35 countries. In addition, Schultz has licensed the Starbucks brand name to marketers of non-coffee products such as ice cream. The company is also diversifying into movies and recorded music.

However, coffee remains Starbucks core business; to reach the ambitious goal of 40,000 shops worldwide,

Starbucks is expanding aggressively in key countries (see Exhibit 9-1). For example, at the end of 2006, Starbucks had 67 branches in 21 German cities; that number is expected to reach 100 within just a few years. Starbucks had set a higher growth target for Germany; those plans had to be revised, however, after a joint venture with retailer Karstadt-Quelle was dissolved. Now Starbucks intends to pursue further expansion independently. Despite competition from local chains such as Café Einstein, Cornelius Everke, the head of Starbucks' German operations, says, "We see the potential of several hundred coffee shops in Germany."

Starbucks' relentless pursuit of new market opportunities illustrates the fact that most firms face a broad range of

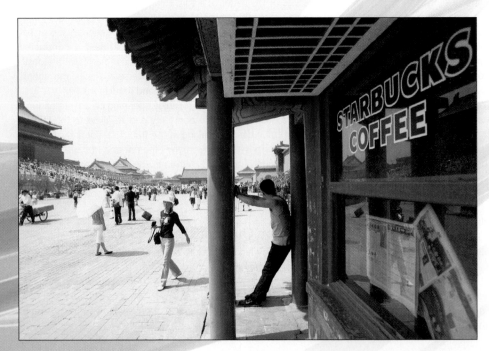

Exhibit 9-1: Starbucks opened a small coffee café in Beijing's Forbidden City in 2000. In 2007, bowing to criticism that the presence of a Western brand near the former imperial palace was disrespectful, Starbucks closed the shop. The company still has more than 600 other locations in China.
Source: Cancan Chu/Getty Images, Inc.

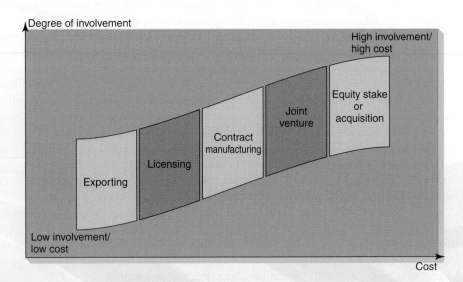

FIGURE 9-1

Investment Cost of Market Entry Strategies

strategy alternatives. In the last chapter, we examined exporting and importing as one way to exploit global market opportunities. However, for Starbucks and other companies whose business models include a service component or store experience, exporting (in the conventional sense) is not the best way to "go global." In this chapter, we go beyond exporting to discuss several additional entry mode options that form a continuum. As shown in Figure 9-1, the level of involvement, risk, and financial reward increases as a company moves from market entry strategies such as licensing to joint ventures and, ultimately, various forms of investment.

When a global company seeks to enter a developing country market, there is an additional strategy issue to address: whether to replicate the strategy that served the company well in developed markets without significant adaptation. You will learn more about the strategic options available to Howard Schultz in the continuation of Case 9-1 at the end of the chapter. This is the issue that Starbucks is facing. To the extent that the objective of entering the market is to achieve penetration, executives at global companies are well advised to consider embracing a mass-market mind-set. This may well mandate an adaptation strategy.[1] Formulating a **market entry strategy** means that management must decide which option or options to use in pursuing opportunities outside the home country. The particular market entry strategy company executives choose will depend on their vision, attitude toward risk, how much investment capital is available, and how much control is sought.

LICENSING

Licensing is a contractual arrangement whereby one company (the licensor) makes a legally protected asset available to another company (the licensee) in exchange for royalties, license fees, or some other form of compensation.[2] The licensed asset may be a brand name, company name, patent, trade secret, or product formulation. Licensing is widely used in the fashion industry. For example, the namesake companies associated with Bill Blass, Hugo Boss, and other global design icons typically generate more revenue from licensing deals for jeans, fragrances, and watches than from their high-priced couture lines. Organizations as diverse as Disney, Caterpillar Inc., the National Basketball Association, and Coca-Cola also make extensive use of licensing. None is an

[1]David Arnold, *The Mirage of Global Markets: How Globalizing Companies Can Succeed as Markets Localize* (Upper Saddle River, NJ: Prentice Hall, 2004), pp. 78–79.
[2]Franklin R. Root, *Entry Strategies for International Markets* (New York: Lexington Books, 1994), p. 107.

apparel manufacturer; however, licensing agreements allow them to leverage their brand names and generate substantial revenue streams. As these examples suggest, licensing is a global market entry and expansion strategy with considerable appeal. It can offer an attractive return on investment for the life of the agreement, provided that the necessary performance clauses are included in the contract. The only cost is signing the agreement and policing its implementation.

There are two key advantages associated with licensing as a market entry mode. First, because the licensee is typically a local business that will produce and market the goods on a local or regional basis, licensing enables companies to circumvent tariffs, quotas, or similar export barriers discussed in Chapter 8. Second, when appropriate, licensees are granted considerable autonomy and are free to adapt the licensed goods to local tastes. Disney's success with licensing is a case in point. Disney licenses trademarked cartoon characters, names, and logos to producers of clothing, toys, and watches for sale throughout the world. Licensing allows Disney to create synergies based on its core theme park, motion picture, and television businesses. Its licensees are allowed considerable leeway to adapt colors, materials, or other design elements to local tastes (see Exhibit 9-2).

In China, licensed goods were practically unknown until a few years ago; by 2001, annual sales of all licensed goods totaled $600 million. Industry observers expect that figure to more than double by 2010. Similarly, yearly worldwide sales of licensed Caterpillar merchandise are running at $900 million as consumers make a fashion statement with boots, jeans, and handbags bearing the distinctive black-and-yellow Cat label. Stephen Palmer is the head of London-based Overland Ltd., which holds the worldwide license for Cat apparel. He notes, "Even if people here don't know the brand, they have a feeling that they know it. They have seen Caterpillar tractors from an early age. It's subliminal, and that's why it's working."[3]

Licensing is associated with several disadvantages and opportunity costs. First, licensing agreements offer limited market control. Because the licensor typically does not become involved in the licensee's marketing program, potential returns from marketing may be lost. The second disadvantage is that the agreement may have a short life if the licensee develops its own know-how and begins to innovate in the licensed product or technology area. In a worst-case scenario (from the licensor's point of view), licensees—especially those working with process technologies—can develop into strong competitors in the local market and, eventually, into industry leaders. This is because licensing, by its very nature, enables a company to "borrow"— that is, leverage and exploit—another company's resources. A case in point is Pilkington, which has seen its leadership position in the glass industry erode as Glaverbel, Saint-Gobain, PPG, and other competitors have achieved higher levels of production efficiency and lower costs.[4]

Exhibit 9-2: Licensed merchandise generates nearly $30 billion in annual revenues for the Walt Disney Company. Thanks to the popularity of the company's theme parks, movies, and television shows, Mickey Mouse, Winnie the Pooh, and other popular characters are familiar faces throughout the world. The president of Disney Consumer Products recently predicted that the company's license-related revenues will eventually reach $75 billion.
Source: The Image Works.

[3]Cecilie Rohwedder and Joseph T. Hallinan, "In Europe, Hot New Fashion for Urban Hipsters Comes from Peoria," *The Wall Street Journal* (August 8, 2001), p. B1.
[4]Charis Gresser, "A Real Test of Endurance," *Financial Times—Weekend* (November 1–2, 1997), p. 5.

> **⟱ STRATEGIC DECISION MAKING IN GLOBAL MARKETING**
> **Sony and Apple**

Perhaps the most famous example of the opportunity costs associated with licensing dates back to the mid-1950s, when Sony cofounder Masaru Ibuka obtained a licensing agreement for the transistor from AT&T's Bell Laboratories. Ibuka dreamed of using transistors to make small, battery-powered radios. However, the Bell engineers with whom he spoke insisted that it was impossible to manufacture transistors that could handle the high frequencies required for a radio; they advised him to try making hearing aids. Undeterred, Ibuka presented the challenge to his Japanese engineers who spent many months improving high-frequency output. Sony was not the first company to unveil a transistor radio; a U.S.-built product, the Regency, featured transistors from Texas Instruments and a colorful plastic case. However, it was Sony's high-quality, distinctive approach to styling and marketing savvy that ultimately translated into worldwide success.

Conversely, the *failure* to seize an opportunity to license can also lead to dire consequences. In the mid-1980s, Apple Computer chairman John Sculley decided against a broad licensing program for Apple's famed operating system (OS). Such a move would have allowed other computer manufacturers to produce Mac-compatible units. Meanwhile, Microsoft's growing world dominance in both OS and applications got a boost in 1985 from Windows, which featured a Mac-like graphic interface. Apple sued Microsoft for infringing on its intellectual property; however, attorneys for the software giant successfully argued in court that Apple had shared crucial aspects of its OS without limiting Microsoft's right to adapt and improve it. Belatedly, in the mid-1990s, Apple began licensing its operating system to other manufacturers. However, the global market share for machines running the Mac OS continues to hover in the low single digits.

The return of Steve Jobs and Apple's introduction of the new iMac in 1998 marked the start of a new era for Apple. More recently, the popularity of the company's iPod digital music players, iTunes Music Store, and the iPhone have boosted its fortunes. However, Apple's failure to license its technology in the pre-Windows era arguably cost the company tens of billions of dollars. What's the basis for this assertion? Microsoft, the winner in the operating systems war, had a market capitalization of about $160 billion in 2008. By contrast, Apple's 2008 market capitalization was roughly $95 billion.

Companies may find that the upfront easy money obtained from licensing turns out to be a very expensive source of revenue. To prevent a licensor-competitor from gaining unilateral benefit, licensing agreements should provide for a cross-technology exchange among all parties. At the absolute minimum, any company that plans to remain in business must ensure that its license agreements include a provision for full cross licensing (i.e., that the licensee shares its developments with the licensor). Overall, the licensing strategy must ensure ongoing competitive advantage. For example, license arrangements can create export market opportunities and open the door to low-risk manufacturing relationships. They can also speed diffusion of new products or technologies.

Special Licensing Arrangements

Companies that use **contract manufacturing** provide technical specifications to a subcontractor or local manufacturer. The subcontractor then oversees production. Such arrangements offer several advantages. The licensing firm can specialize in product design and marketing, while transferring responsibility for ownership of manufacturing facilities to contractors and subcontractors. Other advantages include limited commitment of financial and managerial resources and quick entry into target countries, especially when the target market is too small to justify significant investment.[5] One disadvantage, as already noted, is that companies may open themselves to public scrutiny and criticism if workers in contract factories are poorly paid or labor in inhumane circumstances. Timberland and other companies that source in low-wage countries are using image advertising to communicate their corporate policies on sustainable business practices.

Franchising is another variation of licensing strategy. A franchise is a contract between a parent company-franchiser and a franchisee that allows the franchisee to operate a business developed by the franchiser in return for a fee and adherence to franchise-wide policies and practices. Table 9-1 lists several U.S.-based franchisers with an extensive network of overseas locations. Exhibit 9-3 shows an ad for Pollo Campero, a restaurant chain based in Central America that is using franchising to expand operations in the United States.

---

[5]Franklin R. Root, *Entry Strategies for International Markets* (New York: Lexington Books, 1994), p. 138.

TABLE 9-1 Worldwide Franchise Activity

Company	Overseas Sites	Countries
7-Eleven	23,652	18
McDonald's	22,571	110
Yum Brands	14,057	100
Doctor's Associates (Subway)	5,962	85
Domino's Pizza	3,038	55
Jani-King International (commercial cleaning)	2,210	20

Source: Adapted from Richard Gibson, "Foreign Flavors," *The Wall Street Journal* (September 25, 2006), p. R8.

Exhibit 9-3: Executives at Guatemala's Pollo Campero SA know how to spot a market entry opportunity. It came to their attention that passengers flying to the United States from Guatemala City and San Salvador often carried packages of the company's spicy chicken on board the planes. The Campero team also recognized that the chain enjoyed high levels of brand awareness in Los Angeles, where there is a large Guatemalan population.

In short order, Pollo Campero opened several locations in Los Angeles. Today, there are Pollo Campero restaurants in more than a dozen states, plus Washington, D.C.
Source: Used by permission of Campero US.

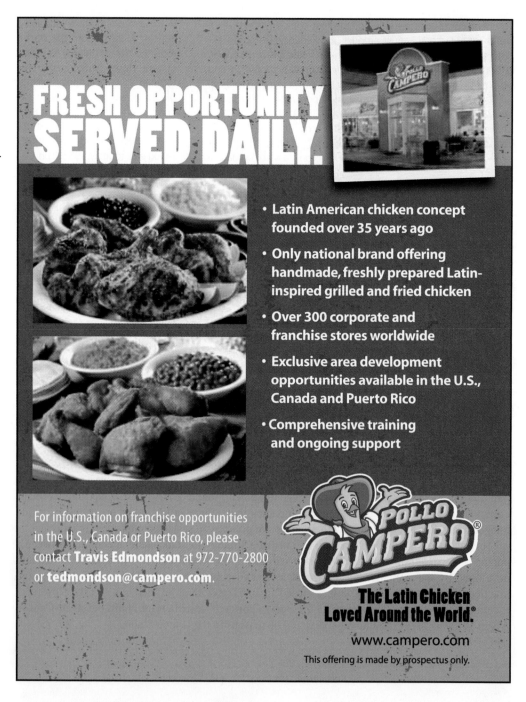

FRESH OPPORTUNITY SERVED DAILY.

- Latin American chicken concept founded over 35 years ago
- Only national brand offering handmade, freshly prepared Latin-inspired grilled and fried chicken
- Over 300 corporate and franchise stores worldwide
- Exclusive area development opportunities available in the U.S., Canada and Puerto Rico
- Comprehensive training and ongoing support

For information on franchise opportunities in the U.S., Canada or Puerto Rico, please contact **Travis Edmondson** at 972-770-2800 or **tedmondson@campero.com**.

POLLO CAMPERO®
The Latin Chicken Loved Around the World.®
www.campero.com
This offering is made by prospectus only.

Franchising has great appeal to local entrepreneurs anxious to learn and apply Western-style marketing techniques. Franchising consultant William Le Sante suggests that would-be franchisers ask the following questions before expanding overseas:

- Will local consumers buy your product?
- How tough is the local competition?
- Does the government respect trademark and franchiser rights?
- Can your profits be easily repatriated?
- Can you buy all the supplies you need locally?
- Is commercial space available and are rents affordable?
- Are your local partners financially sound and do they understand the basics of franchising?[6]

By addressing these issues, franchisers can gain a more realistic understanding of global opportunities. In China, for example, regulations require foreign franchisers to directly own two or more stores for a minimum of one year before franchisees can take over the business. Intellectual property protection is also a concern in China.

The specialty retailing industry favors franchising as a market entry mode. For example, there are more than 1,800 The Body Shop stores around the world; franchisees operate about 90 percent of them. Franchising is also a cornerstone of global growth in the fast-food industry; McDonald's reliance on franchising to expand globally is a case in point. The fast-food giant has a well-known global brand name and a business system that can be easily replicated in multiple country markets. Crucially, McDonald's headquarters has learned the wisdom of leveraging local market knowledge by granting franchisees considerable leeway to tailor restaurant interior designs and menu offerings to suit country-specific preferences and tastes (see Case 1-2). Generally speaking, however, franchising is a market entry strategy that is typically executed with less localization than licensing.

When companies do decide to license, they should sign agreements that anticipate more extensive market participation in the future. Insofar as is possible, a company should keep options and paths open for other forms of market participation. Many of these forms require investment and give the investing company more control than is possible with licensing.

> "One of the key things licensees bring to the business is their knowledge of the local marketplace, trends, and consumer preferences. As long as it's within the guidelines and standards, and it's not doing anything to compromise our brand, we're very willing to go along with it."[7]
>
> Paul Leech, COO, Allied Domecq Quick Service Restaurants

INVESTMENT

After companies gain experience outside the home country via exporting or licensing, the time often comes when executives desire a more extensive form of participation. In particular, the desire to have partial or full ownership of operations outside the home country can drive the decision to invest. **Foreign direct investment (FDI)** figures reflect investment flows out of the home country as companies invest in or acquire plants, equipment, or other assets. Foreign direct investment allows companies to produce, sell, and compete locally in key markets. Examples of FDI abound: Honda built a $550 million assembly plant in Greensburg, Indiana; Hyundai invested $1 billion in a plant in Montgomery, Alabama; IKEA has spent nearly $2 billion to open stores in Russia; and South Korea's LG Electronics purchased a 58 percent stake in Zenith Electronics (see Exhibit 9-4). Each of these represents foreign direct investment.

The final years of the twentieth century were a boom time for cross-border mergers and acquisitions. At the end of 2000, cumulative foreign investment by U.S. companies totaled $1.2 trillion. The top three target countries for U.S. investment were the United Kingdom, Canada, and the Netherlands. Investment in the United States by foreign companies also totaled $1.2 trillion; the United Kingdom, Japan, and the Netherlands were the top three sources of investment.[8] Investment in developing nations also grew rapidly in the 1990s. For example, as noted in earlier chapters, investment interest in the BRIC nations is increasing, especially in the automobile industry and other sectors critical to the countries' economic development.

[6]Eve Tahmincioglu, "It's Not Only the Giants with Franchises Abroad," *The New York Times* (February 12, 2004), p. C4.
[7]Sarah Murray, "Big Names Don Camouflage," *Financial Times* (February 5, 2004), p. 9.
[8]Maria Borga and Raymond J. Mataloni, Jr., "Direct Investment Positions for 2000: Country and Industry Detail," *Survey of Current Business* 81, no. 7 (July 2001), pp. 16–29.

Exhibit 9-4: "Drive your way" is the advertising slogan for Hyundai Motor Company, South Korea's leading automaker. In a press statement, Hyundai chairman Chung Mong Koo noted, "Our new brand strategy is designed to ensure that we reach industry-leading levels, not only in terms of size but also in terms of customer perception and overall brand value." To better serve the U.S. market, Hyundai recently invested $1 billion in an assembly plant in Montgomery, Alabama. The plant produces two models, the popular Sonata sedan and the Santa Fe SUV.
Source: Hyundai Motor America.

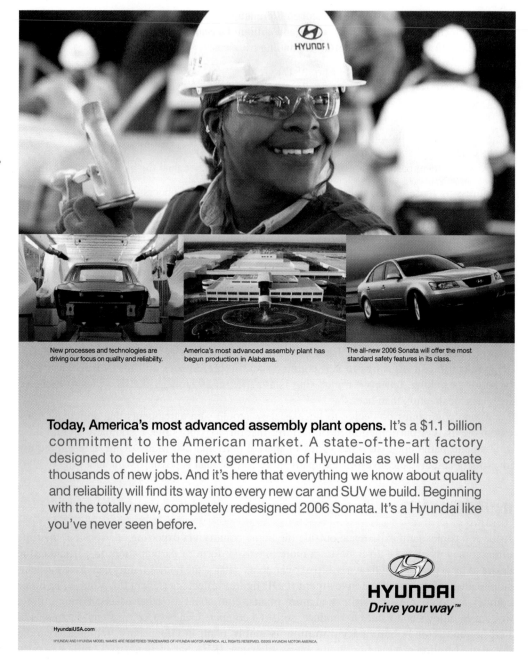

New processes and technologies are driving our focus on quality and reliability.

America's most advanced assembly plant has begun production in Alabama.

The all-new 2006 Sonata will offer the most standard safety features in its class.

Today, America's most advanced assembly plant opens. It's a $1.1 billion commitment to the American market. A state-of-the-art factory designed to deliver the next generation of Hyundais as well as create thousands of new jobs. And it's here that everything we know about quality and reliability will find its way into every new car and SUV we build. Beginning with the totally new, completely redesigned 2006 Sonata. It's a Hyundai like you've never seen before.

HYUNDAI
Drive your way™

HyundaiUSA.com
HYUNDAI AND HYUNDAI MODEL NAMES ARE REGISTERED TRADEMARKS OF HYUNDAI MOTOR AMERICA. ALL RIGHTS RESERVED. ©2005 HYUNDAI MOTOR AMERICA.

Foreign investments may take the form of minority or majority shares in joint ventures, minority or majority equity stakes in another company, or outright acquisition. A company may choose to use a combination of these entry strategies by acquiring one company, buying an equity stake in another, and operating a joint venture with a third. In recent years, for example, UPS has made numerous acquisitions in Europe and has also expanded its transportation hubs.

Joint Ventures

A joint venture with a local partner represents a more extensive form of participation in foreign markets than either exporting or licensing. Strictly speaking, a **joint venture** is an entry strategy for a single target country in which the partners share ownership of a newly created business entity.[9] This strategy is attractive for several reasons. First and foremost is the sharing of risk.

---

[9]Franklin R. Root, *Entry Strategies for International Markets* (New York: Lexington Books, 1994), p. 309.

By pursuing a joint venture entry strategy, a company can limit its financial risk as well as its exposure to political uncertainty. Second, a company can use the joint venture experience to learn about a new market environment. If it succeeds in becoming an insider, it may later increase the level of commitment and exposure. Third, joint ventures allow partners to achieve synergy by combining different value chain strengths. One company might have in-depth knowledge of a local market, an extensive distribution system, or access to low-cost labor or raw materials. Such a company might link up with a foreign partner possessing well-known brands or cutting-edge technology, manufacturing know-how, or advanced process applications. A company that lacks sufficient capital resources might seek partners to jointly finance a project. Finally, a joint venture may be the only way to enter a country or region if government bid award practices routinely favor local companies, if import tariffs are high, or if laws prohibit foreign control but permit joint ventures.

Many companies have experienced difficulties when attempting to enter the Japanese market. Anheuser-Busch's experience in Japan illustrates both the interactions of the entry modes discussed so far and the advantages and disadvantages of the joint venture approach. Access to distribution is critical to success in the Japanese market; Anheuser-Busch first entered by means of a licensing agreement with Suntory, the smallest of Japan's four top brewers. Although Budweiser had become Japan's top-selling imported beer within a decade, Bud's market share in the early 1990s was still less than 2 percent. Anheuser-Busch then created a joint venture with Kirin Brewery, the market leader. Anheuser-Busch's 90 percent stake in the venture entitled it to market and distribute beer produced in a Los Angeles brewery through Kirin's

EMERGING MARKETS BRIEFING BOOK

⟐ Joint Ventures

Joint venture investment in the BRIC nations is growing rapidly. China is a case in point; for many companies, the price of market entry is the willingness to pursue a joint venture with a local partner. Procter & Gamble has several joint ventures in China. China Great Wall Computer Group is a joint venture factory in which IBM is the majority partner with a 51 percent stake. In automotive joint ventures, the Chinese government limits foreign companies to minority stakes. Despite this, Japan's Isuzu Motors has been a joint venture partner with Jiangling Motors for more than a decade. The venture produces 20,000 pickup trucks and one-ton trucks annually.

As indicated in Table 9-2, in 1995 General Motors pledged $1.1 billion for a joint venture with Shanghai Automotive Industry to build Buicks for government and business use. GM was selected after giving high-level Chinese officials a tour of GM's operations in Brazil and agreeing to the government's conditions regarding technology transfer and investment capital. In 1997, GM was chosen by the Chinese government as the sole Western partner in a joint venture in Guangzhou that would build smaller, less expensive cars for the general public. Other global carmakers competing with GM for the project were BMW, Mercedes-Benz, Honda Motor, and Hyundai Motor.

Russia represents a huge, barely tapped market for a number of industries. The number of joint ventures is increasing. In 1997, GM became the first Western automaker to begin assembling vehicles in Russia. To avoid hefty tariffs that pushed the street price of an imported Blazer over $65,000, GM invested in a 25-75 joint venture with the government of the autonomous Tatarstan republic. Elaz-GM assembled Blazer sport utility vehicles

from imported components until the end of 2000. Young Russian professionals were expected to snap up the vehicles as long as the price was less than $30,000. However, after about 15,000 vehicles had been sold, market demand evaporated. At the end of 2001, GM terminated the joint venture.

GM executives are counting on better results with AvtoVAZ, the largest carmaker in the former Soviet Union. AvtoVAZ is home to Russia's top technical design center and also has access to low-cost Russian titanium and other materials. GM originally intended to assemble a stripped-down, reengineered car based on its Opel model. However, market research revealed that a "Made in Russia" car would only be acceptable if it sported a very low sticker price; GM had anticipated a price of approximately $15,000. The same research pointed GM toward an opportunity to put the Chevrolet nameplate on a redesigned domestic model, the Niva. With GM's financial aid, the Chevrolet Niva was launched in the fall of 2002; another model, the Viva, was launched in 2004. In addition to GM, several other automakers are joining with Russian partners. BMW Group AG has already begun the local manufacture of its 5-series sedans; Renault SA is producing Megane and Clio Symbol models at a plant near Moscow. Fiat SpA and Ford also anticipate starting production at joint venture plants. Some other recent joint venture alliances are outlined in Table 9-2.

Sources: Keith Naughton, "How GM Got the Inside Track in China," *Business Week* (November 6, 1995), pp. 56–57; Gregory L. White, "Off Road: How the Chevy Name Landed on SUV Using Russian Technology," *The Wall Street Journal* (February 20, 2001), pp. A1, A8.

TABLE 9-2 **Market Entry and Expansion by Joint Venture**

Companies Involved	Purpose of Joint Venture
GM (United States), Toyota (Japan)	NUMMI, a jointly operated plant in Freemont, California (venture was terminated in 2009).
GM (United States), Shanghai Automotive Industry (China)	50-50 joint venture to build assembly plant to produce 100,000 mid-sized sedans for Chinese market beginning in 1997 (total investment of $1 billion)
GM (United States), Hindustan Motors (India)	Joint venture to build up to 20,000 Opel Astras annually (GM's investment $100 million)
GM (United States), governments of Russia and Tatarstan	25-75 joint venture to assemble Blazers from imported parts and, by 1998, to build a full assembly line for 45,000 vehicles (total investment $250 million)
Ford (United States), Mazda (Japan)	Joint operation of a plant in Flat Rock, Michigan
Ford (United States), Mahindra & Mahindra Ltd. (India)	50-50 joint venture to build Ford Fiestas in Indian state of Tamil Nadu ($800 million)
Chrysler (United States), BMW (Germany)	50-50 joint venture to build a plant in South America to produce small-displacement 4-cylinder engines ($500 million)

Source: Compiled by authors.

channels. Anheuser-Busch also had the option to use some of Kirin's brewing capacity to brew Bud locally. For its part, Kirin was well positioned to learn more about the global market for beer from the world's largest brewer. By the end of the decade, however, Bud's market share hadn't increased and the venture was losing money. On January 1, 2000, Anheuser-Busch dissolved the joint venture and eliminated most of the associated job positions in Japan; it reverted instead to a licensing agreement with Kirin. The lesson for consumer products marketers considering market entry in Japan is clear. It may make more sense to give control to a local partner via a licensing agreement rather than making a major investment.[10]

The disadvantages of joint venturing can be significant. Joint venture partners must share rewards as well as risks. The main disadvantage associated with joint ventures is that a company incurs very significant costs associated with control and coordination issues that arise when working with a partner. (However, in some instances, country-specific restrictions limit the share of capital help by foreign companies.)

A second disadvantage is the potential for conflict between partners. These often arise out of cultural differences, as was the case in a failed $130 million joint venture between Corning Glass and Vitro, Mexico's largest industrial manufacturer. The venture's Mexican managers sometimes viewed the Americans as too direct and aggressive; the Americans believed their partners took too much time to make important decisions.[11] Such conflicts can multiply when there are several partners in the venture. Disagreements about third-country markets where partners face each other as actual or potential competitors can lead to "divorce." To avoid this, it is essential to work out a plan for approaching third-country markets as part of the venture agreement.

A third issue, also noted in the discussion of licensing, is that a dynamic joint venture partner can evolve into a stronger competitor. Many developing countries are very forthright in this regard. Yuan Sutai, a member of China's Ministry of Electronics Industry, told the *Wall Street Journal*, "The purpose of any joint venture, or even a wholly-owned investment, is to allow Chinese companies to learn from foreign companies. We want them to bring their technology to the soil of the People's Republic of China."[12] GM and South Korea's Daewoo Group formed a joint venture in 1978 to produce cars for the Korean market. By the mid-1990s, GM had helped Daewoo improve its competitiveness as an auto producer, but Daewoo chairman

---

[10]Yumiko Ono, "Beer Venture of Anheuser, Kirin Goes Down Drain on Tepid Sales," *The Wall Street Journal* (November 3, 1999), p. A23.

[11]Anthony DePalma, "It Takes More Than a Visa to Do Business in Mexico," *The New York Times* (June 26, 1994), sec. 3, p. 5.

[12]David P. Hamilton, "China, With Foreign Partners' Help, Becomes a Budding Technology Giant," *The Wall Street Journal* (December 7, 1995), p. A10.

Kim Woo-Choong terminated the venture because its provisions prevented the export of cars bearing the Daewoo name.[13]

As one global marketing expert warns, "In an alliance you have to learn skills of the partner, rather than just see it as a way to get a product to sell while avoiding a big investment." Yet, compared with U.S. and European firms, Japanese and Korean firms seem to excel in their ability to leverage new knowledge that comes out of a joint venture. For example, Toyota learned many new things from its partnership with GM—about U.S. supply and transportation and managing American workers—that have been subsequently applied at its Camry plant in Kentucky. However, some American managers involved in the venture complained that the manufacturing expertise they gained was not applied broadly throughout GM. An example of a successful alliance is Ericsson's cell phone alliance with Sony (see Exhibit 9-5).

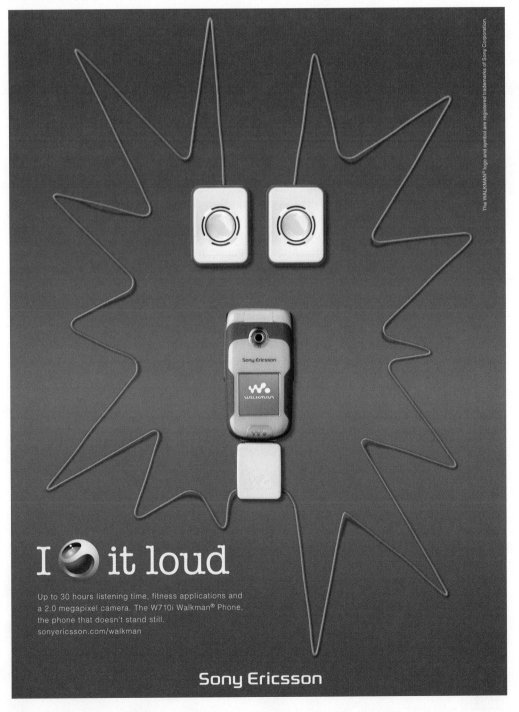

Exhibit 9-5: Sony Ericsson is a 50-50 joint venture between Sweden's Telefonaktiebolaget LM Ericsson, the world's leading manufacturer of wireless telecom equipment, and Japanese consumer electronics giant Sony Corporation. Sony Ericsson's logo is a green circular symbol that is used as a "verb" in print ads for a new line of Walkman phones. Headlines include "I [logo] music," "I [logo] my long commute," and "I [logo] it loud."

Source: Used by permission of Sony Ericsson.

Investment via Equity Stake or Full Ownership

The most extensive form of participation in global markets is investment that results in either an equity stake or full ownership. An **equity stake** is simply an investment; if the investor owns fewer than 50 percent of the shares, it is a minority stake; ownership of more than half the shares makes it a majority. **Full ownership**, as the name implies, means the investor has 100 percent control. This may be achieved by a start-up of new operations, known as **greenfield investment**, or by merger or acquisition of an existing enterprise. For example, in 2008 the largest merger and acquisition (M&A) deal in the pharmaceutical industry was Roche's acquisition of Genentech for $43 billion. Prior to the onset of the global financial crisis, the media and telecommunications industry sectors were among the busiest for M&A worldwide. Ownership requires the greatest commitment of capital and managerial effort and offers the fullest means of participating in a market. Companies may move from licensing or joint venture strategies to ownership in order to achieve faster expansion in a market, greater control, or higher profits. In 1991, for example, Ralston Purina ended a 20-year joint venture with a Japanese company to start its own pet food subsidiary. Monsanto and Bayer AG, the German pharmaceutical company, are two other companies that have also recently disbanded partnerships in favor of wholly owned subsidiaries in Japan. Home Depot is using acquisition to expand in China; the home improvement giant recently acquired the HomeWay chain (see Exhibit 9-6).

If government restrictions prevent majority or 100 percent ownership by foreign companies, the investing company will have to settle for a minority equity stake. In Russia, for example, the government restricts foreign ownership in joint ventures to a 49 percent stake. A minority equity stake may also suit a company's business interests. For example, Samsung was content to purchase a 40 percent stake in computer maker AST. As Samsung manager Michael Yang noted, "We thought 100 percent would be very risky, because any time you have a switch of ownership, that creates a lot of uncertainty among the employees."[14]

In other instances, the investing company may start with a minority stake and then increase its share. In 1991, Volkswagen AG made its first investment in the Czech auto industry by purchasing a 31 percent share in Skoda. By 1995, Volkswagen had increased its equity stake to 70 percent (the government of the Czech Republic owns the rest). Today the Czech automaker is evolving from a regional company to a global one, with sales in 100 countries and more than $5 billion in

Exhibit 9-6: When U.S. Commerce Secretary Carlos Gutierrez visited China for trade talks in 2006, Home Depot announced it would acquire the HomeWay do-it-yourself chain. China's home-improvement market generates an estimated $50 billion in annual sales and is growing at double-digit rates. Home Depot, which also has operations in Mexico and Canada, is experiencing a business slowdown in the U.S. market. According to Annette Verschuren, president of Home Depot's Asian operations, the company's China strategy will include further acquisitions to fuel revenue growth.
Source: Jason Lee/ Reuters/Landov Media.

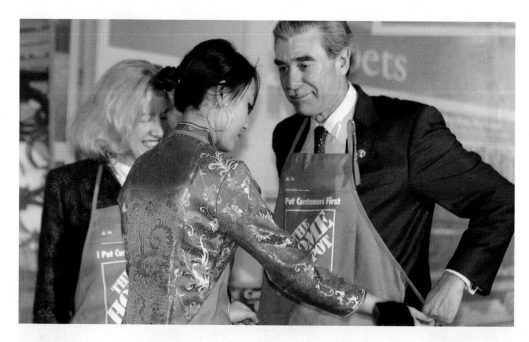

---

[14]Ross Kerber, "Chairman Predicts Samsung Deal Will Make AST a Giant," *The Los Angeles Times* (March 2, 1995), p. D1.

annual revenues.[15] Similarly, Ford purchased a 25 percent stake in Mazda in 1979; in 1996, Ford spent another $408 million to raise its stake to 33.4 percent. However, in contrast to the Volkswagen/Skoda alliance, Ford has been forced to scale back its investment. At the end of 2008, the economic crisis prompted Ford to sell 20 percent of its Mazda holdings; the sale raised more than $500 million.

Large-scale direct expansion by means of establishing new facilities can be expensive and require a major commitment of managerial time and energy. However, political or other environmental factors sometimes dictate this approach. For example, Japan's Fuji Photo Film Company invested hundreds of millions of dollars in the United States after the U.S. government ruled that Fuji was guilty of dumping (i.e., selling photographic paper at substantially lower prices than in Japan). As an alternative to greenfield investment in new facilities, acquisition is an instantaneous—and sometimes less expensive—approach to market entry or expansion. Although full ownership can yield the additional advantage of avoiding communication and conflict of interest problems that may arise with a joint venture or coproduction partner, acquisitions still present the demanding and challenging task of integrating the acquired company into the worldwide organization and coordinating activities.

Tables 9-3, 9-4, and 9-5 provide a sense of how companies in the automotive industry utilize a variety of market entry options discussed previously, including equity stakes, investments to establish new operations, and acquisition. Table 9-3 shows that GM favors minority stakes in non-U.S. automakers; from 1998 through 2000, the company spent $4.7 billion on such deals. Ford spent twice as much on acquisitions. Despite the fact that GM losses from the deals resulted in substantial write-offs, the strategy reflects management's skepticism about making big mergers work. As former GM chairman and CEO Rick Wagoner said, "We could have bought

TABLE 9-3 Investment in Equity Stake

Investing Company (Home Country)	Investment (Share, Amount, Date)
General Motors (United States)	Fuji Heavy Industries (Japan, 20% stake, $1.4 billion, 1999)
	Saab Automobiles AB (Sweden, 50% stake, $500 million, 1990; remaining 50%, 2000; following bankruptcy filing, sold Saab to Swedish consortium in 2009)
Volkswagen AG (Germany)	Skoda (Czech Republic, 31% stake, $6 billion, 1991; increased to 50.5%, 1994; currently owns 70% stake)
Ford (USA)	Mazda Motor Corp. (Japan, 25% stake, 1979; increased to 33.4%, $408 million, 1996; decreased stake to 13%, 2008)
Renault SA (France)	AvtoVaz (Russia, 25% stake, $1.3 billion, 2008); Nissan Motors (Japan, 35% stake, $5 billion, 2000)
Proton (Malaysia)	Lotus Cars (Great Britain, 80% stake, $100

TABLE 9-4 Investment to Establish New Operations

Investing Company (Headquarters Country)	Investment (Location)
Honda Motor (Japan)	$550 million auto assembly plant (Indiana, United States, 2006)
Hyundai (South Korea)	$1.1 billion auto assembly and manufacturing facility producing Sonata and Santa Fe models (Georgia, United States, 2005)
Bayerische Motoren Werke AG (Germany)	$400 million auto assembly plant (South Carolina, United States, 1995)
Mercedes-Benz AG (Germany)	$300 million auto assembly plant (Alabama, United States, 1993)
Toyota (Japan)	$3.4 billion manufacturing plant producing Camry, Avalon, and minivan models (Kentucky, United States); $400 million engine plant (West Virginia, United States)

---

[15]Gail Edmondson, "Skoda, Volkswagen's Hot Growth Engine," *Business Week* (September 14, 2007), p. 30.

TABLE 9-5 Market Entry and Expansion by Acquisition

Acquiring Company	Target (Country, Date, Amount)
Tata Motors (India)	Jaguar and Land Rover (UK, $2.3 billion 2008)
Volkswagen AG (Germany)	Sociedad Española de Automoviles de Turisme (SEAT, Spain, $600 million, purchase completed in 1990)
Ford Motor Company (USA)	Volvo car unit (Sweden, $6.5 billion, 1999)
Paccar (USA)	DAF Trucks (Netherlands, $543 million, 1996)

100 percent of somebody, but that probably wouldn't have been a good use of capital." Meanwhile, the investments in minority stakes are finally paying off: The company enjoys scale-related savings in purchasing, it has gained access to diesel technology, and Saab produced a new model in record time with the help of Subaru.[16] Following its bankruptcy filing in 2009, GM divested itself of several non-core businesses and brands, including Saab.

What is the driving force behind many of these acquisitions? It is globalization. In cases like Gerber, management realizes that the path to globalization cannot be undertaken independently. Management at Helene Curtis Industries came to a similar realization and agreed to be acquired by Unilever. Ronald J. Gidwitz, president and CEO, said, "It was very clear to us that Helene Curtis did not have the capacity to project itself in emerging markets around the world. As markets get larger, that forces the smaller players to take action."[17] Still, management's decision to invest abroad sometimes clashes with investors' short-term profitability goals. Although this is an especially important issue for publicly held U.S. companies, there is an increasing trend toward foreign investment by U.S. companies.

Several of the advantages of joint ventures also apply to ownership, including access to markets and avoidance of tariff or quota barriers. Like joint ventures, ownership also permits important technology experience transfers and provides a company with access to new manufacturing techniques. For example, The Stanley Works, a tool maker with headquarters in New Britain, Connecticut, has acquired more than a dozen companies. Among them is Taiwan's National Hand Tool/Chiro Company, a socket wrench manufacturer and developer of a "cold-forming" process that speeds up production and reduces waste. Stanley is now using that technology in the manufacture of other tools. Former chairman Richard H. Ayers presided over the acquisitions and envisioned such global cross-fertilization and "blended technology" as a key

> "We used to go into talks saying 'acquisition' with joint ventures a distant second choice, but now we see joint ventures as a great way to dip a toe into a new market."[18]
>
> Pamela Daley, senior vice president for corporate business development, GE

Exhibit 9-7: As we have seen in previous chapters, China's growing economic clout has contributed to increased antiglobalization sentiment in various parts of the world. For example, China offsets its huge trade surplus with the United States by investing in American securities and companies. As this cartoon implies, business schools may be next!
Source: Cartoon Features Syndicate.

Cable

"OK, but just suppose China *did* make a takeover move on our B-school."

---

[16]James Mackintosh, "GM Stands By Its Strategy for Expansion," *Financial Times* (February 2, 2004), p. 5.
[17]Richard Gibson and Sara Calian, "Unilever to Buy Helene Curtis for $770 Million," *The Wall Street Journal* (February 19, 1996), p. A3.
[18]Claudia Deutsch, "The Venturesome Giant," *The New York Times* (October 5, 2007), p. C1.

benefit of globalization.[19] In 1998, former GE executive John Trani succeeded Ayers as CEO; Trani brought considerable experience with international acquisitions, and his selection was widely viewed as evidence that Stanley intended to boost global sales even more.

The alternatives discussed here—licensing, joint ventures, minority or majority equity stake, and ownership—are points along a continuum of alternative strategies for global market entry and expansion. The overall design of a company's global strategy may call for combinations of exporting-importing, licensing, joint ventures, and ownership among different operating units. Avon Products uses both acquisition and joint ventures to enter developing markets. A company's strategy preference may change over time. For example, Borden Inc. ended licensing and joint venture arrangements for branded food products in Japan and set up its own production, distribution, and marketing capabilities for dairy products. Meanwhile, in nonfood products, Borden has maintained joint venture relationships with Japanese partners in flexible packaging and foundry materials.

⮞ STRATEGIC DECISION MAKING IN GLOBAL MARKETING
Gerber

Gerber Products is the undisputed leader in the U.S. baby food market. Despite a 70 percent market share, Gerber faces a mature market and stagnant growth at home. Because 9 out of 10 births take place outside the United States, Gerber executives hoped to make international sales a greater proportion of the company's $1.17 billion in annual revenues. Overall, Gerber's international sales increased 150 percent between 1989 and 1993, from $86.5 million to $216.1 million.

Still, for two decades a combination of changing market conditions, management inconsistency, and decisions that didn't pay off slowed Gerber's globalization efforts. Gerber entered the Latin American market in the 1970s, but then closed operations in Venezuela in the wake of government-imposed price controls. Management's focus on the U.S. market resulted in a series of diversifications into nonfood categories that were not successful. Meanwhile, management was not willing to sacrifice short-term quarterly earnings growth to finance an international effort. As Michael A. Cipollaro, Gerber's former president of international operations, remarked, "If you are going to sow in the international arena today to reap tomorrow, you couldn't have that [earnings] growth on a regular basis." In the 1980s, Gerber pursued a strategy of licensing the manufacture and distribution of its baby food products to other companies. In France, for example, Gerber selected CPC International as a licensee.

Unfortunately, Gerber couldn't force its licensees to make baby food a priority business. In France, for example, baby food represented a meager 2 percent of CPC's European revenues. When CPC closed its French plant, Gerber had to find another manufacturing source. It bought a stake in a Polish factory, but production was held up for months while quality improvements were made. The delay ended up costing Gerber its market position in France.

Belatedly, Gerber discovered that strong competitors already dominated many markets around the globe. Heinz has about one-third of the $1.5 billion baby food market outside the United States; Gerber's share of the global market is 17 percent. Competitors with less global share than Gerber—including

France's BSN Group (15 percent market share) and Switzerland's Nestlé SA (8 percent)—have been aggressively building brand loyalty. In France, for example, parents traveling with infants can get free baby food and diapers through Nestlé's system of roadside changing stations. Another barrier is that many European mothers think homemade baby food is healthier than food from a jar.

Meanwhile, Gerber's global efforts were interrupted by the resignations of several key executives. Cipollaro, the chief of international operations, left, as did the vice president for Europe and the international director of business development. Gerber's management team was forced to rethink its strategy: In May 1994, it agreed to an acquisition by Sandoz AG, a $10.3 billion Swiss pharmaceutical and chemical company. As market analyst David Adelman noted, "It was very expensive for Gerber to build business internationally. This was one of the driving reasons why Gerber wanted to team up with a larger company."

Some industry analysts expressed doubts about the logic behind the acquisition. London broker Peter Smith said, "I'm sorry: Baby food and anticancer drugs don't really come together." Nevertheless, the deal gave Gerber immediate access to a global marketing and distribution network that is particularly strong in developing countries such as China and India. Sandoz, which faces expiring patents for some of its most profitable drugs, instantly assumed a strong position in the U.S. nutrition market. In 2007, Nestlé acquired Gerber for $5.5 billion; plans call for increasing Gerber's market share both at home and abroad.

Sources: Jennifer Reingold, "The Pope of Basel," *Financial World* (July 18, 1995), pp. 36–38; Margaret Studer, "Sandoz AG Is Foraging for Additional Food Holdings," *The Wall Street Journal* (February 21, 1995), p. B4; Richard Gibson, "Growth Formula: Gerber Missed the Boat in Quest to Go Global, So It Turned to Sandoz," *The Wall Street Journal* (May 24, 1994), pp. A1, A7; Leah Rickard and Laurel Wentz, "Sandoz Opens World for Gerber," *Advertising Age* (May 30, 1994), p. 4; Margaret Studer and Ron Winslow, "Sandoz, Under Pressure, Looks to Gerber for Protection," *The Wall Street Journal* (May 25, 1994), p. B3.

---

[19]Louis Uchitelle, "The Stanley Works Goes Global," *The New York Times* (July 23, 1989), sec. 3, pp. 1, 10.

Competitors within a given industry may pursue different strategies. For example, Cummins Engine and Caterpillar both face very high costs—in the $300 to $400 million range—for developing new diesel engines suited to new applications. However, the two companies vary in their strategic approaches to the world market for engines. Cummins management looks favorably on collaboration; also, the company's relatively modest $6 billion in annual revenues presents financial limitations. Thus, Cummins prefers joint ventures. The biggest joint venture between an American company and the Soviet Union linked Cummins with the KamAZ truck company in Tatarstan. The joint venture allowed the Russians to implement new manufacturing technologies while providing Cummins with access to the Russian market. Cummins also has joint ventures in Japan, Finland, and Italy. Management at Caterpillar, by contrast, prefers the higher degree of control that comes with full ownership. The company has spent more than $2 billion on purchases of Germany's MaK, British enginemaker Perkins, and others. Management believes that it is often less expensive to buy existing firms than to develop new applications independently. Also, Caterpillar is concerned about safeguarding proprietary knowledge that is basic to manufacturing in its core construction equipment business.[20]

GLOBAL STRATEGIC PARTNERSHIPS

In Chapter 8 and the first half of this chapter, we surveyed the range of options—exporting, licensing, joint ventures, and ownership—traditionally used by companies wishing either to enter global markets for the first time or to expand their activities beyond present levels. However, recent changes in the political, economic, sociocultural, and technological environments of the global firm have combined to change the relative importance of those strategies. Trade barriers have fallen, markets have globalized, consumer needs and wants have converged, product life cycles have shortened, and new communications technologies and trends have emerged. Although these developments provide unprecedented market opportunities, there are strong strategic implications for the global organization and new challenges for the global marketer. Such strategies will undoubtedly incorporate—or may even be structured around—a variety of collaborations. Once thought of only as joint ventures with the more dominant party reaping most of the benefits (or losses) of the partnership, cross-border alliances are taking on surprising new configurations and even more surprising players.

Why would any firm—global or otherwise—seek to collaborate with another firm, be it local or foreign? For example, despite commanding a 37 percent share of the global cellular handset market, Nokia recently announced that it would make the source code for its proprietary Series 60 software available to competing handset manufacturers such as Siemens AG. Why did Nokia's top executives decide to collaborate, thereby putting the company's competitive advantage with software development (and healthy profit margins) at risk? As noted, a "perfect storm" of converging environmental forces is rendering traditional competitive strategies obsolete.

Today's competitive environment is characterized by unprecedented degrees of turbulence, dynamism, and unpredictability; global firms must respond and adapt quickly. To succeed in global markets, firms can no longer rely exclusively on the technological superiority or core competence that brought them past success. In the twenty-first century, firms must look toward new strategies that will enhance environmental responsiveness. In particular, they must pursue "entrepreneurial globalization" by developing flexible organizational capabilities, innovating continuously, and revising global strategies accordingly."[21] In the second half of this chapter, we will focus on global strategic partnerships. In addition, we will examine the Japanese *keiretsu* and various other types of cooperation strategies that global firms are using today.

---

[20]Peter Marsh, "Engine Makers Take Different Routes," *Financial Times* (July 14, 1998), p. 11.
[21]Michael Y. Yoshino and U. Srinivasa Rangan, *Strategic Alliances: An Entrepreneurial Approach to Globalization* (Boston: Harvard Business School Press, 1995), p. 51.

THE NATURE OF GLOBAL STRATEGIC PARTNERSHIPS

The terminology used to describe the new forms of cooperation strategies varies widely. The phrases **strategic alliances, strategic international alliances**, and **global strategic partnerships (GSPs)** are frequently used to refer to linkages between companies from different countries to jointly pursue a common goal. This terminology can cover a broad spectrum of interfirm agreements, including joint ventures. However, the strategic alliances discussed here exhibit three characteristics (see Figure 9-2).[22]

1. The participants remain independent subsequent to the formation of the alliance.
2. The participants share the benefits of the alliance as well as control over the performance of assigned tasks.
3. The participants make ongoing contributions in technology, products, and other key strategic areas.

According to estimates, the number of strategic alliances has been growing at a rate of 20 to 30 percent since the mid-1980s. The upward trend for GSPs comes in part at the expense of traditional cross-border mergers and acquisitions. Since the mid-1990s, a key force driving partnership formation is the realization that globalization and the Internet will require new inter-corporate configurations (see Exhibit 9-8). Table 9-6 lists examples of GSPs.

Like traditional joint ventures, GSPs have some disadvantages. Partners share control over assigned tasks, a situation that creates management challenges. Also, there are potential risks associated with strengthening a competitor from another country.

First, high product development costs in the face of resource constraints may force a company to seek one or more partners; this was part of the rationale for Sony's partnership with Samsung to produce flat-panel TV screens. Second, the technology requirements of many contemporary products mean that an individual company may lack the skills, capital, or know-how to go it alone.[23] Third, partnerships may be the best means of securing access to national and regional markets. Fourth, partnerships provide important learning opportunities; in fact, one expert regards GSPs as a "race to learn." Professor Gary Hamel of the London Business School has observed that the partner that proves to be the fastest learner can ultimately dominate the relationship.

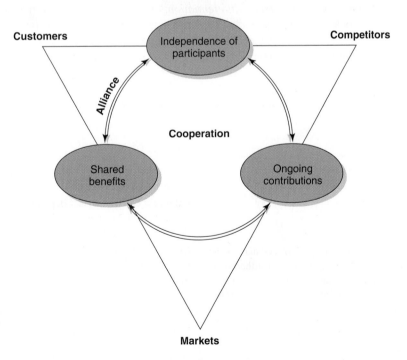

FIGURE 9-2

Three Characteristics of Strategic Alliances

---

[22]Michael Y. Yoshino and U. Srinivasa Rangan, *Strategic Alliances: An Entrepreneurial Approach to Globalization* (Boston: Harvard Business School Press, 1995), p. 5. For an alternative description see Riad Ajami and Dara Khambata, "Global Strategic Alliances: The New Transnationals," *Journal of Global Marketing* 5, no. 1/2, (1991), pp. 55–59.
[23]Kenichi Ohmae, "The Global Logic of Strategic Alliances," *Harvard Business Review* 67, no. 2 (March–April 1989), p. 145.

Exhibit 9-8: The Star Alliance is a global network that brings together United Airlines and carriers in a number of different countries. Passengers booking a ticket on any Alliance member can easily connect with other carriers for smooth travel to more than 130 countries. A further benefit for travelers is the fact that frequent-flyer miles earned can be redeemed on any Alliance member.
Source: Getty Images, Inc. AFP.

As noted earlier, GSPs differ significantly from the market entry modes discussed in the first half of the chapter. Because licensing agreements do not call for continuous transfer of technology or skills among partners, such agreements are not strategic alliances.[24] Traditional joint ventures are basically alliances focusing on a single national market or a specific problem. The Chinese joint venture described previously between GM and Shanghai Automotive fits this description; the basic goal is to make cars for the Chinese market. A true global strategic partnership is different; it is distinguished by five attributes.[25] S-LCD, Sony's strategic alliance with Samsung, offers a good illustration of each attribute.[26]

1. *Two or more companies develop a joint long-term strategy aimed at achieving world leadership by pursuing cost leadership, differentiation, or a combination of the two.* Samsung and Sony are jockeying with each other for leadership in the global television market. One key to profitability in the flat-panel TV market is being the cost leader in panel production. S-LCD is a $2 billion joint venture to produce 60,000 panels per month.

TABLE 9-6 Examples of Global Strategic Partnerships

Name of Alliance or Product	Major Participants	Purpose of Alliance
S-LCD	Sony Corp., Samsung Electronics Co.	Produce flat-panel LCD screens for high-definition televisions
Beverage Partners Worldwide	Coca-Cola and Nestlé	Offer new coffee, tea, and herbal beverage products in "rejuvenation" category
Star Alliance	Air Canada, Air China, Air New Zealand, ANA, Asiana Airlines, Austrian, bmi, EGYPTAIR, LOT Polish Airways, Lufthansa, Scandinavian Airlines, Shanghai Airlines, Singapore Airlines, South African Airways, Spanair, SWISS, TAP Portugal, THAI, Turkish Airlines, United, US Airways	Create a global travel network by linking airlines and providing better service for international travelers

[24]Michael A. Yoshino and U. Srinivasa Rangan, *Strategic Alliances: An Entrepreneurial Approach to Globalization* (Boston: Harvard Business School Press, 1995), p. 6.
[25]Howard V. Perlmutter and David A. Heenan, "Cooperate to Compete Globally," *Harvard Business Review* 64, no. 2 (March–April 1986), p. 137.
[26]Discussion is adapted from Phred Dvorak and Evan Ramstad, "TV Marriage: Behind Sony-Samsung Rivalry, An Unlikely Alliance Develops," *The Wall Street Journal* (January 3, 2006), pp. A1, A6.

2. *The relationship is reciprocal. Each partner possesses specific strengths that it shares with the other; learning must take place on both sides.* Samsung is a leader in the manufacturing technologies used to create flat-panel TVs. Sony excels at parlaying advanced technology into world-class consumer products; its engineers specialize in optimizing TV picture quality. Jang Insik, Samsung's chief executive, says, "If we learn from Sony, it will help us in advancing our technology."

3. *The partners' vision and efforts are truly global, extending beyond home countries and the home regions to the rest of the world.* Sony and Samsung are both global companies that market global brands throughout the world.

4. *The relationship is organized along horizontal, not vertical, lines. Continual transfer of resources laterally between partners is required, with technology sharing and resource pooling representing norms.* Jang and Sony's Hiroshi Murayama speak by telephone on a daily basis; they also meet face-to-face each month to discuss panel making.

5. *When competing in markets excluded from the partnership, the participants retain their national and ideological identities.* Samsung markets a line of high-definition televisions that use digital light processing (DLP) technology. Sony does not produce DLP sets. When developing a DVD player and home theater sound system to match the TV, a team headed by head TV designer Yunje Kang worked closely with the audio/video division. At Samsung, managers with responsibility for consumer electronics and computer products report to digital media chief Gee-sung Choi. All the designers work side-by-side on open floors. As noted in a recent company profile, "the walls between business units are literally nonexistent."[27] By contrast, in recent years Sony has been plagued by a time-consuming, consensus-driven communication approach between divisions that have operated largely autonomously.

SUCCESS FACTORS

Assuming that a proposed alliance has these five attributes, it is necessary to consider six basic factors deemed to have significant impact on the success of GSPs: mission, strategy, governance, culture, organization, and management.[28]

1. *Mission.* Successful GSPs create win-win situations, where participants pursue objectives on the basis of mutual need or advantage.

2. *Strategy.* A company may establish separate GSPs with different partners; strategy must be thought out up front to avoid conflicts.

3. *Governance.* Discussion and consensus must be the norms. Partners must be viewed as equals.

4. *Culture.* Personal chemistry is important, as is the successful development of a shared set of values. The failure of a partnership between Great Britain's General Electric Company and Siemens AG was blamed in part on the fact that the former was run by finance-oriented executives, the latter by engineers.

5. *Organization.* Innovative structures and designs may be needed to offset the complexity of multi-country management.

6. *Management.* GSPs invariably involve a different type of decision making. Potentially divisive issues must be identified in advance and clear, unitary lines of authority established that will result in commitment by all partners.

Companies forming GSPs must keep these factors in mind. Moreover, the following four principles will guide successful collaborators. First, despite the fact that partners are pursuing mutual goals in some areas, partners must remember that they are competitors in others. Second, harmony is not the most important measure of success—some conflict is to be

---

[27]Frank Rose, "Seoul Machine," *Wired* (May 2005).
[28]Howard V. Perlmutter and David A. Heenan, "Cooperate to Compete Globally," *Harvard Business Review* 64, no. 2 (March–April 1986), p. 137.

expected. Third, all employees, engineers, and managers must understand where cooperation ends and competitive compromise begins. Finally, as noted earlier, learning from partners is critically important.[29]

The issue of learning deserves special attention. As one team of researchers notes,

> The challenge is to share enough skills to create advantage vis-à-vis companies outside the alliance while preventing a wholesale transfer of core skills to the partner. This is a very thin line to walk. Companies must carefully select what skills and technologies they pass to their partners. They must develop safeguards against unintended, informal transfers of information. The goal is to limit the transparency of their operations.[30]

Alliances with Asian Competitors

Western companies may find themselves at a disadvantage in GSPs with an Asian competitor, especially if the latter's manufacturing skills are the attractive quality. Unfortunately for Western companies, manufacturing excellence represents a multifaceted competence that is not easily transferred. Non-Asian managers and engineers must also learn to be more receptive and attentive—they must overcome the "not-invented-here" syndrome and begin to think of themselves as students, not teachers. At the same time, they must learn to be less eager to show off proprietary lab and engineering successes. To limit transparency, some companies involved in GSPs establish a "collaboration section." Much like a corporate communications department, this department is designed to serve as a gatekeeper through which requests for access to people and information must be channeled. Such gatekeeping serves an important control function that guards against unintended transfers.

A 1991 report by McKinsey and Company shed additional light on the specific problems of alliances between Western and Japanese firms.[31] Often, problems between partners had less to do with objective levels of performance than with a feeling of mutual disillusionment and missed opportunity. The study identified four common problem areas in alliances gone wrong. The first problem was that each partner had a "different dream"; the Japanese partner saw itself emerging from the alliance as a leader in its business or entering new sectors and building a new basis for the future; the Western partner sought relatively quick and risk-free financial returns. Said one Japanese manager, "Our partner came in looking for a return. They got it. Now they complain that they didn't build a business. But that isn't what they set out to create."

A second area of concern is the balance between partners. Each must contribute to the alliance and each must depend on the other to a degree that justifies participation in the alliance. The most attractive partner in the short run is likely to be a company that is already established and competent in the business with the need to master, say, some new technological skills. The best long-term partner, however, is likely to be a less competent player or even one from outside the industry.

Another common cause of problems is "frictional loss," caused by differences in management philosophy, expectations, and approaches. All functions within the alliance may be affected, and performance is likely to suffer as a consequence. Speaking of his Japanese counterpart, a Western businessperson said, "Our partner just wanted to go ahead and invest without considering whether there would be a return or not." The Japanese partner stated that "the foreign partner took so long to decide on obvious points that we were always too slow." Such differences often lead to frustration and time-consuming debates that stifle decision making.

Last, the study found that short-term goals can result in the foreign partner limiting the number of people allocated to the joint venture. Those involved in the venture may perform only two- or three-year assignments. The result is "corporate amnesia," that is, little or no corporate memory is built up on how to compete in Japan. The original goals of the venture will be lost as each new group of managers takes their turn. When taken collectively, these four problems will almost ensure that the Japanese partner will be the only one in it for the long haul.

---

[29]Gary Hamel, Yves L. Doz, and C. K. Prahalad, "Collaborate with Your Competitors—and Win," *Harvard Business Review* 67, no. 1 (January–February 1989), pp. 133–139.
[30]Hamel, Doz, Prahalad, p. 136.
[31]Kevin K. Jones and Walter E. Schill, "Allying for Advantage," *The McKinsey Quarterly,* no. 3 (1991), pp. 73–101.

CFM International, GE, and Snecma: A Success Story

Commercial Fan Moteur (CFM) International, a partnership between GE's jet engine division and Snecma, a government-owned French aerospace company, is a frequently cited example of a successful GSP. GE was motivated, in part, by the desire to gain access to the European market so it could sell engines to Airbus Industrie; also, the $800 million in development costs was more than GE could risk on its own. While GE focused on system design and high-tech work, the French side handled fans, boosters, and other components. In 2004, the French government sold a 35 percent stake in Snecma; in 2005, Sagem, an electronics maker, acquired Snecma. The combined companies are known as Safran. Today, the Snecma division has more than 300 commercial and military customers worldwide, including Boeing, Airbus, and the United States Air Force. In 2006, Snecma generated sales of €3.4 billion.

The alliance got off to a strong start because of the personal chemistry between two top executives, GE's Gerhard Neumann and the late General René Ravaud of Snecma. The partnership thrives despite each side's differing views regarding governance, management, and organization. Brian Rowe, senior vice president of GE's engine group, has noted that the French like to bring in senior executives from outside the industry, whereas GE prefers to bring in experienced people from within the organization. Also, the French prefer to approach problem solving with copious amounts of data, and Americans may take a more intuitive approach. Still, senior executives from both sides of the partnership have been delegated substantial responsibility.

Boeing and Japan: A Controversy

In some circles, GSPs have been the target of criticism. Critics warn that employees of a company that becomes reliant on outside suppliers for critical components will lose expertise and experience erosion of their engineering skills. Such criticism is often directed at GSPs involving U.S. and Japanese firms. For example, a proposed alliance between Boeing and a Japanese consortium to build a new fuel-efficient airliner, the 7J7, generated a great deal of controversy. The project's $4 billion price tag was too high for Boeing to shoulder alone. The Japanese were to contribute between $1 billion and $2 billion; in return, they would get a chance to learn manufacturing and marketing techniques from Boeing. Although the 7J7 project was shelved in 1988, a new wide body aircraft, the 777, was developed with about 20 percent of the work subcontracted out to Mitsubishi, Fuji, and Kawasaki.[32]

Critics envision a scenario in which the Japanese use what they learn to build their own aircraft and compete directly with Boeing in the future—a disturbing thought since Boeing is a major exporter to world markets. One team of researchers has developed a framework outlining the stages that a company can go through as it becomes increasingly dependent on partnerships:[33]

Step 1 Outsourcing of assembly for inexpensive labor

Step 2 Outsourcing of low-value components to reduce product price

Step 3 Growing levels of value-added components move abroad

Step 4 Manufacturing skills, designs, and functionally related technologies move abroad

Step 5 Disciplines related to quality, precision manufacturing, testing, and future avenues of product derivatives move abroad

Step 6 Core skills surrounding components, miniaturization, and complex systems integration move abroad

Step 7 Competitor learns the entire spectrum of skills related to the underlying core competence

Yoshino and Rangan have described the interaction and evolution of the various market entry strategies in terms of cross-market dependencies (Figure 9-3).[34] Many firms start with an export-based approach as described in Chapter 8. For example, the success of Japanese firms in the

---

[32]John Holusha, "Pushing the Envelope at Boeing," *The New York Times* (November 10, 1991), sec. 3, pp. 1, 6.

[33]David Lei and John W. Slocum Jr., "Global Strategy, Competence-Building and Strategic Alliances," *California Management Review* 35, no. 1 (Fall 1992), pp. 81–97.

[34]Michael A. Yoshino and U. Srinivasa Rangan, *Strategic Alliances: An Entrepreneurial Approach to Globalization* (Boston: Harvard Business School Press, 1995), pp. 56–59.

FIGURE 9-3

**Evolution and
Interaction of
Entry Strategies**

Source: Adapted from
Michael Y. Yoshino and
U. Srinivasa Rangan,
*Strategic Alliances: An
Entrepreneurial Approach to
Globalization* (Boston:
Harvard Business School
Press, 1995), p. 51.

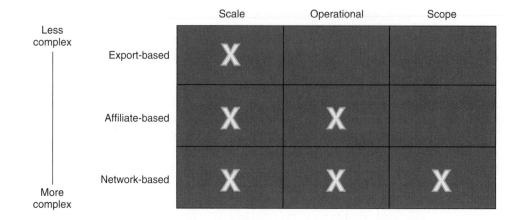

automobile and consumer electronics industries can be traced back to an export drive. Nissan, Toyota, and Honda initially concentrated production in Japan, thereby achieving economies of scale. Eventually, an export-driven strategy gives way to an affiliate-based one. The various types of investment strategies described previously—equity stake, investment to establish new operations, acquisitions, and joint ventures—create operational interdependence within the firm. By operating in different markets, firms have the opportunity to transfer production from place to place, depending on exchange rates, resource costs, or other considerations. Although at some companies foreign affiliates operate as autonomous fiefdoms (the prototypical multinational business with a polycentric orientation), other companies realize the benefits that operational flexibility can bring. The third and most complex stage in the evolution of a global strategy comes with management's realization that full integration and a network of shared knowledge from different country markets can greatly enhance the firm's overall competitive position. As implied by Figure 9-3, as company personnel opt to pursue increasingly complex strategies, they must simultaneously manage each new interdependency as well as preceding ones. The stages described here are reflected in the evolution of Taiwan's Acer Group as described in Case 1-3.

INTERNATIONAL PARTNERSHIPS IN DEVELOPING COUNTRIES

Central and Eastern Europe, Asia, India, and Mexico offer exciting opportunities for firms that seek to enter gigantic and largely untapped markets. An obvious strategic alternative for entering these markets is the strategic alliance. Like the early joint ventures between U.S. and Japanese firms, potential partners will trade market access for know-how. Other entry strategies are also possible; in 1996, for example, Chrysler and BMW agreed to invest $500 million in a joint venture plant in Latin America capable of producing 400,000 small engines annually. While then-Chrysler chairman Robert Eaton was skeptical of strategic partnerships, he believed that limited forms of cooperation such as joint ventures make sense in some situations. Eaton said, "The majority of world vehicle sales are in vehicles with engines of less than 2.0 liters, outside of the United States. We have simply not been able to be competitive in those areas because of not having a smaller engine. In the international market, there's no question that in many cases such as this, the economies of scale suggest you really ought to have a partner."[35]

Assuming that risks can be minimized and problems overcome, joint ventures in the transition economies of Central and Eastern Europe could evolve at a more accelerated pace than past joint ventures with Asian partners. A number of factors combine to make Russia an excellent location for an alliance: There is a well-educated workforce, and quality is very important to Russian consumers. However, several problems are frequently cited in connection with joint ventures in Russia; these include organized crime, supply shortages, and outdated regulatory and legal systems in a constant state of flux. Despite the risks, the number of joint ventures in Russia

---

[35]Angelo B. Henderson, "Chrysler and BMW Team Up to Build Small-Engine Plant in South America," *The Wall Street Journal* (October 2, 1996), p. A4.

→ CULTURE WATCH
Will Beer Drinkers Toast SABMiller's Global Strategy?

South African Breweries PLC had a problem. The company owned more than 100 breweries in 24 countries. South Africa, where the company had a commanding 98 percent share of the beer market, accounted for about 14 percent of annual revenues (see Exhibit 9-9). However, most of the company's brands, which include Castle Lager, Pilsner Urquell, and Carling Black Label, were sold on a local or regional basis; none had the global status of Heineken, Amstel, or Guinness. Nor were the company's brands well known in the key U.S. market, where a growing number of the "echo boom"—the children of the nation's 75 million baby boomers—were reaching drinking age.

In 2002, a solution presented itself: South African Breweries had an opportunity to buy the Miller Brewing unit from Philip Morris. The $3.6 billion deal created SABMiller, a new company that ranks as the world's number two brewer in terms of production volume; Anheuser-Busch InBev ranks first. Miller operates nine breweries in the United States, where its flagship brand, Miller Lite, had been losing market share for a number of years. The challenge facing Graham McKay, SABMiller's CEO, is to revitalize the Miller Lite brand in the United States and then launch Miller in Europe as a premium brand.

SABMiller and its competitors are also making strategic investment in China, the world's largest beer market with $6 billion in annual sales. As Sylvia Mu Yin, an analyst with Euromonitor, noted, "Local brewers are keen to explore strategic alliances with large multinational companies. At the same time, foreign companies are eager to sell to the 1.3 billion Chinese, but lack local knowledge." SAB Miller has partnerships with more than two dozen Chinese breweries. In 2003, SABMiller purchased a 29 percent equity share of Harbin Brewery Group, China's oldest

and fourth-largest brewer. The brand is popular in northeast China, and SABMiller hoped to expand the brand in other regions. In 2004, Anheuser-Busch announced that it was also buying 29 percent of Harbin. That, in turn, triggered a bid by SABMiller to buy the rest of Harbin's shares. When the resulting bidding war was over, Anheuser-Busch emerged as the victor.

Meanwhile, some of SABMiller's local brands are being introduced in the United States. The company hopes to build Pilsner Urquell, the number one beer in the Czech Republic, into a national brand in the United States. If that effort succeeds, it can be the foundation for building Urquell into a global premium brand that rivals Heineken. SABMiller is also launching Tyskie, a popular Polish brand, in cities such as Chicago that are home to large Polish immigrant communities. The company hopes to successfully position Miller Genuine Draft as a premium global brand in Eastern Europe. Some industry observers predict it will be a hard sell. As one analyst noted, "American beer has a bad reputation in Eastern Europe, because beer drinkers think it tastes like water." Will all these efforts succeed? SABMiller's chief harbors no doubts; if the Miller acquisition does *not* pay off, he says, "I'll fall on my sword."

Sources: Chris Buckley, "Battle Shaping Up for Chinese Brewery," *The New York Times* (May 6, 2004), pp. W1, W7; Maggie Urry and Adam Jones, "SABMiller Chief Preaches the Lite Fantastic," *Financial Times* (November 21, 2003), p. 22; Dan Bilefsky and Christopher Lawton, "SABMiller Has U.S. Hangover," *The Wall Street Journal* (November 20, 2003), p. B5; Christopher Lawton and Dan Bilefsky, "Miller Lite Now: Haste Great, Less Selling," *The Wall Street Journal* (October 4, 2002), pp. B1, B6; Nicol Deglil Innocenti, "Fearless Embracer of Challenge," *Financial Times Special Report—Investing in South Africa* (October 2, 2003), p. 6; David Pringle, "Miller Deal Brings Stability to SAB," *The Wall Street Journal* (May 31, 2002), p. B6; John Willman, "Time for Another Round," *Financial Times* (June 21, 1999), p. 15.

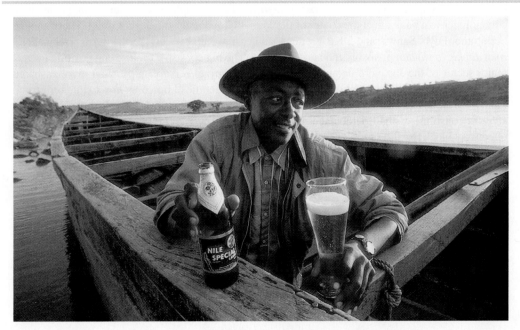

Exhibit 9-9: A few years ago, South African Breweries was a local company that dominated its domestic market. Using joint ventures and acquisitions, the company expanded into the rest of Africa as well as key emerging markets such as China, India, and Central Europe. Today, following the acquisition of Miller, SABMiller is the world's second largest brewer with a strong presence in the U.S. market.
Source: SABMiller plc.

is growing, particularly in the service and manufacturing sectors. In the early-post Soviet era, most of the manufacturing ventures were limited to assembly work, but higher value-added activities such as component manufacture are now being performed.

A Central European market with interesting potential is Hungary. Hungary already has the most liberal financial and commercial system in the region. It has also provided investment incentives to Westerners, especially in high-tech industries. Like Russia, this former communist economy has its share of problems. Digital's recent joint venture agreement with the Hungarian Research Institute for Physics and the state-supervised computer systems design firm Szamalk is a case in point. Although the venture was formed so Digital would be able to sell and service its equipment in Hungary, the underlying importance of the venture was to stop the cloning of Digital's computers by Central European firms.

COOPERATIVE STRATEGIES IN JAPAN: *KEIRETSU*

Japan's *keiretsu* represent a special category of cooperative strategy. A **keiretsu** is an interbusiness alliance or enterprise group that, in the words of one observer, "resembles a fighting clan in which business families join together to vie for market share."[36] *Keiretsu* exist in a broad spectrum of markets, including the capital, primary goods, and component parts markets.[37] *Keiretsu* relationships are often cemented by bank ownership of large blocks of stock and by cross-ownership of stock between a company and its buyers and nonfinancial suppliers. Further, *keiretsu* executives can legally sit on each other's boards, share information, and coordinate prices in closed-door meetings of "presidents' councils." Thus, *keiretsu* are essentially cartels that have the government's blessing. While not a market entry strategy per se, *keiretsu* played an integral role in the international success of Japanese companies as they sought new markets.

Some observers have disputed charges that *keiretsu* have an impact on market relationships in Japan and claim instead that the groups primarily serve a social function. Others acknowledge the past significance of preferential trading patterns associated with *keiretsu* but assert that the latter's influence is now weakening. Although it is beyond the scope of this chapter to address these issues in detail, there can be no doubt that, for companies competing with the Japanese or wishing to enter the Japanese market, a general understanding of *keiretsu* is crucial. Imagine, for example, what it would mean in the United States if an automaker (e.g., GM), an electrical products company (e.g., GE), a steelmaker (e.g., USX), and a computer firm (e.g., IBM) were interconnected, rather than separate, firms. Global competition in the era of *keiretsu* means that competition exists not only among products, but between different systems of corporate governance and industrial organization.[38]

As the hypothetical example from the United States suggests, some of Japan's biggest and best-known companies are at the center of *keiretsu*. For example, several large companies with common ties to a bank are at the center of the Mitsui Group and Mitsubishi Group. These and the Sumitomo, Fuyo, Sanwa, and DKB groups together make up the "big six" *keiretsu* (in Japanese, *roku dai kigyo shudan* or six big industrial groups). The big six strive for a strong position in each major sector of the Japanese economy; because intra-group relationships often involve shared stockholdings and trading relations, the big six are sometimes known as *horizontal keiretsu*.[39] Annual revenues in each group are in the hundreds of billions of dollars. In absolute terms, *keiretsu* constitute a small percentage of all Japanese companies. However, these alliances can effectively block foreign suppliers from entering the market and result in higher prices to Japanese consumers, while at the same time resulting in corporate stability, risk sharing, and long-term employment. The Mitsubishi Group's *keiretsu* structure is shown in detail in Figure 9-4.

---

[36]Robert L. Cutts, "Capitalism in Japan: Cartels and Keiretsu," *Harvard Business Review* 70, no. 4 (July–August 1992), p. 49.
[37]Michael L. Gerlach, "Twilight of the *Keiretsu*? A Critical Assessment," *Journal of Japanese Studies* 18, no. 1 (Winter 1992), p. 79.
[38]Ronald J. Gilson and Mark J. Roe, "Understanding the Japanese Keiretsu: Overlaps Between Corporate Governance and Industrial Organization," *The Yale Law Journal* 102, no. 4 (January 1993), p. 883.
[39]Kenichi Miyashita and David Russell, *Keiretsu: Inside the Hidden Japanese Conglomerates* (New York: McGraw-Hill, 1996), p. 9.

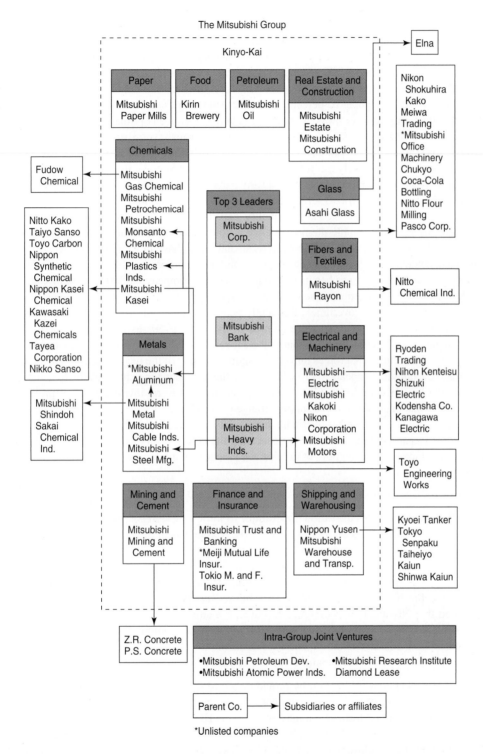

FIGURE 9-4

Mitsubishi Group's *Keiretsu* Structure

Source: Courtesy of the Mitsubishi Group, from Collins and Doorley, *Teaming Up for the 90s,* Deloitte & Touche, 1991.

In addition to the big six, several other *keiretsu* have formed, bringing new configurations to the basic forms previously described. *Vertical* (i.e., supply and distribution) *keiretsu* are hierarchical alliances between manufacturers and retailers. For example, Matsushita controls a chain of 25,000 National stores in Japan through which it sells its Panasonic, Technics, and Quasar brands. About half of Matsushita's domestic sales are generated through the National chain, 50 to 80 percent of whose inventory consists of Matsushita's brands. Japan's other major consumer electronics manufacturers, including Toshiba and Hitachi, have similar alliances. (Sony's chain of stores is much smaller and weaker by comparison.) All are fierce competitors in the Japanese market.[40]

---

[40]The importance of the chain stores is eroding due to increasing sales at mass merchandisers not under the manufacturers' control.

Another type of manufacturing *keiretsu* consists of vertical hierarchical alliances between automakers and suppliers and component manufacturers. Intergroup operations and systems are closely integrated, with suppliers receiving long-term contracts. Toyota, for example, has a network of about 175 primary and 4,000 secondary suppliers. One supplier is Koito; Toyota owns about one-fifth of Koito's shares and buys about half of its production. The net result of this arrangement is that Toyota produces about 25 percent of the sales value of its cars, compared with 50 percent for GM. Manufacturing *keiretsu* show the gains that can result from an optimal balance of supplier and buyer power. Because Toyota buys a given component from several suppliers (some are in the *keiretsu*, some are independent), discipline is imposed down the network. Also, since Toyota's suppliers do not work exclusively for Toyota, they have an incentive to be flexible and adaptable.[41]

The *keiretsu* system ensured that high-quality parts were delivered on a just-in-time basis, a key factor in the high quality for which Japan's auto industry is well known. However, as U.S. and European automakers have closed the quality gap, larger Western parts makers are building economies of scale that enable them to operate at lower costs than small Japanese parts makers. Moreover, the stock holdings that Toyota, Nissan, and others have in their supplier network ties up capital that could be used for product development and other purposes. At Nissan, for example, a new management team from France began divesting some of the company's 1,300 *keiretsu* investments.[42]

Some observers have questioned whether *keiretsu* violate antitrust laws. As many observers have noted, the Japanese government frequently puts the interests of producers ahead of the interests of consumers. The *keiretsu* were formed in the early 1950s as regroupings of four large conglomerates—*zaibatsu*—that dominated the Japanese economy until 1945. *Zaibatsu* were dissolved after the occupational forces introduced antitrust as part of the reconstruction. Today, Japan's Fair Trade Commission appears to favor harmony rather than pursuing anticompetitive behavior. As a result, the U.S. Federal Trade Commission has launched several investigations of price fixing, price discrimination, and exclusive supply arrangements. Hitachi, Canon, and other Japanese companies have also been accused of restricting the availability of high-tech products in the U.S. market. The Justice Department has considered prosecuting the U.S. subsidiaries of Japanese companies if the parent company is found guilty of unfair trade practices in the Japanese market.[43]

How *Keiretsu* Affect American Business: Two Examples

Clyde Prestowitz provides the following example to show how *keiretsu* relationships have a potential impact on U.S. businesses. In the early 1980s, Nissan was in the market for a supercomputer to use in car design. Two vendors under consideration were Cray, the worldwide leader in supercomputers at the time, and Hitachi, which had no functional product to offer. When it appeared that the purchase of a Cray computer was pending, Hitachi executives called for solidarity; both Nissan and Hitachi were members of the same big six *keiretsu*, the Fuyo group. Hitachi essentially mandated that Nissan show preference to Hitachi, a situation that rankled U.S. trade officials. Meanwhile, a coalition within Nissan was pushing for a Cray computer; ultimately, thanks to U.S. pressure on both Nissan and the Japanese government, the business went to Cray.

Prestowitz describes the Japanese attitude toward this type of business practice:[44]

> . . . It respects mutual obligation by providing a cushion against shocks. Today Nissan may buy a Hitachi computer. Tomorrow it may ask Hitachi to take some of its redundant workers. The slightly lesser performance it may get from the Hitachi computer is balanced against the broader considerations. Moreover, because the decision to buy Hitachi would be a favor, it would bind Hitachi closer and guarantee slavish service and future Hitachi loyalty to Nissan products. . . . This attitude of sticking together is what the Japanese mean by the long-term view; it is what enables them to withstand shocks and to survive over the long term.[45]

---

[41]"Japanology, Inc.—Survey," *The Economist* (March 6, 1993), p. 15.

[42]Norihiko Shirouzu, "U-Turn: A Revival at Nissan Shows There's Hope for Ailing Japan Inc.," *The Wall Street Journal* (November 16, 2000), pp. A1, A10.

[43]Carla Rappoport, "Why Japan Keeps on Winning," *Fortune* (July 15, 1991), p. 84.

[44]For years, Prestowitz has argued that Japan's industry structure—*keiretsu* included—gives its companies unfair advantages. A more moderate view might be that any business decision must have an economic justification. Thus, a moderate would caution against overstating the effect of *keiretsu*.

[45]Clyde Prestowitz, *Trading Places: How We Are Giving Our Future to Japan and How to Reclaim It* (New York: Basic Books, 1989), pp. 299–300.

Because *keiretsu* relationships are crossing the Pacific and directly affecting the American market, U.S. companies have reason to be concerned with *keiretsu* outside the Japanese market as well. According to 1991 data compiled by Dodwell Marketing Consultants, in California alone *keiretsu* own more than half of the Japanese-affiliated manufacturing facilities. But the impact of *keiretsu* extends beyond the West Coast. Illinois-based Tenneco Automotive, a maker of shock absorbers and exhaust systems, does a great deal of worldwide business with the Toyota *keiretsu*. In 1990, however, Mazda dropped Tenneco as a supplier to its U.S. plant in Kentucky. Part of the business was shifted to Tokico Manufacturing, a Japanese transplant and a member of the Mazda *keiretsu*; a non-*keiretsu* Japanese company, KYB Industries, was also made a vendor. A Japanese auto executive explained the rationale behind the change: "First choice is a *keiretsu* company, second choice is a Japanese supplier, third is a local company."[46]

COOPERATIVE STRATEGIES IN SOUTH KOREA: *CHAEBOL*

South Korea has its own type of corporate alliance groups, known as *chaebol*. Like the Japanese *keiretsu*, **chaebol** are composed of dozens of companies, centered around a central bank or holding company, and dominated by a founding family. However, *chaebol* are a more recent phenomenon; in the early 1960s, Korea's military dictator granted government subsidies and export credits to a select group of companies. By the 1980s, Daewoo, Hyundai, LG, and Samsung had become leading producers of low-cost consumer electronics products. The *chaebol* were a driving force behind South Korea's economic miracle; GNP increased from $1.9 billion in 1960 to $238 billion in 1990. Since the economic crisis of 1997, however, South Korean President Kim Dae Jung has pressured *chaebol* leaders to initiate reform. Prior to the crisis, the *chaebol* had become bloated and heavily leveraged; today some progress has been made in improving corporate governance, changing corporate cultures, and reducing debt levels.[47]

TWENTY-FIRST CENTURY COOPERATIVE STRATEGIES: TARGETING THE DIGITAL FUTURE

Increasing numbers of companies in all parts of the world are entering into alliances that resemble *keiretsu*. The phrase *digital keiretsu* is frequently used to describe alliances between companies in several industries—computers, communications, consumer electronics, and entertainment—that are undergoing transformation and convergence. These processes are the result of tremendous advances in the ability to transmit and manipulate vast quantities of audio, video, and data and the rapidly approaching era of a global electronic "superhighway" composed of fiber optic cable and digital switching equipment.

One U.S. technology alliance, Sematech, is unique in that it is the direct result of government industrial policy. The U.S. government, concerned that key companies in the domestic semiconductor industry were having difficulty competing with Japan, agreed to subsidize a consortium of 14 technology companies beginning in 1987. Sematech was originally comprised of 700 employees, some permanent and some on loan from IBM, AT&T, Advanced Micro Devices, Intel, and other companies. The task facing the consortium was to save the U.S. chipmaking equipment industry, whose manufacturers were rapidly losing market share in the face of intense competition from Japan. Although initially plagued by attitudinal and cultural differences between different factions, Sematech eventually helped chipmakers try new approaches with their equipment vendors. By 1991, the Sematech initiative, along with other factors such as the economic downturn in Japan, reversed the market share slide of the semiconductor equipment industry. Sematech's creation heralded a new era in cooperation among technology companies. As the company has expanded internationally, its membership roster has expanded to include Agere Systems, Conexant, Hewlett-Packard, Hynix, Infineon, Motorola, Philips, STMicroelectronics, and Taiwan Semiconductor. Companies in a variety of industries are pursuing similar types of alliances.

---

[46]Carla Rappoport, "Why Japan Keeps on Winning," *Fortune* (July 15, 1991), p. 84.
[47]"The Chaebol Spurn Change," *The Economist* (July 27, 2000), pp. 59–60.

Beyond Strategic Alliances

The "relationship enterprise" is said to be the next stage of evolution of the strategic alliance. In a relationship enterprise, groupings of firms in different industries and countries will be held together by common goals that encourage them to act as a single firm. Cyrus Freidheim, former vice chairman of the Booz Allen Hamilton consulting firm, outlined an alliance that, in his opinion, might be representative of an early relationship enterprise. He suggests that, within the next few decades, Boeing, British Airways, Siemens, TNT, and Snecma might jointly build several new airports in China. As part of the package, British Airways and TNT would be granted preferential routes and landing slots, the Chinese government would contract to buy all its aircraft from Boeing/Snecma, and Siemens would provide air traffic control systems for all 10 airports.[48]

More than the simple strategic alliances we know today, relationship enterprises will be super-alliances among global giants, with revenues approaching $1 trillion. They would be able to draw on extensive cash resources, circumvent antitrust barriers, and, with home bases in all major markets, enjoy the political advantage of being a "local" firm almost anywhere. This type of alliance is not driven simply by technological change but by the political necessity of having multiple home bases.

Another perspective on the future of cooperative strategies envisions the emergence of the "virtual corporation." As described in a *Business Week* cover story, the virtual corporation "will seem to be a single entity with vast capabilities but will really be the result of numerous collaborations assembled only when they're needed."[49] On a global level, the virtual corporation could combine the twin competencies of cost effectiveness and responsiveness; thus, it could pursue the "think globally, act locally" philosophy with ease. This reflects the trend toward "mass customization." The same forces that are driving the formation of the digital *keiretsu*—high-speed communication networks, for example—are embodied in the virtual corporation. As noted by William Davidow and Michael Malone in their book *The Virtual Corporation*, "The success of a virtual corporation will depend on its ability to gather and integrate a massive flow of information throughout its organizational components and intelligently act upon that information."[50]

Why has the virtual corporation suddenly burst onto the scene? Previously, firms lacked the technology to facilitate this type of data management. Today's distributed databases, networks, and open systems make possible the kinds of data flow required for the virtual corporation. In particular, these data flows permit superior supply chain management. Ford provides an interesting example of how technology is improving information flows among the far-flung operations of a single company. Ford's $6 billion "world car"—known as the Mercury Mystique and Ford Contour in the United States and the Mondeo in Europe—was developed using an international communications network linking computer workstations of designers and engineers on three continents.[51]

MARKET EXPANSION STRATEGIES

Companies must decide whether to expand by seeking new markets in existing countries or, alternatively, seeking new country markets for already identified and served market segments.[52] These two dimensions in combination produce four **market expansion strategy** options, as shown in Table 9-7. Strategy 1, **country and market concentration**, involves targeting a limited number of customer segments in a few countries. This is typically a starting point for most companies.

---

[48]"The Global Firm: R.I.P." *The Economist* (February 6, 1993), p. 69.

[49]John Byrne, "The Virtual Corporation," *Business Week* (February 8, 1993), p. 103.

[50]William Davidow and Michael Malone, *The Virtual Corporation: Structuring and Revitalizing the Corporation for the 21st Century* (New York: HarperBusiness, 1993), p. 59.

[51]Julie Edelson Halpert, "One Car, Worldwide, with Strings Pulled from Michigan," *The New York Times* (August 29, 1993), sec. 3, p. 7.

[52]This section draws on I. Ayal and J. Zif, "Market Expansion Strategies in Multinational Marketing," *Journal of Marketing* 43 (Spring 1979), pp. 84–94; and "Competitive Market Choice Strategies in Multinational Marketing," *Columbia Journal of World Business* (Fall 1978), pp. 72–81.

TABLE 9-7 Market Expansion Strategies

		MARKET	
		Concentration	Diversification
COUNTRY	**Concentration**	1. Narrow Focus	2. Country Focus
	Diversification	3. Country Diversification	4. Global Diversification

It matches company resources and market investment needs. Unless a company is large and endowed with ample resources, this strategy may be the only realistic way to begin.

In Strategy 2, **country concentration and market diversification**, a company serves many markets in a few countries. This strategy was implemented by many European companies that remained in Europe and sought growth by expanding into new markets. It is also the approach of the American companies that decide to diversify in the U.S. market as opposed to going international with existing products or creating new global products. According to the U.S. Department of Commerce, the majority of U.S. companies that export limit their sales to five or fewer markets. This means that U.S. companies typically pursue Strategies 1 or 2.

Strategy 3, **country diversification and market concentration**, is the classic global strategy whereby a company seeks out the world market for a product. The appeal of this strategy is that, by serving the world customer, a company can achieve a greater accumulated volume and lower costs than any competitor and therefore have an unassailable competitive advantage. This is the strategy of the well-managed business that serves a distinct need and customer category.

Strategy 4, **country and market diversification**, is the corporate strategy of a global, multi-business company such as Matsushita. Overall, Matsushita is multi-country in scope and its various business units and groups serve multiple segments. Thus, at the level of corporate strategy, Matsushita may be said to be pursuing Strategy 4. At the operating business level, however, managers of individual units must focus on the needs of the world customer in their particular global market. In Table 9-7, this is Strategy 3—country diversification and market concentration. An increasing number of companies all over the world are beginning to see the importance of market share not only in the home or domestic market but also in the world market. Success in overseas markets can boost a company's total volume and lower its cost position.

Summary

Companies that wish to move beyond exporting and importing can avail themselves of a wide range of alternative **market entry strategies**. Each alternative has distinct advantages and disadvantages associated with it; the alternatives can be ranked on a continuum representing increasing levels of investment, commitment, and risk. **Licensing** can generate revenue flow with little new investment; it can be a good choice for a company that possesses advanced technology, a strong brand image, or valuable intellectual property. **Contract manufacturing** and **franchising** are two specialized forms of licensing that are widely used in global marketing.

A higher level of involvement outside the home country may involve **foreign direct investment**. This can take many forms. **Joint ventures** offer two or more companies the opportunity to share risk and combine value chain strengths. Companies considering joint ventures must plan carefully and communicate with partners to avoid "divorce." Foreign direct investment can also be used to establish company operations outside the home country through **greenfield investment**, acquisition of a minority or majority **equity stake** in a foreign business, or taking **full ownership** of an existing business entity through merger or outright acquisition.

Cooperative alliances known as **strategic alliances**, **strategic international alliances**, and **global strategic partnerships (GSPs)** represent an important market entry strategy in the twenty-first century. GSPs are ambitious, reciprocal, cross-border alliances that may involve business partners in a number of different country markets. GSPs are particularly well suited to emerging markets in Central and Eastern Europe, Asia, and Latin America.

Western businesspeople should also be aware of two special forms of cooperation found in Asia, namely Japan's *keiretsu* and South Korea's *chaebol*.

To assist managers in thinking through the various alternatives, **market expansion strategies** can be represented in matrix form: **country and market concentration, country concentration and market diversification, country diversification and market concentration**, and **country and market diversification**. The preferred expansion strategy will be a reflection of a company's stage of development (i.e., whether it is international, multinational, global, or transnational). The Stage 5 transnational combines the strengths of the prior three stages into an integrated network to leverage worldwide learning.

Discussion Questions

1. What are the advantages and disadvantages of using licensing as a market entry tool? Give examples of companies from different countries that use licensing as a global marketing strategy.

2. The president of XYZ Manufacturing Company of Buffalo, New York, comes to you with a license offer from a company in Osaka. In return for sharing the company's patents and know-how, the Japanese company will pay a license fee of 5 percent of the ex-factory price of all products sold based on the U.S. company's license. The president wants your advice. What would you tell him?

3. What is foreign direct investment (FDI)? What forms can FDI take?

4. What is meant by the phrase *global strategic partnership*? In what ways does this form of market entry strategy differ from more traditional forms such as joint ventures?

5. What are *keiretsu*? How does this form of industrial structure affect companies that compete with Japan or that are trying to enter the Japanese market?

6. Which strategic options for market entry or expansion would a small company be likely to pursue? A large company?

Starbucks has also been successful in other European countries, including the United Kingdom and Ireland. This success comes despite competition from local rivals such as Ireland's Insomnia Coffee Company and Bewley's and the fact that per capita consumption of roasted coffee in the two countries is the lowest in Europe. In January 2004, Starbucks opened its first outlets in Paris. CEO Howard Schultz acknowledged that the decision to target France was a gutsy move; relations between the United States and France had been strained because of political differences regarding President Bush's Iraq policy. Moreover, café culture has long been an entrenched part of the city's heritage and identity. The French prefer dark espresso, and the conventional wisdom is that Americans don't know what good coffee is. As one Frenchman put it, "American coffee, it's only water. We call is *jus des chaussette*—'sock juice.'"

Not surprisingly, Greater China—including the mainland, Hong Kong, and Taiwan—represents another strategic growth market for Starbucks. Starting with one store in Beijing at the China World Trade Center that opened in 1999, Starbucks now has more than 600 locations. Starbucks has faced several different types of challenges in this part of the world. First of all, government regulations forced the company to partner with local firms. After the regulations were eased, Starbucks stepped up its rate of expansion, focusing on metropolises such as Beijing and Shanghai.

Another challenge comes from the traditional Chinese teahouse. Indeed one rival, Real Brewed Tea, aims to be "the Starbucks of tea." A related challenge is the perceptions and preferences of the Chinese, who do not care for coffee. Those who had tasted coffee were only familiar with the instant variety. Faced with one of global marketing's most fundamental questions—adapt offerings for local appeal or attempt to change local tastes—Starbucks hopes to educate the Chinese about coffee.

Chinese consumers exhibit different behavior patterns than in Starbucks' other locations. For one thing, most orders are consumed in the cafés; in the United States, by contrast, most patrons order drinks for carryout. (In the United States, Starbucks is opening hundreds of new outlets with drive-through service.) Also, store traffic in China is heaviest in the afternoon. This behavior is consistent with Starbucks' research findings, which suggest that the number-one reason the Chinese go to cafés is to have a place to gather.

Meanwhile, as a result of the global economic downturn, cash-strapped consumers were cutting back on non-essential purchases. The notion of a "$4 latte" seemed out of step with the times, and some perceived Starbucks' premium brand image as a liability. Even before the economy nosedived, Schultz had circulated a memo to senior executives titled "The Commoditization of the Starbucks Experience." In the memo, Schultz warned that over-aggressive market expansion was compromising the company's brand experience.

In part, the memo was a response to unofficial Web sites and blogs such as starbucksgossip.com where customer and employee complaints and company information were circulated. To better connect with its customers, Starbucks created a social media Web site known as MyStarbucksIdea.com (MSI). Within months of MSI's launch in 2008, nearly 75,000 ideas had been submitted. Forrester Research recognized Starbucks' social media initiative with a Grandswell award in the "Embracing" category. But Starbucks also stepped up efforts to communicate with the general public using traditional media. Working with the BBDO advertising agency, Starbucks launched a corporate branding campaign that was timed to coincide with a major revamping of its food offerings. Full-page print ads in *The New York Times* and *USA Today* were keyed to the tagline "It's Not Just Coffee. It's Starbucks."

Sensing a window of opportunity, McDonald's executives are proceeding with plans to roll out McCafé, a new branded coffee concept featuring cappuccino and other coffee drinks at prices that are significantly lower than Starbucks'. At a Starbucks in Paris, for example, a cappuccino is €4.00 ($6.00); a comparable drink at McCafé is €2.00 or €2.50. McCafés feature sophisticated brewing equipment and special coffee blends.

In Europe, Starbucks currently has about 1,300 locations. McDonald's plans call for a total of 1,200 McCafés by the end of 2009. McCafés can currently be found in Ireland, Germany, Russia, and Italy; France and Austria are next. Some McCafés are located inside existing McDonald's stores; others are freestanding locations near the regular restaurants.

Case 9-1 Discussion Questions

1. In the United States, about two-thirds of Starbucks outlets are company owned; the remaining one-third are operated by licensees. Outside the United States, the proportions are reversed: about two-thirds are run by licensees or partnerships in which Starbucks has equity stakes. What is the explanation for the two different market expansion strategies?

2. In response to the economic downturn, Starbucks recently launched a new line of instant coffee called VIA Ready Brew. The company also developed a breakfast value meal that costs less than $4. Do you agree with these decisions?

3. In the long run, which company is more likely to win the global "coffee wars," Starbucks or McDonald's?

Sources: Andrew Ward, "Why Schultz Has Caused a Stir at Starbucks," *Financial Times* (February 26, 2007), p. 21; Janet Adamy, "Different Brew: Eyeing a Billion Tea Drinkers, Starbucks Pours It on in China," *The Wall Street Journal* (November 29, 2006), pp. A1, A12; Gerhard Hegmann and Birgit Dengel, "Starbucks Looks to Step Up Openings in Germany," *Financial Times* (September 5, 2006), p. 23; Steven Gray, "'Fill 'Er Up—With Latte,'" *The Wall Street Journal* (January 6, 2006), pp. A9, A10; John Murray Brown and Jenny Wiggins, "Coffee Empire Expands Reach by Pressing Its Luck in Ireland," *Financial Times* (December 15, 2005), p. 21; Gray and Ethan Smith, "New Grind: At Starbucks, a Blend of Coffee and Music Creates a Potent Mix," *The Wall Street Journal* (July 19, 2005), pp. A1, A11; Noelle Knox, "Paris Starbucks Hopes to Prove U.S. Coffee Isn't 'Sock Juice,'" *USA Today* (January 16, 2004), p. 3B.

In 2008, Tata Motors paid the Ford Motor Company $2.3 billion for UK-based automakers Land Rover and Jaguar. The deal came about as Detroit's automakers faced one of the worst business environments in decades. The Big Three posted losses in the billions of dollars; by 2008, with the global recession and credit crunch causing a sharp decline in demand, executives from GM and Chrysler appealed to Washington for a bailout. Meanwhile industry observers had been calling for Ford to shed some of its luxury brands. Speaking of Jaguar, Charles Lemonides, an institutional investor, said, "Ford doesn't necessarily get a halo effect from the brand, nor does it get a significant marketplace presence from the brand. It's not clear what Ford gains from having it. It will never be big enough to be important to Ford."

When Ford acquired Jaguar in 1989, the American company lacked a high-end luxury model. Executives were betting that they could leverage an exclusive nameplate by launching a new, less expensive line of Jaguars and selling it to more people. The challenge was to execute this strategy without diminishing Jaguar's reputation. Daniel Jones, a professor at the University of Cardiff and an auto industry expert, noted that the Ford name is synonymous with "bread and butter" cars. Meanwhile, Ford's Japanese competitors, including Honda, Nissan, and Toyota, pursued a different strategy: They launched new nameplates and upgraded their dealer organizations. Status- and quality-conscious car buyers embraced Lexus, Infiniti, and other new luxury sedans that offer high performance and outstanding dealer organizations.

In 2006, Jaguar launched the 420 hp XKR luxury sports car. The company, which is now owned by India's Tata Motors, faces strong competition in Europe from Toyota.
Source: Luke MacGregor/Reuters/Landov Media.

Jaguar's S-type represented the venerable automaker's bid to become a mainstream luxury nameplate and double its North American sales to 80,000 cars each year. In terms of styling, the $45,000 S-Type recalls the classic Jaguar designs of the 1950s and 1960s. Worldwide, Jaguar executives hoped to quadruple sales from 50,000 units to 200,000 by 2003. Unfortunately, that goal proved to be unrealistic.
Source: Jaguar.

Despite Jaguar's classy image and distinguished racing heritage, the cars were also legendary for their unreliability. Gears sometimes wouldn't shift, headlights wouldn't light, and the brakes sometimes caught fire. Part of the problem could be traced to manufacturing. To remedy the situation, Ford invested heavily to update and upgrade Jaguar's plant facilities and improve productivity. As a benchmark, Ford's manufacturing experts knew that German luxury carmakers could build a vehicle in 80 hours; in Japan, the figure was 20 hours. If Jaguar were ever to achieve world-class status, Jaguar's assembly time of 110 hours per car had to be drastically reduced. Jaguar's chief executive, Sir Nicholas Scheele, attacked the quality problem on a number of different fronts. For example, line employees made telephone calls to Jaguar owners who were experiencing problems with their vehicles.

As the 1990s came to an end, Jaguar introduced several new vehicles. In 1997, amid industry estimates that Ford's cumulative investment had reached $6 billion, Jaguar launched the $64,900 XK8 coupe and roadster. Styling cues clearly identified this model as the successor to Jaguar's legendary XK-E, or E-Type. In the spring of 1999, the S-Type sedan was introduced to widespread acclaim. One observer called the S-Type a "handsome car, instantly recognizable as a Jaguar, yet totally contemporary." In 2001, the long-awaited "baby Jaguar," the $30,000 X-Type compact sport sedan, was unveiled. Company executives hoped to attract a new generation of drivers and capture a significant share of the entry-level luxury market dominated by the BMW 3-series and the Mercedes C-Class. The X-Type was built on the same platform as the Ford Contour.

The early signs were positive. In 2002, first-year sales of the X-Type boosted Jaguar's worldwide sales to a record 130,000 vehicles, a 29 percent increase. Unfortunately, the company was not able to sustain the momentum. A backlash began to develop. For example, critics of the X-Type derided it as a "warmed-over Ford." Critics also found fault with Ford for failing to move Jaguar's styling forward enough. As one long-time Jaguar owner explained, "They lost their way in what the public wanted. Instead of making Jaguar a niche player, where it should be, they tried to go the mass-production route. That may very well work for the Ford Fusion, but that's not Jaguar's forte." In 2005, bowing to pressures to move the venerable nameplate upmarket again, it was announced that the least expensive Jaguar model, the 2.5 liter X-Type, would be discontinued.

By 2008, the curtain came down on Jaguar's two decades under American ownership. Jaguar's new owners face challenges of their own. Some have criticized the acquisition on the grounds that the brands are not compatible with the low-cost cars, trucks, and commercial vehicles that have long been Tata's mainstays. The company became embroiled in a dispute with displaced farmers over plans to build a new plant in West Bengal. Meanwhile, the global economic crisis has led to a slump in demand for cars in India; many automakers were forced to suspend production at some Indian production facilities. Jaguar's new models sold well despite the economic downturn; by contrast, Land Rover sales were down significantly. Management at both Jaguar and Land Rover were expected to leverage their ties to Tata and set up dealer networks in India.

Discussion Questions

1. Assess Ford's decision to introduce the X-Type to broaden Jaguar's appeal from niche player to major competitor in the luxury segment.
2. Tata Motors recently introduced the Nano, the world's least-expensive car. The Nano fits Tata's strategic goal of building a low-cost car for the Indian market. Can Tata succeed in targeting both the very low end of the auto market as well as the high end?
3. Do you think Jaguar and Land Rover will prosper under the ownership of Tata Motors?

Sources: Gordon Fairclough, "Bill Ford Jr.: For Auto Makers, China Is the New Frontier," *The Wall Street Journal* (October 27, 2006), p. B5; James Mackintosh, "Ford's Luxury Unit Hits Problems," *Financial Times* (October 24, 2006), p. 23; Sharon Silke Carty, "Will Ford Make the Big Leap?" *USA Today* (August 31, 2006), pp. 1B, 2B; James Macintosh, "Jaguar Still Aiming to Claw Back Market Share," *Financial Times* (July 20, 2006), p. 14; Reinventing a '60s Classic, " *The Wall Street Journal* (May 5, 2006), p. W9; James R. Healy, "Cheapest Jags Get Kicked to the Curb," *USA Today* (March 29, 2005), p. 1B; Danny Hakim, "Restoring the Heart of Ford," *The New York Times* (November 14, 2001), pp. C1, C6; Haig Simonian, "Jag's Faces for the Future," *Financial Times* (November 7–8, 1998), p. 12; Joann S. Lublin and Craig Forman, "Going Upscale: Ford Snares Jaguar, But $2.5 Billion Is High Price for Prestige," *The Wall Street Journal* (November 3, 1989), pp. A1, A4; Steven Prokesch, "Jaguar Battle at a Turning Point," *The New York Times* (October 29, 1990), p. C1; Prokesch, "Ford's Jaguar Bet: Payoff Isn't Close," *The New York Times* (April 21, 1992) p. C1; Robert Johnson, "Jaguar Owners Love Company and Sharing Their Horror Stories," *The Wall Street Journal* (September 28, 1993), p. A1.

Brand and Product Decisions in Global Marketing

Case 10-1
Suzlon Energy

A worldwide, consumer-driven movement toward renewable energy solutions has created global market opportunities for entrepreneurial companies. In 1995, after facing rising electricity costs for his family's

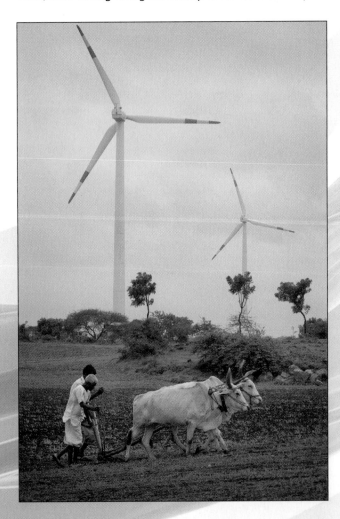

textile factory in Pune, India, Tulsi Tanti decided to build two wind turbines to power the facility. Tanti soon realized that he had stumbled upon a promising opportunity. As he explained, "I had a very clear vision: If Indians start consuming power like the Americans, the world will run out of resources. Either you stop India from developing, or you find some alternate solution." Within a few years' time, Tanti had converted his factory from textiles to the manufacturing of wind turbine generators, gearboxes, towers, rotor blades, and wind turbines. Tanti's company, now called Suzlon Energy Limited, was well positioned to take advantage of the growing demand for alternative energy sources (see Exhibit 10-1).

Moving into the U.S. market, Suzlon enjoyed the promising prospects of a booming industry; however, numerous problems with product quality and negative publicity, in addition to economic turbulence and regulatory restrictions, have raised concerns about the potential of Suzlon and other green-energy companies. To learn more about the challenges and opportunities facing Tanti's company, turn to the continuation of Case 10-1 Suzlon Energy: The Assignment, at the end of the chapter.

Tulsi Tanti's success at Suzlon Energy illustrates the point that products—and the companies and brands

Exhibit 10-1: India's Suzlon Energy has become a major player in the wind-turbine industry. Historically, India's power distribution system has been inefficient and inconsistent; users pay high prices for electricity but still must endure blackouts on a regular basis. Moreover, burning coal to generate electricity can have serious environmental consequences. For these reasons, industrial users in India seeking alternative sources of energy are Suzlon's primary customers. Suzlon is also thinking globally: The company has opened a turbine-blade factory in Minnesota, where it also operates a wind farm.
Source: Scott Eells/Redux Pictures.

associated with them—are arguably the most crucial element of a company's marketing program; they are integral to the company's value proposition. In Part 3, we surveyed several topics that directly impact product strategy as a company approaches global markets. Input from a company's business intelligence network and market research studies guides the product development process. The market must be segmented, one or more target markets selected, and a strong positioning established. Global marketers must also make decisions about exporting and sourcing; other market entry strategies such as licensing and strategic alliances may be considered as well.

As we will see in Part 4, every aspect of a firm's marketing program, including pricing, distribution, and communication policies, must fit the product. This chapter examines the major dimensions of global product and brand decisions. First is a review of basic product and brand concepts, followed by a discussion of local, international, and global products and brands. Product design criteria are identified, and attitudes toward foreign products are explored. The next section outlines strategic alternatives available to global marketers. Finally, new product issues in global marketing are discussed.

BASIC PRODUCT CONCEPTS

The product P of the marketing mix is at the heart of the challenges and opportunities facing global companies today: Management must develop product and brand policies and strategies that are sensitive to market needs, competition, and company ambitions and resources on a global scale. Effective global marketing often entails finding a balance between the payoff from extensively adapting products and brands to local market preferences and the benefits that come from concentrating company resources on relatively standardized global products and brands.

A **product** is a good, service, or idea with both tangible and intangible attributes that collectively create value for a buyer or user. A product's *tangible* attributes can be assessed in physical terms such as weight, dimensions, or materials used. Consider, for example, a flat-panel TV with an LCD screen that measures 42 inches across. The unit weighs 100 pounds, is 4 inches deep, is equipped with four high-definition media interface (HDMI) connections, has a built-in tuner capable of receiving high-definition TV signals over the air, and delivers a screen resolution of 1080p. These tangible, physical features translate into benefits that enhance the enjoyment of watching HDTV broadcasts and DVD movies. Accessories such as wall mounts and floor stands enhance the value offering by enabling great flexibility in placing the set in a living room or home theater. *Intangible* product attributes, including the status associated with product ownership, a manufacturer's service commitment, and a brand's overall reputation or mystique, are also important. When shopping for a new TV, for example, many people want "the best": They want a TV loaded with features (tangible product elements), as well as one that is "cool" and makes a status statement (intangible product element).

Product Types

A frequently used framework for classifying products distinguishes between consumer and industrial goods. For example, Sharp offers products and services to both consumers and businesses worldwide. Consumer and industrial goods, in turn, can be further classified on the basis of criteria such as buyer orientation. Buyer orientation is a composite measure of the amount of effort a customer expends, the level of risk associated with a purchase, and buyer involvement in the purchase. The buyer orientation framework includes such categories as convenience, preference, shopping, and specialty goods. Electronics products are often high involvement purchases, and many shoppers will compare several brands before make a decision. Products can also be categorized in terms of their life span (durable, nondurable, and disposable). Sharp and other electronics companies market products that are meant to last for many years; in other words, they are durable goods. As these examples from the electronics industry suggest, traditional product classification frameworks are fully applicable to global marketing.

Brands

A **brand** is a complex bundle of images and experiences in the customer's mind. Brands perform two important functions. First, a brand represents a promise by a particular company about a particular product; it is a type of quality certification. Second, brands enable customers to better organize their shopping experience by helping them seek out and find a particular product. Thus, an important brand function is to differentiate a particular company's offering from all others.

Customers integrate all their experiences of observing, using, or consuming a product with everything they hear and read about it. Information about products and brands comes from a variety of sources and cues, including advertising, publicity, word of mouth, sales personnel, and packaging. Perceptions of service after the sale, price, and distribution are also taken into account. The sum of impressions is a **brand image**, defined as perceptions about a brand as reflected by brand associations that consumers hold in their memories.[1]

Brand image is one way that competitors in the same industry sector differentiate themselves. Take Apple and Nokia, for example. Both market music phones. Apple CEO Steve Jobs is a constant media presence who is a master at generating buzz; the iPhone has received stellar reviews for its sleek look, large screen, and user-friendly features. Apple's retail stores reinforce the brand's hip, cool image. By contrast, Nokia's brand image is more heavily skewed toward technology; few Nokia users are likely to know the name of the company's chief executive. Key products have alphanumeric names that might charitably be described as bland; the N96 is a case in point.[2]

Another important brand concept is **brand equity**, which represents the total value that accrues to a product as a result of a company's cumulative investments in the marketing of the brand. Just as a homeowner's equity grows as a mortgage is paid off over the years, brand equity grows as a company invests in the brand. Brand equity can also be thought of as an asset representing the value created by the relationship between the brand and customers over time. The stronger the relationship, the greater the equity. For example, the value of global megabrands such as Coca-Cola and Marlboro runs in the tens of *billions* of dollars.[3] As outlined by branding expert Kevin Keller, the benefits of strong brand equity include:

- Greater loyalty
- Less vulnerability to marketing actions
- Less vulnerability to marketing crises
- Larger margins
- More inelastic consumer response to price increases
- More elastic consumer response to price decreases
- Increased marketing communication effectiveness[4]

Warren Buffett, the legendary American investor who heads Berkshire Hathaway, asserts that the global power of brands such as Coca-Cola and Gillette permits the companies that own

[1]Kevin Lane Keller, *Strategic Brand Management: Building, Measuring, and Managing Brand Equity* (Upper Saddle River, NJ: Prentice Hall, 1998), p. 93.
[2]Cassell Bryan-Low, "Apple, Nokia Face Off in UK Music-Phone Clash," *The Wall Street Journal* (October 18, 2007), p. B3.
[3]For a complete discussion of brand equity, see Kevin Lane Keller, *Strategic Brand Management* (Upper Saddle River, NJ: Prentice Hall, 1998), Chapter 2.
[4]Kevin Lane Keller, *Strategic Brand Management: Building, Measuring, and Managing Brand Equity* (Upper Saddle River, NJ: Prentice Hall, 1998), p. 93.

them to set up a protective moat around their economic castles. As Buffett once explained, "The average company, by contrast, does battle daily without any such means of protection."[5] That protection often yields added profit because the owners of powerful brand names can typically command higher prices for their products than can owners of lesser brands. In other words, the strongest global brands have tremendous brand equity.

Companies develop logos, distinctive packaging, and other communication devices to provide visual representations of their brands. A logo can take a variety of forms, starting with the brand name itself. For example, the Coca-Cola brand is expressed in part by a *word mark* consisting of the words *Coke* and *Coca-Cola* written in a distinctive white script. The "wave" that appears on red Coke cans and bottle labels is an example of a *nonword mark logo*, sometimes known as a *brand symbol*. Nonword marks such as the Nike swoosh, the three-pronged Mercedes star, and McDonald's golden arches have the great advantage of transcending language and are therefore especially valuable to global marketers. To protect the substantial investment of time and money required to build and sustain brands, companies register brand names, logos, and other brand elements as trademarks or service marks. As discussed in Chapter 5, safeguarding trademarks and other forms of intellectual property is a key issue in global marketing.

> "We have to shift to high value-added products, and to do that we need to improve our brand."[6]
>
> Noboru Fujimoto, President, Sharp Electronics Corporation

Local Products and Brands

A **local product** or **local brand** is one that has achieved success in a single national market. Sometimes a global company creates local products and brands in an effort to cater to the needs and preferences of particular country markets. For example, Coca-Cola has developed several branded drink products for sale only in Japan, including a noncarbonated, ginseng-flavored beverage; a blended tea known as Sokenbicha; and the Lactia-brand fermented milk drink. In India, Coca-Cola markets Kinely brand bottled water. The spirits industry often creates brand extensions to leverage popular brands without large marketing expenditures. For example, Diageo PLC markets Gordon's Edge, a gin-based ready-to-drink beverage in the United Kingdom. Allied Domecq created TG, a brand flavored with Teacher's Scotch and guaraná, in Brazil.[7]

> "There is a strong local heritage in the brewing industry. People identify with their local brewery, which makes beer different from detergents or electronic products."[8]
>
> Karel Vuursteen, Chairman, Heineken

Local products and brands also represent the lifeblood of domestic companies. Entrenched local products and brands can represent significant competitive hurdles to global companies entering new country markets. In China, for example, a sporting goods company started by Olympic gold medalist Li Ning sells more sneakers than global powerhouse Nike. In developing countries, global brands are sometimes perceived as overpowering local ones. Growing national pride can result in a social backlash that favors local products and brands. In China, a local TV manufacturer, Changhong Electric Appliances, has built its share of the Chinese market from 6 percent to more than 22 percent by cutting prices and using patriotic advertising themes such as "Let Changhong hold the great flag of revitalizing our national industries."

White-goods maker Haier Group has also successfully fought off foreign competition and now accounts for 40 percent of China's refrigerator sales. In addition, Haier enjoys a 30 percent share of both the washing machine and air conditioner markets. Slogans stenciled on office walls delineate the aspirations of company president Zhang Ruimin: "Haier—Tomorrow's Global Brand Name," and "Never Say 'No' to the Market."[9] In 2002, Haier Group announced a strategic alliance with Taiwan's Sampo Group. The deal, valued at $300 million, called for each company to manufacture and sell the other's refrigerators and telecommunications products both globally and locally.

---

[5]John Willman, "Labels That Say It All," *Financial Times—Weekend Money* (October 25–26, 1997), p. 1.
[6]Peter Landers, "Sharp Covets the Sony Model: A Sexy, High-end Image," *The Wall Street Journal* (March 11, 2002), p. A13.
[7]Deborah Ball, "Liquor Makers Go Local," *The Wall Street Journal* (February 13, 2003), p. B3.
[8]John Willman, "Time for Another Round," *Financial Times* (June 21, 1999), p. 15.
[9]John Ridding, "China's Own Brands Get Their Acts Together," *Financial Times* (December 30, 1996), p. 6; Kathy Chen, "Global Cooling: Would America Buy a Refrigerator Labeled 'Made in Quingdao'?" *The Wall Street Journal* (September 17, 1997), pp. A1, A14.

International Products and Brands

International products and **international brands** are offered in several markets in a particular region. For example, a number of "Euro products" and "Euro brands" such as Daimler's two-seat Smart car are available in Europe; the Smart was recently launched in the United States as well. The experience of GM with its Corsa model in the early 1990s provides a case study in how an international product or brand can be taken global. The Opel Corsa was a new model originally introduced in Europe. GM then decided to build different versions of the Corsa in China, Mexico, and Brazil. As David Herman, chairman of Adam Opel AG, noted, "The original concept was not that we planned to sell this car from the tip of Tierra del Fuego to the outer regions of Siberia. But we see its possibilities are limitless." GM calls the Corsa its "accidental world car."[10] Honda had a similar experience with the Fit, a five-door hatchback built on the company's Global Small Car platform. Following Fit's successful Japanese launch in 2001, Honda rolled out the vehicle in Europe (where it is known as Jazz). Over the next few years, Fit was rolled out in Australia, South America, South Africa, and China. The Fit made its North American market debut in 2006.

Global Products and Brands

Globalization is putting pressure on companies to develop global products and to leverage brand equity on a worldwide basis. A **global product** meets the wants and needs of a global market. A true global product is offered in all world regions, including the Triad and in countries at every stage of development. A **global brand** has the same name and, in some instances, a similar image and positioning throughout the world. Some companies are well established as global brands. For example, when Nestlé asserts that it "Makes the very best," the quality promise is understood and accepted globally. The same is true for Gillette ("The best a man can get"), BMW ("The ultimate driving machine"), GE ("Imagination at work"), Harley-Davidson ("An American legend"), Visa International ("Life takes Visa"), and many other global companies (see Exhibit 10-2).

Former Gillette CEO Alfred Zeien explained his company's approach as follows:

> A multinational has operations in different countries. A global company views the world as a single country. We know Argentina and France are different, but we treat them the same. We sell them the same products, we use the same production methods, we have the same corporate policies. We even use the same advertising—in a different language, of course.[11]

Zeien's remarks reflect the fact that Gillette creates competitive advantage by marketing global products and utilizing global branding strategies. Gillette reaps economies of scale associated with creating a single ad campaign for the world and the advantages of executing a single brand strategy. All global companies are trying to increase the visibility of their brands, especially in key markets such as the United States and China. Examples include Philips with its "Sense and simplicity" global image advertising and Siemens' recent "Siemens Answers" campaign.

In the twenty-first century, global brands are becoming increasingly important. As one research team noted:

> People in different nations, often with conflicting viewpoints, participate in a shared conversation, drawing upon shared symbols. One of the key symbols in that conversation is the global brand. Like entertainment stars, sports celebrities, and politicians, global brands

---

[10]Diana Kurylko, "The Accidental World Car," *Automotive News* (June 27, 1994), p. 4.
[11]Victoria Griffith, "As Close as a Group Can Get to Global," *Financial Times* (April 7, 1998), p. 21.

Exhibit 10-2: In French ("La perfection au masculin"), German ("Für das Beste im Mann"), Italian ("Il meglio di un uomo"), Portuguese ("O melhor para o homem"), or any other language, Gillette's trademarked brand promise is easy to understand.
Source: Stephen Cherin/Getty Images, Inc.

have become a lingua franca for consumers all over the world. People may love or hate transnational companies, but they can't ignore them.[12]

These researchers note that brands that are marketed around the world are endowed with both an aura of excellence and a set of obligations. Worldwide, consumers, corporate buyers, governments, activists, and other groups associate global brands with three characteristics; consumers use these characteristics as a guide when making purchase decisions.

- *Quality signal.* Global brands compete fiercely with each other to provide world-class quality. A global brand name differentiates product offerings and allows marketers to charge premium prices.
- *Global myth.* Global brands are symbols of cultural ideals. As noted in Chapter 7, marketers can use global consumer culture positioning (GCCP) to communicate a brand's global identity and link that identity to aspirations in any part of the world.
- *Social responsibility.* Customers evaluate companies and brands in terms of how they address social problems and how they conduct business (see Exhibit 10-3).

Note that a global brand is not the same thing as a global product. For example, personal stereos are a category of global product; Sony is a global brand. Many companies, including Sony, make personal stereos. However, Sony created the category 30 years ago when it introduced the Walkman in Japan. The Sony Walkman is an example of **combination** or **tiered branding**, whereby a corporate name (Sony) is combined with a product brand name

---

[12]Douglas B. Holt, John A. Quelch, and Earl L. Taylor, "How Global Brands Compete," *Harvard Business Review* 82, no. 9 (September 2004), p. 69.

Exhibit 10-3: Nucor is a steel company best known for its pioneering use of the minimill. Minimills produce steel by melting scrap in electric arc furnaces. This process is much more efficient than that used by traditional integrated steel producers. Nucor uses print and online media for an integrated general branding campaign featuring the tagline "It's our nature." The campaign is designed to raise awareness about the company's stance on a variety of issues, including the environment, energy conservation, and the importance of creating a strong corporate culture. *Source:* Courtesy of Nucor.

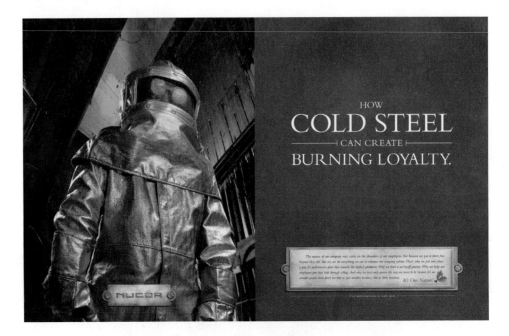

(Walkman). By using combination branding, marketers can leverage a company's reputation while developing a distinctive brand identity for a line of products. The combination brand approach can be a powerful tool for introducing new products. Although Sony markets a number of local products, the company also has a stellar track record as a global corporate brand, a creator of global products, and a marketer of global brands. For example, using the Walkman brand name as a point of departure, Sony created the Discman portable CD player and the Watchman portable TV. Sony's recent global product brand offerings include Bravia brand HDTVs and the PlayStation family of video game consoles and portables.

Co-branding is a variation on combination branding in which two or more *different* company or product brands are featured prominently on product packaging or in advertising. Properly implemented, co-branding can engender customer loyalty and allow companies to achieve synergy. However, co-branding can also confuse consumers and dilute brand equity. The

---

➔ STRATEGIC DECISION MAKING IN GLOBAL MARKETING
The Sony Walkman

The history of the Sony Walkman illustrates the fact that it is up to visionary marketers to create global brands. Initially, Sony's personal stereo was to be marketed under three brand names. In their book *Breakthroughs!*, Ranganath Nayak and John Ketteringham describe how the global brand as we know it today came into being when famed Sony Chairman Akio Morita realized that global consumers were one step ahead of his marketing staffers:

> At an international sales meeting in Tokyo, Morita introduced the Walkman to Sony representatives from America, Europe, and Australia. Within two months, the Walkman was introduced in the United States under the name "Soundabout"; two months later, it was on sale in the United Kingdom as "Stowaway." Sony in Japan had consented to the name changes because their English-speaking

marketing groups had told them the name "Walkman" sounded funny in English. Nevertheless, with tourists importing the Walkman from Japan and spreading the original name faster than any advertising could have done, Walkman became the name most people used when they asked for the product in a store. Thus, *Sony managers found themselves losing sales because they had three different names for the same item.* Morita settled the issue at Sony's United States sales convention in May 1980 by declaring that, "funny or not," Walkman was the name everybody had to use.

Source: P. Ranganath Nayak and John M. Ketteringham, *Breakthroughs! How Leadership and Drive Create Commercial Innovations That Sweep the World* (San Diego, CA: Pfeiffer & Company, 1994), pp. 128–129.

approach works most effectively when the products involved complement each other. Credit card companies were the pioneers, and today it is possible to use cards to earn frequent-flyer miles and discounts on automobiles. Another well-known example of co-branding is the Intel Inside campaign promoting both the Intel Corporation and its Pentium-brand processors in conjunction with advertising for various brands of personal computers.

Global companies can also leverage strong brands by creating **brand extensions**. This strategy entails using an established brand name as an umbrella when entering new businesses or developing new product lines that represent new categories to the company. British entrepreneur Richard Branson is an acknowledged master of this approach: The Virgin brand has been attached to a wide range of businesses and products (www.virgin.com). Virgin is a global brand, and the company's businesses include an airline, a railroad franchise, retail stores, movie theaters, financial services, and soft drinks. Some of these businesses are global, and some are local. For example, Virgin Megastores are found in many parts of the world, while Virgin Rail Group and Virgin Media operate only in the United Kingdom. The brand has been built on Branson's shrewd ability to exploit weaknesses in competitors' customer service skills, as well as a flair for self-promotion. Branson's business philosophy is that brands are built around reputation, quality, innovation, and price rather than image. Although Branson is intent on establishing Virgin as *the* British brand of the new millennium, some industry observers wonder if the brand has been spread too thin. Branson's newest ventures include Virgin America Airlines and Virgin Galactic.

Table 10-1 shows the four combinations of local and global products and brands in matrix form. Each represents a different strategy; a global company can use one or more strategies as appropriate. Some global companies pursue Strategy 1 by developing local products and brands for individual country or regional markets. Coca-Cola makes extensive use of this strategy; Georgia canned coffee in Japan is one example. Coca-Cola's flagship cola brand is an example of Strategy 4. In South Africa, Coca-Cola markets Valpre brand bottled water (Strategy 2). The global cosmetics industry makes extensive use of Strategy 3; the marketers of Chanel, Givenchy, Clarins, Guerlain, and other leading cosmetics brands create different formulations for different regions of the world. However, the brand name and the packaging may be uniform everywhere.

Global Brand Development

Table 10-2 shows global brands ranked in terms of their economic value as determined by analysts at the Interbrand consultancy and Citigroup. To be included in the rankings, the brand had to generate about one-third of sales outside the home country; brands owned by privately held companies such as Mars are not included. Not surprisingly, Coca-Cola tops the list. However, one of the telling findings of the rankings is that strong brand management is now being practiced by companies in a wide range of industries, not just by consumer packaged-goods marketers. As illustrated in Exhibit 10-4, Nokia's top-5 ranking is due in part to its success in building a successful global brand.

Developing a global brand is not always an appropriate goal. As David Aaker and Erich Joachimsthaler note in the *Harvard Business Review,* managers who seek to build global brands must first consider whether such a move fits well with their company or their markets. First,

"We believe strongly that there isn't a so-called global consumer, at least not when it comes to food and beverages. People have local tastes based on their unique cultures and traditions—a good candy bar in Brazil is not the same as a good candy bar in China. Therefore, decision making needs to be pushed down as low as possible in the organization, out close to the markets. Otherwise, how can you make good brand decisions? A brand is a bundle of functional and emotional characteristics. We can't establish emotional links with consumers in Vietnam from our offices in Vevey."[13]

Peter Brabeck-Letmathe, former CEO, Nestlé

TABLE 10-1 Product/Brand Matrix for Global Marketing

		Product	
		Local	Global
BRAND	**Local**	1. Local product/local brand	2. Global product/local brand
	Global	3. Local product/global brand	4. Global product/global brand

---

[13]Suzy Wetlaufer, "The Business Case Against Revolution," *Harvard Business Review* 79, no. 2 (February 2001), p. 116.

TABLE 10-2 **The World's Most Valuable Brands**

Rank	Value ($ millions)	Rank	Value ($ millions)
1. Coca-Cola	66,667	14. Gillette	22,069
2. IBM	59,031	15. American Express	21,940
3. Microsoft	59,007	16. Louis Vuitton	21,602
4. GE	53,086	17. Cisco	21,306
5. Nokia	35,942	18. Marlboro	21,300
6. Toyota	34,050	19. Citi	20,174
7. Intel	31,261	20. Honda	19,079
8. McDonald's	31,049	21. Samsung	17,689
9. Disney	29,251	22. H&M	13,840
10. Google	25,590	23. Oracle	13,831
11. Mercedes-Benz	25,577	24. Apple	13,724
12. Hewlett-Packard	23,509	25. Sony	13,583
13. BMW	23,298		

Source: Adapted from "The 100 Top Brands," *Business Week* (September 29, 2008), pp. 60–61.

managers must realistically assess whether anticipated scale economies will actually materialize. Second, they must recognize the difficulty of building a successful global brand team. Finally, managers must be alert to instances in which a single brand cannot be imposed on all markets successfully. Aaker and Joachimsthaler recommend that companies place a priority on creating strong brands in *all* markets through **global brand leadership**:

> Global brand leadership means using organizational structures, processes, and cultures to allocate brand-building resources globally, to create global synergies, and to develop a global brand strategy that coordinates and leverages country brand strategies.[14]

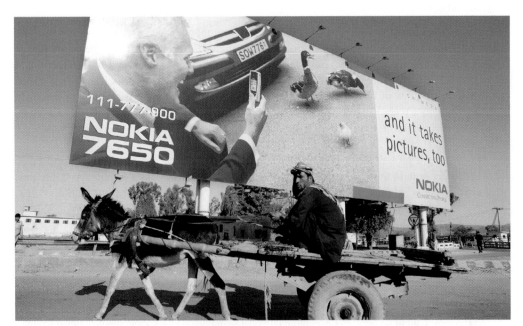

Exhibit 10-4: Annual global cell phone sales have passed the one-billion-unit mark. Now, faced with saturated markets in the West, Nokia and its competitors are looking to emerging markets for new customers. Robust economic growth and rising incomes mean that consumers in China, India, and other emerging markets can buy cell phones as status symbols. As indicated by this billboard on the Grand Trunk Highway outside of Islamabad, Pakistan, many users are upgrading to new handsets with fashionable designs and the latest features, including color screens, cameras, and digital music players.
Source: Robert Nickelsberg/Getty Images, Inc.

[14]David Aaker and Erich Joachimsthaler, "The Lure of Global Branding," *Harvard Business Review* 77, no. 6 (November–December 1999), pp. 137–144.

CULTURE WATCH
Nintendo's Wii Captures Hearts and Minds Around the World

Nintendo and Sony are locked in a marketing battle that might be called *Clash of the Titans*. In November 2006, after months of delays, Sony launched PlayStation 3 (PS3) in the United States. PS3's advanced graphics capability was provided by a built-in high-definition DVD player using a format known as Blu-ray. PS3 was initially available in two models—one with a 20-gigabyte hard drive and the other with 60 gigabytes—priced at $499 and $599, respectively. In December, Nintendo launched Wii, its latest video game console, in the United States and Europe. Priced at $250, €249 (eurozone), and £179 (United Kingdom), the Wii features a wireless controller that allows players to simulate such activities as fishing, golfing, and fencing. The new game consoles began arriving in stores about one year after Microsoft's Xbox 360; worldwide, approximately 10 million Xbox 360 units had been sold by the end of 2006.

Industry observers noted that Nintendo and Sony's strategies for their respective game consoles entailed major risks. Nintendo was defying orthodox wisdom in the industry, according to which each new generation of machines has to be faster and more powerful than the preceding generation. Nintendo's designers deliberately chose a different path: They created a machine that is simpler to use and less costly to manufacture. The designers were also guided by the sense that many video games had gotten so complicated to learn that they appealed mainly to advanced gamers. As Satoru Iwata, president and director at Nintendo, noted, "Everyone thought that consumers would continue to buy new consoles as long as you could play more real and more impressive games. There were also people who would quietly walk away because they got too complex." With the Wii, Nintendo hoped to appeal to veteran players addicted to games like *Mario Brothers* and *Zelda* as well as inexperienced or novice players.

Sony had enjoyed massive worldwide success with the PlayStation (1994) and PlayStation 2 (PS2) (2000), each of which had sold more than 100 million units. PS2 commanded an impressive 70 percent share of the console market. Sony's designers intended to "up the ante" with PS3. For one thing, the company spent nearly $2 billion on a new processing chip called Cell that packs as much speed as a supercomputer and offers superior graphics quality. Another component, a laser diode that plays next-generation high-definition DVDs, was intended to drive adoption of a new video format called Blu-ray that Sony had developed. However, the diode proved to be difficult to produce in mass quantities, contributing to product shortages at the holiday launch.

In March 2007, PS3 finally went on sale in Europe. Some industry observers believe that the success or failure of the European launch will ultimately determine the outcome of the video console war. As Paul Jackson, an analyst with Forrester Research, explained, "I think Europe is viewed by Microsoft and Sony as the most important territory. Microsoft is almost certainly going to win in the United States and Sony is almost certainly going to win in Japan, eventually, depending on whether the Wii's appeal as a novelty item is going to peter out. Europeans, however, are pretty agnostic and tend to buy whatever has the coolest games."

Sources: Joseph Pereira and Nick Wingfield, "Wii! Wii! Wii! This Holiday Season Has Been a Wild Ride for Nintendo," *The Wall Street Journal* (December 12, 2006), p. B1; Chris Nuttal, "Console Makers Go for a Slam Dunk," *Financial Times* (November 17, 2006), p. 8; Michiyo Nakamoto and Leo Lewis, "Sony Prepares for Big Game Battle," *Financial Times* (November 10, 2006), p. 21; John Gapper, "Sony Is Scoring Low at Its Own Game," *Financial Times* (November 6, 2006), p. 8; Yukari Iwatani Kane and Nick Wingfield, "Out of the Box: Amid Videogame Arms Race, Nintendo Slows Things Down," *The Wall Street Journal* (November 2, 2006), pp. A1, A10; Robert Levine, "En Garde! Fight Foes Using a Controller Like a Sword," *The New York Times* (October 30, 2006), p. C5.

The following six guidelines can assist marketing managers in their efforts to establish global brand leadership:[15]

- Create a compelling value proposition for customers in every market entered, beginning with the home-country market. A global brand begins with this foundation of value.
- Before taking a brand across borders, think about all elements of brand identity and select names, marks, and symbols that have the potential for globalization. Give special attention to the Triad and BRIC nations.
- Develop a company-wide communication system to share and leverage knowledge and information about marketing programs and customers in different countries.
- Develop a consistent planning process across markets and products. Make a process template available to all managers in all markets.
- Assign specific responsibility for managing branding issues to ensure that local brand managers accept global best practices. This can take a variety of forms, ranging from a

---

[15]Warren J. Keegan, "Global Brands: Issues and Strategies," Center for Global Business Strategy, Pace University, Working Paper Series, 2002.

STRATEGIC DECISION MAKING IN GLOBAL MARKETING
Mars

Mars Inc. confronted the global brand issue with its chocolate-covered caramel bar that was sold under a variety of national brand names such as Snickers in the United States and Marathon in the United Kingdom. Management decided to transform the candy bar—already a global product—into a global brand. This decision entailed some risk, such as the possibility that consumers in the United Kingdom would associate the name Snickers with knickers, the British slang for a woman's undergarment. Mars also changed the name of its successful European chocolate biscuit from Raider to Twix, the same name used in the United States. In both instances, a single brand name gives Mars the opportunity to leverage all of its product communications across national boundaries. Managers were forced to think globally about the positioning of Snickers and Twix, something that they were not obliged to

do when the candy products were marketed under different national brand names. The marketing team rose to the challenge; as Lord Saatchi described it:

> Mars decided there was a rich commercial prize at stake in ownership of a single human need: hunger satisfaction. From Hong Kong to Lima, people would know that Snickers was "a meal in a bar." Owning that emotion would not give them 100 percent of the global confectionery market but it would be enough. Its appeal would be wide enough to make Snickers the number one confectionery brand in the world, which it is today.

Source: Lord Saatchi, "Battle for Survival Favours the Simplest," *Financial Times* (January 5, 1998), p. 19. Reprinted by permission.

---

business management team or a brand champion (led by senior executives) to a global brand manager or brand management team (led by middle managers).
- Execute brand-building strategies that leverage global strengths and respond to relevant local differences.

Coke is arguably the quintessential global product and global brand. Coke relies on similar positioning and marketing in all countries; it projects a global image of fun, good times, and enjoyment. The product itself may vary to suit local tastes; for example, Coke increased the sweetness of its beverages in the Middle East where customers prefer a sweeter drink. Also, prices may vary to suit local competitive conditions, and the channels of distribution may differ. In 2009, Coke adopted the global advertising theme "Open Happiness." The previous slogan, "The Coke Side of Life," was also global but required adaptation in emerging markets such as Russia and China.[16] However, the basic, underlying strategic principles that guide the management of the brand are the same worldwide. The issue is not exact uniformity but rather: Are we offering *essentially* the same product and brand promise? As discussed in the next few chapters, other elements of the marketing mix—for example, price, communications appeal and media strategy, and distribution channels—may also vary.

EMERGING MARKETS BRIEFING BOOK

GM in China

General Motors' experience in China provides a good example of how a company's global brand strategy must be adapted to the needs of the market. In the Chapter 9 discussion of GM's joint venture in China it was noted that, in the mid-1990s, the American automaker was selected to produce Buick sedans for government and business. Why was the Buick nameplate chosen from among GM's various vehicle brands? In an interview with *Fortune*, GM CEO Rick Wagoner related the following story:

> There is a straightforwardness to the way the Chinese negotiate things. What they are interested in becomes

clear quickly. When we were ready to go into the China market, they said, "Okay, we will choose GM, and we want you to use Buick." We said, "It is not really one of our global brands. We'd probably rather use something else." They said, "We'd like you to use Buick." We said, "We'll use Buick." And it has worked great.

Source: Alex Taylor III, "China Would Rather Have Buicks," *Fortune* (October 4, 2004), p. 98.

---

[16]Betsy McKay and Suzanne Vranica, "Coca-Cola to Uncap 'Open Happiness' Campaign," *The Wall Street Journal* (January 14, 2009), p. B6.

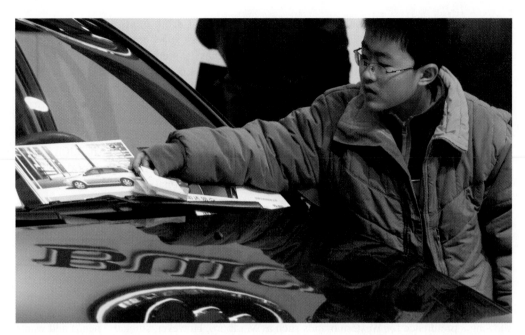

Exhibit 10-5: As General Motors sought aid from the U.S. government, the Obama administration asked CEO Rick Wagoner to step down. The company will be forced to cut costs; among other concessions and remedies, the Saturn and Pontiac brands will be discontinued. Meanwhile, GM's Buick brand is one of the top-selling nameplates in China. GM's Chinese sales totaled more than one million vehicles in 2008.
Source: The Eng Koon/AFP/Newscom.

Local Versus Global Products and Brands: A Needs-Based Approach

Coca-Cola, McDonald's, Singapore Airlines, Mercedes-Benz, and Sony are a few of the companies that have transformed local products and brands into global ones. The essence of marketing is finding needs and filling them. **Maslow's needs hierarchy,** a staple of sociology and psychology courses, provides a useful framework for understanding how and why local products and brands can be extended beyond home-country borders. Maslow proposed that people's desires can be arranged into a hierarchy of five needs.[17] As an individual fulfills needs at each level, he or she progresses to higher levels (Figure 10-1). At the most basic level of human existence, physiological and safety needs must be met. People need food, clothing, and shelter, and a product that meets these basic needs has potential for globalization.

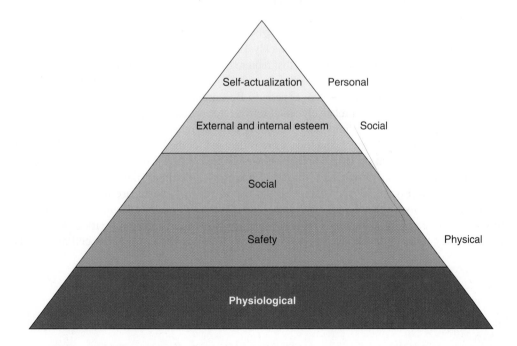

FIGURE 10-1

Maslow's Hierarchy of Needs

Source: A. H. Maslow, "A Theory of Human Motivation," in *Readings in Managerial Psychology,* Harold J. Levitt and Louis R. Pondy, eds. (Chicago: University of Chicago Press, 1964), pp. 6–24. Original— *Psychological Review* 50 (1943).

---

[17]A. H. Maslow, "A Theory of Human Motivation," in *Readings in Managerial Psychology,* eds. Harold J. Levitt and Louis R. Pondy (Chicago: University of Chicago Press, 1964), pp. 6–24.

However, the basic human need to consume food and drink is not the same thing as wanting or preferring a Big Mac or a Coke. Before the Coca-Cola Company and McDonald's conquered the world, they built their brands and business systems at home. Because their products fulfilled basic human needs and because both companies are masterful marketers, they were able to cross geographic boundaries and build global brand franchises. At the same time, Coca-Cola and McDonald's have learned from experience that some food and drink preferences—China is a case in point—remain deeply embedded in culture.[18] Responding to those differences has meant creating local products and brands for particular country markets. Sony has prospered for a similar reason. Audio and video entertainment products fulfill important social functions. Throughout its history, Sony's corporate vision has called for developing new products such as the transistor radio and the Walkman personal stereo that fulfill the need for entertainment.

Mid-level needs in the hierarchy include self-respect, self-esteem, and the esteem of others. These social needs, which can create a powerful internal motivation driving demand for status-oriented products, cut across the various stages of country development. Gillette's Alfred Zeien understood this. Marketers in Gillette's Parker Pen subsidiary are confident that consumers in Malaysia and Singapore shopping for an upscale gift will buy the same Parker pen as Americans shopping at Neiman Marcus. "We are not going to come out with a special product for Malaysia," Zeien has said.[19] In Asia today, young women are taking up smoking as a status symbol—and showing a preference for Western brands such as Marlboro. However, smokers' needs and wants may be tempered by economic circumstances. Recognizing this, companies such as BAT create local brands that allow individuals to indulge their desire or need to smoke at a price they can afford to pay.

Luxury goods marketers are especially skilled at catering to esteem needs on a global basis. Rolex, Louis Vuitton, and Dom Perignon are just a few of the global brands that consumers buy in an effort to satisfy esteem needs. Some consumers flaunt their wealth by buying expensive products and brands that others will notice. Such behavior is referred to as *conspicuous consumption* or *luxury badging*. Any company with a premium product or brand that has proven itself in a local market by fulfilling esteem needs should consider devising a strategy for taking the product global.

Products can fulfill different needs in different countries. Consider the refrigerator as used in industrialized, high-income countries. The *primary function* of the refrigerator in these countries is related to basic needs as fulfilled in that society. These include storing frozen foods for extended periods; keeping milk, meat, and other perishable foods fresh between car trips to the supermarket; and making ice cubes. In lower-income countries, by contrast, frozen foods are not widely available. Homemakers shop for food daily rather than weekly. People are reluctant to pay for unnecessary features such as icemakers. These are luxuries that require high income levels to support. The function of the refrigerator in a lower-income country is to store small quantities of perishable food for one day and to store leftovers for slightly longer periods. Because the needs fulfilled by the refrigerator are limited in these countries, a relatively small refrigerator is quite adequate. In some developing countries, refrigerators have an important *secondary purpose* related to higher-order needs: They fulfill a need for prestige. In these countries, there is demand for the largest model available, which is prominently displayed in the living room rather than hidden in the kitchen (see Exhibit 10-6).

Hellmut Schütte has proposed a modified hierarchy to explain the needs and wants of Asian consumers (Figure 10-2).[20] Although the two lower-level needs are the same as in the traditional hierarchy, the three highest levels emphasize social needs. *Affiliation needs* in Asia are satisfied when an individual has been accepted by a group. Conformity with group norms becomes a key force driving consumer behavior. For example, when a cool new cell phone hits

"For Asians, face is very important, so you have to show you are up to date with the latest available product."[21]

Alan Chang, View Sonic (Taiwan), explaining the popularity of flat-panel TVs in Japan

---

[18]Jeremy Grant, "Golden Arches Bridge Local Tastes," *Financial Times* (February 9, 2006), p. 10.

[19]Louis Uchitelle, "Gillette's World View: One Blade Fits All," *The New York Times* (January 3, 1994), p. C3.

[20]Hellmut Schütte, "Asian Culture and the Global Consumer," *Financial Times–Mastering Marketing* (September 21, 1998), p. 2.

[21]Andrew Ward, Kathrin Hille, Michiyo Nakamoto, Chris Nuttal, "Flat Out for Flat Screens: The Battle to Dominate the $29 bn Market Is Heating Up but the Risk of Glut Is Growing," *Financial Times* (December 24, 2003), p. 9.

Exhibit 10-6: In India, Vietnam, and other emerging markets, many people cannot afford the kinds of durable goods that consumers in developed countries take for granted. In India, for example, refrigerators are found in less than 20 percent of households. That means that refrigerators, flush toilets, and other amenities are considered status symbols.

Now, some Indian companies are developing innovative new products that the country's poorest consumers can afford. For example, one company has created the Little Cool refrigerator. Selling for the equivalent of $70, the device is small and portable. It only has about 20 parts, about one-tenth the number of parts that are found in conventional full-sized units.

Source: David Turnley/Corbis–NY.

the market, every teenager who wants to fit in buys one. Knowing this, managers at Japanese companies develop local products specifically designed to appeal to teens. The next level is *admiration*, a higher-level need that can be satisfied through acts that command respect within a group. At the top of the Asian hierarchy is *status*, the esteem of society as a whole. In part, attainment of high status is character driven. However, the quest for status also leads to luxury badging. Support for Schütte's contention that status is the highest-ranking need in the Asian hierarchy can be seen in the geographic breakdown of the $35 billion global luxury goods market. Fully 20 percent of industry sales are generated in Japan alone, with another 22 percent of sales occurring in the rest of the Asia-Pacific region. Nearly half of all sales revenues of Italy's Gucci Group are generated in Asia.

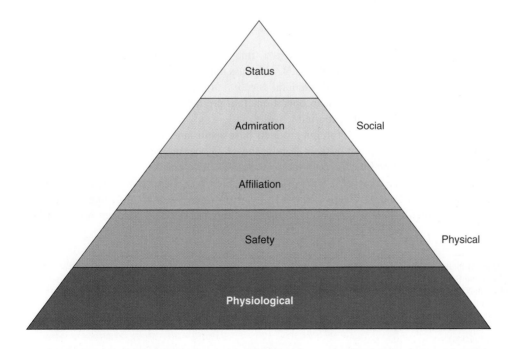

FIGURE 10-2

Maslow's Hierarchy: The Asian Equivalent

Source: A. H. Maslow, "A Theory of Human Motivation," in *Readings in Managerial Psychology,* Harold J. Levitt and Louis R. Pondy, eds. (Chicago: University of Chicago Press, 1964), pp. 6–24. Original—*Psychological Review* 50 (1943).

"COUNTRY OF ORIGIN" AS BRAND ELEMENT

One of the facts of life in global marketing is that perceptions about and attitudes toward particular countries often extend to products and brands known to originate in those countries. Such perceptions contribute to the **country-of-origin effect;** they become part of a brand's image and contribute to brand equity. This is particularly true for automobiles, electronics, fashion, beer, recorded music, and certain other product categories. Perceptions and attitudes about a product's origins can be positive or negative. On the positive side, as one marketing expert pointed out in the mid-1990s, "'German' is synonymous with quality engineering, 'Italian' is synonymous with style, and 'French' is synonymous with chic."[22] A quarter century later, those associations are still evident. Within a given country, consumers are likely to differ in terms of both the importance they ascribe to a product's country of origin and their perceptions of different countries. Moreover, as industries and markets globalize, the origin issue is becoming more complex. Country of design, country of manufacture, and country sources for parts can all become relevant considerations.

The manufacturing reputation of a particular country can change over time. Studies conducted during the 1970s and 1980s indicated that the "made in the USA" image lost ground to the "made in Japan" image. Today, however, U.S. brands are finding renewed acceptance globally. Examples include the Jeep Cherokee, clothing from Lands' End and American Apparel, and Budweiser beer, all of which are being successfully marketed with strong "USA" themes. Korea's image has improved greatly in recent years, thanks to the reputations of global companies such as Daewoo, Hyundai, and Samsung. Industry observers expect other Asian corporate megabrands to emerge in the coming years.

Finland is home to Nokia, which rose in stature from a local company to a global one in little more than a decade. However, as brand strategy expert Simon Anholt points out, other Finnish companies need to move quickly to capitalize on Nokia's success if Finland is to become a valuable nation-brand. For example, Raisio Oy's Benecol brand margarine has been proven to lower cholesterol levels. If large numbers of health-conscious consumers around the world embrace so-called nutraceutical products, Raisio and Benecol may become well-known brands and further raise Finland's profile on the global scene. Anholt also notes that Slovenia and other countries are "launch brands" in the sense that they lack centuries of tradition and foreign interaction upon which to build their reputations (see Exhibit 10-7):

> For a country like Slovenia to enhance its image abroad is a very different matter than for Scotland or China. Slovenia needs to be launched: Consumers around the world first must be taught where it is, what it makes, what it has to offer, and what it stands for. This in itself represents a powerful opportunity: The chance to build a modern country brand, untainted by centuries of possibly negative associations.[24]

Since the mid-1990s, the "made in Mexico" image has gained in stature as local companies and global manufacturers have established world-class manufacturing plants in Mexico to supply world demand. For example, Ford, General Motors, Nissan, Volkswagen, and other global automakers have established Mexican operations that produce nearly two million vehicles per year, three-fourths of which are exported.[25]

In some product categories, foreign products have a substantial advantage over their domestic counterparts simply because of their "foreign-ness." Global marketers have an opportunity to capitalize on the situation by charging premium prices. The import segment of the beer industry is a case in point. In one study of American attitudes about beer, subjects who were asked to taste beer with the labels concealed indicated a preference for domestic beers over imports. The same subjects were then asked to indicate preference ratings for beers in an open test with labels

[22]Dana Milbank, "Made in America Becomes a Boast in Europe," *The Wall Street Journal* (January 19, 1994), p. B1.
[23]Bertrand Benoit and Geoff Dyer, "The Mittelstand Is Making Money in the Middle Kingdom," *Financial Times* (June 6, 2006), p. 13.
[24]Simon Anholt, "The Nation as Brand," *Across the Board* 37, no. 10 (November–December 2000), pp. 22–27.
[25]Elliot Blair Smith, "Early PT Cruiser Took a Bruisin'," *USA Today* (August 8, 2001), pp. 1B, 2B; see also Joel Millman, "Trade Wins: The World's New Tiger on the Export Scene Isn't Asian; It's Mexico," *The Wall Street Journal* (May 9, 2000), pp. A1, A10.
[26]Christopher A. Bartlett and Sumantra Ghoshal, "Going Global: Lessons from Late Movers," *Harvard Business Review* 78, no. 2 (March–April 2000), p. 133.

Exhibit 10-7: Countries, like products, can be branded and positioned. For example, Slovenija, which recently joined the euro zone, is positioned as "The green piece of Europe."
Source: Embassy of the Republic of Slovenia.

attached. In this test, the subjects preferred imported beer. Conclusion: The subjects' perceptions were positively influenced by the knowledge they were drinking an import. In 1997, thanks to a brilliant marketing campaign, Grupo Modelo's Corona Extra surpassed Heineken as the best-selling imported beer in America. With distribution in 150 countries, Corona is a textbook example of a local brand that has been built into a global powerhouse.

Scotland provides an interesting case study of a country that enjoys strong brand equity but is somewhat misunderstood. A study titled "Project Galore" was undertaken to discover which aspects of Scotland's equity could be leveraged for commercial advantage. Among other things, the researchers learned that high-quality goods and services such as whisky, wool, salmon, and golf courses were perceived as Scotland's core industries. In fact, Scotland's top export category is information technology! The researchers created a perceptual map that identified Scotland's four key values: Integrity, tenacity, inventiveness, and spirit.[27] In order to better position Scotland relative to Ireland and other neighboring countries, Scottish Development International recently launched an advertising campaign that incorporated some of the study's findings (see Exhibit 10-8).

PACKAGING

In many instances, packaging is an integral element of product-related decisions. Packaging is an important consideration for products that are shipped to markets in far-flung corners of the world. Moreover, the phrase "consumer packaged goods" applies to a wide variety of products whose packaging is designed to protect or contain the product during shipping, at retail locations, and at the point of use or consumption. "Eco-packaging" is a key issue today, and package designers must address environmental issues such as recycling and biodegradability. In Germany, for example, product packaging must conform to Green Dot regulations. Packaging also serves important communication functions: Packages (and labels attached to them) offer communication cues that provide consumers with a basis for making a purchase decision. Today, many industry experts agree that packaging must engage the senses, make emotional connections, and enhance a consumer's brand experience. According to Bernd Schmitt, director of Columbia University's Center on Global Brand Leadership, "Packages are creating an experience for the customer that goes beyond the functional benefits of displaying and protecting the object."[28] Absolut vodka, Altoids breath mints, and Godiva chocolates are a few examples of brands whose value proposition includes "experiential packaging."

Brewers, soft drink marketers, distillers, and other beverage firms typically devote considerable thought to ensuring that packages speak to consumers or provide some kind of benefit beyond simply holding liquid. For example, a critical element in the success of Corona Extra beer in export markets was management's decision to retain the traditional package design that consisted of a tall transparent bottle with "Made in Mexico" etched directly on the glass. At the time, the conventional wisdom in the brewing industry was that export beer bottles should be short, green or brown in color, with paper labels. In other words, the bottle should resemble Heineken's! The fact that consumers could see the beer inside the Corona Extra bottle made it seem more pure and natural. Today, Corona is the top-selling imported beer brand in the United States, Australia, Belgium, the Czech Republic, and several other countries.[29]

Coca-Cola's distinctive (and trademarked) contour bottle comes in both glass and plastic versions and helps consumers seek out the "real thing." The Coke example also illustrates the point that packaging strategies can vary by country and region. In North America, where large

---

[27]Kate Hamilton, "Project Galore: Qualitative Research and Leveraging Scotland's Brand Equity," *Journal of Advertising Research* 40, nos. 1/2 (January–April 2000), pp. 107–111. "Galore" is one of two English words that are taken from Gaelic. The other is "whisky."
[28]Queena Sook Kim, "The Potion's Power Is in Its Packaging," *The Wall Street Journal* (December 21, 2000), p. B12.
[29]Sara Silver, "Modelo Puts Corona in the Big Beer League," *Financial Times* (October 30, 2002), p. 26.

Exhibit 10-8: The body copy in this print ad positions Scotland in a positive light: "If there's one thing Scotland is known for, it's bold innovation. The television. The telephone. The steam engine. The fax machine. Penicillin. Insulin. The ATM. Dolly the sheep. They all got their start in Scotland. In fact, there are far too many Scottish innovations to name. Which is why more companies are doing business in Scotland. Where they can get the innovative thinking and practical solutions they need to develop new products."
Source: Scottish Development International.

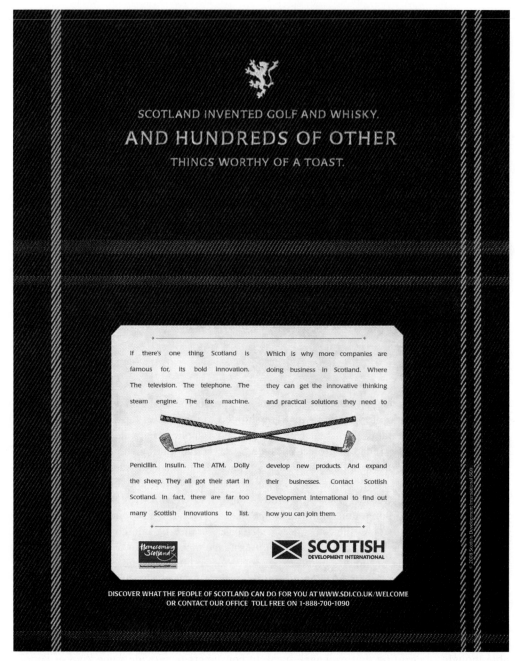

refrigerators are found in many households, Coca-Cola's latest packaging innovation is the Fridge Pack, a long, slender carton that holds the equivalent of 12 cans of soda. The Fridge Pack fits on a refrigerator's lower shelf and includes a tap for easy dispensing. In Latin America, by contrast, Coca-Cola executives intend to boost profitability by offering Coke in several different sized bottles. Until recently, for example, 75 percent of Coke's volume in Argentina was accounted for by 2-liter bottles priced at $0.45 each. Coke has introduced cold, individual-serving bottles priced at $0.33 that are stocked in stores near the front; unchilled, 1.25-liter returnable glass bottles priced at $0.28 are available on shelves further back in the store.[30] Other examples include:

- Grey Goose, the world's top-selling super premium vodka brand, is the brainchild of Sidney Frank. The owner of an importing business in New Rochelle, New York, Frank first devised the bottle design and name. Only then did he approach a distiller in Cognac, France, to create the actual vodka.[31]

[30]Betsy McKay, "Coke's Heyer Finds Test in Latin America," *The Wall Street Journal* (October 15, 2002), p. B4.
[31]Christina Passariello, "France's Cognac Region Gives Vodka a Shot," *The Wall Street Journal* (October 20, 2004), p. B1.

- Nestlé has packaging teams throughout the world that are required to contribute packaging improvement suggestions on a quarterly basis. Implemented changes include a new plastic lid to make ice cream containers easier to open; slightly deeper indentations in the flat end of candy wrappers in Brazil that make them easier to rip open; and deeper notches on single-serve packets of Nescafé in China. Nestlé also asked suppliers to find a type of glue to make the clicking sound louder when consumers snap open a tube of Smarties brand chocolate candies.[32]

Labeling

One hallmark of the modern global marketplace is the abundance of multi-language labeling that appears on many products. In today's self-service retail environments, product labels may be designed to attract attention, to support a product's positioning, and to help persuade consumers to buy. Labels can also provide consumers with various types of information. Obviously, care must be taken that all ingredient information and use and care instructions are properly translated. The content of product labels may also be dictated by country- or region-specific regulations. Regulations regarding mandatory label content vary in different parts of the world; for example, the European Union now requires mandatory labeling for some foods containing genetically modified ingredients.

Regulators in Australia, New Zealand, Japan, Russia, and several other countries have also proposed similar legislation. In the United States, the Nutrition Education and Labeling Act that went into effect in the early 1990s was intended to make food labels more informative and easier to understand. Today, virtually all food products sold in the United States must present information regarding nutrition (e.g., calories and fat content) and serving size in a standard format. The use of certain terms such as *light* and *natural* is also restricted. Other examples of labeling in global marketing include:

- Mandatory health warnings on tobacco products are required in most countries.
- The American Automobile Labeling Act clarifies the country of origin, the final assembly point, and percentages of the major sources of foreign content of every car, truck, and minivan sold in the United States (effective since October 1, 1994).
- Since mid-2004, the EU has required labels on all food products that include ingredients derived from genetically modified crops.
- Responding to pressure from consumer groups, in 2006 McDonald's began posting nutrition information on all food packaging and wrappers in approximately 20,000 restaurants in key markets worldwide. Executives indicated that issues pertaining to language and nutritional testing would delay labeling in 10,000 additional restaurants in smaller country markets.[33]
- Nestlé introduced Nan, an infant-formula brand that is popular in Latin America, in the American market. Targeted at Hispanic mothers, Nestlé Nan's instructions are printed in Spanish on the front of the can. Other brands have English-language labeling on the outside; Spanish-language instructions are printed on the reverse side.[34]
- In 2008, the United States enacted a country-of-origin labeling (COOL) law. The law requires supermarkets and other food retailers to display information that identifies the country that meat, poultry, and certain other food products come from.[35]

Aesthetics

In Chapter 4, the discussion of aesthetics included perceptions of color in different parts of the world. Global marketers must understand the importance of *visual aesthetics* embodied in the

---

[32]Deborah Ball, "The Perils of Packaging: Nestlé Aims for Easier Openings," *The Wall Street Journal* (November 17, 2005), p. B1.

[33]Steven L. Gray and Iian Brat, "Read It and Weep? Big Mac Wrapper to Show Fat, Calories," *The Wall Street Journal* (October 26, 2005), p. B1.

[34]Miriam Jordan, "Nestlé Markets Baby Formula to Hispanic Mothers in U.S.," *The Wall Street Journal* (March 4, 2004), p. B1.

[35]David Kesmodel and Julie Jargon, "Labels Will Say If Your Beef Was Born in the USA," *The Wall Street Journal* (September 23, 2008), p. B1.

color or shape of a product, label, or package. Likewise, *aesthetic styles*, such as the degree of complexity found on a label, are perceived differently in different parts of the world. For example, it has been said that German wines would be more appealing in export markets if the labels were simplified. Aesthetic elements that are deemed appropriate, attractive, and appealing in one's home country may be perceived differently elsewhere. In some cases, a standardized color can be used in all countries; examples include the distinctive yellow color on Caterpillar's earth-moving equipment and its licensed outdoor gear and the red Marlboro chevron. In other instances, color choices should be changed in response to local perceptions. It was noted in Chapter 4 that white is associated with death and bad luck in some Asian countries; recall that when GM executives were negotiating with China for the opportunity to build cars there, they gave Chinese officials gifts from upscale Tiffany & Company in the jeweler's signature blue box. The Americans astutely replaced Tiffany's white ribbons with red ones because red is considered a lucky color in China and white has negative connotations.

Packaging aesthetics are particularly important to the Japanese. This point was driven home to the chief executive of a small U.S. company that manufactures an electronic device for controlling corrosion. After spending much time in Japan, the executive managed to secure several orders for the device. Following an initial burst of success, Japanese orders dropped off; for one thing, the executive was told, the packaging was too plain. "We couldn't understand why we needed a five-color label and a custom-made box for this device, which goes under the hood of a car or in the boiler room of a utility company," the executive said. While waiting for the bullet train in Japan one day, the executive's local distributor purchased a cheap watch at the station and had it elegantly wrapped. The distributor asked the American executive to guess the value of the watch based on the packaging. Despite all that he had heard and read about the Japanese obsession with quality, it was the first time the American understood that, in Japan, "a book is judged by its cover." As a result, the company revamped its packaging, seeing to such details as ensuring that strips of tape used to seal the boxes were cut to precisely the same length.[36]

PRODUCT WARRANTIES

A warranty can be an important element of a product's value proposition. An **express warranty** is a written guarantee that assures the buyer is getting what he or she has paid for or that provides recourse in case a product's performance falls short of expectations. In global marketing, warranties can be used as a competitive tool to position a company in a positive way. For example, in the late 1990s, Hyundai Motor America chief executive Finbarr O'Neill realized that many American car buyers perceived Korean cars as "cheap" and were skeptical about the Hyundai nameplate's reliability. The company had made significant improvements in the quality and reliability of its vehicles, but consumer perceptions of the brand had not kept pace with the changes. O'Neill instituted a 10-year, 100,000-mile warranty program that represents the most comprehensive coverage in the auto industry. Concurrently, Hyundai launched several new vehicles and increased expenditures for advertising. The results are impressive: Hyundai's U.S. sales jumped from about 90,000 vehicles in 1998 to more than 350,000 vehicles in 2009.

EXTEND, ADAPT, CREATE: STRATEGIC ALTERNATIVES IN GLOBAL MARKETING

To capitalize on opportunities outside the home country, company managers must devise and implement appropriate marketing programs. Depending on organizational objectives and market needs, a particular program may consist of extension strategies, adaptation strategies, or a combination of the two. A company that has developed a successful local product or brand can implement an **extension strategy** that calls for offering a product virtually unchanged

---

[36]Nilly Landau, "Face to Face Marketing Is Best," *International Business* (June 1994), p. 64.

(i.e., "extending" it) in markets outside the home country. A second option is an **adaptation strategy**; this involves changing elements of design, function, or packaging in response to needs or conditions in particular country markets. These product strategies can be used in conjunction with extension or adaptation communication strategies. This is the type of strategic decision facing executives at a company such as Starbucks who build a brand and a product/service offering in the home-country market before expanding into global markets. A third strategic option, **product invention**, entails developing new products "from the ground up" with the world market in mind.

Laws and regulations in different countries frequently lead to obligatory product design adaptations. This may be seen most clearly in Europe, where one impetus for the creation of the single market was the desire to dismantle regulatory and legal barriers that prevented pan-European sales of standardized products. These were particularly prevalent in the areas of technical standards and health and safety standards. In the food industry, for example, there were 200 legal and regulatory barriers to cross-border trade within the EU in 10 food categories. Among these were prohibitions or taxes on products with certain ingredients and different packaging and labeling laws. As these barriers are dismantled there will be less need to adapt product designs and many companies will be able to create standardized "Euro-products."

Despite the trend toward convergence, many product standards that remain on the books have not been harmonized. This situation can create problems for companies not based in the EU. Dormont Manufacturing, appropriately based in Export, Pennsylvania, makes hoses that hook up to deep-fat fryers and similar appliances used in the food industry. Dormont's gas hose is made of stainless-steel helical tubing with no covering. British industry requirements call for galvanized metal annular tubing and a rubber covering; Italian regulations specify stainless steel annual tubing with no covering. The cost of complying with these regulations effectively shuts Dormont out of the European market.[37]

Moreover, the European Commission continues to set product standards that force many non-EU companies to adapt product or service offerings that satisfy domestic market regulations. For example, consumer safety regulations mean that McDonald's cannot give away soft-plastic toys with its Happy Meals in Europe. Microsoft has been forced to modify contracts with European software makers and Internet service providers to ensure that consumers in the EU have access to a wide range of technologies. The commission has also set stringent guidelines on product content as it affects recyclability. As Maja Wessels, a Brussels-based lobbyist for United Technologies Corporation (UTC), noted, "Twenty years ago, if you designed something to U.S. standards you could pretty much sell it all over the world. Now the shoe's on the other foot." Engineers at UTC's Carrier division are redesigning the company's air conditioners to comply with pending European recycling rules, which are tougher than U.S. standards.[38]

As noted in Chapter 1, the extension/adaptation/creation decision is one of the most fundamental issues addressed by a company's global marketing strategy. Although it pertains to all elements of the marketing mix, extension/adaptation is of particular importance in product and communications decisions. Earlier in the chapter, Table 10-1 displayed product and brand strategic options in matrix form. Figure 10-3 expands on those options: All aspects of promotion and communication—not just branding—are considered. Figure 10-3 shows four strategic alternatives available to Starbucks or any other company seeking to expand from its domestic base into new geographic markets.

Companies in the international, global, and transnational stages of development all employ extension strategies. The critical difference is one of execution and mind-set. In an international company, for example, the extension strategy reflects an ethnocentric orientation and the *assumption* that all markets are alike. A global company such as Gillette does not fall victim to such assumptions; the company's geocentric orientation allows it to thoroughly understand its markets and consciously take advantage of similarities in world markets. Likewise, a multinational company utilizes the adaptation strategy because of its polycentric orientation and the assumption that all markets are different. By contrast, the geocentric orientation of managers and

---

[37]Timothy Aeppel, "Europe's 'Unity' Undoes a U.S. Exporter, " *The Wall Street Journal* (April 1, 1996), p. B1.

[38]Brandon Mitchener, "Standard Bearers: Increasingly, Rules of Global Economy Are Set in Brussels," *The Wall Street Journal* (April 23, 2002), p. A1.

FIGURE 10-3

Global Product Planning: Strategic Alternatives

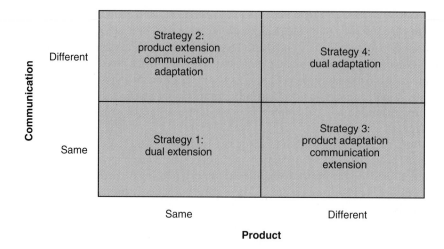

executives in a global company has sensitized them to actual, rather than assumed, differences between markets. The key, as one executive has noted, is to avoid being either "hopelessly local" or "mindlessly global."

Strategy 1: Product-Communication Extension (Dual Extension)

Many companies employ the **product-communication extension** strategy when pursuing global market opportunities. Under the right conditions, this is a very straightforward marketing strategy; it can be the most profitable one as well. Companies pursuing this strategy sell the same product with virtually no adaptation, using the same advertising and promotional appeals used domestically, in two or more country markets or segments. For this strategy to be effective, the advertiser's message must be understood across different cultures, including those in emerging markets. Examples of the dual-extension strategy include the following:

- Apple launched its iPhone in the United States in mid-2007. In the following months, it was gradually rolled out in several more markets, including France and the United Kingdom. When Apple brought its second-generation iPhone to market one year later, it was launched in 21 countries simultaneously.
- Henkel KGaA's family of Loctite-brand adhesive products are marketed globally using the dual-extension strategy.

As a general rule, extension/standardization strategies are utilized more frequently with industrial (business-to-business) products than with consumer products. The reason is simple: Industrial products tend to be less deeply rooted in culture than consumer goods. If this is so, how can Apple, a consummate consumer brand, utilize the dual-extension reason to such good effect? One explanation is that, as discussed in Chapter 7, the brand's high-tech, high-touch image lends itself to global consumer culture positioning (GCCP). As these examples show, technology companies and industrial goods manufacturers should be especially alert to dual-extension possibilities. However, Henkel also markets hundreds of other glues, detergents, and personal care products with different formulas and different brand names. Speaking about Loctite, Henkel CEO Ulrich Lehner explains, "There aren't many products like that. Usually, you have to adapt to local tastes. You have to balance between local insight and centralized economies of scale. It's a constant battle."[39]

Strategy 2: Product Extension-Communication Adaptation

In some instances, a product or brand can be successfully extended to multiple country markets with some modification of the communication strategy. Research may have revealed that consumer perceptions about one or more aspects of the value proposition are different from

"I can think of very few truly global ads that work. Brands are often at different stages around the world, and that means there are different advertising jobs to do."[40]
Michael Conrad, Chief Creative Officer, Leo Burnett Worldwide

---

[39]Gerrit Wiesmann, "Brands That Stop at the Border," *Financial Times* (October 6, 2006), p. 10.
[40]Vanessa O'Connell, "Exxon 'Centralizes' New Global Campaign," *The Wall Street Journal* (July 11, 2001), p. B6.

country to country. It may also turn out that a product fills a different need, appeals to a different segment, or serves a different function in a particular country or region. Whatever the reason, extending the product while adapting the marketing communications program may be the key to market success. The appeal of the **product extension-communication adaptation** strategy is its relatively low cost of implementation. Because the product itself is unchanged, expenditures for R&D, manufacturing setup, and inventory are avoided. The biggest costs associated with this approach are in researching the market and revising advertising, sales promotion efforts, point-of-sale material, and other communication elements as appropriate.

- In Hungary, Slovakia, and other Central European countries, SABMiller positions Miller Genuine Draft as an international lifestyle brand (GCCP) rather than an American brand (FCCP). The communication adaptation strategy was chosen after focus group research showed that many Europeans have a low regard for American beer.[41]
- Before executives at Ben & Jerry's Homemade launched their ice cream in the United Kingdom, the company conducted extensive research to determine whether the package design effectively communicated the brand's "super premium" position. The research indicated that British consumers perceived the colors differently than U.S. consumers. The package design was changed, and Ben & Jerry's was launched successfully in the UK market.
- To promote its Centrino wireless chip, Intel launched a global ad campaign that features different combinations of celebrities. In print, TV, and online ads, one of the celebrities sits on the lap of a mobile computer user. The celebrities—including comedian John Cleese, actress Lucy Liu, and skateboard king Tony Hawk—were chosen because they are widely recognized in key world markets.[42]
- In the United States, Sony's TV ads for its Bravia high-definition TVs encourage viewers to log onto the Internet and choose different endings. In Europe, the ads are completely different: They feature bright images such as colored balls bouncing in slow motion. As Mike Fasulo, chief marketing officer at Sony Electronics, explains, "Consumer adoption as well as awareness of high-definition products, including our line of Bravia televisions, differs dramatically from region to region.[43]
- Targeting the 300 million farmers in India who still use plows harnessed to oxen, John Deere engineers created a line of relatively inexpensive, no-frills tractors. The Deere team then realized that the same equipment could be marketed to hobby farmers and acreage owners in the United States—a segment that they had previously overlooked.[44]

Marketers of premium American bourbon brands such as Wild Turkey have found that images of Delta blues music, New Orleans, and Route 66 appeal to upscale drinkers outside the United States. However, images that stress bourbon's rustic, backwoods origins do not appeal to Americans. Likewise, Jägermeister schnapps is marketed differently in key country markets. Chief executive Hasso Kaempfe believes that a diversity of images has been a key element in the success of Jägermeister outside of Germany, where the brown herb-based concoction originated. In the United States, Jägermeister was "discovered" in the mid-1990s by bar patrons, particularly college students. Eschewing traditional media advertising, Kaempfe's marketing team has capitalized on the brand's cult status by hiring "Jägerettes" girls to pass out free samples; the company's popular T-shirts and orange banners are also distributed at rock concerts. By contrast, in Italy, the brand's second-largest export market, Jägermeister is considered an up-market digestive to be consumed after dinner. In Germany, Austria, and Switzerland, where beer culture predominates, Jägermeister and other brands of schnapps have more traditional associations as a remedy for coughs, stomachaches, or as a "morning after" elixir.[45]

---

[41]Dan Bilefsky and Christopher Lawton, "In Europe, Marketing Beer as 'American' May Not Be a Plus," *The Wall Street Journal* (July 21, 2004), p. B1.

[42]Geoffrey A. Fowler, "Intel's Game: Play It Local, but Make It Global," *The Wall Street Journal* (September 30, 2005), p. B4.

[43]Jorge Valencia, "Sony Paints Lavish Hues to Sell LCDs," *The Wall Street Journal* (August 3, 2007), p. B3.

[44]Jenny Mero, "John Deere's Farm Team," *Fortune* (April 14, 2008), pp. 119–126.

[45]Bettina Wassener, "Schnapps Goes to College," *Financial Times* (September 4, 2003), p. 9.

Jägermeister is an example of **product transformation**: The same physical product ends up serving a different function or use than that for which it was originally designed or created. In some cases a particular country or regional environment will allow local managers a greater degree of creativity and risk taking when approaching the communication task.

Strategy 3: Product Adaptation-Communication Extension

A third approach to global product planning is to adapt the product to local use or preference conditions while extending, without minimal change, the basic home-market communications strategy or brand name. This third strategy option is known as **product adaptation-communication extension**. For example:

- A new Cadillac model, the BLS, is built in Sweden; it is 6 inches shorter than the current CTS. A four-cylinder engine is standard; buyers can also choose an available diesel engine.
- For many years, Ford has sold the Escort, Focus, and other nameplates worldwide. However, the vehicles themselves often varied from region to region. In 2010, Ford plans to launch a new Focus model in the United States that has 80 percent shared content with the European Focus. The 20 percent adapted content reflects regulations such as bumper crash test standards.[47]
- When Kraft Foods launched Oreo brand cookies in China in 1996, it used a product extension approach. Following several years of flat sales, Kraft's in-country marketing team launched a research study. The team learned that Oreos were too sweet for the Chinese palate and that the price—14 cookies for 72 cents—was too high. Oreos were reformulated as a less-sweet, chocolate-covered, four-layer wafer filled with vanilla and chocolate cream. Packages of the new wafer Oreos contain fewer cookies but sell for about 29 cents. Today, Oreos are the best-selling cooking brand in China.[48]

Kraft's experience with Oreos in China is an example of changing from a product extension to a product adaptation strategy when an extension strategy does not yield the desired results. Conversely, managers at Ford, faced with strong competition from Toyota, Honda, and other automakers, are now seeking alternatives to product adaptation; in 2008, Ford unveiled the latest version of its Fiesta. It is designed to be manufactured in high volumes—as many as one million units annually—that can be sold worldwide with minimal adaptation. As Ford executive Mark Shields explained, "This is a real shift point for us in that it's a real global car."[49] In the case of GM's Cadillac, managers intend to achieve annual sales of 20,000 vehicles outside the United States by 2010. Doing so required considerable adaptation to European driving preferences and conditions. The BLS is only sold in Europe; as James Taylor, general manager of GM's Cadillac division, noted, "There's no Cadillac guy in the U.S. who is going to buy a four-cylinder low-displacement engine."[50]

Strategy 4: Product-Communication Adaptation (Dual Adaptation)

A company may also utilize the **product-communication adaptation (dual adaptation)** strategy. As the name implies, both the product and one or more promotional elements are adapted for a particular country or region. Sometimes marketers discover that environmental conditions or consumer preferences differ from country to country; the same may be true of the function a product serves or consumer receptivity to advertising appeals. In cases where country managers who have been granted considerable autonomy order adaptations, they may be simply exercising

[46]Kimberly Palmer, "Rustic Bourbon: A Hit Overseas, Ho-Hum in the U.S." *The Wall Street Journal* (September 2, 2003), p. B1.

[47]Joseph B. White, "One Ford for the Whole World," *The Wall Street Journal* (March 17, 2009), p. D2.

[48]Julie Jargon, "Kraft Reformulates Oreo, Scores in China," *The Wall Street Journal* (May 1, 2008), pp. B1, B7.

[49]Bill Vlasic, "Ford Introduces One Small Car for a World of Markets," *The Wall Street Journal* (February 15, 2008), p. C3.

[50]Mark Landler, "Europe, Meet Cadillac and Dodge," *The Wall Street Journal* (March 2, 2005), p. C3.

their power to act independently. If headquarters tries to achieve inter-country coordination, the result can be, in the words of one manager, "like herding cats." Consider the following:

- Unilever's Italian country managers discovered that, although Italian women spend more than 20 hours each week doing cleaning, ironing, and other tasks, they are not interested in labor-saving conveniences. The final result—a really clean, shiny floor, for example—is more important than saving time. For the Italian market, Unilever reformulated its Cif brand spray cleaner to do a better job on grease; several different varieties were also rolled out, as were bigger bottles. Television commercials portray Cif as strong rather than convenient.[51]
- Unilever's Rexona deodorant once had 30 different package designs and 48 different formulations. Advertising and branding were also executed on a local basis.[52]

In the case of Cif in Italy, managers boosted sales by making product and promotion improvements based on business intelligence findings. By contrast, the multiple formulations of the Rexona brand were, for the most part, redundant and unnecessary. To address such issues, in 1999, Unilever initiated Path to Growth. This was a program designed to reduce country-by-country tinkering with product formulations and packaging.

As noted previously, the four alternatives are not mutually exclusive. In other words, a company can simultaneously utilize different product-communication strategies in different parts of the world. For example, Nike has built a global brand by marketing technologically advanced, premium-priced athletic shoes in conjunction with advertising that emphasizes U.S.-style in-your-face brashness and "Just Do It" attitude. In the huge and strategically important China market, however, this approach had several limitations. For one thing, Nike's "bad boy" image is at odds with ingrained Chinese values such as respect for authority and filial piety. As a general rule, advertisements in China do not show disruption of harmony; this is due in part to a government that discourages dissent. Price was another issue: A regular pair of Nike shoes cost the equivalent of $60–$78 while average annual family income ranges from about $200 in rural areas to $500 in urban areas. In the mid-1990s, Nike responded by creating a shoe that could be assembled in China specifically for the Chinese market using less expensive material and sold for less than $40. After years of running ads designed for Western markets by longtime agency Wieden & Kennedy, Nike hired Chinese-speaking art directors and copywriters working in WPP Group's J. Walter Thompson ad agency in Shanghai to create new advertising featuring local athletes that would appeal to Chinese nationalistic sentiments.[53]

"You can't just import cosmetics here. Companies have to understand what beauty means to Chinese women and what they look for, and product offerings and communication have to be adjusted accordingly. It's a lot harder than selling shampoo or skin care."[54]

Daisy Ching, Regional Group Account Director for Procter & Gamble, Grey Global Group

Strategy 5: Innovation

Extension and adaptation strategies are effective approaches to many but not all global market opportunities. For example, they do not respond to markets where there is a need but not the purchasing power to buy either the existing or adapted product. Global companies are likely to encounter this situation when targeting consumers in India, China, and other emerging markets. When potential customers have limited purchasing power, a company may need to develop an entirely new product designed to address the market opportunity at a price point that is within the reach of the potential customer. The converse is also true: Companies in low-income countries that have achieved local success may have to go beyond mere adaptation by "raising the bar" and bringing product designs up to world-class standards if they are to succeed in high-income countries. **Innovation**, the process of endowing resources with a new capacity to create value, is a demanding but potentially rewarding product strategy for reaching mass markets in less developed countries as well as important market segments in industrialized countries.

---

[51]Deborah Ball, "Women in Italy Like to Clean but Shun the Quick and Easy," *The Wall Street Journal* (April 25, 2006), pp. A1, A12.
[52]Deborah Ball, "Too Many Cooks: Despite Revamp, Unwieldy Unilever Falls behind Rivals," *The Wall Street Journal* (January 3, 2005), pp. A1, A5.
[53]Sally Goll Beatty, "Bad-Boy Nike Is Playing the Diplomat in China," *The Wall Street Journal* (November 10, 1997), p. B1.
[54]Laurel Wentz, "P&G Launches Cover Girl in China," *Advertising Age* (October 31, 2005), p. 22.

Two entrepreneurs working independently recognized that millions of people around the globe need low-cost eyeglasses. Robert J. Morrison, an American optometrist, created Instant Eyeglasses. These glasses utilize conventional lenses, can be assembled in minutes, and sell for about $20 per pair. Joshua Silva, a physics professor at Oxford University, took a more high-tech approach: glasses with transparent membrane lenses filled with clear silicone fluid. Using two manual adjusters, users can increase or decrease the power of the lenses by regulating the amount of fluid in them. Professor Silva hopes to sell the glasses in developing countries for about $10 per pair.[55] Another example of the innovation strategy is the South African company that licensed the British patent for a hand-cranked, battery-powered radio. The radio was designed by an English inventor responding to the need for radios in low-income countries. Consumers in these countries do not have electricity in their homes, and they cannot afford the cost of replacement batteries. His invention is an obvious solution: a hand-cranked radio. It is ideal for the needs of low-income people in emerging markets. Users simply crank the radio, and it will play on the charge generated by a short cranking session for almost an hour.

Sometimes manufacturers in developing countries that intend to go global also utilize the innovation strategy. For example, Thermax, an Indian company, had achieved great success in its domestic market with small industrial boilers. Engineers developed a new design for the Indian market that significantly reduced the size of the individual boiler unit. However, the new design was not likely to succeed outside India because installation was complex and time consuming. In India, where labor costs are low, relatively elaborate installation requirements are not an issue. The situation is different in higher-wage countries where industrial customers demand sophisticated integrated systems that can be installed quickly. The managing director at Thermax instructed his engineers to revise the design for the world market with ease of installation as a key attribute. The gamble paid off: Today, Thermax is one of the world's largest producers of small boilers.[56]

The winners in global competition are the companies that can develop products offering the most benefits, which in turn create the greatest value for buyers anywhere in the world. In some instances, value is not defined in terms of performance, but rather in terms of customer perception. Product quality is essential—indeed, it is frequently a given—but it is also necessary to support the product quality with imaginative, value-creating advertising and marketing communications. Most industry experts believe that a global appeal and a global advertising campaign are more effective in creating the perception of value than a series of separate national campaigns.

How to Choose a Strategy

Most companies seek product-communications strategies that optimize company profits over the long term. Which strategy for global markets best achieves this goal? There is no general answer to this question. For starters, the considerations noted before must be addressed. In addition, it is worth noting that managers run the risk of committing two types of errors regarding product and communication decisions. One error is to fall victim to the **"not invented here" (NIH) syndrome**, *ignoring* decisions made by subsidiary or affiliate managers. Managers who behave in this way are essentially abandoning any effort to leverage product-communication policies outside the home-country market. The other error has been to *impose* policies upon all affiliate companies on the assumption that what is right for customers in the home market must also be right for customers everywhere.

To sum up, the choice of product-communication strategy in global marketing is a function of three key factors: (1) the product itself, defined in terms of the function or need it

"Designing a Harley-Davidson motorcycle for international markets requires constant collaboration among design teams around the world. We use video-conferencing, phone calls, e-mail, and on-site meetings to enhance communications. We advise our engineers to stay close to the customers in the markets in which the customers are located so we can quickly react to changing customer desires and international regulations.[57]
Bruce Roberts, Harley-Davidson mechanical design engineer

---

[55]Amy Borrus, "Eyeglasses for the Masses," *Business Week* (November 20, 1995), pp. 104–105; Nicholar Thompson, "Self-Adjusted Glasses Could Be Boon to Africa," *The New York Times* (December 10, 2002), p. D6.
[56]Christopher A. Bartlett and Sumantra Ghoshal, "Going Global: Lessons from Late Movers," *Harvard Business Review* 78, no. 2 (March–April 2000), p. 137.
[57]Bruce Wiebusch, "Deere, Hogs, and International Design," *Design News* (November 18, 2002).

TABLE 10-3 Product Markets Compared: United States and EU Versus BRIC

United States/EU	Brazil	Russia	India	China
Product Development and Intellectual Property Rights (IPR)				
Sophisticated product-design capabilities are available. Governments enforce IPR and protect trademarks so R&D investments yield competitive advantages.	Local design capability exists. IPR disputes have arisen in some sectors.	Russia possesses a strong local design capability but exhibits an ambivalent attitude about IPR. Sufficient regulatory authority exists, but enforcement is inconsistent.	Some local design capability is available. IPR problems with the United States exist in some industries. Regulatory bodies monitor product quality and fraud.	Imitation and piracy abound. Punishment for IPR theft varies across provinces and by level of corruption.
Brand Perceptions and Management				
Markets are mature and have strong local and global brands. The profusion of brands clutters consumer choice. Numerous ad agencies are available.	Consumers accept both local and global brands. Global as well as local ad agencies are present.	Consumers prefer global brands in automobiles and high tech. Local brands thrive in the food and beverage businesses. Both local and global ad agencies are available.	Consumers buy both local and global brands. Global ad agencies are present, but they have been less successful than local ad agencies.	Consumers prefer to buy products from American, European, and Japanese companies. Global ad agencies dominate the business.

Source: Adapted from Tarun Khanna, Krishna G. Palepu, and Jayant Sinha, "Strategies That Fit Emerging Markets," *Harvard Business Review* 83, no. 6 (June 2005), p. 69. Reprinted by permission.

serves; (2) the market, defined in terms of the conditions under which the product is used, the preferences of potential customers, and the ability and willingness to buy; and (3) adaptation and manufacturing costs to the company considering these product-communication approaches. Only after analysis of the product-market fit and of company capabilities and costs can executives choose the most profitable strategy. Table 10-3 identifies important product and communication strategy issues in the United States and EU and compares and contrasts them with the BRIC countries.

NEW PRODUCTS IN GLOBAL MARKETING

The matrix shown in Figure 10-3 provides a framework for assessing whether extension or adaptation strategies can be effective. However, the four strategic options described in the matrix do not necessarily represent the best possible responses to global market opportunities. To win in global competition, marketers, designers, and engineers must think outside the box and create innovative new products that offer superior value worldwide. In today's dynamic, competitive market environment, many companies realize that continuous development and introduction of new products are keys to survival and growth. That is the point of Strategy 5, product invention. Similarly, marketers should look for opportunities to create global advertising campaigns to support the new product or brand.

Identifying New-Product Ideas

What is a new product? A product's newness can be assessed in terms of its relation to those who buy or use it. Newness may also be organizational, as when a company acquires an already existing product with which it has no previous experience. Finally, an existing product that is not new to a company may be new to a particular market. The starting point for an effective worldwide new-product program is an information system that seeks new-product ideas from all potentially useful sources and channels these ideas to relevant screening and decision centers within the organization. Ideas can come from many sources, including customers, suppliers, competitors, company salespeople, distributors and agents, subsidiary executives, headquarters executives, documentary sources (e.g., information service reports and publications), and, finally, actual firsthand observation of the market environment.

The product may be an entirely new invention or innovation that requires a relatively large amount of learning on the part of users. When such products are successful, they create new markets and new consumption patterns that literally represent a break with the past; they are sometimes called **discontinuous innovations**.[58] For example, the VCR's revolutionary impact can be explained by the concept of time shifting: The device's initial appeal was that it freed TV viewers from the tyranny of network programming schedules. For the first time, it was possible to record television programming for viewing at a later time. The VCR's market growth and acceptance was also driven by the video rental industry, which sprang up to serve the needs of VCR owners. Likewise, the personal computer revolution that began two decades ago has resulted in the democratization of technology. When they were first introduced, PCs were a continuous innovation that dramatically transformed the way users live and work.

An intermediate category of newness is less disruptive and requires less learning on the part of consumers; such products are called **dynamically continuous innovations**. Products that embody this level of innovation share certain features with earlier generations while incorporating new features that offer added value such as a substantial improvement in performance or greater convenience. Such products cause relatively smaller disruptions of previously existing consumption patterns. The Sensor, SensorExcel, and MACH3 shaving systems represent Gillette's ongoing efforts to bring new technology to bear on wet shaving, an activity that is performed today much as it has been for decades. The consumer electronics industry has been the source of many dynamically continuous innovations. Personal stereos such as Sony's Walkman provide music on the go, something that people had grown accustomed to since the transistor radio was introduced in the 1950s; the innovation was a miniaturized cassette playback system. The advent of the compact disc in the early 1980s provided an improved music listening experience but didn't require significant behavioral changes. Similarly, much to the delight of couch potatoes everywhere, widescreen TVs with flat-panel LCD and plasma displays offer viewers significantly improved performance without enabling or requiring new behaviors.

Most new products fall into a third category, **continuous innovation**. Such products are typically "new and improved" versions of existing ones and require less R&D expenditure to develop than dynamically continuous innovations. Continuous innovations cause minimal disruption of existing consumption patterns and require the least amount of learning on the part of buyers. As noted previously, newness can be evaluated relative to a buyer or user. When a current PC user seeking an upgrade buys a new model with a faster processor or more memory, the PC can be viewed as a continuous innovation. However, to a first-time user, the same computer represents a discontinuous innovation. Consumer packaged goods companies and food marketers rely heavily on continuous innovation when rolling out new products. These often take the form of **line extensions** such as new sizes, flavors, and low-fat versions. The three degrees of product newness can be represented in terms of a continuum as shown in Figure 10-4.

FIGURE 10-4

New Product Continuum

---

[58]The terminology and framework described here are adapted from Thomas Robertson, "The Process of Innovation and the Diffusion of Innovation," *Journal of Marketing* 31, no. 1 (January 1967), pp. 14–19.

New-Product Development

A major driver for the development of global products is the cost of product R&D. As competition intensifies, companies discover they can reduce the cost of R&D for a product by developing a global product design. Often the goal is to create a single **platform**, or core product design element or component, that can be quickly and cheaply adapted to various country markets. As Christopher Sinclair noted during his tenure as president and CEO of PepsiCo Foods and Beverages International, "What you really want to do is look at the four or five platforms that can allow you to cut across countries, become a scale operator, and do the things that global marketers do."[59]

Even automobiles, which must meet national safety and pollution standards, are now designed with global markets in mind. With a global product platform, automakers can offer an adaptation of a global design as needed instead of creating unique designs for individual countries or geographic regions. The Ford Focus, launched in Europe at the end of 1998 and in the United States in 1999, is being marketed globally with a minimum of adaptation. The chief program engineer on the Focus project was from Great Britain, the chief technical officer was German, the project manager was Irish, and an Anglo-Australian was chief designer. Under Ford 2000, about $1,000 per vehicle was cut out of the development cost.[60]

A standardized platform was also a paramount consideration when GM set about the task of redesigning its minivan. GM's globally minded board directed the design team to create a vehicle that would be popular in both the United States and Europe. Because roads in Europe are typically narrower and fuel is more expensive, the European engineers lobbied for a vehicle that was smaller than the typical minivan. In the end, interior designers were able to provide ample interior space in a slightly smaller body. By using lightweight metals such as magnesium for some components, vehicle weight was minimized, with a corresponding improvement in fuel economy. In the United States, the minivans are marketed as the Chevrolet Venture, Pontiac Transport, and Oldsmobile Silhouette. The Opel Sentra version will be exported to Germany; the right-hand-drive Vauxhall Sintra is destined for the British market.[61]

Other design-related costs, whether incurred by the manufacturer or the end user, must also be considered. *Durability* and *quality* are important product characteristics that must be appropriate for the proposed market. In the United States and Europe, car buyers do not wish to incur high service bills. Ironically, the new Ford Focus was designed to be less expensive to maintain and repair. For example, engine removal takes only about 1.5 hours, about half the time required to remove the engine in the discontinued Escort. In addition, body panels are bolted together rather than welded, and the rear signal lights are mounted higher so they are less likely to be broken in minor parking lot mishaps.

The International New-Product Department

As noted previously, a high volume of information flow is required to scan adequately for new-product opportunities, and considerable effort is subsequently required to screen these opportunities to identify candidates for product development. The best organizational design for addressing these requirements is a new-product department. Managers in such a department engage in several activities. First, they ensure that all relevant information sources are continuously tapped for new-product ideas. Second, they screen these ideas to identify candidates for investigation. Third, they investigate and analyze selected new-product ideas. Finally, they ensure that the organization commits resources to the most likely new-product candidates and is continuously involved in an orderly program of new-product introduction and development on a worldwide basis.

---

[59]"Fritos 'Round the World," *Brandweek* (March 27, 1995), pp. 32, 35.

[60]Robert L. Simison, "Ford Hopes Its New Focus Will Be a Global Bestseller," *The Wall Street Journal* (October 8, 1998), p. B10.

[61]Rebecca Blumenstein, "While Going Global, GM Slips at Home," *The Wall Street Journal* (January 8, 1997), pp. B1, B4.

With the enormous number of possible new products, most companies establish screening grids in order to focus on those ideas that are most appropriate for investigation. The following questions are relevant to this task:

1. How big is the market for this product at various prices?
2. What are the likely competitive moves in response to our activity with this product?
3. Can we market the product through our existing structure? If not, what changes will be required, and what costs will be incurred to make the changes?
4. Given estimates of potential demand for this product at specified prices with estimated levels of competition, can we source the product at a cost that will yield an adequate profit?
5. Does this product fit our strategic development plan? (a) Is the product consistent with our overall goals and objectives? (b) Is the product consistent with our available resources? (c) Is the product consistent with our management structure? (d) Does the product have adequate global potential?

For example, the corporate development team at Virgin evaluates more than a dozen proposals each day from outside the company, as well as proposals from Virgin staff members. Brad Rosser, Virgin's former Group Corporate Development Director, headed the team for several years. When assessing new-product ideas, Rosser and his team looked for synergy with existing Virgin products, pricing, marketing opportunities, risk versus return on investment, and whether the idea "uses or abuses" the Virgin brand. Examples of ventures that have been given the green light are Virgin Jeans, a denim clothing store chain; Virgin Bride, a wedding consulting service; and Virgin Net, an Internet service provider.[62]

Testing New Products

The major lesson of new-product introduction outside the home market has been that whenever a product interacts with human, mechanical, or chemical elements, there is the potential for a surprising and unexpected incompatibility. Because virtually *every* product matches this description, it is important to test a product under actual market conditions before proceeding with full-scale introduction. A test does not necessarily involve a full-scale test-marketing effort. It may be simply observing the actual use of the product in the target market.

Failure to assess actual use conditions can lead to big surprises, as Unilever learned when it rolled out a new detergent brand in Europe without sufficient testing. Unilever spent $150 million to develop the new detergent, which was formulated with a stain-fighting manganese complex molecule intended to clean fabrics faster at lower temperatures than competing products such as Procter & Gamble's Ariel. Backed by a $300 million marketing budget, the detergent was launched in April 1994 as Persil Power, Omo Power, and other brand names. After a restructuring, Unilever had cut the time required to roll out new products in Europe from 3 years to 16 months. In this particular instance, the increased efficiency combined with corporate enthusiasm for the new formula resulted in a marketing debacle. Consumers discovered that some clothing items were damaged after being washed with Power. P&G was quick to capitalize on the situation; P&G ran newspaper ads denouncing Power and commissioned lab tests to verify that the damage did, in fact, occur. Unilever chairman Sir Michael Perry called the Power fiasco, "the greatest marketing setback we've seen." Unilever reformulated Power, but it was too late to save the brand. The company lost the opportunity to gain share against P&G in Europe.[63]

---

[62]Elena Bowes, "Virgin Flies in Face of Conventions," *Ad Age International* (January 1997), p. i4.
[63]Laurel Wentz, "Unilever's Power Failure a Wasteful Use of Haste," *Advertising Age* (May 6, 1995), p. 42.

Summary

The product is the most important element of a company's marketing program. Global marketers face the challenge of formulating coherent product and brand strategies on a worldwide basis. A **product** can be viewed as a collection of tangible and intangible attributes that collectively provide benefits to a buyer or user. A **brand** is a complex bundle of images and experiences in the mind of the customer. In most countries, **local brands** compete with **international brands** and **global brands**. A **local product** is available in a single country; an **international product** is available in several countries; a **global product** meets the wants and needs of a global market.

A global brand has the same name and a similar image and positioning in most parts of the world. Many global companies leverage favorable **brand images** and high **brand equity** by employing **combination (tiered) branding**, **co-branding**, and **brand extension** strategies. Companies can create strong brands in all markets through **global brand leadership**. **Maslow's needs hierarchy** is a needs-based framework that offers a way of understanding opportunities to develop local and global products in different parts of the world. Some products and brands benefit from the **country-of-origin effect**. Product decisions must also address packaging issues such as **labeling** and **aesthetics**. Also, **express warranty** policies must be appropriate for each country market.

Product and communications strategies can be viewed within a framework that allows for combinations of three strategies: **extension strategy**, **adaptation strategy**, and **creation strategy**. Five strategic alternatives are open to companies pursuing geographic expansion: **product-communication extension**, **product extension-communication adaptation**, **product adaptation-communication extension**, **product-communication adaptation (dual adaptation)**, and **product invention (innovation)**. The strategic alternative(s) that a particular company chooses will depend on the product and the need it serves, customer preferences and purchasing power, and the costs of adaptation versus standardization. **Product transformation** occurs when a product that has been introduced into new country markets serves a different function or is used differently than originally intended. When choosing a strategy, management should consciously strive to avoid the **"not invented here" syndrome**.

Global competition has put pressure on companies to excel at developing standardized product **platforms** that can serve as a foundation for cost-efficient adaptation. New products can be classified as **discontinuous**, **dynamically continuous**, or **continuous innovations**. A successful product launch requires an understanding of how markets develop: sequentially over time or simultaneously. Today, many new products are launched in multiple national markets as product development cycles shorten and product development costs soar.

Discussion Questions

1. What is the difference between a product and a brand?
2. How do local, international, and global products differ? Cite examples.
3. What are some of the elements that make up a brand? Are these elements tangible or intangible?
4. What criteria should global marketers consider when making product design decisions?
5. How can buyer attitudes about a product's country of origin affect marketing strategy?
6. Identify several global brands. What are some of the reasons for the global success of the brands you chose?
7. Each August, *Business Week* magazine features a survey of global brands as a cover story. The top-ranked brands for 2008 are shown in Table 10-2. Browse through the list and choose any brand that interests you. Compare its 2008 ranking with the most recent ranking, which you can find either by referring to the print version of *Business Week* or by accessing the article online. How has the brand's ranking changed? Consult additional

sources (e.g., articles from print media, annual reports, the company's Web site) to enhance your understanding of the factors and forces that contributed to the brand's move up or down in the rankings.

8. Hofstede's social values framework can be used to help explain the Asian version of Maslow's hierarchy. Which dimension from Table 4-3 (p. 155) is most relevant? In Chapter 4, we also noted the differences between innovation diffusion processes in Asia and the West. Review the discussion on pages 162 and 163. Can you relate it to Figure 10-1?

9. Briefly describe various combinations of product-communication strategies available to global marketers. When is it appropriate to use each?

10. Compare and contrast the three categories of innovation discussed in the chapter. Which type of innovation do flat-panel widescreen HDTVs represent? The iPhone?

Product problems initially made headlines in 2008 after a turbine blade manufactured by Suzlon and financed by John Deere Wind Energy cracked and broke off a tower in Illinois. Although this was the sole reported incident of a blade actually falling, the incident raised concerns about the quality of Suzlon's products. The company had attempted to address the quality problem. It announced a program to strengthen or replace 1,251 blades—almost the entire number it had sold in the United States—after cracks were found on more than 60 blades on turbines run by Deere and Edison International's Edison Mission Energy.

Despite Suzlon's efforts to address the quality issue, problems continued. Edison claimed blades were splitting and planned to delay their wind-generation development. Edison refused to make further purchases and announced it would consider switching to one of Suzlon's competitors. In response, Suzlon spokesperson Vivek Kher claimed the cracks were not due to faulty blades. Instead, he blamed the Midwest's unexpectedly violent changes in wind direction. However, these problems are not limited only to the U.S. market. Suzlon's products in India appear to have similar flaws. One of Suzlon's largest Indian customers claimed that Suzlon's products "are not fit to handle the wind."

While battling product reliability and durability problems, other product development issues arose. The turbines manufactured by Suzlon failed to create as much energy as originally promised due to differences in the U.S. electrical grid and the power grid in India. To address the problem, Suzlon quickly converted turbines to work in the United States. In addition, some turbines installed in Minnesota broke down during the winter due to the region's extremely cold winter temperatures. Electrical heaters were installed to keep the control panels from freezing; however, the placement of the heaters has created electrical problems for the turbines.

The fact that doubts have been raised about the reliability and durability of Suzlon's products suggests that the company's research and technology-update programs have not kept pace with customer needs. One member of Suzlon's management team acknowledged as much; Ashish Dhawan, an independent director on Suzlon's board stated: "It's not that their technology is bad [. . .] but they've been a laggard." Would a company that once prided itself on rapid innovation and design changes be able to stay ahead of competitors? Or, would the company fall victim to unfavorable publicity?

While the short-term outlook for Suzlon may be bleak, the long-term outlook is becoming clouded as well. Policymakers in many parts of the world realize the importance of reducing dependence on imported oil and cutting greenhouse gas emissions. However, the collapse in oil prices and the global economic downturn mean that it will be difficult for Suzlon's customers to obtain financing for wind-energy generation projects.

In an interview in April 2008, Suzlon's chairman and managing director was asked about the concerns with the economy and the product. Tanti responded with confidence. "There are no companies growing the way we are growing. Within four years we will feed product technology to the whole world," Tanti said. He was confident that Suzlon would double its annual production capacity by 2010, insisting that the cracked-blade problem doesn't stem from any fundamental design flaw.

However, critics and others are not convinced that Tanti's optimism is well founded. Only time will tell, but one thing is clear: Suzlon needs to fix the problems with its product quality.

Case 10-1 Discussion Questions

1. Assess the global market opportunity for sustainable energy sources such as wind turbines.
2. Do you think Suzlon can address the quality control issue before the company's brand image is damaged?
3. What impact do you think the global economic downturn and credit crunch will have on a company like Suzlon?

Sources: Saritha Rai, "Bulls Are Running to India, Raising Fears of a Bubble," *The New York Times* (April 18, 2008), p. C6; Keith Bradsher, "Indian Turbine Maker Becomes World Class as Rising Economies Discover New Source of Wealth," *The New York Times* (September 28, 2008), p. C2; Tom Wright, "Winds Shift for Renewable Energy as Oil Price Sinks, Money Gets Tight," *The Wall Street Journal* (October 20, 2008), p. B1; Wright, "India's Suzlon Energy Encounters Headwinds at Home; Turbine Maker Says Electricity Shortfall Due to Power Grid Problems, Wind Speeds," *The Wall Street Journal* (August 25, 2008), p. B1; Wright, "Edison Unit Cancels Suzlon Order," *The Wall Street Journal* (June 10, 2008), p. B2.

Case 10-2
Godiva Chocolatier and Godiva Gems

Godiva Chocolatier, a Belgium chocolate manufacturer renowned for its premium quality handcrafted chocolates, was founded in 1926 in Brussels by the master chocolatier Joseph Draps. The company makes and sells premium chocolate delights including bonbons, truffles, flavored coffee, cocoa mixes, cookies, ice cream, and liqueurs. Godiva has always been an admired brand with an upscale appeal in the market supported by its "golden boxes."

As the success of Godiva grew in Belgium, it started to expand into international markets by opening exclusive Godiva stores in Paris, France, in 1958, followed by the United Kingdom, Germany, Italy, and many more European countries. The Godiva brand then expanded to North America in 1966 as an importer and distributor of Godiva chocolates from Belgium in one of the most elegant department stores in Philadelphia. The first Godiva store was opened on New York's Fifth Avenue in 1972. The expansion then continued in Asia by the opening of a corner shop at one of the prestigious department stores in Tokyo in 1972. In 1988, the first Godiva store was opened in Hong Kong, followed by store openings in Taiwan and Singapore.

Presently, Godiva's products are available worldwide in over 80 countries around the world, at 450 exclusive Godiva stores as well as at finer department and specialty stores. The company also issues mail-order catalogs in North America and accepts phone and Internet orders.

In 1967, New Jersey–based Campbell Soup Company acquired Godiva Chocolatier and invested heavily to turn it into a worldwide renowned brand. However, in August 2007, Campbell Soup

Godiva Chocolatier, a Belgium chocolate maker, operates 450 shops worldwide and their products are available in over 10,000 other retailers. The business, founded in 1926, is now owned by a major Turkish company, despite the fact that many of the largest and best-known confectionery and food manufacturers in the world were bidding to purchase Godiva. Ulker, the new owners, began as a small biscuit baker in 1944; they now sell over 700 products under 132 brand names. In Turkey Ülker has 60 percent of the chocolate market.
Source: © Jeffrey Blackler/Alamy

Company announced that it was looking for strategic alternatives for its Godiva business. The company decided to sell Godiva when a strategic review reported that luxuries like chocolates were strategically unfit for the Campbell Soup Company, which was focusing on simple meals and engaging in mass-market products. The company decided to focus more on its traditional business of soups, baked snacks, and vegetable-based beverages, which are increasingly being marketed as part of a healthy lifestyle, to which chocolate did not fit.

Major international food giants and conglomerates such as Hershey, Mars, Nestlé, and Lindt made bids for Godiva. On December 20, 2007, Campbell announced that it entered into an agreement to sell Godiva to Ülker Group, one of the largest consumer goods companies in the Turkish food industry. The acquisition was completed on March 18, 2008, and Godiva was officially sold to Yildiz Holding, the owner of Ülker Group, for $850 million. The 61-year-old Ülker Group is a conglomerate offering a wide assortment of biscuits, cookies, chocolates, confectioneries, beverages, and dairies to its customers. Ülker Group has a solid position in the local food market with its high profitability, strong financial metrics, and adequate liquidity position. The company is reported to be the market leader in the Turkish chocolate industry, holding a market share of 60 percent in 2009.

The acquisition of Godiva is a definite achievement for Ülker Group and represents a strategic fit with Ülker Group's portfolio. This business deal is expected to help the company to diversify its product offerings by entering the premium-luxury chocolate market and is in line with its business strategies of expanding vertically through mergers and acquisitions rather than growing horizontally. The company aims to position its brand image through an international name in the regional and global markets. Ülker's Biscuits, Chocolate and Cake Division President Ali Ülker also reported that the purchase of the world-renowned Godiva brand was a step toward the company becoming a regional power. The company already dominates the Turkish market and exports its products internationally to 95 countries; it has strong roots and brand presence in the Middle East and Turkish Republics. The Godiva takeover will allow Ülker Group to enter into the global markets and take a serious step in its attempts to be a global company. Besides, this deal is being viewed as a success story for the Turkish economy since $850 million is the largest amount of money a Turkish firm has ever paid in acquisition of a foreign firm.

Godiva Gems: A "Little" Taste of Godiva Anytime, Anywhere

The acquisition has worked out well, and Godiva has grown into a $500 million business with upscale products sold at more than 10,400 stores around the world. In fall 2009, the chocolatier decided to go mass market and introduced a lower-priced line named "Godiva Gems," intended to help consumers perceive the premium Godiva brand as more affordable or accessible. Gems are marketed as ideal for enjoying a "little taste of Godiva chocolates anytime and anywhere." Perfect for the consumers who appreciate the highest quality chocolate at an affordable price, the launch of

Godiva Gems is defined as a groundbreaking moment in the world's leading premium chocolate producer's history.

Godiva Gems are individually wrapped packages of smaller pieces of chocolates so that they can be shared. The collection features three varieties: Solid Gems, Caramel Gems, and Truffle Gems, all are available in rich milk or dark chocolate. Made with the finest cocoa and in keeping with Godiva's Belgian heritage, Solid Gems are a treat for any chocolate lover, Caramel Gems are soft chewy centers of caramel enrobed in chocolate, and Truffle Gems feature a smooth filling crafted in the tradition of Godiva's world-renowned truffles. Godiva Gems are available in packages containing a single variety of truffles, caramels, or solids. Consumers can purchase Gems bags for as low as $4.99 for a range of 12 to 18 chocolates or $9.99 for a bag of 20 to 29 chocolates. These products are offered for sale in Godiva stores, newsstands, duty-free shops, and select premium grocers like Safeway, Publix, and Wegmans, making it possible for consumers to easily obtain these chocolates.

Although one may question whether these Gems may damage Godiva's premium chocolate brand image, this attempt is actually seen as an excellent adaptation of the chocolatier to the challenges in the marketing environment. Jim Goldman, president and CEO of Godiva Chocolatier Worldwide, states that Godiva Chocolatier has been known for over 80 years as the leader in the premium chocolate category. He also asserts that Godiva's delicious chocolates have traditionally been packaged and sold primarily as gifts, and have been available only in exclusive stores and department stores. With the launch of the new Godiva Gems, the chocolatier has broadened the availability and accessibility of its high-quality chocolate. This exciting move for Godiva and its consumers is in line with the changes in the consumer behavior brought on by the sluggish economy. Goldman, who has managed Godiva since 2004, also asserts that this expansion became possible only with the support of the new owner, Ülker Group. He further states that this new downmarket move aims to meet the needs of today's consumers who have given up many luxury goods but are still treating themselves with lower-priced impulse purchases like chocolates. With the sales of Godiva Gems, the company is trying to play a different game, other than its offering of its famous gold boxes of Godiva chocolate. Already, Gems have accounted for 10 percent of sales in its 423 company stores since the early-September 2009 introduction. The company also forecasts that Gems will be in 2,000 supermarkets by year-end.

Many consumers may think that there's a risk in this new product introduction decision and if Godiva's widely available Gems will turn out to be as good as its golden-boxed chocolates, this could lead to cannibalization. Also, there is still the question of whether the company is risking the Godiva brand in consumers' minds. Goldman reported that the company is not compromising the quality of its chocolates, and with the introduction of Godiva Gems the company aims to appeal to more consumers who will consume just more Godiva every day.

Godiva is not abandoning the high-end market either. Alongside the Gems selling on the supermarket shelves, the company also introduced "Legacy Truffles," which retail for $54 for 20 pieces. Godiva executives also report that baked goods like cakes will soon be available from the company's Web site. These new product offerings are forecasted to help double the $500 million revenue of the company by 2014. Finally, Yildiz Holding, the parent company of Godiva, continues investments to grow the Godiva brand in different markets. The company is preparing to enter China with two store openings and is also planning to open two stores in its home country of Turkey in the beginning of 2010.

Visit the Web site

www.godiva.com and www.godiva.com/gems

Discussion Questions

1. Define "the product" offered by Godiva. Identify the different levels of the product. Discuss the attempts made by the management to come up with an augmented product.
2. Do you think that the Godiva brand could be damaged after the introduction of the new product to the lower end of the market? Do you see any risk of cannibalization of this line extension for the existing product line? Why or why not? Discuss.
3. Is "Godiva Gems" an international or a global product/brand? Discuss whether the brand holds global brand characteristics.
4. What are the possible impacts of the "country-of-origin" and "packaging" in motivating consumers to purchase Godiva chocolates.
5. Godiva is entering new markets like China and Turkey. What strategy would you offer to the company in its global product planning decisions in term of standardization versus adaptation?

Sources: "Campbell Soup Sells Godiva for $850 Million," *The New York Times* (December 20, 2007): "New Product: 'Godiva Chocolatier Gems (TM)' Individually Wrapped Chocolates by Godiva Chocolatier, Inc.," *FoodBiz Daily* (August 27, 2009), www.foodbizdaily.com. Accessed November 1, 2009; Stuart Elliott, "Godiva Rides in a New Direction," *The New York Times* (November 16, 2009); Şükrü Andaç, "Godiva 2010 başında Nişantaşı ve Cadde'de," *Milliyet Newspaper* (October 27, 2009), p.11; "Ülker'in 'Kaşıkçı Elması,'" *Fortune* (July 1, 2008), pp. 149–152; Venessa Wong, "Godiva Goes to the Supermarket," *BusinessWeek* Special Report (October 14, 2009); Zainab Mansoor, "Ülker Group Strikes with Belgian Chocolatier GODIVA's Acquisition—Belgian Chocolates to Resurface as Turkish Delights," *Dinar Standard* (January 26, 2008); www.godiva.com. Accessed November 1, 2009; www.ulker.com.tr. Accessed November 2, 2009.

Pricing Decisions

Case 11-1
Low-Cost Logan: The Race to Build the World's Cheapest Car

In the 1950s and 1960s, the space race pitted the Soviet Union against the United States in an effort to explore outer space. Half a century later, the International Space Station is a collaborative effort involving Russia, the United States, and other nations. Meanwhile, a new race is underway. This one is much more "down to earth," and does not involve superpowers in different hemispheres jostling for geopolitical advantage. Rather, this twenty-first-century competition involves efforts by leading automakers in Asia, Europe, and the United States to create inexpensive cars that can be sold in huge volumes to consumers in India and other developing countries.

Renault, the French automotive group, was a pioneer in the low-price segment with its Logan; launched in 2004, more than a half million units have been sold (see Exhibit 11-1). Initially, the Logan was produced at a single plant operated by Renault's Dacia affiliate in Romania. As Dacia Chairman Luc-Alexandre Ménard explained, "At the time, we weren't too sure of what we would do with this car. It was meant to be a one-off, a Trojan horse to penetrate new markets in developing countries." Today, Logans are manufactured in seven countries, including Iran, India, and Brazil; the cars are available for sale in more than 50 countries.

In general, two basic factors determine the boundaries within which prices should be set. The first is product cost, which establishes a *price floor*, or minimum price. Although pricing a product below the cost

Exhibit 11-1: The Dacia Logan is at the center of Renault chief Carlos Ghosn's low-price strategy. The Logan doesn't have power steering or air conditioning; even so, it has proven to be very popular in both emerging and developed countries. The Logan's success demonstrates a very simple marketing idea: Price sells cars. Many first-time buyers have discovered that they can own a new Logan for about the same price as a motorcycle. In 2009, government stimulus programs in France, Germany, and elsewhere that included "cash-for-clunkers" incentives kept demand high.
Source: Pierre Verdy/AFP/Newscom.

boundary is certainly possible, few firms can afford to do this over the long run. Moreover, as we saw in Chapter 8, low prices in export markets can invite dumping investigations.

Second, prices for comparable substitute products create a *price ceiling*, or maximum price. In many instances, global competition puts pressure on the pricing policies and related cost structures of domestic companies. The imperative to cut costs—especially fixed costs—is one of the reasons for the growth of outsourcing. In some cases, local market conditions such as low incomes force companies to innovate by creating new products that can be profitably sold at low prices. For more on the auto industry's efforts to create low-cost cars, turn to the continuation of Case 11-1 at the end of the chapter.

Between the lower and upper boundary for every product there is an *optimum price*, which is a function of the demand for the product as determined by the willingness and ability of customers to buy. In this chapter we will review basic pricing concepts, and then discuss several pricing topics that pertain to global marketing. These include target costing, price escalation, and environmental considerations such as currency fluctuations and inflation. In the second half of the chapter, we will discuss gray market goods, dumping, price fixing, transfer pricing, and countertrade.

BASIC PRICING CONCEPTS

Generally speaking, international trade results in lower prices for goods. Lower prices, in turn, help keep a country's rate of inflation in check. In a true global market, the **law of one price** would prevail: All customers in the market could get the best product available for the best price. As Lowell Bryan and his collaborators note in *Race for the World*, a global market exists for certain products such as crude oil, commercial aircraft, diamonds, and integrated circuits: All other things being equal, a Boeing 787 costs the same worldwide. By contrast, beer, compact discs, and many other products that are available around the world are actually being offered in markets that are national rather than global in nature. That is, these are markets where national competition reflects differences in factors such as costs, regulation, and the intensity of the rivalry among industry members.[1] The beer market is extremely fragmented; even though Budweiser is the leading global brand, it commands less than 4 percent of the total market. The nature of the beer market explains why; for example, a six-pack of Heineken varies in price by as much as 50 percent (adjusted for purchasing power parity, transportation, and other transaction costs) depending on where it is sold. In Japan, for example, the price is a function of the competition between Heineken, other imports, and five national producers—Kirin, Asahi, Sapporo, Suntory, and Orion—that collectively command 60 percent of the market.

Because of these differences in national markets, the global marketer must develop pricing systems and pricing policies that take into account price floors, price ceilings, and optimum prices. A firm's pricing system and policies must also be consistent with other uniquely global opportunities and constraints. For example, many companies that are active in the 15 nations of the euro zone are adjusting to the new cross-border transparency of prices. Similarly, the Internet has made price information for many products available around the globe. Companies must carefully consider how customers in one country or region will react if they discover they are paying significantly higher prices for the same product as customers in other parts of the world.

There is another important internal organizational consideration besides cost. Within the typical corporation, there are many interest groups and, frequently, conflicting price objectives. Divisional vice presidents, regional executives, and country managers are each concerned about

---

[1]Lowell Bryan, *Race for the World: Strategies to Build a Great Global Firm* (Boston: Harvard Business School Press, 1999), pp. 40–41.

profitability at their respective organizational levels. Similarly, the director of global marketing seeks competitive prices in world markets. The controller and financial vice president are concerned about profits. The manufacturing vice president seeks long production runs for maximum manufacturing efficiency. The tax manager is concerned about compliance with government transfer pricing legislation. Finally, company counsel is concerned about the antitrust implications of global pricing practices. Ultimately, price generally reflects the goals set by members or the sales staff, product managers, corporate division chiefs, and/or the company's chief executive.

GLOBAL PRICING OBJECTIVES AND STRATEGIES

Whether dealing with a single home country market or multiple country markets, marketing managers must develop pricing objectives as well as strategies for achieving those objectives. However, a number of pricing issues are unique to global marketing. The pricing strategy for a particular product may vary from country to country; a product may be positioned as a low-priced, mass-market product in some countries and a premium-priced, niche product in others. Stella Artois beer is a case in point: As noted in Chapter 7, it is a low-priced, "everyday" beer in Belgium but a premium-priced brand in export markets. Pricing objectives may also vary depending on a product's life-cycle stage and the country-specific competitive situation. In making global pricing decisions, it is also necessary to factor in external considerations such as the added cost associated with shipping goods long distances across national boundaries. The issue of global pricing can also be fully integrated in the product-design process, an approach widely used by Japanese companies.

Market Skimming and Financial Objectives

Price can be used as a strategic variable to achieve specific financial goals, including return on investment, profit, and rapid recovery of product development costs. When financial criteria such as profit and maintenance of margins are the objectives, the product must be part of a superior value proposition for buyers; price is integral to the total positioning strategy. The **market skimming** pricing strategy is often part of a deliberate attempt to reach a market segment that is willing to pay a premium price for a particular brand or for a specialized or unique product. Companies that seek competitive advantage by pursuing differentiation strategies or positioning their products in the premium segment frequently use market skimming. LVMH and other luxury goods marketers that target the global elite market segment use skimming strategies (see Case 11-2). For years, Mercedes-Benz utilized a skimming strategy; however, this created an opportunity for Toyota to introduce its luxury Lexus line and undercut Mercedes.

The skimming pricing strategy is also appropriate in the introductory phase of the product life cycle when both production capacity and competition are limited. By setting a deliberately high price, demand is limited to innovators and early adopters who are willing and able to pay the price. When the product enters the growth stage of the life cycle and competition increases, manufacturers start to cut prices. This strategy has been used consistently in the consumer electronics industry; for example, when Sony introduced the first consumer VCRs in the 1970s, the retail price exceeded $1,000. The same was true when compact disc players were launched in the early 1980s. Within a few years, prices for these products dropped well below $500. Today, both products are considered commodities.

A similar pattern is evident with HDTVs; in the fall of 1998, HDTVs went on sale in the United States with prices starting at about $7,000. This price maximized revenue on limited volume and matched demand to available supply. Now prices for HDTVs are dropping significantly as consumers become more familiar with HDTV and its advantages and as next-generation factories in Asia bring lower costs and increased production capacity. In 2005, Sony surprised the industry by launching a 40-inch HDTV for $3,500; by the end of 2006, comparable HDTVs were selling for about $2,000. The challenge facing manufacturers now is to hold the line on prices; if they do not succeed, HDTVs may also become commoditized.

Penetration Pricing and Nonfinancial Objectives

Some companies are pursuing nonfinancial objectives with their pricing strategy. Price can be used as a competitive weapon to gain or maintain market position. Market share or other sales-based objectives are frequently set by companies that enjoy cost-leadership positions in their industry. A **market penetration pricing strategy** calls for setting price levels that are low enough to quickly build market share. Historically many companies that used this type of pricing were located in the Pacific Rim. Scale-efficient plants and low-cost labor allowed these companies to blitz the market.

It should be noted that a first-time exporter is unlikely to use penetration pricing. The reason is simple: Penetration pricing often means that the product may be sold at a loss for a certain length of time. Unlike Sony, many companies that are new to exporting cannot absorb such losses, nor are they likely to have the marketing system in place (including transportation, distribution, and sales organizations) that allows global companies like Sony to make effective use of a penetration strategy. Many companies, especially those in the food industry, launch new products that are not innovative enough to qualify for patent protection. When this occurs, penetration pricing is recommended as a means of achieving market saturation before competitors copy the product.

Companion Products: "Razors and Blades" Pricing

One crucial element is missing from the discussion of video game console pricing in the Strategic Decision Making in Global Marketing box: the video games themselves. The biggest profits in the video industry come from sales of game software; even though Sony and Microsoft may actually

---

STRATEGIC DECISION MAKING IN GLOBAL MARKETING
Sony Sets a Price for the Walkman

When Sony was developing the Walkman in 1979, initial plans called for a retail price of ¥50,000 ($249) to achieve breakeven. However, it was felt that a price of ¥35,000 ($170) was necessary to attract the all-important youth market segment. After the engineering team conceded that they could trim costs to achieve breakeven volume at a price of ¥40,000, Chairman Akio Morita pushed them further and insisted on a retail price of ¥33,000 ($165) to commemorate Sony's 33rd anniversary. At that price, even if the initial production run of 60,000 units sold out, the company would lose $35 per unit. The marketing department was convinced the product would fail: Who would want a tape recorder that couldn't record? Even Yasuo Kuroki, the project manager, hedged his bets: He ordered enough parts for 60,000 units but had only 30,000 produced. Although sales were slow immediately following the Walkman's launch in July 1979, they exploded in late summer. The rest, as the saying goes, is history.[2]

Sony has used penetration strategies with numerous other product introductions. When the portable CD player was in development in the mid-1980s, the cost per unit at initial sales volumes was estimated to exceed $600. Realizing that this was a

"no-go" price in the United States and other target markets, Chairman Morita instructed management to price the unit in the $300 range to achieve penetration. Because Sony was a global marketer, the sales volume it expected to achieve in these markets led to scale economies and lower costs.

It is not unusual for a company to change its objectives as a product proceeds through its life cycle and as competitive conditions change. For example, in 2000, Sony rolled out its next-generation game console, the PlayStation 2 (PS2), for $299; competing systems from Microsoft (Xbox) and Nintendo (GameCube) were launched one year later. By March 2001, Sony had shipped 10 million units to Asia, Europe, and the United States. As of 2004, Sony had sold more than 100 million PS2 units worldwide; according to industry estimates, one out of three American households owned a PlayStation.[3]

Sony launched the PlayStation 3 in November 2006; it is equipped with a chip that is capable of performing more than 200 billion calculations per second. The development cost of the chip alone was nearly $2 billion. Two different models were available, priced at $499 and at $599. Industry observers estimate that, initially, Sony lost $100 on each PS3 unit sold.

---

[2]P. Ranganath Nayak and John M. Ketteringham, *Breakthroughs! How Leadership and Drive Create Commercial Innovations That Sweep the World* (San Diego, CA: Pfeiffer, 1994), pp. 124–127.

[3]Lauren J. Flynn, "Deep Price Cuts Help Nintendo Climb to No. 2 in Game Sales," *The New York Times* (January 26, 2004), p. C3.

lose money on each console, sales of hit video titles generate substantial revenues and profits. Sony, Microsoft, and Nintendo receive licensing fees from the companies that create the games. Moreover, the typical households own one or two consoles but dozens of games. Since launching the first PlayStation in 1994, Sony has sold more than 200 million game consoles worldwide. During the same time period, however, sales of PlayStation games have exceeded 880 million units.

This illustrates the concept of *companion products*: a video game console has no value without software, and a DVD player has no value without movies. Additional examples abound; a razor handle has no value without blades, and Gillette can sell a single Mach3 razor for less than $5—or even give the razor away for free. Over a period of years, the company will make significant profits from selling packages of replacement blades. As the saying goes, "If you make money on the blades, you can give away the razors."

Companion products-pricing has long been the preferred strategy of Vodaphone, AT&T, and other cellular service providers. They buy handsets at prices set by Motorola, Nokia, and other manufacturers, and then subsidize the cost by offering significant discounts on (or even giving away) handsets to subscribers who sign long-term contracts. The carriers make up the price difference by charging additional fees for extras such as roaming, text messaging, and so on. However, this approach does not always work globally. For example, in most markets, Apple's iPhone is priced at the equivalent of $199. In India, however, consumers don't like to be locked in to long-term contracts, and the iPhone sells for the equivalent of $600. Moreover, Apple distributes the iPhone in India exclusively through stores operated by Airtel, an Indian carrier, and Vodaphone. Indian sales of the iPhone have been slow as consumers choose lower-priced models from Nokia and Samsung that are distributed through more retailers. Also, a significant number of $199 iPhones are making the trip from the United States to India in tourist luggage![4]

> "Nobody buys a piece of hardware because they like hardware. They buy it to play movies or music content."[5]
> Howard Stringer, CEO, Sony Corporation

Target Costing[6]

Japanese companies have traditionally approached cost issues in a way that results in substantial production savings and products that are competitively priced in the global marketplace. Toyota, Sony, Olympus, and Komatsu are some of the well-known Japanese companies that use target costing. The process, sometimes known as *design to cost*, can be described as follows:

> Target costing ensures that development teams will bring profitable products to market not only with the right level of quality and functionality but also with appropriate prices for the target customer segments. It is a discipline that harmonizes the labor of disparate participants in the development effort, from designers and manufacturing engineers to market researchers and suppliers. . . . In effect, the company reasons backward from customers' needs and willingness to pay instead of following the flawed but common practice of cost-plus pricing.[7]

Western companies are beginning to adopt some of these money-saving ideas. For example, target costing was used in the development of Renault's Logan, a car that retails for less than $10,000 in Europe (see Case 11-1). According to Luc-Alexandre Ménard, chief of Renault's Dacia unit, the design approach prevented technical personnel from adding features that customers did not consider absolutely necessary. For example, the Logan's side windows have relatively flat glass; curved glass is more attractive but it adds to the cost. The Logan was originally targeted at consumers in Eastern Europe; to the company's surprise, it has also proven to be popular in Germany and France.[8]

---

[4]Brian Caulfield, "IPhone's Pricing Problem in India," *Forbes.com* (November 18, 2008).
[5]Phred Dvorak and Merissa Marr, "Shock Treatment: Sony, Lagging Behind Rivals, Hands Reins to a Foreigner," *The Wall Street Journal* (March 7, 2005), p. A8.
[6]This section is adapted from Robin Cooper and W. Bruce Chew, "Control Tomorrow's Costs Through Today's Designs," *Harvard Business Review* 74, no. 1 (January–February 1996), pp. 88–97. See also Robin Cooper and Regine Slagmulder, "Develop Profitable New Products with Target Costing," *Sloan Management Review* 40, no. 4 (Summer 1999), pp. 23–33.
[7]Robin Cooper and W. Bruce Chew, "Control Tomorrow's Costs Through Today's Designs," *Harvard Business Review* 74, no. 1 (January–February 1996), pp. 88–97.
[8]Norihiko Shirouzu and Stephen Power, "Unthrilling but Inexpensive, the Logan Boosts Renault in Emerging Markets," *The Wall Street Journal* (October 14, 2006), pp. B1, B18.

The target costing approach can be used with inexpensive consumer nondurables as well. For example, in Mexico and other emerging markets, Procter & Gamble managers know that workers are often paid a daily wage; that's why its Mexican customers generally carry 5- and 10-peso coins. To keep prices of shampoo and detergent below, say, 11 or 12 pesos, and still ensure satisfactory profit margins, P&G uses target costing (P&G calls it "reverse engineering"). Rather than create an item and then assign a price to it—the traditional cost-plus approach—the company first estimates what consumers in emerging markets can afford to pay. From there, product attributes and manufacturing processes are adjusted to meet various pricing targets. For example, to hold down the cost of its Ace Natural detergent, used to hand-wash clothes in Mexico, P&G reduced the product's enzyme content. The result: a product that costs a peso less than a single-use packet of regular Ace. Plus, the reformulated product is gentler on the skin.[9]

As shown in Figure 11-1, the target costing process begins with market mapping and product definition and positioning; this requires using concepts and techniques discussed in Chapters 6 and 7. The marketing team must do the following:

- Determine the segment(s) to be targeted, as well as the prices that customers in the segment will be willing to pay. Using market research techniques such as conjoint analysis, the team seeks to better understand how customers will perceive product features and functionalities.
- Compute overall target costs with the aim of ensuring the company's future profitability.
- Allocate the target costs to the product's various functions. Calculate the gap between the target cost and the estimated actual production cost. Think of debits and credits in accounting: Because the target cost is fixed, additional funds allocated to one subassembly team for improving a particular function must come from another subassembly team.
- Obey the cardinal rule: If the design team can't meet the targets, the product should not be launched.

Only at this point are design, engineering, and supplier pricing issues dealt with; extensive consultation between all value chain members is used to meet the target. Once the necessary negotiations and trade-offs have been settled, manufacturing begins, followed by continuous cost reduction. In the U.S. process, cost is typically determined after design, engineering, and marketing decisions have been made in sequential fashion; if the cost is too high, the process cycles back to square one—the design stage.

Calculating Prices: Cost-Plus Pricing and Export Price Escalation

The laptop computer exemplifies many characteristics of today's global marketplace: No matter what the brand—Acer, Apple, Dell, or Hewlett-Packard, for example—components are typically sourced in several different countries and the computers themselves are assembled in China,

FIGURE 11-1

The Target Costing Process

Source: Robin Cooper and W. Bruce Chew, "Control Tomorrow's Costs Through Today's Designs," *Harvard Business Review* 74, no. 1 (January–February 1996), p. 95.

---

[9]Ellen Byron, "Emerging Ambitions: P&G's Global Target: Shelves of Tiny Stores," *The Wall Street Journal* (July 16, 2007), p. A1.

TABLE 11-1 Sourcing a Laptop Computer

Component	Country of Manufacture
Hard-disk drive	Japan, China, Singapore, United States
Power supplies	China
Magnesium casings	China
Memory chips	South Korea, Taiwan, United States, Germany
Liquid-crystal displays	South Korea, Taiwan, Japan, China
Microprocessors	United States
Graphics processors	Designed in the United States, Canada; made in Taiwan

Source: Jason Dean and Pui-Wing Tam, "The Laptop Trail," *The Wall Street Journal* (June 9, 2005), p. B1.

Taiwan, or Japan (see Table 11-1). Within two days, the computers are sent via airfreight to the countries where they will be sold. As anyone who has studied managerial accounting knows, finished goods have a cost associated with the actual production. In global marketing, however, the total cost will depend on the ultimate market destination, the mode of transport, tariffs, and various fees, handling charges, and documentations costs. **Export price escalation** is the increase in the final selling price of goods traded across borders that reflects these factors. The following is a list of eight basic considerations for persons whose responsibility includes setting prices on goods that cross borders.[10]

1. Does the price reflect the product's quality?
2. Is the price competitive given local market conditions?
3. Should the firm pursue market penetration, market skimming, or some other pricing objective?
4. What type of discount (trade, cash, quantity) and allowance (advertising, trade-off) should the firm offer its international customers?
5. Should prices differ with market segment?
6. What pricing options are available if the firm's costs increase or decrease? Is demand in the international market elastic or inelastic?
7. Are the firm's prices likely to be viewed by the host-country government as reasonable or exploitative?
8. Do the foreign country's dumping laws pose a problem?

Companies frequently use a method known as cost-plus or cost-based pricing when selling goods outside their home-country markets. **Cost-based pricing** is based on an analysis of internal (e.g., materials, labor, testing) and external costs. As a starting point, firms that comply with Western cost accounting principles typically use the *full absorption cost method*; this defines per-unit product cost as the sum of all past or current direct and indirect manufacturing and overhead costs. However, when goods cross national borders, additional costs and expenses such as transportation, duties, and insurance are incurred. If the manufacturer is responsible for them, they too must be included. By adding the desired profit margin to the cost-plus figure, managers can arrive at a final selling price. It is important to note that, in China and some other developing countries, many manufacturing enterprises are state run and state subsidized. This makes it difficult to calculate accurate cost figures and opens a country's exporters to charges that they are selling products for less than the "true" cost of producing them.

Companies using *rigid cost-plus pricing* set prices without regard to the eight considerations previously listed. They make no adjustments to reflect market conditions outside the home country. The obvious advantage of rigid cost-based pricing is its simplicity: Assuming that both internal and external cost figures are readily available, it is relatively easy to arrive at a quote. The disadvantage is that this approach ignores demand and competitive conditions in target

---

[10]Adapted from "Price, Quotations, and Terms of Sale Are Key to Successful Exporting," *Business America* (October 4, 1993), p. 12.

Exhibit 11-2: Canada's Imax Corporation is the world's premier provider of large-format motion picture projection technology. The company has identified 900 potential markets for new Imax theaters; two-thirds of those are global. Imax has developed a lower-cost projection system called Imax MPX that fits in existing movie theaters; by improving the economics for movie exhibitors, this innovation will expand the number of available market opportunities. In China, for example, 25 Imax theaters were expected to be operating by 2008.
Source: © Morton Beebe/Corbis. All Rights Reserved.

markets; the risk is that prices will either be set too high or too low. If the rigid cost-based approach results in market success, it is only by chance. Rigid cost-plus pricing is attractive to inexperienced exporters, who are frequently less concerned with financial goals than with assessing market potential. Such exporters are typically responding to global market opportunities in a reactive manner, not proactively seeking them.

An alternative method, *flexible cost-plus pricing*, is used to ensure that prices are competitive in the context of the particular market environment. This approach is frequently used by experienced exporters and global marketers. They realize that the rigid cost-plus approach can result in severe price escalation, with the unintended result that exports are priced at levels above what customers can pay. Managers who utilize flexible cost-plus pricing are acknowledging the importance of the eight criteria listed earlier. Flexible cost-plus pricing sometimes incorporates the *estimated future cost method* to establish the future cost for all component elements. For example, the automobile industry uses palladium in catalytic converters. Because the market price of heavy metals is volatile and varies with supply and demand, component manufacturers might use the estimated future cost method to ensure that the selling price they set enables them to cover their costs.

Terms of the Sale

Every commercial transaction is based on a contract of sale, and the trade terms in that contract specify the exact point at which the ownership of merchandise is transferred from the seller to the buyer and which party in the transaction pays which costs. The following activities must be performed when goods cross international boundaries:

1. Obtaining an export license if required (in the United States, nonstrategic goods are exported under a general license that requires no specific permit)
2. Obtaining a currency permit if required
3. Packing the goods for export
4. Transporting the goods to the place of departure (this would normally involve transport by truck or rail to a seaport or airport)
5. Preparing a land bill of lading
6. Completing necessary customs export papers

7. Preparing customs or consular invoices as required by the country of destination
8. Arranging for ocean freight and preparation
9. Obtaining marine insurance and certificate of the policy

Who is responsible for performing these tasks? It depends on the terms of the sale. The internationally accepted terms of trade are known as International Commercial Terms (**Incoterms**). Incoterms are classified into four categories. **Ex-works (EXW)**, the sole "E-Term" or "origin" term among Incoterms, refers to a transaction in which the buyer takes delivery at the premises of the seller; the buyer bears all risks and expenses from that point on. In principle, ex-works affords the buyer maximum control over the cost of transporting the goods. Ex-works can be contrasted with several "D-Terms" ("post-main-carriage" or "arrival" terms). For example, under **delivered duty paid (DDP)**, the seller has agreed to deliver the goods to the buyer at the place he or she names in the country of import, with all costs, including duties, paid. Under this contract, the seller is also responsible for obtaining the import license if one is required.

Another category of Incoterms is known as "F-Terms" or "pre-main-carriage terms." Because it is suited for all modes of transport, **free carrier (FCA)** is widely used in global sales. Under FCA, transfer from seller to buyer is effected when the goods are delivered to a specified carrier at a specified destination. Two additional F-terms apply to sea and inland waterway transportation only. **Free alongside ship (FAS) named port** is the Incoterm for a transaction in which the seller places the shipment alongside, or available to, the vessel upon which the goods will be transported out of the country. The seller pays all charges up to that point. The seller's legal responsibility ends once the goods have been cleared for export; the buyer pays the cost of actually loading the shipment. FAS is often used with *break bulk cargo*, which is non-containerized, general cargo such as iron, steel, or machinery (often stowed in the hold of a vessel rather than in containers on the deck). With **free on board (FOB) named port**, the responsibility and liability of the seller do not end until the goods—typically in containers—have cleared the ship's rail. As a practical matter, access to the terminal and harbor areas in many modern ports may be restricted; in such an instance, FCA should be used instead.

Several Incoterms are known as "C-Terms" or "main-carriage" terms. When goods are shipped **cost, insurance, freight (CIF) named port**, the risk of loss or damage to goods is transferred to the buyer once the goods have passed the ship's rail. In this sense, CIF is similar to FOB. However, with CIF, the seller has to pay the expense of transportation for the goods up to the port of destination, including the expense of insurance. If the terms of the sale are **CFR (cost and freight)**, the seller is not responsible for risk or loss at any point outside the factory.

Table 11-2 is a typical example of the kind of export price escalation that can occur when some of these costs are added to the per-unit cost of the product itself. In this example, a Des Moines–based distributor of agricultural equipment is shipping a container load of agricultural tires to Yokohama, Japan, through the port of Seattle. A shipment of tires that costs ex-works $45,000 in Des Moines ends up with a total retail price in excess of $66,000 in Yokohama. A line-by-line analysis of this shipment shows how price escalation occurs. First, there is the total shipping charge of $2,715.00, which is 6 percent of the ex-works Des Moines price. The principal component of this shipping charge is a combination of land and ocean freight totaling $2,000.00.

All import charges are assessed against the landed price of the shipment (CIF value). Note that there is no line item for duty in this example; no duties are charged on agricultural equipment sent to Japan.[11] Duties may be charged in other countries. A nominal distributor markup of 10 percent ($4,925.46) actually represents 12 percent of the CIF Yokohama price because it is a markup not only on the ex-works price but on freight and VAT (value-added tax) as well. Finally, a dealer markup of 25 percent adds up to $12,313.64 (27 percent) of the CIF Yokohama price. Like distributor markups, dealer markup is based on the total landed cost.

The net effect of this add-on accumulating process is a total retail price in Yokohama of $66,493.67, or 147 percent of the ex-works Des Moines price. This is price escalation. The example provided here is by no means an extreme case. Indeed, longer distribution channels or channels that require a higher operating margin, as are typically found in export marketing, can contribute to

---

[11]Since the Uruguay Round of GATT negotiations, Japan has lowered or eliminated duties on thousands of categories of imports. Japan's simple average duty rate for 2003 was 2.5 percent; approximately 60 percent of tariff lines (including most industrial products) were rated 5 percent or lower.

TABLE 11-2 Price Escalation: A 20-ft. Container of Agricultural Equipment Shipped from Des Moines to Yokohama*

Item			Percentage of Ex-works Price
Ex-works Des Moines		$45,000	100%
Inland and ocean freight from DSM to CY Yokohama	$1,475.00		4.44%
Bunker adjustment fee	300.00		0.67%
Destination charges	240.00		0.53%
Freight forwarding fee	150.00		0.33%
AES filing fee	25.00		0.06%
Total shipping charges	$2,715.00	$ 2,715.00	6.03%
Insurance (110% of CIF value) – $0.20 per $100		104.97	0.23%
Total CIF Yokohama value		$47,819.97	106.27%
VAT (3% of CIF value)		1,434.60	3.19%
Landed cost		49,254.57	109.45%
Distributor markup (10%)		4,925.46	10.95%
Dealer markup (25%)		12,313.64	27.36%
Total retail price		$66,493.67	147.76%

*This was loaded at the manufacturer's door, shipped by stack train to Seattle, and then transferred via ocean freight to Yokohama. Total transit time from factory door to foreign port is about 30 days. The authors are indebted to Terri Carter, Manager, Export Services, Bridgestone Americas Tire Operations LLC, for her assistance in creating this table.

price escalation. Because of the layered distribution system in Japan, the markups in Tokyo could easily result in a price that is 200 percent of the CIF value. An example of price escalation for a single product is shown in Table 11-3. A right-hand drive Jeep Grand Cherokee equipped with a V8 engine ends up costing ¥5 million—roughly $50,000—in Japan (see Exhibit 11-3). The final price represents 167 percent of the U.S. sticker price of $30,000.

These examples of cost-plus pricing show an approach that a beginning exporter might use to determine the CIF price. This approach could also be used for differentiated products such as

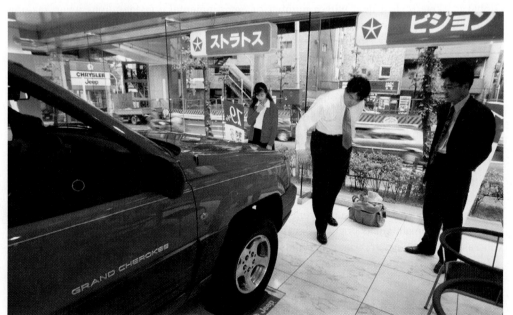

Exhibit 11-3: Chrysler began exporting right-hand drive Jeeps to Japan in 1996. However, the country was in a deep recession at the time, forcing many American marketers—including Coca-Cola, J.Crew, Microsoft, and Jeep—to cut prices. Ten years later, Japan's economy rebounded, and consumers started buying. Jeep is enjoying double-digit sales growth at the 60-plus dealerships that sell Chrysler and Jeep vehicles.
Source: © TWPhoto/Corbis. All Rights Reserved.

TABLE 11-3 An American-Built Jeep Grand Cherokee Goes to Japan (estimates)

Item	Amount of Price Escalation	Total
Ex-works price	0	$30,000
Exchange rate adj.	$2,100	$32,100
Shipping	$ 300	$32,400
Customs fees	$1,000	$33,400
Distributor margin	$3,700	$37,100
Inspection, accessories	$1,700	$38,800
Added options, prep	$3,000	$41,800
Final sticker price	$8,200	$50,000

the Jeep Cherokee for which buyers are willing to pay a premium. However, as noted earlier, experienced global marketers are likely to take a more flexible approach and view price as a strategic variable that can help achieve marketing and business objectives.

From a practical point of view, a working knowledge of Incoterms can be a source of competitive advantage to anyone seeking an entry-level job in global marketing. Beth Dorrell, an export coordinator at a U.S.-based company that markets industrial ink products, explains how terms of the sale affect price:

> We actually use different Incoterms as incentives for larger orders. Instead of offering a "price break" price, we offer a better Incoterm based upon the size of a customer's order. We adhere to some general guidelines: Any order less than one ton is sold on an ex-works basis. Anything one ton or more is sold CIF port. All air freight is ex-factory. We will, of course, go to great lengths to ensure that our customers are happy. So, even though a product is sold ex-works, we'll often arrange shipping to destination port (CIF) or airport (CIP), or to the domestic port (FOB) and simply tag the freight cost onto the invoice. We end up with an ex-factory price, but a CIF or FOB invoice total. Sounds complicated, doesn't it? It keeps me busy arranging shipping.

ENVIRONMENTAL INFLUENCES ON PRICING DECISIONS

Global marketers must deal with a number of environmental considerations when making pricing decisions. Among them are currency fluctuations, inflation, government controls and subsidies, and competitive behavior. Some of these factors work in conjunction with others; for example, inflation may be accompanied by government controls. Each is discussed in detail in the following paragraphs.

Currency Fluctuations

In global marketing, fluctuating exchange rates complicate the task of setting prices. As we noted in Chapter 2, currency fluctuations can create significant challenges and opportunities for any company that exports. Management faces different decision situations, depending on whether currencies in key markets have strengthened or weakened relative to the home-country currency. A weakening of the home-country currency swings exchange rates in a favorable direction: A producer in a weak-currency country can choose to cut export prices to increase market share or maintain its prices and reap healthier profit margins. Overseas sales can result in windfall revenues when translated into the home-country currency.

It is a different situation when a company's home currency strengthens; this is an unfavorable turn of events for the typical exporter because overseas revenues are reduced when translated into the home-country currency. Now, suppose the U.S. dollar weakens relative to the Japanese yen. This is good news for American companies such as Boeing, Caterpillar, and GE but bad news for Canon and Olympus (and Americans shopping for cameras). Indeed, according to Teruhisa Tokunaka, chief financial officer of Sony, a 1-yen shift in the yen-dollar exchange rate can raise or lower the company's annual operating profit by eight billion yen (see Figure 11-2).[12] These examples underscore the point that "roller-coaster" or "yo-yo"–style swings in currency values, which may move in a favorable direction for several quarters and then abruptly reverse, characterize today's business environment.

The degree of exposure varies among companies. For example, Harley-Davidson exports all of its motorcycles from the United States. In every export market, the company's pricing decisions must take currency fluctuations into account. Similarly, 100 percent of German automaker Porsche's production takes place at home; Germany serves as its export base. However, for exports within the euro zone, Porsche is insulated from currency fluctuations.

In responding to currency fluctuations, global marketers can utilize other elements of the marketing mix besides price. Table 11-4 provides several guidelines. In some instances, slight upward price adjustments due to the strengthening of a country's currency have little effect on export performance, especially if demand is relatively inelastic. The first two strategies in the right-hand column of Table 11-4 call for focusing attention on competitive issues besides price as well as productivity and cost reduction efforts. Companies in the strong-currency country can also choose to absorb the cost of maintaining international market prices at previous levels—at least for a while. Companies using the rigid cost-plus pricing method described earlier may be forced to change to the flexible approach. The use of the flexible cost-plus method to reduce prices in response to unfavorable currency swings is an example of a **market holding strategy** and is adopted by companies that do not want to lose market share. If, by contrast, large price increases are deemed unavoidable, managers may find their products can no longer compete.

FIGURE 11-2

Value of U.S. Dollar Versus Japanese Yen

Source: Based on data gathered by the Board of Governors of the Federal Reserve (www.federalreserve.gov).

---

[12]Robert A. Guth, Michael M. Phillips, and Charles Hutzler, "On the Decline: As the Yen Keeps Dropping, a New View of Japan Emerges," *The Wall Street Journal* (April 24, 2002), pp. A1, A8.

TABLE 11-4 Global Pricing Strategies

When Domestic Currency Is Weak	When Domestic Currency Is Strong
1. Stress price benefits.	1. Engage in nonprice competition by improving quality, delivery, and after-sale service.
2. Expand product line and add more costly features.	2. Improve productivity and engage in cost reduction.
3. Shift sourcing to domestic market.	3. Shift sourcing outside home country.
4. Exploit market opportunities in all markets.	4. Give priority to exports to countries with stronger currencies.
5. Use full-costing approach, but employ marginal-cost pricing to penetrate new or competitive markets.	5. Trim profit margins and use marginal-cost pricing.
6. Speed repatriation of foreign-earned income and collections.	6. Keep the foreign-earned income in host country; slow down collections.
7. Minimize expenditures in local (host-country) currency.	7. Maximize expenditures in local (host-country) currency.
8. Buy advertising, insurance, transportation, and other services in domestic market.	8. Buy needed services abroad and pay for them in local currencies.
9. Bill foreign customers in their own currency.	9. Bill foreign customers in the domestic currency.

Source: S. Tamer Cavusgil, "Pricing for Global Markets," *Columbia Journal of World Business* 31, no. 4 (Winter 1996), p. 69.

In the three years immediately after the euro zone was established, the euro declined in value more than 25 percent relative to the dollar. This situation forced American companies, in particular small exporters, to choose from among the options associated with strong currencies listed in Table 11-4. The strategy chosen varies according to a company's particular circumstances. For example, Vermeer Manufacturing of Pella, Iowa, with annual sales of $650 million, prices its products in euros for the European market. As 2000 came to an end, Vermeer had been forced to raise its European prices four times since the euro's introduction. Its subsidiary in the Netherlands pays employees in euros and also buys materials locally, illustrating strategies number 7 and 8.

By contrast, Stern Pinball of Melrose Park, Illinois, prices its machines in dollars in export markets; this represents strong-currency strategy number 9. Company president Gary Stern's product strategy also reflects strong-currency strategy number 1 in Table 11-4: To offset the higher cost to European customers who must convert euros before paying in dollars, the company developed new features such as pinball machines that "speak" several European languages. It has also produced new products such as a soccer game themed to European interests as well as an Austin Powers game targeted at the United Kingdom. As Stern commented, "If I were bright enough to know which way the euro was going, I sure wouldn't be making pinball machines. I'd be trading currency."[13]

As noted earlier, price discrepancies across the euro zone should gradually disappear because manufacturers will no longer be able to cite currency fluctuations as a justification for the discrepancies. **Price transparency** means that buyers will be able to comparison shop easily because goods will be priced in euros as opposed to marks, francs, or lira. The European Commission publishes an annual report comparing automobile price differences in the EU. Table 11-5 shows prices from the late 1990s (pre-euro zone) and prices from November 2003. A comparison of the figures shows that, although price discrepancies for some models have narrowed, prices for a Volkswagen Passat are as much as 39 percent higher depending on the country of purchase. Not surprisingly, these differences encourage cross-border shopping

Some automobile price differences in Europe are due to different standards for safety equipment and different tax levels. For example, Denmark and Sweden have a value-added tax (VAT)

"The car industry is going to be hurt. There will be greater price transparency. Prices are higher in northern Europe and once consumers there get wind of this there will be a move down in prices towards the southern countries."[14]

Marcie Krempel, AT Kearney

---

[13]Christopher Cooper, "Euro's Drop Is Hardest for the Smallest," *The Wall Street Journal* (October 2, 2000), p. A21.
[14]Graham Bowley, "On the Road to Price Convergence," *Financial Times* (November 12, 1998), p. 29.

TABLE 11-5 Automobile Price Differences in the EU, 1998/2003

Small Segment		Medium Segment		Large Segment	
Opel Corsa	24.0%/13.6%	VW Golf	43.5%/28.0%	BMW 318I	12.0%/12.7%
Ford Fiesta	44.7%/23.1%	Opel Astra	26.0%/17.6%	Audi A4	13.0%/9.1%
Renault Clio	33.8%/17.3%	Ford Escort/Focus	33.8%/22.7%	Ford Mondeo	58.5%/21.0%
Peugeot 106/206	21.1%/24.6%	Renault Mégane	27.9%/19.6%	Opel Vectra	18.2%/16.0%
VW Polo	36.7%/19.3%	Peugeot 306/307	46.2%/16.9%	VW Passat	36.4%/39.0%

Source: European Commission (europa.eu/press releases). Accessed March 2004.

of 25 percent, the highest rates in the EU. Moreover, Denmark taxes luxury goods heavily. Taxes are also high in Finland, Belgium, Ireland, Austria, and Italy. Volkswagen has already begun to harmonize its wholesale prices for vehicles distributed in Europe.

EMERGING MARKETS BRIEFING BOOK

➡ Pricing Reeboks in India

When Reebok, the world's number two athletic shoe company, decided to enter India in 1995, it faced several basic marketing challenges. For one thing, Reebok was creating a market from scratch. Upscale sports shoes were virtually unknown, and the most expensive sneakers available at the time cost 1,000 rupees (about $23). Reebok officials also had to select a market entry mode. The decision was made to subcontract with four local suppliers, one of which, the Phoenix Group, became a joint venture partner. To reinforce Reebok's high-tech brand image, company officials decided to establish their own retail infrastructure. There were two other crucial pieces of the puzzle: product and price. Should Reebok create a line of mass-market shoes specifically for India and priced at Rs1,000? The alternative was to offer the same designs sold in other parts of the world and price them at Rs2,500 ($58), a figure that represents the equivalent of a month's salary for a junior civil servant.

In the end, Reebok decided to offer Indian consumers about 60 models chosen from the company's global offerings. The decision was based in part on a desire to sustain Reebok's brand image of high quality. Management realized that the decision could very well limit the size of the market; despite estimates that as many as 300 million Indians could be classified as "middle class," the number of people who could afford premium-priced products was estimated to be about 30 million.

Reebok's least expensive shoes were priced at about Rs2,000 per pair; for the same amount of money, a farmer could buy a dairy cow or a homeowner could buy a new refrigerator. Nevertheless, consumer response was very favorable, especially among middle-class youths. As Muktesh Pant, a former regional manager who became the first CEO of Reebok India, noted, "For Rs2,000 to Rs3,000, people feel they can really make a statement. It's cheaper than buying a new watch, for instance, if you want to make a splash at a party. And though our higher-priced shoes put us in competition with things like refrigerators and cows, the upside is that we're now being treated as a prestigious brand."

Sneakers represented just one aspect of the larger marketing of professional sports and sports culture to Indian youth. India's

middle-class households were spending more time in the living room watching cricket matches on TV, a trend that created an opportunity for sports sponsorships and sports-related ads. In the late 1990s, Reebok spent more than $1.5 million on event marketing and sponsoring teams such as the East Bengal Football Club.

Reebok quickly discovered that demand was strong outside of key metropolitan markets such as Delhi, Mumbai, and Chennai. The cost of living is lower in small towns, so consumers have more disposable income to spend. Reebok appointed distributors in each of India's 26 states to distribute lower-priced shoe models in a network of about 1,500 multi-brand footwear and apparel shops. One problem, however, is that knockoff versions of Reebok, Adidas, and Nike shoes were widely available. Reebok conducted several raids on outlets that were selling the counterfeit goods.

Reebok's agreement with the Phoenix Group called for the latter to create 50-plus stores. However, after the first 10 stores were opened, management at Phoenix decided to concentrate on marketing the company's own brands. Accordingly, Reebok began to identify individual partners to run stores in major cities; there are currently about 90 branded franchise stores in 50 cities. By establishing exclusive stores, promoting Reebok as a lifestyle brand, and offering a unique "sports fashion" shopping experience, Reebok was able to offer a taste of Western-style capitalist consumption for those so inclined. Between 1996 and 1999, Reebok's retail sales in India more than tripled, increasing from Rs250 million to Rs900 million.

Today, Reebok India exports hundreds of thousands of pairs of Indian-made shoes to Europe and the United States. CEO Pant was promoted to vice president of global brand marketing at Reebok International headquarters in Stoughton, Massachusetts. Reflecting on Reebok's Indian launch, he observed, "At first we were embarrassed about our pricing. But it has ended up serving us well" (see Exhibit 11-4).

Sources: Bernard D'Mello, "Reebok and the Global Footwear Sweatshop," *Monthly Review* 54, no. 9 (February 2003), pp. 26–41; Mark Nicholson, "Where a Pair of Trainers Costs as Much as a Cow," *Financial Times* (August 18, 1998), p. 10.

Exhibit 11-4: Reebok dominates the footwear market in India, where its cricket shoes are a top seller. In an effort to attract foreign investment, India's leaders approved legislation in 2006 that will make it easier for Reebok and other global marketers to establish single-brand retail chains. Previously, market entry and expansion was done primarily through franchisees. Now, Reebok is stepping up its efforts to expand outside of large metropolitan areas such as Mumbai. Some three dozen Indian cities have populations exceeding one million people, including a rapidly growing base of middle-class consumers.
Source: Dibyangshu Sarkar/Getty Images, Inc. AFP.

Inflationary Environment

Inflation, or a persistent upward change in price levels, is a problem in many country markets. An increase in the money supply can cause inflation; as noted in the previous section, inflation is often reflected in the prices of imported goods for a country whose currency has been devalued. For example, in the Dominican Republic, the peso lost one-third of its value in 2002; suddenly, shoppers were faced with price increases of 40 to 50 percent. The situation in the Dominican Republic is extreme; overall, in 2000, the average rate of inflation in the world's advanced economies stood at a low 2.3 percent. In developing countries, inflation averaged about 6 percent. By comparison, inflation in 2000 was much higher in the transitional economies in Central and Eastern Europe with Russia experiencing inflation of 20 percent.

An essential requirement for pricing in an inflationary environment is the maintenance of operating profit margins. When present, inflation requires price adjustments, for a simple reason: Increased selling prices must cover rising costs. Regardless of cost accounting practices, if a company maintains its margins, it has effectively protected itself from the effects of inflation. This, in turn, requires manufacturers and retailers of all types to become more technologically adept. In Brazil, where the inflation rate was as high as 2,000 percent during the late 1980s, retailers sometimes changed prices several times each day. Shelf pricing, rather than individual unit pricing, became the norm throughout the retailing sector nearly 15 years before Walmart arrived in the region. Because their warehouses contained goods that had been bought at different prices, local retailers were forced to invest in sophisticated computer and communications systems to help them keep pace with the volatile financial environment. They utilized sophisticated inventory management software to help them maintain financial control. As Walmart came to Brazil in the mid-1990s, it discovered that local competitors had the technological infrastructure that allowed them to match its aggressive pricing policies.[15]

Low inflation presents pricing challenges of a different type. With inflation in the United States in the low single digits in the late 1990s and strong demand forcing factories to run at or near capacity, companies should have been able to raise prices. However, the domestic economic situation was not the only consideration. In the mid-1990s, excess manufacturing capacity in many industries, high rates of unemployment in many European countries, and the lingering recession in Asia made it difficult for companies to increase prices. As John Ballard, CEO of a California-based engineering firm, noted in 1994, "We thought about price increases. But our

---

[15]Pete Hisey, "Walmart's Global Vision," *Retail Merchandiser* 41, no. 4 (April 2001), pp. 21–49.

research of competitors and what the market would bear told us it was not worth pursuing." By the end of the decade, globalization, the Internet, a flood of low-cost exports from China, and a new cost-consciousness among buyers were also significant constraining factors.[16]

Government Controls, Subsidies, and Regulations

Governmental policies and regulations that affect pricing decisions include dumping legislation, resale price maintenance legislation, price ceilings, and general reviews of price levels. Government action that limits management's ability to adjust prices can put pressure on margins. Under certain conditions, government action poses a threat to the profitability of a subsidiary operation. In a country that is undergoing severe financial difficulties and is in the midst of a financial crisis (for example, a foreign exchange shortage caused in part by runaway inflation), government officials are under pressure to take some type of action. This was true in Brazil for many years. In some cases, governments take expedient steps such as selective or broad price controls.

When selective controls are imposed, foreign companies are more vulnerable to control than local ones, particularly if the outsiders lack the political influence over government decisions that local managers have. For example, Procter & Gamble encountered strict price controls in Venezuela in the late 1980s. Despite increases in the cost of raw materials, P&G was granted only about 50 percent of the price increases it requested; even then, months passed before permission to raise prices was forthcoming. As a result, by 1988, detergent prices in Venezuela were less than what they were in the United States.[17]

Government control can also take other forms. As discussed in Chapter 8, companies are sometimes required to deposit funds in a noninterest-bearing escrow account for a specified period of time if they wish to import products. For example, Cintec International, an engineering firm that specializes in restoring historic structures, spent eight years seeking the necessary approval from Egyptian authorities to import special tools to repair a mosque. In addition, the country's port authorities required a deposit of nearly $25,000 before allowing Cintec to import diamond-tipped drills and other special tools. Why would Cintec's management accept such conditions? Cairo is the largest city in the Muslim world, and there are hundreds of centuries-old historic structures in need of refurbishment. By responding to the Egyptian government's demands with patience and persistence, Cintec is positioning itself as a leading contender for more contract work.[18]

Cash deposit requirements such as the one described here clearly create an incentive for a company to minimize the stated value of the imported goods; lower prices mean smaller deposits. Other government requirements that affect the pricing decision are profit transfer rules that restrict the conditions under which profits can be transferred out of a country. Under such rules, a high transfer price paid for imported goods by an affiliated company can be interpreted as a device for transferring profits out of a country.

Also discussed in Chapter 8 were government subsidies. As noted earlier, the topic of agricultural subsidies is a sensitive one in the current round of global trade talks. Brazil and a bloc of more than 20 other nations are pressing Washington to end agricultural subsidies. For example, Washington spends between $2.5 and $3 billion per year on cotton subsidies (the EU spends about $700 million), a fact that has contributed to delays in completing the Doha round. Benin, Chad, Burkina Faso, and others complain that the subsidies keep U.S. cotton prices so low that it costs the African nations $250 million each year in lost exports.[19] Brazil recently won its WTO complaint against U.S. cotton subsidies.

---

[16]Lucinda Harper and Fred R. Bleakley, "Like Old Times: An Era of Low Inflation Changes the Calculus for Buyers and Sellers," *The Wall Street Journal* (January 14, 1994), p. A1. See also Jacob M. Schlesinger and Yochi J. Dreazen, "Counting the Cost: Firms Start to Raise Prices, Stirring Fear in Inflation Fighters," *The Wall Street Journal* (May 16, 2000), pp. A1, A8.

[17]Alecia Swasy, "Foreign Formula: Procter & Gamble Fixes Aim on Tough Market: The Latin Americans," *The Wall Street Journal* (June 15, 1990), p. A7.

[18]Scott Miller, "In Trade Talks, the Gloves Are Off," *The Wall Street Journal* (July 15, 2003), p. A12. See also James Drummond, "The Great Conservation Debate," *Financial Times Special Report—Egypt* (October 22, 2003), p. 6.

[19]Neil King, Jr. and Scott Miller, "Trade Talks Fail amid Big Divide over Farm Issues," *The Wall Street Journal* (September 15, 2003), pp. A1, A18.

Government regulations can affect prices in other ways. In Germany, for example, price competition was historically severely restricted in a number of industries. This was particularly true in the service sector. The German government's recent moves toward deregulation have improved the climate for market entry by foreign firms in a range of industries, including insurance, telecommunications, and air travel. Deregulation is also giving German companies their first experience with price competition in the domestic market. In some instances, deregulation represents a *quid pro quo* that will allow German companies wider access to other country markets. For example, the United States and Germany recently completed an open-skies agreement that will allow Lufthansa to fly more routes within the United States. At the same time, the German air market has been opened to competition. As a result, air travel costs between German cities have fallen significantly. Change is slowly coming to the retail sector as well. The Internet and globalization have forced policymakers to repeal two archaic laws. The first, the

⮞ CULTURE WATCH
Hollywood Battles Video Piracy

Twentieth Century Fox, the film entertainment unit of Rupert Murdoch's News Corporation, has a problem: Video pirates are siphoning off profits from the studio's hit movies. In many parts of the world, lax enforcement of intellectual property laws creates an opportunity for unscrupulous merchants to sell counterfeit DVDs at rock-bottom prices. In emerging markets such as Mexico, Russia, and China, piracy costs Fox and rival movie studios hundreds of millions of dollars each year (see Exhibit 11-5). These losses reflect both decreased ticket sales at movie theaters and decreased sales of legitimate DVD releases. It is not uncommon for counterfeit copies of Hollywood's latest blockbuster to hit the streets before the movie has even opened in local cinemas. The Motion Picture Association of America estimates that, in China alone, losses totaled $244 billion in 2005. In China and elsewhere, the movie studios take legal action against the counterfeiters. Despite such efforts, Chinese merchants do a brisk trade in DVDs that sell for as little as Rmb10—the equivalent of about $1.20. Now Fox is adopting a new approach in China: charging less than Rmb30 for new DVD releases. The studio is hoping that, at this price, Chinese movie lovers will be motivated to buy an official version rather than a counterfeit.

Pirated movies are found in other emerging country markets as well. In Russia, for example, customs duties and tariffs contribute to retail prices equivalent to $20 or $30 for an authentic DVD; pirated versions sell for about $4. Columbia TriStar has responded to the situation in Russia by cutting prices to the equivalent of $10; as Vyacheslav Dobychin, director of Columbia TriStar's licensee in Russia, explained, "The idea is to get Russian consumers used to buying licensed material, but at a price that most of the population can afford. We're changing distribution from the 'exclusive model' to the 'mass model' in Russia."

A similar situation exists in Mexico, where a movie ticket costs a day's pay and pirated DVDs sell for about $5.50. Videomax, Quality Films, and other Mexican distributors have

responded by cutting retail prices for DVDs to about $4.50. As Carlos Cayon, vice president of Videomax, noted, "If we don't do something drastic, our business is finished." Another tactic is to bundle several older movie titles on individual DVDs that sell for $23 at Blockbuster, Sam's Club, and Walmart stores in Mexico. Videomax is also experimenting with innovative distribution channels such as street vendors, many of whom previously sold pirated movies. These vendors set up stands in high-traffic areas such as public plazas and subway station entrances.

The video piracy problem isn't confined to emerging markets: In the United States, losses from piracy exceed $1 billion each year for the movie industry as a whole. In the United States, Europe, and Japan, DVDs of hit movies such as *X-Men Origins: Wolverine* sell for $20 to $24. For years, Hollywood studios have relied on a business model that calls for DVDs to be released several months after a movie's theatrical run; DVD sales generate substantial profits for the studios and can equal or exceed a movie's take at the box office.

Hollywood studios are trying a new approach to marketing home videos: bundling several video formats into "triple-play" releases that combine a standard DVD, a high-definition Blu-ray disc, and a digital copy that can be loaded onto a computer or iPod. The triple-play release typically costs about $10 more than a stand-alone DVD, for example, $39.98 for the bundle versus $29.98 for a single-format DVD. As Lexine Wong, an executive at Sony Pictures, explains, "Our goal is to continue to build on the value proposition of Blu-ray and offer Blu-ray customers the flexibility to view the titles they purchase not just on their high-def home televisions but also on the go."

Sources: Thomas K. Arnold, "Combo Pack Protects Studios Against Piracy," *USA Today* (March 31, 2009), p. 11D; Mure Dickie, "Fox in DVD Distribution Deal with China Partner," *Financial Times* (November 13, 2006), p. 23; Ross Johnson, "Good News in Hollywood. Shhh," *The New York Times* (January 31, 2005), pp. C1, C8; Erin Arvedlund, "To Combat Rampant DVD Piracy, U.S. Film Companies Cut Prices," *The New York Times* (April 7, 2004), p. E1; Ken Bensinger, "Film Companies Take to Mexico's Streets to Fight Piracy," *The Wall Street Journal* (December 17, 2003), p. B1.

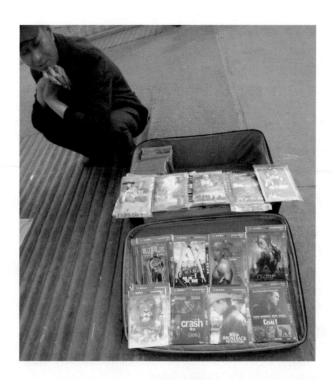

Exhibit 11-5: Home video piracy—including DVDs and VHS tapes—is rampant in many parts of the world. The Motion Picture Association of America claims that Hollywood loses $3.5 billion each year due to piracy; according to another estimate, the figure is more than $6 billion.
Source: Stephen Shaver/Bloomberg News.

Rabattgesetz or Discount Law, limited discounts on products to 3 percent of the list price. The second, the *Zugabeverordung* or Free Gift Act, banned companies from giving away free merchandise such as shopping bags.[20]

Competitive Behavior

Pricing decisions are bounded not only by cost and the nature of demand but also by competitive action. If competitors do not adjust their prices in response to rising costs, management—even if acutely aware of the effect of rising costs on operating margins—will be severely constrained in its ability to adjust prices accordingly. Conversely, if competitors are manufacturing or sourcing in a lower-cost country, it may be necessary to cut prices to stay competitive.

In the United States, Levi Strauss & Company is under price pressure from several directions. First, Levi faces stiff competition from the Wrangler and Lee brands marketed by VF Corporation. A pair of Wrangler jeans retails for about $20 at JCPenney and other department stores, compared with about $30 for a pair of Levi 501s. Second, Levi's two primary retail customers, JCPenney and Sears, are aggressively marketing their own private label brands. Finally, designer jeans from Calvin Klein, Polo, and Diesel are enjoying renewed popularity. Exclusive fashion brands such as Seven and Lucky retail for more than $100 per pair. Outside the United States, thanks to the heritage of the Levi brand and less competition, Levi jeans command premium prices—$80 or more for one pair of 501s.

To support the prestige image, Levi's are sold in boutiques. Levi's non-U.S. sales represent about one-third of revenues but more than 50 percent of profits. In an attempt to apply its global experience and enhance the brand in the United States, Levi has opened a number of Original Levi's Stores in select American cities. Despite such efforts, Levi rang up only $4.1 billion in sales in 2003 compared with $7.1 billion in 1996. In 2002, officials announced plans to close six plants and move most of the company's North American production offshore in an effort to cut costs.[21]

---

[20]Greg Steinmetz, "Mark Down: German Consumers Are Seeing Prices Cut in Deregulation Push," *The Wall Street Journal* (August 15, 1997), pp. A1, A4; David Wessel, "German Shoppers Get Coupons," *The Wall Street Journal* (April 5, 2001), p. A1.
[21]Leslie Kaufman, "Levi Strauss to Close 6 U.S. Plants and Lay Off 3,300," *The New York Times* (April 9, 2002), p. C2.

Using Sourcing as a Strategic Pricing Tool

The global marketer has several options for addressing the problem of price escalation or the environmental factors described in the last section. Product and market competition, in part, dictate the marketer's choices. Marketers of domestically manufactured finished products may be forced to switch to offshore sourcing of certain components to keep costs and prices competitive. In particular, China is quickly gaining a reputation as "the world's workshop." U.S. bicycle companies such as Huffy are relying more heavily on production sources in China and Taiwan.

Another option is a thorough audit of the distribution structure in the target markets. A rationalization of the distribution structure can substantially reduce the total markups required to achieve distribution in international markets. Rationalization may include selecting new intermediaries, assigning new responsibilities to old intermediaries, or establishing direct marketing operations. For example, Toys 'R' Us successfully targets the Japanese toy market by bypassing layers of distribution and adopting a warehouse style of selling similar to its U.S. approach. Toys 'R' Us was viewed as a test case of the ability of Western retailers—discounters in particular—to change the rules of distribution.

GLOBAL PRICING: THREE POLICY ALTERNATIVES

What pricing policy should a global company pursue? Viewed broadly, there are three alternative positions a company can take on worldwide pricing.

Extension or Ethnocentric

The first can be called an *extension* or *ethnocentric* pricing policy. An **extension** or **ethnocentric pricing policy** calls for the per-unit price of an item to be the same no matter where in the world the buyer is located. In such instances, the importer must absorb freight and import duties. The extension approach has the advantage of extreme simplicity because it does not require information on competitive or market conditions for implementation. The disadvantage of the ethnocentric approach is that it does not respond to the competitive and market conditions of each national market and, therefore, does not maximize the company's profits in each national market or globally. When toymaker Mattel adapted U.S. products for overseas markets, for example, little consideration was given to price levels that resulted when U.S. prices were converted to local currency prices. As a result, Holiday Barbie and some other toys were overpriced in global markets.[22]

> "In the past, Mercedes vehicles would be priced for the European market, and that price was translated into U.S. dollars. Surprise, surprise: You're 20 percent more expensive than the Lexus LS 400, and you don't sell too many cars."
>
> Joe Eberhardt, Chrysler Group Executive Vice President for Global Sales, Marketing and Service

Similarly, Mercedes executives recently moved beyond an ethnocentric approach to pricing. As Dieter Zetsche, chairman of Daimler AG, noted, "We used to say that *we* know what the customer wants, and he will have to pay for it . . . we didn't realize the world had changed."[23] Mercedes got its wake-up call when Lexus began offering "Mercedes quality" for $20,000 less. After assuming the top position in 1993, Mercedes CEO Helmut Werner boosted employee productivity, increased the number of low-cost outside suppliers, and invested in production facilities in the United States and Spain in an effort to move toward more customer- and competition-oriented pricing. The company also rolled out new, lower-priced versions of its E Class and S Class sedans. *Advertising Age* immediately hailed management's new attitude for transforming Mercedes from "a staid and smug purveyor into an aggressive, market-driven company that will go bumper-to-bumper with its luxury car rivals—even on price."[24]

Adaptation or Polycentric

The second policy, **adaptation** or **polycentric pricing**, permits subsidiary or affiliate managers or independent distributors to establish whatever price they feel is most appropriate in their market environment. There is no requirement that prices be coordinated from one country to the next.

[22]Lisa Bannon, "Mattel Plans to Double Sales Abroad," *The Wall Street Journal* (February 11, 1998), pp. A3, A11.
[23]Alex Taylor III, "Speed! Power! Status!" *Fortune* (June 10, 1996), pp. 46–58.
[24]Raymond Serafin, "Mercedes-Benz of the '90s Includes Price in Its Pitch," *Advertising Age* (November 1, 1993), p. 1.

IKEA takes a polycentric approach to pricing: While it is company policy to have the lowest price on comparable products in every market, managers in each country set their own prices. These depend in part on local factors such as competition, wages, taxes, and advertising rates. Overall, IKEA's prices are lowest in the United States, where the company competes with large retailers. Prices are higher in Italy where local competitors tend to be smaller, more upscale furniture stores than those in the U.S. market. Generally, prices are higher in countries where the IKEA brand is strongest. When IKEA opened its first stores in mainland China, the young professional couples who are the company's primary target segment considered the prices to be too high. Ian Duffy, an Englishman in charge of the stores, quickly increased the amount of Chinese-made furniture in the stores so that he could lower prices; today, the average Chinese customer spends ¥300—about $36—per visit.[25]

One recent study of European industrial exporters found that companies utilizing independent distributors were the most likely to utilize polycentric pricing. Such an approach is sensitive to local market conditions; however, valuable knowledge and experience within the corporate system concerning effective pricing strategies are not brought to bear on each local pricing decision. Because the distributors or local managers are free to set prices as they see fit, they may ignore the opportunity to draw upon company experience. Arbitrage is also a potential problem with the polycentric approach; when disparities in prices between different country markets exceed the transportation and duty costs separating the markets, enterprising individuals can purchase goods in the lower-price country market and then transport them for sale in markets where higher prices prevail.

This is precisely what has happened in both the pharmaceutical and textbook publishing industries. Discounted drugs intended for AIDS patients in Africa have been smuggled into the European Union and sold at a huge profit. Similarly, Pearson (which publishes this text), McGraw-Hill, Thomson, and other publishers typically set lower prices in Europe and Asia than in the United States. The reason is that the publishers use polycentric pricing: They establish prices on a regional or country-by-country basis using per capita income and economic conditions as a guide.

> "The practice of selling U.S. products abroad at prices keyed to the local market is longstanding. It's not unusual, it doesn't violate public policy, and it's certainly not illegal."[26]
> Allen Adler, American Association of Publishers

Geocentric

The third approach, geocentric pricing, is more dynamic and proactive than the other two. A company using **geocentric pricing** neither fixes a single price worldwide, nor allows subsidiaries or local distributors to make independent pricing decisions. Instead, the geocentric approach represents an intermediate course of action. Geocentric pricing is based on the realization that unique local market factors should be recognized in arriving at pricing decisions. These factors include local costs, income levels, competition, and the local marketing strategy. Price must also be integrated with other elements of the marketing program. The geocentric approach recognizes that price coordination from headquarters is necessary in dealing with international accounts and product arbitrage. The geocentric approach also consciously and systematically seeks to ensure that accumulated national pricing experience is leveraged and applied wherever relevant.

Local costs plus a return on invested capital and personnel fix the price floor for the long term. In the short term, however, headquarters might decide to set a market penetration objective and price at less than the cost-plus return figure by using export sourcing to establish a market. This was the case described earlier with the Sony Walkman launch. Another short-term objective might be to arrive at an estimate of the market potential at a price that would be profitable given local sourcing and a certain volume of production. Instead of immediately investing in local manufacture, a decision might be made to supply the target market initially from existing higher-cost external supply sources. If the market accepts the price and product, the company can then build a local manufacturing facility to further develop the identified

---

[25]Mei Fong, "IKEA Hits Home in China," *The Wall Street Journal* (March 3, 2006), pp. B1, B4. See also Eric Sylvers, "IKEA Index Indicates the Euro Is Not a Price Equalizer Yet," *The New York Times* (October 23, 2003), p. W1; and Paula M. Miller, "IKEA with Chinese Characteristics," *The China Business Review* (July–August 2004), pp. 36–38.
[26]Tamar Lewin, "Students Find $100 Textbooks Cost $50, Purchased Overseas," *The New York Times* (October 21, 2003), p. A16.

TABLE 11-6 How Managers Calculate Export Prices for Industrial Products

Statement by Management	Implication/Interpretation
"We have the competitors' price list on our desk. I may speak frankly—who does not? We know exactly what our competitors charge for certain products, and we calculate accordingly."	When calculating prices for foreign markets, managers benchmark competitors' prices.
"An interesting way of evaluating whether a product will fit requirements of the market has emerged. You give some machines to an auction house and set a very low price limit. Your products are then auctioned off. That way, you get a feel for the right price level as well as the potential demand for the product. It is a very easy and cost-effective method."	As a practical matter, some companies use innovative, trial-and-error approaches to determine price elasticity.
"At trade shows, we go directly to our customers and try to find out what prices we can charge. We scan our price limits sensitively. This is how we get to a price list in the end."	Some companies take a methodical approach to determining price elasticity.
"We differentiate simply because there are some countries where we can get a better price. Then there are countries where we can't."	Rationale for differentiating prices using either polycentric or geocentric approach.
"I decided not to listen to people who advise me to differentiate prices. Wherever we are active, we want to have the image and the reputation of calculating our prices correctly and honestly."	Rationale for using standardized pricing.

Source: Adapted from Barbara Stöttinger, "Strategic Export Pricing: A Long and Winding Road," *Journal of International Marketing* 9, no. 1 (2001), pp. 40–63.

market opportunity in a profitable way. If the market opportunity does not materialize, the company can experiment with the product at other prices because it is not committed to a fixed sales volume by existing local manufacturing facilities.

For consumer products, local income levels are critical in the pricing decision. If the product is normally priced well above full manufacturing costs, the global marketer should consider accepting reduced margins and price below prevailing levels in low-income markets. *The important point here is that in global marketing there is no such thing as a "normal" margin.* Of the three methods described, the geocentric approach is best suited to global competitive strategy. A global competitor will take into account global markets and global competitors in establishing prices. Prices will support global strategy objectives rather than the objective of maximizing performance in a single country. Table 11-6 lists some comments by European exporters that provide insights into the real-world process of setting prices.

GRAY MARKET GOODS

Gray market goods are trademarked products that are exported from one country to another where they are sold by unauthorized persons or organizations. Consider the following illustration:

Suppose that a golf equipment manufacturer sells a golf club to its domestic distributors for $200; it sells the same club to its Thailand distributor for $100. The lower price may be due to differences in overseas demand or ability to pay. Or, the price difference may reflect the need to compensate the foreign distributor for advertising and marketing the club. The golf club, however, never makes it to Thailand. Instead, the Thailand distributor resells the club to a gray marketer in the United States for $150. The gray marketer can then undercut the prices charged by domestic distributors who paid $200 for the club. The manufacturer is forced to lower the domestic price or risk losing sales to gray marketers, driving down the manufacturer's profit margins. Additionally, gray marketers make liberal use of manufacturer's trademarks and often fail to provide warranties and other services that consumers expect from the manufacturer and its authorized distributors.[27]

This practice, known as **parallel importing**, occurs when companies employ a polycentric, multinational pricing policy that calls for setting different prices in different country markets. Gray markets can flourish when a product is in short supply, when producers employ skimming strategies in certain markets, or when the goods are subject to substantial markups. For example, in the European pharmaceuticals market, prices vary widely. In the United Kingdom and the Netherlands, for example, parallel imports account for as much as 10 percent of the sales of some pharmaceutical brands. The Internet is emerging as a powerful new tool that allows would-be gray marketers to access pricing information and reach customers.[28]

Gray markets impose several costs or consequences on global marketers. These include:[29]

- *Dilution of exclusivity.* Authorized dealers are no longer the sole distributors. The product is often available from multiple sources and margins are threatened.
- *Free riding.* If the manufacturer ignores complaints from authorized channel members, those members may engage in *free riding.* That is, they may opt to take various actions to offset downward pressure on margins. These options include cutting back on presale service, customer education, and salesperson training.
- *Damage to channel relationships.* Competition from gray market products can lead to channel conflict as authorized distributors attempt to cut costs, complain to manufacturers, and file lawsuits against the gray marketers.
- *Undermining segmented pricing schemes.* As noted earlier, gray markets can emerge because of price differentials that result from multinational pricing policies. However, a variety of forces—including falling trade barriers, the information explosion on the Internet, and modern distribution capabilities—hamper a company's ability to pursue local pricing strategies.
- *Reputation and legal liability.* Even though gray market goods carry the same trademarks as goods sold through authorized channels, they may differ in quality, ingredients, or some other way. Gray market products can compromise a manufacturer's reputation and dilute brand equity, as when prescription drugs are sold past their expiration dates or electronics equipment is sold in markets where they are not approved for use or where manufacturers do not honor warranties.

Sometimes, gray marketers bring a product produced in a single country—French champagne, for example—into export markets in competition with authorized importers. The gray marketers sell at prices that undercut those set by the legitimate importers. In another type of gray marketing, a company manufactures a product in the home-country market as well as in foreign markets. In this case, products manufactured abroad by the company's foreign affiliate for sales abroad are sometimes sold by a foreign distributor to gray marketers. The latter then bring the products into the producing company's home-country market, where they compete with domestically produced goods.

As these examples show, the marketing opportunity that presents itself requires gray market goods to be priced lower than goods sold by authorized distributors or domestically produced goods. Clearly, buyers gain from lower prices and increased choice. In the United Kingdom alone, for example, total annual retail sales of gray market goods are estimated to be as high as $1.6 billion. A recent case in Europe resulted in a ruling that strengthened the rights of brand owners. Silhouette, an Austrian manufacturer of upscale sunglasses, sued the Hartlauer discount chain after the retailer obtained thousands of pairs of sunglasses that Silhouette had intended for sale in Eastern Europe. The European Court of Justice found in favor of Silhouette. In clarifying

---

[27]Adapted from Perry J. Viscounty, Jeff C. Risher, and Collin G. Smyser, "Cyber Gray Market Is Manufacturers' Headache," *The National Law Journal* (August 20, 2001), p. C3.

[28]Perry J. Viscounty, Jeff C. Risher, and Collin G. Smyser, "Cyber Gray Market Is Manufacturers' Headache," *The National Law Journal* (August 20, 2001), p. C3.

[29]Kersi D. Antia, Mark Bergen, and Shantanu Dutta, "Competing with Gray Markets," *MIT Sloan Management Review* 46, no. 1 (Summer 2004), pp. 65–67.

a 1989 directive, the court ruled that stores cannot import branded goods from outside the EU and then sell them at discounted prices without permission of the brand owner. The *Financial Times* denounced the ruling as "bad for consumers, bad for competition, and bad for European economies."[30]

In the United States, gray market goods are subject to the Tariff Act of 1930. Section 526 of the act expressly forbids importation of goods of foreign manufacture without the permission of the trademark owner. However, because courts have considerable leeway in interpreting the act, one legal expert has argued that the U.S. Congress should repeal Section 526. In its place, a new law should require gray market goods to bear labels clearly explaining any differences between them and goods that come through authorized channels. Other experts believe that, instead of changing the laws, companies should develop proactive strategic responses to gray markets. One such strategy would be improved market segmentation and product differentiation to make gray market products less attractive; another would be to aggressively identify and terminate distributors that are involved in selling to gray marketers.

DUMPING

Dumping is an important global pricing strategy issue. GATT's 1979 antidumping code defined dumping as the sale of an imported product at a price lower than that normally charged in a domestic market or country of origin. In addition, many countries have their own policies and procedures for protecting national companies from dumping. For example, China has retaliated against years of Western antidumping rules by introducing rules of its own. China's State Council passed the Antidumping and Antisubsidy Regulations in March 1997. The Ministry of Foreign Trade and Economic Cooperation and the State Economic and Trade Commission have responsibility for antidumping matters.[32]

The U.S. Congress has defined *dumping* as an unfair trade practice that results in "injury, destruction, or prevention of the establishment of American industry." Under this definition, dumping occurs when imports sold in the U.S. market are priced either at levels that represent less than the cost of production plus an 8 percent profit margin or at levels below those prevailing in the producing country. The U.S. Commerce Department is responsible for determining whether products are being dumped in the United States; the International Trade Commission (ITC) then determines whether the dumping has resulted in injury to U.S. firms. Many of the dumping cases in the United States involve manufactured goods from Asia and frequently target a single or very narrowly defined group of products. U.S. companies that claim to be materially damaged by the low-priced imports often initiate such cases. In 2000, the U.S. Congress passed the so-called Byrd Amendment; this law calls for antidumping revenues to be paid to U.S. companies harmed by imported goods sold at below-market prices.[33]

In Europe, the European Commission administers antidumping policy; a simple majority vote by the Council of Ministers is required before duties can be imposed on dumped goods. Six-month provisional duties can be imposed; more stringent measures include definitive, five-year duties. Low-cost imports from Asia have been the subject of dumping disputes in Europe. Another issue concerns $650 million in annual imports of unbleached cotton from China, Egypt, India, Indonesia, Pakistan, and Turkey. A dispute pitted an alliance of textile importers and wholesalers against Eurocoton, which represents textile weavers in France, Italy, and other EU countries. Eurocoton supports the duties as a means of protecting jobs from low-priced imports; the job issue is particularly sensitive in France. British textile importer Broome & Wellington maintains, however, that imposing duties would drive up prices and cost even more jobs in the textile finishing and garment industries.[34] In January 2005, the global

[30]Peggy Hollinger and Neil Buckley, "Grey Market Ruling Delights Brand Owners," *Financial Times* (July 17, 1998), p. 8.
[31]Ray Marcelo, "Officials See Red Over Handset Sales," *Financial Times* (October 3, 2003), p. 16.
[32]Lester Ross and Susan Ning, "Modern Protectionism: China's Own Antidumping Regulations," *China Business Review* (May/June 2000), pp. 30–33.
[33]Philip Brasher, "Clarinda Plant Takes Hit in Dispute over Imports," *The Des Moines Register* (November 16, 2005), p. D1.
[34]Neil Buckley, "Commission Faces Fight on Cotton 'Dumping,'" *Financial Times* (December 2, 1997), p. 5; Emma Tucker, "French Fury at Threat to Cotton Duties," *Financial Times* (May 19, 1997), p. 3.

system of textile quotas was abolished. Almost overnight, Chinese textile exports to the United States and Europe increased dramatically. Within a few months, the U.S. government had re-imposed quotas on several categories of textiles imports; in the EU, trade minister Peter Mandelson also imposed quotas for a period of two years.

Dumping was a major issue in the Uruguay round of GATT negotiations. Many countries took issue with the U.S. system of antidumping laws, in part because historically the commerce department almost always ruled in favor of the U.S. company that filed the complaint. For their part, U.S. negotiators were concerned that U.S. exporters were often targeted in antidumping investigations in countries with few formal rules for due process. The U.S. side sought to improve the ability of U.S. companies to defend their interests and understand the bases for rulings.

The result of the GATT negotiations was an agreement on interpretation of GATT Article VI. From the U.S. point of view, one of the most significant changes between the agreement and the 1979 code is the addition of a "standard of review" that will make it harder for GATT panels to dispute U.S. antidumping determinations. There are also a number of procedural and methodological changes. In some instances, these have the effect of bringing GATT regulations more in line with U.S. law. For example, in calculating "fair price" for a given product, any sales of the product at below-cost prices in the exporting country are not included in the calculations; inclusion of such sales would have the effect of exerting downward pressure on the fair price. The agreement also brought GATT standards in line with U.S. standards by prohibiting governments from penalizing differences between home market and export market prices of less than 2 percent.

For positive proof that dumping has occurred in the United States, both price discrimination and injury must be demonstrated (see Exhibit 11-6). *Price discrimination* is the practice of setting different prices when selling the same quantity of "like-quality" goods to different buyers. The existence of either one without the other is an insufficient condition to constitute dumping. Companies concerned with running afoul of antidumping legislation have developed a number of

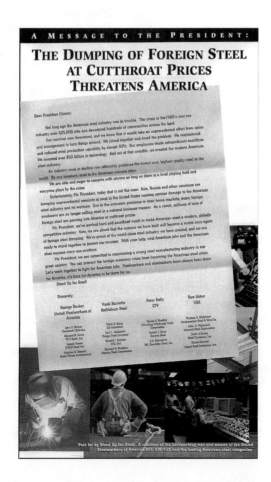

Exhibit 11-6: Representatives of the U.S. steel industry sponsored this 1998 ad to urge President Clinton to get tough on unfairly traded, government-subsidized steel that was sold in the United States by producers in Western Europe, Asia, and Russia. In 2001, the International Trade Commission launched an investigation under the Section 201 provision of the U.S. Foreign Trade Act to determine whether steel imports were hurting American steel producers. Based on the ITC's recommendation, in March 2002 President George W. Bush imposed sweeping tariffs of up to 30 percent on a wide range of steel imports for a three-year period. The European Union responded by drawing up a list of U.S. product imports that would be taxed in retaliation for the president's action. In 2003, President Bush dropped the tariffs.

approaches for avoiding the dumping laws. One approach is to differentiate the product sold from that in the home market so it does not represent "like quality." An example of this is an auto accessory that one company packaged with a wrench and an instruction book, thereby changing the "accessory" to a "tool." The duty rate in the export market happened to be lower on tools, and the company also acquired immunity from antidumping laws because the package was not comparable to competing goods in the target market. Another approach is to make nonprice competitive adjustments in arrangements with affiliates and distributors. For example, credit can be extended and essentially have the same effect as a price reduction.

PRICE FIXING

In most instances, it is illegal for representatives of two or more companies to secretly set similar prices for their products. This practice, known as **price fixing**, is generally held to be an anticompetitive act. Companies that collude in this manner are generally trying to ensure higher prices for their products than would generally be available if markets were functioning freely. In *horizontal price fixing*, competitors within an industry that make and market the same product conspire to keep prices high. For example, in the 1990s, ArcherDanielsMidland (ADM) and several other companies were found guilty of colluding to prop up world prices for an enzyme used in animal feed. The term *horizontal* applies in this instance because ADM and its co-conspirators are all at the same supply chain "level" (i.e., they are manufacturers). *Vertical price fixing* occurs when a manufacturer conspires with wholesalers or retailers (i.e., channel members at different "levels" from the manufacturer) to ensure certain retail prices are maintained. For example, the European Commission recently fined Nintendo nearly $150 million after it was determined that the video game company had colluded with European distributors to fix prices. During the 1990s, prices of Nintendo video game consoles varied widely across Europe. They were much more expensive in Spain than in Britain and other countries; however, distributors in countries with lower retail prices agreed not to sell to retailers in countries with high prices.[35]

Another case of price fixing pits DeBeers SA, the South African diamond company, against the United States. At issue are prices for industrial diamonds, not gemstones; however, DeBeers is a well-known name in the United States thanks to a long-running advertising campaign keyed to the tagline "A Diamond Is Forever." Because the company itself has no American retail presence, DeBeers diamonds are marketed in the United States by intermediaries. DeBeers executives have indicated a willingness to plead guilty and pay a fine in exchange for access to the United States. As a spokesperson said, "The U.S. is the biggest market for diamond jewelry—accounting for 50 percent of global retail jewelry sales—and we would really, really like to resolve these issues."[36]

TRANSFER PRICING

Transfer pricing refers to the pricing of goods, services, and intangible property bought and sold by operating units or divisions of the same company. In other words, transfer pricing concerns *intracorporate exchanges*, which are transactions between buyers and sellers that have the same corporate parent. For example, Toyota subsidiaries both sell to, and buy from, each other. Transfer pricing is an important topic in global marketing because goods crossing national borders represent a sale; therefore, their pricing is a matter of interest both to the tax authorities, who want to collect a fair share of income taxes, and to the customs service, which wants to collect an appropriate duty on the goods. Joseph Quinlan, chief marketing strategist at Bank of America, estimates that U.S. companies have 23,000 overseas affiliates; about 25 percent of U.S. exports represent shipments by American companies to affiliates and subsidiaries outside the United States.

In determining transfer prices to subsidiaries, global companies must address a number of issues, including taxes, duties and tariffs, country profit transfer rules, conflicting objectives of

[35]Paul Meller, "Europe Fines Nintendo $147 Million for Price Fixing," *The Wall Street Journal* (February 24, 2004), p. W1.
[36]John R. Wilke, "DeBeers Is in Talks to Settle Price-Fixing Charge," *The Wall Street Journal* (February 24, 2004), pp. A1, A14.

joint venture partners, and government regulations. Tax authorities such as the Internal Revenue Service (IRS) in the United States, Inland Revenue in the United Kingdom, and Japan's National Tax Administration Agency take a keen interest in transfer pricing policies. Transfer pricing is proving to be a corporate key issue in Europe as the euro makes it easier for tax authorities to audit transfer-pricing policies.

Three major alternative approaches can be applied to transfer pricing decisions. The approach used will vary with the nature of the firm, products, markets, and historical circumstances of each case. A **market-based transfer price** is derived from the price required to be competitive in the global marketplace. In other words, it represents an approximation of an arm's-length transaction. **Cost-based transfer pricing** uses an internal cost as the starting point in determining price. Cost-based transfer pricing can take the same forms as the cost-based pricing methods discussed earlier in the chapter. The way costs are defined may have an impact on tariffs and duties of sales to affiliates and subsidiaries by global companies. A third alternative is to allow the organization's affiliates to determine **negotiated transfer prices** among themselves. This method may be employed when market prices are subject to frequent changes. Table 11-7 summarizes the results of recent studies comparing transfer pricing methods by country. As shown in the table, market-based and cost-based transfer pricing are the two preferred methods in the United States, Canada, Japan, and the United Kingdom.

Tax Regulations and Transfer Prices

Because global companies conduct business in a world characterized by different corporate tax rates, there is an incentive to maximize income in countries with the lowest tax rates and to minimize income in high-tax countries. Governmental regulatory agencies are well aware of this situation. In recent years, many governments have tried to maximize national tax revenues by examining company returns and mandating reallocation of income and expenses. Some companies recently involved in transfer pricing cases include:

- Motorola may owe the IRS as much as $500 million in taxes from earnings from global operations that were booked incorrectly.
- The U.S. Labor Department filed a complaint against Swatch Group alleging that the Swiss watchmaker improperly used transfer pricing to evade millions of dollars in customs duties and taxes.[37]
- The U.S. government spent years attempting to recover $2.7 billion plus interest from pharmaceutical giant GlaxoSmithKline (GSK). The IRS charged that GSK did not pay enough tax on profits from Zantac, its hugely successful ulcer medication. Between 1989 and 1999, U.S. revenues from Zantac totaled $16 billion; the IRS charged that GSK's American unit overpaid royalties to the British parent company, thus reducing taxable U.S. income. The case was scheduled for trial in 2007; however, in September 2006, GSK settled the case by agreeing to pay the IRS approximately $3.1 billion.[38]

TABLE 11-7 **Transfer Pricing Methods Used in Selected Countries**

Methods	United States (%)	Canada (%)	Japan (%)	United Kingdom (%)
1. Market-based	35	37	37	31
2. Cost-based	43	33	41	38
3. Negotiated	14	26	22	20
4. Other	8	4	0	11
	100%	100%	100%	100%

Source: Adapted from Charles T. Horngren, Srikant M. Datar, and George Foster, *Cost Accounting: A Managerial Emphasis* (Upper Saddle River, NJ: Prentice Hall, 2003), p. 767.

---

[37]Leslie Lopez and John D. McKinnon, "Swatch Faces Complaint over Taxes," *The Wall Street Journal* (August 13, 2004), p. B2.
[38]Susannah Rodgers, "GlaxoSmithKline Gets Big Tax Bill," *The Wall Street Journal* (January 8, 2004), p. A8.

Sales of Tangible and Intangible Property

Each country has its own set of laws and regulations for dealing with controlled intracompany transfers. Whatever the pricing rationale, executives and managers involved in global pricing policy decisions must familiarize themselves with the laws and regulations in the applicable countries. The pricing rationale must conform with the intention of these laws and regulations. Although the applicable laws and regulations often seem perplexingly inscrutable, ample evidence exists that most governments simply seek to prevent tax avoidance and to ensure fair distribution of income from the operations of companies doing business internationally.

Even companies that make a conscientious effort to comply with the applicable laws and regulations and that document this effort may find themselves in tax court. Should a tax auditor raise questions, executives should be able to make a strong case for their decisions. Fortunately, consulting services are available to help managers deal with the arcane world of transfer pricing. It is not unusual for large global companies to invest hundred of thousands of dollars and hire international accounting firms to review transfer pricing policies.

COUNTERTRADE

In recent years, many exporters have been forced to finance international transactions by taking full or partial payment in some form other than money.[39] A number of alternative finance methods, known as *countertrade*, are widely used. In a **countertrade** transaction, a sale results in product flowing in one direction to a buyer; a separate stream of products and services, often flowing in the opposite direction, is also created. Countertrade generally involves a seller from the West and a buyer in a developing country; for example, the countries in the former Soviet bloc have historically relied heavily on countertrade. This approach, which reached a peak in popularity in the mid-1980s, is now used in some 100 countries. Within the former Soviet Union, countertrade has flourished in the 1990s, following the collapse of the central planning system.

As one expert notes, countertrade flourishes when hard currency is scarce. Exchange controls may prevent a company from expatriating earnings; the company may be forced to spend money in-country for products that are then exported and sold in third-country markets. Historically, the single most important driving force behind the proliferation of countertrade was the decreasing ability of developing countries to finance imports through bank loans. This trend resulted in debt-ridden governments pushing for self-financed deals.[40] According to Pompiliu Verzariu, former director of the Financial Services and Countertrade Division at the International Trade Administration:

> In the 1990s, countertrade pressures abated in many parts of the world, notably Latin America, as a result of debt reduction induced by the Brady plan initiative, lower international interest rates, policies that liberalized trade regimes, and the emergence of economic blocs such as NAFTA and Mercosur, which integrate regional trade based on free-market principles.[41]

Today, several conditions affect the probability that importing nations will demand countertrade. First is the priority attached to the Western import. The higher the priority, the less likely it is that countertrade will be required. The second condition is the value of the transaction; the higher the value, the greater the likelihood that countertrade will be involved. Third, the availability of products from other suppliers can also be a factor. If a company is the sole supplier of a differentiated product, it can demand monetary payment. However, if competitors are willing to deal on a countertrade basis, a company may have little choice but to agree or risk losing the sale altogether. Overall, the advantages to nonmarket and developing economies are access to Western marketing expertise and technology in the short term, and creation of hard currency export markets in the long term. The U.S. government officially opposes government-mandated countertrade, which represents the type of bilateral trade agreement that violates the free trading system established by GATT.

---

[39]Many of the examples in the following section are adapted from Matt Schaffer, *Winning the Countertrade War: New Export Strategies for America* (New York: John Wiley & Sons, 1989).
[40]Pompiliu Verzariu, "Trends and Developments in International Countertrade," *Business America* (November 2, 1992), p. 2.
[41]Janet Aschkenasy, "Give and Take," *International Business* (September 1996), p. 11.

Two categories of countertrade are discussed here. Barter falls into one category; the mixed forms of countertrade, including counterpurchase, offset, compensation trading, and switch trading, belong in a separate category. They incorporate a real distinction from barter because the transaction involves money or credit.

Barter

The term **barter** describes the least complex and oldest form of bilateral, nonmonetized countertrade. Simple barter is a direct exchange of goods or services between two parties. Although no money is involved, both partners construct an approximate shadow price for products flowing in each direction. Companies sometimes seek outside help from barter specialists. For example, New York–based Atwood Richards engages in barter in all parts of the world. Generally, however, distribution is direct between trading partners, with no intermediary included.

One of the highest-profile companies involved in barter deals is PepsiCo, which has done business in the Soviet and post-Soviet market for decades. In the Soviet era, when the ruble could not be converted to dollars or other "hard" currencies, PepsiCo bartered soft-drink syrup concentrate for Stolichnaya vodka. The vodka was exported to the United States by the PepsiCo Wines & Spirits subsidiary and marketed by M. Henri Wines. In the post-Soviet market economy, Russian rubles are freely convertible and barter is not necessarily required. Today, Stolichnaya is imported into the United States and marketed by Carillon Importers, a unit of Diageo PLC. Venezuelan president Hugo Chávez is currently bartering oil to foster closer relations with other Latin American countries. For example, Cuba sends doctors to Venezuela in exchange for oil; other countries "pay" for oil with bananas or sugar.

Counterpurchase

The **counterpurchase** form of countertrade, also termed *parallel trading* or *parallel barter*, is distinguished from other forms in that each delivery in an exchange is paid for in cash. For example, Rockwell International sold a printing press to Zimbabwe for $8 million. The deal went through, however, only after Rockwell agreed to purchase $8 million in ferrochrome and nickel from Zimbabwe, which it subsequently sold on the world market.

The Rockwell-Zimbabwe deal illustrates several aspects of counterpurchase. Generally, products offered by the foreign principal are not related to the Western firm's exports and cannot be used directly by the firm. In most counterpurchase transactions, two separate contracts are signed. In one the supplier agrees to sell products for a cash settlement (the original sales contract); in the other, the supplier agrees to purchase and market unrelated products from the buyer (a separate, parallel contract). The dollar value of the counterpurchase generally represents a set percentage—and sometimes the full value—of the products sold to the foreign principal. When the Western supplier sells these goods, the trading cycle is complete.

Offset

Offset is a reciprocal arrangement whereby the government in the importing country seeks to recover large sums of hard currency spent on expensive purchases such as military aircraft or telecommunications systems. In effect, the government is saying, "If you want us to spend government money on your exports, you must import products from our country." Offset arrangements may also involve cooperation in manufacturing, some form of technology transfer, placing subcontracts locally, or arranging local assembly or manufacturing equal to a certain percentage of the contract value.[42] In one deal involving offsets, Lockheed Martin Corp. sold F-16 fighters to the United Arab Emirates for $6.4 billion. In return, Lockheed agreed to invest $160 million in the petroleum-related UAE Offsets Group.[43]

---

[42]The commitment to local assembly or manufacturing under the supplier's specifications is commonly termed a *coproduction agreement*, which is tied to the offset but does not, in itself, represent a type of countertrade.
[43]Daniel Pearl, "Arms Dealers Get Creative with 'Offsets,'" *The Wall Street Journal* (April 20, 2000), p. A18.

Offset may be distinguished from counterpurchase because the latter is characterized by smaller deals over shorter periods of time.[44] Another major distinction between offset and other forms of countertrade is that the agreement is not contractual but reflects a memorandum of understanding that sets out the dollar value of products to be offset and the time period for completing the transaction. In addition, there is no penalty on the supplier for nonperformance. Typically, requests range from 20 to 50 percent of the value of the supplier's product. Some highly competitive sales have required offsets exceeding 100 percent of the valuation of the original sale.

Offsets have become a controversial facet of today's trade environment. To win sales in important markets such as China, global companies can face demands for offsets even when transactions do not involve military procurement. For example, the Chinese government requires Boeing to spend 20 to 30 percent of the price of each aircraft on purchases of Chinese goods. As Boeing executive Dean Thornton explained:

> "Offset" is a bad word, and it's against GATT and a whole bunch of other stuff, but it's a fact of life. It used to be twenty years ago in places like Canada or the UK, it was totally explicit, down to the decimal point. "You will buy 20 percent offset of your value." Or 21 percent or whatever. It still is that way in military stuff. [With sales of commercial aircraft], it's not legal so it becomes less explicit.[45]

Compensation Trading

Compensation trading, also called *buyback*, is a form of countertrade that involves two separate and parallel contracts. In one contract, the supplier agrees to build a plant or provide plant equipment, patents or licenses, or technical, managerial, or distribution expertise for a hard currency down payment at the time of delivery. In the other contract, the supplier company agrees to take payment in the form of the plant's output equal to its investment (minus interest) for a period of as many as 20 years.

Essentially, the success of compensation trading rests on the willingness of each firm to be both a buyer and a seller. The People's Republic of China has used compensation trading extensively. Egypt also used this approach to develop an aluminum plant. A Swiss company, Aluswiss, built the plant and also exports alumina (an oxide of aluminum found in bauxite and clay) to Egypt. Aluswiss takes back a percentage of the finished aluminum produced at the plant as partial payment for building the plant. As this example shows, compensation differs from counterpurchase in that the technology or capital supplied is related to the output produced.[46] In counterpurchase, as noted before, the goods taken by the supplier typically cannot be used directly in its business activities.

Switch Trading

Also called *triangular trade* and *swap*, **switch trading** is a mechanism that can be applied to barter or countertrade. In this arrangement, a third party steps into a simple barter or other countertrade arrangement when one of the parties is not willing to accept all the goods received in a transaction. The third party may be a professional switch trader, switch trading house, or a bank. The switching mechanism provides a "secondary market" for countertraded or bartered goods and reduces the inflexibility inherent in barter and countertrade. Fees charged by switch traders range from 5 percent of market value for commodities to 30 percent for high-technology items. Switch traders develop their own networks of firms and personal contacts and are generally headquartered in Vienna, Amsterdam, Hamburg, or London. If a party to the original transaction anticipates that the products received in a barter or countertrade deal will be sold eventually at a discount by the switch trader, the common practice is to price the original products higher, build in "special charges" for port storage or consulting, or require shipment by the national carrier.

---

[44]Patricia Daily and S. M. Ghazanfar, "Countertrade: Help or Hindrance to Less-Developed Countries?" *Journal of Social, Political, and Economic Studies* 18, no. 1 (Spring 1993), p. 65.

[45]William Greider, *One World, Ready or Not: The Manic Logic of Global Capitalism* (New York: Simon & Schuster, 1997), p. 130.

[46]Patricia Daily and S. M. Ghazanfar, "Countertrade: Help or Hindrance to Less-Developed Countries?" *Journal of Social, Political, and Economic Studies* 18, no. 1 (Spring 1993), p. 66.

Summary

Pricing decisions are a critical element of the marketing mix that must reflect costs, competitive factors, and customer perceptions regarding value of the product. In a true global market, the **law of one price** would prevail. Pricing strategies include **market skimming**, **market penetration**, and **market holding**. Novice exporters frequently use the **cost-plus** method when setting prices. International terms of a sale such as **ex-works**, **DDP**, **FCA**, **FAS**, **FOB**, **CIF**, and **CFR** are known as **Incoterms** and specify which party to a transaction is responsible for covering various costs. These and other costs lead to **export price escalation**, the accumulation of costs that occurs when products are shipped from one country to another.

Expectations regarding currency fluctuations, inflation, government controls, and the competitive situation must also be factored into pricing decisions. The introduction of the euro has impacted price strategies in the EU because of improved **price transparency**. Global companies can maintain competitive prices in world markets by shifting production sources as business conditions change. Overall, a company's pricing policies can be categorized as **ethnocentric**, **polycentric**, or **geocentric**.

Several additional pricing issues are related to global marketing. The issue of **gray market goods** arises because price variations between different countries lead to **parallel imports**. **Dumping** is another contentious issue that can result in strained relations between trading partners. **Price fixing** among companies is anticompetitive and illegal. **Transfer pricing** is an issue because of the sheer monetary volume of intra-corporate sales and because country governments are anxious to generate as much tax revenue as possible. Various forms of **countertrade** play an important role in today's global environment. **Barter**, **counterpurchase**, **offset**, **compensation trading**, and **switch trading** are the main countertrade options.

Discussion Questions

1. What are the basic factors that affect price in any market? What considerations enter into the pricing decision?
2. Define the various types of pricing strategies and objectives available to global marketers.
3. Identify some of the environmental constraints on global pricing decisions.
4. Why do price differences in world markets often lead to gray marketing?
5. What is dumping? Why was dumping such an important issue during the Uruguay Round of GATT negotiations?
6. What is a transfer price? Why is it an important issue for companies with foreign affiliates? Why did transfer pricing in Europe take on increased importance in 1999?
7. What is the difference between ethnocentric, polycentric, and geocentric pricing strategies? Which would you recommend to a company that has global market aspirations?
8. If you were responsible for marketing CAT scanners worldwide (average price, $1,200,000), and your country of manufacture was experiencing a strong and appreciating currency against almost all other currencies, what options are available to you to maintain your competitive advantage in world markets?
9. Compare and contrast the different forms of countertrade.

The Logan is a case study in driving down costs. The windshield glass is nearly flat, meaning that it is less expensive to produce. The left and right outside mirrors are identical; the ashtrays are exactly the same as the ones used in another Renault model, the Espace. Similarly, Logan shares an engine and gearbox with Renault's Clio subcompact; for these and other components, high manufacturing volumes translate into economies of scale. The Logan was launched in India in April 2007 with a sticker price of about $10,000; the vehicle is manufactured by a joint venture between Renault and Mahindra & Mahindra, one of India's best-known industrial conglomerates.

The question is: Can the auto companies come up with the optimal value proposition—small, no-frills, four-door cars that are safe to drive, stylish enough to appeal to the aspirations of first-time buyers, and yet sell for *half* the price of a Logan (or less)? Under the best of circumstances, creating such a vehicle would test the prowess of the world's best automotive engineers. However, the challenge is especially daunting in a business environment characterized by record prices for steel, resin, and other commodities and components. As the general manager for a sourcing and procuring company noted, "There are so many legacy costs built into a design, and trying to engineer those out is difficult. It's better to start with a clean sheet of paper and engineer low costs in."

Established automakers based in developed countries are not the only companies racing to develop low-cost vehicles for entry-level buyers. For example, India's Tata Motors recently launched a new model, the Nano, with a rock-bottom sticker price of one Lakh (equivalent to 100,000 rupees or $2,500). The Nano has a rear-mounted, two-cylinder engine that delivers 33 horsepower. The top speed is 60 miles per hour and it delivers 50 miles per gallon of gas. The instrument panel is clustered in the middle of the dashboard so that Tata can offer both right- and left-hand drive versions for export. Tata's target market is consumers in emerging markets who currently travel by scooter. Some environmentalists have warned about the negative impact of hundreds of thousands of new vehicles on India's already congested roads. However, as Chairman Ratan Tata notes, low-income families should be given access to the freedom that a car provides. "Should they be denied the right to independent transport?" he asked recently.

Case 11-1 Discussion Questions

1. What is the key to the Logan's low price?
2. What are the environmental implications of millions of middle-class consumers in emerging markets buying their first automobile?
3. Assess the prospects for Tata's launch of the Nano. Is it likely to be a success?

Sources: Simon Robinson, "The World's Cheapest Car," *Time.com* (January 10, 2008); Heather Timmons, "In India, a $2,500 Pace Car," *The New York Times* (October 12, 2007), pp. C1, C4; David Gauthier-Villars, "Ghosn Bets Big on Low-Cost Strategy," *The Wall Street Journal* (September 4, 2007), p. A8; John Reed and Amy Yee, "Thrills Without Frills," *Financial Times* (June 25, 2007), p. 9; Christopher Condon, "The Birth of a Frankenstein Car," (July 20, 2004).

LVMH Moët Hennessy-Louis Vuitton SA is the world's largest marketer of luxury products and brands. Chairman Bernard Arnault has assembled a diverse empire of more than 60 brands, sales of which totaled $24.2 billion (€17.2 billion) in 2008 (see Figure 1). Arnault, whom some refer to as "the pope of high fashion," recently summed up the luxury business as follows: "We are here to sell dreams. When you see a couture show on TV around the world, you dream. When you enter a Dior boutique and buy your lipstick, you buy something affordable, but it has the dream in it."

Decades ago, the companies that today comprise LVMH were family-run enterprises focused more on prestige than on profit. Fendi, Pucci, and others sold mainly to a niche market comprised of very rich clientele. However, as markets began to globalize, the small luxury players struggled to compete. When Arnault set about acquiring smaller luxury brands, he had three goals in mind. First, he hoped that the portfolio approach would reduce the risk exposure to fashion cycles. According to this logic, if demand for watches or jewelry declined, clothing or accessory sales would offset any losses. Second, he intended to cut costs by eliminating redundancies in sourcing and manufacturing. Third, he hoped that LVMH's stable of brands would translate into a stronger bargaining position when managers negotiated leases for retail space or bought advertising.

Sales of luggage and leather fashion goods, including the 100-year-old Louis Vuitton brand, account for 34 percent of revenues. The company's specialty group includes Duty Free Shoppers (DFS) and Sephora. DFS operates stores in international airports around the world; Sephora, which LVMH acquired in 1997, is Europe's second-largest chain of perfume and cosmetics stores. Driven by such well-known brands as Christian Dior, Givenchy, and Kenzo, perfumes and cosmetics generate nearly 20 percent of LVMH's revenues. LVMH's wine and spirits unit includes such prestigious Champagne brands as Dom Perignon, Moët & Chandon, and Veuve Clicquot.

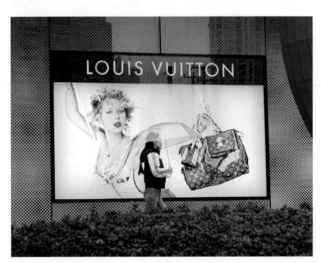

Source: Landov Media.

Despite the high expenses associated with operating elegant stores and purchasing advertising space in upscale magazines, the premium retail prices that luxury goods command translate into handsome profits. The Louis Vuitton brand alone accounts for about 60 percent of LVMH's operating profit. Unscrupulous operators have taken note of the high margins associated with Vuitton handbags, gun cases, and luggage displaying the distinctive beige-on-brown latticework LV monogram. Louis Vuitton SA spends $10 million annually battling counterfeiters in Turkey, Thailand, China, Morocco, South Korea, and Italy. Some of the money is spent on lobbyists who represent the company's interests in meetings with foreign government officials. Yves Carcelle, chairman of Louis Vuitton SA, recently explained, "Almost every month, we get a government somewhere in the world to destroy canvas, or finished products."

Another problem is a flourishing gray market. Givenchy and Christian Dior's Dune fragrance are just two of the luxury perfume brands that are sometimes diverted from authorized channels for sale at mass-market retail outlets. LVMH and other luxury goods marketers recently found a new way to combat gray market imports into the United States. In March 1995, the U.S. Supreme Court let stand an appeals court ruling prohibiting a discount drugstore chain from selling Givenchy perfume without permission. Parfums Givenchy USA had claimed that its distinctive packaging should be protected under U.S. copyright law. The ruling means that Costco, Walmart, and other discounters will no longer be able to sell some imported fragrances without authorization.

Opportunities and Challenges in Asia

Asia—particularly Japan—is a key region for LVMH and its competitors. The financial turmoil of the late 1990s and the subsequent currency devaluations and weakening of the yen translated into lower demand for luxury goods. Because price perceptions are a critical component of luxury goods' appeal, LMVH executives made a number of adjustments in response to changing business conditions. For example, Patrick Choel, president of the perfume

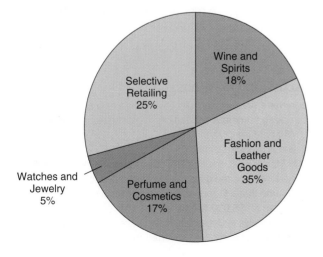

FIGURE 1
LVMH Operating Units by 2008 Net Sales

(Pie chart: Wine and Spirits 18%; Fashion and Leather Goods 35%; Perfume and Cosmetics 17%; Watches and Jewelry 5%; Selective Retailing 25%)

and cosmetics division, raised wholesale prices in individual Asian markets. The goal was to discourage discount retailers from stocking up on designer products and then selling them to down-market consumers. Also, expenditures on perfume and cosmetics advertising were reduced to maintain profitability in the face of a possible sales decline.

Louis Vuitton chairman Yves Carcelle also made adjustments. He canceled plans for a new store in Indonesia, and group managers raised prices to counteract the effect of currency devaluations. Because the DFS chain depends on Japanese tourists in Asia and Hawaii for 75 percent of sales, Louis Vuitton managers also work with tour operators to predict the flow of Japanese tourists. When tourism is at a peak, price increases from 10 to 22 percent help maximize profits on merchandise sales.

Arnault was confident that the Asian crisis would not severely affect his company's performance in the long term. As Arnault explained in the spring of 1998, "One has to distinguish between Japan, where most of our business is, and the rest of Asia. Japan is in a growth slump, but it isn't going to have the same difficulties as Korea or Indonesia. And our business in Japan is doing very well." Because the Louis Vuitton unit controls its own distribution, management has even been able to take advantage of the crisis by renegotiating store leases in key Asian cities. In some instances, the company has secured longer lease terms plus reductions in rates by as much as one third. Arnault's optimism was well founded; with interest rates at record lows and a gloomy outlook for the stock market, Japanese consumers had few other spending options. In 2001, executives actually raised prices at Louis Vuitton's Japanese stores.

> *"One friend of mine has 10 Louis Vuitton bags. In Japan, it's a status symbol. It's very important to have European luxury goods."*
>
> **a 39-year-old flight attendant based in Tokyo**

Strategic Decisions at LVMH

Over the past decade, Arnault has leveraged his multibrand strategy by broadening the company's consumer base. In the late 1990s, Arnault sensed that cosmetics-buying habits were changing in key markets. He opened Sephora stores in New York, Chicago, and San Francisco in conjunction with a new Web site, Sephora.com. Today, there are nearly 100 Sephora stores in the United States; the chain also has a presence in more than one dozen other countries, including China and Russia. Customers who visit Sephora USA stores are encouraged to wander freely and sample products on an open floor without waiting for sales clerks to assist them.

In 2001, Arnault paid more than $600 million for Donna Karan International Inc. and its trademarks. Arnault had tried without success to acquire Giorgio Armani; Donna Karan is LVMH's first American designer label. As Arnault noted, "What appealed to us is the fact that it is one of the best-known brand names in the world."

In January 2008, executives at Louis Vuitton announced a new corporate branding campaign using a 90-second ad that would appear on cable and satellite television and in cinemas. This was something new in the luxury goods sector; generally, advertising budgets are limited and television is viewed as too expensive. In addition, some in the industry believe that TV's status as a mass-marketing medium can undercut a luxury brand's aura of exclusivity. However, Louis Vuitton executives hoped audiences would connect with the brand's travel heritage. To achieve that, the company's ad agency proposed buying time on news channels that business travelers watch such as CNN. As Louis Vuitton marketing chief Pietro Beccari noted, "It is supposed to touch our clientele and viewers in ways that perhaps other media will not touch. This is a way to say Louis Vuitton is different. It is something éphémère, but also something that stays."

Arnault has also turned his attention to emerging markets. Louis Vuitton entered India in 2002 with a boutique at a luxury hotel; now, Fendi, Tag Heuer, and Dior are open for business as well. LVMH has a lock on prime locations at Emporio, an upscale shopping mall that opened recently in New Delhi. Because LVMH has a group presence in the mall, it can negotiate favorable lease rates for retail space. Arnault's expansion coincided with the September 2007 launch of Vogue India. Once again, thanks to LVMH's diverse brand portfolio, the company is able to buy large blocks of advertising space from Condé Nast India at discounted prices.

The global economic crisis that gained traction in 2008 affected many retail sectors, and the luxury goods business was no exception. Overall purchases of luxury goods fell in the key U.S. market; sales slowed in Russia and other emerging markets as well. Although total sales in the luxury segment were expected to reach a record €175 billion ($218 billion) in 2008, industry observers expected that they would drop significantly in 2009. For European-based luxury companies, there was some good news: the dollar was strengthening against the euro. As the 2008 holiday shopping season approached, many luxury goods makers reduced prices in the United States. At Chanel, the cuts ranged from 7 to 10 percent; as John Galantic, president of Chanel's U.S. unit, noted, "The dollar's recent strength has allowed us to pass on greater value to our customers." Louis Vuitton was a notable exception; in fact, during 2008, the company raised prices twice, resulting in an average increase of 10 percent. The price increases did not dampen sales; in fact, sales continued to increase.

Visit the Web site

www.lvmh.com
A complete PowerPoint presentation of the current year's financial results is available on the LVMH Web site.
www.sephora.com

Discussion Questions

1. Bernard Arnault has built LVMH into a luxury goods empire by making numerous acquisitions. What strategy is evident here?
2. What are the possible risks of Louis Vuitton's first-ever television advertising campaign?
3. In March 2008, the euro/dollar exchange rate was €1 = $1.50. By November, the dollar had strengthened to €1 = $1.25. Assume that a European luxury goods marketer cuts the price of an $8,000 tweed suit by 10 percent to maintain holiday sales in December. How will revenues be affected when dollar prices are converted to euros?

4. Louis Vuitton executives raised prices in 2008, and sales continued to increase. What does this say about the demand curve of the typical Louis Vuitton customer?

Sources: Rachel Dodes and Christina Passariello, "In Rare Move, Luxury-Goods Makers Trim Their Prices in U.S." *The Wall Street Journal* (November 14, 2008), p. B1; Eric Pfanner, "Vuitton Is Embracing Medium of the Masses," *The New York Times* (January 30, 2008), p. C3; Christina Passariello, "LVMH Books Passage to India for Vuitton, Dior, Fendi, Celine," *The Wall Street Journal* (May 8, 2007), pp. B1, B2; Lisa Bannon and Alessandra Galloni, "Brand Manager Deluxe," *The Wall Street Journal* (October 10, 2003), p. B1; John Carreyrou and Christopher Lawton, "Napoleon's Nightcap Gets a Good Rap from Hip-Hop Set," *The Wall Street Journal* (July 14, 2003), pp. A1, A7; Teri Agins and Deborah Ball, "Changing Outfits: Did LVMH Commit a Fashion Faux Pas Buying Donna Karan?" *The Wall Street Journal* (March 21, 2002), pp. A1, A8; Deborah Ball, "Despite Downturn, Japanese Are Still Having Fits for Luxury Goods," *The Wall Street Journal* (April 24, 2001), pp. B1, B4; Bonnie Tsui, "Eye of the Beholder: Sephora's Finances," *Advertising Age* (March 19, 2001), p. 20; Lucia van der Post, "Life's Brittle Luxuries," *Financial Times* (July 18–19, 1998), p. I; Gail Edmondson, "LVMH: Life Isn't All Champagne and Caviar," *Business Week* (November 10, 1997), pp. 108+; Jennifer Steinhauer, "The King of Posh," *The New York Times* (August 17, 1997), sec. 3, pp. 1, 10–11; David Owen, "A Captain Used to Storms," *Financial Times* (June 21–22, 1997); Holly Brubach, "And Luxury for All," *The New York Times Magazine* (July 12, 1998), pp. 24–29+; Amy Barrett, "LVMH's Chairman Remains Calm Despite Turbulence," *The Wall Street Journal* (March 16, 1998), p. B4; Amy Barrett, "Gucci's Big Makeover Is Turning Heads," *The Wall Street Journal* (August 26, 1997), p. 12; Stewart Toy, "100 Years of Louis Vuitton," *Cigar Aficionado* (Autumn 1996), pp. 378–379+.

Global Marketing Channels and Physical Distribution

Case 12-1
Tesco Expands in the United States

Tesco is the largest supermarket chain in the United Kingdom. The company's slogan is "Every Little Helps"; it executes on that promise in various ways, including its Clubcard loyalty program and an online grocery retailing operation that fulfills more than 100,000 orders every week. Tesco's supply chain—including relationships with suppliers and distributors—is one of the best in the industry. Despite these strengths, Tesco lags behind retailing giants Walmart and Carrefour in terms of global presence. To address this weakness, Sir Terry Leahy, Tesco's chief executive, is implementing an expansion strategy. For example, his executives initiated negotiations with

India's Bharti Enterprises about possible joint ventures. Tesco is also expanding in China.

But Tesco is also making waves in the United States. Sir Terry has committed hundreds of millions of dollars to open small stores in Los Angeles and Phoenix, a decision that industry observers have described as "one of the most widely watched events in the global retailing sector." The first stores have 15,000 square feet of floor space and bear the name "Tesco Fresh & Easy"; they offer a focused selection of fresh foods, packaged goods, and prepared meals (see Exhibit 12-1). Commenting on the $1 trillion U.S. grocery market, Sir Terry noted, "Demand

Exhibit 12-1: Tesco currently operates more than 100 Fresh & Easy supermarkets in the United States. The first store opened in November 2007; as the economic environment deteriorated, Tesco was forced to adjust its strategy. To appeal to budget-conscious shoppers, Tesco uses aggressive price promotions. It also has "Everything under $1" displays.
Source: Pacific Photo/Newscom.

for convenience shopping is very well developed there. There are lots of wealthy and busy people and it's multicultural. You've got to start somewhere and it's important to do it in bite-sized chunks." For more on Tesco's global expansion, see Case 12-1 at the end of the chapter.

Supermarkets and convenience stores comprise just two of the many elements that make up distribution channels around the globe. The American Marketing Association defines a channel of distribution as "an organized network of agencies and institutions that, in combination, perform all the activities required to link producers with users to accomplish the marketing task."[1] Physical distribution is the movement of goods through channels; as suggested by the definition, channels are made up of a coordinated group of individuals or firms that perform functions that add utility to a product or service.

Distribution channels are one of the most highly differentiated aspects of national marketing systems. Retail stores vary in size from giant hypermarkets to small stores in Latin America called *pulperías*. The diversity of channels and the wide range of possible distribution strategies and market entry options can present challenges to managers responsible for designing global marketing programs. Channels and physical distribution are crucial aspects of the total marketing program; without them, a great product at the right price and effective communications mean very little.

CHANNEL OBJECTIVES

Marketing channels exist to create utility for customers. The major categories of channel utility are **place utility** (the availability of a product or service in a location that is convenient to a potential customer), **time utility** (the availability of a product or service when desired by a customer), **form utility** (the availability of the product processed, prepared, in proper condition and/or ready to use), and **information utility** (the availability of answers to questions and general communication about useful product features and benefits). Because these utilities can be a basic source of competitive advantage and comprise an important element of the firm's overall value proposition, choosing a channel strategy is one of the key policy decisions management must make. For example, the Coca-Cola Company's global marketing leadership position is based in part on its ability to put Coke "within an arm's reach of desire"; in other words, to create place utility.

The starting point in selecting the most effective channel arrangement is a clear focus of the company's marketing effort on a target market and an assessment of the way(s) in which distribution can contribute to the firm's overall value proposition. Who are the target customers, and where are they located? What are their information requirements? What are their preferences for service? How sensitive are they to price? Moreover, each market must be analyzed to determine the cost of providing channel services. What is appropriate in one country may not be effective in another. Even marketers concerned with a single-country program can study channel arrangements in different parts of the world for valuable information and insight into possible new channel strategies and tactics. For example, retailers from Europe and Asia studied self-service discount retailing in the United States and then introduced the self-service concept in their own countries. Similarly, governments and business executives from many parts of the world have examined Japanese trading companies to learn from their success. Walmart's formula has been closely studied and copied by competitors in the markets it has entered.

---

[1]Peter D. Bennett, *Dictionary of Marketing Terms* (Chicago: American Marketing Association, 1988), p. 29.

DISTRIBUTION CHANNELS: TERMINOLOGY AND STRUCTURE

As defined previously, distribution channels are systems that link manufacturers to customers. Although channels for consumer products and industrial products are similar, there are also some distinct differences. In **business-to-consumer marketing** (b-to-c or B2C), consumer channels are designed to put products in the hands of people for their own use. By contrast, **business-to-business marketing** (b-to-b or B2B) involves industrial channels that deliver products to manufacturers or other organizations that use them as inputs in the production process or in day-to-day operations. Intermediaries play important roles in both consumer and industrial channels; a **distributor** is a wholesale intermediary that typically carries product lines or brands on a selective basis. An **agent** is an intermediary who negotiates exchange transactions between two or more parties but does not take title to the goods being purchased or sold.

Consumer Products and Services

Figure 12-1 summarizes six channel structure alternatives for consumer products. The characteristics of both buyers and products have an important influence on channel design. The first alternative is to market directly to buyers via the Internet, mail order, various types of door-to-door selling, or manufacturer-owned retail outlets. The other options use retailers and various combinations of sales forces, agents/brokers, and wholesalers. The number of individual buyers and their geographic distribution, income, shopping habits, and reaction to different selling methods frequently vary from country to country and may require different channel approaches.

Product characteristics such as degree of standardization, perishability, bulk, service requirements, and unit price have an impact as well. Generally speaking, channels tend to be longer (require more intermediaries) as the number of customers to be served increases and the price per unit decreases. Bulky products usually require channel arrangements that minimize shipping distances and the number of times products change hands before they reach the ultimate customer.

The Internet and related forms of new media are dramatically altering the distribution landscape. eBay pioneered the **peer-to-peer marketing** (p-to-p) model whereby individual consumers market products to other individuals. eBay's success was one reason that traditional merchants quickly recognized the Internet's potential. To sustain revenue growth, eBay began

FIGURE 12-1

Marketing Channel Alternatives: Consumer Products

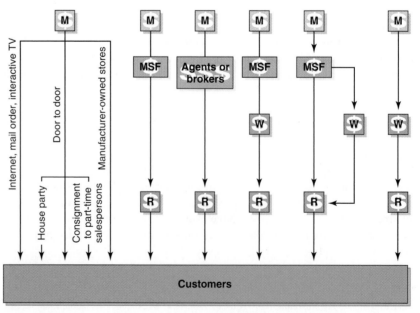

M = Manufacturer   MSF = Manufacturer's sales force
W = Wholesaler   R = Retailer

assisting large companies such as Disney and IBM in setting up online "storefronts" to sell items for fixed prices in addition to conducting b-to-c auctions. "As we evolved from auction-style bidding to adding Buy It Now, the logical next step for us was to give sellers a place to showcase their listings," said Bill Cobb, eBay's senior vice president for global marketing.[2] Some observers predict that interactive television (ITV) will also become a viable direct distribution channel in the coming years as more households are wired with the necessary two-way technology. Time-pressed consumers in many countries are increasingly attracted to the time and place utility created by the Internet and similar new media technologies.

Low-cost, mass-market nondurable products and certain services can be sold door-to-door via a direct sales force (see Exhibit 12-2). Door-to-door selling is mature in the United States; however, it is growing in popularity elsewhere. For example, by the mid-1990s, AIG had 5,000 agents selling insurance policies door-to-door in China. This innovative channel strategy was so successful that domestic Chinese companies such as People's Insurance and Ping An Insurance copied it. Noted one local insurance executive, "We have to adjust ourselves to the rising competition."[3]

In April 1998, China's state council imposed a blanket ban on all types of direct selling. The ban was aimed most directly at illegal pyramid schemes, and several foreign companies, including Amway, Avon, Mary Kay, and Tupperware, were allowed to continue operations in China. However, they were forced to adapt their business models: Their sales representatives had to be affiliated with brick-and-mortar retailers. The ban was lifted in 2005; because it restricted competition, the handful of foreign direct-sales marketers that maintained a presence in China had a unique growth opportunity during the years the ban was in force. Amway is a case in point: Between 1998 and 2004, Amway's Chinese sales tripled, to $2 billion. Today, China is Amway's biggest market.[4]

In Japan, the biggest barrier facing U.S. auto manufacturers isn't high tariffs; rather, it's the fact that half the cars that are sold each year are sold door to door. Toyota and its Japanese competitors maintain showrooms, but they also employ more than 100,000 car salespeople. Unlike their American counterparts, many Japanese car buyers never visit dealerships.

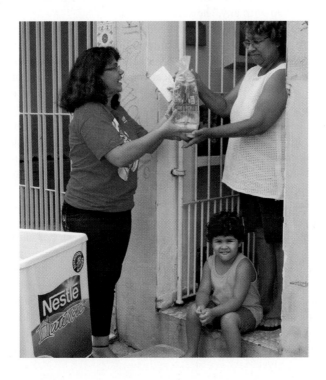

Exhibit 12-2: Nestlé is using an innovative approach to distribution in Brazil with a program of door-to-door selling in low-income neighborhoods. Consumers in these areas often do not have access to supermarkets. Currently, about 4,000 self-employed salespeople sell Nestlé products door-to-door; they often extend credit, giving customers two weeks to pay. The salespeople increase volume by establishing relationships with their customers; as the proprietor of Vita N, a Nestlé distributor with a staff of 400, explains, "In the favelas, you have to be part of the community or you just don't get in."
Source: Magdalena Gutierrez/ Kashmir Servicos Culturais LTDA.

[2]Nick Wingfield, "Ebay Allows Sellers to Set Up Storefronts Online in Bid to Expand Beyond Auctions," *The Wall Street Journal* (June 12, 2001), p. B8.

[3]Craig Smith, "AIG Reshapes China's Insurance Industry," *The Wall Street Journal* (February 9, 1996), p. A8.

[4]Mei Fong, "Avon's Calling, but China Only Opens the Door a Crack," *The Wall Street Journal* (February 26, 2007), p. B1.

EMERGING MARKETS BRIEFING BOOK

Avon Seeks Growth in Asia and Europe

Avon has succeeded with door-to-door sales in dozens of countries identified by company executives as having weak retail infrastructures. Avon's management team recognizes that low discretionary income levels translate into modest expenditures on cosmetics and toiletries. Thus, the role of the sales force is to communicate the benefits of cosmetics and build demand. Avon was the first company permitted to sell door-to-door in China; the company's joint venture with Guangzhou Cosmetics Factory dates to 1990.

However, after the 1998 government ban on direct selling, Avon shifted from a direct-sales model and opened beauty boutiques. Today, the company has more than 5,700 boutiques across China. In 2006, the Ministry of Commerce and the State Administration for Industry and Commerce both gave their approval for Avon to resume direct selling. Avon immediately hired more than 100,000 sales representatives. However, the sales reps can only generate income through product sales; they cannot earn bonuses by recruiting other people to join the sales force. Sales commissions are capped at 30 percent.

Avon is also targeting Romania, Ukraine, and other emerging markets in Europe. For example, Russia represents the most successful new market entry in Avon's history. Between 1997 and 2002, Avon Russia's sales increased from $56 million to $142 million. The company invested in a $40 million production facility in Moscow. Avon's Russian sales force promotes Avon cosmetics in factories, beauty parlors, and, occasionally, in the homes of friends. Avon has aggressively recruited highly qualified women from the ranks of doctors and engineers, offering them the opportunity to achieve financial independence despite Russia's uncertain economic environment.

Source: Based on Andrew Yeh, "Avon Recruits 114,000 in China," *Financial Times* (July 19, 2006), p. 20.

The close, long-term relationships between auto salespersons and the Japanese people can be thought of as a consumer version of the *keiretsu* system discussed in Chapter 9. Japanese car buyers expect numerous face-to-face meetings with a sales representative, during which trust is established. The relationship continues after the deal is closed; sales reps send cards and continually seek to ensure the buyer's satisfaction. American rivals such as Ford, meanwhile, try to generate showroom traffic. Nobumasa Ogura manages a Ford dealership in Tokyo. "We need to come up with some ideas to sell more cars without door-to-door sales, but the reality is that we haven't come up with any," he said.[5]

Another direct selling alternative is the *manufacturer-owned store* or *independent franchise store*. One of the first successful U.S.-based international companies, Singer, established a worldwide chain of company-owned and -operated outlets to sell and service sewing machines. As noted in Chapter 9, Japanese consumer electronics companies integrate stores into their distribution groups. Apple, Levi Strauss, Nike, Sony, well-known fashion design houses, and other companies with strong brands sometimes establish flagship retail stores as product showcases or as a means of obtaining marketing intelligence (see Exhibit 12-3). Nokia and Motorola are among the cell phone marketers to open branded stores in London, Moscow, New York, Paris, and other major cities. The stores are designed to provide an interactive shopping experience and build brand loyalty.[6] Such channels supplement, rather than replace, distribution through independent retail stores.

Other channel structure alternatives for consumer products include various combinations of a manufacturer's sales force and wholesalers calling on independent retail outlets, which in turn sell to customers (retailing is discussed in detail later in the chapter). For mass-market consumer products such as ice-cream novelties, cigarettes, and light bulbs that are bought by millions of consumers, a channel that links the manufacturer to distributors and retailers is generally required to achieve market coverage. A cornerstone of Walmart's phenomenal growth in the United States was its ability to achieve significant economies by buying huge volumes of goods directly from manufacturers. However, individual country customs vary. In Latin America, for example, some vendors refused to sell direct to Walmart. Similarly, Toys 'R' Us faced considerable opposition from Japanese toy manufacturers that refused to bypass intermediaries and supply the company directly.

---

[5]Valerie Reitman, "Toyota Calling: In Japan's Car Market, Big Three Face Rivals Who Go Door-to-Door," *The Wall Street Journal* (September 28, 1994), pp. A1, A6.
[6]Cassell Bryan-Low and Li Yuan, "Selling Cellphone Buzz," *The Wall Street Journal* (February 23, 2006), pp. B1, B5.

Exhibit 12-3: Apple operates more than 200 retail stores in the United States, Canada, Japan, the United Kingdom, China, and several other countries. Each store features a "genius bar" where customers can seek one-on-one technical support with a knowledgeable employee. Many stores, such as this one in London, feature a signature glass staircase that Apple co-founder and CEO Steve Jobs helped design.
Source: Hufton & Crow/Alamy Images.

Perishable products impose special demands on channel members who must ensure that the merchandise is in satisfactory condition (form utility) at the time of customer purchase. In developed countries, a company's own sales force or independent channel members handle distribution of perishable food products; in either case, the distributor organization checks the stock to ensure that it is fresh. In less-developed countries, public marketplaces are important channels; they provide a convenient way for producers of vegetables, bread, and other food products to sell their goods directly.

Sometimes, a relatively simple channel innovation in a developing country can significantly increase a company's overall value proposition. In the early 1990s, for example, the Moscow Bread Company (MBC) needed to improve its distribution system. Russian consumers queue up daily to buy fresh loaves at numerous shops and kiosks. Unfortunately, MBC's staff was burdened by excessive paperwork that resulted in the delivery of stale bread. Andersen Consulting found that as much as one-third of the bread the company produced was wasted. In developed countries, about 95 percent of food is sold packaged; the figure is much lower in the former Soviet Union. Whether a consumer bought bread at an outdoor market or in an enclosed store, it was displayed unwrapped. The consulting team devised a simple solution—plastic bags to keep the bread fresh. Russian consumers responded favorably to the change; not only did the bags guarantee freshness and significantly extend the bread's shelf life, but the bags themselves also created utility. In a country where such extras are virtually unknown, the bags constituted a reusable "gift."[7]

The retail environment in developing countries presents similar challenges for companies marketing nonperishable items. In affluent countries, Procter & Gamble, Unilever, Colgate-Palmolive, and other global consumer products companies are accustomed to catering to a "buy-in-bulk" consumer mentality. By contrast, in Mexico and other emerging markets, many consumers shop for food, soft drinks, and other items several times each day at tiny, independent "mom-and-pop" stores, kiosks, and market stalls. The products available here, including shampoo, disposable diapers, and laundry detergent, are packaged in single-use quantities at a relatively high per-use cost.

At Procter & Gamble, these operations are known as "high-frequency stores"; in Mexico alone, an estimated 70 percent of the population shops at such stores. To motivate shopkeepers to stock more of P&G's products, the company launched a "golden store" program. In exchange for a pledge to carry at least 40 different P&G products, participating stores receive regular visits from P&G representatives who tidy display areas and arrange promotional material in prominent

---

[7]"Case Study: Moscow Bread Company," Andersen Consulting, 1993.

places. Although P&G initially used its own sales force, it has since begun relying on independent agents who buy inventory (paying in advance) and then resell the items to shop operators.[8] P&G's experience illustrates the fact that the channel structures shown in Figure 12-1 represent strategic alternatives; firms can and should vary their strategies as market conditions change.

Industrial Products

Figure 12-2 summarizes marketing channel alternatives for the industrial or business products company. As is true with consumer channels, product and customer characteristics have an impact on channel structure. Three basic elements are involved: the manufacturer's sales force, distributors or agents, and wholesalers. A manufacturer can reach customers with its own sales force, a sales force that calls on wholesalers who sell to customers, or a combination of these two arrangements. A manufacturer can sell directly to wholesalers without using a sales force, and wholesalers, in turn, can supply customers. Finally, a distributor or agent can call on wholesalers or customers for the manufacturer. For vendors serving a relatively small customer base, a shorter channel design with relatively few (or no) intermediaries may be possible. For example, if there are only 10 customers for an industrial product in each national market, these 10 customers must be directly contacted by either the manufacturer or an agent.

Channel innovation can be an essential element of a successful marketing strategy. Dell's rise to a leading position in the global PC industry was based on Michael Dell's decision to bypass conventional channels by selling direct and by building computers to customers' specifications (see Exhibit 12-4). Dell began life as a b-to-b marketer; its business model proved so successful that the company then began marketing direct to the home PC market. Consider Boeing aircraft; given the price, physical size, and complexity of a jet airliner, it is easy to understand why Boeing utilizes its own sales force. Other products sold in this way include mainframe computers and large photocopy systems; these are expensive, complicated products that require both explanation and applications analysis focused on the customer's needs. A company-trained salesperson, sales engineer, or sales team is well-suited for the task of creating information utility for computer buyers.

FIGURE 12-2

Marketing Channel Alternatives: Industrial Products

M = Manufacturer   MSF = Manufacturer's sales force
W = Wholesaler   D or A = Distributor or agent

---

[8]Ellen Byron, "Emerging Ambitions: P&G's Global Target: Shelves of Tiny Stores," *The Wall Street Journal* (July 16, 2007), p. A1.

Exhibit 12-4: Dell rang up $61 billion in direct sales of made-to-order PC systems in 2009. The company experienced phenomenal growth thanks in part to sales generated through the company's Web site. Although Dell originally was a business-to-business marketer, founder Michael Dell guided the company to the consumer market as well. Although the direct sales approach has been effective in more than 100 countries, Dell has recently made its products available through traditional retail channels in response to changing consumer shopping habits.
Source: © 2009 Dell Inc. All Rights Reserved.

ESTABLISHING CHANNELS AND WORKING WITH CHANNEL INTERMEDIARIES

A global company expanding across national boundaries must utilize existing distribution channels or build its own. Channel obstacles are often encountered when a company enters a competitive market where brands and supply relationships are already established. If management chooses *direct involvement*, the company establishes its own sales force or operates its own retail stores. Kodak adopted the direct approach in Japan, where Kodak Japan is a company-owned distributor. The other option is *indirect involvement*, which entails utilizing independent agents, distributors, and retailers. In Asia, for example, Western luxury goods marketers have long relied on independent distributors such as Hong Kong–based Fairton, whose local market knowledge and networks of stores are keys to success. Similarly, as noted in Chapter 11, DeBeers uses independent intermediaries to market its diamonds in the United States.

Channel strategy in a global marketing program must fit the company's competitive position and overall marketing objectives in each national market. Direct involvement in distribution in a new market can entail considerable expense. Sales representatives and sales management must be hired and trained. The sales organization will inevitably be a heavy loser in its early stage of operation in a new market because it will not have sufficient volume to cover its overhead costs. Therefore, any company contemplating establishing its own sales force should be prepared to underwrite its losses for a reasonable period of time.

Channel decisions are important because of the number and nature of relationships that must be managed. Channel decisions typically involve long-term legal commitments and obligations to various intermediaries. Such commitments are often extremely expensive to terminate or change, so it is imperative for companies to document the nature of the relationship with the foreign partner. As the saying goes, "The shortest pencil is better than the longest memory." At a minimum, the written agreement should include a definition of what constitutes "good cause" for termination. Also, as noted in Chapter 5, it is often preferable to settle business disputes through arbitration rather than in a local court. Thus, the distributor or agent agreement should also provide for arbitration in a neutral forum in a third country. In many instances, local laws protect agents and distributors; even in the absence of a formal written agreement, in a civil-law country the law will be applied. In addition to written obligations, commitments must be backed by good faith and feelings of mutual obligation. In short, the selection of distributors and agents in a target market is critically important.

Companies entering emerging markets for the first time must exercise particular care in choosing a channel intermediary. Typically, a local distributor is required because the market entrant lacks knowledge of local business practices and needs a partner with links to potential customers. In addition, newcomers to a particular market generally want to limit their risk and financial exposure. Although initial results may be satisfactory, with time headquarters may become dissatisfied with the local distributor's performance. This is when managers from the global company often intervene and attempt to take control. Harvard professor David Arnold offers seven specific guidelines to help prevent such problems from arising.[9]

- *Select distributors. Don't let them select you.* A company may link up with a distributor by default after being approached by representatives at a trade fair. In fact, such eager candidates may already be serving a company's competitors. Their objective may be to maintain control over the product category in a given market. A proactive market entrant can identify potential distributors by requesting a list from the U.S. Department of Commerce or its equivalent in other countries. The local chamber of commerce or trade association in a country can provide similar information.
- *Look for distributors capable of developing markets, rather than those with a few good customer contacts.* A distributor with good contacts may appear to be the "obvious" choice in terms of generating quick sales and revenues. However, a better choice is often a partner willing to both make the investment necessary to achieve success and draw upon the marketing experience of the global company. Such a partner may, in fact, have no prior experience with a particular product category. In this case, the distributor may devote more effort and assign the new partner a higher priority simply because taking on the product line does not represent the status quo.
- *Treat local distributors as long-term partners, not temporary market entry vehicles.* A contractual agreement that provides strong financial incentives for customer acquisition, new product sales, or other forms of business development is a signal to the distributor that the market entrant is taking a long-term perspective. Such development can be done with the input of managers from the global company.
- *Support market entry by committing money, managers, and proven marketing ideas.* In addition to providing sales personnel and technical support, management should consider demonstrating its commitment early on by investing in a minority equity stake in

---

[9]The following discussion is adapted from David Arnold, "Seven Rules of International Distribution," *Harvard Business Review* 78, no. 6 (November–December 2000), pp. 131–137.

an independent distributor. The risks associated with such investment should be no greater than risks associated with independent distribution systems in the manufacturer's home country. The earlier such a commitment is made, the better the relationship that is likely to develop.

- *From the start, maintain control over marketing strategy.* To exploit the full potential of global marketing channels, the manufacturer should provide solid leadership for marketing in terms of which products the distributor should sell and how to position them. Again, it is necessary to have employees on site or to have country or regional managers monitor the distributor's performance. As one manager noted, "We used to give far too much autonomy to distributors, thinking that they knew their markets. But our value proposition is a tough one to execute, and time and again we saw distributors cut prices to compensate for failing to target the right customers or to sufficiently train salespeople." This is not to say that the intermediary should not be allowed to adapt the distribution strategy to suit local conditions. The point is for the manufacturer to take the lead.

- *Make sure distributors provide you with detailed market and financial performance data.* Distributor organizations are often a company's best source—maybe the only source—of market information. The contract between a manufacturer and distributor should include specific language to the effect that local market information and financial data will be transferred back to the manufacturer. One sign that a successful manufacturer–distributor relationship can be established is the latter's willingness to provide such information.

- *Build links among national distributors at the earliest opportunity.* A manufacturer should attempt to establish links between its networks of national distributors. This can be accomplished by setting up a regional corporate office or by establishing a distributor council. At any point in time, a company may have some excellent agents and distributors, others that are satisfactory, and a third group that is unsatisfactory. By creating opportunities for distributors to communicate, ideas for new product designs based on individual market results can be leveraged, and overall distributor performance can be improved.

When devising a channel strategy, it is necessary to be realistic about the intermediary's motives. On the one hand, it is the intermediary's responsibility to implement an important element of a company's marketing strategy. Left to their own devices, however, middlemen may seek to maximize their own profit rather than the manufacturer's. These agents sometimes engage in *cherry picking*, the practice of accepting orders only from manufacturers with established demand for products and brands. Cherry picking can also take the form of selecting only a few choice items from a vendor's product lines. The cherry picker is not interested in developing a market for a new product, which is a problem for the expanding international company. As noted previously, a manufacturer should provide leadership and invest resources to build the relationship with a desired distributor. A manufacturer with a new product or a product with a limited market share may find it more desirable to set up some arrangement for bypassing the cherry-picking channel member. In some cases, a manufacturer must incur the costs of direct involvement by setting up its own distribution organization to obtain a share of the market. When the company sales finally reach critical mass, management may decide to shift from direct involvement to a more cost-effective independent intermediary.

An alternative method of dealing with the cherry-picking problem does not require setting up an expensive direct sales force. Rather, a company may decide to rely on a distributor's own sales force by subsidizing the cost of the sales representatives the distributor has assigned to the company's products. This approach has the advantage of holding down costs by tying in with the distributor's existing sales management team and physical distribution system. It is possible to place managed direct selling support and distribution support behind a product at the expense of only one salesperson per selling area. The distributor's incentive for cooperating in this kind of arrangement is that he or she obtains a "free" sales representative for a new product with the potential to be a profitable addition to his or her line. This cooperative arrangement is ideally suited to getting a new export-sourced product into distribution in a market. Alternatively, a company may also decide to provide special incentives to independent channel agents.

GLOBAL RETAILING

Global retailing is any retailing activity that crosses national boundaries. For centuries, entrepreneurial merchants have ventured abroad to seek out merchandise and ideas and to establish retail operations. During the nineteenth and early twentieth centuries, British, French, Dutch, Belgian, and German trading companies established retailing organizations in Africa and Asia. International trading and retail store operations were two of the economic pillars of that era's colonial system. In the twentieth century, Dutch apparel and footwear retailer C&A expanded across Europe. In 1909, American Frank Woolworth took his five-and-dime concept across the Atlantic, opening his first British store in Liverpool.

Global retailers serve an important distribution function; when Carrefour, Tesco, and Walmart set up shop in developing countries, they provide customers with access to more products and lower prices than were available previously. As we have noted throughout the text, when global companies expand abroad, they often encounter local competitors. The retail sector is no exception; India is a case in point. *Organized retail*, a term that is used to describe the modern, branded chain stores, currently comprises less than 5 percent of India's market. The sector is expected to exhibit double-digit growth, a fact that has attracted the giants of global retailing. However, they must compete with stores operated by local retail chains. One such company is Reliance Industries; its Reliance Retail division is opening thousands of modern supermarkets across India. What's more, Reliance itself is developing plans for global expansion.[10]

In some instances, it is a local retailer, rather than a global one, that breaks new ground by transforming the shopping experience. Nakumatt, a supermarket chain in Kenya, is a case in point. As Wambui Mwangi, a political science professor at University of Toronto, notes, "Nakumatt is where you go to show you are educated and prosperous and cognizant of larger affairs. It's an aspirational space that appeals to everyone, especially the people who can't really afford to shop there."[11]

Retail business models may undergo significant adaptation outside the country in which they originated. For example, after the first 7-Eleven Japan franchise opened in 1973, the stores quickly attracted customers seeking convenience. Today, "conbinis" are ubiquitous in Japan, with more than 43,000 stores location. Seven & I Holdings, which operates 7-Eleven, is Japan's largest grocer. The convenience store operators use cutting-edge EPOS data to track customer behavior and ensure that perishable products and other merchandise is delivered on a just-in-time basis during high-traffic periods. Even in today's difficult economic environment, convenience store sales have remained strong. Now the operators are moving to further differentiate themselves; for example, 7-Eleven has Seven Bank ATMs in its stores and a lower-priced line of own-brand merchandise, Seven Premium.[12]

Today's global retailing scene is characterized by great diversity (Table 12-1 lists the top five companies by revenue). We will begin the discussion with a brief survey of some of the different forms retailing can take. Retail stores can be divided into categories according to the amount of square feet of floor space, the level of service offered, width and depth of product offerings, or other criteria. Each represents a strategic option for a retailer considering global expansion.

TABLE 12-1 Top Five Global Retailers (2008 Sales; Millions)

Rank	Company	Country	Formats	Sales ($)
1	Walmart Stores	United States	Discount store, Wholesale club	$378,799
2	Carrefour	France	Hypermarket	120,914
3	Metro AG	Germany	Diversified	94,697
4	Tesco PLC	UK	Supermarket/Hypermarket	93,844
5	Home Depot	United States	Home improvement	77,349

---

[10]Eric Bellman, "India's Reliance Looks Abroad," *The Wall Street Journal* (March 16, 2007), p. A8.
[11]Barney Jopson, "Consumerism for Kenya's As and Bs," *Financial Times* (July 8, 2008), p. 14.
[12]Michiyo Nakamoto, "Convenience Stores Pay Price of Success," *Financial Times Special Report—Japan* (October 14, 2008), p. 3. See also Juro Osawa, "Convenience Stores Score in Japan," *The Wall Street Journal* (August 19, 2008), p. B2.

Types of Retail Operations

Department stores literally have several departments under one roof, each representing a distinct merchandise line and staffed with a limited number of salespeople. Departments in a typical store might include men's, women's, children's, beauty aids, housewares, and toys. Table 12-2 lists major department stores that have expanded outside their home-country markets. However, in most instances, the expansion is limited to a few countries. As Maureen Hinton, a retail analyst with a London-based consultancy, notes, "It's quite difficult to transfer a department store brand abroad. You have to find a city with the right demographic for your offer. If you adapt your offer to the locality, you dilute your brand name." Marvin Traub, former chief executive of Bloomingdales, has a different perspective. "Conceptually, department stores are global brands already because we live in a world with an enormous amount of travel between cities and continents," he says.[13]

Specialty retailers offer less variety than department stores. They are more narrowly focused and offer a relatively narrow merchandise mix aimed at a particular target market. Specialty stores offer a great deal of merchandise depth (e.g., many styles, colors, and sizes), high levels of service from knowledgeable staff persons, and a value proposition that is both clear and appealing to consumers. Laura Ashley, The Body Shop, Victoria's Secret, Gap, Starbucks, and the Disney Store are examples of global retail operators that have stores in many parts of the world. In some countries, local companies operate the stores. In Japan, for example, the giant Aeon Group runs Laura Ashley and The Body Shop stores and has a joint venture with Sports Authority.

Supermarkets are departmentalized, single-story retail establishments that offer a variety of food (e.g., produce, baked goods, meats) and nonfood items (e.g., paper products, health and beauty aids), mostly on a self-service basis. On average, supermarkets occupy between 50,000 square feet and 60,000 square feet of floor space. As noted in the chapter introduction, UK-based Tesco is one retailing group that is expanding globally. While home-country sales still account for approximately 80 percent of overall sales, the company has operations in more than a dozen foreign countries. Company officials typically study a country market for several years before choosing an entry strategy. Tesco's initial entry into Japan came via the acquisition of the C Two-Network, a chain of shops in Tokyo. As David Reid, head of international operations, explains, Tesco has succeeded globally because it does its homework and pays attention to details. Although Walmart is generating headlines as it moves around the globe, American retailers lag behind the Europeans in moving outside their home countries. One reason is the sheer size of the domestic U.S. market.[14] In fact, Walmart's lack of experience outside North America undoubtedly contributed to its failures in South Korea and Germany.

Convenience stores offer some of the same products as supermarkets, but the merchandise mix is limited to high-turnover convenience and impulse products. Prices for some products may

TABLE 12-2 Department Stores with Global Branches

Store	Original Store Location	Global Locations
Harvey Nichols	United Kingdom	Saudi Arabia, Hong Kong, Ireland, Dubai
Saks Fifth Avenue	United States	Dubai, Saudi Arabia, Mexico
Barneys New York	United States	Japan
Lane Crawford	Hong Kong	China, Macao Taiwan
Mitsukoshi	Japan	United States, Europe, Asia
H&M (Hennes & Mauritz)	Sweden	Austria, Germany, Kuwait, Slovakia, United States, 20 others

---

[13]Cecilie Rohwedder, "Harvey Nichols's Foreign Affair," *The Wall Street Journal* (February 18, 2005), p. B3.
[14]Michael Flagg, "In Asia, Going to the Grocery Increasingly Means Heading for a European Retail Chain," *The Wall Street Journal* (April 24, 2001), p. A21.

be 15 to 20 percent higher than supermarket prices. In terms of square footage, these are the smallest organized retail stores discussed here. In the United States, for example, the typical 7-Eleven occupies 3,000 square feet. Typically, convenience stores are located in high-traffic locations and offer extended service hours to accommodate commuters, students, and other highly mobile consumers. 7-Eleven is the world's largest convenience store chain; it has a total of 26,000 locations, including franchisees, licensees, and stores the company operates itself. A trend in convenience store retailing is toward smaller stores placed inside malls, airports, office buildings, and in college and university buildings. As Jeff Lenard, spokesperson for the National Association of Convenience Stores, noted recently, "All the good street corners are gone, and the competition is so fierce for the ones that are left."[15]

Discount retailers can be divided into several categories. The most general characteristic that they have in common is the emphasis on low prices. *Full-line discounters* typically offer a wide range of merchandise, including nonfood items and nonperishable food, in a limited-service format. As Table 12-1 clearly shows, Walmart is the reigning king of the full-line discounters (see Exhibit 12-5). Many stores cover 120,000 square feet (or more) of floor space; food accounts for about a third of floor space and sales. Walmart stores typically offer a folksy atmosphere and value-priced brands. Walmart is also a leader in the *warehouse club* segment of discount retailing; shoppers "join" the club to take advantage of low prices on a limited range of products (typically 3,000 to 5,000 different items), many of which are displayed in their shipping cartons in a "no frills" atmosphere.

When Walmart expands into a new country market, local discounters must respond to the competitive threat. In Canada, for example, Hudson Bay's Zellers is the largest discount store chain. After Walmart acquired a bankrupt Canadian chain, Zellers countered by brightening the décor in its stores, widening aisles, and catering to women with young children.[16] French discounter Tati is also going global; in addition to opening a store on New York's Fifth Avenue, Tati currently has stores in Lebanon, Turkey, Germany, Belgium, Switzerland, and the Cote d'Ivoire.

Dollar stores sell a select assortment of products at a single low price. In the United States, Family Dollar Stores and Dollar Tree Stores dominate the industry. However, a recent industry entrant, My Dollarstore, is experiencing rapid international growth. My Dollarstore Inc. has franchises in Eastern Europe, Central America, and Asia. To succeed in global markets, My Dollarstore has adapted its U.S. business model. For example, the typical U.S. dollar store has a

Exhibit 12-5: Walmart's international division currently generates only 20 percent of company sales, but the world's biggest retailer is staking its claim in China, India, and other emerging markets. By the end of 2009, Walmart had 146 stores in China, including 138 supercenters.
Source: Eugene Hoshiko/AP Wide World Photos.

---

[15]Kortney Stringer, "Convenience Stores Turn a New Corner," *The Wall Street Journal* (June 1, 2004), p. B5.
[16]Elena Cherney and Ann Zimmerman, "Canada's Zellers Retools Itself in Bid to Battle Walmart," *The Wall Street Journal* (December 10, 2001), p. B4.

"bargain basement" image. By contrast, in India, My Dollarstore targets affluent, middle-class shoppers who are attracted by the lure of low prices on brands associated with "the good life" in America. Goods are priced at 99 rupees—the equivalent of $2—and the stores are decorated in red, white, and blue with the Statue of Liberty on display. In the United States, dollar stores operate on a self-service basis with lean staffs; My Dollarstore's Indian locations have significantly higher staffing levels, the better to answer questions about new or unfamiliar products.[17]

Hard discounters include retailers such as Aldi, Leader Price ("Le Prix La Qualitié en Plus!"), and Lidl ("Where quality is cheaper!") that sell a tightly focused selection of goods—typically 900 to 1,600 different items—at very low prices. When Walmart entered the German market, hard discounters were already well entrenched. By mid-2006, after years of losses, Walmart decided to pull out of Germany. In the current economic downturn, hard discounters are thriving as cash-strapped consumers seek ways to stretch household budgets. Hard-discount retailers, which account for about 10 percent of grocery sales in Europe, rely heavily on private brands. Some of these sell for half the price of well-known global brands. Carrefour and other large supermarket operators are responding by offering more own-brand products at lower prices. For example, Tesco recently began selling 350 new cheap products under its own brands, including tea bags, cookies, and shampoo. "If there is a war, we will win it," said Tesco's commercial director, Richard Brasher.[18]

Hypermarkets are a hybrid retailing format combining the discounter, supermarket, and warehouse club approaches under a single roof. Size-wise, hypermarkets are huge, covering 200,000 square feet to 300,000 square feet.

Supercenters offer a wide range of aggressively priced grocery items plus general merchandise in a space that occupies about half the size of a hypermarket. Supercenters are an important aspect of Walmart's growth strategy, both at home and abroad. Walmart opened its first supercenter in 1988; today, it operates more than 2,600 supercenters, including hundreds of stores in Mexico and units in Argentina and Brazil. Some prices at Walmart's supercenters in Brazil are as much as 15 percent lower than competitors', and some observers wonder if the company has taken the discount approach too far. Company officials insist that profit margins are in the 20 to 22 percent range.[19]

Superstores (also known as *category killers* and *big-box retail*) is the label many in the retailing industry use when talking about stores such as Toys 'R' Us, Home Depot, and IKEA. The name refers to the fact that such stores specialize in selling vast assortments of a particular product category—toys or furniture, for example—in high volumes at low prices. In short, these stores represent retailing's "900 pound gorillas" that put pressure on smaller, more traditional competitors and prompt department stores to scale down merchandise sections that are in direct competition.

Shopping malls consist of a grouping of stores in one place. Developers such as Simon Property Group assemble an assortment of retailers that will create an appealing leisure destination; typically one or more large department stores serve as anchors. Shopping malls offer acres of free parking and easy access from main traffic thoroughfares. Historically, malls were enclosed, allowing shoppers to browse in comfort no matter what the weather is outside. However, a current trend is toward outdoor shopping centers, now called "lifestyle centers." Food courts and entertainment encourage families to spend several hours at the mall. In the United States, malls sprang up as people moved from city centers to the suburbs. Today, global mall development reflects the opportunity to serve emerging middle-class consumers who seek both convenience and entertainment.

Three of the world's five largest malls are in Asia (see Table 12-3). The reasons are clear-cut: Economic growth led to rising incomes; in addition, tourism is booming in the region. Some industry observers warn that the mega-malls and their glamorous global brand offerings are luring shoppers away from markets that sell goods produced by local craftspersons. Somewhere

[17]Eric Bellman, "A Dollar Store's Rich Allure in India," *The Wall Street Journal* (January 23, 2007), pp. B1, B14.

[18]Christina Passariello and Aaron O. Patrick, "Europe Eats on the Cheap," *The Wall Street Journal* (September 30, 2008), pp. B1, B7.

[19]Matt Moffett and Jonathan Friedland, "Walmart Won't Discount Its Prospects in Brazil, Though Its Losses Pile Up," *The Wall Street Journal* (June 4, 1996), p. A15; Wendy Zellner, "Walmart Spoken Here," *Business Week* (June 23, 1997), pp. 138–139+.

TABLE 12-3 The World's Largest Shopping Malls (ranked by gross leasable retail space)

Rank	Mall	Country	Number of Stores
1	South China Mall	Dongguan, China	1,500
2	Golden Resources Shopping Mall	Beijing, China	1,000
3	SM Mall of Asia	Pasay City, Philippines	NA
4	Dubai Mall	Dubai, UAE	1,200
5	West Edmonton Mall	Edmonton, Alberta, Canada	800

along the way, the thrill of discovering something new has been lost. Emil Pocock, a professor of American studies at Eastern Connecticut State University, is an expert on shopping malls. As he noted recently, "I find it very disconcerting that shopping malls are more or less the same wherever you go in the world. I'm not sure I want 100 international companies determining our choices for consumer goods."[20]

Outlet stores are a variation on the traditional shopping mall: retail operations that allow companies with well-known consumer brands to dispose of excess inventory, out-of-date merchandise, or factory seconds. To attract large numbers of shoppers, outlet stores are often grouped together in **outlet malls**. The United States is home to hundreds of outlet malls such as the giant Woodbury Common mall in Central Valley, New York. Now, the concept is catching on in Europe and Asia as well. The acceptance reflects changing attitudes among consumers and retailers; in both Asia and Europe, brand-conscious consumers are eager to save money.

Trends in Global Retailing

Currently, a variety of environmental factors have combined to push retailers out of their home markets in search of opportunities around the globe. Saturation of the home-country market, recession or other economic factors, strict regulation on store development, and high operating costs are some of the factors that prompt management to look abroad for growth opportunities. Walmart is a case in point; its international expansion in the mid-1990s coincided with disappointing financial results in its home market.

Even as the domestic retailing environment grows more challenging for many companies, an ongoing environmental scanning effort is likely to turn up markets in other parts of the world that are underdeveloped or where competition is weak. In addition, high rates of economic growth, a growing middle class, a high proportion of young people in the population, and less stringent regulation combine to make some country markets very attractive.[21] For example, Laura Ashley, The Body Shop, Disney Stores, and other specialty retailers were lured to Japan by developers who needed established names to fill space in large, suburban, American-style shopping malls.[22] Such malls are being developed as some local and national restrictions on retail development are being eased and as consumers tire of the aggravations associated with shopping in congested urban areas.

However, the large number of unsuccessful cross-border retailing initiatives suggests that anyone contemplating a move into global retailing should do so with a great deal of caution. Among those that have scaled back expansion plans in the face of disappointment are France's Galeries Lafayette and the Shanghai-based Yaohan Group. Galeries Lafayette opened a New York store on fashionable Fifth Avenue; however, the merchandise mix suffered in comparison with offerings at posh competitors such as Henri Bendel and Bonwit Teller. Yaohan has more than 400 stores in 13 countries, including the United States and China. Speaking of global opportunities for U.S.-based retailers, one industry analyst noted, "It's awfully hard to operate across

---

[20]Stan Sesser, "The New Spot for Giant Malls: Asia," *The Wall Street Journal* (September 16/17, 2006), p. P6.
[21]Ross Davies and Megan Finney, "Retailers Rush to Capture New Markets," *Financial Times—Mastering Global Business, Part VII* (1998), pp. 2–4.
[22]Norihiko Shirouzu, "Japanese Mall Mogul Dreams of American Stores," *The Wall Street Journal* (July 30, 1997), pp. B1, B10; Norihiko Shirouzu, "Jusco Bets that U.S.-Style Retail Malls Will Revolutionize Shopping in Japan," *The Wall Street Journal* (April 21, 1997), p. A8.

the water. It's one thing to open up in Mexico and Canada, but the distribution hassles are just too big when it comes to exporting an entire store concept overseas."[23]

The critical question for the would-be global retailer is, "What advantages do we have relative to local competition?" The answer will often be, "Nothing," when competition, local laws governing retailing practice, distribution patterns, or other factors are taken into account. However, a company may possess competencies that can be the basis for competitive advantage in a particular retail market. A retailer has several things to offer consumers, such as selection, price, and the overall manner and condition in which the goods are offered in the store setting. Store location, parking facilities, in-store atmosphere, and customer service also contribute to the value proposition. Competencies can also be found in less visible value chain activities such as distribution, logistics, and information technology. As Thomas Hübner, CEO of Metro Cash & Carry International, noted recently, "Stores are just the tip of the iceberg—90 percent of the work is under water."[24]

For example, Japanese retailers traditionally offered few extra services to their clientele. There were no special orders, no returns, and stock was chosen not according to consumer demand but, rather, according to purchasing preferences of the stores. Typically, a store would

EMERGING MARKETS BRIEFING BOOK

India's Retail Sector

Global retailers that have set their sights on India face special challenges. As noted previously in this chapter, the term *organized retail* is used to describe activity by large branded retail chains such as Woolworths, Tesco, and Walmart. Such stores currently account for only about 5 percent of India's $370 billion in annual retail sales; according to some forecasts, organized retail will comprise 17 percent of the sector by 2011.

The vast majority of Indian retail activity is conducted in cramped stalls with about 50 square feet of floor space. There have been many calls for regulatory reform, and some observers believe organized retailing will grow at a rate of 30 to 35 percent in the next few years. For now, however, some members of the ruling Congress party are concerned about the impact of organized retailing on the millions of small-scale "mom-and-pop" stores.

Modernization of the sector is inevitable, although it may be slow in coming. Walmart and other global retailers that sell multiple brands are barred from participating directly in the Indian market. In 2006, Bharti Enterprises, a local business group that operates India's largest cellular network, announced a joint venture partnership with Walmart. However, because of restrictions, the venture will consist of wholesale stores. When single brand-retailers such as Benetton, Nike, Pizza Hut, Reebok, and Subway first entered the market, they were required to use franchising. Recent regulatory changes will make it easier for such companies to use direct ownership.

Western retailers often have to work with local vendors to help them improve quality. For example, as Germany's Metro opens wholesale cash-and-carry supercenters that serve small retailers, it has to contend with India's poor infrastructure and inefficient supply chains that stem from producers using outdated techniques. Produce is typically transported on open trucks and then transferred to warehouses that are not temperature-controlled. By the time it gets to consumers, the produce has passed through as many as seven intermediaries; much of it is spoiled. Metro works with the farmers and shepherds who supply it to improve quality; in addition, Metro bypasses traditional middlemen by sending its own refrigerated trucks to the farms.

Meanwhile, anticipating the arrival of the global retailers, local operators in India are investing for the future. For example, Pantaloon Retail Ltd., India's largest retailer, operates the Central and Big Bazaar department store chains and Food Bazaar, a supermarket chain. Ironically, Kishore Biyani, Pantaloon's chief executive, has succeeded by giving lower-middle-class shoppers a familiar retail experience: Cramped stores with an environment that Western shoppers would find chaotic. Large business groups such as Reliance Industries, a petroleum refiner, and Birla Group have also entered the retail sector. Meanwhile, Hindustan Lever, the Indian unit of packaged goods giant Unilever, has launched a consultancy service to help the "mom-and-pop" retail operators become more competitive.

Sources: Eric Bellman and Cecilie Rohwedder, "Western Grocer Modernizes Passage to India's Markets," *The Wall Street Journal* (November 28, 2007), pp. B1, B2; Eric Bellman, "Chaos Theory: In India, a Retailer Finds Key to Success Is Clutter," *The Wall Street Journal* (August 8, 2007), p. A8; Eric Bellman, "India's Reliance Looks Abroad," *The Wall Street Journal* (March 16, 2007), pp. A1, A10; Jo Johnson and Jonathan Birchall, "'Mom and Pop' Stores Braced for Challenge," *Financial Times* (November 28, 2006), p. 16; Joe Leahy, "Indian Regulation Hampers Retail Growth," *Financial Times* (October 26, 2006), p. 21; Anita Jain, "The 'Crown Jewel' Sector that's Ripe for Modernization," *Financial Times Special Report—India and Globalization* (January 26, 2006), p. 16.

[23]Neil King, Jr., "Kmart's Czech Invasion Lurches Along," *The Wall Street Journal* (June 8, 1993), p. A11.
[24]Eric Bellman and Cecilie Rohwedder, "Western Grocer Modernizes Passage to India's Markets," *The Wall Street Journal* (November 28, 2007), p. B2.

buy limited quantities from each of its favorite manufacturers and then, when the goods sold out, consumers had no recourse. Instead of trying to capitalize on the huge market, many retailers simply turned a deaf ear to customer needs. From the retailers' point of view, this came out fine in the end, however; most of their stock eventually sold because buyers were forced to purchase what was left over. They had no other choice. Then Gap, Eddie Bauer, and other Western retailers entered Japan, often by means of joint ventures. The stores offered liberal return policies, a willingness to take special orders, and a policy of replenishing stock, and many Japanese consumers switched loyalties. Also, thanks to economies of scale and modern distribution methods unknown to some Japanese department store operators, the foreign retailers offer a greater variety of goods at lower prices. Although upscale foreign competition has hurt Japanese department store operators, Japan's depressed economy is another factor. Traditional retailers are also being squeezed from below as recession-pressed consumers flock to discounters such as the Y100 Shop chain.

JCPenney is expanding retailing operations internationally for a number of the reasons cited here. After touring several countries, Penney executives realized that retailers outside the United States often lack marketing sophistication when grouping and displaying products and locating aisles to optimize customer traffic. For example, a team visiting retailers in Istanbul in the early 1990s noted that one store featured lingerie next to plumbing equipment. As CEO William R. Howell noted at the time, Penney's advantage in such instances was its ability to develop an environment that invites the customer to shop. Although it struggled in Indonesia, the Philippines, and Chile, Penney has met with great success in Brazil. In 1999, the American retailer purchased a controlling stake in Renner, a regional chain with 21 stores. Crucially, Penney maintained the local name and local management team. Meanwhile, Renner, benefiting from Penney's expertise in logistics, distribution, and branding, has become Brazil's fastest-growing chain, with a total of 49 stores.[25]

Figure 12-3 shows a matrix-based scheme for classifying global retailers.[26] One axis represents private- or own-label focus versus a manufacturer brands focus. The other axis differentiates between retailers specializing in relatively few product categories and retailers that offer a wide product assortment. IKEA, in quadrant A, is a good example of a global retailer with a niche focus (assemble-yourself furniture for the home) as well as an own-label focus (IKEA sells its own brand). IKEA and other retailers in quadrant A typically use extensive advertising and product innovation to build a strong brand image.

In quadrant B, the private-label focus is retained, but many more product categories are offered. This is the strategy of Marks & Spencer (M&S), the British-based department store company whose St. Michael private label is found on a broad range of clothing, food, home

FIGURE 12-3

Global Retailing Categories

Source: Adapted from Jacques Horovitz and Nirmalya Kumar, "Strategies for Retail Globalization," *Financial Times—Mastering Global Business, Part VII* (1998), pp. 4–8.

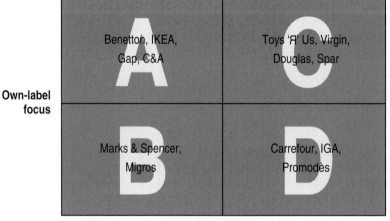

[25]Miriam Jordan, "Penney Blends Two Business Cultures," *The Wall Street Journal* (April 5, 2001), p. A15.
[26]The discussion in this section is adapted from Jacques Horovitz and Nirmalya Kumar, "Strategies for Retail Globalization," *Financial Times—Mastering Global Business, Part VII* (1998), pp. 4–8.

furnishings, jewelry, and other items. Private-label retailers that attempt to expand internationally face a double-edged challenge: They must attract customers to both the store and the branded merchandise. M&S has succeeded by virtue of an entrepreneurial management style that has evolved over the last 100-plus years. M&S opened its first store outside the United Kingdom in 1974; it currently operates in 40 countries. In 1997, then-chairman Sir Richard Greenbury announced an ambitious plan to put M&S "well on its way to establishing a global business." It was his belief that consumer tastes are globalizing, at least with respect to fashion apparel. Food is a different story; because tastes are more localized, M&S executives anticipate that the proportion of revenues from food sales will be lower than they are in Great Britain.[27] The difficulty of today's retailing environment is underscored by Marks & Spencer's recent financial woes. The company's profits and share price plunged in the late 1990s amid a sales slump and infighting between top executives; Sir Richard left the company in 1998. A turnaround strategy called for disposing of non-core properties such as the Brooks Brothers and Kings Super Markets chains in the United States.

Retailers in quadrant C offer many well-known brands in a relatively tightly defined merchandise range. Here, for example, we find Toys 'R' Us, which specializes in toys and includes branded products from Mattel, Nintendo, and other marketers. Additional examples include such category killers as Blockbuster Video and Virgin Megastores. As noted earlier, this type of store tends to quickly dominate smaller established retailers by out-merchandising local competition and offering customers superior value by virtue of extensive inventories and low prices. Typically, the low prices are the result of buyer power and sourcing advantages that local retailers lack.

The retailing environment in which Richard Branson built the Virgin Megastore chain illustrates once again the type of success that can be achieved through an entrepreneurial management style:

> It required little retailing expertise to see that the sleepy business practices of traditional record shops provided a tremendous opportunity. To rival the tiny neighborhood record shops, with their eclectic collections of records, a new kind of record store was coming into being. It was big; it was well-lit, and records were arranged clearly in alphabetical order by artist; it covered most tastes in pop music comprehensively; and it turned over its stock much faster than the smaller record retailer. . . . It was the musical equivalent of a supermarket.[28]

Starting with one megastore location on London's Oxford Street in 1975, Branson's Virgin Retail empire now extends throughout Europe, North America, Japan, Hong Kong, and Taiwan.

Carrefour, Promodès, Walmart, and other retailers in quadrant D offer the same type of merchandise available from established local retailers. What the newcomers bring to a market, however, is competence in distribution or some other value chain element. To date, Walmart's international division has established more than 3,000 stores outside the United States; it is already the biggest retailer in Mexico and Canada. Other store locations include Central America, South America, China, and, until recently, Germany. International revenues for 2009 totaled just under $100 billion.

Global Retailing Market Expansion Strategies

Retailers can choose from four market entry expansion strategies when expanding outside the home country. As shown in Figure 12-4, these strategies can be diagrammed using a matrix that differentiates between (1) markets that are easy to enter versus those that are difficult to enter and (2) culturally close markets versus culturally distant ones. The upper half of the matrix encompasses quadrants A and D and represents markets in which shopping patterns and retail structures are similar to those in the home country. In the lower half of the matrix, quadrants B and C represent markets that are significantly different from the home-country market in terms

"International expansion has proved to be a competitive advantage for us. In Canada, Mexico, and now, China, we've shown we can enter a market, tailor our model to the local customer and see the same sort of growth we saw in our early days here in the U.S."[29]
Frank Blake, CEO, Home Depot

[27]Rufus Olins, "M&S Sets Out Its Stall for World Domination," *The Sunday Times* (November 9, 1997), p. 6. See also Andrew Davidson, "The Andrew Davidson Interview: Sir Richard Greenbury," *Management Today* (November 2001), pp. 62–67; and Judi Bevan, *The Rise and Fall of Marks & Spencer* (London: Profile Books, 2001).
[28]Tim Jackson, *Virgin King: Inside Richard Branson's Business Empire* (London: HarperCollins, 1995), p. 277.
[29]Ann Zimmerman, "Home Depot Chief Renovates," *The Wall Street Journal* (June 5, 2008), p. B2.

STRATEGIC DECISION MAKING IN GLOBAL MARKETING
Retailers Expand Abroad

Retailers may have a difficult time crossing borders if they fail to appreciate differences in retailing environments and consumer behavior and preferences. For example, when Galeries Lafayette opened a location in New York, the store was stocked with women's clothing that was too trendy to be practical. In addition, the clothing was proportioned for the French, rather than American, physique. In London, retailers typically locate their stores on "high streets," which are roughly equivalent to downtown in the United States. However, America is the land of the mall; there are no "high streets" in most American cities. Gap recently closed its 10 stores in Germany as price-conscious consumers shopped at H&M and other stores where prices are lower.

Other obstacles include breaking through to get the consumer's attention. In the United States, fresh product assortments and aggressive pricing drive retailing. Anita Roddick got her Body Shop off to a good start in the United States; in short order, however, The Limited jumped into the category with Bath & Body Works. Bath & Body Works captured The Body Shop's market by constantly changing products, entering as many malls as possible, and by keeping prices lower. Meanwhile, The Body Shop did not even have a formal marketing department. Today, Bath & Body Works dominates the category that The Body Shop created.

Until recently, the companies that avoided these pitfalls were the exceptions to the rule. For example, Richard Branson, the entrepreneurial leader of Virgin, has built the Virgin brand in the United States the American way—by adding more and more products and by being noisy and loud about the brand. Now, however,

increasing numbers of British retailers are changing with the times. Harrods, Harvey Nichols, and other top retailers are improving the décor in key stores and offering shoppers an entertainment experience. For example, visitors to Fifth Floor Harvey Nichols will find a posh restaurant, a wine shop, and a gourmet food hall.

Some of the biggest innovations have been at Selfridges, whose flagship store just off Oxford Street in London is home to Europe's largest cosmetics department. Window displays have featured buzz-building "performances" such as humans in animal costumes modeling lingerie. As Peter Williams, CEO of Selfridges, said," Our competitors are not just other department stores. Our competitors are restaurants, theaters, a weekend away, or other entertainment venues."

Even with these changes, retailers may have difficulty expanding abroad. One challenge facing Saks is lining up popular fashion designers, many of whom are opening their own stores in key country markets.

Sources: Vanessa O'Connell, "Department Stores Are Hard Sell Abroad," *The Wall Street Journal* (May 22, 2008), p. B3; Cecile Rohwedder, "Harvey Nichols's Foreign Affair," *The Wall Street Journal* (February 18, 2005), pp. B1, B3; Erin White, "Dress for Success: After Long Slump, U.S. Retailers Look to Britain for Fashion Tips," *The Wall Street Journal* (April 22, 2004), pp. A1, A8; Rohwedder, "Selling Selfridges," *The Wall Street Journal* (May 5, 2003), p. B1; Ernest Beck, "Marks & Spencer to Focus on Key Brands," *The Wall Street Journal* (July 15, 1999), p. B1; Jennifer Steinhauer, "The British Are Coming, and Going," *The New York Times* (September 22, 1998), pp. C1, C4.

of one or more cultural characteristics. The right side of the matrix, quadrants A and B, represents markets that are difficult to enter because of the presence of strong competitors, location restrictions, excessively high rent or real estate costs, or other factors. In quadrants C and D, any barriers that exist are relatively easy to overcome. The four entry strategies indicated by the matrix are organic, franchise, chain acquisition, and joint ventures and licensing.

FIGURE 12-4

Global Retailing Market Entry Strategy Framework

Source: Adapted from Jacques Horovitz and Nirmalya Kumar, "Strategies for Retail Globalization," *Financial Times–Mastering Global Business, Part VII* (1998), p. 5.

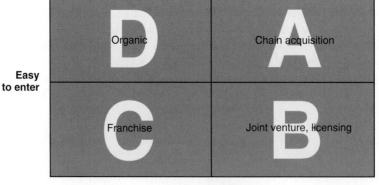

Organic growth occurs when a company uses its own resources to open a store on a greenfield site or to acquire one or more existing retail facilities from another company. In 1997, for example, M&S announced plans to expand from one store to four in Germany via the purchase of three stores operated by Cramer and Meerman. When Richard Branson set up the first Virgin Megastore in Paris, he did so by investing millions of pounds in a spectacular retail space on the Champs-Elysées. From the perspective of M&S and Virgin, the retail environments of Germany and France are both culturally close and easy to enter. The success of this strategy hinges on the availability of company resources to sustain the high cost of the initial investment.

Franchising, shown in quadrant C of Figure 12-4, is the appropriate entry strategy when barriers to entry are low yet the market is culturally distant in terms of consumer behavior or retailing structures. As defined in Chapter 9, franchising is a contractual relationship between two companies. The parent company-franchisor authorizes a franchisee to operate a business developed by the franchisor in return for a fee and adherence to franchise-wide policies and practices. The key to a successful franchise operation is the ability to transfer company know-how to new markets. Benetton, IKEA, and other focused, private-label retailers often use franchising as a market entry strategy in combination with wholly owned stores that represent organic growth. IKEA has more than 100 company-owned stores across Europe and the United States; its stores in the Middle East and Hong Kong are franchise operations.

In global retailing, **acquisition** is a market entry strategy that entails purchasing a company with multiple retail locations in a foreign country. This strategy can provide the buyer with quick growth as well as access to existing brand suppliers, distributors, and customers. Marks & Spencer, for example, had no plans for organic growth in the United States; rather, it acquired the upscale private-label American retailer Brooks Brothers in 1988 for $750 million. Executives at Brooks Brothers spent most of the 1990s trying to expand the brand's customer base, and recent results have been promising. With hindsight, however, it is clear that M&S paid too much for the acquisition. As noted previously, M&S itself is currently in the midst of a financial retrenchment; at the end of 2001, it sold Brooks Brothers to Retail Brand Alliance, a private holding company.

Joint ventures and **licensing** have been examined in detail in Chapter 9. Global retailers frequently use these strategies to limit their risk when targeting unfamiliar, difficult-to-enter markets. For example, Barneys New York licensed its name to Barneys Japan for a period of 10 years; Saks Fifth Avenue has licensed stores in the Middle East. In some countries, local regulations mandate use of joint ventures. For example, prior to 2005, China had regulations that required foreign retailers entering the market to have local partners. Chinese authorities liberalized the country's retail climate in 2005; today, IKEA and other retailers that initially used joint ventures as an entry strategy are shifting to wholly owned stores.

Virgin Group's retail expansion in Asia provides a case study in the appropriateness of the joint venture approach. In Japan, commercial landlords typically require millions in up-front payments before they will lease retail space. Accordingly, in 1992, Virgin established a joint venture called Virgin Megastores Japan with Marui, a local retailer with a good track record of catering to the preferences of young people. The first megastore was set up in the basement of an existing Marui department store in Japan's Shinjuku district. That and subsequent stores have been wildly successful; Virgin has duplicated the joint venture approach elsewhere in Asia, including Hong Kong, Taiwan, and South Korea. In each location, Virgin establishes a joint venture with a leading industrial group.[30]

Achieving retailing success outside the home-country market is not simply a matter of consulting a matrix and choosing the recommended entry strategy. Management must also be alert to the possibility that the merchandise mix, sourcing strategy, distribution, or other format elements will have to be adapted. Management at Crate & Barrel, for example, is hesitant to open stores in Japan. Part of the reason is research indicating that at least half the company's product line would have to be modified to accommodate local preferences. Another issue is the company's ability to transfer its expertise to new country markets.

---

[30]Tim Jackson, *Virgin King: Inside Richard Branson's Business Empire* (London: HarperCollins, 1995), pp. 289–291.

PHYSICAL DISTRIBUTION, SUPPLY CHAINS, AND LOGISTICS MANAGEMENT

In Chapter 1, marketing was described as one of the activities in a firm's value chain. The distribution *P* of the marketing mix plays a central role in a given firm's value chain; after all, Coca-Cola, IKEA, Nokia, Toyota, and other global companies create value by making sure their products are available where and when customers want to buy them. As defined in this chapter, physical distribution consists of activities involved in moving finished goods from manufacturers to customers. However, the value chain concept is much broader, for two basic reasons. First, the value chain is a useful tool for assessing an organization's competence as it performs value-creating activities within a broader **supply chain** that includes *all* the firms that perform support activities by generating raw materials, converting them into components or finished products, and making them available to customers. Second, the particular industry in which a firm competes (for example, automobiles, pharmaceuticals, or consumer electronics) is characterized by a value chain. The specific activities an individual firm performs help define its position in the value chain. If a company is somewhat removed from the final customer, it is said to be *upstream* in the value chain. A company that is relatively close to customers—a retailer, for example—is said to be *downstream* in the value chain. **Logistics**, in turn, is the management process that integrates the activities of all companies—both upstream and downstream—to ensure an efficient flow of goods through the supply chain.

An industry's value chain can change over time. In pharmaceuticals, for example, research, testing, and delivery are the three steps that historically defined the industry from its beginnings in the early nineteenth century. Then, starting in the mid-1960s, after Crick and Watson published their groundbreaking work on DNA, two new upstream steps in the industry's value chain emerged: basic research into genes associated with specific diseases and identification of the proteins produced by those genes. More recently, with the mapping of the human genome largely complete, value in the pharmaceuticals industry is migrating downstream to identifying, testing, and producing molecules that operate on the proteins produced by genes.[31]

The value chain, logistics, and related concepts are extremely important as supply chains stretch around the globe. As export administrator Beth Dorrell notes, "A commodity raw material from Africa can be refined in Asia, then shipped to South America to be incorporated into a component of a final product that is produced in the Middle East and then sold around the world." Table 12-4 compares and contrasts logistics availability in both developed and developing countries. Figure 12-5 illustrates some of these concepts and activities at IKEA, the global furniture marketer. IKEA purchases wood and other raw material inputs from a network of suppliers located in dozens of countries; these suppliers are upstream in the value chain, and the process by which wood is transported to the factories is known as *inbound logistics*. IKEA's factories add value to the inputs by transforming them into furniture kits that are then shipped on to IKEA's stores. The stores are downstream in IKEA's value chain; the activities associated with shipping furniture kits from factory to store are known as *outbound logistics*.[32]

Physical distribution and logistics are the means by which products are made available to customers when and where they want them. The most important distribution activities are order processing, warehousing, inventory management, and transportation.

Order Processing

Activities relating to order processing provide information inputs that are critical in fulfilling a customer's order. **Order processing** includes *order entry*, in which the order is actually entered into a company's information system; *order handling*, which involves locating, assembling, and

---

[31]David Champion, "Mastering the Value Chain: An Interview with Mark Levin of Millennium Pharmaceuticals," *Harvard Business Review* 79, no. 6 (June 2001), pp. 108–115.

[32]A detailed analysis of IKEA's approach to value creation is found in Richard Normann and Rafael Ramirez, "From Value Chain to Value Constellation: Designing Interactive Strategy," *Harvard Business Review* 71, no. 4 (July–August 1993), pp. 65–77.

[33]Ian Bickerton, "'It Is All About the Value Chain,'" *Financial Times* (February 24, 2006), p. 10.

[34]Francesco Guerrera, "GE to Shift Output from U.S." *Financial Times* (July 27, 2006), p. 27.

TABLE 12-4 United States and EU/BRIC Comparison

Country	Supplier Base and Infrastructure/Logistics
United States/EU	Companies use national and international suppliers. Firms outsource and move manufacturing and services offshore instead of integrating vertically. A highly developed infrastructure is in place, but urban areas are saturated.
Brazil	Suppliers are available in the Mercosur region. A good network of highways, airports, and ports exists but port congestion is a chronic problem. Customs clearance time averages eight days. Overall freight costs are 20 percent higher than international average.
Russia	Companies can rely on local suppliers for simple components. Customs clearance time averages eight days, on a par with Brazil. The European region has adequate logistics networks, but trans-Ural Russia is not well developed.
India	Suppliers are available, but quality and dependability varies greatly. Average time to clear customs exceeds two weeks; worse than Brazil or Russia. The transport infrastructure is in poor condition. Truck transport is slowed by toll booths and tax collection checkpoints; heavy congestion slows traffic on the national highway network. Ports and airports are underdeveloped. Power outages are common. Government has budgeted $500 billion for infrastructure improvements.
China	Several suppliers have strong manufacturing capabilities, but few vendors have advanced technical abilities. The road network is well developed. Excellent port facilities. However, transportation/distribution costs are high. Lacks a network of refrigerated and containerized trucks and warehouses to connect farms with grocery retailers.

Source: Adapted from Tarun Khanna, Krishna G. Palepu, and Jayant Sinha, "Strategies That Fit Emerging Markets," *Harvard Business Review* 83, no. 6 (June 2005), p. 69.

moving products into distribution; and *order delivery*, the process by which products are made available to the customer.

In some instances the customer is a consumer, as is the case when you place an order with Amazon.com or Lands' End. In other instances, the customer is a channel member. Pepsi Bottling Group recently overhauled its supply chain in an effort to eliminate inventory out-of-stock problems. The company's handheld computers lacked wireless capability and required hookup to landline telephone service; by upgrading the technology, sales representatives can now enter orders wirelessly. Warehouse workers are equipped with barcode scanners and headsets so they can do a better job of ensuring that each pallet of drink products contains exactly what retailers have ordered.[35]

Warehousing

Warehouses are used to store goods until they are sold; another type of facility, the *distribution center*, is designed to efficiently receive goods from suppliers and then fill orders for individual stores or customers. Modern distribution and warehousing is such an automated, high-tech business today that many companies outsource this function. For example, ODW Logistics Inc. operates

FIGURE 12-5

Supply Chain, Value Chain, and Logistics

[35]Chad Terhune, "Supply-Chain Fix for Pepsi," *The Wall Street Journal* (June 6, 2006), p. B3.

several warehouses on behalf of Deere & Company, Limited Brands, and other customers. Much of ODW's capacity is in Columbus, Ohio, a major U.S. port of entry for textiles. One of the driving forces behind the growth of third-party warehousing is the need to reduce fixed costs and speed up delivery times to customers. ODW adds additional utility by tracking shipments from the time they leave the factory in, say, China, until they reach Columbus. This enables the company to alert retailers of possible delays due to weather or port congestion. In addition, as manufacturers ramp up efforts to use RFID tags on shipments, ODW will split the cost of the new technology with its customers. As consultant John Boyd notes, "Right now, distribution warehousing is the next arena of corporate re-engineering and corporate cost-cutting."[36]

Inventory Management

Proper inventory management ensures that a company neither runs out of manufacturing components or finished goods nor incurs the expense and risk of carrying excessive stocks of these items. Another issue is balancing order-processing costs against inventory-carrying costs. The more often a product is ordered, the higher the order-processing costs associated with unloading, stocking, and related activities. The less frequently a product is ordered, the higher the inventory carrying costs, since more product must be kept in inventory to cover the longer period between orders. As noted in Chapter 6, an important new tool for inventory management is radio frequency identification (RFID). RFID utilizes small tags that are attached to pallets, containers, or individual inventory items.

Transportation

Finally, transportation decisions concern the method or *mode* a company should utilize when moving products through domestic and global channels. The word *mode* implies a choice, and the major transportation mode choices are rail, truck, air, water, pipeline, and the Internet. Each of these modes has its advantages and disadvantages, as summarized in Table 12-5. However, a particular mode may be unavailable in some countries because of an underdeveloped infrastructure or geographic barriers. Pipelines are highly specialized and used by companies transporting energy-related resources such as oil and natural gas.

Rail provides an extremely cost-effective means for moving large quantities of merchandise long distances. In the United States, carriers such as CSX and Burlington Northern Santa Fe (BNSF) account for nearly half of all cargo moved when measured by ton-miles (see Exhibit 12-6). Rail's capability is second only to water in terms of the variety of products that can be transported. However, trains are less reliable than trucks. Poor track maintenance leads to derailments, and bottlenecks on heavily traveled lines can create delays.

TABLE 12-5 **Comparison of Major International Transportation Modes**

Mode	Reliability	Cost	Speed	Accessibility	Capability	Ease of Tracing
Rail	average	average	average	high	high	low
Water	low	low	slow	low	high	low
Truck	high	varies	fast	high	high	high
Air	high	high	fast	low	moderate	high
Pipeline	high	low	slow	low	low	moderate
Internet	high	low	moderate to fast	moderate; increasing	low	high

---

[36]Kris Maher, "Global Goods Jugglers," *The Wall Street Journal* (July 5, 2005), pp. A11, A12.

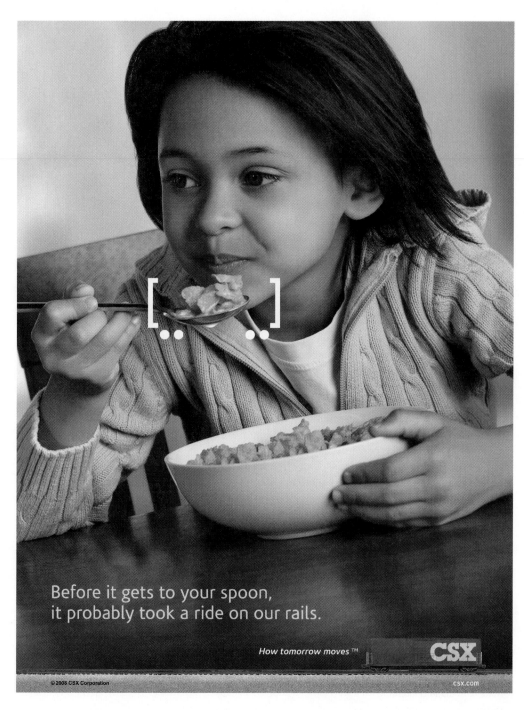

Exhibit 12-6: "How tomorrow moves" is the theme of a corporate brand-image advertising campaign from CSX. The company is one of the largest freight-hauling rail lines in the United States. This ad is a reminder that CSX is a critical link in the supply chain: Products that people use every day travel at least part of the way by rail as they move from producer to consumer.
Source: Photographer: Bruce DeBoer. Used by permission of CSX.

Trucks are an excellent mode for both long-haul, transcontinental transport and local delivery of goods (see Exhibit 12-7). In nations with well-developed highway systems, truck freight combines the advantage of fast delivery times with the highest level of accessibility of any mode. Thanks to modern information technology, truck shipments are also easily traced. However, in countries with poorly developed infrastructures, truck deliveries can move much more slowly. India is a case in point.

There are two main types of water transportation. *Inland water transportation* is an extremely low-cost mode generally used to move agricultural commodities, petroleum, fertilizers, and other goods that, by their nature, lend themselves to bulk shipping via barge. However, inland water transportation can be slow and subject to weather-related delays. Virtually any product can be shipped via *ocean transportation*. The world's deep-water ports can receive a variety of types of

Exhibit 12-7: FedEx Express is a unit of Memphis-based FedEx Corporation. With operations in more than 220 countries, FedEx Express is the world's leading express delivery provider. China is the world's second-largest domestic air-cargo market, and FedEx forecasts that market growth there will average 10 percent annually over the next 15 years. FedEx recently spent $400 million to buy out its Chinese joint venture partner. In addition, FedEx is now offering the first guaranteed overnight express-delivery service in China, with deliveries to more than 100 cities.
Source: FedEx Corporation.

ocean-going vessels, such as container vessels, bulk and break-bulk vessels, and roll-on, roll-off (ro-ro) vessels. Although sailing times are not competitive with air transportation, it is generally more cost effective to ship large quantities of merchandise via ocean than by air. Denmark's Maersk Sealand is the world's largest shipping container line (see Table 12-6).

Why is water rated "low" in reliability? In any given year, approximately 200 freighters sink due to bad weather or other factors. Compounding the tragic loss of human lives is the fact that the cargo ends up on the ocean floor. Cargo can sometimes be lost without a ship sinking. For example, in 1997, a huge wave rocked the freighter *Tokio Express* in the waters off Land's End, England. Several dozen shipping containers were tossed overboard, including one containing nearly 5 million LEGO pieces. The container was bound for Connecticut, where the pieces were to be assembled in kits. One year later, LEGO pieces began washing ashore in Florida!

Losses can occur even when the cargo remains on board and the ship doesn't sink. For example, the *Cougar Ace*, a freighter loaded with 4,700 new Mazdas, narrowly avoided sinking in the Pacific in 2006. The cars were strapped down but the ship listed at a 60° angle for weeks before being righted. Concerned that the cars might not be saleable, management decided to destroy the entire shipment, which was valued at $100 million.[37] Piracy on the high seas is

TABLE 12-6 Leading Shipping Lines

Carrier	Number of Vessels	Capacity 20-ft Units (thousands)
Maersk Sealand (Denmark)	324	816
Evergreen Marine (Taiwan)	209	493
P&O Nedlloyd (United Kingdom)	155	414
Hanjin Shipping (South Korea)	76	414
American President Lines (United States)	78	260
Cosco (China)	136	257
CP Ships (United Kingdom)	85	193
CMA-CGM (France)	74	191
NYK Line (Japan)	61	189

Source: Containerization International.

[37]Joel Millman, "A Crushing Issue: How to Destroy Brand-New Cars," *The Wall Street Journal* (April 29, 2008), pp. A1, A9.

→ CULTURE WATCH
Prince of Ports

Hutchison Port Holdings was established in 1866, when the Hong Kong and Whampoa Dock Company was registered. They are now the world's leading port investor, developer, and operator. Hutchinson runs 49 ports in 25 countries across the Americas, Australasia, Asia, Africa, the Middle East, and Europe. It directly employs more than 30,000 people. One of its latest acquisitions was to become the major shareholder of Amsterdam Port Holdings.

Foreign ownership of ports has become a major concern for many countries. When Dubai Ports World acquired the port's operator, P&O, there were major problems with both the American and the British ports that the company now owned. Concerns over security forced DP World, the world's seventh largest port company, to sell one of P&O's former American ports. In Britain, members of parliament belonging to the Commons Transport Committee warned that foreign companies owning British ports could lead to difficulties. The companies could simply see that the land could be sold off for development, or that they would cease investing in the port as higher profits could be made elsewhere. This would not be in the national interest.

Nonetheless, multinational companies such as Hutchison, which is also the parent company of one of the world's largest shipping companies, have pressed on with acquisitions. In the Baltic alone, Hutchinson has two container terminals, and it is active from Argentina to Thailand and from the Bahamas to Vietnam.

Although Hutchison does not own any ports in the United States, its European acquisitions span Belgium, Germany, Italy, the Netherlands, Poland, Spain, Sweden, and the United Kingdom. It had been believed that the so-called cross-ownership of ports and shipping across the globe would have pushed up charges, particularly since dominant companies such as Hutchison have been acquiring assets at an alarming rate. In fact, the reverse has been true and charges have so far been seen to be at historic lows, primarily due to the strength of commercial shippers, such as importers.

Investment by businesses such as Hutchison has actually given some ports an unexpected competitive advantage. In 2006, Hutchison became involved in the development of the Spanish port of Barcelona. The 20-year strategic plan was nearly 10 years into its plan when Hutchison became involved. The plan was to increase the number of 20-feet equivalent container units handled by the port per year from 2 million to 4.5 million by 2014. Barcelona is ideally placed to handle Hong Kong and Mainland Chinese exporters, as well as the developing markets in Latin America.

The Hutchison Port Holdings' parent company is Hutchison Whampoa Limited. It operates in 54 countries, and the port-related business is just one of its five core areas of activity. The Hutchison Port Holdings operation handles 13 percent of the world's container traffic. The group as a whole reported a turnover of $45 billion for the year ending December 31, 2008, and $18 billion for the six months ending June 30, 2009.

While misgivings over foreign ownership of ports remain, the busiest UK port of Felixstowe was acquired by the business in 1991. Since then it has grown in significance. One of the latest acquisitions was by the Admiral Consortium, which bought the largest British operator, Associated British Ports, in August 2006. It is owned by the U.S. Wall Street bank, Goldman Sachs, the global investment management company handling the Singapore government's foreign reserves, the Canadian pension fund Borealis, and the largely British fund management arm of the Prudential group.

Sources: Hutchison Port Holdings, www.hph.com; Hong Kong Trade Development Council, www.hktdc.com; Hutchison Whampoa Limited, www.hutchison-whampoa.com; Associated British Ports, www.abports.co.uk.

Exhibit 12-8: Hutchison Port Holdings' business spans twenty six countries, including cargo and container handling operations.
Source: © PictureArt #4147868.

another factor affecting the reliability of water as a transport mode. In recent years, pirates operating in the Indian Ocean off the coast of Africa have fired upon and attempted to board dozens of commercial vessels. In some instances, the pirates have succeeded in boarding ships and hijacking the cargo. In one case, pirates captured the captain of an American-flagged ship carrying food aid to East Africa.

Air is the fastest transport mode and the carrier of choice for perishable exports such as flowers or fresh fish, but it is also the most expensive. The size and the weight of an item may determine that it is more cost effective to ship via air than ocean. If a shipment's delivery is time sensitive, such as emergency parts replacement, air is also the logical mode.

Thanks to the digital revolution, the *Internet* is becoming an important transportation mode that is associated with several advantages and one major disadvantage. First, the bad news: the Internet's capability is low. As Nicolas Negroponte of MIT's Media Lab has famously observed, as long as something consists of atoms, it cannot be shipped via the Internet. However, anything that can be digitized—including text, voice, music, pictures, and video—can be sent via the Internet. Advantages include low cost and high reliability. Accessibility is increasing as global PC demand increases; today, it is estimated that approximately one billion households have Internet access. Accessibility is also growing thanks to telecommunications innovations that allow cell phones and other wireless digital devices to access the Internet. Speed depends on several factors, including bandwidth. As broadband technology becomes more widespread and compression technology improves, the speed at which large digital files such as full-length motion pictures can be downloaded will increase dramatically.

Channel strategy involves an analysis of each shipping mode to determine which mode, or combination of modes, will be both effective and efficient in a given situation. A number of firms specializing in third-party logistics are available to help companies with transportation logistics. For example, C.H. Robinson Worldwide matches shippers with trucking companies and other carriers in all parts of the world. An aspect of transportation technology that has revolutionized global trade is containerization—a concept that was first utilized in the United States starting in the mid-1950s. **Containerization** refers to the practice of loading ocean-going freight into steel boxes measuring 20 feet, 40 feet, or longer. Containerization offers many advantages, including flexibility in the product that can be shipped via container, as well as flexibility in shipping modes (see Exhibit 12-9).

Exhibit 12-9: Prior to 1985, the Port of New York was the busiest container port in the world. Then New York went into decline as ports on the West Coast and the South courted freight lines. Now, thanks to a high tide of imports from Asia, the Port of New York is experiencing a resurgence of traffic. Giant freighters leave China and travel through the Panama Canal.
Source: Keith Meyers/*The New York Times*/Redux Pictures.

Intermodal transportation of goods involves a combination of land and water shipping from producer to customer.[38] In the United States alone, railroads handle more than $150 billion in seaport goods, a statistic that is a testament to intermodal transportation's growing importance. Unfortunately, lack of investment in America's rail infrastructure has resulted in delays at seaports. As Bernard LaLonde, a professor of transportation and logistics, noted recently, "It's the Achilles' heel of global distribution. The ships keep getting bigger and faster. Trade keeps growing. But we don't have the rail links we need."[39]

The decision about which mode of transportation to use may be dictated by a particular market situation, by the company's overall strategy, or by conditions at the port of importation. For example, every November, winemakers from France's Beaujolais region participate in a promotion celebrating the release of the current vintage. Although wine destined for European markets may travel by rail or truck, U.S.-bound wine is shipped via air freight. Normally, owing to weight and bulk considerations, French wine makes the transatlantic journey by water. Similarly, Acer Group ships motherboards and other high-tech components from Taiwan via air freight to ensure that the latest technology is incorporated into its computers. Bangladesh's primary port, Chittagong, is subject to frequent delays and strikes, which forces Gap and other clothing companies to ship via air.

Every Christmas, supplies of the season's hottest-selling toys and electronics products are shipped via air from factories in Asia to ensure just-in-time delivery by Santa Claus. Sony's PS3 is a case in point; in the fall of 2006, the company shipped hundreds of thousands of units by air to the United States. Likewise, in 2007, the first shipments of Apple's highly anticipated iPhone arrived from Asia via air freight. An estimated $1 billion is added to U.S. shipping costs each year because companies are forced to compensate for railway delays by keeping more components or parts in inventory or by shipping via air.

Logistics Management: A Brief Case Study

The term **logistics management** describes the integration of activities necessary to ensure the efficient flow of raw materials, in-process inventory, and finished goods from producers to customers. JCPenney provides a case study in the changing face of logistics, physical distribution, and retail supply chains in the twenty-first century. Several years ago, Penney's management team made a key decision to outsource most elements of its private-label shirt supply chain to TAL Apparel Ltd. of Hong Kong. Penney's North American stores carry virtually no extra inventory of house-brand shirts; when an individual shirt is sold, EPOS scanner data is transmitted directly to Hong Kong. TAL's proprietary computer model then determines whether to replenish the store with the same size, color, and style. Replacement shirts are sent directly to stores without passing through Penney's warehouse system; sometimes the shirts are sent via air, sometimes by ship. This approach represents a dramatic departure from past practices; Penney typically carried six months' worth of inventory in its warehouses and three months' inventory in stores. By working more closely with TAL, Penney can lower its inventory costs, reduce the quantity of goods that have to be marked down, and respond more quickly to changing consumer tastes and fashion styles. As Wai-Chan Chan of McKinsey & Company Hong Kong noted, "You are giving away a pretty important function when you outsource your inventory management. That's something that not a lot of retailers want to part with."[40]

---

[38]For an excellent case study of the evolution of intermodal technology in the United States, see Jon R. Katzenback and Douglas K. Smith, *The Wisdom of Teams: Creating the High-Performance Organization* (New York: HarperBusiness, 1994), Chapter 2.

[39]Daniel Machalaba, "Cargo Hold: As U.S. Seaports Get Busier, Weak Point Is a Surprise: Railroads," *The Wall Street Journal* (September 19, 1996), p. A1.

[40]Alexandra Harney, "Technology Takes the Wrinkles out of Textiles Manufacturing," *Financial Times* (January 11, 2006), p. 11. See also Gabriel Kahn, "Made to Measure: Invisible Supplier Has Penney's Shirts All Buttoned Up," *The Wall Street Journal* (September 11, 2003), pp. A1, A9.

Summary

A **channel of distribution** is the network of agencies and institutions that links producers with users. **Physical distribution** is the movement of goods through channels. **Business–to-consumer marketing** uses consumer channels; **business-to-business marketing** employs industrial channels to deliver products to manufacturers or other types of organizations. **Peer-to-peer** marketing via the Internet is another channel. **Distributors** and **agents** are key intermediaries in both channel types. Channel decisions are difficult to manage globally because of the variation in channel structures from country to country. Marketing channels can create **place utility**, **time utility**, **form utility**, and **information utility** for buyers. The characteristics of customers, products, middlemen, and environment all affect channel design and strategy.

Consumer channels may be relatively direct, utilizing direct mail or door-to-door selling, as well as manufacturer-owned stores. A combination of manufacturers' sales forces, agents/brokers, and wholesalers may also be used. Channels for industrial products are less varied, with manufacturer's sales force, wholesalers, and dealers or agents used.

Global retailing is a growing trend as successful retailers expand around the world in support of growth objectives. Retail operations take many different forms, including **department stores**, **specialty retailers**, **supermarkets**, **convenience stores**, **discount stores**, **hard discounters**, **hypermarkets**, **supercenters**, **superstores**, **shopping malls**, **outlet stores**, and **outlet malls**. Selection, price, store location, and customer service are a few of the competencies that can be used strategically to enter a new market. It is possible to classify retailers in a matrix that distinguishes companies offering few product categories with an own-label focus, many categories with an own-label focus, few categories with a manufacturer-brand focus, and many categories with a manufacturer-brand focus. Global retail expansion can be achieved via **organic growth**, **franchising**, **acquisition**, **joint venture**, and **licensing**.

Transportation and physical distribution issues are critically important in a company's value chain because of the geographical distances involved in sourcing products and serving customers in different parts of the world. A company's **supply chain** includes all the firms that perform support activities such as generating raw materials or fabricating components. **Logistics** and **logistics management** integrate the activities of all companies in a firm's value chain to ensure an efficient flow of goods through the supply chain. Important activities include **order processing**, **warehousing**, and **inventory management**. To cut costs and improve efficiency, many companies are reconfiguring their supply chains by outsourcing some or all of these activities. Six transportation modes—air, truck, water, rail, pipeline, and Internet—are widely used in global distribution. **Containerization** was a key innovation in physical distribution that facilitates **intermodal transportation**.

Discussion Questions

1. In what ways can channel intermediaries create utility for buyers?
2. What factors influence the channel structures and strategies available to global marketers?
3. What is *cherry picking*? What approaches can be used to deal with this problem?
4. Compare and contrast the typical channel structures for consumer products and industrial products.
5. Identify the different forms of retailing, and cite an example of each. Identify retailers from as many different countries as you can.
6. Identify the four retail market expansion strategies discussed in the text. What factors determine the appropriate mode?
7. Many global retailers are targeting China, India, and other emerging markets. In terms of the strategies described in Figure 12-4, what would be the most likely entry strategies for these countries?
8. Briefly discuss the global issues associated with physical distribution and transportation logistics. Cite one example of a company that is making efficiency improvements in its channel or physical distribution arrangements.
9. What special distribution challenges exist in Japan? What is the best way for a non-Japanese company to deal with these challenges?

In its home market, Tesco operates more than 2,300 stores in four formats: supercenters (large stores with a limited range of nonfood items), regular supermarkets, and Tesco Express convenience stores. While the U.S. market entry will be limited to small neighborhood markets, Tesco has raised eyebrows with an ambitious plan to establish its own distribution network as well. Management expects prepared foods such as salads and chicken-based dishes to be big sellers. To execute, Tesco is bringing two suppliers across the Atlantic: Natures Way Foods, which specializes in salads, and 2 Sisters Food Group, a leading UK poultry purveyor.

Will Tesco succeed with its strategy for entering the U.S. market? Management is confident it has identified an opportunity. The small-store format makes it unlikely that Tesco will encounter the type of backlash that has been directed at Walmart in some communities. Speaking about the U.S. retail environment, Tim Mason, director of marketing and property at Tesco, notes, "Generally, shopping either means the big-box model, where you get in your car once a week and drive out of town to do your shopping, or the convenience store at the end of the street. We found that the [U.S.] market for convenience stores at the end of your street is not very well served. There is more consumer opportunity and more retail opportunity."

The company does have an impressive track record outside the United Kingdom; Tesco has even penetrated markets that have proven to be difficult for Walmart and Carrefour. For example, Tesco entered South Korea in 1999; today it is the number two retailer behind E-Mart, a local chain. Samsung Tesco, an 89-11 joint venture, operates Homeplus "value store" hypermarkets. Homeplus is known for more than just shopping: The stores also feature coffee shops and restaurants. As one analyst noted, the joint venture approach has served Tesco well. "Thanks to its local partner, Tesco has tailored its service well to local tastes, while Walmart and Carrefour have struggled to win over consumers with their focus on prices," the analyst said.

Tesco has also been successful in Japan, although on a limited scale. Before entering the market, a team was dispatched to live with Japanese consumers, accompany them on shopping trips, and observe their food preparation customs. As David Reid, chairman and head of Tesco's international operations, explained, "In America you have big cars, you can drive several miles in five minutes, you can buy in bulk and store it in your double garage. Chalk and cheese compared to Japan.[41] In Japan we learned that some housewives shop on bikes and shop daily. They visit six or seven shops looking for deals." Armed with these insights, Tesco acquired C-Two, a small discount convenience store chain with stores in Tokyo.

Case 12-1 Discussion Questions

1. What are the keys to Tesco's success in the competitive retailing industry?
2. In view of the tough retailing environment, what changes do you think Tesco might be forced to make to the "Fresh & Easy" concept?
3. Which of the market entry strategies identified in the chapter is Tesco using in the United States? Do you think this is the appropriate strategy?

Sources: Cecilie Rohwedder, "Tesco Tries to Hit a U.S. Curveball," *The Wall Street Journal* (March 2, 2009), p. B1; Cecilie Rohwedder, "Stores of Knowledge: No. 1 Retailer in Britain Uses 'Clubcard' to Thwart Walmart," *The Wall Street Journal* (June 6, 2006), pp. A1, A16; Jonathan Birchall, "Tesco Will Launch in LA and Phoenix," *Financial Times* (May 18, 2006), p. 17; Elizabeth Rigby, "Tesco Seeks to Gain Weight Abroad," *Financial Times* (May 2, 2006), p. 17; Song Jung-a, "One-Stop Model Gives Tesco Edge in Korea," *Financial Times* (March 22, 2006), p. 17; Sophy Buckley and Jonathan Birchall, "Tesco Plans to Build Brand in US," *Financial Times* (February 10, 2006), p. 19; Cecilie Rohwedder, "Tesco Jumps the Pond," *The Wall Street Journal* (February 10, 2006), p. B2; Susanna Voyle, "Tesco's Tough Act: With Record Profits, Britain's Biggest Retailer Prepares for Further Challenges at Home and Abroad," *Financial Times* (April 20, 2004), p. 13; Alastair Ray, "Own-brand Broadcaster Tunes In," *Financial Times* (March 16, 2004), p. 10; Bayan Rahman, "Tesco's Japanese Shopping without the Hype," *Financial Times* (January 16, 2004), p. 20.

---

[41]The British English expression "as [different as] chalk and cheese" is the equivalent of the American English expression "as different as night and day."

Case 12-2
LIDL Explores Further Expansion in Global Retailing

Hardly anyone could deny the popularity and relevance of discount stores in recent times. Essentially, the prevailing credit crunch has turned retailers such as Lidl into household names in the United Kingdom and other parts of the world where they have successfully established branches to serve the price-sensitive consumer segment of the society. Although there are many other characteristics of discount stores such as offering a wide range of products—food, nonfood, perishables, and nonperishable items—to their customers, the most general characteristic common to them is their consistent emphasis on low prices. This key feature has been on top of the list of major strengths of Lidl since it started its operations in the United Kingdom in 1994. In its marketing communications, Lidl does not mince words in emphasizing that it is the place where quality is cheaper. Besides, it also emphasizes in its customer philosophy that it holds customer satisfaction as core to its businesses in relation to its product assortment, the prompt response to customers' queries, and the dedication of the staff to customer satisfaction. For example, in terms of its product assortment, Lidl offers its customers a wide range of products from its private-labeled bread to organic items, and provides its customers with nutritional guides so that they have an overview of their eating habits and know the most important nutrients and calories. Furthermore, in order to achieve all of this, the discounter has the recruitment policy that attracts people of all ages and backgrounds, and is committed to their welfare knowing fully that its success is inextricably linked to the quality of people who work for the company.

The close relationship between Lidl and its increasing customer base is not without threats. Other discounters like Aldi also woo customers with a low-price strategy. Even retailing giants like Tesco and ASDA pose major threats to Lidl with their relentless efforts on improving their value-range items, which are sold using their own brand names. But this "war" is not surprising as the retail industry generally suffered a major blow due to the recession. People are now more conscious of how they spend their hard-earned money. Hence, competition among the retailers has now become stiffer than it used to be several years ago. To add to this, a recent study suggests that low-income consumers are not loyal to brands of grocery items but are merely loyal to the price. They buy value-range items as long as the price remains the cheapest but can switch immediately if they notice that another brand offers a better price deal. So, Lidl keeps a close eye on its competitors daily so as not to trivialize the threats to its main strength—low price.

The first Lidl stores opened in Germany in 1973 and they are now active in over 20 countries worldwide. The chain continues to expand, with branches opening in Romania and Bulgaria in 2010, Canada in 2012, and Serbia in 2015. It is owned by the German holding company, Schwarz.

Source: © Alex Segre/Alamy.

Nonetheless, Lidl is strongly committed to spreading its relevance to other parts of the world. It emphasizes this clearly to the public as stated on its Web site: "We are a successful chain of grocery stores, expanding strongly throughout Europe and beyond its borders." It becomes obvious that different sets of strategies will be applicable now that its core business is in retailing than when it started in the 1930s as Lidl and Schwarz Grocery Wholesale in Germany. So far, it now has branches in virtually all countries in Europe with about 500 stores in the United Kingdom alone. Yet, the intention is to keep playing a key role in the retail industry in these countries and beyond. As it expands beyond Europe, it is important to get it right as a host of factors influence success in global retailing. While maintaining its key strategy of low price, other crucial factors that will drive its operations include the locals' sensitivity to cultural values, understanding the legal frameworks associated with its line of business, exploring the competitive dynamics, and many others. The intention to expand sounds fine, but how well Lidl could explore it remains a major challenge.

Discussion Questions

1. As Lidl intensifies its effort to increase its presence in the global marketplace, what are the major likely opportunities it could explore and the threats it should be prepared to confront?
2. What are the key success factors of Lidl in the United Kingdom, and could these be replicated in the new territories being targeted for future expansion?

Sources: This case was prepared by Dr. Tunji Gbadamosi, Senior Lecturer in Marketing, University of East London, London, UK. *Additional*

Sources: A. Diepenbrock, "Channel Watch: Will Recession Prompt a Discount Breakthrough in Western Europe?" *Euromonitor* (October 1, 2008); "Lidl Ireland Gmbh—Retailing—Ireland," *Euromonitor* (June 30, 2009), www.portal.euromonitor. Accessed November 11, 2009; "Budget Beauty Brands Are the New Black. But for How Long?" *Euromonitor* (September 23, 2009); A. Gbadamosi, "Cognitive Dissonance: The Implicit Explication in Low-Income Consumers' Shopping Behaviour for 'Low-Involvement' Grocery Products," *International Journal of Retail and Distribution Management*, 37, no. 12 (2009), pp. 1077–1095; www. lidl.co.uk/uk/home.nsf/pages/c.services.au.campany.index. Accessed November 15, 2009.

Global Marketing Communications Decisions I: Advertising and Public Relations

Case 13-1
2008 Beijing Olympics: An Advertising and PR Bonanza

The Chinese government left nothing to chance in its quest to host the 2008 Olympic Games. After narrowly losing its 1993 hosting bid, the Chinese government hired several public relations (PR) firms and consultants, including U.S.-based Weber Shandwick and Bell Pottinger, a British firm. The investment in PR paid off: The International Olympics Committee named China as the host of the 2008 games.

Premier Wen Jiabao, President Hu Jintao, and other government officials were fully aware that the Games would provide a window through which the rest of the world could see China up close. Beijing intended to take full advantage of the opportunity to showcase the progress China has made in the three decades since

economic reforms were launched. The Beijing Organizing Committee for the Olympic Games (Bocog) served as the liaison between government agencies and corporate sponsors; it was also responsible for developing an overall PR strategy.

Beijing hired another PR firm, Hill & Knowlton, to work on the games. It's a good thing, too: various non-governmental groups (NGOs) such as Students for a Free Tibet and Dreams for Darfur had their own agendas. These activists were also thoroughly steeped in modern PR tactics; using text messaging, blogs, and other tools, they spread messages and organized protests that threatened to undermine and overshadow the carefully cultivated image of Olympic harmony (see Exhibit 13-1).

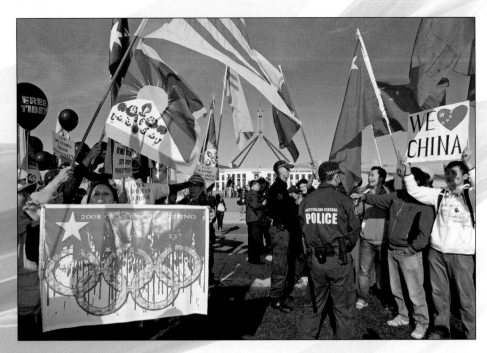

Exhibit 13-1: Police attempt to separate pro-Tibet protesters (L) and thousands of Chinese supporters (R) outside Parliament House during the Beijing 2008 Olympic torch relay through Canberra on April 24, 2008.
Source: Torsten Blackwood/AFP/Newscom.

The protests were staged to call attention to a number of policy issues, including Beijing's crackdown in Tibet and its economic ties with the government of Sudan, the North African country where a deadly civil war has been raging in the Darfur region. Bocog also had pressing issues closer to home, such as concerns among some Olympic athletes about air pollution in the Chinese capital. The rest of Case 13-1, including discussion questions, is at the end of the chapter.

Advertising, public relations, and other forms of communication are critical tools in the marketing program. Marketing communications—the promotion *P* of the marketing mix—refers to all forms of communication used by organizations to inform, remind, explain, persuade, and influence the attitudes and buying behavior of customers and others. The primary purpose of marketing communications is to tell customers about the benefits and values that a company, nation, product, or service offers. The elements of the promotion mix are advertising, public relations, personal selling, and sales promotion. Global marketers can use all of these elements, either alone or in varying combinations. Beijing's experience with the 2008 Olympics Games highlights the critical importance of PR to any entity—be it a nation or a business enterprise—that finds itself spotlighted on the world stage. This chapter examines advertising and public relations from the perspective of the global marketer. Chapter 14 covers sales promotion, personal selling, event marketing, and sponsorships. As you study these chapters, remember: All the communication tools described here should be used in a way that reinforces a consistent message.

GLOBAL ADVERTISING

The environment in which marketing communications programs and strategies are implemented varies from country to country. The challenge of effectively communicating across borders is one reason that global companies and their advertising agencies are embracing a concept known as **integrated marketing communications (IMC)**. Adherents of an IMC approach explicitly recognize that the various elements of a company's communication strategy must be carefully coordinated.[1] For example, Nike has embraced the IMC concept. Trevor Edwards is Nike's vice president for global brand and category management. He notes:

> We create demand for our brand by being flexible about how we tell the story. We do not rigidly stay with one approach. . . . We have an integrated marketing model that involves all elements of the marketing mix from digital to sports marketing, from event marketing to advertising to entertainment, all sitting at the table driving ideas.[2]

Advertising is one element of an IMC program. **Advertising** may be defined as any sponsored, paid message that is communicated in a nonpersonal way. Some advertising messages are designed to communicate with persons in a single country or market area. Regional or pan-regional advertising is created for audiences across several country markets such as Europe or Latin America. **Global advertising** may be defined as messages whose art, copy, headlines, photographs, taglines, and other elements have been developed expressly for their worldwide suitability. Companies that have used global themes include McDonald's ("I'm lovin' it"), IBM ("Solutions for a small planet"), De Beers ("A diamond is forever"), BP ("Beyond Petroleum"),

---

[1]Thomas R. Duncan and Stephen E. Everett, "Client Perception of Integrated Marketing Communications," *Journal of Advertising Research* (May–June 1993), pp. 119–122; see also Stephen J. Gould, Dawn B. Lerman, and Andreas F. Grein, "Agency Perceptions and Practices on Global IMC," *Journal of Advertising Research* 39, no. 1 (January–February 1999), pp. 7–20.
[2]Gavin O'Malley, "Who's Leading the Way in Web Marketing? It's Nike, Of Course," *Advertising Age* (October 26, 2006), p. D3.

and Vodafone ("Your voice"). In Chapter 10, we noted that some global companies simultaneously offer local, international, and global products and brands to buyers in different parts of the world. The same is true with advertising: A global company may use single-country advertising in addition to campaigns that are regional and global in scope.

A global company possesses a critical marketing advantage with respect to marketing communications: It has the opportunity to successfully transform a domestic advertising campaign into a worldwide one. Alternatively, it can create a new global campaign from the ground up. The search for a global advertising campaign should bring together key company and ad agency personnel to share information, insights, and experience. McDonald's "I'm lovin' it" tagline is a case in point; it was developed after global marketing chief Larry Light called a meeting of representatives from all of McDonald's ad agencies. Global campaigns with unified themes can help to build long-term product and brand identities and offer significant savings by reducing the cost associated with producing ads. Regional market areas such as Europe are experiencing an influx of standardized global brands as companies align themselves for a united region by making acquisitions and evaluating production plans and pricing policies. From a marketing point of view, there is a great deal of activity going on that will make brands truly pan-European in a short period of time. This phenomenon is accelerating the growth of global advertising.

The potential for effective global advertising also increases as companies recognize and embrace new concepts such as "product cultures." An example is the globalization of beer culture, which can be seen in the popularity of German-style beer halls in Japan and Irish-style pubs in the United States. Similarly, the globalization of coffee culture has created market opportunities for companies such as Starbucks. Companies also realize that some market segments can be defined on the basis of global demography—youth culture or an emerging middle class, for example—rather than ethnic or national culture. Athletic shoes and other clothing items, for instance, can be targeted to a worldwide segment of 18- to 25-year-old males. William Roedy, global chairman of MTV Networks, sees clear implications of such product cultures for advertising. MTV is just one of the media vehicles that enable people virtually anywhere to see how the rest of the world lives and to learn about products that are popular in other cultures.

According to data compiled by ZenithOptimedia, worldwide advertising expenditures in 2005 exceeded $400 billion. Because advertising is often designed to add psychological value to a product or brand, it plays a more important communications role in marketing consumer products than in marketing industrial products. Frequently purchased, low-cost products generally require heavy promotional support, which often takes the form of reminder advertising. Consumer products companies top the list of big global advertising spenders. P&G, Unilever, L'Oréal, and Nestlé are companies whose "globalness" can be inferred from the significant proportion of advertising expenditures outside the home-country markets.

Advertising Age magazine's ranking of global marketers in terms of advertising expenditures is shown in Table 13-1.[3] The top 100 advertisers spent $107.6 billion in 2007; as a group, the top 100 spent $46.6 billion on U.S. advertising. A close examination of Table 13-1 provides clues to the extent of a company's globalization efforts. For example, packaged-goods giants P&G and Unilever spend significant amounts in all major world regions. By contrast, the table shows that the geographic scope of France's Peugeot Citroën is largely limited to Europe with additional presence in Asia and Latin America.

Global advertising also offers companies economies of scale in advertising as well as improved access to distribution channels. Where shelf space is at a premium, a company has to convince retailers to carry its products rather than those of competitors. A global brand supported by global advertising may be very attractive because, from the retailer's standpoint, a global brand is less likely to languish on the shelves. Landor Associates, a company specializing in brand identity and design, recently determined that Coke has the number one brand-awareness and esteem position in the United States, number two in Japan, and number six in Europe. However, standardization is not always required or even advised. Nestlé's Nescafé coffee is marketed as a global brand, even though advertising messages and product formulation vary to suit cultural differences.

---

[3]To be included in the rankings, companies must report media spending on at least three continents.

TABLE 13-1 Top 25 Global Marketers, 2007 ($ millions)

Company/ Headquarters	Worldwide Ad Spending	U.S. Ad Spending	Asia Ad Spending*	Europe Ad Spending	Latin America Ad Spending
1. Procter & Gamble (United States)	9,358	$3,700	$1,943	$3,113	$251
2. Unilever (United Kingdom, Netherlands)	5,295	910	1,504	2,285	397
3. L'Oréal (France)	3,426	782	393	2,048	88
4. General Motors Corp. (United States)	3,345	2,062	79	926	114
5. Toyota Motor Corp. (Japan)	3,202	1,072	1,221	735	55
6. Ford Motor Co. (United States)	2,902	1,653	118	895	108
7. Johnson & Johnson (United States)	2,192	1,421	317	486	54
8. Nestlé (Switzerland)	2,181	693	236	1,091	102
9. Coca-Cola Co. (United States)	2,177	411	538	999	131
10. Honda Motor Co. (Japan)	2,047	849	926	197	18
11. Time Warner (United States)	2,022	1,738	8	210	33
12. Reckitt Benckiser	1,983	469	200	1,172	70
13. Sony Corp. (Japan)	1,886	973	248	548	40
14. Kraft Foods	1,853	1,083	25	643	43
15. Nissan Motor Co. (Japan)	1,826	953	396	361	43
16. GlaxoSmithKline (United Kingdom)	1,802	1,187	126	390	59
17. McDonald's (United States)	1,740	809	317	509	32
18. Volkswagen (Germany)	1,729	201	101	1,309	67
19. Mars Inc. (United States)	1,708	570	210	843	23
20. Walt Disney Company (United States)	1,677	1,387	30	212	10
21. PepsiCo (United States)	1,583	890	193	283	110
22. Chrysler	1,319	1,148	23	68	30
23. Danone Group (France)	1,306	100	56	993	131
24. PSA Peugeot Citroën (France)	1,292	0	30	1,190	56
25. General Electric Co. (United States)	1,277	1,057	22	163	1

*Asia includes Australia and New Zealand.
Source: Advertising Age (December 8, 2008), p. 4.

Global Advertising Content: The "Standardization" Versus "Adaptation" Debate

Communication experts generally agree that the overall requirements of effective communication and persuasion are fixed and do not vary from country to country. The same thing is true of the components of the communication process: The marketer is the source of the message; the message must be encoded, conveyed via the appropriate channel(s), and decoded by a member of the target audience. Communication takes place only when the intended meaning transfers from the source to the receiver. Four major difficulties can compromise an organization's attempt to communicate with customers in any location:

1. The message may not get through to the intended recipient. This problem may be the result of an advertiser's lack of knowledge about appropriate media for reaching certain types of audiences.
2. The message may reach the target audience but may not be understood or may even be misunderstood. This can be the result of an inadequate understanding of the target audience's level of sophistication or improper encoding.

3. The message may reach the target audience and may be understood but still may not compel the recipient to take action. This could result from a lack of cultural knowledge about a target audience.

4. The effectiveness of the message can be impaired by *noise*. Noise in this case is an external influence such as competitive advertising, other sales personnel, and confusion at the receiving end. These factors can detract from the ultimate effectiveness of the communication.

The key question for global marketers is whether the *specific* advertising message and media strategy must be changed from region to region or country to country because of environmental requirements. Proponents of the "one world, one voice" approach to global advertising believe that the era of the global village has arrived and that tastes and preferences are converging worldwide. According to the standardization argument, people everywhere want the same products for the same reasons. This means that companies can achieve significant economies of scale by unifying advertising around the globe. Advertisers who prefer the localized approach are skeptical of the global village argument. Instead, they assert that consumers still differ from country to country and must be reached by advertising tailored to their respective countries. Proponents of localization point out that most blunders occur because advertisers have failed to understand— and adapt to—foreign cultures. A decade ago, Nick Brien, managing director of Leo Burnett, explained the situation this way:

> As the potency of traditional media declines on a daily basis, brand building locally becomes more costly and international brand building becomes more cost effective. The challenge for advertisers and agencies is finding ads that work in different countries and cultures. At the same time as this global tendency, there is a growing local tendency. It's becoming increasingly important to understand the requirements of both.[4]

During the 1950s, the widespread opinion among advertising professionals was that effective international advertising required assigning responsibility for campaign preparation to a local agency. In the early 1960s, this idea of local delegation was repeatedly challenged. For example, Eric Elinder, head of a Swedish advertising agency, wrote: "Why should three artists in three different countries sit drawing the same electric iron and three copywriters write about what, after all, is largely the same copy for the same iron?"[5] Elinder argued that consumer differences between countries were diminishing and that he would more effectively serve a client's interest by putting top specialists to work devising a strong international campaign. The campaign would then be presented with insignificant modifications that mainly entailed translating the copy into language well suited for a particular country.

As the decade of the 1980s began, Pierre Liotard-Vogt, then-CEO of Nestlé, expressed similar views in an interview with *Advertising Age*.

> *Advertising Age:* Are food tastes and preferences different in each of the countries in which you do business?
>
> *Liotard-Vogt:* The two countries where we are selling perhaps the most instant coffee are England and Japan. Before the war they didn't drink coffee in those countries, and I heard people say that it wasn't any use to try to sell instant coffee to the English because they drink only tea and still less to the Japanese because they drink green tea and they're not interested in anything else.
>
> When I was very young, I lived in England and at that time, if you spoke to an Englishman about eating spaghetti or pizza or anything like that, he would just look at you and think that the stuff was perhaps food for Italians. Now on the corner of every road in London you find pizzerias and spaghetti houses.

---

[4]Meg Carter, "Think Globally, Act Locally," *Financial Times* (June 30, 1997), p. 12.
[5]Eric Elinder, "International Advertisers Must Devise Universal Ads, Dump Separate National Ones, Swedish Ad Man Avers," *Advertising Age* (November 27, 1961), p. 91.

So I do not believe [preconceptions] about "national tastes." They are "habits," and they're not the same. If you bring the public a different food, even if it is unknown initially, when they get used to it, they will enjoy it too.

To a certain extent we know that in the north they like a coffee milder and a bit acid and less roasted; in the south, they like it very dark. So I can't say that taste differences don't exist. But to believe that those tastes are set and can't be changed is a mistake.[6]

The "standardized versus localized" debate picked up tremendous momentum after the 1983 publication, noted in earlier chapters, of Professor Ted Levitt's *Harvard Business Review* article, "The Globalization of Markets." Recently, global companies have embraced a technique known as **pattern advertising**. This is analogous to the concept of global product platforms discussed in Chapter 10. Representing a middle ground between 100 percent standardization and 100 percent adaptation, a pattern strategy calls for developing a basic pan-regional or global communication concept for which copy, artwork, or other elements can be adapted as required for individual country markets. For example, ads in a European print campaign for Boeing shared basic design elements, but the copy and the visual elements were localized on a country-by-country basis.

Much of the research on this issue has focused on the match between advertising messages and local culture. For example, Ali Kanso surveyed two different groups of advertising managers; those adopting localized approaches to advertising and those adopting standardized approaches. One finding was that managers who are attuned to cultural issues tended to prefer the localized approach, whereas managers less sensitive to cultural issues preferred a standardized approach.[7] Bruce Steinberg, ad sales director for MTV Europe, discovered that the people responsible for executing global campaigns locally can exhibit strong resistance to a global campaign. Steinberg reported that he sometimes had to visit as many as 20 marketing directors from the same company to get approval for a pan-European MTV ad.[8]

As Kanso correctly notes, the long-standing debate over advertising approaches will probably continue for years to come. Kanso's conclusion: What is needed for successful international advertising is a global commitment to local vision. In the final analysis, the decision of whether to use a global or localized campaign depends on recognition by managers of the trade-offs involved. A global campaign will result in the substantial benefits of cost savings, increased control, and the potential creative leverage of a global appeal. It is also true that localized campaigns can focus on the most important attributes of a product or brand in each nation or culture.

As a practical matter, marketing managers may choose to run *both* global *and* local ads rather than adopt an "either/or" stance. For example, marketing and advertising managers at Pioneer Hi-Bred International frequently use both global and localized advertising executions. It is management's belief that some messages lend themselves to straight translation, while others need to be created in a way that best suits the farmers, marketplace, and style of the particular country or region. Of the ads shown in Exhibit 13-2, the top ad is for the United States, and the ad at the bottom was created for Québec.

The question of *when* to use each approach depends on the product involved and a company's objectives in a particular market. The following generalizations can serve as guidelines:

- Standardized print campaigns can be used for industrial products or for technology-oriented consumer products. Example: Apple iPhone
- Standardized print campaigns with a strong visual appeal often travel well. Example: Chivas Regal ("This is the Chivas Life")
- TV commercials that use voice-overs instead of actors or celebrity endorsers speaking dialogue can use standardized visuals with translated copy for the voice-over. Examples: Gillette ("The best a man can get"); GE ("Imagination at work")

"I can think of very few truly global ads that work. Brands are often at different stages around the world, and that means there are different advertising jobs to do."[9]
Michael Conrad, Chief Creative Officer, Leo Burnett Worldwide

"If we could find one message on a global basis it could be effective, but so far there are different needs in different countries. We have been in Sweden for 60 years and in China for only four or five so our feeling is that retail is local. It is important to take advantage of local humor, and the things on people's minds."[10]
Nils Larsson, Manager, External Communications, IKEA

"Eighteen-year-olds in Paris have more in common with 18-year-olds in New York than with their own parents. They buy the same products, go to the same movies, listen to the same music, sip the same colas. Global advertising merely works on that premise."[11]
William Roedy, Director, MTV Europe

[6]"A Conversation with Nestlé's Pierre Liotard-Vogt," *Advertising Age* (June 30, 1980), p. 31.
[7]Ali Kanso, "International Advertising Strategies: Global Commitment to Local Vision," *Journal of Advertising Research* 32, no. 1 (January–February 1992), pp. 10–14.
[8]Ken Wells, "Selling to the World: Global Ad Campaigns, After Many Missteps, Finally Pay Dividends," *The Wall Street Journal* (August 27, 1992), p. A1.
[9]Vanessa O'Connell, "Exxon 'Centralizes' New Global Campaign," *The Wall Street Journal* (July 11, 2001), p. B6.
[10]Emma Hall and Normandy Madden, "IKEA Courts Buyers with Offbeat Ideas," *Advertising Age* (April 12, 2004), p. 1.
[11]Ken Wells, "Selling to the World: Global Ad Campaigns, after Many Missteps, Finally Pay Dividends," *The Wall Street Journal* (August 27, 1992), p. A1.

ADVERTISING AGENCIES: ORGANIZATIONS AND BRANDS

Advertising is a fast-paced business, and the ad agency world is fluid and dynamic. New agencies are formed, existing agencies are dismantled, and cross-border investment, spin-offs, joint ventures, and mergers and acquisitions are a fact of life. There is also a great deal of mobility in the industry as executives and top talent move from one agency to another. The 20 largest global **advertising organizations** ranked by 2008 gross income are shown in Table 13-2. The key to understanding the table is the word *organization*; each firm identified in Table 13-2 is an umbrella corporation or holding company that includes one or more "core" advertising agencies, as well as units specializing in direct marketing, marketing services, public relations, or research. A close inspection of the table reveals that Microsoft and IBM have gotten into the advertising business. Not surprisingly, both Razorfish (Microsoft) and IBM Interactive are digital specialists.

TABLE 13-2 Top 20 Global Advertising Organizations

Organization and Headquarters Location	Worldwide Revenue 2008 (millions)
1. WPP Group (London)	$13,598
2. Omnicom Group (New York)	13,360
3. Interpublic Group of Cos. (New York)	6,963
4. Publicis Groupe (Paris)	6,900
5. Dentsu (Tokyo)	3,296
6. Aegis Group (London)	2,490
7. Havas (Suresnes, France)	2,307
8. Hakuhodo DY Holdings (Tokyo)	1,560
9. MDC Partners (Toronto/New York)	585
10. Asatsu-DK (Tokyo)	503
11. Alliance Data Systems (Dallas)	491
12. Media Consula (Dallas)	427
13. Microsoft Corp. (IRazorfish; Redmond, WA)	409
14. Photon Group (Sydney)	383
15. Carlson Marketing (Minneapolis)	367
16. Cheil Worldwide (Seoul)	340
17. IBM Corp. (IBM Interactive; Armonk, NY)	313
18. Sapient Corp. (Sapient Interactive; Cambridge, MA)	306
19. inVentiv Health (inventive Communications; Westerville, OH)	280
20. Grupo ABC (ABC Group; São Paulo)	280

Source: "World's Top 25 Agency Companies," *Advertising Age* (April 27, 2009), p. 12.

As shown in Figure 13-1, the family tree of Omnicom Group is quite complex. The group includes three core agencies: BBDO Worldwide, DDB Worldwide Communications, and TBWA Worldwide; each agency, in turn, has a global network. Omnicom's other agencies provide services in various specialty areas such as recruitment, health care, digital, and direct marketing. Omnicom generates about 43 percent of annual revenues from advertising and media; public relations accounts for 9.5 percent, and customer relationship management (CRM) for 38 percent. Specialty services such as health care advertising account for the remaining 9.5 percent of revenues.

Table 13-3 presents the rankings of individual agencies (agency "brands") by 2008 worldwide income. Most of the agency brands identified in Table 13-3 are *full-service agencies*: In addition to creating advertising, they provide other services such as market research, media buying, and direct marketing. The agencies listed in Table 13-3 are all owned by larger holding companies.

Selecting an Advertising Agency

Companies can create ads in-house, use an outside agency, or combine both strategies. For example, Chanel, Benetton, H&M, and Diesel rely on in-house marketing and advertising staffs for creative work; Coca-Cola has its own agency, Edge Creative, but also uses the services of outside agencies such as Leo Burnett. When one or more outside agencies are used, they can serve product accounts on a multi-country or even global basis. It is possible to select a local agency in each national market or an agency with both domestic and overseas offices. Like Coca-Cola, Levi Strauss and Polaroid also use local agencies. Today, however, there is a growing tendency for Western clients to designate global agencies for product accounts to support the integration of the marketing and advertising functions; Japan-based companies are less inclined to use this approach. For example, in 1995, Colgate-Palmolive consolidated its $500 million in global

FIGURE 13-1

**Omnicom Group
"Family Tree"**

Source: Advertising Age.

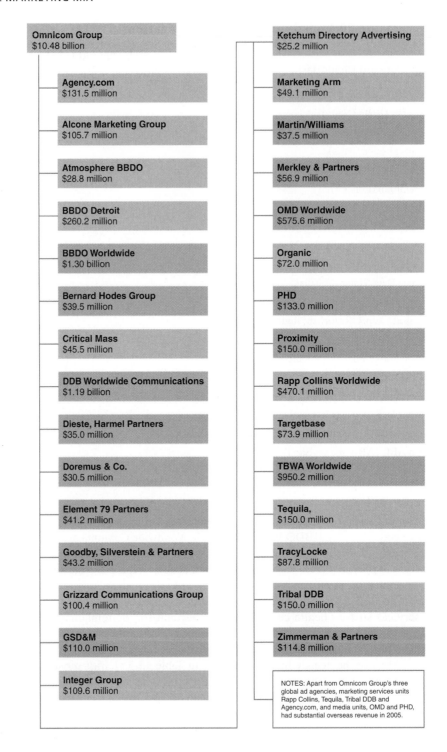

billings with Young & Rubicam. That same year, IBM consolidated its ad account with Ogilvy & Mather for the launch of the "Solutions for a small planet" global campaign. Similarly, Bayer AG consolidated most of its $300 million consumer products advertising with BBDO Worldwide; Bayer had previously relied on 50 agencies around the globe. Agencies are aware of this trend and are themselves pursuing international acquisitions and joint ventures to extend their geographic reach and their ability to serve clients on a global account basis. In an effort to remain competitive, many small independent agencies in Europe, Asia, and the United States belong to the Transworld Advertising Agency Network. TAAN allows member agencies to tap into worldwide resources that would not otherwise be available to them.

TABLE 13-3 Top 10 Global Advertising Agency Brands

Agency	Estimated Worldwide Revenue 2008 (millions)
1. Dentsu (Dentsu)	$2,472
2. BBDO Worldwide (Omnicom)	1,986
3. McCann-Erickson Worldwide (Interpublic)	1,741
4. DDB Worldwide (Omnicom)	1,509
5. TBWA Worldwide (Omnicom)	1,357
6. JWT (WPP)	1,157
7. Publicis (Publicis)	1,071
8. Leo Burnett Worldwide (Publicis)	795
9. Saatchi & Saatchi (Publicis)	790
10. Ogilvy & Mather Worldwide (WPP)	771

Source: Adapted from "Top 15 Consolidated Agency Networks," *Advertising Age* (April 27, 2009), p. 14.

In selecting an advertising agency, the following issues should be considered:

Company organization. Companies that are decentralized may want to leave the choice to the local subsidiary.

National responsiveness. Is the global agency familiar with local culture and buying habits in a particular country or should a local selection be made?

Area coverage. Does the candidate agency cover all relevant markets?

Buyer perception. What kind of brand awareness does the company want to project? If the product needs a strong local identification, it would be best to select a national agency.

Despite an unmistakable trend toward using global agencies to support global marketing efforts, companies with geocentric orientations will adapt to the global market requirements and select the best agency or agencies accordingly. Western agencies still find markets such as China and Japan very complex; similarly, Asian agencies find it just as difficult to establish local agency presence in Western markets.

As noted later in the chapter, advertising professionals face escalating pressure to achieve new heights of creativity. Some critics of advertising complain that agencies sometimes try to create advertising that will win awards and generate acclaim and prestige rather than advertising that serves clients' needs. The search for fresh answers to promotion challenges has prompted some client companies to look to new sources for creative ideas. For example, McDonald's historically relied on American agencies for basic creative direction. However, Larry Light, global marketing chief, staged a competition that included agencies from all over the world. A German agency devised the "I'm lovin' it" tagline.[12] Leo Burnett China's ideas included a hand signal for McDonald's global campaign. As Light noted, "China just blew our minds. We didn't expect that kind of expression and joy. Our expectation was for more conservatism, much less individuality, and more caution."[13]

---

[12]Erin White and Shirley Leung, "How Tiny German Shop Landed McDonald's," *The Wall Street Journal* (August 6, 2003), pp. B1, B3.

[13]Geoffrey A. Fowler, "Commercial Break: The Art of Selling," *Far Eastern Economic Review* (October 30, 2003), pp. 30–33.

In 1994, the Chinese government banned tobacco advertising from television and radio; the ban also extended to newspaper, magazine, and cinema ads. With a population of 1.3 billion people, including one-third of the world's smokers, China is a massive potential market for cigarette manufacturers at a time when Western markets are shrinking. The ban was part of China's first law of advertisements. The WHO has asked Chinese leaders to launch antismoking campaigns and impose tougher controls on cigarette smuggling and higher taxes on domestic cigarette producers. China agreed to ratify the UN's Framework Convention on Tobacco Control.

In the European Union, a tobacco ad ban proposal was introduced in mid-1991 with the aim of fulfilling single-market rules of the Maastricht Treaty. The directive would have prohibited tobacco advertising on billboards as of July 2001; newspaper and magazine advertising was slated to end by 2002, with sports sponsorship banned by 2003 (such "world level" sports as Formula One racing would be excluded until 2006). Tobacco companies and advertising associations opposed the proposed ban. The European Commission justified the directive on the grounds that various countries had or were considering restrictions on tobacco advertising and that there was a need for common rules on cross-border trade.

Prior to the directive's implementation date, however, the German government took the issue to the European Court of Justice. The Germans argued that the directive was illegal because tobacco advertising is a health issue; thus, the directive could only be adopted if the member states agreed unanimously. The EU's advocate general concurred with the German government. On October 5, 2000, the court ruled that the directive prohibiting tobacco ads should be annulled. A revised directive concerning cross-border tobacco advertising was adopted in December 2002;

it went into effect in August. However, the German government challenged the new directive at the European Court of Justice on the grounds that it would restrict single-country print advertisements for local cigarette brands. Even so, by 2006 the German government was working on a bill to ban tobacco advertising.

For RJ Reynolds International, Philip Morris International, B.A.T., and other tobacco marketers, the receding threat of a pan-European ban on tobacco ads comes as welcome news. The industry spends between $600 million and $1 billion on advertising in the EU annually. An EU ban would have hurt them most in the countries where they compete with entrenched state tobacco monopolies, namely, France, Italy, and Spain.

Tobacco companies in Central Europe face the prospect of tougher marketing regulations as countries in the region work to meet requirements for entry into the EU. In Lithuania, authorities began to enforce the country's three-year-old tobacco advertising ban on May 1, 2000; some newspapers printed blank pages in protest. Jurga Karmanoviene, media director for Saatchi & Saatchi Lithuania, interprets the enforcement as evidence that the government is sending a signal that it is beginning to meet EU requirements. Similar developments are occurring in Poland, Hungary, Bulgaria, and Romania.

Sources: Geoffrey A. Fowler, "Treaty May Stub Out Cigarette Ads in China," *The Wall Street Journal* (December 2, 2003), pp. B1, B6; Joyce-Ann Gatsoulis, "EU Aspirants Shake Up Tobacco Marketing Scene," *Advertising Age International* (July 2000), p. 15; Tony Koenderman and Paul Meller, "EU Topples Tobacco Ad Rules," *Advertising Age* (October 9, 2000), pp. 4, 97; Juliana Koranteng, " EU Ad Ban on Tobacco Under Fire as Illegal," *Advertising Age* (July 10, 2000), pp. 4, 49; "Australia's Ad Ban Is Fought," *The New York Times* (June 7, 1994), p. 19; Marcus Brauchli, "China Passes Law in Move to Prohibit Ads for Tobacco," *The Wall Street Journal* (October 31, 1994), p. B10; Lili Cui, "Mass Media Boycott Tobacco Ads," *Beijing Review* (June 6, 1994), p. 8; "Tobacco Adverts: Fuming," *The Economist* (February 5, 1994), pp. 60–61.

CREATING GLOBAL ADVERTISING

As suggested earlier in the discussion of the adaptation versus standardization debate, the *message* is at the heart of advertising. The particular message and the way it is presented will depend on the advertiser's objective. Is the ad designed to inform, entertain, remind, or persuade? Moreover, in a world characterized by information overload, ads must break through the clutter, grab the audience's attention, and linger in their minds. This requires developing an original and effective **creative strategy**, which is simply a statement or concept of what a particular message or campaign will say. Advertising agencies can be thought of as "idea factories"; in industry parlance, the Holy Grail in creative strategy development is something known as the **big idea**. Legendary ad man John O'Toole defined the *big idea* as "that flash of insight that synthesizes the purpose of the strategy, joins the product benefit with consumer desire in a fresh, involving way, brings the subject to life, and makes the reader or audience stop, look, and listen."[14] In his book about Subaru of America, Randall Rothenberg describes the big idea in the following way:

> The Big Idea is easier to illustrate than define, and easier to illustrate by what it is not than by what it is. It is not a "position" (although the place a product occupies in the consumer's mind may be a part of it). It is not an "execution" (although the writing or graphic style of an ad certainly contributes to it). It is not a slogan (although a tagline may encapsulate it).
>
> The Big Idea is the bridge between an advertising strategy, temporal and worldly, and an image, powerful and lasting. The theory of the Big Idea assumes that average consumers are at best bored and more likely irrational when it comes to deciding what to buy.[15]

Some of the world's most memorable advertising campaigns have achieved success because they originate from an idea that is so "big" that the campaign offers opportunities for a seemingly unlimited number of new executions. Such a campaign is said to have *legs* because it can be used for long periods of time. The print campaign for Absolut vodka is a perfect example: Over the course of two decades, Absolut's agency created hundreds of two-word puns on the brand name linked with various pictorial renderings of the distinctive bottle shape. Other campaigns based on Big Ideas include MSN ("Life's better with the butterfly") and MasterCard ("There are some things in life money can't buy"). In 2003, McDonald's executives launched a search for an idea "big" enough to be used in multiple country markets even as the company faced disapproval in some countries from consumers who link it to unpopular U.S. government policies (see Case 1-2).

The **advertising appeal** is the communications approach that relates to the motives of the target audience. For example, ads based on a **rational appeal** depend on logic and speak to the audience's intellect. Rational appeals are based on consumers' needs for information. The Pioneer Hi-Bred ads inform farmers about the attributes of pest-resistant seed varieties that will boost yields (see Exhibit 13-2). By contrast, ads using an **emotional appeal** may tug at the heartstrings or tickle the funny bone of the intended audience and evoke a feeling response that will direct purchase behavior. For example, a recent global campaign for IKEA, the Swedish home furnishings retailer, positioned houses as homes: "It's a place for love . . . a place for memories . . . a place for laughter. Home is the most important place in the world."[16]

The message elements in a particular ad will depend in part on which appeal is being employed. The **selling proposition** is the promise or claim that captures the reason for buying the product or the benefit that ownership confers. Because products are frequently at different stages in their life cycle in various national markets, and because of cultural, social, and economic differences that exist in those markets, the most effective appeal or selling proposition for a product may vary from market to market.

Effective global advertising may also require developing different presentations of the product's appeal or selling proposition. The way an appeal or proposition is presented is called the **creative execution**. In other words, there can be differences between *what* one says and *how* one says it. Ad agency personnel can choose from a variety of executions including straight sell, scientific evidence, demonstration, comparison, testimonial, slice of life, animation, fantasy, and dramatization. The responsibility for deciding on the appeal, the selling proposition, and the appropriate execution lies with *creatives*, a term that applies to art directors and copywriters.

Art Direction and Art Directors

The visual presentation of an advertisement—the "body language"—is a matter of **art direction**. The individual with general responsibility for the overall look of an ad is known as an *art director.* This person chooses graphics, pictures, type styles, and other visual elements that appear in an ad. Some forms of visual presentation are universally understood. Revlon, for example, has used a French producer to develop television commercials in English and Spanish for use in international markets.

---

[14]John O'Toole, *The Trouble with Advertising* (New York: Random House, 1985), p. 131.
[15]Randall Rothenberg, *Where the Suckers Moon* (New York: Vintage Books, 1995), pp. 112–113.
[16]Suzanne Vranica, "IKEA to Tug at Heartstrings," *The Wall Street Journal* (September 18, 2007), p. B6.

A creative challenge presented to Ogilvy & Mather in China illustrates the relationship between creative strategy, appeal, and execution. The client, Coca-Cola's Fanta, wanted a national TV ad that would communicate to consumers that Fanta is an antidote to everyday pressures on Chinese youth. This was the overall creative strategy; in other words, what the message should say. What type of appeal would be appropriate? Not surprisingly, soft drinks lend themselves especially well to emotional appeals; that was the appeal Ogilvy & Mather preferred.

The next step was to choose a specific execution. Soft drink marketers often utilize slice-of-life and fantasy executions, usually injected with an element of fun or humor. As Jeff Delkin, Ogilvy's regional business director in Shanghai, notes, for a U.S. ad, the creative strategy could be executed with a teen's fantasy or images of revenge on a mean teacher. However, in China, it is not acceptable to challenge or undermine the position of authority figures. The completed ad shows that drinking Fanta can create a fun experience in a classroom. When a student opens a can of Fanta, oranges begin to rain down. The teacher catches the oranges and juggles them—much to the delight of the students.

Another example is a Nike campaign created by Wieden & Kennedy in China. Nike's "Just Do It" ads typically showcase famous athletes and sports heroes and are legendary for their inspirational appeals. The selling proposition is universal—Nike is a "cool" brand. However, a localized execution of a Nike ad that featured Chinese superstar Wang Zhizhi did not connect with consumers; they prefer to draw inspiration from the world's best players rather than a national star who has yet to prove himself in the global arena. Nike tried a different execution with the theme "Chamber of Fear" featuring NBA star LeBron James defeating a kung fu master. This spot was banned after consumer complaints.

In 2006, Nike launched a new campaign that featured Chinese youth who had overcome personal obstacles to excel at sports. Young people were encouraged to share their stories at Nike stores or at a Web site, nike.com.cn/justdoit. Visitors to the Web site can also view short, three- to four-minute films featuring Chinese youth playing sports in well-known locales. Shortened versions of the clips are used as TV ads. As Jesse Lin, Wieden's managing director in Shanghai, said, "China's younger generation is in the midst of forming its own style, mixing together Chinese elements and influences they've absorbed from the West, but they don't think they need to learn from the West. Nike realized this and wants to be a part of this new generation, rather than telling them what to do."

McDonald's also used a localized campaign for the Chinese launch of the Quarter Pounder sandwich; ironically, the campaign came as the fast-food giant removed menu items such as an Asian-style chicken or beef wrap with rice created to appeal to Chinese tastes. Beef is considered a luxury, upscale item in China; beef also is perceived to boost energy and heighten sex appeal. In Chinese, the word *beef* connotes manliness, strength, and skill. Television commercials for the Quarter Pounder have sex appeal: They include close-ups of a woman's neck and mouth juxtaposed with images of fireworks and spraying water. The voice-over says, "You can feel it. Thicker. You can taste it. Juicier."

Print ads also conveyed sexual innuendo. One execution features a "beauty shot" of a Quarter Pounder with an extreme close up of a woman's mouth in the background. The copy reads, "Part of your body will be excited. You will feel 100 percent of the beef." As Jeffrey Schwartz, the head of McDonald's Chinese operations, explains, "Our customers are young, modern, and bilingual. If we're not edgy in communications, out front in technology, this consumer is going to blow right by us."

Sources: Gordon Fairclough and Janet Adamy, "Sex, Skin, Fireworks, Licked Fingers—It's a Quarter Pounder Ad in China," *The Wall Street Journal* (September 21, 2006), pp. B1, B2; Geoffrey A. Fowler, "Commercial Break: The Art of Selling," *Far Eastern Economic Review* (October 30, 2003), p. 32; Normandy Madden, "Nike Drops Its American Idols," *Advertising Age* (March 20, 2006), p. 12.

These commercials are filmed in Parisian settings but communicate the universal appeals and specific benefits of Revlon products. By producing its ads in France, Revlon obtains effective television commercials at a much lower cost than it would have paid for commercials produced in the United States. PepsiCo has used four basic commercials to communicate its advertising themes. The basic setting of young people having fun at a party or on a beach has been adapted to reflect the general physical environment and racial characteristics of North America, South America, Europe, Africa, and Asia. The music in these commercials has also been adapted to suit regional tastes, ranging from rock 'n' roll in North America to bossa nova in Latin America to high life in Africa.

The global advertiser must make sure that visual executions are not inappropriately extended into markets. In the mid-1990s, Benetton's United Colors of Benetton campaign generated considerable controversy. The campaign appeared in scores of countries, primarily in print and on billboards. The art direction focused on striking, provocative interracial juxtapositions—a white hand and a black hand handcuffed together, for example. Another version of the campaign, depicting a black woman nursing a white baby, won advertising awards in France and Italy. However, because the image evoked the history of slavery in the United States, that particular creative execution was not used in the U.S. market.

Copy and Copywriters

The words that are the spoken or written communication elements in advertisements are known as **copy**. *Copywriters* are language specialists who develop the headlines, subheads, and body copy used in print advertising and the scripts containing the words that are delivered by spokespeople, actors, or hired voice talents in broadcast ads. As a general rule, copy should be relatively short and avoid slang or idioms. Languages vary in terms of the number of words required to convey a given message; thus the increased use of pictures and illustrations. Some global ads feature visual appeals that convey a specific message with minimal use of copy. Low literacy rates in many countries seriously compromise the use of print as a communications device and require greater creativity in the use of audio-oriented media.

It is important to recognize overlap in the use of languages in many areas of the world (e.g., the EU, Latin America, and North America). Capitalizing on this, global advertisers can realize economies of scale by producing advertising copy with the same language and message for these markets. The success of this approach will depend in part on avoiding unintended ambiguity in the ad

> "There is a tradition in France of advertising as an extension of the arts, and the arts have always been seen as a sacrosanct area of free expression. You get the feeling that copywriters and photographers have the same extent of protected expression that Michelangelo or Andy Warhol might have claimed."[17]
>
> Seth Goldschlager, Publicis Groupe, Paris

➔ STRATEGIC DECISION MAKING IN GLOBAL MARKETING
Adidas Hopes Beckham Will Score with Americans

In spring 2004, Adidas launched a $50 million global print and TV campaign keyed to the tagline "Nothing is impossible." Some of the ads featured boxing legend Muhammad Ali and told a "past and present" story linking sports figures from earlier eras with modern-day stars. In May, marketing chief Erich Stamminger announced the fruits of a secret, three-year development effort: the $250 Adidas 1, a shoe with an onboard microchip that adjusts the cushioning level to an athlete's weight and performance needs. In a press release, Stamminger noted, "This is the world's first intelligent shoe. It senses, understands, and adapts."

In 2007, Adidas ramped up its efforts to unseat Nike as the leader in the U.S. sportswear market. Soccer superstar David Beckham, who had been a worldwide Adidas endorser for more than a decade, was at the center of the new promotional campaign.

Following Beckham's highly publicized move from the Real Madrid to the Los Angeles Galaxy, he signed a five-year, $250 million contract (see Exhibit 13-3). Beckham was featured prominently in a variety of media, including billboards and prime-time television ads. Adidas executives expected Beckham's endorsement to lead to increased sales of a variety of branded merchandise. As Stephen Pierpoint, vice president for brand marketing at Adidas, said, "The U.S. market has a real opportunity to grow. Football [soccer] has always been a core sport for Adidas. We hope David will be the catalyst for growth."

Sources: David Owen, "Brand Beckham Kicks Off Soccer's American Appeal," *Financial Times* (March 20, 2007), p. 7; Matthew Karnitschnig and Stephanie Kang, "Leap Forward: For Adidas, Reebok Deal Caps Push to Broaden Urban Appeal," *The Wall Street Journal* (August 4, 2005), pp. A1, A6.

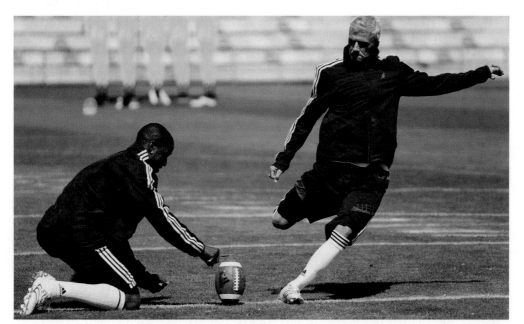

Exhibit 13-3:
New Orleans Saints running back Reggie Bush holds an "American" football as soccer legend David Beckham prepares to kick off. Both athletes endorse Adidas; in 2006, Bush was fined several thousand dollars for wearing Adidas cleats during a preseason football game. The reason? The NFL has partnership agreements with Nike and Reebok; players aren't allowed to wear other shoe brands.
Source: REUTERS/Adidas/HO/Landov.

---

[17]Elaine Sciolino, "Advertising: A Campaign to Shock the Bourgeoisie in France," *The Wall Street Journal* (January 21, 2003), p. C14.

copy. Then again, in some situations, ad copy must be translated into the local language. Translating copy has been the subject of great debate in advertising circles. Advertising slogans often present the most difficult translation problems. The challenge of encoding and decoding slogans and taglines in different national and cultural contexts can lead to unintentional errors. For example, the Asian version of Pepsi's "Come alive" tagline was rendered as a call to bring ancestors back from the grave.

Advertising executives may elect to prepare new copy for a foreign market in the language of the target country or to translate the original copy into the target language. A third option is to leave some (or all) copy elements in the original (home-country) language. In choosing from these alternatives, the advertiser must consider whether the intended foreign audience can receive and comprehend a translated message. Anyone with knowledge of two or more languages realizes that the ability to think in another language facilitates accurate communication. To be confident that a message will be understood correctly after it is received, one must understand the connotations of words, phrases, and sentence structures, as well as their translated meaning.

The same principle applies to advertising—perhaps to an even greater degree. A copywriter who can think in the target language and understands the consumers in the target country will be able to create the most effective appeals, organize the ideas, and craft the specific language, especially if colloquialisms, idioms, or humor are involved. For example, in southern China, McDonald's is careful not to advertise prices with multiple occurrences of the number four. The reason is simple: In Cantonese, the pronunciation of the word *four* is similar to that of the word *death*.[18] In its efforts to develop a global brand image, Citicorp discovered that translations of its slogan "Citi never sleeps" conveyed the meaning that Citibank had a sleeping disorder such as insomnia. Company executives decided to retain the slogan but use English throughout the world.[19]

Cultural Considerations

Knowledge of cultural diversity, especially the symbolism associated with cultural traits, is essential for creating advertising. Local country managers can share important information, such as when to use caution in advertising creativity. Use of colors and man-woman relationships can often be stumbling blocks. For example, in Japan, intimate scenes between men and women are in bad taste; they are outlawed in Saudi Arabia. Veteran adman John O'Toole offers the following insights to global advertisers:

> Transplanted American creative people always want to photograph European men kissing women's hands. But they seldom know that the nose must never touch the hand or that this rite is reserved solely for married women. And how do you know that the woman in the photograph is married? By the ring on her left hand, of course. Well, in Spain, Denmark, Holland, and Germany, Catholic women wear the wedding ring on the right hand.
>
> When photographing a couple entering a restaurant or theater, you show the woman preceding the man, correct? No. Not in Germany and France. And this would be laughable in Japan. Having someone in a commercial hold up his hand with the back of it to you, the viewer, and the fingers moving toward him should communicate "come here." In Italy it means "good-bye."[20]

Ads that strike viewers in some countries as humorous or irritating may not necessarily be perceived that way by viewers in other countries. American ads make frequent use of spokespeople and direct product comparisons; they use logical arguments to try to appeal to the reason of audiences. Japanese advertising is more image oriented and appeals to audience sentiment. In Japan, what is most important frequently is not what is stated explicitly but, rather, what is implied. Nike's U.S. advertising is legendary for its irreverent, "in your face" style and relies heavily on celebrity sports endorsers such as Michael Jordan. In other parts of the world, where soccer is the top sport, some Nike ads are considered to be in poor taste and its spokespeople have less relevance. Nike has responded by adjusting its approach; as Geoffrey Frost, former director of global advertising at Nike, noted over a decade ago, "We have to root ourselves in the

---

[18]Jeanne Whalen, "McDonald's Cooks Worldwide Growth," *Advertising Age International* (July–August 1995), p. I4.
[19]Stephen E. Frank, "Citicorp's Big Account Is at Stake as It Seeks a Global Brand Name," *The Wall Street Journal* (January 9, 1997), p. B6.
[20]John O'Toole, *The Trouble with Advertising* (New York: Random House, 1985), pp. 209–210.

passions of other countries. It's part of our growing up."[21] Some American companies have canceled television ads created for the Latin American market portraying racial stereotypes that were offensive to persons of color. Nabisco, Goodyear, and other companies are also being more careful about the shows during which they buy airtime; some very popular Latin American programs feature content that exploits class, race, and ethnic differences.[22]

There are also widely varying standards for use of sexually explicit or provocative imagery. Partial nudity and same-sex couples are frequently seen in ads in Latin America and Europe. In the U.S. market, network television decency standards and the threat of boycotts by conservative consumer activists constrain advertisers. Some industry observers note a paradoxical situation in which the programs shown on U.S. TV are frequently racy, but the ads that air during those shows are not. As Marcio Moreira, worldwide chief creative officer at the McCann-Erickson agency, noted, "Americans want titillation in entertainment but when it comes to advertising they stop being viewers and become consumers and critics."[23] However, it is certainly not the case that anything goes outside the United States. Women in Monterrey, Mexico, recently complained about billboards for the Playtex unit of Sara Lee Corporation that featured supermodel Eva Herzegova wearing a Wonderbra. The campaign was created by a local agency, Perez Munoz Publicidad. Playtex responded by covering up the model on the billboards in some Mexican cities. French Connection UK made waves in the United States recently with print ads that prominently featured the British company's initials, that is, FCUK. Public outcry prompted the company to tone down the ads by spelling out the name.

Food is the product category most likely to exhibit cultural sensitivity. Thus, marketers of food and food products must be alert to the need to localize their advertising. A good example of this is the effort by H. J. Heinz Company to develop the overseas market for ketchup. Heinz's strategy called for adapting both the product and advertising to target country tastes.[24] In Greece, for example, ads show ketchup pouring over pasta, eggs, and cuts of meat. In Japan, they instruct Japanese homemakers on using ketchup as an ingredient in Western-style food such as omelets, sausages, and pasta. Barry Tilley, London-based general manager of Heinz's Western Hemisphere trading division, says Heinz uses focus groups to determine what foreign consumers want in the way of taste and image. Americans like a sweet ketchup, but Europeans prefer a spicier, more piquant variety. Significantly, Heinz's foreign marketing efforts are most successful when the company quickly adapts to local cultural preferences. In Sweden, the made-in-America theme is so muted in Heinz's ads that "Swedes don't realize Heinz is American. They think it is German because of the name," says Tilley. In contrast to this, American themes still work well in Germany. Kraft and Heinz are trying to outdo each other with ads featuring strong American images. In one of Heinz's TV ads, American football players in a restaurant become very angry when the 12 steaks they ordered arrive without ketchup. The ad ends happily, of course, with plenty of Heinz ketchup to go around.[25]

Much academic research has been devoted to the impact of culture on advertising. For example, Tamotsu Kishii identified seven characteristics that distinguish Japanese from American creative strategy:

1. Indirect rather than direct forms of expression are preferred in the messages. This avoidance of directness in expression is pervasive in all types of communication among the Japanese, including their advertising. Many television ads do not mention what is desirable about the brand in use and let the audience judge for themselves.
2. There is often little relationship between ad content and the advertised product.
3. Only brief dialogue or narration is used in television commercials, with minimal explanatory content. In the Japanese culture, the more one talks, the less others will perceive him or her as trustworthy or self-confident. A 30-second advertisement for young menswear shows five models in varying and seasonal attire, ending with a brief statement from the narrator: "Our life is a fashion show!"

[21]Roger Thurow, "Shtick Ball: In Global Drive, Nike Finds Its Brash Ways Don't Always Pay Off," *The Wall Street Journal* (May 5, 1997), p. A10.
[22]Leon E. Wynter, "Global Marketers Learn to Say 'No' to Bad Ads," *The Wall Street Journal* (April 1, 1998), p. B1.
[23]Melanie Wells and Dottie Enrico, "U.S. Admakers Cover It Up; Others Don't Give a Fig Leaf," *USA Today* (June 27, 1997), pp. B1, B2.
[24]Gary Levin, "Ads Going Global," *Advertising Age* (July 22, 1991), pp. 4, 42.
[25]Gabriella Stern, "Heinz Aims to Export Taste for Ketchup," *The Wall Street Journal* (November 20, 1992), p. B1.

4. Humor is used to create a bond of mutual feelings. Rather than slapstick, humorous dramatizations involve family members, neighbors, and office colleagues.
5. Famous celebrities appear as close acquaintances or everyday people.
6. Priority is placed on company trust rather than product quality. Japanese tend to believe that if the firm is large and has a good image, the quality of its products should also be outstanding.
7. The product name is impressed on the viewer with short, 15-second commercials.[26]

Green, Cunningham, and Cunningham conducted a cross-cultural study to determine the extent to which consumers of different nationalities use the same criteria to evaluate soft drinks and toothpaste. Their subjects were college students from the United States, France, India, and Brazil. Compared to France and India, the U.S. respondents placed more emphasis on the subjective, as opposed to functional, product attributes. The Brazilian respondents appeared even more concerned with the subjective attributes than the Americans were. The authors concluded that advertising messages should not use the same appeal for these countries if the advertiser is concerned with communicating the most important attributes of its product in each market.[27]

In another study, Zandpour and Harich combined Hofstede's social values framework with a culture's perceptions of time (monochronic cultures focus on one thing at a time, while members of a polychronic culture do not display a preference for sequential schedules or presentation of information). Several relevant market factors were also studied, including advertising expenditures per capita, the presence or absence of U.S. advertising agencies or their affiliates, the availability of qualified advertising professionals, and the degree of government control over advertising. The researchers used these factors to group countries into "think" and "feel" clusters and predict whether rational or emotional appeals used in television advertising for food and beverage, personal care, and several other product categories would be most prevalent in a given country market.

The researchers divided rational appeals into *argument* (the ad relates facts or reasons why the purchase should be made) and *lecture* (ads are devoid of fictional characters or plot elements; rather, they include narration that directly addresses the audience and provides an explicit conclusion). Emotional appeals were classified as *dramatic* (narration, character, and plot are key message elements) and *psychological* (explicit statements of how the product will benefit the consumer; desire is created by appealing to a consumer's self-interest). The findings are summarized in Figure 13-2 and Table 13-4. Figure 13-2 places the countries studied in a matrix

FIGURE 13-2

"Think" and "Feel" Country Clusters

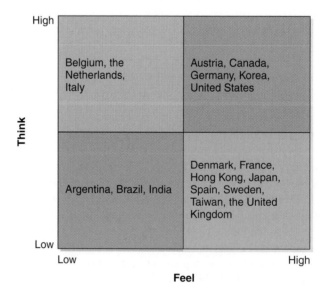

---

[26]C. Anthony di Benedetto, Mariko Tamate, and Rajan Chandran, "Developing Creative Advertising Strategy for the Japanese Marketplace," *Journal of Advertising Research* (January–February 1992), pp. 39–48. A number of recent studies have been devoted to comparing ad content in different parts of the world, including Mary C. Gilly, "Sex Roles in Advertising: A Comparison of Television Advertisements in Australia, Mexico, and the United States," *Journal of Marketing* (April 1988), pp. 75–85; and Marc G. Weinberger and Harlan E. Spotts, "A Situation View of Information Content in TV Advertising in the U.S. and UK," *Journal of Advertising* 53 (January 1989), pp. 89–94.
[27]Robert T. Green, William H. Cunningham, and Isabella C. M. Cunningham, "The Effectiveness of Standardized Global Advertising," *Journal of Advertising* (Summer 1975), pp. 25–30.

TABLE 13-4 Effective Advertising Appeal Alternatives

Type of Appeal	Cultural/Market Factors	Countries Where Appeal Is Appropriate
Rational/argument	Monochronic cultures with low power distance, high uncertainty avoidance, and a good supply of marketing professionals.	Austria, Belgium, Germany, Italy, United States
Rational/lecture	Collectivist cultures with high power distance and high uncertainty avoidance.	Belgium, Italy, Mexico
Emotional/psychological	Collectivist cultures with high power distance, high advertising expenditures, and strict government control.	Hong Kong, Taiwan, France, United States, South Korea, Spain
Emotional/dramatic	Cultures with high power distance, high advertising expenditures, and a limited supply of advertising professionals.	Hong Kong, France, Japan

Source: Adapted from Fred Zandpour and Katrin R. Harich, "Think and Feel Country Clusters: A New Approach to International Advertising Standardization," *International Journal of Advertising* 15, no. 4 (1996), pp. 325–344.

classifying them in terms of the dimensions "think" and "feel." For example, the researchers rank Austria, Canada, Germany, Korea, and the United States high on both dimensions; consumers in these countries are presumed to be receptive to television advertising employing either rational or emotional appeals.[28] Table 13-4 is intended to be a guide to creating standardized appeals in terms of the clusters; for example, a standardized ad employing a rational/argument appeal could be translated as appropriate and used to good effect in Austria, Belgium, Italy, and the United States. Many German companies, for example, prefer ads that contain plenty of copy that presents a rational argument for a product's superiority. This is typical of ads for beer, automobiles, and food products. However, many creative campaigns are based on the understanding that sometimes the best approach is to disregard guidelines and break some so-called rules. German ads for the Mini Cooper are definitely offbeat when compared to mainstream auto ads.[29]

GLOBAL MEDIA DECISIONS

The next issue facing advertisers is which medium or media to use when communicating with target audiences. Media availability can vary from country to country. Some companies use virtually the entire spectrum of available media; Coca-Cola is a good example. Other companies prefer to utilize one or two media categories. In some instances, the agency that creates advertising also makes recommendations about media placement; however, many advertisers use the services of specialized media planning and buying organizations. Omnicom's OMD Worldwide, the Starcom Media Vest Group unit of Publicis, and WPP's MindShare Worldwide are three of the top media specialists.

The available alternatives can be broadly categorized as print media, electronic media, and other. Print media range in form from local daily and weekly newspapers to magazines and business publications with national, regional, or international audiences (see Exhibit 13-4). Electronic media include broadcast television, cable television, radio, and the Internet. Additionally, advertisers may utilize various forms of outdoor, transit, and direct mail advertising. Globally, media decisions must take into account country-specific regulations. For example, France bans retailers from advertising on television.

Global Advertising Expenditures and Media Vehicles

Each year, more money is spent on advertising in the United States than anywhere else in the world. According to data compiled by TNS Media Intelligence, U.S. ad spending in 2008 totaled $141.7 billion. To put this figure in perspective, consider that 2008 ad spending in Japan, the

[28]Fred Zandpour and Katrin R. Harich, "Think and Feel Country Clusters: A New Approach to International Advertising Standardization," *International Journal of Advertising* 15, no. 4 (1996), pp. 325–344.
[29]Erin White, "German Ads Get More Daring, but Some Firms Aren't Pleased," *The Wall Street Journal* (November 22, 2002), p. B6.

number two advertising market, totaled ¥6.6 billion (approximately $60 billion). In addition, as one might expect, the largest per capita ad spending occurs in highly developed countries. However, much of the current growth in advertising expenditures—as much as one-third—is occurring in the BRIC countries. Russia alone represents a $5 billion advertising market; ad expenditures are growing at about 30 percent annually, compared with a rate of 4 or 5 percent in the United States and Europe. The WPP Group recently announced an alliance with Video International, Russia's largest ad agency.[30]

Worldwide, television is the number one advertising medium; with estimated ad revenues of $176 billion in 2008, television captured slightly more than one-third of global expenditures. Newspapers rank second on a worldwide basis, accounting for about 27 percent of advertising spending. However, media consumption patterns vary from country to country. For example, television is the number one medium in both the United States and Japan. By contrast, newspapers are the leading medium in Germany; television ranks second. In Germany, outlays for newspaper advertising surpass those for television by a ratio of two to one. In real terms, television spending in the EU increased by 78 percent between 1990 and 2000, compared with 26 percent for newspapers and 11 percent for magazines during the same period. This trend is likely to continue as digital broadcasting gains acceptance in Europe.

Television is also important in the Latin American market. In Brazil, expenditures on television advertising are nearly three times higher than those for newspapers. The availability of media and the conditions affecting media buys also vary greatly around the world. In Mexico, an advertiser that can pay for a full-page ad may get the front page, while in India, paper shortages may require booking an ad six months in advance. In some countries, especially those where the electronic media are government owned, television and radio stations can broadcast only a restricted number of advertising messages. In Saudi Arabia, no commercial television advertising was allowed prior to May 1986; currently, ad content and visual presentation are restricted.

Worldwide, radio continues to be a less important advertising medium than print and television. However, in countries where advertising budgets are limited, radio's enormous reach can provide a cost-effective means of communicating with a large consumer market. Also, radio can be effective in countries where literacy rates are low. One clear trend that is gaining traction throughout the world: Spending on CRM and Internet advertising is gaining ground at the expense of TV and print.

> "The U.S. online advertising market is much bigger than Europe's, but it is a crowded market and the room for growth is shrinking. In Europe, online advertising is growing much faster and portals like Yahoo want to tap into that."[31]
>
> Jupiter Research

Exhibit 13-4: Two trends are driving the globalization of the magazine industry. First, marketers of global brands need a way to communicate with consumers in all parts of the world. Second, brand-conscious consumers are seeking out Western titles. For example, Hearst Corporation's *Cosmopolitan* is available in more than 50 foreign-language editions.

In South Korea, readers can choose from a wide variety of magazines from local and global publishers. To encourage young women to purchase the Korean edition of *Cosmo Girl*, this in-store promotion offered several free gifts.

Source: Otto Pohl/*The New York Times*/Redux Pictures.

[30]Guy Chazan, "Moscow, City of Billboards," *The Wall Street Journal* (July 18, 2005), p. B1.
[31]Dan Bilefsky, "Yahoo Tightens Control in Europe and Asia," *The New York Times* (November 8, 2005), p. C18.

Media Decisions

The availability of television, newspapers, and other forms of broadcast and print media varies around the world. Moreover, patterns of media consumption differ from country to country as well. In many developed countries, for example, newspapers are experiencing circulation and readership declines as consumers devote more time to new media options such as the Internet. In India, by contrast, print media are enjoying a revival as redesigned newspaper formats and glossy supplements lure a new generation of readers (see Figure 13-3). India is home to nearly 300 daily newspapers, including the *Times of India* and the *Hindustan Times*; the price per copy is only 5 rupees—about 10 cents. Additional critical factors in India's media environment include the lack of penetration by cable television and the fact that only about four million Indians currently subscribe to an Internet service.[32] By contrast, billboards are the medium of choice in Moscow. As Thomas L. Friedman has pointed out, Moscow is a city built for about 30,000 cars; during the past decade, the number of cars has grown from 300,000 to 3 million.[33] The result is massive traffic jams and commuting delays; affluent businesspeople spend hours in traffic and have little time to read the newspaper or watch TV.

Even when media availability is high, its use as an advertising vehicle may be limited. For example, in Europe, television advertising is very limited in Denmark, Norway, and Sweden. Regulations concerning content of commercials vary; Sweden bans advertising to children younger than 12 years of age. In 2001, when Sweden headed the EU, its policymakers tried to extend the ban to the rest of Europe. Although the effort failed, Sweden retained its domestic ban. This helps explain why annual spending on print media in Sweden is three times the annual spending for television.[34]

As noted earlier, cultural considerations often affect the presentation of the advertising message. One study comparing the content of magazine advertisements in the United States with those in the Arab world found the following:

- People are depicted less often in Arabic magazine ads. However, when people do appear, there is no difference in the extent to which women are depicted. Women appearing in ads in Arab magazines wear long dresses; their presence generally is relevant to the advertised product.
- U.S. ads tend to have more information content; by contrast, brevity is considered a virtue in the Arab world. Context plays a greater role in interpreting an Arab message than in the United States.
- U.S. ads contain more price information, and are more likely to include comparative appeals than Arabic ads.[35]

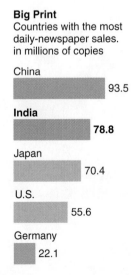

Big Print
Countries with the most daily-newspaper sales. in millions of copies

China — 93.5
India — **78.8**
Japan — 70.4
U.S. — 55.6
Germany — 22.1

FIGURE 13-3

Leading Countries for Daily Newspaper Sales (millions of copies)

Source: World Association of Newspapers.

[32]John Larkin, "Newspaper Nirvana? 300 Dailies Court India's Avid Readers," *The Wall Street Journal* (May 5, 2006), pp. B1, B3.

[33]Thomas L. Friedman, "The Oil-Addicted Ayatollahs," *The New York Times* (February 2, 2007), p. A19.

[34]John Tylee, "EC Permits Sweden to Continue Child Ad Ban," *Advertising Age* (July 11, 2003), p. 6.

[35]Fahad S. Al-Olayan and Kiran Karande, "A Content Analysis of Magazine Advertisements from the United States and the Arab World," *Journal of Advertising* 29, no. 3 (Fall 2000), pp. 69–82. See also Mushtag Luqmani, Ugur Yavas, and Zahir Quraeshi, "Advertising in Saudi Arabia: Content and Regulation," *International Marketing Review* 6, no. 1 (1989), pp. 59–72.

PUBLIC RELATIONS AND PUBLICITY

Public relations (PR) is the department or function responsible for evaluating public opinion about, and attitudes toward, the organization and its products or brands. Public relations personnel also are responsible for fostering goodwill, understanding, and acceptance among a company's various constituents and publics. Like advertising, PR is one of four variables in the promotion mix. One of the tasks of the PR practitioner is to generate favorable **publicity**. By definition, publicity is communication about a company or product for which the company does not pay. (In the PR world, publicity is sometimes referred to as "earned media," and advertising and promotions are known as "unearned media.") PR personnel also play a key role in responding to unflattering media reports or controversies that arise because of company activities in different parts of the globe. In such instances, PR's job is to make sure that the company responds promptly and gets its side of the story told (see Exhibit 13-5). The basic tools of PR include news releases, newsletters, media kits, press conferences, tours of plants and other company facilities, articles in trade or professional journals, company publications and brochures, TV and radio talk show interviews, special events, social media, and corporate Web sites.

Caterpillar's recent activities in China are a textbook example of the power of public relations. The Chinese market for industrial machinery is booming because the government is spending billions of dollars on infrastructure improvements. Caterpillar hopes to sell giant wheel tractor-scrapers that are more efficient to operate than the hydraulic excavators and trucks currently in wide use. However, a business intelligence team that contacted 100 customers and dealers across China found low levels of awareness and acceptance of Caterpillar's machines. Survey respondents were not persuaded by data from other countries about the machines' cost savings. To gain traction, Mike Cai, Cat's man in China, staged product demonstrations—road shows—around the country. "Word-of-mouth is the best form of publicity for the construction industry in China," he says. Scott Kronick, president for Ogilvy Public Relations Worldwide/China, agrees. "Chinese customers are being introduced to a lot of products and services for the first time, so you can't advertise something that's intangible," he said. Reporters from the local and national media were invited to the demonstrations; in one instance, China Central Television ran a story that featured a clip of the tractor-scraper at work.[36]

Senior executives at some companies relish the opportunity to generate publicity. For example, Benetton's striking print and outdoor ad campaigns keyed to the "United Colors of

Exhibit 13-5: Because of its size and presence in more than 200 countries, the Coca-Cola Company is often the target of antiglobalization protests. The Indian villagers shown here were protesting the company's water consumption in areas severely affected by drought. Coca-Cola chairman and CEO E. Neville Isdell has responded to this type of negative publicity by guiding the company toward greater transparency in its global operations. Isdell also wants to make sure that the public perceives Coke as a global leader in corporate social responsibility. To do this, he is forging relationships and partnerships with nongovernmental organizations (NGOs).
Source: Raveendran/Getty Images, Inc. AFP.

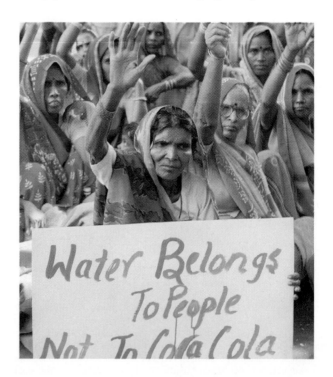

[36]Jason Leow, "In China, Add a Caterpillar to the Dog and Pony Show," *The Wall Street Journal* (December 10, 2007), p. B1.

Benetton" generated both controversy and wide media attention. Richard Branson, the flamboyant founder of the Virgin Group, is a one-man publicity machine. His personal exploits as a hot-air balloon pilot have earned him and his company a great deal of free ink. The company does employ traditional media advertising; however, as Will Whitehorn, Virgin's head of brand development and corporate affairs, noted, "PR is the heart of the company. If we do things badly, it will reflect badly on the image of the brand more than most other companies." At Virgin, Whitehorn says, "Advertising is a subset of PR, not the other way around."[37]

As noted earlier, a company exerts complete control over the content of its advertising and pays for message placement in the media. However, the media typically receive many more press releases and other PR materials than they can use. Generally speaking, a company has little control over when, or if, a news story runs; nor can the company directly control the spin, slant, or tone of the story. To compensate for this lack of control, many companies utilize **corporate advertising** that, despite the name, is generally considered part of the PR function. As with "regular" advertising, a company or organization identified in the ad pays for corporate advertising. However, unlike regular advertising, the objective of corporate advertising is not to generate demand by informing, persuading, entertaining, or reminding customers. In the context of integrated marketing communications, corporate advertising is often used to call attention to the company's other communications efforts. In addition to the examples discussed in the following pages, Table 13-5 summarizes several instances of global publicity involving well-known firms.

Image advertising enhances the public's perception of a company, creates goodwill, or announces a major change, such as a merger, acquisition, or divestiture. In 2008, for example, Anheuser-Busch InBev placed full-page ads in the business press to announce their merger. Global companies frequently use image advertising in an effort to present themselves as good corporate citizens in foreign countries. BASF uses advertising to raise awareness about the company's innovative products that are used in the automotive, home construction, and pharmaceutical industries. Similarly, a recent campaign from Daimler AG announced an eco-friendly fuel called Sun Diesel (see Exhibit 13-6). In **advocacy advertising**, a company presents its point of view on a particular issue. The ad in Chapter 11 with the headline "The Dumping of Foreign Steel at Cutthroat Prices

TABLE 13-5 Negative Publicity Affecting Global Marketers

Company or Brand (home country)	Nature of Publicity
Hyundai (South Korea)	Hyundai Motor Company Chairman Chung Mong Koo was convicted of embezzlement and fraud.
Samsung (South Korea)	Samsung officials allegedly bribed candidates in Korea's 1997 presidential elections. It was also revealed that the children of Samsung chairman Lee Kun-hee broke the law when purchasing securities of a Samsung affiliate.
Coca-Cola (United Kingdom) and **PepsiCo** (United Kingdom)	In India, allegations that soft drink products from both companies were contaminated with pesticide residue led to sharp sales drops in late summer 2003.
Halliburton (United Kingdom)	Allegations that the company overcharged the U.S. government for supplies and services rendered in Iraq.
Ford Motor Company (United Kingdom) and **Bridgestone/Firestone** (Japan/United Kingdom)	A rash of tire failures on Ford vehicles prompted a recall in 2000 of several tire models. Ultimately, Ford severed its decades-old relationship with Firestone.
Nike (United States)	Since the mid-1990s, Nike has been responding to the criticism that its subcontractors operate factories in which sweatshop conditions prevail (see Exhibit 13-7). Filmmaker Michael Moore featured an interview with Nike CEO Phil Knight in the antiglobalization documentary *The Big One*.
McDonald's (United Kingdom)	Extensive media reporting linking fast food to obesity has been an ongoing public relations challenge for the fast-food giant.

---

[37]Elena Bowes, "Virgin Flies in Face of Conventions," *Ad Age International* (January 1997), p. I.

Exhibit 13-6: Daimler AG is one of the world's leading producers of diesel automobiles. This corporate image advertisement is not about the company's cars; rather, it is about the company's ongoing efforts to create more eco-friendly diesel fuels for its cars to run on.

Translated, the headline reads, "If you invent the car, you're also committed to Energy for the Future." The ad positions Daimler both as an innovator and as a responsible corporate citizen. Because the message and the associated image have worldwide appeal, this ad lends itself to an extension strategy.
Source: Courtesy of Daimler Corporation.

Threatens America" is an example of advocacy advertising. Other examples of image and advocacy advertising by global marketers include the following:

- Japan's Fuji Photo Film asked its advertising agency to develop an advocacy campaign for the United States. At the time, Fuji was embroiled in a trade dispute with Kodak. Fuji had also invested more than $1 billion in U.S. production facilities and had won a long-term photo-finishing contract with Walmart. The campaign was designed to appeal both to Walmart and to the giant retailer's customers; as a Walmart spokesman said, "We've long said we buy American when we can. The more people understand how American Fuji is, the better."[38]

---

[38]Wendy Bounds, "Fuji Considers National Campaign to Develop All-American Image," *The Wall Street Journal* (October 1, 1996), p. B8.

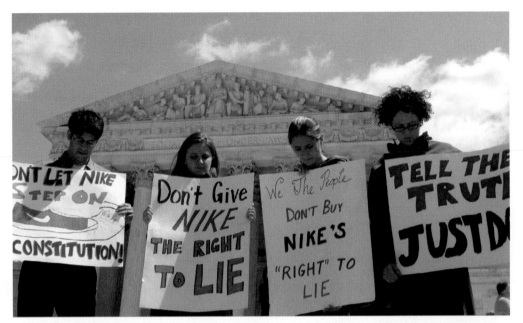

Exhibit 13-7: When making public appearances, Nike chairman Phil Knight and other executives frequently defend labor practices and policies in the Asian factories where the company's shoes are made. In the late 1990s, a protester filed a lawsuit against Nike alleging that the company's public assertions about working conditions constituted false advertising. Attorneys for Nike argued that statements made by executives constitute free commercial speech, are part of a public policy debate and are protected by the First Amendment.
Source: Chuck Kennedy/ Newscom.

- In 1995, the American International Automobile Dealers Association (AIADA) hired Hill & Knowlton to create a PR campaign designed to convince then-President Bill Clinton, Congress, the media, and the general public that a proposed plan to impose a 100 percent tariff on 13 luxury cars was ill-advised. The campaign's central message was that foreign automakers account for a good number of U.S. jobs that would be jeopardized if the sanctions were enacted. Nissan and other companies also sent position papers and information packets to dealers and the media. Interviews with representatives from auto dealers were carried by both print and electronic media. Within a few weeks, the Clinton administration announced that the United States and Japan had reached an agreement. No sanctions were imposed, and the AIADA was able to claim an important PR victory.

These examples notwithstanding, most global companies attempt to create an overall balance of promotion mix elements. PepsiCo made good use of IMC when it undertook an ambitious global program to revamp the packaging of its flagship cola. To raise awareness of its new blue can, Pepsi spent $500 million on advertising and public relations; to generate publicity, Pepsi leased a Concorde jet and painted it in the new blue color. Pepsi also garnered free ink by spending $5 million to film an ad with two Russian cosmonauts holding a giant replica of the new can while orbiting the earth in the Mir space station. As Massimo d'Amore, PepsiCo's head of international marketing, told reporters, "Space is the ultimate frontier of global marketing. The cola wars have been fought all over the place, and it's time to take them to space."[39]

Sometimes a company generates publicity simply by going about the business of global marketing activities. As noted in Table 13-5, Nike and other marketers have received a great deal of negative publicity regarding alleged sweatshop conditions in factories run by subcontractors. Today, Nike's PR team is doing a better job of counteracting the criticism by effectively communicating the positive economic impact Nike has had on the nations where it manufactures its sneakers (see Exhibit 13-7).

Any company that is increasing its activities outside the home country can utilize PR personnel as boundary spanners between the company and employees, unions, stockholders, customers, the media, financial analysts, governments, or suppliers. Many companies have their own in-house PR staff. Companies may also choose to engage the services of an outside PR firm. During the past few years, some of the large advertising holding companies discussed previously

[39]Melanie Wells, "Pepsi, Coke Go into Orbit," *USA Today* (May 22, 1996), p. 1B.

have acquired PR agencies. For example, Omnicom Group bought Fleishman-Hillard, WPP Group acquired Canada's Hill & Knowlton, and Interpublic Group bought Golin/Harris International. Other PR firms, including the London-based Shandwick PLC and Edelman Public Relations Worldwide, are independent. Several independent PR firms in the United Kingdom, Germany, Italy, Spain, Austria, and the Netherlands have joined together in a network known as Globalink. The purpose of the network is to provide members with various forms of assistance such as press contacts, event planning, literature design, and suggestions for tailoring global campaigns to local needs in a particular country or region.[40]

The Growing Role of PR in Global Marketing Communications

Public relations professionals with international responsibility must go beyond media relations and serve as more than a company mouthpiece; they are called upon to simultaneously build consensus and understanding, create trust and harmony, articulate and influence public opinion, anticipate conflicts, and resolve disputes.[41] As companies become more involved in global marketing and the globalization of industries continues, company management must recognize the value of international PR. One recent study found that, internationally, PR expenditures are growing at an average of 20 percent annually. Fueled by soaring foreign investment, industry privatization, and a boom in initial public offerings (IPOs), PR expenditures in India are reported to be growing by 200 percent annually.

The number of international PR associations is growing as well. The new Austrian Public Relations Association is a case in point; many European PR trade associations are part of the Confédération Européenne des Relations Publiques and the International Public Relations Association. Another factor fueling the growth of international PR is increased governmental relations between countries. Governments, organizations, and societies are dealing with broad-based issues of mutual concern such as the environment and world peace. Finally, the technology-driven communication revolution that has ushered in the information age makes public relations a profession with truly global reach. Faxes, satellites, high-speed modems, and the Internet allow PR professionals to be in contact with media virtually anywhere in the world.

In spite of these technological advances, PR professionals must still build good personal working relationships with journalists and other media representatives, as well as with leaders of other primary constituencies. Therefore, strong interpersonal skills are needed. One of the most basic concepts of the practice of PR is to know the audience. For the global PR practitioner, this means knowing the audiences in both the home country and the host country or countries. Specific skills needed include the ability to communicate in the language of the host country and familiarity with local customs. A PR professional who is unable to speak the language of the host country will be unable to communicate directly with a huge portion of an essential audience. Likewise, the PR professional working outside the home country must be sensitive to nonverbal communication issues in order to maintain good working relationships with host-country nationals. Commenting on the complexity of the international PR professional's job, one expert notes that, in general, audiences are "increasingly more unfamiliar and more hostile, as well as more organized and powerful . . . more demanding, more skeptical and more diverse." International PR practitioners can play an important role as "bridges over the shrinking chasm of the global village."[42]

How PR Practices Differ around the World

Cultural traditions, social and political contexts, and economic environments in specific countries can affect public relations practices. As noted earlier in the chapter, the mass media and the

---

[40]Joe Mullich, "European Firms Seek Alliances for Global PR," *Business Marketing* 79 (August 1994), pp. 4, 31.
[41]Karl Nessman, "Public Relations in Europe: A Comparison with the United States," *Public Relations Journal* 21, no. 2 (Summer 1995), p. 154.
[42]Larissa A. Grunig, "Strategic Public Relations Constituencies on a Global Scale," *Public Relations Review* 18, no. 2 (Summer 1992), pp. 127–136.

written word are important vehicles for information dissemination in many industrialized countries. In developing countries, however, the best way to communicate might be through the gongman, the town crier, the market square, or the chief's courts. In Ghana, dance, songs, and storytelling are important communication channels. In India, where half of the population cannot read, writing press releases will not be the most effective way to communicate.[43] In Turkey, the practice of PR is thriving in spite of that country's reputation for harsh treatment of political prisoners. Although the Turkish government still asserts absolute control as it has for generations, corporate PR and journalism are allowed to flourish so that Turkish organizations can compete globally.

Even in industrialized countries, there are some important differences between PR practices. In the United States, the hometown news release comprises much of the news in a small, local newspaper. In Canada, on the other hand, large metropolitan population centers have combined with Canadian economic and climatic conditions to thwart the emergence of a local press. The dearth of small newspapers means that the practice of sending out hometown news releases is almost nonexistent.[44] In the United States, PR is increasingly viewed as a separate management function. In Europe that perspective has not been widely accepted; PR professionals are viewed as part of the marketing function rather than as distinct and separate specialists in a company. In Europe, fewer colleges and universities offer courses and degree programs in PR than in the United States. Also, European coursework in PR is more theoretical; in the United States, PR programs are often part of mass communication or journalism schools and there is more emphasis on practical job skills.

A company that is ethnocentric in its approach to PR will extend home-country PR activities into host countries. The rationale behind this approach is that people everywhere are motivated and persuaded in much the same manner. This approach does not take cultural considerations into account. A company adopting a polycentric approach to PR gives the host-country practitioner more leeway to incorporate local customs and practices into the PR effort. Although such an approach has the advantage of local responsiveness, the lack of global communication and coordination can lead to a PR disaster.[45]

The ultimate test of an organization's understanding of the power and importance of public relations occurs during a time of environmental turbulence, especially a potential or actual crisis. When disaster strikes, a company or industry often finds itself thrust into the spotlight. A company's swift and effective handling of communications during such times can have significant implications. The best response is to be forthright and direct, reassure the public, and provide the media with accurate information.

China's ongoing trade-related friction with the United States highlights the need for a better PR effort on the part of the Chinese Foreign Ministry. Some sources of this friction have been discussed in earlier chapters, such as estimates that Chinese counterfeiting of copyrighted material alone costs U.S. companies $800 million annually or that 98 percent of the computer software used in China is pirated. Such revelations reflect poorly on China. Hong Kong businessman Barry C. Cheung notes, "China lacks skills in public relations generally and crisis management specifically, and that hurts them."[46] Part of the problem stems from the unwillingness of China's Communist leaders to publicly explain their views on these issues, to admit failure, and to accept advice from the West.

---

[43]Carl Botan, "International Public Relations: Critique and Reformulation," *Public Relations Review* 18, no. 2 (Summer 1992), pp. 150–151.
[44]Melvin L. Sharpe, "The Impact of Social and Cultural Conditioning on Global Public Relations," *Public Relations Review* 18, no. 2 (Summer 1992), pp. 103–107.
[45]Carl Botan, "International Public Relations: Critique and Reformulation," *Public Relations Review* 18, no. 2 (Summer 1992), p. 155.
[46]Marcus W. Brauchli, "A Change of Face: China Has Surly Image, but Part of the Reason Is Bad Public Relations," *The Wall Street Journal* (June 16, 1996), p. A1.

Summary

Marketing communications—the promotion *P* of the marketing mix—includes advertising, public relations, sales promotion, and personal selling. When a company embraces **integrated marketing communications** (**IMC**), it recognizes that the various elements of a company's communication strategy must be carefully coordinated. **Advertising** is a sponsored, paid message that is communicated through nonpersonal channels. **Global advertising** consists of the same advertising appeals, messages, artwork, and copy in campaigns around the world. The effort required to create a global campaign forces a company to determine whether or not a global market exists for its product or brand. The trade-off between standardized and adapted advertising is often accomplished by means of **pattern advertising**, which can be used to create localized global advertising. Many advertising agencies are part of larger **advertising organizations**. Advertisers may place a single global agency in charge of worldwide advertising; it is also possible to use one or more agencies on a regional or local basis.

The starting point in ad development is the **creative strategy**, a statement of what the message will say. The people who create ads often seek a **big idea** that can serve as the basis for memorable, effective messages. The **advertising appeal** is the communication approach—rational or emotional—that best relates to buyer motives. **Rational appeals** speak to the mind; **emotional appeals** speak to the heart. The **selling proposition** is the promise that captures the reason for buying the product. The **creative execution** is the way an appeal or proposition is presented. **Art direction** and **copy** must be created with cultural considerations in mind. Perceptions of humor, male-female relationships, and sexual imagery vary in different parts of the world. Media availability varies considerably from country to country. When selecting media, marketers are sometimes as constrained by laws and regulations as by literacy rates.

A company utilizes **public relations (PR)** to foster goodwill and understanding among constituents both inside and outside the company. In particular, the PR department attempts to generate favorable **publicity** about the company and its products and brands. The PR department must also manage corporate communications when responding to negative publicity. The most important PR tools are press releases, media kits, interviews, and tours. Many global companies make use of various types of **corporate advertising**, including **image advertising** and **advocacy advertising**. Public relations is also responsible for providing accurate, timely information, especially in the event of a crisis.

Discussion Questions

1. In what ways can global brands and global advertising campaigns benefit a company?
2. How does the "standardized versus localized" debate apply to advertising?
3. What is the difference between an advertising appeal and creative execution?
4. Starting with Chapter 1, review the ads that appear in this text. Can you identify ads that use emotional appeals? Rational appeals? What is the communication task of each ad? To inform? To persuade? To remind? To entertain?
5. When creating advertising for world markets, what are some of the issues that art directors and copywriters should take into account?
6. How do the media options available to advertisers vary in different parts of the world? What can advertisers do to cope with media limitations in certain countries?
7. How does public relations differ from advertising? Why is PR especially important for global companies?
8. What are some of the ways public relations practices vary in different parts of the world?

In addition to targeting the Chinese government, activists also set their sights on Carrefour, Coca-Cola, Lenovo, McDonald's, and other global companies that spent tens of millions of dollars on advertising and public relations campaigns associated with the Games and the Olympic torch relay. These A-list Olympics sponsors were forced to take a proactive approach to PR as well.

E. Neville Isdell, chief executive of the Coca-Cola Company, responded to activists' concerns at Coke's annual shareholder meeting and in newspaper opinion-page letters. China is an important market for the soft drink and beverage giant: It is currently Coke's fourth-largest market, accounting for an estimated 5 percent of total annual revenues. Isdell noted, "We are neither a government nor the United Nations, but we can and must be a catalyst for change through actions that are appropriate for a business to take." Those actions include committing resources to ensure that relief supplies reach Darfur and addressing the pressing need for fresh water and sanitation for residents who have been displaced by the fighting.

China represents the second-largest market for Adidas, the German sportswear company; sales are expected to reach $1.5 billion by 2010. The United States is still Adidas's top market, but China ranks number 1 in terms of profitability. Overall, China's sportswear market in 2009 was worth more than $7 billion, almost twice the figure in 2006.

Adidas leveraged its status as official sportswear provider for the 2008 Games by opening a giant new flagship store in Beijing's entertainment district. Ironically, the new store is just a few blocks from a popular market that sells counterfeit Adidas goods. Even so, the store was designed to attract heavy foot traffic with novel features such as an interactive area that allows shoppers to test their fitness skills on precision exercise machines.

Adidas executives hoped that the publicity generated by the new store would help offset the widespread perception in China that archrival Nike was an official Olympic sportswear sponsor. Nike has endorsement contracts with a number of high-profile Chinese athletes and sponsored 22 Chinese federations for the Games. It also developed a line of shoes for Olympic athletes.

Adidas allocated most of its Olympics advertising budget to China. Research indicated that 90 percent of the Chinese population had an interest in the games. Adidas's media strategy included TV, outdoor, retail, mobile, and online ads. The central theme was Chinese nationalism and pride at hosting the games. The slogan "Impossible is Nothing" appeared in both English and Chinese, and the ads featured Chinese athletes and fans. The ad compaign was created by Omnicom Group's TBWA/Shanghai agency. Commented an executive at a New York-based sports-marketing firm, "Is there a risk that Adidas faces more of a backlash than other marketers because of its China-centric marketing? Yes."

Lenovo, the world's fourth-largest computer maker, also had a lot riding on the 2008 Games. Its design for the Olympic torch, ten months in the making, was chosen from among three hundred submitted to a competition sponsored by Bocog. Lenovo spent about $100 million for a full sponsorship and related Olympics-themed marketing activities. It was the only Chinese company among the 12 major Olympics sponsors; Lenovo's computers and servers provided the core of the Games' technology infrastructure.

In China, Lenovo is a well-known brand name and commands about one-third of the PC market. Ads timed to coincide with the Games utilized emotional appeals designed to tap into nationalistic fervor. Ads for Australia, France, and the United States featured well-known Olympic athletes such as Misty May-Treanor, a member of the U.S. beach volleyball team, and Australian swimmer Lisbeth Lenton. Chief Marketing Officer Deepak Advani hoped Lenovo's Olympics-themed communications program would build brand recognition and position the company as a global brand. "You don't say 'Samsung, the Korean phone company,'" he said. "You can't deny Lenovo has roots in China, but we've become very global. We don't define ourselves by geographical boundaries."

France's Carrefour, the world's second-largest retailer, operates more than 100 stores in China. Although Carrefour was not an official sponsor of the Games, executives nevertheless found themselves caught up in a barrage of negative publicity as well. What happened? When the Olympic torch relay passed through Paris, a pro-Tibet protester tried to grab a torch from the hands of a Chinese torch bearer who was in a wheelchair. The incident received extensive press coverage; meanwhile, rumors circulated that Carrefour supported Tibet's independence movement.

The result was an outburst of nationalistic emotion in China that was fueled by an Internet campaign directed against French companies. Crowds of protesters gathered outside several of Carrefour's Chinese stores. In a run-up to a final protest on May Day, the government-run media urged citizens to express their national price "in a more rational way." For its part, Carrefour executives issued public apologies for the disruptions of the torch relay that occurred on French soil.

Case 13-1 Discussion Questions

1. Why did the Chinese government hire a Western public relations firm to work on the 2008 Beijing Olympics?
2. Why do protesters and activists target events such as the Olympics?
3. Does the opportunity to reach a global audience by advertising during the Olympics offset the potential for bad publicity?
4. Do you think the companies identified in this case did a good job anticipating and responding to the protests?

Sources: Mei Fong, "Adidas Bets Big on Beijing," *The Wall Street Journal* (July 3, 2008), pp. B1, B2; Stephanie Kang, "Adidas Ad Campaign Invokes Chinese Nationalism," *The Wall Street Journal* (July 3, 2008), p. B6; Geoff Dyer, "Angry Chinese Target French Supermarkets," *Financial Times* (April 21, 2008), p. 6; Neville Isdell, "We Help Darfur but Do Not Harm the Olympics," *Financial Times* (April 18, 2008); Stephanie Clifford, "Coca-Cola Faces Critics of Its Olympics Support," *The New York Times* (April 17, 2008), p. C3; Jane Spencer, "Olympic Torch Uproar Could Burn Lenovo," *The Wall Street Journal* (April 14, 2008), p. B1.

In February 2008, Pepsi launched its new healthy option Pepsi Raw in the United Kingdom. The claim was that it was made from natural ingredients and contained no artificial preservatives, colorings, flavorings, or sweeteners.

It was a major new move as it was the first time that Pepsi has added a new drink to its product line in more than 10 years. Pepsi claimed that by simply replacing the corn syrup with cane sugar it had managed to drive down the calorie content of a 300 milliliter bottle from 120 calories to around 90 calories. Traditionally, Pepsi had always used fructose corn syrup, artificial flavorings, caffeine, citric acid, phosphoric acid, and natural flavorings. Pepsi Raw changed all of that with apple extract, caramel coloring, coffee leaf, tartaric acid from grapes, cane sugar, gum Arabic from acacia trees, and sparkling water. A year later, Pepsi Natural, almost identical to Pepsi Raw, was launched in the United States.

There were two major differences between the new version and regular Pepsi: it was paler and less fizzy. However, Pepsi claimed that it was responding to consumer demand for a premium, yet more natural soft drink. The UK cola market is estimated to be worth more than $9.7 billion per year. The market is dominated by Coca-Cola and Pepsi who have been fierce rivals for more than a hundred years. Coca-Cola remains the most valuable grocery brand in the United Kingdom.

Initially Pepsi Raw was launched in bars and clubs. The venues were carefully selected in seven cities: London, Manchester, Glasgow, Brighton, Birmingham, Leeds, and Liverpool. Once this initial launch was successful, the product was rolled out across the country.

PepsiCo brought forward the national launch of the cola brand in up-market chains such as Waitrose, supported by sampling and promotional activity. Its initial launch in the on-trade market was supported by a $2.4 million integrated campaign created by Abbott Mead Vickers BBDO.

One of the innovative ideas in marketing the new product was that Pepsi included a Twitter tag on its Pepsi Raw cans. It asked consumers to log on to the microblogging Web site and share their thoughts on the soda in 140 characters or less. The innovation was launched in May, and the @PepsiRaw account is part of a major sampling drive, which included 1.4 million cans across the United Kingdom. This idea was created by the digital agency Graphico DMG. The purpose of the initiative was to increase the dialogue with consumers and also featured a Pepsi Raw Facebook page. This page had a competition and downloadable coupons. By early June, Pepsi Raw had attracted 150 Twitter fans (over 1,000 by November 2009) and 1,250 Facebook fans (nearly 2,000 by November 2009). Over 95 percent of the Pepsi Raw tweets were positive, and any negative ones are quickly responded to and transformed into positive ones.

For their convention print advertising, Pepsi Raw used the concept of "stripped-back cola," showing naked people in front of a cityscape. On city buses, the advertising featured the tagline "Natural Born Cola."

Pepsi Raw is aimed at a sophisticated urban market and was created to provide consumers with a choice of premium cola, complementing the existing Pepsi range with a more subtle-tasting cola

and distinctive brand image. Graphico DMG was given a clear brief with Pepsi Raw positioned as a "stripped back" cola. The client wanted them to make that proposition live and breathe online.

The agency's solution was to dovetail their campaign with the fact that the product was going to be introduced to consumers in a limited number of bars and clubs in the United Kingdom. The agency created a Web site that started with a visually appealing short film that could also be run in the bars and clubs. The film is, in fact, an animated dance sequence. Everything in the film is stripped back to the essentials to mirror the product. Bar codes of light suggest dancing figures; the idea is to challenge the viewer to fill in gaps in what they see. The film was shot using technology more closely associated with sports science. The dancers wore reflective nodes, which were picked up by the cameras. Each of the nodes was triangulated, meaning that the movement of the dancers rather than the dancers themselves was recorded in 3D. Animators then worked to create the bodies of the dancers and inserted a light source.

Packaging was another key issue and designed to complement Pepsi Raw as a natural and up-market drink. A glass bottle with an old-fashioned crimped crown cap was used. It had a positive reception, so much so that this helped to accelerate the rollout to the home market.

Pepsi as a whole brand in the United Kingdom has seen its sales value rise from $349 million in 2006 to $410 million in 2008. This

PepsiCo and Coca Cola are the two cola market leaders in the United Kingdom with a combined market share of 60 percent. Each time one of them launches a new initiative or product line, the other counters it to retain its market position.
Source: © Irochka–Fotolia.com

equated to a market share of 11 percent and 12 percent respectively. Its major competitor, Coca-Cola, again looking at cola sales alone, also rose from a sales value of $1,520 billion in 2006 to $1,575 billion in 2008. Again there was a rise in market share of 47 percent to 48 percent, respectively.

Advertising spending is not necessarily the solitary reason behind the disparity in the sales and market share of Coca-Cola compared to PepsiCo. However in 2008, Coca-Cola as a brand, including all of its products, spent nearly $57 million on advertising in the United Kingdom. Over the same period, PepsiCo spent just under $18 million.

The two cola giants seem set for another major advertising and marketing war, this time in the natural sugar market. In 2008, just as PepsiCo was launching Pepsi Raw, Coca-Cola announced a partnership with U.S. conglomerate Cargill to create a stevia-based product called Truvia. PepsiCo beat its rival to market with its version, PureVia. Both are stevia based, some 300 times sweeter than sugar. According to Lou Imbrgno, the senior vice president of Pepsi Worldwide Technical Operations, its version is more natural and extracted from the stevia plant leaf and not synthetic in any way. Both companies believe that this is the way forward for artificial sweeteners, but at a time when Pepsi has just launched a product that is at the other end of the extreme.

Each new product launch and new advertising campaign simply reignites the so-called "Cola Wars" between the two main cola producers, and Pepsi Raw is just the latest move in this hundred-year battle for dominance.

Discussion Questions

1. Why might PepsiCo be willing to launch this brand in the United Kingdom rather than its home market, the United States?
2. Why was the positioning and ultimately the correct choice of advertising so important to this product's success?
3. To what extent might it be the case that PepsiCo's relative sales turnover and market share is simply a reflection of its relatively small advertising budget compared to its larger rival Coca-Cola?

Sources: Graphico New Media Limited, Digital Marketing Group plc., www. graphicodmg.co.uk; Britvic, www.britvic.com; PepsiCo, www.pepsi. co.uk; Pepsi Raw, www.pepsiraw.co.uk.

14

Global Marketing Communications Decisions II: Sales Promotion, Personal Selling, Special Forms of Marketing Communication

Case 14-1
Lenovo

In 2005, China's Lenovo Group acquired IBM's personal computer (PC) business for $1.25 billion. The acquisition vaulted China's top computer company into third place among the world's PC marketers, behind Dell and Hewlett-Packard. With annual revenues of $15 billion generated by sales in more than 60 countries, Lenovo now has almost an 8 percent share of the world's PC market. The crown jewel in the acquisition was the popular ThinkPad, a laptop that features an exceptionally well-designed keyboard. President and CEO William J. Amelio was tasked with gradually eliminating the IBM logo as Lenovo built a global brand identity.

As noted in the previous chapter, Amelio and his marketing team decided to use the Olympics as a vehicle for building awareness about the corporate name and its products. Lenovo paid more than $60 million to become China's first Olympic sponsor; it provided several thousand PCs and servers at various competition venues during the 2006 Winter Olympics in Turin, Italy (see Exhibit 14-1). The computers were clearly visible during television broadcasts of Olympic events and were used by Visa, Coca-Cola, and other sponsors. Lenovo also sponsored 11 athletes. Lenovo's status as a sponsor entitled it to invite preferred customers to the games to meet company executives, get hands-on time with some of the company's products, and, of course, view the sporting events.

Lenovo was also the computer provider for the 2008 Beijing Summer Olympics. Speaking about the Olympics,

Exhibit 14-1: In September 2005, with 150 days to go before the opening ceremonies of the 2006 Olympic Winter Games in Torino, Italy, Lenovo Chairman Yuanqing Yang and Vice President of Marketing Philippe Davy kicked off the company's computing equipment sponsorship in New York City. Lenovo was the official computing equipment partner for the 2006 Olympic Winter Games; it was also the partner for the 2008 Olympic Games in Beijing.
Source: Feature Photo Service/AP Wide World Photos.

CEO Amelio said, "It's a great opportunity. It's a coming-out party to say, 'Here's Lenovo, we're a global brand and we're here to stay.'" To find out more about Lenovo's use of sponsorships, turn to Case 14-1 at the end of the chapter.

Sponsorships have been a crucial marketing tool for Lenovo as it rebrands the ThinkPad. When developing IMC solutions and strategies, global companies and advertising agencies are giving sponsorship and other forms of promotion an increasingly prominent role; in the first decade of the twenty-first century, worldwide expenditures on sales promotion are growing at double-digit rates. Sales promotion, direct marketing, and specialized forms of marketing communication such as infomercials and the Internet are also growing in importance. Personal selling remains an important promotional tool as well. Taken together, the marketing mix elements discussed in this chapter and Chapter 13 can be used to create highly effective integrated promotional campaigns that support global brands.

SALES PROMOTION

Sales promotion refers to any paid consumer or trade communication program of limited duration that adds tangible value to a product or brand. In a *price promotion*, tangible value may take the form of a price reduction, coupon, or mail-in refund. *Nonprice promotions* may take the form of free samples, premiums, "buy one, get one free" offers, sweepstakes, and contests. **Consumer sales promotions** may be designed to make consumers aware of a new product, to stimulate nonusers to sample an existing product, or to increase overall consumer demand. **Trade sales promotions** are designed to increase product availability in distribution channels. At many companies, expenditures for sales promotion activities have surpassed expenditures for media advertising. At any level of expenditure, however, sales promotion is only one of several marketing communication tools. Sales promotion plans and programs should be integrated and coordinated with those for advertising, PR, and personal selling.

Worldwide, there are several explanations for the increasing popularity of sales promotion as a marketing communication tool. In addition to providing a tangible incentive to buyers, sales promotions also reduce the perceived risk buyers may associate with purchasing the product. From the point of view of the marketer, sales promotion provides accountability; the manager in charge of the promotion can immediately track the results of the promotion. Overall, promotional spending is increasing at many companies as they shift advertising spending away from traditional print and broadcast advertising. Exhibit 14-2 shows how marketing managers responsible for M&M's brand candy use sales promotions; additional examples are listed in Table 14-1.

Sweepstakes, rebates, and other promotional tools may require consumers to divulge personal information that companies can add to their databases. For example, the French Ministry of Agriculture recently launched a global promotion aimed at boosting exports of French wine and cheese. Acknowledging that some consumers are intimidated by France's culinary heritage, the Ministry sponsored the promotion to demonstrate that French cuisine can be relaxed and laid back. Spoexa, a food-marketing company, was hired to organize cocktail parties in 19 countries, including Canada, Spain, and the United States. House Party Inc., an American marketing firm, promoted the U.S. parties through its Web site. Would-be hosts registered online; from that applicant pool, House Party chose 1,000 people. The winners received discount coupons good for purchases of French wine; they also were entitled to free gifts when ordering French cheeses from select Web sites. Each winner also received a basket of party supplies, including a corkscrew and an apron. In return, the hosts agreed to take photos and blog about their party. After the parties, the hosts answered questionnaires to provide sponsors with feedback about the featured food and wine. Finally, in-store promotions on party-related French goods were featured at various shops and supermarkets.[1]

---

[1]Max Colchester, "French Recipe for Launching 1,000 Parties," *The Wall Street Journal* (April 24, 2009), p. B7.

Exhibit 14-2: Masterfoods USA, a unit of Mars, Inc., uses contests and other promotions to generate excitement about its M&M'S® brand chocolate candies. For example, on New Year's Eve 2003, Masterfoods launched the Great Candy Quest promotion. Black and white M&M'S® replaced the traditional colored versions, and consumers were invited to hunt for orange, brown, red, and other favorite colors.

In March 2004, contest winners took part in a celebrity-filled ceremony in Los Angeles and M&M'S® were reintroduced with brighter colors, new packaging, and an updated, larger M logo.

Source: Bloomberg News.

A global company can sometimes leverage experience gained in one country market and use it in another market. For example, PepsiCo experienced great success in Latin America with its Numeromania contest. When soft drink sales stalled in Poland in the mid-1990s, Pepsi rolled out Numeromania there; lured by the promise of big cash prizes, many economically squeezed Poles rushed out to buy Pepsi so they could enter the contest.[2] International managers can learn about American-style promotion strategies and tactics by attending seminars such as those offered by the Promotional Marketing Association of America (PMAA). Sometimes adaptation to country-specific conditions is required; for example, TV ads in France cannot have movie tie-ins. Ads must be designed to focus on the promotion rather than the movie. Such regulations would have an impact on Disney, for example.

As with other aspects of marketing communication, a key issue is whether headquarters should direct promotion efforts or leave them to local country managers. The authors of one study noted that Nestlé and other large companies that once had a polycentric approach to consumer and trade sales promotion have redesigned their efforts. Kashani and Quelch identify

TABLE 14-1 Sales Promotions by Global Marketers

Company and Country Market for Promotion	Promotion
Walt Disney Company/China	To fight counterfeiting, "Disney Magical Journey" promotion was keyed to mail-in hologram stickers on genuine Disney products. Participants could win Disney DVDs, TV sets, and trips to Hong Kong Disneyland.[*]
Mars/global	Global Color Vote promotion invited consumers in 200 countries to vote whether a new M&M candy should be purple, aqua, or pink. Purple won.
Wm. Wrigley Co./United States	U.S. launch of European Orbit brand gum with "Orbit Institute" advertising tied to Orbit Institute Sampling Initiative that included "field research teams" who distributed 7 million gum samples while dressed like the characters in the ads.
Guinness/Malaysia, Singapore, Hong Kong	Promotion to select new bottle shape from four different design options for Guinness, e.g., "bullhorn" shape and guitar shape. Contest was advertised in magazines, billboards, and table tent cards.

*Geoffrey A. Fowler, "Disney Fires a Broadside at Pirates," *The Wall Street Journal* (May 31, 2006), p. B3.

---

[2]Roderick Oram, "Brand Experiences," *Financial Times* (October 30, 1996), FT Survey, p. III.

four factors that contribute to more headquarters involvement in the sales promotion effort: cost, complexity, global branding, and transnational trade:[3]

1. As sales promotions command ever-larger budget allocations, headquarters naturally takes a greater interest.
2. The formulation, implementation, and follow-up of a promotion program may require skills that local managers lack.
3. The increasing importance of global brands justifies headquarters involvement to maintain consistency from country to country and ensure that successful local promotion programs are leveraged in other markets.
4. As mergers and acquisitions lead to increased concentration in the retail industry and as the industry globalizes, retailers will seek coordinated promotional programs from their suppliers.

The level of headquarters involvement notwithstanding, in most cases, local managers in the market know the specific local situation. They should be consulted before a promotion is launched. A number of factors must be taken into account when determining the extent to which the promotion must be localized:

- In countries with low levels of economic development, low incomes limit the range of promotional tools available. In such countries, free samples and demonstrations are more likely to be used than coupons or on-pack premiums.
- Market maturity can also be different from country to country; consumer sampling and coupons are appropriate in growing markets, but mature markets might require trade allowances or loyalty programs.
- Local perceptions of a particular promotional tool or program can vary. Japanese consumers, for example, are reluctant to use coupons at the checkout counter. A particular premium can be seen as a waste of money.
- Local regulations may rule out the use of a particular promotion in certain countries. Table 14-2 lists regulations governing coupon distribution in several countries.

TABLE 14-2 Coupon Promotion Regulation in Select Countries

Country	Coupons by Mail	Home Delivery Coupons	On-Pack Coupons	In-Pack Coupons
England	Legal	Legal	Legal	Legal
France	Legal for discount on same product. No cross coupons.	Legal for discount on same product. No cross coupons.	Legal for discount on same product. No cross coupons.	Legal for discount on same product. No cross coupons.
Germany	Legal for samples only. Price-off coupons not allowed.	Legal for samples only. Price-off coupons not allowed.	Price reduction cannot be made by retailer. Consumers mail coupon with on-pack code directly to manufacturer.	Prohibited in most cases.
Sweden	Legal to persons age 16 and older; illegal to send to persons younger than 16. Restrictions when sending to parents of new baby.	Legal to persons age 16 and older; illegal to send to persons younger than 16. Restrictions when sending to parents of new baby.	Legal	Legal
USA	Legal. Restrictions on alcohol, tobacco, and drugs.	Legal. Restrictions on alcohol, tobacco, and drugs.	Legal; all terms must be disclosed. Minimum 6-month redemption period required.	Legal; all terms must be disclosed. Minimum 6-month redemption period required.

Source: Adapted from *Promo* magazine.

---

[3]Kamran Kashani and John A. Quelch, "Can Sales Promotion Go Global?" *Business Horizons* 33, no. 3 (May–June 1990), pp. 37–43.

- Trade structure in the retailing industry can affect the use of sales promotions. For example, in the United States and parts of Europe, the retail industry is highly concentrated (i.e., dominated by a few key players such as Walmart). This situation requires significant promotional activity at both the trade and consumer level. By contrast, in countries where retailing is more fragmented—Japan is a case in point—there is less pressure to engage in promotional activities.

Sampling

Sampling is a sales promotion technique that provides potential customers with the opportunity to try a product or service at no cost. As Marc Pritchard, vice president of global cosmetics and personal care at Procter & Gamble, noted recently, "The most fundamental thing that consumers want to do is try before they buy."[4] A typical sample is an individual portion of a consumer packaged good such as breakfast cereal, shampoo, cosmetics, or detergent distributed through the mail, door-to-door, or at a retail location. For example:

- Fifty years ago, Kikkoman brand soy sauce was unknown in the United States. Yuzaburo Mogi, now Kikkoman's CEO, initiated a sampling program in American supermarkets. Mogi and his employees passed out free samples of food seasoned with Kikkoman; today, the U.S. market accounts for 85 percent of Kikkoman's profit from international operations (see Exhibit 14-3).[5]
- When Unilever launched Axe deodorant body spray in the United States in 2002, the promotion strategy called for print ads and in-store sampling. Unilever hired attractive female models to offer samples to male shoppers at Walmart and Costco stores. The successful U.S. launch helped propel Axe's global growth rate to 22 percent.[6]

The average cost per sample for such promotional programs can range from $0.10 to $0.50; 2 to 3 million samples are distributed in a typical sampling program. Cost is one of the major disadvantages associated with sampling; another problem is that it is sometimes difficult for marketing managers to assess the contribution a sampling program makes to return on investment. Today, many companies utilize *event marketing* and *sponsorships* to distribute samples at concerts, sports events, or special events such as food and beverage festivals attended by large numbers of people. In the information age, sampling may also consist of a week's free viewing of a cable TV channel or a no-cost trial subscription to an online computer service; Internet users can also request free samples through a company's Web site.

Compared with other forms of marketing communication, sampling is more likely to result in actual trial of the product. To ensure trial, consumer products companies are increasingly using a technique known as "point-of-use" sampling. For example, Starbucks dispatches "chill patrols" in the summertime to pass out samples of ice-cold Frappucino to overheated commuters during rush hour in busy metropolitan areas. In an example of "point-of-dirt" sampling, Unilever recently hired a promotional marketing firm to pass out Lever2000 hand wipes in food courts and petting zoos. As Michael Murphy, director of home and personal-care promotions at Unilever, noted, "We're getting smarter. You must be much more precise in what, where, and how you deliver samples."[7] Sampling can be especially important if consumers are not persuaded by claims made in advertising or other channels. In China, for example, shoppers are reluctant to buy full-sized packages of imported consumer products that they haven't tried—especially because the price may be several times higher than the price of local brands. Procter & Gamble's dominance in China's shampoo market can be attributed to the company's skillful use of market segmentation coupled with an aggressive sampling program. P&G offers four shampoo brands in China: Rejoice ("soft and beautiful hair"), Pantene ("nutrition"), Head & Shoulders (dandruff relief), and Vidal Sassoon (fashion).[8] P&G distributed millions of free samples of its shampoo products; after the no-risk trial, many consumers became adopters.

---

[4]Sarah Ellison, "Taking the 'Free' out of Free Samples," *The Wall Street Journal* (September 25, 2002), p. D1.

[5]Mariko Sanchanta, "Soy Sauce Seeps into the Culture," *Financial Times* (August 10, 2006), p. 6.

[6]Deborah Ball, "Consumer Goods Firms Duel for Shelf Space," *The Wall Street Journal* (October 22, 2004), p. B3.

[7]Geoffrey A. Fowler, "When Free Samples Become Saviors," *The Wall Street Journal* (August 14, 2001), p. B1.

[8]"Winning the China FMCG Market," ATKearney, 2003.

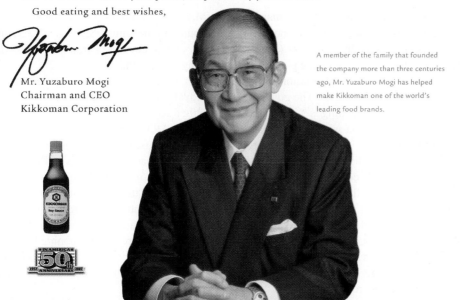

Couponing

A **coupon** is a printed certificate that entitles the bearer to a price reduction or some other special consideration for purchasing a particular product or service. In the United States and Great Britain, marketers rely heavily on newspapers to deliver coupons; nearly 90 percent of all coupons are distributed in a printed ride-along vehicle known as a *free-standing insert* (FSI). Sunday papers carry the vast majority of FSIs. *On-pack coupons* are attached to, or part of, the product package; they can frequently be redeemed immediately at checkout. *In-pack coupons* are placed inside the package. Coupons can also be handed out in stores, offered on a self-service basis from on-shelf dispensers, delivered to homes by mail, or distributed electronically at the checkout counter. Also, the number of coupons distributed via the Internet is growing. *Cross coupons* are distributed with one product but redeemable for a different product. For example, a toothpaste coupon might be distributed with a toothbrush. The United States leads the world in

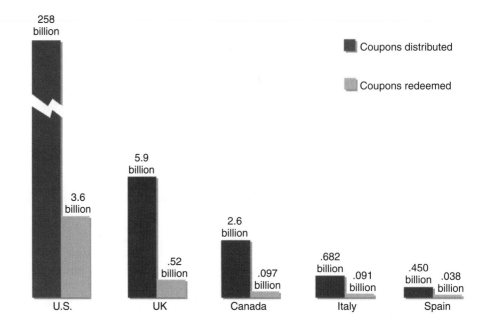

FIGURE 14-1

Coupon Distribution, U.S. Versus Select Country Markets

Source: Used by permission of NCH Marketing Services.

number of coupons issued, by a wide margin. NCH Marketing Services, which tracks coupon trends, reports that about 300 billion coupons are distributed in the United State each year; only about 1 percent are actually redeemed (see Figure 14-1). Online coupon distribution is growing at a rapid rate; Google is among the players experimenting with them.[9]

Coupons are a favorite promotion tool of consumer packaged goods companies such as Procter & Gamble and Unilever. The goal is to reward loyal users and stimulate product trial by nonusers. In the EU, couponing is widely used in the United Kingdom and Belgium. Couponing is not as prevalent in Asia where saving face is important. Although Asian consumers have a reputation for thriftiness, some are reluctant to use coupons because doing so might bring shame upon them or their families. According to Joseph Potacki, who teaches a "Basics of Promotion" seminar for the PMAA, couponing is the aspect of the promotion mix for which the practices in the United States differ the most from those in other countries. In the United States, couponing accounts for 70 percent of consumer promotion spending. Elsewhere, the percentage is much lower. As Potacki explains, "It is far less—or nonexistent—in most other countries simply because the cultures don't accept couponing." Potacki notes that one reason couponing is gaining importance in countries such as the United Kingdom is because retailers are learning more about its advantages.[10] Table 14-2 on page 463 gives an overview of regulations concerning coupon promotions in selected countries.

Sales Promotion: Issues and Problems

As noted earlier, many companies are being more strategic in targeting their sampling programs. In the case of coupons, retailers must bundle the redeemed coupons together and ship them to a processing point. Many times, coupons are not validated at the point of purchase; fraudulent redemption costs marketers hundreds of millions of dollars each year. Fraud can take other forms as well. For example, during the 2004 Super Bowl broadcast, PepsiCo launched a joint promotion with Apple Computer's iTunes Music Store. Apple planned to give away 100 million songs for free (regular price: $0.99); consumers could obtain a code from the caps of Pepsi bottles and enter the code online to qualify for the download. The promotion was designed so that anyone purchasing a bottle of Pepsi had a one-in-three chance of being a winner. However, many people discovered that, by tilting the bottles to one side, they could tell whether the bottle was a winner. Moreover, they could read the code without having to pay for the Pepsi!

[9]Steve Lohr, "Clip and Save Holds Its Own Against Point and Click," *The New York Times* (August 30, 2006), p. C1.
[10]Leslie Ryan, "Sales Promotion: Made in America," *Brandweek* (July 31, 1995), p. 28.

Companies must take extreme care when formulating and executing sales promotions. In some emerging markets, sales promotion efforts can raise eyebrows if companies appear to be exploiting regulatory loopholes and lack of consumer resistance to intrusion. Sales promotion in Europe is highly regulated. Sales promotions are popular in Scandinavia because of restrictions on broadcast advertising, but promotions in the Nordic countries are subject to regulations. If such regulations are relaxed as the single market develops in Europe and regulations are harmonized, companies may be able to roll out pan-European promotions.

A recent study examined coupon usage and attitudes toward both coupons and sweepstakes in Taiwan, Thailand, and Malaysia. The study has particular relevance to global companies that are targeting these and other developing nations in Asia where consumers have relatively little experience with coupons. The study utilized Hofstede's social values framework as a guide. All three countries in the studies are collectivist, and the researchers found that positive attitudes of family members and society as a whole influenced an individual's positive attitude toward coupons and coupon usage. However, the three nations show some differences in value orientation. For example, Malaysia has a higher power distance and lower uncertainty avoidance than the others. For Malaysians, the fear of public embarrassment was a constraint on coupon usage. In all three countries, media consumption habits were also a factor; persons who were not regular readers of magazines or newspapers were less likely to be aware that coupons were available. Consumers in Taiwan and Thailand look more favorably upon coupons than sweepstakes. The impact of religion surprised the researchers. In Malaysia, where the population is primarily Muslim, the researchers assumed that consumers would avoid sweepstakes promotions. Sweepstakes can be compared to gambling, which is frowned on by Islam. However, Malaysians showed a preference for sweepstakes over coupons. In Taiwan, where Buddhism, Confucianism, and Taoism are all practiced, religion appeared to have little impact on attitudes toward promotions. One implication for marketing in developing countries is that, despite cultural differences, increased availability of promotions will result in higher levels of consumer utilization.[11]

PERSONAL SELLING

Personal selling is person-to-person communication between a company representative and a prospective buyer. The seller's communication effort is focused on informing and persuading the prospect, with the short-term goal of making a sale and with a longer-term goal of building a relationship with that buyer. The salesperson's job is to correctly understand the buyer's needs, match those needs to the company's product(s), and then persuade the customer to buy. Because selling provides a two-way communication channel, it is especially important in marketing industrial products that may be expensive and technologically complex. Sales personnel can often provide headquarters with important customer feedback that can be utilized in design and engineering decisions.

Effective personal selling in a salesperson's home country requires building a relationship with the customer; global marketing presents additional challenges because the buyer and seller may come from different national or cultural backgrounds. Despite such challenges, it is difficult to overstate the importance of a face-to-face, personal selling effort for industrial products in global markets. For example, when Spain's Iberia Airlines was modernizing its long-haul fleet, salespeople from Boeing and rival Airbus met numerous times with Enrique Dupuy de Lome, Iberia's chief financial officer. At stake was a 12-plane order worth about $2 billion. The aircraft under consideration were the Boeing 777-300ER ("Extended Range") and the Airbus A340-600. After each sales team presented initial bids the negotiations began; Toby Bright, Boeing's top salesman for jets, faced off against John Leahy of Airbus. Iberia's demands included discounts off list prices and resale value guarantees for the aircraft. After months of meetings and revised proposals, Airbus was awarded the contract.[12]

---

[11]Lenard C. Huff and Dana L. Alden, "An Investigation of Consumer Response to Sales Promotions in Developing Markets: A Three Country Analysis," *Journal of Advertising Research* 38, no. 3 (May/June 1998), pp. 47–57.
[12]Daniel Michaels, "Dogfight: In the Secret World of Airplane Deals, One Battle Up Close," *The Wall Street Journal* (March 10, 2003), pp. A1, A9.

Personal selling is also a popular marketing communication tool in countries with various restrictions on advertising. As noted in Chapter 13, it is difficult to obtain permission to present product comparisons in any type of advertising in Japan. In such an environment, selling is the best way to provide hard-hitting, side-by-side comparisons of competing products. Personal selling is also used frequently in countries where low wage rates allow large local sales forces to be hired. For example, Home Box Office built its core of subscribers in Hungary by selling door-to-door. The cost effectiveness of personal selling in certain parts of the world has been a key driver behind the decision at many U.S.-based firms to begin marketing products and services overseas. A company is more likely to test a new territory or product if the entry price is relatively low. For example, some high-tech firms have utilized lower-cost sales personnel in Latin America to introduce new product features to their customers. Only if the response is favorable do the firms commit major resources to a U.S. rollout.

The challenge to companies that wish to pursue low-cost personal selling overseas, however, is to establish and maintain acceptable quality among members of the sales team. The old saying, "You get what you pay for" has come to haunt more than one company that has undertaken global expansion. When MCI Communications first entered Latin America several decades ago, it was attracted in part by the prospect of achieving inexpensive market penetration for its large multinational client companies. Management's initial enthusiasm quickly gave way to an alarming realization that the quality of support in this part of the world was not on a level with what MCI's major accounts were used to in the United States. As a result, there was a period when both MCI and its competition chose the costlier sales approach of using U.S.-based personnel to provide remote, but higher quality, support to the Latin American sites of their respective global customer bases. However, MCI's upper management ultimately decided to invest more to create in-country sales and service teams whose output more closely mirrored that of their U.S. counterparts.

The risks inherent in establishing a personal selling structure overseas remain today. The crucial issue is not whether in-country sales and marketing people can provide more benefit than a remote force. It's a given that, in the vast majority of scenarios, they can. The issue is whether the country team should consist of in-country nationals or **expatriates** (also known as expats); that is, employees who are sent from their respective home countries to work abroad. It should be noted that many of the environmental issues and challenges identified in earlier chapters often surface as a company completes the initial stages of implementing a personal selling strategy. These include:

- *Political risks.* Unstable or corrupt governments can completely change the rules for the sales team. Establishing new operations in a foreign country is especially tricky if a coup is imminent or if a dictator demands certain "considerations" (which has been the case in many developing countries). For example, Colombia offers great market potential and its government projects an image of openness. However, many companies have found the unspoken rules of the cabal to be inordinately burdensome. In a country ruled by a dictatorship, the target audience and accompanying message of the sales effort tend to be far narrower and restricted because government planners mandate how business will be conducted. Firms selling in Hong Kong were concerned that China would impose its will and dramatically alter the selling environment after the transfer of power in 1997. In response to such concerns, British Telecom brought many members of its Hong Kong sales staff back to London prior to the changeover. However, to the great relief of Hong Kong's business community, Chinese officials ultimately recognized that a policy of minimal intervention would be the wisest approach.
- *Regulatory hurdles.* Governments sometimes set up quota systems or impose tariffs that affect entering foreign sales forces. In part, governments consider such actions to be an easy source of revenue, but, even more importantly, policymakers want to ensure that sales teams from local firms retain a competitive edge in terms of what they can offer and at what price. Regulations can also take the form of rules that restrict certain types of sales activities. In 1998, for example, the Chinese government banned door-to-door selling, effectively blocking Avon's business model. Avon responded by establishing a network of store representatives; today, China is Avon's fastest growing global market. CEO Andrea Jung expects that, within just a few years, China will be adding $1 billion a year to Avon's bottom line.

- *Currency fluctuations.* There have been many instances where a company's sales effort has been derailed not by ineffectiveness or lack of market opportunity but by fluctuating currency values. In the mid-1980s, for example, Caterpillar's global market share declined when the dollar's strength allowed Komatsu to woo U.S. customers away. Then, while Caterpillar's management team was preoccupied with domestic issues, competitors chipped away at the firm's position in global markets.

- *Market unknowns.* When a company enters a new region of the world, its selling strategy may unravel because of a lack of knowledge of market conditions, the accepted way of doing business, or the positioning of its in-country competitors. When a game plan is finally crafted to counter the obstacles, it is sometimes too late for the company to succeed. However, if management devotes an inordinate amount of time conducting market research prior to entry, it may discover that its window of opportunity has been lost to a fast-moving competitor that did not fall victim to the "analysis paralysis" syndrome. Thus, it is difficult to make generalizations about the optimal time to enter a new country.

If all of these challenges can be overcome, or at least minimized, the personal selling endeavor can be implemented with the aid of a tool known as the Strategic/Consultative Selling Model.

The Strategic/Consultative Selling Model

Figure 14-2 shows the **Strategic/Consultative Selling Model**, which has gained wide acceptance in the United States. The model consists of five interdependent steps, each with three prescriptions that can serve as a checklist for sales personnel.[13] Many U.S. companies have begun developing global markets and have established face-to-face sales teams either directly, using their own personnel, or indirectly, through contracted sales agents. As a result, the Strategic/Consultative Selling Model is increasingly used on a worldwide basis. The key to ensuring that the model produces the desired outcome—building quality partnerships with customers—is to have it implemented and followed on a consistent basis. This is far more difficult to achieve with international sales teams than it is with U.S.-based units that are much more accessible to corporate headquarters.

First, a sales representative must develop a **personal selling philosophy**. This requires a commitment to the marketing concept and a willingness to adopt the role of problem solver or partner in helping customers. A sales professional must also be secure in the belief that selling is a valuable activity. The second step is to develop a **relationship strategy**, which is a game plan for establishing and maintaining high-quality relationships with prospects and customers. The relationship strategy provides a blueprint for creating the rapport and mutual trust that will serve as the basis of a lasting partnership. This step connects sales personnel directly to the concept of *relationship marketing*, an approach that stresses the importance of developing long-term partnerships with customers. Many U.S.-based companies have adopted the relationship marketing approach to selling in the American market; it is equally relevant—and perhaps even more so— to any company hoping to achieve success in global marketing.

In developing personal and relationship strategies on an international level, the representative is wise to take a step back and understand how these strategies will likely fit in the foreign environment. For example, an aggressive "I'll do whatever it takes to get your business" is the worst possible approach in some cultures, even though in many large U.S. cities it would be viewed as a standard, even preferred, practice. This is why it is prudent for a company's sales management and sales rep teams to invest the time and energy necessary to learn about the global market in which they will be selling. In many countries, people have only a rudimentary understanding of sales techniques; acceptance of those techniques may be low as well. A sophisticated sales campaign that excels in the United States may never hit the mark in other countries. In-country experts such as consultants or agents can be excellent sources of real-world intelligence that can help a sales rep create an effective international relationship strategy. Such people are especially helpful if the

---

[13]This discussion of the Strategic/Consultative Selling Model is adapted from Gerald L. Manning and Barry L. Reece, *Selling Today: Creating Customer Value,* 10th ed. (Upper Saddle River, NJ: Prentice Hall, 2007), Chapter 1. The authors are also indebted to Larry Sirhall, a marketing consultant based in Bend, Oregon.

FIGURE 14-2

**The Strategic/
Consultative
Selling Model**

Source: Gerald L. Manning
and Barry L. Reece, *Selling
Today: Creating Customer
Value,* 10th ed. © 2007,
pp. 15, 18, 238. Reprinted/
Adapted by permission of
Pearson Education, Inc.,
Upper Saddle River, NJ.

Strategic/Consultative Selling Model

Strategic Step	Prescription
Develop a Personal Selling Philosophy	☐ Adopt Marketing Concept ☐ Value Personal Selling ☐ Become a Problem Solver/Partner
Develop a Relationship Strategy	☐ Adopt Win-Win Philosophy ☐ Project Professional Image ☐ Maintain High Ethical Standards
Develop a Product Strategy	☐ Become a Product Expert ☐ Sell Benefits ☐ Configure Value-Added Solutions
Develop a Customer Strategy	☐ Understand Buyer Behavior ☐ Discover Customer Needs ☐ Develop Prospect Base
Develop a Presentation Strategy	☐ Prepare Objectives ☐ Develop Presentation Plan ☐ Provide Outstanding Service

Strategic/consultative selling evolved in response to increased competition, more complex products, increased emphasis on customer needs, and growing importance of long-term relationships.

sales force will include many expatriates who will not have resident nationals as colleagues whom they can turn to for advice. Sales representatives must understand that patience and a willingness to assimilate host-country norms and customs are important attributes in developing relationships built on respect.

The third step, developing a **product strategy**, results in a plan that can assist the sales representative in selecting and positioning products that will satisfy customer needs. A sales professional must be an expert who possesses not only a deep understanding of the features and attributes of each product he or she represents but also an understanding of competitive offerings. That understanding is then used to position the product and communicate benefits that are relevant to the customer's wants and needs. As with the selling philosophy and relationship strategy, this step must include comprehension of the target market's characteristics and the fact that prevailing needs and wants may mandate products that are different than those offered in the home country.

Until recently, most American companies engaged in international selling offered products rather than services. For example, John Deere did a marvelous job of increasing its global market share by supplying high quality but relatively mundane farming equipment to countries where agriculture remains a mainstay of local economies. Today, however, with exploding worldwide demand for technology-related services, the picture is changing. For example, in 2008, IBM's two Global Services Segments—Global Technology Services and Global Business Services—together accounted for 57 percent of revenues and 42 percent of pretax profits.

Next comes a **customer strategy**, a plan that ensures that the sales professional will be maximally responsive to customer needs. Doing so requires a general understanding of consumer behavior; in addition, the salesperson must collect and analyze as much information as possible about the needs of each customer or prospect. The customer strategy step also includes building a prospect base, consisting of current customers as well as potential customers (or leads). A qualified lead is someone whose probability of wanting to buy the product is high. Many sales organizations diminish their own productivity by chasing after too many nonqualified leads. This issue can be extremely challenging for an international sales unit because customer cues or "buying signs" may not coincide with those that have been proven in the sales rep's home country.

The final step, the actual face-to-face selling situation, requires a **presentation strategy**. This consists of setting objectives for each sales call and establishing a presentation plan to meet those objectives. The presentation strategy must be based on the sales representative's commitment to provide outstanding service to customers. As shown in Figure 14-3, when these five strategies are integrated with an appropriate personal selling philosophy, the result is a high-quality partnership.

The **presentation plan** that is at the heart of the presentation strategy is typically divided into six stages: approach, presentation, demonstration, negotiation, closing, and servicing the sale (Figure 14-4). The relative importance of each stage can vary by country or region. As mentioned several times already, the global salesperson *must* understand cultural norms and proper protocol, from proper exchange of business cards to the volume of one's voice during a discussion to the level of eye contact made with the decision maker. In some countries, the approach is drawn out as the buyer gets to know or takes the measure of the salesperson on a personal level with no mention of the pending deal. In such instances, the presentation comes only after rapport has been firmly established. In some regions of Latin America and Asia, rapport development may take weeks, even months. The customer may place more importance on what occurs *following* work than on what is accomplished during the formal work hours of 8 A.M. to 5 P.M.

In the six-step presentation plan, the first step, *approach*, is the sales representative's initial contact with the customer or prospect. The most crucial element of the step is to completely understand the decision-making process and the roles of each participant, such as decision maker, influencer, ally, or blocker. In some societies, it is difficult to identify the highest-ranking individual based on observable behavior during group meetings. This crucial bit of strategic information often is uncovered only after the rep has spent considerable time developing rapport and getting to know the overall customer organization from various perspectives and in various contexts.

In the *presentation* step, the prospect's needs are assessed and matched to the company's products. To communicate effectively with a foreign audience, the style and message of the presentation must be carefully thought out. In the United States, the presentation is typically designed to sell and persuade, whereas the intent of the international version should be to educate and inform. High-pressure tactics rarely succeed in global selling, despite the fact that they are natural components of many American sales pitches. The message is equally critical because what may be regarded as fully acceptable in U.S. discussions may either offend or

FIGURE 14-3

Building a High-Quality Sales Partnership

Source: Gerald L. Manning and Barry L. Reece, *Selling Today: Creating Customer Value,* 10th ed. © 2007, pp. 15, 18, 238. Reprinted/Adapted by permission of Pearson Education, Inc., Upper Saddle River, NJ.

FIGURE 14-4

**The Six-Step
Presentation Plan**

Source: Gerald L. Manning
and Barry L. Reece, *Selling
Today: Creating Customer
Value,* 10th ed. © 2007,
pp. 15, 18, 238. Reprinted/
Adapted by permission of
Pearson Education, Inc.,
Upper Saddle River, NJ.

Step One: Approach	☐ Review Strategic/Consultative Selling Model ☐ Initiate customer contact
Step Two: Presentation	☐ Determine prospect needs ☐ Select product or service ☐ Initiate sales presentation
Step Three: Demonstration	☐ Decide what to demonstrate ☐ Select selling tools ☐ Initiate demonstration
Step Four: Negotiation	☐ Anticipate buyer concerns ☐ Plan negotiating methods ☐ Initiate win-win negotiations
Step Five: Close	☐ Plan appropriate closing methods ☐ Recognize closing clues ☐ Initiate closing methods
Step Six: Servicing the Sale	☐ Suggestion selling ☐ Follow through ☐ Follow-up calls

Service, retail, wholesale, and manufacturer selling

confuse the overseas sales audience. A humorous example of this occurred during a session between representatives from Adolph Coors Company and a foreign prospect. The first slide in the presentation contained a translation of Coors's slogan "Turn It Loose," but within seconds of this slide being shown, the audience began to chuckle. As translated, the slogan described diarrhea—obviously something that the presenter had no desire to convey to this group!

Next comes the *sales demonstration*, during which the salesperson has the opportunity to tailor the communication effort to the customer and alternately tell and show how the product can meet the customer's needs. This step represents one of selling's important advantages as a promotional tool. The prospect's senses become involved, and he or she can actually see the product in action, touch it, taste it, or hear it, as the case may be.

During the presentation, the prospect may express concerns or objections about the product itself, the price, or some other aspect of the sale. Dealing with objections in an international setting is a learned art. In some cases, this is simply part of the sales ritual and the customer expects the representative to be prepared for a lively debate on the pros and cons of the product in question. In some instances, it is taboo to initiate an open discussion where any form of disagreement is apparent; such conversations are to be handled in a one-to-one situation or in a small group with a few key individuals present. A common theme in sales training is the concept of *active listening*; naturally, in global sales, verbal and nonverbal communication barriers of the type discussed in Chapter 4 present special challenges. When objections are successfully overcome, serious negotiations can begin.

Negotiation is required to ensure that both the customer and the salesperson come away from the presentation as winners. Experienced American sales representatives know that persistence during the negotiation stage is one tactic often needed to win an order in the United States. However, some foreign customers consider American-style persistence (inferring tenacity) or arm-twisting can be considered rude and offensive. This can end the negotiations quickly—or, in the worst case, such behavior can be taken as a display of self-perceived American superiority, which then must be countered aggressively or brought to an immediate end. Inappropriate application of American-style negotiation tactics has plagued some U.S. sales representatives attempting to assertively close deals with Canadian companies. Conversely, in other countries, persistence often means endurance, a willingness to patiently invest months or years before the effort results in an actual sale. For example, a company wishing to enter the Japanese market must be prepared for negotiations to take several years.

Having completed the negotiation step, the sales representative is able to move on to the *close* and thus asks for the order. Attitudes toward the degree of bluntness that is acceptable in making this request vary among countries. In Latin America, a bold closing statement is respected, whereas in Asia, it is something that must be done with more deference toward the decision maker. As with objection handling and negotiation, the close is a selling skill that comes with both knowledge and experience in global business and sales.

The final step is *servicing the sale.* A successful sale does not end when the order is written; to ensure customer satisfaction with the purchase, an implementation process (which may include delivery and installation) must be outlined and a customer service program established (see Exhibit 14-4). Implementation can be complicated because of logistical and transportation issues as well as potential problems with the in-country resources to handle all the necessary

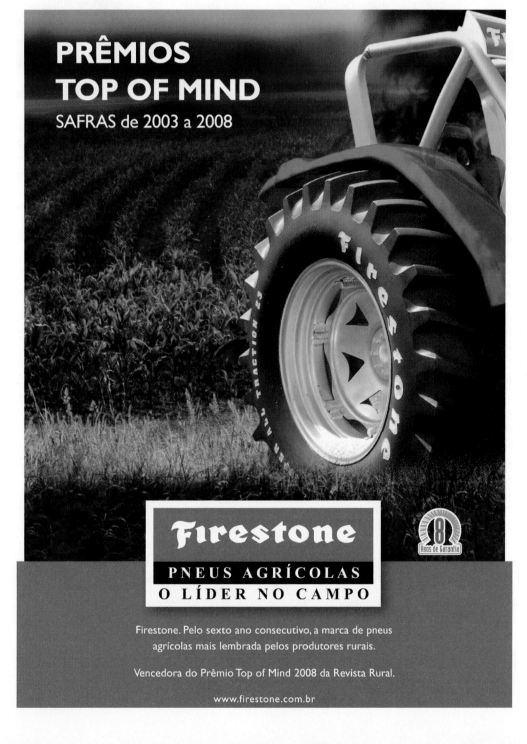

Exhibit 14-4: This print advertisement for Bridgestone Firestone Brazil communicates the fact that the company's extensive dealer network is dedicated to top-notch customer service. Worldwide, the Firestone brand is associated with expert in-store service as well as quick in-field service. It is important for farmers to have the right tires on their equipment, and sales representatives at each dealership match the right tire to a particular application. In addition, dealers are able to replace damaged tires on-site to minimize downtime for the farmer. This ad campaign also incorporates "Leader in the Field," the corporate-wide slogan that is a very appropriate positioning for an agricultural products company.

Exhibit 14-5: In global marketing, sales meetings and presentations typically involve people from various nationalities. These may include expatriates (from the headquarters country), host-country nationals, and third-country nationals. A successful salesperson takes the time to adapt the Strategic/Consultative Model to the specific selling situation. The various elements of the six-step presentation plan may also need to be adapted. Table 4-1 (Chapter 4, p. 118) lists several characteristics of "typical" American communication patterns that may require adaptation.

Source: © Harry Meynard zefa/Corbis. All Rights Reserved.

steps. Transportation alternatives were discussed in Chapter 12. Decisions regarding resources for implementation and after-sale service are similar to decisions about the personal selling structure described in the following paragraphs. There are cost benefits to using in-country nationals for implementation, but quality control is more difficult to guarantee. Establishing expatriates for the primary function of implementation is costly and normally cannot be justified until international operations are more mature and profitable. But sending an implementation team to the host country creates a variety of expense and regulatory concerns. Even when implementation has been adequately addressed, the requirement for sold customer service raises all of the same questions again: in-country nationals, expatriates, or third-country nationals?

Sales Force Nationality

As noted previously, a basic issue for companies that sell globally is the composition of the sales force in terms of nationality. It is possible to utilize expatriate salespersons, hire host-country nationals, or recruit third-country sales personnel (see Exhibit 14-5). The staffing decision is contingent on several factors, including management's orientation, the technological sophistication of the product, and the stage of economic development exhibited by the target country. Table 14-3 summarizes these decisions. Not surprisingly, a company with an ethnocentric orientation is likely to prefer expatriates and adopt a standardized approach without regard to technology or the level of economic development in the target country. Polycentric companies selling in developed countries should opt for expatriates to sell technologically sophisticated products; a host-country sales force can be used when technological sophistication is lower. In less-developed countries, host-country

TABLE 14-3 Contingency Factors in Selecting Sales Force Nationality

| | Management Orientation | | | | | |
| | Ethnocentric | | Polycentric | | Regiocentric | |
Technology Level	Developed	Less Developed	Developed	Less Developed	Developed	Less Developed
High	Expatriates	Expatriates	Expatriates	Host-country nationals	Expatriates	Third-country nationals
Low	Expatriates	Expatriates	Host-country nationals	Host-country nationals (agents)	Third-country nationals	Third-country nationals (agents)

Source: Earl D. Honeycutt Jr. and John B. Ford, "Guidelines for Managing an International Sales Force," *Industrial Marketing Management* 24 (March 1995), p. 139.

TABLE 14-4 **Advantages and Disadvantages of Different Sales Types**

Category	Advantages	Disadvantages
Expatriates	Superior product knowledge	Highest cost
	Demonstrated commitment to high customer service standards	High turnover
		Cost for language and cross-cultural training
	Train for promotion	
	Greater HQ control	
Host country	Economical	Need product training
	Superior market knowledge	May be held in low esteem
	Language skills	Language skills may not be important
	Superior cultural knowledge	Difficult to ensure loyalty
	Implement actions sooner	
Third country	Cultural sensitivity	Face identity problems
	Language skills	Blocked promotions
	Economical	Income gaps
	Regional sales coverage	Need product or company training
		Loyalty not assured

Source: Adapted from Earl D. Honeycutt Jr. and John B. Ford, "Guidelines for Managing an International Sales Force," *Industrial Marketing Management* 24 (March 1995), p. 138.

nationals should be used for products in which technology is a factor; host-country agents should be used for low-tech products. The widest diversity of sales force nationality is found in a company in which a regiocentric orientation prevails. Except in the case of high-tech products in developed countries, third-country nationals are likely to be used in all situations.

In addition to the factors just cited, management must also weigh the advantages and disadvantages of each nationality type (Table 14-4). First, because they come from the home country, expatriates often possess a high level of product knowledge and are likely to be thoroughly versed in their company's commitment to after-sales service. They come with corporate philosophies and culture well engrained. Also, they are better able to institute the acceptable practices and follow the policies of the home office and, generally, there is less potential for control or loyalty issues to arise. Finally, a foreign assignment can also provide employees with valuable experience that can enhance promotion prospects.

There are also several disadvantages to utilizing expatriates. If the headquarters mind-set is *too* firmly ingrained, the expat may have a difficult time understanding the foreign environment and assimilating into it. This can eventually lead to significant losses; the sales effort may be poorly received in the market, or homesickness can lead to a costly reversal of the relocation process. Maintaining expat sales personnel is extremely expensive; the average annual cost to post employees and their families overseas exceeds $250,000. In addition to paying expat salaries, companies must pay moving expenses, cost-of-living adjustments, and host-country taxes. Despite the high investment, many expats fail to complete their assignments because of inadequate training and orientation prior to the cross-border transfer. In the case of U.S. expats, studies have shown that one-quarter leave their companies within a year of returning home.

An alternative is to build a sales force with host-country personnel. Locals offer several advantages, including intimate knowledge of the market and business environment, language skills, and superior knowledge of local culture. The last consideration can be especially important in Asia and Latin America. In addition, because in-country personnel are already in place in the target country, there is no need for expensive relocations. However, host-country nationals may possess work habits or selling styles that do not mesh with those of the parent company. Furthermore, the firms' corporate sales executives tend to have less control over an operation that is dominated by host-country nationals. Headquarters executives may also experience difficulty cultivating loyalty, and host-country nationals are likely to need hefty doses of training and education regarding both the company and its products.

A third option is to hire persons who are not natives of either the headquarters country or the host country; such persons are known as *third-country nationals*. For example, a U.S.-based company might hire someone from Thailand to represent it in China. This option has many advantages in common with the host-country national approach. In addition, if conflict, diplomatic tension, or some other form of disagreement has driven a wedge between the home country and the target sales country, a sales representative from a third country may be perceived as sufficiently neutral or at "arm's length" to enable the company to continue its sales effort. However, there are several disadvantages of the third-country option. For one thing, sales prospects may wonder why they have been approached by someone who is neither a local national nor a native of the headquarters country. Third-country nations may lack motivation if they are compensated less generously than expats or host-country sales personnel; also, they may find themselves passed over for promotions as coveted assignments go to others.

After much trial and error in creating sales forces, most companies today attempt to establish a hybrid sales force comprised of a balanced mix of expatriates and in-country nationals. The operative word for this approach is *balanced* because there always remains the potential for conflict between the two groups. It is also the most expensive proposition in terms of up-front costs because both relocation of expats and extensive training of in-country nationals are required. However, the short-term costs are usually deemed necessary in order to do business and conduct personal selling overseas.

After considering the options shown in Table 14-4, management may question the appropriateness of trying to create personal selling units made up of their own people. A fourth option is to utilize the services of **sales agents**. Agents work under contract rather than as full-time employees. In the United States, companies have used sales agents for many years, often with mixed results. From a global perspective, it often makes a great deal of sense to set up one or more agent entities to at least gain entry to a selected country or region. In some cases, because of the remoteness of the area or the lack of revenue opportunity (beyond servicing satellite operations of customers headquartered elsewhere), agents are retained on a fairly permanent level. To this day, the majority of U.S., Asian and European companies with an Africa-based sales presence maintain agent groups to represent their interests.

Agents are less expensive than full-time, in-country national sales representatives; at the same time, they possess the same market and cultural knowledge. If agents are used initially and the sales effort gains traction, they can be phased out and replaced by the manufacturer's sales force. Conversely, a company may use its own sales force initially and then convert to agents. Procter & Gamble's Golden Store program in Mexico is an excellent illustration of the various sales force options. As discussed in Chapter 12, company representatives visit participating stores to tidy display areas and arrange promotional material in prominent places. At first, P&G used its own sales force; now it relies on independent agents who buy inventory (paying in advance) and then resell the items to shopkeepers.

Other international personal selling approaches that fall somewhere between sales agents and full-time employee teams include:

- *Exclusive license arrangements* in which a firm will pay commissions to an in-country company's sales force to conduct personal selling on its behalf. For example, when Canada's regulatory agency prevented U.S. telephone companies from entering the market on their own, AT&T, MCI, Sprint, and other firms crafted a series of exclusive license arrangements with Canadian telephone companies.
- *Contract manufacturing or production* with a degree of personal selling made available through warehouses or showrooms that are open to potential customers. Sears has employed this technique in various overseas markets, with the emphasis placed on the manufacturing and production but with the understanding that opportunities for some sales results do exist.
- *Management-only agreements* through which a corporation will manage a foreign sales force in a mode that is similar to franchising. Hilton Hotels has these types of agreements all over the world; not only for hotel operations but also for personal selling efforts aimed at securing conventions, business meetings, and large group events.
- *Joint ventures* with an in-country (or regional) partner. Because many countries place restrictions on foreign ownership within their borders, partnerships can serve as the best way for a company to obtain both a personal sales capability as well as an existing base of customers.

SPECIAL FORMS OF MARKETING COMMUNICATIONS: DIRECT MARKETING, SUPPORT MEDIA, EVENT SPONSORSHIP, AND PRODUCT PLACEMENT

The Direct Marketing Association defines **direct marketing** as any communication with a consumer or business recipient that is designed to generate a response in the form of an order, a request for further information, and/or a visit to a store or other place of business. Companies use direct mail, telemarketing, television, print, and other media to generate responses and build databases filled with purchase histories and other information about customers. By contrast, mass marketing communications are typically aimed at broad segments of consumers with certain demographic, psychographic, or behavioral characteristics in common. Table 14-5 shows other differences between direct marketing and "regular" marketing. Although direct marketing dates back decades, more sophisticated techniques and tools are being used today. For example, Don Peppers and Martha Rogers advocate an approach known as **one-to-one marketing**. Building on the notion of customer relationship management (CRM), one-to-one marketing calls for treating different customers differently based on their previous purchase history or past interactions with the company. Peppers and Rogers describe the four steps in one-to-one marketing as follows:[14]

1. *Identify* customers and accumulate detailed information about them.
2. *Differentiate* customers and rank them in terms of their value to the company.
3. *Interact* with customers and develop more cost-efficient and effective forms of interaction.
4. *Customize* the product or service offered to the customer (e.g., by personalizing direct mail offers).

Worldwide, the popularity of direct marketing has been steadily increasing in recent years. One reason is the availability of credit cards—widespread in some countries, growing in others—as a convenient payment mechanism for direct response purchases. (Visa, American Express, and MasterCard generate enormous revenues by sending direct mail offers to their cardholders.) Another reason is societal: Whether in Japan, Germany, or the United States, dual-income families have money to spend but less time to shop outside the home. Technological advances have made it easier for companies to reach customers directly. Cable and satellite television allow advertisers to reach specific audiences on a global basis. As noted in Case 7-3, MTV reaches hundreds of millions of households worldwide and attracts a young viewership. A company wishing to reach businesspeople can buy time on CNN, Fox News Network, or CNBC.

Direct marketing's popularity in Europe increased sharply during the 1990s. The European Commission expects investment in direct marketing to surpass expenditures for traditional advertising in the near future. One reason is that direct marketing programs can be readily made to conform to the "think global, act local" philosophy. As Tony Coad, managing director of a

TABLE 14-5 Comparison of Direct Marketing and Mass Marketing

Direct Marketing	Mass Marketing
Marketer adds value (creates place utility) by arranging for delivery of product to customer's door.	Product benefits do not typically include delivery to customer's door.
Marketer controls the product all the way through to delivery.	Marketer typically loses control as product is turned over to distribution channel intermediaries.
Direct response advertising is used to generate an immediate inquiry or order.	Advertising is used for cumulative effect over time to build image, awareness, loyalty, and benefit recall. Purchase action is deferred.
Repetition is used within the ad/offer.	Repetition is used over a period of time.
Customer perceives higher risk because product is bought unseen. Recourse may be viewed as distant or inconvenient.	Customer perceives less risk due to direct contact with product. Recourse is viewed as less distant.

Source: Adapted from Direct Marketing Association.

---

[14]Don Peppers, Martha Rogers, and Bob Dorf, "Is Your Company Ready for One-to-One Marketing?" *Harvard Business Review* 77, no. 1 (January–February 1999).

London-based direct marketing and database company, noted more than a decade ago, "Given the linguistic, cultural, and regional diversity of Europe, the celebrated idea of a Euro-consumer is Euro-baloney. Direct marketing's strength lies in addressing these differences and adapting to each consumer."[15] Obstacles still remain, however, including the European Commission's concerns about data protection and privacy, high postal rates in some countries, and the relatively limited development of the mailing list industry. Rainer Hengst of Deutsche Post offers the following guidelines for U.S.-based direct marketers that wish to go global:[16]

- The world is full of people who are not Americans. Be sure not to treat them like they are.
- Like politics, all marketing is local. Just because your direct mail campaign worked in Texas, do not assume it will work in Toronto.
- Although there may be a European Union, there is no such thing as a "European."
- Pick your target, focus on one country, and do your homework.
- You'll have a hard time finding customers in Paris, France, if your return address is Paris, Texas. Customers need to be able to return products locally or at least believe there are services available in their country.

Direct Mail

Direct mail uses the postal service as a vehicle for delivering a personally addressed offer to a prospect targeted by the marketer. Direct mail is popular with banks, insurance companies, and other financial services providers. As customers respond to direct mail offers, the marketer adds information to its database. That information, in turn, allows the marketer to refine subsequent offers and generate more precisely targeted lists. The United States is home to a well-developed mailing list industry. A company can rent a list to target virtually any type of buyer; naturally, the more selective and specialized the list, the more expensive it is. The availability of good lists and the sheer size of the market are important factors in explaining why Americans receive more direct mail than anyone else. However, on a per capita basis, German consumers are world-leader mail-order shoppers, buying more than $500 each in merchandise annually. Americans rank second, with annual per capita spending of $379.

Compared with the United States, list availability in Europe and Japan is much more limited. The lists that are available may be lower in quality and contain more errors and duplications than lists from the United States. Despite such problems, direct mail is growing in popularity in some parts of the world. In Europe, for example, regulators are concerned about the extent that children are exposed to, or even targeted by, traditional cigarette advertising. Faced with the threat of increased restrictions on its advertising practices, the tobacco industry is making a strategy shift toward direct mail. As David Robottom, development director at the Direct Marketing Association, noted, "Many of the promotions on cigarette packets are about collected data. [The tobacco companies] are working very hard at building up loyalty."

Following the economic crisis in Asia, a number of companies in that region have turned to direct mail in an effort to use their advertising budgets more effectively. Historically, the Asian direct marketing sector has lagged behind its counterparts in the United States and Europe. Grey Global Group established a Kuala Lumpur office of Grey Direct Interactive in 1997; OgilvyOne Worldwide is the Malaysian subsidiary of Ogilvy & Mather Group specializing in direct marketing. Companies in the banking and telecommunications sectors have been to the forefront of direct marketing initiatives in Asia, using their extensive databases to target individual consumers by mail or Internet.

Catalogs

A **catalog** is a magazine-style publication that features photographs, illustrations, and extensive information about a company's products. (The term "magalog" is sometimes used to describe this communication medium.) The global catalog retail sector generated revenues of nearly $380 billion in 2005.[17] Catalogs have a long and illustrious history as a direct marketing tool in both Europe and

---

[15]Bruce Crumley, "European Market Continues to Soar," *Advertising Age* (February 21, 1994), p. 22.
[16]Rainer Hengst, "Plotting Your Global Strategy," *Direct Marketing* 63, no. 4 (August 2000), pp. 52–57.
[17]"Global Catalog Retail: Industry Profile," Datamonitor (April 2006), p. 7.

EMERGING MARKETS BRIEFING BOOK

⇄ Nestlé Uses Direct Mail in Asia

In 2000, Nestlé launched a successful direct mail campaign in Malaysia that offered cat owners free samples of Friskies brand cat food, coupons for discounts on purchases of Friskies, and the opportunity to join the Friskies Cat Club. Nestlé expanded its existing database of 450,000 names by placing newspaper ads offering coupons to readers who wrote to the company, distributing questionnaires in conjunction with in-store sampling, and hosting contests on its Web site. The 20 percent response rate to the Friskies mailing was well above the single-digit rates typical of

direct mail campaigns in the United States. As Leong Ming Chee, marketing and communications director for Nestlé Products, noted, "You can spend 100,000 ringgit ($26,320) on TV ads for a product like this and have no idea how many viewers have cats and so how much of it goes to waste. This way, you can target those exact consumers directly."

Source: Cris Prystay, "In Malaysia, Advertisers Adopt Direct Mail to Keep Sales Purring," *Asian Wall Street Journal* (March 26–April 1, 2001), p. 12.

the United States. The European catalog market flourished after World War II as consumers sought convenience, bargain prices, and access to a wider range of goods. U.S.-based catalog marketers include JCPenney, Lands' End, L.L.Bean, and Victoria's Secret; in Europe, Otto GmbH & Co KG (Germany) is the leading catalog retailer. Catalogs are widely recognized as an important part of an IMC program, and many companies use catalogs in tandem with traditional retail distribution and e-commerce channels. The catalog retail sector in the United States represents about one-third of the total global market; more than 17 billion catalogs were mailed in 2008.

Historically, catalogers in the United States benefited from the ability to ship goods from one coast to the other, crossing multiple state boundaries with relatively few regulatory hurdles. By contrast, prior to the advent of the single market, catalog sales in Europe were hindered by the fact that mail-order products passing through customs at national borders were subject to value-added taxes (VAT). Because VAT drove up prices of goods that crossed borders, a particular catalog tended to be targeted at intracountry buyers. In other words, Germans bought from German catalogs, French consumers bought from French catalogs, and so on. Market-entry strategies were also affected by the customs regulations; catalogers grew by acquiring existing companies in various countries. For example, Otto GmbH & Co KG distributes hundreds of different catalogs in 20 countries (see Exhibit 14-6).

Exhibit 14-6: German supermodel Tatjana Patitz poses with Otto's spring/summer 2007 catalog, which features her photo on the cover. Shoppers can choose from Pure Wear, Kind To Your Skin, and other eco-friendly fashion lines made from organic cotton. As Otto Group CEO Dr. Michael Otto explains, "Conscious buying and consumption behavior are an important contribution toward promoting environmentally friendly and socially compatible ways of manufacturing goods worldwide."
Source: Fabian Bimmer/AP Wide World Photos.

Today, the single market means that mail-order goods can move freely throughout the EU without incurring VAT charges. Also, since January 1993, VAT exemptions have been extended to goods bound for the European Free Trade Area countries (Norway, Iceland, Switzerland, and Liechtenstein). Some predict robust growth in Europe's mail-order business, thanks to the increased size of the potential catalog market and the VAT-free environment. The single market is also attracting American catalog retailers, who will be faced with higher costs for paper, printing, and shipping as well as the familiar issue of whether to adapt their offerings to local tastes. Stephen Miles, director of international development, Lands' End, said, "The most difficult thing is to know in which areas to be local. We're proud that we're an American sportswear company, but that doesn't mean your average German consumer wants to pick up the phone and speak English to someone."[18]

In Japan, the domestic catalog industry is well developed. Leading catalog companies include Cecile, with $1 billion in annual sales of women's apparel and lingerie; Kukutake Publishing, which sells educational materials; and Shaddy, a general merchandise company. As noted in Chapter 12, Japan's fragmented distribution system represents a formidable obstacle to market entry by outsiders. An increasing number of companies use direct marketing to circumvent the distribution bottleneck. Annual revenues for all forms of consumer and business direct response advertising in Japan passed the $1 trillion mark in the mid-1990s; they declined to $525 billion in 2000 as Japan's economic difficulties continued. Success can be achieved using different strategies. For example, Patagonia dramatically increased sales after publishing a Japanese-language catalog, whereas L.L.Bean offers a Japanese-language insert in its traditional catalog.

Even as they continue to develop the Japanese market, Western catalogers are now turning their attention to other Asian countries. In Hong Kong and Singapore, efficient postal services, highly educated populations, wide use of credit cards, and high per capita income are attracting the attention of catalog marketers. Notes Michael Grasee, the former director of international business development at Lands' End, "We see our customer in Asia as pretty much the same customer we have everywhere. It's the time-starved, traveling, hardworking executive."[19] Catalogers are also targeting Asia's developing countries. Otto GmbH & Co KG, with 2009 revenues of $13.6 billion and about 6 percent of global mail-order sales, is planning to enter China, Korea, and Taiwan. Because these countries have few local mail-order companies that could be acquisition targets, executives at Otto have mapped out an entry strategy based on acquiring a majority stake in joint ventures with local retailers.

Infomercials, Teleshopping, and Interactive Television

An **infomercial** is a form of paid television programming in which a particular product is demonstrated, explained, and offered for sale to viewers who call a toll-free number shown on the screen. Thomas Burke, president of Saatchi & Saatchi's infomercial division, calls infomercials "the most powerful form of advertising ever created." The cost of producing a single infomercial can reach $3 million; advertisers then pay as much as $500,000 for time slots on U.S. cable and satellite systems and local TV channels. Because infomercials are typically 30 minutes in length and often feature studio audiences and celebrity announcers, many viewers believe they are watching regular talk show–type programming. Although originally associated with personal care, fitness, and household products such as those from legendary direct-response pitchman Ron Popeil, infomercials have gone up-market in recent years. For example, Lexus generated more than 40,000 telephone inquiries after launching its used-car program with an infomercial; 2 percent of respondents ultimately purchased a Lexus automobile.

In Asia, infomercials generate several hundred million dollars in annual sales. Costs for a late-night time slot range from $100,000 in Japan to $20,000 in Singapore. Infomercials are also playing a part in the development of China's market sector. The government has given its blessing by allowing China Central Television, the state-run channel, to air infomercials and give Chinese consumers access to Western goods. Despite low per capita incomes, Chinese

---

[18]Cacilie Rohwedder, "U.S. Mail-Order Firms Shake Up Europe," *The Wall Street Journal* (January 6, 1998), p. A15.
[19]James Cox, "Catalogers Expand in Asia," *USA Today* (October 18, 1996), p. 4B.

consumers are thought to achieve a savings rate as high as 40 percent because housing and health care are provided by the state. China Shop-A-Vision is in the vanguard, signing up 20,000 "TV shopping members" in its first year of airing infomercials. As these and other pioneers in Chinese direct-response television have learned, however, many obstacles remain, including the limited number of private telephones, low penetration of credit cards, and problems with delivery logistics in crowded cities such as Shanghai.[20]

With **teleshopping**, home-shopping channels such as QVC and the Home Shopping Network (HSN) take the infomercial concept one step further; the round-the-clock programming is *exclusively* dedicated to product demonstration and selling (see Exhibit 14-7). Worldwide, home shopping is a multibillion-dollar industry. The leading home shopping channels are also leveraging the Internet. For example, in addition to operating home shopping channels in the United States, China, Germany and Japan, HSN Inc. also offers an online shopping experience at www.hsn.com.

QVC's agreement with Rupert Murdoch's British Sky Broadcasting (BSkyB) satellite company enables it to reach Germany and the United Kingdom; it is also available in Japan. As QVC executive Francis Edwards explained, "European customers respond in different ways, though the basic premise and concept is the same. The type of jewelry is different. German consumers wouldn't buy 14-karat gold. They go for a higher karat. We can sell wine in Germany, but not in the U.S."[21] A number of local and regional teleshopping channels have sprung up in Europe. Germany's HOT (Home Order Television) is a joint venture with Quelle Schickedanz, a mail-order company. Sweden's TV-Shop is available in 15 European countries. Typically, Europeans are more discriminating than the average American teleshopping customer.

Industry observers expect the popularity of home shopping to increase during the next few years as **interactive television** (ITV or t-commerce) technology is introduced into more households. As the term implies, ITV allows television viewers to interact with the programming content that they are viewing. ITV has a greater presence in Europe than in the United States; in the United Kingdom alone, more than half of all pay-TV subscribers make use of ITV services. The remote control units provided by pay-TV service providers in the United Kingdom have a red button that viewers press to order products from home-shopping channels, choose different

Exhibit 14-7: QVC ("Quality, Value, and Convenience"), the home shopping channel, is available in 166 million homes worldwide. Shoppers can order jewelry, housewares, clothing, and other merchandise around the clock, both on QVC's cable TV channels and online.

The company recently introduced a new logo, redesigned its Web site, and brightened up its shipping boxes. In the new logo, the oversized "Q" is intended to signify a ribbon on a gift box. As Jeff Charney, chief marketing officer at QVC, noted, "The essence of the brand is the feeling you get when you open the package."
Source: Ian Waldie/Reuters/Landov Media.

---

[20]Jon Hilsenrath, "In China, a Taste of Buy-Me TV," *The New York Times* (November 17, 1996), Sec. 3, pp. 1, 11.
[21]Michelle Pentz, "Teleshopping Gets a Tryout in Europe but Faces Cultural and Legal Barriers," *The Wall Street Journal* (September 9, 1996), p. A8.

"Infomercials represent a powerful marketing vehicle that is not limited by geographic borders. U.S. manufacturers are in a fierce competition to create brands and infomercials that can create shelf space for products in consumers' homes on a global basis. Down the road, we'll be able to put a product simultaneously into the homes of 300 to 500 million people around the globe. Now *that's* powerful."[23]

Mark Hershorn, former President and CEO, E4L

TABLE 14-6 Expenditures for Outdoor Advertising as Percentage of Total Ad Spending

Country	Percentage
France	11.7%
United Kingdom	5.8
Spain	5.4
Italy	4.3
Canada	4.2
United States	4.0
Germany	4.0
Worldwide	5.9

camera angles during sports broadcasts, vote during audience participation shows such as "Big Brother," or order free samples of advertised products. In 2005, Diageo tested an interactive ad for Smirnoff vodka; after the first 60 seconds, viewers were required to press the button two more times to see the ad in its entirety. Comparing traditional TV ads with the new format, James Pennefather, Smirnoff brand manager for the United Kingdom, noted, "Interactive advertising is a lot more unproven and untested, and it is a calculated risk for us. We have to do this kind of thing to learn if it will be a success or not."[22]

Support Media

Traditional support media include transit and billboard advertising. As shown in Table 14-6, in most parts of the world, outdoor advertising is growing at a faster rate than the overall advertising market. Exhibit 14-8 illustrates how, as governments in China and other emerging markets add mass transportation systems and build and improve their highway infrastructures, advertisers are utilizing more indoor and outdoor posters and billboards to reach the buying public. Japan's population relies heavily on public transportation; the average Tokyo resident spends 70 minutes commuting to work. Consequently, spending on outdoor and transit advertising in Japan is much

Exhibit 14-8: The popularity of transit and billboard advertising is boosting the fortunes of JCDecaux, the outdoor advertising group. The market leader in Europe, the company operates in about 45 different countries. Outdoor advertising is experiencing explosive growth in China, where JCDecaux competes with Tom Group, Clear Media, and thousands of other local companies. This is especially true in large cities such as Beijing, Shanghai, and Guangzhou. The same trend is evident in Russia, especially in Moscow.
Source: Alamy Images.

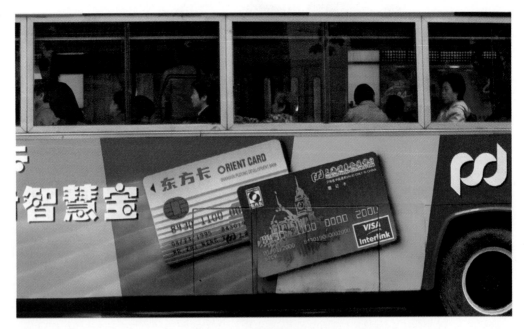

[22]Aaron O. Patrick, "Selling Vodka with an Interactive Twist," *The Wall Street Journal* (October 11, 2005), p. B3. See also "Europe Wants Its ITV," *Chain Store Age 77*, no. 7 (July 2001), pp. 76–78.
[23]Kim Cleland, "Infomercial Audience Crosses over Cultures," *Advertising Age International* (January 15, 1996), p. I8.

情熱を制す者が、ゲームを制す。

adidas

Exhibit 14-9: Advertising clutter is a problem in Japan's fiercely competitive marketplace, so advertisers and ad agencies must use creativity to stand out amid all the neon signs and electronic video billboards. In 2003, Omnicom Group's TBWA Japan developed this billboard featuring a vertical soccer game for Adidas. Players suspended from ropes kick a ball from side to side as pedestrians gather on the sidewalk below. *Source:* Itsuo Inouye/AP Wide World Photos.

higher than in most other countries; an estimated $4.4 billion annual expenditures on outdoor media amounts to as much as 12 percent of total ad spending (see Exhibit 14-9).[24]

Worldwide spending on outdoor advertising amounts to about 6 percent of total ad spending; in Europe, 6.4 percent of advertising spending is allocated to outdoor, compared with 4 percent in the United States. The two largest players in the industry are Texas-based Clear Channel Outdoor Holdings, with more than 900,000 outdoor and transit displays worldwide, and France's JCDecaux.

↪ CULTURE WATCH
Promoting Cigarettes in Indonesia

As noted in Chapter 13, tobacco advertising is banned in many parts of the world. One exception is Indonesia, the world's fifth largest market for cigarettes. Capitalizing on the size of the market opportunity and the absence of strict antismoking laws, global giants (e.g., Philip Morris International) and PT Gudang Garam, PT HM Sampoerna, and other local companies spend heavily on advertising and other forms of promotion. Two-thirds of adult males smoke in Indonesia, and cigarette brands are advertised on television, in print, on billboards, and on banners in public parks. The tobacco companies also sponsor sports events and rock concerts, where they distribute free samples.

There are some restrictions; for example, ads cannot show cigarettes or people in the act of smoking; however, the relatively unregulated environment results in a lot of clutter. This means that advertisers have to take creative risks in order to ensure that individual brand names stand out. Sampoerna's advertising agency, the Bates Asia unit of WPP Group, creates humorous ads that send up various aspects of Indonesian society, including police corruption. As Andrew White, an executive at Sampoerna, explained, "Indonesians have a very good sense of humor."

Do the ads work? Sampoerna's sales have been growing faster than the industry average. The company's light cigarettes are especially popular with Indonesia's middle class. Another indicator that the satirical ads work is the fact that competitors such as PT Djarum have also begun using humorous police-themed ads. Meanwhile, some companies continue to use more traditional male-oriented themes such as hunting and sports. The slogan for PT Gudang Garam is "The real man's taste."

Source: Tom Wright, "Indonesian Tobacco Ads Pack in Humor," *The Wall Street Journal* (March 8, 2007), p. B4.

---

[24]Geoffrey A. Fowler and Sebastian Moffett, "Adidas's Billboard Ads Give a Kick to Japanese Pedestrians," *The Wall Street Journal* (August 29, 2003), pp. B1, B4.

Sponsorship

Sponsorship is an increasingly popular form of marketing communications whereby a company pays a fee to have its name associated with a particular event, team or athletic association, or sports facility. Sponsorship combines elements of PR and sales promotion. From a PR perspective, sponsorship generally ensures that a corporate or brand name will be mentioned numerous times by on-air or public-address commentators. Large-scale events also draw considerable media attention that typically includes multiple mentions of the sponsoring company or brand in news reports or talk shows. Because event sponsorship typically provides numerous contact points with large numbers of people, it is a perfect vehicle for sampling and other sales promotion opportunities. As suggested by Exhibit 14-10, an Olympic Games or World Cup soccer sponsorship can help the Coca-Cola Company reach a global audience; sponsors are also drawn to events that reach national or regional audiences, such as professional team sports, car racing, hot air balloon competitions, rodeos, and music concerts.

Sony recently became an official U.S. sponsor of the NBA with the signing of a $10 million per year deal. One part of the deal calls for recordings by musicians on the Sony Music label—Aerosmith, Pearl Jam, and Mariah Carey, for example—to get priority consideration for air time during games. Hoping to achieve higher levels of brand awareness in the United States, Nokia sponsors the Sugar Bowl; Ericsson paid to have its name emblazoned on the new stadium where the Carolina Panthers football team plays. In 1997, Fila and Adidas engaged in a bidding war for sponsorship rights to the New York Yankees baseball team. Adidas eventually won a 10-year deal with a total value of $100 million; Adidas recently announced that the sponsorship would be extended through the 2013 season. Although the Adidas–Yankees deal set a record for sponsorship of an American sport, it was dwarfed by Nike's $200 million deal to sponsor the Brazilian national soccer team.

Sponsorship can be an effective component of an integrated marketing communications program. It can be used in countries where regulations limit the extent to which a company can use advertising or other forms of marketing communication. In China, for example, where tobacco advertising is prohibited, B.A.T. and Philip Morris spent tens of millions of dollars sponsoring events such as a Hong Kong–Beijing car rally and China's national soccer tournament. However, in 2005, Chinese authorities ratified the WHO's Framework Convention on Tobacco Controls. This means that all forms of tobacco promotion and sponsorship will be phased out by 2010. Sponsorship was also popular in the United Kingdom, where Benson & Hedges paid £4 million for a five-year contract to sponsor cricket matches and Rothman's spent £15 million annually to sponsor a Formula One racing team. However, to comply with the EU directive on tobacco advertising, tobacco sponsorship of all sports—including Formula One racing—has been phased out.

Exhibit 14-10: Neville Isdell, former chairman and CEO of the Coca-Cola Company, and International Olympic Committee (IOC) President Jacques Rogge shake hands on the Tower of the Great Wall outside the Chinese capital city of Beijing on August 1, 2005. Isdell and Rogge met in China to announce their partnership for the 2008 Olympic Games in Beijing.
Source: Jason Lee/Reuters/Landov Media.

Product Placement: Motion Pictures, Television Shows, and Public Figures

Companies can achieve a unique kind of exposure by using **product placement:** arranging for their products and brand names to appear in popular television programs, movies, and other types of performances. Marketers can also lend or donate products to celebrities or other public figures; the products get publicity when the celebrity appears in public using the product (see Exhibit 14-11). This tactic is especially popular with auto manufacturers and fashion designers and is often used in conjunction with popular annual television events such as the Academy Awards and the Grammys that garner media attention. For example, Celeste Atkinson is a lifestyle and entertainment manager for Audi. Her job is to create buzz by ensuring that vehicles such as the Audi A8L, the 12-cylinder A8L, and the S8 sports sedan figure in paparazzi photos.[25] For the premiere of *Superman Returns* in 2006, Atkinson arranged for 35 Audis to chauffer Kevin Spacey and other stars to the event.

Worldwide audience figures for a blockbuster movie hit can equal tens of millions of people. In many instances, product placements generate considerable media interest and result in additional publicity. Placements can be arranged in several different ways. Sometimes companies pay a fee for the placement; alternatively, a show's producers will write the product into the script in exchange for marketing and promotion support of the new production. A brand's owners can also strike a barter agreement whereby the company (Sony, for example) supplies the filmmakers with products that serve as props in exchange for licensing rights to the James Bond name in retail promotions (see Exhibit 14-12). Product placement agencies such as Propaganda, Hero Product Placement, and Eon function like talent agencies for products. As such, the agencies fulfill several important functions such as obtaining legal clearances from a brand's owners, promoting their clients' products to producers, and arranging for products to be delivered to a soundstage.

In the case of television placement, the blurring of advertising and programming content comes as companies increasingly question the effectiveness of traditional advertising. In fact, there is research evidence suggesting that a prominent product placement in a television program

Exhibit 14-11: Some global marketers are able to generate publicity for their brands from an unlikely source: Pope Benedict XVI. In this photo taken during the pope's installment mass, for example, His Holiness was wearing red shoes supplied by Italian shoemaker Geox. The pope also has been seen wearing Serengeti sunglasses, and he travels in a customized sport-utility vehicle with a bulletproof bubble that Mercedes-Benz donated to the Vatican. One global branding consultant notes that the pope's devoted following— one billion Catholics— makes a brand's association with him far more valuable than association with even an A-list celebrity.
Source: Jasper Juinen/AP Wide World Photos.

---

[25]Chris Woodyard, "Audi Works the Ropes to Put Stars in Its Cars," *USA Today* (February 22, 2007), p. 3B.

Exhibit 14-12: A legendary secret agent deserves a legendary car, so it is not surprising that the latest two James Bond films paired 007 with a new Aston Martin model, the DBS. Built by hand in England, Aston Martin cars offer "performance without compromise." The CoolBrands Council recently named Aston Martin "the UK's coolest brand."

Source: Starstock/Photoshot/Newscom.

leads to better recall than a traditional ad. Moreover, many viewers use digital video recorders such as TiVo to "zip" commercials; consumers are, in effect, ignoring commercials. This trend forces advertisers to find new ways to expose viewers to their messages. Sometimes called *branded entertainment*, the effective integration of products and brands with entertainment can be seen on the monster TV hit *American Idol*. The branded entertainment trend is so important that *Advertising Age* magazine sponsors an annual "Madison + Vine" conference to bring together key players from the advertising and Hollywood entertainment industries.

In addition to the effectiveness issue, prop masters and set dressers facing budget pressures are compelled to obtain props for free whenever possible. Moreover, as the cost of marketing major feature films has increased—it is not unusual for a studio to spend $20 to $30 million on marketing alone—studios are increasingly looking for partnerships to share the cost and attract the broadest possible viewing audience. Product placement raises an interesting issue for global marketers, especially consumer packaged-goods companies. This tactic virtually dictates a product standardization approach, because once footage of a scene is shot and incorporated into a movie or television program, the image of the product is "frozen" and will be seen without adaptation everywhere in the world.[26]

For better or for worse, product placements have even reached the world of live theater and opera: In fall 2002, a new Broadway production of Puccini's *La Bohème* was set in Paris circa

It's only until tourism picks up.

[26]Stephen J. Gould, Pola B. Gupta, and Sonja Grabner-Krauter, "Product Placements in Movies: A Cross-Cultural Analysis of Austrian, French and American Consumers' Attitudes Toward this Emerging, International Promotional Medium," *Journal of Advertising* 29, no. 4 (Winter 2000) pp. 41–58.

➔ STRATEGIC DECISION MAKING IN GLOBAL MARKETING
Products Star in Bond Films

The James Bond films are well known for integrating well-known brand names into the action. The 22 films featuring the suave British agent have grossed nearly $5 billion in worldwide ticket sales. However, the most recent films in the series, *Die Another Day, Casino Royale,* and *Quantum of Solace,* each cost nearly $100 million to produce. The series' popularity, plus the high cost of making the films, make Bond a perfect vehicle for showcasing products and brands.

Many companies are eager to be associated with a high-profile project like a Bond film. In 1996, when BMW introduced a sporty new Z3 convertible, it wanted to make a major global splash. BMW garnered extensive publicity by placing the Z3 in *GoldenEye,* the eighteenth James Bond film. In the film, gadget chief Q gives 007 a Z3 in place of his Aston Martin; the Z car also figured prominently in movie previews and print ads. BMW dealers were provided with "BMW 007 kits" that allowed prospective buyers to learn more about both the movie and the car before either was available. As *Advertising Age* observed, "BMW has shaken, not just stirred, the auto industry with unprecedented media exposure and awareness for the Z3 and BMW in the U.S."

Tomorrow Never Dies, the follow-up to *GoldenEye,* featured global brand promotional tie-ins worth an estimated $100 million. Ericsson, Heineken, Omega, Brioni, and Visa International all placed products in the film. Bond star Pierce Brosnan also appeared as Agent 007 in specially filmed television commercials. When *Die Another Day,* the twentieth installment in the series, was released at the end of 2002, BMW took a backseat to Ford. The U.S. automaker persuaded the producers to bring back the Aston Martin (the nameplate was owned by Ford at the time); Jaguars and the new Thunderbird were also prominent in the film.

The twenty-first Bond film, *Casino Royale,* featured actor Daniel Craig in the role of 007. To avoid a backlash from fans and marketing executives, the film's producers deliberately limited the number of official global partners in the film to six: Sony Electronics, Sony Ericsson, Omega, Heineken, Ford, and Smirnoff. As Myles Romero, Ford's global brand entertainment director, noted, "It's great for brand awareness. The film takes us where we don't have marketing."

The producers' decision to cast Craig as the sixth Bond proved to be a brilliant choice. *Casino Royale* raked in nearly $600 million at the box office, making it the number one money-maker in the franchise. For the next installment, 2008's *Quantum of Solace,* several companies hitched their brands to Bond for the first time. These included Coke Zero and Avon. Speaking of Coke Zero, Derk Hendriksen explained, "We're in more than 100 markets. We thought the tie-in would be very appropriate for two irreverent and global personalities." For its part, Avon coordinated the launch of Bond Girl 007 Fragrance with the film's release. Tracy Haffner, global vice president for marketing, called the film "a great platform to develop a beautiful fragrance and connect with women worldwide."

Sources: Theresa Howard, "Brands Cozy Up to Bond," *USA Today* (October 20, 2008), p. 3B; Emiko Terazono, "Brand New Bond has a License to Sell," *Financial Times* (November 14, 2006), p. 10; Tim Burt, "His Name's Bond, and He's Been Licensed to Sell," *Financial Times* (October 5–6, 2002), p. 22; Jon Rappoport, "BMW Z3," *Advertising Age* (June 24, 1996), p. S37.

1957. The stage set included billboards for luxury pen maker Montblanc and Piper-Heidsieck champagne; during a crowd scene at Café Momus, Piper-Heidsieck was served. Some industry observers warn of a backlash. Ethical concerns are sometimes raised when controversial products such as cigarettes are featured prominently or glamorized. When advertising appears in conventional forms such as broadcast commercials, most consumers are aware of the fact that they are being exposed to an ad. This is not necessarily the case with product placement; in effect, viewers are being marketed to subliminally without their consent. What constitutes proper use of product placement? As Joe Uva, an executive of Omnicom's media planning group, noted, "It shouldn't be forced; it shouldn't be intrusive. If people say 'It's a sell out, it's product placement,' it didn't work." Eugene Secunda, a media studies professor at New York University, is skeptical. "I think it's a very dangerous plan. The more you get the audience to distrust the content of your programming, to look at it with suspicion in terms of your real agenda, the less likely they are to be responsive to the message because they're going to be looking at everything cynically and with resistance."[27]

---

[27]Richard Tompkins, "How Hollywood Brings Brands into Your Home," *Financial Times* (November 5, 2002), p. 15.

Summary

Sales promotion is any paid, short-term communication program that adds tangible value to a product or brand. **Consumer sales promotions** are targeted at ultimate consumers; **trade sales promotions** are used in business-to-business marketing. **Sampling** gives prospective customers a chance to try a product or service at no cost. A **coupon** is a certificate that entitles the bearer to a price reduction or other value-enhancing consideration when purchasing a product or service.

Personal selling is face-to-face communication between a prospective buyer and a company representative. The **Strategic/Consultative Selling Model** that is widely used in the United States is also being utilized worldwide. The model's five strategic steps call for developing a **personal selling philosophy**, a **relationship strategy**, a **product strategy**, a **customer strategy**, and a **presentation strategy**. The six steps in the **presentation plan** are approach; presentation; demonstration; negotiation; close; and servicing the sale. Successful global selling may require adaptation of one or more steps in the presentation plan. An additional consideration in global selling is the composition of the sales force, which may include **expatriates**, host-country natives, or **sales agents**.

Several other forms of communication can be used in global marketing. These include **direct marketing**, a measurable system that uses one or more media to start or complete a sale. **One-to-one marketing** is an updated approach to direct marketing that calls for treating each customer in a distinct way based on his or her previous purchase history or past interactions with the company. **Direct mail**, **catalogs**, **infomercials**, **teleshopping**, and **interactive television** are some of the direct marketing tools that have been successfully used on a global basis. Global marketers frequently try to place their products in blockbuster movies that will reach global audiences. **Sponsorships** and **product placement** are also becoming vital communication tools that can be used on a global basis.

Discussion Questions

1. Briefly review how the main tools of sales promotion (e.g., sampling and couponing) can be used in global markets. What issues and problems can arise in different country markets?
2. What potential environmental challenges must be taken into account by a company that uses personal selling as a promotional tool outside the home country?
3. Identify the six steps in the Strategic/Consultative Selling Model and the outlined six-step presentation plan. Do these steps have global applicability or are they used only for selling in the home-country market? What special challenges face a sales representative outside his or her home country?
4. How does management's orientation (e.g., ethnocentric, polycentric, or regiocentric) correlate with decisions about sales force nationality? What other factors affect sales force composition?
5. Procter & Gamble (P&G) has a "golden store" program in Mexico and other emerging markets. P&G's representatives visit participating stores to tidy display areas and arrange promotional material in prominent places. At first, P&G, used its own manufacturer's sales force; now it relies on independent agents who buy inventory (paying in advance) and then resell the items to shopkeepers. Is this approach in line with the recommendations in Table 14-4?
6. What role does direct marketing have in a global company's promotion mix? Name three companies that have successfully used direct mail or other forms of direct-response advertising.
7. Why are infomercials, sponsorship, and product placement growing in importance for global marketers?

Lenovo is also using other sports to raise its profile. For example, Lenovo has joined forces with the National Basketball Association (NBA) by becoming the "Official PC Partner of the NBA." The opportunity arose when Dell, which had a previous agreement with the NBA, chose not to renew it. Also, Brazilian soccer star Ronaldinho signed a one-year contract to serve as Lenovo's global brand ambassador.

Some observers have suggested that Lenovo is moving too quickly to distance itself from the IBM brand name. For example, University of Pennsylvania Professor David Reibstein says, "What Lenovo is trying to do is get itself established with credibility in this market, but it feels like a premature transition. Lenovo may be strong in China, but it is a non-name in the West." Deepak Advani, Lenovo's chief marketing officer, responds by noting, "The IBM brand is a double-edged sword for us. It gives customers a sense of comfort and safety and provides some instant credibility. But the longer we hold on to a well-established brand like IBM, the more difficult it becomes for us to be known as Lenovo."

At least one industry analyst applauds the rebranding effort. Simon Yates, an analyst with technology consultancy Forrester Research, says, "The IBM brand says 'third place finisher, high-priced.' Lenovo needs to get rid of the IBM brand quickly because it came with a lot of baggage. It's not appealing to the market they want to grab in the future: small business. The ThinkPad has a reputation for industrial strength and being IT friendly, but as an IBM product it was expensive. Now people can get it at close to Dell prices."

Today, Lenovo's headquarters are in the United States, although most of its employees are in China. While the rebranding effort is ongoing, Amelio faces additional challenges, such as bridging cultural differences among the company's far-flung employees and maintaining profitability despite a worldwide slow-down in PC sales. In a recent interview with the *Financial Times*, a reporter asked Amelio, "How hard has it been to bring together the Chinese and U.S. parts of the company?" Amelio responded as follows:

I'll give you an example. We had two design teams from the east and west . . . and they were working well together but all of a sudden the meetings stopped dead, they weren't communicating effectively. Finally someone said, "Let's look at this one word that somebody used when it seemed like it stopped the meeting. That one word was, we needed to have a 'common' design element across our two different design languages. Well, when it's translated into Mandarin, 'common' means 'uninteresting' and 'boring.'"

Amelio also embarked on a $100 million restructuring program that resulted in an 11 percent workforce reduction. Substantial investment is also being made in sales and distribution channels. Will the result be market success? As one observer noted, "If you look at HP and Compaq, they took four or five years to integrate a Texas culture and a California culture. When you try to merge a U.S. company and a Chinese company, it is going to take a lot longer to make it successful."

Case 14-1 Discussion Questions

1. In the third quarter of 2008, Lenovo posted a loss of nearly $100 million. Do you think that Olympic sponsorships pay off for companies such as Lenovo?
2. What is the biggest global marketing challenge facing Lenovo today?
3. In 2009, as his three-year contract came to an end, Bill Amelio resigned as president and CEO of Lenovo. What nationality will the new chief executive likely be?

Sources: Richard Waters and Chrystia Freeland, "View from the Top," *Financial Times* (August 3, 2007), p. 8; Jane Spencer and Geoffrey A. Fowler, "Lenovo Goes for Its Own Olympic Medal," *The Wall Street Journal* (March 27, 2007), p. B4; Justine Lau and Mure Dickie, "Lenovo Shows How China Is Able to Take on the World," *Financial Times* (November 9, 2006), p. 19; Jane Spencer, "Lenovo Takes a Shot at Building Brand Awareness with NBA Deal," *The Wall Street Journal* (October 24, 2006), p. B4; Evan Ramstad, "Lenovo Still Chewing on Its Byte of IBM," *The Wall Street Journal* (May 11, 2006), p. B4; Glenn Rifkin and Jenna Smith, "Quickly Erasing 'I' and 'B' and 'M,'" *The New York Times* (April 12, 2006), p. C9; Steve Lohr, "Lenovo Evolves with Its IBM PC Unit in Tow," *The New York Times* (August 30, 2005), p. C1.

Management at a large manufacturer located in Gothenburg, in the Swedish state of Västra Götaland County, have decided to improve productivity at one of its subsidiaries by investing several million krona in state-of-the-art production equipment. As word circulated about the planned investment, vendors in Asia, Europe, and North America put together proposals.

One such vendor was a Singaporean company that had an excellent global reputation for quality products and service. Management at the Singaporean firm reviewed the size of the order and decided to bypass its regular Northern European representative, a Dutchman, and send its international sales manager instead. The following describes what took place.

The sales manager is a Singaporean Chinese, and when he arrived in Gothenburg he checked into the Elite Plaza Hotel, in the center of the city. He had some difficulty in discovering exactly who he needed to speak to at the Swedish firm. In fact it seemed that six or seven people would be involved in the purchasing decision.

After a few days without any success he called the Northern European representative to see if he could provide him with any tips on what to do next. Understandably the representative was a little frosty, feeling that the business opportunity had been his and it had been usurped by the international sales manager. Nonetheless he agreed to meet him at the hotel and provide whatever help he could in arranging a meeting. The representative did tell him, however, that the purchasing manager was the key individual, but that it was the Swedish way for decisions to be made by consensus and therefore several people would be involved in the decision.

The representative's advice ran somewhat as follows:

1. "If you are planning to do business here in Sweden you should really make your appointments at least two weeks in advance."
2. "It is early March; this is one of the popular times that the Swedish go on holiday. You'll be lucky to be able to organize a meeting at this time of the year because not everyone that needs to be involved will be at work."
3. "You have got the advantage that you know your business. In Sweden they like people with knowledge and experience. They are very detail orientated. I hope that you've got your presentation well planned and organized."
4. "Don't expect great things out of the first meeting; it is probably going to be very low key at least that is my experience. They will be very matter of fact; just don't expect them to make a decision at the first meeting. They will be sizing you up. They'll be looking at our company and at what you are saying. I would expect you to have to attend several meetings before all the details are covered and you've answered any questions they might have."
5. "I expect you've got an expensive and impressive gift for the top man in the business. I would not bother if I were you. Don't channel all your energies into one person. In Sweden consensus is the way they prefer to make their decisions. In fact ultimately the decisions might fall to the middle managers, who will have to actually implement the improvements."
6. "Try to remain calm, cool, collected, and controlled. They are not ones to show a great deal of emotion during negotiations. I know we are used to making quick decisions in our company, but don't try and push them; they'll want to listen to everyone's point of view, and they'll value those views, so stay calm because you might find the process very frustrating."
7. "Don't try and play one of the managers or departments against one another. Swedish companies are very open; information flows well and there is less social distance between the managers in the hierarchy. So watch what you say to one that you wouldn't want any of the others to hear."

The Presentation

The international sales manager still wanted to take the lead, but was happy for the Northern European representative to try and set up a meeting. The purchasing manager finally agreed to meet him for 10 minutes in a café close to the head office. The international sales manager arrived early, having been warned that punctuality is of enormous importance in Sweden and that lateness is indefensible. He had carefully chosen a table near the window, with two seats. Promptly, at 11 A.M., the Swedish purchasing manager arrived, along with four other people. There were a few moments of embarrassment as tables were switched and chairs pulled up. They had only just seated themselves when their mobiles began to ring. So far they had not even introduced themselves.

It was the international sales manager's nature to be cautious. He liked to do business with the right person, he was happy to take things slowly and to spend time forging a good relationship and showing what he could do. This situation did not suit him at all. There were five of them and he was struggling to understand who was who.

The meeting lasted barely five minutes. They agreed to arrange a meeting for the day after tomorrow. In his normal way, the international sales manager asked the purchasing manager directly, "Would you care to have dinner tonight or not?" The reply was a no and the Singaporean laughed and simply added, "I will see you in two days then."

An hour or so later, the Swedish purchasing manager telephoned the Singaporean, "I apologize if I may have sounded rude when I turned down your offer of dinner tonight. I can now make it. Shall we say I'll meet you in the hotel restaurant at 7?"

The Singaporean was delighted, although he thought it a little early to be sitting down for an evening meal. He let the Swedish buyer choose the dish; it was a huge plate of meat and potatoes, with beer and wine. No matter how many times he tried to steer the conversation in the direction of the order, the buyer did not seem to be happy to talk about it very much and it was obvious that no firm decisions were going to be made. He found the Swede quite direct and in his own opinion a little rude and aggressive. There were long periods of silence, which he did not understand. The Swede's body language was quite hard for him to read; he often appeared disinterested and aloof. He also did not have a great sense of humor. The Singaporean was also shocked when the Swede asked him to e-mail him all the points that he had brought up. It was something else that he could not quite understand.

The evening went off fairly well, although the Singaporean did not feel that he had actually made any great progress. After saying goodnight, the Singaporean went up to his room and decided to telephone the Dutch representative, who was by now back at his home in Amsterdam.

"So you met him then? How did it go?" asked the Dutchman.

"I'm not sure. I found him abrupt and he was silent for what seemed like ages. I'm not sure I know how to read him. Am I missing something?" replied the Singaporean.

"They are plain speakers; directness is a prized asset, and as for the silence that's fairly common too. It doesn't mean they are disinterested, they just don't always think it is necessary to speak."

"So why did he ask me to write down everything that we'd talked about?" queried the Singaporean.

"They put more emphasis on the written than the spoken word. They prefer you to follow things up in writing." The Dutchman explained.

The Singaporean spent the next hour composing an e-mail. He thought about sending it immediately, but decided it would be better to send it in the morning. He received a curt but courteous reply, but along with it was an invitation to make his presentation that very afternoon at 4.

Although the Singaporean had spoken to large crowds of workers, he had also attended awards ceremonies and was used to public speaking. He was a little taken aback when he was ushered into a large meeting room with no fewer than 12 people sitting around a large, oval table. He was invited to make his presentation, which he made in a measured and considered way, handing out copies of his proposals and details of his company. As he sat down, ready to take questions, the purchasing manager slid an agenda in front of him. They had obviously done quite a lot of homework on this and against each agenda point was someone's name. The meeting went on for three hours. There was little interruption when someone had the floor, and each time someone around the table raised their hand to attract the attention of the purchasing manager, who was acting as the chair, the Singaporean's heart sank that there would be more questions and more debate. There seemed to be no emotion; everything was carefully debated, everyone had a point of view, and nobody seemed to make a point without referring to facts, figures, and tables. The meeting broke up with a series of handshakes and a promise of a debriefing meeting and, perhaps, a decision the following day. In the meantime the purchasing manager offered to walk to a nearby bar with the Singaporean.

They walked across Gustaf Adolf's square and there was a statue standing outside the Gothenburg City Hall.

"That's Gustaf II Adolf," the Swede said.

"Who?" replied the Singaporean

"He was a solider, a statesman, and our king. He founded the postal service, newspapers, and universities. He is the father of the modern Swedish state," replied the Swede.

"Never heard of him," dismissed the Singaporean.

This was the last time the Singaporean ever saw the purchasing manager. The Singaporean company won the contract, but it was the Dutchman who managed to secure the signatures on the contract.

Discussion Questions

1. What impression do you think the international sales manager made on the purchasing manager?
2. How would you critique the quality of the communication between all parties in this case?
3. Is a high-context culture or a low-context culture at work in this case? Explain your answer.

Sources: The Local—Sweden's News in English, www.thelocal.se; Kwintessential, www.kwintessential.co.uk; World Business Culture, www.worldbusinessculture.com; Embassy of Sweden (Singapore), www. swedenabroad.com.

Global Marketing and the Digital Revolution

Case 15-1
Global Marketers Discover Social Media

What do Chris Anderson, Sir Richard Branson, George Colony, and Tony Hsieh have in common? Besides being influential and successful business leaders, thinkers, and public figures, they all use the micro-blogging Web site known as Twitter. Twitter is one of many social media Web sites that have burst onto the scene and quickly gone global within the span of just a few short years. Other popular social networking Web sites include Facebook, MySpace, and YouTube; LinkedIn is a social network for professionals. These sites, which are sometimes collectively referred to as Web 2.0, enable individuals and companies to interact using the Internet. Twitter users post short messages ("tweets") of 140 characters or less from computers and mobile devices such as cell phones, BlackBerries, and iPods. Once an individual has signed up for Twitter, he or she can attract "followers" who read the tweets. So, how, exactly, are global marketers using Web 2.0? To help answer that question, many companies are turning to social media consultancies for help in navigating the new digital landscape (see Exhibit 15-1). To find out more, turn to Case 15-1 at the end of the chapter.

The digital revolution is driving the creation of new companies, industries, and markets in all parts of the world. It is also contributing to the transformation and, in some cases, destruction of companies, industries, and markets. In short, the revolution is dramatically

Exhibit 15-1: Nathan Wright and Hillary Brown are social media strategists at Lava Row, a consultancy based in Des Moines, Iowa. Nathan and Hillary help companies of all sizes formulate and implement online engagement strategies. At a typical workshop, the partners explain best practices that illustrate how companies should behave and participate within online social channels and what to expect in terms of ROI.
Source: Garrett Cornelison.

transforming the world in which we live. As the revolution gains traction and picks up speed, global marketers will be forced to adapt to an evolutionary world in which new social media tools such as Twitter play an important role.

This chapter appears after the five-chapter sequence devoted to the marketing mix. Why? Because all the elements of the marketing mix—the 4Ps—converge in the world of Internet connectivity and commerce. For example, the product "P" includes Google, Twitter, Wikipedia, and the myriad other Web sites that can be accessed worldwide. The Web also functions as a distribution channel, and a very efficient one at that. Case in point: Apple's iTunes, the digital-only entertainment retailer that has rewritten the rules of music and film distribution. The Internet is also a communication channel. Today, virtually every company and organization has a presence in the online space. The Internet can be used as an advertising channel, as a PR tool, as a means for running a contest or sales promotion, and as support for the personal selling effort. Finally, there is price. Comparison-shopping Web sites make it easy to check and compare prices for products and services. Moreover, the marginal cost of warehousing and distributing digitized products—music files, for example—is practically nothing. This has led to some interesting pricing strategy experiments. For example, Radiohead, the innovative rock band from Oxford, England, harnessed the efficiency of the Web to offer downloads of *In Rainbows* for free.

We begin by briefly reviewing the key innovations that served as precursors to the digital revolution. In the next two sections, convergence, the disruptive nature of Internet technology, and their effects on global companies are discussed. Next, key e-commerce issues that face global marketers are examined and a typology of Web site categories is introduced. The discussion continues with an overview of Web site design issues as they pertain to global marketing. The final section of the chapter examines some of the new products and services made possible by the digital revolution.

THE DIGITAL REVOLUTION: A BRIEF HISTORY

The **digital revolution** is a paradigm shift resulting from technological advances that allow for the digitization (i.e., conversion to binary code) of analog sources of information, sounds, and images. The origins of the digital revolution can be traced back to the mid-twentieth century. Over a five-year period between 1937 and 1942, John Vincent Atanasoff and Clifford Berry developed the world's first electromechanical digital computer at Iowa State University. The Atanasoff-Berry Computer (ABC) incorporated several major innovations in computing including the use of binary arithmetic, regenerative memory, parallel processing, and separation of the memory and computing functions.

In 1947, William Shockley and two colleagues at AT&T's Bell Laboratories invented a "solid state amplifier," or **transistor**, as it became known. This was a critical innovation because the vacuum tubes used in computers and electronics products at that time were large, consumed a large amount of power, and generated a great deal of heat. Shockley and collaborators John Bardeen and William Brattain were awarded the Nobel Prize in physics in 1956 for their invention.

In 1948, a Bell Labs researcher named Claude Shannon wrote a technical report titled "A Mathematical Theory of Communication" in which he proposed that all information media could be encoded in *binary digits*, or bits. Earlier, in 1940, Shannon had argued in his doctoral dissertation that the logical values "true" and "false" could be denoted by "1" and "0," respectively, and that streams of 1s and 0s could transmit media over a wire.

In the mid-1950s, Sony licensed the transistor from Bell Labs; Sony engineers boosted the yield of the transistor and created the market for transistor radios. The sound was "lo-fi" but the devices were portable and stylish, which is what consumers—especially teenagers—wanted. Also during the 1950s, Robert Noyce and Jack Kilby independently invented the silicon chip (also known as the **integrated circuit** or IC).[1] In essence, the IC put the various parts of an electrical circuit—including resistors, diodes, and capacitors—on a single piece of material. The IC gave the transistor its modern form and allowed its power to be harnessed in a reliable, low-cost way.

The IC and the concept of binary code permitted the development of the **personal computer (PC)**, a compact, affordable device whose appearance marked the next phase of the digital revolution. Many of the events and people associated with this era have become the stuff of legend. Some observers credit Alan Kay with research that permitted the development of the first PCs. During the 1970s, Kay was director of the Learning Research Group at the Xerox Palo Alto Research Center (PARC). Then, between 1981 and 1983, Kay worked at Atari which, along with other pioneering PC companies such as Osborne and Commodore, has long since disappeared from the scene.

Kay's work at Xerox PARC had a strong impact on Steve Jobs who, with partner Steve Wozniak, started Apple Computer in a garage in the late 1970s. The company's Apple II is widely regarded as the first "true" PC; the Apple II's popularity received a big boost in 1979 when a spreadsheet program known as VisiCalc was introduced. A computer **spreadsheet** is an electronic ledger that automatically calculates the effect of a change to one figure on other figures across rows and down columns; previously, these changes had to be done manually. While such powerful, time-saving functionality is taken for granted today, VisiCalc was a true milestone in the digital revolution.[2]

IBM brought its first PC to market in 1981; Bill Gates initially declined an offer to create an **operating system**—the software code that provides basic instructions—for IBM's new machine. Gates later changed his mind and developed the Microsoft Disk Operating System (MS-DOS). In 1984, Apple introduced the revolutionary Macintosh, with its user-friendly graphical interface and point-and-click mouse. A few years, later, Microsoft replaced MS-DOS with Windows. Meanwhile, component manufacturers were innovating as well; Intel began marketing the 286 microprocessor in 1982. This was followed in quick succession by the 386 and 486 versions; in 1993, Intel unveiled the Pentium.

The rise of the Internet and the World Wide Web marks the next phase of the digital revolution. The Internet's origins can be traced back to an initiative by the **Defense Advanced Research Projects Agency (DARPA)**, which created a computer network that could maintain lines of communication in the event of a war. In 1969, the ARPANET was unveiled; this was a network linking computer research centers at colleges and universities. E-mail within a computer network was made possible by the creation of a file-transfer program in 1972. There was a problem, however; it was not possible to send e-mail that was created on one network to a computer on a different network. This problem was solved the following year when Vinton Cerf and Robert Kahn created a software framework known as TCP/IP ("Transmission Control Protocol/Internet Protocol"). Launched in 1973, this cross-network protocol paved the way for a "network of networks," and the **Internet** was born (see Exhibit 15-2).

The ability to exchange e-mail messages on the Internet had a revolutionary impact on society, as technology guru Stewart Brand noted in the mid-1980s:

> Marshall McLuhan used to remark, "Gutenberg made everybody a reader. Xerox made everybody a publisher." Personal computers are making everybody an author. E-mail, word processing programs that make revising as easy as thinking, and laser printers collapse the whole writing-publishing-distributing process into one event controlled entirely by the individual. If, as alleged, the only real freedom of the press is to own one, the fullest realization of the First Amendment is being accomplished by technology, not politics.[3]

Of course, the Internet revolution does not end with the advent of e-mail. More innovations were yet to come. In 1990, a software consultant named Tim Berners-Lee invented the **uniform**

---

[1]Noyce founded Fairchild Semiconductor and later, Intel. His Intel cofounder was Gordon Moore, who is famous for formulating "Moore's Law," according to which computer power doubles every 18 months. Kilby was the founder of Texas Instruments. See Evan Ramstad, "At the End of an Era, Two Tech Pioneers Are Remembered," *The Wall Street Journal* (August 15, 2005), p. B1.

[2]For more on the development of VisiCalc, see Dan Bricklin, "Natural Born Entrepreneur," *Harvard Business Review* 79, no. 8 (September 2001), pp. 53–59.

[3]Stewart Brand, *The Media Lab: Inventing the Future at MIT* (New York: Penguin Books, 1988), p. 253.

Exhibit 15-2: Internet pioneers Bob Khan and Vint Cerf were among those in attendance at the first Internet Governance Forum (IGF) held in Athens, Greece, in 2006. The IGF will guide "the development and application by governments, the private sector, and civil society, in their respective roles, of shared principles, norms, rules, decision-making procedures, and programs that shape the evolution and use of the Internet." Many in the global Internet community are concerned about the inclusion of the word "governments" in this statement.
Source: Louisa Gouliamaki/Getty Images, Inc. AFP.

resource locator (URL), an Internet site's address on the World Wide Web; **hypertext markup language (HTML)**, a format language that controls the appearance of Web pages; and **hypertext transfer protocol (http)**, which enables hypertext files to be transferred across the Internet.[4] These innovations allowed Web sites to be linked and visually rich content to be posted and accessed. In short, Berners-Lee is the father of the **World Wide Web**.

In the mid-1990s, a computer scientist at the University of Illinois named Marc Andreesen developed a Web browser; called Mosaic, it combined images and words together on the same screen and allowed users to search and view resources on the Web. Andreesen joined forces with Jim Clark, one of the founders of Silicon Graphics, to form Mosaic Communications. Renamed Netscape Communications, the company became one of the brightest stars in the dot-com era as commercial demand for the Netscape browser software exploded. As Thomas L. Friedman notes, "Marc Andreessen did not invent the Internet, but he did as much as any single person to bring it alive and popularize it."[5]

Within five years of the Web's debut, the number of users increased from 600,000 to 40 million. In the following decade, search engines such as Yahoo! and Google were created and encryption and security features were built into the Web. Search engines have also been dramatically improved; for example, Google's novel "page ranking" superseded an earlier technology known as "link analysis." Today Google has a commanding 64 percent share of the U.S. search market; second-place Yahoo! has a 20 percent share. Surprisingly, Microsoft has not been a major player in search. To remedy the situation, in 2009 the software giant unveiled Bing. The service is designed to provide a superior search experience in shopping, travel, health, and local businesses.

Today, more than 1.5 billion people—one-quarter of the world's population—are using the Internet. The technology's powerful capabilities and increasing importance have resulted in a backlash that manifests itself in various ways. For example, the Chinese government, alarmed by the free flow of information across the Internet, closely monitors the content on Web sites that its citizens access. In addition, policymakers in some countries are concerned about U.S. control of the Internet. The nonprofit Internet Corporation for Assigned Names and Numbers (Icann) is based in Marina del Ray, California. Icann maintains a database of Web addresses, approves new suffixes for Web addresses (e.g., .info and .tv) and performs other behind-the-scenes procedures

"There are certain limitations that are part of the network, and we are struggling with that. We're worried that in the zeal to address localization that people will not be able to communicate any more. If someone gives you a business card with the e-mail address in Chinese, what are you to do?"[6]
Vinton G. Cerf, Internet pioneer and Chairman, Icann

---

[4]Hypertext is any text that contains links to other documents.
[5]Thomas L. Friedman, *The World Is Flat* (New York: Farrar, Straus and Giroux, 2005), p. 58.
[6]John Markoff, "Control the Internet? A Futile Pursuit, Some Say," *The New York Times* (November 24, 2005), p. C4.

that are critical for keeping the Internet functioning properly. Icann's advisory body includes international members, but the U.S. Department of Commerce retains veto power over all decisions. For example, after Icann tentatively approved the domain name .xxx for pornography sites, the Department of Commerce blocked the decision.

Recently, China, India, Brazil, and the EU have taken the position that, because the Internet is global, no single country should be in control. Accordingly, these nations are seeking to have

↔ CULTURE WATCH
South Korea and France Embrace the Digital Revolution

According to a recent "digital opportunity index" published by the United Nations, South Korea leads the world in providing its citizens with access to information and communications technologies (ICT). The country's high-tech infrastructure takes a variety of forms. The availability of broadband Internet connections is one example. In South Korea, 90 percent of households are broadband subscribers.

As Stephen Ward, a consultant with Deloitte, explains, "Koreans tend to be early adopters of technology and, more significantly, are fast followers. They are always conscious of the need not to get left behind by the Japanese and the young have a great desire to conform with the gadget-carrying norm of their peers" (see Exhibit 15-3). Ninety percent of Koreans in their teens and early 20s regularly log on to Cyworld ("Cyber World"), South Korea's leading social network site. Subscribers create virtual worlds and blog in a rich 3-D environment. Although the site is free, users pay for virtual furniture, BGM (BackGroundMusic), and other items to customize their "rooms." Cyworld is extremely profitable for host SK Communications, a unit of SK Telecom.

The desire for speed also seems to be engrained in South Korea's culture; as one university student noted, Koreans tend to be "fast, fast, and fast." To bring the speed, South Korea's government is committing significant financial resources. It budgeted $50 billion in an effort to link 80 major cities and towns via broadband; moreover, South Korea's network is extremely fast, offering standard speeds of up to 100 megabits per second (Mbps). By comparison, much of Europe's broadband network currently operates at less than 1 Mbps; in the United States, the average speed is 5 Mbps. Korea's Communication Commission plans to boost the network's speed to 1 gigabit per second (Gbps) by 2012.

However, South Korea's digital future includes much more than simply broadband connections. For example, policymakers are aggressively pursuing applications for radio frequency identification tags (RFID); the South Korean government is spending nearly $300 million to build an RFID research center. This initiative is the source of controversy; some observers warn about possible abuses from the invasion of privacy.

The RFID center will be part of an even more ambitious effort: the construction of a ubiquitous city on a 1,500-acre man-made island near the Incheon Free Economic Zone. What makes New Songdo City a "ubiquitous city" (U-city for short)? For one

thing, all major information systems—commercial, residential, and government—share data, and computers are designed into all buildings. With an estimated price tag of $25 billion, New Songdo City is scheduled for completion in 2014. Complementing its high-tech features will be high-touch elements inspired by the world's major cities. These elements include a central park (inspired by New York) and a canal system similar to that in Venice.

John Kim is in charge of planning for the U-city, which he says will exemplify "U-life." Kim explains, "U-life will become its own brand, its own lifestyle." Residents will be able to communicate via video conferencing and everyone will have access to video on demand. Smart-card house keys will also function as payment devices for subways, parking meters, movie tickets, and myriad other uses. The challenge now is to make sure that all Koreans—even those who don't live in U-city—can benefit from the development's innovations.

Korea is not alone in embracing the digital future. In France, for example, industry deregulation has resulted in vastly improved broadband service for consumers. The changes have shaken up France Telecom and other established firms and paved the way for newcomers such as Iliad, a company that offers a "triple play" service package. Carrying the brand name Free, the service includes broadband Internet service at 24 Mbps, 81 television channels, and Internet telephone service. The price? €29.95 per month—about $36. As Illiad chief executive Michaël Bouzoba says, "Entrepreneurship exists in France, but we're a rare example. I also say to French politicians, 'Stop focusing on national champions. Innovation's not coming from national champions.'" An analyst at eMarketer noted, "France's quick shift to broadband and the oncoming storm of Internet calling and digital television make it the country to watch as a model of market transformation."

Sources: Leila Abboud, "French Rivals Wire Nation Together," *The Wall Street Journal* (February 7, 2008), p. B3; Tom Braithwaite, "The Young Guns of Broadband," *Financial Times* (May 29, 2006), p. 8; Leila Abboud, "How France Became a Leader in Offering Faster Broadband," *The Wall Street Journal* (March 28, 2006), pp. B1, B4; Pamela Licalzi O'Connell, "Korea's High-Tech Utopia, Where Everything Is Observed," *The New York Times* (October 5, 2005), p. 6; Andrew Ward, "Where High-Speed Access Is Going Mainstream," *Financial Times FT-IT Review: Next-Generation Broadband* (June 9, 2004), p. 4; Jim Hopkins, "Other Nations Zip by USA in High-Speed Net Race," *USA Today* (January 19, 2004), pp. 1B, 2B.

Exhibit 15-3: South Koreans in traditional scholar costumes use laptop computers at the digital version of a state examination at Sungkyunkwan University in Seoul. The event commemorates the traditional means for selecting government officers during the Chosun Dynasty, which dates back to the fourteenth century. Several hundred participants competed by composing Korean, Chinese, and English poems; demonstrating foreign language skills; and playing Internet games.
Source: Kim Kyang-Hoon/Reuters/Landov Media.

the United Nations assume a role in Internet governance.[7] Privacy is another issue. As companies become more adept at using the Internet to gather, store, and access information about customers, privacy issues are becoming a focal point of concern among policymakers and the general public. In the EU, for example, a privacy protection directive was established in 1995; in 2002, the EU adopted a privacy and electronic communications directive.

CONVERGENCE

The digital revolution is causing dramatic changes in industry structure. **Convergence** is a term that refers to the coming together of previously separate industries and product categories (see Figure 15-1). New technologies affect the business sector(s) in which a company competes. What business is Sony in? Originally, Sony was a consumer electronics company best known for innovative products such as transistor radios, Trinitron televisions, VCRs and other stereo components, and the Walkman line of personal music players. Then, Sony entered new businesses by acquiring a record company and a motion picture studio. These acquisitions themselves did not represent convergence, because they occurred in the early days of the digital revolution. Motion pictures, recorded music, and consumer electronics were still separate industries. Today, however, Sony is in the "bits" business: Its core businesses incorporate digital technology and involve digitizing and distributing sound, images, and data. Now, Sony's competitors include Dell (computers and consumer electronics), Kodak (digital cameras), and Nokia (cell phones).

What kind of challenges does convergence present? Consider the challenges facing Kodak, the undisputed leader in photography-related products for more than a century. The company has been struggling to remake its business model as its sales of digital-related products grew from zero to $1 billion in 5 years (see Case 16-2). Because of convergence, Kodak's competitors include companies such as Dell and Hewlett-Packard. However, competition also comes from the telecommunications industry. The cell phone camera was invented in 1997; a key benefit was the ability to download digital photos from the camera and post them on the Web or e-mail them to friends. Ironically, Motorola, a key player in the cell phone business, could have been one of the first companies to market with a cell phone camera. However, management's attention

---

[7]Christopher Rhoads, "EU, Developing Nations Challenge U.S. Control of Internet," *The Wall Street Journal* (October 25, 2005), pp. B1, B2. See also "A Free Internet," *Financial Times* (November 14, 2003), p. 15.

FIGURE 15-1

Industry Convergence

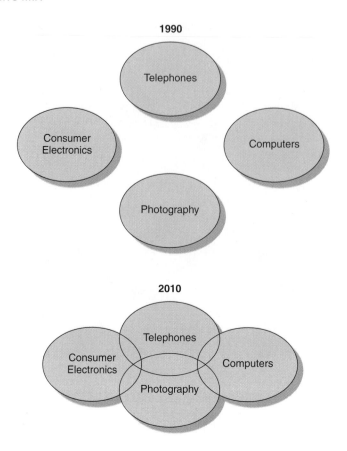

was distracted by the ill-fated launch of the Iridium satellite phone business (see Chapter 6). As a result, inventor Philippe Kahn took his idea to Japan where the first cell phone cameras were introduced in 1999. According to industry estimates, by 2010, annual sales of camera-equipped cell phones will reach 1 billion.[8]

VALUE NETWORKS AND DISRUPTIVE TECHNOLOGIES[9]

As noted in the chapter introduction, the digital revolution creates both opportunities and threats. IBM, Kodak, Xerox, and Motorola are examples of global companies that have struggled to remake their businesses in the face of technological innovation. IBM missed out on the minicomputer market, in part because management believed minicomputers promised lower margins and represented a smaller market. DEC, Data General, and Prime created the minicomputer market, but these companies, in turn, missed the PC revolution. This time, however, IBM's executive team demonstrated that it had learned its lesson: It set up an independent organizational unit to create the company's first PC. However, IBM subsequently was slow to recognize growing market demand for laptops; new entrants included Toshiba, Sharp, and Zenith. Recently, IBM exited the PC market altogether.

In an era when environmental scanning, strategic planning, and other conceptual tools of the type discussed in Chapter 16 are widely known and used, how is it that managers at many companies have failed to respond to change in a timely manner? According to Harvard professor Clayton Christensen, the problem is that executives become so committed to a current, profitable

[8]Kevin Maney, "Baby's Arrival Inspires Birth of Cell Phone Camera—and Societal Evolution," *USA Today* (January 24, 2007), p. 3B.
[9]Much of the material in this section is adapted from Clayton Christensen, *The Innovator's Dilemma* (New York: HarperBusiness, 2003). See also Simon London, "Digital Discomfort: Companies Struggle to Deal With the 'Inevitable Surprise' of the Transition from Atoms to Bits," *Financial Times* (December 17, 2003), p. 17.

technology that they fail to provide adequate levels of investment in new, apparently riskier technologies. Ironically, companies fall into this trap by adhering to prevailing marketing orthodoxy, namely, listening to and responding to the needs of established customers. Christensen calls this situation the **innovator's dilemma**.

In every industry, companies are embedded in a **value network**. Each value network has a cost structure associated with it that dictates the margins needed to achieve profitability. The boundaries of the network are defined, in part, by the unique rank ordering of the importance of various product performance attributes. Parallel value networks, each built around a different definition of what makes a product valuable, may exist within the same broadly defined industry. Each network has its own "metrics of value" (e.g., for laptop computers, the metrics are small size, low weight and power consumption, and rugged design). For example, during the 1980s, customers who bought portable computers were willing to pay a premium for smaller size; buyers of mainframe computers did not value this attribute. Conversely, mainframe buyers valued (i.e., were willing to pay more for) memory capacity as measured by megabytes; portable computer buyers placed less value on this attribute. In short, the value networks for mainframe computers and portable computers are different.

As firms gain experience within a given network, they are likely to develop capabilities, organizational structures, and cultures tailored to the distinctive requirements of their respective value networks. The industry's dominant firms—typically with reputations as "well managed" firms—lead in developing and/or adopting **sustaining technologies**, that is, incremental or radical innovations that improve product performance. According to Christensen, most new technologies developed by established companies are sustaining in nature; indeed, the vast majority of innovations are of this type. However, new entrants to an industry lead in developing **disruptive technologies** that redefine performance. The benefits associated with disruptive technologies go beyond enhancing product performance; disruptive technologies enable something to be done that was previously deemed impossible. Disruptive technologies typically enable new markets to emerge. As Christensen explains, "An innovation that is disrupting to one firm can be sustaining to another firm. The Internet was sustaining technology to Dell, which already sold PCs via direct marketing channels. But it was disruptive technology to Compaq, whose major distribution channel was retailers."[10]

To help managers recognize the innovator's dilemma and develop appropriate responses to environmental change, Christensen has developed five principles of disruptive innovations:

1. Companies depend on customers and investors for resources. As management guru Rosabeth Moss Kanter points out, the best innovations are user-driven; paradoxically, however, if management listens to established customers, opportunities for disruptive innovation may be missed.[11]
2. Small markets don't solve the growth needs of large companies. Small organizations can most easily respond to the opportunities for growth in a small market. This fact may require large organizations to create independent units to pursue new technologies, as IBM did in developing its PC.
3. Markets that don't exist can't be analyzed. Christensen recommends that companies embrace *agnostic marketing*. This is the explicit assumption that *no one*—not company personnel, not the company's customers—can know whether, how, or in what quantities a disruptive product can or will be used before they have experienced using it.
4. An organization's capabilities define its disabilities.
5. Technology supply may not equal market demand. Some products offer a greater degree of sophistication than the market requires. For example, developers of accounting software for small businesses overshot the functionality required by the market, thus creating an opportunity for a disruptive software technology that provided adequate, not superior, functionality and was simple and more convenient to use. This was the opportunity seized by Scott Cook, developer of Quicken and QuickBooks.

[10]Simon London, "Why Disruption Can Be Good for Business," *Financial Times* (October 3, 2003), p. 8.
[11]Rosabeth Moss Kanter, John Kao, and Fred Wiersema, *Innovation: Breakthrough Thinking at 3M, DuPont, GE, Pfizer, and Rubbermaid* (New York: HarperBusiness, 1997), p. 24.

GLOBAL E-COMMERCE

The term **e-commerce** refers to the general exchange of goods and services using the Internet or similar online network as a marketing channel. The U.S. Census Bureau estimates that 2008 e-commerce revenues totaled $133 billion, a figure that represents about 3.5 percent of total U.S. retail sales. Internet penetration in the United States is currently 75 percent of the population; however, South Korea leads the world in Internet penetration with 76.1 percent of the population having Internet access (see the Culture Watch box in this chapter).[12] Consider the following:

- Every 48 hours, Yahoo! records more than 24 terabytes of data about its users' online activities. That is the equivalent of all the information contained in all the books in the Library of Congress.[13]
- Between 2003 and 2008, the number of Internet users in China increased from 68 million to nearly 300 million. This makes China the world's largest e-commerce market; in Shanghai, Beijing, and Guangzhou, more than one-third of all residents use the Internet. Local companies such as Dangdang.com are proving to be formidable competitors against global rivals such as Yahoo!, Google, and eBay.[14]
- According to Forrester Research, online retail and travel sales in Western Europe will grow at a compound annual rate of 8 percent between 2008 and 2014. In 2008, 37 percent of European adults—136 million people—shopped online.[15]

TECHNOLOGY FORECAST

Travel booked over the Internet represents the largest e-commerce category. Revenues totaled $68 billion in 2005 and are expected to reach $104 billion by 2010.[16]

Jupiter Research

E-commerce activities can be divided into three broad categories: business-to-consumer (B2C or b-to-c), business-to-business (B2B or b-to-b), and consumer-to-consumer (or peer-to-peer or P2P). Many people associate e-commerce with well-known consumer-oriented sites such as Amazon.com, iTunes, and eBay. Overall, however, B2B commerce constitutes the biggest share of the Internet economy and will likely continue to do so for the foreseeable future. About three-fourths of 2001 b-to-c revenue was generated in North America; that figure is expected to drop to 50 percent as online sales in Europe and elsewhere increase over the next few years (see Table 15-1).

Problems can arise when a transaction site that is not designed to serve foreign customers nevertheless attracts them. Customer service can be a problem when customers are located in different time zones. For example, BlueTie is a small company based in Rochester, New York, that markets e-mail and office-software applications by subscription. The company's servers continually update customer calendars and e-mail. When non-U.S. orders began to come in,

TABLE 15-1 Forecast, Online Retail and Travel Sales, Select European Countries, 2008–2014 (millions)

Country	2008	2009	2010	2011	2012	2013	2014
Germany[a]	€27,581	€31,311	€34,021	€37,131	€39,662	€41,901	€43,723
France[b]	14,795	16,990	19,594	22,334	24,373	26,256	27,948
Spain[c]	5,961	6,976	9,031	11,281	13,247	15,286	17,353
Western Europe[d]	116,009	128,606	146,636	164,046	177,781	190,960	202,799

[a]Forrester Research, *German Online Retail and Travel Sales, 2008–2014* (March 2, 2009), p. 8.
[b]Forrester Research, *French Online Retail and Travel Sales, 2008–2014* (March 2, 2009), p. 8.
[c]Forrester Research, *Spanish Online Retail and Travel Sales, 2008–2014* (March 6, 2009), p. 9.
[d]Forrester Research, *Western European Online Retail and Travel Sales, 2008–2014* (March 16, 2009), p. 8.
Data is for EU-17: Austria, Belgium, Denmark, Finland, France, Germany, Greece, Ireland, Italy, Luxembourg, the Netherlands, Norway, Portugal, Spain, Sweden, Switzerland, and the United Kingdom.

---

[12]Internet World Stats, www.internetworldstat.com (accessed June 1, 2009).
[13]Kevin J. Delaney, "Lab Test: Hoping to Overtake Its Rivals, Yahoo Stocks Up on Academics," *The Wall Street Journal* (August 26, 2006), p. A8.
[14]Jason Dean, "China's Web Retailers Beat U.S. Rivals at Their Own Game," *The Wall Street Journal* (August 22, 2006), p. B1.
[15]Forrester Research, *Western European Online Retail and Travel Sales, 2008–2014* (March 16, 2009), p. 2.
[16]Amy Yee, "Integrating New Assets the Way to Go," *Financial Times* (January 3, 2006), p. 17.

BlueTie managers found it challenging to deliver correct times and dates. Fixing the problem required spending tens of thousands of dollars and tied up precious employee time.

Web sites can be classified by purpose: **promotion sites** provide marketing communications about a company's goods or services, **content sites** provide news and entertainment and support a company's PR efforts, and **transaction sites** are cyberspace retail operations that allow customers to purchase goods and services. In many instances, Web sites combine the three functions. Web sites can also be categorized in terms of content and audience focus.

In quadrant 1 of Figure 15-2, the focus is on providing information and service to domestic or local-country customers. Quadrant 2 companies maintain transaction-oriented e-commerce sites with a domestic focus. Companies in both quadrants 1 and 2 do attract international traffic, but the focus is still local. For example, international students at your college or university may have learned about your school via the Internet, even though home-country prospective students constitute the primary target audience for the Web site. Similarly, Netflix, the online movie rental service, only serves American subscribers. Companies that initially fall into quadrants 1 and 2 can transition into quadrants 3 and 4; for example, Apple's iTunes Music Store began as a U.S.-only retailer. During the past several years, the service has been rolled out in Germany, France, the United Kingdom, and elsewhere.

Procter & Gamble Far East Inc., the consumer products company's operation in Japan, is using the Web to build its portfolio of brands in the region. The company has launched shufufufu.com, Japan's first virtual community for women. The Web address combines *shufu* ("housewife") and *fu-fu-fu* (the sound of a woman's laughter); the P&G logo has been de-emphasized. The site was created by the digital division of Beacon Communications K.K. As Fergus Kibble, digital director at Beacon, noted, "Our research showed that Japanese housewives often feel very isolated."[17] The site's success can be attributed in part to the popularity of Harumi Kurihara, the "Japanese Martha Stewart" who writes a weekly essay on the site and provides tips on cooking, homemaking, and personal care.

In quadrant 3, the audience focus is global. Companies such as Federal Express and Gucci are already global in scope, and the Internet constitutes a powerful, cost-effective communication tool. Similarly, the interactive marketing staff at Unilever PLC understands that the Web represents an important low-cost medium for promoting products. Unilever's vast archive of TV commercials has been digitized; Web surfers can download the videos for products such as Salon Selectives shampoo and watch them anytime. Recently, Unilever launched a 12-week series on Yahoo! Food titled "In Search of Real Food." Hosted by Food Network TV star David

"Increased broadband penetration is opening up possibilities that didn't exist even two years ago. . . . We need to realize that online is now an important part of the overall communications mix. . . . We are not an online business. We're a beverage business. But we have to develop compelling marketing platforms that are relevant to the lives of young people."[18]
Tim Kopp, Vice President of Global Interactive Marketing, Coca-Cola

Web Site Content

FIGURE 15-2

Categories of Web Sites

Source: Adapted from "The Internet and International Marketing," by John A. Quelch and Lisa R. Klein, *MIT Sloan Management Review* 37, no. 3 (Spring 1996), p. 65.

[17] Tom Boatman, "Interactive Marketing Strategies in Japan," *Japan Inc.* (June 2001).
[18] Andrew Ward, "Coke Taps into Brand New Internet Craze," *Financial Times* (August 8, 2006), p. 15.

Lieberman, the show was created around Hellman's mayonnaise. As Doug Scott, executive director of entertainment at the Ogilvy & Mather ad agency explained, "Content for broadband costs significantly less than TV productions and it allows you to distribute to a much larger audience."[19]

Procter & Gamble also has ambitious plans for exploiting the Internet as a global promotional and informational tool. P&G has registered a number of Internet domains based on brand names, including www.covergirl.com, www.oldspice.com, and www.sunnyd.com. Another P&G site, Pampers.com, represents a new conceptualization of the brand. Previously, brand managers viewed Pampers as a way of keeping babies happy; the new view is that the Pampers brand is a child development aid. By mid-2006, Pampers.com was receiving 400,000 hits per month. Visitors to the site can read advice from the Pampers Parenting Institute as well as tips from mothers. Discount coupons are also available from the site.[20] P&G has also registered scores of other generic domains that relate to its various product lines, including cakemix.com, laundry.com, and nails.com. P&G's actions have sent a signal to other consumer packaged-goods marketers that it is striving for a first-mover advantage on the Internet.

In quadrant 4, companies seek e-commerce transactions with customers on a worldwide basis. Amazon.com is perhaps the most successful example of the global audience-transaction business model. Online book shoppers can chose from more than 2.5 million titles; many titles carry discounted prices. After assessing a number of potential products in terms of their suitability for online sales, company founder Jeffrey Bezos settled on books for two reasons. First, there are too many titles for any one "brick-and-mortar" store to carry. The second reason is related to industry structure: The publishing industry is highly fragmented, with 4,200 publishers in the United States alone. That means that no single publisher has a high degree of supplier power. Bezos's instincts proved sound: Sales exploded after Amazon.com's Web site became operational in mid-1995. Within a year, orders were coming in from 66 countries. Today, Amazon.com's sites in China, France, Germany, Japan, and the United Kingdom generate nearly 50 percent of total sales.

As noted earlier, online retail in the United States totaled $133 billion in 2008. This figure includes orders from abroad; Abercrombie & Fitch, Timberland, Coach, and Saks Fifth Avenue are just some of the U.S. retailers targeting foreign buyers. The trend has been fueled by a variety of factors, including the slowdown in U.S. consumer spending and a weak dollar that translates into savings for shoppers paying in euros or other currencies. Saks has discovered that shoppers in Canada and the United Kingdom spend 20 to 30 percent more money than American online shoppers. To keep shipping costs and import duties down, some retailers are considering opening distribution centers in Europe and elsewhere.[21]

Some products are inherently not suitable candidates for sale via the Internet: McDonald's doesn't sell hamburgers from its Web site, and Procter & Gamble does not sell shampoo. In some instances, global marketers make the strategic decision to establish a presence on the Web without offering transaction opportunities even though the product could be sold that way. Rather, such companies limit their Web activities to promotion and information in support of offline retail distribution channels. There are several reasons for this. First, many companies lack the infrastructure necessary to process orders from individual customers. Second, it can cost anywhere from $20 million to $30 million to establish a fully functioning e-commerce site. There may be other, product-specific reasons. The Web site for Godin Guitars, for example, provides a great deal of product information and a directory of the company's worldwide dealer network. Company founder Robert Godin believes that the best way for a person to select a guitar is to play one, and that requires a visit to a music store.

Likewise, visitors to Web sites for some luxury goods purveyors, including Burberry, Prada, and Gucci, are not given the opportunity to buy. Top design houses strive to create an overall retail shopping experience that enhances the brand; this objective is basically at odds with e-commerce. As a spokesperson for Prada noted recently, "Miuccia Prada is trying to combine

[19]Susanne Vranica, "Hellman's Targets Yahoo for Its Spread," *The Wall Street Journal* (June 27, 2007), p. B4.
[20]Gary Silverman, "How May I Help You?" *Financial Times* (February 4–5, 2006), p. W2.
[21]Vanessa O'Connell and Rachel Dodes, "Going Online to Lure Foreign Shoppers," *The Wall Street Journal* (February 8, 2008), p. B1.

fashion with architecture and design. It's a 360-degree experience."[22] One notable exception is LVMH, whose www.eluxury.com Web site offers a limited selection of ready-to-wear items by Marc Jacobs and other designers.

As the Internet has developed into a crucial global communication tool, decision makers in virtually all organizations are realizing that they must include this new medium in their communications planning. Many companies purchase banner ads on popular Web sites; the ads are linked to the company's home page or product- or brand-related sites. Advertisers pay when users click on the link. Although creative possibilities are limited with banner ads and **click-through rates**—the percentage of users who click on an advertisement that has been presented—are typically low, the number of companies that use the Web as a medium for global advertising is expected to increase dramatically over the next few years.

An important trend is **paid search advertising**, whereby companies pay to have their ads appear when users type certain search terms. Yahoo! recently paid $1.6 billion to acquire Overture, a company specializing in paid search advertising. As a Yahoo! spokesman person noted, "Paid search is just starting to take off globally. So this acquisition wasn't just part of our strategy for search, it was important for our international strategy as well."[23]

One of the most interesting aspects of the digital revolution has been noted by Chris Anderson, the editor of *Wired* magazine and author of *The Long Tail*. The book's title refers to the use of the efficient economics of online retail to aggregate a large number of relatively slow-selling products. *The Long Tail* helps explain the success of eBay, Amazon.com, and iTunes, all of which offer far more variety and choice than traditional retailers can. As Anderson explains, "The story of the Long Tail is really about the economics of abundance—what happens when the bottlenecks that stand between supply and demand in our culture start to disappear and everything becomes available to everyone." Anderson notes that "below-the–radar" products—for example, obscure books, movies, and music—are driving revenues at e-commerce merchants such as Amazon.com, Netflix, and iTunes. He says, "These millions of fringe sales are an efficient, cost-effective business. . . . For the first time in history, hits and niches are on equal economic footing."[24]

WEB SITE DESIGN AND IMPLEMENTATION[25]

To fully exploit the Internet's potential, company executives must be willing to integrate interactive media into their marketing mixes. Web sites can be developed in-house, or an outside firm can be contracted to do the job. During the past few years, a new breed of interactive advertising agency has emerged to help companies globalize their Internet offerings (see Table 15-2). Some of these agencies are independent; others are affiliated with other advertising agency brands and holding companies. Whether Web development is handled in-house or by an outside agency,

TABLE 15-2 Top Five Interactive Agencies by 2008 Interactive Marketing Revenue

Agency/HQ Location	Clients
Digitas (Boston)	American Express, Royal Bank of Scotland, Saab, FedEx
Razorfish (Seattle)	AstraZeneca, Oxfam, Red Bull, Singapore Airlines
Sapient Interactive (Cambridge, Mass.)	Audi, Avis Europe, Deutsche Telekom, Volkswagen
OgilvyInteractive (New York)	IBM, Cisco Systems, Dove, BP
IBM Interactive (Chicago)	NA

Source: Adapted from "Top U.S. Agencies in Ten Specialties," *Advertising Age* (April 27, 2009), p. 16.

---

[22]Sally Beatty, "Fashion Tip: Get Online," *The Wall Street Journal* (October 31, 2003), pp. B1, B3.
[23]Bob Tedeschi, "E-Commerce Report," *The New York Times* (January 12, 2004), p. C6.
[24]Chris Anderson, *The Long Tail: Why the Future of Business Is Selling Less of More* (Hyperion, 2006), p. 13.
[25]Much of the discussion in this section is adapted from Alexis D. Gutzman, *The E-Commerce Arsenal* (New York: Amacom, 2001).

TABLE 15-3 Amazon.com Domain Names

Domain Name	Country
amazon.co.uk	United Kingdom
amazon.de	Germany
amazon.fr	France
amazon.co.jp	Japan
amazon.at	Austria

several issues must be addressed when setting up for global e-commerce. These include choosing domain names, arranging payment, localizing sites, addressing privacy issues, and setting up a distribution system.

A critical first step is registering a country-specific domain name. Thus, Amazon.com has a family of different domain names, including one for each country in which it operates (see Table 15-3). Although it is certainly possible for European consumers to browse Amazon.com's U.S. site, they may prefer a direct link to a site with a local domain name. From both a marketing and consumer perspective, this makes sense: The Web site of choice will be one that quotes prices in euros rather than dollars, offers a product selection tailored to local tastes, and ships from local distribution points. However, as noted earlier, the weak dollar may make it less expensive for shoppers in, say, Europe, to order from U.S. online retailers.

Moreover, research suggests that visitors spend more time at sites that are in their own language; they also tend to view more pages and make more purchases. Many people will seek information about sites on local versions of well-known search engines. For example, in France, Yahoo!'s local site is fr.Yahoo.com. The same principle applies to non-U.S. companies targeting the American online consumer market. Waterford Wedgwood PLC, Harrods, and other well-known companies have acquired U.S. domain names and created sites with prices listed in dollars.[26]

While registering a ".com" domain name is a relatively straightforward procedure in the United States, requirements can vary elsewhere. In some countries, for example, a company must establish a legal entity before it can register a site with a local domain-name extension. **Cybersquatting**—the practice of registering a particular domain name for the express purpose of reselling it to the company that should rightfully use it—is also a problem. Avon, Panasonic, and Starbucks are some of the companies that have been victims of cybersquatting.

Payment can be another problem; in some countries, including China, credit card use is low. In such situations, e-commerce operators must arrange payment by bank check or postal money order; cash on delivery is also an option. Another issue is credit card fraud; Indonesia, Russia, Croatia, and Bosnia are among the countries where fraud is rampant. Extra identity measures may have to be taken, such as requiring buyers to fax the actual credit card they are using as well as photo IDs.[27] In Japan, consumers pay for online purchases at convenience stores (*konbini*). After selecting an item online, the buyer goes to a nearby convenience store (e.g., a 7-Eleven) and pays cash for the item; the clerk transfers the money to the online seller's account. However, foreign companies can't participate in the *konbini* system; this means that a foreign online retailer must establish an alliance with a local company.

Ideally, each country-specific site should reflect local culture, language usage, customs, and aesthetic preferences. Logos and other elements of brand identity should be included on the site, with adjustments for color preferences and meaning differences when necessary. For example, the shopping cart icon is familiar to online shoppers in the United States and many European countries. However, online companies must determine whether that icon is

"Shopping on the Internet is no different than traditional sales channels. It's all about trusting the brand and having a strong relationship with one's customers."[28]

Ron Fry, Internet Business Manager, Lands' End

[26]Jessica Vascellaro, "Foreign Shopping Sites Cater to U.S. Customers," *The Wall Street Journal* (October 12, 2005), pp. D1, D14.

[27]Peter Loftus, "Internet Turns Firms into Overseas Businesses," *The Wall Street Journal* (December 16, 2003), p. B4. See also Matt Richtel, "Credit Card Theft Is Thriving Online as Global Market," *The New York Times* (May 13, 2002), p. A1.

[28]Christopher Price, "Fashion Suits the Internet Shopper," *Financial Times* (June 24, 1998), p. 23.

appropriate in all country markets. Subtle but important language differences can occur even in English-speaking countries. For example, figleaves.com and figleaves.com/uk are, respectively, the American and British Web addresses for a UK-based lingerie marketer. However, the U.S. site refers to "panties" while the UK site has a listing for "briefs." When two or more different languages are involved, translators should be used to ensure that copy reflects current language usage. It is also important not to "reinvent the wheel" by translating the same terms over and over again. Local translators should have access to an in-house dictionary that contains preferred translations of company-specific terms. The system should be capable of identifying content that has already been translated and then reusing that content. Product descriptions may also vary from country to country; as noted in Chapter 4, American-themed merchandise is very popular in Japan. Table 15-4 compares sample product descriptions in English and Japanese.

After Yao Ming joined the Houston Rockets in 2002, nba.com/china was launched in conjunction with SOHU.com, China's leading Internet portal. Written entirely in Chinese characters, nba.com/china is designed to capitalize on basketball's increasing popularity in the world's largest market. The NBA has also launched several other country- and language-specific sites, including nba.com/uk, nba.com/canada, and nba.com/espanol. As Jon Belmonte, chief executive of the Active Network sports marketing firm, told the *New York Times*:

> NBA.com has done a great job of building a community. The NBA is very personality- and stats-driven, and the Web sites do a great job of packaging all of that information and making it accessible to the rabid fan. Building and deepening that core customer relationship is one of the most important things you can do online.[29]

As the NBA's Chinese site illustrates, it is not enough to simply translate a Web site from the home-country language into other languages. Thus, another basic step is localizing a Web site in the native language and business nomenclature of the target country. From a technical point of view, Web sites designed to support English, French, German, and other languages that use the Latin alphabet only store a maximum of 256 characters in the American Standard Code for Information Interchange (ASCII) format. Even so, there are language-specific needs; for example, a German language Web site requires more than double the capacity of an English language site because German copy takes more space.[30] However, languages such as Japanese and

TABLE 15-4 Product Description: An English Versus Japanese Comparison

English	Japan
"New York Yankees hat with white stitching on black canvas."	"Authentic baseball hat for the New York Yankees baseball team. Just like they wear in New York City! White stitching on black canvas reflects the team's colors."
These warm-weather cargos are made from our popular tropic-weight cotton. The 6 oz. cloth is dyed with rich pigment color that weathers gradually. Garment-washed to feel comfortably broken-in right away. Our Natural Fit offers extra room at the seat and thighs. Quarter front pockets, two flapped back pockets and roomy cargo pockets on legs. Double-needle stitching at stress seams. Fit belts up to $1\frac{3}{4}$". Imported. Machine wash and dry. (L.L.Bean)	Cargo Pants have high breathability for hot weather. This garment is made from tropic-weight cotton and dyed with rich pigment color and weathers gradually. Enjoy the way this cargo's fabric feels comfortably broken in. This fits you naturally for the way you move. Front pockets for both sides, two flapped back pockets and roomy cargo pockets on legs. Double-needle stitching at stress seams. Fit belts up to 4 cm. 100% Cotton. Washable by machine.

Source: Adapted from Alexis D. Gutzman, *The E-Commerce Arsenal* (New York: Amacom, 2001), p. 165.

---

[29]Marc Weingarten, "Site by Site, N.B.A. Takes on the World," *The New York Times* (November 14. 2002), p. G2.
[30]Patricia Riedman, "Think Globally, Act Globally," *Advertising Age* (June 19, 2000), p. 48.

Chinese require a database that supports double-ASCII. For this reason, it is wise to start with a double-ACSII platform when designing a Web site's architecture. The site's architecture should also be flexible enough to allow different date, currency, and money formatting. For example, to someone living in the United Kingdom, "7/10/10" means October 7, 2010. To an American, it means July 10, 2010.

Another critical global e-commerce issue is privacy. The European Union's regulations are among the world's strictest; companies are limited in terms of how much personal information—a customer's age, marital status, and buying patterns, for example—can be gathered and how long the information can be retained. Customers have the right to view the information contained in company databases and correct errors. Moreover, the EU's standards have been adopted in other parts of the world, including Canada, Australia, and Asia. Spain's regulations are particularly stringent; taking advantage of a common language, Chile and Argentina have copied the Spanish drafts of Spain's laws. By contrast, Washington's reluctance to protect privacy stems is due in part to First Amendment issues as well as to national security concerns stemming from the terror attacks of 2001. To help ensure compliance with privacy laws, American companies have created a new executive-level job position: chief privacy officer.[31]

A number of issues are related to physical distribution decisions. As online sales increase in a particular country or region, it may be necessary to establish local warehouse facilities to

---

➡ STRATEGIC DECISION MAKING IN GLOBAL MARKETING
Open Source Software

Global software sales have been very, very good to Microsoft. The company's Windows operating system is found in more than 90 percent of the world's PCs, and popular software programs such as Office Suite are used virtually everywhere. Because of its dominant position in the industry, Microsoft has a global pricing policy that calls for charging approximately the same amount in every world market. Today, however, Microsoft's pricing structure faces a threat from open source software that is distributed for free.

The term *open source software* is used to describe a software program for which the source code—the original program instructions—is made available so that users can make modifications. In the mid-1970s, a programmer named Richard Stallman wrote a macro editor for Unix that he called Emacs. Other programmers wanted to use Emacs, so Stallman published the GNU ("GNU's not Unix") Public License (GPL) in association with the concept of "copyleft" (a play on the notion of copyright). In essence, Stallman granted permission for others to run, copy, modify, and distribute his operating system software, with one caveat: No one could place restrictions on their modifications. In 1991, a 21-year-old Helsinki University student named Linus Torvalds developed a Unix-compatible operating system that he called Linux (a combination of Linus and Minix, a Unix clone widely used by college students; see Exhibit 15-4). Today, numerous free versions of Linux are available, including Mandrakelinux. Worldwide, 25 percent of servers run Linux software; increasingly, Linux is being used on PCs as well.

What does the Linux phenomenon mean for Microsoft? In short, it means that the software giant's virtual monopoly on PC

operating systems may be at risk. In developing countries such as Malaysia and Thailand, government initiatives are aimed at putting as many PCs as possible into the hands of ordinary citizens and small business owners. Government agencies are looking for the best price, making free Linux software a very attractive choice. For example, working with the Association of Thai Computer Manufacturers, the Thai government made Linux-equipped "People's PCs" available for about 10,900 baht ($260). Microsoft responded by creating a Thai-language version of Windows XP and bundling it with Microsoft Office for a price of about $36. By mid-2003, roughly one quarter of the 134,000 PCs ordered by Thais were equipped with Windows. Similarly, in Malaysia, PCs running Linux are available at prices as low as about $263. Microsoft has responded by making a Malaysian version of Windows XP available on a PC for about $302.

Developing countries are not the only ones hoping to find cheaper alternatives to Microsoft. France, for example, needs to reduce its deficit to be in compliance with eurozone regulations. To do so, the French government is considering open source options such as OpenOffice, a version of Sun Microsystem's Star-Office, Mozilla, a Web browser, and other open source programs. In Asia, representatives from Japan and South Korea are holding meetings in an effort to set joint policies regarding information technology.

Sources: Rebecca Buckman, "Microsoft's Malaysia Policy," *The Wall Street Journal* (May 20, 2004), p. B1; Buckman, "Face-Off Over People's PC," *The Wall Street Journal* (August 14, 2003), p. B1; www.gnu.org (accessed June 2004).

---

[31]David Scheer, "For Your Eyes Only: Europe's New High-Tech Role: Playing Privacy Cop to the World," *The Wall Street Journal* (October 10, 2003), p. A1.

Exhibit 15-4: The Linux open source operating system was created by Linus Tovalds, shown here with the software's iconic penguin mascot. Although Linux is distributed for free, annual sales of Linux-related software, hardware, and support services total about $15 billion. The Linux Foundation was created to deal with competitive issues pertaining to Microsoft and its Windows operating system. It also deals with technical, legal, and standards issues.
Source: Paul Sakuma/AP Wide World Photos.

speed delivery and reduce shipping costs. In the United States, such a step has tax implications; the marketer may have to collect sales tax. To allay consumer concerns about ordering merchandise online, companies may opt to waive shipping fees and offer free returns and money-back guarantees.

NEW PRODUCTS AND SERVICES

The digital revolution has spurred innovation in many different industries. Companies in all parts of the world are developing a new generation of products, services, and technologies. These include broadband networks, mobile commerce, wireless connectivity, and smart phones.

Broadband

A **broadband** communication system is one that has sufficient capacity to carry multiple voice, data, or video channels simultaneously. *Bandwidth* determines the range of frequencies that can pass over a given transmission channel. For example, traditional telephone networks offered quite limited bandwidth compared with state-of-the art digital telephone networks. As a result, a traditional telephone call sounds "lo-fi." Bandwidth is measured in bits-per-second (Bps); a full page of English text is about 16,000 bits. For example, a 56Kbs modem connected to a conventional telephone line can move 16,000 bits in less than one second; by comparison, a broadband Internet connection that utilizes coaxial cable can move up to 10 gigabits per second. Consumer broadband service is typically available from cable TV companies or telephone companies via digital subscriber lines (DSL). In addition to faster download times and greater capacity, broadband offers other advantages. For example, it is always on (in other words, there is no need to access the Internet via phone dial-up service).

Broadband offers a variety of marketing opportunities to companies in a variety of industries. Broadband Internet allows users to access streaming audio, streaming video, and streaming media. **Streaming audio** allows users to listen to Internet radio stations. Many radio stations offer free Web-based online streams as a complement to their regular over-the-air broadcasts. Some audio streams are built around popular shows rather than stations per se. For example, *Hearts of Space*, a popular show that is heard on many National Public Radio stations in North America, has its own Web site, www.hos.com. An obvious advantage of online radio streams is that persons outside a terrestrial-based station's listening area can still tune in. Personalized radio services, such as Pandora.com, allow users to list their favorite artists and songs. Pandora uses a proprietary technology called the Music Genome Project to make recommendations for new music that is similar to a listener's current favorites.

Streaming video is a sequence of moving images that are sent in compressed form over the Internet and displayed by the viewer as they arrive. **Streaming media** combines streaming video with sound. With streaming video or streaming media, a Web user does not have to wait to download a large file before seeing the video or hearing the sound. Instead, the media is sent in a continuous stream and is played as it arrives. Streaming media is having a profound impact on the television industry, as many households use hulu.com and other Web sites to view their favorite TV shows online. Streaming video also promises to revolutionize the home video industry, as iTunes, Amazon.com, and Netflix offer movie downloads as a home viewing option.

Streaming media represents huge market opportunity for the video game industry, which includes electronics companies (e.g., Microsoft and Sony), game publishers (e.g., Electronic Arts), and Internet portals (e.g., Yahoo!). Another trend in online gaming: Gamers in different locations, even different countries, compete against each other using PCs, Xbox, or Play-Station consoles. These are sometimes known as massively multiplayer online games (MMOG); the most popular title is *World of Warcraft*. As of mid-2008, Microsoft's Xbox Live service had attracted 10 million subscribers worldwide. Consumer interest in online gaming has been fueled by powerful next-generation game consoles, Microsoft's Xbox 360 and the PlayStation 3 from Sony.

However, the promise of broadband goes far beyond entertainment. It is a key productivity tool that allows employees to save time by tapping online resources and by sharing electronic documents on desktop PCs in real time. Broadband provides opportunities for online education, medical diagnosis and treatment, and, of course, e-commerce.

Mobile Commerce

Mobile commerce (m-commerce) is the term for conducting commercial transactions using wireless handheld devices such as personal digital assistants (PDAs) and cell phones. Many companies are developing ways to provide Internet access without the need for a wired broadband connection. For example, **Wi-Fi** (wireless fidelity) permits laptop and PDA users to establish high-speed wireless connections to the Internet and corporate intranets via "hotspots" located in airports, cafés, or other public places (see Exhibit 15-5). One reason for the popularity of hotspots is the need for so-called knowledge workers or "laptop warriors" to maintain high levels of productivity during business trips.

Wi-Fi networks have a limited range; an improved technology known as **World Interoperability for MicroWave Access (WiMax)** is being deployed in many parts of the world. A WiMax network can have a range of several miles, making it superior to traditional Wi-Fi. Fixed WiMax doesn't work with mobile devices; an improved technology called mobile WiMax does. Because mobile WiMax offers greater capacity and faster speeds than current mobile data networks, it is well suited for streaming music or video.[32] As noted in this chapter's Culture Watch box, South Korea is home to the world's largest Wi-Fi network. Next up on South Korea's tech horizon is wireless broadband, or Wibro.

Another mobile communication technology, **Bluetooth**, has the advantage of consuming less power than Wi-Fi. This makes Bluetooth well-suited to use with cell phones.[33] However, Bluetooth works over shorter distances than Wi-Fi. Bluetooth technology has been incorporated into automobiles and home appliances such as refrigerators and microwave ovens. Currently, British Telecommunications (BT) has several thousand Bluetooth hotspots in place. In addition,

---

[32]Sarmand Ali, "New and (Soon) Improved," *The Wall Street Journal* (November 27, 2006), p. R8.
[33]"Bluetooth" is the English translation of Harald Blatand, a Danish Viking and king who lived in the tenth century.

Exhibit 15-5: Wi-Fi zones such as this one in Paris are becoming more common in Europe. UK- based Cloud Networks operates public access Wi-Fi networks for laptop users in select towns and cities in the United Kingdom, France, Germany, the Netherlands, and Sweden. Some industry observers have identified Wi-Fi as a disruptive technology because its faster download speeds pose a threat to slower cellular networks. However, Nokia and other manufacturers are developing next-generation handsets with Wi-Fi capabilities.
Source: MEIDNEUX/SIPA Press.

BT is testing a service called Blue Phone that will allow Bluetooth users to connect to BT's phone line network from a mobile unit.[34]

Wi-Fi connections require a subscription to a service provider; one problem is getting a connection in a hotspot supported by a different provider than the one to which a user subscribes.[35] In the United States, Starbucks is partnering with T-Mobile USA (the American arm of Deutsche Telekom's T-Mobile International) to offer Wi-Fi service; the strategy is to encourage patrons to stay in its coffee shops longer and, presumably, spend more money on coffee and other items. In the United States, T-Mobile also has deals with Border's bookstores, FedEx Kinko's business centers, Texaco service stations, and major airports. Current Wi-Fi technology can only handle data, not voice. However, many industry observers expect that in the near future, hotspots will allow cell phones to switch to the Internet for telephone calls.

Wireless technology is being used in other ways. In the automotive world, there is a trend toward **telematics**, which is a car's ability to exchange information about the vehicle's location or mechanical performance. Cars are also being equipped with online access; BMW Assist, BMW Online, and BMW TeleServices illustrate some of telematics' potential. The system provides access to a wide range of information and services, including the availability of parking spaces. The service also assists users who wish to book hotel rooms or make restaurant reservations. Mercedes-Benz is rolling out a similar service.[36] Similarly, Microsoft's SYNC is a voice-activated communication system that is available on Ford and Mercury vehicles. It can be used in conjunction with Bluetooth-equipped cell phones.

Smart Phones

Cell phones have been one of the biggest new product success stories of the digital revolution. Worldwide, 1 billion cellular handsets are sold each year. The popularity of cell phone handsets has boosted the fortunes of manufacturers such as Nokia, Motorola, Samsung, and Ericsson as well as service providers such as Deutsche Telekom, U.S. Cellular, Verizon, and others. New

---

[34]Jonathan Moules, "Bluetooth and the Quest for a Wireless World," *Financial Times* (December 3, 2003), p. 9.
[35]Dennis K. Berman and Jesse Drucker, "Wi-Fi Industry Bets 'Roaming' Will Lure Users," *The Wall Street Journal* (November 6, 2003), p. B1.
[36]Chris Reiter, "Web-Rigged Cars Get Second Look," *The Wall Street Journal* (December 11, 2003), p. D2.

EMERGING MARKETS BRIEFING BOOK

⇢ New Media in China and India

China is home to the largest population of Internet users, so it is no surprise that companies are allocating more of their ad budgets to this emerging medium. Although television is still the most important medium, online ad revenue is growing at double-digit annual rates. Clients comprise A-list global marketers including Samsung, Mazda, Nike, and Coca-Cola. One recent promotion for Coke Zero on social networking site Xiaonei.com had the theme "Be Bond for a Day." Coke invited users to upload photos that demonstrated why they should be chosen as the next James Bond. Winners were treated to helicopter flights and rides in 007's iconic Aston Martin sports car.

China also enjoys the distinction of the world's largest population of mobile phone subscribers. However, cell phone usage is exploding in India. As Manoj Dawane, CEO of Mumbai software company People Infocom, explains, "In India, mobile phone penetration is high compared to other forms of media like television or the Internet. You can't have a better place than India for mobile advertising." Overall advertising revenues in India have been growing at 20 percent annually. Total worldwide spending for mobile ads was only about $1 billion in 2007, but industry experts expect that figure could reach $10 billion to $20 billion by 2013.

One factor driving mobile ads in India is the low rates that subscribers pay—as little as two cents per minute. Demographics play an important role, too. About two-thirds of the Indian population lives in rural areas where television ownership and newspaper readership are low. Cellular operators such as BPL Mobile have built networks that reach tens of thousands of Indian villages. Arif Ali, head of brand communications at BPL, has ideas that will keep subscriber costs low. "We are thinking of providing 30- to 60-second commercials over the phone where we will pass on some kind of benefit," he said.

Sources: Loretta Chao, "Online Advertising Gets Boost in China," *The Wall Street Journal* (December 11, 2008), p. B6; Eric Bellman and Tariq Engineer, "India Appears Ripe for Cell Phone Ads," *The Wall Street Journal* (March 10, 2008), p. B3.

---

features such as color displays and cameras give consumers a reason to upgrade their handsets on a regular basis; a new generation of **smart phones** gives phones some of the capabilities of computers. Case in point: Apple's wildly successful iPhone comes equipped with a full-blown Web browser. The marketing possibilities of cell phone–based e-commerce are suggested by the following:

- In Australia, a thirsty traveler can pay for a Coke at Central Station in Sydney by calling "Dial-a-Coke," making a beverage selection, and then collecting his or her selection from a vending machine. Charges for the purchase appear on the customer's cell phone bills.
- In Norway, mobile operator Telenor ASA has teamed with a finance group to offer mobile purchases of flowers, compact discs, bus tickets and food.[37]
- In 2009, Apple's iTunes store sold its one-billionth iPhone application ("app").

While these and other new mobile services are in development, individuals are already using their cell phones for a variety of tasks besides calling. For example, text messaging has exploded in popularity. Now, advertisers are taking advantage of this capability by using **short message service (SMS)**, a globally accepted wireless standard for sending alphanumeric messages of up to 160 characters. SMS is the technology that is the basis for Twitter's micro-blogging service (see Case 15-1). Industry experts expect marketers to integrate SMS with communication via other digital channels such as interactive digital TV, the Internet, and e-mail.

"Wireless phone booths are the Starbucks of telephony in South America."[39]

Ralph de la Vega, BellSouth Latin America

Some smart phones are equipped with a **global positioning system (GPS)** that allows users to determine their exact geographic position. This capability is also opening new opportunities for *location-based advertising*. For example, Alcatel-Lucent, the French telecommunications equipment manufacturer, has just launched a service that sends tailored text messages when cell phone users are near a specific location such as a store, hotel, or restaurant. The service provides addresses and telephone numbers of the businesses and can also provide links to coupons or other types of sales promotions.[38]

---

[37]Gren Manuel, "Dialing for Dollars," *The Wall Street Journal—E-Commerce* (October 20, 2003), p. R3.
[38]Sara Silver and Emily Steel, "Alcatel Gets Into Mobile Ads," *The Wall Street Journal* (May 21, 2009), p. B9.
[39]Almar Latour, "Latin Lessons: BellSouth Finds Pocket of Growth in an Odd Place," *The Wall Street Journal* (November 20, 2003), p. A8.

One might ask whether spam—unsolicited "junk" promotional messages sent to large numbers of people—will start cluttering text message inboxes. (The term *spam* is borrowed from a famous Monty Python comedy routine in which the brand name of Hormel Foods Corporation's canned meat product is used so often that it crowds everything else out.) The Mobile Marketing Association is the global industry trade group that has the responsibility for addressing this and other issues. Because of privacy concerns, mobile advertisers often give users the opportunity to "opt in or opt out" by choosing whether or not they want to receive such promotional communications. This is a classic "pull" marketing strategy that allows marketers to target high-value consumers with relevant messages.

Mobile Music: Ringtones, Truetones, and Full-Track Music Downloads

Because of rampant illegal sharing of music files, record companies are searching for new sources of revenue. Thanks to technology convergence, a new generation of cell phones is leading to changes in the mobile music industry. **Mobile music** is music that is purchased and played on a cell phone. One opportunity is to license the rights to popular songs for use as cell phone ringtones or as ringback tones. (Ringback tones are songs that the caller hears when he or she places a call to another mobile subscriber.) According to Gartner Research, ringtone sales peaked in 2006 with worldwide revenues totaling $6 billion.

At first, the primary beneficiaries of this growing market were music publishers and songwriters. The reason is simple: Many ringtones are rerecordings and thus represent instrumental "soundalike" or "cover" versions rather than the original versions by the original recording artists; therefore, a song's publisher and writer receive royalties of approximately 15 percent each time a tone is downloaded. The situation has changed, however, as record companies and artists recognize an important new revenue stream. Truetones, also known as realtones and mastertones, are digitized clips of original songs by the original recording artists. Licensing fees for truetones are typically higher, because they include master recording royalties of 30 to 50 percent. As John Rose, former executive vice president of EMI Group, noted, "This is quite an attractive market to us. We think it'll be a significant multi-billion-dollar market over the next couple of years as the new handsets roll out."[41]

The market for paid, legal, full-track music downloads is dominated by Apple's iTunes Store. Music purchased from iTunes can be played back on computers and mobile devices such as the Apple iPod and iPhone. Downloaded song files can also be burned onto CDs. In 2006, iTunes reached a milestone of 1 billion song downloads. Apple's competitors have tried, without much success, to develop their own music players and download services to rival the iPod/iTunes combination. For example, Microsoft has a device called Zune; Dell also has a player in development. Besides the iTunes store, other online music services are available, including Amazon.com, Napster 2.0, RealNetworks' Rhapsody and RealPlayer Music Store, and Microsoft's ZunePass.

These online music services use a variety of pricing strategies. Rhapsody is primarily a subscription service, with rates starting at $12.99 per month. Napster charges $9.99 per month, and also has a "Napster to Go" plan for $5. By contrast, iTunes uses "al a carte" pricing, charging for each song track or album download. Originally, iTunes sold individual songs for $0.99 each. Recently, however, Apple introduced a variable pricing policy; new hits from the Top 100 are $1.29 each, while millions of "back catalog" titles are $0.69. Other songs will still sell for $0.99. The new pricing policy coincided with Apple's decision to abandon digital rights management (DRM) copy protection on the files it sells. This change means that songs purchased on iTunes can be played back on devices other than the iPod and iPhone.

TECHNOLOGY FORECAST

Sales of cell phones with cameras reached 460 million units in 2006. By 2010, the number sold per year will exceed 1 billion.[40]

Gartner, Inc.

TECHNOLOGY FORECAST

By 2011, annual worldwide mobile music purchases will total $14 billion. Asia is expected to account for 40 percent of the market.[42]

Juniper Research

TECHNOLOGY FORECAST

Online music spending in the United States is forecast to reach $2.5 billion (22 percent of music sales) in 2011. Ringtones will account for an additional 12 percent.

Jupiter Research

[40]Kevin Maney, "Baby's Arrival Inspires Birth of Cell Phone Camera—and Societal Evolution," *USA Today* (January 24, 2007), p. 3B.
[41]Bob Tedeschi, "E-Commerce Report," *The Wall Street Journal* (February 23, 2004), p. C5.
[42]Bob Ibison, "Deal Could Be Music to Nokia's Ears," *Financial Times* (August 14, 2006), p. 14.

Mobile Gaming

There is a growing trend toward mobile gaming; eMarketer estimates that nearly 300 million cell phone subscribers play games that they have downloaded on their handsets. Revenues from mobile games totaled $1.7 billion in 2007; eMarketer predicts that figure will increase to $7 billion by 2012. Popular categories include puzzles such as Sudoku; solitaire, blackjack, and other card and casino games; and board games such as Monopoly. Some games are available for free; others sell for the equivalent of a few dollars. However, the word "free" can be misleading, as network operators typically charge fees for downloading games.

Because cell phones have small screens and limited storage space and computing power, mobile gaming originally appealed more to occasional users such as commuters rather than hard-core gamers. Industry growth was also slowed by the varying technical standards incorporated into different brands of telephones. However, mobile games are quickly becoming more sophisticated as phone makers improve compatibility and add more features and functionality. GPS capability will lead to location-based games in which players compete by trying to physically approach their opponents.

Currently, the economics of mobile gaming do not favor game developers; cell phone service providers keep 10 to 70 percent of the selling price of each game downloaded. Moreover, for games based on popular motion pictures, game developers are required to pay licensing fees to the film studios.[43] John du Pre Gaunt, an eMarketer analyst, explains why mobile gaming is growing more slowly in the United States than elsewhere. "The United States will never become a gigantic mobile game market on a par with India and China (with their huge populations) or Japan (with its fanatical gaming user base), but the U.S. mobile gaming market does exist in the world's largest interactive advertising economy. That, combined with advanced handsets and an increase in unlimited mobile data plans, could cause marketers to look at U.S. mobile gaming in a new light," he said.[44]

Internet Phone Service

For the telecommunications industry, Internet telephone service is the "next big thing." **Voice over Internet protocol (VoIP)** technology allows the human voice to be digitized and broken into data packets that can be transmitted over the Internet and converted back into normal speech. If a call is placed to a conventional phone, it must be switched from the Internet to a traditional phone network; local telephone companies generally own the lines into residences and businesses. However, if the call is made between two subscribers to the same VoIP provider, it bypasses the traditional network altogether. The implications are clear: VoIP has the potential to render the current telecommunications infrastructure—consisting primarily of twisted copper and fiber optic cable—obsolete.

Currently, VoIP accounts for only a small percentage of global calling. However, it has the potential to be a disruptive innovation that will upset the balance of power in the telecommunications industry. The promise of a global growth market resulted in soaring stock values for start-up companies. In Europe, Niklas Zennström, the co-founder of the KaZaA music file sharing service, started Skype Ltd. to offer Internet telephone service. As hundreds of thousands of new users—many in China, India, and Sweden—joined each day, Skype became a global phenomenon. In 2005, eBay acquired Skype for $2.6 billion. However, despite the fact that Skype currently has more than 400 million users, eBay struggled to create synergies between the communication system and the company's core auction business. In 2009, eBay announced plans to spin off Skype as a separate company.

Digital Books and Electronic Reading Devices

The digital revolution has had a dramatic impact on traditional print media properties such as newspapers and magazines. Publishers are experiencing dramatic downturns in readership as people spend more time online. At the same time, the global recession has forced many

---

[43]David Pringle, "Making Games for Cell Phones Is No Easy Play," *The Wall Street Journal* (October 17, 2003), p. B1.
[44]*The eMarketer Daily* (August 26, 2008).

companies to cut back on print advertising. Caught in a squeeze, magazines are folding and newspaper companies are declaring bankruptcy. Electronic readers such as the Kindle from Amazon.com and Sony's Reader Digital Book may help lure subscribers back.

Amazon sold the first Kindle for $359; the new, larger Kindle DX costs $489, holds 3,500 books, and has a 9.7-inch display screen (see Exhibit 15-6). Industry observers also believe colleges and universities may be instrumental in building awareness and encouraging adoption of electronic readers. The reason is simple: electronic versions of textbooks represent a huge market opportunity. As Amazon.com founder and CEO Jeff Bezos explains:

> Physical textbooks get resold as used textbooks five or six times after the initial sale. The publisher has to capture all that value on that first sale. There's a real opportunity here to have a very good business for textbook publishers, and at the same time lower the prices of textbooks for students.[45]

For example, the textbook you are reading is available direct from the publisher in the form of an electronic "subscription" at www.coursesmart.com. The online version requires users to be connected to the Internet; the text can be accessed from an unlimited number of computers. Buyers can use the e-book for 180 days before the subscription expires. The price is approximately half of what bookstores charge for a new copy of the physical textbook. Usually, students can print as many as 10 pages at a time; it is also possible to cut and paste, highlight, and take notes directly on the computer. Industry insiders and Steve Jobs watchers predict that Apple will enter the e-book market with its own reader. Meanwhile, Amazon has taken the Kindle global with the launch of a small, less expensive version that can be used in more than 100 countries.

As is the case with music and movies, digital piracy is a growing problem with electronic editions of books. A number of Web sites and file-sharing services distribute unauthorized copies of popular copyrighted material. What do the authors themselves think of the problem? Some view digital piracy as a way to gain new readers. Others say that they simply want fair compensation for their work. A third camp includes authors who don't think pursuing the pirates is worth the effort. As best-selling author Stephen King said recently, "The question is, how much time and energy do I want to spend chasing these guys? And to what end? My sense is that most of them live in basements floored with carpeting remnants, living on Funions and discount beer."[46]

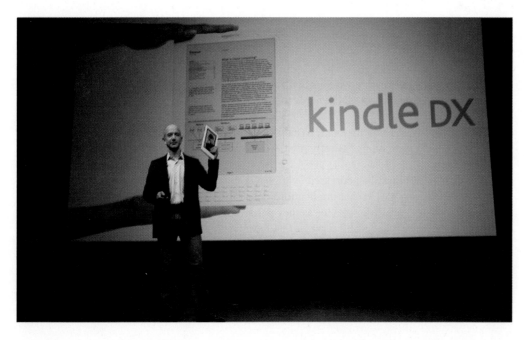

Exhibit 15-6: Amazon.com founder and CEO Jeff Bezos unveils the Kindle DX, the latest version of his company's wireless reading device. Bezos is hoping that the Kindle will gain acceptance among college students.
Source: John Angelillo/UPI/Newscom.

[45]Edward C. Baig, "Larger Kindle Lands with Larger Price," *USA Today* (May 7, 2009), p. 3B.
[46]Motoko Rich, "New Target for Digital Pirates: The Printed Word," *The New York Times* (May 12, 2009), p. A1.

Summary

The **digital revolution** has created a global electronic marketplace. The revolution has gained momentum over the course of 70-plus years, during which time technological breakthroughs included the digital mainframe computer; the **transistor**; the **integrated circuit; the personal computer**; the **spreadsheet**, the PC **operating system**; and the **Internet,** which originated as an initiative of the Defense Advanced Research Projects Agency (**DARPA**). Three key innovations by Tim Berners-Lee, the **URL, http**, and **HTML**, led to the creation in the early 1990s of the **World Wide Web**.

The digital revolution has resulted in a process known as **convergence**, meaning that previously separate industries and markets are coming together. In this environment, the **innovator's dilemma** means that company management must decide whether to invest in current technologies or try to develop new technologies. Although leading firms in an industry often develop **sustaining technologies** that result in improved product performance, the revolution has also unleashed a wave of **disruptive technologies** that are creating new markets and reshaping industries and **value networks**.

E-commerce is growing in importance for both consumer and industrial goods marketers. Generally, commercial Web sites can have a domestic or global focus; in addition, they can be classified as **promotion sites**, **content sites**, and **transaction sites**. Global marketers must take care when designing Web sites. Country-specific domain names must be registered and local-language sites developed. In addition to addressing issues of technology and functionality, content must reflect local culture, customs, and aesthetic preferences. **Cybersquatting** can hinder a company's effort to register its corporate name as an Internet destination.

The Internet is a powerful tool for advertisers; **click-through rates** are one measure of effectiveness. Another trend is **paid search advertising**. New products and services spawned by the digital revolution include: **broadband,** which permits transmission of **streaming media** over the Internet; **mobile commerce (m-commerce)**, which is made possible by **Wi-Fi, Bluetooth, WiMax,** and other forms of wireless connectivity; **telematics** and **global positioning systems (GPS)**; and **short message service (SMS). Smart phones** are creating new markets for **mobile music** downloads, including ringtones, truetones, and full-track music files; they can also be used for mobile gaming and Internet phone service using **VoIP**.

Discussion Questions

1. Briefly review the key innovations that culminated in the digital revolution. What is the basic technological process that made the revolution possible?
2. What is convergence? How is convergence affecting Sony? Kodak? Nokia?
3. What is the innovator's dilemma? What is the difference between sustaining technology and disruptive technology? Briefly review Christensen's five principles of disruptive innovation.
4. What key issues must be addressed by global companies that engage in e-commerce?
5. What is the Long Tail? What implications does this have for market segmentation?
6. Briefly outline Web design issues as they pertain to global marketing.
7. Review the key products and services that have emerged during the digital revolution. What are some new products and services that are not mentioned in the chapter?
8. You have the option of purchasing an electronic edition of *Global Marketing* and other textbooks. Is this something that you are interested in doing?
9. Which pricing model do you think is the best for music downloads, iTunes Store's "pay-per-track" or Rhapsody's subscription service? Why?

In the chapter opening, you were introduced to several prominent individuals who use the Twitter social media Web site. For example, Sir Richard Branson is the charismatic founder and chairman of the Virgin Group. Two of his companies, Virgin Atlantic and Virgin America, have their own presence on Twitter (www.twitter.com/virginatlantic and www.twitter.com/virginamerica, respectively). As Sir Richard told *BusinessWeek*, "With more than 200 Virgin companies worldwide, my days and nights are filled with exciting service launches, product announcements, parties, events, and consumer opportunities. I'm regularly asked what a day in the life of Richard Branson looks like, and Twitter helps me answer that. It also enables communication no matter where I am."

Other corporate chiefs report similar experiences. Mozilla's John Lilly says, "Mozilla is a huge community of people all around the world—different time zones, countries, companies—and Twitter lets me follow both the mood and the substance of the community sort of in my peripheral vision." Tony Hsieh, CEO of Internet shoe retailer Zappos.com, confesses that he is hooked on Twitter as well. Hsieh uses Twitter as a media-sharing device; many Twitter postings include links to articles of interest from various news sources. "I generally get all my news through Twitter," Hsieh says.

Despite such enthusiastic endorsements, many people aren't sure what Twitter is, why they would want to use it, and how it is different from, say, Facebook. This is understandable; as noted in the *Financial Times*, "Operating at the juncture of blogging, texting, and social networking, the service defies easy categorization." Descriptions of Twitter often include "community," "conversation," "engagement," and similar words. However, some companies have been quick to harness Twitter's potential as a sales promotion tool. For example, a quick look at Dell's Web site, www.dell.com/twitter, reveals that the computer marketer's Twitter streams offer online shoppers discount codes that they can use when buying refurbished computers or "scratch and dent" closeouts. Dell is also involved with community sites (e.g., Digital_Nomads) and blogs in various languages, including Japanese and Chinese.

Twitter was launched in 2006 by Silicon Valley entrepreneurs Biz Stone and Evan Williams. The founders created the service with some interesting features. For example, Twitter is integrated with Facebook, so users can choose to have their status update tweets automatically appear on their Facebook page. Twitter was also designed to work with third-party applications, or "apps." For example, TwitPic is an app that allows users to share photos via a link in their tweets. Twitterific is an app from the iTunes store that gives iPod users direct access to Twitter.

Users must master some new terms and symbols. Members of Twitter's online community are known as "tweeps." "Tweet" can be both a noun and a verb; when users update their pages, they are "tweeting"; each individual entry is a "tweet." It is possible to "retweet" ("RT"); that is, forward someone else's tweet. Each Twitter user can choose other users to follow. Twitter is searchable; entries marked with a "#" symbol ("hashtag") are a group of tweets about a particular subject. The "@" symbol is used to link a tweet to another user.

In keeping with Twitter's status as a social medium and community, users in a particular geographic area can meet face-to-face in "tweetups." Attendees wear tweetup badges, which can be equipped with QR ("quick response") codes. The codes are scannable; an app is available that enables a smart phone's camera to read the code and directly access the Twitter page of the person wearing the badge.

Twitter's success has been accompanied by some major challenges. So far, the company has raised $55 million in venture capital and is attracting millions of new users. Even so, it is unclear whether Twitter will achieve the levels of global popularity enjoyed by YouTube and Facebook. One issue is the number of users who quit using the service after trying it. Then there is the issue of making money. Although the founders insist that they will never charge for the basic service, they may ultimately charge business users for access to premium services. Stone and Williams are also weighing partnership opportunities with Microsoft and Google. A redesign of Twitter's home page is in the works; the new design will help people understand how they can use the site to discover what is happening around them. As Stone explains, "In the long run, we need to make Twitter the product more relevant to more people."

Case 15-1 Discussion Questions

1. Twitter seems to have a polarizing effect on people; some are excited by it, others seem angry or even scared. What is the explanation for this?
2. You have just been hired as director of social media at a global company. This is a newly created position. What will you do during your first week on the job?
3. In the long run, how will Twitter generate revenues? Will it be through advertising, subscriptions, or some other source?

Sources: Jessica E. Vascellaro, "Twitter Trips on Its Rapid Growth," *The Wall Street Journal* (May 26, 2009), p. B1; Jessica E. Vascellaro, "Firms Seek Profits in Twitter's Chatter," *The Wall Street Journal* (March 25, 2009), p. B1; Richard Waters, "Sweet to Tweet," *Financial Times* (February 27, 2009), p. 8.

Case 15-2
eBay in Asia

eBay, the company whose name is synonymous with online auctions in the United States, is one of the legendary success stories of the digital revolution. Today the company is a cultural phenomenon, boasting 230 million registered users who can bid on 45,000 different categories of goods at any given time, customers are engaged in 100 million auctions. The company also hosts more than 250,000 online stores. In 2006, eBay generated $5.9 billion in revenues; this represents an increase of more than 100 percent from 2003. To sustain this type of growth, eBay's executive team has set its sights on international expansion. Today, the company has successfully established a presence in several countries, including Australia, Brazil, Spain, and Switzerland.

However, one of eBay's first forays outside the United States ended in defeat. Yahoo! opened its Internet portal in Japan in April 1996, four years ahead of eBay's entry. Yahoo! Japan was a joint venture between Yahoo! Inc. and Japan's Softbank Corp. Yahoo! Japan was modeled on its U.S. parent; a variety of free services was available, including news, chat rooms, and e-mail. As more users logged on, increasing numbers of advertisers paid to post banner ads on the site. In due course, Yahoo! founder Jerry Yang and Softbank chairman Masayoshi Son encouraged Yahoo! Japan chief Masahiro Inoue to start offering online auctions. Yang had been blindsided by eBay's U.S. success and did not want to repeat the mistake a second time. Inoue resisted, noting that the Japanese have little experience with auctions of any kind. He was also skeptical that status-conscious Japanese consumers would buy products from complete strangers. However, Yang continued to press his case, stressing that eBay was gearing up for a Japanese launch. Moreover, with advertising providing 80 percent of Yahoo!'s revenues in the United States, Yang was anxious to diversify the venture's revenue stream.

In the end, Inoue relented; his team of engineers had Yahoo! Japan's auction site operational in September 1999. eBay launched its Japanese service in February 2000. Taking its cue from eBay's early development in the United States, management stressed used collectibles. This turned out to be a mistake; Japanese users showed more interest in bidding on new goods. eBay also erred by charging a commission on each transaction; initially, Yahoo! Japan users did not pay commissions or monthly fees. By the end of 2001, between 20,000 and 25,000 items were listed on eBay's Japanese site; by contrast, Yahoo! Japan had more than 3 million items. As eBay CEO Meg Whitman noted, "We're definitely in catch-up mode." In March 2001, after barely more than a year, eBay closed down the service.

Despite the setback in Japan, eBay continues to expand in Asia. In 2003, the company paid $180 million to acquire Eachnet, a popular Chinese consumer auction site. Once again, eBay faces competition from Yahoo!, whose entry strategy included investing in a Chinese language search development company and forming a joint venture auction site with Sina.com. In 2005, Yahoo! bought a 40 percent stake in Alibaba, a company founded by Chinese Internet entrepreneur Jack Ma that operates an auction site called Taobao.com. Initially, Taobao.com users were not charged sales commissions or listing fees.

Ma believes that global Internet companies are prone to making three types of mistakes in approaching China: They underestimate the differences between China and the U.S. market; they incur higher costs than local companies; and they go global too quickly. In 2004, Ma summarized the situation by observing, "[eBay and Yahoo!] are the sharks in the ocean, and we are the crocodiles in the Yangtze River. When they fight in the Yangtze River, they will be in trouble. The smell of the water is different." Now that Ma has joined forces with Yahoo!, he has changed his tune slightly. "I know the Chinese user market and users better than Meg Whitman. Once we start to charge, we can be profitable in 18 months," Ma said.

Ma's words were prescient: In September 2006, Martin Wu, head of eBay China, resigned. At the end of the year, eBay announced that it had spent $40 million for a 49 percent stake in Tom Online, a Chinese Internet portal and wireless operator. eBay shut down its main Chinese Web site and launched a new auction site using the Eachnet brand name. By the end of 2008, Taobao was China's number one auction site, with a market share of approximately 76 percent. Eachnet had about 8 percent. Meanwhile, Baidu.com, the Chinese Internet search company, announced that it would launch its own e-commerce site.

Discussion Questions

1. Why has eBay struggled in Japan, China, and other Asian markets?
2. eBay is making a strategic shift by giving control of its main China operation to Tom Online. What does this shift signify?

Sources: Sky Canaves, "Sites Battle for Chinese Web Users," *The Wall Street Journal* (October 9, 2008), p. B4; Chris Nuttal and Mure Dickie, "EBay Tries to Fix Its Strategy in China," *Financial Times* (December 20, 2006), p. 15; Moon Ihlwan and Rob Hof, "Out-eBaying eBay in Korea," *Business Week* (July 17, 2006), p. 74; Mylene Mangalindan, "Hot Bidding: In a Challenging China Market, eBay Confronts a Big New Rival," *The Wall Street Journal* (August 12, 2005), pp. A1, A6; Jason Dean and Jonathan Cheng, "Meet Jack Ma, Who Will Guide Yahoo in China," *The Wall Street Journal* (August 12, 2005), p. B1; Mure Dickie, "China's Crocodiles Ready for a Fight," *Financial Times* (July 14, 2004), p. 18; Nick Wingfield, "eBay, Conceding Missteps, Will Close Its Site in Japan," *The Wall Street Journal* (February 27, 2002), p. B4; Ken Belson, Rob Hof, and Ben Elgin, "How Yahoo! Japan Beat eBay at Its Own Game," *Business Week* (June 4, 2001), p. 58; Robert A. Guth, "Yahoo Japan Learns from Parent's Achievements and Errors," *The Wall Street Journal* (December 11, 2000), p. A28.

Case 15-3
Barry Diller and IAC/InterActiveCorp

Barry Diller has always been a man with big plans. He began his career in the mailroom at the fabled William Morris talent agency. His next stop was ABC Television, where his programming innovations included the *Movie of the Week* and the miniseries. Television proved to be a stepping-stone to Hollywood; in 1974, at the age of 34, Diller became chairman of Paramount Pictures. In 1984, he moved on to 20th Century Fox. Cable television was next; Diller took the top spot at QVC, the home shopping channel. After resigning from QVC in the mid-1990s, Diller began building a media company that he named USA Networks. He bought the Home Shopping Network (HSN) and a family of TV stations.

During the next few years, however, the burgeoning dot-com scene caught his eye. He was intrigued by the possibilities for e-commerce, especially online retailing. In 2001, only one year after the dot-com bubble had burst, he bought a 64 percent stake in Expedia, the online travel service.

To raise additional money to invest, he sold USA Networks to Vivendi Universal, the French media company, for $11 billion. Diller's vision was to make his new company, IAC/InterActiveCorp, the world's largest e-commerce enterprise. By 2006 IAC was the world's largest provider of online travel services through its Hotels.com and Expedia.com Web sites. IAC also owned Ticketmaster, the world's leading ticketing service, and online personals listing services Match.com and uDate.com.

The travel industry experienced a steep downturn in the aftermath of the terror attacks of September 11. In an effort to put "heads in beds," InterContinental, Marriott, and other major hotel chains sold excess room inventory at a discount to Hotels.com and other online services. When a traveler books a room through, say, Hotels.com, the price he or she pays is 20 to 30 percent more than Hotels.com's cost; thus, each transaction nets a tidy gross margin for Hotels.com. According to estimates compiled by Smith Travel Research, in the United States alone, online services redirected $1 billion in revenues away from the hotel operators.

Hotel operators took notice and began developing their own online services. InterContinental has been especially aggressive, launching brand-neutral sites such as "Accommodations.info" and "DealsonHotels.com" that direct users to various hotel properties run by InterContinental. The company has also launched Web sites in French, German, Spanish, and Chinese. As Eric Pearson, vice president of e-commerce at InterContinental, noted, "There's a huge demand from consumers traveling abroad. That shows proof positive that if you're a global company, you need to provide services around the world."

Recently, Diller has begun sharpening his focus on Internet search. Diller spun off the Expedia.com business; Hotels.com is a subsidiary. Diller retained a controlling 60-percent stake. His next move was to divest Ticketmaster. He also acquired the Ask Jeeves search engine for $1.7 billion and renamed it Ask.com.

Why did Diller break up IAC? In a recent interview, he said that the company had become overly complex and unmanageable. He also conceded that it was very difficult to understand Internet advertising. Going forward, Diller has set clear parameters for IAC: advertising-based Internet businesses that leverage the company's strengths at marketing and distribution.

Discussion Questions

1. Why did Barry Diller divest several of IAC's businesses and acquire Ask Jeeves?
2. Which search engine do you use most frequently? Why?
3. What acquisition do you think Diller will make next?

Sources: Shira Ovide, "Barry Diller's Breakup: Why IAC Didn't Work," *The Wall Street Journal* (October 7, 2008), p. B4; Aaron O. Patrick, "Ask.Com's 'Revolt' Risks Costly Clicks," *Wall Street Journal* (April 5, 2007), p. B8; Peter Grand and Sara Silver, "Diller Retools IAC to Compete with Web Stars," *The Wall Street Journal* (August 31, 2006), pp. C1, C5; Grant, "Diller's IAC, AOL to Invest in Web-TV Company," *The Wall Street Journal* (November 22, 2005), p. B4; Dennis K. Berman and Kevin J. Delaney, "Diller's IAC Nears Deal for Jeeves," *The Wall Street Journal* (March 21, 2005), p. A3; Tim Burt and Peter Thal Larsen, "The Negotiator-in-Chief," *Financial Times* (April 27, 2004), p. 11; Betty Liu and Amy Lee, "Hoteliers Try to Evict an Unwelcome Visitor," *Financial Times* (April 19, 2004), p. 6; Timothy J. Mullaney and Ronald Grover, "The Web Mogul" (Cover Story), *Business Week* (October 13, 2003), pp. 62–66+; Tim Burt and Peter Thal Larsen, "Inside Barry Diller's Hive of Interactivity," *Financial Times* (September 19, 2003), p. 10.

Barry Diller has been described as a no-nonsense, cut-to-the-chase kind of businessperson. Hailed by some as a visionary, Diller laid the groundwork for a successful e-commerce empire by investing in companies with strong business plans and services that are well matched to the Internet.
Source: IAC/InterActiveCorp.

Strategic Elements of Competitive Advantage

Case 16-1
IKEA

The first few years of the twenty-first century were difficult for IKEA, the $31 billion global furniture powerhouse based in Sweden. The euro's strength dampened financial results, as did an economic downturn in Central Europe. The company faces increasing competition from hypermarkets, "do-it-yourself" retailers such as Walmart, and supermarkets that are expanding into home furnishings. Looking to the future, CEO Anders Dahlvig is stressing three areas for improvement: product assortment, customer service, and product availability.

With stores in 38 countries, the company's success reflects founder Ingvar Kamprad's "social ambition" of selling a wide range of stylish, functional home furnishings at prices so low that the majority of people can afford to buy them. The store exteriors are painted bright blue and yellow: Sweden's national colors. Shoppers view furniture on the main floor in scores of realistic settings arranged throughout the cavernous showrooms. In a departure from standard industry practice, IKEA's furniture bears names such as "Ivar" and "Sten" instead of model numbers.

At IKEA, shopping is a self-service activity; after browsing and writing down the names of desired items, shoppers can pick up their furniture on the lower level. There they find "flat packs" containing the furniture in kit

Exhibit 16-1: Global marketing experts cite IKEA as an illustration of several key strategic principles. IKEA exemplifies the concept of the flagship firm: The company has built a network of more than 2,000 suppliers in 50 countries. This arrangement has helped IKEA achieve and maintain a low-cost position in the global furniture industry. IKEA reaps further economies by minimizing transportation and delivery costs. Furniture is shipped to the stores in flat packaging; customers assemble the finished pieces themselves.

In its quest for cost leadership, IKEA's management team is mindful of the need for ethical corporate citizenship. In 2000, IKEA launched an initiative in India designed to ensure that the companies that supply it with carpets do not use child labor.
Source: Mark Antman/The Image Works.

form; one of the cornerstones of IKEA's strategy is having customers take their purchases home in their own vehicles and assemble the furniture themselves. The lower level of a typical IKEA store also contains a restaurant, a grocery store called the Swede Shop, a supervised play area for children, and a baby care room. After reading this chapter, turn to Case 16-1 and apply key concepts to an analysis of IKEA's global marketing strategy.

The essence of marketing strategy is successfully relating the strengths of an organization to its environment. As the horizons of marketers have expanded from domestic to regional and global, so too have the horizons of competitors. The reality in almost every industry today, including home furnishings, is global competition. This fact of life puts an organization under increasing pressure to master techniques for conducting industry analysis and competitor analysis, and understanding competitive advantage at both the industry and national levels. This chapter covers these topics in detail.

INDUSTRY ANALYSIS: FORCES INFLUENCING COMPETITION

A useful way of gaining insight into competitors is through industry analysis. As a working definition, an industry can be defined as a group of firms that produce products that are close substitutes for each other. In any industry, competition works to drive down the rate of return on invested capital toward the rate that would be earned in the economist's "perfectly competitive" industry. Rates of return that are greater than this so-called "competitive" rate will stimulate an inflow of capital either from new entrants or from existing competitors making additional investment. Rates of return below this competitive rate will result in withdrawal from the industry and a decline in the levels of activity and competition.

Harvard University's Michael E. Porter, a leading theorist of competitive strategy, developed a **five forces model** that explains competition in an industry: the threat of new entrants, the threat of substitute products or services, the bargaining power of buyers, the bargaining power of suppliers, and the competitive rivalry among current members of the industry. In industries such as soft drinks, pharmaceuticals, and cosmetics, the favorable nature of the five forces has resulted in attractive returns for competitors. However, pressure from any of the forces can limit profitability, as evidenced by the recent fortunes of some competitors in the PC and semiconductor industries. A discussion of each of the five forces follows.

Threat of New Entrants

New entrants to an industry bring new capacity, a desire to gain market share and position, and, quite often, new approaches to serving customer needs. The decision to become a new entrant in an industry is often accompanied by a major commitment of resources. New players mean prices will be pushed downward and margins squeezed, resulting in reduced industry profitability in the long run. Porter describes eight major sources of barriers to entry, the presence or absence of which determines the extent of threat of new industry entrants.[1]

The first barrier, *economies of scale*, refers to the decline in per-unit product costs as the absolute volume of production per period increases. Although the concept of scale economies is frequently associated with manufacturing, it is also applicable to R&D, general administration, marketing, and other business functions. Honda's efficiency at engine R&D, for example, results

---

[1]Michael E. Porter, *Competitive Strategy* (New York: Free Press, 1980), pp. 7–33.

from the wide range of products it produces that feature gasoline-powered engines. When existing firms in an industry achieve significant economies of scale, it becomes difficult for potential new entrants to be competitive.

Product differentiation, the second major entry barrier, is the extent of a product's perceived uniqueness; in other words, whether or not it is a commodity. Differentiation can be achieved as a result of unique product attributes or effective marketing communications, or both. Product differentiation and brand loyalty "raise the bar" for would-be industry entrants who would be required to make substantial investments in R&D or advertising. For example, Intel achieved differentiation and erected a barrier in the microprocessor industry with its "Intel Inside" advertising campaign and logo that appear on many brands of PCs.

A third entry barrier relates to *capital requirements*. Capital is required not only for manufacturing facilities (fixed capital) but also for financing R&D, advertising, field sales and service, customer credit, and inventories (working capital). The enormous capital requirements in such industries as pharmaceuticals, mainframe computers, chemicals, and mineral extraction present formidable entry barriers.

A fourth barrier to entry are the one-time *switching costs* caused by the need to change suppliers and products. These might include retraining, ancillary equipment costs, the cost of evaluating a new source, and so on. The perceived cost to customers of switching to a new competitor's product may present an insurmountable obstacle preventing industry newcomers from achieving success. For example, Microsoft's huge installed base of PC operating systems and applications presents a formidable entry barrier.

A fifth barrier to entry is access to *distribution channels*. If channels are full, or unavailable, the cost of entry is substantially increased because a new entrant must invest time and money to gain access to existing channels or to establish new channels. Some Western companies have encountered this barrier in Japan.

Government policy is frequently a major entry barrier. In some cases, the government will restrict competitive entry. This is true in a number of industries, especially those outside the United States, that have been designated as "national" industries by their respective governments. Japan's postwar industrialization strategy was based on a policy of preserving and protecting national industries in their development and growth phases. The result was a market that proved difficult for non-Japanese competitors to enter, an issue that was targeted by the Clinton administration. American business executives in a wide range of industries urged adoption of a government policy that would reduce some of these barriers and open the Japanese market to more U.S. companies.

Established firms may also enjoy *cost advantages independent of scale economies* that present barriers to entry. Access to raw materials, a large pool of low-cost labor, favorable locations, and government subsidies are several examples.

Finally, expected *competitor response* can be a major entry barrier. If new entrants expect existing competitors to respond strongly to entry, their expectations about the rewards of entry will certainly be affected. A potential competitor's belief that entry into an industry or market will be an unpleasant experience may serve as a strong deterrent. Bruce Henderson, former president of the Boston Consulting Group, used the term "brinkmanship" to describe a recommended approach for deterring competitive entry. Brinkmanship occurs when industry leaders convince potential competitors that any market entry effort will be countered with vigorous and unpleasant responses. This is an approach that Microsoft has used many times to maintain its dominance in software operating systems and applications.

In the three decades since Porter first described the five forces model, the digital revolution appears to have altered the entry barriers in many industries. First and foremost, technology has lowered the cost for new entrants. For example, Barnes & Noble watched an entrepreneurial upstart, Amazon.com, storm the barriers protecting traditional "brick-and-mortar" booksellers. Amazon.com founder Jeff Bezos identified and exploited a glaring inefficiency in book distribution: Bookstores ship unsold copies of books back to publishers to be shredded and turned into pulp. Amazon's centralized operations and increasingly personalized online service enable customers to select from millions of different titles at discount prices and have them delivered to their homes within days. For a growing number of book-buying consumers, Amazon.com eclipses the value proposition of local bookstores that offer "only" a few thousand titles and gourmet coffee bars. Since Bezos founded Amazon.com in 1995, sales have grown to $19.1 billion and the company has expanded into new product lines including CDs, DVDs, and music, movie, and e-book downloads. The company serves tens of millions of customers in more than 160 countries. Barnes & Noble responded by entering the online book market itself even as it continues to be profitable in its traditional bricks-and-mortar business. In the meantime, Bezos has repositioned Amazon.com as an Internet superstore selling electronics and general merchandize.

Threat of Substitute Products

A second force influencing competition in an industry is the threat of substitute products. The availability of substitute products places limits on the prices market leaders can charge in an industry; high prices may induce buyers to switch to the substitute. Once again, the digital revolution is dramatically altering industry structures. In addition to lowering entry barriers, the digital era means that certain types of products can be converted to bits and distributed in pure digital form. For example, the development of the MP3 file format for music was accompanied by the increased popularity of peer-to-peer (p-to-p) file swapping among music fans. Napster and other online music services offered a substitute to consumers who are tired of paying $15 or more for a CD. Although a U.S. court severely curtailed Napster's activities, other services—including several outside the United States—have sprung up in its place. The top players in the music industry were taken by surprise, and even now Sony BMG, Warner Music, EMI, and Universal Music Group are struggling to develop new strategies in response to the changing business environment.

Bargaining Power of Buyers

In Porter's model, "buyers" refers to manufacturers (e.g., GM) and retailers (e.g., Walmart) rather than consumers. The ultimate aim of such buyers is to pay the lowest possible price to obtain the products or services that they require. Usually, therefore, if they can, buyers drive down profitability in the supplier industry. To accomplish this, the buyers have to gain leverage over their vendors. One way they can do this is to purchase in such large quantities that supplier firms are highly dependent on the buyers' business. Second, when the suppliers' products are viewed as commodities—that is, as standard or undifferentiated—buyers are likely to bargain hard for low prices because many firms can meet their needs. Buyers will also bargain hard when the supplier industry's products or services represent a significant portion of the buying firm's costs. A fourth source of buyer power is the willingness and ability to achieve backward integration.

For example, because it purchases massive quantities of goods for resale, Walmart is in a position to dictate terms to any vendor wishing to distribute its products at the retail giant's stores. The Coca-Cola Company and PepsiCo are two of the companies that cater to the retailer's demands, creating new products and altering delivery systems. Walmart's influence also extends to the recorded music industry; Walmart refuses to stock CDs bearing parental advisory stickers for explicit lyrics or violent imagery. Recording artists who want their recordings available at Walmart have the option of altering lyrics and song titles or deleting offending tracks. Likewise, artists are sometimes asked to change album cover art if Walmart deems it offensive (see Exhibit 16-2). Recently, Walmart launched Soundcheck, which consists of performances by up-and-coming recording artists that are broadcast every Friday night on the in-house television network found in each store. Exclusive tracks featuring special versions of songs by the Soundcheck sessions' artists are also available at http://soundcheck.walmart.com.[2]

"Walmart is the 800-pound gorilla. You're going to want to do more things for a customer who is growing as fast as Walmart is."[3]
Ted Taft, Meridian Consulting Group

Bargaining Power of Suppliers

Supplier power in an industry is the converse of buyer power. If suppliers have enough leverage over industry firms, they can raise prices high enough to significantly influence the profitability of their organizational customers. Several factors determine suppliers' ability to gain leverage over industry firms. Suppliers will have the advantage if they are large and relatively few in number.

[2]Jonathan Birchall, "Walmart, the Record Label," *Financial Times* (January 31, 2006), p. 17.
[3]Melanie Warner, "Its Wish, Their Command," *The New York Times* (March 3, 2006), p. C1.

Exhibit 16-2: In the late 1990s, "big-box retail" only accounted for about 20 percent of recorded music sales; a few years later, the figure was about 65 percent. Much of the discounters' growth in this area came at the expense of specialty music stores. One way that Walmart exercises its buying power is by refusing to stock CDs bearing "Parental Advisory" stickers. Until recently, Walmart was the biggest music retailer in the United States. In 2008, data compiled by NPD MusicWatch confirmed that Apple's iTunes Music Store had surpassed Walmart to become number one.
Source: David Young-Wolff/ PhotoEdit Inc.

Second, when the suppliers' products or services are important inputs to user firms, are highly differentiated, or carry switching costs, the suppliers will have considerable leverage over buyers. Suppliers will also enjoy bargaining power if alternative products do not threaten their business. A fourth source of supplier power is the willingness and ability of suppliers to develop their own products and brand names if they are unable to get satisfactory terms from industry buyers.

In the tech world, Microsoft and Intel are two companies with substantial supplier power. Because about 90 percent of the world's nearly 1 billion PCs run on Microsoft's operating systems and 80 percent use Intel's microprocessors, the two companies enjoy a great deal of leverage relative to Dell, Hewlett-Packard, and other computer manufacturers. Microsoft's industry dominance prompted both the U.S. government and the European Union to launch separate antitrust investigations. Today, the shift is on to new electronic devices such as smart phones and netbook computers that run the Linux operating system instead of Windows and that use chips from competitors such as Qualcomm and Texas Instruments. As these trends take hold, Microsoft and Intel will find their supplier power diminishing.[4]

Rivalry Among Competitors

Rivalry among firms refers to all the actions taken by firms in the industry to improve their positions and gain advantage over each other. Rivalry manifests itself in price competition, advertising battles, product positioning, and attempts at differentiation. To the extent that rivalry among firms forces companies to rationalize costs, it is a positive force. To the extent that it drives down prices, and therefore profitability, and creates instability in the industry, it is a negative factor. Several factors can create intense rivalry. Once an industry becomes mature, firms focus on market share and how it can be gained at the expense of others. Second, industries characterized by high fixed costs are always under pressure to keep production at full capacity to cover the fixed costs. Once the industry accumulates excess capacity, the drive to fill capacity will push prices—and profitability—down. A third factor affecting rivalry is lack of differentiation or an absence of switching costs, which encourages buyers to treat the products or services as commodities and shop for the best prices. Again, there is downward pressure on prices and profitability. Fourth, firms with high strategic stakes in achieving success in an industry generally are destabilizing because they may be willing to accept below-average profit margins to establish themselves, hold position, or expand.

---

[4]Olga Kharif, Peter Burrows, and Cliff Edwards, "Windows and Intel's Digital Divide," *Business Week* (February 23, 2009), p. 58.

EMERGING MARKETS BRIEFING BOOK

⮫ Cemex

Mexico's S.A. de C.V. Cemex is a global building solutions company with operations in more than 50 countries. Chief executive Lorenzo Zambrano, the grandson of the company's founder, holds an MBA degree from Stanford University. To help drive sales in Mexico, where Cemex commands more than 50 percent of the market, the company devised an innovative payment method. Migrant workers in the United States can pay for cement that their friends and relatives in Mexico can pick up at a local store.

Zambrano introduced sophisticated technology to the company's operations. For example, satellites and computer software allows company engineers in Mexico to monitor temperatures in kilns across the ocean in Spain. As Zambrano explained, "A cement company is not supposed to be high-tech, but we showed it can be. It is supposed to be boring, but we showed it is not." Under Zambrano's leadership, Cemex had 2007 revenues of $21 billion.

Starting in the early 1990s, Zambrano began extending Cemex's global reach by acquiring Spain's two largest cement companies for $1 billion. Other acquisitions followed in Indonesia, Panama, the Philippines, the United States, Venezuela, and elsewhere. Unfortunately, after a string of successes, one recent acquisition turned out to be disastrous. In 2007, Zambrano paid more than $15 billion to acquire Australia's Rinker Materials Corp. Rinker was a major supplier to the U.S. housing market; as the economic crisis worsened, sales to the United States declined.

There was more bad news; the global credit crunch made it very difficult for Zambrano to refinance some of the debt burden that Cemex had taken on. Moreover, as investors sought security by holding dollars, the greenback's value rose while other currencies weakened. The weaker peso meant that Cemex's dollar-denominated debt was even more of a burden. Rossana Fuentes Berain, author of a biography of the Cemex chief, summed up Zambrano's predicament this way: "For 20 years, he managed Cemex flawlessly. Now people are obviously asking why such brilliant people like Lorenzo could not see this coming. Why weren't they more cautious? Why didn't they ask the right questions?"

Source: Adapted from Joel Millman, "Hard Times for Cement Man," *The Wall Street Journal* (December 11, 2008), pp. A1, A14.

The PC industry is a case in point. For years, demand for PCs grew at an annual rate of 15 percent. When the tech bubble burst in early 2000, however, the computer industry experienced a worldwide slowdown in demand; recent growth has been in the single digits. Dell responded by aggressively cutting prices in a bid to boost share. With profit margins collapsing, competitors struggled to adjust. Dell is legendary for its lean operating philosophy; just $.115 cents of every sales dollar go toward overhead, compared with $0.16 at Gateway, $0.21 at Compaq, and $0.225 cents at Hewlett-Packard.

Dell's factories can assemble a complete PC in 3 minutes. With a build-to-order strategy at the heart of its business model, Dell's sales staff maintains close ties with customers. This approach gives Dell a great deal of flexibility when making pricing decisions.[5] The price war has claimed two victims already; in mid-2001, key rival Compaq was acquired by Hewlett-Packard. Then, in 2007, Taiwan's Acer acquired Gateway. Today, Dell faces new competitive threats as the global recession slams the brakes on industry growth. Businesses are ordering fewer computers and consumers are shopping for laptops in traditional brick-and-mortar stores.[6]

> "Our goal is to shrink the profit pool and take the biggest slice."[7]
>
> Kevin Rollins, President and COO, Dell Inc.

COMPETITIVE ADVANTAGE

Competitive advantage exists when there is a match between a firm's distinctive competencies and the factors critical for success within its industry. Any superior match between company competencies and customers' needs permits the firm to outperform competitors. There are two basic ways to achieve competitive advantage. First, a firm can pursue a low-cost strategy that enables it to offer products at lower prices than competitors. Competitive advantage may also be gained by a strategy of differentiating products so that customers perceive unique benefits, often accompanied by a premium price. Note that both strategies have the same effect: They both

---

[5]Gary McWilliams, "Lean Machine: How Dell Fine-Tunes Its PC Pricing to Gain Edge in a Slow Market," *The Wall Street Journal* (June 8, 2001), p. A1.
[6]Justin Scheck, "Dell's Revival Strategy Runs into Trouble," *The Wall Street Journal* (November 28, 2008), p. A1.
[7]Richard Waters, "Dell Aims to Stretch Its Way of Business," *Financial Times* (November 13, 2003), p. 8.

contribute to the firm's overall value proposition. Michael E. Porter explored these issues in two landmark books, *Competitive Strategy* (1985) and *Competitive Advantage* (1990); the latter is widely considered to be one of the most influential management books in recent years.

Ultimately, customer perception decides the quality of a firm's strategy. Operating results such as sales and profits are measures that depend on the level of psychological value created for customers: The greater the perceived consumer value, the better the strategy. A firm may market a better mousetrap, but the ultimate success of the product depends on customers deciding for themselves whether or not to buy it. Value is like beauty; it's in the eye of the beholder. In sum, creating more value than the competition achieves competitive advantage, and customer perception defines value.

Two different models of competitive advantage have received considerable attention. The first offers "generic strategies," four routes or paths that organizations choose to offer superior value and achieve competitive advantage. According to the second model, generic strategies alone did not account for the astonishing success of many Japanese companies in the 1980s and 1990s. The more recent model, based on the concept of "strategic intent," proposes four different sources of competitive advantage. Both models are discussed in the following paragraphs.

> "The only way to gain lasting competitive advantage is to leverage your capabilities around the world so that the company as a whole is greater than the sum of its parts. Being an international company—selling globally, having global brands or operations in different countries—isn't enough."[8]
> David Whitwam, former CEO, Whirlpool

Generic Strategies for Creating Competitive Advantage

In addition to the "five forces" model of industry competition, Michael Porter has developed a framework of so-called generic business strategies based on the two types or sources of competitive advantage mentioned previously: *low-cost* and *differentiation*. The relationship of these two sources with the scope of the target market served (narrow or broad) or product mix width (narrow or wide) yields four **generic strategies**: *cost leadership*, *product differentiation*, *cost focus*, and *focused differentiation*.

Generic strategies aiming at the achievement of competitive advantage or superior marketing strategy demand that the firm make choices. The choices concern the *type of competitive advantage* it seeks to attain (based on cost or differentiation) and the *market scope* or *product mix width* within which competitive advantage will be attained.[9] The nature of the choice between types of advantage and market scope is a gamble, and it is the nature of every gamble that it entails *risk*: By choosing a given generic strategy, a firm always risks making the wrong choice.

BROAD MARKET STRATEGIES: COST LEADERSHIP AND DIFFERENTIATION   Cost leadership is competitive advantage based on a firm's position as the industry's low-cost producer, in broadly defined markets or across a wide mix of products. This strategy has gained widespread appeal in recent years as a result of the popularization of the experience curve concept. In general, a firm that bases its competitive strategy on overall cost leadership must construct the most efficient facilities (in terms of scale or technology) and obtain the largest share of market so that its cost per unit is the lowest in the industry. These advantages, in turn, give the producer a substantial lead in terms of experience with building the product. Experience then leads to more refinements of the entire process of production, delivery, and service, which leads to further cost reductions.

Whatever its source, cost leadership advantage can be the basis for offering lower prices (and more value) to customers in the late, more-competitive stages of the product life cycle. In Japan, companies in a range of industries—photography and imaging, consumer electronics and entertainment equipment, motorcycles, and automobiles—have achieved cost leadership on a worldwide basis.

Cost leadership, however, is a sustainable source of competitive advantage only if barriers exist that prevent competitors from achieving the same low costs. In an era of increasing technological improvements in manufacturing, manufacturers constantly leapfrog over one another in pursuit of lower costs. At one time, for example, IBM enjoyed the low-cost advantage in the production of computer printers. Then the Japanese took the same technology and, after reducing production costs and improving product reliability, gained the low-cost advantage. IBM fought back with a

---

[8]Regina Fazio Maruca, "The Right Way to Go Global: An Interview with Whirlpool CEO David Whitwam," *Harvard Business Review* 72, no. 2 (March–April 1994), p. 135.
[9]Michael E. Porter, *Competitive Advantage: Creating and Sustaining Superior Performance* (New York: Free Press, 1985), p. 12.

highly automated printer plant in North Carolina, where the number of component parts was slashed by more than 50 percent and robots were used to snap many components into place. Despite these changes, IBM ultimately chose to exit the business; the plant was sold.

When a firm's product has an actual or perceived uniqueness in a broad market, it is said to have achieved competitive advantage by **differentiation**. This can be an extremely effective strategy for defending market position and obtaining superior financial returns; unique products often command premium prices (see Exhibit 16-3). Examples of successful differentiation include Maytag in large home appliances, Caterpillar in construction equipment, and almost any successful branded consumer product. Maytag has been called "the Rolls-Royce of washers and dryers;" half the washers sold in the United States are priced at $399 or less, and Maytag

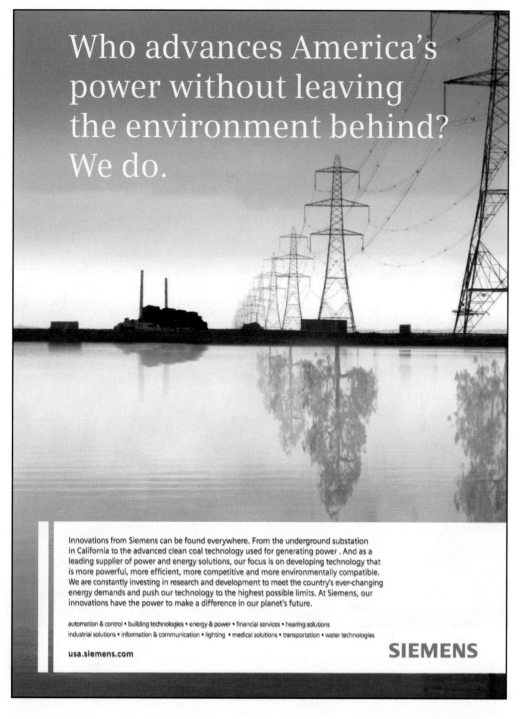

Exhibit 16-3: With annual revenues of $111.7 billion, Munich-based Siemens AG is a key global player in a variety of engineering sectors. Worldwide, public interest in energy-related issues has increased significantly. This advertisement for Siemens' U.S. unit underscores the company's commitment to innovation in power generation, transmission, and distribution to ensure that the nation's energy needs are met.
Source: Courtesy of Siemens Corporation.

does offer a model at that price point. However, Maytag also markets Neptune, a high-tech, water-saving machine; the Neptune line is priced substantially higher than "regular" washers. IBM traditionally has differentiated itself with a strong sales/service organization and the security of the IBM standard in a world of rapid obsolescence. Among athletic shoe manufacturers, Nike has positioned itself as the technological leader thanks to unique product features found in a wide array of shoes.

NARROW TARGET STRATEGIES: COST FOCUS AND FOCUSED DIFFERENTIATION The preceding discussion of cost leadership and differentiation considered only the impact on broad markets. By contrast, strategies to achieve a narrow focus advantage target a narrowly defined market or customer. This advantage is based on an ability to create more customer value for a narrowly targeted segment and results from a better understanding of customer needs and wants. A narrow-focus strategy can be combined with either cost- or differentiation-advantage strategies. In other words, while a *cost focus* means offering low prices to a narrow target market, a firm pursuing *focused differentiation* will offer a narrow target market the perception of product uniqueness at a premium price.

German's *Mittelstand* companies have been extremely successful pursuing **focused differentiation** strategies backed by a strong export effort. The world of "high-end" audio equipment offers another example of focused differentiation. A few hundred small companies design speakers, amplifiers, and related hi-fi gear that costs thousands of dollars per component. While audio components represent a $21 billion market worldwide, annual sales in the high-end segment are only about $1.1 billion. American companies such as Audio Research, Conrad-Johnson, Krell, Mark Levinson, Martin-Logan, and Thiel dominate the segment, which also includes hundreds of smaller enterprises with annual sales of less than $10 million (see Exhibit 16-4). The state-of-the-art equipment these companies offer is distinguished by superior craftsmanship and performance and is highly sought after by audiophiles in Asia (especially Japan and Hong Kong) and Europe. Industry growth is occurring as companies learn more about overseas customers and build relationships with distributors in other countries.[10]

The final strategy is **cost focus**, when a firm's lower cost position enables it to offer a narrow target market and lower prices than the competition. In the shipbuilding industry, for example, Polish and Chinese shipyards offer simple, standard vessel types at low prices that reflect low production costs.[11] Germany's Aldi, a no-frills "hard discounter" with operations in numerous

Exhibit 16-4: In keeping with the design aesthetics of high-end audio gear, Aragon's 7-channel surround sound home theatre preamp and matching amplifier are the epitome of classic, minimalist design. The amplifier alone (bottom unit) retails for about $3,000.
Source: Klipsch Audio Technologies.

---

[10]Personal communication from Kerry Moyer, Senior Director, Industry Programs, Consumer Electronics Association, Arlington, Virginia.
[11]Michael E. Porter, *The Competitive Advantage of Nations* (New York: Free Press, 1990), p. 39.

Exhibit 16-5: Indian pharmaceutical companies such as Ranbaxy and Dr Reddy's Laboratories specialize in low-cost, generic versions of drugs to treat cancer, AIDS, and other diseases. Despite the fact that India passed new patent legislation in 2005 intended to limit the manufacture of generics, Western pharmaceutical companies are concerned about lack of clarity in the laws. Meanwhile, India's pharmaceutical sector is becoming more global; some industry experts expect Indian companies to have at least a 30 percent share of the worldwide generics market.
Source: Amit Bhargava/ Bloomberg News.

countries, offers a very limited selection of household goods at extremely low prices. Indian pharmaceutical manufacturers have taken advantage of patent loopholes to create low-cost generic drugs (see Exhibit 16-5). IKEA, the Swedish furniture company described in the chapter introduction, has grown into a successful global company by combining both the focused differentiation and cost focus strategies. As George Bradley, president of Levitz Furniture in Boca Raton, Florida, noted, "[IKEA] has really made a splash. They're going to capture their niche in every city they go into." Such a strategy can be risky. As Bradley explains, "Their market is finite because it is so narrow. If you don't want contemporary, knock-down furniture, it's not for you. So it takes a certain customer to buy it. And remember, fashions change."[12]

The issue of sustainability is central to this strategy concept. As noted, cost leadership is a sustainable source of competitive advantage only if barriers exist that prevent competitors from achieving the same low costs. Sustained differentiation depends on continued perceived value and the absence of imitation by competitors.[13] Several factors determine whether or not focus can be sustained as a source of competitive advantage. First, a cost focus is sustainable if a firm's competitors are defining their target markets more broadly. A focuser doesn't try to be all things to all people: Competitors may diminish their advantage by trying to satisfy the needs of a broader market segment—a strategy which, by definition, means a blunter focus. Second, a firm's differentiation focus advantage is only sustainable if competitors cannot define the segment even more narrowly. Also, focus can be sustained if competitors cannot overcome barriers that prevent imitation of the focus strategy, and if consumers in the target segment do not migrate to other segments that the focuser doesn't serve.

The Flagship Firm: The Business Network with Five Partners[15]

According to Professors Alan Rugman and Joseph D'Cruz, Porter's model is too simplistic given the complexity of today's global environment. Rugman and D'Cruz have developed an alternative framework based on business networks that they call the **flagship model** (Figure 16-1). Japanese vertical *keiretsu* and Korean *chaebol* have succeeded, Rugman and D'Cruz argue, by adopting

"We're living in a very polarized world now. You're either an absolute price leader—you're a Ryanair, a Southwest Airlines, a Walmart and you're just hugely efficient and you will not be touched on price or cost. Or you're over on the quality end of the market with the Guccis and the Pradas and you're a quality leader."[14]
Steve Ridgway, Chief Executive Officer, Virgin Atlantic Airways

[12]Jeffrey A. Trachtenberg, "Home Economics: IKEA Furniture Chain Pleases with Its Prices, Not with Its Service," *The Wall Street Journal* (September 17, 1991), pp. A1, A5.
[13]Michael E. Porter, *Competitive Advantage: Creating and Sustaining Superior Performance* (New York: Free Press, 1985), p. 158.
[14]Daniel Michaels, "No, the CEO Isn't Sir Richard Branson," *The Wall Street Journal* (July 30, 2007), pp. B1, B3.
[15]The following discussion is adapted from Alan M. Rugman and Joseph R. D'Cruz. *Multinationals as Flagship Firms* (Oxford, England: Oxford University Press, 2000).

FIGURE 16-1

The Flagship Model

Source: Alan M. Rugman and Joseph R. D'Cruz. *Multinationals as Flagship Firms* (Oxford, England: Oxford University Press, 2003), p. 9. By permission of Oxford University Press.

strategies that are mutually reinforcing within a business system and by fostering a collective long-term outlook among partners in the system. Moreover, the authors note, "long-term competitiveness in global industries is less a matter of rivalry between firms and more a question of competition between business systems." A major difference between their model and Porter's is that Porter's is based on the notion of corporate individualism and individual business transactions. For example, as discussed previously, Microsoft's tremendous supplier power allows it to dictate to, and even prosper at the expense of, the computer manufacturers it supplies with operating systems and applications. The flagship model is evident in the strategies of Ford, Volkswagen, and other global automakers; Sweden's IKEA and Italy's Benetton are additional examples (see Exhibit 16-6).

As shown in Figure 16-1, the flagship firm is at the center of a collection of five partners; together, they form a business system that consists of two types of relationships. The flagship firm provides the leadership, vision, and resources to "lead the network in a successful global strategy." *Key suppliers* are those that perform some value-creating activities, such as manufacturing of critical components, better than the flagship. The double-headed arrows that penetrate the flagship and key suppliers in Figure 16-1 indicate that this is a network relationship, with a sharing of strategies, resources, and responsibility for the success of the network. Other suppliers are kept at "arm's length"; these traditional commercial relationships are depicted diagrammatically by arrows that stop at the border of the flagship. Likewise, the flagship has network relationships with *key customers* and more traditional, arm's length commercial relationships with *key consumers*. In the case of Volkswagen, for example, dealers are its key customers while individual car buyers are key consumers; similarly, Benetton's key customers are its retail outlets while the individual clothes shopper is the key consumer. *Key competitors* are companies with which the flagship develops alliances such as those described at the end of Chapter 9. The fifth partner is the *nonbusiness infrastructure* (NBI), comprised of universities, governments, trade unions, and other entities that can supply the network with intangible inputs such as intellectual property and technology. In the flagship model, flagship firms often play a role in the development of a country's industrial policy.

Benetton's success in the global fashion industry illustrates the flagship model. Benetton is the world's largest purchaser of wool, and its centralized buying enables the company to reap

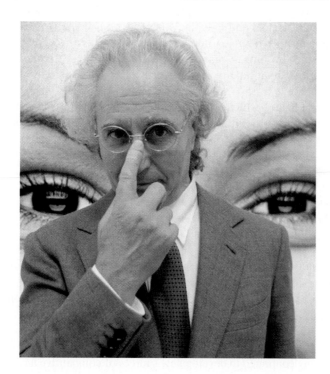

Exhibit 16-6: Luciano Benetton is one of four siblings who founded the Italian fashion company that bears the family's name. Luciano recently stepped down as chairman of the Benetton Group and turned over control of the company to son Alessandro. The change comes as Benetton faces increased competition from fleet-footed global rivals such as Sweden's Hennes & Mauritz (H&M) and Spain's Zara. Some industry observers note that Benetton's business model, which involves partnerships with regional sales agents, will need to be adjusted to reflect the business environments in key emerging markets such as China and India.
Source: Marcelo del Pozo/ Reuters/Corbis—NY.

scale economies. The core activities of cutting and dyeing are retained in-house, and Benetton has made substantial investments in computer-assisted design and manufacturing. However, Benetton is linked to approximately 400 subcontractors that produce finished garments in exclusive supply relationships with the company. In turn, a network of 80 agents who find investors, train managers, and assist with merchandising link the subcontractors to the 5,000 Benetton retail shops. As Rugman and D'Cruz note, "Benetton is organized to reward cooperation and relationship building and the company's structure has been created to capitalize on the benefits of long-term relationships."

Creating Competitive Advantage via Strategic Intent

An alternative framework for understanding competitive advantage focuses on competitiveness as a function of the pace at which a company implants new advantages deep within its organization. This framework identifies **strategic intent**, growing out of ambition and obsession with winning, as the means for achieving competitive advantage. Writing in the *Harvard Business Review*, Gary Hamel and C. K. Prahalad note:

> Few competitive advantages are long lasting. Keeping score of existing advantages is not the same as building new advantages. The essence of strategy lies in creating tomorrow's competitive advantages faster than competitors mimic the ones you possess today. An organization's capacity to improve existing skills and learn new ones is the most defensible competitive advantage of all.[16]

This approach is founded on the principles of W. E. Deming, who stressed that a company must commit itself to continuing improvement in order to be a winner in a competitive struggle. For years, Deming's message fell on deaf ears in the United States, while the Japanese heeded his message and benefited tremendously. Japan's most prestigious business award is named after him. Finally, however, U.S. manufacturers are starting to respond.

---

[16]Gary Hamel and C. K. Prahalad, "Strategic Intent," *Harvard Business Review* 67, no. 3 (May–June 1989), pp. 63–76. See also Hamel and Prahalad, "The Core Competence of the Corporation," *Harvard Business Review* 68, no. 3 (May–June 1990), pp. 79–93.

The significance of Hamel and Prahalad's framework becomes evident when comparing Caterpillar and Komatsu. As noted earlier, Caterpillar is a classic example of differentiation: The company became the largest manufacturer of earthmoving equipment in the world because it was fanatical about quality and service. Caterpillar's success as a global marketer has enabled it to achieve a 35 percent share of the worldwide market for earthmoving equipment, more than half of which represents sales to developing countries. The differentiation advantage was achieved with product durability, global spare parts service (including guaranteed parts delivery anywhere in the world within 48 hours), and a strong network of loyal dealers.

Caterpillar faced a very challenging set of environmental forces during the last several decades. Many of Caterpillar's plants were closed by a lengthy strike in the early 1980s; a worldwide recession at the same time caused a downturn in the construction industry. This hurt companies that were Caterpillar customers. In addition, the strong dollar gave a cost advantage to foreign rivals.

Compounding Caterpillar's problems was a new competitive threat from Japan. Komatsu was the world's number two construction equipment company and had been competing with Caterpillar in the Japanese market for years. Komatsu's products were generally acknowledged to offer a lower level of quality. The rivalry took on a new dimension after Komatsu adopted the slogan "*Maru-c*," meaning "encircle Caterpillar." Emphasizing quality and taking advantage of low labor costs and the strong dollar, Komatsu surpassed Caterpillar as number one in earthmoving equipment in Japan and made serious inroads in the United States and other markets. However, the company continued to develop new sources of competitive advantage even after it achieved world-class quality. For example, new-product development cycles were shortened and manufacturing was rationalized. Caterpillar struggled to sustain its competitive advantage because many customers found that Komatsu's combination of quality, durability, and lower price created compelling value. Yet even as recession and a strong yen put new pressure on Komatsu, the company sought new opportunities by diversifying into machine tools and robots.[17]

The Komatsu/Caterpillar saga illustrates the fact that global competitive battles can be shaped by other factors than the pursuit of generic strategies. Many firms have gained competitive advantage by *disadvantaging* rivals through "competitive innovation." Hamel and Prahalad define *competitive innovation* as "the art of containing competitive risks within manageable proportions" and identify four successful approaches used by Japanese competitors. These are *building layers of advantage*, *searching for loose bricks*, *changing the rules of engagement*, and *collaborating*.

LAYERS OF ADVANTAGE A company faces less risk in competitive encounters if it has a wide portfolio of advantages. Successful companies steadily build such portfolios by establishing layers of advantage on top of one another. Komatsu is an excellent example of this approach. Another is the TV industry in Japan. By 1970, Japan was not only the world's largest producer of black-and-white TV sets but was also well on its way to becoming the leader in producing color sets. The main competitive advantage for such companies as Matsushita at that time was low labor costs.

Because they realized that their cost advantage could be temporary, the Japanese also added an additional layer of *quality and reliability* advantages by building plants large enough to serve world markets. Much of this output did not carry the manufacturer's brand name. For example, Matsushita Electric sold products to other companies such as RCA that marketed them under their own brand names. Matsushita was pursuing a simple idea: A product sold was a product sold, no matter whose label it carried.[18]

In order to build the next layer of advantage, the Japanese spent the 1970s investing heavily in marketing channels and Japanese brand names to gain recognition. This strategy added yet

---

[17]Robert L. Rose and Masayoshi Kanabayashi, "Komatsu Throttles Back on Construction Equipment," *The Wall Street Journal* (May 13, 1992), p. B4.
[18]James Lardner, *Fast Forward: Hollywood, The Japanese, and the VCR Wars* (New York: New American Library, 1987), p. 135.

another layer of competitive advantage: the *global brand franchise*; that is, a global customer base. By the late 1970s, channels and brand awareness were established well enough to support the introduction of new products that could benefit from global marketing—VCRs and photocopy machines, for example. Finally, many companies have invested in *regional manufacturing* so their products can be differentiated and better adapted to customer needs in individual markets.

The process of building layers illustrates how a company can move along the value chain to strengthen competitive advantage. The Japanese began with manufacturing (an upstream value activity) and moved on to marketing (a downstream value activity) and then back upstream to basic R&D. All of these sources of competitive advantage represent mutually reinforcing layers that are accumulated over time.

LOOSE BRICKS A second approach takes advantage of the "loose bricks" left in the defensive walls of competitors whose attention is narrowly focused on a market segment or a geographic area to the exclusion of others. For example, Caterpillar's attention was focused elsewhere when Komatsu made its first entry into the Eastern Europe market. Similarly, Taiwan's Acer prospered by following founder Stan Shih's strategy of approaching the world computer market from the periphery. Shih's inspiration was the Asian board game Go, in which the winning player successfully surrounds opponents. Shih gained experience and built market share in countries overlooked by competitors such as IBM and Compaq. By the time Acer was ready to target the United States in earnest, it was already the number one PC brand in key countries in Latin America, Southeast Asia, and the Middle East.[19]

Intel's loose brick was its narrow focus on complex microprocessors for PCs. Even as it built its core business—it currently commands about 80 percent of the global market for PC processors—demand for non-PC consumer electronics products was exploding in the late 1990s. The new products, which include set-top boxes for televisions, digital cameras, and smart phones, require chips that are far cheaper than those produced by Intel. Competitors such as NEC Corp and LSI Logic recognized the opportunity and beat Intel into an important new market.[20]

CHANGING THE RULES A third approach involves changing the so-called "rules of engagement" and refusing to play by the rules set by industry leaders. For example, in the copier market, IBM and Kodak imitated the marketing strategies used by market leader Xerox. Meanwhile Canon, a Japanese challenger, wrote a new rulebook.

While Xerox built a wide range of copiers, Canon built standardized machines and components, reducing manufacturing costs. While Xerox employed a huge direct sales force, Canon chose to distribute through office-product dealers. Canon also designed serviceability, as well as reliability, into its products so that it could rely on dealers for service rather than incurring the expense required to create a national service network. Canon further decided to sell rather than lease its machines, freeing the company from the burden of financing the lease base. In another major departure, Canon targeted its copiers at secretaries and department managers rather than at the heads of corporate duplicating operations.[21]

Canon introduced the first full-color copiers and the first copiers with "connectivity"— the ability to print images from such sources as video camcorders and computers. The Canon example shows how an innovative marketing strategy—with fresh approaches to the product, pricing, distribution, and selling—can lead to overall competitive advantage in the marketplace. Canon is not invulnerable, however; in 1991 Tektronix, a U.S. company, leapfrogged past Canon in the color copier market by introducing a plain-paper color copier that offered sharper copies at a much lower price.[22]

---

[19]Dan Shapiro, "Ronald McDonald, Meet Stan Shih," *Sales & Marketing Management* (November 1995), p. 86.

[20]Dean Takahashi, "Hand-Held Combat: How the Competition Got Ahead of Intel in Making Cheap Chips," *The Wall Street Journal* (February 12, 1998), pp. A1, A10.

[21]Gary Hamel and C. K. Prahalad, "Strategic Intent," *Harvard Business Review* 67, no. 3 (May–June 1989), p. 69.

[22]G. Pascal Zachary, "Color Printer Gives Tektronix Jump on Canon," *The Wall Street Journal* (June 14, 1991), p. B1.

→ CULTURE WATCH
Jollibee Takes on Ronald McDonald

Quick! What's the most popular fast-food operator in the Philippines? If you answered "McDonald's," then you're probably not familiar with Jollibee. Jollibee operates some 1,700 restaurant locations in the Philippines, more than McDonald's. In the late 1970s, company president Tony Tan decided against acquiring the local McDonald's franchise. Instead, he studied the American fast-food icon, then built a regional empire from the ground up by tailoring menus, advertising, and store atmospherics to the preferences of the 70 million people who live in the Philippines. Even Jollibee's marketing vice president concedes that McDonald's provided the basic blueprint. "They have playlands, we have playgrounds. They have a mascot, we have a mascot. In terms of service and execution, we are all the same."

However, at Jollibee, sweet and spicy flavors predominate in the burgers and chicken dishes, and Jollibee's menu offerings are much more varied than competitors'. Advertising stresses interaction among closely knit family members and national pride; a 1998 ad campaign theme was the centennial anniversary of the nation's independence from Spain. Restaurant interiors are kid-friendly, with play areas and decorations reflecting a cheerful, carnival theme.

In 1989, Jollibee got an unexpected boost when the threat of a military coup prompted McDonald's to temporarily suspend operations. Jollibee even managed to ride out the Asian currency crisis. Manolo Tingzon, the general manager for the international division explained, "People will cut back on everything except food. And even when they do cut back on food spending, they usually will skip fancy and expensive restaurants in times of crisis. We therefore expect fast-food sales to go up." Tan's formula has been so well received that Jollibee commands a 56 percent of the hamburger fast-food segment.

Tan has also applied his fast-food know-how to other dining concepts. Noting the impact of Chinese culture in the Philippines and the rest of Asia, Tan acquired the Chowking and Yonghe King quick-service Asian food chains. As Tan explained, "We Filipinos like Chinese food. It was just a case of finding the right way to present it." Other acquisitions include Greenwich Pizza, Red Ribbon bakeries, and Delifrance French-style cafés. The company currently has about 50 Jollibee restaurants in the United States, Brunei, Vietnam, Saudi Arabia, and Hong Kong.

Sources: James Hookway, "Fast-Food Maven in the Philippines Raises the Ante," *The Wall Street Journal* (October 4, 2002), p. A11; Gertrude Chavez, "The Buzz: Jollibee Hungers to Export Filipino Tastes, Dominate Asian Fast Food," *Advertising Age* (March 9, 1998), p. 14; William McGurn, "Home Advantage: Local Chain Upstages McDonald's in the Philippines," *Far Eastern Economic Review* (November 20, 1997), p. 70; Andrew Tanzer, "Bee Bites Clown," *Forbes* (October 20, 1997), pp. 182–183; Hugh Filman, "Happy Meals for a McDonald's Rival," *Business Week* (July 29, 1996), p. 77.

COLLABORATING A final source of competitive advantage is using know-how developed by other companies. Such *collaboration* may take the form of licensing agreements, joint ventures, or partnerships. History has shown that the Japanese have excelled at using the collaborating strategy to achieve industry leadership. As noted in Chapter 9, one of the legendary licensing agreements of modern business history is Sony's licensing of transistor technology from AT&T's Bell Labs subsidiary in the 1950s for $25,000. This agreement gave Sony access to the transistor and allowed the company to become a world leader. Building on its initial successes in the manufacturing and marketing of portable radios, Sony has grown into a superb global marketer whose name is synonymous with a wide assortment of high-quality consumer electronics products.

More recent examples of Japanese collaboration are found in the aircraft industry. Today, Mitsubishi Heavy Industries Ltd. and other Japanese companies manufacture airplanes under license to U.S. firms and also work as subcontractors for aircraft parts and systems. Many observers fear that the future of the American aircraft industry may be jeopardized as the Japanese gain technological expertise. The next section discusses various examples of "collaborative advantage."[23]

---

[23]Hamel and Prahalad have continued to refine and develop the concept of strategic intent since it was first introduced in their groundbreaking 1989 article. During the 1990s, the authors outlined five broad categories of resource leverage that managers can use to achieve their aspirations: Concentrating resources on strategic goals via convergence and focus; accumulating resources more efficiently via extracting and borrowing; complementing one resource with another by blending and balancing; conserving resources by recycling, co-opting, and shielding; and rapid recovery of resources in the marketplace. Gary Hamel and C. K. Prahalad, "Strategy as Stretch and Leverage," *Harvard Business Review* 71, no. 2 (March–April 1993), pp. 75–84.

GLOBAL COMPETITION AND NATIONAL COMPETITIVE ADVANTAGE[24]

An inevitable consequence of the expansion of global marketing activity is the growth of competition on a global basis. In industry after industry, global competition is a critical factor affecting success. As Yoshino and Rangan have explained, **global competition** occurs when a firm takes a global view of competition and sets about maximizing profits worldwide, rather than on a country-by-country basis. If, when expanding abroad, a company encounters the same rival in market after market, then it is engaged in global competition.[25] In some industries, global companies have virtually excluded all other companies from their markets. An example is the detergent industry, in which three companies—Colgate, Unilever, and Procter & Gamble—dominate an increasing number of detergent markets in Latin America and the Pacific Rim. Many companies can make a quality detergent, but brand-name muscle and the skills required for quality packaging overwhelm local competition in market after market.[26]

The automobile industry has also become fiercely competitive on a global basis. Part of the reason for the initial success of foreign automakers in the United States was the reluctance—or inability—of U.S. manufacturers to design and manufacture high-quality, inexpensive small cars. The resistance of U.S. manufacturers was based on the economics of car production: the bigger the car, the higher the list price. Under this formula, small cars meant smaller unit profits. Therefore, U.S. manufacturers resisted the increasing preference in the U.S. market for smaller cars, a classic case of ethnocentrism and management myopia. European and Japanese manufacturers' product lines have always included cars smaller than those made in the United States. In Europe and Japan, market conditions were much different: less space, high taxes on engine displacement and on fuel, and greater market interest in functional design and engineering innovations. First Volkswagen, then Japanese automakers such as Nissan and Toyota discovered a growing demand for their cars in the U.S. market. It is noteworthy that many significant innovations and technical advances—including radial tires, antilock brakes, and fuel injection—also came from Europe and Japan. Airbags are a notable exception.

The effect of global competition has been highly beneficial to consumers around the world. In the two examples cited, detergents and automobiles, consumers have benefited. In Central America, detergent prices have fallen as a result of global competition. In the United States, foreign companies have provided consumers with the automobile products, performance, and price characteristics they wanted. If smaller, lower-priced imported cars had not been available, it is unlikely that Detroit manufacturers would have provided a comparable product as quickly. What is true for automobiles in the United States is true for every product class around the world. Global competition expands the range of products and increases the likelihood that consumers will get what they want.

The downside of global competition is its impact on the producers of goods and services. Global competition creates value for consumers, but it also has the potential to destroy jobs and profits. When a company offers consumers in other countries a better product at a lower price, this company takes customers away from domestic suppliers. Unless the domestic supplier can create new values and find new customers, the jobs and livelihoods of the domestic supplier's employees are threatened.

This section addresses the following issue: Why is a particular nation a good home base for specific industries? Why, for example, is the United States the home base for the leading competitors in PCs, software, credit cards, and movies? Why is Germany the home of so many world leaders in printing presses, chemicals, and luxury cars? Why are so many leading pharmaceutical, chocolate/confectionery, and trading companies located in Switzerland? Why are the world leaders in consumer electronics based in Japan?

---

[24]This section draws heavily on Chapter 3, "Determinants of National Competitive Advantage," and Chapter 4, "The Dynamics of National Advantage," in Porter, *The Competitive Advantage of Nations,* 1990. For an extended country analysis based on Porter's framework, see Michael Enright, Antonio Francés, and Edith Scott Assavedra, *Venezuela: The Challenge of Competitiveness* (New York: St. Martins Press, 1996).

[25]Michael Y. Yoshino and U. Srinivasa Rangan, *Strategic Alliances: An Entrepreneurial Approach to Globalization* (Boston: Harvard Business School Press, 1995), p. 56.

[26]See Joseph Kahn, "Cleaning Up: P&G Viewed China as a National Market and Is Conquering It," *The Wall Street Journal* (September 12, 1995), pp. A1, A6.

FIGURE 16-2

National Diamond

Source: Reprinted with permission of *Business Review.* Table from Michael E. Porter, "The Competitive Advantage of Nations," *Business Review*, 90, no. 2 (March–April 1990), p. 77. Copyright © 2004 by Business School Publishing Corporation. All rights reserved.

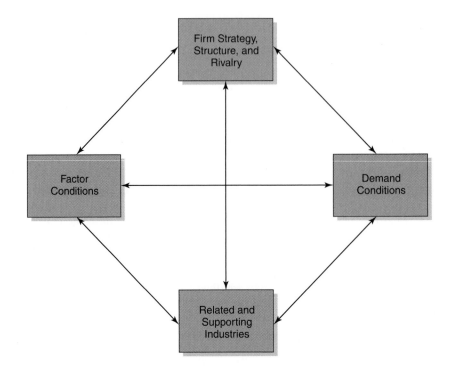

Harvard professor Michael E. Porter addressed these issues in his landmark 1990 book *The Competitive Advantage of Nations*. Many observers hailed the book as a groundbreaking guide for shaping national policies on competitiveness. According to Porter, the presence or absence of particular attributes in individual countries influences industry development, not just the ability of individual firms to create core competences and competitive advantage.[27] Porter describes these attributes—factor conditions, demand conditions, related and supporting industries, and firm strategy, structure, and rivalry—in terms of a national "diamond" (Figure 16-2). The diamond shapes the environment in which firms compete. Activity in any one of the four points of the diamond impacts on all the others and vice versa.

Factor Conditions

Factor conditions refers to a country's endowment with resources. Factor resources may have been created or inherited. *Basic factors* may be inherited or created without much difficulty; because they can be replicated in other nations, they are not sustainable sources of national advantage. Specialized factors, by contrast, are more advanced and provide a more sustainable source for advantage. Porter describes five categories of factor conditions: human, physical, knowledge, capital, and infrastructure.

HUMAN RESOURCES The quantity of workers available, the skills possessed by these workers, the wage levels, and the overall work ethic of the workforce together constitute a nation's human resource factor. Countries with a plentiful supply of low-wage workers have an obvious advantage in the production of labor-intensive products. On the other hand, such countries may be at a *disadvantage* when it comes to the production of sophisticated products requiring highly skilled workers capable of working without extensive supervision.

PHYSICAL RESOURCES The availability, quantity, quality, and cost of land, water, minerals, and other natural resources determine a country's physical resources. A country's size and location are also included in this category, because proximity to markets and sources of supply, as well as transportation costs, are strategic considerations. These factors are important advantages or disadvantages to industries dependent on natural resources.

---

[27]Michael E. Porter, *The Competitive Advantage of Nations* (New York: Free Press, 1990).

KNOWLEDGE RESOURCES The availability within a nation of a significant population having scientific, technical, and market-related knowledge means that the nation is endowed with knowledge resources. The presence of this factor is usually a function of the number of research facilities and universities—both government and private—operating in the country. This factor is important to success in sophisticated products and services, and to doing business in sophisticated markets. This factor relates directly to Germany's leadership in chemicals; for some 160 years, Germany has been home to top university chemistry programs, advanced scientific journals, and apprenticeship programs.

CAPITAL RESOURCES Countries vary in the availability, amount, cost, and types of capital available to the country's industries. The nation's savings rate, interest rates, tax laws, and government deficit all affect the availability of this factor. The advantage enjoyed by industries in countries with low capital costs versus those located in nations with relatively high capital costs is sometimes decisive. Firms paying high capital costs are frequently unable to stay in a market where the competition comes from a nation with low capital costs. The firms with the low cost of capital can keep their prices low and force the firms paying high costs to either accept low returns on investment or leave the industry.

INFRASTRUCTURE RESOURCES Infrastructure includes a nation's banking system, health care system, transportation system, and communications system, as well as the availability and cost of using these systems. More sophisticated industries are more dependent on advanced infrastructures for success.

Competitive advantage accrues to a nation's industry if the mix of factors available to the industry is such that it facilitates pursuit of a generic strategy (i.e., low-cost production or the production of a highly differentiated product or service). Nations that have selective factor *disadvantages* may also indirectly create competitive advantage. For example, the absence of suitable labor may force firms to develop forms of mechanization or automation that give the nation an advantage. High transportation costs may motivate firms to develop new materials that are less expensive to transport.

Demand Conditions

The nature of home demand conditions for the firm's or industry's products and services is important because it determines the rate and nature of improvement and innovation by the firms in the nation. **Demand conditions** are the factors that either train firms for world-class competition or that fail to adequately prepare them to compete in the global marketplace. Three characteristics of home demand are particularly important to the creation of competitive advantage: the composition of home demand, the size and pattern of growth of home demand, rapid home market growth, and the means by which a nation's home demand pulls the nation's products and services into foreign markets.

COMPOSITION OF HOME DEMAND This demand element determines how firms perceive, interpret, and respond to buyer needs. Competitive advantage can be achieved when the home demand sets the quality standard and gives local firms a better picture of buyer needs, at an earlier time, than is available to foreign rivals. This advantage is enhanced when home buyers pressure the nation's firms to innovate quickly and frequently. The basis for advantage is the fact that the nation's firms can stay ahead of the market when firms are more sensitive to and more responsive to home demand and when that demand, in turn, reflects or anticipates world demand.

SIZE AND PATTERN OF GROWTH OF HOME DEMAND These are important only if the composition of the home demand is sophisticated and anticipates foreign demand. Large home markets offer opportunities to achieve economies of scale and learning while dealing with familiar, comfortable markets. There is less apprehension about investing in large-scale production facilities and expensive R&D programs when the home market is sufficient to absorb the increased capacity. If the home demand accurately reflects or anticipates foreign demand, and if the firms do not become content with serving the home market, the existence of large-scale facilities and programs will be an advantage in global competition.

RAPID HOME MARKET GROWTH This is yet another incentive to invest in and adopt new technologies faster, and to build large, efficient facilities. The best example of this is in Japan, where rapid home market growth provided the incentive for Japanese firms to invest heavily in modern automated facilities. *Early home demand*, especially if it anticipates international demand, gives local firms the advantage of getting established in an industry sooner than foreign rivals. Equally important is *early market saturation*, which puts pressure on a company to expand into international markets and innovate. Market saturation is especially important if it coincides with rapid growth in foreign markets.

MEANS BY WHICH A NATION'S PRODUCTS AND SERVICES ARE PUSHED OR PULLED INTO FOREIGN COUNTRIES The issue here is whether a nation's people and businesses go abroad and then demand the nation's products and services in those second countries. For example, when the U.S. auto companies set up operations in foreign countries, the auto parts industry followed. The same is true for the Japanese auto industry. Similarly, when overseas demand for the services of U.S. engineering firms skyrocketed after World War II, those firms in turn established demand for U.S. heavy construction equipment. This provided an impetus for Caterpillar to establish foreign operations.

A related issue is that of a nation's people going abroad for training, pleasure, business, or research. After returning home, they are likely to demand the products and services with which they became familiar while abroad. Similar effects can result from professional, scientific, and political relationships between nations. Those involved in the relationships begin to demand the products and services of the recognized leaders.

It is the interplay of demand conditions that produces competitive advantage. Of special importance are those conditions that lead to initial and continuing incentives to invest and innovate, and to continuing competition in increasingly sophisticated markets.

Related and Supporting Industries

A nation has an advantage when it is home to globally competitive companies in business sectors that comprise **related and supporting industries**. Globally competitive supplier industries provide inputs to downstream industries. The latter, in turn, are likely to be globally competitive in terms of price and quality and thus gain competitive advantage from this situation. Downstream industries will have easier access to these inputs and the technology that produced them, and to the managerial and organizational structures that have made them competitive. Access is a function of proximity both in terms of physical distance and cultural similarity. It is not the inputs in themselves that give advantage. It is the *contact* and *coordination* with the suppliers, the opportunity to structure the value chain so that linkages with suppliers are optimized. These opportunities may not be available to foreign firms.

Similar advantages are present when there are globally competitive, related industries in a nation. Opportunities are available for coordinating and sharing value chain activities. Consider, for example, the opportunities for sharing between computer hardware manufacturers and software developers. Related industries also create "pull through" opportunities as described previously. For example, non-U.S. sales of PCs from Hewlett-Packard, Lenovo, Dell, Acer, and others have bolstered demand for software from Microsoft and other U.S. companies. Porter notes that the development of the Swiss pharmaceuticals industry can be attributed in part to Switzerland's large synthetic dye industry; the discovery of the therapeutic effects of dyes in turn led to the development of pharmaceutical companies.[28]

Firm Strategy, Structure, and Rivalry

The **nature of firm strategy, structure, and rivalry** is the final determinant of a nation's diamond. Domestic rivalry in a single national market is a powerful influence on competitive advantage. The PC industry in U.S. industry is a good example of how a strong domestic rivalry keeps an industry dynamic and creates continual pressure to improve and innovate.

---

[28]Michael E. Porter, *The Competitive Advantage of Nations* (New York: Free Press, 1990), p. 324.

The rivalry between Dell, Hewlett-Packard, and Apple forces all the players to develop new products, improve existing ones, lower costs and prices, develop new technologies, and continually improve quality and service to keep customers happy. Rivalry with foreign firms may lack this intensity. Domestic rivals have to fight each other not just for market share, but also for employee talent, R&D breakthroughs, and prestige in the home market. Eventually, strong domestic rivalry will push firms to seek international markets to support expansions in scale and R&D investments, as Japan amply demonstrates. The absence of significant domestic rivalry can lead to complacency in the home firms and eventually cause them to become noncompetitive in the world markets.

It is not the number of domestic rivals that is important; rather, it is the intensity of the competition and the quality of the competitors that make the difference. It is also important that there be a fairly high rate of new business formations to create new competitors and safeguard against the older companies becoming comfortable with their market positions and products and services. As noted earlier in the discussion of the five forces model, new industry entrants bring new perspectives and new methods. They frequently define and serve new market segments that established companies have failed to recognize.

Differences in management styles, organizational skills, and strategic perspectives also create advantages and disadvantages for firms competing in different types of industries, as do differences in the intensity of domestic rivalry (see Exhibit 16-7). In Germany, for example, company structure and management style tends to be hierarchical. Managers tend to come from technical backgrounds and to be most successful when dealing with industries that demand highly disciplined structures, like chemicals and precision machinery. Italian firms, on the other hand, tend to look like, and be run like, small family businesses that stress customized over standardized products, niche markets, and substantial flexibility in meeting market demands.

There are two final external variables to consider in the evaluation of national competitive advantage—chance and government.

Chance

Chance events play a role in shaping the competitive environment. Chance events are occurrences that are beyond the control of firms, industries, and usually governments. Included in this category are such things as wars and their aftermaths, major technological breakthroughs, sudden dramatic shifts in factor or input cost, like an oil crisis, dramatic swings in exchange rates, and so on.

Exhibit 16-7: India's Tata Group participates in a variety of industries, including heavy vehicles, cars, department stores, and tea. Now the group's management team is hoping to maintain that brand image as an international strategy is implemented. Historically, Tata Group's competitive advantage was based on scouring the globe to find the lowest-cost, highest-quality production inputs and then selling them in the global marketplace at a substantial profit. In 2006, the Group's Taj Hotels Resorts and Palaces subsidiary announced plans to buy the Ritz-Carlton Hotel in Boston.
Source: Kuni/AP Wide World Photos.

Chance events are important because they create major discontinuities in technologies that allow nations and firms that were not competitive to leapfrog over old competitors and become competitive, even leaders, in the changed industry. For example, the development of microelectronics allowed many Japanese firms to overtake U.S. and German firms in industries that had been based on electromechanical technologies—areas traditionally dominated by the Americans and Germans.

From a systemic perspective, the role of chance events lies in the fact that they alter conditions in the diamond. The nation with the most favorable "diamond," however, will be the one most likely to take advantage of these events and convert them into competitive advantage. For example, Canadian researchers were the first to isolate insulin, but they could not convert this breakthrough into a globally competitive product. Firms in the United States and Denmark were able to do that because of their respective national "diamonds."

Government

Although it is often argued that government is a major determinant of national competitive advantage, government is not a determinant but rather an influence on determinants. Government influences determinants by virtue of its role as a buyer of products and services, and by its role as a maker of policies on labor, education, capital formation, natural resources, and product standards. It also influences determinants by its role as a regulator of commerce—for example, by telling banks and telephone companies what they can and cannot do.

By reinforcing determinants in industries where a nation has competitive advantage, government improves the competitive position of the nation's firms. Governments devise legal systems that influence competitive advantage by means of tariffs and nontariff barriers and laws requiring local content and labor. In the United States, for example, the dollar's decline over the past decade has been due in part to a deliberate policy to enhance U.S. export flows and stem imports. In other words, government can improve or lessen competitive advantage, but it cannot create it.

◆〉 STRATEGIC DECISION MAKING IN GLOBAL MARKETING
IBM

IBM originally succeeded in the data-processing industry by focusing on customer needs and wants better than Univac. After decades of success, however, IBM remained focused on mainframe computers, despite the fact that customers were increasingly turning to PCs. IBM was a key player in the early days of the PC revolution, but its corporate culture was still oriented toward mainframes. Big Blue faltered in the early 1990s—it lost more than $8 billion in 1993—in part because competitors specializing in PCs had become even *more* clearly focused on what PC customers needed and wanted; namely, low prices and increased speed.

Within a few years, however, then-CEO Lou Gerstner succeeded in refocusing the company's PC business and broadening IBM's scope to include higher-margin products such as servers for electronic commerce. Gerstner and e-business marketing chief Abby Kohnstamm also leveraged IBM's reputation for providing expertise-based solutions for its customers. IBM became even more tightly focused with the sale of its personal computer business to China's Lenovo. Global services currently account for 60 percent of revenues.

In 2004, IBM employed 34,000 people in Brazil, Russia, India, and China. Today, its payroll includes 113,000 people in the BRIC nations. Even so, management knows that it must seek new sources of competitive advantage besides low labor costs. As Mike Daniels, head of global technology services at IBM, noted recently, "There are always going to be labor pools that offer some amount of arbitrage. But we never saw that as sustainable advantage, or the best business model."

IBM's hardware manufacturing business had already formulated and implemented a successful global marketing strategy by spreading component sourcing and computer assembly around the globe. Now, the same approach is being applied to services as well: In each of IBM's country markets, a consistent, integrated process is used to determine how to carry out a given assignment. Says Daniels, "The real scale comes out of doing the work in a codified way. The key breakthrough was to ask, 'How do you do the work at the lowest-level components?'"

Source: Richard Waters, "Big Blueprint for IBM Services," *Financial Times* (March 3, 2009), p. 12.

CURRENT ISSUES IN COMPETITIVE ADVANTAGE

Porter's work on national competitive advantage has stimulated a great deal of further research. The Geneva-based World Economic Forum issues an annual report ranking countries in terms of their competitiveness. A decade ago, Morgan Stanley used the Porter framework to identify 238 companies with a sustainable competitive advantage worldwide. "National advantage" was then assessed by analyzing how many of these companies were headquartered in a particular country. The United States ranked first, with 125 companies identified as world leaders (see Table 16-1). Among the world's automakers, Morgan Stanley's analysts considered only BMW, Toyota, and Honda to have worldwide competitive advantage.[29]

Hypercompetitive Industries

In a book published in the mid-1990s, Dartmouth College professor Richard D'Aveni suggests that the Porter strategy frameworks fail to adequately address the dynamics of competition in the 1990s and the new millennium.[30] D'Aveni takes a different approach. He notes that, in today's business environment, short product life cycles, short product design cycles, new technologies, and globalization undermine market stability. The result is an escalation and acceleration of competitive forces. In light of these changes, D'Aveni believes the goal of strategy has shifted from sustaining to disrupting advantages. The limitation of the Porter models, D'Aveni argues, is that they are static; that is, they provide a snapshot of competition at a given point in time. Acknowledging that Hamel and Prahalad broke new ground in recognizing that few advantages are sustainable, D'Aveni aims to build upon their work in order to shape "a truly dynamic approach to the creation and destruction of traditional advantages." D'Aveni uses the term **hypercompetition** to describe a dynamic competitive world in which no action or advantage can be sustained for long. In such a world, D'Aveni argues, "everything changes" because of the dynamic maneuvering and strategic interactions by hypercompetitive firms such as Microsoft and Gillette.

According to D'Aveni's model, competition unfolds in a series of dynamic strategic interactions in four arenas: cost/quality, timing and know-how, entry barriers, and deep pockets. Each of these arenas is "continuously destroyed and recreated by the dynamic maneuvering of hypercompetitive firms." According to D'Aveni, the only source of a truly sustainable competitive advantage is a company's ability to manage its dynamic strategic interactions with competitors by means of frequent movements and countermovements that maintain a relative position of strength in each of the four arenas (see Table 16-2).

TABLE 16-1 Location of Companies with Global Competitive Advantage

Country	Number of Companies
1. United States	125
2. United Kingdom	21
3. Japan	19
4. France	12
5. Germany	10
6. Netherlands	7
7. Canada	6
8. Switzerland	6
9. Sweden	3
10. Finland	3

---

[29]Tony Jackson, "Global Competitiveness Observed from an Unfamiliar Angle," *Financial Times* (November 21, 1996), p. 18.
[30]Richard D'Aveni, *Hypercompetition: Managing the Dynamics of Strategic Maneuvering* (New York: Free Press, 1994).

TABLE 16-2 Dynamic Strategic Interactions in Hypercompetitive Industries

Arena	Dynamic Strategic Interaction
1. Cost/Quality	1. Price wars 2. Quality and price positioning 3. "The middle path" 4. "Cover all niches" 5. Outflanking and niching 6. The move toward an ultimate value marketplace 7. Escaping from the ultimate value marketplace by restarting the cycle
2. Timing and know-how	1. Capturing first-mover advantages 2. Imitation and improvement by followers 3. Creating impediments to imitation 4. Overcoming the impediments 5. Transformation or leapfrogging 6. Downstream vertical integration
3. Entry barriers	1. Building a geographic stronghold by creating and reinforcing entry barriers 2. Targeting the product market strongholds of competitors in other countries 3. Incumbents make short-term counter-responses to guerrilla attacks 4. Incumbents realize they must respond fully to the invaders by making strategic responses to create new hurdles 5. Competitors react to new hurdles 6. Long-run counter-responses via defensive or offensive moves 7. Competition between the incumbent and entrant is exported to entrant's home turf 8. An unstable standoff between the competitors is established
4. Deep pockets	1. "Drive 'em out" 2. Smaller competitors use courts or Congress to derail deep-pocketed firm 3. Large firm thwarts antitrust suit 4. Small firms neutralize the advantage of the deep pocket 5. The rise of a countervailing power

COST/QUALITY Competition in the first arena, cost/quality, occurs via seven dynamic strategic interactions: price wars, quality and price positioning, "the middle path," "cover all niches," outflanking and niching, the move toward an ultimate value marketplace, and escaping from the ultimate value marketplace by restarting the cycle. D'Aveni cites the global watch industry as an example of hypercompetitive behavior in the cost/quality arena. In the 1970s, the center of the industry shifted from Switzerland to Japan as the Japanese created high-quality quartz watches that could be sold cheaply. In the early 1980s, the merger of two Swiss companies into Société Suisse Microelectronique et d'Horlogerie SA (SMH) was followed by a highly automated manufacturing innovation that allowed a quartz movement to be integrated into a stylish plastic case. As a result of this innovation and a strong marketing effort in support of the Swatch brand, the center of the watch industry shifted back to Switzerland. Today, the Swatch Group is the world's second largest watch maker; the watch industry continues to be highly segmented, with prestige brands competing on reputation and exclusivity; as with many other luxury goods, higher prices are associated with higher perceived quality. In the low-cost segment, brands compete on price and value (see Exhibit 16-8).

TIMING AND KNOW-HOW The second arena for hypercompetition is based on organizational advantages derived from timing and know-how. As described by D'Aveni, a firm that has the skills to be a "first mover" and arrive first in a market has achieved a *timing advantage*. A *know-how*

Exhibit 16-8: Swatch Group provided sports timing systems and services worth nearly $40 million for the 2008 Beijing Olympics. Prior to the Games, Swatch Group CEO Georges Nicolas Hayek, Jr., noted, "We will ship 500 tons of equipment and 300 professional engineers from Switzerland to different competition venues in Beijing to measure and transmit results and scores." Hayek, the son of Swatch founder Nicolas Hayek, expected that the company's annual sales in China would reach five to six million watches by 2008. Swatch products were available at several hundred Chinese stores and sales counters; the majority were in Shanghai.
Source: Courtesy of Swatch.

advantage is the technological knowledge—or other knowledge of a new method of doing business—that allows the firm to create an entirely new product or market.[31]

D'Aveni identifies six dynamic strategic interactions that drive competition in this arena: capturing first-mover advantages, imitation and improvement by followers, creating impediments to imitation, overcoming the impediments, transformation or leapfrogging, and downstream vertical integration. As the consumer electronics industry has globalized, Sony and its competitors have exhibited hypercompetitive behavior in this second arena. Sony has an enviable history of first-mover achievements based on its know-how in audio technology: first pocket-sized transistor radio, first consumer VCR, first portable personal stereo, and first compact disc player.

Although each of these innovations literally created an entirely new market, Sony has fallen victim to the risks associated with being a first mover. The second dynamic strategic interaction—imitation and improvement by followers—can be seen in the successful efforts of JVC and Matsushita to enter the home VCR market a few months after Sony's Betamax launch. VHS technology offered longer recording times and was the dominant consumer format worldwide until the advent of the DVD era.

After years of moves and countermoves between Sony and its imitators, Sony progressed to downstream vertical integration with the 1988 purchase of CBS Records for $2 billion and then,

---

[31]Richard D'Aveni, *Hypercompetition: Managing the Dynamics of Strategic Maneuvering* (New York: Free Press, 1994), p. 71.

later, the purchase of Columbia Pictures. The acquisitions, which represent the sixth dynamic strategic interaction, were intended to complement Sony's core "hardware" businesses (e.g., TVs, VCRs, and hi-fi equipment) with "software" (e.g., videocassettes and CDs). However, Matsushita quickly imitated Sony by paying $6 billion for MCA Inc. Initially, neither Sony nor Matsushita proved successful at managing the acquisitions. More recently, however, Sony Pictures Entertainment has enjoyed huge successes with the *Spider-Man* movies and *Casino Royale* and *Quantum of Solace*, the latest James Bond films.

Sony is also facing serious challenges to its core electronics businesses. The digital revolution rendered Sony's core competences in analog audio technology obsolete. Chief executive Howard Stringer must develop new know-how resources if the company is to continue to lead in the information age. Sony has found technological leaps harder to achieve, as evidenced by the fact that Apple's iPod is now the world's best-selling portable music player. Sony was also slow to grasp the speed with which consumers would embrace flat-panel TV technology.

Hypercompetition is showing up in other ways, too. For example, after 20 years, sales of Sony's Handycam camcorders started to decline. Meanwhile, an inexpensive device called the Flip from start-up Pure Digital Technologies quickly became a best-seller after its launch in 2006. Belatedly, Sony rolled out the Webbie Internet-ready camcorder. During the product's development, the U.S.-based marketing director for the design team asked Tokyo for permission to make the camcorder available in orange and purple.[32] More competitive challenges loom. Although Sony's Blu-Ray high-definition DVD format triumphed over Toshiba's HD-DVD to become the industry standard, the victory may be fleeting as on-demand video downloads gain in popularity. And, Sony is learning that technological breakthroughs are not necessarily the key to market leadership. For example, Sony's PlayStation 3 (PS3) has a powerful chip that provides new levels of realism; PS3 also contains a Blu-Ray DVD player. However, the less complex, less expensive Nintendo Wii has been outselling Sony's game system by a margin of 3-to-1.

ENTRY BARRIERS Industries in which barriers to entry have been built up comprise the third arena in which hypercompetitive behavior is exhibited. As described earlier in the chapter, these barriers include economies of scale, product differentiation, capital investments, switching costs, access to distribution channels, cost advantages other than scale, and government policies. D'Aveni describes how aggressive competitors erode these traditional entry barriers via eight strategic interactions. For example, a cornerstone of Dell's global success in the PC industry is a direct-sales approach that bypasses dealers and other distribution channels. Similarly, in the long-distance industry, ring-back services based in the United States and elsewhere enabled people making long-distance calls from Europe to sidestep exorbitant rates charged by government-owned telecoms.

The first dynamic strategic interaction comes as a company builds a geographic "stronghold" by creating and reinforcing barriers. After securing a market—especially the home-country market—competitors begin to seek markets outside the stronghold. Thus, the second dynamic strategic interaction takes place when companies target the product market strongholds of competitors in other countries. Honda's geographic expansion outside Japan with motorcycles and automobiles—a series of forays utilizing guerrilla tactics—is a case in point. The third dynamic strategic interaction comes when incumbents make short-term counter-responses to the guerrilla attacks. Strong incumbents may try to turn back the invader with price wars, factory investment, or product introductions, or they may adopt a wait-and-see attitude before responding. In the case of both Harley-Davidson and the Detroit-based U.S. auto industry, management originally underestimated and rationalized away the full potential of the threat from Honda and other Japanese companies. Realizing that their company was a weak incumbent, Harley-Davidson management had little choice but to appeal for government protection. The resulting "breathing room" allowed Harley to put its house in order. Similarly, the U.S. government heeded Detroit's pleas for relief and imposed tariffs and quotas on Japanese auto imports. This gave the Big Three time to develop higher-quality, fuel-efficient models to offer U.S. consumers.

The fourth dynamic strategic interaction occurs when the incumbent realizes it must respond fully to the invader by making strategic responses to create new hurdles. U.S. automakers, for

---

[32]Daisuke Wakabayashi and Christopher Lawton, "At Sony, Culture Shift Yields a Low-Cost Video Camera," *The Wall Street Journal* (April 16, 2009), p. B1.

example, waged a PR campaign urging U.S. citizens to "Buy American." The fifth dynamic strategic interaction takes place when competitors react to these new hurdles. In an effort to circumvent import quotas as well as co-opt the "Buy American" campaign, the Japanese automakers built plants in the United States. The sixth dynamic strategic interaction consists of long-run counter-responses to the attack via defensive moves or offensive moves. GM's 1990 introduction of Saturn is a good illustration of a well-formulated and executed defensive move. As the first decade of the twenty-first century continues, GM is launching another defensive move; in an effort to defend its Cadillac nameplate from Lexus, Acura, and Infiniti, GM is developing a global strategy for Cadillac. Competition in the third arena continues to escalate; in the seventh dynamic strategic interaction, competition between the incumbent and entrant is exported to the entrant's home turf. President Clinton's threat of trade sanctions against Japanese automakers in 1995 was intended to send a message that Japan needed to open its auto market. In 1997, GM intensified its assault on Japan with the introduction of Saturn. The eighth and final dynamic strategic interaction in this arena consists of an unstable standoff between the competitors. Over time the stronghold erodes as entry barriers are overcome, leading competitors to the fourth arena.

As the preceding discussion shows, the irony and paradox of the hypercompetition framework is that, in order to achieve a sustainable advantage, companies must seek a series of *unsustainable* advantages! D'Aveni is in agreement with the late Peter Drucker, who long counseled that the role of marketing is innovation and the creation of new markets. Innovation begins with abandonment of the old and obsolete. Sumantra Ghoshal and Christopher Bartlett make a similar point in *The Individualized Corporation*:

> Managers are forced to refocus their attention from a preoccupation with defining defensible product-market positions to a newly awakened interest in how to develop the organizational capability to sense and respond rapidly and flexibly to change. . . . Managers worldwide have begun to focus less on the task of forecasting and planning for the future and more on the challenge of being highly sensitive to emerging changes. Their broad objective is to create an organization that is constantly experimenting with appropriate responses, then is able to quickly diffuse the information and knowledge gained so it can be leveraged by the entire organization. The age of strategic planning is fast evolving into the era or organizational learning.[33]

Likewise, D'Aveni urges managers to reconsider and reevaluate the use of what he believes are old strategic tools and maxims. He warns of the dangers of commitment to a given strategy or course of action. The flexible, unpredictable player may have an advantage over the inflexible, committed opponent. D'Aveni notes that, in hypercompetition, pursuit of generic strategies results in short-term advantage at best. The winning companies are the ones that successfully move up the ladder of escalating competition, not the ones that lock into a fixed position. D'Aveni is also critical of the five forces model. The best entry barrier, he argues, is maintaining the initiative, not mounting a defensive attempt to exclude new entrants.

Additional Research on Comparative Advantage

Other researchers have challenged Porter's thesis that a firm's home-base country is the main source of core competencies and innovation. For example, Indiana University Professor Alan Rugman argues that the success of companies based in small economies such as Canada and New Zealand stems from the "diamonds" found in a particular set or combination of home and related countries. For example, a company based in an EU nation may rely on the national "diamond" of one of the 26 other EU members. Similarly, one impact of NAFTA on Canadian firms is to make the U.S. "diamond" relevant to competency creation. Rugman argues that, in such cases, the distinction between the home nation and the host nation becomes blurred. He proposes that Canadian managers must look to a "double diamond" and assess the attributes of both Canada and the United States when formulating corporate strategy.[34] In other words,

---

[33]Sumantra Ghoshal and Christopher Bartlett, *The Individualized Corporation* (New York: HarperBusiness, 1997), p. 71.
[34]Alan M. Rugman and Lain Verbeke, "Foreign Subsidiaries and Multinational Strategic Management: An Extension and Correction of Porter's Single Diamond Framework," *Management International Review* 3, no. 2 (1993), pp. 71–84.

he argues that, for smaller countries, the nation is not the relevant unit of analysis in formulating strategy. Rather, corporate strategists must look beyond the nation to the region or to sets of closely linked countries. Other critics have argued that Porter generalized inappropriately from the American experience, while confusing industry-level competition with trade at the national level. In the *Journal of Management Studies,* Howard Davies and Paul Ellis assert that nations can, in fact, achieve sustained prosperity without becoming innovation driven; the authors also note the absence of strong diamonds in the home bases of many global industries.[35]

As for Michael Porter, his views on corporate strategy and competitive advantage have evolved during the last quarter century. In a recent interview, he emphasized the difference between operational efficiency and strategy. The former, in Porter's view, concerns improvement via time-based competition or total quality management; the latter entails "making choices." Porter explains, "'Choice' arises from doing things differently from the rival. And strategy is about trade-offs, where you decide to do this and not that. Strategy is the deliberate choice not to respond to some customers, or choosing which customer needs you are going to respond to." Porter is not convinced of the validity of competitive advantage models based on core competency or hypercompetitive industries. A nation has an advantage when it is home to globally competitive companies in business sectors that are related and supporting industries. As for core competencies, Porter notes:

> Any individual thing that a company does can usually be imitated. The whole notion that you should rest your success on a few core competencies is an idea that invites destructive competition. Successful companies don't compete that way. They fit together the things they do in a way that is very hard to replicate. [Competitors] have to match everything, or they've basically matched nothing.

On the subject of hypercompetition, Porter says:

> I don't think we're moving towards a hypercompetitive world in which there are no trade-offs. We're probably moving in the other direction. There are more customer segments than ever before, more technological options, more distribution channels. That ought to create lots of opportunities for unique positions.[36]

Summary

In this chapter we focus on factors that help industries and countries achieve **competitive advantage**. According to Porter's **five forces model**, industry competition is a function of the threat of new entrants, the threat of substitutes, the bargaining power of suppliers and buyers, and rivalry among existing competitors. Managers can use Porter's **generic strategies** model to conceptualize possible sources of competitive advantage. A company can pursue broad market strategies of **cost leadership** and **differentiation** or the more targeted approaches of **cost focus** and **focused differentiation**. Rugman and D'Cruz have developed a framework known as the **flagship model** to explain how networked business systems have achieved success in global industries. Hamel and Prahalad have proposed an alternative framework for pursuing competitive advantage, growing out of a firm's **strategic intent** and use of competitive innovation. A firm can build *layers of advantage*, search for *loose bricks* in a competitor's defensive walls, *change the rules of engagement*, or *collaborate with competitors* and utilize their technology and know-how.

Today, **global competition** is a reality in many industry sectors. Thus, competitive analysis must also be carried out on a global scale. Global marketers must also have an understanding of national sources of competitive advantage. Porter has described four determinants of *national*

[35]Howard Davies and Paul Ellis, "Porter's Competitive Advantage of Nations: Time for the Final Judgment?" *Journal of Management Studies* 37, no. 8 (December 2000) pp. 1189–1213.
[36]Tony Jackson, "Why Being Different Pays," *Financial Times* (June 23, 1997), p. 14.

advantage. **Factor conditions** include human, physical, knowledge, capital, and infrastructure resources. **Demand conditions** include the composition, size, and growth pattern of home demand. The rate of home market growth and the means by which a nation's products are pulled into foreign markets also affect demand conditions. The final two determinants are the presence of **related and supporting industries** and the **nature of firm strategy, structure, and rivalry**. Porter notes that chance and government also influence a nation's competitive advantage. Porter's work has been the catalyst for promising new research into strategy issues, including D'Aveni's work on **hypercompetition** and Rugman's recent **double-diamond framework** for national competitive advantage.

Discussion Questions

1. How can a company measure its competitive advantage? How does a firm know if it is gaining or losing competitive advantage? Cite a global company and its source of competitive advantage.
2. Outline Porter's five forces model of industry competition. How are the various barriers to entry relevant to global marketing?
3. How does the five partners, or flagship model, developed by Rugman and D'Aveni differ from Porter's five forces model?
4. Give an example of a company that illustrates each of the four generic strategies that can lead to competitive advantage: overall cost leadership, cost focus, differentiation, and focused differentiation.
5. Briefly describe Hamel and Prahalad's framework for competitive advantage.
6. How can a nation achieve competitive advantage?
7. According to current research on competitive advantage, what are some of the shortcomings of Porter's models?
8. What is the connection, if any, between *national* competitive advantage and *company* competitive advantage? Explain and discuss.

IKEA's unconventional approach to the furniture business has enabled it to rack up impressive growth in a $30 billion industry in which overall sales have been flat. Sourcing furniture from a network of more than 1,600 suppliers in 55 countries helps the company maintain its low-cost, high-quality position. During the 1990s, IKEA expanded into Central and Eastern Europe. Because consumers in those regions have relatively low purchasing power, the stores offer a smaller selection of goods; some furniture was designed specifically for the cramped living styles typical in former Soviet bloc countries.

Throughout Europe, IKEA benefits from the perception that Sweden is the source of high-quality products and efficient service. Currently, Germany and the United Kingdom are IKEA's top two markets. The United Kingdom represents the fastest-growing market in Europe; although Britons initially viewed the company's less-is-more approach as cold and "too Scandinavian," they were eventually won over. IKEA currently has 18 stores in the United Kingdom and plans call for opening more in the next decade. As Allan Young, creative director of London's St. Luke's advertising agency, noted, "IKEA is anti-conventional. It does what it shouldn't do. That's the overall theme for all IKEA ads: liberation from tradition."

In 2005, IKEA opened two stores near Tokyo; more stores are on the way as the company expands in Asia. IKEA's first attempt to develop the Japanese market in the mid-1970s resulted in failure. Why? As Tommy Kullberg, chief executive of IKEA Japan, explains, "In 1974, the Japanese market from a retail point of view was closed. Also, from the Japanese point of view, I do not think they were ready for IKEA, with our way of doing things, with flat packages and asking the consumers to put things together and so on." However, demographic and economic trends are much different today. After years of recession, consumers are seeking alternatives to paying high prices for quality goods. Also, IKEA's core customer segment—post–baby boomers in their 30s—will grow by nearly 10 percent between 2000 and 2010. In Japan, IKEA will offer home delivery and an assembly service option.

"To succeed in Japan, I think we have to tell the whole story of why we can sell our products at affordable prices."

Tommy Kullberg

Industry observers predict that North America will eventually rise to the number one position in terms of IKEA's worldwide sales. The company opened its first U.S. store in Philadelphia in 1985; as of 2009, IKEA operated stores in 37 U.S. states and Canada. Plans call for opening at least several more U.S. stores each year between now and 2015. As Goran Carstedt, president of IKEA North America, explains, "Our customers understand our philosophy, which calls for each of us to do a little in order to save a lot. They value our low prices. And almost all of them say they will come back again." As one industry observer noted, "IKEA is on the way to becoming the Walmart Stores of the home-furnishing industry. If you're in this business, you'd better take a look."

Case 16-1 Discussion Questions

1. Review the characteristics of global and transnational companies in Chapter 1. Now consider, as noted in the case, IKEA both sources from the world and markets to the world. Company executives are all Swedish, and the company signals its national origin by using Sweden's national colors—blue and yellow—in its stores and serving Swedish meatballs with lingonberry sauce in its cafés. Based on this evidence, would IKEA be described as a global firm or a transnational firm?

2. At the end of Chapter 11, it was noted that managers of IKEA stores have a great deal of discretion when it comes to setting prices. In terms of the ethnocentric/polycentric/regiocentric/geocentric (EPRG) framework, which management orientation is in evidence at IKEA?

3. What does it mean to say that, in terms of Porter's generic strategies, IKEA pursues a strategy of "cost focus?"

Sources: Mei Fong, "IKEA Hits Home in China," *The Wall Street Journal* (March 3, 2006), pp. B1, B4; Richard Tomkins, "How IKEA Has Managed to Treat Us Mean and Keep Us Keen," *Financial Times* (January 14/January 15, 2006), p. 7; Kerry Capell, "IKEA: How the Swedish Retailer Became a Global Cult Brand," *Business Week* (November 14, 2005), pp. 96–106; Theresa Howard, "IKEA Builds on Furnishings Success," *USA Today* (December 29, 2004), p. 3B; Mariko Sanchanta, "IKEA's Second Try at Japan's Flat-Pack Fans," *Financial Times* (March 4, 2004), p. 11; Paula M. Miller, "IKEA with Chinese Characteristics," *The China Business Review* (July–August, 2004), pp. 36–38; Christopher Brown-Humes, "An Empire Built on a Flat Pack," *Financial Times* (November 24, 2003), p. 8; Christopher Brown-Humes, "IKEA Aims to Fill Up Homes One Catalogue at a Time," *Financial Times* (August 14, 2003), p. 14; Alan M. Rugman and Joseph R. D'Cruz, *Multinationals as Flagship Firms* (Oxford: Oxford University Press, 2000), Chapter 3; Ernest Beck, "IKEA Sees Quirkiness as Selling Point in UK," *The Wall Street Journal* (January 4, 2001), pp. A1, A5; Loretta Roach, "IKEA: Furnishing the World," *Discount Merchandiser* (October 1994), pp. 46, 48; "Furnishing the World," *The Economist* (November 19, 1994), pp. 79–80.

Case 16-2
Kodak in the Twenty-First Century: The Search for New Sources of Competitive Advantage

Eastman Kodak Company is at a crossroads. After inventing the famous Brownie camera in 1900, Kodak reigned as the undisputed leader in the silver-halide chemical processes that formed the basis of the photography industry throughout the twentieth century. Kodak's yellow boxes of film were iconic symbols of the brand. Once, the company's color film business was a classic cash cow, accounting for as much as 70 percent of Kodak's revenues.

Sadly, the company's long-entrenched conservative corporate culture, bureaucratic organizational structure, and go-slow approach to innovation resulted in sluggish, ill-fated responses to changes in the photography market. Although management understood that the digital revolution was changing the way consumers take, store, and access photos, the speed of the changeover from film-based photography to digital came as a shock. In the late 1990s, Kodak invested $1 billion in an alternative film-based format known as Advanced Photo System. It flopped. Meanwhile, the company maintained a premium pricing strategy, allowing competitors such as Fuji to undercut it and gain market share.

Now, management is attempting to remake the company's business model in fundamental ways. After being named president and CEO in 2000, Daniel Carp replaced most of Kodak's executive team with newcomers who worked at technology-oriented companies such as Hewlett-Packard, Lexmark International, and General Electric. To shore up its core film business, Kodak will make private-label film for sale outside the United States. Kodak has also vowed to fight more aggressively for market share with its branded film by cutting prices. Perhaps the most dramatic move is the decision to stop selling film-based cameras for the consumer market in the United States, Canada, and Europe. The only exception is a popular line of disposable single-use cameras. The company continues to market film cameras in China, India, Eastern Europe, and Latin America, where management believes the traditional photography format still has potential for growth.

"The trick is to get the cost structure of the traditional consumer business down. We are a business in transition."

Daniel Carp, former CEO, Eastman Kodak

By 2005, the year Carp retired and Antonio Perez was named chairman and CEO, the digital camera market in the United States became a key battleground. Canon ranked number one in digital camera sales. Although Canon's cameras are designed and manufactured in Japan, company engineers regularly visit the United States to absorb insights about consumer needs. One analyst noted, "Canon has built on its camera heritage and has been able to get people to believe in them as a digital company." The same analyst was also impressed by Kodak. Although the company's traditional sources of competitive advantage were in film and processing, "In a short period of time they've transitioned into a strong hardware company. They've done an amazing job," he said.

Managing the transition away from film is also requiring Kodak to redefine relationships with key business partners. For example, Kodak was for many years the exclusive supplier of traditional photo processing services for the Walgreens drugstore chain. The relationship, which includes one-hour services, generates about $500 million in annual revenue for Kodak. Archrival Fuji, which has a close partnership with Walmart, is now making inroads at Walgreens as well. Kodak's minilabs were subject to frequent breakdowns; despite the fact that Walgreens was bound by long-term leases, the retailer began installing Fuji minilabs at a cost of $115,000 per unit. Presently, about one-third of Walgreens' stores use Fuji's one-hour minilab equipment. The Walgreens photo processing Web site also uses Fuji to process prints.

Not to be outdone, at the 2006 Photo Marketing Association trade show, Kodak unveiled the DSP900, a modular replacement for the minilab that can produce 900 prints per hour at half the price of previous models. Kodak currently has installed about 60,000 self-service photo kiosks in the United States that allow customers to print photos from their digital cameras. Fuji also supplies in-store kiosks bearing the Aladdin brand name.

Now, Hewlett-Packard has entered the retail photo services market as well; it has begun installing $15,000 PhotoStudio kiosks at stores in the Long's Drugs chain. Kodak has responded by targeting H-P's highly profitable consumer printer business. A new ad campaign is keyed to the theme "Print and Prosper." Print ads proclaim, "The world's most expensive liquid isn't found in the Middle East. It is found in ink-jet printer cartridges." Matt Troy, an analyst with Citigroup Investment Research, summed up the situation by saying, "Kodak has been very successful in cultivating an ecosystem in the digital world. H-P's motivation is to sell more ink." Concludes Troy, "H-P is trying to be the next Kodak."

Discussion Questions

1. Assess Kodak's situation in terms of Porter's five forces model and generic strategies. Which forces are driving competition in the photo industry? What has happened to Kodak's traditional sources of competitive advantage?

2. Do you think the digital photography revolution will spread to China and India more quickly than Kodak's management expects?

3. For decades, Kodak has been known as the world's largest consumer photography company. Today, the company's strategy calls for a shift toward business-to-business marketing with an emphasis on such products as medical imaging systems and digital printing systems. What risks does this change in strategic direction present?

Sources: Suzanne Vranica, "Kodak Ads Get More Aggressive," *The Wall Street Journal* (March 20, 2009), p. B5; Francesca Guerrera, "Kodak Refocuses on Digital Age," *Financial Times* (November 29, 2006), p. 11; William M. Bulkeley, "Kodak Revamps Walmart Kiosks," *The Wall Street Journal* (September 6, 2006), p. B2; Damon Darlin, "Hewlett-Packard Decides Store Photo Printing Is Its Turf," *The New York Times* (February 23, 2006), pp. C1, C17; Jefferson Graham, "Canon, Kodak Face Off in Digital Arena," *USA Today* (February 23, 2006), p. 3B; James Bandler, "Losing Focus: As Kodak Eyes, Digital Future, A Big Partner Starts to Fade," *The Wall Street Journal* (January 23, 2004), pp. A1, A8; Bandler, "Ending Era, Kodak Will Stop Selling Most Film Cameras," *The Wall Street Journal* (January 14, 2004), pp. B1, B4; Bandler, "Kodak Shifts Focus from Film, Betting Future on Digital Lines," *The Wall Street Journal* (September 29, 2003), pp. A1, A12.

Case 16-3
LEGO

The LEGO Company is a $1.6 billion global business built out of the humblest of materials: interlocking plastic toy bricks. From its base in Denmark, the family-owned LEGO empire extends around the world and came to include theme parks, clothing, and computer-controlled toys. Each year, the company produces about 14 billion plastic blocks as well as tiny human figures to populate towns and operate gizmos that spring from the imaginations of young people. LEGO products, which are especially popular with boys, are available in more than 130 countries; in the key North American market, the company's overall share of the construction-toy market has been as high as 80 percent. Kjeld Kirk Kristiansen, the grandson of the company's founder as well as the main shareholder, served as CEO from 1979 until 2004. Kristiansen says that LEGO products stand for "exuberance, spontaneity, self-expression, concern for others, and innovation." (The company's name comes from the Danish phrase *leg godt*, which means "play well.") Kristiansen also attributes his company's success to the esteem the brand enjoys among parents. "Parents consider LEGO not as just a toy company but as providing products that help learning and developing new skills," he says.

Source: AP Wide World Photos.

For the past several years, however, some of those parents have been switching loyalties. Mega Bloks Inc., a rival company in Montreal, Canada, has been aggressively gaining market share with its own colorful plastic blocks. Some are compatible with LEGO products, and all generally cost less than comparable LEGO products. LEGO executives believe that LEGO's proprietary mix of resin results in a higher quality toy. By contrast, Mega Bloks holds costs down by using commodity-grade resin. While LEGO dominates the 7- to 12-year-old segment, Mega Bloks is the number one player in the preschool market. Because the bricks in Mega Bloks' original line are larger and softer than LEGO, some parents believe they are easier for very young children to use. LEGO responded by introducing a Duplo line of oversized blocks made of the same material as the company's core brick line.

In recent years, Mega Bloks has introduced a midsized line as well as a line called Micro for the elementary school set. Micro bricks can be used interchangeably with LEGOs. LEGO filed a lawsuit alleging that the Micro line copied the "look" of the knobs on LEGO bricks, and thus violated Canadian trademark law. Canada's Federal Court of Appeal dismissed the claim in 2003, concluding that the bricks' design is functional and not entitled to trademark protection. In 2004, Canada's Supreme Court announced that it would hear LEGO's appeal.

"For many people, the biggest part of the brand equity is the brick—which is why we must ensure a significant proportion of the business stays in the brick arena."

Francesco Ciccolella, Senior Vice President for Corporate Development, LEGO Company

In short, Mega Bloks has prospered at LEGO's expense. Mega Bloks' sales doubled between 2000 and 2003; by contrast, the Danish company reported its first loss ever—$44 million—in 1988. Meanwhile, Hasbro and other competitors are also targeting the $600 million market for construction toys. In the 1990s, LEGO's strategy called for new sources of growth beyond the core block category. The company developed its own line of original robot action figures. Known as Bionicles, the figures can be integrated with the traditional construction materials. Currently, the Bionicle line is LEGO's best seller; in 2003, a direct-to-DVD animated feature, *Bionicle—Mask of Light*, was released by Miramax. Another new product, Mybots, was a $70 toy set that included blocks with computer chips embedded to provide lights and sound. A $200 Mindstorms Robotics Invention System allowed users to build computer-controlled creatures. To further leverage the LEGO brand, the company also formed alliances with Walt Disney Company and Lucasfilms, creator of the popular *Star Wars* series. For several years, sales of licensed merchandise relating to the popular Harry Potter and Star Wars movie franchises sold extremely well.

More recently, however, although the Harry Potter movie series continued to enjoy great success, interest in the Potter-themed play sets was waning. After a disappointing Christmas 2003 season, LEGO was left with millions of dollars worth of unsold goods. The difficult retail situation was compounded by the dollar's weakness relative to the Danish krone; LEGO posted a record loss of $166 million for 2003. The company unveiled a number of new initiatives aimed at restoring profitability. Its new Quattro line of large, soft bricks is targeted directly at the preschool market. Clikits is a line for pastel-colored bricks targeted at young girls who want to create jewelry.

In 2004, after several years of losses, Jørgen Vig Knudstorp succeeded Kristiansen as LEGO's chief executive. Acknowledging that the company's forays into theme parts, children's clothing, and software games had been the wrong strategy, Knudstorp launched a restructuring initiative. Production was outsourced to a Singapore company with production facilities in Mexico and the Czech Republic; in the past few years, more than 2,000 jobs have been eliminated. In 2006, LEGO launched a new generation of programmable robots in the Mindstorms line. As Knudstorp noted, "Mindstorms is as close to the core as you can come other than a bucket of bricks, which is the core of the core."

Discussion Questions

1. Jørgen Vig Knudstorp became CEO in 2004. Assess the key strategic decisions he has made, including outsourcing, divesting the theme parks, and launching new toys in the Mindstorms line.

2. In 2004, LEGO continued its entertainment promotional and product tie-ins with new Harry Potter and Spiderman movies. Do you think this is the right strategy?

3. Using Porter's generic strategies framework, compare and contrast LEGO and Mega Bloks in terms of their respective pursuit of competitive advantage.

Sources: John Tagliabue, "Taking Their Blocks and Playing Toymaker Elsewhere," *The New York Times* (November 20, 2006), p. A4; Lauren Foster and David Ibison, "Spike the Robot Helps LEGO Rebuild Strategy," *Financial Times* (June 22, 2006), p. 18; Ian Austen, "Building a Legal Case, Block by Block," *The New York Times* (February 2, 2005), p. C6; Joseph Pereira and Christopher J. Chipello, "Battle of the Block Makers," *The Wall Street Journal* (February 4, 2004), pp. B1, B4; Clare MacCarthy, "Deputy Chief Sacked as LEGO Tries to Rebuild," *Financial Times* (January 9, 2004), p. 19; Majken Schultz and Mary Jo Hatch, "The Cycles of Corporate Branding: The Case of the LEGO Company," *California Management Review* 46, no. 1 (Fall 2003), pp. 6–26; Meg Carter, "Building Blocks of Success," *Financial Times* (October 30, 2003), p. 8; Peter Marsh, "LEGO Builds Its Future," *Financial Times* (March 16–17, 1996), p. 9.

Leadership, Organization, and Corporate Social Responsibility

Case 17-1
Unilever

Unilever, the global food and consumer packaged-goods powerhouse, markets a brand portfolio that includes such well-known names as Axe, Ben & Jerry's, Dove, Hellmann's, and Lipton. The company has approximately 200,000 employees and annual sales of $57 billion; Unilever can trace its roots, in part, to the northern English town of Port Sunlight on the River Mersey. There, in 1888, Lever Brothers founder William Hesketh Lever created a garden village for the benefit of his employees. Before retiring at the end of 2008, Unilever Group Chief Executive Patrick Cescau wanted to reconnect the company with its heritage of sustainability and concern for the environment (see Exhibit 17-1). These and other values reflect Unilever's philosophy of "doing well by doing good".

One example: the Campaign for Real Beauty that was launched by managers at the company's Dove brand. To prepare for their first presentation to management, Dove team members videotaped interviews with girls who talked about the pressure they felt to conform to a certain look and body style. The interviewees included Cescau's daughter as well as daughters of Unilever's directors. Later, when the CEO recalled watching the video, he explained, "It suddenly becomes personal. You realize your own children are impacted by the beauty industry, and how stressed they are by this image of unattainable beauty which is imposed on them every day." The Dove team was given the green light to launch a new advertising campaign based on this insight; in the years since, Dove has won numerous awards and accolades.

Exhibit 17-1: Patrick Cescau was CEO of Unilever from 2005 to 2008. Unilever Chairman Michael Treschow spoke very highly of the retiring executive's achievements, noting, "Patrick has had an outstanding career. We are greatly in his debt for the transformation he has brought about over the last four years. The performance of the business has improved markedly under his leadership. Liked and admired in equal measure, Patrick leaves a substantial record on which to build." *Source:* Unilever/AFP/Newscom.

Cescau's vision of "doing well by doing good" manifested itself in other ways, too. For example, he guided the company's detergent business toward using fewer chemicals and less water, plastic, and packaging. In addition, he recognized that today's "conscience consumers" look to a company's reputation when deciding which brands to purchase. Paul Polman, Cescau's successor, will build on another of the outgoing chief executive's priorities: business opportunities in emerging markets such as India and China. To find out more about Unilever's commitment to global social responsibility, turn to Case 17-1 at the end of the chapter.

This chapter focuses on the integration of each element of the marketing mix into a total plan that addresses opportunities and threats in the global marketing environment. Patrick Cescau's achievements as the head of Unilever illustrate some of the challenges facing business leaders in the twenty-first century: They must be capable of articulating a coherent global vision and strategy that integrates global efficiency, local responsiveness, and leverage. The leader is also the architect of an organization design that is appropriate for the company's strategy. For large global enterprises such as ABB, GE, Royal Philips Electronics, Toyota, and Unilever, the leader must ensure that size and scale are assets that can be leveraged rather than encumbrances that slow response times and stifle innovation. Finally, the leader must ensure that the organization takes a proactive approach to corporate social responsibility.

LEADERSHIP

Global marketing demands exceptional leadership. As noted throughout this book, the hallmark of a global company is the capacity to formulate and implement global strategies that leverage worldwide learning, respond fully to local needs and wants, and draw on the talent and energy of every member of the organization. This daunting task requires global vision and sensitivity to local needs. Overall, the leader's challenge is to direct the efforts and creativity of everyone in the company toward a global effort that best utilizes organizational resources to exploit global opportunities. As Carly Fiorina, former CEO of Hewlett-Packard, said in her 2002 commencement address at the Massachusetts Institute of Technology:

> Leadership is not about hierarchy or title or status: It is about having influence and mastering change. Leadership is not about bragging rights or battles or even the accumulation of wealth; it's about connecting and engaging at multiple levels. It's about challenging minds and capturing hearts. Leadership in this new era is about empowering others to decide for themselves. Leadership is about empowering others to reach their full potential. Leaders can no longer view strategy and execution as abstract concepts, but must realize that both elements are ultimately about people.[1]

An important leadership task is articulating beliefs, values, policies, and the intended geographic scope of a company's activities. Using the mission statement or similar document as a reference and guide, members of each operating unit must address their immediate responsibilities and at the same time cooperate with functional, product, and country experts in different locations. However, it is one thing to spell out the vision and another thing entirely to secure commitment to it throughout the organization. As noted in Chapter 1, global marketing entails engaging in significant business activities outside the home country. This means exposure to different languages and cultures. In addition, global marketing involves skillful application of specific concepts, insights, and strategies. Such endeavors may represent substantial change,

---

[1]Carleton "Carly" S. Fiorina, Commencement Address, Massachusetts Institute of Technology, Cambridge, MA, June 2, 2000. See also "It's Death if You Stop Trying New Things," *Financial Times* (November 20, 2003), p. 8.

especially in U.S. companies with a long tradition of domestic focus. When the "go global" initiative is greeted with skepticism, the CEO must be a change agent who prepares and motivates employees.

Former Whirlpool CEO David Whitwam described his own efforts in this regard in the early 1990s after he approved the acquisition of Royal Philips Electronics' European home appliance division:

> When we announced the Philips acquisition, I traveled to every location in the company, talked with our people, explained why it was so important. Most opposed the move. They thought, "We're spending a billion dollars on a company that has been losing money for 10 years? We're going to take resources we could use right here and ship them across the Atlantic because we think this is becoming a 'global' industry? What the hell does that mean?"[2]

Jack Welch encountered similar resistance at GE. "The lower you are in the organization, the less clear it is that globalization is great," he said. As Paolo Fresco, a former GE vice chairman, explained:

> To certain people, globalization is a threat without rewards. You look at the engineer for X-ray in Milwaukee and there is no upside on this one for him. He runs the risk of losing his job, he runs the risk of losing authority—he might find his boss is a guy who does not even know how to speak his language.[3]

In addition to "selling" their visions, top management at Whirlpool, GE, Nokia, Boeing, Tata Group, and other companies face the formidable task of building a cadre of globally oriented managers. Similar challenges are facing corporate leaders in all parts of the world. For example, Uichiro Niwa, former president of Japan's ITOCHU Corp., took steps to ensure that more of the trading company's $115 billion in annual transactions are conducted online.[4] He also radically changed the way he communicated with employees. He began relying more on e-mail, a practice that until recently was virtually unknown in Japan. He also convened face-to-face meetings and conferences with employees to solicit suggestions and to hear complaints. This too represented a dramatic change in the way some Japanese companies were being led; traditionally, low-level employees were expected to accept the edicts of top management without questioning them.

Top Management Nationality

Many globally minded companies realize that the best person for a top management job or board position is not necessarily someone born in the home country. Speaking of U.S. companies, Christopher Bartlett of the Harvard Business School has noted:

> Companies are realizing that they have a portfolio of human resources worldwide, that their brightest technical person might come from Germany, or their best financial manager from England. They are starting to tap their worldwide human resources. And as they do, it will not be surprising to see non-Americans rise to the top.[5]

The ability to speak foreign languages is one difference between managers born and raised in the United States and those born and raised elsewhere. For example, the U.S. Department of Education recently reported that 200 million Chinese children are studying English; by contrast, only 24,000 American children are studying Chinese! Roberto Goizueta, the Cuban-born CEO of Coca-Cola who died in 1997, spoke English, Spanish, and Portuguese. Sigismundus W. W. Lubensen, the former president and CEO of Quaker Chemical Corporation, is a good example of today's cosmopolitan executive. Born in the Netherlands and educated in Rotterdam as well as New York, Lubensen, who speaks Dutch, English, French, and German, says, "I was lucky to be born in a

---

[2]William C. Taylor and Alan M. Webber, *Going Global: Four Entrepreneurs Map the New World Marketplace* (New York: Penguin Books USA, 1996), p. 12.
[3]Noel M. Tichy and Stratford Sherman, *Control Your Destiny or Someone Else Will* (New York: HarperBusiness, 1994), p. 227.
[4]Robert Guth, "Facing a Web Revolution, a Mighty Japanese Trader Reinvents Itself," *The Wall Street Journal* (March 27, 2000), p. B1.
[5]Kerry Peckter, "The Foreigners Are Coming," *International Business* (September 1993), p. 53.

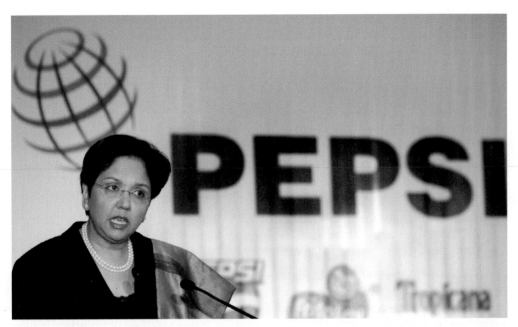

Exhibit 17-2: Indra Nooyi, chairman and chief executive of PepsiCo, is faced with rising prices for raw materials and weak demand for carbonated soft drinks in the United States. Despite these threats, Nooyi believes the snack-and-beverage giant's current strategy is on track. In recent quarters, the strongest results have come from PepsiCo's fast-growing international division. Snack sales are particularly strong in Mexico and Russia; international sales volume for beverage brands is also increasing, particularly in the Middle East, Argentina, China, and Brazil.
Source: Manish Swarup/AP Wide World Photos.

place where if you drove for an hour in any direction, you were in a different country, speaking a different language. It made me very comfortable traveling in different cultures."[6] PepsiCo's Indra Nooyi is also bilingual (see Exhibit 17-2). Table 17-1 shows additional examples of corporate leaders who are not native to the headquarters country.

As noted in this chapter's Culture Watch box, Howard Stringer is the chief executive at Sony. Generally speaking, however, Japanese companies have been reluctant to place non-Japanese nationals in top positions. For years, only Sony, Mazda, and Mitsubishi had foreigners on their boards. In March 1999, however, after Renault SA bought a 36.8 percent stake in Nissan Motor, the French company installed a Brazilian, Carlos Ghosn, as president. An outsider, Ghosn was required to move aggressively to cut costs and make drastic changes in Nissan's structure.

TABLE 17-1 Who's in Charge? Executives of 2010

Company (Headquarters Country)	Executive/Nationality	Position
Cadbury PLC (Great Britain)	Todd Stitzer (United States)	CEO
Carrefour (France)	Lars Olofsson (Sweden)	CEO
Citigroup (United States)	Vikram Pandit (India)	CEO
Eastman Kodak (United States)	Antonio Perez (Spain)	Chairman and CEO
L'Oréal SA (France)	Lindsay Owen-Jones (Great Britain)	Chairman
Monsanto (United States)	Hugh Grant (United Kingdom–Scotland)	Chairman, CEO, and President
Motorola (United States)	Sanjay Jha (India)	Co-CEO
Nissan Motor (Japan)	Carlos Ghosn (Brazil)	Chairman, President, and CEO
Pearson PLC (Great Britain)	Marjorie Scardino (United States)	Chairman and CEO
PepsiCo (United States)	Indra K. Nooyi (India)	CEO
Reuters Media (Great Britain)	Tom Glocer (United States)	CEO and Director
Samsung Electronics (Korea)	David Steel (Great Britain)	Vice President of Business Development
Schering-Plough (United States)	Fred Hassan (Pakistan)	Chairman and CEO
Sony (Japan)	Howard Stringer (United Kingdom–Wales)	Chairman and CEO
Sual (Russia)	Chris Norval (South Africa)	CEO
Wolters Kluwer NV (Netherlands)	Nancy McKinstry (United States)	Chairman and CEO

---

[6]Peckter, p. 58.

He also introduced two new words into Nissan's lexicon: *speed* and *commitment*. Ghosn's turn-around effort was so successful that his life story and exploits have been celebrated in *Big Comic Story*, a comic that is popular with Japan's salarymen.[7]

Leadership and Core Competence

Core competence, a concept developed by global strategy experts C. K. Prahalad and Gary Hamel, was introduced in Chapter 16. In the 1980s, many business executives were assessed on their ability to reorganize their corporations. In the 1990s, Prahalad and Hamel believed executives were judged on their ability to identify, nurture, and exploit the core competencies that make growth possible. Simply put, **core competence** is something that an organization can do better than competitors. Prahalad and Hamel note that a core competence has three characteristics:

- It provides potential access to a wide variety of markets.
- It makes a significant contribution to perceived customer benefits.
- It is difficult for competitors to imitate.

Few companies are likely to build world leadership in more than five or six fundamental competencies. In the long run, an organization will derive its global competitiveness from its ability to bring high-quality, low-cost products to market faster than its competitors. To do this, an organization must be viewed as a portfolio of competencies rather than as a portfolio of businesses. In some instances, a company has the technical resources to build competencies, but key executives lack the vision to do so. As Jorma Ollila, chairman of Finland's Nokia, noted, "Design is a fundamental building block of the [Nokia] brand. It is central to our product creation and is a core competence integrated into the entire company."[9] Ollila's comment underscores the fact that today's executives must rethink the concept of the corporation if they wish to operationalize the concept of core competencies. In addition, the task of management must be viewed as building both competencies and the administrative means for assembling resources spread across multiple businesses.[10] Table 17-2 lists some of the individuals responsible for global marketing at select companies.

TABLE 17-2 Responsibility for Global Marketing

Company (Headquarters Country)	Executive	Position/Title
Adidas (Germany)	Erich Stamminger	Senior Vice President of Global Marketing
Apple Computer (United States)	Greg Joswiak	Vice President of Worldwide iPod Product Marketing
Calvin Klein (United States)	Kim Vernon	Senior Vice President, Global Advertising, Marketing and Communications
Coca-Cola (United States)	Joseph Tripodi	Chief Marketing and Commercial Officer
Haier (China)	Larry Rinaldi	Global Chief Brand Officer
Kodak (United States)	Jeff Hayzlett	Chief Marketing Officer
Kraft Foods (United States)	Betsy D. Holden	President, Global Marketing and Category Development
McDonald's (United States)	Mary Dillon	Global Chief Marketing Officer
Procter & Gamble (United States)	Marc Pritchard	Global Marketing Officer
Reebok International (United States)	Muktesh Pant	Vice President of Global Brand Marketing
SAP AG (Germany)	Martin Homlish	Global Chief Marketing Officer
Warner Music (United States)	John Reid	Executive Vice President, Warner Music International

[7]Norihiko Shirouzu, "U-Turn: A Revival at Nissan Shows There's Hope for Ailing Japan Inc.," *The Wall Street Journal* (November 16, 2000), pp. A1, A10. See also Todd Zaun, "Look! Up in the Sky! It's Nissan's Chief Executive!" *The Wall Street Journal* (December 27, 2001), p. B1.

[8]Todd Zaun, "Now at the Helm, Eckrodt Must Produce Results at Mitsubishi," *The Wall Street Journal* (March 29, 2002), p. A11.

[9]Neil McCartney, "Squaring Up to Usability at Nokia," *Financial Times—IT Review Telecom World* (October 13, 2003), p. 4.

[10]C. K. Prahalad and Gary Hamel, "The Core Competence of the Corporation," *Harvard Business Review* 68, no. 3 (May–June 1990), pp. 79–86.

⟫ STRATEGIC DECISION MAKING IN GLOBAL MARKETING
Managing Global Growth

The beginning of the twenty-first century has challenged deal-making top executives at several global companies. In 1998, Edgar Bronfman, Jr., the CEO of Montreal-based Seagram Company, paid $1 billion for music giant PolyGram NV and sold Seagram's Tropicana orange juice unit to PepsiCo. Bronfman then sold Chivas Regal, several other major spirits brands, and Seagram's wine business to Diageo PLC and Pernod-Ricard SA.

Collectively, these transactions shifted Seagram's focus from beverages to entertainment; the combination of PolyGram with Seagram's MCA record unit created a global music powerhouse. In 2000, Bronfman agreed to a $32 billion takeover by France's Vivendi. The resulting company, Vivendi Universal, was tightly focused in two industry sectors: environmental services and communications. The strategic plan for the communications businesses called for distributing Universal's entertainment content via an Internet portal that PCs, wireless phones, and other electronic devices could access. However, Vivendi Universal had taken on too much debt, and chairman Jean-Marie Messier was forced to resign in 2002. In 2003, the theme park, movie, and television businesses were sold to GE. Today, the company is known simply as Vivendi.

ABB Inc., the Swiss and Swedish electrical and engineering firm that was once comprised of 1,300 companies in 140 countries, is another global giant that has been forced to restructure. During the 1990s, ABB was frequently cited as a textbook example of a successful transnational company. Former Chief Executive Percy Barnevik was legendary in business circles for his charismatic and visionary leadership. However, one of his acquisitions, Combustion Engineering, an American producer of powerplant boilers, proved disastrous because of asbestos-related liability claims. Although his decentralized management structure helped the company grow, it also resulted in conflict and breakdowns in communication between far-flung management units.

Between 1997 and 2003, two chief executives—Göran Lindahl and Jörgen Centerman—came and went in quick succession. The company lost nearly $700 million in 2001; also in 2001, Barnevik, who had remained with the company as a non-executive chairman, was forced to resign after a scandal involving pension benefits. The following year, losses totaled nearly $800 million. ABB's next chief executive, Jürgen Dormann, sold the finance unit and other non-core assets in an effort to reduce debt; the slimmed-down company's two core businesses are focused around automation and power technologies. Commenting on Barnevik's legacy, Dormann noted, "We had a lack of focus as Percy went on an acquisition spree. . . . The company wasn't disciplined enough."

Sources: Dan Bilefsky and Anita Raghavan, "Blown Fuse: How 'Europe's GE' and Its Star CEO Tumbled to Earth," *The Wall Street Journal* (January 23, 2003), pp. A1, A8; John Carreyrou and Martin Peers, "Damage Control: How Messier Kept Cash Crisis at Vivendi Hidden for Months," *The Wall Street Journal* (October 31, 2002), pp. A1, A15; Bruce Orwall, "Universal Script: Vivendi-Seagram Deal Has the Former MCA Playing Familiar Role," *The Wall Street Journal* (June 20, 2000), pp. A1, A8.

ORGANIZING FOR GLOBAL MARKETING

The goal in **organizing** for global marketing is to find a structure that enables the company to respond to relevant market environment differences while ensuring the diffusion of corporate knowledge and experience from national markets throughout the entire corporate system. The pull between the value of centralized knowledge and coordination and the need for individualized response to the local situation creates a constant tension in the global marketing organization. A key issue in global organization is how to achieve balance between autonomy and integration. Subsidiaries need autonomy to adapt to their local environment, but the business as a whole needs integration to implement global strategy.[11]

When management at a domestic company decides to pursue international expansion, the issue of how to organize arises immediately. Who should be responsible for this expansion? Should product divisions operate directly or should an international division be established? Should individual country subsidiaries report directly to the company president or should a special corporate officer be appointed to take full-time responsibility for international activities? After the decision of how to organize initial international operations has been reached, a growing company is faced with a number of reappraisal points during the development of its international business activities. Should a company abandon its international division, and, if so, what alternative structure should be adopted? Should it form an area or regional headquarters? What should be the relationship of staff executives at corporate, regional, and subsidiary offices? Specifically, how should it organize the marketing function? To what extent should regional and corporate marketing executives become involved in subsidiary marketing management?

---

[11]George S. Yip, *Total Global Strategy* (Upper Saddle River, NJ: Prentice Hall, 1992), p. 179.

Even companies with years of experience competing around the globe find it necessary to adjust their organizational designs in response to environmental change. It is perhaps not surprising that, during his tenure at Quaker Chemical, Sigismundus Lubensen favored a global approach to organizational design over a domestic/international approach. He advised Peter A. Benoliel, his predecessor CEO, to have units in Holland, France, Italy, Spain, and England report to a regional vice president in Europe. "I saw that it would not be a big deal to put all of the European units under one common denominator," Lubensen recalled.[12]

As markets globalize and as Japan opens its own market to more competition from overseas, more Japanese companies are likely to break from traditional organization patterns. Many of the Japanese companies discussed in this text qualify as global or transnational companies because they serve world markets, source globally, or do both. Typically, however, knowledge is created at headquarters in Japan and then transferred to other country units. For example, Canon enjoys a high reputation for world-class, innovative imaging products such as bubble-jet printers and laser printers. In recent years, Canon has shifted more control to subsidiaries, hired more non-Japanese staff and management personnel, and assimilated more innovations that were not developed in Japan. In 1996, R&D responsibility for software was shifted from Tokyo to the United States, responsibility for telecommunication products to France, and computer language translation to Great Britain. As Canon President Fujio Mitarai explained, "The Tokyo headquarters cannot know everything. Its job should be to provide low-cost capital, to move top management between regions, and come up with investment initiatives. Beyond that, the local subsidiaries must assume total responsibility for management. We are not there yet, but we are moving step by step in that direction." Toru Takahashi, director of R&D, shares this view. "We used to think that we should keep research and development in Japan, but that has changed," he said. Despite these changes, Canon's board of directors includes only Japanese nationals.[13]

No single correct organizational structure exists for global marketing. Even within a particular industry, worldwide companies have developed different strategic and organizational responses to changes in their environments.[14] Still, it is possible to make some generalizations. Leading-edge global competitors share one key organizational design characteristic: Their corporate structure is flat and simple, rather than tall and complex. The message is clear: The world is complicated enough, so there is no need to add to the confusion with a complex internal structuring. Simple structures increase the speed and clarity of communication and allow the concentration of organizational energy and valuable resources on learning, rather than on controlling, monitoring, and reporting.[15] According to David Whitwam, CEO of Whirlpool, "You must create an organization whose people are adept at exchanging ideas, processes, and systems across borders, people who are absolutely free of the 'not-invented-here' syndrome, people who are constantly working together to identify the best global opportunities and the biggest global problems facing the organization."[16]

A geographically dispersed company cannot limit its knowledge to product, function, and the home territory. Company personnel must acquire knowledge of the complex set of social, political, economic, and institutional arrangements that exist within each international market. Many companies start with ad hoc arrangements such as having all foreign subsidiaries report to a designated vice president or to the president. Eventually, such companies establish an international division to manage their geographically dispersed new businesses. It is clear, however, that the international division in the multiproduct company is an unstable organizational arrangement. As a company grows, this initial organizational structure frequently gives way to various alternative structures.

---

[12]Kerry Peckter, "The Foreigners Are Coming," *International Business* (September 1993), p. 58.

[13]William Dawkins, "Time to Pull Back the Screen," *Financial Times* (November 18, 1996), p. 12. See also Sumatra Ghoshal and Christopher A. Bartlett, *The Individualized Corporation* (New York: Harper Perennial, 1999), pp. 179–181.

[14]Christopher Bartlett and Sumantra Ghoshal, *Managing Across Borders: The Transnational Solution* (Boston: Harvard Business School Press, 1989), p. 3.

[15]Vladimir Pucik, "Globalization and Human Resource Management," in V. Pucik, N. Tichy, and C. Barnett (eds.), *Globalizing Management: Creating and Leading the Competitive Organization* (New York: J. Wiley & Sons, 1992), p. 70.

[16]Regina Fazio Maruca, "The Right Way to Go Global: An Interview with Whirlpool CEO David Whitwam," *Harvard Business Review* 72, no. 2 (March–April 1994), p. 137.

In the fast-changing competitive global environment of the twenty-first century, corporations will have to find new, more creative ways to organize. New forms of flexibility, efficiency, and responsiveness are required to meet the demands of globalizing markets. The need to be cost effective, to be customer driven, to deliver the best quality, and to deliver that quality quickly are some of today's global realities. Recently, several authors have described new organization designs that represent responses to today's competitive environment. These designs acknowledge the need to find more responsive and flexible structures, to flatten the organization, and to employ teams. There is the recognition of the need to develop networks, to develop stronger relationships among participants, and to exploit technology. These designs also reflect an evolution in approaches to organizational effectiveness. At the turn of the twentieth century, Frederick Taylor claimed that all managers had to see the world the same way. Then came the contingency theorists who said that effective organizations design themselves to match their conditions. These two basic theories are reflected in today's popular management writings. As Henry Mintzberg has observed, "To Michael Porter, effectiveness resides in strategy, while to Tom Peters it is the operations that count—executing any strategy with excellence."[17]

Kenichi Ohmae has written extensively on the implications of globalization on organization design. He recommends a type of "global superstructure" at the highest level that provides a view of the world as a single unit. The staff members of this unit are responsible for ensuring that work is performed in the best location and coordinating efficient movement of information and products across borders. Below this level, Ohmae envisions organizational units assigned to regions "governed by economies of service and economies of scale in information." In Ohmae's view of the world, there are 30 regions with populations ranging from 5 million to 20 million people. For example, China would be viewed as several distinct regions; the same is true of the United States. The first task of the CEO in such an organization is to become oriented to the single unit that is the borderless business sphere, much as an astronaut might view the earth from space. Then, zooming in, the CEO attempts to identify differences. As Ohmae explains,

> A CEO has to look at the entire global economy and then put the company's resources where they will capture the biggest market share of the most attractive regions. Perhaps as you draw closer from outer space you see a region around the Pacific Northwest, near Puget Sound, that is vibrant and prosperous. Then you recognize the region stretching from New York to Boston that is still doing awful. You might see a booming concentration of computer companies and software publishers around Denver, and similar concentrations around Dallas-Fort Worth. Along the coast of California and in parts of New England you will see regions that are strong centers for health care and biotechnology. As a CEO, that's where you put your resources and shift your emphasis.[18]

Your authors believe that successful companies, the real global winners, must have both good strategies and good execution.

Patterns of International Organizational Development

Organizations vary in terms of the size and potential of targeted global markets and local management competence in different country markets. Conflicting pressures may arise from the need for product and technical knowledge; functional expertise in marketing, finance, and operations; and area and country knowledge. Because the constellation of pressures that shape organizations is never exactly the same, no two organizations pass through organizational stages in exactly the same way, nor do they arrive at precisely the same organizational pattern. Nevertheless, some general patterns hold.

A company engaging in limited export activities often has a small in-house export department as a separate functional area. Most domestically oriented companies undertake initial

[17]Henry Mintzberg, "The Effective Organization: Forces and Forms," *Sloan Management Review* 32, no. 2 (Winter 1991), pp. 54–55.

[18]William C. Taylor and Alan M. Webber, *Going Global: Four Entrepreneurs Map the New World Marketplace* (New York: Penguin, 1996), pp. 48–58.

Sony Corporation is a legend in the global consumer electronics industry. Its reputation for innovation and engineering has made it the envy of rivals. For decades, quality-conscious consumers paid premium prices for the company's Trinitron color televisions. Sony was a key player in the development of the VCR and virtually invented the personal stereo with its Walkman product line. Sony was a co-developer of the compact disc music format. The PlayStation 2 enjoyed a commanding 70 percent market share of the videogame console market.

By the turn of the millennium, however, Sony's vaunted innovation and marketing machine was faltering. The company had not anticipated the rapid consumer acceptance of flat-panel, widescreen LCD and plasma TV sets, and the Walkman was eclipsed by Apple's iPod and iTunes Music Store. In 2005, a tumbling stock price resulted in the resignation of chairman and CEO Nobuyuki Idei. Sir Howard Stringer, a Welsh-born American who had been knighted in 2000, was named as Idei's replacement (see Exhibit 17-3).

Although Stringer had been in charge of Sony's U.S. operations, his appointment to the top position came as a surprise to some observers: He was neither Japanese nor an engineer. One of his first priorities was to bridge the divide between Sony's media businesses, which included music, games, and motion pictures, and its hardware businesses. As Stringer himself declared, "We've got to get the relationship between content and devices seamlessly managed."

Management writers often use terms like *silos*, *stovepipes*, or *chimneys* to describe an organization in which autonomous business units operate with their own agendas and a minimum of horizontal interdependence. This was the situation at Sony, where the internal rivalries between different engineering units—the PC and Walkman groups, for example—were ingrained in the corporate culture and regarded as healthy.

The intracorporate rivalries were especially evident as Sony ramped up for the 2004 launch of Connect, a paid music download service positioned to compete with Apple's iTunes. Sony's PC group developed the software; it was to be played on next-generation Walkman devices from the company's portable audio unit. Meanwhile, the music division insisted on strict copy-protection measures because of concerns about piracy. As head of Sony's U.S. operations, Sir Howard championed the service; however, he was not able to compel Sony's different divisions to

work together. Little surprise, then, that consumers gave Connect a lukewarm reception.

Because Sony's consumer electronics business accounts for more than two-thirds of Sony's worldwide sales, breathing new life into the unit is important. To do this, Sir Howard developed a restructuring plan that called for cutting 10,000 jobs, reducing the number of manufacturing sites from 65 to 54, and eliminating some unprofitable products. In an effort to improve horizontal communication, he also merged some of the electronics business's units

Cost cutting is only part of the story. Boosting revenues with new products is also crucial to Sony's recovery. Sir Howard believes that Sony's TV business will recover, thanks in part to the new Bravia line of HDTVs. The company has also launched an e-book reader. Although Sir Howard had high hopes for the launch of the PlayStation 3 game console in mid-2006, production issues delayed the introduction until November. By the time the crucial Christmas shopping season was over, industry observers were pronouncing Nintendo's Wii the victor in the videogame console wars. In 2008, Wii outsold PS3 by a ratio of three to one.

Will Sir Howard succeed in effecting a turnaround at Sony? While some consider him to be an outsider, he is known for his nonconfrontational style. Because of Sony's complexity, Sir Howard will be heavily reliant on the skills of his Japanese management team. Sir Howard explains, "I had to do two things: develop those relationships and convince them that the kind of changes I had in mind would be worthwhile." William Ouchi, author of *Triad Power* and *Theory Z*, says, "Sony is going through the major repositioning that Intel has gone through and AOL is going through. From hardware to software to communications to content, every segment of these industries is being turned topsy-turvy."

60 Minutes, *the CBS news magazine, recently aired a profile of Sir Howard. The DVD of the program makes an excellent companion to the text discussion.*

Sources: Yukari Iwatani Kane, "Sony Expects to Trim PS3 Losses, Plans More Games, Online Features," *The Wall Street Journal* (May 18, 2007), p. B4; Phred Dvorak, "Sony Aims to Cut Costs, Workers to Revive Its Electronics Business," *The Wall Street Journal* (September 23, 2005), p. A5; Dvorak, "Out of Tune: At Sony, Rivalries Were Encouraged; Then Came iPod," *The Wall Street Journal* (June 29, 2005), pp. A1, A6; Lorne Manly and Andrew Ross Sorkin, "Choice of Stringer Aims to Prevent Further Setbacks," *The New York Times* (March 8, 2005), pp. C1, C8; Dvorak and Merissa Marr, "Shock Treatment: Sony, Lagging Behind Rivals, Hands Reins to a Foreigner," *The Wall Street Journal* (March 7, 2005), pp. A1, A8.

foreign expansion by means of foreign sales offices or subsidiaries that report directly to the company president or other designated company officer. This person carries out his or her responsibilities without assistance from a headquarters staff group. This is a typical initial arrangement for companies getting started in international marketing operations.

INTERNATIONAL DIVISION STRUCTURE As a company's international business grows, the complexity of coordinating and directing this activity extends beyond the scope of a single

Exhibit 17-3: When Sir Howard Stringer was named chairman and chief executive of Sony in 2005, he became the first non-Japanese executive in the consumer electronics giant's history. He praised Nintendo's latest videogame console, the Wii, calling it, "a very good business model."

On the subject of executive compensation, Sir Howard believes that, by American standards, "Japanese executives are astonishingly underpaid." But, he added in another interview, "Most executives in Japan don't work for money, pure and simple. They are motivated by something else."[19]
Source: Koji Sasahara/AP Wide World Photos.

person. Pressure is created to assemble a staff that will take responsibility for coordination and direction of the growing international activities of the organization. Eventually, this process leads to the creation of the international division, as illustrated in Figure 17-1. Best Buy, Hershey, Levi Strauss, Walt Disney, and Walmart are some examples of companies whose structures include international divisions. When Hershey announced the creation of its international division in 2005, J.P. Bilbrey, the division's senior vice president, noted that Hershey will no longer utilize the extension strategy of exporting its chocolate products from the United States. Instead, the

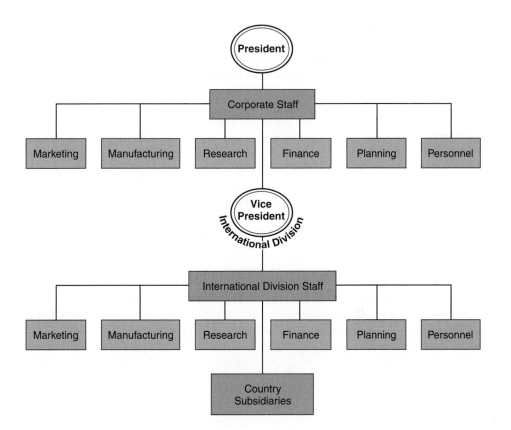

FIGURE 17-1

Functional Corporate Structure, Domestic Corporate Staff Orientation, International Division

[19]Aline van Duyn, "View from the Top: Sir Howard Stringer," *Financial Times* (June 15, 2007), p. 10.

company will tailor products to local markets and also manufacture locally. As Bilbrey explained, "We're changing our business model in Asia. The product was not locally relevant and it also got there at an unattractive cost."[20]

Four factors contribute to the establishment of an international division. First, top management's commitment to global operations has increased enough to justify an organizational unit headed by a senior manager. Second, the complexity of international operations requires a single organizational unit whose management has sufficient authority to make its own determination on important issues such as which market entry strategy to employ. Third, an international division is frequently formed when the firm has recognized the need for internal specialists to deal with the special demands of global operations. A fourth contributing factor is management's recognition of the importance of strategically scanning the global horizon for opportunities and aligning them with company resources rather than simply responding on an ad hoc basis to situations as they arise.

REGIONAL MANAGEMENT CENTERS When business is conducted in a single region that is characterized by similarities in economic, social, geographical, and political conditions, there is both justification and need for a management center. Thus, another stage of organizational evolution is the emergence of an area or regional headquarters as a management layer between the country organization and the international division headquarters. The increasing importance of the EU as a regional market has prompted a number of companies to change their organizational structures by setting up regional headquarters there. In the mid-1990s, Quaker Oats established its European headquarters in Brussels; Electrolux, the Swedish home appliance company, has also regionalized its European operations.[21] A regional center typically coordinates decisions on pricing, sourcing, and other matters. Executives at the regional center also participate in the planning and control of each country's operations with an eye toward applying company knowledge on a regional basis and optimally utilizing corporate resources on a regional basis. This organizational design is illustrated in Figure 17-2.

Regional management can offer a company several advantages. First, many regional managers agree that an on-the-scene regional management unit makes sense where there is a real need for coordinated, pan-regional decision making. Coordinated regional planning and control are becoming necessary as the national subsidiary continues to lose its relevance as an independent operating unit. Regional management can probably achieve the best balance of geographical, product, and functional considerations required to implement corporate objectives effectively. By shifting operations and decision making to the region, the company is better able to maintain an insider advantage.[22]

A major disadvantage of a regional center is its cost. The cost of a two-person office could exceed $600,000 per year. The scale of regional management must be in line with the scale of operations in a region. A regional headquarters is inappropriate if the size of the operations it manages is inadequate to cover the costs of the additional layer of management. The basic issue with regard to the regional headquarters is "Does it contribute enough to organizational effectiveness to justify its cost and the complexity of another layer of management?"

GEOGRAPHICAL AND PRODUCT DIVISION STRUCTURES As a company becomes more global, management frequently faces the dilemma of whether to organize by geography or by product lines. The geographical structure involves the assignment of operational responsibility for geographic areas of the world to line managers. The corporate headquarters retains responsibility for worldwide planning and control, and each area of the world—including the "home" or base market—is organizationally equal. For the company with French origins, France is simply another geographic market under this organizational arrangement. This structure is most common in companies with closely related product lines that are sold in similar end-use markets around the world. For example, the major international oil companies utilize the geographical

[20]Jeremy Grant, "Hershey Chews Over Growth Strategy," *Financial Times* (December 14, 2005), p. 23.
[21]"... And Other Ways to Peel the Onion," *The Economist* (January 7, 1995), pp. 52–53.
[22]Allen J. Morrison, David A. Ricks, and Kendall Roth, "Globalization Versus Regionalization: Which Way for the Multinational?" *Organizational Dynamics* (Winter 1991), pp. 17–29.

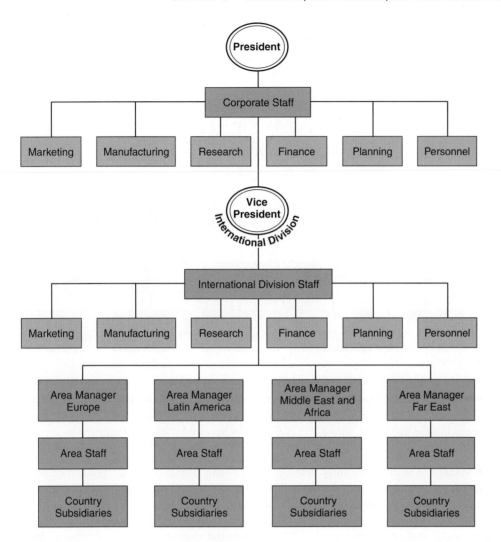

FIGURE 17-2

Functional Corporate Structure, Domestic Corporate Staff Orientation, International Division, Area Divisions

structure, which is illustrated in Figure 17-3. McDonald's organizational design integrates the international division and geographical structures. McDonald's U.S. is organized into five geographical operating divisions and McDonald's International has four.

When an organization assigns regional or worldwide product responsibility to its product divisions, manufacturing standardization can result in significant economies. For example, Whirlpool recently reorganized its European operations, switching from a geographic or country orientation to one based on product lines. One potential disadvantage of the product approach is that local input from individual country managers may be ignored with the result that products will not be sufficiently tailored to local markets. The essence of the Ford 2000 reorganization initiated in 1995 was to integrate North American and European operations. Over a three-year period, the company saved $5 billion in development costs. However, by 2000, Ford's European market share had slipped nearly 5 percent. In a shift back toward the geographic model, then-CEO Jacques Nasser returned to regional executives some of the authority they had lost.[23]

The challenges associated with devising the structure that is best suited to improving global sales can be seen in Procter & Gamble's ambitious Organization 2005 plan. Initiated by CEO Durk Jager in 1999, this reorganization entailed replacing separate country organizations with five global business units for key product categories such as paper products and feminine hygiene. A number of executives were reassigned; in Europe alone, 1,000 staff members were

---

[23]Joann S. Lublin, "Division Problem: Place vs. Product: It's Tough to Choose a Management Model," *The Wall Street Journal* (June 27, 2001), pp. A1, A4.

FIGURE 17-3

Geographic Corporate Structure, World Corporate Staff Orientation, Area Divisions Worldwide

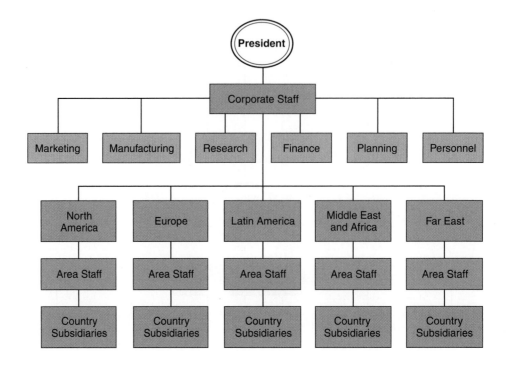

> "GE is managing its worldwide organization as a network, not a centralized hub with foreign appendages."[25]
> Christopher A. Bartlett

transferred to Geneva. Many managers, upset about the transfers and news that P&G intended to cut 15,000 jobs worldwide, quit the company; the resulting upheaval cost CEO Jager his job. To appease middle managers, new CEO A.G. Lafley restored some of the previous geographic focus.[24]

THE MATRIX DESIGN In the fully developed large-scale global company, product or business, function, area, and customer know-how are simultaneously focused on the organization's worldwide marketing objectives. This type of total competence is a **matrix organization**. Management's task in the matrix organization is to achieve an organizational balance that brings together different perspectives and skills to accomplish the organization's objectives. In 1998, both Gillette and Ericsson announced plans to reorganize into matrix organizations. Ericsson's matrix is focused on three customer segments: network operators, private consumers, and commercial enterprises.[26] Gillette's new structure separates product-line management from geographical sales and marketing responsibility.[27] Likewise, Boeing has reorganized its commercial transport design and manufacturing engineers into a matrix organization built around five platform or aircraft model-specific groups. Previously, Boeing was organized along functional lines; the new design is expected to lower costs and quicken updates and problem solving. It will also unite essential design, engineering, and manufacturing processes between Boeing's commercial transport factories and component plants, enhancing product consistency.[28] Why are executives at these and other companies implementing matrix designs? The matrix form of organization is well-suited to global companies because it can be used to establish a multiple-command structure that gives equal emphasis to functional and geographical departments.

Professor John Hunt of the London Business School suggests four considerations regarding the matrix organizational design. First, the matrix is appropriate when the market is demanding and dynamic. Second, employees must accept higher levels of ambiguity and understand that

[24]Emily Nelson, "Rallying the Troops at P&G: New CEO Lafley Aims to End Upheaval by Revamping Program of Globalization," *The Wall Street Journal* (August 31, 2000), pp. B1, B4.

[25]Claudia Deutsch, "At Home in the World," *The New York Times* (February 14, 2008), p. C1.

[26]"Ericsson to Simplify Business Structure," *Financial Times* (September 29, 1998), p. 21.

[27]Mark Maremont, "Gillette to Shut 14 of Its Plants, Lay Off 4,700," *The Wall Street Journal* (September 29, 1998), pp. A3, A15.

[28]Paul Proctor, "Boeing Shifts to 'Platform Teams,'" *Aviation Week & Space Technology* (May 17, 1999) pp. 63–64.

policy manuals cannot cover every eventuality. Third, in country markets where the command-and-control model persists, it is best to overlay matrices on only small portions of the workforce. Finally, management must be able to clearly state what each axis of the matrix can and cannot do. However, this must be accomplished without creating a bureaucracy.[29]

Having established that the matrix is appropriate, management can expect the matrix to integrate four basic competencies on a worldwide basis:

1. *Geographic knowledge.* An understanding of the basic economic, social, cultural, political, and governmental market and competitive dimensions of a country is essential. The country subsidiary is the major structural device employed today to enable the corporation to acquire geographical knowledge.

2. *Product knowledge and know-how.* Product managers with a worldwide responsibility can achieve this level of competence on a global basis. Another way of achieving global product competence is simply to duplicate product management organizations in domestic and international divisions, achieving high competence in both organizational units.

3. *Functional competence in such fields as finance, production, and, especially, marketing.* Corporate functional staff with worldwide responsibility contributes toward the development of functional competence on a global basis. In some companies, the corporate functional manager, who is responsible for the development of his or her functional activity on a global basis, reviews the appointment of country subsidiary functional managers.

4. *A knowledge of the customer or industry and its needs.* Certain large and extremely sophisticated global companies have staff with a responsibility for serving industries on a global basis to assist the line managers in the country organizations in their efforts to penetrate specific customer markets.

Under this arrangement, instead of designating national organizations or product divisions as profit centers, both are responsible for profitability—the national organization for country profits and the product divisions for national and worldwide product profitability. Figure 17-4 illustrates the matrix organization. This organization chart starts with a bottom section that represents a single-country responsibility level, moves to representing the area or international level, and finally moves to representing global responsibility from the product divisions to the corporate staff, to the chief executive at the top of the structure.

At Whirlpool, North American operations are organized in matrix form. CEO David Whitwam expects to extend this structure into Europe and other regional markets. Whirlpool managers from traditional functions such as operations, marketing, and finance also work in teams devoted to specific products, such as dishwashers or ovens. To encourage interdependence and integration, the cross-functional teams are headed by "brand czars" such as the brand chief for Whirlpool or Kenmore. As Whitwam explains, "The Whirlpool-brand czar still worries about the Whirlpool name. But he also worries about all the refrigerator brands that we make because he heads that product team. It takes a different mind-set."[30]

The key to successful matrix management is ensuring that managers are able to resolve conflicts and achieve integration of organization programs and plans. The mere adoption of a matrix design or structure does not create a matrix organization. The matrix organization requires fundamental changes in management behavior, organizational culture, and technical systems. In a matrix, influence is based on technical competence and interpersonal sensitivity, not on formal authority. In a matrix culture, managers recognize the absolute need to resolve issues and choices at the lowest possible level and do not rely on higher authority.

Some companies are moving away from the matrix in response to changing competitive conditions. Heineken is one example; ABB is another. For nearly a decade, ABB was a matrix organized along regional lines. Local business units—factories that make motors or power generators, for example—reported both to a country manager and to a business area manager who set strategy for the whole world. This structure allowed ABB to execute global strategies while still thriving in local markets. However, in 1998, new chairman Göran Lindahl dissolved

---

[29]John W. Hunt, "Is Matrix Management a Recipe for Chaos?" *Financial Times* (January 12, 1998), p. 10.
[30]William C. Taylor and Alan M. Webber, *Going Global: Four Entrepreneurs Map the New World Marketplace* (New York: Penguin USA, 1996), p. 25.

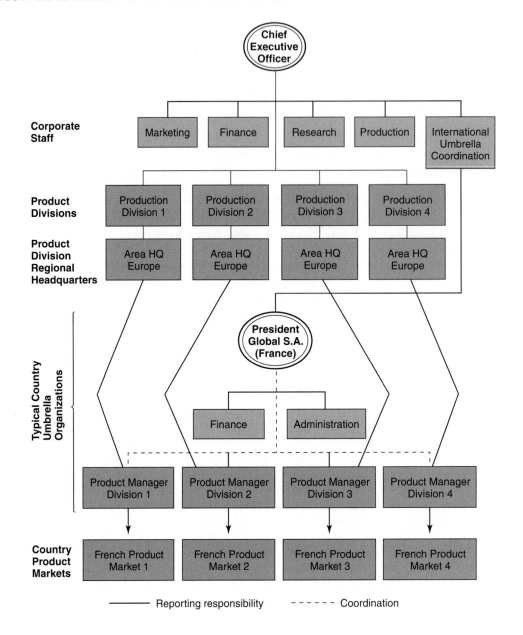

FIGURE 17-4

The Matrix Structure

——— Reporting responsibility   - - - - - Coordination

the matrix. As the chairman explained in a press release, "This is an aggressive move aimed at greater speed and efficiency by further focusing and flattening the organization. This step is possible now thanks to our strong, decentralized presence in all local and global markets around the world." In January 2001, Lindahl stepped down and his successor, Jorgen Centerman, revamped the organizational structure yet again. The new design was intended to improve the focus on industries and large corporate customers; Centerman wanted to ensure that all of ABB's products were designed to the same systems standards. However, in 2002, with the chief executive under pressure to sell assets, ABB's board replaced Centerman with Jürgen Dorman.[31]

In the twenty-first century, an important task of top management is to eliminate a one-dimensional approach to decisions and encourage the development of multiple management perspectives and an organization that will sense and respond to a complex and fast-changing world. By thinking in terms of changing behavior rather than changing structural design, management can free itself from the limitations of the structural chart and focus instead on achieving the best possible results with available resources.

[31]David Woodruff, "New ABB Chairman Unveils Overhaul, Reacting to Rival GE," *The Wall Street Journal* (January 12, 2001), p. A16. A detailed discussion of ABB's matrix structure is found in Sumatra Ghoshal and Christopher A. Bartlett, *The Individualized Corporation* (New York: Harper Perennial, 1999), pp. 183–190.

LEAN PRODUCTION: ORGANIZING THE JAPANESE WAY

In the automobile industry, a comparison of early craft production processes, mass production, and modern "lean" production provides an interesting case study of the effectiveness of new organizational structures in the twentieth century.[32] Dramatic productivity differences existed between craft and mass producers in the first part of the twentieth century. The mass producers—most notably Ford Motor Company—gained their substantial advantage by changing their value chains so that each worker was able to do far more work each day than the craft producers. The innovation that made this possible was the moving assembly line, which required the originators to conceptualize the production process in a totally new way. The assembly line also required a new approach to organizing people, production machinery, and supplies. By rearranging their value chain activities, the mass producers were able to achieve reductions in effort ranging from 62 to 88 percent over the craft producers. These productivity improvements provided an obvious competitive advantage.

The advantage of the mass producers lasted until the Japanese auto companies further revised the value chain and created **lean production**, thereby gaining for themselves the kinds of dramatic competitive advantages that mass producers had previously gained over craft producers. For example, the Toyota Production System (TPS), as the Japanese company's manufacturing methods are known, achieves efficiencies of about 50 percent over typical mass production systems. Even with the reduced assembly time, the lean producer's vehicles have significantly fewer defects than the mass-produced vehicles. The lean producer is also using about 40 percent less factory space and maintaining only a fraction of the inventory stored by the mass producer. Again, the competitive advantages are obvious. Whether the strategy is based on differentiation or low cost, the lean producer has the advantage.

To achieve these gains at Toyota, production gurus Taiichi Ohno and Shigeo Shingo challenged several assumptions traditionally associated with automobile manufacturing. They made changes to operations within the auto company itself such as reducing setup times for machinery. The changes also applied to operations within supplier firms and the interfaces between Toyota and its suppliers and to the interfaces with distributors and dealers. Ohno and Shingo's innovations have been widely embraced in the industry; as a result, individual producers' value chains have been modified, and interfaces between producers and suppliers have been optimized to create more effective and efficient value systems (see Table 17-3).

Assembler Value Chains

Employee ability is emphasized in a lean production environment. Before being hired, people seeking jobs with Toyota participate in the Day of Work, a 12-hour assessment test to determine who has the right mix of physical dexterity, team attitudes, and problem-solving ability. Once

TABLE 17-3 Five Assumptions about Mass Production Versus Toyota Production System

Traditional Assumptions	Ohno and Shingo's Insights
1. Maximize machine utilization	Labor is more costly than machines
2. Fixed setup times	Can reduce setup time
3. Build to inventory to reduce unit cost	Minimize inventory to cut costs, waste
4. Inspect at end of process	Inspect to prevent defective production
5. Maximize backwards integration	Outsource from supplier specialists

Source: Adapted from Adrian Slywotzky, *Value Migration* (Cambridge, MA: Harvard Business School Press, 1996), pp. 31–33.

---

[32]This section is adapted from the following sources: James P. Womack, Daniel T. Jones, and Daniel Roos, *The Machine That Changed the World: The Story of Lean Production* (New York: HarperCollins, 1990); Ranganath Nayak and John M. Ketteringham, *Breakthroughs!* (San Diego, CA: Pfeiffer, 1994), Chapter 9; and Michael Williams, "Back to the Past: Some Plants Tear Out Long Assembly Lines, Switch to Craft Work," *The Wall Street Journal* (October 24, 1994), pp. A1, A4.

hired, workers receive considerable training to enable them to perform any job in their section of the assembly line or area of the plant, and they are assigned to teams in which all members must be able to perform the functions of all other team members. Workers are also empowered to make suggestions and to take actions aimed at improving quality and productivity. Quality control is achieved through *kaizen*, a devotion to continuous improvement that ensures that every flaw is isolated, examined in detail to determine the ultimate cause, and then corrected (see Exhibit 17-4).

Mechanization, and particularly flexible mechanization, is a hallmark of lean production. For example, a single assembly line in Georgetown, Kentucky, that produces Toyota's Camry sedan also produces the Sienna minivan. The Sienna and Camry share the same basic chassis and 50 percent of their parts. Of the 300 different stations on the line, only 26 stations require different parts to assemble minivans. Similarly, Honda has invested hundreds of millions of dollars to introduce flexible production technology in its U.S. plants. In an era of volatile gasoline prices and fluctuating exchange rates, production flexibility becomes a source of competitive advantage. For example, when the weak dollar put pressure on margins for vehicles imported into the United States, Honda shifted production of CR-V crossovers from the United Kingdom to a plant in Ohio. Within a matter of minutes, Honda can switch from producing Civic compacts to CR-V crossovers as demand or other market conditions dictate.[33]

In contrast to the lean producers, U.S. mass producers typically maintain operations with greater direct labor content, less mechanization, and much less flexible mechanization. They also divide their employees into a large number of discrete specialties with no overlap. Employee initiative and teamwork are not encouraged. Quality control is expressed as an acceptable number of defects per vehicle.

Even when the comparisons are based on industry averages, the Japanese lean producers continue to enjoy substantial productivity and quality advantages. Again, these advantages put the lean producers in a better position to exploit low cost or differentiation strategies. They are getting better productivity out of their workers and machines, and they are making better use of their factory floor space. The relatively small size of the repair area reflects the higher quality of their products. A high number of "suggestions per employee" provides some insight into why lean producers outperform mass producers. First, they invest a great deal more in the training of their workers. They also rotate all workers through all jobs for which their teams are responsible. Finally, all workers are encouraged to make suggestions, and management

Exhibit 17-4: The Toyota Production System (TPS) is based on two concepts. First is *jidoka*, which involves visualizing potential problems. *Jidoka* also means that quality is built into the company's vehicles during the manufacturing process. "Just-in-time," the second pillar of the TPS, means that Toyota only produces what is needed, when it is needed, in the amount that is needed. Toyota's training programs ensure that all employees understand the Toyota Way. Future factory workers attend the Toyota Technical Skills Academy in Toyota City, Japan. Executive training takes place at the Toyota Institute.
Source: Ko Sasaki/*The New York Times*/Redux Pictures.

[33]Kate Linebaugh, "Honda's Flexible Plants Provide Edge," *The Wall Street Journal* (September 23, 2008), p. B1.

acts on those suggestions. These changes to the value chain translate into major improvements in the value of their products.

It should come as no surprise that many of the world's automakers are studying lean production methods and introducing them in both existing and new plants throughout the world. In 1999, for example, GM announced plans to spend nearly $500 million to overhaul its Adam Opel plant in Germany. Pressure for change came from several sources, including increasing intense rivalry in Europe's car market, worldwide overcapacity, and a realization that price transparency in the euro zone will exert downward pressure on prices. GM's goal was to transform the plant into a state-of-the-art lean production facility with a 40 percent workforce reduction. As GM Europe President Michael J. Burns said at the time, "Pricing is more difficult today. . . . You have to work on product costs, structural costs . . . everything."[34]

Downstream Value Chains

The differences between lean producers and U.S. mass producers in the way they deal with their respective dealers, distributors, and customers are as dramatic as the differences in the way they deal with their suppliers. U.S. mass producers follow the basic industry model and maintain an "arm's length" relationship with dealers that is often characterized by a lack of cooperation and even open hostility. There is often no sharing of information because there is no incentive to do so. The manufacturer is often trying to force on the dealer models the dealer knows will not sell. The dealer, in turn, is often trying to pressure the customer into buying models he or she does not want. All parties are trying to keep information about what they really want from the others. This does little to ensure that the industry is responsive to market needs.

The problem starts with the market research, which is often in error. It is compounded by lack of feedback from dealers regarding real customer desires. It continues to worsen when the product planning divisions make changes to the models without consulting the marketing divisions or the dealers. This process invariably results in production of models that are unpopular and almost impossible to sell. The manufacturer uses incentives and other schemes to persuade the dealers to accept the unpopular models, such as making a dealer accept one unpopular model for every five hot-selling models it orders. The dealer then has the problem of persuading customers to buy the unpopular models.

Within the mass assembler's value chain, the linkage between the marketing elements and the product planners is broken. The external linkage between the sales divisions and the dealers is also broken. The production process portion of the value chain is also broken in that it relies on the production of thousands of unsold models that then sit on dealer lots, at enormous cost, while the dealer works to find customers. Within the dealerships, there are even more problems. The relationship between the salesperson and the customer is based on sparring and trying to outsmart each other on price. When the salesperson gets the upper hand, the customer gets stung. It is very much like the relationship between the dealer and the manufacturer. Each is withholding information from the other in the hope of outsmarting the other. Too often, salespeople do not investigate customers' real needs and try to find the best product to satisfy those needs. Rather, they provide only as much information as is needed to close the deal. Once the deal is closed, the salesperson has virtually no further contact with the customer. No attempt is made to optimize the linkage between dealers and manufacturers or the linkage between dealers and customers.

The contrast with the lean producer is again striking. In Japan, the dealer's employees are true product specialists. They know their products and deal with all aspects of the product, including financing, service, maintenance, insurance, registration and inspection, and delivery. A customer deals with one person in the dealership, and that person takes care of everything from the initial contact through eventual trade-in and replacement and all the problems in between. Dealer representatives are included on the manufacturer's product development teams and provide continuous input regarding customer desires. The linkages between dealers, marketing divisions, and product development teams are totally optimized.

The stress caused by large inventories of finished cars is also absent. A car is not built until there is a customer order for it. Each dealer has only a stock of models for the customer to view.

---

[34]Joseph B. White, "GM Plans to Invest $445 Million, Cut Staff," *The Wall Street Journal* (May 27, 1999), p. A23.

Once the customer has decided on the car he or she wants, the order is sent to the factory and in a matter of a couple of weeks the salesperson delivers the car to the customer's house.

Once a Japanese dealership gets a customer, it is absolutely determined to hang on to that customer for life. It is also determined to acquire all of the customer's family members as customers. A joke among the Japanese says that the only way to escape from the salesperson who sold a person a car is to leave the country. Japanese dealers maintain extensive databases on actual and potential customers. These databases deal with demographic data and preference data. Customers are encouraged to help keep the information in the database current and they cooperate in this. This elaborate store of data becomes an integral part of the market research effort and helps ensure that products match customer desires. The fact that there are no inventories of unpopular models because every car is custom ordered for each customer and the fact that the dealer has elaborate data on the needs and desires of its customers change the whole nature of the interaction between the customer and the dealer. The customer literally builds the car she or he wants and can afford. There is no need to try to outsmart each other.

The differences between U.S. mass producers and the Japanese lean producers reflect their fundamental differences in business objectives. The U.S. producers focus on short-term income and return on investment. Today's sale is a discrete event that is not connected to upstream activities in the value chain and has no value in tomorrow's activities. Efforts are made to reduce the cost of the sales activities. The Japanese see the process in terms of the long-term perspective. There are two major goals of the sales process. The first is to maximize the income stream from each customer over time. The second is to use the linkage with the production processes to reduce production and inventory costs and to maximize quality and therefore differentiation.

EMERGING MARKETS BRIEFING BOOK

⇒〉 Volkswagen AG

German automaker Volkswagen has a great deal of experience in emerging markets. One example is the 1991 purchase of a 31 percent stake in Skoda from the Czechoslovak government. Located northeast of Prague in the city of Mlada Boleslav, the Skoda works enjoyed distinction as the most efficient plant in the former Soviet bloc. However, product quality was low and the plant was a major source of pollution. With an eye to doubling production to 450,000 cars, VW pledged to invest $5 billion by the end of the 1990s (see Exhibit 17-5).

In 1992, the Czech Republic split from Slovakia. VW's presence drew TRW, Rockwell International, and other parts suppliers to the region. However, to maintain their low-cost position and ensure quality control, VW and Skoda executives went a step beyond the Japanese-style "lean production" system that emphasizes just-in-time delivery from nearby suppliers. Several different suppliers manufacture components such as seats, instrument panels, and rear axles *inside* the plant itself.

As Skoda CFO Volkhard Kohler explained in 1994, "We have to organize better than in the Western world and use supplier integration. Wages will increase, so we have to find other ways of being cost-effective. Supplier integration is part of the new thinking and what we do here can be a model for the West." Professor Daniel Jones of the Cardiff University Business School supports the effort. "It's physically integrated, but in terms of management and performance each runs his own show. It makes a lot of sense because you have the direct integration of people making the parts and the people putting them in the car," he said in an interview.

During the communist era the citizens of East Germany had a "choice" of basically one car: the notoriously low-quality Trabant. After unification, VW built a $1.9 billion factory that employed 6,500 workers and produced a quarter of a million Golf and Polo models each year. The investment was justified in part by forecasts that East Germans would buy 750,000 cars each year; VW aimed to capture a third of the market, equal to its share in West Germany.

At VW's General Pachecho plant in Buenos Aires, VW subcontracts various aspects of production to a dozen outside companies. VW workers build a few crucial parts such as the chassis and power train; suppliers are responsible for various other tasks such as assembling instrument panels.

Maryann Kellar, author of a book about VW, calls the Czech and Argentine experiment "something that has been talked about for years as the next great productivity and cost enhancement move by the industry." In 1996, Skoda rolled out the Octavia, the first new car developed by the Czech plant during the Volkswagen era and the first to use a VW chassis platform.

Sources: Stephen Power, "Aggressive Driver: Top Volkswagen Executive Tries U.S.-Style Turnaround Tactics," *The Wall Street Journal* (July 18, 2006), pp. A1, A11; Joseph B. White and Stephen Power, "VW Chief Confronts Corporate Culture," *The Wall Street Journal* (September 19, 2005), p. B2; James Mackintosh, "Volkswagen Misfires: The Carmaker Counts the Cost of Its High Spending and Its Faltering Search for Luxury," *Financial Times* (March 9, 2004), p. 9.

Exhibit 17-5: 2006 was a turbulent year for Bernd Pischetsrieder. After five years as the chief executive of Volkswagen, he lost a boardroom battle with Chairman Ferdinand Piech concerning the German automaker's ongoing efforts to cut costs and remain competitive in the face of increased competition from Asian nameplates. At the beginning of 2007, another Volkswagen executive resigned. Wolfgang Bernhard, chairman of the Volkswagen brand group, had initiated a series of cost-cutting measures; both Germany's powerful labor unions and Chairman Piech were opposed to some of his actions.
Source: Marcus Brandt/Getty Images, Inc. AFP.

ETHICS, CORPORATE SOCIAL RESPONSIBILITY, AND SOCIAL RESPONSIVENESS IN THE GLOBALIZATION ERA

Today's chief executive must be a proactive steward of the reputation of the company he or she is leading. This entails, in part, understanding and responding to the concerns and interests of a variety of stakeholders. A **stakeholder** is any group or individual that is affected by, or takes an interest in, the policies and practices adopted by an organization (see Exhibit 17-6).[35] Top management, employees, customers, persons or institutions that own the company's stock, and suppliers constitute a company's *primary stakeholders*. *Secondary stakeholders* include the

Exhibit 17-6: U2 singer Bono and Bobby Shriver are co-founders of Product (RED)™, a partnership with global companies to raise money to fight disease in Africa. Apple, American Express, Emporio Armani, Converse, Dell, Gap, Hallmark, and Starbucks all offer (RED)-themed merchandise and services to their customers. The partners donate a percentage of the profits to the Global Fund to Fight AIDS, Tuberculosis, and Malaria.

To launch its (RED) line, Gap's ad campaign used celebrities and one-word headlines consisting of verbs that end in "-red." One ad featured the word "INSPI(RED)" superimposed over a photo of director Steven Spielberg wearing a Product (RED) leather jacket.
Source: Tony Cenicolo/*The New York Times*/Redux Pictures.

---

[35]The English term "stakeholder" is sometimes hard to convey in different languages, especially in developing countries. See Neil King Jr. and Jason Dean, "Untranslatable Word in U.S. Aide's Speech Leaves Beijing Baffled," *The Wall Street Journal* (December 7, 2005), pp. A1, A8.

media, the general business community, local community groups, and **nongovernmental organizations (NGOs)**. The latter focus on human rights, political justice, and environmental issues; examples include Global Exchange, Greenpeace, Oxfam, and others. **Stakeholder analysis** is the process of formulating a "win-win" outcome for all stakeholders.[36]

The leaders of global companies must practice **corporate social responsibility (CSR)**, which can be defined as a company's obligation to pursue goals and policies that are in society's best interests. Organizations can demonstrate their commitment to CSR in a variety of ways including cause-marketing efforts or a commitment to sustainability. In some companies, such policies play an important internal role with primary stakeholders, especially employees drawn from the ranks of Generation Y. As Kevin Havelock, president of Unilever U.S., noted recently,

> We are seeing, particularly with the new generation of young business people and young marketers, that they are only attracted to companies that fit with their own value set. And the value set of the new generation is one that says this company must take a positive and global view on the global environment. . . . The ethical positions we take on brands like Dove, the positions we take on not using [fashion] models of size zero across any of our brands, the positions we take in terms of adding back to communities . . . these all underpin an attractive proposition for marketers."[37]

Similarly, Starbucks founder and CEO Howard Schultz's enlightened human resources policies have played a key part in the company's success. Partners, as the company's employees are known, who work 20 hours or more per week are offered health benefits; partners can also take advantage of an employee stock option plan known as Bean Stock. As noted on the company's Web site:

> Consumers are demanding more than "'product" from their favorite brands. Employees are choosing to work for companies with strong values. Shareholders are more inclined to invest in businesses with outstanding corporate reputations. Quite simply, being socially responsible is not only the right thing to do; it can distinguish a company from its industry peers.

As noted in Chapter 1, one of the forces restraining the growth of global business and global marketing is resistance to globalization. In a wired world, a company's reputation can quickly be tarnished if activists target its policies and practices. The antiglobalization movement constitutes an important secondary stakeholder for global companies; the movement takes a variety of forms and finds expression in various ways. In developed countries, the movement's concerns and agenda include cultural imperialism (e.g., the French backlash against McDonald's), the loss of jobs due to offshoring and outsourcing (e.g., the furniture industry in the United States), and a distrust of global institutions (e.g., anti-WTO protesters in Hong Kong). In developing countries, globalization's opponents accuse companies of undermining local cultures, placing intellectual property rights ahead of human rights, promoting unhealthy diets and unsafe food technologies, and pursuing unsustainable consumption.[38] Environmental degradation and labor exploitation are also key issues (see Exhibit 17-7).

In a socially responsible firm, employees conduct business in an ethical manner. In other words, they are guided by moral principles that enable them to distinguish between right and wrong. At many companies, a formal statement or **code of ethics** summarizes core ideologies, corporate values, and expectations. GE, Boeing, and United Technologies Corp. are some of the American companies offering training programs that specifically address ethics issues. For many years, Jack Welch, the legendary former CEO of GE, challenged his employees to take an informal "mirror test." The challenge: "Can you look in the mirror every day and feel proud of what you're doing?"[39] Today, GE uses more formal approaches to ethics and compliance; it has

[36]Archie B. Carroll and Ann K. Buchholtz, *Business and Society: Ethics and Stakeholder Management,* 5th ed. (Cincinnati: South-Western, 2003).

[37]Jack Neff, "Unilever, P&G War Over Which Is Most Ethical," *Advertising Age* (March 3, 2008), p. 67.

[38]Terrence H. Witkowski, "Antiglobal Challenges to Marketing in Developing Countries: Exploring the Ideological Divide," *Journal of Public Policy and Marketing* 24, no. 1 (Spring 2005), pp. 7–23.

[39]Stratford Sherman and Noel Tichy, *Control Your Destiny or Someone Else Will* (New York: HarperBusiness, 2001), Chapter 9, "The Mirror Test."

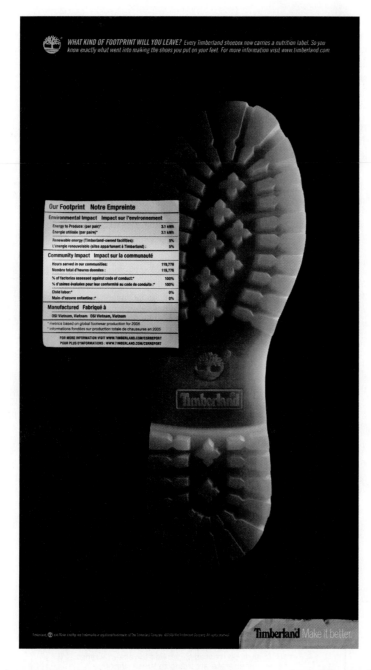

Exhibit 17-7: The Timberland Company, based in Stratham, New Hampshire, is best known for its popular hiking boots and work boots. Timberland is a truly global brand; each year, the company sells outdoor gear, accessories, and apparel (2008 revenue was 1.4 billion) through a network of 200 franchised and company-owned stores as well as department and sporting goods stores.

However, the company stands for more than just rugged authenticity; Timberland is a mission-centered company as well. CEO Jeff Swartz, the grandson of Timberland's founder, is deeply concerned with social justice issues. In 2006, Timberland unveiled a "nutritional label" on its footwear boxes as a means of communicating its CSR commitment to consumers. The label (in both English and French) addresses issues of interest to many con- sumers, including "Percent of factories assessed against Code of Conduct—100%" and "Child labor—0%."
Source: Used with permission of Timberland.

produced training videos, instituted an online training program, and provides employees with a guide to ethical conduct titled *Spirit and Letter* (see Table 17-4). At Johnson & Johnson, the ethics statement is known as "Our Credo"; first introduced in 1945, the credo has been translated into dozens of languages for J&J employees around the world (see Exhibit 17-8 and Appendix).

For the global company with operations in multiple markets, the issue of corporate social responsibility becomes complicated. When the chief executive of a global firm in a developed country or government policymakers attempt to act in "society's best interests," the question arises: Which society? That of the home-country market? Other developed countries? Developing countries? For example, in the late 1990s, in an effort to address the issue of child labor, the U.S. government threatened trade sanctions against the garment industry in Bangladesh. After thousands of child workers lost their jobs, their plight worsened. Whose inter- ests were served by this turn of events? In addition, as noted in Chapter 1, companies that do business around the globe may be in different stages of evolution. Thus, a multinational firm may

"Perhaps we have the opportunity to be a different type of global company, a global brand that can build a different model, a company that is a global business, that makes a profit, but at the same time demonstrates a social conscience and gives back to the local market."[40]
Howard Schultz, CEO, Starbucks

---

[40]John Murray Brown and Jenny Wiggins, "Coffee Empire Expands Reach by Pressing Its Luck in Ireland," *Financial Times* (December 15, 2005), p. 21.

TABLE 17-4 Ethics Questions from GE

Q: A new customer wants to place a big order with GE, provided the equipment can be shipped to them overnight. That doesn't give us enough time for the terrorist watchlist screening required of GE customers. Can I ship the equipment and check the watchlists tomorrow?

A: No, don't ship the equipment until the screening is done. GE cannot agree to do business with a customer until the required watchlist screening has been completed.

Q: An overseas customer has been invited to travel to our training facility at GE's expense. The customer wants to add a weekend side trip to Universal Studios. Can we fund the whole trip?

A: It depends on many factors including whether the customer is a government official, local law, the customer's policies, and your business's guidelines. Consult with GE general counsel and your manager.

Source: Kathryn Kranhold, "U.S. Firms Raise Ethics Focus," *The Wall Street Journal* (November 28, 2005), p. B4.

Exhibit 17-8: As management guru Jim Collins notes in his book *Built to Last*, Johnson & Johnson's credo is a "codified ideology" that guides managerial action. J&J operationalizes the credo in various ways, including its organizational structure and its planning and decision processes. The credo also serves as a crisis management guide. For example, during the Tylenol crisis of the early 1980s, J&J's adherence to the credo enabled the company to mount a swift, decisive, and transparent response.

Our Credo

We believe our first responsibility is to the doctors, nurses and patients, to mothers and fathers and all others who use our products and services. In meeting their needs everything we do must be of high quality. We must constantly strive to reduce our costs in order to maintain reasonable prices. Customers' orders must be serviced promptly and accurately. Our suppliers and distributors must have an opportunity to make a fair profit.

We are responsible to our employees, the men and women who work with us throughout the world. Everyone must be considered as an individual. We must respect their dignity and recognize their merit. They must have a sense of security in their jobs. Compensation must be fair and adequate, and working conditions clean, orderly and safe. We must be mindful of ways to help our employees fulfill their family responsibilities. Employees must feel free to make suggestions and complaints. There must be equal opportunity for employment, development and advancement for those qualified. We must provide competent management, and their actions must be just and ethical.

We are responsible to the communities in which we live and work and to the world community as well. We must be good citizens – support good works and charities and bear our fair share of taxes. We must encourage civic improvements and better health and education. We must maintain in good order the property we are privileged to use, protecting the environment and natural resources.

Our final responsibility is to our stockholders. Business must make a sound profit. We must experiment with new ideas. Research must be carried on, innovative programs developed and mistakes paid for. New equipment must be purchased, new facilities provided and new products launched. Reserves must be created to provide for adverse times. When we operate according to these principles, the stockholders should realize a fair return.

Johnson & Johnson

"Mr. Schultz recognized ahead of most executives that customers today vote with their dollars and will spend more money at companies with values they admire."[41]

Professor Nancy Koehn, Harvard Business School

rely on individual country managers to address CSR issues on an ad hoc basis, while a global or transnational may create a policy at headquarters.

Consider the following:

- Nike came under fire from critics who alleged poor working conditions in the factories that make the company's athletic shoes.
- In 2005, Walmart became the target of criticism for a variety of reasons. Well-publicized lawsuits put the company's compensation policies in the public spotlight. A documentary

---

[41]Carol Hymowitz, "Big Companies Become Big Targets Unless They Guard Images Carefully," *The Wall Street Journal* (December 12, 2005), p. B1.

film titled *The High Cost of Low Prices* examined the social repercussions of the retailer's presence in American communities. Two separate Web sites—WakeUp WalMart.com and WalMartWatch.com—were established by organizations representing U.S. labor unions.

- As retail gasoline prices soared in the United States following the devastation of Hurricane Katrina, BP, Royal Dutch Shell, and other companies were accused of gouging. The American Petroleum Institute, the industry's trade group, launched a national TV advertising campaign aimed at explaining its business and urging conservation.[42]
- CEO pay in the United States is rising faster than average salaries and much faster than inflation. One study found that in 2004, CEOs were paid 431 times more than the average worker.

What is the best way for a global firm to respond to such issues? Using Starbucks as a case study, Paul A. Argenti explains how global companies can work collaboratively with NGOs to arrive at a "win-win" outcome. As previously noted, with no external prompting, Starbucks CEO Howard Schultz used enlightened compensation and benefit packages to attract and retain employees. Despite the fact that Starbucks is widely admired for such forward-thinking management policies, Global Exchange pressed the company to further demonstrate its commitment to social responsibility by selling Fair Trade coffee. Schultz was faced with three options: Ignore Global Exchange's demands, fight back, or capitulate. In the end, Schultz pursued a middle ground: He agreed to offer Fair Trade coffee in Starbucks' company-owned U.S. stores. He also launched several other initiatives, including establishing long-term direct relationships with suppliers. Argenti offers seven lessons from the Starbucks case study:[43]

- Realize that socially responsible companies are likely targets but also attractive candidates for collaboration.
- Don't wait for a crisis to collaborate.
- Think strategically about relationships with NGOs.
- Recognize that collaboration involves some compromise.
- Appreciate the value of the NGOs' independence.
- Understand that building relationships with NGOs takes time and effort.
- Think more like an NGO by using communication strategically.

In a recent article in *Business Ethics Quarterly*, Arthaud-Day proposed a three-dimensional framework for analyzing the social behavior of international, multinational, global, and transnational

> "Companies should be addressing some of the problems facing the world, not in a philanthropic way but in a core, strategic way. But we seem to be among the least-trusted institutions, so there's a dilemma."[44]
> John Manzoni, head of refining and marketing, BP

> "Coke has become a whipping boy for globalization, just as Nike and McDonald's have been for years."[45]
> Tom Pirko, President, BevMark

TABLE 17-5 Global Marketing and Corporate Social Responsibility

Company/Headquarters Country	Nature of CSR Initiative
IKEA/Sweden	IKEA's primary carpet supplier in India monitors subcontractors to ensure they do not employ children (see Exhibit 17-9). IKEA also helps lower-caste Indian women reduce their indebtedness to money-lenders. In an effort to create a more child-friendly environment in Indian villages, IKEA sponsors "bridge schools" to increase literacy so young people—including girls and untouchables—can enroll in regular schools.*
Avon/USA	The company's Breast Cancer Awareness Crusade has raised hundreds of millions of dollars for cancer research. The money funds research in 50 countries.

*Edward Luce, "Ikea's Grown-Up Plan to Tackle Child Labor," *Financial Times* (September 15, 2004), p. 7.

---

[42]Jean Halliday, "Slick: Big Oil Tries Image Makeover," *Advertising Age* (November 7, 2005), pp. 1, 56.
[43]Paul A. Argenti, "Collaborating with Activists: How Starbucks Works with NGOs," *California Management Review* 47, no. 1 (Summer 2004), pp. 91–116.
[44]Alison Maitland, "Four Questions for Tomorrow's Leviathans," *Financial Times* (July 25, 2006), p. 7.
[45]Andrew Ward, "Coke Struggles to Defend Positive Reputation," *Financial Times* (January 6, 2006), p. 15.

Exhibit 17-9: In India's carpet belt, IKEA operationalizes the concept of corporate global responsibility by sponsoring bridge schools. The school programs are intended to reduce child labor in India's carpet industry by preparing village children to enroll in mainstream schools. To date, the bridge school program has helped an estimated 21,000 children learn to read and write.
Source: © Pallava Bagla/Corbis.

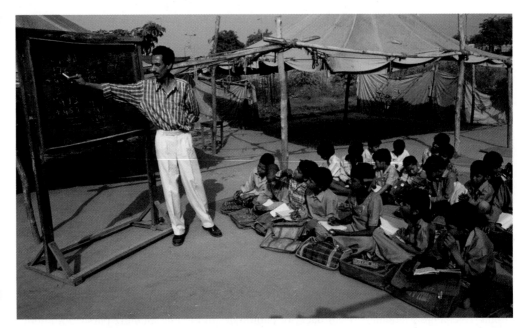

"There are tensions in a multinational company between what I call the financial fundamentalists, who just want to stress short-term profits, and the ethical fundamentalists, who don't think we should make profits at all. . . . As stewards of large amounts of capital, both monetary and human, the unique role of business—and what no other institution can duplicate— is to create social, economic and environmental value for the countries where we operate. But this most challenging goal—of creating value for society—can only be successful in the long run if it has a relationship to creating shareholder value."[47]
Peter Brabeck, Chairman and CEO, Nestlé

FIGURE 17-5

Source of Conflict in Global CSR

Source: Business Ethics Quarterly 15, no. 1 (2005). Used with permission of *Business Ethics Quarterly.*

firms.[46] The second dimension of the model includes CSR's three "content domains": human rights, labor, and the environment. These are the universal concerns for global companies established by the United Nations Global Compact. The third dimension in Arthaud-Day's framework consists of three perspectives. The *ideological dimension* of CSR pertains to the things a firm's management believes it should be doing. The *societal dimension* consists of the expectations held by the firm's external stakeholders. The *operational dimension* includes the actions and activities actually taken by the firm. As illustrated in Figure 17-5, the interaction between the dimensions can result in several

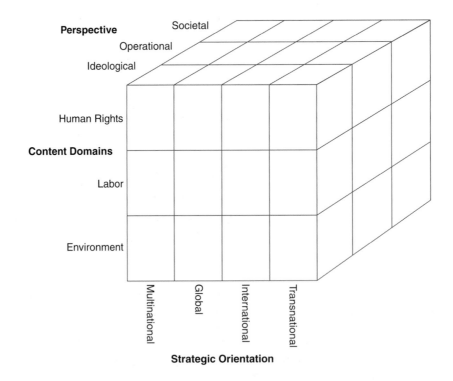

---

[46]Marne Arthaud-Day, "Transnational Corporate Social Responsibility: A Tri-Dimensional Approach to International CSR Research," *Business Ethics Quarterly* 15, no. 1 (January 2005), pp. 1–22.
[47]Haig Simonian, "Nestle Charts Low-Income Territory," *Financial Times* (July 14, 2006), p. 15.

conflict scenarios. Conflict may arise if there is an incongruity between those things a company's leadership believes it should be doing and the expectations of stakeholders. Conflict can also arise when there is an incongruity between those things a company's leadership believes it should be doing and the things it actually is doing. A third scenario is conflict that arises from an incongruity between society's expectations and actual corporate practices and activities.

Summary

To respond to the opportunities and threats in the global marketing environment, organizational leaders must develop a global vision and strategy. Leaders must also be able to communicate that vision throughout the organization and build **core competencies** on a worldwide basis. Global companies are increasingly realizing that the "right" person for top jobs is not necessarily a home-country national.

In **organizing** for the global marketing effort, the goal is to create a structure that enables the company to respond to significant differences in international market environments and to extend valuable corporate knowledge. Alternatives include an international division structure, regional management centers, geographical structure, regional or worldwide product division structure, and the **matrix organization**. Whichever form of organization is chosen, balance between autonomy and integration must be established. Many companies are adopting the organizational principle of **lean production** that was pioneered by Japanese automakers.

Many global companies are paying attention to the issue of **corporate social responsibility (CSR)**. A company's **stakeholders** may include **nongovernmental organizations**; **stakeholder analysis** can help identify others. Consumers throughout the world expect that the brands and products they buy and use are marketed by companies that conduct business in an ethical, socially responsible way. Socially conscious companies should include human rights, labor, and environmental issues in their agendas. These values may be spelled out in a **code of ethics**. Ideological, societal, and organizational perspectives can all be brought to bear on CSR.

Discussion Questions

1. Are top executives of global companies likely to be home-country nationals?
2. In a company involved in global marketing, which activities should be centralized at headquarters and which should be delegated to national or regional subsidiaries?
3. Identify some of the factors that lead to the establishment of an international division as an organization increases its global business activities.
4. "A matrix structure integrates four competencies on a worldwide scale." Explain.
5. In the automobile industry, how does "lean production" differ from the traditional assembly line approach?
6. Identify some of the ways the global companies discussed in this text demonstrate their commitment to CSR.
7. Identify and explain the three dimensions that provide different perspectives on CSR.

After Cescau was elevated to the top job, Unilever's board streamlined the company's management structure. Now there is a single chief executive; previously, there had been two. In a recent interview, Cescau said, "I enjoy being the only chief executive. It does really simplify things in terms of decisions." As noted, many of those decisions concern "doing good." However, some observers were skeptical of Cescau's determination to operationalize a responsible business philosophy. Cescau recalled, "The company was not doing well. There was an article saying that I was draping myself in a flag of corporate social responsibility to excuse poor performance. I was so angry with that."

Cescau's commitment was put to the test in 2008. Greenpeace launched an advertising campaign alleging that Unilever's purchases of Indonesian palm oil were contributing to rainforest destruction. Palm oil, a key ingredient in Dove's beauty bar, comes from oil palm trees that grow in Indonesia and Malaysia. Rising world prices for the commodity prompted Indonesian farmers to cut down large swaths of old-growth rain forest and plant fast-growing oil palms. The Greenpeace campaign included newspaper ads in London and a video on YouTube. Fliers parodied Unilever's Campaign for Real Beauty; for example, they showed pictures of orangutans juxtaposed with the headline "Gorgeous or gone?" (see Exhibit 17-10). John Sauven, executive director of Greenpeace, explained why his organization had targeted Unilever. "Everyone has heard of those brands. They are the public face of the company."

Cescau responded to the protest by calling for a moratorium on rain forest destruction by Indonesian oil producers. The Unilever chief also pledged that the company would only buy palm oil from producers who could prove that the rain forest had not been sacrificed to produce the oil. A spokesperson also indicated that, although the company was aware of the protests, the proposed change in its palm-oil sourcing strategy had been in the works for months. Nevertheless, Greenpeace and other nongovernmental organizations claimed victory.

As Cescau's remark makes clear, "doing well" is also part of the leadership equation. Cescau understood the importance of improving Unilever's profitability. To this end, he continued a restructuring drive that was initiated by his predecessor, co-chairman Niall FitzGerald. Specific actions include reducing Unilever's bureaucracy by removing several management layers. Cescau has also reduced the top management head count from 25 people to 7, and narrowed the vertical distance between management and marketing. The company has also shed hundreds of brands and closed dozens of factories in France, Germany, and elsewhere. In Cescau's view, the new, leaner structure will translate into more rapid response to changing market trends and consumer preferences and ensure quicker rollouts of new products.

Cescau also bet heavily on emerging markets to jump-start sales growth. According to company forecasts, by 2010, one-sixth of the world's population—some 1.2 billion people—will buy packaged goods for the first time. According to this scenario, as increasing numbers of people in developing countries buy their first washing machines, they will upgrade to detergent. Cescau shifted budgetary resources out of mature markets such as Europe; those funds are now being used to support research in India and

Exhibit 17-10

Source: Courtesy of Greenpeace.

other emerging markets. Brands managers have been instructed to innovate by taking a "clean slate" approach to developing new products for emerging markets. As Steph Carter, packaging director for deodorant brands, said recently, "Traditionally, we would have taken existing products and then tried to fathom how to adapt them for the developing world. Our thinking has changed."

Case 17-1 Discussion Questions

1. If a company such as Unilever has to make trade-offs between being a good corporate citizen and making a profit, which should have the highest priority?
2. Assess Cescau's response to the Greenpeace palm-oil protest. Was it appropriate? What type of relationships should Unilever cultivate with Greenpeace and other NGOs in the future?
3. Do you think that a streamlined management structure and emphasis on emerging markets will enable new CEO Paul Polman to lead Unilever to improved performance?

Sources: Michael Skapinker, "Taking a Hard Line on Soft Soap," *Financial Times* (July 7, 2008), p. 12; Aaron O. Patrick, "After Protests, Unilever Does an About-Face on Palm Oil," *The Wall Street Journal* (May 2, 2008), p. B1; Jenny Wiggins, "Unilever to Go Under 'The Knife,'" *Financial Times* (May 16, 2007), p. 19; Deborah Ball, "As Its Brands Lag at Home, Unilever Makes a Risky Bet," *The Wall Street Journal* (March 27, 2007), pp. A1, A12; Deborah Ball, "Too Many Cooks: Despite Revamp, Unwieldy Unilever Falls Behind Rivals," *The Wall Street Journal* (January 3, 2005), pp. A1, A5; Adam Jones, "No Nimble Giant: The Stumbling Blocks Unilever Faces on Its Path to Growth," *Financial Times* (August 23, 2004), p. 11.

What a difference a year makes! At the end of 2005, Airbus, the European aircraft manufacturer, reported that it had booked 1,055 orders for new airplanes in the preceding 12 months. By contrast, archrival Boeing Company had recorded only 1,002 orders. Moreover, for the third year in a row, Airbus delivered more airplanes to customers than Boeing. Airbus had also stolen a step in the PR arena in April with the maiden flight of its new double-decker super-jumbo jet, the 555-passenger A-380. The new jet, which was scheduled to go into service in 2006, had taken 10 years to develop at a cost of $12 billion.

The strategic decision to develop the A-380 was based on projections of large increases in air passenger traffic but a limited amount of new airport construction. The conclusion: Airlines—the industry's main customers—would need a new super jumbo to carry more passengers while reducing the number of flights between key city hubs. Airbus executives believed the A-380 would revolutionize air travel in the twenty-first century.

By mid-2006, however, production of the A-380 was running six months behind schedule and $2.5 billion over budget. Then came an announcement of an additional six months' delay due to unanticipated difficulties in wiring the giant airliner. Airbus was facing trouble on another front as well: A second new plane in the design phase, the A-350, was being criticized by Singapore Airlines and other potential customers for offering less comfort, less speed, and less operating efficiency than a rival Boeing plane, the 787 Dreamliner. As originally designed, the A-350 was essentially an upgrade of an existing model, the A-330, outfitted with new engines.

Boeing: A History of Innovation

Executives at Boeing, the world's largest manufacturer of commercial aircraft, might have been forgiven if they took time to savor the reversal of fortune at Airbus. However, they were busy booking orders for the new Dreamliner. Boeing has a stellar track record with "bet the company"–type product decisions. In the 1950s, when the company was best known for military aircraft such as the B-52 bomber, Boeing single-handedly created the commercial market for jet aircraft with the introduction of the 707. In the mid-1960s, Boeing gambled that the world's airlines would be enthusiastic about a new wide-body aircraft. The gamble paid off handsomely: Since its first passenger flight in 1970, the Boeing 747 jumbo jet has generated more than $130 billion in sales. In 2001, Boeing made headlines again when it announced plans for a revolutionary new delta-wing aircraft called the Sonic Cruiser. The new jet would carry between 100 and 300 passengers and fly just below the speed of sound (Mach 1) with a range of up to 10,000 miles.

> *"We spent a great deal of time on product strategy and trying to come up with airplanes that were pleasant for customers and profitable for the airlines."*
>
> Larry Dickenson, Senior Vice President, Boeing

Strategic Decision Making and the 7E7/787

By 2002, Boeing was backpedaling on the Sonic Cruiser plan. The airline industry was retrenching in the wake of the 9/11 terror attacks; United Airlines, a key Boeing customer, was in bankruptcy. Moreover, airline passengers appeared to be more concerned with ticket prices than with travel time. Accordingly, Boeing began assessing customer reaction to an alternative design for a more conventional aircraft. As one airline executive said in mid-2002, "The folks over at Boeing are sort of pulling their hair out right now trying to figure out which is the right avenue to take." In the past, Boeing had canceled new-product development programs such as a proposed fuel-efficient model 7J7. Alan Mulally, Boeing's top executive at its commercial airplane division, defended that record, saying that Boeing is a nimble, customer-driven company. "What a neat thing it is to look at your customers and the market and make your investments accordingly. The fact that Boeing is listening and flexible is a great thing," he said.

By the fall of 2003, the suspense was over: As some industry observers had predicted, Boeing announced it was scrapping plans for the Sonic Cruiser. Instead the company would develop a new 200-seat model, the 7E7 Dreamliner, that would offer passengers improved comfort in the air. The new aircraft features arched ceilings and "mood-enhancing lighting"; larger windows than those on the 777; and seats in economy class will be arranged 3-2-3 across rather than 2-4-2. This configuration will make it less likely that passengers will be stuck in a "bad" seat. Boeing's new baby would also represent a powerful value proposition for the airlines: The "E" stands for "efficiency." With new engines and a body comprised of carbon-enhanced plastic, the new aircraft would cost airlines 20 percent less to operate than existing aircraft.

In mid-2004, All Nippon Airlines ordered 50 7E7s valued at $6 billion; the order represented the largest product launch in

Source: Francois Mori/AP Wide World Photos.

Boeing's history. In January 2005, with the announcement that China had placed an order for 60 planes, Boeing officials gave the new plane the official model designation 787. The designation brought the new plane into line with Boeing's tradition of using a succession of 7-7 numberings such as 747, 767, and 777. Moreover, as Mulally noted in a press release, "Incorporating the '8' at the time of the China order is also significant because in many Asian cultures the number 8 represents good luck and prosperity." In April, Air Canada announced it would replace its entire fleet of Airbus models with the Dreamliner; in the following months, more orders poured in.

The 787: Cost Savings and Global Sourcing

The first 787s were scheduled to go into service in 2008. Boeing's production strategy for the 787 included dispersing design work to Russia, China, and Japan. Thanks to the Internet, engineers in these nations can collaborate in real time. Moreover, by tapping talent resources in key countries, Boeing hoped to increase the likelihood of booking orders from airlines and governments in those nations. Composite materials would not only lower the 787's operating costs, but would also enable Boeing to reconfigure its supply chain. For example, the wings and most of the fuselage would be manufactured in Japan and transported to Seattle in specially modified 747-400 freightliners. Previously, parts from Japan had been transported by water, rail, and, finally, truck, a journey that could take one month. Boeing expected that, by cutting transport time to one day, it could save 40 percent in shipping and inventory expenses. Companies that wish to bid on parts of the 787 would not communicate directly with Boeing headquarters. Instead, they would deal with Boeing's new 787 Council, a group made up of top executives from several outside suppliers.

Boeing's strategy for the 787 created some controversy. In the two years leading up to the 787 announcement, Boeing had cut 35,000 jobs in the United States. The company had previously outsourced some aircraft production to other countries; for example, Japanese companies supply about one-fifth of the 777. One

reason for outsourcing was that airlines would be more likely to buy aircraft that had some local content. However, that strategy had not always paid off. For example, Boeing has a design center in Russia that employs more than 700 engineers. In 2002, however, Russia's largest airline, AeroFlot, ordered twice as many aircraft from Airbus than it did from Boeing. Similarly, Boeing helped establish a small plant in South Africa to perform work that had previously been done in Seattle. In 2002, South African Airways ordered 41 jets from Airbus.

In the eyes of some critics, there is more at stake than just orders for new airplanes: The 787 project marks the first time that Boeing is sharing its proprietary technology for wing design and manufacture. Jennifer MacKay is president of the Society of Professional Engineering Employees in Aerospace, a union that represents Boeing engineers and other technical workers. She is deeply concerned about the long-term consequences of sharing technology with other countries. "In the end, if we teach everybody how to make the major parts, why is Boeing even needed?" she asks. Mike Blair, senior vice president of the 787, has an answer. "Figuring out what the wings look like, figuring out how to put them on the airplane, understanding whether that's something our customers will buy, understanding how to integrate that stuff, that's the magic Boeing brings to this process," he said.

TABLE 1 787 Suppliers

Supplier	Percent of Project
Boeing	35%
Mitsubishi Heavy Industries/Fuji Heavy Industries/Kawasaki Heavy Industries	35%
Vought Aircraft Industries (Dallas, Texas)/ Alenia Aeronautica (Rome)	26%
Others	4%

Source: Lord Saatchi, "Battle for Survival Favours the Simplest," *Financial Times* (January 5, 1998).

Production Delays and Management Restructuring at Airbus

Meanwhile, at Airbus, the management team that had previously dismissed Boeing's claims about the 787's efficiency and downplayed customer concerns was in turmoil. In part, the problems could be traced to the complicated corporate structure of European Aeronautic Defence and Space Company (EADS), the corporate parent of Airbus. Germany's DaimlerChrysler owns 22.5 percent, Sogeade (a corporate entity owned by the French government and the Lagardère Group), holds a 30 percent stake, and Spain owns 5.4 percent through a holding company known as Sepi. (The remaining shares are listed on major European stock exchanges.) EADS, in turn, owns an 80 percent share in Airbus; BAE Systems, a British company, controls the remaining 20 percent.

Tensions were growing because of attempts by DaimlerChrysler to maintain control over the chief executive of Airbus, Noël Forgeard, who happened to be French. Observers also noted that the crisis stemmed partly from political infighting and power struggles between the French executives at EADS and their compatriots at the Airbus unit. The interpersonal dynamics had been stabilized by Jean-Luc Lagardère, the chief executive of the French company that was a key shareholder in EADS. After Lagardère died suddenly in 2003, however, the rivalries got out of hand.

The crisis was also rooted in the autonomy granted to the manufacturing locations, particularly those in France and Germany; lack of integration between those locations resulted in delays. Moreover, in an attempt to raise his profile with the EADS board, Forgeard had driven his team to deliver on-time results in the face of tight development windows. Unfortunately, this resulted in a "green-light" corporate culture that downplayed potential problems or delays. For example, the German team in Hamburg was using different computer design software than the French team in Toulouse; this led to delays in installing the complex cable system in the cabin of the A-380. In the opinion of some observers, the lack of investment in new software was the result of top management's desire to boost profits. In interviews, Forgeard asserted that he had not been alerted to the seriousness of the mounting problems. Meanwhile, Forgeard used his political connections to win a promotion to the position of co-chief executive of EADS. In June 2005, Gustav Humbert was named to replace Forgeard as Airbus CEO.

In addition to headaches with the A380 program, the Airbus management team was facing another issue: customer complaints about the new A-350. A crisis management team was assembled and given a mandate to redesign the A-350. The jet's top speed was increased slightly to .85 mach to match the 787, and the cabin was widened to allow seating nine passengers in each row instead of eight as originally planned. The redesign means that the new model will not be introduced until 2012.

In July 2006, after barely a year on the job, Humbert resigned as CEO of Airbus. Almost simultaneously, Noël Forgeard resigned as well. Christian Streiff, a Frenchman, was named as Humbert's replacement. One of Streiff's first acts was to fire Charles Champion, the head of the A380 program. He also launched a restructuring program dubbed Power8. However, Streiff himself resigned after only 100 days on the job. Louis Gallois was named chief executive of Airbus and co-CEO of EADS; a German, Thomas Enders, will share the top job at EADS.

As he settled into the job, Gallois faced a number of challenges and questions stemming from the crisis at Airbus. Would the French and German investors and management be able to set aside their differences? Should he close some of Airbus' 16 assembly plants—spread across the United Kingdom, Spain, France and Germany—and transfer production out of Europe? Would key customers such as Virgin Atlantic Airways cancel orders for the A380? Would the euro's strength relative to the dollar translate into a significant cost advantage for Boeing?

Discussion Questions

1. What key mistakes did Airbus make with its A-350 and A-380 product development programs?
2. What are some of the factors contributing to the success of Boeing's 787 Dreamliner?
3. Assess Boeing's plans to subcontract out significant portions of the Dreamliner's manufacture.
4. EADS is not the only global company to revamp its dual management structure. For example, until recently, Unilever had a tradition of two co-chairmen, one in Great Britain and one in the Netherlands. In 2005, Unilever named a single chief executive; the company still maintains separate headquarters in the two countries. Also in 2005, Royal Dutch/Shell Group abolished its dual management structure. Conduct some exploratory research to learn more about the management changes at Unilever and Shell. Should similar changes be made at EADS?

Sources: J. Lynn Lunsford and Daniel Michaels, "New Course: Under Pressure, Airbus Redesigns a Troubled Plane," *The Wall Street Journal* (July 14, 2006), pp. A1, A7; Lunsford and Michaels, "Rapid Descent: Bet on Huge Plane Trips Up Airbus," *The Wall Street Journal* (June 15, 2006), pp. A1, A11; Roger Yu, "Airbus Sneaks Past Boeing in 11th Hour," *USA Today* (January 18, 2006), p. 6B; J. Lynn Lunsford, "Boeing's New Baby," *The Wall Street Journal* (November 18, 2003), pp. B1, B8; Caroline Daniel, "Airbus Takes on Boeing with More than Banter," *Financial Times* (November 14, 2003), p. 23; Byron Acohido, "Boeing Rips a Page out of Airbus' Book," *USA Today* (October 22, 2003), p. 3B; J. Lynn Lunsford, "Boeing Explores Plan 'B'", *The Wall Street Journal* (June 11, 2002), p. D5; J. Lynn Lunsford, "Lean Times: With Airbus on Its Tail, Boeing Is Rethinking How It Builds Planes," *The Wall Street Journal* (September 5, 2001), pp. A1, A16; J. Lynn Lunsford, "Navigating Change: Boeing, Losing Ground to Airbus, Faces Key Choice," *The Wall Street Journal* (April 21, 2003), p. A1; Alan Levin, "Boeing's Sonic Cruiser: Gambling on Speed," *USA Today* (June 18, 2001), pp. 1A, 2A; Laurence Zuckerman, "Boeing Plays an Aerial Wild Card," *The New York Times* (June 17, 2001), Sec. 3, pp. 1, 11; Daniel Michaels, "New Approach: Airbus Revamp Brings Sense to Consortium, Fuels Boeing Rivalry," *The Wall Street Journal* (April 3, 2001), pp. A1, A8; Jeff Cole, "Wing Commander: At Boeing, an Old Hand Provides New Tricks in Battle with Airbus," *The Wall Street Journal* (January 10, 2001), pp. A1, A12.

Johnson & Johnson Credos: Brazil, Russia, India, and China

Nosso Credo

Cremos que nossa primeira responsabilidade é para com os médicos, enfermeiras e pacientes,
para com as mães, pais e todos os demais que usam nossos produtos e serviços.
Para atender suas necessidades, tudo o que fizermos deve ser de alta qualidade.
Devemos constantemente nos esforçar para reduzir nossos custos,
a fim de manter preços razoáveis.
Os pedidos de nossos clientes devem ser pronta e corretamente atendidos.
Nossos fornecedores e distribuidores devem ter a oportunidade
de auferir um lucro justo.

Somos responsáveis por nossos empregados,
homens e mulheres que conosco trabalham em todo o mundo.
Todos devem ser considerados em sua individualidade.
Devemos respeitar sua dignidade e reconhecer o seu mérito.
Eles devem se sentir seguros em seus empregos.
A remuneração pelo seu trabalho deve ser justa e adequada
e o ambiente de trabalho limpo, ordenado e seguro.
Devemos ter em mente maneiras de ajudar nossos empregados
a atender às suas responsabilidades familiares.
Os empregados devem se sentir livres para fazer sugestões e reclamações.
Deve haver igual oportunidade de emprego, desenvolvimento
e progresso para os qualificados.
Devemos ter uma administração competente,
e suas ações devem ser justas e éticas.

Somos responsáveis perante as comunidades nas quais vivemos e trabalhamos,
bem como perante a comunidade mundial.
Devemos ser bons cidadãos – apoiar boas obras sociais e de caridade
e pagar corretamente os tributos.
Devemos encorajar o desenvolvimento do civismo e a melhoria da saúde e da educação.
Devemos manter em boa ordem
as propriedades que temos o privilégio de usar,
protegendo o meio ambiente e os recursos naturais.

Nossa responsabilidade final é para com os acionistas.
Os negócios devem proporcionar lucros adequados.
Devemos experimentar novas idéias.
Pesquisas devem ser levadas avante. Programas inovadores desenvolvidos
e os erros corrigidos.
Novos equipamentos devem ser adquiridos, novas fábricas construídas
e novos produtos lançados.
Reservas devem ser criadas para enfrentar tempos adversos.
Ao operarmos de acordo com esses princípios,
nossos acionistas devem
receber justa recompensa.

Johnson & Johnson

Наше Кредо

Наша основная ответственность – перед врачами и медицинскими сестрами,
перед пациентами, перед отцами и матерями, перед всеми,
кто пользуется нашей продукцией и услугами. В соответствии с их
потребностями мы должны обеспечивать высокие стандарты качества во всем,
что мы делаем. Мы должны постоянно стремиться к снижению затрат,
чтобы поддерживать приемлемый уровень цен. Заказы клиентов должны
выполняться точно и в срок. Наши поставщики и дистрибьюторы
должны иметь возможность получать достойную прибыль.

Мы несем ответственность перед нашими сотрудниками,
мужчинами и женщинами, которые работают у нас по всему миру.
Мы должны ценить индивидуальность в каждом из них.
Мы должны уважать их достоинство и признавать их заслуги:
нам важно поддерживать в них чувство уверенности в завтрашнем дне.
Вознаграждение должно быть справедливым и соразмерным,
а условия труда обеспечивать чистоту, порядок и безопасность.
Нам важно, чтобы сотрудники имели возможность заботиться о семье.
Сотрудники должны чувствовать, что они могут свободно
выступать с предложениями и замечаниями.
У всех квалифицированных специалистов должны быть
равные возможности для получения работы, развития и продвижения.
Мы должны обеспечивать компетентное управление,
действия руководителей должны быть справедливыми и этичными.

Мы несем ответственность перед обществом,
в котором живем и работаем, а также перед мировым сообществом.
Мы должны выполнять свой гражданский долг:
поддерживать добрые начинания и благотворительные акции,
честно платить налоги. Мы должны содействовать улучшениям
в социальной сфере, здравоохранении и образовании.
Мы должны бережно относиться к вверенной нам собственности,
сохраняя природные ресурсы и защищая окружающую среду.

И, наконец, мы несем ответственность перед нашими акционерами.
Бизнес должен приносить существенную прибыль.
Мы должны экспериментировать с новыми идеями,
вести научно-исследовательскую работу,
внедрять инновации, учиться на своих ошибках.
Мы должны приобретать новое оборудование, обеспечивать современные
условия работы и выводить на рынок новую продукцию.
Мы должны быть готовы к сложным ситуациям и иметь резервы
для их решения. Придерживаясь этих принципов,
мы обеспечим нашим акционерам достойный доход.

हमारी नीति

हम यह मानते हैं कि हमारी पहली जिम्मेदारी डाक्टरों, नर्सों, रोगियों, माताओं, पिताओं तथा
उन सभी लोगों के प्रति है जो हमारे उत्पादनों और सेवाओं का उपयोग करते हैं।
उनकी आवश्यकताओं की पूर्ति के लिए जो कुछ भी हम करें, वह उत्तम दर्जे का हो।
हमें अपने उत्पादनों की कीमत घटाने की लगातार कोशिश करनी चाहिए
ताकि वे उचित कीमतों में उपलब्ध हों।
ग्राहकों की माँगी सही तौर पर तथा तत्परता से पूरी की जानी चाहिए।
हमारे विक्रेताओं और वितरकों को उचित लाभ मिलने का अवसर मिले।

हम अपने उन स्त्री और पुरुष कर्मचारियों के प्रति
जिम्मेदार हैं जो हमारे साथ संसार के हर देश में काम करते हैं।
हर व्यक्ति को व्यक्तिगत रूप से देखा जाय।
हमें उनकी प्रतिष्ठा और योग्यता का आदर करना चाहिए।
उन्हें अपनी नौकरी की सुरक्षा का विश्वास रहे।
उनका वेतन उचित और पर्याप्त हो।
काम करने का वातावरण स्वच्छ, सुव्यवस्थित और सुरक्षित हो।
पारिवारिक जिम्मेदारियाँ निभानेके लिए हमें अपने कर्मचारियोंको दक्षतापूर्वक मार्ग दिखाने चाहिए।
कर्मचारियों को उनके सुझाव और शिकायतें उचित ढंग से प्रस्तुत करने की स्वतंत्रता हो।
योग्य लोगों को सेवा, प्रगति और विकास का समान अवसर मिले।
हमारा व्यवस्थापन निपुण हो और प्रबंधकों की कृति उचित और न्यायपूर्ण हो।

हम जिस समाज में रहते और काम करते हैं और जिस विश्व समाज के हम भाग हैं
उस समाज के प्रति हमारी जिम्मेदारी है।
हमें अच्छा नागरिक होना चाहिए – दान, धर्म और दूसरे अच्छे कार्यों में
भाग लेना चाहिए तथा अपने हिस्से के कर बराबर देते रहना चाहिए।
हम नगर-सुधार, स्वास्थ्य और शिक्षा को प्रोत्साहित करें।
वातावरण और नैसर्गिक उपलब्धियों को सुरक्षित रखते हुए, जिस संपत्ति का उपयोग
करने का हमें सुअवसर मिला है इसे हम अच्छी तरह संभाल कर रखें।

हमारी आखरी जिम्मेदारी भागधारकों के प्रति है।
व्यापार में पर्याप्त लाभ होना चाहिए।
हमें नये-नये विचारों को अमल में लाना चाहिए।
अनुसंधान किए जाय, आन्वेषिक योजनाओं का विकास किया जाय और
भूलों से हुई हानि का मूल्य चुकाया जाय।
नये यंत्र खरीदे जाय, नई सुविधाएँ उपलब्ध हों और नये उत्पादनों का
निर्माण किया जाय ताकि बुरे दिनों के लिए प्रबंध हो।
यदि हम उन सिद्धांतों के अनुसार कार्य करते हैं तो
भागधारकों को पर्याप्त लाभ मिल सकता है।

जॉनसन ऑण्ड जॉनसन

我们的信条

我们相信我们首先要对医生、护士和病人，
对父母亲以及所有使用我们的产品和接受我们服务的人负责。
为了满足他们的需求，我们所做的一切都必须是高质量的。
我们必须不断地致力于降低成本，以保持合理的价格。
客户的订货必须迅速而准确地供应。
我们的供应商和经销商应该有机会获得合理的利润。

我们要对世界各地和我们一起共事的男女同仁负责。
每一位同仁都应视为独立的个体。
我们必须维护他们的尊严，赞赏他们的优点。
要使他们对其工作有一种安全感。
薪酬必须公平合理。
工作环境必须清洁、整齐和安全。
我们必须设法照顾好员工履行他们对家庭的责任。
必须让员工在提出建议和申诉时畅所欲言。
对于合格的人必须给予平等的雇用、发展和升迁的机会，
我们必须具备称职的管理人员，
他们的行为必须公正并符合道德。

我们要对我们所生活和工作的社会，对整个世界负责。
我们必须做好公民－支持对社会有益的活动和慈善事业，
缴纳我们应付的税款。
我们必须鼓励全民进步，促进健康和教育事业，
我们必须很好地维护我们所使用的财产，
保护环境和自然资源。

最后，我们要对全体股东负责。
企业经营必须获取可靠的利润。
我们必须尝试新的构想。
必须坚持研究工作，开发革新项目，
承担错误的代价并加以改正。
必须购置新设备，提供新设施，推出新产品。
必须设立储备金，以备不时之需。
如果我们依据这些原则进行经营，
股东们就会获得合理的回报。

Johnson & Johnson

Source: Courtesy of Johnson & Johnson.

Glossary

The chapter number follows the definition.

80/20 rule   In behavioral market segmentation, the rule of thumb that 20 percent of a company's products or customers account for 80 percent of revenues or profits. (7)

acquisition   A market entry strategy that entails investing in assets outside the home country. (12)

adaptation approach   Management's use of highly localized marketing programs in different country markets. (1)

adaptation strategy   A global market approach that involves changing elements of design, function, or packaging in response to needs or conditions in particular country markets. (10)

adopter categories   In the adoption process developed by Everett Rogers, a typology of buyers at different stages of the "adoption" or product life cycle. The categories are innovators, early adopters, early majority, late majority, and laggards. (4)

adoption process   A model developed by Everett Rogers that describes the "adoption" or purchase decision process. The stages consist of awareness, interest, evaluation, trial, and adoption. (4)

ad valorem duty   A duty that is expressed as a percentage of the value of goods. (8)

advertising   Any sponsored, paid message that is communicated through a nonpersonal channel. Advertising is one of the four variables in the promotion mix. (13)

advertising appeal   The communications approach that relates to the motives of the target audience. (13)

advertising organization   A corporation or holding company that includes one or more "core" advertising agencies, as well as units specializing in direct marketing, marketing services, public relations, or research. (13)

advocacy advertising   A form of corporate advertising in which a company presents its point of view on a particular issue. (13)

aesthetics   A shared sense within a culture of what is beautiful as opposed to ugly and what represents good taste as opposed to tastelessness. (4)

agent   An intermediary who negotiates transactions between two or more parties but does not take title to the goods being purchased or sold. (12)

Andean Community   A customs union comprised of Bolivia, Colombia, Ecuador, Peru, and Venezuela. (3)

antidumping duties   Duties imposed on products whose prices government officials deem too low. (8)

arbitration   A negotiation process between two or more parties to settle a dispute outside of the court system. (5)

art direction   The visual presentation of an advertisement. (13)

art director   An ad agency "creative" with general responsibility for the overall look of an advertisement. The art director chooses graphics, pictures, type styles, and other visual elements. (13)

Association of Southeast Asian Nations (ASEAN)   A trade bloc comprised of Brunei, Cambodia, Indonesia, Malaysia, Laos, Myanmar, the Philippines, Singapore, Thailand, and Vietnam. (3)

attitude   In culture, a learned tendency to respond in a consistent way to a given object or entity. (4)

balance of payments   The record of all economic transactions between the residents of a country and the rest of the world. (2)

barter   The least complex and oldest form of bilateral, nonmonetized countertrade consisting of a direct exchange of goods or services between two parties. (11)

behavior segmentation   The process of performing market segmentation utilizing user status, usage rate, or some other measure of product consumption. (7)

belief   In culture, an organized pattern or knowledge that an individual holds to be true about the world. (4)

benefit segmentation   The process of segmenting markets on the basis of the benefits sought by buyers. (7)

big idea   A concept that can serve as the basis for a memorable, effective advertising message. (13)

bill of exchange   A written order from one party directing a second party to pay to the order of a third party. (8)

Bluetooth   Technology that permits access to the Internet from a cell phone when the user is within the range of a hotspot. (15)

brand   A representation of a promise by a particular company about a particular product; a complex bundle of images and experiences in the customer's mind. (10)

brand equity   The reflection of the brand's value to a company as an intangible asset. (10)

brand extensions   A strategy that uses an established brand name as an umbrella when entering new businesses or developing new product lines that represent new categories to the company. (10)

brand image   A single, but often complex, mental image about both the physical product and the company that markets it. (10)

bribery   The corrupt business practice of demanding or offering some type of consideration—typically cash payment—when negotiating a cross-border deal. (5)

BRIC   Brazil, Russia, India, and China; the four fastest-growing markets that represent important opportunities. (2)

broadband   A digital communication system with sufficient capacity to carry multiple voice, data, or video channels simultaneously. (15)

business-to-business marketing   Marketing products and services to other companies and organizations. Contrasts with business-to-consumer (b-to-c or B2C) marketing. (12)

business-to-consumer marketing Marketing products and services to people for their own use. Contrasts with business-to-business (b-to-b or B2B) marketing. (12)

Byrd Amendment Law that calls for antidumping revenues to be paid to U.S. companies harmed by imported goods sold at below-market prices. (11)

call centers Sophisticated telephone operations that provide customer support and other services to in-bound callers from around the world. May also provide outsourcing services such as telemarketing. (8)

call option The right to buy a specified amount of foreign currency at a fixed price, up to the option's expiration date. (2)

capital account In a country's balance of payments, the record of all long-term direct investment, portfolio investment, and other short- and long-term capital flows. (2)

CARICOM (Caribbean Community and Common Market) Formed in 1973, a free trade area whose members include Antigua and Barbuda, Bahamas, Barbados, Belize, Dominica, Grenada, Guyana, Haiti, Jamaica, Montserrat, St. Kitts and Nevis, St. Lucia, St. Vincent and the Grenadines, and Trinidad and Tobago. (3)

cartel A group of separate companies or countries that collectively set prices, control output, or take other actions to maximize profits. (5)

catalog A magazine-style publication that features photographs, illustrations, and extensive information about a company's products. (14)

category killer A store that specializes in a particular product category and offers a vast selection at low prices. (12)

Central American Integration System A customs union comprised of El Salvador, Honduras, Guatemala, Nicaragua, Costa Rica, and Panama. (3)

centrally planned capitalism An economic system characterized by command resource allocation and private resource ownership. (2)

centrally planned socialism An economic system characterized by command resource allocation and state resource ownership. (2)

CFR (cost and freight) A contract in which the seller is not responsible for risk or loss at any point outside the factory. (11)

chaebol In South Korea, a type of corporate alliance group composed of dozens of companies and centered around a central bank or holding company and dominated by a founding family. (9)

changing rules of engagement A strategy for creating competitive advantage that involves breaking these rules and refusing to play by the rules set by industry leaders. (16)

channel of distribution An organized network of agencies and institutions that, in combination, perform all the activities required to link producers with users to accomplish the marketing task. (12)

cherry picking In distribution, a situation in which a channel intermediary such as a distributor accepts new lines only from manufacturers whose products and brands already enjoy strong demand. (12)

CIF (cost, insurance, freight) named port of destination The Incoterm for a contract requiring the seller to retain responsibility and liability for goods until they have physically passed over the rail of a ship. (11)

civil-law country A country in which the legal system reflects the structural concepts and principles of the Roman Empire in the sixth century. (5)

click-through rate The percentage of visitors to an Internet site who click on an advertisement link presented on the computer screen. (15)

cluster analysis In market research, a quantitative data analysis technique that groups variables into clusters that maximize within-group similarities and between-group differences. Can be used in psychographic segmentation. (6)

co-branding A variation of tiered branding in which two or more different company or product brands are featured prominently on product packaging or in advertising. (10)

code of ethics A formal statement that summarizes a company's core ideologies, corporate values, and expectations. (17)

collaborative agreements Linkages between companies from different countries for the purpose of pursuing common goals. (9)

collectivist culture In Hofstede's social values typology, a culture in which group cohesiveness and harmony are emphasized. A shared concern for the well-being of all members of society is also evident. (4)

combination branding A strategy in which a corporate name is combined with a product brand name; also called tiered or umbrella branding. (10)

Common Agricultural Policy (CAP) Legislation adopted by European countries after World War II to aid and protect the interests of farmers. (8)

common external tariff (CET) A tariff agreed upon by members of a preferential trading bloc. Implementation of a CET marks the transition from a free trade area to a customs union. (3)

common-law country A country in which the legal system relies on past judicial decisions (cases) to resolve disputes. (5)

common market A preferential trade agreement that builds on the foundation of economic integration provided by a free trade area and a customs union. (3)

Common Market of the South (Mercosur) A customs union comprised of Argentina, Brazil, Paraguay, Uruguay, and Venezuela. (3)

compensation trading (buyback) A countertrade deal typically involving the sale of plant equipment or technology licensing in which the seller or licensor agrees to take payment in the form of the products produced using the equipment or technology for a specified number of years. (11)

competitive advantage The result of a match between a firm's distinctive competencies and the factors critical for creating superior customer value in an industry. (1, 16)

concentrated global marketing The target market strategy that calls for creating a marketing mix to reach a niche segment of global consumers. (7)

confiscation Governmental seizure of a company's assets without compensation. (5)

conjoint analysis In market research, a quantitative data analysis technique that can be used to gain insights into the combination of product features that will be attractive to potential buyers. (6)

consumer panel Primary data collection using a sample of consumers or households whose behavior is tracked over time; frequently used for television audience measurement. (6)

consumer sales promotions Promotion designed to make consumers aware of a new product, to stimulate nonusers to sample an existing product, or to increase overall consumer demand. (14)

containerization In physical distribution, the practice of loading ocean-going freight into steel boxes measuring 20 feet, 40 feet, or longer. (12)

content site A Web site that provides news and entertainment and supports a company's PR efforts. (15)

continuous innovation A product that is "new and improved" but requires little R&D expenditure to develop, causes minimal disruption of existing consumption patterns, and requires the least amount of learning on the part of buyers. (10)

contract manufacturing A licensing arrangement in which a global company provides technical specifications to a subcontractor or local manufacturer. (9)

convenience stores A form of retail distribution that offers some of the same products as supermarkets, but the merchandise mix is limited to high turnover convenience products. (12)

convergence The aspect of the digital revolution that pertains to the merging, overlapping, or coming together of previously distinct industries or product categories. (15)

cooperative exporter An export organization of a manufacturing company retained by other independent manufacturers to sell their products in some or all foreign markets. (8)

copy The words that are the spoken or written communication elements in advertisements. (13)

copyright The establishment of ownership of a written, recorded, performed, or filmed creative work. (5)

core competence Something that an organization can do better than competitors. (17)

corporate advertising Advertising that is not designed to directly stimulate demand for a specific product. Image advertising and advocacy advertising are two types of corporate advertising. (13)

corporate social responsibility (CSR) A company's obligation and commitment to the pursuit of goals and policies that are in society's best interests. (17)

cost-based pricing Pricing based on an analysis of internal costs (e.g., material, labor, etc.) and external costs. (11)

cost-based transfer pricing A transfer pricing policy that uses costs as a basis for setting prices in intracorporate transfers. (11)

cost focus In Porter's generic strategies framework, one of four options for building competitive advantage. When a firm that serves a small (niche) market has a lower cost structure than its competitors, it can offer customers the lowest prices in the industry. (16)

cost leadership A competitive advantage based on a firm's position as the industry's low-cost producer. (16)

counterfeiting The unauthorized copying and production of a product. (5)

counterpurchase A monetized countertrade deal in which the seller agrees to purchase products of equivalent value that it must then sell in order to realize revenue from the original deal. (11)

countertrade An export transaction in which a sale results in product flowing in one direction to a buyer, and a separate stream of products and services, often flowing in the opposite direction. (11)

countervailing duties (CVDs) Additional duties levied to offset subsidies granted in the exporting country. (8)

country and market concentration A market expansion strategy that involves targeting a limited number of customer segments in a few countries. (9)

country and market diversification The corporate market expansion strategy of a global, multibusiness company. (9)

country concentration and market diversification A market expansion strategy in which a company serves many markets in a few countries. (9)

country diversification and market concentration A market expansion strategy whereby a company seeks out the world market for a product. (9)

country-of-origin effect Perceptions of, or attitudes toward, products or brands on the basis of the country of origin or manufacture. (10)

coupon A sales promotion tool consisting of a printed certificate that entitles the bearer to a price reduction or some other value-enhancing consideration when purchasing a particular product or service. (14)

creative execution In advertising, the way an appeal or selling proposition is presented. Creative execution is the "how," and creative strategy is the "what." (13)

creative strategy A statement or concept of what a particular advertising message or campaign will say. (13)

culture A society's ways of living transmitted from one generation to another. Culture's manifestations include attitudes, beliefs, values, aesthetics, dietary customs, and language. (4)

current account   A record of all recurring trade in merchandise and services, private gifts, and public aid transactions between countries. (2)

customer relationship management (CRM)   The process of storing and analyzing data collected from customer "touchpoints" for the purpose of identifying a firm's best customers and serving their needs as efficiently, effectively, and profitably as possible. (6)

customer strategy   A sales representative's plan for collecting and analyzing information about the needs of each customer or prospect. (14)

customs union   A preferential trade bloc whose members agree to seek a greater degree of economic integration than is provided by a free trade agreement. In addition to reducing tariffs and quotas, a customs union is characterized by a common external tariff (CET). (3)

cybersquatting   The practice of registering a particular domain name for the express purpose of reselling it to the company that should rightfully use it. (15)

data warehouse   A database, part of a company's MIS, that is used to support management decision making. (6)

Defense Advanced Research Projects Agency (DARPA)   Agency that created a computer network which could maintain lines of communication in the event of a war. (15)

delivered duty paid   A type of contract in which the seller has agreed to deliver the goods to the buyer at the place he or she names in the country of import, with all costs, including duties, paid. (11)

demand conditions   Conditions that determine the rate and nature of improvement and innovations by the firms in the nation. (15)

demographic segmentation   The process of segmenting markets on the basis of measurable characteristics such as country income, population, age, or some other measure. (7)

department store   A category of retail operations characterized by multiple sections or areas under one roof, each representing a distinct merchandise line and staffed with a limited number of salespeople. (12)

devaluation   The decline in value of a currency relative to other currencies. (2)

developed countries   Countries that can be assigned to the high-income category. (2)

developing countries   Countries that can be assigned to the upper ranks of the low-income category, the lower-middle income category, or the upper-middle-income category. (2)

differentiated global marketing   A strategy that calls for targeting two or more distinct market segments with multiple marketing mix offerings. (7)

differentiation   In Porter's generic strategies framework, one of four options for building competitive advantage. Differentiation advantage is present when a firm serves a broad market and its products are perceived as unique; this allows the firm to charge premium prices compared with the competition. (16)

diffusion of innovations   A framework developed by Everett Rogers to explain the way that new products are adopted by a culture over time. The framework includes the five stage innovation adoption process, characteristics of innovations, and innovation adopter categories. (4)

digital revolution   The paradigm shift resulting from technological advances allowing for the digitization (i.e., conversion to binary code) of analog sources of information, sounds, and images. (15)

direct mail   A direct marketing technique that uses the postal service as a vehicle for delivering an offer to prospects targeted by the marketer. (14)

direct marketing   Any communication with a consumer or business recipient that is designed to generate a response in the form of an order, a request for further information, and/or a visit to a store or other place of business. (14)

discontinuous innovation   A new product that, when it is widely adopted, creates new markets and new consumption patterns. (10)

discount retailers   A category of retail operations that emphasizes low merchandise prices. (12)

discriminatory procurement policies   Policies that can take the form of government rules and administrative regulations, as well as formal or informal company policies that discriminate against foreign suppliers. (8)

disruptive technology   A technology that redefines product or industry performance and enables new markets to emerge. (15)

distribution   One of the four Ps of the marketing mix; the physical flow of goods through channels. (12)

distribution channels   A barrier to entry into an industry created by the need to create and establish new channels. (12)

domestic company   A company that limits the geographic scope of its resource commitment and marketing activities to opportunities in the home country. (1)

domestic market   A company's "home turf," generally the country or countries in which the organization's headquarters is located. (1)

double-diamond framework   A framework for understanding national competitive advantage in terms of a "double diamond" instead of the single diamond found in Michael Porter's national advantage model. (16)

draft   A payment instrument that transfers all the risk of nonpayment onto the exporter-seller. (8)

dumping   The sale of a product in an export market at a price lower than that normally charged in the domestic market or country of origin. (8, 11)

duties   Rate schedule; can sometimes be thought of as a tax that punishes individuals for making choices of which their government disapproves. (8)

dynamically continuous innovation   An intermediate category of newness that is somewhat disruptive and requires a moderate amount of learning on the part of consumers. (10)

e-commerce   The general exchange of goods and services using the Internet or similar online network as a marketing channel. (15)

Economic Community of West African States (ECOWAS) An association of 16 nations that includes Benin, Burkina Faso, Cape Verde, Gambia, Ghana, Guinea, Guinea-Bissau, Ivory Coast, Liberia, Mali, Mauritania, Niger, Nigeria, Senegal, Sierra Leone, and Togo. (3)

economic freedom index A table of country rankings based on key economic variables such as trade policy, taxation policy, government consumption, monetary policy, capital flows and foreign investment, etc. (2)

economic union A highly evolved form of cross-border economic integration involving reduced tariffs and quotas, a common external tariff, reduced restrictions on the movement of labor and capital, and the creation of unified economic policies and institutions such as a central bank. (3)

economies of scale The decline in per-unit product costs as the absolute volume of production per period increases. (16)

efficient consumer response (ECR) An MIS tool that enables retailers to work more closely with vendors to facilitate stock replenishment. (6)

electronic data interchange (EDI) An MIS tool that allows a company's business units to submit orders, issue invoices, and transact business electronically with other company units as well as outside companies. (6)

electronic point of sale (EPOS) Purchase data gathered by checkout scanners that help retailers identify product sales patterns and the extent to which consumer preferences vary with geography. (6)

emic analysis Global market research that analyzes a country in terms of its local system of meanings and values. (6)

emotional appeal In advertising, an appeal intended to evoke a feeling response (as opposed to an intellectual response) that will direct purchase behavior. (13)

enabling conditions Structural market characteristics whose presence or absence can determine whether the marketing model can succeed. (7)

environmental sensitivity A measure of the extent to which products must be adapted to the culture-specific needs of different country markets. Generally, consumer products show a higher degree of environmental sensitivity than industrial products. (4)

EPRG framework A developmental framework for analyzing organizations in terms of four successive management orientations: ethnocentric, polycentric, regiocentric, and geocentric. (1)

equity stake Market entry strategy involving foreign direct investment for the purpose of establishing partial ownership of a business. (9)

ethnocentric orientation The first level in the EPRG framework: the conscious or unconscious belief that one's home country is superior. (1)

ethnocentric pricing policy The practice of extending a product's home-country price to all country markets. Also known as extension pricing policy. (11)

etic analysis Global market research that analyzes a country from an outside perspective. (6)

euro zone Sixteen countries that use the euro: Austria, Belgium, Cyprus, Finland, Ireland, the Netherlands, France, Germany, Greece, Italy, Luxembourg, Malta, Portugal, Slovakia, Slovenia, and Spain. (3)

expanded Triad The dominant economic centers of the world: the Pacific region, North America, and Europe. (2)

expatriate An employee who is sent from his or her home country to work abroad. (14)

export broker A broker who receives a fee for bringing together the seller and the overseas buyer. (8)

export commission representative Representative assigned to all or some foreign markets by the manufacturer. (8)

export distributor An individual or organization that has the exclusive right to sell a manufacturer's products in all or some markets outside the country of origin. (8)

export management company (EMC) Term used to designate an independent export firm that acts as the export department for more than one manufacturer. (8)

export marketing Exporting using the product offered in the home market as a starting point and modifying it as needed to meet the preferences of international target markets. (8)

export merchants Merchants who seek out needs in foreign markets and make purchases in world markets to fill these needs. (8)

export price escalation The increase in an imported product's price due to expenses associated with transportation, currency fluctuations, etc. (11)

export selling Exporting without tailoring the product, the price, or the promotional material to suit individual country requirements. (8)

express warranty A written guarantee that assures a buyer that he or she is getting what was paid for or provides recourse in the event that a product's performance falls short of expectations. (10)

expropriation Governmental seizure of a company's assets in exchange for compensation that is generally lower than market value. (5)

extension approach Management's use of domestic country marketing programs and strategies when entering new country markets. (1)

extension strategy A global strategy of offering a product virtually unchanged (i.e., "extending" it) in markets outside the home country. (10)

ex-works (EXW) A type of contract in which the seller places goods at the disposal of the buyer at the time specified in the contract. (11)

factor analysis In market research, a computerized quantitative data analysis technique that is used to perform data reduction. Responses from questionnaires that contain multiple items about a product's benefits serve as input; the computer generates factor loadings that can be used to create a perceptual map. (6)

factor conditions A country's endowment with resources. (16)

FAS (free alongside ship) named port of destination The Incoterm for a contract that calls for the seller to place goods alongside, or available to, the vessel or other mode of transportation and pay all charges up to that point. (11)

femininity In Hofstede's social values framework, the extent to which the social roles of men and women overlap in a culture. (4)

first-mover advantage Orthodox marketing wisdom suggesting that the first company to enter a country market has the best chance of becoming the market leader. (7)

five forces model Model developed by Michael E. Porter that explains competition in an industry: the threat of new entrants, the threat of substitute products or services, the bargaining power of buyers, the bargaining power of suppliers, and the competitive rivalry among current members of the industry. (16)

flagship model A model of competitive advantage developed by Alan Rugman that describes how networked business systems can create competitive advantage in global industries. (16)

FOB (free on board) The Incoterm for a contract in which the responsibility and liability of the seller do not end until the goods have actually been placed aboard a ship. (11)

focus The concentration of resources on a core business or competence. (1)

focus group Primary data collection method involving a trained moderator who facilitates discussion among the members of a group at a specially equipped research facility. (6)

focused differentiation In Porter's generic strategies framework, one of four options for building competitive advantage. When a firm serves a small (niche) market and its products are perceived as unique, the firm can charge premium prices. (16)

foreign consumer culture positioning (FCCP) A positioning strategy that seeks to differentiate a product, brand, or company by associating it with its country or culture of origin. (7)

Foreign Corrupt Practices Act (FCPA) A law that makes it illegal for U.S. corporations to bribe an official of a foreign government or political party to obtain or retain business. (5)

foreign direct investment (FDI) The market entry strategy in which companies invest in or acquire plants, equipment, or other assets outside the home country. (9)

foreign purchasing agents Purchasing agents who operate on behalf of, and are remunerated by, an overseas customer. (8)

foreign sales corporation (FSC) Provision in the U.S. tax code that allowed American exporters to exclude 15 percent of international sales from reported earnings. (8)

form utility The availability of the product processed, prepared, in proper condition and/or ready to use. (12)

forward market A mechanism for buying and selling currencies at a preset price for future delivery. (2)

franchising A contract between a parent company franchisor and franchisee that allows the franchisee to operate a business developed by the franchisor in return for a fee and adherence to franchise-wide policies and practices. This is an appropriate entry strategy when barriers to entry are low yet the market is culturally distant in terms of consumer behavior or retailing structures. (9, 12)

free carrier (FCA) The Incoterm for a contract where transfer from seller to buyer is effected when the goods are delivered to a specified carrier at a specified destination. (11)

free trade agreement (FTA) An agreement that leads to the creation of a free trade area (also abbreviated FTA). A free trade agreement represents a relatively low level of economic integration. (3)

free trade area (FTA) A preferential trade bloc whose members have signed a free trade agreement (also abbreviated FTA) that entails reducing or eliminating tariffs and quotas. (3)

free trade zone (FTZ) A geographical entity that may include a manufacturing facility and a warehouse. (8)

freight forwarders Specialists in traffic operations, customs clearance, and shipping tariffs and schedules. (8)

full ownership Market entry strategy involving foreign direct investment for the purpose of establishing 100 percent control of a business. (9)

General Agreement on Tariffs and Trade (GATT) The organization established at the end of World War II to promote free trade; also, the treaty signed by member nations. (3)

generic strategies Michael Porter's model describing four different options for achieving competitive advantage: cost leadership, differentiation, cost focus, focused differentiation. (16)

geocentric orientation The fourth level in the EPRG framework: the understanding that the company should seek market opportunities throughout the world. Management also recognizes that country markets may be characterized by both similarities and differences. (1)

geocentric pricing The practice of using both extension and adaptation pricing policies in different country markets. (11)

global advertising An advertising message whose art, copy, headlines, photographs, tag lines, and other elements have been developed expressly for their worldwide suitability. (13)

global brand A brand that has the same name and a similar image and positioning throughout the world. (10)

global brand leadership The act of allocating brand-building resources globally with the goal of creating global synergies and developing a global brand strategy that coordinates and leverages country brand strategies. (10)

global company A company exhibiting a geocentric orientation that pursues marketing opportunities in all parts of the world using one of two strategies: either serving world markets by exporting goods manufactured in the home-country market or by sourcing products from a variety of different countries with the primary goal of serving the home-country market. Global operations are integrated and coordinated. (1)

global competition A success strategy in which a firm takes a global view of competition and sets about maximizing profits worldwide, rather than on a country-by-country basis. (15)

global consumer culture positioning (GCCP) A positioning strategy that seeks to differentiate a product, brand, or company as a symbol of, or associated with, global culture or a global market segment. (4, 7)

global elite A global market segment comprised of well-traveled, affluent consumers who spend heavily on prestige or luxury products and brands that convey an image of exclusivity. (7)

global industry An industry in which competitive advantage can be achieved by integrating and leveraging operations on a worldwide scale. (1)

global marketing The commitment of organizational resources to pursuing global market opportunities and responding to environmental threats in the global marketplace. (1)

global market research The project-specific gathering and analysis of data on a global basis or in one or more markets outside the home country. (6)

global market segmentation The process of identifying specific segments of potential customers with homogeneous attributes who are likely to exhibit similar buying behavior irrespective of their country of residence. (7)

global marketing strategy (GMS) A firm's blueprint for pursuing global market opportunities that addresses four issues: whether a standardization approach or localization approach will be used; whether key marketing activities will be concentrated in relatively few countries or widely dispersed around the globe; guidelines for coordinating marketing activities around the globe; and the scope of global market participation. (1)

global positioning system (GPS) A digital communication system that uses satellite feeds to determine the geographic position of a mobile device. (15)

global product A product that satisfies the wants and needs of buyers in all parts of the world. (10)

global retailing Engaging in or owning retail operations in multiple national markets. (12)

global strategic partnerships (GSPs) A sophisticated market entry strategy via an alliance with one or more business partners for the purpose of serving the global market. (9)

global teens A global market segment comprised of persons 12 to 19 years old whose shared interest in fashion, music, and youth lifestyle issues shapes purchase behavior. (7)

gray market goods Products that are exported from one country to another without authorization from the trademark owner. (11)

greenfield investment A market entry strategy that entails foreign direct investment in a factory, retail outlet, or some other form of new operations in a target country. Also known as greenfield operations. (9)

gross domestic product (GDP) A measure of a nation's economic activity, calculated by adding consumer spending (C), investment spending (I), government purchases (G), and net exports (NX): $C + I + G + NX = GDP$. (2)

gross national income (GNI) A measure of a nation's economic activity that includes GDP plus income generated by nonresident sources. (2)

Group of Eight (G-8) Eight nations—the United States, Japan, Germany, France, Great Britain, Canada, Italy, and Russia—whose representatives meet regularly to deal with global economic issues. (2)

Group of Seven (G-7) Seven nations—the United States, Japan, Germany, France, Great Britain, Canada, and Italy—whose representatives meet regularly to deal with global economic issues. (2)

Gulf Cooperation Council (GCC) An association of oil-producing states that includes Bahrain, Kuwait, Oman, Qatar, Saudi Arabia, and the United Arab Emirates. (3)

hard discounter A retailer that sells a tightly focused selection of goods at very low prices, often relying heavily on private brands. (12)

Harmonization The coming together of varying standards and regulations that affect the marketing mix. (3)

Harmonized Tariff System (HTS) A system in which importers and exporters have to determine the correct classification number for a given product or service that will cross borders. (8)

hedging An investment made to protect a company from possible financial losses due to fluctuating currency exchange rates. (2)

high-context culture A culture in which a great deal of information and meaning resides in the context of communication, including the background, associations, and basic values of the communicators. (4)

high-income country A country in which per capita GNI is $11,456 or greater. (2)

hypercompetition A strategy framework developed by Richard D'Aveni that views competition and the quest for competitive advantage in terms of the dynamic maneuvering and strategic interactions of firms in an industry. (16)

hypermarket A category of retail operations characterized by very large-scale facilities that combine elements of discount store, supermarket, and warehouse club approaches. (12)

hypertext markup language (HTML) A format language that controls the appearance of Web pages. (15)

hypertext transfer protocol (http) A protocol that enables hypertext files to be transferred across the Internet. (15)

image advertising A type of corporate advertising that informs the public about a major event, such as a name change, merger, etc. (13)

incipient market A market in which demand will materialize if particular economic, political, or sociocultural trends continue. (6)

Incoterms Internationally accepted terms of trade that impact prices. (11)

individualist culture In Hofstede's social values typology, a society in which each member is primarily concerned with his or her interests and those of the immediate family. (4)

infomercial A form of paid television programming in which a particular product is demonstrated, explained, and offered for sale to viewers who call a toll-free number shown on the screen. (14)

information technology (IT) An organization's processes for creating, storing, exchanging, using, and managing information. (6)

information utility The availability of answers to questions and general communication about useful product features and benefits. (12)

innovation The process of endowing resources with a new capacity to create value. (10)

innovation adoption process In Rogers' diffusion of innovation framework, a five-stage hierarchy that a person goes through when deciding to buy a new product: awareness, interest, evaluation, trial, and adoption. (4)

innovator's dilemma Executives become so committed to a current, profitable technology that they fail to provide adequate levels of investment in new, apparently riskier technologies. (15)

integrated circuit (IC) The silicon chip that gave modern form to the transistor and represented a milestone in the digital revolution. (15)

integrated marketing communications (IMC) An approach to the promotion element of the marketing mix that values coordination and integration of a company's marketing communication strategy. (13)

interactive television (ITV) Allows television viewers to interact with the programming content that they are viewing. (14)

intermodal transportation The aspect of physical distribution that involves transferring shipping containers between land and water transportation modes. (12)

international brand A brand that is available throughout a particular world region. Also known as an international product. (10)

international company A company that pursues market opportunities outside the home country via an extension strategy. (1)

international law The body of international law that pertains to noncommercial disputes between nations. (5)

Internet A network of computer networks across which e-mail and other digital files can be sent. (15)

intranet An electronic system that allows authorized company personnel or outsiders to share information electronically in a secure fashion while reducing the amount of paper generated. (6)

Islamic law A legal system used in the Middle East that is based on a comprehensive code known as sharia. (5)

joint venture A market entry strategy in which two companies share ownership of a newly created business entity. (9, 12)

jurisdiction The aspect of a country's legal environment that deals with a court's authority to rule on particular types of controversies arising outside of a nation's borders or exercise power over individuals or entities from different countries. (5)

keiretsu In Japan, an enterprise alliance consisting of businesses that are joined together in mutually reinforcing ways. (9)

latent market An undiscovered market segment in which demand for a product would materialize if an appropriate product were offered. (6)

law of one price A market in which all customers have access to the best product at the best price. (11)

lean production An extremely effective, efficient, and streamlined manufacturing system such as the Toyota Production System. (17)

least-developed countries (LDCs) Terminology adopted by the United Nations to refer to the 50 countries that rank lowest in per capita GNP. (2)

legal environment A nation's system of laws, courts, attorneys, legal customs, and practices. (5)

letter of credit (L/C) A payment method in export/import in which a bank substitutes its creditworthiness for that of the buyer. (8)

leverage Some type of advantage—for example, experience transfers, leverage, or scale economies—that a company enjoys by accumulating experience in multiple country markets. (1)

licensing A contractual market entry strategy whereby one company makes an asset available to another company in exchange for royalties or some other form of compensation. (9, 12)

line extension A variation of an existing product such as a new flavor or new design. (10)

local brand A brand that is available in a single country market. Also known as a local product. (10)

local consumer culture positioning A positioning strategy that seeks to differentiate a product, brand, or company in terms of its association with local culture, local production, or local consumption. (7)

localization (adaptation) approach The pursuit of global market opportunities using an adaptation strategy of significant marketing mix variation in different countries. (1)

logistics The management process that integrates the activities of various suppliers and distribution intermediaries to ensure an efficient flow of goods through a firm's supply chain. (12)

long-term orientation (LTO) The fifth dimension in Hofstede's social values framework, LTO is a reflection of a society's concern with immediate gratification versus persistence and thrift over the long term. (4)

loose bricks A strategy for creating competitive advantage by taking advantage of a competitor whose attention is narrowly focused on a market segment or geographic area to the exclusion of others. (16)

low-context culture A culture in which messages and knowledge are more explicit and words carry most of the information in communication. (4)

low-income country A country with per capita GNI of less than $935. (2)

lower-middle-income country A country with GNI per capita between $936 and $3,705. (2)

Maastricht Treaty The 1991 treaty that set the stage for the transition from the European monetary system to an economic and monetary union. (3)

Madrid Protocol A system of trademark protection that allows intellectual property registration in multiple countries with a single application and fee. (5)

management information system (MIS) A system that provides managers and other decision makers with a continuous flow of information about company operations. (6)

manufacturer's export agent (MEA) representatives One who can act as an export distributor or as an export commission representative. (8)

marginal-cost pricing A pricing strategy that sets the selling price equal to the variable costs of producing one additional unit of output. (11)

market People or organizations with needs and wants and both the ability and willingness to buy. (2)

market-based transfer price A transfer pricing policy that sets prices for intracorporate transactions at levels that are competitive in the global market. (11)

market capitalism An economic system characterized by market allocation of resources and private resource ownership. (2)

market entry strategy The manner in which company management decides to pursue market opportunities outside the home country. (9)

market expansion strategy The particular combination of product-market and geographic alternatives that management chooses when expanding company operations outside the home country. (9)

market holding strategy A pricing strategy that allows management to maintain market share; prices are adjusted up or down as competitive or economic conditions change. (11)

marketing An organizational function and a set of processes for creating, communicating, and delivering value to customers and for managing customer relationships in ways that benefit the organization and its stakeholders. (1)

market penetration pricing strategy A pricing strategy that calls for setting price levels that are low enough to quickly build market share. (11)

market research The project-specific, systematic gathering of data in the search scanning mode. (6)

market segmentation An effort to identify and categorize groups of customers and countries according to common characteristics. (7)

market skimming A pricing strategy designed to reach customers willing to pay a premium price for a particular brand or for a specialized product. (11)

market socialism An economic system characterized by limited market resource allocation within an overall environment of state ownership. (2)

marketing model drivers Key elements or factors that must be taken into account when evaluating countries as potential target markets. (7)

masculinity In Hofstede's social values framework, the extent to which a culture's male population is expected to be assertive, competitive, and concerned with material success. (4)

Maslow's needs hierarchy A classic framework for understanding how human motivation is linked to needs. (10)

matrix organization A pattern of organization design in which management's task is to achieve an organizational balance that brings together different perspectives and skills to accomplish the organization's objectives. (17)

merchandise trade In balance of payments statistics, entries that pertain to manufactured goods. (2)

mobile commerce (m-commerce) Conducting commercial transactions using wireless handheld devices such as personal digital assistants (PDAs) and cell phones. (15)

mobile music Music that is purchased and played on a cell phone. (15)

multidimensional scaling (MDS) In market research, a quantitative data analysis technique that can be used to create perceptual maps. MDS helps marketers gain insights into consumer perceptions when a large number of products or brands are available. (6)

multinational company A company that pursues market opportunities outside the home country market via an adaptation strategy (i.e., different product, price, place, and/or promotion strategy than used in the domestic market). In a typical multinational, country managers are granted considerable autonomy; there is little integration or coordination of marketing activities across different country markets. (1)

multisegment targeting A marketing strategy that entails targeting two or more distinct market segments with multiple marketing mix offerings. (7)

national advantage Strategy guru Michael E. Porter's competitive advantage framework for analysis at the nation-state level. The degree to which a nation develops competitive advantage depends on four elements: factor conditions, demand conditions, the presence of related and supporting industries, and the nature of firm strategy. (16)

nationalization Broad transfer of industry management and ownership in a particular country from the private sector to the government. (5)

nature of firm strategy, structure, and rivalry In Michael Porter's framework for national competitive advantage, the fourth determinant of a national "diamond." (16)

negotiated transfer price   A transfer pricing policy that establishes prices for intracorporate transactions on the basis of the organization's affiliations. (11)

newly industrializing economies (NIEs)   Upper-middle-income countries with high rates of economic growth. (2)

niche   A single segment of the global market. (7)

nongovernmental organization (NGO)   A secondary stakeholder that focuses on human rights, political justice, and environmental issues. (17)

nontariff barriers (NTBs)   Any restriction besides taxation that restricts or prevents the flow of goods across borders, ranging from "buy local" campaigns to bureaucratic obstacles that make it difficult for companies to gain access to some individual country and regional markets. (1, 8)

normal trade relations (NTR)   A trading stratus under WTO rules that entitles a country to low tariff rates. (8)

North American Free Trade Agreement (NAFTA)   A free trade area encompassing Canada, the United States, and Mexico. (3)

"not invented here" (NIH) syndrome   An error made in choosing a strategy by ignoring decisions made by subsidiary or affiliate managers. (10)

observation   A method of primary data collection using trained observers who watch and record the behavior of actual or prospective customers. (6)

offset   A countertrade deal in which a government recoups hard-currency expenditures by requiring some form of cooperation by the seller, such as importing products or transferring technology. (11)

one-to-one marketing   An updated framework for direct marketing that calls for treating each customer in a distinct way based on his or her previous purchase history or past interactions with the company. (14)

operating system   A software code that provides basic instructions for a computer. (15)

option   In foreign currency trading, a contract confirming the right to buy or sell a specific amount of currency at a fixed price. (2)

order processing   The aspect of physical distribution that includes order entry, order handling, and order delivery. (12)

organic growth   In global retailing, a market expansion strategy whereby a company uses its own resources to open a store on a greenfield site or to acquire one or more existing retail facilities or sites from another company. (12)

Organization for Economic Cooperation and Development (OECD)   A group of 30 nations that work together to aid in the development of economic systems based on market capitalism and pluralistic democracy. (2)

organizing   The goal of creating a structure that enables the company to respond to significant differences in international market environments and to extend valuable corporate knowledge. (17)

outlet mall   A grouping of outlet stores. (12)

outlet store   A category of retail operations that allows marketers of well-known consumer brands to dispose of excess inventory, out-of-date merchandise, or factory seconds. (12)

outsourcing   Shifting jobs or work assignments to another company to cut costs. When the work moves abroad to a low-wage country, such as India or China, the term *offshoring* is sometimes used. (8)

paid search advertising   An Internet communication tactic in which companies pay to have their ads appear when users type certain search terms. (15)

parallel importing   The act of importing goods from one country to another without authorization from the trademark owner. Parallel import schemes exploit price differentials between country markets. (11)

patent   A formal legal document that gives an inventor the exclusive right to make, use, and sell an invention for a specified period of time. (5)

pattern advertising   A communication strategy that calls for developing a basic panregional or global concept for which copy, artwork, or other elements can be adapted as required for individual country markets. (13)

peer-to-peer (p-to-p) marketing   A marketing model whereby individual consumers market products to other individuals. (12)

peoplemeter   An electronic device used by companies such as Nielsen to collect national television audience data. (6)

personal computer (PC)   A compact, affordable computing device whose appearance marked a turning phase of the digital revolution. (15)

personal interview   Primary data collection via interactive communication (e.g., face-to-face, telephone, etc.) that allows interviewers to ask "why"-type questions. (6)

personal selling   One of four variables in the promotion mix; face-to-face communication between a prospective buyer and a company sales representative. (14)

personal selling philosophy   A sales representative's commitment to the marketing concept coupled with a willingness to adopt the role of problem solver or partner in helping customers. The first step in the Strategic/Consultative Selling Model. (14)

physical distribution   All activities involved in moving finished goods from manufacturers to customers. Includes order processing, warehousing, inventory management, and transportation. (12)

place utility   The availability of a product or service in a location that is convenient to a potential customer. (12)

platform   A core product design element or component that can be quickly and cheaply adapted to various country markets. (10)

political environment   The set of governmental institutions, political parties, and organizations that are the expression of the people in the nations of the world. (5)

political risk   The risk of a change in political environment or government policy that would adversely affect a company's ability to operate effectively and profitably. (5)

polycentric orientation   The second level in the EPRG framework: the view that each country in which a company does business is unique. In global marketing, this orientation results in high levels of marketing mix adaptation, often implemented by autonomous local managers in each country market. (1)

polycentric pricing   The practice of setting different price levels for a given product in different country markets. Also known as adaptation pricing policy. (11)

positioning   The act of differentiating a product or brand in the minds of customers or prospects relative to competing products or brands. (7)

positioning by attribute or benefit   A positioning strategy that seeks to differentiate a company, product, or brand in terms of one or more specific benefits (e.g., reliability) offered to buyers. (7)

positioning by competition   A positioning strategy that seeks to differentiate a company, product, or brand by comparing it to the competition. (7)

positioning by quality/price   A positioning strategy that seeks to differentiate a product, brand, or company in terms expensiveness/exclusivity, acceptable quality/good value, etc. (7)

positioning by use or user   A positioning strategy that seeks to differentiate a product by associating it with users whose expertise or accomplishments potential buyers admire. (7)

power distance   In Hofstede's social values typology, the cultural dimension that reflects the extent to which it is acceptable for power to be distributed unequally in a society. (4)

preferential tariff   A reduced tariff rate applied to imports from certain countries. (8)

preferential trade agreement   A trade agreement between a relatively small number of signatory nations, often on a regional or subregional basis. Different levels of economic integration can characterize such trade agreements. (3)

presentation plan   In personal selling, the heart of the presentation strategy. The plan has six stages: approach, presentation, demonstration, negotiation, closing, and servicing the sale. (14)

presentation strategy   Setting objectives for each sales call and establishing a presentation plan to meet those objectives. (14)

price fixing   Secret agreements between representatives of two or more companies to set prices. (11)

price transparency   Euro-denominated prices for goods and services that enable consumers and organizational buyers to comparison shop across Europe. (11)

primary data   In market research, data gathered through research pertaining to the particular problem, decision, or issue under study. (6)

product   One of the four Ps of the marketing mix: a good, service, or idea with tangible and/or intangible attributes that collectively create value for a buyer or user. (10)

product adaptation-communication extension   A strategy of extending, without change, the basic home-market communications strategy while adapting the product to local use or preference conditions. (10)

product-communication adaptation (dual adaptation)   A dual-adaptation strategy that uses a combination of marketing conditions. (10)

product-communication extension   A strategy for pursuing opportunities outside the home market. (10)

product extension-communications adaptation   The strategy of marketing an identical product by adapting the marketing communications program. (10)

product invention   In global marketing, developing new products with the world market in mind. (10)

product-market   A market defined in terms of a particular product category (e.g., in the automotive industry, "the SUV market," "the sports car market," etc.). (7)

product placement   A marketing communication tool that involves a company paying a fee to have one or more products and brand names appear in popular television programs, movies, and other types of performances. (14)

product saturation level   The percentage of customers or households that own a product in a particular country market; a measure of market opportunity. (2)

product strategy   In personal selling, a sales representative's plan for selecting and positioning products that will satisfy customer needs. The third step in the Strategic/Consultative Selling Model. (14)

product transformation   When a product that has been introduced into multiple country markets via a product extension-communication adaptation strategy serves a different function or use than originally intended. (10)

pro forma invoice   A document that sets an export/import transaction into motion. The document specifies the amount and the means by which an exporter wants to be paid; it also specifies the items to be purchased. (8)

promotion site   A Web site that provides marketing communications about a company's goods or services. (15)

psychographic segmentation   The process of assigning people to market segments on the basis of their attitudes, interests, opinions, and lifestyles. (7)

public relations (PR)   One of four variables in the promotion mix. Within an organization, the department or function responsible for evaluating public opinion about, and attitudes toward, the organization and its products and brands. PR personnel also are responsible for fostering goodwill, understanding, and acceptance among a company's various constituents and the public. (13)

publicity   Communication about a company or product for which the company does not pay. (13)

purchasing power parity (PPP)   A concept that permits adjustment of national income measurements in various countries to reflect what a unit of each country's currency can actually buy. (2)

put option The right to sell a specified number of foreign currency units at a fixed price, up to the option's expiration date. (2)

quota Government-imposed limit or restriction on the number of units or the total value of a particular product or product category that can be imported. (8)

rational appeal In advertising, an appeal to the target audience's logic and intellect. (13)

regiocentric orientation The third level in the EPRG framework: the view that similarities as well as differences characterize specific regions of the world. In global marketing, a regiocentric orientation is evident when a company develops an integrated strategy for a particular geographic area. (1)

regulatory environment Governmental and nongovernmental agencies and organizations that enforce laws or establish guidelines for conducting business. (5)

relationship strategy In personal selling, a sales representative's game plan for establishing and maintaining high-quality relationships with prospects and customers. The second step in the Strategic/Consultative Selling Model. (14)

restrictive administrative and technical regulations Regulations that can create barriers to trade; they may take the form of antidumping, size, or safety and health regulations. (8)

revaluation The strengthening of a country's currency. (2)

ringtone A digital sound file for cell phones that is an instrumental version of a song or composition. (15)

rules of origin A system of certification that verifies the country of origin of a shipment of goods. (3)

sales agent An agent who works under contract rather than as a full-time employee. (14)

sales promotion One of the four elements of the promotion mix. A paid, short-term communication program that adds tangible value to a product or brand. (14)

sampling A sales promotion technique that provides potential customers with the opportunity to try a product or service at no cost. (14)

secondary data Existing data in personal files, published sources, and databases. (6)

self-reference criterion (SRC) The unconscious human tendency to interpret the world in terms of one's own cultural experience and values. (4)

selling proposition In advertising, the promise or claim that captures the reason for buying the product or the benefit that product ownership confers. (13)

services trade The buying and selling of intangible, experience-based economic output. (2)

shopping mall A group of stores in one place, typically with one or more large department stores serving as anchors and with easy access and free parking. (12)

short message service (SMS) A globally accepted wireless standard for sending alphanumeric messages of up to 160 characters. (15)

short-term orientation One of dimension in Hofstede's social values typology. Contrasts with long-term orientation. (4)

single-column tariff A schedule of duties in which the rate applies to imports from all countries on the same basis; the simplest type of tariff. (8)

smart phone A phone that offers some of the capabilities of computers, such as a Web browser. (15)

social values typology A study by Dutch organizational anthropologist Geert Hofstede that classifies national cultures according to five dimensions: individualism versus collectivism, masculinity versus femininity, power distance, uncertainty avoidance, and long-term orientation versus short-term orientation. (4)

sourcing decision A strategic decision that determines whether a company makes a product itself or buys products from other manufacturers as well as where it makes or buys. (8)

Southern African Development Community (SADC) An association whose member states are Angola, Botswana, Democratic Republic of Congo, Lesotho, Malawi, Mauritius, Mozambique, Namibia, Seychelles, South Africa, Swaziland, Tanzania, Zambia, and Zimbabwe. (3)

sovereignty A country's supreme and independent political authority. (5)

special economic zone (SEZ) A geographic entity that offers manufacturers simplified customs procedures, operational flexibility, and a general environment of relaxed regulations. (8)

specialty retailer A category of retail operations characterized by a more narrow focus than a department store and offering a relatively narrow merchandise mix aimed at a particular target market. (8, 12)

sponsorship A form of marketing communication that involves payment of a fee by a company to have its name associated with a particular event, team or athletic association, or sports facility. (14)

spreadsheet A software application in the form of an electronic ledger that automatically recalculates changes made to figures entered in rows and columns. (15)

stakeholder Any group or individual that is affected by, or takes an interest in, the policies and practices adopted by an organization. (17)

stakeholder analysis The process of formulating a "win-win" outcome for all stakeholders. (17)

standardized (extension) approach The pursuit of a global market opportunity using an extension strategy of minimal marketing mix variation in different countries. (1)

standardized global marketing A target market strategy that calls for creating the same marketing mix for a broad mass market of potential buyers. (7)

strategic alliance A partnership among two or more firms created to minimize risk while maximizing leverage in the marketplace. (9)

Strategic/Consultative Selling Model A five-step framework for approaching the personal selling task: personal selling philosophy, relationship strategy, product strategy, customer strategy, and presentation strategy. (14)

strategic intent A competitive advantage framework developed by strategy experts Gary Hamel and C. K. Prahalad. (16)

streaming audio Transmission that allows users to listen to Internet radio stations. (15)

streaming media The transmission of combined audio and video content via a broadband network. (15)

streaming video A sequence of moving images sent in compressed form via the Internet and displayed on a computer screen. (15)

subculture Within a culture, a small group of people with their own shared subset of attitudes, beliefs, and values. (4)

subsidies Direct or indirect financial contributions or incentives that benefit producers. (8)

supercenter A category of retail operations that combines elements of discount stores and supermarkets in a space that occupies about half the size of a hypermarket. (12)

supermarket A category of retail operations characterized by a departmentalized, single-story retail establishment that offers a variety of food and nonfood items on a self-service basis. (12)

superstore A store that specializes in selling vast assortments of a particular product category in high volumes at low prices. (12)

supply chain A group of firms that perform support activities by generating raw materials, converting them into components of finished goods, and making them available to buyers. (12)

survey research Primary data collection via questionnaire-based studies designed to generate qualitative responses, quantitative responses, or both. (6)

sustaining technologies Incremental or radical innovations that improve product performance. (15)

switch trading A transaction in which a professional switch trader, switch trading house, or bank steps into a simple barter arrangement or other countertrade arrangement in which one of the parties is not willing to accept all the goods received in the transaction. (11)

targeting The process of evaluating market segments and focusing marketing efforts on a country, region, or group of people. (7)

tariffs The rules, rate schedules (duties), and regulations of individual countries affecting goods that are imported. (8)

telematics A car's ability to exchange information about the vehicle's location or mechanical performance via a wireless Internet connection. (15)

teleshopping Round-the-clock programming exclusively dedicated to product demonstration and selling. (14)

temporary surcharge Surcharges introduced from time to time to provide additional protection for local industry and, in particular, in response to balance-of-payments deficits. (8)

tiered branding A strategy in which a corporate name is combined with a product brand name; also called combination or umbrella branding. (10)

time utility The availability of a product or service when desired by a customer. (12)

trade deficit A negative number in the balance of payments showing that the value of a country's imports exceeds the value of its exports. (2)

trade mission A state- or federally sponsored show outside the home country organized around a product, a group of products, an industry, or an activity at which company personnel can learn about new markets as well as competitors. (8)

trade sales promotion Promotion designed to increase product availability in distribution channels. (14)

trade show A gathering of company representatives organized around a product, a group of products, or an industry, at which company personnel can meet with prospective customers and gather competitor intelligence. (8)

trade surplus A positive number in the balance of payments showing that the value of a country's exports exceeds the value of its imports. (2)

trademark A distinctive mark, motto, device, or emblem that a manufacturer affixes to a particular product or package to distinguish it from goods produced by other manufacturers. (5)

transaction site A cyberspace retail operation that allows customers to purchase goods and services. (15)

transfer pricing The pricing of goods, services, and intangible property bought and sold by operating units or divisions of a company doing business with an affiliate in another jurisdiction. (11)

transistor A "solid state amplifier" that replaced vacuum tubes in electronics products; it was a milestone in the digital revolution. (15)

transnational company A company exhibiting a geocentric orientation that pursues marketing opportunities in all parts of the world. However, a transnational company differs from a global company by fully integrating and coordinating two strategies: both sourcing products from a variety of different countries and serving multiple country markets across most world regions. (1)

Triad The three regions of Japan, Western Europe, and the United States, which represented the dominant economic centers of the world. (2)

truetone A digital sound file of a song or composition for a cell phone featuring the original recording artist. (15)

two-column tariff General duties plus special duties indicating reduced rates determined by tariff negotiations with other countries. (8)

uncertainty avoidance In Hofstede's social values framework, the extent to which members of a culture are uncomfortable with unclear, ambiguous, or unstructured situations. (4)

uniform resource locator (URL) An Internet site's address on the World Wide Web. (15)

upper-middle-income country A country with GNI per capita between $3,706 and $11,455. (2)

usage rate In behavioral market segmentation, an assessment of the extent to which a person uses a product or service. (7)

user status In behavioral market segmentation, an assessment of whether a person is a present user, potential user, nonuser, former user, etc. (7)

value A customer's perception of a firm's product or service offering in terms of the ratio of benefits (product, place, promotion) relative to price. This ratio can be represented by the value equation: $V = B/P$. (1)

value chain The various activities that a company performs (e.g., research and development, manufacturing, marketing, physical distribution, and logistics) in order to create value for customers. (1)

value equation $V = B/P$, where V stands for "perceived value," B stands for "product, price, and place," and P stands for "price." (1)

value network The cost structure in a particular industry that dictates the margins needed to achieve profitability. A broadly defined industry (e.g., computers) may have parallel value networks, each with its own metrics of value. (15)

values In culture, enduring beliefs or feelings that a specific mode of conduct is personally or socially preferable to another mode of conduct. (4)

variable import levies A system of levies applied to certain categories of imported agricultural products. (8)

voice over Internet protocol (VoIP) Technology that allows the human voice to be digitized and broken into data packets that can be transmitted over the Internet and converted back into normal speech. (15)

warehousing The aspect of physical distribution that involves the storage of goods. (12)

wireless fidelity (Wi-Fi) Technology based on a low-power radio signal that permits access to the Internet from a laptop computer or PDA when the user is within range of a base station transmitter ("hot spot"). (15)

World Interoperability for Microwave Access (WiMax) An improved Wi-Fi technology that can have a range of several miles. (15)

World Trade Organization (WTO) The successor to the General Agreement on Tariffs and Trade. (3)

World Wide Web Global computer network connecting Internet sites that contain text, graphics, and streaming audio and video resources. (15)

Author/Name Index

Subject/Organization Index